# Clinical Neuropsychology

# CLINICAL
# NEUROPSYCHOLOGY

THIRD EDITION

Edited by

## KENNETH M. HEILMAN, M.D.

PROFESSOR OF NEUROLOGY AND CLINICAL PSYCHOLOGY
UNIVERSITY OF FLORIDA COLLEGE OF MEDICINE

## EDWARD VALENSTEIN, M.D.

PROFESSOR OF NEUROLOGY AND CLINICAL PSYCHOLOGY
UNIVERSITY OF FLORIDA COLLEGE OF MEDICINE

New York   Oxford
OXFORD UNIVERSITY PRESS
1993

Oxford University Press

Oxford   New York   Toronto
Delhi   Bombay   Calcutta   Madras   Karachi
Kuala Lumpur   Singapore   Hong Kong   Tokyo
Nairobi   Dar es Salaam   Cape Town
Melbourne   Auckland   Madrid

and associated companies in
Berlin   Ibadan

Copyright © 1979, 1985, 1993 by Oxford University Press, Inc.

Published by Oxford University Press, Inc.,
200 Madison Avenue, New York, New York 10016

Oxford is a registered trademark of Oxford University Press

Library of Congress Cataloging-in-Publication Data
Clinical neuropsychology /
edited by Kenneth M. Heilman, Edward Valenstein. — 3rd ed.
p.   cm.
Includes bibliographical references and index.
ISBN 0-19-508123-4
1. Neuropsychiatry.   2. Clinical neuropsychology.
I. Heilman, Kenneth M., 1938–
II. Valenstein, Edward, 1942–
[DNLM: 1. Behavior.   2. Nervous System Diseases.
3. Neurologic Manifestations.   4. Neuropsychology.
WL 340 C641]  RC341.C693   1993   616.8—dc20
DNLM/DLC   for Library of Congress   92-49919

2 4 6 8 9 7 5 3

Printed in the United States of America
on acid-free paper

*This book is dedicated to*

*Norman Geschwind*
*and*
*Melvin Greer*

# Preface

Continuing advances in our understanding of brain-behavior relationships have necessitated a new edition of this text. Several chapters have been completely rewritten, while others have been updated. New to this edition is a chapter on schizophrenia. The neuropsychological and neuroanatomic approaches that have been so fruitful in the investigation of illnesses traditionally considered to be neurological have recently yielded exciting results when applied to schizophrenia. Our decision not to include chapters on other psychiatric illnesses is based on the lack of evidence to date of morphological abnormalities in these diseases, and the need to limit the size of the book, but we admit that the decision was somewhat arbitrary.

We would like again to acknowledge our debts to contributing authors, many of whom contributed to previous editions, to the editors at Oxford, and to our families.

We have dedicated this edition to two men who have greatly influenced our careers. Dr. Norman Geschwind came to the Boston City Hospital while we were both residents in neurology. On most mornings after work rounds, as residents collected around the coffee pot and Coke machine, Dr. Geschwind would join us and discuss anything of interest. His intellect and knowledge should have intimidated us, but he was always warm and charming, and his enthusiasm was infectious. He taught us that questioning was a virtue, and that no question was either stupid or unworthy of an answer. He not only imparted some of his knowledge to us, but taught us how to question, posit, and test. A generation of behavioral neurologists (several of whom are also contributors to this book) can attest to this. Even after we left Boston, he was always available for advice and guidance. His untimely death in 1984 took from us not only the most original and incisive intellect in the field, but also a valued mentor and friend.

After residency, we came, by separate paths, to the University of Florida, where we have taught for the past two decades. Academia can be treacherous, but not for us. Dr. Melvin Greer, Chief of the Division of Neurology, and, since 1974, Chairman of the Department of Neurology, always believed that an academic department should foster the academic work of its faculty. His leadership and his willingness to take upon his own shoulders the administrative and clinical burdens of the department enabled his faculty to pursue their academic interests. We continue to benefit from his immense energy, his support, and his friendship. Our expression of gratitude can serve to repay only a fraction of what he has given us over these years.

*Gainesville, Florida*                                                      K.M.H.
*December 1992*                                                             E. V.

# Preface to the First Edition

The growth of interest in brain-behavior relationships has generated a literature that is both impressive and bewildering. In teaching neuropsychology, we have found that the reading lists necessary for adequate coverage of the subject have been unwieldy, and the information provided in the reading has been difficult to integrate. We therefore set out to provide a text that comprehensively covers the major clinical syndromes. The focus of the text is the *clinical* presentation of human brain dysfunction. The authors who have contributed to this volume have provided clinical descriptions of the major neuropsychological disorders. They have discussed methods of diagnosis, and have described specific tests, often of use at the bedside. They have also commented upon therapy. Since the study of pathophysiological and neuropsychological mechanisms underlying these disorders is inextricably intertwined with the definition and treatment of these disorders, considerable space has been devoted to a discussion of these mechanisms, and to the clinical and experimental evidence which bears on them.

A multi-authored text has the advantage of allowing authorities to write about areas in which they have special expertise. This also exposes the reader to several different approaches to the study of brain-behavior relationships, an advantage in a field in which a variety of theoretical and methodological positions have been fruitful. We therefore have not attempted to impose our own views on the contributing authors, but where there were conflicts in terminology, we have provided synonyms and cross-references. Much of brain activity is integrative, and isolated neuropsychological disturbances are rare. Discussions of alexia or agraphia must necessarily include more than a passing reference to aphasia, and so on. Since we wanted each chapter to stand on its own, with its author's viewpoint intact, we have generally allowed some overlap between chapters.

We wish to thank all of the persons who devoted their time and effort to this book. Professor Arthur Benton not only contributed two outstanding chapters, but was instrumental in advising us about authors and content, and in leading us to Oxford University Press. We are grateful to all the other contributing authors, who promptly provided high quality manuscripts; to our secretary, Ann Tison, who typed our manuscripts so many times; and to the editors at Oxford University Press, who helped to improve our grammar and syntax, and, not infrequently, the clarity of our thought. Not least, we are grateful to our families, who have endured many evenings of work with this volume with patience and understanding.

*Gainesville, Florida*                                                          K.M.H.
*March 1979*                                                                    E.V.

# Contents

# Contributors

**Martin L. Albert, M.D.**
Professor of Neurology
Clinical Director, Aphasia Research Center
Boston University School of Medicine; and
Chief, Clinical Neurology Section
Neurology Service
Boston Veterans Administration Hospital, Boston

**Steven W. Anderson, Ph.D.**
Assistant Research Scientist
Department of Neurology
Division of Behavioral Neurology & Cognitive Neuroscience
University of Iowa, Iowa City

**Russell M. Bauer, Ph.D.**
Associate Professor of Clinical & Health Psychology and Neurology
University of Florida, Gainesville

**D. Frank Benson, M.D.**
The Augustus S. Rose Professor of Neurology
University of California, Los Angeles

**Arthur Benton, Ph.D., D.Sc.**
Professor Emeritus of Neurology and Psychology
University of Iowa, Iowa City

**Joseph E. Bogen, M.D.**
Clinical Professor of Neurological Surgery
University of Southern California; and
Adjunct Professor of Behavioral Neuroscience
University of California, Los Angeles

**Dawn Bowers, Ph.D.**
Associate Professor of Neurology and Clinical & Health Psychology
University of Florida, Gainesville

**Antonio R. Damasio, M.D., D. Med. Sci.**
Professor and Chairman of Neurology
University of Iowa, Iowa City

**Rhonda B. Friedman, Ph.D.**
Assistant Clinical Professor of Neurology
Department of Neurology
Georgetown University Medical School
Washington, D.C.

**Terry E. Goldberg, Ph.D.**
Chief, Neuropsychology
Clinical Brain Disorders Branch
Intramural Research Program
National Institute of Mental Health
Neuroscience Center at St. Elizabeths
Washington, D.C.

**Felicia C. Goldstein, Ph.D.**
Assistant Professor of Neurology
Department of Neurology
Emory University School of Medicine
Atlanta

**Leslie J. Gonzalez Rothi, Ph.D.**
Speech Pathologist, Gainesville Veterans Administration Medical Center
Adjunct Associate Professor of Neurology and Speech
University of Florida, Gainesville

**Peter Hedera, M.D.**
Fellow, Alzheimer's Center
University Hospitals of Cleveland
Division of Behavioral and Geriatric Neurology
Case Western Reserve University, Cleveland

**Kenneth M. Heilman, M.D.**
The James E. Rooks, Jr. Professor of Neurology
University of Florida, Gainesville

**Andrew Kertesz, M.D., F.R.C.P.(C)**
Professor of Neurology
University of Western Ontario
St. Joseph's Health Centre, London, Ontario

**Alan Lerner, M.D.**
Fellow, Alzheimer's Center
University Hospitals of Cleveland
Division of Behavioral and Geriatric Neurology
Case Western Reserve University, Cleveland

**Harvey S. Levin, Ph.D.**
Professor, Division of Neurosurgery
University of Texas Medical Branch
Galveston, Texas

**Christopher Randolph, Ph.D.**
Staff Fellow
Clinical Brain Disorders Branch
Intramural Research Program
National Institute of Mental Health
Neuroscience Center at St. Elizabeths
Washington, D.C.

**David P. Roeltgen, M.D.**
Associate Professor of Neurology
Hahnemann University, Philadelphia

**Abigail B. Sivan, Ph.D.**
Assistant Scientist, Department of Psychiatry
Rush-Presbyterian-St. Luke's Medical Center
Assistant Professor, Department of Psychology and Social Science
Rush Medical College, Chicago

**Paul A. Spiers, Ph.D.**
Visiting Scientist
Clinical Research Center
Massachusetts Institute of Technology
Cambridge

**Betsy Tobias, Ph.D.**
Post-Doctoral Associate
Department of Clinical and Health Psychology
University of Florida, Gainesville

**Daniel Tranel, Ph.D.**
Associate Professor of Neurology
University of Iowa College of Medicine, Iowa City

**Edward Valenstein, M.D.**
Professor of Neurology and Clinical and Health Psychology
University of Florida, Gainesville

**Robert T. Watson, M.D.**
Professor of Neurology
Assistant Dean for Education
University of Florida College of Medicine
Gainesville

**Jon Erik Ween, M.D.**
Resident in Neurology (PGY III)
Aphasia Research Center
Department of Neurology
Boston University School of Medicine and
Boston Veteran's Administration Medical Center, Boston

**Daniel R. Weinberger, M.D.**
Chief, Neurology Division
Clinical Brain Disorders Branch
Intramural Research Program
National Institute of Mental Health
Neuroscience Center at St. Elizabeths
Washington, D.C.

**Peter J. Whitehouse, M.D., Ph.D.**
Director, Alzheimer's Center
University Hospitals of Cleveland
Director, Division of Behavioral and Geriatric Neurology
Case Western Reserve University, Cleveland

# Clinical
# Neuropsychology

# 1
# Introduction

KENNETH M. HEILMAN AND EDWARD VALENSTEIN

Aristotle thought that the mind, with the function of thinking, had no relation to the body or the senses and could not be destroyed. The first attempts to localize mental processes to the brain may nevertheless be traced back to antiquity. In the fifth century B.C., Hippocrates of Croton claimed that the brain was the organ of intellect and the heart the organ of the senses. Herophilus, in the third century B.C., studied the structure of the brain and regarded it as the site of intelligence. He believed that the middle ventricle was responsible for the faculty of cognition and the posterior ventricle was the seat of memory. Galen, in the second century B.C., thought that the activities of the mind were performed by the substance of the brain rather than the ventricles, but it was not until the anatomical work of Vesalius in the sixteenth century A.D. that this thesis was accepted. Vesalius, however, thought that the brains of most mammals and birds had similar structures in almost every respect and differed only in size, attaining the greatest dimensions in humans. In the seventeenth century, Descartes suggested that the soul resided in the pineal. He chose the pineal because of its central location: all things must emanate from the soul.

At the end of the eighteenth century, Gall postulated that various human faculties were localized in different organs, or centers of the brain. He thought that these centers were expansions of lower nervous mechanisms and that, although independent, they were able to interact with one another. Unlike Descartes, Gall conceived brain structures as having successive development, with no central point where all nerves unite. He proposed that the vital forces resided in the brainstem and that the intellectual qualities were situated in various parts of the two cerebral hemispheres. The hemispheres were united by the commissures, the largest being the corpus callosum.

Unfortunately, Gall also postulated that measurements of the skull may allow one to deduce moral and intellectual characteristics, since the shape of the skull is modified by the underlying brain. This hypothesis was the foundation of phrenology. When phrenology fell into disrepute, many of Gall's original contributions were blighted. His teachings, however, are the foundation of modern neuropsychology.

Noting that students with good verbal memory had prominent eyes, Gall suggested that memory for words was situated in the frontal lobes. He studied two patients who

3

had lost their memory for words and attributed their disorder to frontal lobe lesions. In 1825, Bouillard wrote that he also believed cerebral function to be localized. He demonstrated that discrete lesions could produce paralysis in one limb and not others and cited this as proof of localized function. He also believed that the anterior lobe was the center of speech. He observed that the tongue had many functions other than speech and that one function could be disordered (e.g., speech) while others remained intact (e.g., mastication). This observation suggested to him that an effector can have more than one center that controls its actions.

In 1861, Broca heard Bouillaud's pupil Auburtin speak about the importance of the anterior lobe in speech and asked Auburtin to see a patient suffering from right hemiplegia and loss of speech and writing. The patient was able to understand speech but could articulate only one word, "tan." This patient died, and postmortem inspection of the brain revealed that there was a cavity filled with fluid on the lateral aspect of the left hemisphere. When the fluid was drained, there could be seen a large left-hemisphere lesion that included the first temporal gyrus, the insula and the corpus striatum, and the frontal lobe, including the second and third frontal convolutions as well as the inferior portion of the transverse convolution. In 1861, Broca saw another patient who had lost the power of speech and writing but could comprehend spoken language. Autopsy again revealed a left-hemisphere lesion involving the second and third frontal convolutions.

Broca later saw eight patients who suffered a loss of speech (which he called aphemia, but which Trousseau later called aphasia). All eight had left-hemisphere lesions. This was the first demonstration of left-hemisphere dominance for language (Broca, 1865).

Broca's observations produced great excitement in the medical world. Despite his clear demonstration of left-hemisphere dominance, medical opinion appeared to split into two camps, one favoring the view that different functions are exercised by the various portions of the cerebral hemisphere and the other denying that psychic functions are or can be localized.

Following Broca's initial observations, there was a flurry of activity. In 1868, Hughlings Jackson noted that there were two types of aphasic patients—fluent and nonfluent—and, in 1869, Bastian argued that there were patients who had deficits not only in the articulation of words but also in the memory for words. Bastian also postulated the presence of a visual and auditory word center and a kinesthetic center for the hand and the tongue. He proposed that these centers were connected and that information, such as language, was processed by the brain in different ways by each of these centers. Lesions in these centers would thus produce distinct syndromes, depending upon which aspect of the processing was disturbed. Bastian thus viewed the brain as a processor. He was the first to describe word deafness and word blindness.

In 1874, Wernicke published his famous *Der Aphasische Symptomenkomplex*. He was familiar with Meynert's work, which demonstrated that sensory systems project to the posterior portions of the hemispheres whereas the anterior portions appear to be efferent. Wernicke noted that lesions of the posterior portion of the superior temporal region produced an aphasia in which comprehension was poor. He thought that this auditory center contained sound images, while Broca's area contained images for movement. He also thought that these areas were connected by a commissure and that a lesion of this commissure would disconnect the area for sound images from the area for images of movement.

Wernicke's scheme could account for motor, conduction, and sensory aphasia with poor repetition. Lichtheim (1885), however, described patients who were nonfluent but repeated normally and sensory aphasics who could not comprehend but could repeat words. Elaborating on Wernicke's ideas, he devised a complex scheme to explain the mechanism underlying seven types of speech and language disorders.

Following World War I, the localizationist-connectionist approach was abandoned in favor of a holistic approach. Probably there were many factors underlying the change. The localizationist theory was built on the foundation laid by Gall. When phrenology was discredited, other localizationist theories became suspect. Lashley (1938), using experimental methods (as opposed to the case reports of the classical neurologists), found that engrams were not localized in the brain but rather appeared to be diffusely represented. From these observations, he proposed a theory of mass action: the behavioral result of a lesion depends on the amount of brain removed more than on the location of the lesion. Head (1926) studied aphasics' linguistic performance and was not satisfied with the classical neurologists' attempts to deduce schemas from clinical observations. Discussing one of Wernicke's case reports, he wrote, "No better example could be chosen of the manner in which the writers of this period were compelled to lop and twist their cases to fit the Procrustean bed of their hypothetical conceptions." Although Freud studied the relationships between the brain and behavior early in his career, he later provided the scientific world with explanations of behavior based on psychodynamic relationships. The Gestalt psychologists abandoned localization and connectionism in favor of the holistic approach.

Social and political influences, however, were perhaps more important in changing neuropsychological thought than were the newer scientific theories. The continental European scientific community was strongly influenced by Kant's *Critique of Pure Reason*, which held that, although knowledge cannot transcend experience, it is nevertheless in part a priori. According to Kant, the outer world produces only the matter of sensation while the mental apparatus (the brain) orders this matter and supplies the concepts by means of which we understand experience. After World War I, the influence on science on the continent waned while in English-speaking countries it bloomed. The American and English political and social systems were strongly influenced by Locke, the seventeenth-century liberal philosopher who, unlike Kant, believed that behavior and ideas were not innate but rather derived from experience. This conceptual scheme provides little reason to look at the structure of the brain in order to understand behavior.

In the second half of the twentieth century, there has been a reawakening of interest in brain-behavior relationships. Many developments contributed to this. The classical neurologists were rediscovered and their findings replicated. Electronic technology provided researchers with new instruments for observing physiological processes. New statistical procedures enabled them to distinguish random results from significant behavior. New behavioral paradigms, such as dichotic listening and lateral visual half-field viewing, permitted psychologists to explore brain mechanisms in normal individuals as well as in pathological cases. Anatomical studies using new

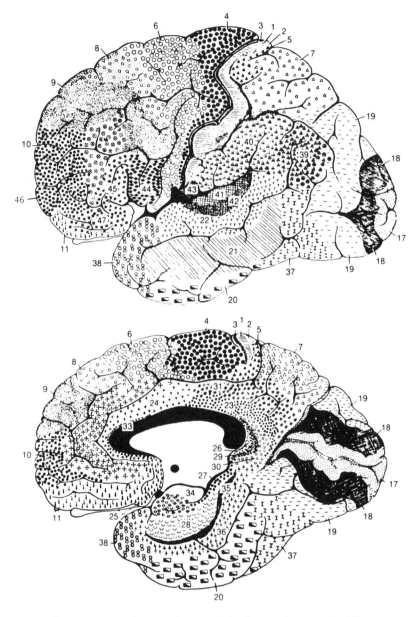

**Fig. 1-1.** Brodmann's cytoarchitectural map of the human brain. The different areas are defined on the basis of subtle differences in cortical cell structure and organization. Broca's area corresponds roughly to areas 44 and 45 and Wernicke's area to the posterior part of area 22.

staining methods permitted more detailed mapping of connections, and advances in neurochemistry and neuropharmacology ushered in a new form of neuropsychology in which, in addition to studying behavioral-structural relationships, investigators can study behavioral-chemical relationships.

## METHODS AND CONCEPTS

The attempt to relate behavior to the brain rests on the assumptions that all behavior is mediated by physical processes and that the complex behavior of higher animals depends upon physical processes in the central nervous system. Changes in complex behavior must therefore be associated with changes in the physical state of the brain. Conversely, changes in the physical state of the brain (such as these associated with brain damage) affect behavior. The genetically determined organization of the nervous system sets limits on what can be perceived and learned. This organization also determines to a great extent the nature of the behavioral changes that occur in response to brain injury.

The understanding of brain-behavior relationships is aided most by the study of behaviors that can be clearly defined and that are likely to be related to brain processes that can be directly or indirectly observed. Behaviors that can be selectively affected by focal brain lesions or by specific pharmacological agents are therefore most often chosen for neuropsychological study. Conversely, behaviors that are difficult to define or that appear unlikely to be correlated with *observable* anatomical, physiological, or chemical processes in the brain are poor candidates for study. As techniques for studying the brain improve, more kinds of behavior should become amenable to study.

Explanations of behavior that are not based on an attempt to understand brain-behavior relationships are of limited interest to the neuropsychologist. Thus, while psychodynamic explanations of behavior may be of considerable clinical utility in the evaluation and treatment of certain behavior disorders, they will be of little interest to neuropsychologists until some correlation with underlying brain processes is demonstrated. Furthermore, psychodynamic explanations of the behavior of brain-damaged patients must be examined critically since the brain damage may have impaired normal emotional mechanisms. Depression, for example, can be seen in brain-damaged persons. The obvious psychodynamic explanation is that the depression is a "normal" reaction to a loss of function the patient has experienced as a result of the brain injury. Evidence that depression correlates less with the severity of functional loss than with the site of the brain lesion, however, suggests that in some patients depression may be a direct result of the brain injury and that in such cases the psychodynamic explanation may be irrelevant. Similar caveats apply to the better-documented association of apathy and denial of illness with lesions in the frontal lobes or in the right hemisphere.

There are many valid approaches to the study of brain-behavior relationships, and no morally and intellectually sound approach should be neglected. We will briefly consider the major approaches, emphasizing those that have been used to greatest advantage.

## Introspection

At times, patients' observations of their own mental state may be not only helpful but necessary. How else can one learn of many sensory abnormalities, hallucinations, or emotional changes? It is conceivable that people's insights into their own mental processes may be of importance in delineating brain mechanisms. For example, persons with "photographic" memory not surprisingly report that they rely on visual rather than verbal memory, and experiments suggest that visual memory has a greater capacity than verbal memory. Patients may have similarly useful insights, and clinicians would do well to listen carefully to what their patients say. This does not mean, however, that they must believe it all. In normal persons, introspection is not always trustworthy. In brain-damaged patients, it may be even less reliable. This is particularly true when the language centers have been disconnected from the region of the brain that processes the information the patient is asked about (Geschwind, 1965). For example, patients with a callosal lesion (separating the left language-dominant hemisphere from the right hemisphere) cannot name correctly an object placed in their left hand. Curiously, such patients do not say that they cannot name the object nor do they explain that their left hand can feel it but they cannot find the right word. Instead, in nearly every such case recorded, the patient confabulates a name. It is clear that in this situation the patient's language area, which is providing the spoken "insight," cannot even appreciate the presence of a deficit (until it is later brought to its attention), let alone explain the nature of the difficulty. In other situations, it is apparent that patients make incorrect assumptions about their deficits. Patients with pure word deafness (who can understand no spoken language but who nevertheless can speak well and can hear) often assume that people are deliberately being obscure; the result of this introspection is often paranoia. Thus, although a patient's introspection at times can provide useful clues for the clinician, this information must always be analyzed critically and used with caution.

## The Black Box Approach

Behavior can be studied without any knowledge of the nervous system. Just as the electrical engineer can study the function of an electronic apparatus without taking it apart (by applying different inputs and studying the outputs), the brain can also be approached as a "black box." The object of the black box approach is to determine laws of behavior. These laws can then be used to predict behavior, which of course is one expressed aim of the study of psychology.

To the extent that laws of behavior are determined by the "hard-wiring" of the brain, the black box approach also yields information about brain function. In this regard, the systematic study of any behavior or set of behaviors is relevant to the study of brain function. Psychology, linguistics, sociology, aesthetics, and related disciplines may all reveal a priori principles of behavior. The study of linguistics, for example, has revealed a basic structure that is common to all languages (Chomsky, 1967). Since there is no logical constraint that gives language this structure and since its generality makes environmental influences unlikely, one can assume that the basic structure of language is hard-wired in the brain. Thus, observations of behavior can constrain theories of brain function without any reference to brain anatomy, chemistry, or physiology (see, for example, Caramazza, 1992).

Although the black box approach yields useful information about brain function, such information is limited because the brain itself is not studied. The study of neuropsychology reflects its origins in nineteenth-century medical science by emphasizing brain anatomy, chemistry, and physiology as relevant variables: purely cognitive studies are but a part of this endeavor.

### Brain Ablation Paradigms

Lesions in specific areas of the brain change behavior in specific ways. Studies correlating these behavioral changes with the site of lesions yield information that can be used to predict from a given behavioral disturbance the site of the lesions, and vice versa. Such information has great clinical utility.

It is another matter, however, to try to deduce from the behavioral effects of an ablative lesion the normal mechanisms of brain function. As Hughlings Jackson pointed out nearly a century ago, the abnormal behavior observed after a brain lesion reflects the functioning of the remaining brain tissue. This remaining brain may react adversely to or compensate for the loss of function caused by the lesion, and thus either add to or minimize the behavioral deficit. Acute lesions often disturb function in other brain areas (termed diaschisis); these metabolic and physiological changes may not be detectable by neuropathological methods and may thus contribute to an overestimate of the function of the lesioned area. Lesions may also produce changes in behavior by releasing other brain areas from facilitation or inhibition. Thus it may be difficult to distinguish behavioral effects caused by an interruption of processing normally occurring in the damaged area from effects due to less specific alterations of function in other areas of the brain.

Possible nonspecific effects of a lesion, such as diaschisis, mass action effects, and reactions to disability or discomfort, can be excluded as major determinants of abnormal behavior by the use of "control" lesions. If lesions of comparable size in other brain areas do not produce similar behavioral effects, one cannot ascribe these effects to nonspecific causes. It is especially elegant to be able to demonstrate that such a control lesion has a different behavioral effect. This has been termed "double-dissociation": lesion A produces behavioral change a but not b, while lesion B produces behavioral change b but not a (Teuber, 1955).

Once nonspecific effects have been excluded, one must take into account the various ways in which a lesion may specifically affect behavior. If a lesion in a particular region results in the loss of a behavior, one must not simply ascribe to that region the normal function of performing that behavior. The first step toward making a meaningful statement about brain-behavior relationships is a scrupulous analysis of the behavior in question. If a lesion in a particular area of the brain interferes with writing, that does not mean that the area is the "writing center" of the brain. Writing is a complex process that requires many other functions: sensory and motor control over the limb must be excellent; there must be no praxic disturbances; language function must be intact; the subject must be mentally alert and able to attend to the task, and so on. One must study every aspect of behavior that is directly related to the task of writing in order to define as closely as possible which aspect of the process of writing is disturbed. It may then be possible to make a correlation between the damaged portion of the brain and the aspect of the writing process that has been disrupted. It is important to distinguish between lesions that destroy areas of the brain involved in processing and lesions that disconnect such areas from one another, disrupting processes which require coordination between two or more such areas (Geschwind, 1965). When a person is writing, for example, the language and motor areas must be coordinated. Lesions that disconnect these areas produce agraphia even though there may be no other language or motor deficit. A lesion in the corpus callosum, for example, may disconnect the language areas in the left hemisphere from the right-hemisphere motor area, thus producing agraphia in the left hand.

Partial recovery of function often occurs after brain lesions and can be attributed to many factors, including resolution of edema, increase in blood supply to ischemic areas, and resolution of diaschisis (see Chapter 17). In addition, the brain is capable of a limited amount of reorganization that may enable remaining structures to take over the functions of the damaged portion. Brain plasticity is greatest in the developing organism and probably decreases with increasing age. This clearly complicates the study of behavioral disorders that follow focal lesions, especially in children.

In addition to these difficulties in interpretation, gross ablations have a further disadvantage in the investigation of brain function. Natural lesions, such as strokes or tumors, do not necessarily respect functional neuroanatomical boundaries. Ischemic strokes occur in the distribution of particular vessels, and the vascular territory often overlaps various anatomical boundaries. The association of two behavioral deficits may thereby result not from a functional relationship but rather from the fact that two brain regions with little anatomical or physiological relation are supplied by the same vessel. The association of a memory disturbance with pure word blindness (alexia without agraphia) merely indicates that the mesial temporal lobe, the occipital lobe, and the splenium of the corpus callosum are all in the distribution of the posterior cerebral artery. Experimental lesions in animals can avoid this problem; even within a specific anatomical region, however, there may be many systems operating, often with contrasting behavioral functions.

Despite all these problems, the study of brain ablations in humans and animals has yielded more information about brain-behavior relationships than any other approach and it has been given renewed impetus by the recent development of powerful methods of neural imaging. Lesions as small as two or three millimeters in diameter can be detected by modern x-ray computerized tomography (CT). Positron emission tomography (PET) has less resolution but can provide images that reflect the metabolic activity of brain regions. Nuclear magnetic resonance imaging (MRI) scanning gives information about brain structure and blood flow and is also beginning to provide information about metabolic activity. Already it can provide information comparable to a CT scan without exposing the patient to x-irradiation. This lessened risk further enlarges the population of subjects for whom neural imaging can be justified.

Abnormalities of development of the nervous system both before and after birth may result in behavioral abnormalities at a much later date. It is difficult to make precise correlations between structural and behavioral abnormalities, since the plasticity of the developing nervous system tends to minimize focal deficits. But there is nevertheless great interest in correlating developmental abnormalities with behavioral syndromes, as evidenced, for example, by the study of brain anomalies in certain children with dyslexia. Another approach is to study the behavioral changes that attend normal development in childhood and to attempt to correlate them with changes within the developing nervous system.

## Brain Stimulation Paradigms

Brain stimulation has been used to map connections in the brain and to elicit changes in behavior. One attraction of this method has been that stimulation, as opposed to ablation, is reversible. (Reversible methods of ablation, such as cooling, have been used, however.) The additional claim that stimulation is more like normal physiological function is open to question: it is highly unlikely that gross electrical stimulation of the brain reproduces any normally occurring physiological state. The stimulation techniques that are usually employed cannot selectively affect only one class of neurons. Furthermore, stimulation disrupts ongoing activity, frequently inhibiting it in a way that resembles the effects of ablation. Some of these objections may be overcome by the use of neurotransmitters or drugs with similar properties to stimulate (or inhibit) specific neurotransmitter systems.

## Neurochemical Manipulations

Neurochemical and immunological methods have identified groups of neurons in the central nervous system which use specific neurotransmitters. The number of neurotransmitters identified continues to increase. Twenty years ago glycine and gamma-aminobutyric acid (GABA) had just been added to the "standard" neurotransmitters—epinephrine, norepinephrine, dopamine, acetylcholine, and serotonin. Now there are a multitude of neurotransmitters (including amino acids such as glutamine, and polypeptides such as the endorphins and enkephalins, substance P, somatostatin, somatomedin, neurotensin, growth hormone, and others), and it is known that one neuron may contain more than one neurotransmitter. The anatomy of major neurotransmitter pathways has been elucidated. Some of these systems can be selectively stimulated by the ontophoresis of neurotransmitters or of drugs with similar properties. Some can be selectively depressed by drugs that block the action of the transmitter (or inhibit its release), and some can be selectively destroyed by drugs that damage the neurons containing a specific transmitter. Brain sections can be analyzed to determine the concentration of transmitters, and the concentrations can be correlated with behavioral data. Imaging techniques for neurotransmitters such as acetylcholine and dopamine are now available for human studies. These and related techniques hold great promise, especially because of their ability to correlate the behavioral effects of pharmacological agents with dysfunction in anatomical areas "redefined" by chemical criteria.

## Electrophysiological Studies

### THE ELECTROENCEPHALOGRAM

Electrophysiological studies of human behavior have been attempted during brain surgery, and depth electrode recording may be justified in the evaluation of a few patients (usually in preparation for epilepsy surgery), but most studies rely on the surface-recorded electroencephalogram (EEG). The raw EEG, however, demonstrates changes in amplitude and frequency that are generally nonspecific and poorly localizing. Computer analysis of EEG frequency and amplitude (power spectra) in different behavioral situations (and from different brain regions) has demonstrated correlations between EEG activity and behavior, but only for certain aspects of behavior (such as arousal) or for broad anatomical fields (e.g., between hemispheres). The use of computer averaging has increased our ability to detect electrical events that are time-locked to stimuli and responses. Thus, cortical evoked potentials to visual, auditory, and somesthetic stimuli have been recorded, as have potentials that precede a response. Certain potentials appear to correlate with expectancy of arousal (the contingent negative variation and the P300 potential). Others correspond to purely mental events, e.g., the nonoccurrence of an expected stimulus. The use of these techniques in behavioral research has been limited by our ignorance of the meaning of the various components of averaged responses and by technical difficulties. The conditions of the experiment must ensure that the stimulus (or the signal to respond) is temporally discrete and reproducible and that extraneous activity does not interfere with the recording of the response. Computers have also been used to trace the spatial and temporal spread of electrical activity associated with specific single events.

### SINGLE-UNIT RECORDING

Discrete activity of individual neurons can be recorded by inserting microelectrodes into the brain. Obviously, this is largely limited to animal experiments. Much has been learned (and remains to be learned) from the use of this technique in alert, responding animals. Responses to well-controlled stimuli can be recorded with precision and analyzed quantitatively. Interpretation of single-unit recording presents its own difficulties. The brain activity related to a behavioral event may occur simultaneously in many cells spatially dispersed over a considerable area. Recording from only one cell may not yield a meaningful pattern. In addition, single-unit recording may be difficult to analyze in relation to complex behaviors.

## Computational Models

The function of the brain is thought to depend principally upon the firing patterns of numerous highly interrelated neurons. This assumption has naturally led to the attempt to describe brain function in terms of computer function, but the typical serially organized computer has not fared well as a model for brain function. Recently, there has been great interest in the properties of computers that use multiple parallel processors arranged in a network (parallel distributed processors, or PDP networks) (see, for example, Rumelhart and McClelland, 1986). Such computers have interesting "brainlike" properties, including the ability, without further programming, to "learn" associations between coincident stimuli, to behave as if "rules" are learned despite being exposed only to data, and to continue to function in the face of damage to a portion of the network ("graceful degradation"). Properties of PDP networks are now often invoked to help explain the nature of neuropsychological deficits occasioned by brain injury, such as interlanguage differences in error rates in aphasics.

Although the brain is highly interconnected, it is not considered to function as a single network, but rather as a collection of many overlapping "modular" networks, each having a specific function. The function of a module depends upon its connections. One can therefore see that network theory can easily be reconciled with the traditional methods of localization of brain function discussed above. It remains to be seen if network theory will generate hypotheses that can lead to a better understanding of brain organization and function.

## ANIMAL VERSUS HUMAN EXPERIMENTATION

Many of the techniques mentioned above are either not applicable to humans or can be applied only with great difficulty. In detailed anatomical studies, for instance, discrete brain lesions are made and the whole brain is studied meticulously soon after the operation. Other anatomical methods entail the injection of substances into the brain. Advances in neurochemistry and neurophysiology, like those in neuroanatomy, rely heavily on animal work. Despite major differences in anatomy between even the subhuman primates and humans (Fig. 1-2), much of this basic research is of direct relevance to human neurobiology. Behavioral studies in animals have also yielded a great deal of information, but the applicability of this information to the study of complex human behavior is not clear-cut. In 1950, nothing in the literature on temporal-lobe lesions in animals would have led to the prediction that bilateral temporal lobectomy in humans would result in permanent impairment of memory; only recently, nearly 20 years after its demonstration in humans, have new testing paradigms demonstrated memory impairment in animals with bitemporal ablations (Mishkin, 1978). Conversely, the applicability of behavioral deficits in animals (and especially in nonhuman primates) to syndromes in humans has also recently been systematically investigated, and some parallels are discernible (Oscar-Berman et al., 1982). Studies of the limbic system and hypothalamus in animals have contributed important information about the relevance of these structures to emotional behavior; however, the emotional content of behavior is difficult to study in animals because they cannot report how they feel. Most obviously, animals cannot be used to study behavior that is uniquely human, such as language. Studies of nonlinguistic communication in animals may relate to some aspects of speech in humans but they do not elucidate the neural mechanisms underlying language. Studies of linguistic

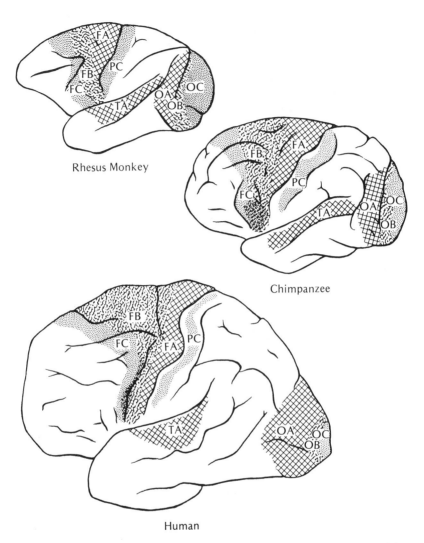

Rhesus Monkey

Chimpanzee

Human

**Fig. 1-2.** The primary motor (FA) and visual (OC) areas and the association areas of the motor, visual, somatosensory (PC), and auditory (TA) systems are compared in these lateral views of the hemispheres of the monkey, chimpanzee, and human. Note the expansion of the unshaded areas of cortex, particulary in the frontal lobe and in the area between TA and OA, as one progresses from monkey to human. The latter area is important for language development (see Chap. 2). The significance of the frontal lobes is discussed in Chap. 12.

behavior in primates are controversial, and their relevance to the study of language in humans remains unclear.

## CONCEPTUAL ANALYSIS

We hear that science proceeds by way of careful observation followed by analysis and then hypothesis on the basis of the observed data (a posteriori hypothesis). In fact, meaningful observations frequently cannot be made without some sort of a priori hypothesis. How else can one decide which observations to make? An observation can be significant only in terms of a conceptual framework.

Some investigators are loathe to put either a priori or posteriori hypotheses in print, feeling that they are too tentative. They report observations with a minimum of interpretation. This may be unfortunate because tentative hypotheses are the seeds of further observations and hypotheses. Other investigators speculate extensively on the basis of only a few observations. These speculations may lead to clearly stated hypotheses which generate further observations, but there is a risk that observations may be honestly and inadvertently distorted to fit the hypotheses. For example, investigators always discard "irrelevant" information either intentionally or not; however, an investigator with an alternative hypothesis may find observations presumed irrelevant by others to be of critical importance. It is important to deal with all hypotheses as though they were tentative so that, as Head (1926) warned, we do not invite observations to sleep in the Procrustean bed of our hypotheses.

We are too far from understanding brain-behavior relationships to be able to state hypotheses entirely without the use of metaphorical terms. Metaphor is not to be taken literally. Diagrams, for example, may be used in a metaphorical way to present a hypothesis. The diagrams found in this book are offered in this spirit: they are meant to be not pictures of the brain but sketches of hypotheses.

Similarly, when we speak of the function of different areas of the brain, it often appears that we assume that the area under discussion operates entirely independently from others. Clearly, this is true only to a limited extent. For the purposes of analysis, however, we must often ignore interactions between brain regions in order to discuss the distinguishing features of these areas. We do not deny that consideration of the brain as a functioning whole may at times be of equal value in explaining behavioral data, as it is in explaining the concept of diaschisis.

Thus, we support a flexible approach to the study of brain-behavior relationships. We know too little about the subject to limit our methods of investigation. We must be prepared to analyze data from many sources and make new hypotheses and test them with the best methods available. Similarly, behavioral testing and methods of treatment must be tailored to the individual situation. Inflexible test batteries, although necessary for obtaining normative data, limit our view of the nervous system if used exclusively. Rigid formulations of therapy similarly limit progress. Changes in testing and therapy, however, should be made not capriciously but rather according to our current understanding of brain-behavior relationships. In this book, therefore, we do not emphasize standardized tests or treatment batteries; instead, we present the existing knowledge on brain-behavior relationships, which should form the basis of diagnosis and treatment.

## REFERENCES

Bastian, H. C. (1869). On the various forms of loss of speech in cerebral disease. *Br. Foreign Medico-Surg. Rev. 43*:470–492.

Bouillaud, J. B. (1825). Récherches cliniques propres a démontrer que la perte de la parole correspond à la lésion de lobules anterieurs du cerveau, et à confirmer l'opinion de M. Gall sur le siege de l'organe du langage articulé. *Arch. Gen. Med. 8*:25–45.

Broca, P. (1865). Sur la faculté du langage articulé. *Bull. Soc. Anthropol. Paris 6*:337–393.

Caramazza, A. (1992). Is cognitive neuropsychology possible? *J. Cognitive Neurosci. 4*:80–95.

Chomsky, N. (1967). The general properties of language. In *Brain Mechanisms Underlying Speech and Language*, C. H. Millikan and F. L. Darley (eds.). New York: Grune and Stratton.

Geschwind, N. (1965). Disconnexion syndrome in animals and men. I and II. *Brain 88*:237–294, 585–644.

Head, H. (1926). *Aphasia and Kindred Disorders of Speech*. Cambridge: Cambridge University Press.

Lashley, K. S. (1938). Factors limiting recovery after central nervous lesions. *J. Nerv. Ment. Dis. 888*:733–755.

Lichtheim, L. (1885). On aphasia. *Brain 7*:433–484.

Mishkin, M. (1978). Memory in monkeys severely impaired by combined but not by separate removal of amygdala and hippocampus. *Nature 273*:297–298.

Oscar-Berman, M., Zola-Morgan, S. M., Oberg, R. G. E., and Bonner, R. T. (1982). Comparative neuropsychology and Korsakoff's syndrome. III: Delayed response, delayed alternation and DRL performance. *Neuropsychologia 20*:187–202.

Rumelhart, D. E., McClelland, J. L., and the PDP Research Group (1986). *Parallel Distributed Processing. Explorations in the Microstructure of Cognition*. Cambridge, Mass.: MIT Press.

Teuber, H. L. (1955). Physiological psychology. *Annu. Rev. Psychol. 6*:267–296.

Wernicke, C. (1874). *Des Aphasische Symptomenkomplex*. Breslau: Cohn and Weigart.

# 2

# Aphasia

D. FRANK BENSON

By definition, aphasia is the loss or impairment of language caused by brain damage; as such, it is a neurologic disorder. But language is involved, so aphasia is a linguistic disorder and, as language is a mental activity, it is also a psychological or, more acurately, a neuropsychological disorder. Further, language impairment demands specialized management so aphasia therapy becomes involved. Each discipline sees language impairment from its own viewpoint, and the result is a confusing nomenclature and a conflicting body of information. The characteristics of disordered language, however, are consistent. The terminology and approaches of neurology and neuropsychology will be used in this chapter.

Two key features of the definition of aphasia deserve emphasis. The first centers on the words "loss or impairment." Aphasia is an acquired disorder: a normally functioning psychological competence has been altered by damage to part of the brain. Failure to develop normal language is excluded from this definition; the term aphasia is not interchangeable with language retardation.

The second feature of the definition concerns the word language, which has diverse connotations. In this chapter language will refer to the symbol system used to exchange information. Table 2-1 presents five distinctly different types of language, each of which can be disordered in aphasia.

The first two, gestural and prosodic language, are relatively universal; they are present in most higher animals, and in humans they can be disordered by damage to either the right or the left hemisphere (Benson, 1985; Ross, 1981). The fifth type, pragmatics, refers to the complex combinations of language symbols needed to transmit complicated ideas and includes additional mental functions such as cognitive manipulation, memory, executive control, and visual imagery. Most descriptions of the disordered language that characterizes aphasia concentrate on semantic and syntactic functions. While it is possible to demonstrate that limited semantic functions can be carried out by the right hemisphere (Sperry and Gazzaniga, 1967; Zaidel, 1985), most semantic and almost all syntactic language functions are performed by the left hemisphere of most humans. It is these predominantly left-hemisphere functions of language that are impaired in aphasia.

17

**Table 2-1.** Language Types

| |
|---|
| Gestural language |
| Prosodic language |
| Semantic language |
| Syntactic language |
| Pragmatic language |

The concentration of two significant psychological functions, syntax and semantics, in the left hemisphere represents one of the more dramatic aspects of language. In no other animal species and in no other human function is hemispheric specialization as dramatic or nearly complete as is the unilateral concentration of language capability in the left hemisphere of the right-handed adult human. Most non-right-handed individuals also have a significant, usually major, portion of their language competency localized to their left hemisphere (Benson, 1985; Gloning et al., 1969; Goodglass and Quadfasel, 1954; Roberts, 1969). While either hemisphere can develop language if the other is damaged early in life—the equipotentiality described by Zangwill (1960)—with maturation most language functions develop in the left hemisphere in the vast majority of humans. Right/left anatomical differences have been proposed to explain the underlying asymmetry of language function (Geschwind and Levitsky, 1968; Scheibel, 1990; Yakovlev and Rakic, 1966). The anatomical differences are subtle, however, and the strong hemispheric specificity of language remains a biological mystery.

## HISTORY

Aphasia was born from a long-simmering debate over localized vs. holistic explanations of psychological functions in the brain and has rarely been free of controversy. The development of aphasiology can be divided into a significant prodrome plus three (and possibly more) major epochs. The four divisions are epitomized by four leading figures (Fig. 2-1), but it must be recognized that each is only a representative, a single individual who stands out among many contemporaries who were also active in the field.

The first major figure, Franz Joseph Gall (Gall and Spurzheim, 1810–1819), best known as the originator of the pseudoscience of phrenology (psychological interpretation through cranial mensuration), ardently espoused localization of mental function within various areas of the brain. Gall subdivided human actions into a number of distinct behaviors (propensities) and proposed separate cortical locations (organs) for each. His proposals (both the behaviors and their postulated anatomical loci) were strongly contested by contemporary scholars and scientists (Young, 1970/1990).

Following a half century of debate over the localization of behavioral propensities, Paul Broca, a Parisian surgeon, presented clinical cases in which focal brain damage was associated with disordered speech/language (Broca, 1861). These demonstrations led to widespread investigation of acquired language dysfunction, additional cases were reported, and aphasia, as a specific brain disorder, was born. Carl Wernicke,

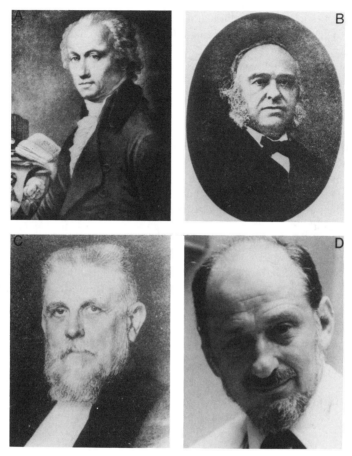

Fig. 2-1. Four individuals of influence in the understanding of aphasia. **A:** Franz Joseph Gall (1758–1828). **B:** Paul Broca (1824–1880). **C:** Pierre Marie (1853–1940). **D:** Norman Geschwind (1926–1984).

adding language comprehension defect to the picture (Wernicke, 1874, 1881), made a division of acquired language disorders that was developed into a theory of linguistic competence (Lichtheim, 1885). The Wernicke-Lichtheim model was followed by many other anatomically based theories of language function; for almost a half century, clinical/pathological correlations leading to new models of brain/language mechanisms appeared in the medical literature, a process that can be considered the first epoch of aphasia research.

Excesses in model making were obvious and the extreme localization schemes evoked strong reactions from many clinicians (Freud, 1891/1953; Jackson, 1868/1915), notably Pierre Marie (1906), who posited a single language function performed by the left hemisphere. Marie's holistic approach became increasingly popular and prevailed for the next half century, the second epoch in the history of aphasia. During this period, brain/language correlations including aphasia became of greater interest to linguists and clinical psychologists, and a new field, language therapy, began to develop. Neurologists and neuropsychologists had relatively little input or influence.

The third epoch, spearheaded by Norman Geschwind (1965), his colleagues, and a rapidly enlarging group of contemporary neurologists and psychologists, followed the original publications of Broca by almost exactly a century and featured rediscovery of the localization of individual language functions to restricted areas of the brain. At this same time, (the 1960s), the field of neuropsychology was undergoing tremendous growth which was related partly to the problem of disordered language. About a decade later, revolutionary technical advances in brain imaging allowed, for the first time, relatively precise localization of intracranial pathology in living subjects capable of performing sophisticated language tests. The improved capabilities of neurologic diagnosis gave both impetus and support to the newly invigorated localization approach.

During this same period linguists developed new models of language functions and used data from the new aphasia investigations to support their theories. In addition, the field of language rehabilitation surged, providing yet another focus for the study of language dysfunction. While controversy remains with us, the knowledge gained from these different approaches has proved complementary.

## ASSESSMENT OF APHASIA

Key to the differentiation of varieties of aphasia are the striking differences in language symptoms. The assessment of individual language functions consistently demonstrates characteristic impairments. Three different diagnostic approaches are currently popular.

Most aphasics undergo one or more formal aphasia assessment procedures, test batteries that feature a variety of interrelated language tests. Some attempt to be diagnostic—Boston Diagnostic Aphasia Examination (Goodglass and Kaplan, 1972), Neurosensory Center Comprehensive Examination for Aphasia (Spreen and Benton, 1969), Western Aphasia Battery (Kertesz, 1980), Aachener Aphasia Test (Huber et al., 1982). Others gauge the severity of the aphasic defect and probe for therapy avenues—Examination for Aphasia (Eisenson, 1954), Language Modalities Test for Aphasia (Wepman, 1961), Minnesota Test for the Differential Diagnosis of Aphasia (Schuell, 1957), Porch Index of Communicative Ability (Porch, 1967). Yet others look at residual functional capability—Functional Communication Profile (Taylor, 1965), Communicative Abilities in Daily Living (Holland, 1980). Each battery provides a replicable, usually numerical, score that categorizes the aphasic patient.

In addition, many tests have been developed to probe a single language function. Most were designed for research but many have proved sufficiently successful that they have been validated and are now used for assessment. Thus, the Token Test (DeRenzi and Vignolo, 1962), Boston Naming Test (Goodglass et al., 1976; Kaplan et al., 1978), and a number of word-fluency tests (Milner, 1964; Spreen and Benton, 1969) are used to supplement many assessment batteries, and many other research-oriented tests are used in selected instances. Techniques for the formal assessment of language disorders are continuously improving.

For the purposes of this chapter the third popular approach, the bedside testing of language competency, will be featured. This approach provides the diagnostic indicators for clinical/anatomical correlations used by neurologists and neuropsychologists.

## Conversational Speech

Disorder of verbal output is obvious in most aphasics. Jackson (1868/1915) described two varieties of aphasia—one with a sparse output (nonfluent) and the other with lots of words but many mistakes (fluent). Nonfluent aphasic output is sparse (under 50 words per minute), produced with considerable effort, poorly articulated, of short phrase length (often only a single word), has notable dysprosody (abnormal rhythm, melody, inflection, and timbre), and features a preferential use of substantive, meaningful words with a relative dearth of syntactically significant functor words (agrammatism). Fluent aphasic output is the opposite—many words, easily produced, well articulated, with normal phrase length and prosodic quality but a tendency to omit the meaningful, semantically significant words; the product is described as empty speech. In addition, paraphasia (substitution of phonemes or words) is excessive in some fluent aphasic output. Fluent paraphasic aphasic ouput is almost invariably linked to pathology located posterior to the fissure of Rolando, while nonfluent aphasia is strongly associated with pathology anterior to this region (Benson, 1967; Poeck et al., 1972; Wagenaar et al., 1975). Merely monitoring aphasic speech reveals an anterior/posterior separation of the left-hemisphere damage site.

## Repetition

Repetition is tested by requesting that the patient repeat digits and single-syllable words, increasing the complexity to multisyllablic words and to complex sentences and verbal sequences. Many aphasics have difficulty repeating but some show remarkably competent repetition, often better than their spontaneous speech. An anatomic correlation is possible. In general, aphasics with impaired repetition have pathology that involves the perisylvian region; when repetition ability is preserved, the perisylvian area is free of pathology. A strong, often mandatory, tendency to repeat (echolalia) almost always indicates an extrasylvian locus of pathology. In general, the extrasylvian areas involved in cases of aphasia without repetition defect lie in vascular border-zone (watershed) areas.

## Comprehension of Spoken Language

The aphasic's ability to comprehend often proves difficult to assess. Both bedside clinical examinations and standardized tests tend to be inadequate and may even produce misleading results. Four procedures are suggested for clinical evaluation: (1) *Conversation*—engaging the patient in ordinary conversation probes the patient's ability to understand the questions and commands presented by the examiner. While excellent as a screening device, the degree of impairment is routinely underestimated as many nonverbal cues are provided (e.g., tone of voice, facial or arm gesture, etc.). (2) *Commands*—a series of single to multistep commands challenges comprehension. Asking the patient to make a fist or clap the hands can be augmented by multistep sequential acts such as asking the patient to pick up a piece of paper, fold it in two, place it in an envelope, and place the envelope on a bedside stand. While such tests can be crudely quantified, apraxia and other motor disorders may cause failure not based on comprehension deficit. (3) *Yes/No*—a more elementary motor response mechanism that can use questions ranging from the obvious (e.g., "Is your name Jones?") to precise syntactical interpretations ("Are the lights turned off in this room?") that can be answered by yes or no. Unfortunately, some aphasics cannot control the yes/no response, producing incorrect verbal or gestural responses or perseverating the same answer for all questions. (4) *Pointing*—another relatively limited motor response is the request to point (point to nose, shoe, window, etc.). If the patient can be put into the set of pointing, single-word comprehension can be tested and, if successful, more difficult requests can be given ("point to the source of illumination in this room"; "point to a receptacle for the residuals of something that has burned"). Despite use of all methods, it is impossible to judge the comprehension competency of some aphasics. In general, however, some degree of comprehension can be demonstrated and, with this accomplished, the degree of comprehension defect gauged. The anatomical correlation of comprehension disturbance is complex with clinically distinct varieties of comprehension defect correlated with pathology involving distinctly different anatomical loci (Benson, 1979a; Luria, 1966).

### Word Finding

Almost every aphasic shows some difficulty in word finding (anomia). Testing should include the patient's ability to name objects, parts of objects, body parts, colors, and, if desired, geometrical figures, actions, mathematical symbols, etc. If the patient fails, a cue such as pronunciation of the initial phoneme of the word by the examiner or the use of an open-ended sentence (e.g., "You pound a nail with a _____.") can be offered. Failure to produce the name is the end point. In addition to standard confrontation naming tasks, attention to the patient's verbal ouput may reveal a lack of substantive words, a lengthy but empty verbal ouput that indicates a word-finding defect. A third, functionally different, naming assessment is the request to produce a list of words in a category suggested by the examiner (e.g., animals, U.S. cities, words beginning with the letter D, etc.).

Distinct differences in word-finding difficulty can be recognized and it is argued that these variations are anatomically based (Benson, 1979c; Luria, 1966). For basic aphasia evaluations, however, it is better to accept that anomia does not provide reliable localizing information (Benson and Geschwind, 1985).

### Reading and Writing

Tests of reading and writing are routinely performed in the bedside aphasia evaluation but, as they are discussed in subsequent chapters, they will not be outlined here.

Valuable localizing information concerning specialized language function can be obtained from these tests (see Chapters 3 and 4).

## SYNDROMES OF APHASIA

Numerous classifications of types of aphasia, based on psychological, linguistic, and philosophic postulates, severity rankings, or language therapy characteristics, have been proposed but all have proved limited. Since the time of Wernicke, clinicians have indulged themselves in the intellectual sport of separating varieties of aphasia on the basis of clusters of language symptoms. The multiple syndromes described over the years represent one of the more confusing aspects of the study of aphasia.

While investigator idiosyncrasy has produced some of the confusion, a basic problem involves misunderstanding of the meaning of the term syndrome. In medicine, a syndrome is a cluster of findings that will lead a physician to suspect the presence of a given disease process. Only the clinically naive would expect a syndrome to represent an invariably fixed grouping of findings. In aphasia, two cases with exactly similar language disorder features are rare. This variability can be interpreted negatively with the suggestion that the syndromes of aphasia lack sufficient validity for use in language research (Caramazza, 1984). Through a long and boisterous history, however, the syndrome descriptions of aphasia have remained relatively stable (Benson, 1988); only the names of the syndromes have been altered.

The syndrome classification originally proposed and developed in the nineteenth century has been replicated, indeed strongly supported, by the new brain-imaging techniques. The following section will describe the syndromes presented by Continental investigators of the nineteenth century and modified in the latter half of the twentieth century. Table 2-2 presents the major aphasic syndromes as clusters of language findings, associated neurological findings, and their most common neuroanatomical loci of pathology. An anatomical division (perisylvian/extrasylvian) is used, but the identical classification is present when a functional division (ability to repeat spoken language) is used.

### Perisylvian Aphasias

BROCA'S APHASIA

Patients with Broca's aphasia have a nonfluent aphasic output, relatively intact comprehension (failing only to understand syntactically crucial information), and disordered repetition which is not as severe as the difficulty in conversational expression. Naming is characteristically poor but is often aided by contextual or phonetic prompting. Several associated neurological features are noteworthy. Most patients with Broca's aphasia have a right hemiplegia and may have sensory loss or visual-field disturbance although these are less common. Ideomotor apraxia affecting the "good" left side is common (Benson and Geschwind, 1985; see Chapter 7).

Broca's aphasia was the first syndrome recognized and is broadly accepted as a specific type, although recent studies, both clinical and neuroimaging, suggest broad

**Table 2-2.** Aphasia Syndromes

| Syndrome | Verbal Output | Paraphasia | Repetition | Comprehension | Naming | Hemiparesis | Hemisensory Defect |
|---|---|---|---|---|---|---|---|
| Broca | Nonfluent | Rare—literal | Poor | Good | Poor | Common | Rare |
| Wernicke | Fluent | Common—mixed | Poor | Poor | Poor | Rare | Occasional |
| Conduction | Fluent | Common—literal | Poor | Good | Poor | Rare | Common |
| Global | Nonfluent | Common—mixed | Poor | Poor | Poor | Common | Common |
| Extrasylvian motor | Nonfluent | Rare | Good | Good | Poor | Occasional | Rare |
| Supplementary motor area | Nonfluent | Rare | Good | Good | Poor | Common/crural | Occasional |
| Extrasylvian sensory | Fluent | Common—mixed | Good | Poor | Poor | Occasional | Common |
| Mixed Extrasylvian | Nonfluent | Rare | Good | Poor | Poor | Common | Common |
| Anomic | Fluent | Rare | Good | Good | Poor | Rare | Rare |
| Subcortical | Fluent or nonfluent | Common | Good | Variable | Poor | Common | Common |

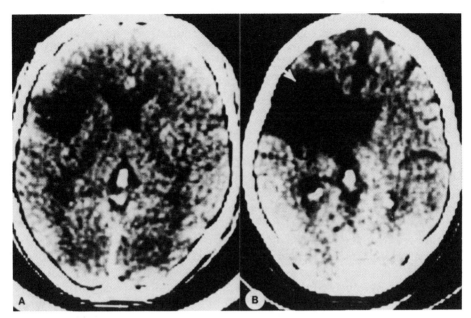

**Fig. 2-2.** CT scans illustrating the larger, deeper lesion producing big Broca's aphasia (**B**) compared to the smaller lesion of little Broca's aphasia (**A**). *Source:* Stuss, D. T., and Benson, D. F. (1986). *The Frontal Lobes.* New York: Raven Press, p. 166, Figure 11-1. Reprinted with permission of the publisher.

variations in the language disorder. The most clinically significant difference can be presented as a simple dichotomy—big Broca's aphasia and little Broca's aphasia. Big Broca's aphasia routinely presents as a severe total aphasia with hemiplegia and slowly improves to eventually produce the syndrome of Broca's aphasia described above. In contrast, little Broca's aphasia starts with the clinical picture of Broca's aphasia and over time improves to a language disorder featuring hesitant output and mild agrammatism. By tradition, Broca's aphasia indicates damage to the dominant hemisphere's frontal opercular region. It is now understood, however, that persistence of the Broca's aphasia language features demands an additional deep-lying lesion, usually involving basal ganglia (Alexander et al., 1989; Mohr, 1973), while the Broca's aphasia that rapidly improves is associated with lesions involving the frontal operculum but not extending as deep (see Fig. 2-2). Correlation of individual clinical features with imaging techniques demonstrates that the Broca's aphasia syndrome can be further subdivided to produce a more exact clinical/structural correlation (Alexander et al., 1989) but the overall picture of Broca's aphasia remains a useful clinical signpost.

WERNICKE'S APHASIA

The language impairment described by Wernicke was dramatically different from Broca's aphasia and is now termed Wernicke's aphasia. The verbal ouput is fluent,

almost always contaminated with paraphasia and neologisms. The key language finding of Wernicke's aphasia, however, is the striking disturbance in comprehension and
a matched disorder of repetition. While considerable variation in the degree of
impairment can be demonstrated, the comprehension and repetition disorders run
parallel. Naming is almost invariably disturbed and, in contrast to Broca's aphasia,
prompting (contextual or phonetic) is rarely helpful.

Two varieties of comprehension defect are described (Hécaen and Albert, 1978;
Hier and Mohr, 1977). In one variety, the ability to comprehend spoken language is
considerably worse than the ability to comprehend written language (predominantly
word deaf), whereas in the other the opposite is true (predominantly word blind).
Wernicke's aphasia features some combination of the two.

Unlike patients with Broca's aphasia, many individuals with Wernicke's aphasia
have no apparent physical or elementary neurologic disability. A superior quadran-
topsia is of localizing significance but may be absent or overlooked. The patient with
severe jargon (verbose, senseless output with copious paraphasic intrusions), poor ability to interrelate, and no obvious basic neurologic defect may be considered psychotic.

The pathology in most cases of Wernicke's aphasia involves the dominant temporal
lobe, particularly the auditory association cortex of the posterior-superior portion of
the first temporal gyrus. When word deafness overshadows word blindness, the
pathology tends to be deeper in the first temporal gyrus involving Heschl's gyrus or
its connections. Predominance of word blindness suggests greater involvement of the
contiguous parietal cortex (primarily angular gyrus), but for most right-handed individuals the presence of Wernicke's aphasia indicates pathology in the left temporal
lobe (Fig. 2-3).

CONDUCTION APHASIA

The third type of perisylvian aphasia, conduction aphasia, features a fluent, paraphasic output (literal paraphasia—primarily substitution of phonemes or syllables),
relatively normal comprehension of spoken language, and a comparatively severe
breakdown in repetition. This disorder is clearly different from Wernicke's aphasia
in that comprehension is much better than repetition and differs from Broca's aphasia
in that the verbal ouput is fluent. Naming is almost always abnormal in conduction
aphasia but the problem tends to be caused by paraphasic contamination. Ideomotor
apraxia that involves buccofacial and limb activities is a common but not constant
finding (Benson et al., 1973; see Chapter 7).

The pathology underlying conduction aphasia most often involves white matter
immediately beneath the supramarginal gyrus (Fig. 2-4). It has been postulated that
the lesion separates (disconnects) the intact language comprehension area from an
equally intact motor speech area (Damasio and Damasio, 1980; Geschwind, 1965;
Mendez and Benson, 1985). Cases with the features of conduction aphasia may, however, have lesions outside this area—left temporal cortex, left parietal cortex, left
white matter lesions, and even right white matter lesions (Benson et al., 1973; Mendez
and Benson, 1985). While there is disagreement concerning the mechanism (Damasio
and Damasio, 1980; Green and Howes, 1977; Hécaen and Albert, 1978), the language

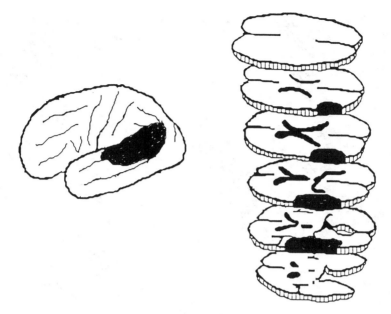

**Fig. 2-3.** Graphic illustration of the left temporal lobe location of structural damage in cases of Wernicke's aphasia. *Source:* Alexander, M. P., and Benson, D. F. (1992). The aphasias and related disturbances. In *Clinical Neurology*, R. J. Joynt (ed.). Philadelphia: Lippincott, Chap. 10, in press. Reprinted with permission of the publisher.

characteristics of conduction aphasia remain consistent and in most instances indicate pathology in the posterior perisylvian region of the dominant hemisphere.

GLOBAL APHASIA

Aphasia in which dysfunction involves all aspects of language is called global or total aphasia. By definition, global aphasia includes a severe nonfluent output, equally severe disruption of comprehension, and little or no ability to repeat. Reading and writing competencies are also disturbed. The degree of language loss and the localization of causative pathology may vary considerably, however. The most common occurrence is a middle cerebral artery territory infarction involving much of the perisylvian language region. Rare cases are reported, however, with a global language disorder but little or no paresis; most often these cases reflect smaller, strategically placed lesions that involve the Broca's and Wernicke's areas (Legatt et al., 1987; Tranel et al., 1987).

### Extrasylvian Aphasias

Aphasia based on damage to dominant-hemisphere extrasylvian territory is characterized by the patient's relatively intact ability to repeat spoken language. Although most extrasylvian aphasias are due to border-zone vascular insufficiency or infarct,

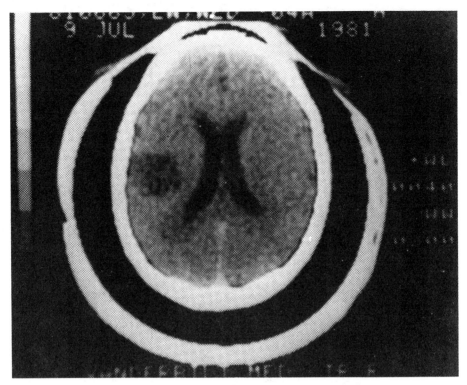

**Fig. 2-4.** CT scan depicting left anterior-inferior parietal structural lesion in a case of conduction aphasia. *Source:* Kirshner, H. S. (1986). *Behavioral Neurology.* New York: Churchill Livingstone, p. 28, Figure 3.6. Reprinted with permission of the publisher.

they may also be caused by tumor, hematoma, and infection. The aphasia of degenerative brain disease, particularly Alzheimer's disease, often fits the extrasylvian pattern (Cummings et al., 1985). The extrasylvian aphasias have been called transcortical aphasia (Goldstein, 1917), based on nineteenth-century postulation of language mechanisms. The theory was discarded but the transcortical terminology remains in the literature.

EXTRASYLVIAN MOTOR APHASIA

Extrasylvian (transcortical) motor aphasia is characterized by a nonfluent verbal ouput except for a considerable ability to echo. Comprehension is relatively well preserved, as is repetition of spoken language. In most cases pathology is located in the frontal/prefrontal regions of the dominant hemisphere, anterior or superior to Broca's area (Fig. 2-5). It is contended that extrasylvian motor aphasia is the result of a separation of the pathways that connect the supplementary motor area with Broca's area (Freedman et al., 1984).

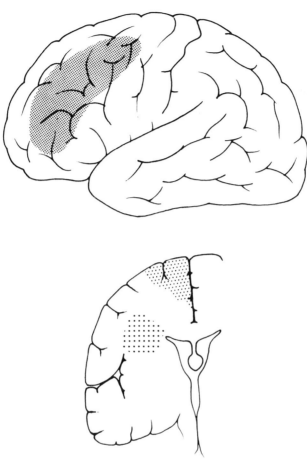

**Fig. 2-5.** Illustration of lesion location in cases of extrasylvian motor aphasia (dorsal convexity and underlying area) and supplementary motor area aphasia (medial frontal structures). *Source:* Stuss, D. T., and Benson, D. F. (1986). *The Frontal Lobes.* New York: Raven Press, p. 166, Figure 11-3. Reprinted with permission of the publisher.

SUPPLEMENTARY MOTOR AREA APHASIA

A language pattern that is basically identical to the extraylvian motor aphasia syndrome (nonfluent verbal output with echolalia, relatively good comprehension and repetition) can be produced by damage to the dominant-hemisphere medial frontal structures (cingulate cortex and supplementary motor area) (Fig. 2-5). Following an initial mutism, patients with this disturbance develop a slow, hypophonic output that improves considerably with repetition. Unlike the patient with extrasylvian motor aphasia, those with supplementary motor area aphasia have a characteristic neurologic disturbance with weakness of the right lower extremity and shoulder but relatively normal strength in the arm and face. A similar pattern of sensory disturbance may or may not be present (Alexander et al., 1989; Damasio and Van Hoesen, 1983).

EXTRASYLVIAN SENSORY APHASIA

Extrasylvian sensory aphasia is a distinct variant that features a fluent, paraphasic output, significant disturbance of comprehension, but intact repetition. These subjects can accurately repeat words that they cannot understand. Echolalia is common. Naming, reading, and writing are usually seriously deficient. The pathology underlying extrasylvian sensory aphasia is most often located in the parietal and temporal areas, posterior to the perisylvian region. Accompanying neurologic findings vary, depending upon the location and depth of the causative lesion. The jargon output coupled with a good ability to repeat suggests difficulty with reality testing (psychosis), and many individuals with extrasylvian sensory aphasia have been mislabeled as schizophrenic.

MIXED EXTRASYLVIAN APHASIA

Mixed extrasylvian aphasia has also been called isolation of the speech area and mixed transcortical aphasia (Geschwind et al., 1968; Goldstein, 1948). It is a combination of the motor and sensory varieties of extrasylvian aphasia with the patient presenting global aphasic features except for preserved ability to repeat spoken language. Both anterior and posterior border-zone cortical areas are involved. While border-zone pathology is rare in pure form, individuals with acute left internal carotid occlusion or the residuals of severe cerebral edema or prolonged hypoxia may show the mixed extrasylvian language pattern. Basic neurologic defects are often present but are not consistent. The striking feature is the relatively preserved ability to repeat spoken language when no other language function appears competent.

ANOMIC APHASIA

Almost all aphasics have some degree of word-finding difficulty and, for some, anomia is the only significant language disturbance. These individuals will have a fluent output, little or no paraphasia, relatively normal ability to comprehend, and excellent ability to repeat. The notable deficiency is demonstrated by tests of naming ability. Patients with anomic aphasia tend to produce lengthy but empty verbal output and they often try to substitute (circumlocute) for the words that they cannot produce. If anomic aphasia is accompanied by alexia and agraphia plus Gerstmann's syndrome (right-left disorientation, finger agnosia, acalculia, agraphia), the pathology almost invariably involves the dominant angular gyrus. Anomia by itself, however, may result from pathology almost anywhere in the language area and can even be seen in some cases of right-hemisphere disorder (Benson, 1979c).

SUBCORTICAL APHASIA

With the advent of brain imaging, particularly computerized tomography (CT), cases that previously were difficult to characterize were found to have pathology affecting subcortical structures, particularly the basal ganglia and the thalamus (Alexander and LoVerme, 1980; Cappa and Vignolo, 1979; Damasio et al., 1982). Considerable variation is seen in the clinical picture, dependent upon the specific subcortical structures involved (Alexander and Benson, 1992), but several general characteristics help define the entity. First, with an acute onset of subcortical aphasia, the patient is almost always mute, recovering slowly to a hypophonic, slow, and poorly articulated (mushy) output. In addition, the output is contaminated with paraphasias which, uncharacteristically, disappear when the patient is asked to repeat spoken language. Most other language features vary, dependent upon the site of subcortical pathology. There is a strong tendency for subcortical aphasia to disappear, and this transient nature can be accepted as a major diagnostic characteristic. If, however, the causative lesion also involves language cortex, a common situation, recovery will be incomplete.

## Disturbances of a Single Language Modality

There are three clearly defined language disorders in which only a single modality is affected. The most dramatic of these, alexia without agraphia, will be discussed in Chapter 3. Two others—aphemia and pure word-deafness—deserve mention here.

### APHEMIA

This disorder, also known as pure word dumbness, or anarthria, usually starts with mutism and recovers to a hypophonic, slow, but grammatically intact verbal output. During the entire course, comprehension of spoken language and the ability to read and write are preserved. Neither agrammatism nor anomia are noted in the written output and the patient rapidly learns to communicate with written language. There may be no major neurologic disabilities, but ideomotor apraxia, particularly affecting buccofacial movements, is often present. The pathology is located in or immediately inferior to Broca's area in the dominant hemisphere (Alexander et al., 1989; Bastian, 1898; Schiff et al., 1983). With recovery, a consistent disorder of prosody (dysprosody) (Monrad-Krohn, 1947) can produce a "foreign accent syndrome," a disorder of rhythm, inflection, and articulation suggesting another language. Aphemia is differentiated from little Broca's aphasia by the absence of agrammatism in the spoken and written output of the aphemic patient.

### PURE WORD DEAFNESS

When the reception of spoken language is the only language function involved, the syndrome is called pure word deafness. Individuals with pure word deafness do not understand spoken language and cannot repeat. They do have, however, adequate hearing and easily identify nonverbal sounds such as a whistle, telephone ring, etc. Verbal output is often normal although paraphasia may be present in the early stage. While these patients do not understand spoken language, their reading is intact and they soon learn to carry a writing tablet for others to use. Two loci of pathology have been demonstrated (Weisenburg and McBride, 1933/1964); about half have a single lesion deep in the dominant superior temporal region damaging the primary auditory cortex and/or the pathways to it from the medial geniculate nucleus. Other cases with the same syndrome, however, show bilateral pathology, most often involving the mid-portion of the superior temporal gyrus of both hemispheres (Auerbach et al., 1982). Not quite pure cases of word deafness are common and can be considered variants of Wernicke's aphasia. The differentiating factor between "pure" and "not quite pure" word deafness is measured by competence in comprehending written language.

## NEUROBEHAVIORAL COMPLICATIONS OF APHASIA

Aphasia almost never occurs in isolation and the complicating behavioral problems not only obscure the language disorder but are of considerable significance in management and rehabilitation. Many of the complicating factors are discussed in subsequent chapters of this volume and will merely be listed here.

Motor and sensory impairments are frequent following brain damage that is sufficient to produce aphasia; paresis and sensory impairment are often amenable to appropriate therapy techniques but are the source of major problems for many aphasics. Visual-field disturbance is a potential complicating factor, and, of considerable importance, a unilateral attention deficit (see Chapter 10) can prove troublesome for therapy measures.

Verbal output abnormalities (speech disorders) such as mutism, dysarthria, stuttering, scanning speech, and palilalia are fairly common complications. To a greater or lesser degree, these disorders can be affected by appropriate speech therapy techniques. Nonetheless, they often cause permanent disability and greatly hinder language therapy efforts. More general disturbances such as confusion, amnesia, dementia, and pseudobulbar palsy are also important as they curtail rehabilitation efforts. More specific behavioral disturbances such as sensory agnosia (visual, auditory, tactile) and motor apraxia may be associated with selected types of aphasia; they are often unnoted or, worse, misinterpreted as willful (hysteric) symptoms.

The combination of any of the above difficulties with a significant aphasia produces a complex and confusing clinical picture that may obscure both the behavioral disturbance and the specific type of aphasia. Awareness of the potential neurobehavioral complications is of great importance to the therapist formulating a therapeutic approach and gauging prognosis.

## REHABILITATION OF APHASIA

Starting with the experience gained during and following World War II, language therapy has developed into a robust formal academic activity. The value of the therapy techniques is not entirely clear, however; many neurologists have contended that aphasia therapy was successful only during the period of spontaneous recovery, a statement that has never been fully disproved (Benson, 1979b). There is, however, fairly strong, albeit not statistically proven, evidence that aphasia therapy does produce worthwhile improvement in language function (Basso et al., 1979; Wertz et al., 1981). Almost all aphasics deserve consideration for language therapy and many will benefit.

## Spontaneous Recovery

A number of investigators have charted the course of spontaneous recovery following the onset of aphasia and have demonstrated reasonably consistent findings. Most agree with Darley et al. (1975), who found that considerable spontaneous recovery occurred in the first month following onset, with ongoing improvement of a lesser degree continuing for several more months. Beyond this, spontaneous recovery was so limited that any notable improvement could be credited to language therapy. Many factors underlie the degree and rapidity of recovery of aphasia. These include the age of the subject (older subjects tend to recover less), type and size of lesion (hemorrhage recovers better than infarction; glioma has a poor prognosis), general health, the presence of complicating neurobehavior factors, etc. Although spontaneous recovery of some degree of language skill is common and may be substantial, most clinicians now agree that language therapy is helpful for most aphasics. The value of early intervention remains uncertain, however.

## Language Therapy

Despite a half century of development, the techniques of aphasia therapy remain remarkably inconsistent. Not only are there distinctly different schools of aphasia therapy but a plethora of specialized techniques exist, gross variations in individual therapist's techniques and competencies are seen, and, most important of all, each aphasic patient has a different problem. In general, rehabilitation techniques to improve verbal output have been more successful than attempts to improve comprehension. On the other hand, the spontaneous recovery of comprehension is considerably greater than that of verbal output. Specialized techniques to improve grammar, naming, reading, writing, articulation, speech melody, use of syntactical structures, etc., are available. The effectiveness of any individual treatment modality remains clouded, however, as blinded studies are literally impossible to perform, and as each aphasic is different, the aphasia therapy program must be modified accordingly. Recovery of language function is rarely complete (the patient will be aware of problems even if the observer is not) and may be severely limited, but any improvement in the ability to communicate is of consequence.

Although frequently overlooked, one of the most significant aspects of aphasia therapy concerns the dedicated interest of a knowledgeable therapist in the treatment of a patient with a devastating and poorly understood impairment. Most aphasics are understandably upset with the sudden loss of one of the most basic of intellectual functions (language); the psychological support provided by the therapist ranks among the strongest weapons in the rehabilitation armamentarium.

## REFERENCES

Alexander, M. P., and Benson, D. F. (1992). The aphasias and related disturbances. In *Clinical Neurology*, R. J. Joynt (ed.). Philadelphia: Lippincott. Volume I (Chap. 10), pp. 1–58.
Alexander M. P., Benson, D. F., and Stuss, D. T. (1989). Frontal lobes and language. *Brain Lang.* 37:656–691.

Alexander, M. P., and LoVerme, S., Jr. (1980). Aphasia after left hemispheric intracerebral hemorrhage. *Neurology* 30:1193–1202.

Auerbach, S. H., Alland, T., Naeser, M., Alexander, M. P., and Albert, M. L. (1982). Pure word deafness: analysis of a case with bilateral lesions and a defect at the prephonemic level. *Brain* 105:271–300.

Basso, A., Capitani, E., and Vignolo, L. A. (1979). Influence of rehabilitation on language skills in aphasia patients. *Arch. Neurol.* 36:190–195.

Bastian, H. C. (1898). *Aphasia and Other Speech Defects.* London: H. K. Lewis.

Benson, D. F. (1967). Fluency in aphasia: correlation with radioactive scan localization. *Cortex* 3:373–394.

Benson, D. F. (1979a). *Aphasia, Alexia, and Agraphia.* New York: Churchill Livingstone.

Benson, D. F. (1979b). Aphasia rehabilitation. *Arch. Neurol.* 36:187–189.

Benson, D. F. (1979c). Neurologic correlates of anomia. In *Studies in Neurolinguistics*, Vol. 4, H. Whitaker and H. A. Whitaker (eds.). New York: Academic Press, pp. 293–328.

Benson, D. F. (1985). Language in the left hemisphere. In *The Dual Brain*, D. F. Benson and E. Zaidel (eds.). New York: Guildford Press, pp. 193–203.

Benson, D. F. (1988). Classical syndromes of aphasia. In *Handbook of Neuropsychology*, Vol. 1, F. Boller and J. Grafman (eds.). Amsterdam: Elsevier, pp. 267–280.

Benson, D. F. and Geschwind, N. (1985). The aphasias and related disturbances. In *Clinical Neurology*, Vol. 1., A. B. Baker and R. J. Joynt (eds.). Philadelphia: Harper and Row.

Benson, D. F., Sheremata, W. A., Buchard, R., Segarra, J., Price, D., and Geschwind, N. (1973). Conduction aphasia. *Arch. Neurol.* 28:339–346.

Broca, P. (1861). Remarques sur le siège de la faculté du langage articulé, suivies d'une observation d'aphemie. *Bull. Soc. Anat. Paris* 2:330–357.

Cappa, S. F., and Vignolo, L. A. (1979). "Transcortical" features of aphasia following left thalamic hemorrhage. *Cortex* 15:121–130.

Caramazza, A. (1984). The logic of neuropsychological research and the problem of patient classification in aphasia. *Brain Lang.* 21:9–20.

Cummings, J. L., Benson, D. F., Hill, M. A., and Read, S. (1985). Aphasia in dementia of the Alzheimer type. *Neurology* 35:394–397.

Damasio, A. R., Damasio, H., Rizzo, M., Varney, N., and Gersh, F. (1982). Aphasia with non-hemorrhagic lesions in the basal ganglia and internal capsule. *Arch. Neurol.* 39:15–20.

Damasio, A. R., and Van Hoesen, G. W. (1983). Emotional disorders associated with focal lesions of the limbic frontal lobe. In *Neuropsychology of Human Emotion*, K. M. Heilman and P. Satz (eds.). New York: Guilford Press, pp. 85-110.

Damasio, H., and Damasio A. (1980). The anatomical basis of conduction aphasia. *Brain* 103:337–350.

Darley, F. L., Aronson, A. E., and Brown, J. R. (1975). *Motor Speech Disorders.* Philadelphia: Saunders.

DeRenzi, E., and Vignolo, L. A. (1962). The token test: a sensitive test to detect receptive disturbances in aphasics. *Brain* 85:665–678.

Eisenson, J. (1954). *Examining for Aphasia.* New York: Psychological Corp.

Freedman, M., Alexander, M. P., and Naeser, M. A. (1984). The anatomical basis of transcortical motor aphasia. *Neurology* 34:409–417.

Freud, S. (1891/1953). *On Aphasia*, E. Stengl (trans.). New York: International Universities Press.

Gall, F., and Spurzheim, G. (1810–1819). *The Anatomy and Physiology of the Nervous System in General and the Brain in Particular*, Vols. 1–4. Paris: F. Schoell.

Geschwind, N. (1965). Disconnexion syndromes in animals and man. *Brain* 88:237–294, 585–644.

Geschwind, N., and Levitsky, W. (1968). Human brain: left-right asymmetries in temporal speech region. *Science 161*:186–187.

Geschwind, N., Quadfasel, F. A., and Segarra, J. (1968). Isolation of the speech area. *Neuropsychologia 6*:327–340.

Gloning, I., Gloning, K., Haub, G., and Quatember, R. (1969). Comparison of verbal behavior in right-handed and non right-handed patients with anatomically verified lesion of one hemisphere. *Cortex 5*:43–52.

Goldstein, K. (1917). *Die Transkortikalen Aphasien.* Jena: Gustav Fischer.

Goldstein, K. (1948). *Language and Language Disturbances.* New York: Grune and Stratton.

Goodglass, H., and Kaplan, E. (1972). *The Assessment of Aphasia and Related Disorders.* Philadelphia: Lea and Febiger.

Goodglass, H., Kaplan, E., and Weintraub, S. (1976). *Boston Naming Test, Experimental Edition.* Boston: Boston VA Hospital.

Goodglass, H., and Quadfasel, F. (1954). Language laterality in left-handed aphasics. *Brain 77*:521–548.

Green, E., and Howes, D. (1977). Conduction aphasia. In *Studies in Neurolinguistics*, Vol. 3, H. Whitaker and H. A. Whitaker (eds.). New York: Academic Press, pp. 123–156.

Hécaen, H., and Albert, M. L. (1978). *Human Neuropsychology.* New York: Wiley, 1978.

Hier, D. B., and Mohr, J. P. (1977). Incongruous oral and written naming: evidence for a subdivision of the syndromes of Wernicke's aphasia. *Brain Lang. 4*:115–126.

Holland, A. L. (1980). *Communicative Abilities in Daily Living.* Baltimore: University Park Press.

Huber, W., Poeck, K., Weniger, D., and Willmer, K. (1982). *Der Aachener Aphasie Test.* Gottingen: Hogrefe.

Jackson, J. H. (1868). On the physiology of language. *Med. Times Gazette II*:275. (Reprinted in *Brain 38*:59–64, 1915.)

Kaplan, E. F., Goodglass, H., and Weintraub, S. (1978). *The Boston Naming Test.* Philadelphia: Lea and Febiger.

Kertesz, A. (1980). *Western Aphasia Battery.* London, Ontario: University of Western Ontario Press.

Kirshner, H. (1986). *Behavioral Neurology.* New York: Churchill Livingstone.

Legatt, A. D., Rubin, M. J., Kaplan, L. R., Healton, E. B., and Brust J.C.M. (1987). Global aphasia without hemiparesis: multiple etiologies. *Neurology 37*:201–205.

Lichtheim, L. (1885). On aphasia. *Brain 7*:434–484.

Luria, A. R. (1966). *Higher Cortical Functions in Man.* New York: Basic Books.

Marie, P. (1906). Revision de la question de l'aphasie: la troisième circonvolution frontale gauche ne joue aucun rôle special dans la fonction du langage. *Sem. Med. 26*:241–247.

Mendez, M. F., and Benson, D. F. (1985). Atypical conduction aphasia—a disconnection syndrome. *Arch. Neurol. 42*:886–891.

Milner, B. (1964). Some effects of frontal lobectomy in man. In *The Frontal Granular Cortex and Behavior*, J. M. Warren and K. Akert (eds.). New York: McGraw-Hill, pp. 313–334.

Mohr, J. P. (1973). Rapid amelioration of motor aphasia. *Arch. Neurol. 28*:77–82.

Monrad-Krohn, G. H. (1947). Dysprosody or altered melody of langauge. *Brain 70*:405–415.

Poeck, K., Kerschensteiner, M., and Hartje, W. (1972). A qualitative study on language understanding in fluent and non-fluent aphasia. *Cortex 8*:299–304.

Porch, B. E. (1967). *Porch Index of Communicative Ability.* Palo Alto, Calif.: Consulting Psychologists Press.

Roberts, L. (1969). Aphasia, apraxia and agnosia in abnornal states of cerebral dominance. In *Handbook of Clinical Neurology*, Vol. 4, P. J. Vinken and G. W. Bruyn (eds.). Amsterdam: North Holland, pp. 312–326.

Ross, E. D. (1981). The aprosodias. *Arch. Neurol. 38*:561–569.

Scheibel, A. B. (1990). Dendritic correlates of higher cognitive function. In *Neurobiology of Higher Cognitive Function*, A. B. Scheibel and A. Wechsler (eds.). New York: Guilford Press, pp. 239–270.

Schiff, H. B., Alexander, M. P., Naeser, M. A., and Galaburda, A. M. (1983). Aphemia. *Arch. Neurol. 40*:720–727.

Schuell, H. (1957). *Minnesota Test for the Differential Diagnosis of Aphasia.* Minneapolis: University of Minnesota Press.

Sperry, R. W., and Gazzaniga, M. S. (1967). Language following surgical disconnection of the hemispheres. In *Brain Mechanisms Underlying Speech and Language*, F. L. Darley (ed.). New York: Grune and Stratton, pp. 108–121.

Spreen, O., and Benton, A. (1969). *Neurosensory Center Comprehensive Examination for Aphasia.* Victoria: University of Victoria Neuropsychology Laboratory.

Stuss, D. T., and Benson, D. F. (1986). *The Frontal Lobes.* New York: Raven Press.

Taylor, M. L. (1965). A measurement of functional communication in aphasia. *Arch. Phys. Med. Rehabil. 46*:101–107.

Tranel, D., Biller, J., Damasio, H., Adams, H. P., and Cornell, S. (1987). Global aphasia without hemiparesis. *Arch. Neurol. 44*:304–308.

Wagenaar, E., Snow, C., and Prins, R. (1975). Spontaneous speech of aphasia patients: a psycholinguistic analysis. *Brain Lang. 2*:281–303.

Weisenburg, T. S., and McBride, K. L. (1933/1964). *Aphasia.* New York: Hafner Publishing Co.

Wepman, J. (1961). *Language Modalities Test for Aphasia.* Chicago: Education Industry Service.

Wernicke, C. (1874). *Das Aphasiche Symptomenkomplex.* Breslau: Cohn and Weigart.

Wernicke, C. (1881). *Lehrbuch der Gehirnkrankheiten. Band I. Tragweite der Aphasie fur das Verstandniss der Tindenfunctionen.* Kassel and Berlin: Theodor Fischer.

Wertz, R. T., Collins, M. J., Weiss, D., Kurtzke, J. F., Friden, T., Brookshire, R. H., Pierce, J., Holtzapple, P., Hubbard, D. J., Porch, B. E., West, J. A., Davis, L., Matovich, V., Morley, G. K., and Resurrection, E. (1981). Veterans Administration cooperative study on aphasia: a comparison of individual and group treatment. *J. Speech Hear. Res. 24*:580–594.

Yakovlev, P. I., and Rakic, P. (1966). Patterns of decussation of bulbar pyramids and distribution of pyramidal tracts on two sides of the spinal cord. *Trans. Am. Neurol. Assoc. 91*:366–367.

Young, R. M. (1970/1990). *Mind, Brain and Adaptation in the Nineteenth Century.* New York: Oxford University Press.

Zaidel, E. (1985). Language in the right hemisphere. In *The Dual Brain*, D. F. Benson and E. Zaidel (eds.). New York: Guilford Press, pp. 205–231.

Zangwill, O. L. (1960). *Cerebral Dominance and Its Relation to Psychological Function.* Springfield, Ill.: Charles C. Thomas.

# 3

# Alexia

RHONDA F. FRIEDMAN, JON ERIK WEEN, AND MARTIN L. ALBERT

Since the last edition of this text, we have witnessed an explosion of interest in acquired disorders of reading. In particular, cognitive and computational theories have added new dimensions to the field. This chapter will review the alexias in the context of a comprehensive model for reading, influenced by cognitive and computational theories. We refer readers to the previous edition of this book and to Friedman (1988) for historical detail and discussions of old controversies. We begin with only a brief historical review to illustrate the emergence of the concept of parallel distributed processing. A summary of our own reading model follows. On the basis of this background, we then provide a neuropsychological account of alexic disorders, together with discussions of clinical assessment, followed by a brief section on therapy.

## HISTORICAL BACKGROUND

Success at providing a coherent explanation of neuropsychological phenomena depends on the adequacy of the underlying theoretical assumptions. Progress in understanding human cognition has depended on continuous refinement of, and challenge to, prior assumptions. For reading disorders the process of refinement and challenge probably began near the end of the nineteenth century when Broca and Wernicke rescued the concept of cerebral localization from the functional holist's derision following the phrenology debacle. Their clinico-anatomical correlations set the stage for Dejerine (1891) to relate reading disorders to a brain-language model consistent with emerging concepts of associationism (see Churchland, 1986, or Gardner, 1985, for excellent discussions).

Various terms were used to label the reading problems observed, based in large measure on associated symptoms, such as alexia with agraphia, etc., indicating that nearby functional centers were also affected. Dejerine's early classification of alexia involved two categories: alexia with and without agraphia. Alternatively, an anatomical bias resulted in such terms as cortical or subcortical alexia (alluded to by Wernicke; 1874). Hinshelwood (1900) raised the issue of whether the alexia involved purely letters or purely words (later dubbed literal and verbal alexia). With Misch and Frankl's (1929) introduction of the terms agnosic and aphasic alexia, a perspective was gained which allowed the separation of alexia due to afferent, visual defects from reading problems linked to disorders of language processing. The issue of discrete processors and their white matter connection pathways came to the fore with the reassertion by Geschwind (1962, 1965) of the associationist theory of brain function.

From the neuropsychological perspective, it had become apparent that reading was not a unitary process, as brain-damaged patients were observed to make a variety of error types in reading. The rise of cognitive neuropsychology in the 1960s and 1970s was a natural outgrowth of the information-processing models gaining eminence in cognitive psychology. Models of reading now contained component processes (e.g., orthographic lexicon, phonologic lexicon) that were linked to each other in a serial fashion. How the discrete processing areas of the brain carried out their specialized function from a computational point of view, however, remained unclear. The search for models that could give computationally sound and testable explanations of reading and alexia was aided by the expansion of cognitive science, with multidisciplinary contributions from neuropsychology, neurology, artificial intelligence, philosophy, and linguistics. This led to a shift away from serial models of brain function, back to models with a more holistic flavor. The result is that parallel distributed processing models (McClelland and Rumelhart, 1986; Rumelhart and McClelland, 1986; Mesulam, 1990) have become strong competitors of the more traditional, serial processing models.

### Parallel Distributed Processing

Most traditional models of brain function assume a serial transfer of information from one region of the brain to another. For example, in reading a single word, the product of the process of visual analysis is passed on to the orthographic lexicon, where the letter string is matched with the corresponding string in memory. Once this orthographic word form is activated, activation passes on to corresponding phonological and semantic representations. In such a system, some sort of localized representation or node is activated at each processing level, and the function of each node is completed before information is sent on to the next level.

The parallel distributed processing (PDP) models challenge assumptions about both information transfer and the representation of information. In this framework a certain processing capacity is thought to be divided among several units linked in parallel. To take neural-type PDP networks as an example, neurons in a given anatomical area may be richly interconnected into an ensemble with certain computational properties. Several such ensembles, often in widely disparate areas of the brain, may then be interconnected, via white matter fiber tracts, into highly complex neural networks. These networks are in turn interconnected hierarchically. It is the combined activity of such a widely distributed, multiply interconnected system which brings about a behavioral function, such as visuospatial orientation or word recognition. The end result is a cross-mapping of information between ensembles (or networks) and it is this cross-mapping that we observe and interpret as "processing" (Churchland, 1986).

Information is represented in patterns of activity within these networks. These patterns are determined by the relative strength of the connections between units and are influenced by the activity of interacting ensembles. Since there can be different levels of organizational complexity depending on how the system is observed, what should be considered "input" or "output" becomes a matter of definition.

Certainly, even in massively parallel systems, some serial "flow" of activity must occur. Hence no system is exclusively parallel in nature. However, in contrast to the strictly sequential processing of serial computers, ensembles composing a PDP network are activated concurrently (Mesulam, 1990) and the activity in one ensemble need not be completed before it affects processing in connected networks. Thus one ensemble may constrain another and these constraints allow a given ensemble, which has its own characteristic set of specific connection strengths, to yield different activity patterns given different configurations of "input." Further flexibility, or variability, in performance is made possible by the existence of noise, or chaotic activity, within the system. Noise prevents the network from settling into activity patterns that are too stable to change (Skarda and Freeman, 1987). Learning may be accomplished in these systems as the connection strengths are changed through experience.

To date, the marriage of cerebral localizationism, classical associationism, and distributed processing remains somewhat uneasy. It is true that mainstream behavioral neurology has been quick to pick up the notion of a parallel division of labor (it is no great leap of faith to accept the posterior half of the brain as contributing afferent elements of processing and the anterior half efferent ones, of Broca's and Wernicke's areas working in concert to permit language, and so forth). Yet the notion of nonpropositional activity patterns as the fundamental currency of brain functioning has yet to take a firm hold in the community of clinical neurobehaviorists.

## A BRIEF OUTLINE OF AN ANATOMICAL FRAMEWORK FOR READING AND LANGUAGE

Primary auditory input for language arrives at Heschl's gyrus on the superior surface of the dominant (left) temporal lobe (see Fig. 3-1). This unimodal cortical area is directly contiguous with the higher-order auditory association cortex which becomes gradually more heteromodal as one moves caudally along the superior temporal gyrus toward the highly heteromodal Wernicke's area, a critical crossroad for much of language input and comprehension. This area is connected via a long white matter tract, the arcuate fasciculus (a component of the superior longitudinal fasciculus), with Broca's area, a crucial way station for language output to primary motor cortex.

Wernicke's area is also directly contiguous posteriorly with the heteromodal cortex of the angular gyrus. The angular gyrus is an essential way station for systems responsible for processing orthographic, abstract word forms (see below) and receives visual input from the primary visual cortex via cortical areas on the inferior, posterior, and lateral surfaces of the temporal lobe. (The secondary visual cortex was once believed to be connected with the angular gyrus via the inferior longitudinal fasciculus, but

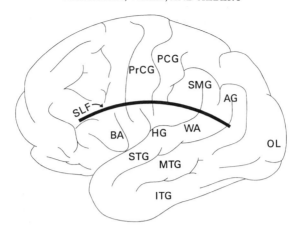

**Fig. 3-1.** PrCg = precentral gyrus; PCG = postcentral gyrus; SMG = supramarginal gyrus; AG = angular gyrus; STG = superior temporal gyrus; HG = Heschl's gyrus (on the superior surface of the STG); MTG = medial temporal gyrus; ITG = inferior temporal gyrus; OL = occipital lobe; BA = Broca's area; WA = Wernicke's area; SLF = superior longitudinal fasciculus (of which the arcuate fasciculus is a part). (Adapted from DeArmond et al., 1974.)

this white matter "tract" turned out to be an artifact of dissection (Tusa and Ungerleider, 1985).)

Thus a large-scale reading and language network is established. Mesulam (1990) conceives of Wernicke's area as lying on the semantic-lexical "pole" of this network. Sandwiched as it is between auditory, visual, and somatosensory association cortices, it can integrate activity in these areas. Broca's area, according to Mesulam (1990), lies on the syntactic and articulatory side, being closely related anatomically to motor output systems. Both areas contribute to input and output processes, however, and probably cooperate extensively in the execution of their individual functions. This contemporary statement is reminiscent of a highly comparable anatomical model of language proposed by Freud in his monograph *On Aphasia* (Freud, 1891). The angular gyrus serves in a similar way to integrate visual and somesthetic information necessary for reading, and along with Wernicke's and Broca's areas makes up the language network of the dominant hemisphere. Hence, it is inappropriate to view the "function" of each area as strictly determined by its own intrinsic properties. Rather, the larger network of close and distant interrelated areas gains functional abilities from this connectivity.

## A MODEL OF READING

The early dichotomy between alexia with and without agraphia has essentially survived newer neuropsychological theorizing, the latter group turning out to be fairly clearly equivalent to the syndrome of letter-by-letter reading, the former group incorporating most of the remaining neuropsychological classifications. As Friedman

(1988) points out, this former group of "aphasic" alexias has not received its fair share of scrutiny until recent times. From careful study of these aphasic alexias, as well as the classical syndromes, the current model of reading has been elaborated. This model may be thought of as a subsection of a model of all language functions, but in itself contains only those aspects that are necessary for the oral reading of single words. (For a more detailed account of how single-word reading might be accomplished in a PDP model, the reader is referred to Seidenberg and McClelland, 1989.)

The basic elements of a reading model must comprise an initial stage of primary visual processing that "feeds" the language system and an "output" system from the language system to spoken words. The primary visual input is thought to be common to all visual perception. Although reading-specific processes are commonly thought to arise "downstream" from this primary system, it is clear from the foregoing discussion that primary visual processing must be strongly affected by these "downstream" systems. How reading-specific language processes are brought to bear on the primary visual input, as opposed to processes involving more abstract visuospatial operations, when viewing a landscape for example, is not yet clear.

Reading-specific language processing is thought to be accomplished within two major networks: one links orthographic information directly to the phonological system. The other accesses phonology from orthography via semantics. When a word is presented in the visual modality, an analysis system specific to visual input extracts visual features and categorizes them. The initial feature analysis can be "tuned" for the presence of features consistent with letter shapes. Recognized letter shapes can be represented as abstract letter identities in which letters of different case, size, font, etc., are not distinguished. This process of letter identification generally occurs in a slow, serial, left-to-right manner in the child who is just learning to read. As the reading process becomes more practiced, letter identification becomes automatic, and the letters of a word are identified rapidly and in parallel (LaBerge and Samuels, 1974). The letter-identification process activates orthographic units. In contrast to more traditional models, in which an individual "orthographic word form" may be represented in lexical memory by a specific item or location, in a PDP model it is represented by a specific pattern of activation in the neural net that subserves this function. Orthographic units are connected to both semantic units and phonological units. Direct connections between orthography and semantics, without intermediary phonological units, enable the reader to comprehend the written words "blue" and "blew," "hymn" and "him" (Barron and Baron, 1977; Bauer and Stanovich, 1980; Coltheart, 1978, 1980b; McCusker et al., 1981; Stanovich and Bauer, 1978). Direct connections between orthography and phonology allow written words to be pronounced even if they are not comprehended. Pronunciations can also be retrieved via semantic mediation, and vice versa.

Many models of reading (Bub et al., 1987; Funnell, 1983; Patterson and Morton, 1985) also include a set of explicit "rules" for translating graphemes or letter groups into phonemes or syllabic units. Such rules are said to enable the reader to pronounce nonwords (which we shall call pseudowords) and unfamiliar real words. These rules are often sketched as a separate component, completely divorced from stored phonological codes for real words, and no lexical influence upon pseudoword pronunciation is expected. On the other hand, the model that we present contains no explicit rules for the transcoding of graphemes into phonemes. The pronunciations of all letter strings, both words and pseudowords, are derived on the basis of the same connections between orthographic units and phonological units. A written pseudoword will activate orthographic units in common with many real words. These orthographic units will activate phonological units based upon the connections that have been established. Thus the pronunciation of the pseudoword will be influenced by the pronunciations of words with which it shares letters.

## THE ALEXIAS

Following Misch and Frankl's (1929) distinction of afferent (sensory) and language-based reading disorders, we begin our discussion of specific alexias with the reading disorders thought to be due primarily to disruption of primary visual processing or visual access to the language system. Much of the primary visual analysis takes place in "prelanguage" systems. Most notably, the work of Hubel and Wiesel (1968) has shown how the geniculostriate and early visual association areas together allow for contrast and border discriminations. These are processes well suited for letter identification. An isolated deficit of letter perception probably does not occur, and the phenomenon of literal alexia described in earlier literature probably represents an anomia.

### Attentional Alexia

An example of attentional alexia was described by Shallice and Warrington in 1977. Their patients could read single words, but had trouble with multiword displays. In this situation, letters tended to "migrate" from words to neighboring words. For example, "pot big hut" was read as "but big hut." A similar phenomenon can be seen in normal readers when words are presented under tachistoscopic, patterned mask conditions (Mozer, 1983). We are aware of no additional reports of such acquired cases, although a related case of an adult developmental dyslexic was reported by Rayner et al. (1989). This case differs in that migration errors per se do not occur, but it is similar in that letters from parafoveal vision do interfere with reading. The underlying problem in attentional alexia is generally attributed to a deficit in selective attention which is not specific to orthographic material.

### Neglect Alexia

Neglect alexia refers to a heterogeneous group of reading disorders thought to be related to the clinical phenomenon of visuospatial neglect. The neglect syndromes are, in turn, thought to arise from lesions affecting different mechanisms, such as premotor programming of ocular scanning, spatial distribution of attention, or construction of abstract visuospatial representations, that cooperate in the encoding and processing of visuospatial information. The reading disorders commonly classified as neglect alexia are of three principal varieties: First, neglect alexia may be seen in some patients with right parietal lobe lesions and left-sided neglect. These cases show neglect of the left side of the page, manifested by the omission of whole words, and neglect of the left side of words, resulting in characteristic substitution errors. This latter effect is sensitive to the orientation of the word in space. The effect is not seen with words oriented vertically, for example. Second, cases have been reported where the above substitution errors within words are seen without other features of neglect. Third, a few cases have been described of neglect for the ends of words, in a manner that is not sensitive to the spatial orientation of word presentation.

Six well-studied cases of left neglect due to right parietal lobe lesions were reported by Kinsbourne and Warrington (1962). All six made visual errors on the leftmost letters of words, even when the entire word fell within the patient's right visual field. This finding rules out a primary left visual-field defect as a cause of the phenomenon. More recent studies of left neglect alexia have further fractionated elements of the disorder (Behrmann et al., 1990b; Ellis et al., 1987; Riddoch, 1990).

The majority of errors in single-word neglect alexia are substitutions, in which overall word length is preserved (e.g., yellow → pillow). Deletions (cage → age) and additions (owl → bowl) are produced as well, but to a lesser extent. The patient reported by Ellis et al. (1987) neglected the entire left half of the page when reading text, but the effects of word neglect were typically seen only with the initial letter. Furthermore, text neglect took the form of omission, while word neglect was manifested as letter substitution. The qualitative differences between neglect of single words and neglect of text led Ellis et al. (1987) to conclude that the two reflect impairments of different mechanisms.

The prevailing wisdom until quite recently was that the symptoms of neglect alexia occur "because visual neglect happens to compromise the reading process" (Ellis et al., 1987). However, there have been several recent reports of cases of pure alexic neglect isolated from other manifestations of neglect (Patterson and Wilson, 1990; Riddoch et al., 1990) and even a case of left neglect alexia in a patient with right visual-field neglect (Costello and Warrington, 1987). These cases do not necessarily rule out the possibility that neglect alexia is a form of primary visual neglect rather than a disorder of the reading system per se. As pointed out by Riddoch (1990), reading places particularly hard demands upon visual processing, and may thus be the first place in which subtle manifestations of visuospatial neglect can be seen.

Whether or not neglect alexia is dissociable from visual neglect, the problem is generally thought to be one of attentional processes within that part of the reading system responsible for the coding of abstract letter identity and position information. When patients with left neglect alexia are asked to read words presented vertically (Behrmann et al., 1990b), neglect is not seen. When reading words presented right to left, as in upside-down writing (Ellis et al., 1987) or mirror-image writing (Riddoch et al., 1990), neglect is again seen on the left, which is now the end of the word. The attentional deficit, then, appears to occur in the lower levels of visual spatial analysis.

However, all patients who produce neglect errors in reading also produce some orthographically related errors that are not restricted to one side. The preponderance of substitution errors has led to the suggestion that information about letter position is retained in neglect alexia, while information about letter identity is lost (Ellis et al., 1987).

The type of neglect alexia that involves right neglect from left-hemisphere lesions raises questions as to the processing level involved in neglect. A questionable case of such right neglect alexia was described by Warrington and Zangwill (1957), and a more definitive case was reported by Friedrich et al. (1985). Caramazza and Hillis (1990) described in great detail the reading of a patient with right neglect alexia. This patient always showed neglect of the end of the word, regardless of orientation. In fact, this patient also neglected the ends of words in spelling. They suggested that their patient's pattern of neglect demonstrated an impairment of an internal representation which serves as input to the orthographic word form. Considering the many differences between their patient and other patients with neglect alexia, they leave open the possibility that other patients' neglect alexias may nonetheless result from attentional deficits at lower levels of visual analysis.

Hence, the ultimate causes of neglect alexia are still unclear. The evidence suggests that there are different types of neglect alexia depending on the area of the brain damaged. They may be the result of disrupted scanning strategies that prevent proper "input" to an otherwise intact representational system, or a disrupted representational system that receives adequate input, or disordered attention with otherwise intact input and representational systems, or some combination of these.

### Pure Alexia

The next level at which we might see brain damage affecting reading is in the processing of information between the visual system and the language system. All aspects of the orthographic lexicon and semantic processing remain intact, hence there is no significant agraphia or aphasia. The integrity of lower levels of visual analysis allows for accurate perception of the visually presented word, but the visual input appears to be unable to activate the appropriate orthographic units. Patients with this form of alexic disorder tend to compensate for the problem by naming the letters of the word in serial order, then using the auditory input to decode the word. As a consequence of this reading problem and compensatory strategy, two features of "letter-by-letter reading" are apparent: (1) The longer the word, the more time it will take the patient to read it, and the greater the probability that it will be misread. (2) Words that are spelled aloud to the patient will be recognized with no particular difficulty.

The precise nature of the functional deficit in letter-by-letter reading is still debated. Patterson and Kay (1982) suggest that the ability to transfer the results of the letter form analysis to the orthographic lexicon is lost. Alternatively, there may be a problem within the visual analysis system, preventing the automatic, parallel identification of letters. This latter alternative would imply disrupted processing of nonletter entities as well. Such a multimodal deficit was indeed observed in a patient with letter-by-letter reading who demonstrated a subtle problem in the identification of pictures as well as words (Friedman and Alexander, 1984). The problem with picture identification was evident only with very brief stimulus durations, however. Under normal viewing conditions the patient's only obvious problem was in reading.

Patients with letter-by-letter reading do not show any lexical effects in reading (but see the sections on letter-by-letter phonological and letter-by-letter surface alexias below). They do not produce reading errors seen in other types of alexia, such as semantic or derivational/inflectional paralexias (see below). Pseudoword reading is not differentially affected, and there are no effects of concreteness or part of speech. The diagnostic criteria include a length effect, as described above, normal or near-normal recognition of orally spelled words, and a tendency to name the letters of written words, either overtly or covertly.

The syndrome of letter-by-letter reading has been fairly well established as equivalent to the syndrome of pure alexia, and the anatomical details of this syndrome have been fairly well worked out. Three major reviews summarize the essential anatomical information regarding the low-level visual processing systems (Damasio and Damasio, 1983; Henderson, 1986; DeRenzi et al. 1987) and a significant contribution has been provided by neurosurgical case studies (Greenblatt, 1973, 1976, 1977, 1983, 1990). The visual language system consists of (1) primary visual circuits from the retina to the calcarine or striate cortex of the occipital lobe, (2) immediately adjacent secondary visual association cortex, and (3) the angular gyrus (see Fig. 3-1). The angular gyrus is part of the frontotemporoparietal language system which also includes Wernicke's and Broca's areas. Lesions that isolate the angular gyrus from its input, but leave the angular gyrus itself intact, cause alexia without agraphia. The patient is able to write well (both spontaneously and to dictation), but has great difficulty reading even what he or she has written. It is therefore thought that the angular gyrus is a central area involved in the processing of orthographic word–forms. Indeed, damage to the angular gyrus itself causes alexia with agraphia (termed angular alexia by Greenblatt, 1983), where both reading and writing are affected.

The angular gyrus may be isolated from its input in two ways: The first is by a lesion in the area immediately subcortical to the angular gyrus, thus affecting very proximal input fibers. The second is through a more complex constellation of lesions, frequently from infarction in the territory of the posterior cerebral artery that simultaneously affects the mesial left occipital cortex and the splenium of the corpus callosum. This damage results in a right visual-field defect (from damage to left primary visual cortex) but preserves vision in the left hemifield since the right calcarine cortex is unaffected. Nevertheless, the patient is alexic even for words presented to the intact left hemifield.

Greenblatt (1990) offers the following account in explanation (see also Henderson, 1986): Information from the right secondary visual cortex is thought to access the left angular gyrus only after obligatory connection with homologous areas in the left hemisphere, and no direct connection between the angular gyrus and the right occipital cortex via the splenium exists. The angular gyrus is connected with secondary occipital visual cortex via the vertical occipital fasciculus. Hence a lesion restricted to the close vicinity of the left subangular area will disconnect both the left and right hemispheres from the reading system by affecting the vertical occipital fasciculus. Lesions more posterior in the occipital lobe, on the other hand, must damage all of the projections from the left occipital association cortex into the vertical occipital fasciculus as well as all the right hemisphere projections to their left occipital homologues. It remains unsettled just which areas of the occipital and posterior temporal association cortex are critical to the integrity of this network. Both lingual and fusiform gyri and inferolateral temporal lobe cortex have been thought to be key areas (see Greenblatt, 1990, and De Renzi, 1987, vs. Henderson, 1986 for contrasting views). In the Japanese literature, the emphasis seems to be on inferolateral temporal areas to maintain the integrity of the occipital-angular neural networks.

The Japanese language provides a unique substrate for study of written language in that two linguistically distinct symbol types are used. One type, Kana, is phonemic (syllabic), somewhat similar to English. The second, Kanji, is morphemic, based on morphograms derived from Chinese (not quite ideograms in that their phonetic value may vary depending on context and they can be combined into complex units with yet new phonemic values). Kanji is used mostly for verb roots, adverbs, adjectives, and nouns, while Kana functions for onomatopoiea, foreign words, inflections, and conjunctions. Homophones of words indistinguishable when written in Kana have unique forms in Kanji (Iwata, 1984). The details of these two writing systems are quite intricate and beyond the scope of this chapter, but of significant interest is the fact that brain damage affects the reading of these two systems in strikingly different ways. A subangular and occipital lesion causes alexia in both systems. However, ability to make semantic judgments regarding Kanji characters is preserved, as are writing and kinesthetically facilitated reading in Kana. A subangular but more inferior and lateral temporal lesion, on the other hand, preserves reading and writing in Kana but abolishes writing in Kanji and the ability to make semantic decisions on these characters. (Some phonological processing of Kanji characters is preserved.) Lastly, an angular gyrus lesion disrupts reading in Kana and all writing in both Kanji and Kana, but preserves reading in Kanji.

These observations point to an anatomical dissociation between phonological (Kana) and semantic (Kanji) processing systems. The phonological system seems to involve more dorsal, occipitoparietal structures that are spared after inferolateral temporal lesions that affect the semantic system (Iwata, 1984). The preservation of some reading ability in Kanji after left angular gyrus lesions has raised the question of right hemispheric, semantic reading ability, a question that is still hotly debated.

Other neurobehavioral deficits are associated with pure alexia, depending on the extent to which the anatomical neighborhood is affected. These "syndromic" considerations have been of great interest to neurologists for decades. Damasio and Damasio (1983, 1986) elaborate three types of pure alexia based on such neighborhood effects. One type includes hemianopia, color anomia, and verbal anomia, primarily from infarctions in the territory of the posterior cerebral artery affecting mesial temporo-occipital cortex. Another type spares visual memory and color perception but includes a right hemianopia secondary to disruption of the left optic radiation. The lesion in this type is more restricted to posterior occipital areas, sparing the mesial temporal cortex. The third type results from infarctions close to the angular gyrus and may or may not include a superior quadrantanopia, depending on involvement of the left optic radiation. These three types correlate well with lesion location and serve as aids in clinical diagnosis. Visual object naming is affected to a variable degree in all cases, and it has been difficult to distinguish deficits of color perception from color anomia. Although there may exist a continuum of visual perception deficits, where visual agnosias and pure alexias overlap (DeRenzi et al., 1987), it appears that letter and word reading can be affected more or less in isolation.

## Surface (Orthographic) Alexia

When a written word activates an established pattern of orthographic units in lexical memory, we say that an orthographic word form has been activated. An impairment in the orthographic lexicon, such that the appropriate word form is not activated, results in a "regularity effect" in languages with alphabetic orthographies such as English; regular words are more likely to be read correctly than irregular words. A "regular" word may be defined as one whose pronunciation corresponds to the typical spelling-to-sound correspondence "rules" of the language (e.g., Venezky, 1970; Wijk, 1967). An "irregular" word breaks one or more of these rules.

In the past two decades there have been several reports of patients whose reading of regular words and pseudowords is significantly better than their reading of irregular words (Coltheart et al., 1983; Deloche et al., 1982; Friedman and Hadley, 1992; Kay and Lesser, 1986; Marshall and Newcombe, 1973; Shallice et al., 1983; Shallice and Warrington, 1980; see also Patterson et al., 1985). This pattern of reading is known as "surface alexia." Patients with a pronounced regularity effect often produce errors known as "regularization" errors, in which irregular words are pronounced with a regular pronunciation (e.g., pint → /pInt/).

Earlier accounts of surface alexia attributed it to a reliance upon a nonlexical rule-guided reading strategy. Yet a qualification had to be made, as many of the errors produced by surface alexic patients did not quite follow the rules (e.g., guest → just). Furthermore, Shallice et al. (1983) demonstrated that the regular/irregular dichotomy was not so clear-cut. Some words are mildly irregular (dread), others are very irregular (business), and surface alexic patients are sensitive to these differences.

A PDP reading model can account for these features of surface alexia. By this account, surface alexia reflects a disturbance within the orthographic system such that an incomplete or inappropriate constellation of orthographic units is activated. In the absence of correct information in orthography, the phonological system can still compute a phonological code on the basis of the remaining functional units. The orthographic units of regular words are well represented in the network because there are many similar words. They will be better preserved than irregular words, which tend to be more weakly represented. Since rules are not strictly applied, but fall out as a by-product of the connection weighting in the network and its "inputs," not all paralexias need be regularizations. Furthermore, mildly irregular words will indeed be better represented in the network than very irregular words, as there will be more similar words sharing connections (dread—bread; business—??)

Semantic units do not fare as well as phonological units when orthographic units are disturbed; partial orthographic information does not map onto partial semantic information. That is, words with similar orthography tend to have similar phonology ("lock" sounds like "dock"). But a "lock" shares precious few semantic features with a "dock." The semantic system in surface alexia, then, must rely upon input from the phonological system: the word is comprehended according to how it is pronounced. Hence, if "pint" were pronounced as /pInt/, it would be deemed a pseudoword. If "come" were pronounced /kom/, a grooming aid would be envisioned. Similarly, if semantic information were obtained strictly on the basis of the sound of the word, then words with homophones would often be interpreted incorrectly, "would" for "wood," etc. (Coltheart et al., 1983). The diagnosis of orthographic (surface) alexia, then, is made when regular words and pseudowords are read significantly better than irregular words matched for length and frequency. If comprehension depends upon the phonological code assigned to the word, homophone confusions are common, and pseudohomophone words (e.g., "phocks") are often accepted as real words, then the surface alexia results from impairment of the orthographic lexicon.

Anatomical correlation in surface alexia is difficult, since the lesions are heterogeneous and extensive, from closed head injuries, intracerebral hemorrhages, tumors, or multifocal cortical degeneration. Fourteen cases are summarized in Table 3-1. The lesions tend to involve temporoparietal cortex and deep white and gray matter of the left hemisphere, usually sparing occipital cortex and white matter (areas affected in pure alexia) and frontal association cortex and Broca's areas (affected in deep alexia). The right hemisphere is involved on occasion, though never in isolation. No region is invariably involved, though the superior temporal gyrus is most frequently affected.

### Alexia from Disconnection of Orthographic and Semantic Systems

Given our model of reading, one could conceive of a situation in which the connections between orthographic units and semantic units are disrupted, while all other connections are intact. Oral reading should be completely unaffected in this circumstance, since the pronunciation of words can be obtained via connections between orthographic units and phonological units. Furthermore, once phonological units are properly activated, they could activate the appropriate semantic units, so that comprehension should also be possible.

How, then, could we detect such a condition, if it were to exist? If semantic activation is possible only by way of phonology, then we might expect to see a selective impairment in the ability to disambiguate written homophones. For example, if the written word "hoarse" were presented in isolation, its pronunciation could be achieved, but it would be impossible to know whether the word referred to an animal or to a condition of the throat. To date there have been no reports of a selective deficit in homophone disambiguation. This does not mean that the condition does not exist. If a patient exhibited no detectable impairment in either oral reading or in reading for comprehension, then why would one test for homophone comprehension?

### Phonological Alexia

What might we expect to happen if the direct connections between orthographic units and phonological units are disturbed? Provided that all other connections remain intact, oral word reading should still be possible: activation of orthographic units would lead to activation of semantic units, which, in turn, would activate the phonological units. However, some problems might be expected. Since there are no patterns of activation of semantic units that correspond to pseudowords, the pronunciation of pseudowords, unlike real words, cannot be attained through this alternate route, and pseudoword reading should therefore be greatly impaired relative to words. Patients have indeed been reported with this pattern of impairment, which is known as "phonological alexia" (Beauvois and Derouesné, 1979; Derouesné and

**Table 3-1.** Surface Alexia

| Subject | Age | Sex | Hand | Insult | Frontal PEF | PEC | POC | Parietal SMG | DWM | Temporal ITG | MTG | STG | AG | DWM | Occipital CTX | DWM | DGM | Reference | Comment |
|---|---|---|---|---|---|---|---|---|---|---|---|---|---|---|---|---|---|---|---|
| MP | 62 | F | ? | CHI | | | | O | | | X | X | O | X | O | | | 1 | Diffuse BL atrophy |
| MS | 18 | M | ? | CHI | | | | | | | | | X | X | | | | 2 | |
| LL | 15 | F | ? | CVA/ICH | | | | | X | | | | X | | | | X | 3 | |
| RF | 39 | F | R | CVA/ICH | X | | X | | X | X | X | X | X | X | | | | 4 | Diffuse BL ENC.MAL. |
| MS | 22 | M | ? | CHI | | | | | | | | | X | X | | | | 5 | |
| HAM | 35 | F | R | CVA/ICH | | | X | X | X | | X | X | X | X | X | | | 6 | |
| SU | 46 | M | ? | CVA/ICH | X | | X | X | X | | | | X | X | X | | | 7 | Also R SUBCTX ICH |
| BF | 32 | F | R | CVA | X | | X | X | | X | X | X | X | X | X | | X | 8 | S/P resection |
| EST | 45 | M | R | Tumor | X | | X | X | X | X | X | X | X | X | X | | X | 9 | Devel. bilingual |
| FE | 28 | M | R | None | X | | | | | | | | | | | | | 10 | Injured at age 20 |
| JC | 58 | ? | ? | OHI | | | | | | | | | | | | | | 11 | Temporal lobe atrophy |
| ATR | 66 | F | ? | Demented | | | | | | | | | | | | | | 12 | Diffuse atrophy |
| KT | 54 | M | ? | Demented | | | | | | | | | | | | | | 13 | Diffuse atrophy |
| PT | 39 | M | R | Migraines | | | | | | | | | | | | | | 14 | Normal CT scan |

Lesions indicated are for the left hemisphere unless otherwise noted.

X = affected area; O = spared area specifically noted; Blank = No data, assumed spared. Must be evaluated based on lesion type. Hand = handedness; PEF = prefrontal cortex; PEC = precentral cortex; POC = postcentral cortex; SMG = supramarginal gyrus; DWM = deep white matter; ITG = inferior temporal gyrus; MTG = middle temporal gyrus; STG = superior temporal gyrus; AG ± = angular gyrus; CTX = cortex; DGM = deep gray matter; S/P = status post; CVA = cerebrovascular accident; ICH = intracerebral hemorrhage; CHI = closed head injury; OHI = open head injury; R = right; BL = bilateral; SUBCTX = subcortical; ENC.MAL. = encephalomalacia.

References: 1. Bub et al., 1985; 2. Newcombe and Marshall, 1985; 3. Saffran, 1985; 4. Margolin et al., 1985; 5. Temple, 1985; 6. Kremin, 1985; 7. Sasanuma, 1985; 8. Goldblum, 1985; 9. Kay and Patterson, 1985; 10. Masterson et al., 1985; 11. Marshall and Newcombe, 1973; 12. Shallice et al., 1983; 13. McCarthy and Warrington, 1986; 14. Kay and Lesser, 1986.

Beauvois, 1985; Funnell, 1983; Glosser and Friedman, 1990; Patterson, 1982; Shallice and Warrington, 1980).

A second consequence is that the ability to activate the appropriate phonological code will depend upon the ability to activate a corresponding semantic code. This should be no problem for words with widespread representation in the semantic network, such as concrete nouns and adjectives (Glosser and Friedman, 1990). Words that are weakly represented may be less likely to succeed in activating the correct phonological representation. Both functor words and affixes should be poorly represented within the semantic system (Glosser and Friedman, 1990; Patterson, 1982), and in fact, many patients whose oral reading exhibits a large advantage for words over pseudowords do indeed read functor words and affixes more poorly than concrete nouns and adjectives (part-of-speech effect) (Friedman, 1988).

If the connections from the orthographic lexicon to the phonological lexicon are intact, but phonological processing itself is impaired, we would, once again, expect to see a pattern of reading in which pseudowords are read poorly relative to real words. In the face of weakened or disturbed patterns of phonological activation, those that are well established (i.e., real words) will fare better. This advantage should extend to other language tasks that involve phonological processing, such as repetition. Part-of-speech effects are not expected, since problems in phonological processing will affect reading regardless of input route. This second type of phonological alexia does indeed exist. The phonological alexic patients reported by Bub et al. (1987), Friedman and Kohn (1990), and Funnell (1983) all exhibited marked pseudoword deficits that extended to pseudoword repetition. Furthermore, unlike other phonological alexics, these patients did not read nouns better than functors.

Thus there are at least two different underlying deficits that result in impaired pseudoword reading. How the disconnection between orthography and phonology is effected anatomically is not at all clear. One would hope to see fairly discrete deficits that disconnect two functionally and anatomically distinct areas (analogous to the disconnection seen in pure alexia). This, unfortunately, is not the case. As can be seen from Table 3-2, lesions causing phonological alexia are extensive. In cases LB and AM, right-hemisphere lesions were responsible. LB, however, was most likely a patient with crossed aphasia and therefore represents an anomaly; case AM seems to be that of a left-hander with true right-hemisphere language lateralization. In general, a large proportion of middle cerebral artery strokes is noted. Damage to the superior temporal lobe and angular and supramarginal gyri is fairly consistent.

### Alexia of Alzheimer's Disease (Semantic Alexia)

The semantic lexicon is the hypothesized network that contains all knowledge about concepts and their relationship to one another. It is one of the components of the reading system that is shared with other language processing systems. An impairment in semantic processing should therefore affect both reading and other aspects of language. If all other aspects of orthographic and phonological processing remain intact, then we should see a patient who reads aloud both real words and pseudowords, but has difficulty comprehending the words. This picture is seen mostly clearly in the dementing illness of Alzheimer's disease. As the disease progresses, patients with

**Table 3-2.** Phonological Alexia

| Subject | Age | Sex | Hand | Insult | Frontal PEF | PEC | POC | Parietal SMG | DWM | Temporal ITG | MTG | STG | AG | DWM | Occipital CTX | DWM | DGM | Reference | Comment |
|---|---|---|---|---|---|---|---|---|---|---|---|---|---|---|---|---|---|---|---|
| LB | 45 | M | R | CVA, R MCA | X | X | | X | X | | X | X | X | | | | X | 1 | |
| MV | 67 | F | R | CVA, L MCA | X | X | X | X | | | | X | | | | | X | 2 | |
| AM | ? | M | L | CVA, R MCA | | | | | | | | | | | | | | 3 | No details |
| HR | 52 | M | R | CVA, L MCA | | | | X | | | | X | X | | | | | 4 | |
| ? | 39 | M | R | CVA/ICH | | | | O | | X | X | | O | | | | | 5 | |
| RG | 64 | M | R | AVM | | | | | | | X | | X | | X | | | 6 | S/P excision |
| GR | 23 | M | R | CHI | | | | | | X | X | | | | | X | | 7 | |
| GRN | ? | F | R | CHI | | | | | | | | | | | | | | 8 | No anatomy |
| BTT | 29 | ? | L | SAH | | | | | | | | | | | | | | 8 | No anatomy |
| ROC | ? | F | L | SAH | | | | | | | | | | | | | | 8 | No anatomy |
| WB | 50 | M | ? | CVA, L MCA | | | | | | | | | | | | | | 9 | No anatomy |
| FL | 66 | F | ? | CVA ? | | | | | | | | | | | | | | 9 | No anatomy |

Lesions indicated are for the left hemisphere unless otherwise noted.

X = affected area; O = spared area specifically noted; Blank = No data, assumed spared. Must be evaluated based on lesion type. Hand = handedness; PEF = prefrontal cortex; PEC = precentral cortex; POC = postcentral cortex; SMG = supramarginal gyrus; DWM = deep white matter; ITG = inferior temporal gyrus; MTG = middle temporal gyrus; STG = superior temporal gyrus; AG = angular gyrus; CTX = cortex; DGM = deep gray matter; S/P = status post; CVA = cerebrovascular accident; MCA = middle cerebral artery; ICH = intracerebral hemorrhage; AVM = arteriovenous malformation; CHI = closed head injury; SAH = subarrachnoid hemorrhage; R = right; L = left.

References: 1. Derouesne and Beauvois, 1985; 2. Bub et al., 1987; 3. Patterson, 1982; 4. Friedman and Kohn, 1990; 5. Rapcsak et al., 1987; 6. Beauvois and Derouesne, 1979; 7. Glosser and Friedman, 1990; 8. Shallice and Warrington, 1980; 9. Funnell, 1983.

51

Alzheimer's disease have increasing difficulty with the comprehension of spoken and written language. Their spoken output also becomes garbled in content, though real words continue to be produced. Yet oral reading remains remarkably well preserved (Cummings et al., 1986), even for pseudowords (Friedman et al., 1992).

An interesting dissociation has been noted in the pseudoword reading of Alzheimer's patients. Although most pseudowords continue to be read well, presumably because the well-established connections between familiar orthographic and phonological units remain intact, pseudowords that contain unfamiliar orthographic sequences (e.g., "scuv") present considerable trouble for Alzheimer's patients compared with normal controls (Friedman et al., 1992). This suggests that an alternative processing mechanism may be required for the phonological decoding of strange or "scuv"-like pseudowords, one that presumably involves a more controlled, metalinguistic processing strategy.

## Deep Alexia

A semantic paralexia is a reading error in which the response resembles the target word in meaning, but not visually or phonologically. Semantic paralexias can be opposites (hot → cold), superordinates (cat → animal), subordinates (fruit → apple), coordinates (arm → leg), synonyms (attorney → lawyer), or associates (sleep → dream). Patients who produce semantic paralexias as more than 5% of their reading errors are said to display the syndrome of "deep alexia" (also called "deep dyslexia"). Deep alexia is a syndrome that is defined by a single feature (production of semantic paralexias) because it has been observed that this feature nearly always guarantees the presence of several other alexic symptoms (Coltheart, 1980a). These include the production of derivational and orthographic paralexias, a part-of-speech effect (nouns and adjectives are read better than verbs, which are read better than functors), a concreteness/imageability effect (concrete/imageable nouns read better than abstract/nonimageable nouns), the production of many functor word substitutions, and the inability to read pseudowords. (An exception can be found in the recent paper by Caramazza and Hillis, 1990; their patients failed to produce orthographic paralexias. We will return to this later.)

Early attempts to account for the syndrome of deep alexia ran to two extremes. At one extreme was the notion that multiple impairments were necessary to account for the multitude of symptoms (Morton and Patterson, 1980). This hypothesis appears untenable given that semantic paralexias are never seen in isolation from the rest of deep alexic symptoms (Coltheart et al. 1987). At the other extreme was the possibility that all symptoms were manifestations of "a disruption of a single underlying mechanism" (Newcombe and Marshall, 1980, p. 20). This account is difficult to reconcile with any current cognitive models of reading, none of which posit a single processing unit that, when impaired, would give all the deep alexic symptoms (Coltheart et al., 1987). Yet another proposal hypothesized that deep alexia reflects the reading of the semantic system when the phonological route is blocked (Newcombe and Marshall, 1980). By this account, the semantic reading route is by its very nature imprecise and requires additional input from phonology to choose between semantically similar words, e.g. "pretty" and "beautiful." However, most semantic paralexias are not synonyms, and the existence of phonological alexia, in which phonological input is unavailable yet semantic paralexias do not occur, makes it unlikely that the latter explanation can satisfactorily account for deep alexia.

We have noted that damage to the semantic reading route is not expected to result in semantic reading errors; the phonological reading route, if intact, can process all words for oral reading, including pseudowords. We have also claimed that damage to the phonological reading route forces reading through the semantic path. Again, if this path is intact, most words will be read correctly, although words with low semantic value such as functors (and pseudowords) may be misread. The production of reading errors known as semantic paralexias may therefore indicate a disturbance within both reading routes, as such semantic paralexias should not occur otherwise.

Accordingly, deep alexia is the expected result of the inability to use the direct orthography-to-phonology route to oral reading, coupled with a deficit within the semantic reading route (Friedman, 1991; Glosser and Friedman, 1990). The deficit in the semantic route may occur within the semantic system itself or within the route from semantics to phonology. These two possibilities can be distinguished in any given patient by having the patient read a word aloud, then point to the corresponding picture from among several semantically related choices (Friedman and Perlman, 1982). If the patient chooses the incorrect picture, a semantic processing deficit is suggested. If the patient produces a semantic paralexia, but then chooses the correct picture (even when the picture corresponding to the paralexia is among the choices) then it is likely that the problem occurs subsequent to semantic processing. The patient described by Friedman and Perlman (1982) showed errors of both types. The patients reported by Caramazza and Hillis (1990) fit the second pattern; they performed well on word-picture matching tasks and they provided correct definitions of words to which they had produced semantic paralexias. These patients' semantic paralexias clearly seemed to emanate from a disturbance beyond the level of semantic processing.

If deep alexia reflects reading from the impaired semantic route when the phonological route is inoperative, then deep alexia should look like phonological alexia, and more. In fact, it has been argued that deep and phonological alexia form points on a continuum (Glosser and Friedman, 1990). The impairment in the phonological route results in poor pseudoword reading in both deep and phonological alexia. Reliance upon the semantic route results in decreased accuracy on functor words and on inflectional/derivational affixes, as both are low in semantic value. With the addition of a deficit in the semantic route (either within the semantic system or in its connections to other systems), concreteness effects and semantic paralexias appear.

The performance of deep alexics has also been noted to resemble the right-hemisphere reading ability of some patients who have undergone transection of the corpus callosum for amelioration of intractable epilepsy (Zaidel and Peters, 1981; Gazzaniga and Hillyard, 1971), and the anatomical lesions causing deep alexia are commonly extensive left-hemisphere insults (Coltheart, 1983; Sevush et al., 1983; Schweiger et al., 1989). These two observations engendered the notion that deep alexic reading represented the functioning of a right-hemispheric reading system.

However, problems with the notion of a right-hemispheric reading system being responsible for deep alexic reading performance are illustrated by three issues: (1) the lack of consistent evidence for right-hemispheric influence in normal readers; (2) the lack of deep alexic reading features in patients with pure alexia who have lexical material presented to their right hemispheres; and (3) the fact that most right-hemisphere reading in callosotomized patients actually does not produce a consistent deep alexia pattern (Gazzaniga, 1983). The first two issues resulted in a postulate of left-hemisphere inhibition of right-hemisphere systems (Coltheart, 1983; Landis et al., 1983). This inhibition should be maximal in normal individuals, less prominent but still present in patients with small left-hemisphere lesions such as in pure alexia, and abolished in subjects with callosotomies. Patterson and Besner (1984a,b) argued against the inhibition theory mostly on intuitive grounds, stating that this would be an inefficient way of engineering a brain (see also Marshall and Patterson, 1983). However, neural science is rife with examples of how one neural system inhibits another, and Coltheart's inhibition theory is therefore not impossible (see also Jones and Martin, 1985, for similar arguments).

## COMBINATION ALEXIAS

### Letter-by-Letter Reading and Phonological Alexia

In a standard serial processing model of reading, if a written word cannot activate an orthographic word form, the word can be neither pronounced nor understood. In pure alexia, it is only after the letters of a word are all identified and an orthographic word form is activated that the word can be comprehended or read aloud. Partial comprehension is not expected, nor is it usually reported. Patterson and Kay (1982) sought evidence for partial semantic activation in four letter-by-letter readers using a category decision task, and found none. Behrmann et al. (1990a), also failed to find such an effect.

However, Coslett and Saffran (1989) and Shallice and Saffran (1986) described letter-by-letter readers who performed above chance on category decision tasks when the written words were presented too fast for the patients to use a letter-by-letter strategy. In addition, under similar (tachistoscopic) viewing conditions, three of the patients read nouns better than functors and read highly imageable words better than words of low imageability. These findings suggest that some activation of semantic units must be occurring.

It has been suggested that a semantically based reading system, perhaps controlled by right-hemispheric mechanisms, may be available under conditions in which letter-by-letter reading cannot be used (Landis et al., 1980). These authors described a patient who demonstrated the ability to match pictures to written words that he could not explicitly identify. The patient lost this ability, however, when he regained the ability to name letters. Thus it is possible that the availability of an accurate, albeit slow, alternative means of identifying words (i.e., letter by letter) preempts the use of the semantic reading mechanism. In support of this notion, a patient described by Friedman et al. (1992) was found to show a marked part of speech effect, and above-chance performance on semantic categorization taks, even with unlimited time to view the written word. This patient, despite constant attempts to use a letter-by-letter strategy, was quite poor at naming letters. Hence, the alternative reading strategy failed, allowing the semantic process to become manifest.

Friedman et al. (1992) noted that activation of semantic information, even when readout from the orthographic word form is not possible, is consistent with PDP models of reading. If, in letter-by-letter reading, the orthographic units are weakly activated, this weak activation may be passed on to the semantic units before it is lost. Semantic information, being more richly interconnected and widely distributed, may be more likely to remain activated long enough to be available for conscious report.

### Letter-by-Letter Reading and Surface Alexia

Among the many possible combinations of deficits to the reading system is one in which there is trouble with the input to the orthographic word forms and trouble with the orthographic word forms themselves. The former deficit would produce letter-by-letter reading. The latter deficit would cause surface alexia. The result would be "letter-by-letter surface alexia," i.e., a patient with letter-by-letter reading who, in addition to the typical letter-length effect, also shows a regularity effect for both written words and words that are spelled aloud to the patient. Patients with this dual alexia have been reported by Patterson and Kay (1982) and Friedman and Hadley (1992).

## ORTHOGRAPHIC PARALEXIAS

The type of paralexia that has been called a visual paralexia is not a visually based error at all. There are two senses in which this is so. First, while the visual paralexia is said to resemble the target word visually, in fact it often does not resemble the target in a strictly visual sense. The resemblance seen is more often an orthographic one; that is, the paralexic error and the target word share many letters in common. For example, if the word "appraise" is read as "arise," this is typically considered to be a visual error. But it is clear that overall shape (two descenders vs. no descenders) and length (eight letters vs. five letters) are quite different. This paralexia may be conceived of as an orthographic paralexia, since the similarity is in shared letters, not in shape or form.

The second sense in which these errors are not visual is in the underlying causes of these paralexias. Only the orthographic paralexias of attentional and neglect alexias are caused by visual problems, which we have outlined above. But orthographic paralexias are produced in all forms of acquired alexia, and for different reasons. For example, letter-by-letter readers sometimes produce paralexias that are orthographically close to the target word. This might, in fact, be more of a memory problem than a visual problem. The letter-by-letter reader must individually identify each letter of a word, then keep the string of letters in memory until all letters in the word are identified. If the word is a long one, then it is not at all unreasonable to expect that on some occasions a letter will be lost or substituted for a similar-sounding letter as the end of the word is decoded. The result would look like an orthographic paralexia: a word that shares many letters with the target word.

Orthographic paralexias are also produced by surface alexic patients, whose orthographic word forms are impaired. For these patients, the orthographic paralexias may reflect those instances in which the correct word form was not activated, but a word form with many shared orthographic features was activated instead.

In patients with phonological/deep alexia, orthographic paralexias may have yet another cause. The processing of a written word results in the activation of a particular pattern within the orthographic lexicon. Within a PDP model, orthographic units spread their activation to semantic units in varying degrees of strength. The word "bread," for example, will activate units for "read" as well, even if the orthographic units are working properly. Within the semantic system, the pattern of activation will be more consistent with "bread," and that is the one that will "win." But if there is damage within the semantic system, the "bread" pattern may not arise; in that case the pattern for "read" may predominate. The result would be an orthographic paralexia. Patients with impaired semantics tend to produce orthographic paralexias for target words that are abstract (Morton and Patterson, 1980). This is what would be expected if the paralexia was occurring at the level of semantics. In patients with deep alexia for whom the problem is not within the semantic system, but occurs subsequent to the correct activation of semantics, we would not expect to see orthographic paralexias of this type. In fact, the patients of Caramazza and Hillis (1990), mentioned earlier, did not produce orthographic paralexias; their deficits were posited to be located beyond the semantic lexicon.

When examining a patient's reading for orthographic paralexias, then, it is important to realize that these errors are not in and of themselves diagnostic of any specific type of alexia. They occur in all types of acquired disorders of reading, and for many different reasons.

## TREATMENT OF THE ALEXIAS

Since the last edition of this book, new approaches to the rehabilitation of acquired alexia have been introduced. Many of these experimental therapies are the direct result of progress made by cognitive neuropsychologists in understanding reading and alexia. Therapies are emerging that are targeted to specific alexic disorders.

A successful treatment program for a patient with deep alexia was described by dePartz (1986). The goal was to retrain the patient to read through the phonological route. By pairing each letter with a common word that begins with the letter, a patient was gradually taught to produce the phoneme corresponding to each letter. By the end of nine months of intensive therapy, the patient's reading was substantially improved.

Patients with surface alexia have been the subject of two recent experimental therapies (Coltheart and Byng, 1989; Friedman and Robinson, 1991). Although patients with surface alexia can read words with unambiguous spelling-to-sound correspondences, Englist contains many graphemes with multiple pronunciations, particularly vowels and vowel digraphs. The goal of both experimental therapies was to teach the patients to read words that contain ambiguous vowels, using a whole-word approach. Coltheart and Byng (1989) paired each written word with a mnemonic device. Friedman and Robinson (1991) used no mnemonic device, but grouped words according to pronunciation. For example, all "ow" words pronounced /o/, such as "mow" and "grow," were taught together; followed by "ow" words pronounced /au/, such as "cow" and "clown." In both studies, the patients' reading of the treatment words showed significant improvement. In the former study, there was significant improvement of untreated words as well; in the latter study, improvement on the control words was equivocal.

Patients with letter-by-letter reading (pure alexia) typically devise their own therapy; they quickly learn that by spelling words aloud one letter at a time, they can circumvent the problems that they experience recognizing the word in the visual modality. For pure alexic patients who experience trouble recognizing individual letters, and thus are unable to use this compensatory strategy, the use of kinesthetic facilitation has been used for many years (from Goldstein, 1948 to Kashiwagi and Kashiwagi, 1989, and many in between). The patient is taught to trace each letter either with a finger or simply with the head or eyes. Feedback provided by the body movements enables the patient to recognize the letter. A new treatment program for pure alexia, which attempts to capitalize on the possibility of partial semantic activation, has met with some initial success (Moss and Rothi, 1987, 1988; Rothi et al., 1986).

The development of experimental therapies of this kind, aimed at specific deficits identified with reference to cognitive models of reading, is encouraging. It is clear that an important step in designing effective treatment programs for alexia will be to identify the precise nature of the cognitive deficit that is producing the disturbance in reading.

## REFERENCES

Barron, R. W., and Baron, J. (1977). How children get meaning from printed words. *Child Dev.* 48:586–594.

Bauer, D. W., and Stanovich, K. E. (1980). Lexical access and the spelling-to-sound regularity effect. *Memory Cognition* 8:424–432.

Beauvois, M. F., and Derouesné, J. (1979). Phonological alexia; three dissociations. *J. Neurol. Neurosurg. Psychiatry* 42:1115–1124.

Behrmann, M., Black, S. E., and Bub, D. (1990a). The evolution of pure alexia: a longitudinal study of recovery. *Brain Lang.* 39: 405–427.

Behrmann, M., Moscovitch, M. Black, S. E., and Mozer, M. (1990b). Perceptual and conceptual mechanisms in neglect dyslexia. *Brain* 113:1163–1183.

Bub, D., Black, S. E., Howell, J., and Kertesz, A. (1987). Speech output processes and reading. In *Cognitive Neuropsychology of Language*, M. Coltheart, G., Sartori, and R. Job (eds.). Hillsdale, N. J.: Erlbaum.

Bub, D., Cancelliere, A., and Kertesz, A. (1985). Whole-word and analytic translation of spelling to sound in a non-semantic reader. In *Surface Dyslexia.*, K. E. Patterson, J. C. Marshall, and M. Coltheart (eds). London: Lawrence Erlbaum Associates.

Caramazza, A., and Hillis, A. E. (1990). Where do semantic errors come from? *Cortex 26*: 95–122.

Churchland, P. S. (1986). *Neurophilosophy, Towards a Unified Theory of Mind.* Cambridge, Mass.: MIT Press.

Coltheart, M. (1978). Lexical access in simple reading tasks. In *Strategies of Information Processing*, G. Underwood (ed.). London: Academic Press.

Coltheart, M. (1980a). Deep dyslexia: a review of the syndrome. In *Deep Dyslexia*, M. Coltheart, K. E. Patterson, and J. Marshall (eds.). London: Routledge and Kegan Paul.

Coltheart, M. (1980b). Reading, phonological recoding and deep dyslexia. In *Deep Dyslexia*, M. Coltheart, K. E. Patterson, and J. Marshall (eds.). London: Routledge and Kegan Paul.

Coltheart, M. (1983). The right hemisphere and disorders of reading. In *Functions of the Right Cerebral Hemisphere*, A. Young (ed.). London: Academic Press.

Coltheart, M. and Byng, S. (1989). A treatment for surface dyslexia. In: *Cognitive Approaches in Neuropsychological Rehabilitation*, X. Seron, and G. Deloche (eds.). Hillsdale, N.J.: Erlbaum.

Coltheart, M., Masterson, J., Byng, S. Prior. M., and Riddoch, J. (1983). Surface dyslexia. *Q. J. Exp. Psychol. 35A:* 469–495.

Coltheart, M., Patterson, K. E., and Marshall, J. C. (1987). Deep dyslexia since 1980. In *Deep Dyslexia*, 2nd. ed. M. Coltheart, K. E. Patterson, and J. Marshall (eds.). London: Routledge and Kegal Paul.

Coslett, H. B., and Saffran, E. M. (1989). Evidence for preserved reading in "pure alexia." *Brain 112:*327–359.

Costello, A.D.L., and Warrington, E. K. (1987). The dissiociation of visuospatial neglect and neglect dyslexia. *J.Neurol. Neurosurg. Psychiatry 50:*1110–1116.

Cummings, J. L., Houlihan, J. P., and Hill, M. A. (1986). The pattern of reading deterioration in dementia of the Alzheimer type. *Brain Lang. 29:*315–323.

Damasio, A. R., and Damasio, H. (1983). The anatomic basis of pure alexia. *Neurology 33:*1573–1583.

Damasio, A. R., and Damasio, H. (1986). Hemianopia, hemichromatopsia and the mechanisms of alexia. *Cortex 22:*161–169.

DeArmond, S. J., Fusco, M. M., and Dewey, M. M. (1974). Structure of the Human Brain, A Photographic Atlas. New York: Oxford University Press.

Déjerine, J. (1891). Sur un cas de cécité verbal avec agraphie suivi d'autopsie. *Mem. Soc. Biol.* 3:197–201.

Deloche, G., Andreewsky, E., and Desi, M. (1982). Surface dyslexia: a case report and some theoretical implications to reading models. *Brain Lang. 15:*12–31.

dePartz, M. -P. (1986). Re-education of a deep dyslexic patient: rationale of the method and results. *Cognitive Neuropsychol. 3:*149–177.

DeRenzi, E., Zambolin, A., and Crisi, G., (1987). The pattern of neuropsychological impairment associated with left posterior cerebral artery infarcts. *Brain 110:* 1099–1116.

Derouesné, J., and Beauvois, M. F. (1985). The 'phonemic' stage in the nonlexical reading process; evidence from a case of phonological alexia. In *Surface Dyslexia*, K. E. Patterson, J. C. Marshall, and M. Coltheart (eds.). London: Lawrence Erlbaum Associates.

Ellis, A. W., Flude, B. M., and Young A. W. (1987). "Neglect dyslexia" and the early visual processing of letters in words and nonwords. *Cognitive Neuropsychol. 4:*439–464.

Freud, S. (1891). *Zur Auffassung der Aphasien.* Vienna: Deuticke.

Friedman, R. B. (1988). Alexia. In *Handbook of Neuropsychology*, F. Boller and J. Grafman (eds.). Amsterdam: Elsevier.

Friedman, R. B. (1991). Is there a continuum of phonological/deep dyslexia? Paper presented at DD12 Conference, London.

Friedman, R. B., and Alexander, M. P. (1984). Pictures, images and pure alexia: a case study. *Cognitive Neuropsychol. 1:*9–23.

Friedman, R. B., Beeman, M., Lott, S., Link, K., Grafman, J., and Robinson, S. (1992). Modality specific phonological alexia. *Cognitive Neuropsychol.*, in press.

Friedman, R. B., Ferguson, S., Robinson, S., and Sunderland, T. (1992). Dissociation of mechanisms of reading in Alzheimer's disease. *Brain Lang.*, *43*:400–413.

Friedman, R. B., and Hadley, J. A. (1992). Letter by letter surface alexia. *Cognitive Neuropsychol. 9*:185–208.

Friedman, R. B., and Kohn, S. E. (1990). Impaired activation of the phonological lexicon: effects upon oral reading. *Brain Lang. 38*: 278–297.

Friedman, R. B., and Perlman, M. B. (1982). On the underlying causes of semantic paralexias in a patient with deep dyslexia. *Neuropsychologia 20*:559–568.

Friedman, R. B., and Robinson, S. R. (1991). Whole-word training therapy in a stable surface alexic patient: it works. *Aphasiology 5:* 1–7.

Friedrich, F. J., Walker, J. A., and Posner, M. I. (1985). Effects of parietal lesions on visual matching; implications for reading errors. *Cognitive Neuropsychol. 2*:253–264.

Funnell, E. (1983). Phonological processes in reading; new evidence from acquired dyslexia. *Br. J. Psychol. 74*:159–180.

Gardner, H. (1985). *The Mind's New Science*. Cambridge, Mass.: MIT Press.

Gazzaniga, M. S. (1983). Right hemisphere language following brain bisection: a 20 year perspective. *Am. Psychologist 38*:525–537.

Gazzaniga, M. S. and Hillyard, S. A. (1971). Language and speech capacity of the right hemisphere. *Neuropsychologia 9*:273–280.

Geschwind, N. (1962). The anatomy of acquired disorders of reading. In: *Reading Disability*, J. Money (ed.). Baltimore: Johns Hopkins Press.

Geschwind, N. (1965). Disconnexion syndromes in animals and man, I and II. *Brain 88*:237–294, 585–644.

Glosser, G., and Friedman, R. B. (1990). The continuum of deep/phonological alexia. *Cortex 26*:343–359.

Goldblum, M. C. (1985). Word comprehension in surface dyslexia. In *Surface Dyslexia*, K. E. Patterson, J. C. Marshall, and M. Coltheart (eds.). London: Lawrence Erlbaum Associates.

Goldstein, K. (1948). *Language and Language Disturbances*. New York: Grune and Stratton.

Greenblatt, S. H. (1973). Alexia without agraphia or hemianopsia. *Brain 96*:307–316.

Greenblatt, S. H. (1976). Subangular alexia without agraphia or hemianopsia. *Brain Lang 3*:229–245.

Greenblatt, S. H. (1977). Neurosurgery and the anatomy of reading: a practical review. *Neurosurgery 1*:6–15.

Greenblatt, S. H. (1983). Localization of lesions in alexia. In *Localization in Neuropsychology*, A. Kertesz (ed.). New York: Academic Press.

Greenblatt, S. H. (1990). Left occipital lobectomy and the preangular anatomy of reading. *Brain Lang. 38*:576–595.

Henderson, V. W. (1986). Anatomy of posterior pathways in reading: a reassessment *Brain Lang. 29*:119–133.

Hinshelwood, J. (1900). *Letter, Word and Mind Blindness*. London: H. K. Lewis.

Hubel, D. H. and Wiesel, T. N. (1968). Receptive fields and functional architecture of monkey striate cortex. *J. Physiol. (Lond.) 195*:215–243.

Iwata, M. (1984). Kanji versus Kana, neuropsychological correlates of the Japanese writing system. *Trends Neural Sci. 7*:290–293.

Jones, G. V., and Martin, M. (1985). Deep dyslexia and the right-hemisphere hypothesis for semantic paralexia; a reply to Marshall and Patterson. *Neuropsychologia 23*:685–688.

Kashiwagi, T. and Kashiwagi, A. (1989). Recovery process of a Japanese alexic without agraphia. *Aphasiology 3*:75–91.

Kay, J. and Lesser, R. (1986). The nature of the phonological processing in oral reading; evidence from surface dyslexia. *Q. J. Exp. Psychol.* 37A:39–81.

Kay, J., and Patterson, K. E. (1985). Routes to meaning in surface dyslexia. In: *Surface Dyslexia*, K. E. Patterson, J. C. Marshall, and M. Coltheart (eds). London: Lawrence Erlbaum Associates.

Kinsbourne, M., and Warrington, E. K. (1962). A variety of reading disability associated with right hemisphere lesions. *J. Neurol. Neurosurg. Psychiatry* 25:339–344.

Kremin, H. (1985). Routes and strategies in surface dyslexia and dysgraphia. In: *Surface Dyslexia*, K. E. Patterson, J. C. Marshall, and M. Coltheart (eds.). London: Lawrence Erlbaum Associates.

LaBerge, D., and Samuels, S. J. (1974). Toward a theory of automatic information processing in reading. *Cognitive Psychol.* 6: 293–322.

Landis, T., Regard, M., and Serrat, A. (1980). Iconic reading in a case of alexia without agraphia caused by a brain tumor; a tachistoscopic study. *Brain Lang.* 11:45–53.

Landis, T., Regard, M., Graves, R., and Goodglass, H. (1983). Semantic paralexia: a release of right hemisphere function from left hemispheric control? *Neuropsychologia* 21:359–364.

Margolin, D. I., Marcel, A. J., and Carlson, N. R. (1985). Common mechanisms in dysnomia and post-semantic surface dyslexia: process defects and selective attention. In: *Surface Dyslexia*, K. E. Patterson, J. C. Marshall, and M. Coltheart (eds.). London: Lawrence Erlbaum Associates.

Marshall, J. C., and Newcombe, F. (1973). Patterns of paralexia; a psycholinguistic approach. *J. Psycholinguist. Res.* 2:175–199.

Marshall, J. C., and Patterson, K. E. (1983). Semantic paralexia and the wrong hemisphere; a note on Landis, Regard, Graves and Goodglass (1983). *Neuropsychologia* 21:425–427.

Masterson, J., Coltheart, M., and Meara, P. (1985). Surface dyslexia in a language with irregularly spelled words. In *Surface Dyslexia*, K. E. Patterson, J. C. Marshall, and M. Coltheart (eds.). London: Lawrence Erlbaum Associates.

McCarthy, R., and Warrington, E. K. (1986). Phonological reading: phenomena and paradoxes. *Cortex* 22:359–380.

McClelland, J. L., Rumelhart, D., and the PDP Research Group (1986). *Parallel distributed processing: explorations in the microstructure of Cognition*, Vol. 2. Cambridge, Mass.: MIT Press.

McCusker, L. X., Hillinger, M. L., and Bias, R. G. (1981). Phonological recoding and reading. *Psychol. Bull.* 89:217–245.

Mesulam, M. M. (1990). Large scale neurocognitive networks and distributed processing for attention, language and memory. *Ann. Neurol.* 28:587–613.

Misch, W., and Frankl, K. (1929). Beitrag zur Alexielehr. *Monatsschr. Psychiatr. Neurol.* 71:1–47.

Morton, J., and Patterson, K. E., (1980). A new attempt at an interpretation, or, an attempt at a new interpretation. In *Deep Dyslexia*, M. Coltheart, K. Patterson, and J. C. Marshall (eds.). London: Routledge and Kegan Paul.

Moss, S. E., and Rothi, L.J.G. (1987). Computerized treatment of alexia without agraphia: a case report. *J. Clin. Exp. Neuropsychol.* 9:39.

Moss, S. E., and Rothi, L. J. G., (1988). Computerized treatment of pure alexia: an advanced treatment program. *J. Clin. Exp. Neuropsychol.* 10:30.

Mozer, M. C. (1983). Letter migration in word perception. *J. Exp. Psychol.: Hum. Percept. Perform.* 9:531–546.

Newcombe, F., and Marshall, J. C. (1980). Transcoding and lexical stabilization in deep dyslexia. In *Deep Dyslexia*, M. Coltheart, K. E. Patterson, and J. C. Marshall (eds.). London: Routledge and Kegan Paul.

Newcombe, F., and Marshall, J. C. (1985). Reading and writing by letter sounds. In *Surface Dyslexia* K. E. Patterson, J. C. Marshall, and M. Coltheart (eds.). London: Lawrence Erlbaum Associates.

Patterson, K. E. (1982). The relation between reading and phonological coding; further neuropsychological observations. In *Normality and Pathology in Cognitive Functions*, A. W. Ellis (ed.). London: Academic Press.

Patterson, K. E., and Besner, D. (1984a). Is the right hemisphere literate? *Cognitive Neuropsychol. 1*:315–341.

Patterson, K. E., and Besner, D. (1984b). Reading from the left: a reply to Rabinowicz and Moscovitch and to Zaidel and Schweiger. *Cognitive Neuropsychol. 1*:365–380.

Patterson, K. E., and Kay, J. (1982). Letter by letter reading; psychological descriptions of a neurological syndrome. *Q. J. Exp. Psychol. 34A*:411–441.

Patterson, K. E., and Morton, J. (1985). From orthography to phonology; an attempt at an old interpretation. In *Surface Dyslexia*, K. E. Patterson, J. C. Marshall, and M. Coltheart (eds.). London: Lawrence Erlbaum Associates.

Patterson, K. E., and Wilson, B., (1990). A ROSE is a ROSE or a NOSE; a deficit in initial letter identification. *Cognitive Neuropsychol. 7*:447–477.

Patterson, K. E., Marshall, J. C., and Coltheart, M. (1985). *Surface Dyslexia*. London: Lawrence Erlbaum Associates.

Rapcsak, S. Z., Rothi, L.J.G., and Heilman, K. M. (1987). Phonological alexia with optic and tactile anomia. *Brain Lang. 31*:109–121.

Rayner, K., Murphy, L. A., Henderson, J. M., and Pollatsek, A. (1989). Selective attentional dyslexia. *Cognitive Neuropsychol. 6*:357–378.

Riddoch, J. (1990). Neglect and the peripheral dyslexias. *Cognitive Neuropsychol. 7*:369–389.

Riddoch, J., Humphreys, G., Cleton, P., and Fery, P. (1990). Interaction of attentional and lexical processes in neglect dyslexia. *Cognitive Neuropsychol. 7*:479–517.

Rothi, L.J.G., Goldstein, L. P., Teas, E., Schoenfeld, D., Moss, S. E., and Ochipa, C. (1986). Treatment of alexia without agraphia: a case report. Presented at the International Neuropsychological Society, Denver.

Rumelhart, D. E., McClelland, J. L., and the PDP Research Group (1986). *Parallel Distributed Processing: Explorations in the Microstructure of Cognition*, Vol. 1. Cambridge, Mass.: MIT Press.

Saffran, E. M. (1985). Lexicalization and reading performance in surface dyslexia. In *Surface Dyslexia*, K. E. Patterson, J. C. Marshall, and M. Coltheart (eds.). London: Lawrence Erlbaum Associates.

Sasanuma, S. (1985). Surface dyslexia and dysgraphia: how are they manifested in Japanese? In: *Surface Dyslexia*, K. E. Patterson, J. C. Marshall, and M. Coltheart (eds.). London: Lawrence Erlbaum Associates.

Schweiger, A., Zaidel, E., Field, T., and Dobkin, B. (1989). Right hemisphere contribution to lexical access in an aphasic with deep dyslexia. *Brain Lang. 37*:73–89.

Seidenberg, M., and McClelland, J. L. (1989). A distributed developmental model of word recognition and naming. *Psychol. Rev. 96*:523–568.

Sevush, S., Roeltgen, D. P., Campanella, M. A., and Heilman, K. M. (1983). Preserved oral reading in Wernicke's aphasia. *Neurology 33*:916–920.

Shallice, T., and Saffran, E. (1986). Lexical processing in the absence of explicit word identification: evidence from a letter-by-letter reader. *Cognitive Neuropsychol. 3*:429–458.

Shallice, T., and Warrington, E. K. (1977). The possible role of selective attention in acquired dyslexia. *Neuropsychologia 15*:31–41.

Shallice, T., and Warrington, E. K., (1980). Single and multiple component central dyslexic syndromes. In *Deep Dyslexia*, M. Coltheart, K. E. Patterson, and J. C. Marshall (eds.). London: Routledge and Kegal Paul.

Shallice, T., Warrington, E. K., and McCarthy, R. (1983). Reading without semantics. *Q. J. Exp. Psychol.* 35A:111–138.

Skarda, C. A., and Freeman, W. J. (1987). Brains make chaos in order to make sense of the world. *Behav. Brain Sci.* 10:161–196.

Stanovich, K. E., and Bauer, K. W. (1978). Experiments on the spelling to sound regularity effect in word recognition. *Memory Cognition* 6:410–415.

Temple, C. M. (1985). Surface dyslexia: variations wtihin a syndrome. In *Surface Dyslexia*, K. E. Patterson, J. C. Marshall, and M. Coltheart (eds.). London: Lawrence Erlbaum Associates.

Tusa, R. J., and Ungerleider, L. G. (1985). The inferior longitudinal fasciculus: a reexamination in humans and monkeys. *Ann Neurol.* 18:583–591.

Venezky, R. L. (1970). *The Structure of English Orthography*. The Hague: Mouton.

Warrington, E. K., and Zangwill, O. L. (1957). A study of dyslexia. *J. Neurol. Neurosurg. Psychiatry* 20:208–215.

Wernicke, C. (1874). *Der aphasische Symptomencomplex*. Breslau: Frank und Weigert.

Wijk, A. (1967). *Rules of Pronunciation for the English Language*. Oxford: Oxford University Press.

Zaidel, E., and Peters, A. M. (1981). Phonological encoding and ideographic reading by the disconnected right hemisphere; two case studies. *Brain Lang.* 14:205–234.

# 4

# Agraphia

DAVID P. ROELTGEN

Benedikt (1865) applied the term agraphia to disorders of writing and was one of the first to describe the relationship of agraphia to aphasia. Ogle (1867) also addressed the relationship of agraphia to aphasia and found that although aphasia and agraphia usually occurred together, they were occasionally separable. He described one patient who was aphasic but not agraphic and a second who was agraphic but not aphasic. Therefore, he concluded that there were distinct cerebral centers for writing and for speaking. Because agraphia and aphasia usually occurred together, he concluded that these centers were close together. Ogle's classification of agraphia included amnemonic agraphia and atactic agraphia. Patients with amnemonic agraphia wrote well-formed, but incorrect letters. Patients with atactic agraphia made poorly formed letters but usually had an element of amnemonic agraphia as well. Ogle's two types of agraphia might be termed linguistic and motor.

In contrast to Ogle, Lichtheim (1885) proposed that disorders of writing usually were the same as disorders of speech. The exception was agraphia due to disruption of the "center from which the organs of writing are innervated." Clinically, that agraphia was similar to Ogle's atactic agraphia. Lichtheim proposed that agraphia and aphasia were similar because the acquisition of writing (and spelling) was superimposed on speech, and therefore utilized previously acquired speech centers.

Head's position (1926) was similar to Lichtheim's. He stressed that the capacity to write was associated with internal speech because writing development was superimposed on speech. Therefore, his classification of the agraphias was the same as his classification of the aphasias. With verbal aphasia the production of language was disturbed and therefore these patients had severe agraphia. Syntactical aphasia led to disruption of phrase structure. Nominal aphasia led to poor word choice and to poor letter choice (misspellings). Semantic aphasia led to the production of incoherent phrases.

Nielson's classification (1946) reflected his view that writing is closely associated with speech but separable from it (a view similar to Ogle's). Nielson described three types of agraphia: apractic (apraxic), aphasic, and isolated. Apractic agraphia was characterized by poorly formed letters and was associated with the various apraxias.

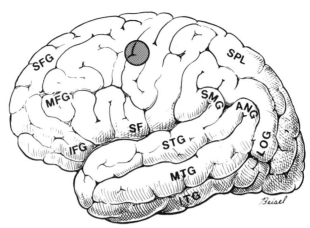

**Fig. 4-1.** Lateral view of the left hemisphere demonstrating the approximate position attributed to Exner's area. ANG = angular gyrus, IFG = inferior frontal gyrus, ITG = inferior temporal gyrus, LOG = lateral occipital gyrus, MFG = middle frontal gyrus, MTG = middle temporal gyrus, SF = sylvian fissure, SFG = superior frontal gyrus, SMG = supramarginal gyrus, SPL = superior parietal lobule, STG = superior temporal gyrus.

Aphasic agraphia was associated with the various aphasias, and the patients' written errors reflected the aphasic disturbance. Agraphia without associated neuropsychological signs (isolated agraphia) resulted from a lesion of the frontal writing center (Exner's area) or of the angular gyrus. Nielson thought that isolated agraphias were rare. He theorized that Exner's area, the foot of the second frontal convolution (Fig. 4-1), worked in close association with the angular gyrus and Wernicke's area to produce writing. He also proposed that the fibers carrying information from the angular gyrus to Exner's area passed close to Broca's speech area. Nielson suggested that these functional and anatomic connections accounted for the frequent association of agraphia and aphasia.

Goldstein (1948) took the position that agraphia is often but not always associated with aphasia. Thus, he described two general types of agraphia: primary, resulting from impairment of the motor act of writing, and secondary, resulting from disturbances of speech. The primary agraphias were divided into five types: (1) poor impulse for writing (with transcortical aphasias); (2) impairment of the abstract attitude, leading to trouble using small words with better production of concrete words; (3) ideatoric agraphia characterized by loss of the idea of letter form; (4) pure or motor agraphia characterized by production of incorrect letters; and (5) agraphia associated with apraxia of the minor hand. In secondary agraphias the letter form is unimpaired but words are misspelled. He described five types of secondary agraphia, corresponding to the five types of aphasia: motor aphasia, central aphasia, pure sensory aphasia, cortical sensory aphasia, and the transcortical aphasias. In most of these the agraphia was thought to parallel the aphasia.

In addition to the dissociations between aphasia and agraphia and the contrast of motor agraphia and linguistic agraphia, as early at the 1880s, two different linguistic abilities were postulated (Roeltgen and Rapcsak, in press). Dejerine (1891) and Pitres (1894) postulated orthographic or visual word images. In contrast, Grashey (1885) and Wernicke (1886) postulated that writing utilized translation of sound units into letters.

## TESTING FOR AGRAPHIA

As discussed above, many investigators have agreed that there are two major components of writing: linguistic and motor. In the evaluation of a patient with agraphia, both components must be evaluated. The linguistic component includes the choice of the correct letters (spelling) and the choice of the correct word (meaning). The motor component includes those neuropsychologic functions necessary for producing the correct letter form and correct word form. In order to evaluate these features it is convenient to divide the test into three types: spontaneous writing, writing to dictation, and copying.

To test spontaneous writing the patient is asked to write sentences or words about a familiar topic. For maximum value the topic should be standard from patient to patient, and controlled. Therefore, we recommend having the patient write about a picture. The same picture can then be used with different patients and at different times with the same patient in order to compare performance. From this spontaneous writing sample it is possible to judge in a general way both the content and form of the patient's writing.

Having the patient write to dictation gives the examiner better stimulus control. This enables the examiner to evaluate some of the specific features of writing. However, writing to dictation is usually limited to single words or phrases. To evaluate the effects of particular variables on writing, the type of word may be varied (e.g., long vs. short, common vs. uncommon). The word type can also be varied to test specific hypotheses based on models of agraphia such as those presented later in this chapter. These models predict, for example, that certain patients may have more difficulty with a word depending on word class (noun, verb, adjective, adverb, or function word, i.e., conjunctions and prepositions), imageability (high or low), abstractness (high or low), regularity (regular or irregular), or lexicality (real or nonword). The type of patient response may also be varied: the patient can be asked to spell orally, type, or spell using anagram letters (blocks with single letters written on them). This enables the examiner to determine if the disorder is only within the writing mechanism or if it is part of a more fundamental linguistic disorder, encompassing not only letter production, but also letter choice.

The third group of writing tests evaluates copying. Depending on the goals of the examination, the task may include copying single letters, words, sentences, and/or paragraphs. When one asks a patient to copy, it is important, but not always possible, to distinguish slavish or "stroke-by-stroke" copying from transcribing. Transcribing is characterized by reading the material and then writing it in an almost spontaneous fashion. It may be possible to distinguish these copying methods by (1) varying the length of material to be copied (increased length usually decreases slavish copying), (2) increasing the distance between the stimulus and the response (it is difficult to slavishly copy material from across the room), (3) having the patient copy nonsense figures (figures which have no symbolic meaning) since it is very difficult to transcribe nonsense symbols, and (4) performing delayed copying (showing the stimulus to the patient, removing the stimulus and then having him or her write it).

After writing (or oral spelling) is produced, important information is frequently gleaned from the analysis of the productions. First, correct performance as related to specific word types is helpful (i.e., comparing frequency of correct performance on regular compared to irregular words) (see the section on lexical agraphia below). Second, the type of error may be important. Patients with one type of agraphia may produce a specific type of error (i.e., semantic errors in deep agraphia or phonologically inaccurate errors in phonological agraphia, see below). Lastly, recent studies have indicated that a level of analysis that has been ignored in most previous studies, analysis of syntax, content, and sentence length in written paragraphs, may be of importance (Rapcsak and Rubens, 1990).

Linguistic error analysis is important in assessing patients with linguistic agraphia. Analysis of handwriting form is necessary in assessing patients with motor agraphia. Such analysis in adult neuropsychology is usually clinical and nonsystematic. However, assessment of developmental dysgraphia in children has at times been performed using a systematic approach (Denckla and Roeltgen, in press). In addition, we (Roeltgen et al., 1991; Denckla and Roeltgen, in press) have developed a computerized system that effectively, efficiently, and accurately measures most of the structural components that are important in printed handwriting (manuscript).

In addition to these detailed tests of writing, it is important to evaluate the patient for neurological disorders that may interfere with writing, oral spelling, or copying. These include disorders of speech, reading, ideomotor praxis, visuoperceptual, visuospatial, and constructional abilities, and elementary motor and sensory functions.

## COMMON NEUROLOGICAL CLASSIFICATIONS OF AGRAPHIA

Among recent classifications of agraphia have been those by Leischner (1969), Hécaen and Albert (1978), Benson (1979), and Kaplan and Goodglass (1981). These classifications, derived from clinical evaluations of agraphic patients, have usually included five general types of agraphia (Table 4-1): pure agraphia, aphasic agraphia, agraphia with alexia (also called parietal agraphia) (Kaplan and Goodglass, 1981), apraxic agraphia, and spatial agraphia.

Pure agraphia is characterized by the presence of agraphia in the absence of any other significant language disturbance. Pure agraphia may result from a focal lesion

**Table 4-1.** Neurological Classification of Agraphia

| |
| --- |
| Pure agraphia |
| Aphasic agraphia |
| Agraphia with alexia (parietal agraphia) |
| Apraxic agraphia |
| Spatial agraphia |

or an acute confusional state. Patients with agraphia from focal lesions make well-formed graphemes (written letters) with spelling errors that vary in type, depending on the lesion location. Pure agraphia has been reported from focal lesions in the second frontal convolution (Exner's area) (Aimard et al., 1975; Hécaen and Albert, 1978; Marcie and Hécaen, 1979; Kaplan and Goodglass, 1981), superior parietal lobule (Basso et al., 1978), the posterior perisylvian region (Rosati and DeBastiani, 1981; Auerbach and Alexander, 1981), and the region of the left caudate and internal capsule (Laine and Martilla, 1981) and other subcortical structures (Tanridag and Kirshner, 1985; Kertesz et al., 1990). Pure agraphia resulting from an acute confusional state (Chedru and Geschwind, 1972) is characterized by poorly formed graphemes, inability to write on a line, and writing over the model when copying. When the letters are well formed, spelling errors may be recognized.

Aphasic agraphia has been described with Broca's aphasia, conduction aphasia, Wernicke's aphasia, and transcortical sensory aphasia (Marcie and Hécaen, 1979; Benson, 1979; Kaplan and Goodglass, 1981; Grossfeld and Clark, 1983). Two distinct subtypes of agraphia have been described in patients with Broca's aphasia. One agraphia is characterized by a difficulty in graphemic production and the second by agrammatism (Marcie and Hécaen, 1979; Kaplan and Goodglass, 1981). Patients with the former make poorly formed graphemes and have severe difficulty spelling. Patients with the latter make well-formed graphemes but produce agrammatic sentence structure. Agraphia with conduction aphasia is characterized by misspellings and overwriting (Marcie and Hécaen, 1979). Wernicke's aphasics make severe spelling errors that are similar to the phonemic and semantic jargon typically heard in their speech (Marcie and Hécaen, 1979; Kaplan and Goodglass, 1981). The lesions causing the aphasic agraphias are usually not different from the lesions that typically cause the associated aphasic disorder.

Agraphia with alexia has also been called parietal agraphia because these two symptoms, in the absence of significant aphasia, usually occur together in patients with parietal lesions (Kaplan and Goodglass, 1981). These patients typically make poorly formed graphemes when writing. When spelling aloud they pronounce letters correctly but have difficulty spelling.

Apraxic agraphia is characterized by difficulty in forming graphemes when writing spontaneously and to dictation (Leischner, 1969; Hécaen and Albert, 1978; Marcie and Hécaen, 1979). Copying and oral spelling may be disturbed as well. "Writing" frequently improves with the use of anagram letters. The lesions causing apraxic agraphia are usually in the parietal lobe opposite the preferred hand.

Lesions in the nondominant parietal lobe may cause spatial agraphia. Patients with this type of agraphia typically duplicate strokes, having trouble writing on a horizontal line, write on only the right side of the paper, and have intrusion of blank spaces between graphemes. It is frequently associated with the neglect syndrome (Hécaen and Albert, 1978; Marcie and Hécaen, 1979; Benson, 1979).

Although we have attempted to classify agraphia into five well-defined groups, detailed analysis of agraphic patients reveals difficulty in classifying many of them (Roeltgen and Heilman, 1985). For example, some patients with Broca's aphasia have agraphias that more closely resemble the agraphias of patients with Wernicke's aphasia than the agraphias of other patients with Broca's aphasia. Also, certain lesion sites may be associated with multiple agraphias. For example, parietal lesions may cause parietal agraphia (agraphia with alexia) but may also cause apraxic agraphia. In some discussions it is not clear whether or not these two syndromes represent the same abnormality seen from two different perspectives. One way that these difficulties may be resolved is by using an alternative approach to classifying the agraphias. Rather than base the classification on clinical descriptions of agraphic patients, the classification can be based on the neuropsychological mechanism within the writing system that is presumed to be disturbed.

## A NEUROPSYCHOLOGICAL MODEL OF WRITING AND SPELLING

In order to develop such a classification one must first appreciate what neuropsychological mechanisms may be involved in writing. It is best to begin with the two general categories of functions necessary for writing that Ogle (1867) delineated: linguistic components and motor components. To these must be added certain visuospatial skills.

In the last decade, numerous information processing or cognitive models have been proposed to explain the ability to write (and spell aloud) (Ellis, 1982; Margolin, 1984; Roeltgen, 1985; Roeltgen and Heilman, 1985; Patterson, 1986; Lesser, 1990; Rapcsak and Rubens, 1990). These models contain many similar components, although the terms used to describe the components, and the subtleties of functional capacity among them, often differ. In the context of these models, there have been occasional attempts at clinical-pathological correlations of the agraphias, but only rarely has there been an attempt to correlate the cognitive components and the brain regions that might be associated with them (Roeltgen, 1985; Roeltgen and Heilman, 1985). The model of writing described here (Fig. 4-2) is a modification of one we have presented before (Roeltgen, 1985; Roeltgen and Heilman, 1985). It defines many of the linguistic and motor components thought to be important for writing and oral spelling. It also addresses the mode of interaction between motor components and visuospatial skills. Lastly, it suggests certain anatomic regions that may be associated with specific types of agraphia. Among the linguistic components, there are at least two parallel systems available for spelling, and a mechanism by which semantics (meaning) interacts with these systems. This interaction enables one to write with meaning. The motor components include mechanisms by which words can be spelled or written. It appears that the parallel spelling systems converge prior to motor output as drawn in Figure 4-2. A detailed discussion of this model follows.

For convenience, this chapter will refer to the general output of both writing and oral spelling systems as "spelling." "Writing" will refer to written production (handwriting) and "oral spelling" will refer to oral production.

### *Linguistic Components*

LEXICAL AGRAPHIA

There are at least two general systems available to adults for spelling words: lexical and phonological (Beauvois and Derouesne, 1981; Ellis, 1982; Roeltgen et al., 1982a,

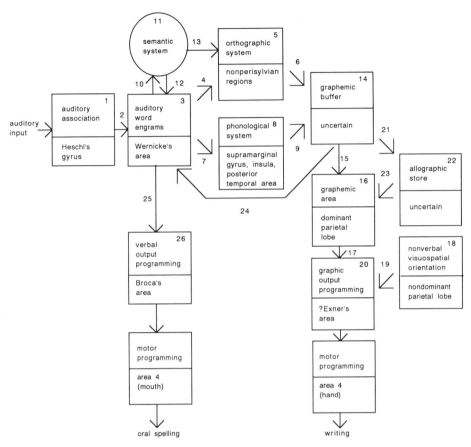

**Fig. 4-2.** An anatomically based neuropsychological model of writing and spelling.

1983a; Hatfield and Patterson, 1983; Roeltgen and Heilman, 1984, 1985; Patterson, 1986; Bub and Chertkow, 1988; Roeltgen and Rapcsak, in press). The lexical system (Fig. 4-2, pathway 4-5-6), probably functionally the more important, has also been called lexical-orthographic (Margolin, 1984) or orthographic (Patterson, 1986; Rapcsak and Rubens, 1990). This system appears to utilize a whole-word retrieval process that may incorporate visual word images. It has been proposed that these visual word images arise from word engrams that are visual rather than phonological (Roeltgen et al., 1983a). In some patients the lexical system may also use whole-word processing that is not entirely based on visual word images but may include certain phonological components, word analogies, and mnemonic rules (Hatfield, 1985). The lexical strategy is necessary for spelling familiar orthographically irregular words (words that cannot be spelled utilizing direct sound-to-letter correspondence rules, e.g., "comb") and ambiguous words (words with sounds that may be represented by multiple letters or letter clusters, e.g., "phone"). The lexical system can also be used for spelling familiar orthographically regular words (words with direct sound-to-letter correspondence, e.g., "animal") that the phonological system can also handle (see below).

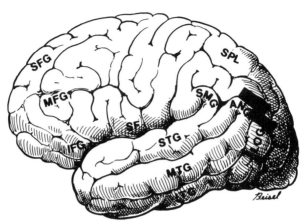

**Fig. 4-3.** Lateral view of the left hemisphere demonstrating the region damaged in four patients with lexical agraphia. (From Roeltgen and Heilman, 1984.) Abbreviations are explained in caption to Figure 4-1.

Dysfunction of the lexical system is called lexical agraphia (Beauvois and Derouesne, 1981; Roeltgen and Heilman, 1984). It has also been called phonological spelling (Hatfield and Patterson, 1983). This disorder is characterized by impaired ability to spell irregular and ambiguous words with preserved ability to spell regular words and nonwords. These patients usually make errors that are phonologically correct (e.g., "gelosy" for "jealousy"). Approximately 20 patients with lexical agraphia have been reported (Beauvois and Derouesne, 1981; Hatfield and Patterson, 1983; Roeltgen and Heilman, 1984; Goodman-Shulman and Caramazza, 1987; Rapcsak et al., 1988, 1990; Friedman and Alexander, 1989; Croisile et al., 1989; Alexander et al., 1990; Roeltgen and Rapcsak, in press).

Previously, Roeltgen and Heilman (1984) attempted to delineate the anatomy underlying lexical agraphia. We studied the computerized tomograms (CT) of four patients with lexical agraphia by plotting the lesions seen on CT on a lateral view of the left hemisphere. Overlap of these plots revealed that the junction of the posterior angular gyrus and the parieto-occipital lobule was lesioned in each patient (Fig. 4-3). In addition, the lesion extended subcortically into the white matter in all patients. This suggested that this area is an important anatomic substrate for lexical agraphia.

Since then there have been reports that some patients with lexical agraphia have lesions at or around the dominant angular gyrus (Roeltgen, 1989; Alexander et al., 1990), while others have lesions outside that region. These have included the right parietal lobe (in a right-hander without aphasia or alexia) (Rothi et al., 1987), the left posterior temporal region (middle temporal gyrus) (Croisile et al., 1989), the left frontal region (Rapcsak et al., 1988), the left caudate (Roeltgen, 1989), and left thalamus (Roeltgen, 1989). Roeltgen and Rapcsak (in press) reviewed reports of previous patients with lexical agraphia and added seven new cases. We concluded that patients with lexical agraphia had lesions that usually spared the immediate perisylvian region, especially the anterior supramarginal gyrus and insula, areas thought to be important for the production of phonological agraphia (see below). We also noted a degree of linguistic heterogeneity that was consistent with the pathological heterogeneity. We concluded that the most striking cases appeared to have lesions of the angular gyrus but that the clinical and pathological heterogeneity were consistent with Hatfield's (1985) position that the lexical system might contain multiple cognitive components.

PHONOLOGICAL AGRAPHIA

The alternative parallel spelling system is the phonological system (Fig. 4-2, pathway 7-8-9). Words and speech sounds must be phonologically decoded and then converted into letters. One way this may occur is through what has been termed sublexical sound-letter or phoneme-grapheme conversion. For this method to occur there are at least two necessary components: segmentation and sound-letter conversion. The former parses the phoneme string into separate phonemes and the latter converts the single phonemes into letters. Alternatively, it has been suggested that the phonological system is lexically based and spells unknown words by an analogy method (Campbell, 1985). An analogy system chooses a spelling for a nonword by associating the phonology of the stimulus with similar-sounding real words and then chooses the best combination of sounds for the response. The phonological system is used for spelling unfamiliar orthographically regular words and pronounceable nonwords (e.g., "flig"). It is probable that this sytem is used to spell familiar regular words only when the lexical system is dysfunctional or when there is no available lexical item for the word that is to be spelled (an unfamiliar word).

    Dysfunction of the phonological system causes phonological agraphia (Shallice, 1981; Roeltgen et al., 1983a). This disorder is characterized by impaired ability to spell nonwords and preserved ability to spell familiar words, both regular and irregular. Spelling errors by patients with phonological agraphia are usually not phonologically correct but may have a high degree of visual resemblance to the stimulus (Fig. 4-4).

    Roeltgen and colleagues (Roeltgen et al., 1983a; Roeltgen and Heilman, 1984) have

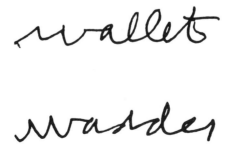

Fig. 4-4. Example of visual similarity of errors made by patients with phonological agraphia. Above, "wallet" written correctly; below, "wallet" written incorrectly. (From Roeltgen, Sevush, and Heilman, 1983a.)

investigated the anatomic basis of phonological agraphia using the methods similar to the methods they used with lexical agraphia. The lesion site common to eight patients with phonological agraphia was the supramarginal gyrus or the insula medial to it (Fig. 4-5). In addition, one patient with isolated phonological agraphia (that is, with no additional language deficits) had a small lesion confined to the insula or possibly extending to the surface of the supramarginal gyrus as revealed by CT scan (Roeltgen et al., 1982). We concluded that lesions of the supramarginal gyrus or the insula medial to it (or both) are the critical anatomic loci for inducing phonological agraphia. Previously, other patients with phonological agraphia had been reported to have lesions that included this area (Shallice, 1981; Bub and Kertesz, 1982; Nolan and Caramazza, 1982).

As in the case of lexical agraphia, subsequent studies of phonological agraphia have yielded patients with lesions that did not precisely correspond to Roeltgen and colleagues' hypothesis. Baxter and Warrington (1986) described a patient with phonological agraphia who had a lesion that appeared to be slightly posterior to that proposed by Roeltgen and colleagues. Bolla-Wilson et al. (1985) described a left-handed patient with phonological agraphia who had a lesion of the right frontal-parietal region (involving the supramarginal gyrus and insula). Also, Roeltgen (1989) described patients with lesions away from those previously described. These lesion sites included the caudate and internal capsule and the thalamus and posterior internal capsule. Based on these data, we have concluded that phonological agraphia is usually associated with lesions of the posterior perisylvian region and certain subcortical structures. In addition, there may be functional diversity similar to that proposed for lexical agraphia, and there are also individual variations in cerebral architecture and functional representation.

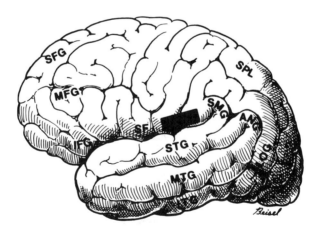

**Fig. 4-5.** A lateral view of the left hemisphere demonstrating the region damaged in eight patients with phonological agraphia. (From Roeltgen and Heilman, 1984.) Abbreviations are explained in caption to Figure 4-1.

## DEEP AGRAPHIA

Bub and Kertesz (1982) and Hatfield (1985) have used the term deep agraphia to describe a syndrome of phonological agraphia with a group of associated findings. Their patients, as well as two others (Roeltgen et al., 1983a) had trouble spelling nonwords but also showed trouble spelling function words compared to nouns, and spelled nouns of high imageability (e.g., arm) better than nouns of low imageability (e.g., law). These patients also made semantic paragraphias. These are spelling errors that consist of real words related in meaning to the target word, but with little phonological or visual resemblance to the target. For example, one patient wrote "flight" when the stimulus was "propeller" (Roeltgen et al., 1983a).

All reported cases of deep agraphia have had phonological agraphia as well and have had lesions of the supramarginal gyrus or insula (Roeltgen et al., 1983a; Bub and Kertesz, 1982; Nolan and Caramazza, 1982). But their lesions have been large, extending well beyond the circumscribed area thought to be important for phonological agraphia. It is possible that deep agraphia reflects right-hemisphere writing processes (Roeltgen and Heilman, 1982). This hypothesis is similar to a proposed explanation for deep dyslexia, a reading disorder that is clinically similar to deep agraphia. Patients with deep dyslexia have trouble reading nonwords and make frequent semantic errors. Also, their reading ability is affected by word class and imageability (Coltheart, 1980; Saffran et al., 1980). The alternative hypothesis is that residual left-hemisphere mechanisms are important for the residual abilities in patients with deep agraphia (Roeltgen and Heilman, 1982). A possible anatomic correlate of this hypothesis is that the left posterior angular gyrus has been spared in patients with deep agraphia.

## SEMANTIC INFLUENCE ON WRITING

The incorporation of meaning into what is written is termed the semantic influence on writing. The classical view of the interaction between semantics and language is that semantics interacts directly with oral language through auditory word images (Heilman et al., 1976, 1981) (Fig. 4-2, pathway 12). Such an interaction enables a writer to incorporate meaning into words utilizing both the lexical strategy and the phonological strategy. With this arrangement the incorporation of meaning into spelling is indirect: it must come through auditory word images. There is evidence to suggest, however, the semantics may directly influence the lexical strategy (Brown and McNeill, 1966; Hier and Mohr, 1977; Morton, 1980; Shallice, 1981; Roeltgen et al., 1983a) Fig. 4-2, pathway 13).

*Semantic agraphia.*    There are clinical disorders that exemplify the interactions of semantics and spelling. A disruption of semantic ability (Fig. 4-2, component 11) or a disconnection of semantics from spelling (disruption of pathways 12 and 13, Fig. 4-2) has been termed semantic agraphia (Roeltgen et al., 1986). Patients with semantic agraphia lose their ability to spell and write with meaning. They may produce semantic jargon in sentence production (Rapcsak and Rubens, 1990). Also, they write and orally spell semantically incorrect but correctly spelled dictated homophones (words that are pronounced the same, but have different meanings dependent on the spelling, such as "doe" and "dough"). For example, when asked to write doe as in "the doe ran through the forest," these patients may write "dough." They may write irregular words and nonwords correctly, demonstrating intact lexical and phonological systems (Fig. 4-2, pathways 4-5-6 and 7-8-9). The pathology of the reported patients with semantic agraphia is inconsistent but frequently involves anatomic substrates important for assessing meaning in speech (Roeltgen and Rapcsak, in press).

*Lexical agraphia with semantic paragraphia.*    Another disorder involving semantic interaction with spelling is a part of the syndrome of lexical agraphia. Many patients with lexical agraphia have difficulty utilizing semantic information when writing (Hatfield and Patterson, 1983; Roeltgen, personal observation). These patients, when asked to spell dictated homophones, frequently spell the semantically incorrect homophone (as do patients with semantic agraphia). They differ from some patients with semantic agraphia in that they are able to comprehend the meaning of the words when they read or hear them. Therefore, general semantic knowledge (Fig. 4-2, component 11) is preserved, but interacts poorly with spelling. This is presumably because there is a disturbance of the direct semantic influence on spelling (through the lexical system).

A TEST OF THE MODEL

The model described here, as well as other similar models of spelling, has been developed from single case reports and small series of patients. Roeltgen (1989, 1991) recently completed a study designed to test whether the model could be generalized to all agraphia patients. To do this, he prospectively studied 43 consecutive right-handed patients with left-hemisphere lesions and compared them with controls matched for handedness, age, and education.

The results of this study provided some support for the model but indicated certain important modifications. Of the 43 patients studied, eight had no agraphia, five had lexical agraphia, four had phonological agraphia, and ten had semantic agraphia. In this study classification as phonological agraphia required a moderately good performance on real words, whereas some previous studies (Roeltgen et al., 1983a; Roeltgen and Heilman, 1984) had less strict criteria, and included patients with less proficient performances on real words. The use of stricter criteria necessitated formulating definitions for additional groups of patients including global agraphia, phonological-plus agraphia, mixed-plus agraphia, and noncompensated lexical agraphia. The first group (global) consisted of six patients with severely impaired performance when spelling all word types. The second group (phonological-plus) consisted of three patients with impaired performance when spelling nonwords and moderately or severely impaired performance when spelling real words. However, they had no difference in performance when spelling regular compared to irregular words. The third group (mixed-plus) consisted of eight patients with impaired performance when spelling nonwords (similar to phonological agraphia), a significant difference in performance when spelling regular compared to irregular words (similar to lexical agraphia), and overall poorer performance than either of the subjects with phonological or lexical agraphia. The fourth group (noncompensated lexical) consisted of eight patients with normal or nearly normal spelling performance when spelling nonwords but impaired performance when spelling real words, with an equal degree of impairment for both regular and irregular words. Although some of the patients in the last group may have had some impairment in the graphemic buffer (see below), accounting for equal impairment on regular and irregular words, the good performance on nonwords makes that explanation unlikely. It is more likely that these patients, like patients with lexical agraphia, had impairment of the lexical system, but, unlike patients with lexical agraphia, they did not use the relatively preserved phonological system to compensate for difficulty spelling real words. This lack of compensation may be explained by the finding that patients with noncompensated lexical agraphia were less likely to have chronic lesions than patients with lexical agraphia.

Attempts were made to correlate the type of agraphia with the locus of the cerebral lesion. Lesion locations of patients with lexical, phonological, and semantic agraphias were similar to those described previously. Patients with lexical agraphia had lesions away from the mid-perisylvian region, specifically the insula, the anterior supramarginal gyrus, and the posterior superior temporal gyrus. In contrast, the patients with phonological agraphia had lesions involving these structures. The patients with semantic agraphia had various left-hemispheric lesions.

Educational level significantly affected spelling performance after stroke. Better-educated subjects had better overall spelling ability after stroke and were less likely to have difficulty spelling nonwords.

In summary, the results from this prospective study supported the general framework of Roeltgen and Heilman's anatomically based information processing model of spelling. However, analysis of the results also indicated that premorbid education level and chronicity of the lesion also had an effect on the outcome. For example, it appears that for patients to develop lexical agraphia after a stroke, they need chronic lesions in the nonperisylvian brain regions, sparing the mid-insula, anterior supramarginal gyrus, and posterior superior temporal region, and usually 12 or more years of premorbid education.

### *Transition from Linguistic Information in Motor Output and the Graphemic Buffer*

Potential spellings produced by the phonological and lexical systems in most circumstances apparently converge prior to motor output, whether it be oral (oral spelling) or graphic (writing). This convergence is evident clinically, since most patients with disorders of either spelling system produce substantially the same errors in oral spelling as in writing.

Since the lexical and phonological systems need not produce the same spellings, there must be some way of choosing which spelling is to be produced. For example, in attempting to spell "comb," the lexical system, if familiar with the word, will produce "c-o-m-b." The phonological system, however, may produce "k-o-m" or "c-o-m," since the silent "b" does not conform to the rules of English orthography. Alternatively, "k-o-m-e" could be produced by analogy with "home." These alternative spellings will converge on the graphemic buffer (see below), which must transfer the correct spelling to the motor output systems. Because the lexical system produces only one response, which is dependent on prior experience, but the phonological system has the potential to produce multiple letter sequences for a single phonetic sequence, it is only reasonable to assume that under normal circumstances the output of the lexical system is preferentially incorporated into written or oral spelling. Data from patients with semantic agraphia support this contention (Roeltgen et al., 1986): patterns of responses obtained from these patients suggest that the phonological system is probably only used for spelling nonwords and unfamiliar regular words. Rarely, normal writers produce "slips of the pen" that are phonologically correct (Hotopf, 1980). These errors (responses such as "k-o-m" for "comb") suggest that although most normal spelling (and writing) utilizes the lexical system, the phonological system continues to function in the background.

GRAPHEMIC BUFFER

The output of the linguistic systems converges on what has been termed the graphemic or orthographic buffer (Fig. 4-2, component 14) (Margolin, 1984; Caramazza et al., 1987; Hillis and Caramazza, 1989; Lesser, 1990). This component of the model is thought to be a temporary working memory store of abstract letters. According to Caramazza and colleagues, disturbances of the graphemic buffer typically produce letter omissions, substitutions, insertions, and transpositions in nonwords and real words in oral and written spelling. Impairment occurs in spontaneous writing, writing to dictation, written naming, and delayed copying. Errors are not affected by linguistic factors (i.e., word class, regularity, and imageability) but are influenced by word length, with errors more common in longer words. Errors also tend to be more prominent at the beginnings and ends of words. Although most patients with impairment of this type show similar disturbances in oral and written spelling, Lesser (1990) has described a dissociation, such that oral spelling was influenced by regularity and written spelling was not. She therefore suggested that there are separate graphemic buffers for oral and written spelling.

Despite the fact that only a few reports have described patients with agraphia due to impairment of the graphemic buffer, the lesion loci have varied widely, including the left frontal parietal region (Hillis and Caramazza, 1989; Lesser, 1990), the left parietal region (Miceli et al., 1985), and the right frontal parietal, and basal ganglia region (Hillis and Caramazza, 1989). We (unpublished observation) and Laine (personal communication) have each observed patients with apparent agraphia due to impairment of the graphemic buffer. These patients had relatively discrete lesions of the left posterior dorsal lateral frontal lobe. Based on the anatomic variability among the lesions in these six patients, we do not feel that a proposed clinical-pathological correlation would be more than speculation.

## Motor Components

Motor output of spelled words may be either manual (writing letters or graphemes) or oral (oral spelling). Writing may be performed by the dominant or nondominant hand. Writing is not a unitary process, but includes motor and visuospatial skills, as well as knowledge of graphemes. Although there is some understanding of the neuropsychological bases of these skills, less is known about the components underlying oral spelling. Oral spelling and writing, however, do appear to be functionally dissociable.

*Apraxic agraphia.* In order to write, motor functions are necessary. In addition to the pyramidal and extrapyramidal motor systems (which will not be discussed here), praxis is necessary for writing (see Chapter 7). Praxis includes the ability to properly hold a pen or pencil as well as the ability to perform the other learned fine-finger movements necessary for forming written letters (graphemes). Apraxia usually results from lesions in the hemisphere opposite the preferred hand. In most right-handers, this is also the hemisphere dominant for language, and consequently apraxia is often associated with aphasia. In aphasic apraxic patients, it may not be possible to separate clearly the aphasic from the apraxic elements of agraphia. Several patients have been described who have had language in the hemisphere ipsilateral to the preferred hand. When the hemisphere opposite the preferred hand was damaged, they developed ideomotor apraxia without aphasia (Heilman et al., 1973, 1974; Valenstein and Heilman, 1979). Patients with such disorders have illegible writing, both spontaneously and to dictation. Their oral spelling is preserved. Their writing typically improves with copying. They should be able to type or use anagram letters (Valenstein and Heilman, 1979). This syndrome may be termed apraxic agraphia with ideomotor apraxia and without aphasia. Lesions in the parietal lobe opposite the hand dominant for writing may be the most common etiology for this disorder.

*Apraxic agraphia without apraxia (ideational agraphia).* The cognitive system necessary for performing handwriting, and thought to be important for knowledge of the features of letters, has been termed the graphemic area (Rothi and Heilman, 1981) (Fig. 4-2, component 16). These space-time or visuokinesthetic-motor engrams for letters may be a subset of the engrams necessary to program other skilled movements. Alternatively, letter engrams may be separate from other motor engrams. A syndrome of abnormal grapheme formation with normal praxis has been described and has been called apraxic agraphia with normal praxis (Roeltgen and Heilman, 1983). Patients produce poorly formed graphemes but have normal praxis, including the ability to imitate holding a pen or pencil. Apraxic agraphia with normal praxis is characterized by the production of illegibly formed graphemes in spontaneous writing and writing to dictation. Grapheme production improves with copying. Oral spelling and reading are intact. However, the initial patients described by Roeltgen and Heilman (1983) and Margolin and Binder (1984) also had disturbed visuospatial skills and therefore copying was moderately impaired. Baxter and Warrington (1986) have termed this disorder ideational agraphia and described a patient with this disorder who had intact visuospatial skills. Because of the good visuospatial skills, their patient's writing improved substantially with copying. A similar patient has been described by Croisile and co-workers (1990). The anatomic substrate for this syndrome appears to be in the parietal lobe, either in the hemisphere contralateral to the hand used for writing (Margolin and Binder, 1984; Baxter and Warrington, 1986) or in the ipsilateral hemisphere (Roeltgen and Heilman, 1983).

*Spatial agraphia.*   Visuospatial skills are also necessary for the proper formation of letters and words. Spatial orientation must interact with graphic output in order that letter components (strokes) can be properly formed by the system of graphic output programming (Fig. 4-2, pathway 18-19-20). Disruption of this ability has been termed visuospatial agraphia, constructional agraphia, or afferent dysgraphia (Ellis et al., 1987). It is characterized by the following features: (1) reiteration of strokes, (2) inability to write on a straight horizontal line, and (3) insertion of blank spaces between graphemes. In patients with this disorder the ability to copy is usually disturbed, but ability to spell orally and pronounce aurally perceived words is preserved. This syndrome is usually due to nondominant parietal lobe lesions. For this reason, it is also frequently associated with the syndrome of unilateral neglect, where the patient's writing may be confined to only one side of the paper, ipsilateral to the lesion (See Chapter 10). Ellis and colleagues (1987) have suggested that errors may relate both to the left-sided neglect and to failure to utilize visual and kinesthetic feedback.

*Agraphia due to an impaired allographic store.*   The allographic store (Fig. 4-2, component 22) is said to be important for directing the handwriting systems in the production of correct case (upper and lower) and style (script [cursive] or manuscript [print]). Its existence was hypothesized by Ellis (1982) based on analysis of slips of the pen (spontaneous errors made by normal subjects when writing). Recently, a few reports have described patients with apparently acquired agraphia due to impairment of the allographic store (Yopp and Roeltgen, 1987; DeBastiani and Barry, 1989; Black et al. 1987). Patients with agraphia due to apparent disruption of the allographic store have better oral spelling than writing, normal praxis, normal visuospatial ability, and normal letter form. However, they make frequent case and style errors. Case errors include difficulty producing a specific case or style or substitution of one particular case or style for another.

*Unilateral (callosal) agraphia.*   In most agraphias the dominant and nondominant hands are equally affected, except when one hand is paretic. The spelling and graphemic systems of the left hemisphere have access via the neocommissures to the right-hemisphere motor system responsible for controlling the nondominant hand. Patients may have this interhemispheric transfer disrupted, resulting in unilateral agraphia (Liepmann and Maas, 1907; Geschwind and Kaplan, 1962; Yamadori et al., 1980; Gersh and Damasio, 1981; Bogen, 1969; Rubens et al. 1977; Levy et al. 1971; Sugishita et al., 1980; Watson and Heilman, 1983). Most of these patients make unintelligible scrawls when they attempt to write with their left hands. Most improve with copying and are able to spell orally and read. Watson and Heilman (1983) have described a patient with left unilateral agraphia who was able to type with her left hand. They termed this syndrome unilateral apraxic agraphia, limited to the left hand. Their patient had a lesion affecting the body of the corpus callosum, sparing the genu and the splenium. Geschwind and Kaplan (1962) described a patient with

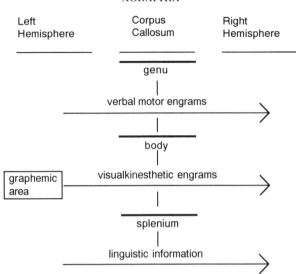

**Fig. 4-6.** Transfer of information across corpus callosum. Evidence suggests that there are at least three separable components necessary for writing and they cross at different levels of the callosum. Verbal motor programs cross in the genu, visuokinesthetic engrams cross in the body, and linguistic information crosses in the splenium.

an acquired callosal lesion and unilateral left agraphia who was unable to type or use anagram letters with his left hand. This patient's lesion affected the entire anterior four-fifths of the corpus callosum. Watson and Heilman (1983) suggested that the difference between their patient and that of Geschwind and Kaplan (1962) was that the genu of the corpus callosum was spared in Watson and Heilman's patient. They hypothesized that the genu is important for the transmission of verbal-motor programs from the left to the right hemisphere. They also hypothesized that the body of the corpus callosum is important for the transmission of visuokinesthetic (space-time) engrams. These engrams are thought to "command the motor systems to adopt the appropriate spatial positions of the relevant body parts over time" (Watson and Heilman, 1983). The disruption of transmission of these engrams was thought to account for the ideomotor apraxia that was also observed in Watson and Heilman's patient (Fig. 4-6).

Some patients with left-sided unilateral agraphia do not have ideomotor apraxia (Sugishita et al., 1980; Yamadori et al., 1980; Gersh and Damasio, 1981). The agraphia of these patients consists of illegible scrawls as well as incorrect letters. The patient of Gersh and Damasio was also unable to write using anagram letters. This syndrome has been called unilateral aphasic agraphia (Watson and Heilman, 1983). The lesions in these patients were confined to the posterior portion of the corpus callosum. Gersh and Damasio suggested that the pathways for ideomotor praxis were more anterior in the callosum than those for writing. Watson and Heilman (1983) further suggested that although the body of the callosum was important for the transfer of visuokinesthetic engrams (ideomotor praxis for writing and other motor tasks), the posterior callosum (especially the splenium) was important for the transmission of linguistic information. This explanation, they felt, accounted for the apraxic agraphia in their patient and the aphasic agraphia in Gersh and Damasio's patient.

Additionally, patients described by Sugushita et al. (1980) and Yamadori et al. (1980) showed a degree of dissociated linguistic agraphia with the left hand in that they wrote Kanji characters (morphograms) better than Kana (phonograms). Rothi et al. (1987) suggested that these results were consistent with the right hemisphere having ability to support both linguistic and motor mechanisms for the more ideographic Kanji characters than for the phonologic Kana.

DISORDERS OF ORAL SPELLING

The mechanisms for oral spelling are not as well defined as those for writing. Two possible mechanisms exist. One mechanism would utilize the area of auditory word engrams (Wernicke's area) to guide the anterior perisylvian speech regions (e.g., Broca's area) to produce oral letters (Fig. 4-2, pathway 25-26). The other mechanism would utilize an independent area of oral motor engrams for letters to guide or program Broca's area. Evidence at this time supports the first possible mechanism. One patient with relatively spared writing but disturbed oral spelling has been well described (Kinsbourne and Warrington, 1965). This patient also had difficulty saying words spelled to him. This finding suggests that the first mechanism is correct and that the system of auditory word images (Wernicke's area) is necessary for both perception of aurally perceived spelled words and the production of oral letters. Alternatively, there may be a close anatomic proximity between the area of auditory word images and the area of oral motor engrams for letters. If this hypothesis is correct, both systems were damaged in the patient of Kinsbourne and Warrington. Additionally, this hypothesis would predict that patients with destruction of auditory word images (Wernicke's aphasia) could have preserved oral spelling. Although patients with Wernicke's aphasia and preserved written spelling have been described (Hier and Mohr, 1977; Roeltgen et al., 1983a), no patients with preserved oral spelling have been described.

## THE RELATIONSHIPS OF THE LINGUISTIC AND MOTOR AGRAPHIAS WITH OTHER NEUROPSYCHOLOGICAL DISORDERS

As discussed, some classifications of agraphia are based on associated findings. Although they are not classified in this manner, the agraphias as defined by the model discussed in this chapter are associated with other neuropsychological disorders, such as aphasia, alexia, the Gerstmann syndrome, and ideomotor apraxia. Although not specific, many of the associations between agraphias and other neuropsychological disorders may have an anatomic or physiologic basis. These anatomic and physiologic mechanisms may also provide a means of understanding why these associations are nonspecific.

## Phonological Agraphia

At least 21 patients with phonological agraphia have been described (Shallice, 1981; Bub and Kertesz, 1982; Roeltgen, 1983; Roeltgen et al., 1983a; Roeltgen and Heilman, 1984; Baxter and Warrington, 1985; Bolla-Wilson et al., 1985; Hatfield, 1985; Goodman-Schulman and Caramazza, 1987). Nineteen of these patients had aphasia: seven Wernicke's, five Broca's, two conduction, two anomic, one global, one transcortical motor, and one transcortical sensory. Except for the transcortical aphasias, each of these aphasias is typically induced by a perisylvian lesion (Benson, 1979). Phonological agraphia is also due to a perisylvian lesion. This shared anatomic relationship, rather than the specific type of aphasia, probably accounts for the association between phonological agraphia and the aphasias.

Not only may phonological agraphia be dissociated from aphasia, but in aphasic patients, writing may be dissociated from speech. Two patients with phonological agraphia (Roeltgen et al., 1983a) wrote better than they spoke. This type of dissociation has been previously described in aphasic patients (Weisenberg and McBride, 1964; Mohr et al., 1973; Hier and Mohr, 1977; Assal et al., 1981). Our evaluation suggested that this dissociation occurs because speech depends on the left-hemisphere phonological systems, whereas writing may be performed nonphonologically by a lexical system using structures outside the left perisylvian area.

Similarly, disorders of writing and disorders of reading are sometimes dissociable. Neuropsychological models have been proposed for reading, similar to the model for writing discussed here (Shallice and Warrington, 1980; Beauvois and Derouesne, 1981). The reading models usually contain both a phonological system and a lexical system. Disruption of the phonological system, phonological alexia (dyslexia), is similar in many ways to phonological agraphia. In each of these disorders there is an inability to transcode nonwords. Also, each of these disorders may be accompanied by effects of imageability and word class with production of semantic paralexias and paragraphias resulting in the syndromes of "deep dyslexia" and "deep dysgraphia." Most patients with phonological agraphia who have alexia, have phonological alexia (Roeltgen, 1983). However, at least one patient had no alexia, and one patient had lexical (or surface) alexia (preserved ability to read nonwords with impaired ability to read irregular words). These findings indicate that phonological agraphia and phonological alexia are dissociable. There are two possible explanations for this dissociation (Fig. 4-7). First, the neuropsychological mechanisms for phonological spelling and phonological reading may represent the same function in opposite directions. The first, phoneme-grapheme conversion, proceeds from sound to sight, and the second, grapheme-phoneme conversion, from sight to sound. This hypothesis suggests that a single lesion affecting the basic phonological system would disrupt both phonological spelling and reading. One of these systems could become dysfunctional in isolation by disruption of information either as it exits the system or enters the system. Alternatively, each system may be dissociable from the other and the association or lack of association between phonological agraphia and the alexias might relate to the anatomic pathology of agraphia and alexia. For example, the anatomic substrate of phonological agraphia appears to be the supramarginal gyrus or insula. Roeltgen (1983) suggested that the mid-perisylvian region had a role in the production of pho-

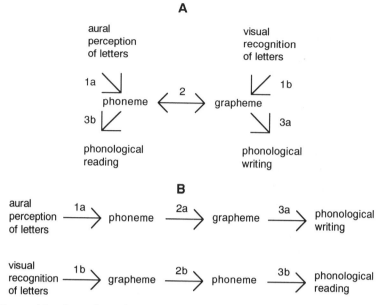

Fig. 4-7. Possible relationships of phonological reading and writing.
A: A common phonological system for both reading and writing

| Lesion site | Syndrome |
|---|---|
| 1 | Phonological agraphia and alexia |
| 2a or 2b | Phonological agraphia |
| 3a or 3b | Phonological alexia |

B: Two separate phonological systems, one for reading and one for writing

| Lesion site | Syndrome |
|---|---|
| Any combination of one "a" lesion and one "b" lesion | Phonological agraphia and alexia |
| 1a, 2a, or 3a | Phonological agraphia |
| 1b, 2b, or 3b | Phonological alexia |

nological alexia. It is possible that proximate structures play an important role in phonological spelling and reading.

In our reported series of 14 patients with phonological agraphia (Roeltgen, 1983) three had other elements of the Gerstmann syndrome (right-left confusion, finger agnosia, or dyscalculia) in addition to agraphia. Also, seven of them had mild or severe ideomotor apraxia. The Gerstmann syndrome has been attributed to lesions in the angular gyrus (Nielson, 1938; Gerstmann, 1940; Roeltgen et al., 1983b), and ideomotor apraxia is frequently attributed to lesions in the dominant parietal lobe (Heilman, 1979). The association of phonological agraphia with these disorders also appears to depend on the anatomic pathology of the lesions. It is probable that phonological agraphia is accompanied by the Gerstmann syndrome and ideomotor apraxia or both when the extent of the lesion is sufficient to involve the anatomic substrates of the Gerstmann functions and praxis.

## Lexical Agraphia

At least 19 patients with lexical agraphia have been described (Beauvois and Der-ouesne, 1981; Roeltgen and Heilman, 1983; Hatfield and Patterson, 1983; Goodman-Schulman and Caramazza, 1987; Rapcsak et al., 1988; Croisile et al., 1989; Rothi et al., 1987; Roeltgen and Rapcsak, in press). For those patients for whom an aphasia diagnosis is known, the frequency of aphasia types differs from that found in phonological agraphia. Two patients had transcortical sensory aphasia, two had Wernicke's aphasia, seven had anomia, one had tactile aphasia, one had phonetic disintegration, and four had no aphasia. Similar to phonological agraphia, the associations of lexical agraphia with aphasia appear to depend on the underlying pathological anatomy of the syndromes. Transcortical sensory aphasia may be caused by lesions of the posterior parietal region (Benson, 1979; Heilman et al., 1981; Roeltgen et al., 1982b), and Wernicke's aphasia is typically caused by lesions in the posterior superior temporal gyrus (Benson, 1979). Anomia may also be caused by lesions of the angular gyrus (Benson, 1979). Therefore, lexical agraphia, a disorder that frequently is caused by an angular gyrus lesion and other nonperisylvian structures, is associated with aphasias caused by lesions in and adjacent to the angular gyrus.

Of the reported patients with lexical agraphia, three had lexical (surface) alexia and had difficulty reading as well as spelling irregular words. Seven patients had phonological alexia and had relatively preserved ability to read irregular words but had difficulty reading nonwords plus trouble spelling irregular words. One patient had a combination of lexical and phonological alexia, one was a letter-by-letter reader, and four had no alexia. Reading results from the other patients are uncertain. As with phonological agraphia, there are at least two explanations for the dissociation between lexical agraphia and lexical alexia. Either the two lexical systems are subserved by two separate neuronal networks, or one network common to reading and spelling is disrupted at different levels causing disruption of spelling or reading. Having separate lexical systems for spelling and reading, similar to the possible separate phonological systems for spelling and reading proposed previously in this chapter, may appear to be redundant. However, Caramazza and Hillis (1991) have provided evidence to support the dissociation of lexical knowledge as it relates to speech and reading. Therefore a similar dissociation between spelling and reading may also exist.

Information about the occurrence of the Gerstmann syndrome and ideomotor apraxia in patients with lexical agraphia is available in only five and four patients, respectively. However, they occur sufficiently often (four of five and three of four) to conclude that these syndromes probably frequently occur together. Given the aforementioned anatomic pathology underlying the Gerstmann syndrome and ideomotor apraxia, it is not unexpected that lexical agraphia, a disorder commonly due to angular gyrus lesions, occurs with them.

### Semantic Agraphia

At least 17 patients with semantic agraphia have been described. It has been associated with transcortical aphasia (motor, two patients; sensory, one patient; mixed, one patient), anomia (seven patients), semantic jargon and global aphasia (one patient each), and no aphasia (three patients). The aphasia diagnosis in one patient was uncertain. The associations are not surprising, given the anatomic diversity of semantic agraphia. It is also not surprising that three patients developed what we termed semantic alexia: fluent, preserved oral reading with absent comprehension (Roeltgen et al., 1986). This pattern of reading plus the semantic agraphia would appear to be secondary to a general disruption of semantics. The alexia in the remaining patients varies and includes phonological, mixed, global, and no alexia.

Other elements of the Gerstmann syndrome, as well as ideomotor apraxia, have been noted in the patients with semantic agraphia. However, because of the severe comprehension disturbance in many of these patients, and the absence of data from others, it is difficult to interpret these results.

*Apraxic Agraphia*

Apraxic agraphia with ideomotor apraxia is typically associated with aphasia as well as alexia and other elements of the Gerstmann syndrome. However, other associations are not constant because ideomotor apraxia, and therefore agraphia with ideomotor apraxia, may be due to dominant parietal lesions or to lesions anterior to this region (Heilman et al., 1982). In those rare patients with crossed dominance (language in one hemisphere and motor in the other), apraxic agraphia with ideomotor apraxia may occur without aphasia (Heilman et al., 1973, 1974; Valenstein and Heilman, 1979).

Agraphia in patients without apraxia has been well described in only a limited number of patients (Roeltgen and Heilman, 1983b; Margolin and Binder, 1984; Baxter and Warrington, 1986; Croisile et al., 1990). Therefore, it is difficult to draw any conclusions regarding the associations of this syndrome with disorders of other neuropsychological functions.

**CONCLUSIONS**

As can be seen from the cases cited, the neuropsychological classification of the agraphias offers a promising method of dealing with these disorders. It complements, rather than supplants, the traditional classifications that rely on associated neurological findings, such as aphasia, apraxia, or visuospatial disorders, rather than on the strict analysis of writing itself. Neuropsychological analysis may be of use not only in classifying agraphias, but also in clarifying the brain mechanisms underlying them and perhaps also in pointing toward rational methods of therapy. An example of this last point is found in a review of a study by Schechter and colleagues (1985). They found that using phoneme analysis as a treatment, patients with acquired agraphia improved. Improvement varied among aphasic subgroups but correlated with phonemic analysis ability. Categorization of patients based on the analysis of the agraphia may have allowed a better understanding of the relationship of treatment response with agraphia.

# REFERENCES

Aimard, G., Devick, Lebel, M., Trouillas, P., and Boisson, D. (1975). Agraphie pure (Dynamique?) D'origine Frontale. *Rev. Neurol. (Paris)* 7:505–512.

Alexander, M. P., Freidman, R., LoVerso, F., and Fisher, R. (1990). Anatomic correlates of lexical agraphia. Presented at the Academy of Aphasia, Baltimore.

Assal, G., Buttet, J., and Jolivet, R. (1981). Dissociations in aphasia: a case report. *Brain Lang.* 13:223–240.

Auerbach, S. H., and Alexander, M. P. (1981). Pure agraphia and unilateral optic ataxia associated with a left superior lobule lesion. *J. Neurol. Neurosurg. Psychiatry* 44:430–432.

Basso, A., Taborelli, A., and Vignollo, L. A. (1978). Dissociated disorders of speaking and writing in aphasia. *J. Neurol. Neurosurg. Psychiatry,* 41:556–563.

Baxter, D. M., and Warrington, E. K. (1985). Category specific phonological dysgraphia. *Neuropsychologia* 23:653–666.

Baxter, D. M., and Warrington, E. K. (1986). Ideational agraphia: a single case study. *J. Neurol. Neurosurg. Psychiatry* 49:369–374.

Beauvois, M. F., and Derouesne, J. (1979). Phonological alexia: three dissociations. *J. Neurol. Neurosurg. Psychiatry* 42:1115–1124.

Beauvois, M. F., and Derouesne, J. (1981). Lexical or orthographic agraphia. *Brain* 104:2–49.

Benedikt, M. (1865). *Uber Aphasie, Agraphie und verwandte pathologische Zustande.* Wiener Medizische Presse, 6.

Benson, D. F. (1979). *Aphasia, Alexia and Agraphia.* New York: Churchill Livingston.

Black, S. E., Bass, K., Behrmann, M., and Hacker, P. (1987). Selective writing impairment: a single case study of a deficit in allographic conversion. *Neurology* 37:174.

Bogen, J. E. (1969). The other side of the brain. I. Dysgraphia and dyscopia following cerebral commissurotomy. *Bull. Los Angeles Neurol. Soc.* 34:3–105.

Bolla-Wilson, K., Speedie, L. J., and Robinson, R. G. (1985). Phonologic agraphia in a left-handed patient after a right-hemisphere lesion. *Neurology* 35:1778–1781.

Brown, R., and McNeill, D. (1966). The "tip of the tongue" phenomenon. *J. Verbal Learning Verbal Behav.* 5:325–337.

Bub, D., and Chertkow, H. (1988). Agraphia. In *Handbook of Neuropsychology,* F. Boller and J. Grafman (eds.). Amsterdam: Elsevier.

Bub, D., and Kertesz, A. (1982). Deep agraphia. *Brain Lang.* 17:146–165.

Campbell, R. (1985). When children write nonwords to dictation. *J. Exp. Child Psychol.* 40:133–151.

Caramazza, A., and Hillis, A. E. (1991). Lexical organization of nouns and verbs in the brain. *Nature* 349:788–790.

Caramazza, A., Miceli, G., Vila, G., and Romani, C. (1987). The role of the graphemic buffer in spelling: evidence from a case of acquired dysgraphia. *Cognition* 26:59–85.

Chedru F., and Geschwind, N. (1972). Writing disturbances in acute confusional states. *Neuropsychologia* 10:343–354.

Coltheart, M. (1980). Deep dyslexia: a review of the syndrome. In *Deep Dyslexia,* M. Coltheart, K. Patterson, and J. C. Marshall (eds.). London: Routledge and Kegan Paul.

Croisile, B., Laurent, B., Michel, D., and Trillet, M. (1990). Pure agraphia from a deep left hemisphere hæmatoma. *J. Neurol., Neurosurg. Psychiatry* 53:263–265.

Croisile, B., Trillet, M., Laurent, B., Latombe, D., and Schott, B. (1989). Agraphie lexicale par hematome temporo-parietal gauche. *Rev. Neurol. (Paris)* 145:287–292.

DeBastiani, K., and Barry, C. (1989). A cognitive analysis of an acquired dysgraphic patient with an "allographic" writing disorder. *Cognitive Neuropsychol.* 6:25–41.

Dejerine, J. (1891). Sur un cas de cecite verbale avec agraphie, suivi d'autopsie. *Mem. Soc. Biol.* 3:197–201.

Denckla, M. B., and Roeltgen, D. P. (in press). Disorders of motor function. In *Handbook of Neuropsychology, Section of Child Neuropsychology*, I. Rapin and S. Segalowitz (eds.). Amsterdam: Elsevier.

Ellis, A. W. (1982). Spelling and writing (and reading and speaking). In *Normality and Pathology in Cognitive Functions*, A. W. Ellis (ed.). London: Academic Press.

Ellis, A. W., Young, A. W., and Flude, B. M. (1987). "Afferent dysgraphia" in a patient and in normal subjects. *Cognitive Neuropsychol.* 4:465–486.

Friedman, R. B., and Alexander, M. P. (1989). Written spelling agraphia. *Brain Lang.* 36:503–517.

Gersh, F., and Damasio, A. R. (1981). Praxis and writing of the left hand may be served by different callosal pathways. *Arch. Neurol.* 38:634–636.

Gerstmann, J. (1940). Syndrome of finger agnosia, disorientation for right and left, agraphia and acalculia. *Arch. Neurol. Psychiatry* 44:398–408.

Geshwind, N., and Kaplan, E. (1962). A human cerebral disconnection syndrome. *Neurology* 12:675–685.

Goldstein, K. (1948). *Language and Language Disturbances*. New York: Grune and Stratton.

Goodman-Schulman, R., and Caramazza, A. (1987). Patterns of dysgraphia and the nonlexical spelling process. *Cortex* 23:143–148.

Grashey, H. (1885). Uber aphasie and und ihre beziehungen zur wahrnehmung. *Arch. Psychiatr. Nervenkr.* 16:654–688.

Grossfield, M. L., and Clark, L. W. (1983). Nature of spelling errors in transcortical sensory aphasia: a case study. *Brain Lang.* 18:47–56.

Hatfield, F. M. (1985). Visual and phonological factors in acquired dysgraphia. *Neuropsychologia* 23:13–29.

Hatfield, F. M. and Patterson, K. E. (1983). Phonological spelling *Q. J. Exp. Psychol.* 35A:451–468.

Head, H. (1926). *Aphasia and Kindred Disorders of Speech*. Cambridge: Cambridge University Press.

Hécaen, H., and Albert, M. L. (1978). *Human Neuropsychology*. New York: John Wiley and Sons.

Heilman K. M. (1979). Apraxia. In *Clinical Neuropsychology*, 1st ed., K. M. Heilman and E. Valenstein (eds.). New York: Oxford University Press.

Heilman, K. M., Coyle, J. M., Gonyea, E. F., and Geschwind, N. (1973). Apraxia and agraphia in a left hander. *Brain* 96:21–28.

Heilman, K. M., Gonyea, E. F., and Geschwind, N. (1974). Apraxia and agraphia in a right-hander. *Cortex* 10:284–288.

Heilman, K. M., Rothi, L., and Valenstein, E. (1982). Two forms of ideomotor apraxia. *Neurology* 32:342–346.

Heilman, K. M., Tucker, D. M., and Valenstein, E. (1976). A case of mixed transcortical aphasia with intact naming. *Brain* 99:415–426.

Heir, D. B., and Mohr, J. P. (1977). Incongruous oral and written naming. *Brain and Language* 4:115–126.

Hillis, A. E., and Caramazza, A. (1989). The graphemic buffer and attentional mechanisms. *Brain Lang.* 36:208–235.

Hotopf, N. (1980). Slips of the pen. In *Cognitive Processes in Spelling*, U. Frith (ed.). London: Academic Press.

Kertesz, A., Latham, N., and McCabe, P. (1990). Subcortical agraphia. *Neurology* 40:172.

Kinsbourne, M., and Warrington, E. K. (1965). A case showing selectively impaired oral spelling. *J. Neurol. Neurosurg. Psychiatry* 28:563–566.

Laine, T. N., and Marttila, R. J. (1981). Pure agraphia: a case study. *Neuropsychologia* 19:311–316.

Leischner, A. (1969). The agraphias. In *Disorders of Speech, Perception, and Symbolic Behavior*, P. J. Vinken and G. W. Bruyn (eds.). Amsterdam: North Holland.

Lesser, R. (1990). Superior oral to written spelling: evidence for separate buffers? *Cognitive Neuropsychol* 7:347–366.

Levy, J., Nebes, R. D., and Sperry, R. W. (1971). Expressive language in the surgically separated minor hemisphere. *Cortex* 71:49–58.

Lichtheim, L. (1885). On aphasia. *Brain* 7:433–485.

Liepmann, H., and Maas, O. (1907). Ein Fall von linksseitiger Agraphie und Apraxie bei rechtsseitiger Lähmung. *J. für Psychologie und Neurologie,* 10:214–227.

Marcie, P., and Hécaen, H. (1979). Agraphia. In *Clinical Neuropsychology*, 1st ed., K. M. Heilman and E. Valenstein (eds.). New York: Oxford University Press.

Margolin, D. I. (1984). The neuropsychology of writing and spelling: semantic, phonological, motor, and perceptual processes. *Q. J. Exp. Psychol.* 36A:459–489.

Margolin, D. I., and Binder, L. (1984). Multiple component agraphia in a patient with atypical cerebral dominance: an error analysis. *Brain Lang.* 22:26–40.

Miceli, G., Silveri, M. C., and Caramazza, A. (1985). Cognitive analysis of a case of pure dysgraphia. *Brain Lang.* 25:187–212.

Mohr, J. P., Sidman, M., Stoddard, L. T., Leichester, J., and Rosenberger, P. B. (1973). Evaluation of the defect of total aphasia. *Neurology* 23:1302–1312.

Morton, J. (1980). The logogen model and orthographic structure. In *Cognitive Processes in Spelling*, U. Frith (ed.). London: Academic Press.

Nielson, J. M. (1946). *Agnosia, Apraxia, Aphasia: Their Value in Cerebral Localization*. New York: Paul B. Hoeber.

Nielson, J. M. (1938). Gerstmann syndrome: finger agnosia, agraphia, confusion of right and left acalculia. *Arch. Neurol. Psychiatry* 39:536–559.

Nolan, K. A., and Caramazza, A. (1982). Modality-indpendent impairments in word processing in a deep dyslexic patient. *Brain Lang.* 16:236–264.

Ogle, J. W. (1867). Aphasia and agraphia. *Rep. Med. Res. Counsel St. George's Hospital (Lond.)* 2:83–122.

Patterson, K. (1986). Lexical but nonsemantic spelling? *Cognitive Neuropsychol.* 3:341–367.

Pitres, A. (1894). *Rapport sur la Question des Agraphies*. Bordeaux: Congres Francais de Medecine Interne.

Rapscak, S. Z., Arthur, S. A., and Rubens, A. B. (1988). Lexical agraphia from focal lesion of the left precentral gyrus. *Neurology* 38:1119–1123.

Rapcsak, S. Z., and Rubens, A. B. (1990). Disruption of semantic influence on writing following a left prefrontal lesion. *Brain Lang.* 38:334–344.

Rapcsak, S. Z., Rubens, A. B., and Laguna, J. F. (1990). From letters to words: procedures for word recognition in letter-by-letter reading. *Brain Lang.* 38:504–514.

Roeltgen, D. P. (1983). The neurolinguistics of writing: anatomic and neurologic correlates. Presented at the International Neuropsychological Society, Pittsburgh.

Roeltgen, D. P. (1985). Agraphia. In *Clinical Neuropsychology*, 2nd ed., K. M. Heilman and E. Valenstein (eds.). New York: Oxford University Press.

Roeltgen, D. P. (1989). Prospective analysis of a model of writing, anatomic aspects. Presented at the Academy of Aphasia, Sante Fe, N.M.

Roeltgen, D. P. (1991). Prospective analysis of writing and spelling. Part II. Results not related to localization. *J. Clin. Exp. Neuropsychol.* 13:48.

Roeltgen, D. P., and Heilman, K. M. (1982). Global aphasia with spared lexical writing. Presented at the International Neuropsychological Society, Pittsburgh.

Roeltgen, D. P., and Heilman, K. M. (1983). Apraxic agraphia in a patient with normal praxis. *Brain Lang.* 18:35–46.

Roeltgen, D. P., and Heilman, K. M. (1984). Lexical agraphia, further support for the two system hypothesis of linguistic agraphia. *Brain* 107:811–827.

Roeltgen, D. P., and Heilman, K. M. (1985). Review of agraphia and proposal for an anatomically-based neuropsychological model of writing. *Appl. Psycholinguist.* 6:205–230.

Roeltgen, D. P., and Rapcsak, S. (in press). Acquired disorders of writing and spelling. In *Linguistic Disorders and Pathologies*, G. Blanken (ed.). Berlin: Walter de Gruyter.

Roeltgen, D. P., Rothi, L.J.G., and Heilman, K. M. (1982). Isolated phonological agraphia from a focal lesion. Paper presented at the Academy of Aphasia, New Paltz.

Roeltgen, D. P., Rothi, L. G., and Heilman, K. M. (1986). Linguistic semantic agraphia. *Brain Lang.* 27:257–280.

Roeltgen, D. P., Sevush, S., and Heilman, K. M. (1983a). Phonological agraphia: writing by the lexical-semantic route. *Neurology* 33:733–757.

Roeltgen, D. P., Sevush, S., and Heilman K. M. (1983b). Pure Gerstmann syndrome from a focal lesion. *Arch. Neurol.* 40:46–47.

Roeltgen, D. P., Siegel, J., and Davis, P. (1991). Influence of task demands on handwriting performance: a computer assisted analysis. Poster presented at TENNET, Montreal.

Rosati, G., and de Bastiani, P. (1981). Pure agraphia: a discreet form of aphasia. *J. Neurol. Neurosurg. Psychiatry* 3:266–269.

Rothi, L., and Heilman, K. M. (1981). Alexia and agraphia with spared spelling and letter recognition abilities. *Brain Lang.* 12:1–13.

Rothi, L.J.G., Roeltgen, D. P., and Kooistra, C. A. (1987). Isolated lexical agraphia in a right-handed patient with a posterior lesion of the right cerebral hemisphere. *Brain Lang.* 301:181–190.

Rubens, A. B., Geschwind, N., Mahowald, M. W., and Mastri, A. (1977). Posttraumatic cerebral hemispheric disconnection syndrome. *Arch. Neurol.* 34:750–755.

Saffran, E. M., Bogeyo, L. C., Schwartz, M. F., and Martin, O.S.M. (1980). Does deep dyslexia reflect right-hemisphere reading? In *Deep Dyslexia*, M. Coltheart, K. E. Patterson, and J. C. Marshall (eds.). London: Routledge and Kegan Paul.

Schechter, I., Bar-Israel, J., Ben-Nun, Y., and Bergman, M. (1985). The phonemic analysis as a treatment method in dysgraphic aphasic patients. *Scand. J. Rehabil. Med.* [Suppl.] 12:80–83.

Shallice, T. (1981). Phonological agraphia and the lexical route in writing. *Brain* 104:412–429.

Shallice, T., and Warrington, E. K. (1980). Single and multiple component central dyslexic syndromes. In *Deep Dyslexia*, M. Coltheart, K. E. Patterson, and J. C. Marshall (eds.). London: Routledge and Kegal Paul.

Sugishita, M., Toyokura, Y., Yoshioka, M., and Yamada, R. (1980). Unilateral agraphia after section of the posterior half of the truncus of the corpus callosum. *Brain Lang.* 9:212–225.

Tanridag, O., and Kirshner, H. S. (1985). Aphasia and agraphia in lesions of the posterior internal capsule and putamen. *Neurology* 35:1797–1801.

Valenstein, E., and Heilman, K. M. (1979). Apraxic agraphia with neglect-induced paragraphia. *Arch. Neurol.* 67:44–56.

Watson, R. T., and Heilman, K. M. (1983). Callosal apraxia. *Brain* 106:391–404.

Weisenberg, T., and McBride, K. E. (1964). Types of aphasia: the expressive. In *Aphasia, a Clinical and Psychological Study*, T. Weisenberg and K. E. McBride (eds.). New York: Hafner.

Wernicke, C. (1886). Nervenheilkunde. Die neuren Arbeiten uber Aphasie. *Fortschr. Med.* 4:463–482.

Yamadori, A., Osumi, Y., Ikeda, H., and Kanazawa, Y. (1980). Left unilateral agraphia and tactile anomia. Disturbances seen after occlusion of the anterior cerebral artery. *Arch. Neurol.* 37:88–91.

Yopp, K. S., and Roeltgen, D. P. (1987). Case of alexia and agraphia due to a disconnection of the visual input to and the motor output from an intact graphemic area. *J. Clin. Exp. Neuropsychol.* 9:42.

# 5

# Acalculia

HARVEY S. LEVIN, FELICIA C. GOLDSTEIN, AND PAUL A. SPIERS

## HISTORICAL BACKGROUND AND CLASSIFICATION OF THE ACALCULIAS

In 1919 Henschen coined the term "Akalkulia" to describe disturbances in computation associated with brain damage. Although his report was the first statistical compilation of a large number of cases, interest in the relationship between calculation ability and the brain was already a century old by the time Henschen's monograph appeared. In 1808 Gall and Spurzheim postulated the existence of a "calculation centre" in the brain which they depicted in their phrenological atlas (see Fig. 5-1). Based on the examination of mathematical prodigies, mathematicians, and cases of dementia or retardation where calculation was preserved, these authors came to the conclusion that "man has an organ which permits him to come into contact with the laws of mathematics" and that this organ is located "in a convolution on the most lateral portion of the external, orbital surface of the anterior lobes." It was not until Broca's work on language in the 1860s that phrenology fell into disfavor and the new methodology emerging for the study of brain-behavior relationships was extended to include research on mathematical ability.

Aphasiologists in the latter half of the nineteenth century recognized that their patients often suffered impaired ability to perform numerical operations, and they interpreted this as an expression of a pervasive linguistic disorder. Lewandowsky and Stadelmann (1908) published the first detailed report of calculation disorder resulting from focal brain damage in a patient who had a right homonymous hemianopsia. The authors attributed the difficulties in written and mental calculation to "gaps" in number reading and to problems in the "optic representation" of numbers, respectively. Lewandowsky and Stadelmann proposed a "specific type of alexia for numbers in which the form and significance of isolated digits are perceived but that at the stage where synthesis is required for the comprehension of several digits the patient fails." This failure was apparently related to an inability to apply the learned rules of the positional system. In the same paper these authors reported that the patient was often unable to recognize arithmetic symbols, though he could still follow the correct pro-

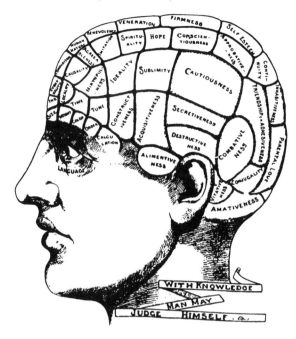

**Fig. 5-1.** Localization of faculties according to the phrenologist Spurzheim. "Calculation" is located above the "language" center. (From Whishaw, 1990.)

cedure for effecting a computation. These observations are notable in that Lewandowsky and Stadelmann focused primarily on disturbances in calculation ability which they considered distinct from aphasia. Similarly, their description of a specific form of number alexia departed from the popular conception that alexia and agraphia for numbers were simply variants of alexia and agraphia for linguistic material. Finally, their paper was important in that it was the first to suggest that calculation disorders should be considered the result of a specific cerebral lesion different from those proposed to account for aphasia. Consistent with their emphasis on visual factors and their patient's right hemianopsia, Lewandowsky and Stadelmann situated the "centre for arithmetic faculties" in the left occipital region.

Henschen (1919) distinguished "akalkulia" from disturbances in reading and writing numbers, "cipher alexia" and "cipher agraphia," respectively. Upon reviewing 305 brain-damaged cases of calculation disturbance reported in the literature and 67 of his own patients, Henschen identified a subgroup of nonaphasic or mildly aphasic patients in whom calculation disorder was the predominant deficit. He inferred the existence of a cerebral substrate for arithmetic operations that is anatomically distinct but proximal to the neural organization of speech and musical capacity. Although Henschen's analysis of a large series provided convincing evidence that acalculia can occur independently of aphasia, he neglected to differentiate defects in oral as opposed to written arithmetic skills and studied only addition and subtraction.

Hans Berger (1926) proposed the distinction between primary and secondary acalculia on the basis of his observations that certain abilities such as short-term memory and capacity for sustained attention are necessary to perform calculation problems. He concluded that primary acalculia cannot be attributed to a more pervasive impairment, though it may occur in association with other deficits which are not suf-ficiently severe to disrupt calculation. Mild word-finding difficulty and paraphasic errors were the principal concomitant neuropsychological symptoms in the patients Berger described as manifesting primary acalculia. Secondary acalculia, as he defined it, is an expression of a severe general disturbance of memory, language, attention, or cognition. Berger reported that the secondary type is the more frequent of the acal-culias and is often among the neuropsychological defects found in patients with dif-fuse cerebral disease and in left-hemisphere-damaged patients with receptive apha-sia.

Hécaen et al. (1961) proposed a classification of acquired calculation disorder based on the mechanisms presumed to be responsible for the acalculia. Although they elucidated the neuropsychological deficits that frequently accompany but do not nec-essarily produce the various types of acalculia, it is important to recognize that there is considerable overlap with respect to the associated symptoms. Their classification includes:

1.  Acalculia associated with alexia and agraphia for numbers which may or may not be accompanied by verbal alexia and agraphia or other aphasic deficits. An exam-ple of this type of impairment is shown in Figure 5-2.
2.  Impaired spatial organization of numbers frequently reflected by misalignment of digits, visual neglect, inversion (e.g., 9 and 6) and reversal errors (e.g., 12 inter-preted as 21), and inability to maintain the decimal place. Hécaen et al. designated this disorder as "acalculia of the spatial type." Inability to correctly solve a math problem due to spatial misalignment of the numbers is displayed in Figure 5-3.

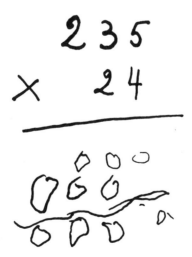

Fig. 5-2. Example of agraphia for numbers. The numbers are arranged correctly for the requested operation, but the patient is unable to write numbers other than zero. (From Hécaen et al., 1961. Reprinted with permission of the publisher.)

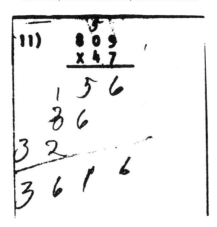

**Fig. 5-3.** Example of spatial dyscalculia. The basic arithmetic is preserved (e.g., 9 × 7 = 56, 4 × 9 = 36) but the columns are misaligned. (From Lezak, M.D., 1983. *Neuropsychological Assessment*. New York: Oxford University Press. Reprinted with permission of the publisher.)

3. Anarithmetria, i.e., impairment of calculation per se. Of these three types of acalculia, this category corresponds most closely to Berger's primary acalculia. The concept of anarithmetria does not imply an isolated deficit but excludes alexia and agraphia for numbers and spatial disorganization as causes for acalculia.

Nonspecific acalculia contributing to the symptom complex of dementia and developmental disturbance of calculation are not encompassed by this scheme, nor is reduced rate of calculation as a consequence of closed head trauma (Gronwall and Wrightson, 1974; Gronwall and Sampson, 1974).

While recognizing that these categories of acalculia are not mutually exclusive, we have organized this review for heuristic purposes according to the classification proposed by Hécaen and his associates. As will become apparent, exceptional cases of acalculia have been reported which do not conform to these global distinctions. More recent formulations (Boller and Grafman, 1985; Caramazza and McCloskey, 1987) will be discussed at the end of this chapter. These conceptualizations are based on information processing models and view calculation as requiring a variety of component processes that can be disrupted at any particular stage.

## VARIETIES OF ACALCULIA

### Alexia and/or Agraphia for Numbers

Although the acalculia arising from alexia and agraphia for numbers has been referred to as "aphasic acalculia" (Benson and Weir, 1972), Hécaen et al. (1961) found that an aphasic disorder was neither a necessary nor a sufficient condition. The relationship between alexia for numbers and impaired reading of words was systematically investigated by Henschen (1919), who found a dissociation in more than 50% of his cases (Table 5-1). Hécaen et al. later confirmed this dissociation and observed

**Table 5-1.** Relationship Between Alexia and Agraphia for
Numbers and Impaired Reading and Writing of Words

| Type of Disorder | Henschen (1919) | | Hécaen et al. (1961) | |
|---|---|---|---|---|
| | Number | % | Number | % |
| | n = 132 | | | n = 101 |
| Verbal alexia | 71 | 54 | 23 | 23 |
| Number alexia | 4 | 3 | 20 | 20 |
| Mixed alexia | 57 | 43 | 58 | 57 |
| | n = 105 | | | n = 108 |
| Verbal agraphia | 33 | 31 | 24 | 22 |
| Number agraphia | 21 | 20 | 13 | 12 |
| Mixed agraphia | 51 | 49 | 71 | 66 |

a greater frequency of number alexia than in Henschen's material. Table 5-1 shows that agraphia confined to words or numbers was also common to both series of patients, though agraphia for numbers with preserved ability to write words was more frequent in Henschen's study. The explanation for the disparity between the Henschen and Hécaen findings remains unclear.

The chief neuropsychological correlates of alexia for numbers (n = 63) found by Hécaen et al. (1961) were aphasia (in 84% of the patients), verbal alexia (79%), ideational or ideomotor apraxia (36.5%), visuoconstructive deficit (68%), and general somatognosia (26%). The latter deficit refers to a basic impairment in appreciation of body schema. It should be noted that aphasia was not confined to the alexic type of acalculia. Visual-field and oculomotor defect and somatosensory impairment were frequent neurological abnormalities, though these often accompanied all three types of acalculia. Hécaen et al. characterized the aphasic disorder associated with alexia for numbers as a general disturbance in verbal formulation, though other authors have emphasized the receptive impairment in these patients (Head, 1926). Paraphasic or paragraphic substitution of numbers may contaminate the calculations by patients with fluent aphasia (Benson and Denckla, 1969) and obscure their relatively preserved capacity for arithmetic operations. Benson and Denckla described a patient with suspected left parietal disease who responded orally to the written problem "4 + 5" with the answer "8." His written answer was 5, and he chose the correct answer when given a multiple-choice format. Clinicopathological correlation has established that either a lesion of the left hemisphere or bilateral cerebral disease may be responsible for number alexia and agraphia (Hécaen, 1962).

A number of studies have examined differences in arithmetic abilities as a function of type of aphasia and task demands (Dahmen et al., 1982; Deloche and Seron, 1982; Rosselli and Ardila, 1989). Deloche and Seron (1982) investigated the ability of Broca's or Wernicke's aphasics to transcode numerals printed in letters (e.g., five hundred and ten) into digits (510). Broca's aphasics were more likely to exhibit "grammatical" mistakes consisting of stack errors (substituting a digit for the one or ten place: fifteen written as 50 or 5) and inserting a "1" to correspond to the one-hundredth or one-

**Table 5-2.** Percentages of Errors in Different Subtests for Left-Hemisphere-Damage Groups

| | Rea | Wri | N-L | L-N | >< | Men | Wop | Com | Sig | Suc | For | Bac | Col | Pro |
|---|---|---|---|---|---|---|---|---|---|---|---|---|---|---|
| Prefrontal (N = 6) | 8.8 | 18.8 | 41.2 | 8.7 | 11.6 | 60.0 | 45.0 | 16.0 | 16.0 | 12.5 | 0.0 | 4.0 | 10.0 | 50.0 |
| Broca (N = 5) | 28.8 | 33.3 | 43.7 | 45.0 | 30.0 | 55.0 | 47.5 | 45.6 | 28.0 | 58.7 | 96.0 | 100.0 | 10.0 | 50.0 |
| Conduction (N = 6) | 33.3 | 31.1 | 75.0 | 48.7 | 26.6 | 68.7 | 52.5 | 56.8 | 34.0 | 68.1 | 11.3 | 48.6 | 21.6 | 76.0 |
| Wernicke (N = 13) | 20.0 | 17.7 | 8.7 | 41.2 | 8.3 | 66.2 | 51.2 | 68.0 | 32.0 | 56.8 | 37.3 | 48.6 | 26.6 | 56.0 |
| Anomic (N = 4) | 13.3 | 13.3 | 7.5 | 46.2 | 0.0 | 75.0 | 56.2 | 72.0 | 50.0 | 3.7 | 0.0 | 14.6 | 8.0 | 44.0 |
| Alexia without agraphia (N = 3) | 17.7 | 0.0 | 66.2 | 100.0 | 0.0 | 57.7 | 52.7 | 82.4 | 52.0 | 25.0 | 0.0 | 0.0 | 33.3 | 20.0 |
| Global (N = 4) | 52.2 | 50.0 | 100.0 | 96.2 | 20.0 | 100.0 | 87.5 | 92.8 | 80.0 | 96.8 | 77.3 | 100.0 | 70.0 | 94.0 |

Reading of numbers (Rea); writing of numbers (Wri); transcoding from numerical to verbal code (N-L); transcoding from verbal to numerical code (L-N); relations "bigger," smaller" (> <); mental arithmetical operations (Men); written arithmetical operations (Wop); complex arithmetical operations (Com); reading arithmetical signs (Sig); successive operations (Suc); counting forward (For); counting backward (Bac); aligning numbers in columns (Col); numerical problems (Pro). (Adapted from Rosselli and Ardila, 1989.)

thousandth place (nine hundred and forty-three written as 9,143). Wernicke's aphasics, in contrast, made more "semantic" or "sequential" errors consisting of displacing numbers (four thousand three written as 3,004). Perseverations were also characteristic (one hundred fifty-three written as 1,553). In their sample, Deloche and Seron found that pure alexic errors were rare in both patient groups. Rosselli and Ardila (1989) examined number processing differences among patients with aphasias classified as prefrontal, Broca's conduction, Wernicke's, anomic, alexia without agraphia, and global. Patients were administered a variety of arithmetic tasks such as reading and writing numbers, transcoding from a numerical to a verbal code or vice versa, and mental arithmetic. Table 5-2 presents the percentage of errors made by the various groups according to type of task. Patients with prefrontal or global aphasia made the least and largest percentage of errors, respectively, on all tasks. For the other groups, the greatest impairment in reading and writing numbers was observed in patients with Broca's or conduction aphasias. Counting forward or backward was particularly impaired in Broca's aphasics. Similar to the observations of Deloche and Seron, the investigators noted differences in the pattern of errors across asphasics. In transcoding from numbers to letters, for example, patients with Wernicke's aphasia were likely to make "decomposition" errors consisting or writing numbers as individual units (47 written as four seven), whereas letter and grammatical omissions were more frequent in patients with Broca's aphasia.

Many investigations of acalculia have assumed a unitary expression of number alexia and agraphia, but few studies have addressed this issue by analyzing the pattern of errors. Based on his case material and review of the literature, Kleist (1934) distinguished two forms of number alexia. The first type was inability to read numbers per se, analogous to literal alexia. In contrast, the second form was confined to multidigit numbers that had positional errors (e.g., 205, 678 read as "two million, five hundred sixty thousand and seventy-eight"). Similarly, he identified two forms of number agraphia. Kleist labeled the first type "ideopraxic" as the patient was totally unable to write numbers or he wrote them in a distorted form. He referred to the second form as "constructive" because the patient had positional or grouping errors (e.g., 54, 38 instead of 5,438) when writing multidigit numbers. McCloskey and Caramazza (1987) more recently have posed a classification of number processing skills based on lexical and syntactic mechanisms. Lexical processing entails the ability to read or write individual numbers, whereas syntactic processing involves the ability to combine numbers into the correct form and quantity. Both mechanisms may be impaired simultaneously or dissociations may occur. Table 5-3 provides an example of the responses of a patient who presented with impaired syntactic but preserved lexical processing in translating verbally presented numbers into digits. As seen below, the patient's numbers were correct but he did not combine them into an appropriate form (e.g., three thousand four hundred written as 3,000,400). McCloskey and Caramazza also observed the opposite pattern in another patient with impaired lexical but preserved syntactic processing (e.g., writing two hundred and twenty-one as 215). The finding of subtypes of errors in number production supports that idea that alexia and agraphia can take on varied forms.

The association between alexia/agraphia for numbers and left-hemisphere disease received ample confirmation in a study of patients manifesting this type of acalculia (Hécaen et al., 1961). In a subsequent study, Hécaen (1962) reported that in a series of unselected cases of left-hemisphere damage, 37% were alexic and agraphic for numbers as compared to 2% of patients with right-hemisphere disease. Figure alexia and agraphia were often found to coexist in patients with bilateral cerebral disease. A recent investigation by Rosselli and Ardila (1989) compared 41 patients with left-hemisphere damage and aphasia against 21 right-hemisphere-damaged patients on

**Table 5-3.** Examples of the Performance of a Patient on a Number-Writing Task

| Stimulus | Response |
| --- | --- |
| One | 1 |
| Eight hundred | 800 |
| Fifty thousand seven hundred two | 50,000,702 |
| Nine thousand | 9,000 |
| One thousand forty | 1,000,40 |
| Eighteen | 18 |
| Three thousand four hundred | 3,000,400 |
| Nine hundred nineteen | 919 |
| Five thousand eleven | 5,000,11 |
| One hundred five thousand five hundred | 100,5000,500 |
| Seven hundred twenty | 720 |

Adapted from McCloskey and Caramazza, 1987.

various calculation measures. The left-hemisphere patients made a higher percentage of errors on tasks requiring them to read numbers (24%) and signs (33%) than right-hemisphere-damaged patients (reading numbers = 8%; signs = 12%). Group differences approached but missed significance in writing numbers, although the performance of the left-hemisphere group was also worse (22% errors vs. 10% for the right-hemisphere group). Acquired aphasia and acalculia were also closely associated in children with left-hemisphere damage (Hécaen, 1976). In a series of 17 left-hemisphere-damaged children of whom 15 were aphasic, 11 patients had a definite acalculia while equivocal acalculia was noted in 3 other aphasic children. Although Hécaen emphasized the persistence of acalculia in these children, he did not elaborate on its qualitative aspects. No child with right-hemisphere damage (n = 6) showed acalculia.

Alexic acalculia can also result from inability to read arithmetical signs despite relatively preserved comprehension of written numbers. Ferro and Botelho (1980) described two aphasic patients (anomic and conduction, respectively) with left-hemisphere lesions who misnamed arithmetical signs and could neither read nor write them to dictation. Although both patients could copy the signs, neither could match them to corresponding words. In contrast, number reading, writing, and naming were relatively spared as was simple oral calculation. The authors suggested that arithmetic signs are similar to ideographic notation because both consist of signs that have unique and universal value and neither combines into more complex symbols. A dissociation between preserved comprehension of numbers but impaired interpretation of signs was also observed by Caramazza and McCloskey (1987). Their patient could not match an operation's sign with its name and used the wrong operation when completing a problem even though the arithmetic was appropriate. For example, the patient pointed to 8 × 5 when asked to indicate which problem involved addition (8 + 5, 8 − 5, 8 × 5). He also provided the answer "45" when asked to add 9 + 5, indicating that he was multiplying. Caramazza and McCloskey suggested that such data demonstrate the independence of processing of operation signs from knowledge of arithmetic facts and ability to perform calculations.

### Acalculia of the Spatial Type

Manifestations of the "spatial" type of acalculia include improper arrangement of numbers during the initial stage of computation or while summing the partial products of multiplication. However, the principle of calculation is retained as reflected by the relatively preserved calculation of numbers presented orally (Benton, 1963, 1966). Table 5-4 displays the features of spatial acalculia in 48 of 183 patients identified by Hécaen. As seen, the majority of patients exhibited visuoconstructive impairments followed next by directional confusion, oculomotor disturbance, and spatial agnosia (unilateral or global). These correlates were corroborated in a smaller series of patients (including four cases of unilateral right-hemisphere disease) described by Cohn (1961), who observed errors in written multiplication resulting from difficulty in horizontal positioning, vertical alignment and transportation of numbers (e.g., "31" instead of "13") even in patients who retained multiplication values. Leleux et al. (1979) described similar errors in a mathematics teacher who exhibited impair-

**Table 5-4.** Correlates of Spatial Acalculia Identified by Hécaen

|  | Percentage of Patients (N = 48) with Deficit |
| --- | --- |
| Visuoconstructive impairment | 95.0 |
| Directional confusion | 78.0 |
| Oculomotor disturbance | 70.0 |
| Unilateral spatial agnosia | 69.0 |
| General spatial agnosia | 62.5 |
| General cognitive deterioration | 46.0 |
| Dressing apraxia | 41.5 |
| Visual-field defect | 56.0 |

ment of advanced quantitative skills (e.g., algebra, geometry) after he developed a right frontoparietal hematoma. The patient's failure to displace an intermediate multiplication, which was associated with neglect of the left visual field, produced incorrect columnar alignment. Selecting patients with the spatial type of acalculia, Hécaen et al. implicated the role of right-hemisphere disease since this disorder was shown to be rare in patients with lesions confined to the left hemisphere. Bilateral brain disease produced the spatial type of acalculia with a frequency comparable to that of right hemisphere lesions.

Spatial deficit of another type may contribute to disorders of calculation in aphasic patients. Dahmen and colleagues (1982) postulated that patients with Wernicke's aphasia associated with lesions in the left temporoparietal region would exhibit a disproportionately severe impairment on calculation tasks emphasizing spatial capacity (e.g., pointing to an orderly linear array of circles which corresponds to the numerical value of a set of randomly distributed geometric symbols) as compared to numeric-symbolic tasks (e.g., matching an array of circles to number words or digits). The authors found that patients with Wernicke's aphasia were markedly impaired across all calculation tasks as compared to Broca's aphasics and deviated most from normal subjects on those calculation tasks which stressed spatial ability. In contrast, there was only a slight nonsignificant trend for the performance of patients with Broca's aphasia and control subjects to decline on the more spatial calculation tasks. By limiting the arithmetic computation to two-digit numbers and omitting presentation of examples in the usual vertical arrangement. Dahmen et al. were unable to differentiate subtypes of acalculia in their series according to Hécaen's classification.

There is general agreement that the spatial type of acalculia is frequently associated with visuoconstructive impairment and directional confusion. As Hartje (1987) has noted, however, symptoms such as spatial confusion and constructional-praxic disturbances are not sufficient to produce spatial dyscalculia. The Hécaen sample found a high proportion of patients with nonspatial dyscalculia who also manifested these disorders. Moreover, Cohn (1961) reported a patient who displayed right-left disorientation but did not exhibit spatial errors in solving written multiplication problems. Collignon and co-workers (1977) found that spatial problems were common in a series of 26 cases of acalculia irrespective of the lateralization of lesion. Furthermore, the authors concluded that spatial deficit (e.g., poor visualization) and visuoconstructive impairment were two of the three "instrumental problems" (aphasia being a third) from which acalculia resulted secondarily. Consequently, the presence of visuospatial deficit per se may not differentiate types of acalculia unless it is a prominent or isolated finding with otherwise minor or no neuropsychological deficit.

## Anarithmetria

Hécaen's definition of anarithmetria excludes impairments in calculation secondary to alexia and agraphia for numbers or spatial disorganization of numbers. Anarithmetria is compatible, however, with other associated neuropsychologic deficits which may directly affect calculation. Hécaen et al. (1961) studied 72 cases of anarithmetria and found a pattern similar to that of patients with acalculia secondary to alexia and agraphia for numbers. The correlates and the corresponding percentage of patients affected were aphasia (62.5%), visuoconstructive impairment (61%), general cognitive deterioration (50%), verbal alexia (39%), and directional confusion (37%). Deficits found on neurological examination included visual-field defect (54.5%), oculomotor disturbance (33%), and sensory impairment (37%). Left-sided lesions and bilateral brain disease predominated in the cases of anarithmetria. For every patient with a lesion confined to the minor hemisphere, there were four patients with unilateral left-hemisphere damage. This pattern of hemispheric involvement is compatible with the principal concomitant deficits found in patients with anarithmetria.

Consistent with the findings of Hécaen et al. demonstrating the presence of general cognitive deterioration in half of their patients with anarithmetria, Cohn (1961) and Grewel (1952) implicated the role of memory impairment in rendering patients unable to carry numbers or retrieve previously learned multiplication table values. Although Benson and Weir (1972) considered the possibility that disruption of memory was responsible for the posttraumatic anarithmetria which they described in a case report, there was no quantitative assessment of memory other than digit span which was intact. Their patient was mildly alexic and agraphic for words, but neither number nor calculation symbols (e.g., "+") were affected. Conversational speech was nonaphasic though naming of visually presented objects was hesitant. Counting both forward and backward was preserved as was counting in series (e.g., by 3's) and in discontinuous groups. While judgment of quantities was mildly impaired (e.g., "36 feet in a yard"), it was unclear whether this resulted from word-finding problems or difficulties with quantity estimation per se. Both oral and written presentation of computational problems disclosed preservation of addition and subtraction, but the patient was unable to perform multiplication or division regardless of the format used or the mode of response. Although the patient produced individual errors at various points of the multiplication process, the more impressive deficit was observed when he attempted to "carry over" from one column to the other in multidigit multiplication. This aspect of calculation was impaired despite intact spatial organization of the numbers in their appropriate columns. Neurologic findings included a right homonymous visual-field cut confined to the temporal area; subtle sensory and motor deficits were present over the right extremities and face. Serial radioisotope brain scans indicated focal left parietal brain damage.

Anarithmetria has been described in a 60-year-old department store executive with a subcortical infarct involving the head of the left caudate nucleus, the superior anterior portion of the putamen, and the anterior limb of the internal capsule extending into the periventricular white matter (Corbett et al., 1986). This patient exhibited syntactic errors in transcoding numbers (e.g., forty thousand one hundred ninety-nine became 40 000 99). She also had difficulty performing serial subtractions and calculating complex problems requiring multiplication and division (substituted other operations, forgot intermediate steps when the problems were not written on paper, etc.). Relatively automatic calculations, such as counting forward or backward by one, or simple addition and multiplication were intact. Neuropsychological testing indicated that language and intellectual functioning were generally preserved. There was also no evidence for spatial difficulties (e.g., inadequate alignment of numbers) in solving written math problems. In contrast, the patient displayed impaired verbal and visual memory, had difficulty performing a task requiring her to sequence numbers or numbers/letters, and could not generate hypotheses and shift response sets on a card sorting task. Corbett and colleagues attributed their patient's anarithmetria to impaired working memory and concentration as well as poor conceptual reasoning skills. Their study indicates the importance of a "process" analysis of the types of errors patients make in order to characterize the nature of their underlying deficits.

Grafman and colleagues (1989) documented a case of dyscalculia presenting as the primary symptom in a 66-year-old president of an engineering firm who was diagnosed with probable Alzheimer's disease. He could perform relatively automatic tasks such as addition and subtraction but had difficulty with multiplication and division. Moreover, mental computations were impaired, whereas performance improved when tasks were presented on paper. The investigators attributed this dissociation to the demands of working memory. Over the course of two years, there was a deterioration in the patient's ability to recognize geometric shapes and symbols, to understand measurements and money, and to read numbers. In contrast, while not totally intact, comprehension of magnitudes (which of two numbers were larger), writing single- and two-digit numbers, and numerosity comparisons (comparing two sets of forms and deciding which was larger) were preserved. Similar to the patient described by Corbett et al. (1986), IQ scores were initially in the average range, but there was evidence for impaired memory and hypothesis testing. Naming was also defective. As the investigators noted, documentation of their patient's decline indicates that selective impairments in subtypes of arithmetic abilities occur.

## LOCALIZATION OF LESION IN THE ACALCULIAS

Clinico-anatomical correlations by Henschen (1919) disclosed that acalculia associated with alexia and agraphia for numbers frequently accompanied global aphasia in patients with extensive left-hemisphere disease. Henschen implicated left angular gyrus lesions in patients with alexia and agraphia for numbers who were not globally aphasic. Consistent with the evidence for behavioral dissociation of alexia and agraphia for numbers from that for words, Hécaen et al. found that left parietal lesions predominated in the former while left temporal and occipital lesions were primarily involved in the latter. Of the patients with alexia and agraphia for numbers studied by Hécaen, bilateral parietal lobe disease was present nearly as often as lesions confined to the dominant hemisphere. Consequently, inability to read and/or write numbers that is not an artifact of presenting figures to the neglected visual field strongly suggests a left parietal lesion but does not exclude involvement of the right hemisphere.

Similarly, alexia for arthimetical signs with preserved reading of numbers and otherwise intact visual recognition is also associated with a focal left-hemisphere lesion (parietal, temporal-occipital). Although the strong association between posterior left-hemisphere lesions and anarithmetria has been corroborated, calculation disorder without spatial deficit has also been reported in rare cases of right-hemisphere damage (Collignon et al., 1977; Grafman et al., 1982). Although the localization of lesions in patients with anarithmetria resembles that of alexia and agraphia for numbers, an important distinction may be drawn.

Parietal disease confined to the right hemisphere is a definite, albeit improbable, etiology of anarithmetria, whereas this circumstance is extremely unlikely to produce figure alexia or agraphia (Hécaen et al., 1961). Hécaen et al. found that focal temporal or occipital lesions of the dominant hemisphere were sufficient to cause anarithmetria, whereas this disorder was not present in patients with right-hemisphere disease unless the parietal lobe was involved.

The localizing features for anarithmetria reported by Hécaen were corroborated by Luria (1973) who described qualitative features of calculation disorder in relation to intrahemispheric locus of lesion. Luria found that patients with parieto-occipital lesions were unable to perform arithmetic word problems because of both calculation disorder and difficulty in processing complex grammatical or numerical features. He reported that patients with temporal lobe lesions had difficulty in retaining the elements of the problem and could not use intermediate speech components in reasoning out the solution, but they were aided by written presentation of the problems because their ability to calculate was intact. Luria observed that patients with frontal lobe damage were unable to solve arithmetic word problems because they frequently failed to perceive the task as a problem and tended to give impulsive responses despite their preserved understanding of the logical-grammatical equations and arithmetical operations. Luria noted that written presentation did not necessarily facilitate performance of patients with frontal lobe lesions. Although he did not specifically investigate the effects of lateralization of injury, the majority of the patients Luria described as exhibiting calculation disturbance had left-hemisphere lesions.

Further support for the contribution of left posterior lesions to calculation disorder was provided by a study of patients with focal brain damage who were initially screened to verify that they could read and write numbers (Grafman et al., 1982). Grafman and colleagues hypothesized that anarithmetria would occur in patients with left-hemisphere lesions whereas visuospatial deficits would be observed in those with right-hemisphere damage. A written test of all four arithmetic operations was administered and was scored not only for total number of errors but also for qualitative aspects. These latter measures entailed errors of spatial configuration (misplacements and rotations), form (size and distortion), and attention (omissions and perseverations). Performance of patients with left- or right-hemisphere, anterior and posterior lesions and normal controls is displayed in Figure 5-4. As shown, patients with left-sided lesions made significantly more total errors than those with right-

**SCORE COVARIED FOR AGE AND EDUCATION**

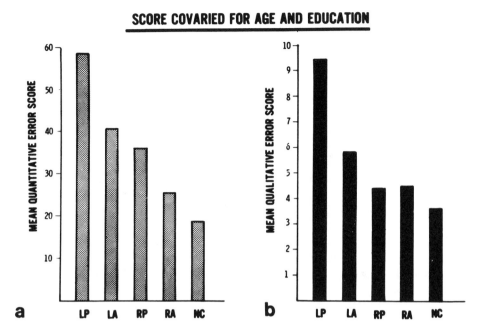

**Fig. 5-4.** Mean quantitative (**a**) and qualitative (**b**) error scores. Each column of the figure on the right represents the mean number of misplacements, size errors, distortions, rotations, omissions, and perseverations for each group. LP = left posterior; LA = left anterior; RP = right posterior; RA = right anterior; NC = controls. (From Grafman et al., 1982. Reprinted with permission of the publisher.)

hemisphere lesions or normal controls. In addition, the left posterior group was dis-proportionately impaired relative to all other groups on the qualitative measure. Errors consisting of spatial configuration were not more common in the patients with right-hemisphere damage. Grafman et al. examined the potential role of language (Token Test), visuospatial/constructional abilities (copying crosses and geometric drawings), and general intellectual functioning (Raven's Progressive Matrices). A selective impairment for the left-hemisphere group in the quantitative score and for the left posterior group in qualitative performance was still observed even when adjusting for group differences on these neuropsychological measures. The research for Grafman and colleagues indicates that left posterior lesions produce calculation disturbances independent of language and visual processing deficits. A potential role of the left angular gyrus was suggested as contributing to anarithmetia (Boller and Grafman, 1985). Replication of their findings with more recent neuroimaging tech-niques would be worthwhile since these investigators did not have neuroradiological data to support their distinctions, and they used patients with mixed etiologies (e.g., vascular, tumors, trauma, and unilateral lobectomies).

The spatial type of acalculia suggests a post-Rolandic lesion of the right hemisphere but does not exclude the possibility of bilateral disease (Hécaen et al., 1961). How-ever, spatial acalculia in a patient without evidence of linguistic defect or general cognitive deterioration most likely indicates the presence of a lesion confined to the right hemisphere (Hécaen et al., 1961).

The aggregate of symptoms including agraphia, finger agnosia, and right-left disorientation in addition to acalculia was interpreted by Gerstmann (1940) as a syndrome characterized by disturbance of body schema arising from left parietal lobe disease. The Gerstmann syndrome was subsequently recognized by neurologists as a clinical entity with localizing significance for the posterior parietal region of the dominant hemisphere. However, there has been no consensus with respect to the type of acalculia manifested by patients with the syndrome. Gerstmann (1940) claimed that anarithmetria was a component of the syndrome, whereas the spatial type of acalculia has been implicated by other authors (Critchley, 1953). The clinical features of patients with finger agnosia described by Kinsbourne and Warrington (1963) suggest that they included both patients with acalculia related to alexia and agraphia for numbers and patients with acalculia of the spatial type. That no specific form of acalculia appears to be consistently associated with the Gerstmann syndrome is understandable in view of systematic studies which have shown that the syndrome is part of a constellation of symptoms predominated by aphasia, impaired visuoconstructive capacity, and general cognitive deterioration (Benton, 1977; Poeck and Orgass, 1966).

Although calculation disturbance without aphasia had been reported by Strub and Geschwind (1974), their patient was diagnosed as having presenile dementia, and without the benefit of standardized intellectual assessment, it is difficult to assess the contribution of general cognitive decline. In a more recent report, however, Roeltgen et al. (1983) described a patient whose initial confusion resolved to Gerstmann's tetrad of symptoms. A discrete cortical lesion was demonstrated on computerized tomography (CT) scan in the superior angular gyrus extending into the superior parietal lobe. Although the authors administered tests which showed that the patient had neither a constructional apraxis nor aphasia, they neither characterized his acalculia nor reported his intellectual functioning.

The debate over the validity of Gerstmann's syndrome is likely to continue so long as patient populations remain unselected in terms of the criteria defining the syndrome and until clearly defined testing procedures are adopted to assess each of the component deficits and to rule out more generalized impairment. More careful analysis and reporting of the calculation disorders in patients supposedly suffering from this syndrome are clearly needed. Similarly, systematic investigations of the other deficits in the Gerstmann tetrad may eventually decide the issue of whether any specific set of symptoms can be associated with a discrete lesion in the dominant angular gyrus.

## HEMISPHERIC SPECIALIZATION FOR CALCULATION

An implication of the foregoing localization studies for hemispheric functional asymmetry is that calculation is primarily subserved by the left hemisphere. This possibility was confirmed by Sperry (1968), who demonstrated in commissurotomized patients that computation of groups of pegs presented in sequence was far superior on the right hand as compared to the left hand. Calculation based on inputs to the left

hand was limited to addition of sums less than five. Acalculia has recently been
reported in three patients who developed interhemispheric disconnection syndromes
as a result of callosal hemorrhages (Leiguarda et al., 1989). These patients were
unable to perform without arithmetic due to spatial difficulties involving misalignment of columns of numbers. Figure 5-5 displays the performance of one patient with
a particularly severe spatial dyscalculia. As seen, the basic calculation of 175 $\times$ 12 is
preserved, but there is improper placement of the numbers, resulting in an incorrect
sum. Mental arithmetic in these patients was relatively preserved. This performance
specifically demonstrates the contribution, unavailable to the patient's right hand, of
the right hemisphere to the calculation process.

Electroencephalographic (EEG) recordings in normal subjects performing calculations have shown greater activation of the left hemisphere than the right hemisphere. Shepherd and Gale (1982) found that cortical arousal, as reflected by the relative abundance of alpha and theta activity, was more strongly related to calculation
performance when analysis was confined to the left-hemisphere recordings as compared to the activity of the nondominant hemisphere. In conformity with the EEG
findings, Papanicolaou et al. (1983) showed that evoked potentials recorded from
parietal and temporal areas reflected greater activation of the left hemisphere (as
compared to a control condition) than the homotopic region of the right hemisphere
while dextral adults were engaged in an arithmetic task. These electrophysiologic
studies lend support to the concept of relative dominance of the left hemisphere in
normal subjects for performing calculation. Further research is necessary to explore
regional cerebral activation during a wider range of calculation and mathematical
operations. Positron emission tomography in particular may provide a useful measure
of cerebral dominance.

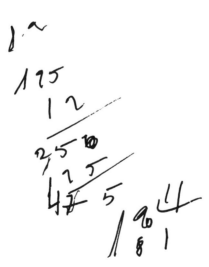

Fig. 5-5. Spatial dyscalculia in a patient with a partial hemispheric disconnection syndrome
resulting from anterior callosal hemorrhage. The patient did not have hemianopia or visual
inattention. (From Leiguarda, R., Starkstein, S., and Berthier, M., 1989. Anterior callosal haemorrhage: a partial interhemispheric disconnection syndrome. *Brain* 112:1019–1037.
Reprinted with permission of the publisher.)

## DEVELOPMENTAL DYSCALCULIA

In comparison with the extensive body of research on developmental dyslexia, relatively few investigators have studied developmental dyscalculia. In fact, there are no widely accepted criteria for the diagnosis of developmental dyscalculia, and there is a dearth of information concerning epidemiology, genetic factors, the presence of congenital or postnatal brain injury, and neuropsychological correlates. Guttman (1936) described neuropsychological findings in four children with dyscalculia, including two cases of normal intelligence who he referred to as "pure arithmetical disability." One child, a ten-year-old boy, could perform simple addition and subtraction but had no concept of division. He was unable to divide a group of objects into equal portions, and he was also deficient in multiplication. The second child, a nine-year-old girl, confused the place values of numbers greater than 100, had difficulty counting in groups greater than 20 and could not accurately estimate the number of objects in a group. Guttman also described other children with calculation disorder who had concomitant neuropsychological and intellectual impairment. He postulated that specific arithmetic disability in children arises from "structural or functional anomalies of the brain."

Since publication of Guttman's findings, investigators have proposed various criteria for diagnosing developmental dyscalculia. The criteria have included the appearance of difficulty in counting and arithmetic at an early age, a profile of psychological test findings which shows a specific disturbance of calculation, and normal intelligence. Slade and Russell (1971) described four adolescents who had long-standing difficulties in all four arithmetic operations, although impaired multiplication was the most prominent defect. The authors found that these patients had a faulty grasp of the multiplication table for which they attempted to compensate by breaking down problems with simpler units, gradually approximating the answer or drawing groups of dots which they counted.

Benson and Geschwind (1970) described two children (ages 12 and 13) whose calculation was effortful, hesitant, and uncertain. One of the patients had superior verbal ability in contrast to his average level of visuospatial capacity. He could perform only simple calculations, exhibiting difficulty in column placement in both addition and multiplication. The second patient, who was of borderline-defective intelligence, could not write multidigit numbers to dictation and could calculate only simple addition problems. Both children exhibited elements of the Gerstmann syndrome in addition to constructional deficit.

Guidelines for identification of dyscalculia in children were advanced by Spellacy and Peter (1978), who reviewed their findings in 430 children referred for assessment of learning disability. The authors defined dyscalculia on the basis of a score on the arithmetic subtest of the Wide Range Achievement Test which fell below the 20th percentile for age in a child who had a Full Scale Wechsler IQ above 80 and no disabling emotional disturbance. Applying this definition, the authors accrued 14 dyscalculics whom they subdivided according to the presence of associated reading disability. They found that dyscalculics who were good readers had poor right-left orientation, whereas dyscalculics who were poor readers evidenced dysgraphia and difficulty in word retrieval (oral word-association test). Both groups performed below expectation for age on three-dimensional block construction, drawing designs, perception of embedded figures, and finger identification. Interestingly, none of the children showed deficits confined to the four elements of the Gerstmann syndrome nor did the presence of all four elements "describe a behaviorally homogeneous group" (p. 202). Although both groups were within the normal range of intelligence, they fell below the median intellectual level for the schools from which they were drawn. This finding, in combination with other features of these children, may indicate "undiagnosed cerebral impairment."

Saxe and Shaheen (1981) described two nine-year-old boys of normal intelligence who were dyscalculic. Neither child could count adequately to compare the number of objects in two arrays nor could they perform "Piagetian concrete operational tasks" such as liquid conservation and serial ordering of sticks according to their length.

Roberts (1968) reported four types of "failure strategies" based on his analysis of children's incorrect responses to calculation problems. Four major error tendencies emerged, which Roberts classifies as wrong operation, obvious computational error, defective algorithm, or random response. Engelhardt (1977) studied the calculation performance of 798 randomly selected third- and sixth-grade pupils on 84 arithmetic computation items drawn from the Stanford Diagnostic Arithmetic Test. From this sample he was able to identify eight separate error types, which included basic fact, defective algorithm, incomplete algorithm, incorrect operation, inappropriate inversion, grouping, identity, and zero errors. Engelhardt also examined the distribution of errors across quartiles within his sample, with rank being determined by the total number of problems correct. He found that the number of errors in a child's performance decreased with increased competence, that basic fact errors were the most common in all quartiles, and that the error type that most clearly determined competent performance was defective algorithm—"Apparently one of the more difficult and critical aspects of computation is executing the correct procedure" (p. 153) (i.e., executing the correct spatial-numerical combinations in the correct sequence required by the algorithm for each operation).

In summary, prospective longitudinal research is necessary to confirm and extend the findings of these studies which implicate a specific developmental disturbance of calculation. The results of case reports and retrospective studies suggest that more than a single type of developmental dyscalculia exists, but a definitive classification and analysis of associated deficits awaits further research.


## CLINICAL ASSESSMENT OF NUMBER OPERATIONS

The literature indicates a lack of standardized measures and methods for analyzing disturbances of calculation. At present, there is no battery of tests with norms that have been systematically employed across a variety of patient populations. In many studies, the stimuli are only briefly described, and the specific errors, if analyzed, are more a function of the investigators' particular orientations than an attempt to work within a theoretical framework (Spiers, 1987). In the following section, we describe approaches to studying acalculia that have proved useful in elucidating the underpinnings of the disorder and that illustrate the minimum data set that should be collected.

The format for presentation of computational problems and the mode of response required by the patient may determine whether acalculia is detected. Oral presentation would be expected to facilitate the performance of a patient with spatial acalculia, whereas utilization of a multiple-choice format would reduce the opportunity for paraphasic errors to contaminate the performance of an aphasic patient with intact computational skill. Benton (1963) found that noteworthy inferiority of written as compared to oral calculation occurred in 2% of non-brain-damaged patients with at least an eighth-grade education, 4.5% of patients with left-hemisphere disease, and 21% of patients with right-hemisphere lesions. Systematic comparison of oral and written modes of presentation and responding is afforded by the examination of number operations devised by Benton (1963) which consists of 12 brief tests:

1. Appreciation of number values when presented with a pair of numbers such as 23 or 31 and asked to state which is greater.
2. Appreciation of number values when presented visually and the response is either oral or pointing to the larger of the two numbers.
3. Reading numbers aloud.
4. Pointing to written numbers which are named by the examiner.
5. Writing numbers to dictation.
6. Writing numbers from copy.

These preliminary six tests serve to estimate the patient's comprehension of numbers when presented in auditory or visual form in order to evaluate an aphasic component. Two additional tests assess counting ability, which is a prerequisite for arithmetic calculation.

7. Counting out loud from 1 to 20, from 20 to 1, and from 1 to 20 by 2's.
8. Estimating the number of items in a series of continuous dots and again in a discontinuous series of dots (e.g., four groups of five dots each arranged horizontally).

It is important to note on test 8 whether the patient utilizes a multiplication strategy in the discontinuous series instead of counting all the dots. Errors may result from severe memory impairment or unilateral visual inattention in which the errors on test 8 are lateralized to one side of the page.

9. Oral arithmetic calculation in which simple examples are given using each of the four basic operations.
10. Written arithmetic calculation in which the examples are similar to those given orally.
11. Arithmetic reasoning ability via the Arithmetic Reasoning subtest of the Wechsler Adult Intelligence Scale Revised (WAIS-R).

12. Immediate memory for calculation problems. This measure is a component of test 9 and serves as a control to ascertain whether a memory deficit is responsible for inability to perform calculation problems given orally.

Assessment of the aphasic component of acalculia is provided by the tests which require the patient to read, aurally comprehend, and write numbers. Furthermore, number alexia and agraphia may be present without major language deficit. A suggested modification of tests 9 and 10 is providing the patient with a multiple-choice format for half of the questions in each test as well as distinguishing between problems which require computation $(42 - 25)$ and those which depend solely on the retrieval of basic number facts $(8 - 3)$ or table values $(4 \times 7, 28/4)$. Studies have indicated that simple arithmetic may be relatively preserved in contrast to problems requiring more complex calculations (Corbett et al., 1986; Grafman et al., 1989). Inclusion of only "rote" calculations may therefore underestimate or miss the presence of acalculia. In addition to the measures recommended by Benton, a number of investigators have examined the ability of patients to transcode letters to numbers (e.g., one hundred and eighty four to 184) and vice versa (Deloche and Seron, 1982; Caramazza and McCloskey, 1987; Rosselli and Ardila, 1989). As reviewed in previous sections, analyses of the performance of patients with different types of aphasias have revealed interesting dissociations between grammatical and semantic errors.

Apart from the quantitative scoring of performance as reflected by the number of correctly solved problems, investigators have obtained qualitative data in order to better characterize the nature of the underlying impairments. Singer and Low (1933) reported a detailed study of a case of calculation disorder following carbon monoxide poisoning. Their procedures for elucidating the patient's acalculia, which are still relevant to investigators and clinicians, are reviewed here. Despite six months of remediation and generally well-preserved speech and reading, their patient was persistently agraphic for all written material and could not perform oral calculations other than addition of single-digit numbers and rote retrieval of multiplication table values. Subtraction and division were totally impaired as the patient failed to enter the digits in proper columns. The authors analyzed the pattern or errors and inferred the presence of several mechanisms contributing to the acalculia:

1. Substitution of one operation for another, e.g., $2 + 3 = 6, 4 + 2 = 8$. The converse error, i.e., substitution of addition for multiplication, was also observed. Subtraction was spontaneously substituted for addition (e.g., $8 + 2 = 6$), whereas the patient could not perform subtraction on request.
2. Substitution of counting for calculation as shown by $15 + 6 = 16$ and $4 + 7 = 8$.
3. Perseveration of the last digit presented as in $5 \times 4 = 24$.
4. Giving a reversal of presented numbers as an answer, e.g., $13 + 6 = 31$.
5. Impaired immediate retention of components of the problem was inferred when the patient failed to repeat it, i.e., "$2 + 6$" was reported as "$2 \times 6$." Further testing indicated that defective repetition could not be attributed entirely to decreased digit span; the context of a calculation problem appeared to accentuate repetition errors. Memory for words exceeded that for numbers.

The patient of Singer and Low could count in a forward sequence whereas backward counting was defective. Counting objects arranged in equal groups (e.g., 5 groups of 4 pills) surpassed counting objects in a discontinuous series (e.g., groups of 3, 6, 6, and 5 pills of different colors) where the sum exceeded 10 objects. However, the patient was unable to utilize multiplication (e.g., 5 × 4) instead of counting objects in the continuous series. Reading and writing figures were limited to two-digit numbers. Number concept was relatively preserved, i.e., the patient could correctly state which of two numbers was greater, 304 or 403. However, he could not integrate orally presented single digits (e.g., 1, 4, 3 into 143) because of spatial errors in "place value."

Analysis of the patient's errors in written calculation can show misidentification of arithmetical signs as the primary source of calculation errors. Inability to read, name, or write arithmetic signs to dictation may be present despite preserved reading and writing of words and numbers (Ferro and Botelho, 1980; Caramazza and McCloskey, 1987). Spatial aspects of acalculia are reflected by reversals in reading or pointing to numbers (e.g., "12" instead of "21"). Columns of numbers are frequently misaligned. Numbers appearing in an area of visual neglect may be omitted by the patient. Patients with parietal disease may produce numbers which drift vertically across the lines and they may have difficulty in writing the digits.

Grafman et al. (1982) proposed an interesting method for scoring calculation errors based on the criteria used in the Benton Visual Retention Test (1974). Errors were classified in the following manner:

1. Misplacement: numbers that were not in the correct column.
2. Size: numbers that were larger or smaller than the size of the printed problem.
3. Distortion: producing an unrecognizable error.
4. Rotation: Rotating a written number.
5. Omission (neglect): omitting one or more numbers from their correct alignments in an answer.
6. Perseveration: replicating a number that was in the immediately preceding problem or space.

Composite scores were then derived for errors of spatial configuration (1 and 4), form (2 and 3), and attention (5 and 6). Table 5-5 displays the average number of

**TABLE 5-5.** Mean Severity of the Three Error Types in the Qualitative Score

|  | LP | LA | RP | RA | NC |
|---|---|---|---|---|---|
| Space (misplacement and rotation errors) | 2.64 | 1.87 | 1.31 | 1.23 | 0.96 |
| Form (size and distortion errors) | 2.73 | 1.60 | 0.85 | 0.82 | 0.76 |
| Attention (omission and perseveration errors) | 3.73 | 2.23 | 2.23 | 2.68 | 2.07 |

LP = left posterior; LA = left anterior; RP = right posterior; RA = right anterior; NC = normal controls. (Adapted from Grafman et al., 1982.)

errors exhibited by patients with various brain lesions and normal controls. As seen, patients with left posterior lesions made more errors of each type than the other patient groups. Attentional errors were comparable across the brain-damaged patients and control subjects whereas errors due to form were more severe in the patients. Further analyses indicated that patients with left posterior lesions made significantly more errors than those with left anterior lesions while the right-lesioned groups did not differ from each other. Errors due to spatial configuration did not differentiate the groups.

More recently, Spiers (1987) has provided a classification system for calculation errors based on his review of the acalculia literature. As shown in Table 5-6, this system divides errors into those involving use of individual numbers (e.g., incorrectly placing numbers in the hundreds, tens, and ones columns), ability to borrow and carry, knowledge of basic facts about numbers (e.g., retrieving an incorrect table value such as $3 \times 4 = 16$), ability to apply algorithms (e.g., using a different operation such as multiplication rather than division), and knowledge of symbols (e.g., writing or using a sign other than that requested). As Spiers notes, the validity of these categories awaits further evaluation.

Warrington (1982) found that response speed (e.g., percent of long latency responses) and activity of oral calculation were sensitive measures of subclinical or mild calculation disorder, particularly when she related these measures to the manipulation required to solve the arithmetic problems (e.g., difference between the whole and remainder or subtrahend). She also tested rapid estimation of two- and three-digit calculation problems and obtained numeric cognitive estimates (e.g., How tall is the average woman?). These procedures can disclose laborious and inaccurate calculations in patients who retain quantitative concepts and knowledge of individual numbers.

Individually administered tests of achievement in mathematics which have been standardized in children and adolescents according to age and grade are available. The Wide Range Achievement Test-Revised (WRAT-R; Jastak and Wilkinson, 1984), Peabody Individual Achievement Test-Revised (PIAT-R; Markwardt, 1989), and Key Math Diagnostic Arithmetic Test (Connolly et al., 1976) are useful if the pattern of errors is examined qualitatively for indications of a particular type of acalculia. The WRAT-R includes preliminary questions to assess counting, number concept, and written calculation problems ranging in difficulty from simple addition to college-level mathematics. In contrast, the PIAT-R utilizes a multiple-choice format to evaluate number concept, counting (e.g., "point to the number which comes just before 100") and number operation presented in an admixture of verbal problems and examples using numbers. Problems on the PIAT-R appear in large print and may be presented concurrently in both written and oral modalities. Although the PIAT-R is less likely to reflect paraphasic errors, it is important to consider any systematic neglect of answers given in one or the other visual half-field and to concurrently obtain oral responses from nonaphasic patients. The Key Math Diagnostic Achievement Test consists of 14 subtests examining areas such as knowledge of numbers and fractions, ability to perform operations such as addition and subtraction, and "real world" skills involving money, measurements, and time. The test does not have adult norms but is useful as a qualitative means of gauging performance in older patients.

**Table 5-6.** Error Analysis Classification

| Error Type | Description |
|---|---|
| Place-holding errors | |
| 1. Number value | Inability to distinguish the larger of two numbers due to a disturbance in the patient's appreciation of units, tens, hundreds, etc. (e.g., 465 vs. 645). |
| 2. Number expansion | Expansion of tens, hundreds, or thousands place-holding representation in number writing without actually violating the place-holding values of the digits (5,614 written as 5000600104). |
| 3. Mirror reversal | Digit sequence is written, copied, or repeated in reverse (564 is written 654). |
| 4. Partial reversal | Same as 3 but only one set of digits is involved in the reversal (5,614 is written 5,641). |
| 5. Transposition | Digit sequence within a number is altered, violating place-holding values (6,325 is 6,523) |
| Digit errors | |
| 1. Simple substitution | The place-holding value of the various digits is maintained but an incorrect digit is present as a result of a paralexia, paraphasia, or paragraphia. In this instance, the patient may or may not arrive at a correct solution as a function of whether the substituted digit is incorporated into the computation. |
| 2. Perseverative computational | A digit is substituted from another number present in the problem and usually incorporated into the computation yielding an incorrect solution (25 $\times$ 12 performed as 25 $\times$ 15). |
| 3. Perseverative solution | A digit is substituted from another number in the problem into the number given as the solution (17 $\times$ 3 = 57). |
| 4. Omission | Failure to use a number or digit present in the problem in the process of computation, leading to an incorrect solution. (This is often a leftmost digit suggesting a neglect error.) |
| Borrow and carry errors | |
| 1. Neglect of carry | The patient fails to use a verbalized or clearly indicated carry in the process of computation. |
| 2. Defective carry | All the digits of an intermediate solution are written and the higher place-holding digits are not carried, though they still may be added to the next column in computation. $$\begin{array}{r} 237 \\ +\ 175 \\ \hline 31112 \end{array}$$ |
| 3. Incorrect placement | Though the carry is made, it then is added to the wrong column. |
| 4. Wrong carry | The patient carries and adds to the next column the smaller rather than the larger place-holding digit from the sum of the previous column. |
| 5. Zero carry/borrow | Confusion of the borrowing of carrying process if there is a zero in the problem. |
| 6. Neglect of borrow | The leftmost or higher place-holding digit is not reduced after a clearly verbalized or indicated borrow. |
| 7. Defective borrow | 1. Adding the borrowed amount to the lesser place-holding digit.<br>2. Borrowing from a lesser to a greater place-holding digit. |

| Error Type | Description |
|---|---|
| Basic fact errors | |
| 1. Table value | Not due to a digit error. Retrieval of an incorrect table value. Solution would often be correct for the next higher or lower multiplicator (7 × 8 = 64). Patients often compensate for this by serial addition, finger counting, or by using rounding-up strategies. |
| 2. Zero/identity | Basic fact errors that appear only when a 0 or 1 is present in the problem being computed. |
| Algorithm errors | |
| 1. Incomplete | Patient initiates the correct operation but fails to carry out all of the steps required to arrive at a solution and leaves the problem or some intermediate step incomplete. |
| 2. Incorrect alignment | The elements of the problem are not spatially disposed on the page in a manner that will lead to correct execution of the problem. |
| 3. Spatial | Misalignment of columns in the intermediate steps of multidigit multiplication or division leading to addition or subtraction of incorrect intermediate products. |
| 4. Incorrect sequence | The patient proceeds from left to right or in some inconsistent manner through the problem, perhaps with correct computations, but the sequence in which they are carried out leads to incorrect carries, borrows, and intermediate products. |
| 5. Subtraction inversion | The minuend and subtrahend are reversed in the act of computation (15 − 6 = 11). |
| 6. Inappropriate | The problem is spatially disposed on the page in the manner of another operation (typically multiplication substituted for division). |
| 7. Substitution | The patient executes an operation other than the one asked for by the problem. For example, a multiplication is added or subtracted instead of multiplied. |
| 8. Confounded | Partial substitution of different operations within the same problem. For example, one column is added and the other multiplied but each correctly computed for the operation applied to it. |
| 9. Defective | Anarithmetia. The patient uses incorrect, inconsistent, or idiosyncratic procedures or fails to access any correct computational strategy. |
| Symbol errors | |
| 1. Loss of symbols | The patient cannot produce the four computation signs upon request or in writing down a problem that has been dictated, but this has no apparent effect on the actual execution of the correct operation. |
| 2. Substitution | An incorrect sign is written by the patient, which then may result in the execution of a different operation from that requested, but this is usually computed correctly. |
| 3. Rotation | A special case of substitution. This involves the perceptual similarity between the addition and multiplication signs where one is easily rotated 90° and becomes the other (+ rotated gives ×). This substitution may or may not affect the operation that is then executed. |

Adapted from Spiers, 1987.

Administration of either the WRAT-R or PIAT-R permits direct comparison of arithmetic calculation and proficiency in reading and spelling. The standardized tests are used for screening purposes, but more qualitative analysis of individualized assessment (both written and oral) is necessary to differentiate various types of errors.

Calculation measures should obviously be complemented with a full neuropsychological battery including tests of attention, expressive and receptive language, memory, and executive functioning in order to ascertain the role of secondary impairments in contributing to acalculia. In addition, it is useful, particularly in children and adolescents, to obtain scholastic records in order to compare current functioning with premorbid abilities.

## OTHER FORMULATIONS OF CALCULATION DISORDER

While Hécan et al's (1961) categories provide a useful schema with which to organize our current knowledge of calculation disorders, they are neither mutually exclusive and exhaustive nor do they represent the only attempt at classification in this field. Grewel (1952, 1969) postulated that disorders of calculation result from disruption of a symbolic-semantic system, the components and principles of which are clearly definable. As such, errors in calculation depend on both the method of calculation and its notation system, as well as on the location and extent of injury to the neural substrate. Grewel, therefore, adopted Berger's (1926) overall classification of primary and secondary acalculia but expanded the former category by postulating asymbolic (inability to use numbers reliably) and asyntactic (inability to combine numbers correctly according to the computational rules governing calculation) forms of primary acalculia. He did not link these to a specific localization. Grewel's formulation emphasizes the contribution of the calculation system itself to the deficits manifested by patients and implies that there is no unitary concept of acalculia or single localization of a cortical lesion which is responsible for calculation disorders.

Mazzuchi and colleagues (1976) proposed a functional hierarchy for calculation abilities. The foundation of the hierarchy is provided by counting and knowledge of basic mathematical table values. Next are the four elementary calculation operations which are divided into two levels: (1) addition and subtraction and (2) multiplication and division. Following this is the level of fixed algebraic and geometric rules which are independent of elementary calculation, and at the highest level is the ability to analyze and program mathematical data in order to solve problems. The authors refer to this hierarchy in their analysis of a residual calculation disorder in a patient who had partially recovered from global aphasia. Because their patient had frequent errors in number reading and writing and exhibited difficulty in retrieving basic number facts and calculations, Mazzuchi et al. inferred the presence of deficits at several levels of the hierarchy. Further study is necessary to characterize the relationship among the levels of function in this hierarchy and to determine whether the deficits exhibited by other thoroughly examined patients may be successfully classified within its categories.

In another study, Collignon and colleagues (1977) concluded that acalculia does not exist in the sense implied by Grewel's (1969) primary category of Hécaen et al.'s

(1961) anarithmetria. Based on an analysis of the calculation abilities of patients with lateralized lesions and the frequency with which they had associated cognitive deficits, Collignon et al. proposed that acalculia is always a secondary problem and falls into three categories. The first is acalculia secondary to one of three "instrumental problems" that include aphasia, spatial disorders, and constructional apraxia. Second is acalculia as a result of some combination of these three problems, and third is acalculia due to generalized intellectual deterioration. In effect, then, Collignon et al.'s classification challenges the notion that calculation be considered a separate cognitive function and reduces it to the level of a skilled performance based on the efficient use of more fundamental, presumably localizable functions. Bresson et al. (1972) embraced a similar strategy in their categorization of calculation errors according to lesion lateralization. They found that errors in number facts and incorrect carrying or borrowing were characteristic of patients with left-hemisphere lesions, whereas errors in place value and misalignment of columns or intermediate product errors in multiplication were most common in cases of right-hemisphere lesions. They found that most other calculation errors occurred with similar frequency in left and right unilateral lesion groups.

Clearly, there is no unitary deficit that warrants the diagnosis of acalculia and that can be specifically lateralized and localized. However, it is probably the case that the calculation system may be disrupted in various ways for which there will be corresponding specifiable lesions. By this definition, calculation is as much a "function" as language. Certainly, there is no unitary aphasia or lesion localization that produces a generalized language disturbance. Rather, this function is differentially disrupted by compromise in its various neural substrates which produce different patterns of language errors. Studies where patients' performances and patterns of errors on calculation tasks have been analyzed in greater detail (Bresson et al., 1972; Benson and Denckla, 1969; Benson and Weir, 1972; Leleux et al., 1979; Rosselli and Ardila, 1989; Warrington, 1982) suggest that such a perspective is also correct for understanding the status of calculation as a higher cognitive function. Most encouraging in this respect is a study by Warrington which deserves to be discussed in some detail. Warrington (1982) studied a physician whose language fully recovered within one month of a left posterior parieto-occipital intracerebral hematoma which had produced an acute aphasia. The patient exhibited a residual decline in efficiency and accuracy of calculation for all oral and written arithmetical operations, whereas his capacity to follow procedural rules (e.g., borrowing) in solutions to mathematical problems, provide numerical cognitive estimates (e.g., How tall is the average English woman?), and select the larger of two numbers were relatively well preserved. Whenever the patient produced errors, they closely approximated the correct response. Warrington concluded that her patient demonstrated a "dissociation between arithmetical processing in general and accurate airthmetical computations" (p. 46). Furthermore, she suggested that this patient had a specific reduction in the accessibility of arithmetical facts despite his use of a processing strategy similar to that of a normal adult.

In her discussion, Warrington refutes any notion that this patient's calculation disorder could be attributed to deficits in language, constructional ability, or fundamental number knowledge. Furthermore, the rules of the calculation operations per se were intact. According to Warrington, then, this case demonstrates several points.

First, it is possible to obtain a dissociation between arithmetical processing in general and accurate retrieval of specific computational values. Second, numeracy (calculation) represents a major category of semantic knowledge within which it is possible to identify various subcategories that may become inoperative. Warrington's report adds to the evidence that the left hemisphere is preferentially involved in mediating the fundamental calculation process.

From a review of the literature, it is clear that acalculia may occur as a relatively isolated deficit or as a result of impairment in other cognitive abilities. A recent model discussed by Boller and Grafman (1985) is based on an information processing framework that views calculation as a skill dependent upon numerous components including verbal processing, perception/recognition of numbers and number-symbol representation, visual-spatial discrimination, short- and long-term memory stores, reasoning, and sustained attention. These components are involved in calculation to varying degrees depending on the type of problem, stage of processing (e.g., addition, carrying, etc.), time demands, complexity, response requirements (e.g., mental calcuation vs. oral or written solution), and instructions. In approaching a problem such as written arithmetic presented in a vertical arrangement, the individual must be able to perceive the spatial alignment of the numbers, comprehend the symbol "$+$", recognize the numbers, and have a plan of action. Attentional demands may be relatively automatic or controlled depending on the individual's level of experience with similar problems. Short-term memory store enables the individual to retain the number to be used in carrying while long-term store contains the procedural rules for completing the problem and the semantic rules for understanding the procedures involved. Acalculia can result from a breakdown in any one of these subprocesses.

McClosky and Caramazza (1987) have focused on a detailed analysis of the calculation system. Their model attempts to account for the numerous dissociations that have been observed across studies such as intact ability to understand numbers but not to read calculation signs (Ferro and Botelho, 1980). Their model distinguishes between number processing and calculation systems. The former consists of the components necessary for understanding and producing numbers while the latter entails mathematical facts and procedures for completing problems. Within the number processing system, McCloskey and Caramazza further posit two subsystems, those for number comprehension and number production. As shown in Figure 5-6, additional distinctions are made between comprehension vs. production of arabic (e.g., 7,040) and verbal numbers (e.g., written or spoken words) as well as lexical processing (ability to comprehend or produce individual elements of a number such as 6 or forty) and syntactic processing (ability to process and produce relations among the elements such as retaining the tens, hundreds, and thousands base). Finally, within the lexical system, their model differentiates between comprehension or production of spoken vs. written numbers. The calculation system, depicted in Figure 5-7, contains the processing mechanisms necessary for interpreting operation symbols, retrieving arithmetic and table facts, and executing the procedures necessary to complete a problem. According to McCloskey and Caramazza's framework, selective impairments in calculation may occur at any level of the system and can therefore account for isolated deficits and dissociations observed in the clinical literature.

In summary, recent contributions to the classification of acalculia show a trend

# NUMBER COMPREHENSION SYSTEM

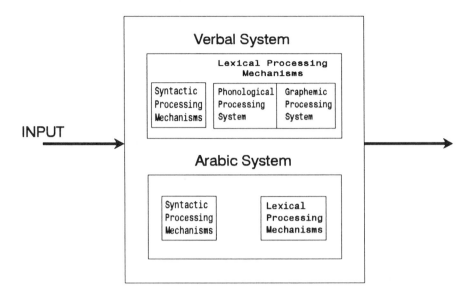

# NUMBER PRODUCTION SYSTEM

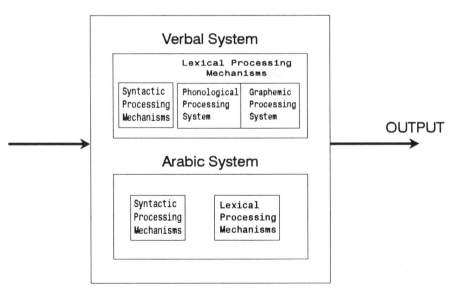

**Fig. 5-6.** Schematic representations of the number comprehension and number productions subsystems. (Adapted from McCloskey and Caramazza, 1987.)

117

CALCULATION SYSTEM

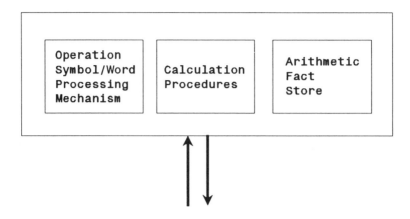

**Fig. 5-7.** Schematic representation of the calculation system. (Adapted from Caramazza and McCloskey, 1987.)

toward more detailed analysis of errors, fine-grained breakdowns of the specific sub-processes involved in normal calculation, and linkage with other processing systems such as memory which can impinge on accurate performance. When combined with improved methods of lesion localization by magnetic resonance imaging and new techniques to measure regional cerebral blood flow and metabolism, the cerebral organization of calculation may be better understood.

## SUMMARY

Since the work of Hécaen et al. (1961), acquired disorders of calculation have been divided into three categories—acalculia secondary to alexia and agraphia for numbers, acalculia resulting from spatial disorganization of numbers, and anarithmetria or impaired calculation in the strict sense. Review of the literature provides empirical confirmation for Hécaen's hypothesis that alexia for words can be dissociated from alexia for numbers and shows that the three types of acalculia are often associated with distinct patterns of cerebral lesions. It is important to recall, however, that these categories were derived empirically and were not intended to become a rigid classification schema. Nevertheless, they have dominated research on acalculia and have often dictated the form which studies on this topic have taken. While this classification continues to be a useful heuristic in clinical practice, more recent research has abandoned this schema and focused on the nature of the calculation itself. Two trends, in particular, can be discerned. The first of these views calculation ability as dependent on various cognitive operations, focuses on the semantic and syntactic aspects of calculation, relies on information processing theory or modeling, and attempts to categorize the performance of acalculic patients within such a frame-work. The second observes the patient's actual productions on various calculation tasks and examines specific errors which then become the point of departure for investigation. Once these error types have been isolated, characterized, and shown not to be dependent on other functions such as memory or language, some attempt is made to correlate them with physiological or neuroanatomical findings.

Both of these approaches have given rise to more refined methods of testing patients with calculation deficits and have helped to elucidate the various component processes required to carry out even simple computations. The cognitive-information processing approach suffers from the invention of a priori categories that may reflect the logical and theoretical structure of calculation much more than its actual neural organization. The error-anatomical correlation method, meanwhile, runs the risk of returning to a phrenological, compartmentalized view of calculation, with table value knowledge in one lobe and spatial schemas in another. Methodological preferences notwithstanding, it is important to remember that, like language, music, and the other major semantic information systems available to humans, calculation is clearly the product of an interactive cerebral network. The network required for this function depends first upon various fundamental structures common to all cognitive activity, such as those which mediate arousal and attention. It also shares structures with overlapping networks which control other semantic systems, such as the spatial-sequential algorithms associated with carrying and borrowing. Such a network must be considered interactive because the structure and task demands of the activity itself will, to some extent, dictate the neuroanatomical structures which can become adapted to subserve this function. For example, Heschl's gyrus, the hippocampus, the supplementary motor cortex, and Broca's area, to name but a few, may contribute nothing to the core abilities underlying calculation. Whereas the superior temporal gyrus, the angular gyrus and portions of the right parietal lobe may be crucial to the acquisition and maintenance of this function.

The more careful methods of examination and more detailed analysis of errors reported in recent studies of calculation disorders have set a standard for future research. Hopefully, the more differentiated, process-error analysis approach that has emerged from these studies will take the place of the more simplistic categorizations that have dominated the literature. More careful investigation of anarithmetria, per se, must also be undertaken in order to identify the component processes and regional localization underlying the fundamental algorithms of calculation. Cerebral activation techniques, meanwhile, are beginning to elucidate hemispheric dominance for calculation in normal adults and may, if coupled with careful testing, help to identify the critical neural substrates of the calculation network.

## ACKNOWLEDGMENT

The inspiration and encouragement for this work were provided by Dr. Edith Kaplan in Boston, Professor Henry Hécaen in Paris, and Gail Hochanadel. We are indebted to Dr. Arthur L. Benton for his review and helpful suggestions regarding an earlier version of this chapter.

## REFERENCES

Benson, D. F., and Denckla, M. B. (1969). Verbal paraphasia as a source of calculation disturbance. *Arch. Neurol.* 21:96–102.

Benson, D. F., and Geschwind, N. (1970). Developmental Gerstmann syndrome. *Neurology*
20:293–298.

Benson, D. F., and Weir, W. F. (1972). Acalculia: acquired anarithmetria. *Cortex* 8:465–472.

Benton, A. L. (1963) *Assessment of Number Operations*. Iowa City: University of Iowa Hospitals, Department of Neurology.

Benton, A. L. (1966). *Problemi di Neuropsicologia*. Firenze: Editrice Universitaria, pp. 147–
159.

Benton, A. L. (1977). Reflections on the Gerstmann syndrome. *Brain Lang.* 4:45–62.

Berger, H. (1926). Ueber rechenstorungen bei herderkrankungen des Grosshirns. *Arch. Psychiat. Nervenk.* 78:238–263.

Boller, F., and Grafman, J. (1985). Acalculia. In *Handbook of Clinical Neurology*, Vol. 1, P. J.
Vinken, G. W. Bruyn, and H. L. Klawans (eds.). Amsterdam: North Holland, pp. 473–
481.

Bresson, F., DeSchonen, S., and Tzortzis, C. (1972). Étude des perturbations dans des performances logico-arithmetiques chez des sujets atteints de diverses lesions cérébrales. *Lan-
gages* 7:108–122.

Caramazza, A., and McCloskey, M. (1987). Dissociations of calculation processes. In *Mathematical Disabilities: A Cognitive Neuropsychological Perspective*, G. Deloche and X.
Seron (eds.). Hillsdale, N.J.: Lawrence Erlbaum Associates, pp. 221–234.

Cohn, R. (1961). Dyscalculia. *Arch. Neurol.* 4:301–307.

Collignon, R., Leclerq, C., and Mahy, J. (1977). Etude de la sémiologie des troubles du calcul
observés au cours des leions corticales. *Acta Neurol. Belg.* 77:257–275.

Connolly, A. J., Nachtman, W., and Pritchett, M. F. (1976). *Key Math Diagnostic Arithmetic
Test*. Circle Pines, Minn.: American Guidance Service.

Corbett, A. J., McCusker, E. A., and Davidson, O. R. (1986). Acalculia following a dominant-
hemisphere subcortical infarct. *Arch. Neurol.* 43: 964–966.

Critchley, M. (1953). *The Parietal Lobes*. London: Arnold.

Dahmen, W., Hartje, W., Bussing, A., and Sturm, W. (1982). Disorders of calculation in aphasic
patients—spatial and verbal components. *Neuropsychologia* 20:145–153.

Deloche, G., and Seron, X. (1982). From three to 3: a differential analysis of skills in transcoding
quantities between patients with Broca's and Wernicke's aphasia. *Brain* 105:719–733.

Engelhardt, J. M. (1977). Analysis of children's computational errors: a qualitative approach.
*Br. J. Educ. Psychol.* 47:149–154.

Ferro, J. M., and Botelho, M.A.S. (1980). Alexia for arithmetical signs. A cause of disturbed
calculation. *Cortex* 16:175–180.

Gall, F. J., and Spurzheim, J. C. (1808). *Recherches sur le Systeme Nerveux en Général et sur
Celui du Cerveau en Particulier*. Amsterdam: E. J. Bonset (1967 reprint).

Gerstmann, J. (1940). Syndrome of finger agnosia, disorientation for right and left, agraphia
and acalculia. *Arch. Neurol. Psychiatry* 44:398–408.

Grafman, J., Kampen, D., Rosenberg, J., Salazar, A. M., and Boller, F. (1989). The progressive
breakdown of number processing and calculation ability: a case study. *Cortex* 25:121–133.

Grafman, J., Passafiume, D., Faglioni, P., and Boller, F. (1982). Calculation disturbances in
adults with focal hemispheric damage. *Cortex* 18:37–50.

Grewel, F. (1952). Acalculia. *Brain* 75:397–407.

Grewel, F. (1969). The acalculias. In *Handbook of Clinical Neurology*, Vol. 3, P. J. Vinken and
G. Bruyn (eds.). Amsterdam: North Holland pp. 181–196.

Gronwall, D. and Sampson, H. (1974). *The Psychological Effects of Concussion*. Auckland: Auckland University Press.

Gronwall, D., and Wrightson, P. (1974). Delayed recovery of intellectual function after minor head injury. *Lancet* 2:606–609.

Guttman, E. (1936). Congenital arithmetic disability and acalculia. *Br. J. Med. Psychol.* 16:16–35.

Hartje, W. (1987). The effect of spatial disorders on arithmetical skills. In *Mathematical Disabilities: A Cognitive Neuropsychological Perspective*, G. Deloche and X. Seron (eds.). Hillside, N.J.: Lawrence Erlbaum Associates, pp. 121–135.

Head, H. (1926). *Aphasia and the Kindred Disorders of Speech*. Cambridge: Cambridge University Press.

Hécaen, H. (1962). Clinical symptomatology in right and left hemispheric lesions. In *Interhemispheric Relations and Cerebral Dominance*, V. B. Mountcastle (ed.). Baltimore: John Hopkins Press, pp. 215–243.

Hécaen, H. (1976). Acquired aphasia in children and the ontogenesis of hemispheric functional specialization. *Brain Lang.* 3:114–134.

Hécaen, H., Angelergues, R., and Houillier, S. (1961). Les varietes cliniques des acalculies au cours des lesions retrorolandiques: approche statistique du probleme. *Rev. Neurol.* 105:85–103.

Henschen, S. E. (1919). Clinical and anatomical contributions on brain pathology. W. F. Schaller (trans.), *Arch. Neurol. Psychiatry* 13:226–249 (1925 reprint).

Jastak, S. R., and Wilkinson, G. S. (1984). *Wide Range Achievement Test-Revised*. Wilmington, Del.: Jastak Associates.

Kinsbourne, M., and Warrington, E. K. (1963). The developmental Gerstmann syndrome. *Arch. Neurol.* 8:490–501.

Kleist, K. (1934). *Gehrinpathologie*. Leipzig:J. Barth.

Kolb, B., and Whishaw, I. Q. (1990). *Fundamentals of Human Neuropsychology*, 3rd ed. New York: W. H. Freeman.

Leiguarda, R., Starkstein, S., and Berthier, M. (1989). Anterior callosal haemorrhage: a partial interhemispheric disconnection syndrome. *Brain* 112:1019–1037.

Leleux, C., Kaiser, G., and LeBrun, Y. (1979). Dyscalculia in a right-handed teacher of mathematics with right cerebral damage. In *Problems of Aphasia. Neurolinguistics*, Vol. 9, R. Hoops and Y. LeBrun (eds.). Lisse: Swets and Zeitlinger.

Lewandowsky, M., and Stadelmann, E. (1908). Ueber einen bemerkenswerten Fall von Himblutung und über Rechenstörungen bei Herderkrankung des Gehirns. *J. Psychol. Neurol.* (Lpz.) 11:249–265.

Lezak, M. D. (1983). *Neuropsychological Assessment*. New York: Oxford University Press.

Luria, A. R. (1973). *The Working Brain: An Introduction to Neuropsychology*, London: Penguin-Allen Lane.

Markwardt, F. C. (1989). *Peabody Individual Achievement Test-Revised*. Circle Pines, Minn.: American Guidance Service.

Mazzuchi, A., Manzoni, G. C., Mainini, P., and Parma, M. (1976). Il problema dell'acalculia: studio di un caso. *Riv. Neurol.* 46:102–115.

McCloskey, M., and Caramazza, A. (1987). Cognitive mechanisms in normal and impaired number processing. In *Mathematical Disabilities: A Cognitive Neuropsychological Perspective*, G. Deloche and X. Seron (eds.). Hillside, N.J.: Lawrence Erlbaum Associates, pp. 201–219.

Papanicolaou, A. C., Schmidt, A. L., Moore, B. D., and Eisenberg, H. J. (1983). Cerebral activation patterns in an arithmetic and a visuospatial processing task. *Int. J. Neurosci.* 20:283–288.

Poeck, K., and Orgass, B. (1966). Gerstmann's syndrome and aphasia. *Cortex* 2:421–437.

Roberts, G. H. (1968). The failure strategies of third grade arithmetic pupils. *Arith. Teacher* 15:442–446.

Roeltgen, D. P., Sevush, S., and Heilman, K. M. (1983). Pure Gerstmann's syndrome from a focal lesion. *Arch. Neurol.* 40:46–47.

Rosselli, M., and Ardila, A. (1989). Calculation deficits in patients with right and left hemisphere damage. *Neuropsychologia* 27:607–617.

Saxe, G. B., and Shaheen, S. (1981). Piagetian theory and the atypical case: an analysis of the developmental Gerstmann's syndrome. *J. Learning Disabil.* 14:131–135.

Shepherd, R., and Gale, A. (1982). EEG correlates of hemisphere differences during a rapid calculation task. *J. Psychol.* 73: 73–84.

Singer, H. D., and Low, A. M. (1933). Acalculia. *Arch. Neurol. Psychiatry* 29:467–498.

Slade, P. D., and Russell, G.F.M. (1971). Developmental dyscalculia: brief report of four cases. *Psychol. Med.* 1:292–298.

Spellacy, F., and Peter, B. (1978). Dyscalculia and elements of the developmental Gerstmann syndrome in school children. *Cortex* 14:197–206.

Sperry, R. W. (1968). Mental unity following surgical disconnection of the cerebral hemispheres. *Harvey Lect.*, 62:293–323.

Spiers, P. A. (1987). Acalculia revisited: current issues. In *Mathematical Disabilities: A Cognitive Neuropsychological Perspective*, G. Deloche and X. Seron (eds.). Hillside, N.J.: Lawrence Erlbaum Associates, pp. 1–25.

Strub, R., and Geschwind, N. (1974). Gerstmann syndrome without aphasia. *Cortex* 10:378–387.

# 6

# Disturbances of the Body Schema

ARTHUR BENTON AND ABIGAIL B. SIVAN

The behavioral deficits discussed in this chapter are conventionally classified as disorders of the "body schema" (or "body image"). A distinction is sometimes made between the two terms, the "body image" referring to a conscious representation (e.g., as in explicit denial of hemiparesis) and the "body schema" to an unconscious representation (e.g., as in unilateral neglect). No doubt the distinction is a meaningful one (cf. Dennis, 1976; Ogden, 1985; Feinberg et al., 1990). However, for the most part, the two terms have been used interchangeably in the literature of clinical neurology.

The concept arose out of diverse neurological and psychiatric observations that seemed to be explained most readily by hypothesizing the existence of a long-standing spatially organized model of one's body that provides a framework within which perceptual, motor, and judgmental reactions directed toward one's body occur. The phantom-limb phenomenon, for example, was interpreted as reflecting the determining influence of an amputee's schema of an intact body on his perceptual responses. Conversely, impairment of the body schema resulting from brain disease was hypothesized by Pick (1908) to explain the gross errors made by some patients in pointing to parts of their body on verbal command (termed autotopagnosia).

Head (1920) explained normal and defective somatosensory localization on the basis of organized representational models of one's body which he called "schemata."

> Such schemata modify the impressions produced by incoming sensory impulses in such a way that the final sensations of position, or of locality, rise into consciousness charged with a relation to something that has happened before. Destruction of such "schemata" by a lesion of the cortex renders impossible all recognition of posture or of the locality of a stimulated spot in the affected part of the body. (Head, 1920, pp. 607–608)

Head postulated the existence of a number of different types of schemata, the main ones being (1) postural schemata that underlie position sense and appreciation of the direction of movement and (2) body surface schemata that furnish the background for tactile point localization and two-point discrimination.

The "body schema" has never been defined in a standard way: each author presents his own view of what he means by it. To some the concept represents the conscious awareness of the body, but to others it is a form of unconscious memory or representation. To some authors (Pick, for example) it was primarily a visual representation, but Head thought in terms of a constantly changing somatosensory organization against which the character of current stimulation was judged. These different emphases testify to the multidimensional nature of the concept.

Nor is it certain that, apart from its application to the phenomenon of the phantom limb, the concept possesses much explanatory value. Decades ago, Oldfield and Zangwill (1942–1943) discussed the many points that were ambiguous and obscure in Head's formulation. Subsequently, the topic was critically evaluated by Benton (1959), Poeck (1963, 1969), Poeck and Orgass (1967), and Denes (1989), who concluded that the "body schema" is merely a label for perceptual and localizing responses related to one's body. Indeed, Poeck (1975) placed disturbances of the body schema in the category of "neuropsychological symptoms without specific significance."

However, recent studies suggest that it may be premature to deny that it is a viable concept. At the very least, the "body schema" is a useful label. Dissociation in level of performance with respect to one's body as compared to objects in external space is often observed. For example, many patients with visuospatial defects, such as inaccurate object localization, show intact capacity to localize the parts of their own body, including the fingers (Hécaen and Angelergues, 1963). Similarly, most patients with impaired right-left discrimination or finger localization show intact orientation to objects in external space (Benton, 1959; De Renzi, 1982). Aphasic patients may show a more severe disability in understanding the names of body parts as compared to their understanding of the names of other classes of objects (Goodglass et al., 1966, 1986; Yamadori and Albert, 1973). Patients who show impaired reaching for objects in external space typically are able to point accurately and without hesitation to their own body parts (Damasio and Benton, 1979; De Renzi, 1982). Thus a distinction between performances relating to the body and those relating to external space is fully justified.

Three types of disturbance of the body schema will be considered in this chapter: autotopagnosia, finger agnosia, and right-left disorientation.

## AUTOTOPAGNOSIA

Inability to identify the parts of one's body, either to verbal command or by imitation, has been the subject of countless case reports since its original description by Badal (1888) and Pick (1898, 1908). The term autotopagnosia is used to designate a more or less complete form of the disability involving most parts of the body. More limited forms of the disability, such as "finger agnosia," "face agnosia," and impairment in discriminating between the right and left sides of the body, are usually considered separately from gross autotopagnosia, which is a fairly uncommon disorder.

Since a number of comprehensive reviews on the topic of autotopagnosia are available (see Benton, 1959; Lhermitte and Cambier, 1960; Frederiks, 1969; Poeck and Orgass, 1971; De Renzi, 1982; Denes, 1989), this section will be restricted to a consideration of some recent contributions that address the question of whether or not impairment in the identification of body parts is a disability that is independent of more general disabilities such as aphasic disorder, pervasive lateral or vertical neglect, and visuomotor directional disturbance.

Pointing to body parts on verbal request obviously demands understanding of the request, and it is only to be expected that patients with seriously impaired verbal comprehension (e.g., aphasics and dements) would perform defectively on this type of task (cf. Selecki and Herron, 1965). Semenza and Goodglass (1985) investigated this and other issues by assessing the performances of aphasic patients in pointing to body parts both to verbal request and on imitation in relation to the frequency of the names of the parts in their language (Italian or English). They found substantial correlation coefficients ($r = .69$ for Italian- and $r = .75$ for English-speaking patients) between accuracy of identification and the frequency of the name of the body part in the respective language. However, the same relationships held for nonverbal tasks involving imitation of the examiner pointing to body parts. Under these conditions, the correlation coefficients between accuracy of identification and name frequency were .60 and .54 for Italian- and English-speaking patients, respectively. Although the verbal tasks generated far more errors, the nonverbal tasks also produced a substantial number of errors. Semenza and Goodglass concluded that neither the global concept of autotopagnosia with its "geographic" implications nor more general formulations in terms of a pervasive inability to locate parts within a configuration are satisfactory explanations of the nature of patients' failure to point to body parts. Instead, they hypothesized that "the strength and precision of the representation" of each body part, as reflected in the relative frequency of its name, might be a prime determinant of performance level. Moreover, they pointed out that both the location and the functional properties of body parts could influence the nature of the errors made by patients.

A second contribution is the case report of Ogden (1985) describing a patient with a large metastatic tumor in the left parietal region who exhibited gross autotopagnosia in the absence of aphasic disorder or a general dementia. He could name body parts and describe their function but made many errors in pointing to both his own body parts and to those on a doll and a photograph. Yet he had no difficulty in pointing on verbal request to parts of an automobile, flower, or elephant. The clinical picture was complicated by ideomotor apraxia as well as dressing dyspraxia, visuoconstructional impairment, and a full Gerstmann syndrome. Ogden concluded that the patient's performance pattern supported the view that autotopagnosia could present as a "disorder that is independent of generalized mental deterioration, visuospatial deficits, aphasic, disorders, apraxia, or a general inability to analyze wholes into parts."

Semenza (1988) has described a 74-year-old mildly aphasic patient with a metastatic tumor in the territory of the left angular gyrus who performed defectively on both verbal and nonverbal body part tasks. In contrast, she had no difficulty in pointing to the parts of a bicycle, a chair, and a shoe both on verbal request and on imitation. It did not appear that her failure could be attributed either to her aphasia or to the full Gerstmann syndrome that she exhibited.

The findings of these recent investigations suggest that, although autotopagnosia invariably appears within the setting of other diabilities (a "pure" autotopagnosia has never been reported), it does possess a certain degree of autonomy. The disability is seen in patients who are neither aphasic nor demented. This fact, together with the observation that at least some autotopagnosic patients are quite capable of pointing to parts of objects, animals, and plants on verbal request, emphasizes the distinctive nature of the disability. The question of the mechanisms underlying its occurrence and its association with other parietal deficits has been addressed. As has been noted, Semenza and Goodglass postulate the existence of a conceptual representation of body parts and their spatial and functional interrelations which is "stored" in the brain, presumably in the posterior parietal region of the left hemisphere. Ogden supports the concept of a neurologically based body schema and advances the possibility that parietal symptomatology, including autotopagnosia, is mediated by interrelated neural circuits. Further, "depending on which circuits are disconnected, and where, different disorders and combinations of disorders result."

## FINGER AGNOSIA

The term finger agnosia was coined by Gerstmann (1924) to denote impairment in the ability to identify the fingers of either one's own hand or those of another person. He regarded the disability as the behavioral expression of a partial dissolution of the body schema and he made it the core symptom in the aggregate of deficits (finger agnosia, agraphia, acalculia, right-left disorientation) that has come to be known as the Gerstmann syndrome.

There is ample evidence that finger agnosia is not a unitary disability but rather a collective term for diverse types of defective performances relating to identification of the fingers (cf. Schilder, 1931; Benton, 1959, 1977; Ettlinger, 1963; Critchley, 1966). These performances can be classified along a number of dimensions, e.g., whether the stimulus is verbal, visual, or tactile, whether the required response is verbal or nonverbal, whether the task involves localizing fingers on one's own hand or their representation on a two-dimensional model of the hand. It is also important to differentiate between bilateral and unilateral disturbances of finger recognition. Gerstmann meant by "finger agnosia" an impairment in finger identification on *both* hands. However, defective localization of tactile stimulation of the fingers of one hand in association with other types of somatosensory impairment in that hand is a recognized sign of unilateral brain disease (cf. Head, 1920; Gainotti, and Tiacci, 1973).

There is also some doubt about the validity of Gerstmann's assumption that finger agnosia represents a partial dissolution of the body schema. As De Renzi (1982) pointed out, autotopagnosic patients, who cannot point to their body parts (e.g., nose, mouth, eyes) on verbal command and who presumably suffer from a gross dissolution of the body schema, may still be able to localize their fingers accurately.

### Developmental Aspects

The development of finger recognition in preschool children was studied in detail by Lefford et al. (1974), who demonstrated that performance level was a function of the

**Fig. 6-1.** Arrangement for tactile localization on fingers on a schematic representation of the hand.

stimulus characteristics and response requirements of the specific tasks that were presented and that, within the age range of three to five years, performance on each task showed a regular developmental course.

The easiest task for the children was pointing to fingers that the examiner touched as the child watched him: 73% of the three-year-old children, 93% of the four-year-olds, and 99% of the five-year-olds showed successful performance. Localizing fingers which the examiner pointed to (but did not touch) was about as easy (63%, 98%, and 99% success at three, four, and five years, respectively). But purely tactile recognition (i.e., identifying touched fingers without the aid of vision) was more difficult for the children (24%, 63%, and 72% success at three, four, and five years, respectively). Still more difficult was tactile localization of touched fingers on a schematic representation of the hand instead of the child's own hand (Fig. 6-1). Only 11% of the three-year-old children, 28% of the four-year-olds, and 52% of the five-year-olds succeeded on this task.

Lefford et al. analyzed the performances of the children in terms of intrasensory differentiation (tactile-visual localization), intersensory integration (tactile localization), and the capacity for representational thinking (localization on a model). Their findings made it evident that different tasks present different age-related cognitive demands.

The normative observations of Benton (1955a, 1959) on school children may be viewed as an extension of those of Lefford et al. Three tasks were presented to children in the age range of six to nine: (1) with the hand visible, identification of single fingers touched by the examiner; (2) with the hand hidden from view, identification of single fingers touched by the examiner; (3) with the hand hidden from view, identification of pairs of fingers simultaneously touched by the examiner. In the purely tactile tasks, an outline drawing of the right or left hand, with the thumb and fingers numbered from 1 to 5, was placed before the child who could identify the stimulated finger or fingers by naming them, pointing to them, or calling out their number (Fig. 6-1).

Virtually all six-year-olds performed adequately on the tactile-visual task. The other two types of finger localization involving identification of touched fingers on a model showed a progressive development with age. The more difficult task was, of course, the identification of simultaneously stimulated pairs of fingers, a task which a substantial proportion of nine-year-old children performed inaccurately. The studies of Wake (cf. Benton et al., 1983) extended these normative observations with the finding that at the age of 12 years, the tactile localization of simultaneously stimulated pairs of fingers had not yet reached the level of performance of adults.

Clearly, there are aspects of finger recognition that call on cognitive skills which reach maturity only after the age of 12 years. One of these skills appears to be visuo-spatial representational thinking, as reflected in making localizations on an external schematic model in place of one's own hand. There are also indications that the verbal encoding of sensory information may play a significant role in the performances of young school children (cf. Stone and Robinson, 1968; Lindgren, 1978; Benton, 1979).

### Behavioral Correlates

Since different tasks having to do with the identification of the fingers make demands on different cognitive capacities, it is evident that there is no such entity as a unitary "finger agnosia." Consequently, in discussing the clinical or pathological correlates of impairment in finger recognition, it is necessary to specify the particular tasks employed to assess the capacity.

Utilizing a nonverbal task in which mentally retarded subjects identified touched fingers (with their hand hidden from view) by pointing to them with the contralateral hand, Matthews et al. (1966) found a closer association between performance level and Wechsler-Bellevue Performance Scale IQ than Verbal Scale IQ. This relationship was confirmed in patients with brain disease by Poeck and Orgass (1969), who assessed diverse aspects of finger recognition with verbal and nonverbal tests. The correlation coefficient of nonverbal tactile localization on a schematic model with the Wechsler Adult Intelligence Scale (WAIS) IQ was .53, while the corresponding correlation coefficient for the WAIS Verbal Scale IQ was .34. On the other hand, performance on verbal tests of finger recognition (identification on verbal command, visual naming, tactile naming) correlated about as closely with the WAIS Verbal Scale IQ (mean $r = .58$) as with the WAIS Performance Scale IQ (mean $r = .52$). Poeck and Orgass found further that the verbal tests of finger recognition formed a highly intercorrelated cluster (mean $r = .72$) while nonverbal test performance showed a more modest association with these verbal tests (mean $r = .47$).

Poeck and Orgass also assessed the relationship between finger recognition performance and scores on other verbal (rote memory, Token Test) and nonverbal (recognition memory for designs) tests. The mean correlation coefficient between verbal finger recognition and the verbal tests was .48, while the correlation coefficient between verbal finger recognition and the nonverbal test was .36. Nonverbal finger recognition did not show this differential relationship with verbal and nonverbal abilities, the correlation coefficient with the verbal tests being .31 and that with the visual memory test being .32.

Studying nine patients with impairment in finger recognition as assessed by nonverbal tests, Kinsbourne and Warrington (1962) found that every patient showed some degree of visuoconstructive disability. Only two patients in the group were clinically aphasic. However, eight of the nine patients were judged to show mild to severe general mental impairment.

Thus the available correlational data indicate that it is useful to distinguish between defects in finger recognition elicited by tasks requiring naming of fingers or their identification when the name is given and those elicited by tasks requiring manual localization of fingers subjected to sensory stimulation. Both types of disability show a significant association with both linguistic and visuoperceptive impairment. But the verbal disability is somewhat more closely correlated with linguistic impairment and the nonverbal disability is somewhat more closely associated with visuoperceptive impairment.

Defective finger recognition may be shown by deviant children in different diagnostic categories. Some mental retardates are grossly defective, performing far below the level that would be predicted from their mental ages (cf. Strauss and Werner, 1938; Benton, 1955b, 1959). Giving a finger localization test to small samples of brain-injured, emotionally disturbed, and normal children who had been matched for age and Wechsler Intelligence Scale for Children (WISC) IQ, Clawson (1962) found that 80% of the brain-injured children performed at a level exceeded by 90% of the normal and emotionally disturbed children.

### Finger Agnosia and Reading Disability

The empirical evidence on the question of a relationship between finger recognition and reading achievement in children is conflicting (cf. Benton, 1975, 1979). To the degree that there is a concurrent association, it is more likely to be stronger among younger school-age children than among older ones (Benton, 1962; Fletcher et al., 1982; Sparrow and Satz, 1970; Hutchinson, 1983). It is possible that lateral differences in finger recognition are related to reading achievement (Fletcher et al., 1982; Reed, 1967). There are indications that the finger localization performances of kindergarten children are a significant predictor of their subsequent reading achievement, particularly in the early school grades (Fletcher et al., 1982; Lindgren, 1978; Zung, 1986). It is not clear why finger recognition should possess this predictive significance and specifically whether it is the body schema component of performance that is the important variable (cf. Benton, 1979). As has been pointed out, "finger recognition" is only a collective name for a series of tasks having to do with the identification of the fingers, each of which may make specific demands on different abilities such as intrasensory discrimination, intersensory integration, perceptual-representational processes, and verbal coding. The analysis of Fletcher et al. (1982) indicates that these different task performances load on different factors and that each may make a specific contribution to the prediction of reading achievement at different grade levels.

### Anatomical Correlates

When Gerstmann first described finger agnosia, he placed the causative lesion for the disability at the parieto-occipital junction around the angular gyrus of the left hemisphere. It was in this area that visual and somatosensory information was integrated to provide the basis for an intact and well-integrated body image. Subsequent clinical study suggested that this localization was more precise than was warranted by the facts; finger agnosia, in one form or another, was encountered in patients with lesions in the temporal and frontal lobes as well as in the posterior parietal area. At the same time, Gerstmann's localization of the responsible lesion in the left hemisphere was generally supported. For example, studying diverse performances in patients with unilateral brain disease. Hécaen (1962) found that finger agnosia was shown by 20% of patients with left-hemisphere lesions, but by only 3% of those with right-hemisphere lesions.

However, later investigative work cast considerable doubt on the assumption of a specific correlation between the disability and left-hemisphere disease. The association of finger agnosia with side-of-lesion seemed to be dependent, first, on whether the disability is manifested in verbal or nonverbal form and, second, on the presence or absence of aphasia and general mental impairment. The findings of studies that have explored these relationships in detail will be described.

Sauguet et al. (1971) assessed both verbal and nonverbal finger recognition in patients with unilateral brain disease. The three verbal tests were naming the fingers, pointing to fingers named by the examiner, and pointing to fingers which the examiner had designated by number. The two nonverbal tests were indicating the fingers touched by the examiner and the interdigital object identification test of Kinsbourne and Warrington (1962). Three groups of right-handed patients were studied: nonaphasic with right-hemisphere lesions, nonaphasic (or only expressive speech disorder without oral comprehension difficulties) with left-hemisphere lesions, and aphasic (with oral comprehension difficulties) with left-hemisphere lesions. Of an original sample of 94 patients, 14 (15%) were excluded from consideration either because they appeared confused or showed clinical and/or psychometric evidence of significant general mental impairment.

The results of the study may be summarized as follows: (1) naming of the fingers and their identification by pointing when their name was called out were closely associated with receptive aphasic disorder; about two-thirds of the patients with receptive language impairment showed defective verbal finger recognition, as compared to about 10% of patients in the other groups; (2) impaired performance on nonverbal tests of finger recognition was shown only by patients with receptive aphasic disorder, the frequency of failure ranging from 20 to 30%. Thus the predominant influence of linguistic impairment on performance in patients who are free from general mental impairment was evident.

Gainotti et al. (1972) studied nonverbal finger recognition in right-handed patients with unilateral brain disease. The relative frequency of bilateral impairment was about equal in the patients with left-hemisphere (18%) and right-hemisphere (16%) lesions. Further analysis showed that most of the patients with left-hemisphere lesions who performed defectively were aphasic and that the patients with right-hemisphere lesions who performed defectively showed clinical and/or psychometric evidence of general mental impairment (Table 6-1).

A third study by Benke et al. (1988) confirmed the high frequency of bilateral finger agnosia in aphasic patients but also noted its occurrence in nonaphasic patients with unilateral lesions. In all the groups, the presence of the disability was related to the severity of defect in visuospatial and linguistic-cognitive functions. The authors concluded that, rather than being the direct expression of a focal lesion, finger agnosia reflects impairment in higher-level cognitive systems.

A number of conclusions emerge when the findings of these studies are considered together. Impairment in finger recognition is closely associated with aphasic disorder or general mental impairment in patients with left-hemisphere disease. Impairment in finger recognition is closely associated with general mental impairment in patients with right-hemisphere disease. Since patients with general mental impairment were excluded from consideration in the study of Sauguet et al., this relationship was not evident in that study but it is quite clear in the results of Gainotti et al. But neither aphasic disorder nor general mental impairment can be considered to be solely responsible for the occurrence of impairment in finger recognition. Many aphasic patients showed intact finger recognition, even on the task of finger naming, as did many mentally deteriorated patients.

On the other hand, two recent case reports, in which the locus and extent of the lesion were documented by computerized tomography scan or magnetic resonance imaging, support Gerstmann's original contention that mechanisms in the angular gyrus–supramarginal gyrus territory of the left hemisphere mediate finger identification. Roeltgen et al. (1983) and Varney (1984) have described nonaphasic, nondemented patients with focal lesions in the posterior parietal region of the left hemisphere who exhibited bilateral finger agnosia as well as the other elements of the Gerstmann syndrome. In addition, confirmation of Gerstmann's localization is provided by the observations reported in an electrocortical stimulation study by Morris et al. (1984) on an epileptic patient. Stimulation of 12 loci in the posterior perisylvian region of the left hemisphere through 3 mm-diameter electrodes elicited the diverse defects associated with lesions in this territory; anomia, agraphia, acalculia alexia,

**Table 6-1.** Finger Agnosia in Patients with Unilateral Lesions

| | |
|---|---|
| Left-hemisphere lesions (n = 88) | 16 (18%) |
|    Mentally deteriorated (n = 30) | 10 (33%) |
|    Not mentally deteriorated (n = 58) | 6 (10%) |
|    Aphasic (n = 34) | 13 (38%) |
|    Not aphasic (n = 54) | 3 (6%) |
| Right-hemisphere lesions (n = 74) | 12 (16%) |
|    Mentally deteriorated (n = 22) | 10 (45%) |
|    Not mentally deteriorated (n = 52) | 2 (4%) |

Adapted from Gainotti et al., 1972.

constructional apraxia, right-left disorientation, and finger agnosia. Stimulation of one (and only one) locus, situated in the transition zone between the angular and supramarginal gyri, produced finger agnosia as well as agraphia and acalculia.

Thus it appears that bilateral finger agnosia, when it is not complicated by basic somatosensory defect, aphasia, or general mental impairment, may well be indicative of a focal lesion in the left posterior parietal region, as Gerstmann postulated. The disability is encountered far more often within a setting of either aphasic disorder or dementia. In these instances it cannot be regarded either as a specific cognitive defect or as having a specific localizing significance. There remains the question as to why some aphasic and mentally impaired patients show the disability in one or another form and others do not. One proposed explanation which has been advanced is that somatosensory defect, interacting with aphasia or mental disability, plays a role in its production. This possibility deserves to be explored by comparative behavioral and neurodiagnostic study of aphasic and demented patients who do or do not show finger agnosia.

## RIGHT-LEFT DISORIENTATION

Inability to identify the right and left sides of one's body or that of the confronting examiner is a familiar symptom to neurologists. First described as one aspect of general mental impairment or defective spatial thinking associated with bilateral disease, the disability attracted greater interest from a diagnostic and theoretical standpoint when Head (1926), Bonhoeffer (1923), and Gerstmann (1924, 1930) showed that it could also occur as a consequence of disease of the left hemisphere. Gerstmann viewed the disability as a limited breakdown of the body schema while Head regarded it as a form of defective symbolic thinking, a conclusion derived from his observation that many aphasic patients were unable to identify lateral parts on their own body or those of the confronting examiner.

Right-left disorientation is a very broad concept, even broader than "finger agnosia." It refers not to one ability, but to a number of performances on different levels of complexity, each making demands on different cognitive abilities and types of response. Naming, executing movements to verbal command, or imitation of movements may be called for. The execution of commands involving the identification of a single lateral body part or of commands involving the identification of more than one lateral body part may be required. The patients may be requested to identify their own body parts, those of the confronting examiner, or a combination of the two. Hence, meaningful assessment of "right-left orientation" requires that it be analyzed into operationally defined components or levels.

An example of such an analysis is presented in Table 6-2, which includes the performances most frequently assessed in clinical examination. Some of the types of performance listed in the table stand in a rather definite hierarchical relationship to each other. The ability to point to single lateral body parts (IB) is prerequisite for success in the execution of double commands (IC, D). The ability to execute double uncrossed commands (IC) is prerequisite for success on crossed commands (ID). The ability to point correctly to the body parts of the confronting examiner (IIIB) is prerequisite for successful combined orientation (IVA). Some performances are qualitatively dif-

**Table 6-2.** Components of Right-Left Orientation

---

I. Orientation Toward One's Own Body
    A. Naming single lateral body parts touched by examiner
    B. Pointing to single lateral body parts on verbal command
    C. Executing double *uncrossed* movements on verbal command (e.g., touching *left* ear with *left* hand)
    D. Executing double *crossed* movements on verbal command (e.g., touching *right* ear with *left* hand)

II. Orientation Toward One's Own Body Without Visual Guidance (Blindfolded or Eyes Closed)
    A. Naming single lateral body parts touched by examiner
    B. Pointing to single lateral body parts on verbal command
    C. Executing double *uncrossed* movements on verbal command (e.g., touching *left* ear with *left* hand)
    D. Executing double *crossed* movements on verbal command (e.g., touching *right* ear with *left* hand)

III. Orientation Toward Confronting Examiner or Picture
    A. Naming single lateral body parts
    B. Pointing to single lateral body parts on verbal command
    C. Imitating *uncrossed* movements of examiner (e.g., *left* hand on *left* ear)
    D. Imitating *crossed* movements of examiner (e.g., *left* hand on *right* ear)

IV. Combined Orientation Toward One's Own Body and Confronting Person
    A. Placing either *left* or *right* hand on specified part of confronting person on verbal command (e.g., placing *right* hand on confronting person's *left* ear)

---

ferent from each other and patients may show dissociation, failing in naming but not in pointing or imitation or vice versa (cf. Sauguet et al., 1971; Dennis, 1976).

There are other testing procedures that are not covered in Table 6-2. For example, the Hands Test of Thurstone (1938; Kao and Li, 1939) requires the patient to identify representations of the right or left hand in different postures. In the Road-Map Test of Direction Sense (Money, 1965), the patient is requested to indicate the direction of moves as the examiner traces a multidirectional path.

Many five-year-old children and the majority of six-year-olds are able to identify single lateral parts of their body in terms of "right" and "left" (Terman, 1916; Benton, 1959; Belmont and Birch, 1963; Clark and Klonoff, 1990). However, they are likely to make errors in the execution of double commands, particularly "crossed" commands. In the latter instance, failure to cross the midline is the most frequent type of error (e.g., the child touches his left ear with his left hand in response to the command to touch his right ear with his left hand). Some children perform decidedly less well with their eyes closed than with their eyes open. Most of them fail to make the necessary 180° reversal in orientation in pointing to lateral body parts of the confronting examiner.

The ability to execute double commands develops rapidly after the age of six years and it is unusual to encounter a nine-year-old who has difficulty in executing these commands. The difference in level of performance under the "eyes open" and "eyes closed" conditions also disappears with advancing age. However, some nine-year-old children evidently are not yet aware of the relativistic nature of the right-left concept, for they fail to make the necessary 180° reorientation in pointing to the lateral body parts of the confronting examiner. Moreover, a majority of them still make errors in executing tasks involving both the "own body" and "confronting persons" systems of orientation, i.e., placing their right (or left) hand on a specified lateral body part of the confronting examiner (cf. Benton and Kemble, 1960). By the age of 12 years, the great majority of children perform successfully in identifying body parts of the confronting examiner and in combined orientation tasks (Clark and Klonoff, 1990).

Occasionally, a child who shows a systematic reversal in response to instructions will be encountered. Such a child will show his left hand when asked to show his right hand and touch his right ear with his left hand when asked to touch his left ear with his right hand. The consistency of his reponses indicates that the child is quite capable of discriminating between the two sides of his body. At the same time, it is clear that he has attached the wrong verbal labels to the two sides. Not surprisingly, many of these children prove to be relatively deficient in the development of language skills (Benton, 1958; Benton and Kemble, 1960).

### Bases of Right-Left Orientation

When one considers the nature of these right-left discrimination tasks, it is evident that they make demands on a number of cognitive abilities. There is a verbal element in performance since the child must understand the verbal labels of "right" and "left" before he can apply them to the sides of his body and he must retain these labels in mind long enough to execute double commands. Of course, right-left orientation can be assessed by nonverbal performances, such as imitation tasks, as well as verbal performance.

(Another form of nonverbal "right-left orientation" is operationally expressed in the localization of stimulation to the right or left side of the body. Disturbances in this capacity, particularly lateral mislocalization of tactile stimulation (allesthesia, allochiria), have been described and a variety of explanations have been proposed to account for them (cf. Bender, 1952; Benton, 1959). However, the relationship between these disturbances and right-left disorientation, as conventionally defined, is a tenuous one. It is true that a few brain-diseased or hysterical patients who showed both types of impairment have been described (Jones, 1907; Seidemann, 1932; Bender, 1952; Hécaen and Ajuriaguerra, 1952). But most patients who show right-left disorientation do not show allesthesia; conversely, allesthesia, particularly when it appears in the context of spinal cord or brainstem disease, is not accompanied by right-left disorientation.)

A second component is sensory in nature. The labels of "right" and "left" are applied (or misapplied, as in systematic reversal) to a distinction between the sides of the body which necessarily involves a sensory discrimination. The basis for this distinction is not immediately obvious. The supposition is that it is primarily of a somesthetic nature, consisting of a continuous asymmetric pattern of sensory excitation from the muscles and joints of the two sides of the body (Benton, 1959; Benton and Kemble, 1960). Presumably this difference in excitation between the two sides of the body provides a right-left gradient of excitation which forms the basis for the intuitive awareness of a difference between the sides which most (but not all) normal persons possess. This awareness if often verbalized in terms of the right side being felt as larger, heavier, and stronger than the left.

When this gradient develops in young children is not known. It is probably related to some degree to the establishment of unilateral manual preference (cf. Elze, 1924; Benton and Menefee, 1957). However, there are normal right-handed adults who admit to having difficulty in the immediate discrimination between right and left and who report a lack of any intuitive feeling of a difference between the two sides of the body. The study of Wolf (1973), in which physicians and their spouses were asked how often they experienced difficulty when they had to identify right and left quickly, provides data on sex differences in "right-left blindness," as Elze (1924) called it. Two percent of the men and 5% of the women reported that they experienced such difficulty "all the time." Another 7% of the men and 13% of the women reported "frequent" difficulty. Similar findings have been reported by Harris and Gitterman (1978).

A third component is of a conceptual nature. Correct identification of the lateral body parts of a confronting person and simultaneous manipulation of the "own body" and "confronting person" orientational systems requires a thorough understanding of the relativistic nature of the right-left concept.

Finally, a fourth element is the visuospatial component which is brought into play when pointing to lateral body parts of a confronting person or to objects on the left or right. Some of the more complex tests of right-left orientation, such as those of Thurstone (1938), Culver (1969), Kao and Li (1939), and Money (1965), make strong demands on visuospatial abilities, especially the capacity for "mental rotation."

### Impairment in Patients with Brain Disease

Apart from the earliest observations of defective performance in demented patients, right-left disorientation has been traditionally associated with the presence of disease of the left hemisphere and aphasic disorders. A particularly important early contribution was that of Bonhoeffer (1923), who described a patient with a left temporoparietal lesion who showed marked right-left disorientation. He was aphasic and showed some impairment in oral language understanding, but his disability in right-left performances was disproportionally severe. However, he also showed a variety of somesthetic disturbances in the right arm and hand—impaired tactile localization, position sense, stereognosis, barognosis, and graphesthesis—raising the question of whether his right-left disorientation might be the product of an interaction between his sensory and linguistic impairments.

As has been mentioned, Head (1926) found that defective performance was so frequent in his aphasic patients that he incorporated both verbal and nonverbal tests of right-left orientation as measures of "symbolic formulation and expression" in his aphasia examination. Later confirmation of the association between left-hemisphere disease and right-left disorientation was provided by the observations of Gerstmann (1930) and McFie and Zangwill (1960). Gerstmann related the disability (along with finger agnosia) to dysfunction of the left parieto-occipital region. McFie and Zangwill found defective right-left orientation in five of eight patients with left-hemisphere lesions; in contrast, not a single patient in the group of 21 with right-hemisphere lesions showed the disability.

Sauguet et al. (1971) investigated the relationship of various forms of right-left disorientation to side-of-lesion and the presence of aphasic disorder in patients with unilateral lesions. The major findings were:

1. With respect to orientation to their own body, nonaphasic patients with lesions in either hemisphere performed adequately while two-thirds of those patients with left-hemisphere disease who had impaired language understanding performed defectively, primarily in the execution of double commands.
2. Identification of single body parts of the confronting examiner was performed defectively by about 50% of the patients with left-hemisphere disease who had impaired language understanding but also by 13% of the nonaphasic patients with right-hemisphere disease; all nonaphasic patients with left-hemisphere disease performed adequately.
3. The imitation of lateral movements (the head-eye-ear items of Head's battery) was performed defectively by aphasic patients with left-hemisphere disease (48%) and by nonaphasic patients with right-hemisphere disease (32%); 14% of the nonaphasic patients with left-hemisphere disease also performed defectively.

Thus the findings indicated that the hemispheric contribution to right-left orientation depends on what aspect of it is assessed. Impairment in "own body" performances is shown by aphasic patients with left-hemisphere disease, but is rarely seen in nonaphasic patients. On the other hand, nonaphasic patients with right-hemisphere lesions, as well as aphasic and demented patients, may show defects both in "confronting person" performances and in imitating right-left movements (cf. Fischer et al., 1990).

The case reports mentioned earlier in the section on finger agnosia that described patients with focal lesions in the angular gyrus–supramarginal gyrus region who exhibited all the elements of the Gerstmann syndrome, including right-left disorientation, indicate that the disability can be produced by a specific lesion in the absence of aphasia or general mental impairment. In the electrocortical stimulation study of Morris et al. (1984), right-left disorientation was elicited by stimulation of two loci adjacent to the locus that, when stimulated, produced finger agnosia.

Right-left disorientation in patients with the syndrome of lateral neglect also needs to be considered. Many of these patients show a unilateral disability, so to speak, in that they will consistently fail to point to body parts on the neglected side or to point to parts of the confronting examiner corresponding spatially to the neglected side of their body.

## CONCLUDING COMMENTS

The occurrence of autotopagnosia in patients who are not aphasic or seriously demented is a striking phenomenon. These patients fail tasks that are easily accomplished by normal two-year-old children and it is reasonable to conclude that there has been a falling out of a specific perceptual-cognitive system. Whether the system is labeled the body schema or the conceptual representation of individual body parts would seem to be of little importance at this time.

It is clear that, in general, both finger agnosia and right-left disorientation are closely associated with impairment in language comprehension in patients with unilateral brain disease. With respect to right-left orientation, this holds for nonverbal performances, such as imitation, as well as for performances that clearly demand verbal understanding of the labels "right" and "left." Perhaps Head (1926) was correct in his assumption that even the imitation of lateralized movements involves verbal mediation. In any case, the performances appear to be mediated by mechanisms that are intimately connected with language processes.

It is equally clear that some forms of right-left disorientation are associated with the presence of right-hemisphere disease. The tasks on which these patients fail are the identification of the body parts of a confronting person and the imitation of lateralized movements. It seems probable that visuospatial disability is the essential basis for failing performance in these nonaphasic patients. This is best regarded as a hypothesis for empirical test.

It cannot be overemphasized that "finger agnosia" and right-left disorientation" are umbrella labels that cover a wide variety of performances of different degrees of complexity and that make different demands on perceptual, cognitive, and linguistic capacities. It is time for both labels to be abandoned in favor of more specific terms that define the tasks presented to a patient. Since a number of abilities are called into play in the performance of complex tasks, it is likely that the simpler tasks will prove to be more fruitful in neuropsychological analysis.

## REFERENCES

Badal, J. (1888). Contribution a l'étude des cécités psychiques: alexie, agraphie, hémianopsie inférieure, trouble de la sens de l'espace. *Arch. Ophtalmol.* 8:97–117.

Belmont, L., and Birch, H. G. (1963). Lateral dominance and right-left awareness in normal children. *Child Dev.* 34:257–270.

Bender, M. B. (1952). *Disorders in Perception.* Springfield, Il.: Charles C. Thomas.

Benke, T., Schelosky, L., and Gerstenbrand, F. (1988). A clinical investigation of finger agnosia. *J. Clin. Exp. Neuropsychol.* 10:335.

Benton, A. L. (1955a). Development of finger-localization capacity in school children. *Child Dev.* 26:225–230.

Benton, A. L. (1955b). Right-left discrimination and finger localization in defective children. *Arch. Neurol. Psychiatry* 74:583–589.

Benton, A. L. (1979). The neurological significance of finger recognition. In M. Bortner (ed.), *Cognitive Growth and Development.* New York: Brunner/Mazel.

Benton, A. L. (1958). Significance of systematic reversal in right-left discrimination. *Acta Psychiatr. Neurol. Scand.* 33:129–137.

Benton, A. L. (1959) *Right-Left Discrimination and Finger Localization: Development and Pathology.* New York: Hoeber-Harper.

Benton, A. L. (1962). Dyslexia in relation to form perception and directional sense. In *Reading Disability,* J. Money (ed.). Baltimore: Johns Hopkins Press.

Benton, A. L. (1975). Developmental dyslexia: neurological aspects. In *Advances in Neurology*, Vol. 7, W. Friedlander (ed.). New York: Raven Press.

Benton, A. L. (1977). Reflections on the Gerstmann syndrome. *Brain Lang.* 4:45–62.

Benton, A. L. (1979). The neuropsychological significance of finger recognition. In *Cognitive Growth and Development*, M. Bortner (ed.). New York: Brunner/Mazel.

Benton, A. L., Hamsher, K., Varney, N. R., and Spreen, O. (1983). *Contributions to Neuropsychological Assessment.* New York: Oxford University Press.

Benton, A. L., and Kemble, J. D. (1960). Right-left orientation and reading ability. *Psychiatr. Neurol. (Basel) 139:*49–60.

Benton, A. L., and Menefee, F. L. (1957). Handedness and right-left discrimination. *Child Dev.* 28:237–242.

Bonhoeffer, K. (1923). Zur klinik und Lokalization des Agrammatismus und der Rechts-Links-Desor%ententierung. *Monatsschr. Psychiatr. Neurol.* 54:11–42.

Clark, C. M., and Klonoff, H. (1990). Right and left orientation in children aged 5 to 13 years. *J. Clin. Exp. Neuropsychol.* 12:459–466.

Clawson, A. (1962). Relationship of psychological tests to cerebral disorders in children. *Psychol. Rep.* 10:187–190.

Critchley, M. (1966). The enigma of Gerstmann's syndrome. *Brain* 89:183–198.

Culver, C. M. (1969). Test of right-left discrimination. *Percept. Mot. Skills* 19:863–867.

Damasio, A. R., and Benton, A. L. (1979). Impairment of hand movements under visual guidance. *Neurology* 29:170–178.

Denes, G. (1989). Disorders of body awareness and body knowledge. In *Handbook of Neuropsychology*, Vol. 2, F. Boller and J. Grafman (eds.). Amsterdam: Elsevier.

Dennis, M. (1976). Dissociated naming and locating of body parts after left temporal lobe resection. *Brain Lang.* 3:147–163.

De Renzi, E. (1982). *Disorders of Space Exploration and Cognition.* New York: Wiley.

Elze, C. (1924). Rechtslinksempfinden und Rechtslinksblindheit. *Z. Angew. Psychol.* 24:129–135.

Ettlinger, G. (1963). Defective identification of fingers. *Neuropsychologia* 1:39–45.

Feinberg, T. E., Haber, L. D., and Leeds, N. E. (1990). Verbal asomatognosia. *Neurology* 40:1391–1394.

Fischer, P., Marterer, A., and Danielczyk, W. (1990). Right-left disorientation in dementia of the Alzheimer type. *Neurology* 40:1619–1620.

Fletcher, J. M., Taylor, H. G., Morris, R., and Satz, P. (1982). Finger recognition skills and reading achievement: a developmental neuropsychological perspective. *Dev. Psychol.* 18:124–132.

Frederiks, J.A.M. (1969). Disorders of the body schema. In *Handbook of Clinical Neurology*, Vol. 4, P. J. Vinken and G. W. Bruyn (eds.). Amsterdam: North-Holland.

Gainotti, G., Cianchetti, C., and Tiacci, C. (1972). The influence of hemispheric side of lesion on nonverbal tests of finger localization. *Cortex* 8:364–381.

Gainotti, G., and Tiacci, C. (1973). The unilateral forms of finger agnosia. *Confin. Neurol.* 35:271–284.

Gerstmann, J. (1924). Fingeragnosie: cine umschriebene Störung der Orientierung am eigenen Körper. *Wien. Klin. Wochenschr.* 37:1010–1012.

Gerstmann, J. (1930). Zur Symptomatologie der Hirnläsionen im Uebergangsgebiet der unteren parietal-und mittleren. Occipitalwindung. *Nervenarzt* 3:691–695.

Goodglass, H., Klein, B., Carey, P., and Jones, K. (1966). Specific semantic word categories in aphasia. *Cortex* 2:74–89.

Goodglass, H., Wingfield, A., Hyde, M. R., and Theurkauf, J. C. (1986). Category specific dissociations in naming and recognition by aphasic patients. *Cortex* 22:87–102.

Harris, L. J., and Gitterman, S. R. (1978). University professors' self-descriptions of left-right confusability: sex and handedness differences. *Percept. Mot. Skills 47*:819–823.

Head, H. (1920). *Studies in Neurology*. London: Oxford University Press.

Head, H. (1926). *Aphasia and Kindred Disorders of Speech*. Cambridge: Cambridge University Press.

Hécaen, H. (1962). Clinical symptomatology in right and left hemispheric lesions. In *Interhemispheric Relations and Cerebral Dominance*, V. B. Mountcastle (ed.). Baltimore: Johns Hopkins Press.

Hécaen, H., and de Ajuriaguerra, J. (1952). *Méconnaissances et Hallucinations Corporelles*. Paris: Masson.

Hécaen, H., and Angelergues, R. (1963). *La Cécité Psychique*. Paris: Masson.

Hutchinson, B. B. (1983). Finger localization and reading ability in three groups of children ages three through twelve. *Brain Lang. 20*:143–154.

Jones, E. (1907). The precise diagnostic value of allochiria. *Brain 30*:490–532.

Kao, C. C., and Li, M. Y. (1939). Tests of finger orientation: methods for testing right-left differentiation and finger identification. In *Neuropsychiatry in China*, R. S. Lyman (ed.). Peking: Henri Vetch.

Kinsbourne, M., and Warrington, E. K. (1962). A study of finger agnosia. *Brain 85*:47–66.

Lefford, A., Birch, H. G., and Green, G. (1974). The perceptual and cognitive bases for finger localization and selective finger movement in preschool children. *Child Dev. 45*:335–343.

Lhermitte, F., and Cambier, J. (1960). *Les Perturbations Somatognosiques en Pathologie Nerveuse*. Paris: Masson.

Lindgren, S. (1978). Finger localization and the prediction of reading disability. *Cortex 14*:87–101.

Matthews, C. G., Folk, E. G., and Zerfas, P. G. (1966). Lateralized finger localization deficits and differential Wechsler-Bellevue results in retardates. *Am. J. Ment. Defic. 70*:695–702.

McFie, J., and Zangwill, O. L. (1960). Visual-constructive disabilities associated with lesions of the left hemisphere. *Brain 83*:243–260.

Money, J. (1965). *A Standardized Road-Map Test of Directional Sense*. Baltimore: John Hopkins Press.

Morris, H. H., Luders, H., Lesser, R. P., Dinner, D. S., and Hahn, J. (1984). Transient neuropsychological abnormalities (including Gerstmann's syndrome) during cortical stimulation. *Neurology 34*:877–883.

Ogden, J. A. (1985). Autotopagnosia. *Brain 108*:1009–1022.

Oldfield, R. C., and Zangwill, O. L. (1942–1943). Head's concept of the schema and its application in contemporary British psychology. *Br. J. Psychol. 32*:267–286; *33*:58–64, 113–129, 143–149.

Pick, A. (1898). *Beiträge zur Pathologie und Pathologische Anatomie des Centralnervensystems*. Berlin: Karger.

Pick, A. (1908). Ueber Störungen der Orientierung am eigenen Körper. *Arb. Dtsch. Psychiatr. Universitäts-Klin. Prag.*

Poeck, K. (1963). Die Modellvorstellung des Körperschemas. *Dtsch. Z. Nervenheilkd. 187*:472–477.

Poeck, K. (1969). Modern trends in neuropsychology. In *Contributions to Clinical Neuropsychology*, A. L. Benton (ed.). Chicago: Aldine.

Poeck, K. (1975). Neuropsychologische Symptomen ohne eigenstaendliche Bedeutung. *Aktuel. Neurol. 2*:199–208.

Poeck, K., and Orgass, B. (1967). Ueber Störungen der Rechts-Links Orientierung. *Nervenarzt 28*:285–291.

Poeck, K., and Orgass, B. (1969). An experimental investigation of finger agnosia. *Neurology* 19:801–807.

Poeck, K., and Orgass, B. (1971). The concept of the body schema. *Cortex* 7:254–277.

Reed, J. C. (1967). Lateralized finger agnosia and reading achievement at ages 6 and 10. *Child Dev.* 38:213–220.

Roeltgen, D. P., Sevush, S., and Heilman, K. M. (1983). Pure Gerstmann's syndrome from a focal lesion. *Arch. Neurol.* 40:46–47.

Sauguet, J., Benton, A. L., and Hécaen, H. (1971). Disturbances of the body schema in relation to language impairment and hemispheric locus of lesion. *J. Neurol. Neurosurg. Psychiatry* 34:496–501.

Schilder, P. (1931). Fingeragnosie, Fingerapraxie, Fingeraphasie. *Nervenarzt* 4:625–629.

Seidemann, H. (1932). Cerebrale Luftembolie mach Pneumothoraxfüllung. (Rechts-Links-Störung. Fingeragnosie, Rechenstorung). *Zentralbl. Neurol. Psychiatr.* 63:729–731.

Selecki, B. R., and Herron, J. T. (1965). Disturbances of the verbal body image: a particular form of sensory aphasia. *J. Nerv. Ment. Dis.*, 141:42–52.

Semenza, C. (1988). Impairment in localization of body parts following brain damage. *Cortex* 24:443–449.

Semenza, C., and Goodglass, H. (1985). Localization of body parts in brain injured subjects. *Neuropsychologia* 23:161–175.

Sparrow, S., and Satz, P. (1970). Dyslexia, laterality and neuropsychological development. In *Specific Reading Disability*, D. J. Bakker and P. Satz (eds.). Rotterdam: Rotterdam University Press.

Stone, F. B., and Robinson, D. (1968). The effect of response mode on finger localization errors. *Cortex* 4:233–244.

Strauss, A. A., and Werner, H. (1938). Deficiency in the finger schema in relation to arithmetic disability. *Am. J. Orthopsychiatry* 8:719–725.

Terman, L. M. (1916). *The Measurement of Intelligence*. Boston: Houghton Mifflin.

Thurstone, L. L. (1938). *Primary Mental Abilities*. Chicago: University of Chicago Press.

Varney, N. R. (1984). Gerstmann syndrome without aphasia: a longitudinal study. *Brain Cognition* 3:1–9.

Wolf, S. M. (1973). Difficulties in right-left discrimination in a normal population. *Arch. Neurol.*, 29:128–129.

Yamadori, A., and Albert, M. L. (1973). Word category aphasia. *Cortex* 9:112–125.

Zung, B. R. (1986). Cognitive-academic correlates of finger localization in right-handed kindergarten girls. *Percept. Mot. Skills* 62:227–234.

# 7

# Apraxia

KENNETH M. HEILMAN AND LESLIE J. GONZALEZ ROTHI

In the 1985 edition of this book we wrote "the definition of apraxic disturbances is more difficult even than the definition of aphasia, since the distinguishing features of movement have not been adequately described. Whereas the aphasic's linguistic errors can be quite precisely described, the abnormalities of movement of the apraxic patient cannot be similarly noted or described. Operationally, therefore, apraxia has been defined by exclusion. It is a disorder of skilled movement not caused by weakness, akinesia, deafferentation, abnormal tone or posture, movement disorders (such as tremors or chorea), intellectual deterioration, poor comprehension, or uncooperativeness." Although apraxia is still in part defined by exclusion, the nature of the abnormal movements has now been described. A variety of errors may characterize the apraxic patient's performance and these errors help define the variety of apraxias seen in the clinic. This chapter will be limited to descriptions of limb-kinetic apraxia, ideomotor apraxia, disconnection and disassociation apraxias, ideational and conceptual apraxias, and buccofacial apraxia. Based on these clinical descriptions, we will also develop a model of how the brain may mediate learned skilled movements. We will not discuss constructional and dressing apraxias. These are discussed in Chapter 8, and apraxic agraphia is discussed in Chapter 4. Gait apraxia is not covered.

## EXAMINATION AND TESTING

### Differential Diagnosis

Since apraxia is in part defined by excluding other disorders of movement that may obscure apraxic errors, a thorough neurological examination is required to exclude weakness or deafferentation (sensory loss). Diseases that affect either the basal ganglia or the cerebellum typically do not cause weakness or sensory change but can be associated with nonapraxic disorders of movement. However, disorders of the basal ganglia and cerebellum are also manifested by changes in posture and tone and by tremors, dysmetria, or stereotypic movements that are evident on neurological examination. If motor, sensory, basal ganglia, or cerebellar signs are limited to one side, the normal side can still be tested for apraxia. If the abnormality is mild enough to permit use of the affected extremity, it should also be tested. In this case, the examiner will make allowance for the underlying disorder in judging whether apraxia is present.

Many apraxic patients are also aphasic, and language disorders are sometimes difficult to distinguish from apraxic disorders. Patients may be thought to be apraxic when they fail to make an appropriate movement in response to a command. However, a patient who also cannot correctly answer yes/no questions or pointing commands probably has a language comprehension disturbace. Conversely, apraxic patients with aphasia are occasionally mistakenly thought to have a comprehension disorder. It is important to test aphasic patients not only with commands such as "stick out your tongue" or "show me how you would throw a ball," but also with questions that can be answered by pointing or with yes/no responses. If patients perform poorly when given limb or buccofacial commands but can answer questions that require yes/no responses or can accurately describe the mvoement tasks they were asked to perform, they may not have a comprehension disturbance, but may be apraxic. Although a portion of the aphasic's abnormal performance may be attributed to aphasia, the clinician should remember that a comprehension disturbance does not preclude the possibility that the patient also has an apraxic disturbance, since both symptoms frequently coexist.

Apraxic patients may use body parts as objects or make spatial and temporal errors, but often these movements can be recognized as having the correct intent. If a patient with a mild langauge comprehension disturbance uses a body part as the object or makes a clumsy but recognizable movement in response to a command, then the errors are of movement formation and are not language related, and hence should not be attributed to comprehension disturbance.

### Methods

Apraxia is common in patients with focal lesions and in patients with degenerative dementias, but patients rarely complain spontaneously of their apraxic disturbances and they often appear unaware of their defect (Rothi et al., 1990). There are several possible explanations for this unawareness. Apraxic patients are often anosognosic for their impairment (Rothi et al., 1990). They frequently have a right hemiparesis, and they may, therefore, attribute their clumsiness to use of their nondominant hand (i.e., they think their left hand is clumsy because they are not accustomed to using it). Furthermore, apraxia is usually mildest when a patient uses actual objects and most severe with pantomime. Since patients at home are rarely called upon to use pantomime, they and their families are often not aware of this disorder. When patients with Alzheimer's disease develop apraxia, it is often attributed either to memory loss (amnesia) or to general intellectual decline. Therefore, in diagnosing apraxia, one cannot rely on history but must test patients.

We suggest the following tests for apraxia:

*Gesture to command.* Gesture to command should involve pantomiming both tool use (transitive movement) such as "Show me how you would use a pair of scissors" as

**Table 7-1.** Tests for Apraxia

| Intransitive limb gestures | Intransitive buccofacial gestures |
|---|---|
| 1. Wave good-bye | 1. Stick out tongue |
| 2. Hitchhike | 2. Blow a kiss |
| 3. Salute | Transitive buccofacial gestures |
| 4. Beckon "come here" | 1. Blow out a match |
| 5. Stop | 2. Suck on a straw |
| 6. Go | Serial acts |
| Transitive limb gestures | 1. Clean pipe, put in tobacco, and light pipe |
| 1. Open a door with a key | 2. Fold letter, put it in envelope, seal envelope, and place stamp on it |
| 2. Flip a coin | |
| 3. Open a catsup bottle | |
| 4. Use a screwdriver | |
| 5. Use a hammer | |
| 6. Use scissors | |

well as emblems (intransitive movement), which are arbitrarily coded nonverbal communications such as waving good-bye. Some of the gestures we use are listed in Table 7-1.

Frequently, when patients pantomime, they use a body part as the object. They may perform in this manner either because they do not understand that they are supposed to pantomime (i.e., they are using the body part as a symbol of the object) or because they cannot perform the task even though they understand it. If a patient uses a body part as the object, his performance should be corrected (e.g., "Do not use your finger as a key. Make believe you are really holding a key."). If verbal instructions do not help, the examiner should demonstrate the correct pantomime. If the patient still uses body part as object, he is making an apraxic error.

*Gesture to imitation.* Although some examiners only test imitation if the patient fails to perform the command correctly, there are patients who cannot imitate who will perform correctly to command.

*Gesture (pantomime) in response to seeing the tool.*

*Gesture (pantomime) in response to seeing object upon which the tool works* (e.g., nail partially driven into block of wood).

*Actual tool use.*

*Imitation of examiner using the tool.*

*Discrimination between correct and incorrect pantomimed movements* (e.g., "Is this the correct way to use a pair of scissors?").

*Gesture comprehension* (e.g., "What tool am I using?" or "Am I using a hammer or a saw?").

*Serial acts* (see Table 7-1).

The examiner should test both hands when possible. If one hand is severely paretic, the nonparetic hand should be tested. The type of errors made by the patient should be noted.

In addition to observing a patient's performance, the clinician should ascertain if a patient is disturbed by his own errors or if he can even recognize these as errors.

When testing aphasic patients, there is always the concern that the failure to per-form correctly is related to a speech-language comprehension error rather than to an apraxic error. Gesturing to command is most likely to be confounded by impaired language comprehension. However, while apraxics make errors, the intent of the ges-ture is often obvious.

Comprehension of movement commands may also be tested by asking the patient to describe what he was asked to do or by having the patient point to the object (from an array of objects) that he would use to perform a specific action)

## VARIETIES OF LIMB APRAXIA

Because of the diverse nature of the apraxias, each will be discussed separately. Although we will use many of the terms used by Liepmann (1920), in order to avoid confusion we have introduced two terms not discussed by Liepmann—disassociation apraxia and conceptual apraxia.

### Limb-Kinetic Apraxia

CLINICAL

Patients with limb-kinetic apraxia are incapable of making fine, precise movements with the limb contralateral to a central nervous system lesion. The disorder is more obvious when testing distal independent movements (finger movements) than prox-imal movements, and is especially evident when the patient makes rapid finger move-ments such as tapping. The movement abnormality can be seen when the patient pantomimes, imitates, or uses objects. In the clinic, we ask patients to pick up a dime from a flat surface. Patients with limb-kinetic apraxia may not be able to perform the necessary pinching movement with their thumb and index finger and instead will slip the dime off the table and grasp the coin between their fingers and their palm.

PATHOPHYSIOLOGY

The neuroanatomic correlates of limb-kinetic apraxia are unclear. Limb-kinetic apraxia is often unilateral (contralateral to the lesioned hemisphere). Liepmann (1920) postulated that lesions in the sensory motor cortex may induce this disorder. It has been demonstrated that pyramidal lesions in monkeys can cause clumsiness and a loss of movement fractionation that is not completely accounted for by weakness or by change in tone or posture (Lawrence and Kuypers, 1968). This suggests that the clumsiness seen in patients with limb-kinetic apraxia may be induced by pyramidal or corticospinal tract lesions. The role of the premotor regions in the pathogenesis of limb-kinetic apraxia is also unclear. However, according to Freund and Hummel-sheim (1985), manual dexterity and the capacity for relatively independent distal movements are unaffected in patients with lesions of convexity premotor cortex. Unfortunately, many patients with lesions of premotor and motor cortex have tone and posture changes that make testing for limb-kinetic apraxia difficult.

## Ideomotor Apraxia

CLINICAL

Unlike patients with limb-kinetic apraxia, patients with ideomotor apraxia may have normal dexterity, especially when they are tested with their ipsilesional arm. Pieczuro and Vignolo (1967) tested the manual dexterity of 35 patients with lesions of the right hemisphere and 70 patients with lesions of the left hemisphere. The severity of the ideomotor apraxia was independent of manual dexterity. In addition, patients with ideomotor apraxia have greatest difficulty when asked to make believe they are making transitive movements (using a tool or instrument) (Goodglass and Kaplan, 1963). They may improve their performance by imitating, but gesture to imitation is frequently defective. Similarly, improvement may be noted when the actual object is used, but performance often remains defective (Poizner et al., 1989).

Patients with ideomotor apraxia make several types of errors. As we have discussed, these patients use a body part as the object despite repeated reminders to act as if they were actually holding and using the object.

Patients with ideomotor apraxia may make perseverative and sequencing errors: for example, when asked to perform a new pantomime, apraxic patients with perseverative errors will execute previously performed pantomimes. When two or more joint movements must be made in a sequence (as, for example, when using a key one needs to extend the arm at the elbow, and *then* rotate the arm at the elbow), the patient who makes sequencing errors may reserve this order (rotate first, and then extend). However, the errors that are most characteristic of ideomotor apraxia are spatial errors. There are three forms of spatial errors; postural, spatial orientation, and spatial movement (Rothi et al., 1988b; Poizner et al., 1990). Patients who make postural errors fail to position the hand as if they were correctly holding the utensil or tool. Therefore, postural errors are seen primarily with pantomiming and imitation tasks and are not usually seen with actual object use. Spatial orientation errors denote hand movements that do not appear to direct the tool toward an imagined object. For example, when asked to pantomime the use of scissors, apraxic patients may orient the scissors in an arc around their own body, or, when asked to cut a slice of bread with a knife, they will not keep the imaginary knife in a constant sagittal plane. Spatial movement errors are made when apraxic patients activate movement at incorrect joints. For example, when asked to pantomime the use of a screwdriver, the normal subject will fix the wrist and shoulder and twist at the elbow. The apraxic patient may fix the wrist and elbow and rotate the shoulder. When one rotates at the elbow, the hand and imaginary screwdriver will each rotate on its own axis. When one rotates the arm at the shoulder, the hand and imaginary screwdriver will move in circles or arcs, which are incorrect movements. Movement errors can also occur when more than one joint needs to be activated. Joint movements may not be produced in coordination with one another or one joint may move more than the other. For example, when cutting a loaf of bread with a knife, at the same time the shoulder is flexed in order to bring the arm forward, the elbow must be extended. When the shoulder is extended (to bring the arm back), the elbow must be flexed. However, with each successive cutting movement, the elbow is flexed less so that the knife moves downward.

Patients with ideomotor apraxia may primarily use one movement, usually the more proximal movement (e.g., shoulder), or may fail to coordinate the two movements (Poizner et al., 1990).

Apraxics also make timing errors (Poizner et al., 1990). There may be a delay in the initiation of the movement or occasional pauses, especially when the spatial trajectory must be changed. Patients may also fail to coordinate speed of movement with spatial components. For example, when cutting bread with an imaginary knife, one normally slows the movement when one is about to reverse the direction of the cut; once the direction has been changed, the speed of movement increases. Patients with ideomotor apraxia do not demonstrate this pattern of movement.

PATHOPHYSIOLOGY

*Callosal lesions—lateralized movement formula.*   Liepmann and Maas (1907) studied a patient with right hemiplegia who performed poorly when attempting to carry out verbal commands with his left hand. On postmortem examination he was found to have a lesion in the left basis pontis, which accounted for his right hemiplegia, and an infarction of the corpus callosum, which spared the splenium. The callosal lesion could produce abnormalities of skilled movement by disconnecting the language areas in the left hemisphere (Wernicke, 1874) from the motor areas in the right hemisphere that control fine movements of the left hand. It was apparent to Liepmann and Maas, however, that their patient's deficit could not be fully explained by a language-motor disconnection since their patient also failed both to imitate skilled movements and to manipulate actual objects properly. Because this patient's primary visual, visual association, primary somesthetic, somesthetic association, and premotor and motor areas in the right hemisphere were all intact he should still have been able to use an object correctly and to imitate. Since he could not imitate or use an object, Liepmann and Maas concluded that the left hemisphere contains not only language but also "movement formulas" that control purposeful skilled movements. Liepmann (1920) proposed that these "movement formulas" contain the "time-space-form picture of the movement" (see Kimura, 1979).

In order to perform a skilled learned act, one must place particular body parts in certain spatial positions in a specific order at specific times. The spatial positions assumed by the relevant body parts depend not only on the nature of the act but also on the position and size of an external object with which the body parts must interact. Skilled acts also require orderly changes in the spatial positions of the body parts over time. These movement formulas command the motor systems to adopt the appropriate spatial positions of the relevant body parts over time.

Lesions of the corupus callosum therefore not only disconnect the language hemisphere from the hemisphere controlling the left hand but also separate these left-hemisphere movement formulas from the motor areas in the right hemisphere. According to Liepmann's postulate, a callosal lesion in a right-handed patient who has both motor language engrams in his left hemisphere would not interfere with the ability of the patient to carry out commands, imitate, and use actual objects correctly with his right hand, but would result in the patient having difficulty with all these tasks when using his left hand.

Until recently there has been little support for this hypothesis. Geschwind and Kaplan (1962) described a patient with a left-hemisphere glioblastoma and a postoperative left anterior cerebral artery infarction that had caused destruction of the anterior four-fifths of the corpus callosum. That patient could not follow commands with his left hand but could correctly imitate and could use actual objects. He was agraphic with the left hand and could not type or use anagram letters with the left hand but performed flawlessly with the right hand. He followed commands with his right hand but not with his left. The aphasic agraphia was interpreted as resulting from a disconnection of the right hemisphere from left-hemisphere language areas, and the apraxic difficulties were attributed to the separation of stimulus (verbal or nonverbal) and response across hemispheres. Similarly, surgical lesions of the corpus callosum (Gazzaniga et al., 1967) were not associated with the type of apraxias proposed by Liepmann and Maas (1907).

Watson and Heilman (1983) and Graff-Radford et al. (1987) reported patients with acute naturally occurring callosal lesions who, unlike the patient of Geschwind and Kaplan (1962), had severe apraxia with imitation and object usage, thereby providing support for Liepmann's callosal motor disconnection hypothesis. It is not known why these patients are apraxic with imitation and object use, while the callosal-lesioned patients of Geschwind and Kaplan (1962) and Gazzaniga et al. (1967) were not. Many of the patients who had surgical callosal lesions had prior seizures and brain injury which may have induced brain reorganization. However, Geschwind and Kaplan's patient did not have long-standing injury, suggesting that the absence of a left-hand ideomotor apraxia cannot be entirely explained by brain reorganization. Extracallosal damage cannot explain the difference, since Geschwind and Kaplan's case had considerable extracallosal damage, but could imitate and use objects, whereas the computer tomographic (CT) scan of Watson and Heilman's case (1983) did not show any extracallosal damage.

Variability in brain organization may explain the difference. In right-handers, right-hemispheric lesions almost never produce apraxia; however, left-hemisphere lesions in areas known to induce both aphasia and apraxia more often induce aphasia. In one study, only 57% (20 of 35) of aphasic patients were also apraxic (Heilman, 1975). The discrepancy between the incidence of aphasia and apraxia suggests that although in right-handers movement formula or space-time movement representations are localized in the left hemisphere, the right hemisphere in many of these persons can substitute for the left (Heilman, 1979). It should therefore not be surprising that callosal damage does not induce apraxia in all patients. The patients of Liepmann and Maas, Watson and Heilman, and Graff-Radford et al. probably had language and movement representations restricted to the left hemisphere, which might represent a more common pattern. The patients reported by Gazzaniga et al. (1967) and Geschwind and Kaplan (1962) were left-hemisphere dominant for language but probably had bilateral movement representations. Geschwind (1965) remarked that the independence of the right hemisphere in nonlanguage function manifested by his patient was unusual and may have been an exception.

The nature of the apraxic deficit seen with callosal lesions depends on the pattern of language and motor dominance in the individual patient. For example, we have seen two left-handed patients who had right-hemisphere lesions and were apraxic

(Heilman et al., 1973; Valenstein and Heilman, 1979). Movement representations in these two patients were stored in the right hemisphere while language was mediated by the left hemisphere. We can speculate that if, prior to their right-hemisphere lesion, these patients had a lesion of their corpus callosum, the right hand, deprived of the movement representations, should perform poorly to command, to imitation, and with the use of the actual object. Their left hand, deprived of language, should perform poorly to gestural command but perform well with imitation and with an actual object.

### Left-hemispheric lesions (intrahemispheric)

*Defect in symbolization vs. motor defects.* In right-handed patients, almost all cases of apraxia are associated with left-hemispheric lesions (Geschwind, 1965; Goodglass and Kaplan, 1963; Hécaen and Ajuriaguerra, 1964; Hécaen and Sanguet, 1971). In right-handers, the left hemisphere is also dominant for language. Apraxia therefore is commonly associated with aphasia. This has led to the suggestion that apraxia and aphasia may both be manifestations of a primary defect in symbolization: aphasia is a disturbance of verbal symbolization, while apraxia is a defect of nonverbal symbolization (e.g., emblem and pantomime) (Goldstein, 1948). The observation that patients with apraxia perform poorly to command and imitation but improve with the use of the actual object (Goodglass and Kaplan, 1963) lends support to Goldstein's postulate. In addition, Dee et al. (1970) and Kertesz and Hooper (1982) found a close relationship between language impairment and apraxia.

However, several studies lend support to Liepmann's hypothesis that the left hemisphere controls skilled movements and that destruction of the movement representations or separation of these representations from the motor areas controlling the extremity causes abnormalities of skilled movement. Goodglass and Kaplan (1963) tested apraxic aphasic patients and control aphasic subjects with the Wechsler Adult Intelligence Scale and used the performance-scaled score as a measure of intellectual ability. They also tested their subjects' ability to gesture and perform simple and complex pantomimes. Although the apraxic aphasics performed less well on these motor skills than did their intellectual counterparts in the control groups, no clear relationship emerged between the severity of aphasia and the degree of gestural deficiency. The apraxic aphasic patients were also less able to imitate than were the nonapraxic controls.

Although Goodglass and Kaplan believed that their results supported Liepmann's hypothesis, they noted that their apraxic subjects did not have any difficulty in handling objects. Liepmann, however, thought apraxic patients were clumsy with objects, and Poizner et al. (1989) observed and quantified the motor and spatial errors with the use of actual objects. Kimura and Archibald (1974) studied the ability of left-hemisphere-impaired aphasics and right-hemisphere-impaired controls to imitate unfamiliar, meaningless motor sequences. The performance of aphasic apraxic patients with left-hemisphere impairment was poorer than that of the controls, again supporting Liepmann's hypothesis.

The strongest support for the postulate that apraxia is a disorder of skilled movement rather than a symbolic defect comes from Liepmann's own observations that only 14 of 20 apraxic patients were aphasic. Goodglass and Kaplan (1963), and Heilman et al. (1973, 1974) have also described similar patients. In addition, aphasic patients are often not apraxic (Heilman, 1975). In summary, because there is a poor correlation between the severity of symbolic disorders (aphasia) and disorders of skilled movements and because even nonsymbolic movements are poorly performed by apraxics, there is little evidence to support the hypothesis that apraxia is a disorder of symbolic behavior.

*Disconnection hypothesis of apraxia.* Geschwind (1965) proposed that language elicits motor behavior by using a neural substrate similar to that proposed by Wernicke (1874) to explain language processing (see Fig. 7-1). Auditory stimuli travel along auditory pathways and reach Heschl's gyrus (primary auditory cortex). From Heschl's gyrus, the auditory message is relayed to the posterior superior portion of the temporal lobe (auditory association cortex). In the left hemisphere, this is called Wernicke's area, and is important in language comprehension. Wernicke's area is connected to premotor areas (motor association cortex) by the arcuate fasciculus, and the motor association area on the left is connected to the left primary motor area. When someone is told to carry out a command with the right hand, this pathway is used. To carry out a verbal command with the left hand, information must be carried to the right premotor cortex. Since it is rare to find fibers that run obliquely in the corpus callosum, fibers either cross from Wernicke's area to the contralateral auditory association area or cross from the premotor area on the left to the premotor area on the right. The information is then conveyed to motor areas on the right side. Geschwind

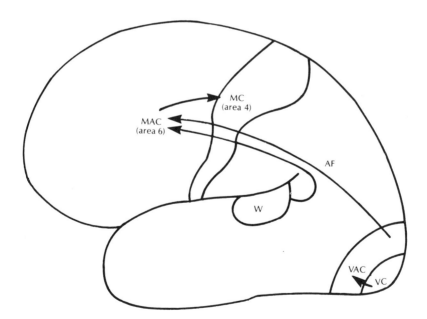

**Fig. 7-1.** Geschwind's schema. Lateral view of the left side of the brain. AF = arcuate fasciculus; MAC = motor association cortex; MC = motor cortex; VAC = visual association cortex; VC = visual cortex. The arrows indicate major connections of the areas shown.

(1965) postulated that the connections between the motor association areas are the active pathways. He believed that disruption of these pathways explained most apraxic disturbances.

As we have already discussed, accordeing to Geschwind, callosal lesions produce unilateral ideomotor apraxia by disconnecting the left premotor region from the right. Lesions that destroy the left premotor cortex also cause ideomotor apraxia, because the cell bodies of neurons that cross the corpus callosum are destroyed. Therefore, a lesion in the left motor association cortex would cause a defect similar to that induced by a lesion in the body of the corpus callosum (sympathetic dyspraxia). Lesions of the left motor association cortex are often associated with right hemiplegia, so the right limb frequently cannot be tested. If these patients were not hemiparetic, however, they would probably be apraxic on the right.

According to Geschwind's schema (1965), lesions of the arcuate fasciculus should disconnect the posterior language areas, important for language comprehension, from the motor association cortex, important for implementing programs. Therefore, patients with parietal (or arcuate fasciculus) lesions that spare motor association cortex should be able to comprehend commands but not perform skilled movements in response to command. More posterior lesions, affecting Herschl's gyrus, Wernicke's area, or the connections between them, cause abnormalities in language comprehension, but not apraxia. These patients fail to carry out commands because they cannot understand the command, not because they have difficulty performing skilled movements.

One problem in Geschwind's interpretation is that patients with arcuate fasciculus lesions should theoretically be able to imitate, but they often cannot. Geschwind attempted to explain this discrepancy by noting that the arcuate fasciculus also contains fibers passing from visual association cortex to premotor cortex. He proposed that the arcuate fasciculus of the left hemisphere is dominant for these visuomotor connections, but there is no evidence to support this hypothesis. Even if one assumes that the left arcuate fasciculus is dominant for visuomotor connections and interruption of this dominant pathway explains why patients cannot imitate, it could not explain why these patients are clumsy when they use objects or perform other somesthetic motor tasks. One would have to assume that the arcuate fasciculus also carries somesthetic-motor impulses and that the left arcuate fasciculus is also dominant for this function.

*Representational hypothesis.* After one learns a skilled motor behavior, the acquired motor skill expedites future behaviors that require that same skill. In addition, even in the absence of specific instruction or cues, one can pantomime learned skilled behaviors. These observations suggest that the nervous system stores knowledge of motor skills. When this knowledge must be called into use, it is retrieved from storage and implemented rather than being constructed de novo. A hypothesis that may explain why patients with parietal lesions cannot properly pantomime, imitate the use of, or use an object postulates that movement formulas or learned time-space movement representations are stored in the dominant parietal cortex (Heilman, 1979; Kimura, 1979). These representations help program the motor association cortex which in turn implements the required movements by selectively activating the motor cortex, which innervates the specific muscle motor neuron pools needed to

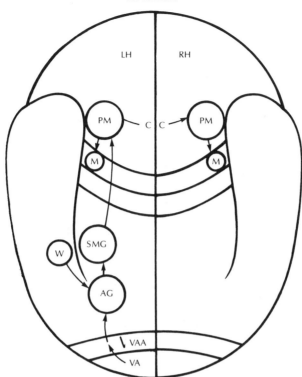

**Fig. 7-2.** Author's schema. View from top of brain. W = Wernicke's area; VA = primary visual area; VAA = visual association area; AG = angular gyrus; SMG = supramarginal gyrus; PM = premotor area (motor association cortex); M = motor cortex; CC = corpus callosum; LH = left hemisphere; RH = right hemisphere. The arrows show major connections of the areas shown.

carry out the skilled act (Fig. 7-2). We call these movement formula or time-space motor representations *praxicons*.

Theoretically, it should be possible to distinguish between dysfunction caused by destruction of parietal areas where praxicons are stored and apraxia which results from disconnection of this parietal area from motor areas that implement these representations. Although patients with either disorder should experience difficulty in performing a skilled act in response to command, imitation of, or use of an object, patients whose representations for skilled acts are retained but whose motor association areas are disconnected (or whose motor association cortex is destroyed) should be able to differentiate a correctly performed skilled act from an incorrectly performed one because they still have these praxic representations (praxicons) and, therefore, have the information characterizing distinctive features of learned skilled movements. Patients with parietal lesions that have destroyed these representations (praxicons) should not be able to perform this analysis.

To test the postulates that praxicons are stored in the dominant parietal lobe and that destruction of these representations induces a discrimination deficit, we (Heilman et al., 1982; Rothi et al., 1985) gave a gestural recognition and discrimination task to apraxic and nonapraxic patients with anterior lesions or nonfluent aphasia and to patients with posterior lesions or fluent aphasia. In the discrimination task, the subject was to select a correctly performed act from a poorly performed act (e.g., using a body part as an object). In the comprehension task, the subject was asked to select the requested (target) act from foils consisting of movements that were correctly executed but not the correct movement. Thus, if the target movement was "open a door with a key," the foil might be using scissors or a screwdriver. On both the discrimination and comprehension task, the posterior/fluent patients performed worse than the other subjects.

Based on these observations, we believe that there are at least two forms of ideomotor apraxia. One is induced by a loss of the praxicons that are stored in the supramarginal or angular gyrus. These patients perform poorly to command, are unable to comprehend gestures, and are also unable to discriminate poorly performed from well-performed acts. The other is induced by lesions anterior to the angular or supramarginal gyrus that either disconnect the praxicons from the premotor and motor areas important in implementing skilled movements or destroy the premotor areas.

If ideomotor apraxia results from destruction of movement representations or praxicons, patients with this disorder should have difficulty acquiring new motor skills and retaining new gestures in memory. In regard to the former, Heilman et al. (1975) studied nine right-handed hemiparetic patients with apraxia and aphasia and eight right-handed hemiparetic controls with aphasia but without apraxia. These subjects were given six trials on a rotary pursuit apparatus (five acquisition trials and one retention trial). All subjects used their left, nonparetic hand. The performance of the control group on the sixth trial was significantly better than on the first trial; however, there was no significant difference between the first and sixth trials in the apraxic group, suggesting that these patients had a defect in motor learning. The defect appeared to be caused by a combined impairment of both acquisition and retention. Wyke (1971), who studied patients with either right- or left-hemisphere lesions, gave her subjects a motor acquisition task that required bimanual coordination. Although patients with left-hemisphere disease demonstrated acquisition, it was below the level of skill in those with right-hemisphere disease. Since Wyke did not separate her left-hemisphere group into apraxic and nonapraxic patients, one could not be certain whether apraxic patients would have demonstrated poorer learning than nonapraxic left-hemisphere-damaged patients.

Rothi and Heilman (1985) used a modified Buschke (1973) paradigm to study apraxic subjects ability to learn a list of gestures. We noted significantly more consolidation errors in the apraxic than control groups, suggesting apraxic patients have a memory consolidation deficit.

Although most patients with ideomotor apraxia imitate transitive gestures better than they can pantomime transitive gestures to command, Ochipa et al. (1990) described a patient whose imitation of learned transitive and symbolic movements was worse than his pantomime of these same movements to command. This patient had no difficulty comprehending the examiners pantomimes and gestures.

Unfortunately, the model we have developed thus far (Fig. 7-3) cannot account for

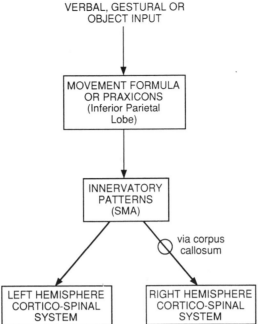

Fig. 7-3. Diagrammatic model of ideomotor apraxia. SMA = supplementary motor area.

these findings. Such findings suggest that there are two independent sets of motor representations or praxicons, one for input (input praxicon) and one for output (output praxicon) (Rothi et al., 1991) (see Fig. 7-4). A preserved ability to comprehend gesture in conjunction with impaired imitation would suggest that the input praxicon remains intact and that the impairment occurs after egress from the input praxicon. Because the patient was better able to pantomime to command, this would suggest that verbal language is capable of activating the output praxicon (bypassing processing by the input praxicon) (see Fig. 7-4).

*Innervatory patterns*

*Supplementary motor area.* The praxicons that are stored in the inferior parietal lobe in a three-dimensional supramodal code have to be transcoded into a motor plan before the target movement can take place. Although Geschwind (1965) thought that the convexity premotor cortex was important for praxis, limb ideomotor apraxia has not been reported from a lesion limited to this cortical area. The convexity premotor cortex may instead be important in developing motor representations or in adapting the motor program to environmental perturbations.

The premotor cortex in the medial frontal lobe is called the supplementary motor area (SMA). Whereas stimulation of the primary motor cortex (Brodmann's area 4) induces simple single movements, SMA stimulation induces complex movements of the fingers, arms, and hands (Penfield and Welch, 1951). SMA receives projections from parietal neurons and projects to primary motor neurons. These SMA neurons

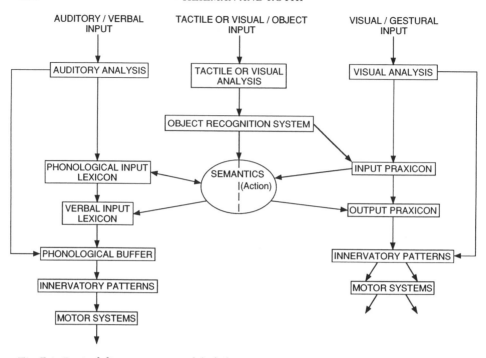

**Fig. 7-4.** Revised diagrammatic model of ideomotor apraxia.

discharge before neurons in the primary motor cortex (Brinkman and Porter, 1979). Studies of cerebral blood flow, an indicator of cerebral metabolism, reveal that a single repetitive movement increases activation of the contralateral motor cortex. However, complex movements increase flow in contralateral motor cortex and bilaterally in the SMA. When subjects think about making complex movements but do not move, blood flow is increased to SMA but not to primary motor cortex. (Orgogozo and Larsen, 1979). Watson et al. (1986) reported several patients with left-sided medial frontal lesions that included the SMA who had bilateral ideomotor apraxia. However, unlike patients with parietal lesions, these patients could both comprehend and discriminate pantomimes.

Because SMA has connections with the primary motor cortex and the parietal lobe, is activated before motor cortex, becomes activated with complex learned movements, and when ablated induces apraxia, we believe SMA is the site of the transcoding of praxic representations into motor programs or innervatory patterns that activate motor cortex.

*Basal ganglia.*    Whereas lesions and dysfunction of the basal ganglia are thought to induce alterations of muscle tone, abnormal movement, decreased spontaneous movements, and slowing of movements, the organization of complex learned purposeful movement has been attributed to cortical networks. However, there have been several reports of patients who demonstrated ideomotor apraxia from lesions that involved the basal ganglia and/or thalamus (Basso et al., 1980; Agostini et al., 1983). Rothi et al. (1988a) described two patients with left-sided lenticular infarctions that did not involve cerebral cortex or associative pathways. Both patients had spatial movement errors that were similar to errors seen in patients with cortical lesions. However, both patients also showed frequent perseverative errors.

Alexander et al. (1986) described five discrete cortical striatal-pallidal-thalamic-cortical circuits. We have already provided evidence that lesions of left SMA are associated with apraxia. SMA is a part of the motor circuit that projects to the putamen. The putamen projects to the globus pallidus and the globus pallidus projects to the ventrolateral nucleus of the thalamus. Finally, the ventrolateral nucleus projects back to SMA. This discrete "motor loop" may control the flow of information into SMA. Therefore, lesions of the loop may cause SMA dysfunction and SMA dysfunction may lead to apraxia.

The network we have described includes the inferior parietal lobe that contains the representations of learned skilled movements (praxicons), the SMA and basal ganglia that are important in transcoding these representations into a motor program, and the motor cortex, which implements these programs. Except for the motor cortex, lesions of these areas may produce ideomotor apraxia. Lesions that disconnect these areas from one another and from the motor cortex that controls limb movement may also produce ideomotor apraxia (see Fig. 7-4).

### Disconnection and Disassociation Apraxias

VERBAL-MOTOR DISASSOCIATION APRAXIA

Heilman (1973) described three patients who, when asked to gesture, hesitated to make any movements and often appeared as if they did not understand the command. They could, however, demonstrate both verbally and by picking out the correct act (from several performed by the examiner) that they understood the command. Unlike patients with ideomotor apraxia, these patients were able to imitate and use actual objects flawlessly. Because imitation and actual object use was performed well, it would seem that their representations of motor skills were intact. What seemed to be defective in these patients was the ability to elicit the correct motor sequences in response to language. Although we hypothesized that the lesions were in, or deep to, the parietal region (angular gyrus), we never learned the exact location of the left-hemisphere lesion that induced this apraxia.

The patients with callosal lesions described by Geschwind and Kaplan (1962) and Gazzaniga et al. (1967) could not perform with their left hand in response to command, but they could imitate and use objects. Performance with the left hand was similar to the performance with both hands of patients with left-hemisphere lesions described above (Heilman, 1973). If normal performance on imitation and use-of-object tasks suggests that movement representations (praxicons) are intact and connected to premotor and primary motor areas, then patients with callosal lesions and patients with angular gyrus or subcortical lesions deep in the parietal lobe must have a dissociation between language areas and the area where motor representations are stored. In patients with callosal lesions, these representations were presumed to be in both hemispheres, whereas comprehension of commands was being mediated by the left hemisphere. In patients with left-hemisphere lesions, both speech comprehension and the learned motor skills were being mediated by the left hemisphere, and the lesion disassociated language areas from these praxicons such that language was not able to activate the appropriate praxicon (see Fig. 7-4). An alternative hypothesis is that in patients with left-hemisphere lesions, the right hemisphere was mediating language comprehension, the left hemisphere contained the praxic representations, and the lesions disconnected the language areas from these representations.

De Renzi et al. (1982) replicated Heilman's (1973) observations and also described a patient who performed in the opposite manner. The patient failed to perform with visual stimuli but performed well to verbal command. Although most patients performed better with tactile stimuli than command, the authors described two patients who performed better with visual and verbal stimuli than with tactile stimuli. The mechanism proposed by De Renzi et al. to explain these modality-specific apraxias was similar to that proposed by Heilman (1973); namely, a disconnection between modality-specific pathways and the center where movements are programmed.

### Pantomime Agnosia

Agnosia is a failure of recognition that cannot be attributed to deafferentation or a naming disorder. Disorders of discrimination and recognition associated with ideomotor apraxia from posterior lesions (described above) may not be considered to be a form of agnosia because of the associated production deficits. Rothi et al. (1986) reported two patients who could not comprehend or discriminate visually presented gestures, but who performed gestures normally. These patients could be considered to have pantomime agnosia.

Both patients could imitate better than they could comprehend or discriminate gestures. Because they could imitate, their inability to discriminate or comprehend gestures could not be accounted for by a defect in vision or perception. The patients had left-sided temporo-occipital lesions that may have disconnected visual input from the input praxicon.

A similar dichotomy can be seen with aphasic patients. Patients with Wernicke's aphasia and pure word deafness can neither comprehend spoken language nor repeat. Whereas the former is thought to be related to destruction of the lexicon (representations of learned word sounds), the latter disorder is thought to be related to an inability of auditory input to gain access to the lexicon. However, patients with transcortical sensory aphasia can repeat (i.e., imitate) in spite of being unable to comprehend, demonstrating that comprehension and imitation are dissociable. This comprehension-imitation disassociation suggests that these two processes are at least in part divergent and are mediated by different parts of the brain. Lichtheim (1885) and Heilman et al. (1976) suggested that while repetition is mediated by a phonological-lexical system that is still functional in transcortical sensory aphasia, comprehension also requires semantic processing. Thus, the systems that mediate semantic processing of language are impaired, or auditory input cannot gain access to these semantic systems (Heilman et al., 1976). The neuropsychological mechanisms underlying impaired gesture comprehension with spared imitation could perhaps be explained in a similar way. These patients can gain access to the input praxicon but the activated praxic representations could not access semantics (see Fig. 7-4).

Several authors have suggested that speech repetition (i.e., imitation) may be performed either by using stored word representations (lexical) or by using a nonlexical route (McCarthy and Warrington, 1984; Coslett et al., 1987). Just as we can repeat words we have not heard, we can also mimic movements we have never seen or previously engaged in. Perhaps imitation, like repetition, can take place without having to access stores of previously learned skilled movement, the praxicon (see Fig. 7-4). Support for this alternative imitation system comes from the observation of a patient whose deficit was limited to the imitation of nonfamiliar limb movement (Mehler, 1987). Because there are no memory stores for unfamiliar movements, the praxicon could not be accessed and the patient had to rely on a nonrepresentational route which was impaired. Perhaps the patients with ideomotor apraxia who improve with imitation can use this nonrepresentational route, whereas those who do not improve may have an additional deficit in this nonrepresentational route.

## Ideational Apraxia

There has been much confusion about the term ideational apraxia. The disassociation apraxias discussed above were unfortunately called ideational apraxia (Heilman, 1973). The inability to carry out a series of acts, an ideational plan, has also been called ideational apraxia Marcuse, 1904; Pick, 1905). These patients have difficulty sequencing acts in the proper order. For example, instead of cleaning the pipe, putting tobacco in, lighting it, and smoking it, the patient with ideational apraxia may first put tobacco in the pipe and then clean it. As noted by Pick (1905), most of the patients with this type of ideational apraxia have had dementing illnesses (such as Alzheimer's disease) or confusional states.

Most patients with ideomotor apraxia improve with actual object use; however, De Renzi et al. (1968) reported patients who made gross errors with the use of actual objects. De Renzi et al. considered the inability to use actual objects a sign of ideational apraxia. While the inability to use actual objects may be induced by a conceptual disorder, Zangwell (1960) noted that failure to use actual objects may be related to a severe production disorder, ideomotor apraxia. However, as we will discuss in the next section, the nature of the error may reveal if the patient is suffering from a production or conceptual disorder. In order to avoid confusion between those patients who cannot sequence acts and are termed ideational apraxics and those who have conceptual disorder, we will term the latter condition conceptual apraxia.

## Conceptual Apraxia

Whereas patients with ideomotor apraxia make production errors (e.g., spatial and temporal errors), patients with conceptual apraxia may make four types of errors. As we briefly discussed above, they may not recall the type of actions associated with specific tools, utensils, or objects (tool-object action knowledge). Therefore, patients with this type of conceptual error make *content errors* (De Renzi and Lucchelli, 1988; Ochipa et al., 1989). For example, when asked to pantomime how to use an actual screwdriver, the patient with the loss of tool-object action knowledge may pantomime a hammering movement or use the screwdriver as if it were a hammer. Patients with ideomotor apraxia may make arcs rather than twisting movements but demonstrate the knowledge of the screw-turning action of screwdrivers. Making content errors (i.e., using a tool as if it were another tool) can also be induced by object agnosia. However, Ochipa et al. (1989) reported a patient who could name tools but used them inappropriately (e.g., used a tube of toothpaste as a toothbrush and a toothbrush as a fork).

Patients with conceptual apraxia may be *unable to recall which tool is associated with an object* (tool-object association knowledge). For example, when shown a nail that has been partially nailed into a piece of wood, they may be unable to select a hammer from an array of tools. Instead, they may select a screwdriver. This conceptual defect may be in the verbal domain: the patient may be unable to name or point to a tool when its function is discussed, even though he can name the actual tool and point to it when named by the examiner. He may also be unable to describe verbally the function of a particular tool.

Patients with conceptual apraxia may also be *unaware of the mechanical advantage* afforded by tools (mechanical knowledge). Therefore, when they are presented with a partially driven-in nail and expected to complete the task without an available hammer, these patients may not select an alternate tool that is hard, rigid, and heavy, such as a wrench or pliers. Instead, they may select an alternate that is flexible and lightweight, such as a handsaw. Lastly, patients with conceptual apraxia may also be *unable to make tools* (tool fabrication).

Because patients with Alzheimer's disease may have impaired semantic memory even early in the course of the disease, Ochipa et al. (1992) studied patients with degenerative dementia of the Alzheimer type for these four components of conceptual apraxia. They found that patients with Alzheimer's disease do have conceptual apraxia. When compared to controls, they were impaired on all four levels discussed above. It was also learned that some elements of conceptual apraxia may even be seen in patients who do not have either ideomotor apraxia or semantic language impairment.

It is not known if conceptual apraxia can be entirely fractionated into four subtypes (tool-object action knowledge, tool-object association knowledge, mechanical knowledge, and tool fabrication knowledge). The lesion associated with conceptual apraxia when testing tool or object use (tool-object action and tool-object association knowledge) has been localized to the posterior regions of the left hemisphere. Liepmann (1920) thought this knowledge was located in the caudal parietal lobe and De Renzi and Lucchelli (1988) placed it in the temporoparietal junction. The subject investigated by Ochipa et al. (1989) was left-handed and rendered conceptually apraxic by a lesion in the right hemisphere, suggesting that both production and conceptual knowledge have lateralized representations and that such representations are contralateral to the preferred hand. Further evidence that these representations are lateralized comes from the observation of a patient who had a callosal disconnection and demonstrated conceptual apraxia of the nonpreferred (left) hand (Watson and Heilman, 1983).

The finding that patients with ideomotor apraxia may not demonstrate conceptual apraxia and that patients with conceptual apraxia may not demonstrate ideomotor apraxia provides evidence for the postulate that the conceptual and production systems are independent. However, in order to perform skilled acts to command or when presented visually with tools or objects, these conceptual and production systems must interact. The recognition and naming of gestures also requires that these systems interact. This is diagrammatically depicted in Figure 7-4 (Rothi et al., 1991).

### Buccofacial Apraxia (Oral Apraxia)

Hughlings Jackson (cited by Taylor, 1932) was the first to describe buccofacial or oral apraxia (nonprotrusion of the tongue). Patients with oral apraxia have difficulty performing learned skilled movements with the face, lips, tongue, cheeks, larynx, and pharynx on command. For example, when they are asked to pretend to blow out a match, suck on a straw, lick a sucker, or blow a kiss, they will make incorrect movements. Poeck and Kerschensteiner (1975) found several types of errors. Verbal descriptions may be substituted for the movement: the oral apraxic asked to pantomime blowing out a match may respond by saying "blow." Other error types include movement substitutions and perseverations. Raade et al. (1991) noted that patients with buccofacial apraxia make content, spatial, and temporal errors. Mateer and Kimura (1977) demonstrated that imitation of meaningless movements was also impaired, providing evidence that oral apraxia is not a form of asymbolia. Although many of these patients do not improve with imitation, they consistently improve dramatically when seeing or using an actual object (e.g., a lighted match). Raade et al. (in preparation) also demonstrated that some patients with buccofacial apraxia also have impaired comprehension of buccofacial gestures.

In order to learn if impairment of the same system could account for both buccofacial and limb ideomotor apraxia, Raade et al. (1991) studied the co-occurrence of these apraxias, the type of errors made by apraxic patients, and lesion sites. Forty percent of their subjects had only one type of apraxia. Basso et al. (1980) reported dissociations in 23% of their subjects, and De Renzi et al. (1968) in 28% of theirs. Raade et al. (1991) also found different error types. Whereas patients with limb apraxia made more errors with transitive than with intransitive movements, Raade and colleagues found no difference in errors between transitive vs. intransitive movements in patients with buccofacial apraxia. Lastly, lesion sites were found to be different.

Tognola and Vignolo (1980) studied patients who were unable to imitate oral gestures. The critical areas for lesions included the frontal and central opercula, anterior insula, and a small area of the first temporal gyrus (adjacent to the frontal and central opercula). Tognola and Vignolo (1980) and Kolb and Milner (1981) found that parietal lesions were not associated with oral apraxia, but they did not test performance to command. Benson et al. (1973), however, described patients with parietal lesions who exhibited oral apraxia to command.

Some authors have classified the phonological selection and sequencing deficit of nonfluent aphasia as "apraxia of speech" (Johns and Darley, 1970; Deal and Darley, 1972). Although Pieczuro and Vognolo (1967) noted that 90% of patients with Broca's aphasia have oral apraxia, it would seem unlikely that buccofacial apraxia causes this phonological disturbance because there are patients with nonfluent aphasia who do not have oral apraxia. It can be argued, however, that oral and verbal apraxias are points along a continuum, sharing a common underlying mechanism. It could be hypothesized that speech requires finer coordination than does response to a command such as "blow out a match"; therefore, the effortful, phonologically inaccurate speech of the nonfluent aphasic may still be caused by an apraxic disturbance affecting speech more than oral, nonverbal movement. Oral apraxia and the speech production deficits associated with Broca's aphasia often coexist, but they can also be completely dissociated (Heilman et al., 1974), suggesting that at least in part the anatomic system that mediates facial praxis is not the same as those that mediate the movements used in speech. Furthermore, because patients may have conduction aphasia with or without oral apraxia (Benson et al., 1973), oral apraxia may coexist with fluent speech. If one attributes the nonfluent disorders of speech in patients with Broca's aphasia to a generalized oral motor programming deficit, one cannot explain how oral apraxia may be associated with the fluent speech seen in conduction aphasia. In addition, we have examined a patient with aphemia (nonfluent speech with intact writing skills) who did not have oral apraxia. If the speech deficits exhibited by left-hemisphere-impaired patients is induced by a motor defect, this motor programming defect is strongly linked to the language and phonological systems and is not a generalized oral motor programming deficit. Without proposing a separate motor programming system for speech, the dependence on the language system and lack of oral motor programming dysfunction call into question the appropriateness of the term apraxia as used in "apraxia of speech."

## RECOVERY FROM APRAXIA AND TREATMENT

Spontaneous recovery from apraxia in right-handed patients may result from the ability of the undamaged right hemisphere's ability to support skilled motor movement programming. (As discussed above, when this ability is sufficient, apraxia may not be seen even with large left-hemisphere lesions.) This hypothesis is similar to the one first proposed by Kleist (1934) to explain why certain patients with lesions of the left hemisphere recover language function.

The association between apraxia and functional disabilities in everyday living has not been extensively studied. It is our clinical impression that ideomotor, ideational, and conceptual apraxias are associated with impaired performance of activities of daily living and instrumental activities. Stroke patients are often anosognosic for their apraxic disability (Rothi et al., 1990) or attribute their disabilities to right hemiparesis and inexperience using their left arm. Therefore, these patients often do not request therapy. In addition, no information is presently available on methods or efficacy of treatment of apraxia. However, information from animal recovery models (Rothi and Horner, 1983) suggests that therapy should be aimed initially at restitution of function: treating the underlying disorder so that maximum function can be achieved within the limits set by the recovery process. Then other therapeutic measures can be attempted to foster substitutive strategies. Apraxic patients should be taught alternative strategies for performing tasks that pose difficulty for them.

## REFERENCES

Agostoni, E., Coletti, A., Orlando, G., and Fredici, G. (1983). Apraxia in deep cerebral lesions. *J. Neurol. Neurosurg. Psychiatry 46*:804–808.

Alexander, G. E., DeLong, M. R., and Strick, P. L. (1986). Parallel organization of functionally segregated circuits linking basal ganglia and cortex. *Annu. Rev. Neurosci. 9*:357–381.

Basso, A., Luzzatti, C., and Spinnler, H. (1980). Is ideomotor apraxia the outcome of damage to well-defined regions of the left hemisphere? Neuropsychological study of CT correlation. *J. Neurol. Neurosurg. Psychiatry 43*:118–126.

Benson, F., Shermata, W., Bouchard, R., Segarra, J., Prie, D., and Geschwin, N. (1973). Conduction aphasia. A clinicopathological study. *Arch. Neurol. 28*:339–346.

Brinkman, C., and Porter, R. (1979). Supplementary motor area in the monkey: activity of neurons during performance of a learned motor task. *J. Neurophysiol. 42*:681–709.

Buschke, H. (1973). Selective reminding for analysis of memory and learning. *J. Verbal Learning Verbal Behav. 12*:543–550.

Coslett, H. B., Roeltgen, D. P., Rothi, L. G., and Heilman, K. M. (1987). Transcortical sensory aphasia: evidence for subtypes. *Brain Lang. 32*:362–378.

Deal, J. L., and Darley, F. L. (1972). The influence of linguistic and situational variables on phonemic accuracy in apraxia of speech. *J. Speech Hear. Res. 15*:639–653.

Dee, H. L., Benton, A., and Van Allen, M. W. (1970). Apraxia in relation to hemisphere locus lesion, and aphasia. *Trans. Am. Neurol. Assoc. 95*:147–150.

De Renzi, E., Faglioni, P., and Sorgato, P. (1982). Modality-specific and supramodal mechanisms of apraxia. *Brain 105*:301–312.

De Renzi, E., and Lucchelli, F. (1988) Ideational apraxia. *Brain 113*:1173–1188.

De Renzi, E., Pieczuro, A., and Vignolo, L. (1968). Ideational apraxia: a quantitative study. *Neuropsychologia 6*:41–52.

Freund, H., and Hummelsheim, H. (1985). Lesions of premotor cortex in man. *Brain 108*:697–733.

Gazzaniga, M., Bogen, J., and Sperry, R. (1967). Dyspraxia following diversion of the cerebral commissures. *Arch. Neurol. 16*:606–612.

Geschwind, N. (1965). Disconnection syndromes in animals and man. *Brain 88*:237–294, 585–644.

Geschwind, N., and Kaplan, E. (1962). A human cerebral disconnection syndrome. *Neurology 12*:65–685.

Goldstein, K. (1948). *Language and Language Disturbances.* New York: Grune and Stratton.

Goodglass, H., and Kaplan, E. (1963). Disturbance of gesture and pantomime in aphasia. *Brain 86*:703–720.

Graff-Radford, N. R., Welsh, K., and Godersky, J. (1987). Callosal apraxia. *Neurology 37*:100–105.

Hécaen, H., and de Ajuriaguerra, J. (1964). *Left Handedness.* New York: Grune and Stratton.

Hécaen, H., and Sanguet, J. (1971). Cerebral dominance in left-handed subjects. *Cortex 7*:19–48.

Heilman, K. M. (1973). Ideational apraxia—a re-definition. *Brain 96*:861–864.

Heilman, K. M. (1975). A tapping test in apraxia. *Cortex 11*:259–263.

Heilman, K. M. (1979). Apraxia. In *Clinical Neuropsychology*, K. M. Heilman and E. Valenstein (eds.). New York: Oxford University Press.

Heilman, K. M., Coyle, J. M., Gonyea, E. F., and Geschwind, N. (1973). Apraxia and agraphia in a left-hander. *Brain 96*:21–28.

Heilman, K. M., Gonyea, E. F., and Geschwind, N. (1974). Apraxia and agraphia in a right-hander. *Cortex 10*:284–288.

Heilman, K. M., Rothi, L. J., and Valenstein, E. (1982). Two forms of ideomotor apraxia. *Neurology 32*:342–346.

Heilman, K. M., Schwartz, H. D., and Geschwind, N. (1975). Defective motor learning in ideomotor apraxia. *Neurology 25*:1018–1020.

Heilman, K. M., Tucker, D. M., and Valenstein, E. (1976). A case of mixed transcortical aphasia with intact naming. *Brain 99*:415–426.

Johns, D. F., and Darley, F. L. (1970). Phonemic variability in apraxia of speech. *J. Speech Hear. Res. 13*:556–583.

Kertesz, A., and Hooper, P. (1982). Praxis and language: the extent and variety of apraxia in aphasia. *Neuropsychologia 20*:275–286.

Kimura, D. (1979). Neuromotor mechanisms in the evolution of human communication. In *Neurobiology of Social Communication in Primates: An Evolutionary Perspective*, H. D. Steklis and M. J. Raleigh (eds.). New York: Academic Press.

Kimura, D., and Archibald, Y. (1974). Motor function of the left hemisphere. *Brain 97*:337–350.

Kleist, K. (1934). *Gehirnpathologie*. Leipzig: Barth.

Kolb, B., and Milner, B. (1981). Performance of complex arm and facial movements after focal brain lesions. *Neuropsychologia 19*:491–503.

Lawrence, D. G., and Kuypers, H.G.J.M. (1968). The functional organization of the motor system in the monkey. *Brain 91*:1–36.

Lichtheim, L. (1885). On aphasia. *Brain 7*:733–784.

Liepmann, H. (1920). Apraxia. *Ergbn. Ges. Med. 1*:516–543.

Liepmann, H., and Mass, O. (1907). Fall von linksseitiger Agraphie und Apraxie bei rechsseitiger Lahmung. *Z. Psychol. Neurol. 10*:214–227.

Marcuse, H. (1904). Apraktiscke Symotome bein linem Fall von seniler Demenz. *Zentralbl. Mervheik. Psychiatr. 27*:737–751.

Mateer, K., and Kimura, D. (1977). Impairment of nonverbal movements in aphasia. *Brain Lang. 4*:262–276.

McCarthy, R., and Warrington, E. K. (1984). A two route model of speech production: evidence from aphasia. *Brain 107*:463–485.

Mehler, M. F. (1987). Visuo-imitative apraxia. *Neurology 37*:129.

Ochipa, C., Rothi, L.J.G., and Heilman, K. M. (1989). Ideational apraxia: a deficit in tool selection and use. *Ann. Neurol. 25*:190–193.

Ochipa, C., Rothi, L.J.G., and Heilman, K. M. (1990). Conduction apraxia. *J. Clin. Exp. Neuropsychol. 12*:89.

Ochipa, C., Rothi, L.J.G., and Heilman, K. M. (1992). Conceptual apraxia in Alzheimer's disease. *Brain 115*:1061–1071.

Orgogozo, J. M., and Larsen, B. (1979). Activation of the supplementary motor area during voluntary movement in man suggests it works as a supramotor area. *Science 206*:847–850.

Penfield, W., and Welch, K. (1951). The supplementary motor area of the cerebral cortex. *Arch. Neurol. Psychiatry 66*:289–317.

Pick, A. (1905). *Sudien uber Motorische Apraxia und ihre Mahestenhende Erscheinungen*. Leipzig: Deuticke.

Pieczuro, A., and Vignolo, L. A. (1967). Studio sperimentale sull'aprassia ideomotoria. *Sisterma Nerv.* 19:131–143.

Poeck, K., and Kerschensteiner, M. (1975). Analysis of the sequential motor events in oral apraxia. In *Otfried Foerster Symposium*, K. Zulch, O. Kreutzfeld, and G. Galbraith (eds.). Berlin: Springer, pp. 98–109.

Poizner, H., Mack, L., Verfaellie, M. Rothi, L.J.G., and Heilman, K. M. (1990). Three dimensional computer graphic analysis of apraxia. *Brain* 113:85–101.

Poizner, H., Soechting, J. F., Bracewell, M., Rothi, L.J.G., and Heilman, K. M. (1989). Disruption of hand and joint kinematics in limb apraxia. *Soc. Neurosc. Abstr.* 15:196.2.

Raade, A. S., Rothi, L.J.G., and Heilman, K. M. (1991). The relationship between buccofacial and limb apraxia. *Brain Cognition* 16:130–146.

Rothi, L.J.G., and Heilman, K. M. (1985). Ideomotor apraxia: gestural learning and memory. In *Neuropsychological Studies in Apraxia and Related Disorders*, E. A. Roy (ed.). New York: Oxford University Press, pp. 65–74.

Rothi, L.J.G., Heilman, K. M., and Watson, R. T. (1985). Pantomime comprehension and ideomotor apraxia. *J. Neurol. Neurosurg. Psychiatry* 48:207–210.

Rothi, L.J.G. and Horner, J. (1983). Restitution and substitution: two theories of recovery with application to neurobehavioral treatment. *J. Clin. Neuropsychol.* 5:73–82.

Rothi, L.J.G., Kooistra, C., Heilman, K. M., and Mack, L. (1988a). Subcortical ideomotor apraxia. *J. Clin. Exp. Neuropsychol.* 10:48.

Rothi, L.J.G., Mack, L., and Heilman, K. M. (1986). Pantomime agnosia. *J. Neurol. Neurosurg. Psychiatry* 49:451–454.

Rothi, L.J.G., Mack, L., and Heilman, K. M. (1990). Unawareness of apraxic errors. *Neurology* 40 (Suppl. 1):202.

Rothi, L.J.G., Mack, L., Verfaellie, M., Brown, P., and Heilman, K. M. (1988b). Ideomotor apraxia: error pattern analysis. *Aphasiology* 2:381–387.

Rothi, L.J.G., Ochipa, C., and Heilman, K. M. (1991). A cognitive neuropsychological model of limb praxis. *Cognitive Neuropsychol.* 8:443–458.

Taylor, J. (1932). *Selected Writings*. London: Hodder and Stoughton.

Tognola, G., and Vignolo, L. A. (1980). Brain lesions associated with oral apraxia in stroke patients: a cliniconeuroradiological investigation with the CT scan. *Neurophysiologica* 18:257–272.

Valenstein, E., and Heilman, K. M. (1979). Apraxic agraphia with neglect induced paragraphia. *Arch. Neurol.* 36:506–508.

Watson, R. T., Fleet, W. S., Rothi, L.J.G., and Heilman, K. M. (1986). Apraxia and the supplementary motor area. *Arch. Neurol.* 43:787–792.

Watson, R. T., and Heilman, K. M. (1983). Callosal apraxia. *Brain* 106:391–403.

Wernicke, E. (1874). *Der Aphasische Symptomenkomplex*. Breslau: Cohn and Weigart.

Wyke, M. (1971). The effects of brain lesions on the learning performance of a bimanual coordination task. *Cortex* 7:59–71.

Zangwell, O. L. (1960) L'apraxie ideatorie. *Nerve Neurol.* 106:595–603.

# 8

# Visuoperceptual, Visuospatial, and Visuoconstructive Disorders

ARTHUR BENTON AND DANIEL TRANEL

The perceptual, perceptuomotor, and perceptuomnemonic disabilities discussed in this chapter are reflected behaviorally in a variety of performance deficits: failure to identify (or discriminate between) objects, pictorial representations, colors, and faces; defective discrimnation of complex stimulus configuration (e.g., nonsense figures, combinations of forms); faulty localization of objects in space and defective topographical orientation; and impaired capacity to organize elements in correct spatial relationships so that they form an entity, as in drawing a house or building a block model. In traditional neurological terminology, many of these deficits are described as one or another form of visual agnosia. The visuoconstructional deficits are usually designated as constructional apraxia or apractagnosia.

Historically there has always been considerable controversy about the fundamental nature of the agnosic disorders. According to one point of view, they represent impairment in either "perceptual-integrative" (apperceptive agnosia) or "associative" (associative agnosia) processes within the context of adequate sensory capacity. The assumption here is that the patient cannot achieve recognition in spite of having received sufficient basic sensory information (Wilbrand, 1887; Lissauer, 1890; Goldstein and Gelb, 1918; Nielsen, 1948). A competing explanation has been that the agnosic disorders result from sensory defects, often coupled with general mental impairment, so that the patient has only incomplete information as a basis for achieving perceptual recognition (Bay, 1953; Critchley, 1953, 1964; Bender and Feldman, 1972). Still another hypothesis which has been advanced is that visual agnosia represents a visual-verbal disconnection symptom and hence is essentially a visual anomia (Geschwind and Fusillo, 1966). The clinical literature includes case reports that fit each of these formulations (cf. Larrabee et al., 1985; Farah, 1990).

Although intellectual impairment per se does not produce agnosia, it is not uncommon for patients with degenerative demential diseases (especially Alzheimer's disease and Pick's disease) to manifest impairment in visual recognition as one part of a more widespread disturbance of memory, i.e., as part of a global amnesic syndrome (cf. Wilson et al., 1982). The distinction between apperceptive and associative agnosia

165

remains problematic, as does the separation of recognition disorders into those that involve a basic perceptual defect and those that do not. One difficulty with these classifications is that they assume a definable point of demarcation between perception and recognition, i.e., a point at which perceptual processes stop and recognition processes take over. Except for some heuristic value, such an assumption is not tenable. Perception and recognition operate on a physiologic continuum, and there is no way to distinguish clearly the "higher" echelons of perception from the "lower" echelons of recognition. For example, it is probable that even so-called "pure" associative agnosics suffer from subtle, higher-order deficiencies of visual perception, relative to certain features or dimensions critical for the recognition of certain stimuli. At most, the statement that visual perception is normal in visual agnosia means that the patient *does* see the stimulus clearly, without blurring or distortion. Moreover, most patients with severe defects of visual perception do not show the cardinal features of visual agnosia. These issues are dealt with at some length in recent reviews (see Damasio et al., 1989a, 1990b).

Irrespective of the precise role of perceptual factors in the development of visual recognition disorders, it is clear that the neural correlates of higher-order visual perceptual disturbances are not the same as those underlying basic deficits in the perception of form, color, texture, motion, and the like. Thus, higher-order perceptual and perceptuomotor disabilities need to be considered separately from "simple" sensory or motor deficits because of their distinctive neurological implications.

Over the years, a large number of specific performance deficits indicative of visuoperceptual, visuospatial, or visuoconstructive disorder have been described. The exact nature of the relationships among these deficits has yet to be worked out, and a definitive classification of neurologically meaningful types of disability remains an unfinished task. However, some fundamental distinctions are generally accepted, for example, that there is a difference between defects in the identification of the formal characteristics of objects and defects in the localization of these objects in space. Both patients with brain disease and experimentally lesioned animals can show dissociated impairment, i.e., defective performances on one type of task but not on the other. A good illustration of this type of dissociation can be found in the literature on prosopagnosia, which indicates that patients with disturbed ability to recognize the identity of faces often have preserved ability to recognize distinctive gaits or postures, i.e., they can recognize identity based on movement information, but not based on form information (Damasio et al., 1982, 1990a,b).

Identification of the neuroanatomical correlates of this dichotomy has led to the postulation of two cortical visual systems, one (inferior occipitotemporal) subserving object recognition and the other (occipitoparietal) subserving the appreciation of spatial relationships (cf. Ungerleider and Mishkin, 1982; Mishkin et al., 1983; Levine et al., 1985). An early study by Newcombe and Russell (1969) will be cited to illustrate both the fact of dissociation and its differential neurological implications.

Newcombe and Russell gave two visual tasks to right-handed patients with penetrating brain wounds and to control subjects. One task was the "face closure" test of Mooney (1957), in which the subject is requested to identify the gender and approximate age of human faces depicted in drawings with exaggerated shadows and highlights. The second task was a visual maze test in which the subject was required to learn a 20-element path over trials. Impairment on this type of spatial learning problem has been shown to be associated with disease of the right hemisphere (Reitan and Tarshes, 1959; Benton et al., 1963; Milner, 1965; Corkin, 1965).

Separate groups of patients with well-localized focal wounds of the left or right hemisphere, as well as control groups matched with the brain-damaged patients for age and vocabulary level, were studied. The performance of the patients with right-hemisphere lesions on both tasks was significantly inferior to that of the left-hemisphere-damaged patients, who were not different in this respect from the controls. However, although both the "closure" and "spatial" task performances proved once again to be associated with right-hemisphere disease, more detailed analysis showed that their relations to locus-of-lesion within the hemisphere and to visual-field defect were quite different.

The perceptual and spatial task performances were not significantly correlated in either the right-hemisphere or the left-hemisphere group, and this lack of correlation was reflected in many instances of dissociation in the right-hemisphere patients. None of the patients with markedly defective "closure" performance showed correspondingly defective "spatial" performance. They were found to have posterior temporal lobe lesions with an associated left upper quadrantic field defect. (Curiously, the men with complete left hemianopia were not particularly severely impaired on this task.) In contrast, the patients with markedly defective spatial performances proved to have high posterior parietal injuries with an associated left hemianopia. Those with an upper quadrantic defect performed quite well, while those with a lower quadrantic defect tended to perform defectively.

This dissociation in performance level on spatial and nonspatial visual tasks on the part of patients with brain disease has been documented in a number of more recent investigations, including a study by Newcombe et al. (1987). The findings provide empirical support for a basic division of visuoperceptive performances into spatial and nonspatial types. However, Ettlinger (1990), reviewing the evidence in both non-human primates and human subjects, has raised questions about the validity of the distinction, particularly as it pertains to neural mechanisms.

A second distinction that can be made is between the loss of ability to identify familiar faces (prosopagnosia or facial agnosia) and impairment in the discrimination of unfamiliar faces. These two deficits, which initially were thought to represent the same underlying disability, are behaviorally dissociable and are produced by the derangement of different anatomic systems (e.g., Damasio et al., 1990b).

In all probability, there are other types of defect, each with its more or less specific neurological implications, that need to be identified. For example, Wasserstein et al. (1984), studying a small sample of patients with focal lesions of the right hemisphere, found that their performances on a test requiring the discrimination of unfamiliar faces and a test of visual synthesis were in fact negatively correlated. A provisional classification of clinically differentiated forms of visuoperceptive, visuospatial, and visuoconstructive disorders is presented in Table 8-1.

**Table 8-1.** Classification of Visuoperceptual, Visuospatial, and Visuoconstructive Disorders

I. Visuoperceptual
    A. Visual object agnosia°
    B. Defective visual analysis and synthesis
    C. Impairment of facial recognition
        1. Facial agnosia (prosopagnosia)
        2. Defective discrimination of unfamiliar faces
    D. Impairment in color recognition

II. Visuospatial
    A. Defective localization of points in space
    B. Defective judgment of direction and distance
    C. Defective topographical orientation
    D. Unilateral visual neglect†
    E. Balint's syndrome°

III. Visuoconstructive
    A. Defective assembling performance
    B. Defective graphomotor performance

°See Chapter 9.
†See Chapter 10.

## HISTORICAL BACKGROUND

Perhaps the earliest explicit description of visuoperceptive defects associated with brain disease was that of Quaglino and Borelli (1867). Their patient showed four persisting symptoms after a stroke: left homonymous hemianopia, inability to recognize family and friends, impairment in color vision, and defective spatial orientation. The authors' diagnosis was hemorrhage in the right hemisphere but the fact that the patient was aphasic and apparently blind directly after his stroke suggested to them that there was bilateral disease.

Hughlings Jackson (1876) was the first neurologist to call special attention to the occurrence of visuoperceptive and visuopractic disabilities in patients with brain disease. Advancing the idea that the posterior region of the right hemisphere played a crucial role in visual recognition and memory, he described a patient with a tumor in this area who showed what he called "imperception"—lack of recognition of familiar persons and places, losing one's way in familiar surroundings, and inability to dress onself. Jackson's observations had little immediate influence. The animal experimentation of Munk made a greater impact on clinical thinking (cf. Benton, 1978).

In 1878, Munk described a condition which he designated as "mindblindness." Following limited bilateral ablation of the upper convex surface of the occipital lobes, his dogs showed a peculiar disturbance in visual behavior. Although they could ambulate freely both indoors and in the garden, avoiding or climbing over obstacles, they seemed to have lost the ability to appreciate the meaning of many visual stimuli. For example, they would merely gaze at a piece of meat instead of snapping at it as would a normal dog. If a threatening gesture was made, they would neither cringe nor bark and they showed no signs of special recognition of their master or other familiar persons as compared to strangers. Munk's explanation of the condition was that the ablation had destroyed their "memory images" of earlier visual experience. As a consequence, they could not relate current perceptions to past experience and hence failed to grasp the meaning of visually perceived stimuli.

"Mindblindness" in patients who did not recognize objects or persons despite seemingly adequate visual acuity was then the subject of many clinical reports. Wilbrand (1887) followed Munk in attributing the disability to a loss of visual memory images and he postulated the existence of a "visual memory center" in the peristriate occipital cortex. Lissauer's (1890) classic case report included a penetrating discussion of the mechanisms underlying mindblindness. According to his formulation, visual recognition involves two processes: accurate perception of an object and association of that perception with past experience. A defect in the first mechanism could lead to an "apperceptive" type of mindblindness, a defect in the second to an "associative" type of disorder.

But other clinicians and experimentalists, while acknowledging the empirical reality of the condition described by Munk, interpreted it as the product of visuosensory defect. Their position was well expressed by Pavlov (1927), who suggested that the classical formula for mindblindness, "the dog sees but does not understand," in fact should read "the dog understands but does not see sufficiently well."

Nomenclature in the field changed with the introduction by Freud (1891) of the term agnosia, to denote disorders of recognition in contrast to disorders of naming, and "visual agnosia" gradually supplanted "mindblindness" as the preferred term for a range of disabilities having to do with the visual apprehension of objects, events, and spatial relations. Various forms of defect were then described. The mindblindness of Munk, Wilbrand, and Lissauer, in which the patient fails to recognize even common objects, was designated as visual object agnosia. Impairment in the discrimination of forms or complex figures with preserved recognition of common objects came to be known as visual form agnosia or geometric form agnosia. The inability to recognize familiar persons on the basis of facial characteristics was described as a specific entity (prosopagnosia), as were symbol agnosia and color agnosia. The inability to grasp the import of a complex pictorial presentation with preserved recognition of its constituent elements was given the designation of stimultanagnosia. The term topographical agnosia was applied to conditions in which patients lost the ability to recognize familiar routes and geographical locales.

Hughlings Jackson's concept of "imperception" involved disturbances in visual orientation as well as lack of recognition of familiar persons and places. Visuospatial disability became a topic of much clinical investigation and discussion in the 1880s, particularly among ophthalmologists (cf. Benton, 1982). An important early contribution was the detailed case report of Badal (1888) describing a patient with preserved central visual acuity who showed spatial disorientation. She could not find her way about the house or the immediate neighborhood and had difficulty in locating objects. She could read letters, numbers, and familiar words, but serial reading was grossly impaired because of directional impairment as she scanned printed material. She recognized objects, but could not estimate their size, distance, or location. Like Jackson's patient, she could not dress herself. Since her disorientation extended to the auditory and somatosensory realms, Badal interpreted her defects as a reflection of a supramodal disability of the "sense of space."

Rather similar cases were described by Foerster (1890), Dunn (1895), and Meyer (1900). The motoric element of "psychic paralysis of gaze" was added to the clinical picture by Balint (1909). On the basis of his observations on younger patients with penetrating brain wounds, Holmes (1918; Holmes and Horrax, 1919) divided visuospatial disabilities into two major types: (1) disturbances in orientation and in size and distance estimation and (2) disturbances in ocular fixation with consequent inability to "find" objects.

The neurological interest of these early observations came from the demonstration that visuospatial disabilities of the types described were produced by focal posterior brain disease. For example, autopsy examination (Sachs, 1895) of Foerster's case disclosed bilteral softening confined to the occipital and temporal lobes, and the brain of Balint's patient showed essentially the same picture. In his cases, Holmes found bilateral lesions involving the angular and supramarginal gyri and extending into adjacent occipital and temporal areas.

Visuoconstructive disabilities were first described under the broader heading of optic apraxia, a term used to designate virtually any disturbance in action referable to defective visual guidance of action. For example, Poppelreuter (1917) described awkwardness in the execution of acts requiring manual dexterity, inability to maintain one's balance in tests of locomotion, and defective imitation of movements, as well as visuoconstructive disabilities, as forms of optic apraxia. Kleist (1923; Strauss, 1924) then singled out constructional apraxia as a separate disorder because of his observation that it could occur independently of other forms of apraxia and his conviction that it possessed a distinctive neuroanatomic significance. He conceived of it as a particular type of visuoconstructive impairment that reflected an inability to translate an adequate visual perception into appropriate action. It was a perceptuomotor, rather than purely visuoperceptual, disability that occurred as a consequence of a break in the connections between visual and kinesthetic processes. Thus, in Kleist's view, constructional apraxia was essentially a disconnection symptom and he placed the locus of the causative lesion in the posterior area of the dominant hemisphere. Yet, at the same time, he emphasized the spatial nature of the disability, defining it as a disturbance "in formative activities such as assembling, building, and drawing, in which the spatial form of the product proves to be unsuccessful, without there being an apraxia of single movements."

After Kleist's description, constructional apraxia was recognized as a form of behavioral disability associated with brain disease. However, his precise formulation that it was neither perceptual nor motor but rather "perceptuomotor" and "executive" in nature was generally ignored and the term was used to designate any visuoconstructive disability, whether or not it appeared within a context of visuoperceptive impairment. Later, Duensing (1953) made a distinction between an "ideational-apractic" type of constructional disability, comparable to Kleist's constructional apraxia, and a "spatio-agnostic" type resulting from visuoperceptive impairment.

## DEFECTIVE VISUAL ANALYSIS AND SYNTHESIS

There is an extensive literature on this topic, describing performance deficits on tasks that make demands on various capacities such as making fine visual discriminations, separating figure from ground in complex configurations, achieving recognition on the basis of incomplete information, and synthesizing disparate elements into a meaningful unity as, for example, when viewing a picture depicting action. Selected aspects of this literature will be reviewed.

### Simple Visual Discrimination

Defects in simple visual discrimination, i.e., altered thresholds for the discrimination of single attributes of a stimulus such as size, brightness, or length, are met with in brain-damaged patients, and the neural correlates of such impairments have been studied at some length. Several representative studies in this area are summarized briefly below.

Taylor and Warrington (1973) assessed the discrimination of size, length, shading, and curvature in groups of patients with focal lesions confined to the left or right hemisphere and a comparable group of control patients. The mean error score of the controls over all tasks was 1.6. Neither the mean error score (1.8) of the left-hemisphere-damaged patients nor that (2.4) of the right-hemisphere-damaged patients was significantly higher than that of the controls. The poorest performances were made by the subgroup of patients with posterior parietal disease of the right hemisphere; however, even their mean error score of 3.7 was not significantly higher than that of the controls. That this failure to find between-group differences was not due to sampling bias is indicated by the fact that the patients with right-hemisphere lesions were inferior to the controls on two other tasks (dot localization, block designs) that were part of the test battery.

A study by Bisiach et al. (1976) approached the problem from the standpoint of signal detection theory and showed that the performances of patients with brain disease were not differentially affected by response biases. Patients with unilateral disease of either hemisphere generally performed at a lower level than controls in the discrimination of length, size, curvature, and brightness. Patients with right-hemisphere disease and with visual-field defects showed the most marked impairment. However, in only one test (discrimination of length) were between-group differences significant. De Renzi (1986a) described two patients who showed a rather extraordinary decline in visuoperceptual abilities without dementia or aphasia and who proved to have a severe deficit in discriminating the length of lines.

The indications are that impairment in simple visual discrimination with its limited demand on information processing is not a particularly frequent occurrence in patients with brain disease. Of all groups of patients, those with posterior parietal disease of the right hemisphere are most likely to show defects of this type. However, the observations of Bertoloni et al. (1978) of a left-field (i.e., right-hemisphere) superiority in the visual discrimination of velocity in normal subjects suggest that there may be other types of "simple" visual discrimination which could be explored with profit in patients with brain lesions. Analogous somesthetic performances seem to present an interesting contrast in this respect. Impairment in tactile two-point discrimination on the side of the body ipsilateral to the side of lesion has been reported by some investigators to occur with notable frequency in patients with unilateral brain disease (Semmes et al., 1960; Vaughan and Costa, 1962; Carmon, 1971). Nebes (1971) found that direct tactile matching of arcs and circles by commissurotomized patients produced markedly poorer performances in the right hand and moderately poorer performances in the left hand, as compared to control subjects. Conversely, disturbances of object recognition in the tactile modality are relatively rare, although it does appear that some patients can exhibit tactile object agnosia in spite of fairly intact basic somatosensory perception (Caselli, 1991; Tranel, 1991a).

In the field of audition, Milner (1962) found that patients with right temporal lobe excisions were inferior to both control patients and those with left temporal lobe excisions in the discrimination of loudness, duration, and pitch; later studies have not been consistently confirmatory (cf. Schulhoff and Goodlgass, 1969; Wyke, 1977). More recently, Hellstrom et al. (1989) reported deviant performance by patients with mild dementia of the Alzheimer's type on a task involving the discrimination of tones of different duration, but not on the analogous visual task of dicriminating the lengths of lines. Finally, Robin et al. (1990) have reported a double dissociation in patients with either left- or right-sided lesions in posterior auditory association cortices, whereby those with left-sided lesions were impaired on auditory perceptual tasks involving temporal demands, but not on tasks involving spectral demands, with the reverse outcome in patients with the right-sided lesions.

### Complex Visual Discrimination

More impressive between-group differences are found when patients are required to discriminate between complex visual stimulus-configurations that differ in one or another subtle characteristic, if the task presented is sufficiently difficult that relatively few subjects make perfect performances. Some examples will be cited to illustrate the point.

Meier and French (1965) studied the visual discrimination of complex figures in patients who had undergone resection of either the right or the left temporal lobe for relief of psychomotor seizures. The two groups were equated for mean age (31–33 years), mean WAIS IQ (96–97), and mean Porteus Maze performance level (13.3–13.5 years). The tasks that were presented assessed the ability to discriminate between fragmented concentric circular patterns on the basis of either a rotational or a structural cue that differentiated one pattern from three other identical patterns. The patients with right-hemisphere lesions were clearly inferior to those with left-hemisphere excisions, their mean error score being 46% higher and the between-group difference in mean error score being significant at the .01 level. Both brain-disease groups performed at levels significantly below that of normal subjects.

Studying patients with penetrating brain wounds, Newcombe (1969) found that those with right-hemisphere wounds performed at a slightly lower level and were slower than those with left-hemisphere lesions on a form matching task; the between-group differences in accuracy and time were not statistically significant. However, the task proved to be a very easy one with many patients making perfect performances. Dee (1970) compared patients with and without visuoconstructional disability and found that defective visual form discrimination was very closely associated with failure on the constructional tests.

Bisiach and Faglioni (1974; Bisiach et al., 1979) employed random shapes of different levels of complexity under diverse conditions of presentation to investigate form discrimination in patients with unilateral hemispheric lesions. Performance differences between control and brain-diseased patients under conditions of simultaneous presentation were generally nonsignificant, patients with left-hemisphere lesions and visual-field defects generating the poorest scores. Under delayed response conditions, between-group differences were more pronounced, with left-hemisphere-lesioned patients (some of whom were aphasic) again making the poorest performances.

In another study, specific relationships were found between performance on a visual form discrimination task and certain aspects of aphasic symptomatology (Varney, 1981). Aphasic alexics (i.e., those with severley defective reading comprehension), who nevertheless still retained the ability to recognize letters, showed a 36% failure on a complex form discrimination task. Aphasic alexics with impaired ability to recognize letters showed an even higher 85% frequency of failure. In contrast, aphasic patients with only mild impairment in reading comprehension and with intact letter recognition showed only a 13% failure in visual form disrimination. It was also noted that, in the course of recovery, the patients' improvement in letter recognition was matched by a corresponding improvement in performance on the test of visual form discrimination.

Benton et al. (1983) assessed the performances of control and brain-diseased patients on a standardized test of complex form discrimination. A remarkably high proportion of the patients with brain lesions performed defectively (as defined by a score exceeded by 98% of the controls). The overall frequency of failure was 53%. Patients with right-hemisphere lesions showed a somewhat higher frequency of failure (58%) than those with lesions of the left hemisphere (47%). Within the right-hemisphere group, the patients with posterior lesions showed the highest frequency of failure (78%). A high proportion (71%) of patients with bilateral disease also performed defectively.

The findings of these studies indicate that, at least with certain types of stimuli and if the task is not too easy, impairment in complex form discrimination is quite frequent in brain-diseased patients. The hemispheric contribution to performance is not clear. Among nonaphasic patients there is a moderate trend toward a higher frequency of failure in those with disease of the right hemisphere. However, a substantial proportion of aphasic patients, particularly those with significant defects in reading comprehension and letter recognition, also produce poor performances.

Given the high sensitivity of certain tasks involving visual form discrimination to the presence of brain disease, it is likely that failing performances often reflect other disabilities as well as specific visuoperceptual defect. Impairments in attention and concentration, visual neglect, and incomplete visual search are distinct possibilities (cf. Teuber, 1964; Tyler, 1969; Heilman et al., 1985). These possibilities need to be considered in clinical assessment to avoid incorrect inferences about the meaning of a defective performance.

### Figure-Ground Differentiation

Impairment in the ability to separate figure from ground in the visual perception of complex stimulus-configurations has long been considered a prominent feature of high-level visuoperceptive defect in patients with brain disease. The ability is typically assessed by tasks requiring the detection of "embedded" or "mixed" figures. The Embedded Figures Test developed by Gottschaldt to investigate the determinants of figure-ground differentiation has been utilized in a number of clinical neuropsychological studies (Teuber and Weinstein, 1956; Weinstein, 1964; Russo and Vignolo, 1967; Orgass et al., 1972; Corkin, 1979). The findings of these studies have indicated that (1) impaired performance is found in a signficant proportion of patients with focal brain disease, independently of locus of lesion; (2) among nonaphasic patients with focal brain disease, those with parieto-occipital lesions of the right hemisphere show the most severe impairment; (3) the performance level of aphasic patients with left-hemisphere disease is inferior to that of nonaphasic patients with left-hemisphere disease and comparable to that of nonaphasic patients with posterior right-hemisphere disease; (4) performance level is not signficantly associated with the presence or absence of visual field defect.

The reasons for the observed association between aphasic disorder and defective performance on this nonverbal visuoperceptive task have not been clearly identified. One possibility is that the aphasic patients have more extensive lesions than their nonaphasic counterparts with left-hemisphere disease and that their defective embedded-figure-test performances reflect general mental impairment associated with a relatively large loss of neuronal tissue. Some empirical findings support this possibility (cf. Corkin, 1979). An argument against it is that, as will be seen, there are other types of visuoperceptive performance that are not related to the presence of aphasia in patients with left-hemisphere disease. A second possibility is that performance on the Gottschaldt test is language dependent in the sense that detection of the target figure embedded in a distracting background is facilitated by implicit verbal mediation processes, i.e., the visual information is verbally coded. If this is so, it would be expected that aphasic patients with disturbances in verbal thinking would perform on a subnormal level. It is perhaps relevant to note that dyslexic children have been found to be deficient on the Gottschaldt test as compared to normal readers with whom they were matched for age and IQ (cf. Goetzinger et al., 1960; Lovell et al., 1964).

The employment of "mixed figures" tests has yielded somewhat different results. Masure and Tzavaras (1976) found that patients with posterior lesions in either hemisphere made the poorest scores. Bisiach et al. (1976) reported that only patients with visual-field defects performed below the level of controls. In neither study was aphasic disorder found to be related to performance level.

### Visual Synthesis

Some patients who can identify and name single stimuli are unable to grasp the interrelations among a number of simultaneously presented stimuli and to integrate the separate elements into a meaningful whole. For example, when presented with an action picture, a patient may enumerate the persons and objects in it but not describe what action is taking place or interpret the implications of the action. A task of this type was introduced by Binet in his intelligence scale and found a place in versions of the Binet Scale developed in different countries. Three levels of performance are typically distinguished: enumeration of elements, depiction of action, and interpretation of the central meaning of the picture.

Binet considered the task to be an appropriate measure of "intelligence," and defective performance by patients with brain disease was at first interpreted as an expression of general mental impairment. However, Wolpert (1924) advanced the view that failure could reflect a modality-specific deficit in visual "integrated apprehension" *(Gesamtauffassung)* which prevented the patient from grasping the import of a complex stimulus situation even though each detail in it was recognized. He regarded the deficit as a form of visual agnosia, for which he coined the term simultaneous agnosia *(Simultanagnosie)*.

The nature and localizing significance of this defect have been the subject of many studies (Brain, 1941; Luria, 1959; Ettlinger, 1960; McFie and Zangwill, 1960; Kinsbourne and Warrington, 1962, 1963; Weigl, 1964; Fogel, 1967; Rizzo and Hurtig, 1987). Failure on picture description and interpretation tasks in patients with brain disease is certainly not rare. Fogel found that 25% of a heterogeneous group of 100 brain-damaged patients performed defectively in the sense that their description of a picture did not go beyond describing elements in it. Fogel also found that failing performance was associated with, but not completely determined by, general mental impairment. When "general mental impairment" was defined as a WAIS IQ score significantly below expectations for the patient's educational background, 32% of the impaired cases showed defective performance as compared to 21% of the unimpaired cases. Some investigators (e.g., Luria; Kinsbourne and Warrington) have related the deficit to either left-sided or bilateral occipital lobe disease. Rizzo and Hurtig (1987), investigating three patients whose main complaint was the "disappearance" of visually fixated stationary stimuli and who also showed the perceptual deficits characteristic of "simultanagnosia," found bilateral occipital lobe lesions in all three cases exhibiting this symptom complex. However, the findings of others have suggested that failure may be associated with lesions in diverse areas. Fogel, in fact, found in his sample that patients with frontal lobe disease made the poorest performances. Nor have comparisons of patients with left- and right-hemisphere lesions shown consistent differences.

This rather confused assemblage of results is understandable when one considers that the task of interpreting a complex meaningful picture makes demands not only on visual integration but also on ideational-associative capacity, verbal encoding, and verbal fluency. Thus a task such as this may be failed by different patients for different reasons. In the light of these considerations, Weigl (1964) questioned the validity of the concept of "simultaneous agnosia" itself, although he did not deny the potential usefulness of picture description tests in the assessment of brain-diseased patients. At the least, the term simultanagnosia is a bad one, and should be replaced by the more accurate descriptor "visual disorientation" (e.g., Damasio, 1985) to avoid the incorrect connotation that the pattern of impairment exhibited by these patients is really a form of agnosia.

The identification of incomplete and mutilated figures and "closure" tasks such as Mooney's (1957) faces and the figure completion test of Street (1931) furnish rather purer measures of the ability to synthesize visual information. As has already been noted, defective performance on the Mooney test is associated with right-hemisphere disease (Newcombe and Russell, 1969). Impaired perception of incomplete figures has also been related to right-hemisphere lesions. Presenting such a task to patients with unilateral brain disease, Warrington and James (1967) found that patients with right-hemisphere lesions performed significantly worse than either controls or patients with left-hemisphere lesions. Within the right-hemisphere group, those patients with lesions involving the posterior parietal region performed most defectively. In contrast, both aphasic and nonaphasic patients with left-hemisphere disease performed at a level comparable to that of controls. Utilizing what seems to have been a rather easy incomplete figures task, Miller (1985) found slightly lower performance levels in patients with right temporal, right frontal, and left frontal lobe excisions. Poor performance on the Street tests has also been found in patients with right-hemisphere disease, particularly those with lesions involving the occipital lobe or with visual-field defects (Orgass et al., 1972).

## IMPAIRMENT IN FACIAL RECOGNITION

There are several reasons why the identification and discrimination of faces have been singled out for particular study in the field of neuropsychology. First, there are patients who present as their primary complaint a loss in the ability to identify familiar faces, a defect that came to be known as prosopagnosia or facial agnosia (cf. Bodamer, 1947). Thus, facial recognition possesses an inherent clinical interest. Second, as Meadows (1974a) and Benton (1980, 1990) have pointed out, facial recognition does occupy a special place in visual experience. Over the course of a lifetime one learns to identify thousands of different faces. Even the faces of persons whom one has met on only one occasion may be recognized instantly at a second encounter years later. There is no other category of nonverbal visual stimulus remotely like it in this respect. It is true that thousands of words can be discriminated, but these are phonologically analyzable and encodable. And finally, faces are used as a highly accurate index of recognition of identity, i.e., physiognomies are used as keys that can unlock a tremendous store of associated information. As such, faces serve a vital and highly efficient role in social interaction.

There are two types of impairment of facial recognition that are essentially independent of each other and that have different neurological implications. The first is facial agnosia or the inability to identify the faces of familiar persons. The second is defective discrimination or matching of unfamiliar faces which makes no demands on memory or past experience.

### *Prosopagnosia (Agnosia for Faces)*

The primary disability in facial agnosia is a patient's incapacity to recognize familiar persons on the basis of visual perception of their faces. It has been reported that the disability is exhibited more frequently by men than by women, even when the higher incidence of stroke in men is taken into account (Mazzucchi and Biber, 1983).

The face recognition defect in prosopagnosia typically covers *both* the retrograde

and anterograde compartments, i.e., patients can no longer recognize the faces of previously known individuals, nor are they able to learn new faces (Damasio et al.,
1990b). The defect is generally profound, patients being unable to recognize the faces
of family members, close friends, and even their own face in a mirror. Upon seeing
those faces, the patients experience no sense of familiarity, no inkling that those faces
are *known* to them, i.e., they fail to conjure up consciously any pertinent information
that would trigger recognition. Prosopagnosia is distinguished from disorders of naming, i.e., it is *not* an inability to name faces of persons who are otherwise recognized
as familiar. There are numerous examples of face *naming* failure, from both brain-
injured populations and from the realm of normal everyday experience, but in such
instances, the unnamed face is invariably recognized as familiar, and the identity of
the possessor of the face may also be apprehended accurately. In prosopagnosia, however, the defect sets in at the level of recognition and, needless to say, the patients will
also manifest a face naming impairment. There are several subtypes of prosopagnosia.

"PURE ASSOCIATIVE" PROSOPAGNOSIA

In this variety, the face recognition impairment is relatively "pure," in the sense that
the defect is confined to the visual modality and occurs in the setting of normal or
near-normal visual perception. Associative prosopagnosia largely conforms to the
classic notion of agnosia, i.e., "a normal percept stripped of its meaning." Thus, the
patients are free of major defects in visual perception, and perform normally or near
normally on standard neuropsychological tests of visuoperceptual discrimination and
visuospatial judgment. Recognition via other modalities is unaffected, e.g., upon
hearing the voices of individuals whose faces go unrecognized, the patient will
instantly recognize the identities of those individuals. Even within the visual modality, the defect is highly circumscribed; for instance, patients may be able to recognize
individuals on the basis of a distinctive feature (e.g., hairstyle) or based up gait or
posture (Damasio et al., 1982, 1990a,b).
   A majority of patients with prosopagnosia also have "central" achromatopsia, i.e.,
an acquired impairment of color perception attributable to cerebral disease (Meadows, 1974b; Damasio et al., 1980). The association of the defects is due to the conti-
guity of visual association areas that are damaged by the lesion. A color perception
defect per se, however, cannot account for the face recognition impairment, since
faces can normally be recognized easily in black and white or color. Another correlate
of face agnosia is defective visual appreciation of texture (e.g., Newcombe, 1979),
although the relationship of this defect to the prosopagnosia is unclear. The ability to
read may or may not be affected in prosopagnosic patients, depending upon the location of the lesion in the left occipital region. When the lesion encompasses both the
left occipitotemporal region *and* the left periventricular region (the white matter
beside, beneath, and behind the occipital horn), reading impairment (alexia) coexists
with prosopagnosia (Damasio and Damasio, 1983).
   "Associative" prosopagnosia is generally produced by bilateral damage in inferior
occipital and temporal visual association cortices, i.e., in the inferior component of
cytoarchitectonic areas 18 and 19, and part of the nearby cytoarchitectonic area 37

(Damasio et al., 1982, 1990b). Most cases are caused by cerebral infarctions due to occlusion in branches of the posterior cerebral arteries. Head injury and cerebral tumors, especially gliomas originating in one occipital lobe and traversing into the opposite hemisphere via the splenium of the corpus callosum, can also produce prosopagnosia, and face recognition impairment is often seen in patients with herpes simplex encephalitis or Alzheimer's disease, as part of a global amnesic condition (see below). Often the lesions are fairly symmetric, involving roughly equivalent portions of the visual association cortices in the left and right hemispheres. Asymmetric damage, however, can also produce the defect, provided either inferior visual association cortices or limbic related structures are involved. Prosopagnosia in connection with bilateral or unilateral lesions located exclusively above the calcarine fissure, in superior visual association cortices, has never been reported.

## "APPERCEPTIVE" PROSOPAGNOSIA

When impaired recognition of familiar faces occurs in the setting of significant visuoperceptual disturbance, it is appropriate to denote such cases as "apperceptive." Unlike the "pure associative" cases described above, apperceptive face agnosics have obvious defects in basic visual perception, demonstrable on neuropsychological testing, which compromise abilities such as matching of unfamiliar faces, judgment of line orientations, and mental manipulation of pictures and picture fragments. In distinguishing between apperceptive and associative forms of face agnosia, it must be emphasized that perceptual processes on the one hand, and recognition/recall processes on the other, cannot be sharply compartmentalized (Damasio et al., 1990a,b). Those processes operate on a continuum, and there is no demarcation point at which perceptual processes stop and recognition processes take over. Even in "pure" cases of associative prosopagnosia, there may be fairly subtle, albeit important, disturbances of high-level integrative abilities, which cannot be detected by available probes. Any explanation of face agnosia tied to perceptual factors must account for the fact that most patients with severe visual perceptual defects do *not* lose their ability to recognize faces. Visuoperceptual disturbance as detected by neuropsychological probes does not necessarily lead to face agnosia.

"Apperceptive" face agnosia is most often associated with damage in right visual association cortices within the occipital and parietal regions. It appears that the damage must involve *both* the inferior and superior components of posterior visual association cortices (areas 18 and 19), mesially and laterally, for severe and lasting face agnosia to develop (Landis et al., 1988; Damasio et al., 1990b). In most cases, parts of areas 39 and 37 on the right are also damaged.

## "AMNESIC ASSOCIATIVE" PROSOPAGNOSIA

In this presentation of prosopagnosia, patients resemble the "pure associative" types in the sense that they have normal visual perception. In amnesic prosopagnosia, however, the face recognition defect is part of a broader recognition impairment that covers multiple sensory channels and multiple categories of stimuli (e.g., Tranel, et al., 1989). Thus, the patient is unable to recognize identity on the basis of information via any sensory channel, so that neither viewing a face nor listening to the appropriate voice will trigger a sense of familiarity or correct recognition. As in other types of prosopagnosia, the face recognition impairment is profound, and may cover virtually all faces from the retrograde compartment, including the faces of family members and the self; the impairment is also severe in the anterograde compartment.

Face agnosia of the "amnesic associative" type is typically associated with bilateral damage in anterior temporal regions (Damasio et al., 1990b). The lesions compromise the hippocampal system (entorhinal cortex, hippocampal formation, and amygdala) and paralimbic and neocortical fields in cytoarchitectonic areas 38, 20/21, and 22. The posterior occipitotemporal cortices, however, are spared. As mentioned above, such damage is very often produced by herpes simplex encephalitis or the neuropathologic destruction associated with Alzheimer's disease.

## "DEVELOPMENTAL" PROSOPAGNOSIA

There are individuals who have never possessed normal capacity for learning faces (McConachie, 1976; Tranel and Damasio, 1989; Ellis and Young, 1988; Young and Ellis, 1989). They have a lifelong deficiency in learning and recognizing faces that ought to have been readily mastered. There are no known neural correlates for this condition, at the level detectable by current techniques, and since the problem begins in early life, it can be labeled "developmental" prosopagnosia. Developmental prosopagnosia has not been widely reported or well studied, but it may not be all that infrequent, its apparent rarity owing to the fact that most affected persons have deliberately concealed their disability. It is probably associated with learning disability for other classes of visual stimuli which, like faces, require individual identification and have many similar exemplars. Developmental prosopagnosics tend to be profoundly embarrassed by their deficiencies, and often evidence adjustment difficulties and related psychological disturbances.

## ADDITIONAL NEUROANATOMICAL CONSIDERATIONS

In general, facial agnosia is seen in combination with the constellation of behavioral defects associated with right-hemisphere disease, leading to the conclusion on clinical grounds that it also is a "right-hemisphere" phenomenon. In support of this conclusion, Hécaen and Angelergues (1963) found in a study of 22 cases of facial agnosia that 16 had right-hemisphere lesions, 4 had bilateral disease, and 2 had left-hemisphere lesions.

However, although clinical evidence favors an association between facial agnosia and right-hemisphere disease, the analyses by Rondot and Tzavaras (1969), Lhermitte et al. (1972), Meadows (1974a), and Damasio et al. (1982) of the anatomic findings in these cases strongly suggest that bilateral lesions are necessary for the appearance of the deficit. Table 8-2 reproduces the listing of autopsied cases originally presented by Lhermitte et al. (1972), augmented by the case studies of Benson et al. (1974), Cohn et al. (1977), and Landis et al. (1988). As will be seen, bilateral lesions

**Table 8-2.** Autopsy Findings in Facial Agnosia

| Author | Etiology | Side of Lesion |
|---|---|---|
| Wilbrand (1892) | Encephalomalacia | Right occipital lobe extending to calcarine fissure; left occipital lobe (smaller lesion) |
| Heidenhain (1927) | Encephalomalacia | Right and left occipital lobes extending to lower aspect of calcarine fissures |
| Arseni et al. (1958) | Spongioblastoma | Left temporal lobe; right tapetum corporis callosi |
| Hécaen and Angelergues (1962) | Glioblastoma | Right parieto-occipital tumor infiltrating splenium and extending slightly into left hemisphere |
| Pevzner et al. (1962) | Encephalomalacia | Left angular gyrus extending to parieto-occipital fissure; inferior lip of right striate cortex |
| Bornstein (1965) | Glioblastoma | Left temporoparieto-occipital tumor infiltrating splenium |
| Gloning et al. (1968) | Encephalomalacia | Left frontal lobe, insula, and fusiform gyrus; right frontal lobe, insula, supramarginal gyrus, and fusiform gyrus |
| Lhermitte et al. (1972) | Encephalomalacia | Left fusiform gyrus; white matter of right fusiform and lingual gyri |
| Benson et al. (1974) | Encephalomalacia | Left medial occipital area; splenium and right inferior longitudinal fasiculus |
| Cohn et al. (1977) | Encephalomalacia | Right precuneus, cingulate, fusiform, and hippocampal gyri, pericalcarine area; left fusiform and lingual gyri, pericalcarine area |
| Cohn et al. (1977) | Encephalomalacia | "Bilateral symmetrical vascular lesions in the distribution of the posterior cerebral arteries, more extensive on the left" |
| Nardelli et al. (1982) | Encephalomalacia | Undersurfaces of both occipitotemporal regions involving fusiform and lingual gyri |
| Landis et al. (1988) | Encephalomalacia | Infarcts in right occipitotemporal and frontal regions; very small infarct in left occipitotemporal region |

were found in all instances, although the left-hemisphere lesion in the most recent case was certainly minimal.

On the other hand, a substantial number of CT-scanned cases of prosopagnosia with lesions apparently confined to the right hemisphere have been reported (Torii and Tamai, 1985; De Renzi, 1986b; Landis et al., 1986b; Michel et al., 1986). Sergent and Villemure (1989) described a patient who had undergone a right hemispherectomy and who was prosopagnosic. Thus the weight of evidence has now shifted in favor of the view that prosopagnosia can be produced by a lesion restricted to the right hemisphere. The right inferior occipitotemporal area, a site where visual information may be transmitted to the mesial and inferior temporal region on the way to being linked to a memory store, appears to be a crucial juncture. However, while a lesion in this region may be a crucial determinant of facial agnosia, it appears that it is not necessarily a sufficient determinant. If it were, the disability would be encountered far more frequently than it is. It is possible that a lesion in the right occipitotemporal region produces facial agnosia only in combination with some atypical condition of the left hemisphere such as might result from acquired disease, congenital weakness, or age-related decline in functional efficiency. This formulation, which is entirely speculative, would account for the finding that prosopagnosia is usually encountered in the setting of bilateral disease but on occasion can be produced by a posterior right-hemisphere lesion alone.

### THE NATURE AND EXTENT OF THE DEFECT

In prosopagnosia, the recognition impairment occurs at the most subordinate level, i.e., at the level of identification of unique faces. Prosopagnosics are fully capable of recognizing faces as *faces*, i.e., at the categorical level, there is no impairment. Also, most prosopagnosics can recognize facial expressions and facial gender, and make accurate estimations of facial age (Tranel et al., 1988). These dissociations highlight the fact that recognizing faces at the level of unique identity is a highly demanding task, which requires the brain to distinguish between numerous different exemplars that bear a high degree of resemblance to one another; breakdown at this level does not imply that other, simpler levels (e.g., recognizing facial expressions) will also be defective.

On the other side of the same coin, although prosopagnosics recognize any number of visual entities at the basic object level, e.g., cars as *cars*, buildings as *buildings*, dogs as *dogs*, they often fail to recognize these items at the more subordinate level of unique identity. Thus, similar to the problem with faces, they are unable to recognize the specific identity of a particular car or a particular building. These related visual recognition impairments are common in prosopagnosia, and help underscore the conclusion that the core defect in face agnosia is the inability to disambiguate fully individual visual stimuli.

### NONCONSCIOUS DISCRIMINATION OF FAMILIAR FACES

Many prosopagnosic patients show accurate covert or nonconscious discrimination of familiar faces, despite their complete inability to recognize those faces at overt level, e.g., based on self-report or verbal ratings of familiarity. For example, it has been shown that prosopagnosics generate large, discriminatory electrodermal responses to familiar faces that are otherwise unrecognized (Bauer, 1984; Tranel and Damasio, 1985, 1988; Bauer and Verfaellie, 1988). Preserved covert face discrimination has been demonstrated in other experimental paradigms, such as reaction time tasks (de Haan et al., 1987; Young and de Haan, 1988) and forced choice procedures (e.g., Tranel et al., 1988). In the electrodermal paradigm, covert face discrimination has even been demonstrated for faces from the anterograde compartment (Tranel and Damasio, 1985, 1988), indicating that the brain can continue to learn new visual information even without conscious influence.

## Defective Discrimination of Unfamiliar Faces

Studies of the capacity of patients to discriminate and identify unfamiliar faces were originally undertaken on the assumption that the abilities which would be assessed were the same as those underlying the identification of familiar faces and with the expectation that the results would elucidate the nature of facial agnosia. Subsequent experiences showed that the assumption was unfounded. If the assumption were correct, then prosopagnosic patients would be expected to show defective discrimination of unfamiliar faces, and patients who failed to discriminate unfamiliar faces should have difficulty in identifying familiar persons. In fact, a number of case reports have described prosopagnosic patients who performed adequately on tests requiring the discrimination of unfamiliar faces (cf. Rondot and Tzavaras, 1969; Assal, 1969; Benton and Van Allen, 1972; Tzavaras et al., 1970). Conversely, failure in the discrimination of unfamiliar faces is not at all rare among brain-diseased patients who show no evidence of prosopagnosia.

Studies of facial discrimination in nonaphasic patients with unilateral brain disease have consistently shown an association between failing performance and the presence of right-hemisphere lesions (De Renzi and Spinnler, 1966; Warrington and James, 1967; Benton and Van Allen, 1968; De Renzi et al., 1968; Tzavaras et al., 1970; Bentin and Gordon, 1979; Hamsher et al., 1979). The observed frequency of defective performance varies from one sample to another, but all studies have found that the relative frequency of defect is more than twice as high in patients with right-hemisphere disease than in those with left-hemisphere lesions. The highest frequency of failure is found in patients with right-hemisphere disease and visual-field defect, the latter pointing to the importance of the retrorolandic localization of the lesion. (That visual-field defect per se is not an important determinant of performance level is indicated by the finding that left-hemisphere-damaged patients with field defects do not perform less well than those without field defects.) Among aphasic patients with left-hemisphere disease, those with posterior lesions and significant impairment in oral language understanding are most likely to show defective performance. Indeed, the frequency of failure in this group of patients is almost as high as that in patients with right posterior lesions (cf. Hamsher et al., 1979).

In summary, studies of facial discrimination in patients with unilateral lesions indicate that failure is prominent in two categories: nonaphasic patients with right posterior lesions and linguistically impaired patients (as reflected in poor oral verbal comprehension) with left-hemisphere lesions. Tachistoscopic visual field studies of normal subjects have found a significant left-field superiority in the accuracy and speed of identification of unfamiliar faces (cf. Rizzolati et al., 1971; Hilliard, 1973; Patterson and Bradshaw, 1975; Hannay and Rogers, 1979; St. John, 1981). Yet it is possible to reconcile these results with the clinical findings, for it is generally the case that a minority of normal right-handed subjects show either no difference between the visual fields or a right-field superiority. The performances of these exceptional subjects can be interpreted as reflecting the participation, or even the preferential use, of left-hemisphere mechanisms in the mediation of facial discrimination. The differential association of holistic and analytical modes of information processing to hemispheric function provides one clue to understanding of the basis of these individual differences (cf. Galper and Costa, 1980; Sergent and Bindra, 1981).

## IMPAIRMENT IN COLOR RECOGNITION

A variety of performance deficits are subsumed under this heading as well as under the terms color imperception, achromatopsia, color agnosia, color anomia, and amnesia for colors found in the clinical literature. For example, a patient may be unable to name colors correctly (even if there is no corresponding impairment in object naming). Or the patient may be unable to point to colors named by the examiner. In another type of impairment, the patient may not be able to give the characteristic colors of common objects, e.g., "red" for blood, "white" for snow, etc. Presented with uncolored line drawings of common objects (e.g., a banana or a fork) and a display of different colors, a patient may make gross errors in matching colors to the drawings, choosing blue for the banana or black for the fork. Presented with a large display of different colors, for example, the Holmgren woolen skeins, the patient may not achieve an adequate sorting of the colors into categories on the basis of hue. The patient may perform defectively on tests for color blindness, such as the Ishihara plates. Finally, a patient may show a visual-field defect for colored targets but not for a white target. These deficits may or may not be the subject of complaint by the patient.

It is obvious that there is no unitary impairment in color recognition. Instead, these diverse performance defects point to the presence of distinctive underlying disabilities of a sensory, perceptual, associative, or linguistic nature, each of which has a different neurological basis. The major forms of deficit are described below.

### Impaired Perception of Colors (Achromatopsia)

It has long been known that defects in the discrimination of colors, roughly analogous to congenital weakness in color discrimination, may occur as a consequence of brain disease. Central or acquired achromatopsia, dyschromatopsia, color blindness, and color imperception are some of the names that have been employed to designate these defects. The defect may be present in the whole visual field, in one half-field (hemi-achromatopsia), or even in just one quadrant. Its presence can be assessed by the same tests, such as the Ishihara plates and the Farnsworth-Munsell 100 Hue test, utilized to probe for congenital color weakness.

The first large-scale study of color imperception in patients with brain disease was undertaken by De Renzi and Spinnler (1967). The capacity was assessed by two tests, the Ishihara plates and a color matching task in which the patients had to abstract pairs of identical colors from two sets of colored squares. Failing performance on the color matching test was shown by 17% of the brain-diseased patients, with a decidedly higher frequency in those with right-hemisphere lesions (23%) than in those with left-hemisphere lesions (12%). Essentially the same findings were obtained from the Ishihara test where failing performance was shown by 9% of the total group, 14% of right-hemisphere-damaged patients, and 6% of left-hemisphere-damaged patients. Further analysis showed that failure was particularly frequent among patients with visual-field defects. In the patients with left-hemisphere disease, aphasics showed a higher frequency of failure than nonaphasics, but it is not clear whether the aphasic patients also had visual-field defects.

A second large-scale study (Scotti and Spinnler, 1970) utilized the Farnsworth-Munsell 100 Hue test to determine whether the observed effects of side-of-lesion and visual-field defect could be confirmed and also to investigate performance along the color spectrum in brain-diseased and control patients. The salient findings were that patients with right-hemisphere disease and visual-field defect performed most poorly and patients with left-hemisphere disease but without visual-field defect performed at a normal level. All groups, including the control patients, showed the same performance profile characterized by a relatively high number of errors in the green-blue section of the spectrum. Essentially similar findings indicating a higher frequency of color imperception in patients with right-hemisphere disease have also been reported by Lhermitte et al. (1969) and Assal et al. (1969). In the latter study, however, the observed between-hemispheres difference was small and nonsignificant.

It should be noted that these large-scale studies defined "color imperception" on a statistical basis as a performance level below that of the great majority of normal subjects and not in terms of gross disability, as reflected in a patient's spontaneous complaints or evident loss of function. In contrast, anatomic investigations have dealt with cases in which loss of color perception was a prominent, if not the primary, complaint.

Anatomic study of cases of color imperception or "central achromatopsia" has a long history dating back to the 1880s (cf. Meadows, 1974b; Damasio et al., 1980). All reports, including those of Green and Lessell (1977), Pearlman et al. (1978), and Damasio et al. (1980), are in agreement that bilateral lesions in the region of the occipitotemporal junction are the basis for full-field achromatopsia. This presentation, however, is relatively rare; more commonly, the color perception defect is present in one hemifield, in association with an occipitotemporal lesion in the contralateral hemisphere (e.g., Damasio, 1985). In fact, probably the most frequent presentation of central achromatopsia involves a combination of a quadrantanopia and quadrantachromatopsia in one hemifield. The former defect (i.e., loss of form vision) is present in the upper quadrant, contralateral to the lesion, and is due to the encroachment of the lesion into primary visual cortex in the inferior bank of the calcarine fissure. The color perception impairment is manifest in the lower quadrant, where form vision is still intact. When this configuration occurs with right-sided lesions (in the left hemifield), it may present in very "pure" form, i.e., the patient may evidence few, if any, associated neuropsychological defects. When the lesion is in the left occipitotemporal region (with the color perception defect being in the right hemifield), it is common for the patient to exhibit alexia in addition to achromatopsia.

A recent study by Damasio et al. (1989b) has provided further evidence regarding the neuroanatomical correlates of achromatopsia. The authors studied 42 patients with posterior lesions, using a comprehensive set of neuropsychological and neuroanatomical techniques. It was found that no patient developed a color perceptual defect following a supracalcarine lesion. Rather, achromatopsia was associated with infracalcarine lesions that damaged the middle third of the lingual gyrus, and also with infracalcarine lesions that damaged the white matter immediately behind the posterior tip of the lateral ventricle. Damasio et al. reported that achromatopsia did not follow infracalcarine lesions in the anterior or posterior thirds of the lingual gyrus, nor was achromatopsia associated with lesions in the fusiform gyrus only and/or in the white matter beneath the ventricle. These findings correlate well with recent data from positron emission tomography (PET) studies, which have indicated a similar "color center" in the brain (Lueck et al., 1989; Corbetta et al., 1990).

## Impairment in Color Association

Failure in tasks requiring a patient to indicate the characteristic colors of familiar objects, within the context of intact color perception, is the primary performance deficit covered by the concept of impaired color association. Provided that the patient understands and can produce the names of colors and familiar objects, an appropriate method to probe for the presence of the defect is to ask the patient what the usual color of an object, such as salt, peas, or a banana, is. Having the patient match colors to uncolored line drawings of objects either by actually coloring the drawing or pointing to the appropriate color in a display is a more desirable procedure since it circumvents overt language demands.

The inability of some patients with brain disease to link colors (or their names) to objects with which they are characteristically associated was noted as early as the 1880s by ophthalmologists and neurologists and was the topic of considerable discussion over the course of subsequent decades. Wilbrand and Saenger (1906) postulated a disconnection between the cortical visual center and the speech area in the left hemisphere as the essential basis for the disability. However, Lewandowsky (1908) pointed out that the failure of these patients on nonverbal coloring tasks (sometimes with preserved ability to give the name of the colors associated with objects) indicated a deficit beyond color anomia. Instead, Lewandowsky advanced the idea that the basic deficit consisted of a "splitting" between the concept of form and that of color, leading to a loss of associations between objects and their characteristic colors. All authors acknowledged the close relationship of the disability to aphasic disorder, and Sittig (1921) emphasized the crucial role of verbal associative functions in performance.

De Renzi and Spinnler (1967) included both verbal and nonverbal color association tests in their study of color imperception. The verbal task consisted of asking the patient to name the characteristic color of familiar objects. In the nonverbal task, the patient was given a choice of ten colored pencils and instructed to color a number of line drawings. Predictably, most of the failures on the verbal color association task were made by aphasic patients. However, a few nonaphasic patients with right-hemisphere disease (about 10%) also failed, most of these showed defects in color perception (Ishihara plates and color matching). No such relationship was evident in the patients with left-hemisphere disease. The results for the nonverbal coloring task were most interesting. About 50% of the aphasics failed the task, i.e., made a score below that of the poorest control. Performance level within the aphasic group showed a modest correlation ($r = .48$) with assessed severity of aphasic disorder. A few nonaphasic patients (11% of those with right-hemisphere disease; 7% of those with left-hemisphere disease) also performed defectively, failure here being closely associated with defective color perception.

A second study by De Renzi et al. (1972) also demonstrated a close relationship between impaired performance on a nonverbal coloring task and aphasic disorder. When attention was restricted to the 18 poorest performances in a sample of 166 patients with unilateral brain disease (60 of whom were aphasic), it was found that 17 of these were made by aphasic patients. Stated in another way, gross failure on the task was shown by 28% of the aphasic but only 1% of the nonaphasic patients.

Varney (1982) found that impaired reading comprehension was closely correlated with defective color-object matching. In a sample of 50 aphasic patients, 15 (30%) performed defectively (below the level of 96% of control patients) on a test requiring the subject to point to the characteristic color of objects depicted in line drawings. All 15 patients also showed defective reading comprehension, while only 10 of the 15 showed impaired oral verbal comprehension as assessed by standardized aphasia tests. Thus it appeared that whatever cognitive disability underlies defective color-object matching also impairs reading comprehension. Other relevant studies are those of Lhermitte et al. (1969) and Tzavaras et al. (1971).

The remarkable frequency with which aphasic patients fail the nonverbal task of matching colors to line drawings is often interpreted as implying that verbal mediational processes must underlie the matching performance. This is a reasonable conclusion but, as De Renzi and his co-workers have pointed out, it has not been securely established. Another possibility is that defective performance reflects impairment in a cognitive function subserved by left-hemisphere mechanisms and hence is likely to be associated with (but not dependent on) aphasic disorder. De Renzi et al. identified the functional impairment as a "general disorder in conceptualisation," while Varney suggested that the color-form matching disability is an expression of "a relatively specific visual information processing disorder."

## Impairment in the Verbal Identification of Colors

The inability to name colors on visual confrontation or to point to them when their names are supplied by the examiner are the major performance deficits subsumed under this heading. Other tasks that have been used to probe for defective verbal identification of colors are the completion of sentences calling for the name of a color (e.g., "The color of an apple is _____."), and controlled world association in which the patient is asked to name as many different colors as she or he can (cf. Wyke and Holgate, 1973).

It is to be expected that aphasic patients will perform defectively on these tasks, the degree of defect being proportional to the severity of their linguistic disabilities. It is also to be expected that patients with impairments in color perception will perform defectively on visuoverbal tasks. In line with these expectations, De Renzi and Spinnler (1967) found that 42% of their group of aphasic patients failed a combined test of color naming and identifying colors when the names were supplied, as compared to 10% of nonaphasic patients. Moreover, five of the six nonaphasic patients with right-hemisphere disease who failed the verbal tests were found to have defective color perception as well. There remained five nonaphasic patients with left-hemisphere disease who failed the verbal tests and who did not show impairment in color perception. These patients showed an apparently specific "color anomia" and/ or "color name amnesia" not attributable to either linguistic impairment or perceptual deficit.

The most striking examples of specific visuoverbal color disability are seen in alexic patients who fail color naming tasks and at the same time show intact (or only mildly impaired) ability to name objects and pictures. This association of incorrect color verbalization with acquired alexia is highly frequent and is often included in the syndrome of pure alexia (i.e., without agraphia) and right hemianopia. Gloning et al. (1968) found evidence of "color agnosia" in 19 of 27 patients with pure alexia. Some insight into the neural mechanisms underlying visuoverbal color disabilities has been gained from clinicopathological studies of individual alexic patients. The findings and implications of two detailed case reports, one dealing with an alexic patient with impairment in verbal color identification and the other with an alexic patient without such impairment, will be considered.

Geschwind and Fusillo (1964, 1966) described a 58-year-old man who, following a vascular accident, manifested pure alexia and right hemianopia as permanent defects after the acute episode. He could not read words aloud or match them to corresponding pictures. He could read a few single letters and some two-digit numbers. He could write to dictation but was not able to read his handwriting. He was able both to spell orally and to identify words spelled to him orally. Speech production, understanding of oral speech, and object naming were intact, as were right-left orientation, finger naming, and oral arithmetic calculation. The single remarkable nonverbal disability was a severe disturbance in topographical orientation, reflected in his inability to give the location of his home or to describe routes in traveling from one place to another.

He was totally unable to name colors (including black, white, and gray) correctly, to identify the colors of pictures of objects where there was no inherent association between the color and the object (e.g., necktie, dress), and even to identify the colors of objects that are associated with specific colors (e.g., white writing paper, red bricks). Nor could he point to colors when their names were supplied by the examiner. In contrast, his performance on nonverbal color tasks was quite adequate. He could match and sort colors and correctly matched colors to uncolored line drawings (e.g., yellow to a banana). His performance on pseudo-isochromatic tests of color vision was normal. He was able to state the usual colors of familiar objects such as an apple or the sky.

Postmortem examination disclosed areas of infarction in the left calcarine cortex, the splenium of the corpus callosum, and the left hippocampus, all within the territory of the left posterior cerebral artery.

Geschwind and Fusillo interpreted this syndrome of alexia, impaired color cognition, and right hemianopia as the functional outcome of a disconnection between the right occipital cortex and the language area of the left hemisphere. The interpretation follows the classic explanation that the failure in naming (and identification) of colors as well as the alexia are due to a break in the connections between the visual cortex and the language area. Thus color anomia comes about because visual information

cannot reach the language zone of the left hemisphere to be encoded. Faulty identification of colors named by the examiner comes about because verbal information
cannot reach the visual cortex to be decoded.

A persisting problem has been how to explain the relatively retained capacity for
object naming and object identification by name shown by patients with alexia and
color anomia since these sensory-verbal performances also would seem to depend on
the same visual mechanisms that are invoked to explain color naming and identification performances. A number of possible explanations have been advanced. One
possibility is that visually presented objects or pictures arouse tactile associative activity in the brain, leading to excitation of anterior areas in the right hemisphere which
is then transmitted to the language zone of the left hemisphere through callosal fibers
anterior to the splenium. Letters, words, and colors do not arouse such tactile associative activity (cf. Geschwind, 1962). Another possibility is that the naming of familiar
objects is such an elementary and automatized performance that (assuming that the
splenial fibers have not been completely destroyed) it can be sustained by meager
interhemispheric connections (cf. Howes, 1962). This explanation implies that the
patient with alexia and color anomia should have difficulty in naming less familiar
objects. The clinical observation that the majority of alexic patients do in fact exhibit
mild word-finding difficulties can be cited to support the implication.

Another possibility, which has become more plausible in light of recent findings
from several laboratories, is that object naming is subserved by neural mechanisms
different from those involved in color naming or reading. Specifically, there is an
increasing convergence of evidence indicating that object naming is dependent upon
structures in the left anterolateral temporal region, including cytoarchitectonic fields
20, 21, and possibly areas 37 (posteriorly) and 38 (anteriorly). Relevant studies in this
regard include those by Damasio et al. (1990c), Graff-Radford et al. (1990), Stafiniak
et al. (1990), and Tranel (1991b). Goodglass et al. (1986) described naming dissociations between different categories of objects (including colors) in a population of
aphasic patients.

As has been noted, color anomia and alexia do not invariably appear in combination. The case report of Greenblatt (1973) describing an alexic patient without
agraphia, hemianopia, or color anomia is instructive because it points to the possible
neural mechanisms underlying each of the two performances. Autopsy study of this
patient disclosed a neoplasm that had invaded the splenium and inferior part of the
left occipital lobe, leaving the left calcarine cortex and optic radiations intact. Thus
there was an interruption in the connection between the left angular gyrus and the
right visual cortex, and a partial interruption between the left angular gyrus and the
left visual cortex, involving the inferior or ventral connections. Greenblatt suggests
that this disconnection was responsible for the patient's isolated alexia and that the
remaining intact dorsal connection from the occipital cortex to the angular gyrus
accounted for the preservation of color naming.

Thus the indications are that specific impairment in verbal operations with colors
is explainable in terms of derangement of specific neural mechanisms and that some
progress has been made in the identification of these mechanisms. Advances in
knowledge depend on the continued accumulation of detailed clinicopathological
correlational data.

## VISUOSPATIAL DEFECTS

Patients with brain disease may show any of a variety of performance deficits indicative of faulty appreciation of the spatial aspects of visual experience. Some of the more prominent deficits and their correlates and interrelations are described below.

### Defective Localization of Points in Space

The defective localization of points in space has long been familiar to clinicians who observed that patients with parieto-occipital injuries exhibited it in particularly severe form (cf. Benton, 1969). In addition, some large-scale studies have assessed its frequency and its association with locus-of-lesion.

Warrington and Rabin (1970) presented two cards containing single dots in a vertical array to patients who were required to state whether or not the position of the dots was the same on the two cards. Both simultaneous and successive presentations were given. The task proved to be rather easy, all groups of patients making relatively low error scores. Nevertheless, it could be shown that the performance of patients with right parietal lesions was significantly poorer than that of patients with left-hemisphere disease or control patients; the latter two groups did not differ from each other.

However, Ratcliff and Davies-Jones (1972; Ratcliff, 1982), using a different procedure for assessing accuracy of visual localization, obtained rather different results. In their study, patients were required to touch point stimuli on a projection perimeter while maintaining fixation of gaze. Defective localization was defined in terms of an average error greater than that made by any control subject. The essential findings were that patients with posterior parietotemporo-occipital lesions in either hemisphere performed defectively while none of the patients with anterior lesions showed defective localization. Visual-field defect was not a significant correlate of performance level.

Thus the results of the two studies were in agreement about the importance of parieto-occipital disease in the production of the deficit but differed in their implications about the role of the right hemisphere in the mediation of visual localization performances. However, a subsequent investigation by Hannay et al. (1976) generated strong evidence of a difference in the performances of patients with right- and left-hemisphere lesions on a visual localization task. In this study the level of difficulty of the task was deliberately augmented by reducing the exposure time and requiring the patient to identify the locations of simultaneously exposed pairs of dots as well as single dots. Under these experimental conditions, 45% of a group of 22 patients with right-hemisphere lesions performed defectively (i.e., below the level of the poorest control patient). None of the 22 patients with left-hemisphere disease performed defectively and the mean score of this group was practically the same as that of the control patient group. In contrast to the Warrington-Rabin findings, visual-field defect was associated with defective performance in this study. And, in contrast to the results of both of the earlier studies, patients with perirolandic lesions of the right hemisphere were found to be impaired as frequently as those with posterior lesions.

All three studies were in agreement that patients with unilateral frontal lesions are likely to perform normally.

Possible reasons for the inconsistency of these findings may be considered. Some clinicians have differentiated between the localization of stimuli within "grasping distance" (thus permitting a reaching or pointing response) and those beyond arm's reach that require a verbal judgment (cf. Brain, 1941; Birkmayer, 1951). In addition, a distinction is sometimes made between the "absolute" localization of a single stimulus in relation to the observer and "relative" localization involving the spatial relationship between two stimuli within grasping distance. The pointing responses made by the patients in the study of Ratcliff and Davies-Jones assessed "absolute" localization of stimuli within grasping distance. In contrast, the judgmental and matching responses called for in the Warrington-Rabin and Hannay-Varney-Benton studies assessed "relative" localization performances. A study in which both types of localization tasks are given to the same group of patients could be done to test this hypothesis, as well as to assess whether the unexpectedly high frequency of defect in the patients with right perirolandic lesions found in the Hannay-Varney-Benton study was a chance finding in a small sample of cases.

### Defective Judgment of Direction and Distance

Appreciation of the directional orientation of lines presented as either tactile or visual stimuli has been the subject of a number of experimental and clinical studies designed to determine whether there is a differential hemispheric contribution in the mediation of this spatial performance (Carmon and Benton, 1969; Newcombe and Russell, 1969; Warrington and Rabin, 1970; Fontenot and Benton, 1971, 1972; Benton et al., 1973, 1975, 1978a,b, 1983; Sasanuma and Koboyashi, 1978). The results of all these studies have been consistent in indicating that perception of directional orientation is mediated primarily by the right hemisphere in right-handed subjects.

The findings of Benton et al. (1983) provide a clear demonstration of this hemispheric asymmetry, as reflected in the high frequency of severe defect in patients with right-hemisphere disease. A test requiring identification of the directional orientation of lines was given to right-handed patients with focal brain disease and a group of control patients. The procedure consisted of presenting pairs of lines in different orientations to the patient and requesting the patient to point to them (or call their number) on a visual display (Fig. 8-1). Scores on this 30-item test were corrected for age and sex on the basis of normative observations. The distributions of these corrected scores in the control and brain-diseased groups are shown in Table 8-3. Severe disability (defined as a performance poorer than than of 98.5% of the controls) was shown by 36% of the patients with right-hemisphere disease but by only 2% of those with left-hemisphere disease, the majority of whom were aphasic. Analysis of the relationship of performance level to intrahemispheric locus of lesion in the patients with right-hemisphere disease indicated that failure was particularly frequent in those with posterior lesions.

Recent investigations by Mehta and colleagues (Mehta et al., 1987; Mehta and Newcombe, 1991) have suggested that the dominant role of the right hemisphere in visuospatial processing is restricted to tasks that make relatively "pure" spatial

Fig. 8-1. Items in test of visuospatial judgment. (From Benton et al., 1983.)

**Table 8-3.** Score Distributions of Control and Brain-Diseased Patients on Test of Judgment of Line Orientation

| Score | Normative Sample ($N = 137$) | Left-Hemisphere Lesions ($N = 50$) | Right-Hemisphere Lesions ($N = 50$) |
|-------|------------|------------|------------|
| 29–30 | 38 | 6  | 2  |
| 27–28 | 22 | 11 | 5  |
| 25–26 | 22 | 8  | 3  |
| 23–24 | 25 | 7  | 3  |
| 21–22 | 18 | 9  | 8  |
| 19–20 | 7  | 4  | 6  |
| 17–18 | 3  | 4  | 5  |
| >17   | 2  | 1  | 18 |

From Benton et al., 1983.

demands, such as matching of angles. For other tasks, including judgment of a line orientation and shape rotations, the left hemisphere may also make an important contribution. It seems likely, however, that the roles of the two hemispheres in such capacities must be quite different, even if both are important for successful performance (see Hamsher et al., 1992).

As was noted, tasks assessing the tactile perception of line direction have generated similar results showing hemispheric asymmetry in the mediation of performance. Thus the indications are that the right hemisphere plays a more important role than the left in subserving behavior requiring the apprehension of spatial relations independently of sensory modality. However, this conclusion does not imply that performances in both the tactile and visual modalities are necessarily mediated by the same neural mechanism in the right hemisphere.

### Defective Topographical Orientation

A variety of performance defects have been placed under the heading of defective topographical orientation. Some, such as inability to describe the spatial arrangement of the rooms in one's house or the disposition of buildings in a public square, to tell how one would travel from one point to another in one's home town, or to indicate the location of cities on a map, implicate failure in representational processes and memory. In these instances the patient is apparently unable to call up the detailed visual schema necessary to describe routes or make localizations. Other defects, such as failure to follow familiar routes or to learn to do so in a new setting (e.g., a hospital), seem to be on a perceptual or attention level. Unilateral visual neglect is not only a demonstrably important determinant of failure in following routes but can also be a factor in failure on representational and memory tasks (cf. De Renzi, 1982). The findings of some pertinent clinical studies are summarized below.

Hécaen and Angelergues (1963) assessed "topographical memory" by requiring patients to describe familiar routes, the arrangement of rooms in their house, the street on which the house is located, or the main square of the city. Studying large samples of patients with unilateral or bilateral retrorolandic disease, the investigators found that loss of topographical memory, as reflected in poor performance on these tasks, was shown only by patients with either bilateral or right-hemisphere disease; even in these groups the deficit occurred rather infrequently. The highest incidence of failure (8%) was found in the bilateral cases. The patients with right-hemisphere disease showed a 6% incidence and those with left-hemisphere disease showed a 1% incidence. Control patients were not studied and it is not made clear how defective performance was defined.

Hécaen and Angelergues also studied geographic orientation (under the heading of "topographical concepts") by having their patients identify the principal cities, regions, and rivers of France on a map. Again, the criteria for judging whether a performance was defective are not explicitly stated. Here the authors found that no less than 21% of the patients with retrorolandic lesions of the right hemisphere performed defectively, as compared to 4% of left-hemisphere cases and 6% of bilateral cases. It is clear from the descriptions in the monograph that failure on this map test was often associated with visual neglect of (i.e., failure to attend to) the left half of the map.

In another study, Landis et al. (1986a) reported 16 patients who had lost the ability to recognize familiar surroundings, in spite of relatively normal verbal memory and visuoperception, a condition termed environmental agnosia. The authors noted several fairly frequent associated defects, including prosopagnosia, central achromatopsia, dressing apraxia, and constructional apraxia. The most common lesion correlate was in the right medial occipitotemporal region, although three patients also had left-sided lesions. A patient with a similar type of defect (i.e., environmental agnosia) was reported by Whiteley and Warrington (1978).

Benton et al. (1974) assessed geographic orientation both with a verbal test (requiring the patient to state the direction she or he would travel in going from one city or state to another) and with a nonverbal test in which patients localized cities and states on a large map of the United States. Since educational background is an obvious determinant of performance level on these tasks, normative data were collected on two separate groups of control patients, one with 12 or more years and the other with fewer than 12 years of education. Defective performance was defined as a score 3 or more standard deviations below the respective group mean on each task. Defective performance on the verbal directions test occurred with equally low frequency (about 5%) in patients with right- or left-hemisphere disease. The frequency of failure on the map localization test was somewhat higher (22%) with only a slight difference between the right- and left-hemisphere groups (25% vs. 20%). However, a "vector" score for the map test, which provided a measure of directional bias in localization, clearly differentiated between the two unilateral groups. The mean "vector" score of the patients with left-hemisphere disease was −3.2, reflecting a systematic shift in localization toward the left or "western" half of the map. The mean "vector" score of the patients with right-hemisphere disease was +4.4, reflecting an even greater systematic shift in localization toward the right or "eastern" half of the map. For the most part, defective performance was shown only by patients with less than a twelfth grade education.

The ability of patients with penetrating brain wounds to follow routes on the basis of maps showing the path to be taken was investigated by Semmes et al. (1955, 1963). Patients with left parietal injury or bilateral parietal injury performed defectively,

while the performances of those with lesions in other sites (including the right posterior parietal area) were comparable to that of control subjects. Among the patients
with left-hemisphere disease, those with aphasic disorder performed most defectively. Employing the same procedure, Ratcliff and Newcombe (1973) found that
only patients with bilateral posterior injury performed defectively on the task.

Our knowledge of the determinants, correlates, and interrelations of defective
topographical orientation, in the sense in which the term has been used in this section,
is still rather scanty. From the anatomic standpoint, it is not clear that there is an
unequal hemispheric contribution to the mediation of these performances. As has
been noted, neglect of the left or right visual field may distort performance and lead
to failure on some tasks. Visual neglect is shown more frequently by patients with
right-hemisphere disease than those with left-hemisphere lesions, thus creating a bias
toward a higher incidence of failure in the first group, as Hécaen and Angelergues
found. These authors also reported an association between impaired topographical
orientation and a number of other defects associated with right-hemisphere disease,
such as constructional apraxia, dressing dyspraxia, and a "spatial" type of dyslexia.

## DEPTH PERCEPTION AND DISTANCE JUDGMENT

A distinction between two types of depth perception can be made: real depth perception of objects in space and the perception of apparent depth produced by binocular disparity in stereoscopic presentation. Impairment in both types of depth perception and concomitant inaccuracy in judging distances have been described in the
clinical literature as sequelae of brain injury (cf. Holmes and Horrax, 1919; Paterson
and Zangwill, 1944; Critchley, 1953; De Renzi, 1982).

A further distinction can be made between two types of stereoscopic perception of
apparent depth (Hamsher, 1978; Ratcliff, 1982). Local stereopsis, or stereoacuity, is
defined as the ability to detect small differences in depth through point-to-point
matching of disparate points in the two retinas, and it is presumably mediated by the
activation of disparity-detecting neurons in the visual cortex. As assessed by performance with stereograms with well-defined forms, impairment in stereoacuity has
been found in some patients with lesions of either the right or left hemisphere (Rothstein and Sacks, 1972; Lehmann and Walchi, 1975; Danta et al., 1978).

The other type of apparent depth perception is called global stereopsis (Julesz,
1971). The term refers to the capacity to achieve depth perception in the absence of
well-defined stimulus forms and is presumed to be mediated by neural mechanisms
other than those involved in stereoacuity. Assessed by the random-dot (or random-
letter) stereograms of Julesz (1964), impairment in global stereopsis appears to be specifically associated with disease of the right hemisphere. This relationship was first
demonstrated by Carmon and Bechtoldt (1969), who found that some patients with
right-hemisphere lesions showed strikingly defective global stereopsis, while patients
with left-hemisphere lesions performed on the same level as control patients. Carmon
and Bechtoldt interpreted their results as supporting the hypothesis that, in the
absence of monocular cues of form and depth, the right hemisphere is "dominant"
for stereopsis in right-handed subjects. Their findings were confirmed by Benton and
Hécaen (1970) and Hamsher (1978). Both of the latter studies found that many

patients who failed the random-letter stereoscopic task were able to perform adequately on a conventional test of stereoscopic vision involving defined forms. Thus it seemed evident that the technique devised by Julesz, in which monocular cues are completely excluded, is required to demonstrate the presence of the defect.

The neural correlates of depth perception and stereopsis have recently been investigated by Rizzo (1989; Rizzo and Damasio, 1985). He found that defective stereoacuity was most reliably associated with lesions in superior visual cortices, particularly the association cortices (areas 18 and 19). Although unilateral lesions to either hemisphere produced a reduction of stereoacuity, the most severe impairments were associated with bilateral damage, and unilateral lesions never abolished stereopsis completely. Inferior lesions, below the calcarine fissure, produced the expected impairments in face recognition, color perception, and reading, but were not associated with impaired stereoacuity. Neuropsychological correlates of defective stereopsis included visual disorientation (simultanagnosia), with bilateral superior lesions, and optic ataxia, with more anterior lesions. These latter manifestations, which comprise core elements of Balint's syndrome, may have an important relationship to defects in motion perception, which have been described in a few isolated cases (e.g., Zihl et al., 1983). Other consistent evidence comes from a PET study by Fox et al., (1987), and from neuroanatomical studies (e.g., Livingstone and Hubel, 1987; De Yoe and Van Essen, 1988).

## VISUOCONSTRUCTIVE DISABILITIES

Constructional praxis refers to any type of performance in which parts are put together or articulated to form a single entity or object, for example, assembling blocks to form a design or drawing four lines to form a square or diamond. Thus it implies organizing activity in which the spatial relations among the component parts must be accurately perceived if these parts are to be synthesized into the desired unity. Following the designation of Kleist (1923), the pathological counterpart of constructional praxis, i.e., a specific defect in spatial-organizational performances, usually has been referred to as constructional apraxia. However, as the historical sketch presented earlier in this chapter indicates, Kleist had a specific idea of what he meant by constructional apraxia and did not think that all forms of contructional failure belonged in that category. For this reason, the neutral and more inclusive term visuoconstructive disability is now more often used to refer to failing performances of this type.

Given the very broad definition of the disability as a disturbance in "organizing" or "constructional" activity, it is inevitable that a variety of tasks should have been employed to probe for its presence. The types of tasks that have been used in clinical and investigative work are listed below:

1. Building in the vertical dimension. An illustrative example of some historical interest is shown in Figure 8-2. It appears in Poppelreuter's monograph published in 1917 and is probably the first pictorial representation of defective block construction by a brain-injured patient.

**Fig. 8-2.** Defective vertical block building. (From Poppelreuter, 1917)

2. Building in the horizontal dimension, as in block design and stick constructions (see Critchley, 1953, for illustrative examples).
3. Three-dimensional block construction, either from a block model or a photograph (see Warrington, 1969, and Benton et al., 1983, for illustrative examples).
4. Copying line drawings (see Benton, 1962, for illustrative examples).
5. Drawing to verbal command, e.g., a house or a person (see Critchley, 1953, and Warrington, 1969, for illustrative examples).

In practice, the level of difficulty of each type of task varies widely. With respect to copying, for example, a patient may be required to reproduce a few single figures, a design comprising several figures in a specific spatial relationship, or an extremely complicated figure containing numerous details, such as the Rey and Taylor complex figures (cf. Lezak, 1983, pp. 396–397). In block construction tasks, the actual block model may be presented to the patient (cf. Benton et al., 1983), or the patient may have to proceed on the basis of a reduced schematic representation, as in the WAIS-R block design subtest. The stimulus for a three-dimensional block construction may be either the actual model or a two-dimensional representation of it. Clearly these diverse tasks are not equivalent in their demands on sustained attention, the capacity for deliberation, perceptual acuity, the apprehension of spatial relationships, judgment of perspective, and motor skill. Yet all are considered to be a measure of constructional praxis.

As has been mentioned, Kleist localized the causative lesion of constructional apraxia in the posterior parietal area of the left hemisphere. Subsequent clinical observation supported this localization, in particular, the frequent association of constructional apraxia with other symptoms referable to posterior left-hemisphere disease, such as aphasic disorder, finger agnosia, and right-left disorientation. However, the fact that patients with right-hemisphere disease also showed visuoconstructive disabilities became increasingly evident and, indeed, the indications were that these patients were likely to be more frequently and more severely impaired that those with left-hemisphere lesions.

Systematic studies generally have supported these indications of a hemispheric difference in the direction of the more frequent and more severe constructional disability in patients with right-hemisphere disease (e.g., Piercy et al., 1960; Benton, 1962, 1967, 1968; Benton and Fogel, 1962; Piercy and Smyth, 1962; Arrigoni and De Renzi, 1964; De Renzi and Faglioni, 1967). However, a substantial number of studies have not found important differences between hemispheres (e.g., Warrington et al., 1966; Benson and Barton, 1970; Benton, 1973; Black and Strub, 1976; Colombo et al., 1976). This inconsistency is only to be expected when one considers the several factors that may determine level of performance on constructional tasks; for the most part, these were not controlled in the studies above.

An important factor is the task used to assess constructional ability. Benton (1967) found that impairment in three-dimensional block building and in copying designs was more than twice as frequent in patients with right-hemisphere lesions than in those with left-hemisphere disease; but an approximately equal proportion of patients in the two unilateral groups performed defectively on the WAIS block design subtest. Similarly, Benson and Barton (1970) found differences in the direction of poorer performance by patients with right-hemisphere lesions on a template matching test and the "token-pattern" test of Arrigoni and De Renzi (1964) but not for three other constructional tasks.

Another factor is intrahemispheric locus of lesion, the general (but not invariable) rule being a trend toward poorer performance on the part of patients with posterior lesions. This trend is probably stronger for the left hemisphere, compared to the right. For example, Black and Strub (1976), investigating performance on three constructional tests in patients with prerolandic and retrorolandic unilateral penetrating brain wounds, found significant between-hemispheres differences in the direction of more defective performance by the patients with right-hemisphere wounds on two of the three tests and a nonsignificant difference in the same direction on the third test. However, more impressive differences were shown in anterior-posterior comparisons, the patients with retrorolandic wounds being consistently poorer than those with prerolandic lesions. Moreover, some studies suggest an interactive effect of side and intrahemispheric locus of lesion on performance. In the Black-Strub study, the patients with right retrorolandic lesions consistently performed less well than did the patients in the other three "quadrant" groups. Benson and Barton (1970) noted a tendency for patients with either left retrorolandic or right prerolandic lesions to perform most defectively. However, their groups were very samll, and this may have been a chance finding.

Still another important correlate of performance level is the presence of sensory aphasic disorder. Benton (1973) compared the performances of nonaphasic patients with right-hemisphere desease on a three-dimensional block construction test with the performances of three discrete groups of patients with left-hemisphere disease: (1) nonaphasics, (2) expressive aphasics with no significant receptive language impairment, and (3) aphasics with significant receptive language impairment. The highest frequency of defect (50%) was shown by the aphasic patients with receptive impairment. The right-hemisphere-damaged patients showed a 36% frequency of defect. The other two groups of patients with left-hemisphere disease (nonaphasics or expressive aphasics only) showed a relatively low frequency of defect (13%).

The study by Arena and Gainotti (1978) of the performances of patients with unilateral lesions on a design-copying task generated similar findings. There was no overall difference in the frequency of defective performance (37% in both the right-hemisphere and left-hemisphere groups). However, within the left-hemisphere group, the frequency of defective performance was 57% in the aphasic patients but only 15% in the nonaphasic patients. Moreover, a highly significant correlation of moderate degree ($r = .59$) was found between scores on the Token Test and the constructional praxis test in the aphasic patients.

Still another variable that needs to be considered as a determinant of performance level is the size of the brain lesion. This factor has been invoked to explain between-hemispheric differences in constructional task performance, the argument being that since patients with right-hemisphere disease have more extensive lesions, their performance is generally poorer than that of left-hemisphere-damaged patients. In fact, no empirical evidence has been adduced to support the contention. In the study of Benson and Barton (1970), the size of lesion was estimated by brain scan in 19 of the 25 cases. The left frontal group showed the largest mean (and median) size and the right frontal group the smallest. But the left frontal patients were superior to the other three "quadrant" groups on all the constructional tasks and, as has been noted, there was a tendency for the right frontal patients to perform particularly poorly.

The fact that such a wide diversity of tasks has been utilized and the observation that different tasks appear to interact in different ways with other factors to determine performance level had led some researchers to conclude that the visuoconstructive disability concept is too broad to be optimally useful in clinical or investigative work (cf. Benton, 1967; Benson and Barton, 1970). Instead, a classification in terms of types of constructional tasks differing in their demands on visuoperceptive, motor, and linguistic capacities offers greater promise of relating performance to cerebral function.

An initial distinction might be made between assembling performances (such as block building and stick construction) and graphomotor performances (such as drawing from a model or to verbal command). Dissociation in performance level on the two types of tasks, with a patient failing one and not the other, is often encountered in clinical evaluation, and large-scale studies also provide justification for the distinction. In a study by Dee (1970), a group of 86 patients with unilateral brain disease were given both a three-dimensional block-construction test and a test of copying

designs. Forty-six patients failed one or both tests. Of these 46 patients, 34 (74%) performed defectively on both tests. Thus 26% of the patients performed defectively on
one test but not the other.

The differentiation first made by Duensing (1953) between an "ideational-apractic" form of constructional disability and a "spatioagnostic" form has been utilized
by some theorists to explain the fact that defective performance may be shown by
patients with lesions of either hemisphere. Following Kleist's original formulation, it
is assumed that a perceptuomotor integrative mechanism in the left hemisphere
mediates the motor aspect of constructional activity and that a lesion impairing this
mechanism will disrupt performance even in the absence of visuospatial disability.
On the other hand, impairment in visuospatial abilities resulting from right-hemisphere disease will also be reflected in defective constructional performance as well
as in failure on nonmotor tasks making demands on spatial thinking. If the theory is
correct, defective constructional performance should be more closely related to perceptual impairment in patients with right-hemisphere disease than in those with left-
hemisphere lesions. But empirical tests of this hypothesis have not confirmed it. The
studies of Piercy and Symth (1962), Dee (1970), and Arena and Gainotti (1978) indicate that visuoconstructional disability is closely associated with visuoperceptive
impairment in patients with lesions of either hemisphere.

One or another form of constructional disability is shown by a remarkably high
proportion of patients with brain disease. One study (Benton, 1967) found that in a
sample of 100 patients, the majority of whom had unilateral lesions, 47 showed defective performance on one or more of four constructional tests (copying designs, three-
dimensional block construction, stick construction, WAIS block designs). Twenty-two
patients performed defectively on at least two tests. Of the 35 patients with right-
hemisphere lesions, 54% were defective on at least one test and 29% on two or more
tests. Of the 43 patients with left-hemisphere lesions, 35% were defective on at least
one test but only 12% on two or more tests. The proportions of patients with bilateral
or diffuse disease (bifrontal tumor or degenerative disease) who performed defectively were about the same as in the right-hemisphere group, 55% failing at least one
test and 36% failing two or more. Thus these tests may be diagnostically useful in that
they often disclose disabilities related to brain disease which are only rarely the subject of complaint on the part of patients. Another interesting observation in this context is that such tasks have been shown to be particularly useful in distinguishing
dementia from "pseudodementia" (Jones et al., 1992), especially early in the presentation, when such a distinction can be quite difficult.


## VISUAL IMAGERY


Visual imagery denotes a process whereby information about a particular entity (e.g.,
object, face, color) is retrieved from memory stores, activated in such a manner that
a coherent "mental percept" is generated in the brain, and can subsequently be
inspected and operated on in its own right, i.e., something that is brought into the
"mind's eye." Although probably not of critical importance from a clinical perspective, visual imagery has been a popular subject of cognitive neuroscience research,

and a number of intriguing findings have emerged which have important implications for theories of higher brain function (cf. Kosslyn, 1987, 1988; Damasio, 1989). Several of the major issues in this area are outlined in recent reviews by Farah (1989) and Sergent (1990). Of particular interest are the questions of (1) whether visual imagery is performed by the same neural regions that perform direct visual perception of external stimuli and (2) whether there are consistent hemispheric asymmetries in the neural substrates of visual imagery. Some recent evidence bearing on these issues is reviewed below. It should be noted that in discussing imagery, the qualifiers of *visual* and *mental* are used virtually interchangeably, although strictly speaking, visual imagery is a narrower concept than mental imagery.

Available evidence indicates that visual imagery is mediated by the same neural structures that subserve direct visual perception of external stimuli. The data come from several different investigative techniques, including cerebral blood flow (e.g., Mazziotta et al., 1983; Goldenberg et al., 1987), electroencephalography (EEG) (e.g., Davidson and Schwartz, 1977; Kaufman et al., 1990), event-related potentials (ERP) (e.g., Farah et al., 1989; Biggins et al., 1990), and the lesion method (e.g., Riddoch, 1990; see review by Sergent, 1990). These studies have come to the same fundamental conclusion, namely, that visual imagery is mediated by the visual association cortices comprised by cytoarchitectonic areas 18 and 19 and by the higher-order visual cortices in the occipitotemporal and occipitoparietal junctions. This is precisely the same location known to subserve visual perception, i.e., the same neural units that operate the fundamental visual perceptive capacities such as perception of form, color, motion, and texture (cf. Livingstone and Hubel, 1987). Such findings fit well with the recent proposal by Damasio (1989), which suggests that recall and recognition of visual information are based on activation of pertinent information in sensory association cortices in the posterior regions of the brain (also see Kosslyn, 1988).

As noted above, there is a good consensus regarding the finding that the same neural units that mediate visual perception also subserve visual imagery. However, the issue of whether one or the other cerebral hemisphere is dominant for visual imagery is considerably more controversial. The initial assumption, based on the intuitively reasonable notion that visual imagery is intimately linked to visuospatial operations (e.g., visuospatial judgment, visuoperceptive discrimination) typically associated with right-hemisphere structures, was that the right hemisphere would be dominant for visual imagery (e.g., Springer and Deutsch, 1981). Early evidence (see review by Ehrlichman and Barrett, 1983) for this position was rather equivocal, however, and Farah (1984) took the position that the left hemisphere was actually the dominant side for visual imagery.

Farah's (1984) initial argument was based on a review of 14 cases in which left- (or dominant-) hemisphere lesions were associated with loss of visual imagery. More recent work in her laboratory, including experiments with normal subjects (Farah, 1986), an investigation of a "split brain" patient (Farah et al., 1985; Kosslyn et al., 1985), and an ERP study in normal subjects (Farah et al., 1989), has supported the left-hemisphere hypothesis, as have a couple of case studies in patients with focal lesions (Farah et al., 1988; Riddoch, 1990). Sergent (1989, 1990), however, has been highly critical of this work, and has pointed out a number of crucial methodological difficulties which render much of the "left-hemisphere" evidence noncontributory or uninterpretable. Additionally, some of Farah's key findings (e.g., 1986) have not been replicated by other investigators (see Biggins et al., 1990). Kosslyn (1988), in fact, has pointed out that it is likely that *both* hemispheres contribute to visual imagery, although the nature of the contributions from the left vs. the right side may be quite different. A detailed critical analysis of the principal work in this area is available in Sergent (1990).

## MENTAL ROTATION

Mental rotation refers to the operation of imagining what a stimulus presented at one orientation would look like if it were presented at another orientation. It is essentially a subprocess related to mental imagery, inasmuch as it refers to an operation on a mental image, but it warrants separate discussion since it has been a frequent topic of investigation. The popularity of the topic can be traced to the nature of the phenomenon—in a seminal paper on the issue, Shepard and Metzler (1971) demonstrated that, as mental images have to be transformed through increasing angles of rotation, there is a related increase (approximately linear) in the time it takes subjects to generate responses to the images, such as making same-different judgments. Thus, for example, the reaction time for a stimulus requiring rotation of 90° might be roughly twice that observed for a stimulus requiring rotation of only 45°. Furthermore, it appears that just as a physical object must pass through a full range of intermediate positions in going from one orientation to another, the mental image also appears to "rotate" through the same range of intermediate positions in making the same shift in orientation (Shepard and Cooper, 1982; Shepard, 1984); hence, the mental rotation phenomenon is an example of a strikingly pure nonverbal analogue cognitive process.

Despite the apparent purity of the phenomenon, there has been remarkably little consensus on which neural regions are crucial for the process of mental rotation, particularly with regard to laterality. Intuitively, the process might be expected to depend most intimately on right posterior structures, especially in the parietal and occipitoparietal regions. Early studies, however, did not provide support for the notion that mental rotation is lateralized to the right hemisphere (De Renzi and Faglioni, 1967; Dee, 1970; Meier, 1970; Butters et al., 1970). More recent studies are similarly inconclusive. Several investigators have provided evidence favoring a dominant role by the right hemisphere (Ratcliff, 1979; Jones and Anuza, 1982; Corballis and Sergent, 1988; Deutsch et al., 1988); other have concluded that the left hemisphere is more important (Hatta, 1978; Mehta et al., 1987; Fischer and Pelligrino, 1988); and still others have found no differences between the two hemispheres (Mayes, 1982; Corballis et al., 1985). Many of these conflicting results may be attributable to methodological differences between studies, especially in the nature of the task used to probe mental rotation; additionally, it has been shown that mental rotation is dependent upon overall level of spatial ability and gender (Voyer and Bryden, 1990). One possibility, suggested by Newcombe and Ratcliff (1989), is that mental rotation deficits related to right-hemisphere lesions might be due to defects in operations on a mental image, while impairments related to left-hemisphere lesions might be due to defects in the generation of mental images. This suggestion is consistent with findings by Farah and colleagues (reviewed in Farah, 1989) indicating that the ability to transform mental images is doubly dissociable from the ability to generate images from memory.

## REFERENCES

Arena, R., and Gainotti, G. (1978). Constructional apraxia and visuoperceptive disabilities in relation to laterality of cerebral lesions. *Cortex 14:*463–473.

Assal, G. (1969). Régression des troubles de la reconnaisance des physionomies et de la mémoire topographique chez un malade operé d'un hématome intracérébral droite. *Rev. Neurol. (Paris) 121:*184–185.

Arrigoni, G., and De Renzi, E. (1964). Constructional apraxia and hemispheric locus of lesion. *Cortex 1:*180–197.

Arseni, C., and Botez, M. I. (1958). Consideraciones sobre un caso de agnosia de fisionomias. *Revista Neuropsiquiatria 21:*583–593.

Assal, G., Eisert, H. G., and Hécaen, H. (1969). Analyse des résultats du Farnsworth D15 chez 155 malades atteints de lésions hémisphériques droites ou gauches. *Acta Neurol. Psychiat. Belg. 69:*705–717.

Badal, J. (1888). Contribution à l'étude des cécités psychiques: alexie, agraphie, hémianopsie inférieure, trouble du sens de l'espace. *Arch. Ophtalmol. 8:*97–117.

Balint, R. (1909). Seelenlähmung des "Schauens," optische Ataxie, räumliche Störung der Aufmerksamkeit. *Monatsschr. Psychiatr. Neurol. 25:*51–81.

Bauer, R. M. (1984). Autonomic recognition of names and faces in prosopagnosia: a neuropsychological application of the Guilty Knowledge Test. *Neuropsychologia 22:*457–469.

Bauer, R. M., and Verfaellie, M. (1988). Electrodermal discrimination of familiar but not unfamiliar faces in prosopagnosia. *Brain Cognition 8:*240–252.

Bay, E. (1953). Disturbances of visual perception and their examination. *Brain 76:*515–550.

Bender, M. B., and Feldman, M. (1972). The so-called "visual agnosias." *Brain 9:*173–186.

Benson, D. F., and Barton, M. I. (1970). Disturbances in constructional ability. *Cortex 6:*19–46.

Benson, D. F., Segarra, J., and Albert, M. L. (1974). Visual agnosia-prosopagnosia. *Arch. Neurol. 30:*307–310.

Bentin, S., and Gordon, H. W. (1979). Assessment of cognitive asymmetries in brain damaged and normal subjects: validation of a test battery. *J. Neurol. Neurosurg. Psychiatry 41:*715–723.

Benton, A. L. (1962). The visual retention test as a constructional praxis task. *Confin. Neurol. 22:*141–155.

Benton, A. L. (1967). Constructional apraxia and the minor hemisphere. *Confin. Neurol. 29:*1–16.

Benton, A. L. (1968). Differential behavioral effects in frontal lobe disease. *Neuropsychologia 6:*53–60.

Benton, A. L. (1969). Disorders of spatial orientation. In *Handbook of Clinical Neurology*, Vol. 3, P. J. Vinken and G. W. Bruyn (eds.). Amsterdam: North-Holland.

Benton, A. L. (1973). Visuoconstructive disability in patients with cerebral disease: its relationship to side of lesion and aphasic disorder. *Doc. Ophthalmol. 34:*67–76.

Benton, A. L. (1978). The interplay of experimental and clinical approaches in brain lesion research. In *Recovery from Brain Damage*, S. Finger (ed.). New York: Plenum Press.

Benton, A. L. (1980). The neuropsychology of facial recognition. *Am. Psychol. 35:*176–186.

Benton, A. L. (1982). Spatial thinking in neurological patients: historical aspects. In *Spatial*

*Abilities: Development and Physiological Foundations*, M. Potegal (ed.). New York: Academic Press.

Benton, A. L. (1990). Facial recognition 1990. *Cortex 26*:491–499.

Benton, A. L., Elithorn, A., Fogel, M. L., and Kerr, M. (1963). A perceptual maze test sensitive to brain damage. *J. Neurol. Neurosurg. Psychiatry 26*:540–543.

Benton, A. L., and Fogel, M. L. (1962). Three-dimensional constructional praxis. *Arch. Neurol. 7*:347–354.

Benton, A. L., Hamsher, K., Varney, N. R., and Spreen, O. (1983). *Contributions to Neuropsychological Assessment*. New York: Oxford University Press.

Benton, A. L., Hannay, J., and Varney, N. R. (1975). Visual perception of line direction in patients with unilateral brain disease. *Neurology 25*:907–910.

Benton, A. L., and Hécaen, H. (1970). Stereoscopic vision in patients with unilateral cerebral disease. *Neurology 20*:1084–1088.

Benton, A. L., Levin, H. S., and Van Allen, M. W. (1974). Geographic orientation in patients with unilateral cerebral disease. *Neuropsychologia 12*:183–191.

Benton, A. L., Levin, H. S., and Varney, N. R. (1973). Tactile perception of direction in normal subjects. *Neurology 23*:1248–1250.

Benton, A. L., and Van Allen, M. W. (1968). Impairment in facial recognition in patients with cerebral disease. *Cortex 4*:344–358.

Benton, A. L., and Van Allen, M. W. (1972). Prosopagnosia and facial discrimination. *J. Neurol. Sci. 15*:167–172.

Benton, A. L., Varney, N. R., and Hamsher, K. (1978a). Visuospatial judgment: a clinical test. *Arch. Neurol. 35*:364–367.

Benton, A. L., Varney, N. R., and Hamsher, K. (1978b). Lateral differences in tactile directional perception. *Neuropsychologia 16*:109–114.

Bertoloni, G., Anzola, G. P., Buchtel, H. A., and Rizzolati, G. (1978). Hemispheric differences in the discrimination of the velocity and duration of a simple visual stimulus. *Neuropsychologia 16*:213–220.

Biggins, C. A., Turetsky, B., and Fein, G. (1990). The cerebral laterality of mental image generation in normal subjects. *Psychophysiology 27*:57–67.

Birkmayer, W. (1951). *Hirnverletzungen*. Vienna: Springer-Verlag.

Bisiach, E., and Faglioni, P. (1974). Recognition of random shapes by patients with unilateral lesions as a function of complexity, association value and delay. *Cortex 10*:101–110.

Bisiach, E., Nichelli, P., and Sala, C. (1979). Recognition of random shapes in unilateral brain damaged patients. *Cortex 15*:491–499.

Bisiach, E., Nichelli, P., and Spinnler, H. (1976). Hemispheric functional asymmetry in visual discrimination between univariate stimuli: an analysis of sensitivity and response criterion. *Neuropsychologia 14*:335–342.

Black, F. W., and Strub, R. L. (1976). Constructional apraxia in patients with discrete missile wounds of the brain. *Cortex 12*:212–220.

Bodamer, J. (1947). Die Prosop-agnosie (die Agnosie des physiognomieerkennens). *Arch. Psychiatr. Nervenkr. 179*:6–53.

Bornstein, B. (1965). Prosopagnosia. Proceedings, 8th International Congress of Neurology, 3:157–160.

Brain, W. R. (1941). Visual disorientation with special reference to lesions of the right cerebral hemisphere. *Brain 64*:224–272.

Butters, N., Barton, M., and Brody, B. A. (1970). Role of the right parietal lobe in the mediation of cross-modal associations and reversible operations in space. *Cortex 6*:174–190.

Carmon, A. (1971). Disturbances in tactile sensitivity in patients with cerebral lesions. *Cortex 7*:83–97.

Carmon, A., and Bechtoldt, H. P. (1969). Dominance of the right cerebral hemisphere for stereopsis. *Neuropsychologia* 7:29–39.

Carmon, A., and Benton, A. L. (1969). Tactile perception of direction and number in patients with unilateral cerebral disease. *Neurology* 19:525–532.

Caselli, R. J. (1991). Rediscovering tactile agnosia. *Mayo Clin Proc.* 66:129–142.

Cohn, R., Neumann, M. S., and Wood, D. H. (1977). Prosopagnosia: a clinicopathological study. *Ann. Neurol.* 1:177–182.

Colombo, A., De Renzi, E., and Faglioni, P. (1976). The occurrence of visual neglect in patients with unilateral cerebral disease. *Cortex* 12:221–231.

Corballis, M. C., Macadie, L., and Beale, I. L. (1985). Mental rotation and visual laterality in normal and reading disabled children. *Cortex* 21:225–236.

Corballis, M. C., and Sergent, J. (1988). Imagery in the commissurotomized patient. *Neuropsychologia* 26:13–26.

Corbetta, M., Miezin, F. M., Dobmeyer, S., Shulman, G. L., and Petersen, S. E. (1990). Attentional modulation of neural processing of shape, color, and velocity in humans. *Science* 248:1556–1559.

Corkin, S. (1965). Tactually-guided maze learning in man: effects of unilateral cortical excisions and bilateral hippocampal lesions. *Neuropsychologia* 3:339–351.

Corkin, S. (1979). Hidden figures performance: lasting effects of unilateral penetrating head injury and transient effects of bilateral cingulotomy. *Neuropsychologia* 17:585–605.

Critchley, M. M. (1953). *The Parietal Lobes*. London: Edward Arnold.

Critchley, M. M. (1964). The problem of visual agnosia. *J. Neurol. Sci.* 1:274–290.

Damasio, A. R. (1985). Disorders of complex visual processing: agnosias, achromatopsia, Balint's syndrome, and related difficulties of orientation and construction. In *Principles of Behavioral Neurology*, M.-M. Mesulam (ed.). Philadelphia: F. A. Davis, Co., pp. 259–288.

Damasio, A. R. (1989). Time-locked multiregional retroactivation: a systems-level proposal for the neural substrates of recall and recognition. *Cognition* 33:25–62.

Damasio, A. R., and Damasio, H. (1983). Anatomical basis of pure alexia. *Neurology* 33:1473–1483.

Damasio, A. R., Damasio, H., and Tranel, D. (1990a). Impairments of visual recognition as clues to the processes of categorization and memory. In *Signal and Sense: Local and Global Order in Perceptual Maps*, G. M. Edelman, W. E. Gall, and W. M. Cowan (eds.). New York: Wiley-Liss, pp. 451–473.

Damasio, A. R., Damasio, H., Tranel, D., and Brandt, J. P. (1990c). Neural regionalization of knowledge access: preliminary evidence. *Cold Spring Harbor Symp. Quant. Biol.* 55:1039–1047.

Damasio, A. R., Damasio, H., Tranel, D., and Rizzo, M. (1989b). Effects of selective visual cortex lesions in humans. *Paper presented at the 12th annual meeting of the European Neurological Association and 21st annual meeting of the European Brain and Behaviour Society*, September 1989, Turin, Italy.

Damasio, A. R., Damasio, H., and Van Hoesen, G. W. (1982). Prosopagnosia: anatomic basis and behavioral mechanisms. *Neurology* 32:331–341.

Damasio, A. R., Tranel, D., and Damasio, H. (1989a). Disorders of visual recognition. In *Handbook of Neuropsychology*, Vol. 2, F. Boller and J. Grafman (eds.). Amsterdam: Elsevier, pp. 317–332.

Damasio, A. R., Tranel, D., and Damasio, H. (1990b). Face agnosia and the neural substrates of memory. *Annu. Rev. Neurosci.* 13:89–109.

Damasio, A. R., Yamada, T., Damasio, H., Corbett, J., and McKee, J. (1980). Central achromatopsia: behavioral, anatomic and physiologic aspects. *Neurology* 30:1064–1071.

Danta, G., Hilton, R. C., and O'Boyle, D. J. (1978). Hemisphere function and binocular depth perception. *Brain 101:*569–590.

Davidson, R. J., and Schwartz, G. E. (1977). Brain mechanisms subserving self-generated imagery: electrophysiological specificity and patterning. *Psychophysiology 14:*598–601.

Dee, H. L. (1970). Visuoconstructive and visuoperceptive deficits in patients with unilateral cerebral lesions. *Neuropsychologia 8:*305–314.

De Haan, E.H.F., Young, A. W., and Newcombe, F. (1987). Face recognition without awareness. *Cognitive Neuropsychol. 4:*385–415.

De Renzi, E. (1982). *Disorders of Space Exploration and Cognition.* New York: Wiley.

De Renzi, E. (1986a). Slowly progressive visual agnosia or apraxia without dementia. *Cortex 22:*171–180.

De Renzi, E. (1986b). Current issues on prosopagnosia. In *Aspects of Face Processing,* H. D. Ellis, M. A. Jeeves, F. Newcombe, and A. Young (eds.). Dordrecht: Martinus Wijhoff.

De Renzi, E., and Faglioni, P. (1967). The relationship between visuospatial impairment and constructional apraxia. *Cortex 3:*327–342.

De Renzi, E., Faglioni, P., and Scotti, G. (1970). Hemispheric contribution to exploration of space through the visual tactile modality. *Cortex 6:*191–203.

De Renzi, E., Faglioni, P., Scotti, G., and Spinnler, H. (1972). Impairment of color sorting behavior after hemispheric damage: an experimental study with the Holmgren skein test. *Cortex 8:*147–163.

De Renzi, E., Faglioni, P., and Spinnler, H. (1968). The performance of patients with unilateral brain damage on face recognition tasks. *Cortex 4:*17–34.

De Renzi, E., and Spinnler, H. (1966). Facial recognition in brain-damaged patients. *Neurology 16:*144–152.

De Renzi, E., and Spinnler, H. (1967). Impaired performance on color tasks in patients with hemispheric damage. *Cortex 3:*194–216.

Deutsch, G., Bourbon, W. T., Papanicolaou, A. C., and Eisenberg, H. M. (1988). Visuospatial tasks compared via activation of regional cerebral blood flow. *Neuropsychologia 26:*445–452.

De Yoe, E. A., and Van Essen, D. C. (1988). Concurrent processing streams in monkey visual cortex. *Trends Neurosci. 11:*219–226.

Duensing, F. (1953). Raumagnostische und ideatorisch-apraktische Störung des gestaltenden Handelns. *Dtsch. Z. Nervenheilk. 170:*72–94.

Dunn, T. D. (1895). Double hemiplegia with double hemianopsia and loss of geographic centre. *Trans. Coll. Physicians Phila. 17:*45–56.

Ehrlichman, H., and Barrett, J. (1983). Right hemispheric specialization for mental imagery: a review of the evidence. *Brain Cognition 2:*55–76.

Ellis, H. D., and Young, A. W. (1988). Training in face-processing skills for a child with acquired prosopagnosia. *Dev. Neuropsychol. 4:*283–294.

Ettlinger, G. (1960). The description and interpretation of pictures in cases of brain lesion. *J. Ment. Sci. 106:*1337–1346.

Ettlinger, G. (1990). "Object vision" and "spatial vision": the neuropsychological evidence for the distinction. *Cortex 26:*319–341.

Farah, M. J. (1984). The neurological basis of mental imagery: a componential analysis. *Cognition 18:*245–272.

Farah, M. J. (1986). The laterality of mental image generation: a test with normal subjects. *Neuropsychologia 24:*541–551.

Farah, M. J. (1989). The neuropsychology of mental imagery. In *Handbook of Neuropsychology,* Vol. 2, F. Boller and J. Grafman (eds.). Amsterdam: Elsevier.

Farah, M. J. (1990). *Visual Agnosia.* Cambridge, Mass.: MIT Press.

Farah, M. J., Gazzaniga, M. S., Holtzman, J., and Kosslyn, S. M. (1985). A left hemisphere basis for mental imagery. *Neuropsychologia 23*:115–118.

Farah, M. J., Levine, D. N., and Calvanio, R. (1988). A case study of mental imagery deficit. *Brain Cognition 8*:147–164.

Farah, M. J., Weisberg, L. L., and Monheit, M. (1989). Brain activity underlying mental imagery: event-related potentials during mental image generation. *J. Cognitive Neurosci. 1*:302–316.

Fischer, S. C., and Pellegrino, J. W. (1988). Hemisphere differences for components of mental rotation. *Brain Cognition 7*:1–15.

Foerster, R. (1890). Ueber Rindenblindheit. *Graefes Arch. Ophthalmol. 36*:94–108.

Fogel, M. L. (1967). Picture description and interpretation in brain-damaged patients. *Cortex 3*:433–448.

Fontenot, D. J., and Benton, A. L. (1971). Tactile perception of direction in relation to hemispheric locus of lesion. *Neuropsychologia 9*:83–88.

Fontenot, D. J., and Benton, A. L. (1972). Perception of direction in the right and left visual fields. *Neuropsychologia 10*:447–452.

Fox, P., Petersen, S., Miezin, S., Raichle, M., and Allman, J. (1987). Superior parietal cortical activation during visual and oculomotor tasks measured with averaged PET images. *Invest. Ophthalmol. Vis. Sci. 28 (Suppl)*:315.

Freud, S. (1891). *Zur Auffassung der Aphasien*. Leipzig: Deuticke. (English translation by E. Stengel (1953). New York: International Universities Press.)

Galper, R. E., and Costa, L. (1980). Hemispheric superiority for recognizing faces depends upon how they are learned. *Cortex 16*:21–38.

Geschwind, N. (1962). The anatomy of acquired disorders in reading. In *Reading Disability*, J. Money (ed.). Baltimore: Johns Hopkins Press.

Geschwind, N., and Fusillo, M. (1964). Color-naming defects in association with alexia. *Trans. Am. Neurol. Assoc. 89*:172–176.

Geschwind, N., and Fusillo, M. (1966). Color-naming defects in association with alexia. *Arch. Neurol. 15*:137–146.

Gloning, I., Gloning, K., and Hoff, H. (1968). *Neuropsychological Symptoms and Syndromes in Lesions of the Occipital Lobe and the Adjacent Areas*. Paris: Gauthier-Villars.

Goetzinger, C. P., Dirks, D. D., and Baer, C. J. (1960). Auditory discrimination and visual perception in good and poor readers. *Ann. Otol. Rhinol. Laryngol. 69*:121–136.

Goldenberg, G., Podreka, I., Steiner, M., and Willmes, K. (1987). Patterns of regional cerebral blood flow related to memorizing of high and low imagery words—an emission computer tomography study. *Neuropsychologia 25*:473–486.

Goldstein, K., and Gelb, A. (1918). Psychologische Analysen Hirnpathologischer Fälle auf Grund von Untersuchungen Hirnverletzter. *Z. Ges. Neurol. Psychiatr. 41*:1–142.

Goodglass, H., Wingfield, A., Hyde, M. R., and Theurkauf, J. C. (1986). Category specific dissociations in naming and recognition by aphasic patients. *Cortex 22*:87–102.

Graff-Radford, N. R., Damasio, A. R., Hyman, B. T., Hart, M. N. Tranel, D., Damasio, H., Van Hoesen, G. W., and Rezai, K. (1990). Progressive aphasia in a patient with Pick's disease: a neuropsychological, radiologic, and anatomic study. *Neurology 40*:620–626.

Green, G. J., and Lessell, S. (1977). Acquired cerebral dyschromatopsia. *Arch. Ophthalmol. 95*:121–128.

Greenblatt, S. H. (1973). Alexia without agraphia or hemianopsia. *Brain 96*:307–316.

Hamsher, K. (1978). Stereopsis and unilateral brain disease. *Invest. Ophthalmol. 4*:336–343.

Hamsher, K., Capruso, D. X., and Benton, A. (1992). Visuospatial judgment and right hemisphere disease. *Cortex 28*:493–495.

Hamsher, K., Levin, H. S., and Benton, A. L. (1979). Facial recognition in patients with focal brain lesions. *Arch. Neurol.* 36:837–839.

Hannay, H. J., and Rogers, J. P. (1979). Individual differences and asymmetry effects in memory for unfamiliar faces. *Cortex* 15:257–267.

Hannay, H. J., Varney, N. R., and Benton, A. L. (1976). Visual localization in patients with unilateral brain disease. *J. Neurol. Neurosurg. Psychiatry* 39:307–313.

Hatta, T. (1978). Visual field differences in a mental transformation task. *Neuropsychologia* 16:637–641.

Hécaen, H., and Angelergues, R. (1962). Agnosia for faces (prosopagnosia). *Arch. Neurol.* 7:92–100.

Hécaen, H., and Angelergues, R. (1963). *La Cécité Psychique.* Paris: Masson.

Heidenhain, A. (1927). Beitrag zur Kenntnis der Seelenblindheit. *Montsschrift für Psychiatrie und Neurologie* 66:61–116.

Heilman, K. M., Watson, R. T., and Valenstein, E. (1985). Neglect and related disorders. In *Clinical Neuropsychology*, 2nd ed., K. M. Heilman and E. Valenstein (eds.). New York: Oxford University Press.

Hellstrom, H., Forssell, L. G., and Fernaeus, S. E. (1989). Early stages of late-onset Alzheimer's disease. V. Psychometric evaluation of perceptual-cognitive processes. *Acta Neurol. Scand. Suppl.* 121:87–92.

Hilliard, R. D. (1973). Hemispheric laterality effects on a facial recognition task in normal subjects. *Cortex* 9:246–258.

Holmes, G. (1918). Disturbances of visual orientation. *Br. J. Ophthalmol.* 2:449–486, 506–516.

Holmes, G., and Horrax, G. (1919). Disturbances of spatial orientation and visual attention, with loss of stereoscopic vision. *Arch. Neurol. Psychiatry* 1:385–407.

Howes, D. H. (1962). A quantitative approach to word blindness. In *Reading Disability*, J. Money (ed.). Baltimore: Johns Hopkins Press.

Jackson, J. H. (1876). Case of large cerebral tumour without optic neuritis and with left hemiplegia and imperception. *R. Ophthalmol. Hosp. Rep.* 8:434–444.

Jones, B., and Anuza, T. (1982). Effects of sex, handedness, stimulus and visual field on "mental rotation." *Cortex* 18:501–514.

Jones, R. D., Tranel, D., Benton, A. L., and Paulsen, J. (1992). Differentiating dementia from "pseudodementia" early in the clinical course: utility of neuropsychological tests. *Neuropsychology* 6:13–21.

Julesz, B. (1964). Binocular depth perception without familiarity cues. *Science* 145:356.

Kaufman, L., Schwartz, B., Salustri, C., and Williamson, S. J. (1990). Modulation of spontaneous brain activity during mental imagery. *J. Cognitive Neurosci.* 2:124–132.

Kinsbourne, M., and Warrington, E. (1962). A disorder of simultaneous form perception. *Brain* 85:461–486.

Kinsbourne, M., and Warrington, E. (1963). The localizing significance of limited simultaneous form perception. *Brain* 86:699–702.

Kleist, K. (1923). Kriegsverletzungen des Gehirns in ihrer Bedeutung für die Hirnlokalisation und Hirnpathologie, In *Handbuch der Ärztlichen Erfahrung im Weltkriege, 1914/1918*, Vol. 4, O. von Schjerning (ed.). Leipzig: Barth.

Kosslyn, S. M. (1987). Seeing and imagining in the cerebral hemispheres: a computational approach. *Psychol. Rev.* 94:148–175.

Kosslyn, S. M. (1988). Aspects of a cognitive neuroscience of mental imagery. *Science* 240:1621–1626.

Kosslyn, S., Holtzman, J., Farah, M. J., and Gazzaniga, M. S. (1985). A computational analysis of mental image generation: evidence from functional dissociations in split-brain patients. *J. Exp. Psychol. [Gen.]* 114:311–341.

Landis, T., Cummings, J. L., Benson, D. F., and Palmer, E. P. (1986a). Loss of topographic familiarity: an environmental agnosia. *Arch. Neurol.* 43:132–136.

Landis, T., Cummings, J. L., Christen, L., Bogen, J. E., and Imhof, H. G. (1986b). Are unilateral posterior cerebral lesions sufficient to cause prosopagnosia? *Cortex* 22:243–252.

Landis, T., Regard, M., Bliestle, A., and Kleihuis, P. (1988). Prosopagnosia and agnosia for non-canonical views: an autopsied case. *Brain* 111:1287–1297.

Larrabee, G. J., Levin, H. S., Huff, J., Kay, M. C., and Guinto, F. C. (1985). Visual agnosia contrasted with visual verbal disconnection. *Neuropsychologia* 23:1–12.

Lehmann, D., and Walchi, P. (1975). Depth perception and location of brain lesions. *J. Neurol.* 209:157–164.

Levine, D. N., Warach, J., and Farah, M. J. (1985). Two visual systems in mental imagery. *Neurology* 35:1010–1018.

Lewandowsky, M. (1908). Ueber Abspaltung des Farbensinnes. *Monatsschr. Psychiatr. Neurol.* 23:488–510.

Lezak, M. D. (1983). *Neuropsychological Assessment.* New York: Oxford University Press.

Lhermitte, F., Chain, F., Aron, D., Leblanc, M., and Jouty, O. (1969). Les troubles de la vision des couleurs dans les lésions postérieures du cerveau. *Rev. Neurol. (Paris)* 121:5–29.

Lhermitte, F., Chain, F., Escourolle, R., Ducarne, B., and Pillon, B. (1972). Etude anatomo-clinique d'un cas de prosopagnosie. *Rev. Neurol. (Paris)* 126:329–346.

Lissauer, H. (1890). Ein Fall von Seelenblindheit nebst einem Beitrag zur Theorie derselben. *Arch. Psychiatr. Nervenkr.* 21:22–70.

Livingstone, M. S., and Hubel, D. H. (1987). Psychological evidence for separate channels for the perception of form, color, movement and depth. *J. Neurosci.* 7:3416–3468.

Lovell, K., Gray, E. A., and Oliver, D. E. (1964). A further study of some cognitive and other disabilities in backward readers of average nonverbal reasoning scores. *Br. J. Educ. Psychol.* 34:275–279.

Lueck, C. J., Zeki, S., Friston, K. J., Deiber, M. P., Cope, P., Cunningham, V. J., Lammertsma, A. A., Kennard, C., and Frackowiak, R. S. (1989). The colour centre in the cerebral cortex of man. *Nature* 340:386–389.

Luria, A. R. (1959). Disorders of simultaneous perception in a case of bilateral occipito-parietal brain injury. *Brain* 82:437–449.

Masure, M. C., and Tzavaras, A. (1976). Perception de figures entrecroisées par des sujets atteints de lésions corticales unilatérales. *Neuropsychologia* 14:371–374.

Mayes, J. T. (1982). Hemisphere function and spatial ability: an exploratory study of sex and cultural differences. *Int. J. Psychol.* 17:65–80.

Mazziotta, J. C., Phelps, M. E., and Halgren, E. (1983). Local cerebral glucose metabolic response to audiovisual stimulation and deprivation: studies in human subjects with positron CT. *Hum. Neurobiol.* 2:11–23.

Mazzucchi, A., and Biber, C. (1983). Is prosopagnosia more frequent in males than females? *Cortex* 19:509–516.

McConachie, H. R. (1976). Developmental prosopagnosia. A single case report. *Cortex* 12:76–82.

McFie, J., and Zangwill, O. L. (1960). Visuo-constructive disabilities associated with lesions of the right cerebral hemisphere. *Brain* 82:243–259.

Meadows, J. C. (1974a). The anatomical basis of prosopagnosia. *J. Neurol. Neurosurg. Psychiatry* 37:489–501.

Meadows, J. C. (1974b). Disturbed perception of colors associated with localized cerebral lesions. *Brain* 97:615–632.

Mehta, Z., and Newcombe, F. (1991). A role for the left hemisphere in spatial processing. *Cortex* 27:153–167.

Mehta, Z., Newcombe, F., and Damasio, H. (1987). A left hemisphere contribution to visuo-spatial processing. *Cortex* 23:447–462.

Meier, M. J. (1970). Effects of focal cerebral lesions on contralateral visuomotor adaptation to reversal and inversion of visual feedback. *Neuropsychologia* 8:269–279.

Meier, M. J., and French, L. A. (1965). Lateralized deficits in complex visual discrimination and bilateral transfer of reminiscence following unilateral temporal lobectomy. *Neuropsychologia* 3:261–272.

Meyer, O. (1900). Ein-und doppelseitige homonyme Hemianopsie mit Orientierungsstörungen. *Monatsschr. Psychiatr. Neurol.* 8:440–456.

Michel, F., Perenin, M. T., and Sieroff, E. (1986). Prosopagnosie sans hémianopsie après lésion unilatérale occipito-temporale droite. *Rev. Neurol. (Paris)* 142:545–549.

Miller, L. (1985). Cognitive risk-taking after frontal or temporal lobectomy—I. The synthesis of fragmented visual information. *Neuropsychologia* 23:359–369.

Milner, B. (1962). Laterality effects in audition. In *Interhemispheric Relations and Cerebral Dominance*, V. B. Mountcastle (ed.). Baltimore: Johns Hopkins Press.

Milner, B. (1965). Visually-guided maze learning in man: effects of bilateral hippocampal, bilateral frontal, and unilateral cerebral lesions. *Neuropsychologia* 3:317–338.

Mishkin, M., Ungerleider, L. G., and Macko, K. A. (1983). Object vision and spatial vision: two cortical pathways. *Trends Neurosci.* 6:414–417.

Mooney, C. M. (1957). Closure as affected by configural clarity and contextual consistency. *Can. J. Psychol.* 11:80–88.

Munk, H. (1878). Weitere Mittheilungen zur Physiologie der Grosshirnrinde. *Arch. Anat. Physiol.* 2:161–178.

Nardelli, E., Buonanno, F., Coccia, G., Fiaschi, A., Terzian, H., and Rizzuto, N. (1982). Prosopagnosia: Report of four cases. *Eur. Neurol.* 21:289–297.

Nebes, R. D. (1971). Superiority of the minor hemisphere in commissurotomized man for the perception of part-whole relationships. *Cortex* 7:333–349.

Newcombe, F. (1969). *Missile Wounds of the Brain*. London: Oxford University Press.

Newcombe, F. (1979). The processing of visual information in prosopagnosia and acquired dyslexia: functional versus physiological interpretation. In *Research in Psychology and Medicine*, D. J. Osborne, M. M. Bruneberg, and J. R. Eiser (eds.). London: Academic Press, pp. 315–322.

Newcombe, F., and Ratcliff, G. (1989). Disorders of visuospatial analysis. In *Handbook of Neuropsychology*, Vol. 2, F. Boller and J. Grafman (eds.). Amsterdam: Elsevier.

Newcombe, F., Ratcliff, G., and Damasio, H. (1987). Dissociable visual and spatial impairments following right posterior cerebral lesions: clinical, neuropsychological and anatomical evidence. *Neuropsychologia* 25:149–161.

Newcombe, F., and Russell, W. R. (1969). Dissociated visual perceptual and spatial deficits in focal lesions of the right hemisphere. *J. Neurol. Neurosurg. Psychiatry* 32:73–81.

Nielsen, J. M. (1948). *Agnosia, Apraxia, Aphasia: Their Value in Cerebral Localization*. New York: Paul B. Hoeber.

Orgass, B., Poeck, K., Kerschensteiner, M., and Hartje, W. (1972). Visuocognitive performances in patients with unilateral hemispheric lesions. *Z. Neurol.* 202:177–195.

Paterson, A., and Zangwill, O. L. (1944). Disorders of visual space perception associated with lesions of the right cerebral hemisphere. *Brain* 67:331–358.

Patterson, K., and Bradshaw, J. L. (1975). Differential hemispheric mediation of nonverbal stimuli. *J. Exp. Psychol. [Hum. Percept.]* 1:246–252.

Pavlov, I. P. (1927). *Conditioned Reflexes*. London: Oxford University Press.

Pearlman, A. L., Birch, J., and Meadows, J. C. (1978). Cerebral color blindness: an acquired defect in hue discrimination. *Ann. Neurol.* 5:153–261.

Pevzner, S., Bornstein, B., and Loewenthal, M. (1962). Prosopagnosia. *J. Neurol. Neurosurg. Psychiatry* 25:336–338.

Piercy, M., Hécaen, H., and de Ajuriaguerra, J. (1960). Constructional apraxia associated with cerebral lesions: left and right cases compared. *Brain* 83:225–242.

Piercy, M., and Smyth, V.O.G. (1962). Right hemisphere dominance for certain nonverbal intellectual skills. *Brain* 85:775–790.

Poppelreuter, W. (1917). *Die psychischen Schädigungen durch Kopfschuss im Kriege 1914– 1916: Die Störungen der neideren und höheren Sehleistungen durch Verletzungen des Okzipitalhirns.* Leipzig: Voss.

Quaglino, A., and Borelli, G. (1867). Emiplegia sinistra con amaurosi; guaragione; perdita totale della percezione dei colori e della memoria della configurazione degli oggetti. *G. Oftalmol. Ital.* 10:106–117.

Ratcliff, G. (1979). Spatial thought, mental rotation and the right cerebral hemisphere. *Neuropsychologia* 17:49–54.

Ratcliff, G. (1982). Disturbances of spatial orientation associated with cerebral lesions. In *Spatial Abilities: Development and Physiological Foundations*, M. Potegal (ed.). New York: Academic Press.

Ratcliff, G., and Davies-Jones, G.A.B. (1972). Defective visual localization in focal brain wounds. *Brain* 95:49–60.

Ratcliff, G., and Newcombe, F. (1973). Spatial orientation in man: effects of left, right and bilateral posterior lesions. *J. Neurol. Neurosurg. Psychiatry* 36:448–454.

Reitan, R. M., and Tarshes, E. L. (1959). Differential effects of lateralized brain lesions on the trail making test. *J. Nerv. Ment. Dis.* 129:257–262.

Riddoch, M. J. (1990). Loss of visual imagery: a generation deficit. *Cognitive Neuropsychol.* 7:249–273.

Rizzo, M. (1989). Asteropsis. In *Handbook of Neuropsychology*, Vol. 2, F. Boller and J. Grafman (eds.). Amsterdam: Elsevier.

Rizzo, M., and Damasio, H. (1985). Impairment of stereopsis with focal brain lesions. *Ann. Neurol.* 18:147.

Rizzo, M., and Hurtig, R. (1987). Looking but not seeing: attention, perception and eye movements in simultanagnosia. *Neurology* 37:1642–1648.

Rizzolati, G., Umiltà, C., and Berlucchi, G. (1971). Opposite superiorities of the right and left cerebral hemispheres in discriminative reaction time of physiognomic and alphabetical material. *Brain* 94:431–442.

Robin, D. A., Tranel, D., and Damasio, H. (1990). Auditory perception of temporal and spectral events in patients with focal left and right cerebral lesions. *Brain Lang.* 39:539–555.

Rondot, P., and Tzavaras, A. (1969). La prosopagnosie après vingt années d'études cliniques et neuropsychologiques. *J. Psychol. Norm. Pathol.* 2:133–165.

Rothstein, T. B., and Sacks, J. (1972). Defective stereopsis in lesions of the parietal lobe. *Am. J. Ophthalmol.* 73:281–284.

Russo, M., and Vignolo, L. A. (1967). Visual figure-ground discrimination in patients with unilateral cerebral disease. *Cortex* 3:113–127.

Sachs, H. (1895). Das Gehirn des Förster'schen Rindenblinden. *Arb. Psychiatr. Klin. Breslau* 2:55–104.

Sasanuma, S., and Koboyashi, Y. (1978). Tachistoscopic recognition of line orientation. *Neuropsychologia* 16:239–242.

Schulhoff, C., and Goodglass, H. (1969). Dichotic listening, site of brain injury and cerebral dominance. *Neuropsychologia* 7:149–160.

Scotti, G., and Spinnler, H. (1970). Colour imperception in unilateral hemisphere-damaged patients. *J. Neurol. Neurosurg. Psychiatry* 33:22–28.

Semmes, J., Weinstein, S., Ghent, L., and Teuber, H.-L. (1955). Spatial orientation in man: I. Analyses by locus of lesion. *J. Psychol. 39*:227–244.

Semmes, J., Weinstein, S., Ghent, L., and Teuber, H.-L. (1960). *Somatosensory Changes After Penetrating Brain Wounds in Man*. Cambridge, Mass.: Harvard University Press.

Semmes, J., Weinstein, S., Ghent, L., and Teuber, H.-L. (1963). Correlates of impaired orientation in personal and extrapersonal space. *Brain 86*:742–772.

Sergent, J. (1989). Image generation and processing of generated images in the cerebral hemispheres. *J. Exp. Psychol.[Hum. Percept.] 15*:170–178.

Sergent, J. (1990). The neuropsychology of visual image generation: data, method and theory. *Brain Cognition 13*:98–129.

Sergent, J., and Bindra, D. (1981). Differential hemispheric processing of faces: methodological considerations and reinterpretation. *Psychol. Bull. 89*:541–554.

Sergent, J., and Villemure, J. G. (1989). Prosopagnosia in a right hemispherectomized patient. *Brain 112*:975–995.

Shepard, R. N. (1984). Kinematics of perceiving, imagining, thinking, and dreaming, *Psychol. Rev. 91*:417–447.

Shepard, R. N., and Cooper, L. A. (1982). *Mental Images and Their Transformations*. Cambridge, Mass.: MIT Press.

Shepard, R. N., and Metzler, J. (1971). Mental rotation of three-dimensional objects. *Science 171*:701–703.

Sittig, O. (1921). Störungen im Verhalten gegenuber Farben bei Aphasischen. *Monatsschr. Psychiatr. Neurol. 49*:63–68, 169–187.

Springer, S., and Deutsch, G. (1981). *Left Brain, Right Brain*. San Francisco: Freeman.

St. John, R. C. (1981). Lateral asymmetry in face perception. *Can. J. Psychol. 35*:213–223.

Stafiniak, P., Saykin, A. J., Sperling, M. R., Kester, M. S., Robinson, L. J., O'Connor, M. J., and Gur, R. C. (1990). Acute naming deficits following dominant temporal lobectomy: prediction by age at 1st risk for seizures. *Neurology 40*:1509–1512.

Strauss, H. (1924). Ueber konstruktiv Apraxie. *Monatsschr. Psychiatr. Neurol. 56*:65–124.

Street, R. F. (1931). *A Gestalt Completion Test*. New York: Bureau of Publications, Teachers College.

Taylor, A. M., and Warrington, E. (1973). Visual discrimination in patients with localized brain lesions. *Cortex 9*:82–93.

Teuber, H.-L. (1964). The riddle of frontal lobe function in man. In *The Frontal Granular Cortex and Behavior*, J. M. Warren and K. Akert (eds.). New York: McGraw-Hill.

Teuber, H.-L., and Weinstein, S. (1956). Ability to discover hidden figures after cerebral lesions. *Arch. Neurol. Psychiatr. 76*:369–379.

Torii, H., and Tamai, A. (1985). The problem of prosopagnosia: report of three cases with occlusion of the right posterior cerebral artery. *J. Neurol. (Suppl.)232*:140.

Tranel, D. (1991a). What has been rediscovered in "Rediscovering tactile agnosia"? *Mayo Clin. Proc. 66*:210–214.

Tranel, D. (1991b). Dissociated verbal and nonverbal retrieval and learning following left anterior temporal damage. *Brain Cognition 15*:187–200.

Tranel, D., and Damasio, A. R. (1985). Knowledge without awareness: an autonomic index of facial recognition by prosopagnosics. *Science 228*:1453–1454.

Tranel, D., and Damasio, A. R. (1987). Evidence for covert recognition of faces in a global amnesic patient. *J. Clin. Exp. Neuropsychol. 9*:15.

Tranel, D., and Damasio, A. R. (1988). Nonconscious face recognition in patients with face agnosia. *Behav. Brain Res. 30*:235–249.

Tranel, D., and Damasio, A. R. (1989). Developmental prosopagnosia: a new form of learning and recognition defect. *Soc. Neurosci. Abstr. 15*:303.

Tranel, D., Damasio, A. R., and Damasio, H. (1988). Intact recognition of facial expression, gender, and age in patients with impaired recognition of face identity. *Neurology* 38:690–696.

Tranel, D., Damasio, A. R., and Damasio, H. (1989). Mechanisms of face recognition. *J. Clin. Exp. Neuropsychol.* 11:55.

Tyler, H. R. (1969). Defective stimulus exploration in aphasic patients. *Neurology* 19:105–122.

Tzavaras, A., Hécaen, H., and LeBras, H. (1970). Le problème de la specificité du déficit de la reconnaissance du visage humain lors les lésions hemisphériques unilatérales. *Neuropsychologia* 8:403–416.

Tzavaras, A., Hécaen, H., and LeBras, H. (1971). Troubles de la vision des couleurs après lésions corticales unilatérales. *Rev. Neurol. (Paris)* 124:396–402.

Ungerleider, L. G., and Mishkin, M. (1982). Two cortical visual systems. In *Analysis of Visual Behavior*, D. J. Ingle and M. A. Goodale (eds.). Cambridge, Mass.: MIT Press.

Varney, N. R. (1981). Letter recognition and visual form discrimination in aphasic alexia. *Neuropsychologia* 19:795–800.

Varney, N. R. (1982). Colour association and "colour amnesia" in aphasia. *J. Neurol. Neurosurg. Psychiatry* 45:248–252.

Vaughan, H. G., and Costa, L. D. (1962). Performances of patients with lateralized cerebral lesions. *J. Nerv. Ment. Dis.* 134:237–243.

Voyer, D., and Bryden, M. P. (1990). Gender, level of spatial ability, and lateralization of mental rotation. *Brain Cognition* 13:18–29.

Warrington, E. K. (1969). Constructional apraxia. In *Handbook of Clinical Neurology*, Vol. 4, P. J. Vinken and G. W. Bruyn (eds.). Amsterdam: North-Holland.

Warrington, E. K., and James, M. (1967). An experimental investigation of facial recognition in patients with unilateral cerebral lesions. *Cortex* 3:317–326.

Warrington, E. K., James, M., and Kinsbourne, M. (1966). Drawing disability in relation to laterality of cerebral lesion. *Brain* 89:53–82.

Warrington, E. K., and Rabin, P. (1970). Perceptual matching in patients with cerebral lesions. *Neuropsychologia* 8:475–487.

Wasserstein, J., Zappula, R., Rosen, J., and Gerstman, L. (1984). Evidence for differentiation of right hemisphere visual-perceptual functions. *Brain Cognition* 3:51–56.

Weigl, E. (1964). Some critical remarks concerning the problem of so-called simultanagnosia. *Neuropsychologia* 2:189–207.

Weinstein, S. (1964). Deficits concomitant with aphasia or lesions of either cerebral hemisphere. *Cortex* 1:151–169.

Whiteley, A. M., and Warrington, E. K. (1978). Selective impairment of topographical memory: a single case study. *J. Neurol. Neurosurg. Psychiatry* 41:575–578.

Wilbrand, H. (1887). *Die Seelenblindheit als Herderscheinung und ihre Beziehungen zur homonymen Hemianopsie.* Wiesbaden: Bergmann.

Wilbrand, H. (1892). Ein Fall von Seelenblindheit und Hemianopsie mit Sectionsbefund. *Deutsche Zeitschrift für Nervenheilkunde* 8:395–402.

Wilbrand, H., and Saenger, A. (1906). *Die Neurologie des Auges*, Vol. 3, Wiesbaden: Bergmann.

Wilson, R. S., Kaszniak, A. W., Bacon, L. D., Fox, J. H., and Kelly, M. P. (1982). Facial recognition memory in dementia. *Cortex* 18:329–336.

Wolpert, I. (1924). Die Simultanagnosie: Störung der Gesamtauffassung. *Z. Ges. Neurol. Psychiatr.* 93:397–425.

Wyke, M. (1977). Musical ability: a neuropsychological interpretation. In *Music and the Brain*, M. Critchley and R. A. Henson (eds.). London: William Heinemann.

Wyke, M., and Holgate, D. (1973). Colour-naming defects in dysphasic patients: a qualitative analysis. *Neuropsychologia 1*:457–461.

Young, A. W., and de Haan, E.H.F. (1988). Boundaries of covert recognition in prosopagnosia. *Cognitive Neuropsychol.* 5:317–336.

Young, A. W., and Ellis, H. D. (1989). Childhood prosopagnosia. *Brain Cognition 9*:16–47.

Zihl, J., Von Cramon, Z., and Mai, N. (1983). Selective disturbances of movement vision after bilateral brain damage. *Brain 106*:313–340.

# 9

# Agnosia

RUSSELL M. BAUER

Agnosia is a relatively rare neuropsychological symptom defined in the classical literature as a failure of recognition that cannot be attributed to elementary sensory defects, mental deterioration, attentional disturbances, aphasic misnaming, or unfamiliarity with sensorially presented stimuli (Frederiks, 1969). Agnosia is most often modality specific; the patient who fails to recognize material presented through a particular sensory channel (e.g., vision) is successful when allowed to handle it or to hear its characteristic sound. Visual, auditory, and tactile agnosias have received the most attention, and will be reviewed here.

One of the most fundamental and seemingly intractable questions that has preoccupied researchers in this field concerns whether agnosia is best thought of as a perceptual or a memory impairment. In his classic definition, Teuber (1968) stated that "two limiting sets of conditions: failure of processing and failure of naming . . . bracket . . . the alleged disorder of recognition per se, which would appear in its purest form as a normal percept that has somehow been stripped of its meaning." Teuber's definition is significant since it "locates" the agnosias at the interface between perception and memory and, in fact, seems to imply that "pure" agnosia is a disorder of memory access. In contrast, others have asserted that such a defect does not exist and that all "so-called agnosics" are are either perceptually impaired, or demented, or both (Bay, 1953; Bender and Feldman, 1972). Proponents on either side of this debate assume that perception and memory are intrinsically separable. As we shall see, this assumption, though intuitively plausible, is not without its complications. In fact, the "perception or memory" question may not be the most useful question to ask in the first place.

An early description of agnosia-like phenomena was provided by Munk (1881), who observed that dogs with bilateral occipital lobe excisions neatly avoided obstacles placed in their paths but failed to react appropriately to objects that previously had frightened or attracted them. Similar observations have been made more recently by Horel and Keating (1969, 1972) in the macaque with lesions of the occipital lobe and its temporal projections. Munk felt that his dogs' behavior resulted from a loss of memory images of previous visual experience and termed the condition *Seelenblin-*

*dheit* (mindblindness). Lissauer (1890) was the first to provide a detailed report of a recognition disturbance in man, and his views on different varieties of the disturbance have had an important historical impact on theory and practice. The term agnosia was introduced by Freud (1891), eventually replacing mindblindness and other terms such as asymbolia (Finkelnburg, 1870) and imperception (Jackson, 1876). As with most neurobehavioral syndromes, significant debate has existed regarding the functional mechanisms responsible for agnosic phenomena. However, unlike most other neuropsychological phenomena, a major point of debate has centered on whether agnosia existed at all. Over the years, interpretation of agnosic syndromes has varied according to the zeitgeist prevailing at the time. In the early twentieth century, when Gestalt psychology guided perceptual theory, published cases of agnosia were conceptualized with gestalt concepts in mind (cf. Goldstein and Gelb, 1918; Goldstein, 1943, vs. Poppelreuter, 1923; Brain, 1941). With the reascendency of "disconnection theory" (Geschwind, 1965), cases of agnosia during the 1960s and 1970s were largely viewed as examples of sensory-verbal or sensory-limbic disconnections. In the past decade, with significant advancements in computational neuroscience and an increased componential understanding of visual cognition, clinical data have been reinterpreted in the language of "cognitive neuropsychology." The history of agnosia contains several striking examples of the interplay between cognitive theory and clinical practice, and represents a good example of how scientific advancement is not always linear or cumulative. There has been a recent "revolution" in the field of agnosia as we have moved primarily from an almost exclusive emphasis on disconnection concepts to a more cognitive neuropsychological perspective. Because conceptualizations of agnosia have always been driven by models of normal perception, a brief review of four broad models will be undertaken before discussing the major agnostic syndromes.

## MODELS OF RECOGNITION

### Stage Models

The earliest neuropsychological ideas about the process of object recognition were embodied in "stage models" which held that the cortex first built up a percept from elementary sensory impressions. Recognition was achieved when the resulting percept was "matched" to stored information about the object. The most famous such model was proposed by Lissauer (1890), who argued that recognition proceeds in two stages: apperception and association. By apperception, Lissauer meant the conscious perception of a sensory impression—the piecing together of separate visual attributes into a whole. By association, he meant the imparting of meaning to the content of perception by matching and linking it to a previous experience. A central idea in Lissauer's work is that object or face recognition depends not just upon the integrity of early perceptual processes, but also upon a later, culminating "gnostic" stage in which the visual impressions are combined in such a way as to access an internal representation. Only after such a stage has been reached will conscious recognition occur. The distinction between apperception and association has had profound implications for clinical testing, since Lissauer felt that the patient with a visual defect at the apperceptive level would be unable to match or copy a misidentified object or picture, while the patient with an associative deficit will be able to copy because he perceives "normally."

Although Lissauer's model has been historically important, recent analyses of normal and disordered perception have raised serious questions about its ability to accommodate the clinical data. The apperceptive stage is itself further divisible into a number of constituent visual abilities that can be selectively impaired with appropriately placed lesions (cf: Farah, 1990; Humphreys and Riddoch, 1986; Kaas, 1989). Also, it is becoming increasingly clear that perception is not entirely normal in the vast majority of so-called associative agnosics (Levine, 1978; Levine and Calvanio, 1989; Humphreys and Riddoch, 1987a,b; Bauer and Trobe, 1984). Despite these problems, the apperceptive-associative distinction remains a useful descriptive framework, and will be used to organize the presentation of clinical material in this chapter.

### Disconnection Models

In his classic paper on "disconnection theory," Geschwind (1965) defined agnosia in a different way. In his view, agnosia resulted from a disconnection between visual and verbal processes. Geschwind cited anatomic evidence from the syndrome of visual object agnosia which, in his view, was occasionally seen in the context of left mesial occipital lobe damage. He thought this lesion not only induced a right homonymous hemianopia, but also prevented information perceived by the intact right hemisphere from reaching the naming area due to impingement of crossing fibers. In advancing this hypothesis, Geschwind described several examples of patients who failed to identify objects who later used or interacted normally with the object. In bringing attention to these phenomena, he made explicit what was known implicitly by clinicians who worked with agnosic patients; that recognition is not a unitary phenomenon.

> A fundamental difficulty has been in the acceptance of a special class of defects of "recognition," lying somewhere between defects of "perception" and "naming." What indeed are the criteria for recognition and is it a single function? I believe that there is no single faculty of recognition, but that the term covers the totality of all the associations aroused by any object. Phrased another way, we "manifest" recognition by responding appropriately; to the extent that any appropriate response occurs, we have shown "recognition." But this view abolishes the notion of a unitary step of "recognition"; instead, there are multiple parallel processes of appropriate response to a stimulus. To describe the behavior correctly we must describe the pattern of loss and preservation of responses to each particular type of stimulus.

Although this idea is crucial to an understanding of agnosia, it is now widely recognized that disconnection theory cannot, by itself, account for the fact that most agnosics show abnormal verbal *and nonverbal* processing of viewed objects. Despite this, the major historical impact of this idea was to point out the fact that "recognition" represents the final common path of many separate components. Thus, an answer to the basic question "Did the patient recognize?" depends on what response is required of the patient in a given task situation.

## Computational Models

The models proposed by Lissauer and Geschwind attempt to explain agnosic symptoms in terms that were consistent with available theoretical constructs. An alternative approach is to begin by accounting for normal perceptual phenomena and to then determine whether such an account can explain recognition failures observed in the clinic. This approach begins by specifying the tasks that sensory/perceptual systems must perform in order to achieve the kind of powerful and flexible recognition abilities we as humans possess. We are able to recognize everyday objects and faces with remarkable ease across wide ranges in viewing distance, orientation, and illumination. We are able to "infer" depth, volume, and structure from relatively impoverished two-dimensional stimuli such as photographs and line drawings. We can determine with immediate certainty whether a pictured and real object are the same or different, or whether they would be used together. Thus, from perceptual analysis, we can derive an enormous amount of structural and semantic information about the world around us.

What is required to perform all these remarkable functions? In his attempt to answer this question, Marr (1982) started with the assumption that the brain must store some form of codified, symbolic description (a "representation") of known objects/faces that is sufficiently flexible to accommodate the perceptual variations inherent in everyday recognition tasks. His analysis led him to postulate three types of representations, which he referred to as (1) the primal sketch, (2) the viewer-centered or 2½-D sketch, and (3) the object-centered or 3-D sketch. The primal sketch represents intensity (brightness) changes across the field of vision, resulting in a way of specifying the two-dimensional geometry (shape) of the image. The 2½-D sketch represents the spatial locations of visible surfaces from the point of view of the observer. The essential feature of this type of representation is that it is computed on the basis of the spatial relationship between viewer and object, and thus would be dependent upon viewpoint. This has also been called a "viewer-centered" or "viewpoint-dependent" description. The 3-D sketch specifies the configuration of surfaces, features, and shapes within an object in an object-centered coordinate frame. An object-centered coordinate frame (in which shapes and features are represented in terms of their location on the object) yields a description that is not dependent upon the observer's point of view since, for example, simple rotation would not alter the spatial relationships among features of the object. Because of this, the 3-D representation has also been referred to as an "object-centered" or "viewpoint-independent" description. Presumably, achieving this kind of description is essential to flexible object recognition, though it is obvious that specific objects could be sometimes be recognized using only a 2½-D sketch (see below).

Marr's theoretical position is important for two reasons. First, it serves as a potent reminder that the various tests used to tap the apperceptive and associative stages of object recognition impose different demands on the recognition apparatus. Second,

it provides an a priori conceptual approach to the study of object recognition disturbances. Indeed, we will see that Marr's ideas about multiple object representations
provides a useful framework within which to understand the various ways that recognition can become disordered. Marr's ideas have led to the development of new,
more refined, clinical assessment tools, and have clarified some of the intractable
problems in this area.

A contemporary computational model set in neural terminology has recently been
proposed by Damasio (1989). Like its ancestors in the parallel-distributed processing
framework (Goldman-Rakic, 1988; McClelland and Rumelhart, 1986; Rumelhart
and McClelland, 1986), Damasio's model suggests that perception involves the evocation of a neural activity pattern in primary and first-order association cortex which
corresponds to the various perceptual features extracted from viewed objects. Downstream, these features are combined in so-called "local convergence zones," which
serve to bind together the pattern of features into an "entity" (e.g., object). Damasio
specifically rejects the view that recognition involves the activation of a "packaged,"
locally stored memory representation of the stimulus. Instead, recognition occurs
when the neural pattern defining a specific entity is reactivated in a time-locked fashion (in response to stimulation). The most important feature of Damasio's model is
that *no fundamental distinction between perception and memory is made.* That is,
information about previously encountered items is stored in a pattern of neural activity, not in a localized representation. In this sense, recognition is indeed "recognition." Because the memory-perception distinction is abolished, this kind of model
avoids many of the problems encountered in answering the question, Is agnosia a perceptual or memory deficit? Damasio's model predicts that there can be no disorder
of object recognition without attendant perceptual dysfunction. As we shall see, this
seems entirely consistent with the behavior of most associative agnosics.

### Cognitive Neuropsychological Models

A fourth class of models has recently emerged in the tradition of the cognitive "box
model" approach. These models attempt to outline, in cognitive terms, the functional
components involved in object recognition. Such models have received significant
attention only in the context of visual recognition, and it remains to be seen how easily
they will map on to the processes involved in recognition of heard or felt objects. One
representative model of object recognition, proposed by Ellis and Young (1988) is
depicted in Figure 9-1. In this model, the initial, viewer-centered, and object-centered representations correspond to Marr's three levels of object description. According to Ellis and Young, the process of recognition begins by comparing viewer-centered and object-centered representations to stored structural descriptions of known
objects (so-called "object recognition units" or ORUs). The ORU acts as an interface
between visual representations (which describes what an object looks like) and semantic information (which describes the object's functional properties and attributes).
According to the model, when information in viewer- and object-centered representations adequately matches structural information in some ORU, the ORU becomes
activated. This, in turn, gives rise to a sense of familiarity and unlocks semantic information about the object. Since the ORU receives independent input from viewer- and

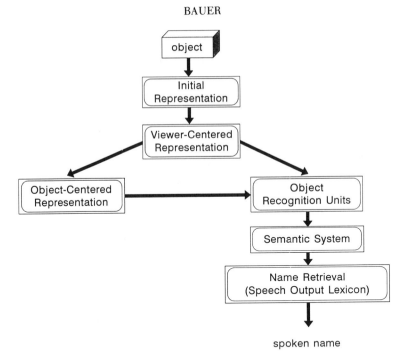

**Fig. 9-1.** A Working Model of Object Recognition. (Adapted from Ellis and Young, 1988)

object-centered representations, it can be activated by either independently if a sufficient match is obtained. Name retrieval occurs in the final stage of the model. Its position at the bottom of the model assumes that the semantic system does not contain a record of the object's name, but can retrieve the name from a separate store or lexicon. There is no direct link between ORU and speech output lexicon; all retrieval of object names occurs via the semantic representation. Deficits prior to the level of the ORU roughly correspond to Lissauer's "apperceptive" agnosics; defects subsequent to this point are more or less "associative."

## CRITERIA OF RECOGNITION

In the literature, three general classes of responses have been used to provide evidence that an object has been recognized. First, the patient's ability to *overtly identify the stimulus* can be assessed. Responses in this category include confrontation naming, pointing, and demonstrating the use of the object in its presence. The second class involves *responses indicative of semantic knowledge about the object*. Tasks eliciting responses of this type include sorting and grouping objects on the basis of functional characteristics. It is obviously important to know whether a patient who has failed a recognition test can group the unrecognized object with other objects with which it is semantically similar. If the patient can do this, some degree of "meaningful" information is being extracted from the stimulus. Third, the presence or absence of *discriminative responses adequate to the stimulus* (e.g., nonverbal, undirected discrimination of the object from others, or spontaneous object use) can be assessed. These three response classes measure different levels of performance in tasks of object recognition, and may be dissociated in specific instances. For example, a patient may "recognize" an object (by emitting a discriminative response to it or by sorting it with other like objects), without being able to identify it.


## CLINICAL PHENOMENA

### Visual Agnosia

The patient with visual agnosia cannot identify visually presented material even though language, memory, and general intellectual functions are preserved at sufficient levels so that their impairment cannot account singly or in combination for the failure to recognize. In the classic cases, the recognition defect is modality specific. Identification is immediate and certain when the patient is presented the stimulus in other sensory modalities.

When the patient fails to name but can indicate visual recognition by verbal description or gesture, the failure is usually considered to be "anomic" in nature. Unlike the agnosic, the anomic generally does not improve when the material is presented through another sensory modality (Goodglass et al., 1968; Spreen et al., 1966), and is less apt to perform normally when asked to produce lists of words in specific categories, to complete open-ended sentences, or to respond to definitions. The conversational speech of the anomic may alert the examiner to the possibility of difficulty on visual confrontation naming because it contains word-finding pauses, circumlocutions, semantic paraphasias, and a general lack of substantives (see Chapter 2). We will later consider a syndrome, called optic aphasia, in which the naming disturbance is disproportionately severe for visually presented objects, and will consider whether this syndrome is agnosic or anomic.

Visual agnosia has been classified in a number of different ways. The most widely known classification is the apperceptive-associative distinction of Lissauer (1890), which is based primarily on the severity of perceptual impairment. Visual agnosia has also been classified according to the specific category of visual material that cannot be recognized. Impairment in the recognition of faces (prosopagnosia), colors (color agnosia), objects (object agnosia), and an agnosic inability to read (agnosic alexia) have been described in isolation and in various combinations (cf. Farah, 1991). The co-occurence of associative visual object agnosia with alexia, color agnosia, and prosopagnosia is common, though not invariant.

Some types of agnosia (e.g., visual object agnosia) involve a defect that prevents the recognition not only of the specific identity of an object, but also of the general semantic class to which it belongs. Other forms of agnosia (e.g., prosopagnosia) are characterized by an ability to recognize the general nature of the object (e.g., a face), but a profound inability to appreciate its individual identity within that class. It remains to be determined whether the distinction between "agnosia for object classes" and "agnosia for specific identities" reflects a feature of brain organization or whether it represents the fact that visual and semantic information play different roles in the recognition of specific classes of objects (see below). It is possible that specific identity discriminations (e.g., "that's my wallet"), are more visually demanding than more general ones (e.g., "a wallet") and that certain classes of objects (e.g., faces) place special demands on sensory/perceptual systems (Damasio et al., 1982; Warrington and Shallice, 1984). We will consider this issue later when we describe some strikingly specific agnosias.

APPERCEPTIVE VISUAL AGNOSIA

The term apperceptive agnosia has been applied to a broad spectrum of patients who have in common some measurable impairment at the perceptual level, but whose elementary sensory functions appear to be relatively intact. Farah (1990) points out that the term has been applied to a heterogeneous range of disabilities from patients whose visual impairments prevent them from negotiating their surroundings (Luria et al., 1963) to those without in vivo impairments in object recognition who fail specialized perceptual tests that require patients to match stimuli across different views (Warrington and Taylor, 1973). The majority of cases have been associated with pathological processes such as carbon monoxide poisoning (Von Hagen, 1941; Adler, 1944; Benson and Greenberg, 1969; Sparr et al., 1991; Milner et al., 1991; Milner and Heywood, 1989; Mendez, 1988), mercury intoxication (Landis et al., 1982), cardiac arrest (Brown, 1972, case II), bilateral strokes (Stauffenburg, 1914), basilar artery occlusion (Caplan, 1980), or bilateral posterior cortical atrophy (Benson et al., 1988; Mendez et al., 1990). The behavior of these patients suggests severe visual difficulties. Many are recovering from a state of cortical blindness. Because of their helplessness in the visual environment, many are considered blind until they report that they can indeed see, but not clearly, or until they are observed avoiding obstacles in their environment. Standard testing then reveals normal or near normal acuity in the spared visual field. Preservation of sufficient field and acuity to allow for recognition distinguishes the apperceptive agnosic from the patient with Anton's syndrome (Anton, 1899), denial of cerebral blindness.

Appreceptive agnosics fail recognition tasks because of defects in perceptual processing. They cannot draw misidentified items or match them to sample. They are generally unable to point to objects named by the examiner. The impairment most often involves elements of the visual environment that require shape and pattern perception (faces, objects, letters). The recognition of even the simplest of line drawings may be impossible. However, bright and highly saturated colors may be better recognized. Some patients can trace outlines of letters, objects, or drawings (Goldstein and Gelb, 1918; Landis et al., 1982), but often retrace them over and over because they lose the starting point. Many patients behave as it they are unaware of, or unconcerned about, their deficit until they are given a visual recognition task. They will then acknowledge that they do not see clearly. Others are aware of their difficulty but try to conceal it.

Many patients complain that their visual environment changes or disappears as they try to scrutinize it. Recognition may improve when visual stimuli are moved (Botez, 1975). Patients may claim they need new glasses, or may complain about poor lighting or the fact that they have not had much prior experience with the particular kind of visual material that they are being asked to identify. One of our patients, a retired architect, condescendingly remarked about the poor quality of our line-drawn stimuli. It has always been difficult to characterize the visual performance of these patients because of large inter- and intraindividual variability. Cognizant of this variability, Farah (1990) attempted to bring order out of chaos by subdividing apperceptive agnosics into the following four behaviorally meaningful categories.

*Narrow apperceptive agnosia.* Representative cases in the category of narrow apperceptive agnosia include patients reported by Adler (1944), Alexander and Albert (1983), Benson and Greenberg (1969), Campion and Latto (1985), Goldstein and Gelb (1918), Landis et al. (1982), and Milner et al. (1991). These patients all have "seemingly adequate" elementary visual function (acuity, visual fields, luminance detection, color vision, depth and movement perception) but display a striking inability to recognize, match, copy, or discriminate simple visual forms. Benson and Greenberg's patient is a case in point.

The patient was a 25-year-old victim of accidental carbon monoxide poisoning. For several months he was thought to be blind and yet was seen one day navigating the corridor in his wheelchair. He could name colors and could often follow moving visual stimuli, but yet could not identify by vision alone objects placed before him. He could occasionally identify the letters "x" and "o" if allowed to see them drawn or if they were moved slowly before his eyes. Visual acuity was at least 20/100 measured by his ability to indicate the orientation of the letter "E," to detect the movement of small objects at standard distances and to reach for fine threads on a piece of paper. Optokinetic nystagmus was elicited bilaterally with fine ⅛" marks on a tape. Visual fields were normal to 3 mm. wide objects with minimal inferior constriction bilaterally to 3 mm. red and green objects. There was an impersistence of gaze with quasi-random searching movements particularly when inspecting an object. His recognition deficit included objects, photographs, body parts, letters, and numbers, but not colors. He could tell which of two objects was larger and could detect very small movements of small targets. He easily identified and named objects tactually and auditorily. He guessed at the names of objects utilizing color, size, and reflectance cues. He was totally unable to match or copy material which he could not identify. However, he was taught to apply a name to each object in a small group of objects which were presented to him one at a time on a piece of white paper. For instance, after he was repeatedly shown the back of a red and white playing card and informed of its identity, he was able on later exposures to identify it. He was thus able to use color and size cues to learn and remember the names of various objects in a closed set. However, when these objects were placed out of context, he was no longer able to name them. His recent and remote memory, spontaneous speech, comprehension of spoken language, and repetition were intact. On psychophysical testing he was able to distinguish small differences in the luminance (0.1 log unit) and wavelength (7–10 microns) of a test aperture subtending a visual angle of approximately 2 degrees, but was unable to distinguish between two objects of the same luminance, wavelength, and area when the only difference between them was shape. The deficit in this patient, therefore, was a low 'specificity' for the attribute of shape while the specificity for the awareness of other stimulus attributes was retained (Efron, 1968). Benson and Greenberg (1969) referred to the patient's defect as a "visual form agnosia."

Many of these patients develop compensatory strategies such as tracing of the outline of stimuli or executing small head movements as they explore their visual environment, perhaps as an attempt to use movement cues to aid form detection. The patient reported by Landis et al. (1982) developed an apperceptive visual agnosia secondary to mercury intoxication and presented with a clinical picture similar to that of the famous patient *Schn.* (Goldstein and Gelb, 1918). The patient developed a strategy whereby he would trace letters, parts of letters, or words with the left hand alone or with both hands. He could trace simple geometric figures if the point of departure for tracing was unimportant. With more complex figures he was misled by unimportant lines. He developed a sophisticated system of codes which aided in the identification of individual letters. Goldstein and Gelb's (1918) patient *Schn.* also developed a tracing strategy by using both his head and hand. Both patients' recognition abilities deteriorated instantly if they were prevented from using kinesthetic feedback.

*Dorsal simultanagnosia.* The term simultanagnosia was introduced by Wolpert (1924) to refer to a condition in which the patient is unable to appreciate the meaning of a whole picture or scene even though the individual parts are "well recognized." Luria (1959) used the term literally to indicate the inability to see or attend to more than one object at a time. Luria's use of the term has more generality since it is debatable, even in mildly impaired cases, whether the parts are recognized normally. Representative cases have been reported by Coslett and Saffran 1991, Hécaen and Ajuriaguerra (1954), Holmes (1918), Holmes and Horrax (1919), Luria (1959), Luria et al. (1963), and Tyler (1968). Most of these patients sustained bilateral parieto-occipital damage, though cases with superior occipital (Rizzo and Hurtig, 1987) or inferior parietal damage (Kase et al., 1977, case 1) have been reported.

As a result of their visual defect, these patients are impaired in counting tasks (Holmes, 1918) and on tasks that require the naming of a number of objects presented together (Luria et al., 1963). The disorder may also be evident in a dramatic inability to interpret the overall meaning of a line drawing or picture, with performance on such tasks being a haphazard, inferred reconstruction of fragmented picture elements. Based on the study of such patients, Luria (1959; Luria et al., 1963) concluded that simultanagnosia represents a complex perceptuomotor breakdown of the active, serial, feature-by-feature analysis necessary for processing elements of a visual scene or pattern. In the most severe cases, prominent features available in the stimulus array may themselves be fragmented and distorted.

Luria equates simultanagnosia with a perceptual defect often found as part of Balint's syndrome (Balint, 1909; Husain and Stein, 1988), which consists of (1) psychic paralysis of fixation with an inability to voluntarily look into the peripheral field (cf. Tyler, 1968; Karpov et al., 1979), (2) optic ataxia, manifested by clumsiness or inability to manually respond to visual stimuli, with mislocation in space when pointing to visual targets (cf. Boller et al., 1975; Damasio and Benton, 1979; Haaxma and Kuypers, 1975; Holmes, 1918; Levine et al., 1978), and (3) a disturbance of visual attention mainly affecting the periphery of the visual field and resulting in a dynamic concentric narrowing of the affective field (cf. De Renzi, 1982; Levine and Calvanio, 1978; Hécaen and Ajuriaguerra, 1954). Balint's syndrome is almost invariably asso-

ciated with large biparietal lesions (but see Watson and Rapcsak, 1987) and is especially severe when frontal lobe lesions are also found (Hécaen and Ajuriaguerra,
1954). Frontal lobe involvement may lead to particularly severe psychic paralysis and
optic ataxia, presumably because of disrumption in visual-motor mechanisms mediated by frontal eye fields and surrounding prefrontal cortex in the control of saccadic
eye movements and visual attention (Lynch and McClaren, 1989).

Visual fields may be normal by standard perimetric testing but shrink to "shaft
vision" when the patient concentrates on the visual environment. Performance may
be worse in one hemifield, more often on the left. A striking example of narrowing
of the "effective visual field" is given by Hécaen and Ajuriaguerra (1954; case 1).
While their patient's attention was focused on the tip of a cigarette held between his
lips, he failed to see a match flame offered him and held several inches away. A good
example of this type of deficit is presented by Tyler (1968), whose patient suddenly
developed visual difficulties after segmental basal artery occlusion:

> Visual acuity was 20/30 with glasses. Visual fields were at first considered normal,
> but careful retesting showed that while the left field was normal to movement of large
> objects, these objects faded from awareness in one or two seconds. With continued
> testing within that field, awareness of even the movement of large objects was lost. In
> the right visual field, the central two degrees around fixation were always normal, the
> surrounding outer 20 degrees fatigued rapidly, and beyond 20 degrees, movement
> was recognized but objects faded rapidly. The patient could see only one object or
> part of one object at a time with her central two to four degrees of vision. She scanned
> normally when looking a predictable objects such as a circle or a square but fre-
> quently lost her place when viewing objects and pictures. Slight movement of the
> page made her lose her place. She reported seeing bits and fragments. For instance,
> when shown a picture of a flag, she said, "I see a lot of lines, now I see some stars."
> When shown a dollar bill, she saw a picture of George Washington. Moments later
> when shown a cup, she said, "A cup with a picture of Washington on it." Eye move-
> ment studies revealed a normal number of visual fixations per unit of time and a nor-
> mal pattern of fixation for small saccades or so-called visual steps. However, there
> were very few, if any, so called long saccades or leaps that relate one part of the pic-
> ture to another.

The three subjects described by Rizzo and Hurtig (1987) reported intermittent disappearance of a light target during electrooculographically (EOG) verified fixation.
Rizzo and Hurtig argue that a disorder of attentional mechanisms that permit sustained awareness of visual targets is involved. Verfaellie et al. (1990), using Posner's
attentional cuing task, found that their Balint's patient had difficulty shifting attention to the left or right visual field, and benefited only from cues directing attention
to the upper visual field. This patient also demonstrated a loss of spontaneous blinking, which may normally participate in a complex system mediating saccadic eye
movement, sensory relay, and attentional deployment (Watson and Rapcsak, 1987;
Gottlieb et al., 1991).

*Ventral simultanagnosia.* A second group of simultanagnosics appears to have
lesions restricted to the left occipitotemporal junction. The primary feature that dis-

tinguishes these patients from "dorsal" simultanagnosics is that they succeed on dot-counting tasks and seem less impaired in negotiating their natural environment. Whether the disorder is one of degree or kind is debatable, though the anatomic pathology of this group is clearly distinct from dorsal simultanagnosia. The patients of Kinsbourne and Warrington (1962), Levine and Calvanio (1978), and Warrington and Rabin (1971), all presenting as letter-by-letter readers, are representative cases.

Kinsbourne and Warrington (1962) described a defect in "simultaneous form perception" which they believed accounted for the reading disturbance in these patients (cf. Levine and Calvanio, 1978; Warrington and Shallice, 1980). Levine and Calvanio (1978) found that patients with simultanagnosia would report only one or two letters when presented with three letters simultaneously. If told in advance which letter to name, they successfully reported any single letter; if told after the exposure which letter to name, they performed poorly. The authors interpreted the defect as an impairment in the perceptual analysis of compound visual arrays. Patients with this form of simulatnagnosia thus do not perceive more than one object at a time. Their problem is compounded by an inability to relate small portions of what they see to the remainder of the stimulus by scanning. Slowing of information processing plays an important, but as yet undetermined role in these defects.

*Perceptual categorization deficit.* Included in the category of perceptual categorization defect are patients who do not have deficits in the "real-life" recognition of objects but whose defect must be elicited experimentally. These patients, most of whom have unilateral posterior right-hemisphere lesions, have difficulties matching two- or three-dimensional objects across different views. Such cases have been reported by De Renzi et al. (1969), Warrington and Taylor (1973), and Warrington and James (1988). Because they may recognize real-life objects, these patients are usually not considered agnosic, but are included in Farah's (1990) classification system because they have a special kind of perceptual defect. In Marr's (1982) terms, these patients fail to achieve a viewpoint-independent description of objects, and thus are impaired whenever an object identification or matching task requires them to match stimuli across views or to recognize a stimulus presented from a highly unconventional or "noncanonical" viewpoint.

Most of the controversy regarding the existence of agnosia has involved the apperceptive types. Given Teuber's classic definition of agnosia as a "normal percept stripped of its meaning," it is reasonable to question whether these patients qualify as agnosic. According to Bay (1953), there exists neither a specific gnostic function nor a specific disorder of gnosis, agnosia. For Bay, apparent cases of agnosia are actually disorders of primary sensory function due to lesions of the primary sensory fields or their connections, and the occasional presence of a generalized dementing process further complicates the interpretation of faulty primary sensory data. Bay reported abnormalities in sensation time (the minimal exposure time sufficient for recognition of portions of the visual field) and local adaptation time (the elapsed time for a visual stimulus to fade from portions of the field) in patients with otherwise normal visual acuity and field. In these patients, visual stimuli tend to drop out of awareness because of abnormal fatiguability, particularly at the periphery (so-called *Funktionswandel*).

Bay applied his tests to a patient with visual agnosia and, finding an abnormality of *Funktionswandel,* attributed the recognition deficit to primary visual sensory impairment.

Similarly, Bender and Feldman (1972) claimed that visual agnosia represented nothing more than a complex interaction between primary visual sensory abnormalities, various degrees of inattention, ocular fixation disturbance, and dementia. In their view, previously reported cases of visual agnosia were insufficently examined. In a retrospective review of agnosia cases, they found perceptuomotor defects and dementia were found in all instances, leading them to conclude that "visual agnosia is a result of a disorder of the total cerebral activity which renders performance of vision and/or other sensory functions inadequate." This kind of argument, of course, begs the question of just how "adequate" vision has to be to for object recognition to occur.

Despite their persistence, these criticisms are weakened by the fact that severe sensory abnormalities in the context of visual-field defects, perceptual derangement, and dementia do not necessarily lead to defects in object recognition (Ettlinger, 1956). The converse also seems true; one of Ettlinger's patients, a prosopagnosic, performed at a higher level on visuosensory tests than did most of the nonagnosic patients. Studies by Levine and Calvanio (1978) suggest that patients with agnosia do not differ from normals in sensation time or susceptibility to "backward masking." It is evident, therefore, that visual sensory abnormalities as measured by tests of sensation time and local adaptation time are not, even in the presence of dementia, sufficient in themselves to produce an agnosia-like recognition defect. It is true, however, that many patients with visual agnosia have elements of this type of disturbance and many also have abnormalities in visual attention, search, and exploration. It seems likely that such defects represent a continuum on which impairment is a necessary, but not sufficient, characteristic of agnosia.

Though each of the four types of apperceptive agnosia has a relatively consistent lesion profile, it would be impossible with our present level of knowledge to fully specify the functional anatomy underlying the various forms of visual apperceptive agnosia. It is clear that there is no singular entity called "apperceptive visual agnosia." Behaviorally, these patients differ along attentional, perceptual, oculomotor, and mnemonic dimensions; the relative contribution of each of these factors remains to be fully elucidated. However, it seems reasonable on clinical and experimental grounds to conclude that complex visual abilities are made up of dissociable ("modular") information processing streams, including form discrimination, color perception, luminance, size, movement, and spatial localization and integration (Berkley and Sprague, 1979; Sprague et al., 1977; Perenin and Jeannerod, 1978; Maunsell and Newsome, 1987; DeYoe and Van Essen, 1988) and that the variability among apperceptive agnosics reflects the fact that in individual cases these streams can be impaired singly or in combination.

ASSOCIATIVE VISUAL AGNOSIA

The major distinguishing feature of associative visual agnosia is the presence of a modality-specific object identification defect in the context of a preserved ability to copy and/or match stimuli presented in the affected modality. Preserved copying or matching has often been taken as evidence of "normal" perception, an assumption that has been called into question by recent evidence (see below). Despite this, it is clear that the perceptual disturbance in this class of patients is different in degree and kind from that seen in apperceptive agnosia. A number of well-documented cases meeting the above criteria have appeared in the literature, leaving no doubt about the existence of this form of agnosia (Albert et al., 1975a; 1979; Benson et al., 1974; Davidoff and Wilson, 1985; Hécaen et al., 1974: Levine and Calvanio, 1989; Lhermitte et al., 1973; Mack and Boller, 1977; McCarthy and Warrington, 1986; Newcombe and Ratcliff, 1974; Pillon et al., 1981; Riddoch and Humphreys, 1987; Rubens and Benson, 1971; Taylor and Warrington, 1971).

Pointing to objects named by the examiner, while characteristically impaired, may be better than identifying objects verbally or by gesture. This may reflect the fact that pointing takes place in the context of a closed set, while naming an object involves an almost infinite list of potential names. It is also possible that pointing to a named object is an easier task because it does not involve speaking and therefore reduces the chances that an incorrect verbal response will adversely affect nonverbal aspects of stimulus recognition. In many patients, picture identification is more impaired than is the identification of real objects, and identification of line drawings is more impaired than either of these. A disturbance in the identification of line drawings or pictures may be the only residual defect after the acute disturbance has cleared. This dissociation is not seen in the naming performance of aphasics (Corlew and Nation, 1975; Hatfield and Howard, 1977), and may serve as a marker for the presence of agnosia in naming tasks.

Impairment of recognition of faces (prosopagnosia), color (so-called "color agnosia"), and written material (alexia) is frequently but not invariably found with associative object agnosia. Object agnosia itself is more rare than these other conditions, each of which may occur in isolation or in various combinations. The agnosic patients of Hécaen and Ajuriaguerra (1956), Lhermitte and Beauvois (1973), and Rubens et al. (1978, cited in Rubens, 1979) had no impairment in facial recognition, and reading was spared in the patients of Davidenkov (1956), Newcombe and Ratcliff (1974), Mack and Boller (1977), and Albert et al. (1975a). Levine's patient and case 1 of Newcombe and Ratcliff had no color agnosia or alexia. Alexia is commonly found alone or with color agnosia (cf. Geschwind and Fusillo, 1966); prosopagnosia is sometimes an isolated recognition disturbance (De Renzi, 1986b), but is often associated with achromatopsia (Critchley, 1965, Pallis, 1955). Much debate has centered around the coexistence of these various signs. Some authors believe that symptom co-occurrence is a "neighborhood sign," while others believe it reflects the fact that certain classes of objects (e.g., objects and faces) overlap in their visual processing demands. Sergent et al. (1992) have provided evidence from a position emission tomography (PET) study in normals that object recognition activated the left temporal region while face identification tasks resulted in bilateral activation of extrastriate cortex and fusiform gyrus with additional activation of the right parahippocampal gyrus and adjacent areas. These data suggest that object and face recognition depend on different anatomic structures and may favor the "neighborhood" view since these regions may all be involved in large, bilateral vascular accidents of the posterior cortex.

Tactile and auditory recognition are typically intact, although two patients of Newcombe and Ratcliff and the patients of Taylor and Warrington (1971) and Feinberg et al. (1986) were unable to identify objects by touch or vision.

The associative agnosic not only cannot identify seen objects, but also typically fails when asked to demonstrate semantic knowledge about the stimulus or its functional properties. The failure to sort objects and pictures into categories (e.g., articles of clothing, tools, etc.) or to match two different representations of the same object (a small line drawing of a wrist watch with a real watch) are typical examples. Some agnosics can classify objects according to their "basic level" (Rosch et al., 1976) category (e.g., prosopagnosics always identify faces as faces) but are unable to identify the object at a more specific, individual level. Others can identify neither the general class nor the individual-within-class. Such differences may signal important differences between agnosic syndromes or may more simply reflect the fact that different recognition tasks demand different levels of specificity. For example, "a key" is often an adequate answer in an object recognition paradigm, while face recognition tasks require the subject to ascertain individual identity.

The role played by perceptual factors has received significant recent attention in analyses of associative agnosia. On the one hand, these patients are capable of remarkable visual achievements given the severity of their object recognition disturbances. The patients of Rubens and Benson, Taylor and Warrington, and Newcombe and Ratcliff (case 1) matched to sample and produced strikingly accurate drawings of pictures and objects they could not identify (Fig. 9-2). The patients of Rubens and Benson and Taylor and Warrington were able to find hidden figures in figure-ground tests. Case 1 of Newcombe and Ratcliff showed no deficits on psychophysical tests of visual function.

On the other hand, two lines of evidence have made it clear that perceptual abilities are not normal in the vast majority of these patients and that such abnormalities may play a causative role in at least some aspects of the recognition disorder. First, though these patients may be capable of earning normal scores on tests of copying and matching, qualitative data suggest remarkably consistent evidence of slow, feature-by-feature, or "slavish" drawing and of a reliance on local detail at the expense of the more global aspects of the stimulus (Farah, 1990; Humphreys and Riddoch, 1987a; Levine, 1978; Levine and Calvanio, 1989). For example, Humphreys and Riddoch (1987a) provide an exquisitely detailed report of a patient H.J.A., who took six hours to complete remarkably accurate drawings of objects he could not identify. Our own experience with the prosopagnosic patient L.F. reveals that performance on difficult facial matching tests (e.g., Benton Test of Facial Recognition), though quantitatively normal, proceeds in a feature-by-feature manner resulting in extremely prolonger examination times. Second, tasks that systematically vary perceptual variables have shown that such factors significantly affect the "recognizability" of stimuli (Levine and Calvanio, 1978, 1989; Riddoch and Humphreys, 1987). Stimulus complexity (e.g., presence of color, morphological similarity between items) appears to exert a strong effect on the frequency of semantic and morphological errors on object naming tasks. Presence of fine-grained visual information as well as the presence in the stimulus of "compound" (multiple) information both appear to contribute to ease of identification (see Levine and Calvanio, 1978). A frequently reported finding is that associative

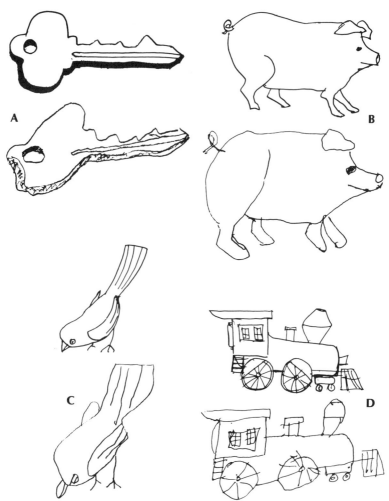

**Fig. 9-2.** Copies of line drawings by patient with associative visual agnosia. After copies were made, the patient still misidentified drawings as follows: **A:** "I still don't know." **B:** "Could be a dog or any other animal." **C:** "Could be a beach stump." **D:** "A wagon or a car of some kind. The larger vehicle is being pulled by the smaller one." (From Rubens and Benson, 1971.)

agnosics appear deficient in "gestalt perception," though they may perceive local details relatively normally. Partially covering an item or placing it in unusual context hinders identification. Levine and Calvanio (1989) reported that their associative agnosic, L.H., was severely impaired on tasks of "visual closure," the ability to perceive shape, and identity of an object that has been degraded by visual noise (cf. also Farah, 1990). H.J.A., the patient reported by Humphreys and Riddoch (1987a), (cf. also Riddoch and Humphreys, 1987a) performed poorly on a feature integration task requiring him to detect an upside-down "T" among a group of upright "T"'s. Unlike normals, H.J.A. did not show faster detection when the stimuli were arranged in a discrete circular configuration (as opposed to random presentation), suggesting a defect in integrating local feature details into an overall 'gestalt." These findings illustrate why there is growing discontent with the apperceptive-associative distinction, at least in its "strong" form. They also illustrate why parallel-distributed models of object recognition which posit no fundamental distinction between perception and memory/association (cf. Damasio, 1989; Goldman-Rakic, 1988) deserve at least a second look by neuropsychologists and behavioral neurologists interested in agnosic phenomena.

The cases of Kertesz (1979) and Wapner et al. (1978) further complicate the apperceptive-associative distinction. Kertesz's patient presents a challenge since she had elements of Balint's syndrome, visual static agnosia (Botez, 1975; Botez and Serbanescu, 1967), simultanagnosia, alexia without agraphia, prosopagnosia, and amnestic syndrome. The patient performed poorly on copying tasks (her reproductions were poorly executed and contained only fragmented elements of the associated target stimuli), but matched real objects, line drawings, colors, letters, and geometric figures better than she named or pointed to them. Verbal responses were marked by perseverations and form confusions. The patient had 20/20 acuity (open E method) and a spiraling visual-field defect. CT scan revealed right frontal and deep left occipital lobe lesions.

Wapner et al. (1978) presented a case report of visual agnosia in an artist in whom drawing skills were specifically assessed. Their patient suffered a CVA with resulting right hemianopia, visual recognition defect, and amnestic syndrome. Brain scan revealed bilateral medial occipital infarctions. Visual acuity was 20/70, and again there was a variable visual-field defect. The patient showed poor visual recognition of objects and drawings in the context of moderately impaired design copying. Interestingly, the patient showed a striking dissociation in qualitative drawing performance between objects he could and could not recognize. With unrecognized objects, his drawings revealed piecemeal, slavish reproduction of recognized elements. Describing his drawing of a telephone dial, he said, "a circle, another circle, a square . . . things keep coming out . . . and this is as though it hooks into something." In contrast, when drawing an object he could identify, the patient relied on preserved structural knowledge of the essential components of the object, producing a sketch that was faithful to the specific target as well as to the general class of objects to which the target belonged. He remarked, "can't help but use your natural knowledge in drawing the thing." These two cases are important for two reasons. First, they both showed *dissociations* among various tests classically used to tap the "apperceptive" level. Second, their combined defects at the levels of "perception" and "recognition" underscore the fact that agnosia is the final outcome of any different defects, and again illustrate that the apperceptive-associative distinction should be viewed as a heuristic and perhaps nothing more.

In addition to the contribution of perceptual factors, there is much evidence that the initial verbalized response to visual presentation can adversely affect recognition ability in at least some of these patients. Identification errors are usually morphological confusions or perseverations, though semantic errors are not uncommon. The tendency to perseverate previous naming errors and the disruptive influence of visual naming on tactile identification are examples of this. One might expect that a visual agnosic patient with normal blindfolded tactile naming would perform at least as well when he simultaneously inspects and handles an object. However, the otherwise superior tactile identification of the patients of Ettlinger and Wyke (1961) and Rubens et al. (1978, cited in Rubens, 1979) fell to the much lower level of visual identification alone when the patients were allowed to simultaneously view and handle the objects. Ettlinger and Wyke's patient, when given two exposures of each of 21 items, made 26 errors with vision alone, only 9 with touch alone, but 16 with vision and touch.

Preventing the contaminating effect of verbal responses is not always easy. Many patients insist on speaking despite strict instructions to remain silent. Case 1 of Oxbury et al. (1969), who was specifically instructed to demonstrate in silence the use of objects shown to her, continued to name them aloud and then to produce an incorrect gesture that corresponded to her verbal misidentification. This same patient, when asked to match a line drawing to one of three real objects, would misname the drawing and then search vainly for an object corresponding to her incorrect name. It has been claimed that perseverations represent verbal reports of a lingering visual sensory experience of previously viewed material (Critchley, 1964; Cummings et al., 1982). However, when patients are asked to draw an object on which such perseverative errors occur, they draw the item they are viewing, not the item whose name has been perseverated (Lhermitte and Beauvois, 1973; Rubens and Benson, 1971; Rubens et al., 1978, cited in Rubens, 1979). Successfully copying a misidentified picture generally does not facilitate identification of that picture. This suggests that the motor system generally does not have the ability to cue the visual identification process in most patients, though requiring the patient to write the name (Lhermitte and Beauvois, 1973) or to supply a description (Newcombe and Ratcliff, 1974) instead of naming aloud normalized "recognition" in one case and enhanced it in the other.

The most common visual field defect in associative agnosia is a dense, right homonymous hemianopia. In the patient of Albert el al. (1975a), the right visual-field defect as confined to the upper quadrant. Two left-handed patients with left homonymous hemianopias have been reported (Newcombe and Ratcliff, 1974, case 2; Levine, 1978). Interestingly, reading was spared in all three of these patients. Normal visual fields have also been reported (Davidenkov, 1956; Newcombe and Ratcliff, 1974, case 1; Taylor and Warrington, 1971).

The marked variability of performance of patients in the natural setting as opposed to the test seeing has been noted by Geschwind (1965), who viewed misidentifications as confabulated responses elaborated by the intact speech area pathologically disconnected from intact visual sensory area. Failure to supply the correct gesture results from concomitant disconnection between motor and sensory areas. The common association of visual object agnosia with right homonymous hemianopia, alexia, and color agnosia, a triad occurring in the context of damage to the mesial left occipital lobe and nearby posterior callosal fibers, supports the visual-verbal disconnection hypothesis. Authors arguing against the disconnection hypothesis cite (1) the occasional finding of normal visual fields or left homonymous hemianopia (Cambier et al., 1980); (2) the occasional absence of color agnosia and alexia in the same patient (Newcombe and Ratcliff, 1974, case 1; Levine, 1978); and (3) the question of why a left occipital-splenial lesion produced the syndrome of alexia without agraphia commonly but object agnosia only rarely. The pathology in some cases is inconsistent with a visual-verbal disconnection view. For example, Levine's (1978) patient with associative agnosia had a unilateral *right* occipital lobe resection.

Strictly speaking, the imperfect correlation between color agnosia, alexia, and visual object agnosia does not, by itself, invalidate the visual-verbal disconnection hypothesis. It remains possible that there may be highly specific forms of visual-verbal disconnection and that unilateral or bilateral intrahemisphere disconnection and/ or selective destruction of independent pathways mediating various elements of visual recognition play a role (cf. Ratcliff and Ross, 1981). There is, for example, evidence for the specificity of neural pathways for color (Meadows, 1974a; Zeki, 1973, 1977). This kind of specificity is also implicit in the classical work of Hubel and Weisel (1977). However, more damaging for the visual-verbal disconnection view is the fact that many associative agnosics fail on tasks which require *nonverbal* skills such as functional classification or gesturing.

Neuropathological data in associative agnosia presents a confusing picture. Some authors (Warrington, 1985) suggest that diffuse damage may be involved, but that a lateralized left-hemisphere lesion may be sufficient. Alexander and Albert (1983) aruge for a bilateral occipitotemporal localization (cf. also Benson et al., 1974). Geschwind's (1965) visual-verbal disconnection model is based on a unilateral left mesial occipital localization, and other left-sided cases include the patients of McCarthy and Warrington (1986) and Feinberg et al. (1986). Levine's (1978) patient shows that associative agnosia can result from a unilateral right occipital lesion. Farah (1990) suggests that this heterogeneity might account for different perceptual impairments in patients with associative agnosia. For example, in the context of the debate regarding the relative significance of cortical and white matter lesions (Ross, 1980b; Albert et al., 1979), it seems possible, even likely, that there are multiple forms of associative visual agnosia representing impairment at different levels of processing. Patients such as those of Taylor and Warrington (1971) and Newcombe and Ratcliff (1974, cases 1 and 2) with diffuse bilateral disease processes, tactile agnosia, and normal visual fields probably form a separate group from those with right homonymous hemianopia associated with infarction in the territory of the left posterior cerebral artery.

## OPTIC APHASIA

The term optic aphasia was introduced by Freund (1889) to describe the deficit of one of his patients with a right homonymous hemianopia and aphasia due to a left parieto-occipital tumor; the patient's naming ability was impaired primarily for objects presented visually. The case report is of little value because of its incompleteness, but Freund's speculations are pertinent. He hypothesized a left speech area–right occipital disconnection as the basis for the visual naming deficit in the intact visual field. In current usage, *optic aphasia* refers to the condition in which patients are unable to name visually presented objects but are able to show that they recognize the object by indicating its use, by pointing to it when it is named, or by otherwise demonstrating knowledge of object meaning. Tactile and auditory naming are preserved. Representative cases have been reported by Lhermitte and Beauvois (1973), Riddoch and Humphreys (1987b), Larrabee et al. (1985), and Coslett and Saffran (1989b). Whether optic aphasia and associative agnosia differ in degree or kind remains a matter of controversy, though the recent trend is to consider it a separate entity.

The patient of Lhermitte and Beauvois (1973) represents a good example of the syndrome of optic aphasia. Their patient suffered a left posterior cerebral artery-distribution stroke and presented with right homonymous hemianopia, moderately severe amnesia, and alexia. The most striking feature of his presentation was an inability to name visually presented objects. Naming errors consisted of perseverations of previously presented objects, semantic errors (in which an object was given the name of a semantically related object), and, less frequently, visual errors. At the same time, he could demonstrate that he knew what the object was by demonstrating how it would be used. Drawing of viewed objects was normal even when the object was misnamed. He showed normal tactile naming in both right and left hands and could name environmental sounds with little difficulty. Also, when given the name of an object he was viewing, he could provide an accurate definition of the object and its functional properties. Although he was aware of his visual field defect and his reading disturbance, he was not aware of his difficulty in visual naming.

What makes optic aphasia so important is that it challenges the widely held view that object naming is based on a common set of semantic representations of known objects that can be accessed from any sensory modality. The problem is this: Why should a patient who shows intact verbal semantics (as evidenced, for example, by his good performance on the definitions task) and intact visual semantics (as evidenced by his accurate miming of object use) be able to name only those objects which are held in the hand? There have been two different answers to this question. Beavois (1982) suggested that, in J.F., different parts of the semantic system became disconnected from each other, and that only tactile input had preserved access to verbal semantics.

Riddoch and Humphreys (1987b) suggest a different answer based on their analysis of another case of optic aphasia. Riddoch and Humphreys presented an "object decision task" in which the patient had to decide whether a series of individual line drawings represented real objects or not. Their patient performed normally on this task, suggesting that he had preserved knowledge of object structure. However, the patient was impaired in grouping semantically related objects (e.g., hammer and nail), and could not draw named objects from memory. Thus, in either direction, the patient could not link semantic and visual information. Based on these results, Riddoch and Humphreys describe optic aphasia as a modality-specific semantic access problem. They further postulate that the knowledge of how to use objects is linked to structural rather than to semantic properties, and suggest that the patient may be able to demonstrate object use by a direct connection between visual object recognition units and motor action systems.

Although optic aphasia appears to be qualitatively different from associative agnosia, the possibility remains that, at least in some patients, the distinction may be a matter of degree. Clinical lore suggests the patients may evolve into optic aphasia during recovery from classical associative visual agnosia. The fact that some patients can be made to oscillate between optic aphasia and visual agnosia by varying the instructions given them on a particular task blurs, at least in some cases, the distinction between a naming disorder and a disturbance of "recognition."

COLOR AGNOSIA

The patient with color agnosia is, by classic definition, unable to name colors shown to him or to point to a color named by the examiner, yet performs normally on non-verbal tasks of color perception. One of the earliest cases was reported by Wilbrand (1887), who referred to the defect as "amnestic color blindness." Wilbrand observed that his patient could not find the appropriate word for a color displayed, that he frequently perseverated names across trials, and that naming the color of a familiar object out of sight was impaired. Wilbrand invoked an "amnestic" disorder because the patient often indicated that he had forgotten the name of the colors he was shown.

The term color agnosia presents something of a conceptual dilemma. Unlike objects, colors cannot be heard or palpated and cannot be shown in use; they can only be known through vision or visual representation (imagery). It is difficult to imagine a clinical tool to assess color recognition in other modalities and thus it is hard to establish the modality specificity of the deficit, though "conceptual" color tasks (e.g., "What color is associated with feelings of envy?") might be useful. Still, acquired anomalies of color vision and color performance do occur as a result of lesions to the posterior cortex. Four syndromes of color disturbance have been described: (1) central achromatopsia/dyschromatopsia (Damasio et al., 1980; Green and Lessell, 1977; MacKay and Dunlop, 1899; Meadows, 1974a; Pearlman et al., 1979; Young and Fishman, 1980); (2) color anomia, found in association with pure alexia and right homonymous hemianopia, and attributable to visual-verbal disconnection (Geschwind and Fusillo, 1966; Meadows, 1974a; Oxbury et al., 1969, case 1; (3) a "specific color aphasia" in which the patient has linguistic defects, but the impairment in utilizing color names is disproportionately severe (Kinsbourne and Warrington, 1964; Oxbury et al., 1969, case 2; and (4) color naming and color association defects concomitant with aphasia (Cohen and Kelter, 1979; De Renzi et al., 1972, 1973; Wyke and Holgate, 1973). We will review the first three of these defects below. A summary of performance defects in patients with these various syndromes is presented in Table 9-1 (Bowers, 1981).

*Central achromatopsia/dyschromatopsia.*   Central achromatopsia refers to a loss of color vision due to central nervous system disease. The causative lesions can be in the optic nerve, chiasm, or in one or both of the cerebral hemispheres (Green and Lessell, 1977). The disorder can be hemianopic (Albert et al., 1975b) or can exist throughout the visual fields. Achromatopsia may be partial, affecting one color more than others. Critchley (1965) described a patient with "xanthopsia" who suddenly felt as if all objects around him were covered with gold paint.

Patients with achromatopsia notice their loss of color vision and describe their visual world as black and white, all gray, washed out, or dirty. Damasio et al. (1980) reported that one of their patients had every drapery in her house laundered because she thought they needed cleaning. Such patients perform poorly on tasks of color perception (Ishihara plates, Munsell-Farnsworth 100 Hue Test, hue discrimination, color matching), but do well on verbal-verbal tasks (e.g., "What color is blood?"; "Name three blue things."). Performance on visual-verbal tasks (naming, pointing, color-object naming and pointing) varies with the severity of the disorder.

There is agreement in the literature that achromatopsia results from unilateral or

**Table 9-1.** Summary of Color Performance Defects in Patients with Various Syndromes

| Tasks | | Achromatopsia | Color Anomia A (visual-verbal d/c) | Color Anomia B (specific color aphasia) | Aphasic Patients |
|---|---|---|---|---|---|
| Visual-visual | Ishihara | ± ° | + | + | + |
| | Hue discrimination | − | + | + | + |
| | Color matching | ± ° | + | + | + |
| | Coloring pictures | ± | + † | − | − |
| | Color absurdities | ± ° | + † | + | ± ‡ |
| | Color sorting | ± ° | + | − | − |
| Verbal-verbal | Color naming | | | | |
| | Blood is ——— | + | + | − | − |
| | What color is grass? | + | + | − | − |
| | Color fluency | + | + | NT | − |
| | Naming items of specific colors | + | + | − | NT |
| Visual-verbal | Color naming | ± ° | − | − | − |
| | Color pointing | ± ° | − | − | − |
| | Color-object naming | ± ° | − | − | − |
| | Color-object pointing | ± ° | − | − | − |

Note: The symbol + refers to intact performance and − refers to impaired performance.
°Performance depends upon severity of achromatopsia. In mild cases, only hue discrimination is impaired.
†Performance on these tasks is unimpaired as long as patient does not attempt to verbalize answers. If patient dies attempt to do so, then verbalizations can interfere with performance.
‡Global and Wernike's aphasics are impaired; all other aphasics are OK.

bilateral lesions in the inferior ventromedial sector of the occipital lobe, involving the lingual and fusiform gyri (Damasio et al., 1980; Green and Lessell, 1977; Meadows, 1974a). Superior field defects are the rule. Prosopagnosia and topographical memory loss are found in the bilateral, but not the unilateral cases (Damasio et al., 1980). Two patients (Green and Lessell, 1977, case 4, and Pearlman et al., 1979) each had two separate unilateral posterior cerebral artery infarctions, and did not become achromatopsic until their second strokes. Visual evoked responses to alternating green and red checkerboard patterns may be abnormal (Damasio et al., 1980).

The physiologic work of Zeki (1973, 1977) has revealed that there exists in rhesus monkey specialized areas (V-4 complex and an additional region in the superior temporal sulcus) containing "color-coded" cells which selectively respond to specific wavelengths of light. Damasio et al. (1980) speculate that the lingual and fusiform gyri in man may be the homologues of area V-4, although the exact location is not currently known. What does seem clear from clinical data is that one single area in each hemisphere (located in the lower visual association cortex) controls color processing for the entire hemifield (Damasio et al., 1980).

*Color anomia.*   The patient with color anomia succeeds on visual-visual and verbal-verbal tasks, but is unable to name colors, a visual-verbal task. The disorder is usually associated with the syndrome of alexia without agraphia (Geschwind and Fusillo, 1966), and frequently exists in the context of right homonymous hemianopia. The underlying neuroanatomic mechanism is a visual-verbal disconnection resulting from infarction in the left PCA distribution. The patients of Geschwind and Fusillo (1966) and Oxbury et al. (1969, case 1) are classic examples of this syndrome.

These patients may show impairment on some tasks related to color perception, such as coloring pictures or detecting errors in wrongly colored stimuli. This impairment is exacerbated if the patient attempts to "verbalize" his answers (Bowers, 1981). Damasio et al. (1979) suggest that the type of stimuli, the demands of the task, and the patient's problem-solving approach can strongly influence the extent of visual-verbal dissociation. In their analysis, visual-verbal dissociation is maximized when, at the perceptual level, stimuli are "purely" visual (such as color), structurally less "rich," or low in association value. At the verbal end, visual-verbal dissociation is maximized when a specific name, rather than the name of a broad category, is involved. If the patient's verbalizations about the stimulus are incorrect, they may interfere with attempts to assign it the correct color.

*Specific color aphasia.*   Patients with specific color aphasia are distinguished from color anomics by their poor performance on verbal-verbal tasks. The patients of Oxbury et al. (1969, case 2) and Kinsbourne and Warrington (1964) are among the best documented cases of this variety. Aphasic symptoms are usually present, but the difficulty with color names and other color-associative skills is disproportionately severe. The patient of Oxbury et al. had head trauma (and probable bilateral lesions) with complete right homonymous hemianopia and mild right hemiparesis. Kinsbourne and Warrington's patient had a left posterior parietal subdural hematoma. These patients can generally sort colors categorically and according to hue, and can appropriately match colors. These deficits are similar to those reported in aphasic patients by De Renzi et al. (1972).

PROSOPAGNOSIA

The term prosopagnosia was formally introduced by Bodamer (1947) to describe the inability to recognize familiar faces. Patients with this disorder may score normally on face discrimination and matching tasks (Benton and Van Allen, 1972; Tzavaras et al., 1970). They almost invariably recognize faces as faces; their defect is in identifying whose face they are viewing. In some cases, the impairment of facial recognition is so striking that the patient is unable to recognize his own face in a mirror. The defect often prevents the recognition of famous personalities by their facial features. Patients learn to identify people by using extrafacial cues including clothing, characteristic gait, length of hair, height, or a distinguishing birthmark. The inability to recognize family members, friends, and hospital staff may lead to the mistaken conclusion that the patient is suffering from a severe memory defect or a generalized dementia. The disorder should be distinguished from Capgras syndrome, a psychiatric disturbance in which the patient believes that familiar persons have been replaced by imposters (Alexander et al., 1979; Shraberg and Weitzel, 1979; Synodinou et al., 1978).

The disorder is frequently associated with central achromatopsia, constructional disability, topographical memory loss, and dressing apraxia, and may exist as part of a more generalized object agnosia (Hécaen and Angelergues, 1962). Some patients (e.g., Gloning et al., 1970; Levine, 1978; Nardelli et al., 1982, case 2 appear to have "apperceptive" forms of the defect, while others (Bauer and Trobe, 1984; Benton and Van Allen, 1972; Pallis, 1955) suffer from a clear "associative" deficit (cf. also De Renzi et al., 1991).

From the beginning, prosopagnosia has attracted much attention because it superficially appears to represent a recognition defect limited to an individual class of stimuli. Several theories have been advanced to explain the nature of the deficit, particularly the associative cases. Some writers have considered the disorder as an "attenuated" form of a general object agnosia, specific to facial material (Beyn and Knyazeva, 1962; Gloning et al., 1970). Others have implicated a limited form of the amnestic syndrome (Benton and Van Allen, 1972; Shuttleworth et al., 1982; Warrington and James, 1967). A third view has been that the defect involves identifying individuality within a class of objects (Faust, 1955; Whiteley and Warrington, 1977). A final hypothesis is that facial recognition is mediated by a special perceptual process (Overman and Doty, 1982) and that prosopagnosia is a defect of this system (Tzavaras et al., 1970; Cohn et al., 1977; Yin, 1970).

Doubt is cast on a purely "material-specific agnosia" view by recent reports of prosopagnosics who concurrently lost the ability to recognize specific chairs (Faust, 1955) or automobiles (Lhermitte and Pillon, 1975). Bornstein and associates (Bornstein, 1963; Bornstein and Kidron, 1959; Bornstein et al., 1969) have reported two prosopagnosics, one a birdwatcher, the other a farmer, who, in addition to their face agnosia, lost the ability to recognize individual birds or cows, respectively. Thus, the defect seems not to be face specific, but involves the identification of individuals within semantic classes whose members are visually similar (Damasio et al., 1982).

The "limited amnestic syndrome" hypothesis is generally consistent with the dissociation seen in prosopagnosic performance on facial matching vs. facial memory tests. Prosopagnosics can match faces, some even at different photographic angles, but fail in any test that requires explicit recent or remote memory for faces (Meadows, 1974b). This view is that ongoing facial percepts cannot be consciously matched with stored visual representations of faces built up from past experience. There is some clinical suport for this hypothesis, including the inability of many prosopagnosics to learn new faces (anterograde defect), the presence of recent memory impairment for other complex nonverbal(izable) stimuli, and the poor performance of many amnesics on famous face recognition tasks (Bauer and Trobe, 1984; Meadows, 1974b; Ross, 1980a, case 1). However, there are three problems with viewing prosopagnosia as exclusively a memory disorder. The first problem is that most prosopagnosics, unlike amnesics, have significant perceptual dysfunction, including impairment in gestalt processing, and apparent defects in analyzing how spatial frequency components of faces (Sergent and Villemure, 1989). Second, patients with full-blown amnesia (e.g., Korsakoff's syndrome) are rarely prosopagnosic, if one adopts the reasonable criterion of equivalent impairment in both anterograde and retrograde face recognition. In most forms of acquired amnesia, there is a relative preservation of remote memory, whereas in prosopagnosia, the recognition of remotely learned faces (friends, family members) is particularly impaired (Meadows, 1974b). Finally, in amnesic states, the impairment in both anterograde and retrograde memory is almost never absolute; such patients have a clinically significant defect in learning new information and in retrieving from the remote store, yet some new learning and remote recall is invariably possible and is accompanied by at least some degree of judged confidence of familiarity. In prosopagnosia, the impairment in face recognition is characteristically absolute and inspection of faces yields no subjective familiarity with the viewed person.

Damasio et al. (1982), drawing on autopsied cases, CT findings, and the work of Benton (1980), suggest that both a visual categorization defect and a material-specific memory defect are necessary for the production of prosopagnosia. Since patients are able to immediately recognize others on the basis of voice or other extrafacial characterics, Damasio et al. argue that the storage of "context is not affected, i.e., the memories pertinent to a given face . . . are intact and are retrievable from all the multimodal sensory storage sites, including the visual one. The disturbance resides in that the visual trigger cannot activate these multimodal memories." They suggest that the defect involves a failure to evoke the context of a particular stimulus. The reason that faces are so strongly affected is that they belong to a category in which differences between category members are so visually subtle and complex. This view supports the notion that prosopagnosia may not be specific to faces, but may involve a defect which could affect any class of visually "ambiguous" stimuli.

The lesions causing prosopagnosia are typically bilateral and involve the cortex and white matter in the occipitotemporal gyrus. In his review of the anatomic evidence, Meadows (1974b) found that superior field defects were frequent, and that the typical finding was a right occipitotemporal lesion coupled with a more variably placed, but usually symmetric, lesion in the left hemisphere. Damasio et al. (1982) found that all pathologically verified cases had functionally symmetric bilateral lesions involving the mesial occipitotemporal region. Although this is still the most widely held view of the pathological anatomy underlying prosopagnosia, there seems to be recent movement toward accepting the fact that prosopagnosia can occur after a unilateral right-hemisphere lesion (Benton, 1990). There are now several well-documented cases of prosopagnosia with CT scan evidence of damage restricted to the right hemisphere (De Renzi, 1986a,b; Michel et al., 1986; Torii and Tamai, 1985). In addition, Sergent and Villemure (1989) described a patient who became prosopagnosic after right hemispherectomy during the developmental period. When taken together with the bilateral cases, the evidence suggests that, though the anatomic substrate for face recognition may normally be bilateral, a crucial lesion involves the right occipitotemporal junction (cf. Benton, 1990).

The occipitotemporal projection system (OTPS), which serves as the functional interface between visual association cortex and temporal lobe, has been particularly implicated in prosopagnosia (Bauer, 1982; Benson et al., 1974; Meadows, 1974b). The regions in temporal lobe served by the OTPS subsequently project to the limbic system. Accordingly, prosopagnosia has been interpreted as a visual-limbic disconnection syndrome (Bauer, 1982; Benson et al., 1974). Evidence that prosopagnosics suffer from reductions in emotional responsivity to visual stimuli seem to support this idea (Bauer, 1982; Habib, 1986). However, the situation seems more complex, because OTPS lesions anterior to the occipitotemporal area (which, if complete, also produce visual-limbic disconnection) do not typically result in prosopagnosia (Meadows, 1974b). Intrinsic damage to occipitotemporal area thus seems important. It is possible that intrinsic damage to the occipitotemporal region destroys or disconnects from visual input the association cortex in which visual representations of faces (or at least the "hardware" for activating such representations) reside (Damasio et al., 1982; Perrett et al., 1982, 1987). Second, occipitotemporal lesions involving the inferior longitudinal fasciculus (ILF) are posterior enough to directly affect portions of inferotemporal cortex, a region which seems particularly critical in recognizing, categorizing, and discriminating visual forms (Gross et al., 1972; Iversen and Weiskrantz, 1964, 1967; Kuypers et al., 1965). This may contribute to the "underspecification" of visual detail which recent authors (Levine, 1978; Shuttleworth et al., 1982) have considered important in the production of the defect.

CATEGORY-SPECIFIC RECOGNITION DEFECTS

Before leaving the topic of visual agnosia, it is important to mention several recent cases in which visual recognition disorders appear to be limited to a specific semantic category or class of objects (Damasio, 1990; Farah et al., 1989; Warrington and Shallice, 1984). As indicated earlier, questions regarding category specificity arose in the context of evaluting other selective forms of agnosia such as prosopagnosia. Although some prosopagnosics have a relatively "pure" face recognition defect (De Renzi, 1986a), others have difficulty in recognizing objects in other semantic classes such as animals (Bornstein and Kidron, 1959; Damasio et al., 1982), plants (Shuttleworth et al., 1982), or foods (Damasio et al., 1982; Michel et al., 1986). When these problems have been considered together, it has been suggested that a "supercategorical" defect in recognizing "living things" might be involved (cf. Farah et al., 1991).

Two general explanations for such "category specificity" have been offered. One, which seems most intuitive on first glance, is that these disorders represent "localized" impairment in a semantic system which is organized taxonomically. Another view suggests that living things are more visually complex (Gloning et al., 1970), more visually similar one to another, or require, for identification, more specific names than do nonliving things (cf. Farah et al., 1991; Warrington and McCarthy, 1987). The former explanation suggests that a selective disruption in the recognition of living things reveals something basic about the structure of semantic memory; the latter implies that such selective disruption results from task, processing, or response factors that have been confounded in the usual clinical tasks of object recognition.

With these alternative explanations in mind, Farah et al. (1991) devised a series of object naming tasks that took account of visual complexity, interitem similarity, and response specificity (e.g., "table" vs. "picnic table") and gave them to two patients who became agnosic after sustaining severe closed head injury. They found that, despite efforts to control for these variables, living things remained selectively impaired relative to nonliving things. Their data do not allow them to specifically discern the locus of impairment (i.e., whether it is in a categorically organized semantic system or within a modularly organized visual system specialized for the recognition of living things), but they concluded that some level of visual or semantic representations specific to living things appeared to be involved.

The patient P.S.D. reported by Damasio (1990) shows a similar, though apparently more complicated dissociation. This patient was able to visually recognized manmade tools, though his recognition of most "natural" stimuli was less than 30% accurate. At the same time, he showed normal recognition of some natural stimuli (e.g., body parts) and poor recognition of some man-made stimuli (e.g., musical instruments).

## *Auditory Agnosia*

The term auditory agnosia refers to impaired capacity to recognize sounds in the presence of otherwise adequate hearing as measured by standard audiometry. The term has been used in a broad sense to refer to impaired capacity to recognize both speech and nonspeech sounds, and in a narrow sense to refer to a selective deficit in the recognition of nonverbal sounds only. If one uses the broader definition, then the disorder is further subdivided into auditory sound agnosia, auditory verbal agnosia, and a mixed group with deficits in both speech and nonspeech sounds. We prefer the more narrow definition, and will discuss pure word deafness (a selective impairment in speech-sound recognition) and auditory agnosia (selective impairment in recognizing nonspeech sounds) separately. The term cortical deafness generally has been applied to those patients whose daily activities and auditory behavior indicate an extreme lack of awareness of those patients whose daily activities and auditory behavior indicate an extreme lack of awareness of auditory stimuli of any kinds, and whose audiometric pure tone thresholds are markedly abnormal. Receptive (sensory) amusia refers to loss of the ability to appreciate various characteristics of heard music.

### CORTICAL AUDITORY DISORDER AND CORTICAL DEAFNESS

In the large majority of cases, impairment of nonverbal sound recognition is accompanied by some degree of impairment in the recognition of speech sounds. The relative severity of these impairments may reflect premorbid lateralization of linguistic processes in the individual patient, and may depend upon which hemisphere is more seriously, or primarily, damaged (Ulrich, 1978). Terminologic confusion has arise with regard to these "mixed" forms, with such terms as cortical auditory disorder (Kanshepolsky et al., 1973; Miceli, 1982), auditory agnosia (Oppenheimer and Newcombe, 1978; Rosati et al., 1982), auditory agnosia and word deafness (Goldstein et al., 1975), and congenital aphasia (Landau et al., 1960) all being used to describe similar phenomena. We will refer to these mixed forms as cortical auditory disorders, and will discuss them together with cortical deafness. Cortical auditory disorders frequently evolve from a state of cortical deafness and, as we shall see, it is often difficult to define a clear separation between the two entities.

Patients with these disorders have difficulty recognizing auditory stimuli of many kinds, verbal and nonverbal (Vignolo, 1969; Lhermitte et al., 1971). Aphasic signs, if present, are mild, and do not prevent the patient from recognizing incoming information provided audition is not required. Difficulties in temporal auditory analysis and localization of sounds in space are common. These disorders are rare, and their underlying neuroanatomic basis is poorly understood (Rosati et al., 1982). Recent case reports have questioned the distinctive nature of "true" cortical deafness (Kanshepolsky et al., 1973; Lhermitte et al., 1971; Vignolo, 1969).

Distinguishing between cortical deafness and auditory agnosia continues to be problematic. One distinction which is frequently cited is that the cortically deaf patient feels deaf and seems to be so, whereas the auditory agnosic insists that he is not deaf (Michel et al., 1980). This turns out to be a poor criterion. Although it was originally believed that bilateral cortical lesions involving the primary auditory cortex resulted in total hearing loss, recent evidence from animal experiments (Massopoust and Wolin, 1967; Neff, 1961), cortical mapping of the auditory area (Celesia, 1976), and clinicopathological studies in man (Mahoudeau et al., 1956; Wohlfart et al., 1952) indicate that complete destruction of primary auditory cortex does not lead to substantial permanent loss of audiometric sensitivity. It is more likely, however, for an asymptomatic patient with old unilateral temporal lobe pathology to suddenly become totally deaf with the occurrence of a second contralateral lesion in the auditory region.

A neuroanatomic distinction between cortical deafness and auditory cortical disorders has been tentatively offered by Michel et al. (1980). Recognizing the hazards of such a dichotomy, they distinguish between lesions of auditory koniocortex (areas 41–52 of Brodmann) and lesions of pro- and parakoniocortex (areas 22 and 52 of Brodmann) respectively. While this distinction may prove useful, naturally occurring lesions do not typically obey architectonic boundaries (Michel et al., 1980).

In their paper on cortical deafness, Michel et al. (1980) considered the possibility that the two syndromes could be differentiated on the basis of auditory evoked potentials (AEPs). Several studies (e.g., Jerger et al., 1969; Michel et al., 1980) have found either totally absent AEPs or absent late components of AEP in patients with cortical auditory disorders. However, AEPs have been found to be present in other cases (Albert et al., 1972 [pure word deafness]; Assal and Despland (1973) [auditory agnosia]), and in at least one case of cortical deafness (Adams et al., 1977), normal late AEPs were found. While results to date are conflicting, this remains a promising area of research. Such variability may be due in part to differing pathologies and recording methods. Michel et al. (1980) offer methodological suggestions designed to increase comparability among patients.

Cortical deafness is most commonly seen in bilateral cerebrovascular disease where the course is commonly biphasic with a transient deficit (often aphasia and hemiparesis) related to unilateral damage followed by a second deficit associated with sudden transient total deafness (Jerger et al., 1969, 1972; Leicester, 1980; Earnest et al., 1977). A biphasic course is also typical of cases of auditory cortical disorder.

In cortical deafness, bilateral destruction of the auditory radiations or the primary auditory cortex has been a constant finding (Leicester, 1980). The anatomic basis of auditory cortical disorder is more variable. Although lesions can be quite extensive (cf. Oppenheimer and Newcombe, 1978), the superior temporal gyrus (i.e., efferent connections of Heschl's gyrus) is frequently involved. Two recent Japanese cases (Kazui et al., 1990; Motomura et al., 1986) suggest that generalized auditory agnosia

can result from bilateral subcortical lesions. The former patient had magnetic resonance imaging (MRI)-verified pathology deep to the left parietal lobe and in the right
temporal stem, insular cortex, and deep white matter underneath Heschl's gyrus. The
latter patient had an old left thalamic infarction involving the medial geniculate and
a recent right thalamic hemorrhage extending to the temporal stem. It is not possible
to tell from the pathology whether auditory cortical disorder was present or not
(Leicester, 1980) since some patients with small lesions do have these problems while
others with similarly placed large lesions do not.

PURE WORD DEAFNESS (AUDITORY AGNOSIA FOR SPEECH, AUDITORY VERBAL AGNOSIA)

The patient with pure word deafness is unable to comprehend spoken language
although he can read, write, and speak in a relatively normal manner (Buchman et
al., 1986). By definition, comprehension of nonverbal sounds is relatively spared. The
syndrome is "pure" in the sense that it is *relatively* free of aphasic symptoms found
with other disorders affecting language comprehension, particularly Wernicke's and
transcortical sensory aphasia. The disorder was first described by Kussmaul (1877).
Lichtheim (1885) defined the disorder as "the inability to understand spoken words
as an isolated deficit unaccompanied by disturbance of spontaneous speech or by
severe disturbance in writing or understanding of the printed word." He used the
term subcortical sensory aphasia, and postulated a subcortical interruption of fibers
from both ascending auditory projections to the left "auditory word center." With
few exceptions, pure word deafness has been associated with bilateral, symmetric cor-
tical-subcortical lesions involving the anterior part of the superior temporal gyri with
some sparing of Heschl's gyrus, particularly on the left. Some patients have unilateral
lesions located subcortically in the dominant temporal lobe, presumably destroying
the ipsilateral auditory radiation as well as callosal fibers from the contralateral auditory region (e.g., Kanter et al., 1986; Liepmann and Storch, 1902; Schuster and
Taterka, 1926). The neuroanatomic substrate is generally conceived, from a functional point of view, as a bilateral disconnection of Wernicke's area from auditory
input (Hécaen and Albert, 1978; Geschwind, 1965). The low incidence of pure word
deafness is due to the fact that it takes an unusually placed, circumscribed lesion of
the superior temporal gyrus to involve Heschl's gyrus or its connections and still selectively spare Wernicke's area.

    Cerebrovascular disease is the most common cause of pure word deafness. The
patient, when first seen, is often recovering from a full-blown Wernicke's aphasia,
though occasionally pure word deafness may actually give way to a Wernicke's aphasia (Albert and Bear, 1974; Klein and Harper, 1956; Gazzaniga et al., 1973; Ziegler,
1952). As the paraphasias and writing and reading disturbances disappear, the patient
still does not comprehend spoken language but can communicate by writing. Deafness can be ruled out by normal pure-tone thresholds on audiometry. At this stage,
the patient may experience auditory hallucinations or exhibit transient euphoric
(Shoumaker et al., 1977) or paranoid (Reinhold, 195) ideation. The inability to repeat
speech stimuli that are not comprehended distinguishes pure word deafness, which
is generally viewed as a disturbance at the perceptual-discriminative level (Jerger et

al., 1969; Kanshepolsky et al., 1973), from transcortical sensory aphasia in which word sounds are perceived normally, but there is an estrangement of sound from meaning. The absence of florid paraphasia and of reading and writing disruption distinguishes the disorder from Wernicke's aphasia. This having been said, it should be recognized that "aphasic" and "agnosic" symptoms may occasionally be difficult to separate in the individual case.

Many patients complain of dramatic, sometimes aversive, changes in their subjective experience of speech (dysacusis; cf. Mendez and Geehan, 1988). The patient with pure word deafness may complain that speech is muffled or sounds like a foreign language. Hemphill and Stengel's patient (1940) stated that "voices come but no words." The patient of Klein and Harper (1956) described speech as "an undifferentiated continuous humming noise without any rhythm" and "like foreigners speaking in the distance." Albert and Bear's (1974) patients said "words come too quickly," and, "they sound like a foreign language." The speech of these patients may contain occasional word-finding pauses and paraphasias and is often slightly louder than normal. Performance on speech perception tests is very inconsistent and highly dependent upon context (Caplan, 1978) and the linguistic structure of the material (Auerbach et al., 1982). Patients do much better when they are aware of the category under discussion, or when they can lip-read. Comprehension often drops suddenly when the topic is changed. Words embedded in sentences are more easily identified than are isolated words. Slowing the presentation rate of words in sentences sometimes facilitates comprehension. Slower speech rates may lessen the impact of abnormally slow temporal auditory analysis or may allow the patient to strategically reconstruct the message and thus make educated guesses about message content (Neisser, 1967, 1976).

Recent studies of patients with pure word deafness have emphasized the role of auditory-perceptual processing in the genesis of the disorder (Albert and Bear, 1974; Auerbach et al., 1982; Jerger et al., 1972; Kanshepolsky et al., 1973; Mendez and Geehan, 1988). Temporal resolution (Albert and Bear, 1974), and phonemic discrimination (Chocholle et al., 1975; Denes and Semenza, 1975; Saffran et al., 1976) have also received attention. In an exceptionally detailed case report and literature review, Auerbach et al. (1982) suggest that the disorder may take two forms: (1) a prephonemic temporal auditory acuity disturbance associated with bilateral temporal lesions or (2) a disorder of phonemic discrimination attributable to left temporal lesions.

Albert and Bear (1974) suggested that the problem in pure word deafness is one of temporal resolution of auditory stimuli rather than specific phonetic impairment. Their patient demonstrated abnormally long click-fusion thresholds (time taken to perceive two clicks as one), and improved in auditory comprehension when speech was presented at slower rates. Saffran et al. (1976), on the other hand, showed that informing their patient of the nature of the topic under discussion (indicating the category of words to be presented or giving the patient a multiple-choice array just before presentation of words) significantly facilitated comprehension. Words embedded in a sentence were better recognized, particularly when they occurred in the latter part of the sentence. Whereas a temporal auditory acuity disorder was likely present in Albert and Bear's (1974) patient, the patient of Saffran et al. (1976) displayed linguistic discrimination deficits which appeared to be independent of a disorder in temporal auditory acuity.

Several studies have reported brainstem and cortical auditory evoked responses in patients with pure word deafness (see Michel et al., 1980, for review). Brainstem evoked potentials (EPs) are almost universally reported as normal, suggesting normal processing up to the level of the auditory radiations (Auerbach et al., 1982; Albert and Bear, 1974; Stockard and Rossiter, 1977). Results from studies of cortical AEPs are more variable, probably consistent with variable pathology (Auerbach et al., 1982). For example, the patient of Jerger et al. (1969) had no appreciable AEP, yet heard sounds. The patient of Auerbach et al. (1982) showed normal P1, N1, and P2 to right-ear stimulation, but minimal response over either hemisphere to left-ear stimulation.

On tests of phonetic discrimination, patients with bilateral lesions tend to show distinctive deficits for the feature of place of articulation (Naeser, 1974; Chocholle et al., 1975; Auerbach et al., 1982). Those with unilateral left-hemisphere disease showed either impaired discrimination for voicing (Saffran et al., 1976) or no distinctive pattern (Denes and Semenza, 1975).

On dichotic listening, some patients show extreme suppression of right-ear perception (Albert and Bear, 1974; Saffran et al., 1976), suggesting the inaccessibility of the left-hemisphere phonetic decoding areas (Wernicke's area) to auditory material that has already been acoustically processed by the right hemisphere. However, the patient of Auerbach et al. (1982) showed marked left-ear extinction, which the authors attribute to spared auditory processing in the left temporal lobe.

Patients with pure word deafness perform relatively well with environmental sounds, although the appreciation of music is sometimes disturbed. Some patients may recognize foreign languages by their distinctive prosodic characteristics, and others can recognize *who* is speaking, but not what is said, suggesting preserved ability to comprehend paralinguistic aspects of speech. Coslett et al. (1984) described a word-deaf patient who showed a remarkable dissociation between the comprehension of neutral and affectively intoned sentences. He was asked to point to pictures of males and females depicting various emotional expressions. When verbal instructions were given in a neutral voice, he performed poorly. When instructions were given with affective intonations appropriate to the target face, he performed significantly better and at a level commensurate to his performance with written instructions. This patient had bilateral destruction of primary auditory cortex with some sparing of auditory association cortex, suggesting at least some direct contribution of the auditory radiations directly to the latter without initial decoding in Heschl's gyrus (Coslett et al., 1984). These authors speculate that one reason why patients with pure word deafness improve their auditory comprehension with lip-reading is that face-to-face contact allows them to take advantage of visual cues (gesture and facial expression) that are processed by different brain systems. An alternative explanation is that lip-reading provides information about place of articulation, a linguistic feature which is markedly impaired at least in the bilateral cases (Auerbach et al., 1982). In either instance, the finding of preserved comprehension of paralinguistic aspects of speech further reinforces the notion that comprehension of speech and nonspeech sounds may represent dissociable abilities.

There is evidence that unilateral left-sided lesions, particularly those producing

Wernicke's aphasia with impaired auditory comprehension, are also associated with impaired ability to match nonverbal sounds with pictures (Vignolo, 1969). However, resulting errors are almost exclusively semantic, not acoustic, and thus do not suggest that unilateral left-hemispheric temporal lobe damage produces a perceptual-discriminative sound recognition disturbance. For that reason, the finding of impaired ability to discriminate nonverbal speech sounds in a patient with pure word deafness suggests bilateral disease, even in the absence of other neurological evidence of bilaterality. Since many of these patients have, by history, successive strokes, the primary and secondary side of damage may be important in producing a picture dominated either by pure word deafness or by auditory sound agnosia (Ulrich, 1978).

## AUDITORY SOUND AGNOSIA (AUDITORY AGNOSIA FOR NONSPEECH SOUNDS)

Auditory agnosia for nonspeech sounds is rare, more uncommon by far than pure word deafness. This may be because such patients are less likely to seek medical advice than are those with a disorder of speech comprehension, and also because nonspecific auditory complaints may be discounted when pure tone audiometric and speech discrimination thresholds are normal. This is unfortunate, since normal or near normal audiometric evaluation does not rule out the possible role played by primary auditory perceptual defects (Buchtel and Stewart, 1989; Goldstein, 1974).

Vignolo (1969) argued that there may be two forms of auditory sound agnosia: (1) a perceptual-discriminative type associated mainly with right-hemisphere lesions and (2) an associative-semantic type associated with lesions of the left hemisphere and closely linked to Wernicke's aphasia. The former group makes predominantly acoustic (e.g., "man whistling" for birdsong) errors on picture-sound matching tasks, while the latter group makes predominantly semantic (e.g., "train" for automobile engine) errors. This division follows the original classification of Kliest (1928) who distinguished between the ability to perceive isolated sounds or noises and the inability to understand the meaning of sounds. It also resembles the apperceptive/associative dichotomy made by Lissauer (1890). In the verbal sphere, the analogous distinction is between pure word deafness (perceptual-discriminative) and transcortical sensory aphasia (semantic-associative).

Relatively few cases of "pure" auditory sound agnosia have been reported in the literature (Albert et al., 1972; Fujii et al., 1990; Nielsen and Sult, 1939; Spreen et al., 1965; Wortis and Pfeffer, 1948). Sometimes a patient evolves into auditory sound agnosia from a more generalized agnosia involving both verbal and nonverbal sounds (Motomura et al., 1986). The patient of Spreen et al. was a 65-year-old right-handed male whose major complaint when seen three years after a left hemiparetic episode was that of "nerves" and headache. Audiometric testing demonstrated moderate bilateral high-frequency loss and speech reception thresholds of 12 dB for both ears. There was no aphasia. The outstanding abnormality was the inability to recognize common sounds; understanding of language was fully retained and there were no other agnosic defects. Sound localization was normal. Scores on the pitch subtest of the Seashore Tests of Musical Talent were at chance level. The patient claimed no experience or talent with music and refused, as many such patients do, to cooperate with further testing of musical ability. The patient was able to match previously heard but misidentified sounds with one of four tape-recorded choices, suggesting an associative defect. Postmortem examination revealed a sharply demarcated old infarct of the right hemisphere centering around the parietal lobe and involving the superior temporal and angular gyri, as well as a large portion of the inferior parietal, inferior and middle frontal, and long and short gyri of the insula. This case represents one of the few examples of auditory sound agnosia with unilateral pathology. The lesion is too large to allow for precise anatomicoclinical correlation. Other cases with unilateral pathology include those reported by Fujii et al. (small posterior right temporal hemorrhagic lesion that involved the middle and superior temporal gyri), Nielsen and Sult (right thalamus and parietal lobe), and Wortis and Pfeffer (large lesion of the right temporo-parietal-occipital junction). The case reported by Fujii et al. (1990) is informative because he was completely free of aphasic symptoms and because of the relatively small size of his lesion. In this patient, pure tone audiometry was within normal limits in spite of a 30 dB high-frequency hearing loss in the left ear. He showed marked suppression of the left ear during dichotic listening tests involving digits and words. Brainstem auditory evoked responses were normal and sound localization was intact. The patient was selectively impaired in identification of nonspeech sounds, and his errors consisted primarily of acoustic confusions ("sound of railroad cross" for telephone ring). His agnosia cleared by the 16th poststroke day.

A more recent case report (Albert et al., 1972) described a patient with auditory sound agnosia with minimal dysphasia. Clinical evidence suggested bilateral involvement. The patient was able to attach meaning to word sounds, but not to nonverbal sounds. Albert et al. also demonstrated marked extinction of the left ear to dichotic listening; impaired perception of pitch, loudness, rhythm, and time; and abnormally delayed and attentuated cortical AEPs, worse on the right. They concluded that the nature of the sound agnosia in their patient resided in "an ability to establish the correspondence between the perceived sound and its sensory or motor associations" (associative defect), and suggested that the dissociation between verbal and nonverbal sound recognition in their patient reflected different processing mechanisms for linguistic and nonlinguistic aspects of acoustic input.

SENSORY (RECEPTIVE) AMUSIA

The subject of amusia has been reviewed in detail by Wertheim (1969), Critchley and Henson (1977), and Gates and Bradshaw (1977). Sensory amusia refers to an inability to appreciate various characteristics of heard music. It occurs to some extent in all cases of auditory sound agnosia and in the majority of cases of aphasia and pure word deafness. As is the case with auditory sound agnosia, the loss of musical perceptual ability is underreported because a specific musical disorder rarely interferes with everyday life. A major obstacle to systematic study of acquired amusia is the extreme variability of preillness musical abilities, interests, and skills. It was Wertheim's (1969) opinion that receptive amusia corresponds more frequently with a lesion of the left hemisphere, while expressive musical disabilities are more apt to be associated with right-hemisphere dysfunction. Recent evidence indicates that cerebral organization of musical ability is dependent on degree of experience, skill, and musical sophistication. Musically skilled and trained individuals may be more likely to perceive music "analytically" and to rely more heavily on the dominant hemisphere. Dichotic listening studies show that the right hemisphere plays a more important role than the left in the processing of musical and nonlinguistic sound patterns (Blumstein and Cooper, 1974; Gordon, 1974). However, the left hemisphere appears to be of major importance in the processing of sequential (temporally organized) material of any kind including musical series. According to Gordon (1974), melody recognition becomes less of a "right-hemisphere task" as time and rhythm factors become more important for distinguishing tone patterns (see also Mavlov, 1980). These factors contribute to a lack of definition of the entity of receptive amusia and the difficulty of localizing the deficit to a particular brain region. Further complicating the picture is the fact that pitch, harmony, timbre, intensity, and rhythm may be affected to different degrees and in various combinations in the individual patient. Furthermore, there is recent evidence that aspects of musical denotation (the so-called "real-world" events referred to by lyrics) and musical connotation (the formal expressive patterns indicated by pitch, timbre, and intensity) are selectively vulnerable to focal brain lesions (Gardner et al., 1977). For instance, on tests of musical denotation, right-hemisphere-damaged patients perform well on items where acquaintence with lyrics is required; in contrast, aphasics with anterior lesions are superior to both right-hemisphere patients and to aphasics with posterior lesions on items where knowledge of lyrics is unnecessary. (Incidentally, Benton (1980) reports that aphasics with posterior lesions and comprehension disturbance are also most impaired among aphasics on tests of face recognition, another ostensibly "configurational" task.) On tests of musical connotation, right-hemisphere patients do better in matching sound patterns to temporally sequenced designs than to simultaneous gestalten. Aphasics with posterior lesions perform relatively well on tests of musical connotation.

## PARALINGUISTIC AGNOSIAS: AUDITORY AFFECTIVE AGNOSIA AND PHONAGNOSIA

Heilman et al. (1975) showed that patients with right temporoparietal lesions and the neglect syndrome were impaired in the comprehension of affectively intoned speech, but showed normal comprehension of speech content. Patients with left temporoparietal lesions and fluent aphasia comprehended both affective (paralinguistic) and content (linguistic) aspects of speech normally. Whether this defect represents a "true" agnosia remains to be determined, since auditory sensory/perceptual skills were not assessed. It is possible that auditory affective agnosia is a variant of auditory sound agnosia, i.e., that it represents a category-specific auditory agnosia.

Recent studies by Van Lancker and associates (Van Lancker and Kreiman, 1988; Van Lancker et al., 1988, 1989) have revealed another type of paralinguistic deficit after right-hemisphere disease. In their studies, patients with unilateral right-hemisphere disease showed deficits in discriminating and recognizing familiar voices, while patients with left-hemisphere disease were impaired only on a task that required a discrimination between two famous voices. CT evidence suggested that right parietal damage was significantly correlated with voice recognition impairment, while temporal lobe damage in either hemisphere led to deficits in voice discrimination. The authors refer to this deficit as "phonagnosia," but, like auditory affective agnosia, it remains to be seen whether it is truly agnosic in nature.

Although the status of these defects vis-à-vis the concept of agnosia is uncertain, the discovery of seemingly specific impairments in the comprehension of affectively intoned speech and speaker identity is important in light of the fact that paralinguistic abilities may be spared in cases of pure word deafness (Coslett et al., 1984). As indicated above, patients with pure word deafness frequently report that they are able to recognize the speaker of the message and, less frequently, the language in which it is transmitted. These findings lend further support to the idea that both linguistic and nonlinguistic processing of auditory signals are based on different neuropsychological mechanisms and in fact may be preferentially processed by different hemispheres. Further research is needed to provide more precise neuroanatomic correlates of auditory affective agnosia and phonagnosia.

### Somatosensory Agnosia

Compared to visual agnosia, somatosensory (tactile) agnosias have received scant attention and are poorly understood. However, it is likely that loss of higher-order tactual recognition in the absence of elementary somatosensory loss is probably at least as common as visual or auditory agnosia. Several distinct disorders have been identified, and many classifications of somatosensory agnosia have been offered. A reasonable descriptive framework was proposed by Delay (1935) who identified (1) impaired recognition of the size and shape of objects ("amorphognosia"), (2) impaired discrimination of the distinctive qualities of objects such as density, weight, texture, and thermal properties ("ahylognosia"), and (3) impaired recognition of the identity of objects in the absence of amorphognosia and ahylognosia ("tactile asymboly"). Delay's scheme is similar to that of Wernicke (1895), who distinguished between primary agnosia involved a loss of primary identification because of a destruction of "tactile images." In contrast, secondary agnosia resulted from the inability of intact tactile images to be associated with other sensory representations, resulting in a loss of appreciation of the object's significance.

The systematic study of tactile recognition disturbances has been beset by terminologic confusion. The terms tactile agnosia and astereognosis have been used interchangeably by some authors, while others draw a sharp distinction between them. Astereognosis has been used to denote (1) loss of the ability to distinguish three-dimensional forms (Hoffman, 1884; cited by Gans, 1916), (2) the inability to make shape or size discriminations (Roland, 1976), and (3) the inability to identify objects by touch (Delay, 1935). This is confusing, since Hoffman and Roland use the term to describe *discrimination* defects, while Delay and others use the term to denote defects of object *identification*. It is clear that defects in two-point discrimination, point localization, and position sense can impair tactile form perception, and thus object identification, without producing concomitant defects in sensitivity to light touch, temperature, or pain (Corkin, 1978; Campora, 1925; Gans, 1916). However, significant defects in discriminative ability need not accompany disorders of tactual identification (Corkin, 1978). Thus, clinical data suggest that tactile discrimination and identification are dissociable. Unfortunately, the vast majority of the physiological and anatomic data on somatosensory agnosia has come from animal research almost exclusively using discrimination, rather than identification paradigms.

With these considerations in mind, we will use the term cortical tactile disorders to refer to a diverse spectrum of defects in somatosensory discrimination or recognition of distinct object qualities. We will reserve the term tactile agnosia for those rare cases in which there is an inability to identify the nature of tactually presented objects despite adequate sensory, attentional, intellectual, and linguistic capacities. Although debatable, we will discuss astereognosis as an apperceptive form of tactile agnosia, recognizing that it represents a failure of complex perceptual processing that has, as an outcome, an impairment in tactile object recognition ability.

Before discussing disorders of tactile recognition, some comments about the functional anatomy of the somatosensory systems are necessary. An exhaustive review of this vast literature will not be undertaken here; the interested reader is referred to excellent reviews by Hécaen and Albert (1978), Corkin (1978), and Werner and Whitsel (1973).

Two relatively "distinct" somatosensory systems have been identified. One is the spinothalamic system: cutaneous nerve endings → spinothalamic tract → reticular formation → intrinsic thalamic nuclei → superior bank of Sylvian fissure (S II) (Hécaen and Albert, 1978; Brodal, 1981). This system is primarily reponsible for the less precise aspects of somesthetic perception, and seems especially important in nocioception and perception of thermal properties. The other system is centered on the medial lemniscus: cutaneous and subcutaneous receptors → medial lemniscal tract → ventroposterolateral thalamic nuclei → postcentral gyrus (S I). The postcentral gyrus corresponds to Brodmann's areas 3, 1, 2. This system appears responsible for more precise discriminative aspects of touch, and carries information regarding form, position, and temporal change (Mountcastle, 1961). The two cortical somatosensory "receiving areas" (S I, S II) contain complex "representations" (homunculi) of body parts, with S I arranged somatotopically, and S II less so. The postcentral gyrus (S I) receives innervation from contralateral body parts, while S II receives bilateral input. It should be noted that other areas of cortex, including supplementary motor area and superior parietal lobe (areas 5, 7), also receive direct input from somatosensory thalamus (Brodal, 1981).

In the sections on visual agnosia, we made mention of the fact that certain visual tasks place strong motor-exploratory demands on the visual system. This "motor" theme is also a striking characteristic of the somatosensory system. In a report of the results of cortical stimulation during craniotomy, Penfield (1958) found significant overlap between "sensory" and "motor" regions, in that 25% of stimulation points giving rise to somatosensory experiences were located in the precentral region. Woolsey (1952) found similar results in his electrophysiological studies of the alert monkey. Because of these and related findings, it has become common to speak of the "sensorimotor" cortex. Anatomic interconnections of S I and S II attest to the sensorimotor nature of these regions. Both S I and S II have reciprocal connections with thalamic nuclei, supplementary motor cortex, area 4, and with each other (Hécaen and Albert, 1978; Brodal, 1981). In addition, S I projects heavily to area 5 (superior parietal lobule) (Jones and Powell, 1969; Corkin, 1978), important for motor pursuit of motivationally relevent targets in extrapersonal space (Mountcastle et al., 1975).

Thus, the functional interconnections of cortical somatensory areas involve regions which, from numerous other studies, have been found to subserve motor, proprio-ceptive, and spatial functions. The existence of such a complex system in the human brain is important for intentional, spatially guided motor movements which bring the organism into contact with tactile stimuli. Reciprocal connections between somato-sensory, motor, proprioceptive, and spatial components of the system provide the mechanisms whereby regulation of the perceptual act can be achieved. The complex functional organization of the somatosensory systems underscores the idea that per-ception is an active process and involves more than the mere passive processing of environmental input.

Though patients with lesions of the afferent somatosensory pathways frequently cannot identify tactually presented objects, this is due to a severe sensory loss, some-times referred to as steroanaesthesia. Lesions of the primary visual and auditory areas produce specific disorders of sensation which can vary in severity depending on the extent and location of the lesion. Total ablation of primary visual and auditory areas results in cortical blindness or deafness, respectively. In contrast, disorders of sensa-tion for touch, temperature, pain, and vibration are rare following cortical lesions (Hécaen and Albert, 1978). Redundancy in representation seems to be an especially important characteristic of somatosensory systems. Paul et al. (1972) explored units in anatomic subdivisons of S I and found multiple representations of the monkey's hand, one in each subdivision (cf. also Powell and Montcastle, 1959; Mountcastle and Powell, 1959a,b). Randolph and Semmes (1974) selectively ablated each of the S I subregions (3b, 2, 1). Area 3b excisions resulted in impairment of all aspects of tactile discrimination learning. Lesions of area 1 produced loss of hard-soft and rough-smooth (texture) discrimination, but spared complex-concave and square-diamond (shape) discriminations. The opposite pattern was seen in area 2 lesions. Thus, the hand appears to be represented and rerepresented within specific subdivisions on somatosensory cortex according to sensory "submodality."

The notion of sensory submodality dates back at least to von Frey (1895), who divided the tactile sense into light touch, pressure, temperature, and pain sensitivity. Head (1918) divided sensory functions into three categories: (1) recognition of spatial relations (passive movement, two-point discrimination, and point localization), (2) relative sensitivity to touch, temperature, and pain, and (3) recognition of similarity and difference (size, shape, weight, and texture). Submodalities may be selectively impaired, while others spared, by circumscribed cortical lesions. Head's (1918) framework, for example, suggests that discriminatory defects are accompanied by defects in the discrimination of texture and weight, but not by impaired perception of spatial relations, touch, temperature, or pain (cf. Corkin, 1978). Head et al. (1905), based on studies of recovery from peripheral nerve injuries, distinguished betwen "protopathic" and "epicritic" sensation. The epicritic system subserves local point sensibility, while the protopathic system is more diffuse. The protopathic-epicritic distinction has been widely accepted by anatomists and physiologists (Rose and Wool-sey; 1949; Mountcastle, 1961), but unlike Head, these authors has emphasized the anatomic implications of this distinction at the cortical and thalamic, rather than at the peripheral level (Hécaen and Albert, 1978, p. 279 ff). As implied previously, the epicritic aspects of touch are more directly subserved by the medical lemniscal–S I system, while the protopathic dimension relates more closely to the functions of the bilaterally represented S II, though there is considerable functional overlap between the two systems.

CORTICAL TACTILE DISORDERS

The brief review of the somatosensory systems has been designed to emphasize the complexity of this sensory modality, and to enable the reader to anticipate the enormous variability with which patients suffering from tactile recognition and identification disorders present. Historically, there have been two views regarding the nature and functional localization of disorders or tactile sensation. The first, more traditional view is that sensory defects are associated with the contralateral primary somatosensory projection area in the postcentral gyrus (Head, 1920). The other perspective is that more diffuse aspects of cortex (e.g., posterior parietal lobe) are involved in somatosensory perception (Semmes et al., 1960). In a series of studies, Corkin and colleagues (Corkin, 1964; Corkin et al., 1970, 1973) administered quantitative tasks of pressure sensitivity, two-point discrimination, point localization, position sense, and tactual object recognition to patients who had been operated on for relief of focal epileptic seizures. The most severe disorders of cortical tactile sensation were produced by lesions in the contralateral postcentral gyrus. Also, clear demonstration was made of the existence of bilateral sensory defects associated with a unilateral cortical lesion, as had been previously reported by Semmes et al. (1960) and Oppenheim (1906).

Corkin found that the most severe defects occurred in patients whose lesions encroached on the hand area. This is consistent with the findings of Roland (1976) in his studies of tactual shape and size discrimination impairment with focal cortical lesions. Corkin et al. (1970) also found that disorders of tactual object recognition were restricted to the contralateral hand in patients with lesions that involved the hand area in S I. Importantly, defects of tactile object recognition were always associated with significant defects in pressure sensitivity, two-point discrimination, and other elementary sensory functions. Patients with parietal lobe lesions sparing S I did not show object identification disturbances.

Twenty of 50 patients with parietal lobe involvement showed additional sensory defects ipsilateral to the damaged hemisphere (Corkin et al., 1970). This effect was found with equal frequency after left- and right-hemisphere excision, in contrast to previous studies which had found the incidence of ipsilateral sensory impairment to be much more frequent following left-hemisphere damage (Semmes et al., 1960). Differences in the extent of lesions in the samples used by Corkin et al. (circumscribed cortical excisions) and Semmes et al. (penetrating missile wounds) may account for some of these discrepancies. An important anatomic fact is that, in patients with bilateral sensory defects of the hand, the postcentral hand area need not be involved (Corkin et al., 1973). The area of damage implicated in these patients was tentatively offered as S II. In summarizing this data, Corkin (1978) suggests that unilateral S I hand area lesions produce severe contralateral sensory defects, while unilateral S II lesions may produce milder defects which affect both hands.

There is growing evidence of hemispheric specialization for certain "higher" somesthetic functions. Data on this issue can be found in cerebral laterality studies, examinations of patients following brain dissection, and in studies of performance on complex somatosensory tasks after unilateral hemispheric lesions (Corkin, 1978; Hécaen and Albert, 1978). While laterality studies have failed to show hemispheric specialization for elementary somesthetic functions such as pressure sensitivity (Fennell et al., 1967), vibration sensitivity (Seiler and Ricker, 1971; cited in Corkin, 1978), two-point discrimination (McCall and Cunningham, 1971), or point localization (Semmes et al., 1960; Weinstein, 1968), results of complex sensory tasks requiring spatial exploration of figures or fine temporal analysis reveal evidence of hemispheric specialization. The left hand–right hemisphere combination appears especially proficient at tasks in which a spatial factor is important, such as in ciphering braille (Rudel et al., 1974) or perceiving the spatial orientation of tactually presented rods (Benton et al., 1973). Results from studies of split-brain patients (reviewed in detail by Corkin, 1978) are consistent with these conclusions; the left hand–right hemisphere combination is better able to perform complex, spatially patterned discriminations, although the right hand–left hemisphere can succeed if familiar stimuli are presented, if a small array of objects is involved, or in other situations in which linguistic processing can be effectively used.

Thus, patients with right-hemisphere disease do worse than left-hemisphere-damaged patients in tasks requiring the perception of complexly organized spatial stimuli, though any patient with elementary somatosensory dysfunction, regardless of hand, can be expected to do poorly in that hand (Corkin, 1978). Semmes (1965) has identified a group of patients without primary sensory tactile impairment who fail in tests of object shape discrimination. These patients were unimpaired in roughness, texture, and size discrimination, but showed profound impairments on tests of spatial orientation and route finding. These patients suffered from lesions of the superior parietal lobe. Semmes concluded that there is a "nontactual" factor in these discriminative defects that transcended sensory modality. According to her view, what is "spatial" for vision is represented in touch by the temporal exploration of object qualities. Teuber (1965a,b) interprets the difficulty as a special form of spatial disorientation rather than one of "agnosia for shape."

To summarize, no hemispheric specialization appears to exist for elementary somatosensory function, though there is growing evidence that the right hemisphere is more strongly involved in processing the highly spatial character of some tactile discrimination and identification tasks. Postcentral gyrus lesions frequently result in severe and long-lasting defects in the contralateral hand, while lesions of S II result in less severe, bilateral defects. A general conclusion from this extensive and complex literature is that the central regions (so-called "sensorimotor" cortex) are more directly involved in elementary somatosensory function, while complex somatosensory tasks possessing strong spatial or motor exploratory components involve additional structures posterior or anterior to the sensorimotor region (Corkin, 1978). This distinction makes it possible to see a "higher" somatosensory disorder in the absence of "elementary" sensory loss. Whether this "higher" disorder deserves to be called an agnosia is a subject to which we now turn.

TACTILE AGNOSIA

The patient with tactile agnosia cannot appreciate the nature or significance of objects placed in the hand despite elementary somatosensory function, intellectual ability, attentional capacity, and linguistic skill adequate to the task of object identification. The terms astereognosis and pure astereognosis have been sometimes used synonymously with tactile agnosia, and sometimes used to describe basic defects in the appreciation of size, shape, and texture. Delay (1935) asserted that astereognosis was a complex disorder comprised of amorphognosis, ahylognosis, *and* tactile agnosia. In our view, astereognosis, as it has been described in the literature, essentially refers to apperceptive tactile agnosia. We will use the term in this fashion, and will reserve the term tactile agnosia for cases in which a deficit of tactile object recognition exists without concomitant sensory-perceptual defects.

Clinical case reports of pure astereognosis are rare (Raymond and Egger, 1906; Bonhoeffer, 1918; Campora, 1925; Hécaen and David, 1945; Newcombe and Ratcliff, 1974). Frequently, obvious sensory defects do appear at some point in the clinical course of these patients, though not necessarily coincident with the indentification disturbance. The astereognosic patient frequently has defects limited to one hand, usually the left, though patients with defects limited to the right hand have been reported (Hécaen and David, 1945). In some cases, the asymbolic hand can eventually achieve recognition of the object, though only after protracted linguistic analysis of the separate features.

Many astereognosic patients do not normally palpate the object when it is placed in the hand for identification (Oppenheim, 1906, 1991). This suggests a defect in the mechanism whereby tactile impressions are collected to form an integrated percept of the whole object, or a defect in stored structural tactile representations. Motor and sensory information is highly integrated in the act of palpating an object; motor commands are issued that direct the hand in ongoing exploration. Roland and Larsen (1976), in a series of experiments using regional cerebral blood flow (rCBF) during astereognostic testing in man, have shown that local rCBF increases occur most strongly in the contralateral sensorimotor hand area and the premotor region. Though sensorimotor integration and proprioception are crucial components in tactile identification, it should be noted that the motor component probably has a complex role and is not obligatory in any simple sense. This conclusion is warranted by two clinical facts: (1) motor paralysis does not necessarily cause tactile identification disturbances (Caselli, 1991b) and (2) objects can often be identified if they are passively moved across the subject's hand, independent of active manipulation. Still, the fact that true astereognosics do not palpate objects suggests that elementary sensory function is not actively brought to bear, nor is it adequately integrated with motor information in the perceptual processing of the stimulus.

Disorders of tactile object recognition (tactile agnosia) without concomitant sensory or higher-order perceptual defects have been rarely reported. Evidence for this kind of associative defect exists when elementary somatosensory defects are either absent or too mild to account for a tactile object recognition disturbance and when the patient can draw or match tactually presented stimuli. For example, the patient of Hécaen and David (1945) could draw an accurate picture of an object placed in the hand and could then name the picture. The patients of Newcombe and Ratcliff (1974) could tactually match to sample even though they had a disturbance in recognition of the nature of objects.

As in other forms of agnosia, there has been significant debate regarding the existence of "true" tactile agnosia. Three general disclaimers have been proposed. The first is the familiar argument that all disturbances of tactile object identification can be traced to defects of elementary somatosensory dysfunction. The second states that the defect is not an agnosia, but instead represents a modality-specific anomia. Third, there are those who do not deny the existence of "higher" defects of tactile identification in the context of normal "elementary" somatosensory function, but who say that the defect of function in astereognosis is "spatial" and supramodal, involving both tactile and visual disturbances. Because one of the hallmarks of the agnosia concept is its modality specificity, this third view rejects the notion that tactile object identification disturbances are agnosic in nature. Each of these views is capable of handling some, but not all, of the data. We will briefly examine the status of each of these arguments below.

The possible role of subtle somatosensory defects in producing disorders of tactile identification has been raised by several authors (Bay, 1944; Head and Holmes, 1911; Corkin et al., 1970). Bay (1944) stated that most putative cases of tactile agnosia had been inadequately tested for elementary somatosensory dysfunction, and specifically implicated labile thresholds and defects in performing complex sensory discriminations. Head and Holmes (1911) also stressed the importance of inconstant thresholds, and found that rapid local fatigue and abnormal persistence of sensations frequently accompanied defects of tactile object identification. Semmes (1953) mentions the possible contributory role of tactile extinction revealed by the method of double simultaneous stimulation, and states that "if one stimulus 'extinguishes' or 'obscures' the perception of another, or displaces the subjective position, the resultant impression might be sufficiently different from normal perception to make recognition impossible" (p. 144).

It has been difficult to fully counter the sensory argument, since historical acceptance of the notion of tactile agnosia has been sufficiently great to cause some authors to be sloppy with respect to evaluations of elementary somatosensory function. One recent exception is a careful study by Caselli (1991b) which examined tactile object recognition (TOR) disturbances in 84 patients with a variety of peripheral and central nervous system diseases. Using an extensive battery of tests of somatosensory function and two tests of TOR, Caselli found a number of patients who, despite normal or only mildly compromised somatosensory function, had disproportionate TOR impairment. According to Caselli, this type of impairment can result from unilateral damage (in either hemisphere) involving parietotemporal cortices, possibly affecting S II. Hécaen (1972) paid careful attention to somatosensory function in examining his patient, revealing neither lability of threshold nor sensory perseveration. Although only one hand was agnosic in this patient, tactile discrimination, touch, and thickness discrimination was equal in both hands. There did appear to be a subtle defect in shape discrimination in the affected hand, as the patient could not accurately judge a series of objects on a continuum from ovoid to sphere, but, like many of Caselli's patients, this defect seemed insufficient in severity to account for the TOR disturbance. Delay (1935) found no differences between the hands for pain, temperature, pressure, kinesthesis, or vibration sense, though tactile localization and position sense were poorer in the affected hand (cf. Hécaen and Albert, 1978). Thus, there are cases in which defects in elementary somatosensory function cannot fully account for the observed defects in object identification.

Although the existence of tactile agnosia seems now established, the possibility that a modality-specific anomia might account for some instances of TOR impairment is raised by the remarkable patient of Geschwind and Kaplan (1962). This patient underwent surgical extirpation of a left-hemisphere glioblastoma and postoperatively developed a left anterior cerebral artery distribution infarction involving the anterior four-fifths of the corpus callosum. He was unable to name or to supply verbal descriptions of items placed in the left hand but could draw misidentified objects with the left hand and could tactually choose a previously presented object from a larger group.

It is important to emphasize the differences between Geschwind and Kaplan's patient and other patients with deficient tactile object identification. First, because their patient could demonstrate recognition "nonverbally," the defect was not a tactile agnosia in the true sense, but instead represented a disconnection of right-hemisphere (left-hand) tactual identification mechanisms from the speech area in the left hemisphere. Second, their patient, who had bilateral lesions, demonstrated an object naming defect confined to the left hand (Geschwind and Kaplan, 1962; Watson and Heilman, 1983; Gazzaniga and Sperry, 1967; Gazzaniga et al. 1963; Lhermitte et al., 1976). This is in contrast to patients with bilateral impairments in TOR after a unilateral lesions insufficient in size or location to cause a complete tactile-verbal disconnection syndrome (e.g., Goldstein, 1916; Oppenheim, 1906; Lhermitte and Ajuriaguerra, 1938). It also contrasts with the patient reported by Beauvois et al. (1978) who, after surgical removal of a large left parieto-occipital tumor, developed a modality-specific inability to name or verbally describe objects placed in either hand. When blindfolded, the patient could demonstrate the use of tactually presented objects. Naming errors were frequently semantic confusions. The authors interpret the deficit as a "bilateral tactile aphasia," and suggest that it represents the tactile analogue of "optic aphasia" (Lhermitte and Beauvois, 1973). Third, Geschwind and Kaplan's patient showed normal tactual exploration of objects, while patients with apperceptive tactile agnosia (astereognosis) show deficient palpation of objects, characterized either by a reluctance to manipulate the object or by a stereotypic pattern of manipulation which is independent of specific object qualities.

"SUPRAMODAL" SPATIAL DEFECTS

Some patients with tactile recognition disorders also have profound defects in spatial localization, route finding, and other visuospatial tasks (Semmes, 1965; Corkin, 1978). In concluding her review of somatosensory function, Corkin (1978) states that it is "possible to observe an impairment of high tactile functions in an individual whose elementary sensory status is preserved. It is inappropriate, however, to call this impairment an agnosia, because the higher-order deficits seen are not specific to somethesis" (p. 145). This is a persuasive and important argument, but should not be taken to mean that tactile agnosia as a modality-specific entity does not exist in some patients. It is possible, for example, that large lesions involving parietal cortex and underlying white matter affect neural systems involved in supramodal spatial and attentional ability in addition to specifically involving the second somatosensory system. What may result from this kind of lesion is a sort of "mixed" defect in which somatosensory, spatial, attentional, and motivational factors combine in unspecified amounts. The fact that such a complex disorder exists does not negate the possibility that, with more restricted lesions, a "purer," modality-specific defect corresponding to tactile agnosia will result.

Although the anatomic and clinical evidence is far from clear, it seems reasonable to distinguish four defects of somatosensory recognition: cortical tactile disorders, astereognosis, tactile agnosia, and disorders of tactile naming secondary to tactile-verbal disconnection. Cortical tactile disorders involve defects in basic and intermediate somatosensory function, the end result of which will be pervasive somatosensory impairment in addition to defects in tactile object recognition. We believe that astereognosis is a more specific defect, that it deserves a designation as an apperceptive tactile agnosia (but see Tranel, 1991), and that it is primarily caused by a lesion in the functional system subserved by the middle third of the postcentral gyrus (the "hand area") and its cortical and subcortical connections. Tactile agnosia, in contrast, seems to result from parietotemporal lesions that primarily involve S II (Caselli, 1991a).

Understanding complex somatosensory function in the individual patient requires a systematic neuropsychological evaluation of the task of tactual object identification as well as an evaluation of elementary and intermediate somatosensory function (Caselli, 1991a,b). When an object is palpated, sensory and proprioceptive cues received by postcentral gyrus interact with premotor region to direct a series of coordinated movements necessary to construct a "tactile image" of the object. Most TOR tasks contain components which could be described as sensory, spatial, proprioceptive, constructive and motor. The functional interconnections between S I, premotor region, and more posterior portions of the parietal cortex highlight the challenges in functionally separating these task dimensions in tasks of tactile object recognition.

## AGNOSIA AND CONSCIOUS AWARENESS

One of the most intriguing and theoretically important recent developments in our understanding of agnosia has been the finding that, despite a profound inability in direct object/face identification, many agnosics are able to demonstrate that some aspect of the stimulus may be recognized if appropriate tests of recognition are used. Generally speaking, such tests have the common characteristic of not requiring the subject to make direct "conscious" reference to the stimulus identity. Instead, such knowledge is embedded in the task and is assessed in an indirect or "implicit" way.

Dissociations of this type have received substantial attention in the literature on acquired amnesia (Schacter, 1987), in which patients with severe impairments in new learning show normal or near normal acquisition of motor (Milner et al., 1968) or cognitive skills (Cohen and Squire, 1980; Moscovitch et al., 1986), and demonstrate intact repetition priming when assessed via word-stem completion (Graf et al., 1984) or perceptual identification tasks (Cermak et al., 1985). Such dissociations have caused some authors (Sherry and Schacter, 1987) to postulate at least two distinct memory systems, one responsible for conscious "explicit" remembering, the other for more automatic or "implicit" aspects of memory, while others (e.g., Roediger, 1990; Roediger and Blaxton, 1987) have emphasized the different processing demands required by explicit and implicit memory tasks (see Chapter 15).

Similar distinctions have been invoked to explain lexical access without awareness in acquired alexia (Coslett and Saffran, 1986b; Landis et al., 1980; Shallice and Saffran, 1986), preserved visual identification capacity in hemianopic fields ("blindsight"; Weiskrantz et al., 1974; Weiskrantz, 1986), and preserved semantic priming in Wernicke's aphasia (Milberg and Blumstein, 1981; Blumstein et al., 1982). In all of these examples, evidence exists that the cognitive system thought to be impaired in these patients is capable of substantial processing. However, the results of such processing do not, or cannot, access conscious awareness (cf. Schacter et al., 1988, for a review).

The best evidence for "covert recognition" in agnosia has emerged from studies of patients with prosopagnosia (cf. Bruyer, 1991, for a review). Such evidence has been found across a number of patients and measures. Bruyer et al. (1983) provided the first behavioral evidence of covert recognition when they showed that their prosopagnosic had more difficulty learning to match unrecognized faces with arbitrary names than he did with real names. DeHaan, et al. (1987b) found that their prosopagnosic, like their normal controls, performed same-different judgments more rapidly when the task involved famous faces than when it involved unknown faces. In these two examples, performance benefited from familiarity even though the patients could not overtly recognize the faces themselves.

In an elegant series of studies, DeHaan et al. (1987a,b) have used the "face-name interference" (FNI) task (Young et al., 1986) to explore preserved processing of semantic information from faces in prosopagnosia (1987a,b). In FNI, subjects are asked to make a semantic classification judgment (e.g., politician-nonpolitician) on a printed word. Presented along with the name, but irrelevant for the name classification task, is a famous face that is either (1) the same identity as the printed name, (2) from the same semantic category as the printed name, or (3) from a different category. In normals, name classification is slowed by the presence of a face from a different semantic category, presumably a Stroop-like phenomenon. Several studies have shown normal face-name interference effects in prosopagnosia (DeHaan, et al. 1987a,b, 1992), suggesting that, at some level, prosopagnosics can extract semantic information from faces and can thus become distracted by it when they perform the name classification task.

Covert recognition in prosopagnosia has also been demonstrated using psychophysiological (Bauer, 1984; Bauer and Verfaellie, 1986; Tranel and Damasio, 1985, 1988), electrophysiological (Debruille et al., 1989; Renault et al., 1989), and oculmotor (Rizzo et al., 1987) measures. Bauer (1984) showed a prosopagnosic a series of faces and read five multiple-choice names, one of which was correct for each. Electrodermal responses were simultaneously recorded. Despite a total inability to identify a single face, the prosopagnosic showed the largest electrodermal response to 60%

of the target names. Bauer and Verfaellie (1986) replicated this basic effect with a second prosopagnosic, but failed to show covert learning of previously unfamiliar faces.

Tranel and Damasio (1985) showed familiar (previously known) and unfamiliar (novel) faces to a prosopagnosic and a second patient with a visual recent memory disorder while recording verbal identification, rated confidence, and electrodermal responses. Both patients showed larger electrodermal responses to previously known than to novel faces.

Renault et al. (1989) asked their prosopagnosic to give familiarity judgments to a series of faces in which the proportion of familiar and unfamiliar faces were varied. They found that, despite poor explicit recognition, P300 amplitude varied inversely with stimulus probability and latency varied with face familiarity.

Finally, Rizzo et al. (1987) evaluated exploratory eye movements in two prosopagnosic patients while they viewed famous and unfamiliar faces. Like normals, these patients examined the whole face when encountering a novel stimulus, but concentrated on the internal features when examining famous faces. Thus, the manner of visual exploration reveals that, at some level, facial familiarity is detected by the visual system although it is not reflected in the patients' verbal report.

Recently, similar techniques have been applied to the question of whether prosopagnosics can demonstrate new episodic learning of faces similar to that seen in amnesic subjects. Sergent and Poncet (1990) asked their prosopagnosic to inspect a series of famous and novel faces for a task of subsequent recognition. Afterward, some of these faces (old) were combined with a series of (new) faces and a new/old judgment was required. Although the patient was generally unable to identify the old or famous face, face familiarity led to increased accuracy in episodic recognition. Remarkably, on some trials, the patient was able to directly recognize the face.

Greve and Bauer (1990) used a variant of Zajonc's "mere exposure" paradigm to demonstrate covert learning of new faces in their prosopagnosic. The patient was shown a series of faces which were later paired with a novel distractor for forced-choice recognition and preference judgments. In the preference-judgment task, the subject was asked which of the two faces he liked better. He performed at chance on forced-choice recognition, but liked significantly more of the target faces than was predicted by chance. Thus, both of these studies suggest that prosopagnosics can learn at least some aspects of new faces provided that such learning is assessed indirectly.

In a few patients, psychophysiological (Bauer, 1986) and behavioral (Newcombe et al., 1989) measures have failed to reveal evidence of covert recognition (cf. Bruyer, 1991, for a more detailed review; Young and DeHaan, 1988). These patients had significant apperceptive defects, suggesting impairment prior to the level of the "face recognition unit." This raises the interesting possibility that covert recognition is primarily a characteristic of "associative" forms of agnosia.

Although much remains to be learned, these findings, and those in the literatures on amnesia, alexia, aphasia, and blindsight, encourage two tentative and somewhat general conclusions. First, they suggest that a significant amount of perceptual and semantic processing must take place relatively "early" in the processing chain, prior to (or independent of) the process that generates contextual or autobiographical recognition (cf. Damasio, 1989; Schacter, 1989). Second, they all seem to imply that conscious or autobiographical recognition (or appreciation) of a stimulus involves mechanisms that are different from the mechanisms that process various attributes of the stimulus itself (Schacter et al., 1988; Dimond, 1976). In more specific terms, Schacter (1989) offers a general account of "explicit"-"implicit" dissociations by proposing that these two domains reflect parallel, nonoverlapping outputs of early, "modular" cortices dedicated to processing specific types of information. In this view, one set of outputs links early cortices' output with motor, verbal, and viscero-autonomic response systems that are, themselves, capable of "reading out" cortical activity without conscious or executive control. Another independent set of outputs links modular cortices with a "conscious awareness system" responsible, in the case of object recognition, for explicit stimulus identification. According to this model, covert recognition in agnosia would result when functional interaction between modular cortices is selectively interrupted while modular outputs to motor, verbal, and autonomic response systems remain intact. This impairment in functional interaction between modular cortices and the consciousness system would lead to precisely the kind of deficit one sees in agnosia: a domain-specific impairment in conscious identification without a global impairment in conscious awareness.

## EXAMINATION OF THE PATIENT WITH AGNOSIA

Two basic principles should guide the examination of the agnosic patient. First, care should be taken to rule out the possibility that the recognition disorder is attributable to sensory-perceptual function, aphasia, generalized memory loss, or dementia. Second, an extensive analysis of the scope and limits of the patient's defect is required to characterize its functional locus.

### *Ruling Out Alternative Explanations*

At the outset, it is important to remember that agnosic recognition failures are most often modality specific. Patients who exhibit multimodal defects are more likely to be suffering from amnesic syndrome, dementia, or, in rare cases, generalized impairments in semantic access. The nonaphasic agnosic patient will not usually manifest word-finding difficulty in spontaneous speech, and will generally succeed in generating lists of words in specific categories, in completing open-ended sentences, and in supplying words that correspond with definitions. Except in the rare case of optic aphasia, the agnosic will not be able to identify the misnamed objects by means of circumlocution, or by indicating function. It is important to determine whether the patient is able to demonstrate the use of objects not in his presence and to follow commands not requiring objects (e.g., salute, wave good-bye, make a fist, etc.). Failures of this type in the presence of otherwise intact auditory comprehension indicate apraxia; subsequent failure to demonstrate the use of objects presented on visual confrontation may therefore be apractic, not agnosic.

In pointing and naming tasks, it is important to be certain that the patient is visually fixating on the objects to be identified and that pointing errors are not due to mislocation in space. Recognition should be examined both in the context of normal surroundings and in the formal test setting, taking care to ensure that the patient is familiar with target objects.

As a start, comprehensive neurologic and neuropsychological assessment of intellectual skill, memory function, language, constructional/perceptual ability, attention, problem solving, and personality/emotional factors should be undertaken to rule out bracketing conditions.

### Characterizing the Nature of the Defect

In the visual sphere, the recognition of objects, colors, words, geometric forms, faces, and emblems and signs should be evaluated. In the event of failure to recognize, the patient should be allowed to match misidentified items to sample and to produce drawings of objects not identified. Quantative achievement *and qualitative performance* on these tasks should be carefully noted, keeping in mind that quantitatively correct matching and accurate drawing does not necessarily suggest intact perceptual processing. Poor drawing does not necessarily implicate an apperceptive defect, since visuomotor or constructional defects may also be present. For this reason, it is important to use tasks in addition to drawing to document intact perception. Cross-modal matching and matching objects across different views should be evaluated. Line drawings to be copied should contain sufficient internal detail so that slavish tracing of an outline can, if present, be elicited.

Other perceptual functions, such as figure-ground perception (hidden figures), closure and synthetic ability, topographical orientation, route finding, and visual counting (counting dots on a white paper, picking up pennies spread over a table top) should also be evaluated. Visual memory for designs, objects, faces, and colors should be assessed by delayed recall (drawing from memory) and multiple-choice recognition tasks. The ability to categorize, sort misidentified objects, and pair similar objects that are not morphologically identical should be tested.

The patient should be asked to identify pictures of well-known people and to identify hospital staff by face. If recognition does not occur, the patient should be asked to determine whether the face is of a male or female or whether the face is of a human or animal. In the acutely hospitalized patient, ability to recognize visiting family can be assessed by dressing the family member in a white coat or other appropriate hospital garb to minimize extrafacial differences between them and hospital personnel. If face recognition impairment exists, it is important to demonstrate intact semantic (nonvisual) knowledge about persons that cannot be recognized visually. Failure to name a particular face should, therefore, be further examined by asking the subject to provide information (e.g., "Who is Margaret Thatcher?") about unrecognized personalities. Discrimination of faces across different viewpoints should be evaluated with matching tasks (e.g., Benton Facial Recognition Test).

Color perception should be tested with pseudoisochromatic plates and with the Munsell-Farnsworth 100 Hue Test ("visual" color tasks). The patient should be asked to respond to verbal tasks such as identifying the color of a banana, to list as many colors as possible in a minute, or to name as many items as possible of a certain color. Other visual tasks, including coloring line drawings with crayons, should be given. Finally, visual-verbal color tasks such as naming colors pointed out by the examiner or pointing to named colors should be routinely presented.

The possibility of confabulation interfering with cognitive and gnostic performance should be kept in mind. Therefore, test performance when the patient is allowed to verbalize should be compared with performance when he is prohibited from verbalizing by asking him to count backward or by having him place his tongue between his teeth. Comparing naming in the tactile modality alone with simultaneous visual and tactile presentation is also important.

Careful visual fields and visual acuity measures are crucial. It may be necessary, in testing patients who cannot read, to construct tests of acuity that use nonverbal targets such as the orientation of lines of various lengths and distances from the viewer, or the detection of two points at variable distances from each other and from the patient. If equipment is available, detailed psychophysical tests should be employed including absolute threshold determination, local adaptation time, flicker fusion, contrast and spatial frequency sensitivity, movement aftereffect, and the tachistoscopic presentation of single and multiple items. In patients with associated alexia without agraphia, tachistoscopic presentation of words and letters, as well as a neurobehaviorally oriented reading battery, should be given. Depth perception using Julesz figures should be tested. Luminance discrimination should also be assessed. The use of an eye-movement monitor may be useful in describing visual scanning behavior. In settings where such sophisticated equipment is not available, careful observational analysis of visual exploratory behavior, manifested in eye movements, head turning, and step-by-step feature comparisons, should nonetheless be conducted.

In the auditory sphere, standard audiometric testing using speech reception and pure tone audiometry should be conducted. The ability to localize sounds in space should also be examined by using both absolute and relative localization tasks. It should be remembered that patients with acquired auditory sound agnosia do not ordinarily complain about their problems. Recognition of nonverbal sounds should be tested preferably with the use of a series of tape-recorded environmental sounds that are sufficiently familiar to unimpaired subjects to yield nearly perfect recognition. The Seashore Tests of Musical Talent may be used with the understanding that in the absence of history of proven musical ability and interest, results may be difficult to interpret.

In the tactile sphere, each hand should be assessed separately in the performance of basic somatosensory function (touch, pain, temperature, vibration, kinesthesia, proprioception, two-point discrimination, double simultaneous stimulation, as well as discrimination of weight, texture, shape, and substance; Caselli, 1991b). In assessing tactile object recognition, verbal, pointing, and matching tasks should be used. Cross-modal matching (tactual-verbal, tactual-visual) is also important in evaluating the scope of the recognition defect. It is important to allow the patient to draw misidentified objects or to after-select them from a group tactually. Tactual exploratory behavior should also be carefully observed.

## CONCLUSION

During the past decade, significant advances have been made toward an understanding of the complex components of recognition processes. It is now clear that "recognition" is not a unitary, or even a two-step process. Much of the age-old debate about the existence of agnosia can be attributed to the fact that our models of recognition have generated some incorrect assumptions about what should happen when the recognition system becomes damaged. The best example is the debate over whether agnosia is a perceptual or memory access problem. The major difficulty with this question has been that it has forced us to assume a sharp distinction between perception and memory, an assumption that has been at the root of most of the major disagreements regarding the ontological status of agnosia. In the past decade, new concepts from computational neuroscience and cognitive neuropsychology have largely resolved this question by questioning the inherent separability of memory and perception and have given us new tools with which to more precisely evaluate and conceptualize disturbances of recognition.

The concept of recognition itself encompasses a broad range of behaviors, including attention, feature extraction, exploratory behavior, pattern and form perception, temporal resolution, and memory. New data on sensory and perceptual systems have revealed the exquisitely complex, "modular" nature of the cortical and subcortical systems that support sensory and perceptual activities. Because of these advances, we have transcended the notion of a two-stage recognition process comprised of "apperception" and "association." Instead, recognition of sensorially presented stimuli is now understood as a complex outcome of parallel processing streams occurring simultaneously at cortical and subcortical levels.

At the same time, new data on "preserved" recognition capacities in agnosics have resulted in renewed interest in how dissociations between "implicit" and "explicit" performances can contribute to a neuropsychology of consciousness and awareness. What has emerged is a general picture in which an extensive amount of "early" processing proceeds relatively normally but does not, or cannot, access mechanisms for conscious, deliberate identification. However, the functional and anatomic loci of this problem remain largely unknown.

These complexities make it extremely unlikely that a "core" defect responsible for all agnosic phenomenon exists. Abandoning the search for the "core agnosia" has been necessary in light of emerging neurophysiological, anatomical, and neuropsychological data. With increasing cross-fertilization among these areas, and with new concepts and methods in hand, a meaningful understanding of the spectrum of agnosic deficits, and of normal recognition abilities, is rapidly emerging.

## REFERENCES

Adams, A. E., Rosenberg, K., Winter, H., and Zollner, C. (1977). A case of cortical deafness. *Arch. Psychiatr. Nervenkr.* 224:213–220.
Adler, A. (1944). Disintegration and restoration of optic recognition in visual agnosia. *Arch. Neurol. Psychiatry* 51:243–259.

Albert, M. L., and Bear, D. (1974). Time to understand: a case study of word deafness with reference to the role of time in auditory comprehension. *Brain* 97:373–384.

Albert, M. L., Reches, A., and Silverberg, R. (1975a). Associative visual agnosia without alexia. *Neurology* 25:322–326.

Albert, M. L., Reches, A., and Silverberg, R. (1975b). Hemianopic colour blindness. *J. Neurol. Neurosurg. Psychiatry* 38:546–549.

Albert, M. L., Soffer, D., Silverberg, R., and Reches, A. (1979). The anatomic basis of visual agnosia. *Neurology (Minneap.)* 29:876–879.

Albert, M. L., Sparks, R., von Stockert, T., and Sax, D. (1972). A case study of auditory agnosia: linguistic and nonlinguistic processing. *Cortex* 8:427–433.

Alexander, M. P., and Albert, M. L. (1983). The anatomical basis of visual agnosia. In *Localization in Neuropsychology*, A. Kertesz (ed.). New York: Academic Press.

Alexander, M. P., Stuss, D. T., and Benson, D. F. (1979). Capgras syndrome: a reduplicative phenomenon. *Neurology* 29:334–339.

Anton, G. (1899). Ueber die Selbstwahrnehmungen der Herderkrankungen des Gehirns durch den Kranken bei Rindenblindheit und Rindentaubheit. *Arch. Psychiatry* 32:86–127.

Assal, G., and Despland, P. A. (1973). Presentation d'un cas d'agnosie auditive. *Otoneuro-ophtalmologie* 45:353–355.

Auerbach, S. H., Allard, T., Naeser, M., Alexander M. P., and Albert M. L. (1982). Pure word deafness: analysis of a case with bilateral lesions and a defect at the prephonemic level. *Brain* 105:271–300.

Balint, R. (1909). Seelenlahmung des "Schauens", optische Ataxie, raumliche Storung der Aufmerksamkeit. *Monatsschr. Psychiatr. Neurol.* 25:57–71.

Bauer, R. M. (1982). Visual hypoemotionality as a symptom of visual-limbic disconnection in man. *Arch. Neurol.* 39:702–708.

Bauer, R. M. (1984). Autonomic recognition of names and faces in prosopagnosia: a neuropsychological application of the Guilty Knowledge Test. *Neuropsychologia* 22:457–469.

Bauer, R. M. (1986). The cognitive psychophysiology of prosopagnosia. In *Aspects of Face Processing*, H. D. Ellis, M. A. Jeeves, F. Newcombe, and A. W. Young (eds.). Dordrecht: Martinus Nijhoff.

Bauer, R. M., and Trobe, J. (1984). Visual memory and perceptual impairments in prosopagnosia. *J. Clin. Neuro-Ophthalmol.* 4:39–46.

Bauer, R. M., and Verfaellie, M. (1986). Electrodermal discrimination of familiar but not unfamiliar faces in prosopagnosia. *Brain Cognition* 8:240–252.

Bay, E. (1953). Disturbances of visual perception and their examination. *Brain* 76:515–550.

Bay, E. (1944). Zum problem der taktilen Agnosie. *Dtsch. Z. Nervenkr.* 156:1–3, 64–96.

Beauvois, M. F. (1982). Optic aphasia: a process of interaction between vision and language. *Philos. Trans. R. Soc. Lond. [Biol.]* 298:35–47.

Beauvois, M. F., Saillant, B., Meininger, V., and Lhermitte, F. (1978). Bilateral tactile aphasia: a tacto-verbal dysfunction. *Brain* 101:381–401.

Bender, M. D., and Feldman, M. (1972). The so-called "visual agnosias." *Brain* 95:173–186.

Benson, D. F., and Greenberg, J. P. (1969). Visual form agnosia. *Arch. Neurol.* 20:82–89.

Benson, D. F., Davis, R. J., and Snyder, B. D. (1988). Posterior cortical atrophy. *Arch. Neurol.* 45:789–793.

Benson, D. F., Segarra, J., and Albert, M. L. (1974). Visual agnosia-prosopagnosia. *Arch. Neurol.* 30:307–310.

Benton, A. L. (1980). The neuropsychology of face recognition. *Am. Psychol.* 35:176–186.

Benton, A. L. (1990). Face recognition 1990. *Cortex* 26:491–499.

Benton, A. L., and Van Allen, M. W. (1972). Prosopagnosia and facial discrimination. *J. Neurol. Sci.* 15:167–172.

Benton, A. L., Levin, A., and Varney, N. (1973). Tactile perception of direction in normal subjects. *Neurology* 23:1248–1250.

Berkley, M. A., and Sprague, J. M. (1979). Striate cortex and visual acuity functions in the cat. *J. Comp. Neurol.* 187:679–702.

Beyn, E. S., and Knyazeva, G. R. (1962). The problem of prosopagnosia. *J. Neurol. Neurosurg. Psychiatry* 25:154–158.

Blumstein, S., and Cooper, W. (1974). Hemispheric processing of intonation contours. *Cortex* 10:146–158.

Blumstein, S. E., Milberg, W., and Shrier, R. (1982). Semantic processing in aphasia: evidence from an auditory lexical decision task. *Brain Lang.* 17:301–315.

Bodamer, J. (1947). Prosopagnosie. *Arch. Psychiatr. Nervenkr.* 179:6–54.

Boller, F., Cole, M., Kim, Y., Mack, J. L., and Patawaran, C. (1975). Optic ataxia: Clinical-radiological correlations with the EMI scan. *J. Neurol. Neurosurg. Psychiatry* 38:954–958.

Bonhoeffer, K. (1918). Partielle reine Tastlahmung. *Monatsschr. Psychiatr. Neurol.* 43:141–145.

Bornstein, B. (1963). Prosopagnosia. In *Problems of Dynamic Neurology*, L. Halpern (ed.). New York: Grune and Stratton.

Bornstein, B., and Kidron, D. P. (1959). Prosopagnosia. *J. Neurol. Neurosurg. Psychiatry* 22:124–131.

Bornstein, B., Sroka, H., and Munitz, H. (1969). Prosopagnosia with animal face agnosia. *Cortex* 5:164–169.

Botez, M. I. (1975). Two visual systems in clinical neurology: readaptive role of the primitive system in visual agnosic patients. *Eur. Neurol.* 13:101–122.

Botez, M. I., and Serbanescu, T. (1967). Course and outcome of visual static agnosia. *J. Neurol. Sci.* 4:289–297.

Bowers, D. (1981). Acquired color disturbances due to cerebral lesions. Presented at the Seventh Annual Course in Behavioral Neurology and Neuropsychology, Florida Society of Neurology, St. Petersburg Beach, Florida.

Brain, W. R. (1941). Visual object agnosia with special reference to the gestalt theory. *Brain* 64:43–62.

Brodal, A. (1981). *Neurological Anatomy in Relation to Clinical Medicine*, 3rd ed. New York: Oxford University Press.

Brown, J. W. (1972). *Aphasia, Apraxia, and Agnosia—Clinical and Theoretical Aspects.* Springfield, Ill. Charles C. Thomas.

Bruyer, R. (1991). Covert face recognition in prosopagnosia: A review. *Brain Cognition* 15:223–235.

Bruyer, R., Laterre, C., Seron, X., Feyereisen, P., Strypstein, E., Pierrard, E., and Rectem, D. (1983). A case of prosopagnosia with some preserved covert remembrance of familiar faces. *Brain Cognition* 2:257–284.

Buchman, A. S., Garron, D. C., Trost-Cardamone, J. E., Wichter, M. D., and Schwartz, M. (1986). Word deafness: one hundred years later. *J. Neurol. Neurosurg. Psychiatry* 49:489–499.

Buchtel, H. A., and Stewart, J. D. (1989). Auditory agnosia: apperceptive or associative disorder? *Brain Lang.* 37:12–25.

Cambier, J., Masson, M., Elghozi, D. (1980). Agnosie visuelle sans hemianopsie droite chez un svjet droitier. *Rev. Neurol.* (Paris) 136:727–740.

Campion, J. and Latto., R. (1985). Apperceptive agnosia due to carbon monoxide poisoning: an interpretation based on critical band masking from disseminated lesions. *Behav. Brain Res.* 15:227–240.

Campora, G. (1925). Astereognosis: its causes and mechanism. *Brain 18*:65–71.

Caplan, L. R. (1978). Variability of perceptual function: the sensory cortex as a categorizer and deducer. *Brain Lang. 6*:1–13.

Caplan, L. R. (1980). "Top of the basilar" syndrome. *Neurology 30*:72–79.

Caselli, R. J. (1991a). Rediscovering tactile agnosia. *Mayo Clin. Proc. 66*:129–142.

Caselli, R. J. (1991b). Bilateral impairment of somesthetically mediated object recognition in humans. *Mayo Clin. Proc. 66*:357–364.

Celesia, G. G. (1976). Organization of auditory cortical areas in man. *Brain 99*:403–414.

Cermak, L. S., Talbot, N., Chandler, K., and Wolbarst, L. R. (1985). The perceptual priming phenomenon in amnesia. *Neuropsychologia 23*:615–622.

Chocholle, R., Chedru, F., Botte, M. C., Chain, F., and Lhermitte, F. (1975). Etude psychoa-coustique dun cas de surdite corticlae. *Neuropsychologia 13*:163–172.

Cohen, N. J., and Squire, L. R. (1980). Preserved learning and retention of pattern-analyzing skill in amnesia: dissociation of "knowing how" and "knowing that." *Science 210*:207–209.

Cohen, R., and Kelter, S. (1979). Cognitive impairment of aphasics in color to picture matching tasks. *Cortex 15*:235–245.

Cohn, R., Neumann, M. A., and Wood, D. H. (1977). Prosopagnosia: a clinico-pathological study. *Ann. Neurol. 1*:177–182.

Corkin, S., (1964). Somesthetic function after focal cerebral damage in man. Unpublished doc-toral dissertation, McGill University.

Corkin, S. (1978). The role of different cerebral structures in somesthetic perception. In *Hand-book of Perception*, Vol. VI B, C. E. Carterette and M. P. Friedman (eds.). New York: Academic Press, pp. 105–155.

Corkin, S., Milner, B., and Rasmussen, T. (1970). Somatosensory thresholds: contrasting effects of postcentral-gyrus and posterior parietal-lobe excision. *Arch. Neurol. 23*:41–58.

Corkin, S., Milner, B., and Taylor, L. (1973). Bilateral sensory loss after unilateral cerebral lesions in man. Presented at the joint meeting of the American Neurological Association and the Canadian Congress of Neurological Sciences, Montreal.

Corlew, M. M., and Nation, J. E. (1975). Characteristics of visual stimuli and naming perfor-mance in aphasic adults. *Cortex 11*:186–191.

Coslett, H. B., and Saffran, E. M. (1989a). Evidence for preserved reading in "pure alexia." *Brain 112*:327–360.

Coslett, H. B., and Saffran, E. M. (1989b). Preserved object recognition and reading compre-hension in optic aphasia. *Brain 112*:1091–1110.

Coslett, H. B., and Saffran, E. (1991). Simultanagnosia: To see but not two see. *Brain 114*:1523–1545.

Coslett, H. B., Brashear, H. R., and Heilman, K. M. (1984). Pure word deafness after bilateral primary auditory cortex infarcts. *Neurology 34*:347–352.

Critchley, M. N. (1964). The problem of visual agnosia. *J. Neurol. Sci. 1*:274–290.

Critchley, M. N. (1965). Acquired anomalies of colour perception of central origin. *Brain 88*:711–724.

Critchley, M. M., and Henson, R. A. (1977). *Music and the Brain: Studies in the Neurology of Music*. Springfield, Ill.: Charles C. Thomas.

Cummings, J. L., Syndulko, K., Goldberg, Z., and Treiman, D. M. (1982). Palinopsia reconsid-ered. *Neurology 32*:331–341.

Damasio, A. R. (1989). Time-locked multiregional coactivation: a systems-level proposal for the neural substrates of recall and recognition. *Cognition 33*:25–62.

Damasio, A. R. (1990). Category-related recognition defects as a clue to the neural substrates of knowledge. *Trends Neurosci. 13*:95–98.

Damasio, A. R., and Benton, A. L. (1979). Impairment of hand movements under visual guidance. *Neurology (Minneap)* 29:170–174.

Damasio, A. R., Damasio H., and Van Hoesen, G. W. (1982). Prosopagnosia: anatomic basis and behavioral mechanisms. *Neurology (N.Y.)* 32:331–341.

Damasio, A. R., Yamada, T., Damasio, H., Corbett, J., and McKee, J. (1980). Central achromatopsia: behavioral, anatomic, and physiologic aspects. *Neurology* 30:1064–1071.

Damasio, H., McKee, H., and Damasio, A. R. (1979). Determinants of performance in color anomia. *Brain Lang.* 7:74–85.

Davidenkov, S. (1956). Impairments of higher nervous activity: Lecture 8, visual agnosias. In *Clinical Lectures on Nervous Diseases*. Leningrad: State Publishing House of Medical Literature.

Davidoff, J., and Wilson, B. (1985). A case of visual agnosia showing a disorder of presemantic visual classification. *Cortex* 21:121–134.

Debruille, B., Breton, F., Robaey, P., Signoret, J. L., and Renault, B. (1989). Potentiels evoques cerebraux et reconnaissance consciente et non consciente des visages: application a l'etude de prosopagnosie. *Neurophysiol. Clin.* 19:393–405.

DeHaan, E.H.F., Bauer, R. M., and Greve, K. W. (1992). Autonomic and behavioral evidence of covert recognition in prosopagnosia. *Cortex.* 28:77–95.

DeHaan, E.H.F., Young, A., and Newcombe, F. (1987a). Faces interfere with name classification in prosopagnosic patient. *Cortex* 23:309–316.

DeHaan, E.H.F., Young, A., and Newcombe, F. (1987b). Face recognition without awareness. *Cognitive Neuropsychol.* 4:385–415.

Delay, J. (1935). *Les Astereognosies. Pathologie due Toucher. Clinique, Physiologie, Topographie*. Paris: Masson.

Denes, G., and Semenza, C. (1975). Auditory modality-specific anomia: evidence from a case of pure word deafness. *Cortex* 11:401–411.

De Renzi, E. (1982). *Disorders of Space Exploration and Cognition*. New York: John Wiley and Sons.

De Renzi, E. (1986a). Prosopagnosia in two patients with CT scan evidence of damage confined to the right hemisphere. *Neuropsychologia* 24:385–389.

De Renzi, E. (1986b). Current issues in prosopagnosia. In *Aspects of Face Processing*, H. D. Ellis, M. A. Jeeves, F. Newcombe, and A. Young (eds.). Dordrecht: Martinus Nijhoff.

De Renzi, E., Faglioni, P., Grossi, D. and Nichelli, P. (1991). Apperceptive and associative forms of prosopagnosia. *Cortex* 27:213–221.

De Renzi, E., Scotti G., and Spinnler, H. (1969). Perceptual and associative disorders of visual recognition. *Neurology* 19:634–642.

De Renzi, E., Faglioni, P., Scotti, G., and Spinnler, H. (1972). Impairment in associating colour to form, concomitant with aphasia. *Brain* 95:293–304.

De Renzi, E., Faglioni, P., Scotti, G., and Spinnler, H., (1973). Impairment of color sorting: an experimental study with the Holmgren Skein Test. *Cortex* 9:147–163.

DeYoe, E. A., and Van Essen, D. C. (1988). Concurrent processing streams in monkey visual cortex. *Trends Neurosci.* 11:219–226.

Dimond, S. J. (1976). Brain circuits for consciousness. *Brain Behav. Evol.* 13:376–395.

Earnest, M. P., Monroe, P. A., and Yarnell, P. A. (1977). Cortical deafness: demonstration of the pathologic anatomy by CT scan. *Neurology* 27:1172–1175.

Ellis, A. W., and Young, A. W. (1988). *Human Cognitive Neuropsychology*. Hillsdale, N.J.: Lawrence Erlbaum.

Ettlinger, G. (1956). Sensory deficits in visual agnosia. *J. Neurol. Neurosurg. Psychiatry* 19:297–307.

Ettlinger, G., and Wyke, M. (1961). Defects in identifying objects visually in a patient with cerebrovascular disease. *J. Neurol. Neurosurg. Psychiatry* 24:254–259.

Farah, M. J. (1990). *Visual Agnosia: Disorders of Object Vision and What They Tell Us About Normal Vision.* Cambridge, Mass.: MIT Press/Bradford.

Farah, M. J. (1991). Patterns of co-occurrence among the associative agnosias: implications for visual object representation. *Cognitive Neuropsychol.* 8:1–19.

Farah, M. J., McCullen, P. A., and Meyer, M. M. (1991). Can recognition of living things be selectively impaired? *Neuropsychologia* 29:185–193.

Farah, M. J., Hammond, K. M., Mehta, Z., and Ratcliff, G. (1989). Category-specificity and modality-specificity in semantic memory. *Neuropsychologia* 27:193-200.

Faust, C. (1955). *Die zerebralen Herderscheinungen bei Hinterhauptsverletzungen und ihre Beurteilung.* Stuttgart: Thieme Verlag.

Feinberg, T. E., Gonzalez-Rothi, L. J., and Heilman, K. M. (1986). Multimodal agnosia after unilateral left hemisphere lesion. *Neurology* 36:864–867.

Fennell, E., Satz, P., and Wise, R. (1967). Laterality differences in the perception of pressure. *J. Neurol. Neurosurg. Psychiatry* 30:337–340.

Finkelnburg, F. C. (1870). Niederrheinische Gesellschaft in Bonn. Medicinische Section. *Berl. Klin. Wochensch.* 7:449–450, 460–461.

Frederiks, J.A.M. (1969). The agnosias. In *Handbook of Clinical Neurology,* vol. 4, P. J. Vinken and G. W. Bruyn (eds.). Amsterdam: North-Holland.

Freud, S. (1891). *Zur Auffasun der Aphasien. Eine Kritische Studie.* Vienna: Franz Deuticke.

Freund, D. C. (1889). Ueber optische Aphasie und Seelenblindheit. *Arch. Psychiatr. Nervenkr.* 20:276–297, 371–416.

Fujii, T., Fukatsu, R., Watabe, S., Ohnuma A., Teramura, K., Kimura, I., Saso, S., and Kogure, K. (1990). Auditory sound agnosia without aphasia following a right temporal lobe lesion. *Cortex* 26:263–268.

Gans, A. (1916). Uber Tastblinheit und uber Storungen der raumlichen Wahrenhmungen der Sensibilitat. *Z. Ges. Neurol. Psychiatr.* 31:303–428.

Gardner, H., Silverman, H., Denes, G., Semenza C., and Rosenstiel, A. K. (1977). Sensitivity to musical denotation and connotation in organic patients. *Cortex* 13:242–256.

Gates, A., and Bradshaw, J. L. (1977). The role of the cerebral hemispheres in music. *Brain Lang.* 4:403–431.

Gazzaniga, M. S., and Sperry, R. W. (1967). Language after section of the cerebral commisures. *Brain* 90:131–148.

Gazzaniga, M. S., Bogen, J. E., and Sperry, R. W. (1963). Laterality effects in somesthesis following cerebral commisurotomy in man. *Neuropsychologia* 1:209–215.

Gazzaniga, M., Glass, A. V., and Sarno, M. T. (1973). Pure word deafness and hemi-spheric dynamics: a case history. *Cortex* 9:136–143.

Geschwind, N. (1965). Disconnexion syndromes in animals and man. *Brain* 88:237–294, 585–644.

Geschwind, N., and Fusillo, M. (1966). Color-naming defects in association with alexia. *Arch. Neurol.* 15:137–146.

Geschwind, N., and Kaplan, E. F. (1962). A human disconnection syndrome. *Neurology (Minneap.)* 12:675–685.

Gloning, I., Gloning, K., Jellinger, K., and Quatember, R. (1970). A case of "prosopagnosia" with necropsy findings. *Neuropsychologia* 8:199–204.

Goldman-Rakic, P. S. (1988). Topography of cognition: parallel distributed networks in primate association cortex. *Annu. Rev. Neurosci.* 11:137–156.

Goldstein, K. (1916). Uber kortikale Sensibilitsstorungen. *Neurol. Zentrabl.* 19:825–827.

Goldstein, K. (1943). Some remarks on Russell Brain's article concerning visual object-agnosia. *J. Nerv. Ment. Dis.* 98:148–153.

Goldstein, K., and Gelb, A. (1918). Psychologische Analysen hirnpathologischer Falle auf Grund von Untersuchungen Hirnverletzter. *Z. Gesamte Neurol. Psychiatr.* 41:1–142.

Goldstein, M. N. (1974). Auditory agnosia for speech ("pure word deafness"): a historical review with current implications. *Brain Lang.* 1:195–204.

Goldstein, M. N., Brown, M., and Holander, J. (1975). Auditory agnosia and word deafness: analysis of a case with three-year follow up. *Brain Lang.* 2:324–332.

Goodglass, H., Barton, M. I., and Kaplan, E. F. (1968). Sensory modality and object-naming in aphasia. *J. Speech Hear. Res.* 11:488–496.

Gordon, H. W. (1974). Auditory specialization of the right and left hemispheres. In *Hemispheric Disconnection and Cerebral Function*, M. Kinsbourne and W. L. Smith (eds.). Springfield, Ill.: Charles C. Thomas.

Gottlieb, D., Calvanio, R., and Levine, D. N. (1991). Reappearance of the visual percept after intentional blinking in a patient with Balint's syndrome. *J. Clin. Neuro-Ophthalmol.* 11:62–65.

Graf, P., Squire, L. R., and Mandler, G. (1984). The information that amnesic patients do not forget. *J. Exp. Psychol. [Learn. Mem. Cognition]* 10:164–178.

Green, G. L., and Lessell, S. (1977). Acquired cerebral dyschromatopsia. *Arch. Ophthalmol.* 95:121–128.

Greve, K. W., and Bauer, R. M. (1990). Implicit learning of new faces in prosopagnosia: an application of the mere-exposure paradigm. *Neuropsychologia* 28:1035–1041.

Gross, C. G., Rocha-Miranda, C. E., and Bender, D. B. (1972). Visual properties of neurons in inferotemporal cortex of the macaque. *J. Neurophysiol.* 35:96–111.

Haaxma, R., and Kuypers, H.G.J.M. (1975). Intrahemispheric cortical connections and visual guidance of hand and finger movements in the rhesus monkey. *Brain* 98:239–260.

Habib, M. (1986). Visual hypoemotionality and prosopagnosia associated with right temporal lobe isolation. *Neuropsychologia* 24:577–582.

Hatfield, F. M., and Howard, D. (1977). Object naming in aphasia—the lack of effect of context or realism. *Neuropsychologia* 15:717–727.

Head, H. (1920). *Studies in Neurology*, vol. 2. London: Oxford University Press.

Head, H. (1918). Sensation and the cerebral cortex. *Brain* 41:57–253.

Head, H., and Holmes, G. (1911). Sensory disturbances from cerebral lesions. *Brain* 34:102–254.

Head, H., Rivers, W.H.R., and Sherren, J. (1905). The afferent system from a new aspect. *Brain* 28:99.

Hécaen, H. (1972). *Introduction a la Neuropsychologie.* Paris: Larousse.

Hécaen, H., and Ajuriaguerra, J. (1954). Balint's syndrome (psychic paralysis of visual fixation) and its minor forms. *Brain* 77:373–400.

Hécaen, H., and Ajuriaguerra, J. (1956). Agnosie visuelle pour les objets inanimes par lesion unilaterale gauche. *Rev. Neurol. (Paris)* 94:222–233.

Hécaen, H., and Albert, M. L. (1978). *Human Neuropsychology.* New York: John Wiley and Sons.

Hécaen, H., and Angelergues, R. (1962). Agnosia for faces (prosopagnosia). *Arch. Neurol.* 7:92–100.

Hécaen, H., and David, M. (1945). Syndrome parietale traumatique: asymbolie tactile et hemiasomatognosie paroxystique et douloureuse. *Rev. Neurol. (Paris)* 77:113–123.

Hécaen, H., Goldblum, M. C., Masure, M. C., and Ramier, A. M. (1974). Une nouvelle observation dagnosie dobjet. Deficit de lassociation ou de la categorisation, specifique de la modalite visuell? *Neuropsychologia* 12:447–464.

Heilman, K. M., Scholes, R., and Watson, R. T. (1975). Auditory affective agnosia. Disturbed comprehension of affective speech. *J. Neurol. Neurosurg. Psychiatry* 38:69–72.

Hemphill, R. C., and Stengel, E. (1940). A study of pure word deafness. *J. Neurol. Psychiatry* 3:251–262.

Holmes, G. (1918). Disturbances of visual orientation. *Br. J. Ophthalmol.* 2:449–468.

Holmes, G., and Horrax, G. (1919). Disturbances of spatial orientation and vidual attention with loss of stereoscopic vision. *Arch. Neurol. Psychiatry* 1:385–407.

Horel, J. A., and Keating, E. G. (1969). Partial Kluver-Bucy syndrome produced by cortical disconnection. *Brain Res.* 16:281–284.

Horel, J. A., and Keating, E. G. (1972). Recovery from a partial Kluver-Bucy syndrome induced by disconnection. *J. Comp. Physiol. Psychol.* 79:105–114.

Hubel, D. H., and Weisel, T. N. (1977). Functional architecture of macaque monkey visual cortex. *Proc. R. Soc. Lond. [Biol]* 198:1–59.

Humphreys, G. W., and Riddoch, M. J. (1987a). *To See But Not to See: A Case Study of Visual Agnosia*. London: Lawrence Erlbaum.

Humphreys, G. W., and Riddoch, M. J. (1987b). The fractionation of visual agnosia. In *Visual Object Processing: A Cognitive Neuropsychological Approach*, G. W. Humphreys and M. J. Riddoch (eds.). London: Lawrence Erlbaum.

Husain, M., and Stein, J. (1988). Rezso Balint and his most celebrated case. *Arch. Neurol.* 45:89–93.

Iversen, S. D., and Weiskrantz, L. (1967). Perception of redundant cues by monkeys with infer-otemporal lesions. *Nature* 214:241–243.

Iversen, S. D., and Weiskrantz, L. (1964). Temporal lobe lesions and memory in the monkey. *Nature* 201:740–742.

Jackson, J. H. (1876). Case of large cerebral tumour without optic neuritis and with left hemi-plegia and imperception. *R. Lond. Ophthal. Hosp. Rep.* 8:434. Reprinted 1932 in *Selected Writings of John Hughlings Jackson*, Vol. 2, I. Taylor (ed.). London: Hodder and Stough-ton.

Jerger, J., Lovering, L., and Wertz, M. (1972). Auditory disorder following bilateral temporal lobe insult: report of a case. *J. Speech Hear. Dis.* 37:523–535.

Jerger, J., Weikers, N., Sharbrough, F., and Jerger, S. (1969). Bilateral lesions of the temporal lobe. A case study. *Acta Otolaryngol. (Stockh.) [Suppl.]* 258:1–51.

Jones, E. G., and Powell, T.P.S. (1969). Connections of the somatic sensory cortex of the rhesus monkey. I. Ipsilateral cortical connections. *Brain* 92:477–502. II. Contralateral connections. *Brain* 92:717–730.

Kaas, J. H. (1989). Why does the brain have so many visual areas? *J. Cognitive Neurosci.* 1:120–135.

Kanshepolsky, J., Kelley, J., and Waggener, J. (1973). A cortical auditory disorder. *Neurology* 23:699–705.

Kanter, S. L., Day, A. L., Heilman, K. M., and Gonzalez-Rothi, L. J. (1986). Pure word deafness: a possible explanation of transient-deterioration after extracranial-intracranial bypass grafting. *Neurosurgery* 18:186–189.

Kase, C. S., Troncoso, J. F., Court, J. E., Tapia, F. J., and Mohr, J. P. (1977). Global spatial disorientation. *J. Neurol. Sci.* 34:267–278.

Karpov, B. A., Meerson, Y. A., and Tonkonogii, I. M. (1979). On some peculiarities of the visuo-motor system in visual agnosia. *Neuropsychologia* 17:231–294.

Kazui, S., Naritomi, H. Sawada, T., and Inque, N. (1990). Subcortical auditory agnosia. *Brain Lang.* 38:476–487.

Kertesz, A. (1979). Visual agnosia: the dual deficit of perception and recognition. *Cortex* 15:403–419.

Kinsbourne, M., and Warrington, E. K. (1962). A disorder of simultaneous form perception. *Brain* 85:461–486.

Kinsbourne, M., and Warrington, E. K. (1964). Observations on color agnosia. *J. Neurol. Neurosurg. Psychiatry* 27:296–299.

Klein, R., and Harper, J. (1956). The problem of agnosia in the light of a case of pure word deafness. *J. Ment. Sci.* 102:112–120.

Kliest, K. (1928). Gehirnpathologische und lokalisatorische Ergebnisse uber Horstorungen, Geruschtaubheiten und Amusien. *Monatsschr. Psychiatr. Neurol.* 68:853–860.

Kliest, K. (1934). *Gelurnpathologie Vornehinlich auf Grund der Kriegerfahrungen.* Leipzig: Barth.

Kussmaul, A. (1877). Disturbances of speech. In *Cyclopedia of the Practice of Medicine*, H. VonZiemssien (ed.). New York: William Wood and Co.

Kuypers, H.G.J.M., Szwarcbart, M. K., Mishkin, M., and Rosvold, H. E. (1965). Occipitotemporal corticocortical connections in the rhesus monkey. *Exp. Neurol.* 11:245–262.

Landau, W. U., Goldstein, R., and Kleffner, F. R. (1960). Congenital aphasia: a clinicopathologic study. *Neurology* 10:915–921.

Landis, T., Regard, M., and Serrant, A. (1980). Iconic reading in a case of alexia without agraphia caused by a brain tumor: a tachistoscopic study. *Brain Lang.* 11:45–53.

Landis, T., Graves, R., Benson, D. F., and Hebben, N. (1982). Visual recognition through kinaesthetic mediation. *Psychol. Med.* 12:515–531.

Larrabee, G. J., Levin, H. S., Huff, F. J., Kay, M. C., and Guinto, F. C. (1985). Visual agnosia contrasted with visual-verbal disconnection. *Neuropsychologia* 23:1–12.

Leicester, J. (1980). Central deafness and subcortical motor aphasia. *Brain Lang.* 10:224–242.

Levine, D. N. (1978). Prosopagnosia and visual object agnosia: a behavioral study. *Brain Lang.* 5:341–365.

Levine, D. N., and Calvanio, R. (1978). A study of the visual defect in verbal alexia-simultanagnosia. *Brain* 101:65–81.

Levine, D. N., and Calvanio, R. (1989). Prosopagnosia: a defect in visual configural processing. *Brain Cognition* 10:149–170.

Levine, D. N., Kaufman, K. J., and Mohr, J. P. (1978). Inaccurate reaching associated with a superior parietal lobe tumor. *Neurology* 28:556–561.

Lhermitte, F., and Ajuriaguerra, I. (1938). Asymbolie tactile et hallucinations du toucher. Etude anatomoclinique. *Rev. Neurol. (Paris)* 70:492–495.

Lhermitte, F., and Beauvois, M. F. (1973). A visual-speech disconnection syndrome. *Brain* 96:695–714.

Lhermitte, F., and Pillon, B. (1975). La prosopagnosie: role de lhemisphere droit dans la perception visuelle. *Rev. Neurol. (Paris)* 131:791–812.

Lhermitte, F., Chedru, J., and Chain, F. (1973). A propos d'une cas d'agnosie visuelle. *Rev. Neurol. (Paris)* 128:301–322.

Lhermitte, F., Chain, F., Chedru, J., and Penet, C. (1976). A study of visual processes in a case of interhemispheric disconnexion. *J. Neurol. Sci.* 25:317–330.

Lhermitte, F., Chain, F., Escourolle, R., Ducarne, B., Pillon, B., and Chedru, F. (1971). Etude des troubles perceptifs auditifs dans les lesions temporales bilaterales. *Rev. Neurol. (Paris)* 128:329–351.

Lichtheim, L. (1885). On aphasia. *Brain* 7:433–484.

Liepmann, H., and Storch, E. (1902). Der mikroskopische Gehirnbefund bei dem Fall Gorstelle. *Monatsschr. Psychiatr. Neurol.* 11:115–120.

Lissauer, H. (1890). Ein Fall von Seelenblindheit nebst conem Beitrage zur Theorie derselben. *Arch. Psychiatr.* 21:222–270.

Luria, A. R. (1959). Disorders of "simultaneous perception" in a case of bilateral occipitoparietal brain injury. *Brain* 83:437–449.

Luria, A. R., Pravdina-Vinarskaya, E. N., and Yarbus, A. L. (1963). Disorders of ocular movement in a case of simultanagnosia. *Brain* 86:219–228.

Lynch, J. C., and McClaren, J. W. (1989). Deficits of visual attention and saccadic eye movements after lesions of parietooccipital cortex in monkeys. *J. Neurophysiol.* 61:74–90.

Mack, J. L., and Boller, F. (1977). Associative visual agnosia and its related deficits: the role of the minor hemisphere in assigning meaning to visual perceptions. *Neuropsychologia* 15:345–349.

MacKay, G., and Dunlop, J. C. (1899). The cerebral lesions in a case of complete acquired colour-blindness. *Scott. Med. Surg. J.* 5:503–512.

Mahoudeau, D., Lemoyne, J., Dubrisay, J., and Caraes, J. (1956). Sur un cas dagnosie auditive. *Rev. Neurol. (Paris)* 95:57.

Marr, D. (1982). *Vision.* New York: W. H. Freeman and Co.

Massopoust, L. C., and Wolin, L. R. (1967). Changes in auditory frequency discrimination thresholds after temporal cortex ablation. *Exp. Neurol.* 19:245–251.

Maunsell, J.H.R., and Newsome, W. T. (1987). Visual processing in monkey extrastriate cortex. *Annu. Rev. Neurosci.* 10:363–401.

Mavlov, L. (1980). Amusia due to rhythm agnosia in a musician with left hemi-sphere damage: a non-auditory supramodel defect. *Cortex* 16:331–338.

McCarthy, R. A., and Warrington, E. K. (1986). Visual associative agnosia: a clinico-anatomical study of a single case. *J. Neurol. Neurosurg. Psychiatry* 49:1233–1240.

McClelland, J. L., and Rumelhart, D. E. (1986). *Parallel Distributed Processing: Explorations in the Microstructure of Cognition,* Vol. 2., Cambridge, Mass.: MIT Press.

Meadows, J. C. (1974a). Disturbed perception of colours associated with localized cerebral lesions. *Brain* 97:615–632.

Meadows, J. C. (1974b). The anatomical basis of prosopagnosia. *J. Neurol. Neurosurg. Psychiatry* 37:489–501.

Mendez, M. F. (1988). Visuoperceptual function in visual agnosia. *Neurology* 38:1754–1759.

Mendez, M. F., and Geehan, G. R. (1988). Cortical auditory disorders: clinical and psychoacoustic features. *J. Neurol. Neurosurg. Psychiatry* 51:1–9.

Mendez, M. F., Mendez, M. A., Martin, R., Smyth, K. A., and Whitehouse, P. J. (1990). Complex visual disturbances in Alzheimer's disease. *Neurology* 40:439–443.

Miceli, G. (1982). The processing of speech sounds in a patient with cortical auditory disorder. *Neuropsychologia* 20:5–20.

Michel, J., Peronnet, F., and Schott, B. (1980). A case of cortical deafness: clinical and electrophysiological data. *Brain Lang.* 10:367–377.

Michel, F., Pernin, M. T., and Sieroff, E. (1986). Prosopagnosie sans hemianopsie apres lesion unilateralie occipito-temporale droite. *Rev. Neurol. (Paris)* 142:545–549.

Milberg, W., and Blumstein, S. E. (1981). Lexical decision and aphasia: evidence for semantic processing. *Brain Lang.* 14:371–385.

Milner, A. D., and Heywood, C. A. (1989). A disorder of lightness discrimination in a case of visual form agnosia. *Cortex* 25:489–494.

Milner, A. D., Perrett, D. I., Johnston, R. S., Benson, P. J., Jordan, T. R., Heeley, D. W., Betucci, D., Mortara, F., Mutani, R., Terazzi, D., and Davidison, D. L. W. (1991). Perception and action in "visual form agnosia." *Brain* 114:405–428.

Milner, B., Corkin, S., and Teuber, H.-L. (1968). Further analysis of the hippocampal amnesic syndrome: 14-year follow-up study of H. M. *Neuropsychologia* 6:215–234.

Moscovitch, M., Winocur, G., and McLachlan, D. (1986). Memory as assessed by recognition and reading time in normal and memory-impaired people with Alzheimer's disease and other neurological disorders. *J. Exp. Psychol.* [*Gen.*] *115*:331–347.

Motomura, N., Yamadori, A., Mori, E., and Tamaru, F. (1986). Auditory agnosia: analysis of a case with bilateral subcortical lesions. *Brain 109*:379–391.

Mountcastle, V. B. (1961). Some functional properties of the somatic afferent system. In *Sensory Communication*, W.A. Rosenblith (ed.). Cambridge, Mass.: MIT Press, pp. 403–436.

Mountcastle, V. B., and Powell, T. P. S. (1959a). Neural mechanisms subserving cutaneous sensibility, with special reference to the role of afferent inhibition in sensory perception and discrimination. *Bull. Johns Hopkins Hosp. 105*:201–232.

Mountcastle, V. B., and Powell, T. P. S. (1959b). Central nervous mechanisms subserving position sense and kinesthesis. *Bull. Johns Hopkins Hosp. 105*:173–200.

Mountcastle, V. B., Lynch, J. C., Georgopoulos, A., Sakata, H., and Acuna, C. (1975). Posterior parietal association cortex of the monkey: command functions for operations within extrapersonal space. *J. Neurophysiol. 38*:871–908.

Munk, H. (1881). *Ueber die Functionen der Grosshirnrinde. Gesammelte Mittheilungenaus den Iahren 1877–80.* Berlin: Hirschwald.

Naeser, M. (1974). The relationship between phoneme discrimination, phoneme/picture perception, and language comprehension in aphasia. Presented at the Twelfth Annual Meeting of the Academy of Aphasia, Warrenton, Virginia.

Nardelli, E., Buonanno, F., Coccia, G., Fiaschi, A., Terzian, H., and Rizzuto, N. (1982). Prosopagnosia: report of four cases. *Eur. Neurol. 21*:289–297.

Neff, W. D. (1961). Neuronal mechanisms of auditory discrimination. In *Sensory Communication*, N. A. Rosenblith (ed.). Cambridge, Mass.: MIT Press.

Neisser, U. (1967). *Cognitive Psychology*. New York: Appleton-Century-Crofts.

Neisser, U. (1976). *Cognition and Reality*. San Francisco: W. H. Freeman.

Newcombe, F., and Ratcliff, G. (1974). Agnosia: a disorder of object recognition. In *Les Syndromes de Disconnexion Calleuse chez L'homme*, F. Michel and B. Schott (eds.). Colloque International de Lyon.

Newcombe, F., Young, A. W., and De Haan, E.H.F. (1989). Prosopagnosia and object agnosia without covert recognition. *Neuropsychologia 27*:179–191.

Nielsen, J. M., and Sult, C. W., Jr. (1939). Agnosia and the body scheme. *Bull. Los Angeles Neurol. Soc. 4*:69–81.

Oppenheim, H. (1906). Uber einen bemerkenswerten Fall von Tumor cerebri. *Berl. Klin. Wochenschr. 43*:1001–1004.

Oppenheim, H. (1911). *Textbook of Nervous Diseases for Physicians and Students.* Edinburgh: Darien Press.

Oppenheimer, D. R., and Newcombe, F. (1978). Clinical and anatomic findings in a case of auditory agnosia. *Arch. Neurol. 35*:712–719.

Overman, W. H., and Doty, R. W. (1982). Hemispheric specialization displayed by man but not macaque for analysis of faces. *Neuropsychologia 20*:113–128.

Oxbury, J., Oxbury, S., and Humphrey, N. (1969). Varieties of color anomia. *Brain 92*:847–860.

Pallis, C. A. (1955). Impaired identification of faces and places with agnosia for colors. *J. Neurol. Neurosurg. Psychiatry 18*:218–224.

Paul, R. L., Merzenich, M., and Goodman, H. (1972). Representation of slowly and rapidly adapting cutaneous mechanoreceptors of the hand in Brodmanns areas 3 and 1 of Macaca mulatta. *Brain Res. 36*:229–249.

Pearlman, A. L., Birch, J., and Meadows, J. C. (1979). Cerebral color blindness: an acquired defect in hue discrimination. *Ann. Neurol. 5*:253–261.

Penfield, W. (1958). *The Excitable Cortex in Conscious Man.* Springfield, Ill.: Charles C. Thomas.

Perenin, M. T., and Jeannerod, M. (1978). Visual function within the hemianopic field following early cerebral hemidecortication in man. I. Spatial localization. *Neuropsychologia 16:*1–13.

Perrett, D. I., Mistlin, A. J., and Chitty, A. J. (1987). Visual cells responsive to faces. *Trends Neurosci. 10:*358–364.

Perrett, D. I., Rolls, E. T., and Caan, W. (1982). Visual neurons responsive to faces in the monkey temporal cortex. *Exp. Brain Res. 47:*329–342.

Pillon, B., Signoret, J. L., and Lhermitte, F. (1981). Agnosie visuelle associative. Role del hemisphere gauche dans la perception visuelle. *Rev. Neurol. (Paris) 137:*831–842.

Poppelreuter, W. (1923). Zur Psychologie und Pathologie der optischen Wahrehmung. *Z. Gesamte Neurol. Psychiatr. 83:*26–152.

Powell, T.P.S., and Mountcastle, V. B. (1959). Some aspects of the functional organization of the cortex of the postcentral gyrus of the monkey: a correlation of findings obtained in a single unit analysis with cyto-architecture. *Bull. Johns Hopkins Hosp. 105:*123–162.

Randolph, M., and Semmes, J. (1974). Behavioral consequences of selective subtotal ablations in the postcentral gyrus of Macaca mulatta. *Brain Res. 70:*55–70.

Ratcliff, G., and Ross, J. E. (1981). Visual perception and perceptual disorder. *Br. Med. Bull. 37:*181–186.

Raymond, F., and Egger, M. (1906). Un cas d'aphasie tactile. *Rev. Neurol. (Paris) 14:*371–375.

Reinhold, M. (1950). A case of auditory agnosia. *Brain 73:*203–223.

Renault, B., Signoret, J. L., Debruille, B., Breton, F., and Bolgert, F. (1989). Brain potentials reveal covert facial recognition in prosopagnosia. *Neuropsychologia 27:*905–912.

Riddoch, M. J., and Humphreys, G. W. (1987a). A case of integrative visual agnosia. *Brain 110:*1431–1462.

Riddoch, M. J., and Humphreys, G. W. (1987b). Visual object processing in optic aphasia: A case of semantic access agnosia. *Cognitive Neuropsychology 4:*131–185.

Rizzo, M., and Hurtig, R. (1987). Looking but not seeing: attention, perception, and eye movements in simultanagnosia. *Neurology 37:*1642–1648.

Rizzo, M., Hurtig, R., and Damasio, A. R. (1987). The role of scanpaths in facial recognition and learning. *Ann. Neurol. 22:*41–45.

Roediger, H. L. (1990). Implicit memory: retention without remembering. *Amer. Psychol. 45:*1043–1056.

Roediger, H. L., and Blaxton, T. A. (1987). Effects of varying modality, surface features, and retention interval on priming in word fragment completion. *Mem. Cognition 15:*379–388.

Roland, P. E. (1976). Astereognosis. *Arch. Neurol. 33:*543–550.

Roland, P. E., and Larsen, B. (1976). Focal increase of cerebral blood flow during stereognostic testing in man. *Arch. Neurol. 33:*551–558.

Rosati, G., DeBastiani, P., Paolino, E., Prosser, S., Arslan, E., and Artioli, M. (1982). Clinical and audiological findings in a case of auditory agnosia. *J. Neurol. 227:*21–27.

Rosch, E., Mervis, C. B., Gray, W., Johnson, D., and Boyes-Braem, P. (1976). Basic objects in natural categories. *Cognitive Psychol. 8:*382–439.

Rose, J. E., and Woolsey, C. N. (1949). Organization of the mammalian thalamus and its relationship to the cerebral cortex. *Electroencephalogr. Clin. Neurophysiol. 1:*391–400.

Ross, E. D. (1980a). Sensory-specific and fractional disorders of recent memory in man. I. Isolated loss of visual recent memory. *Arch. Neurol. 37:*193–200.

Ross, E. D. (1980b). The anatomic basis of visual agnosia [letter]. *Neurology (N.Y.) 30:*109–110.

Rubens, A. B. (1979). Agnosia. In *Clinical Neuropsychology*, K. M. Heilman and E. Valenstein (eds.). New York: Oxford University Press.

Rubens, A. B., and Benson, D. F. (1971). Associative visual agnosia. *Arch. Neurol.* 24:304–316.

Rudel, R. G., Denckla, M. B., and Spalten, E. (1974). The functional asymmetry of Braille letter learning in normal, sighted children. *Neurology* 24:733–738.

Rumelhart, D. E., and McClelland, J. L. (1986). *Parallel Distributed Processing: Explorations in the Microstructure of Cognition*, Vol. 1. Cambridge, Mass.: MIT Press.

Saffran, E. B., Marin, O.S.M., and Yeni-Komshian, G. H. (1976). An analysis of speech perception in word deafness. *Brain Lang.* 3:255-256.

Schacter, D. L. (1987). Implicit memory: history and current status. *J. Exp. Psychol* [*Learn. Mem. Cognition*] 13:501–518.

Schacter, D. L. (1989). On the relation between memory and consciousness: dissociable interactions and conscious experience. In *Varieties of Memory and Consciousness: Essays in Honour of Endel Tulving*, H. L. Roediger and F. I. M. Craik (eds.). Hillsdale, N.J.: Lawrence Erlbaum.

Schacter, D. L., McAndrews, M. P., and Moscovitch, M. (1988). Access to consciousness: dissociations between implicit and explicit knowledge in neuropsychological syndromes. In *Thought Without Language*, L. Weiskrantz (ed.). Oxford: Clarendon Press.

Schuster, P., and Taterka, H. (1926). Beitrag zur Anatomie und Klinik der reinen Worttaubbeit. *Z. Gesamte Neurol. Psychiatr.* 105:494.

Seiler, J., and Ricker, K. (1971). Das Vibrationsempfinden. Eine apparative Schwellenbestimmung. *Z. Neuro.* 200:70–79.

Semmes, J. (1965). A non-tactual factor in astereognosis. *Neuropsychologia* 3:295–314.

Semmes, J. (1953). Agnosia in animal and man. *Psychol. Rev.* 60:140–147.

Semmes, J., Weinstein, S., Ghent, L., and Teuber, H.-L. (1960). *Somatosensory Changes After Penetrating Brain Wounds in Man*. Cambridge, Mass.: Harvard University Press.

Sergent, J., and Poncet, M. (1990). From covert to overt recognition of faces in a prosopagnosic patient. *Brain* 113:989–1004.

Sergent, J., and Villemure, G. (1989). Prosopagnosia in a right hemispherectomized patient. *Brain* 112:975–995.

Sergent, J., Ohta, S., and MacDonald, B. (1992). Functional neuroanatomy of face and object processing: a positron emission tomography study. *Brain.* 115:15–36.

Shallice, T., and Saffran, E. (1986). Lexical processing in the absence of explicit word identification: evidence from a letter-by-letter reader. *Cognitive Neuropsychol.* 3:429–458.

Sherry, D. F., and Schacter, D. L. (1987). The evolution of multiple memory systems. *Psychol. Rev.* 94:439–454.

Shoumaker, R. D., Ajax, E. T., and Schenkenberg, T. (1977). Pure word deafness (auditory verbal agnosia). *Dis. Nerv. Sys.* 38:293–299.

Shraberg, D., and Weitzel, W. D. (1979). Prosopagnosia and the Capgras syndrome. *J. Clin. Psychiatry* 40:313–316.

Shuttleworth, E. C., Syring, V., and Allen, N. (1982). Further observations on the nature of prosopagnosia. *Brain Cognition* 1:307–322.

Sparr, S. A., Jay, M., Drislane, F. W., and Venna, N. (1991). A historic case of visual agnosia revisited after 40 years. *Brain* 114:789–800.

Sprague, J. M., Levy, J. D., and Berlucci, C. (1977). Visual cortical areas mediating form discrimination in the rat. *J. Comp. Neurol.* 172:441–448.

Spreen, O., Benton, A. L., and Fincham, R. (1965). Auditory agnosia without aphasia. *Arch. Neurol.* 13:84–92.

Spreen, O., Benton, A. L., and Van Allen, M. W. (1966). Dissociation of visual and tactile naming in amnesic aphasia. *Neurology (Minneap.)* 16:807–814.

Stauffenburg, V. (1914). *Uber Seelenblindheit. Arbeiten aus dem Hirnatomischen Institut in Zurich Heft 8.* Wiesbaden: Bergman.

Stockard, J. J., and Rossiter, V. S. (1977). Clinical and pathologic correlates of brainstem auditory response abnormalities. *Neurology (Minneap.)* 27:316–325.

Synodinou, C., Christodoulou, G. N., and Tzavaras, A. (1978). Capgras syndrome and prosopagnosia [letter]. *Br. J. Psychiatry* 132:413–414.

Taylor, A., and Warrington, E. K. (1971). Visual agnosia: a single case report. *Cortex* 7:152–164.

Teuber, H.-L. (1965a). Somatosensory disorders due to cortical lesions. *Neuropsychologia* 3:287–294.

Teuber, H.-L. (1965b). Postscript: some needed revisions of the classical views of agnosia. *Neuropsychologia* 3:371–378.

Teuber, H.-L. (1968). Alteration of perception and memory in man. In *Analysis of Behavioral Change*, L. Weiskrantz (ed.). New York: Harper and Row.

Torii, H., and Tamai, A. (1985). The problem of prosopagnosia: report of three cases with occlusion of the right posterior cerebral artery. *J. Neurol. (Suppl.)* 232:140.

Tranel, D. T. (1991). What has been rediscovered in "rediscovering tactile agnosia"? *Mayo Clin. Proc.* 66:210–214.

Tranel, D. T., and Damasio, A. R. (1985). Knowledge without awareness: an autonomic index of facial recognition by prosopagnosics. *Science* 228:1453–1454.

Tranel, D. T., and Damasio, A. R. (1988). Non-conscious face recognition in patients with face agnosia. *Behav. Brain Res.* 30:235–249.

Tyler, H. R. (1968). Abnormalities of perception with defective eye movements (Balint's syndrome). *Cortex* 4:154–171.

Tzavaras, A., Hécaen, H., and LeBras, H. (1970). Le probleme de la specificite du deficit de la reconnaisance du visage humans lors des lesions hemispheriques unilaterales. *Neuropsychologia* 8:403–416.

Ulrich, G. (1978). Interhemispheric functional relationships in auditory agnosia: an analysis of the preconditions and a conceptual model. *Brain Lang.* 5:286–300.

Van Lancker, D. R., and Kreiman, J. (1988). Unfamiliar voice discrimination and familiar voice recognition are independent and unordered abilities. *Neuropsychologia* 25:829–834.

Van Lancker, D. R., Kreiman, J., and Cummings, J. (1989). Voice perception deficits: Neuroanatomical correlates of phonagnosia. *J. Clin. Exp. Neuropsychol.* 11:665–674.

Van Lancker, D. R., Cummings, J. L., Kreiman, L., and Dobkin, B. H. (1988). Phonagnosia: a dissociations between familiar and unfamiliar voices. *Cortex* 24:195–209.

Verfaellie, M. Rapcsak, S. Z. and Heilman, K. M. (1990). Impaired shifting of attention in Balint's syndrome. *Brain Cognition* 12:195–204.

Vignolo, L. A. (1969). Auditory agnosia: a review and report of recent evidence. In *Contributions to Clinical Neuropsychology*, A. L. Benton (ed.). Chicago: Aldine.

Von Frey, M. (1895). Bietrage zur Sinnes physiologie der Haut Berichle u.d. Verhandlungen d.k. Sachs. *Ges. Wiss.* 2S:166.

Von Hagen, K. O. (1941). Two cases of mind blindness (visual agnosia), one due to carbon monoxide intoxication, one due to a diffuse degenerative process. *Bull. Los Angeles Neurol. Soc.* 6:191–194.

Wapner, W., Judd, T., and Gardner, H, (1978). Visual agnosia in an artist. *Cortex* 14:343–364.

Warrington, E. K. (1985). Agnosia: the impairment of object recognition. In *Handbook of Clinical Neurology*, P. J. Vinken, G. W. Gruyn, and H. L. Klawans (eds.). Amsterdam: Elsevier.

Warrington, E. K., and James, M. (1967). An experimental investigation of facial recognition in patients with unilateral cerebral lesions. *Cortex* 3:317–326.

Warrington, E. K., and James, M. (1988). Visual apperceptive agnosia: a clinico-anatomical study of three cases. *Cortex* 24:13–32.

Warrington, E. K., and McCarthy, R. (1987). Categories of knowledge: Further fractionation and an attempted integration. *Brain* 110:1273–1296.

Warrington, E. K., and Rabin, P. (1971). Visual span of apprehension in patients with unilateral cerebral lesions. *Q. J. Exp. Psychol.* 23:423–431.

Warrington, E. K., and Shallice, T. (1984). Category-specific semantic impairments. *Brain* 107:829–854.

Warrington, E. K., and Shallice, T. (1980). Word-form dyslexia. *Brain* 103:99–112.

Warrington, E. K., and Taylor, A. M. (1973). The contribution of the right parietal lobe to visual object recognition. *Cortex* 9:152–164.

Watson, R. T., and Heilman, K. M. (1983). Callosal apraxia. *Brain* 106:391–403.

Watson, R. T., and Rapcsak, S. Z. (1987). Loss of spontaneous blinking in a patient with Balint's syndrome. *Arch. Neurol.* 46:567–570.

Weinstein, S. (1968). Intensive and extensive aspects of tactile sensitivity as a-function of body part, sex, and laterality. In *The Skin Senses*, D. R. Kenshalo (ed.). Springfield, Ill.: Charles C. Thomas, pp. 195–222.

Weiskrantz, L. (1986). *Blindsight: A Case Study and Implications.* New York: Oxford University Press.

Weiskrantz, L., Warrington, E. K., Sanders, M. D., and Marshall, J. (1974). Visual capacity in the hemianopic field following a restricted occipital ablation. *Brain* 97:709–728.

Werner, G., and Whitsel, B. (1973). Functional organization of the somatosensory cortex. In *Somatosensory Systems, Handbook of Sensory Physiology*, Vol. 2, A. Iggo (ed.). New York: Springer-Verlag, pp. 621–700.

Wernicke, C. (1895). Swei Falle von Rindenlasion. *Arb. Psychiatr. Klin. Breslau* 11:35.

Wertheim, N. (1969). The amusias. In *Handbook of Clinical Neurology*, Vol. 4, P. J. Vinken and G. W. Bruyn (eds.). Amsterdam: North-Holland.

Whiteley, A. M., and Warrington, E. K. (1977). Prosopagnosia: a clinical, psychological, and anatomical study of three patients. *J. Neurol. Neurosurg. Psychiatry* 40:395–403.

Wilbrand, H. (1887). *Die Seelenblindheit als Herderscheinung. Wiesbaden: Bergmann.*

Wolhfart, G., Lindgren, A., and Jernelius, B. (1952). Clinical picture and morbid anatomy in a case of "pure word deafness." *J. Nerv. Ment. Dis.* 116:818–827.

Wolpert, I. (1924). Die Simultanagnosie: storung der gesamtauffassung. *Z. Gesamte Neurol. Psychiatr.* 93:397–413.

Woolsey, C. N. (1952). Cortical localization as defined by evoked potential and electrical stimulation studies. In *Cerebral Localization and Organization*, G. Schaltenbrand and C. N. Woolsey (eds.). Madison: University of Wisconsin Press, pp. 17–26.

Wortis, S. B., and Pfeffer, A. Z. (1948). Unilateral auditory-spatial agnosia. *J. Nerv. Ment. Dis.* 108:181–186.

Wyke, M., and Holgate, D. (1973). Color naming defects in dysphasic patients—a qualitative analysis. *Neuropsychologia* 8:451–461.

Yin, R. K. (1970). Face recognition by brain-injured patients: a dissociable ability? *Neuropsychologia* 8:395–402.

Young, A. W. and DeHaan, E.H.F. (1988). Boundaries of covert recognition in prosopagnosia. *Cog. Neuropsychol.* 5:317–336.

Young, A. W., Ellis, A. W., Flude, B. M., McWeeny, K. H., and Hay, D. C. (1986). Face-name interference. *J. Exp. Psychol.* [*Hum. Percept.*] 12:466–475.

Young, R. S., and Fishman, G. A. (1980). Loss of colour vision and Stiles II, mechanism in a patient with cerebral infarction. *J. Opt. Soc. Am. 170*:1301–1305.

Zeki, S. M. (1973). Colour coding in rhesus monkey prestriate cortex. *Brain Res. 53*:422–427.

Zeki, S. M. (1977). Colour coding in the superior temporal sulcus of rhesus monkey visual cortex. *Proc. R. Soc. Lond. [Biol.] 197*:195–223.

Ziegler, D. K. (1952). Word deafness and Wernicke's aphasia: report of cases and discussion of the syndrome. *Arch. Neurol. Psychiatry 67*:323–331.

# 10
# Neglect and Related Disorders

KENNETH M. HEILMAN, ROBERT T. WATSON,
AND EDWARD VALENSTEIN

Neglect is the failure to report, respond, or orient to novel or meaningful stimuli presented to the side opposite a brain lesion, when this failure cannot be attributed to either sensory or motor defects (Heilman, 1979). Neglect may be spatial or personal: one may be inattentive to stimuli in space or on the person and one may fail to act in a portion of space, in a spatial direction, or on a portion of one's body. Many specific disorders have been described, distinguished by their presumed underlying mechanism, the distribution of the abnormal behavior, and the means of eliciting the behavior. Different behavioral manifestations may occur at different times, and in some patients certain manifestations are never seen.

The major behavioral manifestations include (1) inattention or sensory neglect (2) extinction to simultaneous stimuli (3) motor neglect (4) spatial neglect (5) personal neglect (6) allesthesia and allokinesia and (7) anosognosia (denial of illness, including hemiplegia). The first section of this chapter will define specific disorders and describe clinical tests that may be used to assess them. The second section will discuss pathophysiology, and the third, recovery and treatment.

## DEFINITIONS AND TESTS

### Inattention (Sensory Neglect) and Extinction

Sensory neglect or inattention refers to a deficit in awareness of contralateral stimuli in patients and animals with lesions in locations other than primary sensory areas or sensory projection systems. In some cases, one may be unable to distinguish severe inattention from an afferent defect (such as hemianesthesia or hemianopia) without knowing the site of the lesion. But patients with inattention can be distinguished from patients with afferent defects if they can detect stimuli when aided by instructional cues, novel stimuli, or stimuli with motivational value.

Auditory inattention is easier to distinguish from an afferent defect than visual or somatosensory inattention because unilateral hearing loss is not seen with cerebral hemisphere lesions. This is because the auditory pathways that ascend from the brain-stem to the cortex are bilateral: each ear projects to both hemispheres. Furthermore, since sound presented from one side of the body projects to both ears, patients with unilateral hearing loss from a peripheral lesion will usually perceive a unilateral audi-tory stimulus, unless it is very close to the deaf ear. Therefore, patients who neglect or are inattentive to unilateral auditory stimuli most often have unilateral inattention, rather than a primary afferent defect.

The distribution of attentional deficits varies from patient to patient, and may vary in the same patient depending on the method of testing. Patients may fail to attend to visual or auditory stimuli, or to tactile stimuli, and thus their inattention may be to stimuli in space or to stimuli on the body. To make matters more complex, the dis-tribution of attention in space may depend not only on the position of the stimulus in the visual field, but also on the relative position of the stimulus to the patient's body. The visual field and the spatial fields defined by head or body position are only con-gruent when the subject is looking straight ahead. Moving the eyes to one side will result in the visual field being different from the head or body spatial field, and mov-ing the head *and* eyes will result in three noncongruent fields. Hemianopia is not influenced by eye movements, but in some patients unilateral visual inattention varies with direction of gaze. For example, patients with egocentric (body-centered) inat-tention may fail to detect stimuli when they gaze straight ahead or to contralesional hemispace, but when their gaze is directed to ipsilesional hemispace, placing the con-tralateral visual field within the ipsilesional head or body hemispace, they may be able to detect stimuli, even though the stimuli remain at the same locations in their visual field (Kooistra and Heilman, 1989; Nadeau and Heilman, 1991). Some patients who appear to have tactile anesthesia may be able to detect contralesional stimuli when cold water is injected into their ipsilesional ear, suggesting that they have sen-sory neglect (Valler et al., 1990).

Patients with unilateral neglect are most inattentive to stimuli contralateral to their lesion, but it is not unusual for them also to be inattentive to ipsilateral stimuli, although ipsilateral neglect is not as severe (personal observation).

In addition to being unaware of stimuli, patients with hemispheric lesions may also be impaired at shifting their attention, especially in a contralesional directions. Pos-ner et al. (1984) posited three stages in the movement of attention: disengagement, shifting, and engagement. Posner et al. (1984) provided evidence that patients with parietal lesions have difficulty disengaging from ipsilesional stimuli. Kinsbourne (1970) proposed that patients with neglect have an ipsilesional attentional bias.

Most patients who initially have inattention from a stable lesion improve. Whereas initially they ignore stimuli presented to the side opposite their lesion, they eventually become able to correctly detect and lateralize these stimuli. When given bilateral simultaneous stimulation, however, they often fail to report the stimulus presented to the contralesional side. This phenomenon was first noted by Loeb (1885) and Oppen-heim (1885) in the tactile modality and by Anton (1899) and Poppelreuter (1917) in the visual modality; it has been termed extinction to double simultaneous stimulation. It may also be seen in the auditory modality (Bender, 1952; Heilman et al., 1970). A patient may have extinction in several modalities (multimodal extinction) or in one modality. Extinction is usually mildest in the auditory modality. Although extinction is most severe when a stimulus presented to the side contralateral to the lesion is paired with a stimulus on the other side, extinction may also occur when both stimuli are on the same side, even when they are both ipsilateral to the lesion (Rapscak et al., 1987).

*Examination:* Inattention and extinction are detected by asking patients where they were stimulated. Language-impaired patients may respond nonverbally, but failure to respond nonverbally may reflect akinesia rather than inattention. Stimuli should be given in each of three modalities: (1) somesthetic, (2) visual, and (3) auditory.

To test for somesthetic neglect at the bedside, the patient can be touched with a finger, a cotton applicator, or, if better control of stimulus intensity is desired, a Von Frei hair. More elaborate equipment can be used for even better control of stimulus intensity, if this is needed for research purposes. Stimuli of other somatosensory modalities (pin, temperature, etc.) can also be used.

Auditory stimuli for bedside testing may consist of rubbing or snapping the fingers. Audiometric techniques are preferable for rigorous testing.

For testing visual fields, perimetry and tangent screen should be used when possible; however, for beside testing, confrontation techniques are adequate. Either a cotton-tipped applicator or a finger can be used as the stimulus. For bilateral simultaneous testing, finger movements are excellent stimuli. Testing for visual neglect should take place when the patient gazes in the midsagittal plane, looks away from the lesion, and looks toward the lesion.

These somesthetic, auditory, and visual stimuli should be presented to the abnormal (contralesional) side and to the normal side of the body in random order. If the patient responds normally to unilateral stimulation, bilateral simultaneous stimulation should be used. Unilateral stimuli should be interspersed with bilateral simultaneous stimuli. Bender (1952) noted that normal subjects may show extinction to simultaneous stimulation when the stimuli are delivered to two different (asymmetrical) parts of the body (simultaneous bilateral heterologous stimulation). For example, if the right side of the face and the left hand are stimulated simultaneously, normal subjects sometimes report only the stimulus on the face. Normal subjects do not extinguish symmetrical simultaneous stimuli (simultaneous bilateral homologous stimulation). Simultaneous bilateral heterologous stimulation can sometimes be used to test for milder defects in patients with neglect. For example, when the right face and left hand are stimulated, the patient with left-sided neglect does not report the stimulus on the left hand, but when the left face and right hand are stimulated, he reports both stimuli.

### Action-Intentional Disorders (Motor Neglect)

Although sensory loss and inattention may account for unawareness of stimuli, patients can be seen in the clinic who fail to respond even though they are aware of the stimulus. Although weakness may be the most common cause of response failures, one can see response failures that are not caused by weakness. We term these disorders action-intentional disorders. In the section below, we will discuss four types: akinesia, motor extinction, hypokinesia, and motor impersistence.

Failure to initiate movements is most often associated with dysfunction of the motor system, including the motor unit (lower motor neuron, neuromuscular junction, and muscle) and the upper motor neuron (corticospinal system). Akinesia is a failure of initiation that cannot be attributed to dysfunction in these upper and lower motor systems, but rather to dysfunction of the systems necessary to activate motor neurons.

Akinesia may involve different body parts: the eys, the head, a limb, or the whole body. It may vary depending upon where in space the body part is moved, or in what direction it is moved. In *directional akinesia,* there is a reluctance to move in a direction that is contralateral to the lesion. Certain forms of gaze palsy are directional akinesias, and there are directional akinesias of the head and even of the arms. Directional akinesia may be associated with a *directional motor bias:* they eyes may deviate toward the side of the lesion, and, when the patient is asked to point to a spot opposite the sternum with the eyes closed, the arm may also deviate to the side of the lesion (Heilman et al., 1983b).

Meador et al. (1986) described *spatial akinesia* involving the arm. The arm contralateral to a lesion was less akinetic in ipsilesional than in contralesional hemispace, independent of the direction of movement.

Movements can be produced in response to an external stimulus or they can occur independently of a stimulus. The former we call exogenously evoked (exo-evoked) and the latter, endogenously evoked (endo-evoked). Exo-evoked akinesia is also called motor neglect. A patient may have both exo- and endo-evoked akinesia.

*Examination:* Akinesia may be observed in one or more body parts: eyes, head, trunk or limbs. When testing for akinesia, one may therefore want to assess various body parts. To determine if someone has endo-evoked akinesia, it is important to observe spontaneous behavior. Patients with endo-evoked akinesia often have symptoms of abulia (decreased drive, with psychomotor retardation). If the akinesia is principally endo-evoked, they may respond normally to external stimuli. Endo-evoked akinesia is frequently associated with Parkinson's disease, where it has been called akinesia paradoxica.

The failure to move in response to a stimulus, despite the presence of spontaneous movements and good strength, is often attributed to an elemental sensory defect or to sensory inattention. These may be easily confused with exo-evoked akinesia (motor neglect), which can also cause a failure to respond. The *crossed response task* (Watson et al., 1978) was originally designed to distinguish sensory defects and sensory neglect from exo-evoked akinesia in monkeys, but it can also be used with humans. Watson, et al. had monkeys respond with the right arm to a left-sided stimulus and with the left arm to a right-sided stimulus. An animal was considered to have a sensory deficit or sensory neglect if it did not respond to a contralesional stimulus using the "normal" (ipsilesional) arm. It was considered to have exo-evoked akinesia if it failed to move the contralesional extremity in response to stimulation of the "normal" (ipsilesional) side, despite intact spontaneous movements and normal strength of the contralesional arm. One can use the crossed response task to test the limbs, the eyes, or the head.

To assess whether the spatial coordinates of actions influence akinesia, one needs to observe both directional and hemispatial movements that are both endo-evoked (spontaneous) and exo-evoked (in response to stimuli). When attempting to determine if there is an endo-evoked directional akinesia of the eyes, one should observe spontaneous eye movements to detect eye deviation or bias toward the side of the lesion, or a paresis of gaze to the side opposite the lesion (a failure to look spontaneously into contralesional space). An exo-evoked directional akinesia of the eyes can be assessed by a modification of the Watson, et al. (1978) paradigm in which the patient must look both toward and away from an ipsi- and contralesional stimulus. The examiner stands directly in front of a patient and positions one hand in the patient's right visual field and the other in the left visual field, at eye level. The patient is instructed to fixate on the examiner's nose, and to look away from a finger if it moves downward and toward it if it moves upward. A failure to look at the contralesional finger when it moves upward may be related to sensory defect (e.g., hemianopsia), sensory neglect, or directional akinesia. However, failure to look toward the contralesional finger when the ipsilesional finger moves downward suggests an exo-evoked directional akinesia of the eyes (Butter et al., 1988b).

Similar tests can be used to detect directional and hemispatial akinesia of the head or arm. To test for a directional bias of an arm (similar to eye deviation), one asks a patient to close his eyes and point to his sternum. If he is able to point to the sternum, he is then asked to point with the index finger to a point in space perpendicular to his sternum (the midsagittal plane). Patients with a motor (intentional) bias will point toward their lesioned hemisphere (Heilman et al., 1983b).

De Renzi et al. (1970) developed a task than can be used to test for endo-evoked directional limb akinesia. In our modification, the patient is blindfolded and small objects such as pennies are randomly scattered on a table to the left and right of the midsagittal plane (both hemispatial fields) within arm's reach. The patient is asked to retrieve as many pennies as possible. The task is endo-evoked because the patient cannot see the pennies and must initiate exploratory behavior in the absence of an external stimulus. Patients with an endo-evoked directional akinesia of the arm may fail to move their arm fully into contralateral hemispace to explore for pennies.

The line bisection paradigm used by Coslett et al. (1990) can be used to test for exo-evoked directional akinesia. The spatial positions of the stimulus feedback (the patient's view of his hand) and the motor activity can be dissociated by preventing the patient from directly viewing his hand, but instead providing this feedback via a TV monitor. Both the line (where the action takes place) and the TV monitor can be independently placed in either hemispace. If line bisection is not affected by the spatial position of the monitor but mis-bisection of the line toward ipsilesional hemispace increases as the line is brought into contralesional hemispace, it would suggest that the patient has an exo-evoked directional akinesia of the arm.

To test for hemispatial akinesia of the arm, one must test the patient with arms crossed and uncrossed. In uncrossed conditions, each hand is placed on a table in compatible hemispace. In the crossed condition, each hand is placed in the opposite hemispace. The patient is instructed to lift the hand on the same side as the moving finger if he sees the examiner's finger move up, but to move the hand on the opposite side if he sees the examiner's finger move down. The examiner randomly moves his right or left index finger up or down. When a patient fails to move the contralesional arm when it is incontralesional hemispace but moves the arm when it crosses into ipsilesional hemispace, the patient is considered to have hemispatial limb akinesia (Meador et al., 1986).

## MOTOR EXTINCTION

Some patients who do not demonstrate akinesia when they move one limb may demonstrate contralesional akinesia when they must simultaneously move both their extremities (Valenstein and Heilman, 1981). We call this motor extinction.

Motor extinction is tested by using a method similar to that used to test for sensory extinction; however, the examiner not only requests verbal report as to where the patient was stimulated (e.g., right, left, both), but in other trials requests that the subject move the body part (e.g., hand or arm) on the same side that was stimulated (right, left, both). Patients with sensory extinction will fail to report the contralesional stimulus with simultaneous stimulation and will also fail to move the contralesional limb. Patients with motor extinction will report stimulation of both sides but will move only the ipsilateral limb.

## HYPOKINESIA

Patients with mild defects in action-intentional systems may not fail to initiate responses, but initiate responses after an abnormally long delay. We have termed this delay hypokinesia. Since the patient must respond to a stimulus in order to judge whether or not the response is slow, hypokinesia is by definition exo-evoked.

The same paradigms that are used to test for akinesia of the eyes and limbs can be used to test for hypokinesia. While some patients with hypokinesia have such markedly slowed initiation times that hypokinesia can be detected easily, others have more subtle defects, necessitating reaction-time paradigms to observe their defects. Reaction times can be slowed for a variety of reasons, including impaired attention, bradyphrenia, or hypokinesia. To detect hypokinesia, one should use simple reaction times that do not require cognition and cannot, therefore, be impaired by bradyphrenia. Similarly, in order to test for hypokinesia, one has to use stimulus parameters that ensure that inattention cannot masquerade as hypokinesia.

Hypokinesia can be seen both in the limbs and eyes and may be either independent of direction or directionally specific such that there is a greater delay initiating movements in a contralesional direction than in an ipsilesional direction (Heilman et al., 1985). Hypokinesia can also be hemispatial: movements with the same limb may be slower in contralesional hemispace than in the ipsilesional hemispace (Meador et al., 1986).

## MOTOR IMPERSISTENCE

Motor impersistence is the inability to sustain an act. It is the intentional equivalent of the attentional disorder termed distractibility. It can be demonstrated using a variety of body parts, including the limbs, eyes, eyelids, jaw, and tongue. Like akinesia, it may also be directional (Kertesz et al., 1985) or hemispatial (Roeltgen et al., 1989).

To test for impersistence, ask the patient to maintain a position for 20 seconds.

Common tasks are keeping the eyes closed, keeping the mouth open, or protruding the tongue. Patients who can persist in these acts may be further stressed by asking them to persist in two movements simultaneously.

Limb impersistence can be tested by asking a patient to maintain a limb posture such as an arm extension for 20 seconds. Since limb impersistence can be hemispatial (Roeltgen et al., 1989), one can test each limb in its own and in opposite hemispace.

To test for directional impersistence, one requests the patient keep the eyes directed, or the head turned, to the left or right for 20 seconds. Directional impersistence may be worse in one hemispace than the other. Directional impersistence of the arm has not been described.

Patients with directinal impersistence usually have more difficulty in maintaining motor acitivation in contralesional hemispace or in the contralesional direction. While all persistence tasks are exo-evoked, one can use a signal or instructions to initiate the activity, and then either withdraw the stimulus or allow it to persist throughout the trial. The performance of patients is better in the latter condition than it is in the former, except when the stimulus and persistent action take place in opposite directions. These errors, however, may be related to defective response inhibition rather than to motor impersistence.

### Allesthesia and Allokinesia

Patients touched on the side opposite their lesion may report that they were touched on the extremity ipsilateral to their lesion (Obersteiner, 1882). This has been called allesthesia. A similar defect may be seen in other sensory modalities. A similar phenomenon can be seen in movement. If patients move the ipsilesional extremity when the task requires that they move the contralesional extremity, the error is called allokinesia. Allokinesia can also be directional. For example, a patient addressed from the side opposite a lesion may orient his head and eyes to the wrong (ipsilesional) side.

### Spatial Neglect

When patients with spatial neglect are asked to perform a variety of tasks in space, they neglect the hemispace contralateral to their lesion. For example, when asked to draw a picture of a flower, they may draw only half of the flower (Fig. 10-1). When asked to bisect a line, they may quarter it instead (Fig. 10-2), or they may fail to cross out lines distributed over a page (Fig. 10-3). The patients appear to be neglecting onehalf of visual space. This has been variously termed hemispatial neglect, visuospatial agnosia, hemispatial agnosia, visuospatial neglect, and unilateral spatial neglect. Patients with spatial neglect may fail to act in contralesional body centered space, or they may fail to act on the left side of stimuli (object centered or allocentric spatial neglect). They may demonstrate both body-centered and object-centered (allocentric) spatial neglect (Rapscak et al., 1989).

Although several authors (Battersby et al., 1956; Gainotti et al., 1972) have attributed the original description of hemispatial neglect to Holmes (1918), Holmes actually reported six patients with disturbed visual orientation from bilateral lesions. It

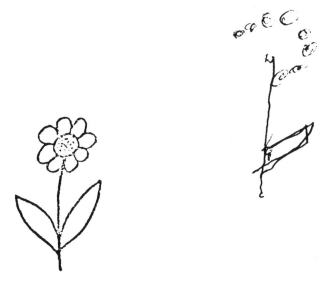

Fig. 10-1. An example of hemispatial neglect (visuospatial agnosia). Drawing on left performed by examiner. Drawing on right performed by patient.

was Riddoch (1935) who reported two patients without any disturbance of central vision who had visual disorientation limited to homonymous half-fields. Brain (1941) also described three patients who had visual disorientation limited to homonymous half-fields not caused by defects in visual acuity. Brain attributed this disorder to inattention of the left half of external space and thought it was similar to the "amnesia" for the left half of the body which may follow a lesion of the right parietal lobe. Paterson and Zangwill (1944), McFie et al. (1950), and Denny-Brown and Banker (1954) demonstrated that patients with unilateral inattention (spatial neglect) not only had visual disorientation limited to a half-field but also omitted material on one side of drawings and failed to eat from one side of their plate.

Patients with neglect may also fail to read part of a word or a portion of a sentence (i.e., they may read the word "cowboy" as "boy"). This has been termed paralexia (Benson and Geschwind, 1969). Patients may write on only one side of a page (see Chapter 4) or, when using a typewriter, they may fail to type letters correctly which are on the side of the keyboard contralateral to their lesion (Fig. 10-4). This has been termed paragraphia (Valenstein and Heilman, 1978).

In addition to horizontal neglect, neglect of lower (Rapcsak et al., 1988) and upper (Shelton et al., 1990) vertical space and neglect of radial space (Shelton et al., 1990)

Fig. 10-2. Performance of patient with hemisptial neglect on line bisection task.

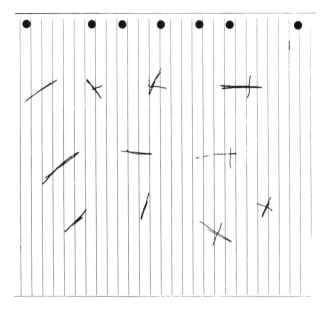

**Fig. 10-3.** Performance by patient with hemispatial neglect on crossing out task.

A

B

C  1  FOUR   SVORQ   ND 40   YER   DGO ..

2  zbrqha  mlincoln

3  AM   IN T THE   HOSPITLW  GWINEV ILLLLL  E    .  FL

4  I   AM   IN   THE   HOSPITL   AT   GAINSVILLLLE

D     Q W E R T Y U I O P °
      A S D F G H J K L : "
      Z X C V B N M , . ?

**Fig. 10-4. A:** Attempting to write, "You are a doctor." **B:** Copying. **C:** Typing. (1–3) Typewriter directly in front of patient; (4) typewriter moved to patient's right. **D:** The typewriter keyboard. Note that the letters missed (A, S, E) are at the left of the keyboard.

287

have been reported. Neglect may be viewer- (body-) centered or object-centered (allocentric) or environmentally centered. Experimental paradigms that change the position of the body in relation to gravity may be able to dissociate the body and environmentally centered reference systems. When a person is standing or sitting, a sheet of paper with stimuli on it is perpendicular to both the body's midsagittal plane and the pull of gravity. If a patient who neglects left-sided stimuli in the upright position lies on this right side and neglects stimuli to the left of his body, he would have body-centered neglect, but if he neglects stimuli in the left side of the environment, he would have environmentally centered neglect. Patients neglect stimuli both to the left of the body (body or viewer centered) and on the left side of the environment (environmentally centered) (Ladavas 1987; Farah et al., 1990).

*Testing:* There are many tests that can be used to determine if a patient has spatial neglect. In the cancellation test and reported by Albert (1973), lines are drawn in random positions on a sheet of paper. The patient is asked to cancel or cross out all the lines (Fig. 10-3). Patients with spatial neglect may fail to cancel lines on the contralesional side of the page. The cancellation task can be made more difficult and sensitive by asking patients to discriminate between targets and distractors. The more difficult it is to discriminate targets from background distractors, the more sensitive the task (see Rapcsak et al., 1989).

The line bisection task is also commonly used. A line six to ten inches long is drawn on a sheet of paper that is placed before the patient. The patient is then asked to bisect this line ("Cross the line out in the middle."). Patients with spatial neglect will usually displace their mark to the ipsilesional side. Neglect may be more apparent when using longer lines (Bisiach et al., 1983; Butter et al., 1988a) or when the line is placed in contralesional hemispace (Heilman and Valenstein, 1979).

Spatial neglect can also be assessed by asking patients to copy a drawing (Fig. 10-1) or to draw spontaneously. If patients fail to draw one side of the object, they may have spatial neglect. Since patients with right-hemisphere lesions commonly have visuospatial defects and associated constructional apraxia, they may have difficulty with spontaneous drawing. An alternative test is to have patients place numbers on a clock. Frequently, patients with neglect will write only on one side of the clock. They may write in only the numbers that belong on that side, or they may write all 12 numbers on one side.

## Personal Neglect

Patients with personal neglect (hemi-asomatognosia) may fail to recognize that their contralesional extremities are their own. They may complain that someone else's arm or leg is in bed with them. When confronted with objective evidence, they may still deny that their own extremities belong to them. Patients with milder neglect may be aware that their extremities belong to them (because they are attached) but still refer to their extremities as though they were objects.

Frequently, patients with this disorder also fail to dress or groom the abnormal side. Although this may be considered a form of dressing apraxia, the pathophysiology may be different from that seen with other forms of apraxia (see Chapter 7) or that seen in patients with profound visuospatial disorders (see Chapter 8).

## Memory and Representational Defects

ANTEROGRADE

We demonstrated that patients with neglect have a unilateral memory defect for auditory stimuli. We randomly presented consonants through earphones to patients on either the neglected or nonneglected side and asked them to report the stimulus either immediately or after a distraction-filled interval. We found that distraction induced more of a defect in the neglected ear than in the normal ear (Heilman et al., 1974).

Samuels et al. (1971) tested patients with right parietal lesions and found a similar phenomenon in the visual modality. Unfortunately, they did not evaluate their subjects for neglect.

RETROGRADE

Denny-Brown and Banker (1954) described a patient who could not from memory describe the details of a room when those details were located on the side opposite her cerebral lesion. Bisiach and Luzzatti (1978) also described patients with neglect who were unable to recall left-sided details when imagining themselves facing the cathedral in a square in Milan. However, when asked to imagine that they were facing away from the cathedral, they could recall details that had been on the left side but now were on the right. In testing patients for a retrograde hemispatial memory defect, patients can be asked to recall the stores one may see when driving down a familiar street. The examiner then compares the number of items recalled for each side of the street. To verify that there is a hemispatial defect, one can ask the patient to imagine driving in the opposite direction.

### Anosognosia and Anosodiaphoria

Patients with the neglect syndrome may be unaware of or deny their hemiparesis. This phenomenon has been termed anosognosia (Babinski, 1914). Patients may also deny sensory loss or hemianopia. More frequently, patients may admit that they have a neurological impairment but they appear unconcerned about it. This has been termed anosodiaphoria (Critchley, 1966). Anosognosia and anosodiaphoria may be associated with conditions other than neglect, such as cortical blindness (Anton's syndrome).

## MECHANISMS UNDERLYING NEGLECT

Most of the defects associated with neglect can be attributed to one or more of three basic mechanisms: disorders of attention, disorders of action or intention, and representational or memory disorders. Although the various behavioral manifestations of the neglect syndrome often coexist, different manifestations may be present at different times in the same patient, and some may not appear at all in certain patients.

For example, severe inattention may be replaced by sensory extinction as a patient improves, and patients with akinesia may not manifest inattention (Valenstein and Heilman, 1981). The mechanisms of inattention, extinction, akinesia, representational deficits, hemispatial neglect, and anosognosia will therefore be discussed separately.

## Mechanisms Underlying Inattention (Sensory Neglect)

As noted above, patients with neglect may be unaware of novel or meaningful stimuli. This has been attributed to disorders of sensation, to abnormalities of the "body schema" or to other complex perceptual deficits, and to disorders of attention.

### SENSORY HYPOTHESES

Battersby and associates (1956) thought that neglect in humans resulted from decreased sensory input superimposed on a background of decreased mental function. Sprague et al. (1961) concluded that neglect was caused by loss of patterned sensory input to the forebrain, particularly to the neocortex. Eidelberg and Schwartz (1971) similarly proposed that neglect (extinction) was a passive phenomenon due to quantitatively asymmetrical sensory input to the two hemispheres. They based this conclusion on the finding that neglect resulted from neospinothalamic lesions but not from medial lemniscal lesions. They claimed that the neospinothalamic tract carries more tactile information to the hemisphere than does the medial lemniscus. However, since lesions in primary and secondary sensory cortex could also produce neglect, they postulated that the syndrome could also be caused by a reduced functional mass of one cortical area concerned with somatic sensation relative to another.

### BODY SCHEMA

Brain (1941) believed that the parietal lobes contained the body schema and mediated spatial perception. Parietal lesions therefore caused a patient to fail to recognize not only half of his body but also half of space. Brain thought that allesthesia resulted from severe damage to the schema for one-half of the body, causing events occurring on that half, if perceived at all, to be related in consciousness to the surviving schema representing the normal half.

### AMORPHOSYNTHESIS

Denny-Brown and Banker (1954) proposed that the parietal lobes were important in cortical sensation and that the phenomenon of inattention belonged to the whole class of cortical disorders of sensation:"a loss of fine discrimination. . .an inability to synthesize more than a few properties of a sensory stimulus and a disturbance of synthesis of multiple sensory stimuli." The neglect syndrome was ascribed to a defect in spatial summation that they called amorphosynthesis.

ATTENTIONAL HYPOTHESIS

Some of the first references in the neglect syndrome literature referred to defects of attention. Poppelreuter (1917) introduced the word inattention. Brain (1941) and Critchley (1966) were also strong proponents of this view. However, Bender and Furlow (1944, 1945) challenged the attentional theory; they felt that inattention could not be important in the pathophysiology of the syndrome because neglect could not be overcome by having the patient "concentrate" on the neglected side.

Heilman and Valenstein (1972) and Watson and associates (1973, 1974) again postulated an attention-arousal hypothesis. These authors argued that the sensory and perceptual hypotheses could not explain all cases of neglect, since neglect was often produced by lesions outside the traditional sensory pathways. Evoked potential studies in animals with unilateral neglect have demonstrated a change in late waves (that are known to be influenced by changes in attention and stimulus significance) but no change in the early (sensory) waves (Watson et al., 1977). Furthermore, neglect is often multimodal and therefore cannot be explained by a defect in any one sensory modality.

*Anatomical basis of attention.* Unilateral neglect in humans and monkeys can be induced by lesions in many different brain regions. These include cortical areas such as the temporoparietal-occipital junction (Critchley, 1966; Heilman et al., 1970, 1983a) (Fig. 10-5), limbic areas such as the cingulate gyrus (Heilman and Valenstein, 1972; Watson et al., 1973), and subcortical areas such as the thalamus (Fig. 10-6) and

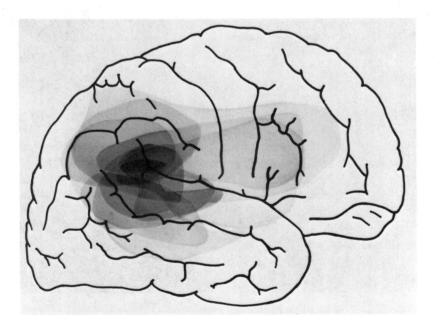

**Fig. 10-5.** Lateral view of the right hemisphere. Lesions (as determined by CT scan) of ten patients with the neglect syndrome are superimposed.

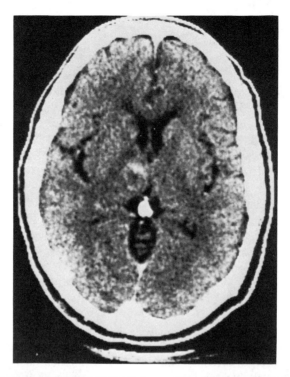

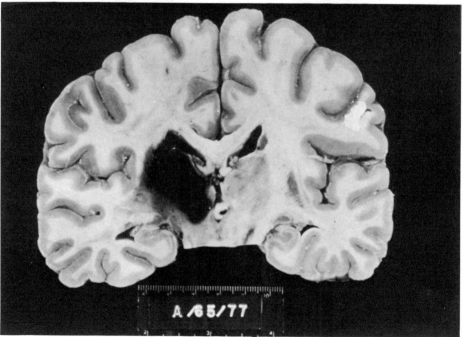

Fig. 10-6. Top: CT scan demonstrating a contrast-enhancing right thalamic infarction in a patient with the neglect syndrome. Bottom: Right thalamic hemorrhage at postmortem examination of a patient who had the neglect syndrome.

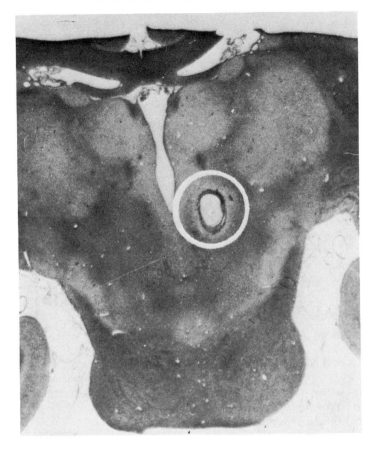

**Fig. 10-7.** Electrolytic lesion in the mesencephalic reticular formation of a monkey who had developed unilateral neglect after the lesion was made.

mesencephalic reticular formation (Fig. 10-7) (Watson et al., 1974). As we will discuss below, these subcortical areas have been shown to be important in mediating arousal and attention, and the cortical areas are regions that are probably specifically involved in the analysis of the behavioral significance of stimuli. We have proposed that inattention or sensory neglect is an attentional-arousal disorder induced by dysfunction in a corticolimbic reticular formation network (Heilman and Valenstein, 1972; Watson et al., 1973, 1981; Heilman, 1979). Mesulam (1981) has put forth a similar proposal. We will review the evidence for our view, and propose a model or schema to explain the neglect syndrome (Figs. 10-8, 10-9).

In monkeys and cats, profound sensory neglect results from discrete lesions of the mesencephalic reticular formation (MRF) (Reeves and Hagaman, 1971; Watson et al., 1974). Stimulation of the MRF is associated with behavioral arousal and also with desynchronization of the electroencephalogram (EEG), a physiological measure of arousal (Moruzzi and Nagoun, 1949). Unilateral stimulation induces greater EEG desynchronization in the ipsilateral than in the contralateral hemisphere (Moruzzi

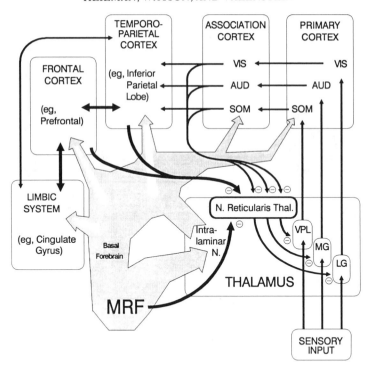

**Fig. 10-8.** Schematic representation of pathways important in sensory attention and tonic arousal. See text for details. MRF = mesencephalic reticular formation; VIS = visual; AUD = auditory; SOM = somasthetic. Within the thalamus, sensory relay nuclei are indicated: VPL = ventralis posterolateralis; MG = medial geniculate; LG = lateral geniculate.

and Magoun, 1949). Arousal is a physiological state that prepares the organism for sensory and motor processing. Bilateral MRF lesions result in coma. Unilateral lesions result in contralateral neglect, which is probably due to unilateral hemispheric hypoarousal (Watson et al., 1974).

*MRF influence on the cortex: major neurotransmitter pathways.* Many neurons that ascend from the mesencephalic reticular activating system and its environs are monoaminergic. The locus coeruleus norepinephrine system projects diffusely to cortical structures. The area of the mesencephalon stimulated by Moruzzi and Magoun (1949) contains ascending catecholamine systems, including the noradrenergic system. Although this norepinephrine system would appear to be ideal for mediating cortical arousal (Jouvet, 1977), destruction of most of the locus coeruleus does not profoundly affect behavioral arousal, nor does it change EEG patterns (Jacobs and Jones, 1978). As mentioned above, Moruzzi and Magoun (1949) demonstrated that unilateral stimulation of the mesencephalic reticular activating system induced greater desynchronization ipsilaterally than contralaterally. We have shown that unilateral lesions in the region of the MRF induce EEG and behavioral changes suggestive of unilateral coma (Watson et al., 1974). Unilateral locus coeruleus lesions do not induce similar behavioral or EEG changes (Deuel, personal communication).

Although the dopaminergic system may be critical for mediating intention (see section below on intention), dopamine does not appear to be important in arousal because blockade of dopamine synthesis or of dopamine receptors does not appear to affect desynchronization (Robinson et al., 1977).

Acetylcholine appears to have a more promising role in the mediation of arousal. Shute and Lewis (1967) described an ascending cholinergic reticular formation. Stimulation of the midbrain mesencephalic reticular activating system not only induces the arousal response but also increases the rate of acetylcholine release from the neocortex (Kanai and Szerb, 1965). Acetylcholine makes some neurons more responsive to sensory input (McCormick, 1989). Cholinergic agonists induce neocortical desynchronization, while antagonists abolish desynchronization (Bradley, 1968). Unfortunately, however, while cholinergic blockers such as atropine interfere with EEG desynchronization, they do not dramatically affect behavioral arousal. Vanderwolf and Robinson (1981) suggested that there may be two types of cholinergic input to the neocortex from the reticular formation, only one of which is atropine sensitive. Therefore, the other cholinergic input may be responsible for behavioral arousal. It is believed that the cholinergic projections from the nucleus basalis are responsible for increasing neuronal responsivity (Sato et al., 1987). The cuneiform area of the mesencephalon could influence the nucleus basalis via the peripeduncular area of the mesencephalon which receives projections from the cuneiform nucleus and projects to the nucleus basalis (Arnault and Roger, 1987).

*Polysynaptic MRF pathway to cortex via the thalamus.* The mesencephalic reticular activating system may project to the cortex in a diffuse polysynaptic fashion (Schiebel and Schiebel, 1967) (see Fig. 10-8) and thereby influences cortical processing of sensory stimuli. Steriade and Glenn (1982) found that the centralis lateralis and paracentralis thalamic nuclei also project to widespread cortical regions. Other neurons from these thalamic areas project to the caudate. Thirteen percent of neurons with cortical or caudate projections could be activated by mesencephalic reticular activating system stimulation.

*MRF influence on the nucleus reticularis of the thalamus.* There is, however, an alternative means whereby the mesencephalic reticular activating system may affect cortical processing of sensory stimuli. Sensory information that reaches the cortex is relayed through specific thalamic nuclei: somatosensory information is transmitted from the ventralis posterolateralis (VPL) to the postcentral gyrus (Brodmann's areas 3, 1, 2); auditory information is transmitted through the medial geniculate nucleus (MGN) to the supratemporal plane (Heschl's gyrus); and visual information is transmitted through the lateral geniculate nucleus (LGN) to the occipital lobe (area 17) (Fig. 10-8). The nucleus reticularis thalami, a thin reticular necleus enveloping the thalamus, projects to the thalamic relay nuclei and appears to inhibit thalamic relay to the cortex (Schiebel and Schiebel, 1966) (Fig. 10-8). The mesencephalic reticular activating system also projects to the nucleus reticularis. Rapid mesencephalic reticular activating system stimulation or behavioral arousal inhibits the nucleus reticularis (NR) and is thereby associated with enhanced thalamic transmission to the cerebral cortex (Singer, 1977). Therefore, unilateral lesions of MRF may induce neglect not only because the cortex is not prepared for processing sensory stimuli in the absence of MRF-mediated arousal, but also because the thalamic sensory relay nuclei are being inhibited by the nucleus reticularis.

*Unimodal sensory association cortex.* Lesions of the thalamic relay nuclei or primary sensory cortex induce a sensory defect rather than neglect. Primary cortical sensory areas project to unimodal association cortex (see Fig. 10-8). Association cortex synthesizes multiple features of a complex simulus within a single sensory modality. Lesions of unimodal association cortex may induce perceptual deficits in a single modality (for example, apperceptive agnosia). Modality-specific association areas may also be detecting stimulus novelity (modeling) (Sokolov, 1963). When a stimulus is neither novel nor significant, corticofugal projections to the NR may allow habituation to occur by selectively influencing thalamic relay. When a stimulus is novel or significant, corticofugal projections might inhibit the NR and thereby allow the thalamus to relay additional sensory input. This capacity for selective control of sensory input is supported by a study revealing that stimulation of specific areas within NR related to specific thalamic nuclei (e.g., NR lateral geniculate, NR medial geniculate, or NR ventrobasal complex) results in abolition of corresponding (visual, auditory, and tactile) cortically evoked responses (Yingling and Skinner, 1977). Recent physiologic imaging studies reveal that selectively attending to tactile stimuli may activate primary (somesthetic) cortex (Meyer et al., 1991). This activation may be mediated by corticofugal projections that inhibit the inhibition NR exerts on thalamic relay nuclei such as ventral posterior lateral (VPL).

*Polymodal and supramodal association areas.* Unimodal association areas converge upon polymodal association areas (Fig. 10-8). In the monkey, these are the prefrontal cortex (periarcuate, prearcuate, orbitofrontal) and both banks of the superior temporal sulcus (STS) (Pandya and Kuypers, 1969). Unimodal association areas may also project directly to the caudal inferior parietal lobule (IPL) or, alternatively, may reach the IPL after a synapse in polymodal convergence areas (e.g., prefrontal cortex and both banks of the STS) (Mesulam et al., 1977). Polymodal convergence areas may subserve cross-modal associations and polymodal sensory synthesis. Polymodal sensory synthesis may also be important in "modeling" (detecting stimulus novelty) and detecting significance. In contrast to the unimodal association cortex that projects to specific parts of the NR and thereby gates sensory input in one modality, these multimodal convergence areas may have a more general inhibitory action on NR and provide further arousal after cortical analysis. These convergence areas also may project directly to the MRF, which either may induce a general state of arousal because of diffuse multisynaptic connections to the cortex or may increase thalamic transmission via connections with NR, as discussed above, or both. Evidence that polymodal areas of cortex are important in arousal comes from neurophysiological studies showing that stimulation of select cortical sites induces a generalized arousal response. These sites include the prearcuate region and both banks of the STS (Segundo et al., 1955). When similar sites are ablated, there is EEG evidence of ipsilateral hypoarousal (Watson et al., 1977).

*Limbic and frontal input.* Although determination of stimulus novelty may be mediated by sensory associaton cortex, stimulus significance is determined in part by the needs by the organism (motivational state). Limbic system input into brain regions important for determining stimulus significance might provide information about biological needs. The frontal lobes might provide input about needs related to goals that are neither directly stimulus dependent nor motivated by an immediate biological need, since the frontal lobes do play a critical role in goal-mediated behavior and in developing sets (see Chapter 12).

Polymodal (e.g., STS) and supramodal (IPL) areas have prominent limbic and frontal connections. The polymodal cortices project to the cingulate gyrus (a portion of the limbic system), and the cingulate gyrus projects to the IPL (Fig. 10-8). The prefrontal cortex, STS, and IPL have strong reciprocal connections. The posterior cingulate cortex (Brodmann's area 23) has more extensive connections with polymodal association areas (prefrontal cortex, and exlusively for STS) and the IPL than does the anterior cingulate cortex (Brodmann's area 24) (Vogt et al., 1979; Baleydier and Maugierre, 1980). These connections may provide an anatomic substrate by which motivational states (e.g., biological needs, sets, and long-term goals) may influence stimulus processing.

*Physiological properties of neurons in the IPL.* In the past decade, investigators have been able to study the physiological function of specific areas of the nervous system by recording from single neurons in awake animals. In this experimental situation, the firing characteristics of individual neurons can be measured in relation to specific sensory stimulation or motor behavior. For example, a single neuron in the visual cortex may respond maximally to a contrast border in a specific region of the visual field, sometimes in a specific orientation. By varying the nature of the stimulus and by training the animal to respond in specific ways, the characteristic patterns of firing of individual neurons can be defined in terms of the optimal stimulus and/or response parameters that cause a maximal change in firing rate. In this fashion, investigators have defined the properties of neurons in the IPL (area 7) of the monkey (Lynch, 1980; Motter and Mountcastle, 1981; Mountcastle et al., 1975, 1981; Goldberg and Robinson, 1977; Robinson et al., 1978; Bushnell et al., 1981). Unlike single cells in primary sensory cortex, the activity of many neurons in the IPL correlates best with stimuli or responses of importance to the animal, while similar stimuli or responses that are unimportant are associated with either no change or a lesser change in neuronal activity. Several types of neurons have been described.

*Projection neurons.* Some neurons are active in relation to limb projection or hand manipulation. Projection neurons are active when an animal reaches toward an object of significance in immediate extrapersonal space, for example, food (when the animal is hungry ) or water (when thirsty). Similar cells are found in the superior parietal lobule (area 5); but the cells in the IPL are more likely to be related to activity of both arms or of the ipsilateral arm, instead of only to the contralateral arm.

*Visual fixation neurons.* Visual fixation neurons are active when the animal fixates an object of interest within arm's reach. If the animal fixates a target to which it must attend in order to perform for a reward, these neurons remain active until the animal is rewarded. Visual fixation cells are also active during smooth pursuit of moving visual stimuli, independent of direction. Most fixation cells are active only when the biologically significant target is placed in one-half or one-quarter of the visual field contralateral to the active cells. A minority of fixation cells is active when the stimulus is placed anywhere in the visual field. Eye position (direction of gaze) is also important: these partial fixation neurons are active when the direction of gaze is toward a specific half or quadrant of the visual field. To summarize, the activity of partial fixation cells depends on (1) the biological significance of the stimulus, (2) the distance of the stimulus from the animal, (3) the region of the retina stimulated, and (4) the direction of gaze.

*Visual tracking neurons.*   Visual tracking neurons do not discharge with fixation but only when the animal's eyes are smoothly pursuing an object of interest that is within arm's reach and is moving in a given direction.

*Saccade neurons.*   When a monkey makes a saccade, the activity of the fixation and tracking neurons abates. Saccade neurons have little activity during fixation or slow pursuit, but become active just (75 msec) before a saccade. Like fixation and tracking neurons, these cells become active with biologically significant stimuli: spontaneous saccades do not induce activity in these cells. Some saccade neurons become active with saccades in all directions, whereas others appear to be directionally dependent. Of these direction-dependent saccade neurons, most are more active before saccades in the contralateral hemifield.

*Enhancement.*   Goldberg and Robinson (1977) and Robinson et al. (1978) have shown that the activity of some posterior parietal neurons is enhanced by motivationally significant visual stimuli independent of behavior. This enhancement is spatially selective. If an animal attends to a visual stimulus, then any response to that stimulus is enhanced, whether it be a saccade, reaching, or using the stimulus as a cue for behavior not requiring a targeted movement. These parietal neurons respond to aversive as well as rewarding stimuli, and their activity may therefore be more dependent on selective attention than specific motivational significance, although motivational aspects are included in a general attentional mechanism.

*Light-sensitive neurons.*   Mountcastle and co-workers (1981) have identified light-sensitive neurons (formerly called "visual space" neurons) of the monkey IPL having large response areas that do not include the fovea. The response areas may be distributed in both halves of the visual fields. These neurons are sensitive to stimulus direction and movement over a wide velocity range. A neuron with bilateral receptive fields will respond to movement in one direction in one visual field and will respond only to movement in the opposite direction in the other visual field, a property called opponent vector organization. During an act of attentive fixation, these neurons have an enhanced response to peripheral visual stimuli. These parietal neurons may play a role in the residual visual function of destriate primates and may be the projection target of the "second" visual system of retinocollicular origin. The facilitation of this system during foveal attention presumably allows the subject to be prepared to shift attention to novel, threatening, or aversive stimuli appearing in the periphery.

*Nonvisual cells.*   The inattention to contralateral stimuli seen in humans and monkeys after lesions in the temporoparietal regions, however, is not limited to the visual modality. Meaningful somesthetic and auditory stimuli are also neglected. Hyvarinen and Poranen (1974) noted that the inferior parietal lobule also contained cells that exhibited enhanced activity when animals manipulated biologically significant objects. Some inferior parietal lobule cells seem to be activated by stimuli in both the visual and the somesthetic modalities.

*Interpretation of physiological studies.*   Mountcastle and co-workers have concluded that the posterior parietal cortex contains sets of neurons serving a command function for manual and visual exploration of immediate extrapersonal space. Deficits after lesions of this area would be explained by a lack of volition to explore with the hand and eye the contralateral side of space. Very few neurons were found that appeared to converge visual information with body position and movement—so few that it seemed unlikely that the posterior parietal cortex could be the region producing a neural model of the orientation and movement of the body in space. It was suggested that the region of the superior temporal sulcus might perform this function since it receives input from area 7.

Goldberg, Robinson, and co-workers have emphasized the importance of the IPL in directing attention. They saw no evidence that the IPL contained cells that programmed responses. While this differs from the view of Mountcastle and co-workers who assign a command function to this area, there are more similarities than differences in the two interpretations, and an analysis of these studies provides insight into the role of the IPL in behavior. This area is not simply a sensory association region. It acts in parallel with the retinostriate system and functions as an interface between attention to, reception of, and response to significant events in extrapersonal space. The retinostriate system is important for discriminating shape, color, and size when a subject concentrates on foveal work. The light-sensitive neurons of the IPL provide continual updating of the neural image of extrapersonal space and therefore allow for the attraction of attention toward events in peripheral vision. Fixation neurons maintain attention on a significant fixated object. Oculomotor neurons, such as the saccade neurons described above, subserve the motor events of shifting visual attention. Projection and manipulation neurons are active during limb movements directed toward an object in extrapersonal space. Neurons in the inferior parietal lobule are movement independent (Bushnell et al., 1981). They are probably not only subserving attention to extrapersonal space but also processing information to determine its emotional or motivational significance.

*Summary of the attentional model.* The attentional model we have discussed is summarized in Figure 10-8. Unilateral inattention will follow unilateral mesencephalic reticular activatng system lesions because loss of inhibition of the ipsilateral nucleus reticularis by the mesencephalic reticular activating system decreases thalamic transmission of sensory input to the cortex or because the MRF does not prepare the cortex for sensory processing, or both. Unilateral lesions of the primary or association cortices cause contralateral unimodal sensory loss or inability to synthesize contralateral unimodal sensory input. Corticothalamic collaterals from the association cortex to the NR may serve unimodal habituation and attention. Unilateral lesions of multimodal sensory convergence areas (e.g., the STS) that project to mesencephalic reticular activating system and NR induce contralateral inattention because the subject cannot be aroused to, or process, multimodal contralateral stimuli. A lesion of the IPL, because of its reciprocal connections with polymodal areas (prefrontal lobes, STS) and the limbic system, may impair the subject's ability to determine the significance of a stimulus.

## Mechanisms Underlying Extinction

Extinction is said to occur when an organism is able to report or respond to a stimulus presented in isolation but unable to report this same stimulus presented simultaneously with another stimulus (usually on the other side of the body). Extinction also may be induced by stimuli in different modalities. The nature and complexity of a stimulus may also affect extinction.

Extinction can be seen in normal subjects as well as in patients with central nervous system lesions (Benton and Levin, 1972; Kimura, 1967). The lesions causing extinction are often in the same areas as lesions that cause inattention, and extinction is more commonly associated with right- than left-hemisphere dysfunction (Meador et al., 1988). However, certain forms of extinction may also occur after lesions of the corpus callosum (Sparks and Geschwind, 1968; Milner et al., 1968), and left-sided extinction has even been reported to follow left-hemisphere lesions (Schwartz et al., 1979). Extinction in normal subjects, extinction in patients with callosal lesions, and extinction in patients with hemisphere lesions may all differ. In this section we will discuss mainly the extinction seen after hemisphere lesions.

Patients with cerebral dysfunction, particularly in the temporoparietal region, may show extinction (Heilman et al., 1983). Multimodal extinction may also occur in monkeys with temporoparietal lesions (Heilman et al., 1970). Unlike the ipsilateral extinction reported by Schwartz et al. (1979) that only occurred with the use of complex stimuli, extinction after parietal lobe lesions can be demonstrated using simple stimuli.

In general, despite many published reports, especially about dichotic listening in normal subjects, the mechanisms underlying extinction are poorly understood. We will discuss several hypotheses that have been advanced to explain extinction.

## SENSORY THEORIES

Extinction has been reported to be induced by lesions that affect purely sensory systems. Because patients with partial deafferentation may exhibit extinction, several authors have postulated a sensory mechanism to explain inattention and extinction. Psychophysical methods have been used to demonstrate that in normal subjects sensory threshold increases on one side when the opposite side is stimulated (obscuration). If this obscuration phenomenon (perhaps induced by reciprocal inhibition) occurs in patients with an elevated threshold from an afferent lesion, it would appear similar to extinction in patients without deafferentation.

## SUPPRESSION AND RECIPROCAL INHIBITION

Nathan (1946) and Reider (1946) suggested that extinction results from suppression: the normal hemisphere inhibits the damaged hemisphere more than the damaged hemisphere inhibits the normal hemisphere. Consequently, stimuli contralateral to the damaged hemisphere are not perceived when the normal side is stimulated. The notion of transcallosal inhibition thus has bearing on theories of inattention. Kinsbourne (1970) postulated a similar mechanism.

To explain extinction and obscuration we can postulate a reciprocal gating mechanism involving the NR, which normally inhibits sensory transmission to the ipsilateral cortex. Each association cortex inhibits the ipsilateral NR, decreasing inhibition of ipsilateral sensory input, and simultaneously facilitates the contralateral NR, gating out sensory input to the contralateral cortex. Therefore, even under normal conditions, a stimulus on one side would induce an increase of threshold for stimuli on the other side. With a lesion of associaton cortex, there would be less inhibition of NR, which in turn would inhibit the thalamic sensory nuclei, thus making the thalamus less sensitive to contralateral stimuli. With bilateral simultaneous stimuli, activated attentional cells in the intact hemisphere would further increase contralateral NR activity, further inhibiting the thalamic sensory nuclei and thereby inducing extinction. The means by which one association cortex may influence the contralateral NR is not known, and this theory remains unproven.

INTERFERENCE THEORY

Birch et al. (1967) proposed that the damaged hemisphere processes information more slowly than the intact hemisphere. Because of this inertia, the damaged side is more subject to interference from the normal side. To support their hypothesis, the authors demonstrated that stimulating the abnormal side (contralesional side) before stimulating the normal side (ipsilateral side) reduced extinction; however, stimulating the normal side before the abnoraml side had no effect on extinction.

LIMITED ATTENTION OR CAPACITY THEORY

According to the limited attention or capcity theory, bilateral simultaneous stimuli are normally processed simultaneously, each hemisphere processing the contralateral stimulus and having an attentional bias toward contralateral space or body. However, a damaged hemisphere (usually the right) may be unable to attend to contralateral stimuli. Recovery from unilateral inattention may be mediated by the normal (left) hemisphere. This hemisphere, however, may not only have an attentional bias toward contralateral space and body, but also may have a limited attentional capacity. Therefore, with bilateral simultaneous stimulation, the normal hemisphere's attentional mechanism, biased toward the contralateral stimulus, may be unable to attend to an ipsilateral stimulus (Heilman, 1979).

EVIDENCE BEARING ON THEORIES OF EXTINCTION

We will briefly review studies which have some bearing on the various theories of extinction. We should note that these theories may not be mutually exclusive: because extinction can be caused by lesions in a variety of anatomically and functionally different areas, the reciprocal inhibition, limited attention, and interference theories could each be correct, but for different lesions.

Benton and Levin (1972) reported that in normal subjects, threshold is raised by presenting a simultaneous stimulus. Because normal persons do not have lesions, Benton and Levin's findings cannot be explained readily by the limited attention or interference models. Their findings appear to support the reciprocal inhibition model. The findings of Birch et al. (1967) that extinction is reduced when a contralateral stimulus precedes an ipsilateral stimulus, but not when an ipsilateral stimulus precedes a contralateral stimulus, are compaitble with both the reciprocal inhibition and limited attention theories. Sevush and Heilman (1981) and Kaplan et al. (1990) showed that a unilateral stimulus preceding a trial with simultaneous stimuli may alter the pattern of extinction in patients with unilateral hemisphere lesions. The subject is more likely to show extinction when a bilateral trial is preceded by a contralateral (e.g., left) stimulus than when a bilateral trial is preceded by an ipsilateral (e.g., right) stimulus. In addition, Rapscak, et al. (1987) observed that extinction can occur even within a visual field. These findings cannot be explained by the interference model.

Heilman et al. (1984) provided additional support for the limited attention or capacity theory model. Patients who exhibited extinction were asked to report where they were given a tactile stimulus: on the right, the left, both, or neither (in the "neither" situation, the subject was not stimulated, but was still asked to give a response). Subjects erred by reporting "both" when the arm ipsilateral to the damaged hemisphere was stimulated more than they reported "both" when the contralateral arm was stimulated. One interpretation of these results is that these patients were not sufficiently attentive to their contralesional extremities to realize when the had *not* been touched. Since the errors consisted of reporting a stimulation that did not occur rather than failing to report a stimulus, these results cannot be explained by the suppression, reciprocal inhibition, or interference theories and are most compatible with the limited attention or capacity theory. Rapscak et al. (1987) demonstrated that capacity is most limited in the contralesional field and becomes progressively reduced as one moves laterally in that field. However, with right-hemisphere lesions, capacity may be so reduced that even when two stimuli are given ipsilaterally either visually (Rapscak et al., 1987) or via the tactile modality (Feinberg, 1991), one is extinguished.

## Mechanisms Underlying Action-Intentional Disorder

Unilateral neglect has been described following unilateral dorsolateral frontal lesions in monkeys (Bianchi, 1895; Kennard and Ectors, 1938; Welch and Stuteville, 1958) and man (Heilman and Valenstein, 1972). Watson et al. (1978) recognized that in most testing paradigms, the animal is required to respond to a stimulus contralateral to the lesion either by orienting to the stimulus or by moving the limbs on the side of the stimulus. Since animals with frontal lobe lesions were not weak, it was assumed that their failure to make the appropriate response resulted from sensory neglect. Watson et al. (1978) suggested that it could be explained equally well by unilateral akinesia. They therefore trained monkeys to use the left hand to respond to a tactile stimulus on the right leg, and the right hand to respond to a left-sided tactile stimulus. After a unilateral frontal arcuate lesion, the monkeys showed contralateral neglect, but when stimulated on their neglected side, they responded normally with the limb on the side of the lesion. When stimulated on the side ipsilateral to the lesion, however, they often failed to respond, or responded by moving the limb ipsilateral to the lesion. These results cannot be explained by sensory or perceptual hypotheses, and are thought to reflect a defect in intention to make a correct response.

### ANATOMIC AND PHYSIOLOGICAL MECHANISM

The region of the arcuate gyrus (periarcuate region) in monkeys contains the frontal eye field. Stimulation of the frontal eye field elicits contralateral eye movement, head rotation, and pupillary dilation resembling attentive orienting (Wagman and Mehler, 1972). The connections of the periarcuate region are important in understanding its possible role in attention and intention to multimodal sensory and limbic inputs. The periarcuate region has reciprocal connections with auditory, visual, and somesthetic association cortex (Chavis and Pandya, 1976). Evoked potential studies have confirmed this as an area of sensory convergence (Bignell and Imbert, 1969). The periarcuate region is also reciprocally connected with STS, another site of multimodal sensory convergence, and with the intraparietal sulcus, an area of somatosensory and visual convergence. There are also connections with prearcuate cortex. The periarcuate cortex has reciprocal connections with subcortical areas: the paralamellar portion of dorsomedial nucleus (DM) and the adjacent centromedian-parafascicularis (CM-Pf) complex (Kievet and Kuypers, 1977; Akert and Von Monakow, 1980). Just as the periarcuate region is transitional in architecture between agranular motor cortex and granular prefrontal cortex, the paralamellar–CM-Pf complex is situated between medial thalamus, which projects to granular cortex, and lateral thalamus, which projects to agranular cortex. Projections to MRF (Kuypers and Lawrence, 1967) as well as nonreciprocal projections to caudate also exist. Last, the periarcuate region also receives input from the limbic system, mainly from the anterior cingulate gyrus (Baleydier and Mauguiere, 1980).

The neocortical sensory association and sensory convergence area connections may provide the frontal lobe with information about external stimuli that may call the individual to action. The limbic connections (anterior cingulate gyrus) may provide the frontal lobe with motivational information. Connections with the MRF may be important in arousal.

Because the dorsolateral frontal lobe has sensory association cortex, limbic, and reticular formation connections, it would appear to be an ideal candidate for mediating a response to a stimulus to which the subject is attending (Fig. 10-9). While this area may not be critical for mediating *how* to respond (e.g., providing instruction for the spatial trajectory and temporal patterns), it may control *when* one responds. There is evidence from physiological studies to support this hypothesis. Recordings from single cells in the posterior frontal arcuate gyrus reveal responses similar to those of the superior colliculus, a structure also important in oculomotor control (Goldberg and Bushnell, 1981). These visually responsive neurons show enhanced activity time-locked to the onset of stimulus and preceding eye movement. This differs from IPL neurons that respond to visual input independent of behavior: an IPL neuron whose activity enhances in a task that requires a saccade also enhances with tasks that do not require a saccade. Therefore, the IPL neurons seem to be responsible for selective spatial attention, which is independent of behavior, and any neuron that is enhanced to one type of behavior will also be enhanced to others (Bushnell et al., 1981). The frontal eye-field neurons, however, are linked to behavior, but only to movements that have motivational significance. Responses to other stimulus modalities (e.g., audition) may be controlled by another group of nearby neurons in the arcuate gyrus (Whittington and Hepp-Reymond, 1977).

The dorsolateral frontal lobe has extensive connections with CM-Pf, one of the "nonspecific" intralaminar thalamic nuclei. Nonsensory neglect has also been reported in monkeys after CM-Pf lesions (Watson et al, 1978) and in a patient with an intralaminar lesion (Bogousslavsky et al., 1986), and an akinetic state (akinetic mutism) is seen with bilateral CM-Pf lesions in humans (Mills and Swanson, 1978). We have postulated a possible role for CM-Pf in behavior (Watson et al., 1981). This role is based on behavioral, anatomic, and physiological evidence that CM-Pf and periarcuate cortex are involved in mediating the response of an individual to meaningful stimuli.

Low-frequency stimulation of CM-Pf induces cortical recruiting responses (Jasper, 1949) and activates the inhibitory NR through a CM-Pf–frontocortical–NR system (Yingling and Skinner, 1975). This NR activation elicits inhibitory postsynaptic potentials in the ventrolateral thalamic nucleus (VL), and thus blocks VL transmission to motor cortex (Purpura, 1970). Transmission in VL has been shown to be inversely proportional to NR activity (Filion et al., 1971). VL projects to motor cortex, and may be important in the control of movement initiation.

High-frequency stimulation of the CM-Pf or MRF induces inhibition of NR, EEG desynchronization, and behavioral arousal (Moruzzi and Magoun, 1949; Yingling and Skinner, 1975). These manifestations elicited by high-frequency CM-Pf stimulation are predominantly mediated via the MRF-NR system, since they are blocked by a lesion between the CM-Pf and MRF (Weinberger et al., 1965). A lesion of the CM-Pf–frontocortical–NR system also prevents inhibition of the NR response to rapid CM-Pf stimulation, whereas rapid MRF stimulation during this blockade will continue to inhibit the NR (Yingling and Skinner, 1977). This indicates that the NR can be inhibited by either an MRF-NR system or a CM-Pf–frontocortical–NR system and suggests that different types of behavior may be mediated independently by these systems.

Novel or noxious stimuli, or anticipation of a response to a meaningful stimulus, produce inhibition of the NR and a negative surface potential over the frontal cortex (Yingling and Skinner, 1977). This surface-negative potential occurs if a stimulus has acquired behavioral significance (Walter, 1973). Specifically, when a warning stimulus precedes a second stimulus that requires a motor response, a negative waveform appears between stimuli and has been called the "contingent negative variation" (CNV) and is thought to reflect motivation, attention, or expectancy.

Skinner and Yingling (1976) demonstrated that in a conditional tone/shock expectancy paradigm, both the frontal negative wave and inhibition of NR elicited by the tone were abolished by blockade of the CM-Pf–frontocortical–NR system, although primitive orienting persisted. Novel or noxious stimuli or rapid MRF stimulation continued to inhibit NR. In an operant task involving alternate bar press for reward, cooling of the CM-Pf–frontocortical–NR loop sufficient to block cortical recruitment-induced incorrect responses to the previously reinforced bar press (i.e., perseveration) (Skinner and Yingling, 1977). Further cooling caused the subject to cease responding altogether. These behavioral observations demonstrated that an appropriate response to a meaningful stimulus in an aroused subject requires an intact CM-Pf–frontocortical–NR system, whereas primitive behavioral orienting elicited by novel or noxious stimuli depends on an intact MRF-NR system. Responding to basic survival stimuli (e.g., food when hungry) may also depend on an MRF-NR system.

Skinner and Yingling (1977) interpreted their data as supporting a role for the MRF-NR system in tonic arousal and the CM-Pf–frontocortical–NR system in "selective" attention. We agree with the hypothesized role of the MRF-NR system in tonic arousal but suggest that the role of the CM-Pf–frontocortical–NR system is preparing the aroused organism to respond to a meaningful stimulus. The demonstration that intralaminar neurons have activity time-locked to either sensory or motor events, depending on the experimental condition, supports the pivotal role of this structure in sensory-motor integration (Schlag-Rey and Schlag, 1980).

The periarcuate region and thalamic zone around the lateral aspect of the dorso-medial nucleus and intralaminar nucleus share common anatomic features. In addition to reciprocal connections, there is a complex arc from periarcuate cortex, motor cortex, and CM-Pf to the neostriatum (caudate and putamen), from the neostriatum to globus pallidus to CM-Pf and VL, and from CM-Pf and VL back to premotor and motor cortex. Not surprisingly, lesions of structures within this loop, including arcuate gyrus (Watson et al., 1978), basal ganglia (Valenstein and Heilman, 1981), VL (Velasco and Velasco, 1979), and CM-Pf (Watson et al., 1978), have induced a deficit in responding to multimodal sensory stimuli (Fig. 10-9).

NEUROPHARMACOLOGY OF INTENTIONAL DISORDERS

Much evidence suggests dopaminergic neurons mediate aspects of intention. Intentional deficits are prominent in patients with Parkinson's disease, which is characterized pathologically by degeneration of ascending dopaminergic neurons. In animals, unilateral lesions in these pathways cause unilateral neglect, while stimulation of dopamine pathways reinforces ongoing behavior (Olds and Milner, 1954; Corbett and Wise, 1980).

Three related pathways have been defined. The nigrostriatal pathway originates in the pars compacta of the substantia nigra (SN), and projects to the neostriatum (caudate and putamen). The mesolimbic and mesocortical pathways originate principally in the ventral tegmental area (VTA) of the midbrain, just medial to the SN, and terminate in the limbic areas of the basal forebrain (nucleus accumbens septi and olfactory tubercle) and the cerebral cortex (frontal and cingulate cortex), respectively (Ungerstedt, 1971a; Lindvall et al., 1974).

These dopaminergic (DA) fibers course through the lateral hypothalamus (LH) in the median forebrain bundle. Bilateral lesions in the lateral hypothalamus of rats induce an akinetic state (Teitelbaum and Epstein, 1962). Unilateral LH lesions cause unilateral neglect: these rats transiently circle toward the side of their lesion; after they recover to the point where spontaneous activity appears symmetrical, they still tend to turn toward their lesioned side when stimulated (e.g., by pinching their tails), and they fail to respond to sensory stimuli delivered to the contralateral side (Marshall et al., 1971). There is considerable evidence the LH lesions cause neglect by damaging DA fibers passing through the hypothalamus. Neglect occurs with 6-hydroxy-dopamine (6-OHDA) lesions of LH that damage DA fibers relatively selectively (Marshall et al., 1974), but not with kainic acid lesions that damage cell bodies but not fibers of passage (Grossman et al., 1978). Unilateral damage to the same DA fibers closer to their site of origin in the midbrain also causes unilateral neglect (Ljungberg and Ungerstedt, 1976; Marshall, 1979). Conversely, unilateral stimulation in the area of ascending DA fibers (Arbuthnott and Ungerstedt, 1975) or of the striatum (Pycock, 1980) causes animals to turn away from the side of stimulation, as if they are orienting

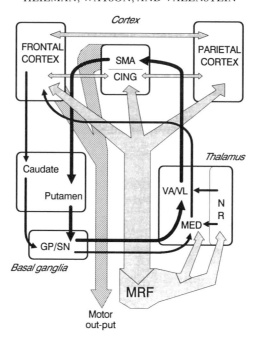

**Fig. 10-9.** Schematic representation of pathways important for motor activation and preparation to respond. See text for details. Two basal ganglia "loops" are indicated: one (thick black arrows) from the supplementary motor area (SMA) to putamen to globus pallidus (GP)/substantia nigra (SN) to VA/VL (ventralis anterior and ventralis lateralis) of thalamus back to the SMA; the other (thin black arrows) from prefrontal cortex to caudate to GP/SN to the medial thalamic nuclei (MED) back to prefrontal cortex. NR = nucleus reticularis thalami; CING = cingulate gyrus.

to the opposite side. Normal (nonlesioned) rats spontaneously turn more in one direction. They also have an asymmetry in striatal dopamine concentration and their direction of turning is generally away from the side of the brain with more dopamine (Glick et al., 1975).

Lesions of the ascending dopaminergic pathways affect the areas of termination of these pathways in at least two ways. First, degeneration of dopamine-containing axons depletes these areas of dopamine. Marshall (1979) has shown that the neglect induced in rats by ventral tegmental 6-OHDA lesions is proportional to the depletion of dopamine in the neostriatum and, to a lesser extent, in the olfactory tubercle and nucleus accumbens. Second, the target areas attempt to compensate for the depletion of DA afferents by increasing their responsiveness to dopamine. This is mediated, at least in part, by an increase in the number of DA receptors (Heikkila et al., 1981), which correlates with behavioral recovery from neglect (Neve et al., 1982).

Changes in DA innervation and in DA receptor sensitivity can explain many effects of pharmacological manipulation in animals with unilateral lesions of the ascending DA pathways. Such lesions result in degeneration of DA axon terminals on the side of the lesion. Drugs such as L-dopa or amphetamines that increase the release of dopamine from normal DA terminals will therefore cause more dopamine to be released on the unlesioned side than on the lesioned side, resulting in orientation or turning toward the lesioned side (Ungerstedt, 1971b, 1974). Several days after the lesion, when DA receptor concentration on the side of the lesion begins to increase, drugs that directly stimulate DA receptors, such as apomorphine, cause the animal to turn away from the side of the lesion (Ungerstedt; 1971b, 1974).

Although rats have been used in most studies, lesions that probably involve the ascending DA systems have also induced unilateral neglect in cats (Hagamen et al., 1977) and monkeys (Deuel, 1980). As mentioned above, bilateral degeneration of the nigrostriatal fibers in humans is associated with Parkinsonism, in which akinesia and hypokinesia are prominent symptoms. Ross and Stewart (1981) described a patient with akinetic mutism secondary to bilateral damage to the anterior hypothalamus. This patient responded to treatment with bromocriptine, a direct DA-receptor agonist. Since the lesion was probably anterior to the site at which nigrostriatal fibers diverge from the median forebrain bundle, the authors suggested that damage to the mesolimbic and mesocortical pathways was critical in causing their patient's hypokinesia.

The evidence summarized above indicates the importance of DA pathways in mediating intention. Although the neglect induced by LH or VTA lesions has been called "sensory" neglect or inattention, rats trained to respond to unilateral stimulation by turning to the side opposite the side of stimulation respond well to stimulation of their "neglected" side (the side opposite the lesion) but fail to turn when stimulated on their "normal" side (Hoyman et al., 1979). This paradigm is similar to that used by Watson et al. (1978), and demonstrates that lesions in ascending DA pathways cause a defect of intention. (Some authors, however, have argued that the defect in orientation to sensory stimuli is not intentional—see Feeney and Weir, 1979.)

The mechanism by which the ascending DA systems produce their effect is not known, even though much has been learned about the circuitry of the DA projections to the striatum (Grofova, 1979; Fonnum and Walaas, 1979). The striatum projects strongly via the globus pallidus and thalamus to the motor cortex, but motor cortex lesions do not abolish drug-induced turning in animals with lesions in the ascending DA pathways (Crossman et al., 1977). The nucleus accumbens and striatum project via the globus pallidus to the intralaminar nuclei of the thalamus (Mehler, 1966). The striatum also projects to the SN, in part providing feedback to DA neurons, but also connecting the striatum with the targets of SN projections; the intralaminar nuclei of the thalamus, the superior colliculus, and portions of the reticular formation (Anderson and Yoshida, 1977; Herkenham, 1979; Dalsass and Krauthamer, 1981). The intralaminar thalamus, the superior colliculus, and the MRF are all areas that have been implicated in the mediation of attention, and in which lesions can induce unilateral neglect. It appears likely that striatal input into these areas, regulated in part by activity in the ascending DA pathways, provides information about the intentional state of the organism.

The frontal neocortex and cingulate cortex receive DA input from the ventral tegmental area (Brown et al., 1979), and the entire neocortex projects strongly to the striatum. This corticostriatal projection is at least in part glutaminergic (Divac et al., 1977). Stimulation in the motor or visual areas of the cat's cortex causes a release of dopamine in the striatum and substantia nigra (Nieoullon et al., 1978). But in rats, 6-OHDA lesions of the mesial prefrontal cortex resulted, after 30 days, in an increase of both striatal dopamine content and of striatal DA receptor concentration (Pycock et al., 1980). The pharmacological effects of cortical lesions are not well described or understood. Several studies have shown that bilateral frontal cortical ablations in the rat increase locomotor response to amphetamine (Lynch et al., 1969; Iversen et al., 1971; Glock, 1972). Rats with unilateral frontal cortical ablations may turn toward the side of their lesion, and amphetamines initially increase this turning (Avemo et al., 1973). After one week, amphetamines induce contralateral turning, while apomorphine causes turning toward the side of the lesion (that is, the opposite of the pharmacological effects seen after unilateral lesions of the ascending DA pathways). Rats subjected to a previous unilateral 6-OHDA lesion of the ascending DA pathways and then a unilateral frontal lesion initially reverse their direction of spontaneous turning, but do not change their turning response to amphetamine or apomorphine (Crossman et al., 1977). Monkeys that have recovered from neglect induced by unilateral frontal arcuate lesions do not show asymmetrical behavior when given L-dopa, amphetamine, haloperidol, scopolamine, physostigmine, or bromocriptine, but do show dramatic turning toward the side of their lesion when given apomorphine (Valenstein et al., 1980). This turning is blocked by prior administration of haloperidol. Following unilateral frontal lesions, rats demonstrated contralateral neglect that was reversed by the dopamine agonist apomorphine (Corwin et al., 1986). This apomorphine-induced reduction of neglect was blocked by the prior administration of the dopamine blocker spiropiridol. While all these studies are difficult to reconcile, they do serve to indicate that frontal lesions influence DA systems, but the site and mechanism of these effects are not fully known.

### Mechanisms Underlying Memory and Representational Defects

The hemispatial antegrade memory defect may be related to an attentional defect. William James (1890) noted that "an object once attended will remain in the memory whilst one inattentively allowed to pass will leave no trace behind." The concept of arousal and its relation to learning and retention has received considerable attention (for a review see Eysenck, 1976). For example, direct relationships have been found between phasic skin conductance response amplitude during learning and accuracy of immediate and delayed recall (Stelmack et al., 1983). As discussed in an earlier section, neglect may be associated with an attention-arousal deficit. Stimuli presented in the hemispace contralateral to a hemispheric lesion may be associated with less arousal than stimuli presented in ipsilateral hemispace. Because these stimuli are poorly attended and do not induce arousal, they may be poorly encoded. The attentional arousal systems discussed earlier may, therefore, also be important in hemispatial memory.

As discussed in the testing section, Bisiach and Luzzatti (1978) asked two patients with right-hemisphere damage to describe from memory a familiar scene (the main square in Milan) from two different spatial perspectives, one facing the cathedral and the other facing away from the cathedral. Regardless of the patients' orientation, left-sided details were omitted. On the basis of these findings and those of a second study

(Bisiach et al., 1979), these investigators postulated that the mental representation of the environment is structured topographically and is mapped across the brain. That is, the mental picture of the environment may be split between the two hemispheres (like the projection of a real scene). With right-hemisphere damage there is a representational disorder for the left half of this image. The representational map postulated by Bisiach may be hemispatially organized so that left hemispace is represented in the right hemisphere and right hemispace is represented in the left hemisphere.

There are at least three reasons why the mental image could not be envisioned: (1) the representation may have been destroyed. A failure to represent stimuli may cause both antegrade and retrograde amnesia. (2) The representation may have been intact but could not be activated so that an image was formed. (3) The image was formed, but it was not correctly inspected. If the representation is destroyed, attentional manipulation should not affect retrieval, but if patients with neglect have an activational or attentional deficit, attentional manipulation may affect retrieval. Meador et al. (1987) replicated Bisiach and Luzzatti's observations and also provided evidence that behavioral manipulations could affect performance. It has been shown that when normal subjects are asked to recall objects in space, they move their eyes to the position that object occupied in space (Kahneman, 1973). Although it is unclear why normal subjects move their eyes during this type of recall task, having patients move their eyes toward neglected hemispace may aid recall because the eye movement induces hemispheric activation or helps direct attention. Meador et al. (1987) asked a patient with left hemispatial neglect and defective left hemispatial recall to move his eyes to either right or left hemispace while recalling. The patient's recall of left-side detail was better when he was looking toward the left than toward the right. Although this finding provides evidence that hemispatial retrograde amnesia may be induced by an exploratory-attentional deficit or an activation deficit, it does not differentiate between these possibilities. It also does not exclude the possibility that in other cases the representation had been destroyed.

### Mechanisms Underlying Hemispatial Neglect

Patients with hemispatial neglect fail to perform in the side of space opposite their lesion, even when using their "normal" ipsilesional hand. For example, they may draw only half a clock or daisy, or bisect lines to one side (see Figs. 10-1, 10-2). Although hemianopia may enhance the symptoms of hemispatial neglect, hemianopia by itself cannot entirely account for the deficit, because some patients with hemispatial neglect are not hemianopic (McFie et al., 1950), and some hemianopic patients do not demonstrate hemispatial neglect. Although neglect can be allocentric (left half of stimuli can be neglected even in ipsilateral hemispace), it is also environmental or viewer or body centered (Heilman and Valenstein, 1979). The abnormal performance of patients in egocentric contralateral space suggests that brain mechanisms relating to the opposite hemispace have been disturbed. It suggests that each hemisphere is responsible not only for receiving stimuli from contralateral space and for controlling the contralateral limbs, but also for attending and intending in contralateral hemispace independent of which hand is used (Heilman, 1979; Bowers and Heilman, 1980).

Hemispace is a complex concept, since it can be defined according to the visual half-field (eye position), head position, or trunk position. With the eyes and head facing directly ahead, the hemispaces defined in these three ways are congruent. But if the eyes are directed to the far right, for example, the left visual field falls in large part in the right hemispace, as defined by the head and body midline. Similarly, if the head and eyes are turned far to the right, left head and eye hemispace can both be in body right hemispace. There is evidence to suggest that head and body hemispace are of importance in determining the symptoms of hemispatial neglect (Heilman and Valenstein, 1979; Bowers and Heilman, 1980).

Experimental evidence in normal subjects supports the hypothesis that each hemisphere is organized at least in part to mediate activity in contralateral hemispace. If a subject fixes his gaze at a midline object, keeps his right arm in right hemispace and his left arm in left hemispace, and receives a stimulus delivered in his right visual half-field, he will respond more rapidly with his right hand than with his left hand. Similarly, if a stimulus is delivered in his left visual half-field, he will respond more rapidly with his left hand than with his right (Anzola et al., 1977). These results were traditionally explained by an anatomic pathway transmission model: the reaction time is longer when the hand opposite the stimulated field responds because in this situation information must be transmitted between hemispheres, and this takes more time than when information can remain in the same hemisphere. But if a choice reaction time paradigm is used, and the hands are crossed so that the left hand is in right hemispace and the right hand is in left hemispace, then the faster reaction times are made by the hand positioned in the same side of space as the stimulus (Anzola et al., 1977), even though in this situation the information must cross the corpus callosum. Clearly, these results cannot be explained by a pathway transmission model.

Cognitive theorists have attributed the stimulus-response compatibility in the crossed-hand studies to a "natural" tendency to respond to a lateralized stimulus with the hand that is in a corresponding spatial position (Craft and Simon, 1970). Alternatively, each hemisphere may be important for intending in the contralateral hemispatial field independent of which hand is used to respond (Heilman and Valenstein, 1979; Heilman, 1979). According to this hemispatial hypothesis, when each hand works in its own hemispace, the same hemisphere mediates both the sensorimotor system and the intentional system; however, when a hand works in the opposite hemispace, different hemispheres mediate the sensorimotor and intentional systems.

If the cerebral hemispheres are organized hemispatially, a similar compatibility may exist between the visual half-field in which a stimulus is presented and the side of hemispace in which the visual half-field is aligned. Our group (Bowers et al., 1981) has found a hemispace-visual half-field compatibility suggesting that each hemisphere may not only be important for intending to the contralateral hemispatial field, independent of hand, but may also be important in attending or perceiving stimuli in contralateral hemispace independent of the visual field to which these stimuli are presented.

According to this hemispatial attention-intentional hypothesis, when each hand works in its own spatial field, the same hemisphere mediates both the sensorimotor systems and the attentional-intentional systems. However, when a hand operates in the opposite spatial field, the hemisphere that is contralateral to this hand controls the sensorimotor apparatus, but the hemisphere ipsilateral to the hand mediates attention and intention. Under these conditions, the sensorimotor and attention-intentional system must communicate through the corpus callosum. When patients with callosal disconnection bisect lines in opposite hemispace, each hand errs by gravitating toward its "own" or compatible hemispace (Heilman et al., 1984).

Microelectrode studies in alert monkeys support the hypothesis that the brain may be hemispatially organized. Researchers have identified cells with high-frequency activity while the monkey is looking at an interesting target (fixation cells). The activity of these cells depends not only on an appropriate motivational state, but also on an appropriate oculomotor state. That is, certain cells become active only when the animals are looking into contralateral hemispace (Lynch, 1980).

These studies support the hypothesis that each hemisphere mediates attention and intention in contralateral egocentric hemispace independent of the sensory hemifield or the extremity used. The neural substrate underlying this egocentric hemispatial organization of the hemispheres remains unknown. One would expect, for example, that on right lateral gaze there should be a corollary discharge to alert left-hemisphere attentional cells to process stimuli that enter the left visual field.

To determine if patients with neglect had egocentric hemispatial deficit, we required patients with left-sided neglect to identify a letter at either the right or left end of a line before bisecting the line. The task was given with the lines placed in either right, center, or left hemispace. Even when subjects were required to look to the left before bisecting a line, ensuring that they saw the entire line, performance was significantly better when the line was placed in the right hemispace than in the left hemispace (Heilman and Valenstein, 1979). These observations indicate that patients with hemispatial neglect have a hemispatial defect rather than a hemifield defect.

Several neuropsychological mechanisms have been hypothesized to account for hemispatial neglect: attentional, intentional, exploratory gaze, and representational map.

ATTENTIONAL HYPOTHESES

There are at least four attentional hypotheses that have been proposed to explain spatial neglect: (1) inattention or unawareness; (2) ipsilesional attention bias; (3) inability to disengage from right-sided stimuli; and (4) reduced sequential attentional capacity or early habituation. These four hypotheses are not necessarily mutually contradictory.

The *inattention hypothesis* states that patients with left hemispatial neglect fail to act in left hemispace because they are unaware of stimuli in left hemispace. In the cancellation task, for example, they fail to cancel targets in left hemispace because they are unaware of them. In the line bisection task they are unaware of a portion of the left side of the line and only bisect the portion of line of which they are aware. The brain mechanisms that mediate attention have been discussed. There are several observations that support the attentional hypothesis. The severity of left-sided neglect may be decreased by instructions to attend to a contralesional stimulus, and increased by instructions to attend to an ipsilesional stimulus (Riddoch and Humphreys, 1983). These instructions may modify attention in a "top down" manner. The severity of neglect may also be modified by novelty, that may influence attention in a "bottom up" manner. Butter et al. (1990) showed that novel stimuli presented on the contralesional side also reduced spatial neglect. Cues may also be intrinsic to the stimulus. Kartsounis and Warrington (1989) have shown that neglect is less when one is drawing meaningful pictures than when drawing meaningless pictures.

On the line cancellation task, patients with left-sided neglect begin on the right side of the page (controls usually begin on the left). Ladavas et al. (1990) demonstrated that patients with right parietal lesions have shorter reaction times to right-sided stimuli than to left-sided stimuli providing evidence of an attentional bias. Kinsbourne (1970) posited that each hemisphere inhibits the opposite himisphere. When one hemisphere is injured, the other becomes hyperactive, and attention is biased contralaterally. Heilman and Watson (1977) agree that there is an ipsilesional bias, but believe that the bias is not being induced by a hyperactive hemisphere. If normally each hemisphere orients attention in a contralateral direction and one hemisphere is hypoactive there will also be an attentional bias. A seesaw or teeter-totter may tilt one way because one child is either too heavy (hyperactive hypothesis) or because the other child is too light (hypoactive hypothesis).

Support for the hypoactive (vs. Kinsbourne's hyperactive) hemisphere hypothesis comes from both behavioral and physiological studies. Ladavas et al. (1990) found that attentional shifts between vertically aligned stimuli were slower when stimuli were in left (contralesional) hemispace than when they were in right (ipsilesional) hemispace. This slowing cannot be explained by the hyperactive hemisphere hypothesis, which predicts only slowing in the horizontal axis (i.e., left directional shifts of attention should be slower than right shifts) and is therefore supportive of the hypoactive hemisphere theory. Additional support for the hypoactive hypothesis comes from the finding of EEG slowing in the nonlesioned (left) hemisphere (Heilman, 1979) of patients with neglect, and from positron emission tomography studies that show lower energy metabolism in the hemisphere contralateral to the lesion inducing neglect (Fiorelli et al., 1991). In summary, hemispatial neglect may be induced by an attention defect. This deficit leads not only to attention bias toward stimuli in ipsilesional space but also to a reduced capacity. Reduction of attentional capacity leads to limited awareness in both the spatial and temporal dimensions.

Posner et al. (1984) proposed a three-stage model of attention. When one is called upon to shift attention, one must first diengage attention from the stimulus one is currently attending, move attention to the new stimulus, and then engage that stimulus. Posner et al. (1984) studied patients with parietal lesions providing visual cues as to which side of extrapersonal space the imperative (reaction time) stimulus would appear. The cues could be either valid, indicating the side that the stimulus would actually appear, or invalid, indicating the opposite side. In normal subjects valid cues reduce reaction times and invalid cues increase reaction times. Posner et al. found that in patients with parietal lobe lesions, invalid cues indicating that the reaction time stimulus is to appear ipsilesionally resulted in abnormal prolongation of reaction times to contralesional stimuli. These results suggest that one of the functions of the parietal lobe is to disengage attention. Patients may have spatial neglect because they cannot disengage from right-sided (ipsilesional) stimuli.

Mark et al. (1988) tested the disengagement and bias hypothesis of spatial neglect by comparing the performance of patients on a cancellation task in which the subject marked each detected target with their performance on another cancellation task in which the subject erased the targets. If a target is erased, the subject should have no difficulty disengaging from the target. In addition, erasing targets should also systematically reduce bias. They observed that on the standard cancellation task, subjects with neglect would first start canceling targets on the side of the sheet that is ipsilateral to their lesion (right side). Although they could disengage from specific targets, they often returned to these targets and canceled them again. When erasing targets, patients' performance improved. They canceled more targets; however, they continued to neglect some targets on the left. These observations suggest not a problem with the "disengage" operation but rather a bias. Although the bias hypothesis may account for *where* in space stimuli are neglected and may partially explain neglect, it cannot entirely explain why subjects fail to cancel left-sided targets. However, one could argue that the bias is primarily a "top down" process, and while right-sided stimuli are more likely to "draw" attention than left-sided stimuli, even in the absence of stimuli the subject with left neglect continues to have a right-sided attention bias and is unable to move attention fully leftward.

Chatterjee et al. (1992) requested that a patient who demonstrated left-sided neglect on standard cancellation tasks alternately cancel targets on the right and left side of an array. Using this procedure, the patient was able to overcome her right-sided bias. However, she did not cancel more targets than when she performed the cancellation test in the traditional way, because she neglected targets in the center. These results suggest that a limited sequential intentional capacity or inappropriately rapid habituation may lead to spatial neglect.

In summary, hemispatial neglect may be induced by an attentional deficit. It appears that patients with neglect have difficulty directing their attention toward contralesional egocentric space and this attentional deficit induces an ipsilesional attention bias.

MOTOR INTENTIONAL HYPOTHESES

Sensory attention and motor intention should be closely linked, since when one is attending in a direction one should also be prepared to act in that direction. However, a patient tested by Heilman and Howell (1980) provides evidence that these processes may be dissociable. This patient with intermittent right parieto-occipital seizures was monitored by an EEG while he received right, left, and bilateral stimuli. Interictally the patient did not have inattention or extinction; however, while the seizure focus was active, he had left-sided extinction and allesthesia. When asked to bisect lines during two focal seizures, however, rather than neglecting left space the patient attempted to make a mark to the left of the entire sheet of paper. When asked to bisect lines immediately after a seizure, he tended to bisect the line to the right of midline, which suggested left hemispatial neglect. However, no sensory extinction was present. This case illustrates that attention to contralateral stimuli and intention to perform in this contralateral hemispatial field may be dissociable.

The action-intention hypothesis of hemispatial neglect states that while patients may be aware of stimuli in contralateral hemispace, they fail to act on these stimuli because they have either a reduced ability to act (or sustain action) in contralesional hemispace or they have an action-intentional bias to act rightward. There are several observations that support these hypotheses.

Heilman and Valenstein (1979) asked patients to read a letter on the left side of a line prior to bisecting the line. This strategy ensures that the subjects were aware of the entire line. In spite of using this strategy, patients did better when the line was in right (ipsilesional) than left (contralesional) hemispace, suggesting a reduced ability to act in contralesional hemispace. De Renzi et al. (1970) asked blindfolded patients with hemispatial neglect to search a maze for a target by tough. The subjects failed to explore the left side of the maze. When using the tactile modality to explore, one can only attend to stimuli in a new spatial position *after* one has moved. Therefore the failure to explore the left (contralesional) side of the maze cannot be attributed to an attentional deficit and may provide evidence for a spatial action-intentional deficit.

To learn if defective attention or defective intention was primarily responsible for the abnormal performance of patients with spatial neglect Coslett et al. (1990) had patients bisect a line that they could not directly see. Instead they saw their hand and the line by viewing a TV monitor that was connected to a video camera which was focused on the patient's hand and line. Using this technique, the action and feedback could be dissociated such that the action could take place in left hemispace but the feedback could take place in right hemispace or vice versa. Independent of the position of the line, two of the four subjects improved when the monitor was moved from left (contralesional) to right (ipsilesional) hemispace, suggesting their primary disturbance was attentional. The two other subjects were not improved by moving the monitor into right hemispace but were primarily affected by the hemispace in which the action took place, performing better when the line was in right (ipsilesional) hemispace than in left (contralesional hemispace), suggesting that they had primarily a motor-intentional deficit.

The bias we previously discussed may not be purely attentional. The results of a study by Heilman et al. (1983b) supports a rightward motor-intentional bias. Control subjects and patients with left-sided hemispatial neglect were asked to close their eyes, point their right index finger to their sternum, and then point to an imaginary spot in space in the midsagittal plane (perpendicular to their chest). The patients with neglect pointed to the right of midline, whereas the controls pointed slightly to the left of midline. Because this task did not require visual or somesthetic input from left hemispace, the defective performance could not be attributed to hemispatial inattention or as attentional bias. Heilman et al. (1983b) also tested the ability of patients with left-sided hemispatial neglect to move a lever toward or away from the side of their lesion. These subjects needed more time to initiate movement toward the neglected left hemispace than to initiate movement toward right hemispace, thus demonstrating a directional hypokinesia. These asymmetries were not found in brain-lesioned controls without neglect. This directional hypokinesia may be related to a motor intentional bias or to an inability for the motor-intentional system to disengage from the right.

A motor-intentional bias is also supported by the work of Bisiach et al. (1990). They used a loop of string stretched around two pulleys. The string was positioned horizontally, with one pulley on the left and the other on the right. A screen was placed horizontally, so that only the segment of string on the top could be seen. An arrow was attached to the top segment of string. Subjects with neglect and control subjects were asked to place the arrow midway between the two pulleys. In the congruent condition, the subject held the arrow on the upper string to move it. In the noncongruent condition, the subject moved the arrow by lateral displacement of the lower string. The movements of the lower string were opposite to the direction of arrow movement. If neglect was caused by sensory attention, there would be no difference between the congruent and noncongruent conditions. If neglect was caused by a directional hypokinesia, the error in the congruent and noncongruent conditions should be in opposite directions, and if the sensory and motor neglect were equal, there should be no deviation from midline in the noncongruent condition. Six of 13 subjects showed a significant reduction of neglect in the noncongruent condition, suggesting that they had a significant motor-intentional bias on the congruent line bisection task.

REPRESENTATIONAL HYPOTHESIS

We have already discussed Denny-Brown's and Bisiach's observations that patients may have a body-centered hemispatial memory defect that Bisiach attributed to destruction of the representation of left space stored in the right hemisphere. Destruction of a representation may not only account for a defect in imagery and memory but also may account for spatial neglect.

The construct of attention derives from the knowledge that the human brain has a limited capacity to simultaneously process information. The organism therefore must select what stimuli to process and how far to process them. Except for novel stimuli of undetermined significance, attention is directed in a "top down" fashion. Therefore knowledge or representations must direct the selection process. There are at least two representations that are needed to perform a spatial task such as a cancellation task: a representation of the target and a representation of space. Because patients with left-sided spatial neglect are able, in a cancellation task, to detect target stimuli on the right side, their failure to detect stimuli on the left cannot be attributed to a loss of the representation of the target. If the knowledge of left space is stored in the right hemisphere and these representations are destroyed, attention may not be directed to left space.

In a similar fashion, mental representations may also direct action. The number of independent actions one can simultaneously perform is also limited. Therefore, just as one selects stimuli to process, one must also select actions to perform. There are at least two pieces of knowledge that guide action: how to move, and where to act. Since patients with spatial neglect know *how* to act in ipsilesional space, their failure to act in contralesional space cannot be attributed to a loss of the "how" representation. However, if knowledge of contralesional space is lost, one may fail to act in or toward that portion of space.

Therefore, both intentional and attentional defects may be induced by a representational defect. The loss of a representation (knowledge) of one-half of space should be manifested by all the signs we discussed: an attentional deficit, an intentional deficit, a memory deficit, and an imagery deficit. Unless a patient has *all* these deficits, hemispatial neglect cannot be attributed to a loss of the spatial representation. As we have already discussed, in the clinic we see patients who have primarily a motor-intentional disorder as well as others who have primarily a sensory-attentional disorder. Not all patients with neglect have imagery-memory defects. Therefore, a representational deficit cannot account for all cases of spatial neglect. A representational defect also cannot account for the attentional and intentional bias we have discussed. However, there are patients who are severely inattentive to contralesional stimuli, fail to explore contralesional space, and have a profound contralesional spatial memory defect. Although these patients may have defects in multiple systems, their representation for contralesional space may be destroyed so that they no longer know of its existence.

EXPLORATORY HYPOTHESIS

Chedru et al. (1973) recorded the eye movements of patients with left-sided spatial neglect and demonstrated a failure to explore the left side of space. This failure to explore could not be accounted for by paralysis, since these patients could voluntarily look leftward. If patients fail to explore the left side of a line, they may never learn the full extent of the line, bisecting only the portion they have explored. Similarly, if they do not fully explore the left side of a sheet, they may fail to cancel targets on the part of the sheet they have failed to explore. However, these defects of visual exploration may all be attributed to the attentional, intentional, or representational defects previously discussed.

## *Mechanisms Underlying Anosognosia for Hemiplegia*

There have been many explanations of this dramatic behavioral disorder. Weinstein and Kahn (1955) studied the premorbid personalities of patients with anosognosia and found that even before they had their strokes, they used denial mechanisms to deal with stressful situations more frequently than did controls. Although premorbid personality may affect a patient's response to his own illness, this theory by itself could not account for the observation that denial of hemiplegia is more frequently associated with right than with left-hemisphere lesions.

Geschwind (1965) posited a disconnection hypothesis to explain anosognosia associated with right-hemisphere disease. There are two sensory feedback systems that may provide information that a limb is not working: somatosensory (proprioceptive) and visual. A large right-hemisphere lesion may not only disconnect these inputs and destroy the areas that monitor them, but it may also disconnect them from the left hemisphere that mediates language and speech. However, if the left hand is moved to the right so it can be seen in the right visual field, the left hemisphere should be able to gain the information that the hand is not working. In many cases of denial of hemiplegia, moving the paralyzed left arm into the right visual field does not influence anosognosia, suggesting that disconnection from speech-language areas cannot entirely explain this form of anosognosia.

Patients with right-hemisphere dysfunction often demonstrate flattening of affect or even euphoria. In part, this flattening of affect may be related to a reduced ability to communicate emotion. For example, patients with right-hemisphere damage are impaired in making emotional faces and emotional inflections of their voice (see Chapter 13.) Patients with right-hemisphere injury also have reduced autonomic activation. Although indifference to a motor or a sensory disability (anosodiaphoria) may be related to an affective communicative disorder and defective arousal, these emotional disorders cannot account for the verbal explicit denial of illness termed anosognosia.

As we have discussed, neglect may be spatial, personal, or both, and is more commonly associated with right- than with left-hemisphere lesions. If a patient has personal neglect, he may be unaware of a hemiplegia. Although in certain cases anosognosia may be related to personal neglect, Bisiach et al. (1986) have demonstrated that neglect of the left side of the body or limbs is not always associated with denial of hemiplegia.

Head and Holmes (1911) proposed that a defect in the body schema was responsible for anosognosia. Their proposal is similar to the personal neglect postulate (i.e., with damage to the body schema, one loses awareness of a body part), and neglect of body parts has also been attributed to a defective body schema. The work of Bisiach et al. also refutes this explanation of anosognosia.

Studies of Mark and Heilman suggested that patients with right-hemisphere lesions are inattentive to their own bodies (1988). Normal subjects were asked to place a mark on a horizontal line directly across from the midline of their body (i.e., in the midsagittal plane) without regard to the midpoint of the line. Their bodies were hidden from view. When the line was in right or left hemispace, control subjects tended to err toward the spatial position of the line, and their performance improved when they could see their bodies. Patients with right-hemisphere lesions erred in the same directions as the controls, but were more influenced by lines on the right than by lines on the left. Unlike controls, their performance did not improve when they were allowed to see their bodies. These results suggest that not only are right-hemisphere-damaged patients inattentive to the left (or attentionally biased toward the right) side of their bodies, but also that they are, in general, inattentive toward their own bodies.

The theories of anosognosia discussed so far are related to false feedback due to sensory defects, sensory disconnection, and inattention. In contrast to these feedback hypotheses, there is also a "feed-foward" or "intentional" theory of anosognosia (Heilman, 1991).

The feed-forward model deals with expectations. If you decide to relax your arm entirely, and if you then became paretic, you will be unaware of the deficit. Theoretically, one's confidence that one's arm is voluntarily resting rather than paretic is based on comparator functions. There is no afferent input into the comparator that indicates movement, and the intentional and premotor systems also have not fed into the comparator the "expectation" that movement should be felt. Because there is no mismatch, you are unaware of the deficit. As soon as you attempt to move your arm, however, the intentional systems or premotor areas would feed the goal of the movement to the comparator. Because you cannot move the arm, no sensory feedback indicating movement would reach the comparator. The mismatch in the comparator between the expectation and the sensory feedback would make you aware that you were paralyzed.

Whereas paralysis is caused by lesions of the upper and lower motor neurons, akinesia is caused by an inability of the intentional system to activate these motor neurons. This intention system may be responsible not only for activating motor systems but also for feeding information about motor expectations to comparator systems. If there are no expectations of movement, the failure to move is not regarded to be abnormal, hence the patient fails to acknowledge the deficit. Unfortunately, the portion of this intention system that feeds into the comparator is unknown, as is the site of the comparator.

This "feed-forward" postulate does not explain why anosognosia of hemiplegia is more common after right than left-hemisphere lesions. Studies in brain-damaged subjects, however, have demonstrated that limb akinesia is more frequently associated with right- than with left-hemisphere lesions (Coslett and Heilman, 1989), suggesting that unilateral lesions of the right hemisphere are more likely to induce intentional deficits than are homologous lesions of the left hemisphere. These intentional deficits may lead not only to akinesia but also to anosognosia of hemiplegia.


## HEMISPHERIC ASYMMETRIES OF NEGLECT

Many early investigators noted that the neglect syndrome was more often associated with right- than left-hemisphere lesions (Brain, 1941; McFie et al., 1950; Critchley, 1966). Although Battersby et al. (1956) thought this preponderance of right-hemisphere-lesioned patients was the result of a sampling artifact caused by the exclusion of aphasic subjects, more recent studies confirm that lesions in the right hemisphere more often induce elements of the neglect syndrome. Albert (1973), Gainotti et al. (1972), and Costa et al. (1969) demonstrated that hemispatial neglect is more frequent and more severe after right than after left-hemisphere lesions. Meador et al. (1988) showed that inattention (extinction) is more common in right- than in left-hemisphere dysfunction. Studies of the limbs by Coslett et al. (1989) and studies of the eyes by De Renzi et al. (1982) and Meador et al. (1989) revealed that limb akinesia and directional akinesia are more common after right than after left-hemisphere lesions.


### Inattention

The attentional cells (or comparator neurons) found in the parietal lobe of monkeys by Lynch (1980) and Robinson et al. (1978) usually had contralateral receptive fields, but some of these neurons had bilateral receptive fields, and thus responded to stimuli presented in either visual half-field. To account for a hemispheric asymmetry of attention in humans, we suggested that the temporoparietal regions of the human brain also have attentional or comparator neurons, but that the cells in the right hemisphere are more likely to have bilateral receptive fields than cells in the left hemisphere (Heilman and Van Den Abell, 1980). Thus, cells in the left hemisphere would be activated predominantly by novel or significant stimuli in the right hemispace or hemifield, but cells in the right hemisphere would be activated by novel or significant stimuli in either visual field or on either side of hemispace (or both). If this were the case, right-hemisphere lesions would cause contralateral inattention more often than left-hemisphere lesions. When the left hemisphere is damaged, the right can attend to ipsilateral stimuli, but the left hemisphere cannot attend to ipsilateral stimuli after right-sided damage. If activation of comparator neurons induces local EEG desynchronization (Sokolov, 1963), and if the right hemisphere is dominant for attention, the right hemisphere should desynchronize to stimuli presented in either field, whereas the left hemisphere would desynchronize only to right-sided stimuli. We therefore gave lateralized visual stimuli to normal subjects while recording the EEG. We found that the right parietal lobe desynchronized equally to right- or left-sided stimuli while the left parietal lobe desynchronized mainly to right-sided stimuli. These observations are compatible with the hypothesis that the right hemisphere (parietal lobe) dominates the comparator, or attentional, processes (Heilman and Van Den Abell, 1980). A similar phenomenon has been demonstrated using positron emission tomography (Pardo, et al. 1991). These electrophysiological and imaging studies provide evidence for a special role of the right hemisphere in attention and may also help explain why inattention is more often caused by right-hemisphere lesions.

Neglect of spatial stimuli may occur even ipsilateral to right-hemisphere lesions (Albert, 1973; Heilman and Valenstein, 1979; Weintraub and Mesulam, 1987). Although less severe and less frequent, extinction within ipsilesional visual and tactile fields may be seen with right-hemisphere lesions (Rapcsak et al. 1987; Feinberg, 1990). These results suggest that although the left hemisphere can attend rightward, when compared to the right hemisphere, the left hemisphere's attentional capacity is limited even contralaterally.

### Arousal

Using the galvanic skin response as a measure of arousal, it has been demonstrated that patients with right temporoparietal lesions have a reduced response when compared to patients with left temporoparietal lesions (Heilman et al. 1978; Schrandt et al. 1989). Yokoyama et al. (1987) obtained similar results using heart rate as a measure of arousal. We also compared the EEG from the nonlesioned hemisphere of awake patients with right or left temporoparietal infarctions. Patients with right-sided lesions showed more theta and delta activity over their nonlesioned hemisphere than patients with left-sided lesions. These studies suggest that the right hemisphere may have a special role in mediating both central and peripheral arousal.

### Intentional Deficits

Patients with right-hemisphere lesions more often have contralateral limb akinesia than patients with left-hemisphere lesions (Coslett and Heilman, 1989). Hypokinesia, however, is not always limited to the contralateral extremities. Although patients with cerebral lesions confined to a single hemisphere have slower reaction times with the hand contralateral to a lesion than with the hand ipsilateral to a lesion, they also have slower reaction times using the hand ipsilateral to the lesion than do nonlesioned controls using the same hand (Benton and Joynt, 1959). De Renzi and Faglioni (1965) also used a simple reaction time task to study patients with unilateral cerebral lesions. Although lesions of either hemisphere slowed the reaction times of the hand ipsilateral to the lesion, right-hemisphere lesions caused greater slowing than left-hemisphere lesions. Howes and Boller (1975) confirmed that patients with right-hemisphere lesions had slower reaction times, and found that the right-hemisphere lesions associated with these deficits were not larger than the left-hemisphere lesions. Although Howes and Boller alluded to a loss of topographical sense as perhaps being responsible, they did not draw any conclusions about why right-hemisphere lesions produced slower reaction times. Unfortunately, they did not mention whether the patients with profound ipsilateral slowing had unilateral neglect.

In monkeys, no hemispheric asymmetries in the production of the neglect syndrome have been noted; however, we (Valenstein et al., 1987) found that monkeys with lesions inducing neglect had slower ipsilateral reaction times than monkeys with equalsized lesions that did not induce neglect.

It has been shown that warning stimuli may prepare an individual for action and thereby reduce reaction times (Lansing et al., 1959). Pribram and McGuiness (1975) used the term activation to define the physiological readiness to respond to environmental stimuli. Because patients with right-hemisphere lesions have been shown to have reduced behavioral evidence of activation, we have postulated that in humans, the right hemisphere may dominate in mediating the activation process. That is, the left hemisphere prepares the right extremities for action and the right prepares both. Therefore, with left-sided lesions, left-side limb akinesia is minimal, but with right-sided lesions there is severe left-limb akinesia. In addition, because the right hemisphere is more involved than the left hemisphere in activating ipsilateral extremities, with right-hemisphere lesions there will be more ipsilateral hypokinesia than wtih left-hemisphere lesions.

If the right hemisphere dominates mediation of activation or intention (physiological readiness to respond), normal subjects may show more activation (measured behaviorally by the reaction time) with warning stimuli delivered to the right hemisphere than with warning stimuli delivered to the left hemisphere. We therefore gave normal subjects lateralized warning stimuli followed by central reaction time stimuli. Warning stimuli projected to the right hemisphere reduced reaction times of the right hand more than warning stimuli projected to the left hemisphere reduced left-hand reaction times. Warning stimuli projected to the right hemisphere reduced reaction times of the right hand even more than did warning stimuli projected directly to the left hemisphere. These results support the hypothesis that the right hemisphere dominates activation (Heilman and Van Den Abell, 1979). As we have discussed, motor bias, direction akinesias, and hypokinesia are more common with right- than with left-hemisphere lesions. This would suggest that the right hemisphere can prepare movement in both directions, but the left hemisphere prepares only for right-sided movements.

### Hemispatial Neglect

Gainotti et al. (1972), Albert (1973), and Costa et al. (1969) have shown that hemispatial neglect is both more frequent and more severe with right-sided lesions than with left-sided lesions. In the preceding sections we discussed some of the mechanisms that may underlie hemispatial neglect. The same hypotheses we put forward to explain attentional and intentional asymmetries may also be extended to a representational hypothesis such that the right hemisphere contains representations for both sides of space and the left hemisphere for right space. The right hemisphere has a special role in visuoperceptive, visuospatial, and visuoconstructive processes (see Chapter 8 for a review), and several authors (McFie et al., 1950; Albert, 1973) have proposed that the asymmetries of hemispatial neglect are related to disorders of these processes.

Kinsbourne (1970) proposed that language-induced left-hemisphere activation makes neglect more evident with right- than with left-hemisphere lesions. Behavioral and psychophysiological studies have shown that language may induce left-hemisphere activation (Kinsbourne, 1974; Bowers and Heilman, 1976). Patients are usually tested for hemispatial neglect using verbal instructions, and, not being aphasic, they usually think and communicate verbally. To test Kinsbourne's hypothesis, we (Heilman and Watson, 1978) presented patients with left-sided hemispatial neglect a crossing-out task in which the subject was asked either to cross out words or to cross out lines oriented in a specific direction (e.g., horizontal). In the verbal condition, the target words were mixed with two others that were foils, and in the visuospatial condition, the target lines were mixed with other lines (e.g., vertical and diagonal) that acted as foils. All the subjects tested crossed out more lines and went farther to the left on the paper in the nonverbal condition than in the verbal condition. These results give partial support to Kinsbourne's hypothesis. However, Caplan (1985) cold not obtain similar results, suggesting the difference found by Heilman and Watson may be related to differences in attentional demands (see Rapcsak et al., 1989). However, additional support of Kinsbourne's hypothesis comes from the observation that use of the left hand in cancellation tasks may reveal less neglect than use of the right hand (Halligan and Marshall, 1989).

It has also been proposed that hemispatial neglect could be induced by hemispatial or directional akinesia, or by hemispatial or directional inattention. In the preceding section, we postulated that the right hemisphere is dominant for intention and attention. That hemispatial neglect occurs more often after right-hemisphere lesions may be explained by a similar phenomenon.

## NEUROPATHOLOGY OF NEGLECT

Neglect in man can accompany lesions in the following areas: (1) IFL (Critchley, 1966), (2) dorsolateral frontal lobe (Heilman and Valenstein, 1972), (3) cingulate gyrus (Heilman and Valenstein, 1972), (4) neostriatum (Heir et al., 1977), (5) thalamus and MRF (Watson and Heilman, 1979), and (6) posterior limb of the internal capsule. On the basis of CT scan localization, Heilman et al. (1989) concluded that neglect is probably seen more frequently after temporoparietal lesions.

The most common cause of neglect from cortical lesions is cerebral infarction (from either thrombosis or embolus), and the most common cause of subcortical neglect is intracerebral hemorrhage. Neglect can also be seen with tumors. Rapidly growing malignant tumors (e.g., metastatic or glioblastoma) are more likely to produce neglect than are slowly growing tumors. It is unusual to see neglect as the result of a degenerative disease, because the degeneration is most often bilateral and insidious. However, we have seen neglect with focal atrophy. The akinesia seen with degenerative diseases may be bilateral neglect (Heilman and Valenstein, 1972; Watson et al., 1973), which we believe is the cause of akinetic mutism. We have also seen a transient neglect syndrome as a postictal phenomenon in a patient with idiopathic right temporal lobe seizures, and the transient bilateral akinesia seen with other types of seizures may also be induced by similar mechanisms (Watson et al., 1974). Neglect may also be seen after unilateral (right) electroconvulsive therapy (ECT) (Sackeim, personal communication, 1983).

## RECOVERY OF FUNCTION AND TREATMENT

### Natural History

After a cerebral infarction, some patients acutely demonstrate a characteristic syndrome that includes neglect of their extremities, limb akinesia, profound inattention or allesthesia, hemispatial neglect, head and eye deviation, and an explicit (verbal) denial of illness. In a period of weeks to months, profound inattention and allesthesia abate, but extinction can be demonstrated with bilateral simultaneous stimulation. Hemispatial neglect also diminishes, and although an explicit denial of illness disappears, patients continue to show a flattening of affect and anosodiaphoria. Extinction, emotional flattening, and anosodiaphoria may persist for years. In our experience, intentional deficits are the most persistent disabling aspect of neglect.

Unlike humans, who recover from the neglect syndrome slowly and often incompletely, monkeys rarely show evidence of neglect after one month. The neural mechanisms underlying this recovery are poorly understood. One hypothesis is that the undamaged hemisphere plays a role in recovery. It may receive sensory information from the side of the body opposite the lesion, either via ipsilateral sensory pathways or from the damaged hemisphere via the corpus callosum. The uninjured hemisphere might also enhance the injured hemisphere's ability to attend to contralateral sensory information and to initiate contralateral limb movements. If the uninjured hemisphere is processing sensorimotor information delivered from the injured hemisphere or enhancing the injured hemisphere's capacity to process sensorimotor activity, then a corpus callosum transection should worsen symptoms of neglect. Crowne et al. (1981) showed that neglect from frontal ablations was worse if the corpus callosum was simultaneously transected than if the callosum was intact. Watson et al. (1984) showed that monkeys receiving a frontal arcuate gyrus ablation several months after a corpus callosum transection also had worse neglect than did animals with intact callosums. These results suggest that the hemisphere are mutually excitatory or compensatory through the corpus callosum.

Although callosal section worsened the severity of neglect, both groups of investigators found that it did not influence the rate of recovery. Subjects with callosal transections recovered completely. This suggests that recovery is an intrahemispheric process. If the intact hemisphere is responsible for the recovery, then a callosal transection after recovery should not reinstate neglect. Crowne et al. (1981) did reinstate neglect in three animals undergoing corpus callosum transections. It is possible, however, that extracallosal damage might be responsible for reinstating neglect. We performed a similar callosal section after a monkey recovered from neglect and did not reinstate neglect. Furthermore, if the intact hemisphere is responsible for recovery in an animal with divided hemispheres, the recovery would have to be mediated through ipsilateral pathways. We have made a unilateral spinal cord lesion to interrupt ipsilateral sensory pathways in one of our recovered subjects without reinstating neglect. Our observations suggest that recovery is occurring within the injured hemisphere.

Hughlings Jackson (1932) postulated that certain functions could be mediated at several levels of the nervous system (hierarchical representation). Lesions of higher areas (e.g., cortex) would release phylogenetically more primitive areas, which may assume some of the function of the lesioned cortical areas. Perhaps after cortical lesions disrupt the corticolimbic-reticular network, a subcortical area takes over function and is responsible for mediating responses. Ideally, the area which substitutes for the lesioned area must have similar characteristics. It must have multimodal afferent input and must not only have reticular connections, but also be capable of inducing activation with stimulation. Lastly, ablation of this area should induce the neglect syndrome, even if transiently. The superior colliculus not only receives optic fibers but also receives somesthetic projections from the spinotectal tract (Sprague and Meikle, 1965) as well as fibers from the medial and lateral lemnisci and the inferior colliculus (Truex and Carpenter, 1964). Sprague and Meikle believe that the colliculus is more than a reflex center controlling eye movements, they think it is a sensory integrative center. Tectoreticular fibers project to the mesencephalic reticular formation and ipsilateral fibers are more abundant than contralateral fibers (Truex and Carpenter, 1964). Stimulation of the colliculus (like stimulation of the arcuate gyrus or the IPL) produces an arousal response (Jefferson, 1958). Unilateral lesions of the superior colliculus produce a multimodal unilateral neglect syndrome, and combined cortical-collicular lesions produce a more profound disturbance regardless of the order of removal (Sprague and Meikle, 1965). Therefore, it is possible that in the absence of the corticoreticular system, a collicular-reticular system takes over function.

Unlike the neglect induced by cortical lesions in monkeys, the neglect associated with lesions of ascending dopamine projections in rats can be permanent (Marshall, 1982). The severity and persistence of neglect induced by 6-OHDA injections into the VTA of rats is correlated with the amount of striatal dopamine depletion: those with more than 95% loss of striatal dopamine have a permanent deficit. The extent of recovery of these animals is also directly related to the quantity of neostriatal dopamine present at sacrifice. Nonrecovered rats show pronounced contralateral turning after injections of apomorphine, a dopamine receptor stimulant. Recovered rats given methyl-p-tyrosine, a catecholamine synthesis inhibitor, or spiroperidol, a dopamine receptor blocking agent, had their deficits reappear. These results suggest that restoration of dopaminergic activity in dopamine-depleted rats is sufficient to reinstate orientation (Marshall, 1979). Further investigation of these findings indicates that a proliferation of dopamine receptors may contribute to pharmacological supersensitivity and recovery of function (Neve et al., 1982). Finally, implanting dopaminergic neurons from the ventral tegmental area of fetal rats adjacent to the ipsilesional striatum will induce recovery in rats having unilateral neglect from a 6-OHDA lesion in the ascending dopamine tracts (Dunnett et al., 1981). This recovery is related to growth of dopamine-containing neurons into the partially denervated striatum. Corwin et al. (1986) induced neglect in rats by ablating frontal cortex unilaterally. After the rats had recovered from neglect, spiroperidol reinstituted their neglect.

[$^{14}$C]2-deoxyglucose (2-DG) incorporation permits one to measure metabolic activity. In rats with 6-OHDA lesions of the VTA that had shown no recovery from neglect, the uptake of [$^{14}$C]2-DG into the neostriatum, nucleus accumbens septi, olfactory tubercle, and central amygdaloid nucleus was significantly less on the denervated side than on the normal side. Rats recovering by six weeks showed equivalent [$^{14}$C]2-DG uptake in the neostriatum and central amygdaloid nucleus on the two sides. Recovery is therefore associated with normalization of neostriatal metabolic activity (Kozlowski and Marshall, 1981).

Similar results have been found in monkeys recovering from frontal arcuate gyrus-induced neglect Deuel et al., 1979). Animals with neglect showed depression of [$^{14}$C]2-DG in ipsilateral subcortical structures, including the thalamus and basal ganglia. Recovery from neglect occurred concomitantly with a reappearance of symmetrical metabolic activity.

It is possible that cortical lesions in animals induce only transient neglect because these lesions affect only a small portion of a critical neurotransmitter system. Critically placed small subcortical lesions, on the other hand, can virtually destroy all of a transmitter system, and can cause a permanent syndrome.

Recovery from cortically induced neglect might also depend on the influence of cortical lesions on subcortical structures. It is likely that just as certain homologous cortical structures are thought to be mutually inhibitory via the corpus callosum, certain pairs of subcortical structures may also be mutally inhibitory. For example, in the study of Watson et al. (1984), a prior corpus callosal lesion worsened neglect from a frontal arcuate lesion. Although this could be explained by loss of an excitatory or compensatory influence from the normal frontal arcuate region on the lesioned hemisphere, it could also be interpreted as a loss of excitation from cortex on a subcortical structure such as the basal ganglia that in turn inhibits the contralateral basal ganglia. The latter is supported by a study showing that anterior callosal section in rats enhances the normal striatal dopamine asymmetry and increases amphetamine-induced turning (Glick et al., 1975). In addition, Sprague (1966) showed that the loss of visually guided behavior in the visual field contralateral to occipitotemporal lesions in cats could be restored by a contralateral superior colliculus removal or by transection of the collicular commissure. The only way to explain this observation is to assume that the superior colliculi are mutually inhibitory.

The two hemispheres are clearly cooperating in our daily activities. However, it appears that recovery from a central nervous system insult can occur within the injured hemisphere. For the neglect syndrome, this may be secondary to alteration in dopamine systems. An understanding of interhemispheric cortical and subcortical interactions, and intrahemispheric cortical and subcortical interactions in the normal state and during recovery of function, is one of the most intriguing aspects of the neglect syndrome and holds great promise for pharmacological and possibly even surgical intervention in this syndrome.

## Treatment

The neglect syndrome is a behavioral manifestation of underlying cerebral disease. The evaluation and treatment of the underlying disease are of primary importance.

There are several things that can be done to manage the symptoms of the neglect syndrome. The patient with neglect should have his bed placed so that his "good" side faces the area where interpersonal actions are most likely to take place. When he must interact with people or things, these interactions should take place on his good side. When discharged home, his environment should be adjusted in a similar manner. So long as a patient has the neglect syndrome, he should not be allowed to drive, or to work with anything that, if neglected, could cause injury to himself or to others.

During the acute stages when patients have anosognosia, rehabilitation is difficult; however, in most patients, anosognosia is transient. In addition, because patients with neglect remain inattentive to their left side and in general are poorly motivated, training is laborious and in many cases unrewarding. Diller and Weinberg (1977) were able to train patients with neglect to look to their neglected side; however, it was not clear that these treatment effects generalized to other situations.

As we discussed, Coslett et al. (1990) demonstrated that patients with spatial neglect induced by attentional disorders improved when feedback was presented to the ipsilesional side. Rossi et al. (1990) used 15-diopter Fresnel prisms to shift images from the neglected side toward the normal side. After using the prisms for four weeks, the treated group performed better than the control group in tasks such as line bisection or cancellation. However, activities of daily living did not improve.

As we discussed, brainstem structures such as the superior colliculus may play an important role in recovery from neglect. Butter et al. (1990) recognized that since dynamic stimuli readily summon attention in normal subjects and are potent activators of brain structures such as the colliculi, perhaps they could be used to reduce neglect. He tested patients with neglect on a line bisection task and demonstrated that dynamic stimuli presented on the contralesional (left) side reduced neglect. Neglect patients with hemianopsia also improved, suggesting that these stimuli affect brainstem structures.

As we also discussed, neglect associated with cortical lesions may be reduced by destroying the ipsilateral colliculus or the intercollicular commissure (Sprague, 1966). These findings suggest that the normal colliculus may inhibit the damaged colliculus. Each colliculus get greater ipsilateral input from the retina than it does from contralateral input. Posner and Rafal (1987) suggest that patching the ipsilesional eye may reduce neglect because it would deprive the superior colliculus ipsilateral to the intact hemisphere of retinal input. The reduced input may reduce collicular activation.

Lastly, we discussed the role of dopamine in neglect and recovery. Corwin et al. (1986) induced neglect in rats with unilateral frontal lesions. Apomorphine, a dopamine agonist, significantly reduced neglect in these animals. Spiroperidol, a dopamine receptor blocking agent, blocked the therapeutic effect of apomorphine. Fleet et al. (1987) treated two neglect patients with bromocriptine, a dopamine agonist. Both showed dramatic improvements. However, a double-blind crossover study has not been performed. Although neuropharmacological therapy appears to be promising, further studies must be performed.

# REFERENCES

Akert, K., and Von Monakow, K. H. (1980). Relationship of precentral, premotor, and prefrontal cortex to the mediodorsal and intralaminar nuclei of the monkey thalamus. *Acta Neurobiol. Exp. (Warsz.)* 40:7–25.

Albert, M. D. (1973). A simple test of visual neglect. *Neurology* 23:658–664.

Anderson, M., and Yoshida, M. (1977). Electrophysiological evidence for branching nigral projections to the thalamus and superior colliculus. *Brain Res.* 137:361—364.

Anton, G. (1899). Uber die Selbstwahrnehmung der Herderkrankungen des Gehirns durch den Kranken der Rindenblindheit und Rindentaubheit. *Arch. Psychiatr.* 32:86–127.

Anzola, G. P., Bertoloni, A., Buchtel, H. A., and Rizzolatti, G. (1977). Spatial compatibility and anatomical factors in simple and choice reaction time. *Neuropsychologia* 15:295–302.

Arbuthnott, G. W., and Ungerstedt, U. (1975). Turning behavior induced by electrical stimulation of the nigro-striatal system of the rat. *Exp. Neurol.* 27:162–172.

Arnault, P., and Roger, M (1987). The connections of the peripeduncular area studied by retrograde and anterograde transport in the rat. *J. Comp. Neurol.* 258:463–478.

Avemo, A., Antelman, S., and Ungerstedt, U. (1973). Rotational behavior after unilateral frontal cortex lesions in the rat. *Acta Physiol. Scand. [Suppl.]*396:77.

Babinski, J. (1914). Contribution a l'etude des troubles mentaux dans l'hemiplegie organique cerebrale (agnosognosie). *Rev. Neurol. (Paris)* 27:845–847.

Baleydier, C., and Mauguiere, F. (1980). The duality of the cingulate gyrus in monkey—neuroanatomical study and functional hypothesis. *Brain* 103:525–554.

Battersby, W. S., Bender, M. B., and Pollack, M. (1956). Unilateral spatial agnosia (inattention) in patients with cerebral lesions. *Brain* 79:68–93.

Bender, M. B. (1952). *Disorders of Perception*. Springfield, Ill.: C. C. Thomas.

Bender, M. B., and Furlow, C. T. (1944). Phenomenon of visual extinction and binocular rivalry mechanism. *Trans. Am. Neurol. Assoc.* 70:87–93.

Bender, M. B., and Furlow, C. T. (1945). Phenomenon of visual extinction and homonymous fields and psychological principals involved. *Arch. Neurol. Psychiatry* 53:29–33.

Benson, F., and Geschwind, N. (1969). The alexias. In *Handbook of Neurology*, Vol. 4, P. J. Vinken and G. W. Bruyn (eds.). Amsterdam: North-Holland.

Benton, A. L., and Joynt, R. J. (1959). Reaction times in unilateral cerebral disease. *Confin. Neurol.* 19:147–256.

Benton, A. L., and Levin, H. S. (1972). An experimental study of obscuration. *Neurology* 22:1176–1181.

Bianchi, L. (1895). The functions of the frontal lobes. *Brain* 18:497–522.

Bignall, K. E., and Imbert, M. (1969). Polysensory and cortico-cortical projections to frontal lobe of squirrel and rhesus monkey. *Electroencephalogr. Clin. Neurophysiol* 26:206–215.

Birch, H. G., Belmont, I., and Karp, E. (1967). Delayed information processing and extinction following cerebral damage. *Brain* 90:113–130.

Bisiach, E., and Luzzatti, C. (1978). Unilateral neglect of representational space. *Cortex* 14:29–133.

Bisiach, E., Luzzatti, C., and Perani, D. (1979). Unilateral neglect, representational schema and consciousness. *Brain* 102:609–618.

Bisiach, E., Bulgarelli, C., Sterzi, R., and Vallar, G. (1983). Line bisection and cognitive plasticity of unilateral neglect of space. *Brain Cognition* 2:32–38.

Bisiach, E., Geminiani, G., Berti, A., and Rusconi, M. L. (1990). Perceptual and premotor factors of unilateral neglect. *Neurology* 40:1278–1281.

Bisiach, E., Vallar, G., Perani, D., Papagno, C., and Buti, A. (1986). Unawareness of disease following lesions of the right hemisphere: anosognosia for hemiplegia and anosognosia for hemianopsia. *Neuropsychologia 24*:471–482.

Bogosslavsky, J., Miklossy, J., Deruaz, J. P., Regli, F., and Assai, G. (1986). Unilateral left paramedian infarction of thalamus and midbrain: a clinico-pathological study. *J. Neurol. Neurosurg. Psychiatry 49*:686–694.

Bowers, D., and Heilman, K. M. (1976). Material specific hemispheric arousal. *Neuropsychologia 14*:123–127.

Bowers, D., and Heilman, K. M. (1980). Effects of hemispace on tactile line bisection task. *Neuropsychologia 18*:491–498.

Bowers, D., Heilman, K. M., and Van Den Abell, T. (1981). Hemispace-visual half field compatibility. *Neuropsychologia 19*:757–765.

Bradley, P. B. (1968). The effect of atropine and related drugs on the EEG and behavior. *Prog. Brain Res. 28*:3–13.

Brain, W. R. (1941). Visual disorientation with special reference to lesions of the right cerebral hemisphere. *Brain 64*:224–272.

Brown, R. M., Crane, A. M., and Goldman, P. S. (1979). Regional distribution of monamines in the cerebral cortex and subcortical structures of the rhesus monkey: concentrations and in vivo synthesis rates. *Brain Res. 168*:133–150.

Bushnell, M. C., Goldberg, M. E., and Robinson, D. L. (1981). Behavioral enhancement of visual responses in monkey cerebral cortex: I. Modulation if posterior parietal cortex related to selected visual attention. *J. Neurophysiol 46*:755–772.

Butter, C. M., Kirsch, N. L., and Reeves, G. (1990). The effect of lateralized dynamic stimuli on unilateral spatial neglect following right hemisphere lesions. *Restorative Neurol. Neurosci. 2*:39–46.

Butter, C. M., Mark, V. W., and Heilman, K. M. (1988a). An experimental analysis of factors underlying neglect in line bisection. *J. Neurol. Neurosurg. Psychiatry 51*:1581–1583.

Butter, C. M., Rapcsak, S. Z., Watson, R. T., and Heilman, K. M. (1988b). Changes in sensory inattention, direction hypokinesia, and release of the fixation reflex following a unilateral frontal lesion: a case report. *Neuropsychologia 26*:533–545.

Caplan, B. (1985). Stimulus effects in unilateral neglect. *Cortex 21:* 69–80.

Chatterjee, A., Mennemeier, M., and Heilman, K. M. (1992). Search patterns in neglect. *Neuropsychogia 30:* 657–672.

Chavis, D. A., and Pandya, D. N. (1976). Further observations on corticofrontal connections in the rhesus monkey. *Brain Res. 117*:369–386.

Chedru, F., Leblanc, M., and Lhermitte, F. (1973). Visual searching in normal and brain-damaged subjects. *Cortex 9*:94–111.

Corbett, D., and Wise, R. A. (1980). Intracranial self-stimulation in relation to the ascending dopaminergic systems of the midbrain: moveable electrode mapping study. *Brain Res. 185*:1–15.

Corwin, J. V., Kanter, S., Watson, R. T., Heilman, K. M., Valenstein, E., and Hashimoto, A. (1986). Apomorphine has a therapeutic effect on neglect produced by unilateral dorsomedial prefrontal cortex lesions in rats. *Exp. Neurol. 36*:683–698.

Coslett, H. B., and Heilman, K. M. (1989). Hemihypokinesia after right hemisphere strokes. *Brain Cognition 9*:267–278.

Coslett, H. B., Bowers, D., Fitzpatrick, E., Haws, B., and Heilman, K. M. (1990) Directional hypokinesia and hemispatial inattention in neglect. *Brain 113*:475–486.

Costa, L. D., Vaughan, H. G., Horowitz, M., and Ritter, W. (1969). Patterns of behavior deficit associated with visual spatial neglect. *Cortex 5*:242–263.

Craft, J., and Simon, J. (1970). Processing symbolic information from a visual display: interference from an irrelevant directional clue. *J. Exp. Psychol. 83*:415–420.

Critchley, M. (1966). *The Parietal Lobes*. New York: Hafner.

Crossman, A. R., Sambrook, M. A., Gergies, S. W., and Slater, P. (1977). The neurological basis of motor asymmetry following unilateral 6-hydroxdopamine lesions in the rat: the effect of motor decortication. *J. Neurol. Sci. 34*:407–414.

Crowne, D. P., Yeo, C. H., and Russell, I. S. (1981). The effects of unilateral frontal eye field lesions in the monkey: visual-motor guidance and avoidance behavior. *Behav. Brain Res. 2*:165–185.

Dalsass, M., and Karuthamer, G. M. (1981). Behavioral alterations and loss of caudate modulation in the CM-PF complex of the cat after electrolytic lesions of the substantia nigra. *Brain Res. 208*:67–79.

De Renzi, E., Colombo, A., Faglioni, P., and Gilbertoni, M. (1982). Conjugate gaze paralysis in stroke patients with unilateral damage. *Arch. Neurol 39*:482–486.

De Renzi, E., Faglioni, P., and Scott, G. (1970). Hemispheric contribution to the exploration of space through the visual and tactile modality. *Cortex 1*:410–433.

De Renzi, E., and Faglioni, P. (1965). The comparative efficiency of intelligence and vigilance test detecting hemispheric change. *Cortex 1*:410–433.

Denny-Brown, D., and Banker, B. Q. (1954). Amophosynthesis from left parietal lesions. *Arch. Neurol. Psychiatry 71*:302–313.

Deuel, R. K. (1980). Sensorimotor dysfunction after unilateral hypothalamic lesions in rhesus monkeys. *Neurology 30*:358.

Deuel, R. K., Collins, R. C., Dunlop N., and Caston, T. V. (1979). Recovery from unilateral neglect: behavioral and functional anatomic correlations in monkeys. *Soc. Neurosci. Abstr. 5*:624.

Diller, L., and Weinberg, J. (1977). Hemi-inattention in rehabilitation: the evolution of a rational remediation program. In *Advances in Neurology*, Vol. 18, E. A. Weinstein and R. R. Friedland (eds.). New York: Raven Press.

Divac, I., Fonnum, F., and Storm-Mathison, J. (1977). High affinity uptake of glutamate in terminals of corticostriatal axons. *Nature 266*:377–378.

Dunnet, S. B., Bjorklund, A. Stenevi, U., and Iverson, S. D. (1981). Behavioral recovery following transplantation of substantia nigra in rats subjected to 6-OHDA lesions of the nigrostriatal pathway. I. Unilateral lesions. *Brain Res. 215*:147–161.

Eidelberg, E., and Schwartz, A. J. (1971). Experimental analysis of the extinction phenomenon in monkeys. *Brain 94*:91–108.

Eysenck, M. W. (1976). Arousal, learning and memory. *Psychol. Bull. 83*:389–404.

Farah, M. J., Brunn, J. L., Wong, A. B., Wallace, M. A., and Carpenter, P. A. (1990). Frames of reference for locating attention to space: evidence from neglect syndrome. *Neuropsychologia 28*:335–347.

Feeney, D. M. and Wier, C. S. (1979). Sensory neglect after lesions of substania nigra on lateral hypothalamus: differential severity and recovery of function. *Brain Res. 178*:329–346.

Feinberg, T. E., Habor, L. D., Stacy, C. B. (1990). Ipsilateral extinction in the hemineglect syndrome. *Arch Neurol. 47*:803–804.

Filion, M., Lamarre, Y., and Cordeau, J. P. (1971). Neuronal discharges of the ventrolateral nucleus of the thalamus during sleep and wakefulness in the cat. Evoked activity. *Exp. Brain Res. 12*:499–508.

Fiorelli, M., Blin, J., Bakchine, S., LaPlane, D., and Baron, J. C. (1991). PET studies of cortical diaschisic in patients with motor hemi-neglect. *J. Neurol. Sci. 104*:135–142.

Fleet, W. S., Valenstein, E., Watson, R. T., and Heilman, K. M. (1987). Dopamine agonist therapy for neglect in humans. *Neurology 37*:1765–1771.

Fonnum, F., and Walaas, I. (1979). Localization of neurotransmitter candidates in neostriatum.

In *The Neostriatum*, I. Divac and R. G. E. Oberg (eds.). Oxford: Pergamon Press, pp. 53–69.

Gainotti, G., Messerli, P., and Tissot, R. (1972). Qualitative analysis of unilateral and spatial neglect in relation to laterality of cerebral lesions. *J. Neurol. Neurosurg. Psychiatry* 35:545–550.

Geschwind, N. (1965). Disconnexion syndromes in animals and man. *Brain* 88:237–294.

Glick, S. D. (1972). Changes in amphetamine sensitivity following cortical damage in rats and mice. *Eur. J. Pharmacol. 20:*351–356.

Glick, S. D., Cran, A. M., Jerussi, T. P., Fleisher, L. N., and Green, J. P. (1975). Functional and neurochemical correlates to potentiation of striatal asymmetry by callosal section. *Nature* 254:616–617.

Goldberg, M. E., and Bushnell, M. C. (1981). Behavioral enhancement of visual responses in monkey cerebral cortex: II. Modulation in frontal eye fields specifically related saccades. *J. Neurophysiol. 46:*773–787.

Goldberg, M. E., and Robinson, D. C. (1977). Visual responses of neurons in monkey inferior parietal lobule. The physiological substrate of attention and neglect. *Neurology* 27:350.

Grofova, I. (1979). Extrinsic connections of neostriatum. In *The Neostriatum*, I. Divak and R. G. E. Oberg (eds.). Oxford: Pergamon Press, pp. 37–51.

Grossman, S. P., Dacey, D., Halaris, A. E., Collier, T., and Routtenberg, A. (1978). Aphagia and adipsia after preferential destruction of nerve cell bodies in the hypothalamus. *Science* 202:537–539.

Hagamen, T. C., Greeley, H. P., Hagamen, W. D., and Reeves, A. G. (1977). Behavioral asymmetries following olfactory tubercle lesions in cats. *Brain Behav. Evol. 14:*241–250.

Halligan, P. W., and Marshall, J. C. (1989). Laterality of motor response in visuo-spatial neglect: a case study. *Neuropsychologia* 27:1301–1307.

Head, H. and Holmes, G. (1911). Sensory disturbances from cerebral lesions. *Brain 34:*102–254.

Heikkila, R. E., Shapiro, B. S., and Duvoisin, R. C. (1981). The relationship between loss of dopamine nerve terminals, striatal $^3$H spiroperidol binding and rotational behavior in unilaterally 6-hydroxdopamine-lesioned rats. *Brain Res. 211:*285–307.

Heilman, K. M. (1979). Neglect and related disorders. In *Clinical Neuropsycology*, K. M. Heilman and E. Valenstein (eds.). New York: Oxford University Press, pp. 268–307.

Heilman, K. M. (1991). Anosognosia: possible neuropsychological mechanisms. In *Awareness of Defect After Brain Injury*, G. Prigatano and D. Schacter (eds.). New York: Oxford University Press.

Heilman, K. M., Bowers, D., and Watson, R. T. (1983b). Performance on hemispatial pointing task by patients with neglect syndrome. *Neurology* 33:661–664.

Heilman, K. M., Bowers, D., and Watson, R. T. (1984). Pseudoneglect in patients with partial callosal disconnection. *Brain* 107:519–532.

Heilman, K. M., Bowers, D., Coslett, H. B., Whelan, H., and Watson, R. T. (1985). Directional hypokinesia: prolonged reaction times for leftward movements in patients with right hemisphere lesions and neglect. *Neurology* 35:855–860.

Heilman, K. M., and Howell, F. (1980). Seizure-induced neglect. *J. Neurol. Neurosurg. Psychiatry* 43:1035–1040.

Heilman, K. M. Odenheimer, G. L. Watson, R. T., and Valenstein, E. (1984). Extinction of nontouch. *Neurology 34 (suppl. 1):*188.

Heilman, K. M., Pandya, D. N., and Geschwind, N. (1970). Trimodal inattention following parietal lobe ablations. *Trans. Am. Neurol. Assoc.* 95:259–261.

Heilman, K. M., Schwartz, H. D., and Watson, R. T. (1978). Hypoarousal in patients with neglect syndrome and emotional indifference. *Neurology* 28:229–232.

Heilman, K. M., and Valenstein, E. (1972). Frontal lobe neglect in man. *Neurology* 22:660–664.

Heilman, K. M., and Valenstein, E. (1979). Mechanisms underlying hemispatial neglect. *Ann. Neurol.* 5:166–170.

Heilman, K. M., Valenstein, E., and Watson, R. T. (1983). Localization of neglect. In *Localization in Neurology*, A. Kertesz (ed.). New York: Academic Press, pp. 471–492.

Heilman, K. M., and Van Den Abell, T. (1979). Right hemispheric dominance for mediating cerebral activation. *Neuropsychologia* 17:315–321.

Heilman, K. M., and Van Den Abell, T. (1980). Right hemisphere dominance for attention: the mechanisms underlying hemispheric asymmetries of inattention (neglect). *Neurology* 30:327–330.

Heilman, K. M., and Watson, R. T. (1977). The neglect syndrome—a unilateral defect of the orienting response. In *Lateralization in the Nervous System*, S. Hardned, R. W. Doty, L. Goldstein, J. Jaynes, and G. Kean Thamer (eds.). New York: Academic Press.

Heilman, K. M., and Watson, R. T. (1978). Changes in the symptoms of neglect induced by changes in task strategy. *Arch. Neurol.* 35:47–49.

Heilman, K. M., Watson, R. T., and Schulman, H. (1974). A unilateral memory deficit. *J. Neurol. Neurosurg. Psychiatry* 37:790–793.

Heir, D.B., Davis, K. R., Richardson, E. T., et al. (1977). Hypertensive putaminal hemorrhage. *Ann. Neurol.* 1:152–159.

Herkenham, M. (1979). The afferent and efferent connections of the ventromedial thalamic nucleus in the rat. *J. Comp. Neurol.* 183:487–518.

Holmes, G. (1918). Disturbances of vision from cerebrel lesions. *Br. J. Opthalmol.* 2:253–384.

Howes, D., and Boller, F. (1975). Evidence for focal impairment from lesions of the right hemisphere. *Brain* 98:317–332.

Hoyman, L., Weese, G. D., and Frommer, G. P. (1979). Tactile discrimination performance deficits following neglect-producing unilateral lateral hypothalamic lesions in the rat. *Physiol. Behav.* 22:139–147.

Hyvarinen, J., and Poranen, A. (1974). Function of the parietal associative area 7 as revealed from cellular discharge in alert monkeys. *Brain* 97:673–692.

Iverson, S. D., Wilkinson, S., and Simpson, B. (1971). Enhanced amphetamine responses after frontal cortex lesions in the rat. *Eur. J. Pharmacol.* 13:387–390.

Jackson, J. Hughlings (1932). *Selected Writings of John Hughlings Jackson*, J. Taylor (ed.). London: Hodder and Stoughton.

James, W., (1890). *The Principles of Psychology*, Vol. 2. New York: Holt.

Jasper, H. H. (1949). Diffuse projection systems: the intergrative action of the thalamic reticular system. *Electroencephalogr. Clin. Neurophysiol.* 1:405–419.

Jefferson, G. (1958). Substrates for intergrative patterns in the reticular core. In *Reticular Formation* M. N. E. Scheibel and A. B. Scheibel (eds.). Boston: Little, Brown.

Jouvet, M. (1977). Neuropharmacology of the sleep waking cycle. In *Handbook of Psychopharmacology*, L. L. Iverson, S. D. Iverson, And S. H. Snyder (eds.). New York: Plenum Press, pp. 233–293.

Kahneman, D. (1973). *Eye Movement Attention and Effort*. Englewood Cliffs, N.J.: Prentice-Hall.

Kaplan, R. F., Verfaellie, M., DeWitt, D., and Caplan, L. R. (1990). Effects of changes in stimulus contingency on visual extinction. *Neurology* 40:1299–1301.

Kanai, T., and Szerb, J. C. (1965). Mesencephalic reticular activating system and cortical acetylcholine output. *Nature* 205:80–82.

Kartsounis, L. D., and Warrington, E. K. (1989). Unilateral visual neglect overcome by ones implicit in stimulus arrays. *J. Neurol. Neurosurg. Psychiatry* 52:1253–1259.

Kennard, M. A., and Ectors, L. (1938). Forced circling movements in monkeys following lesions of the frontal lobes. *J. Neurophysiol.* 1:45–54.

Kertesz, A., Nicholson, I., Cancelliere, A., Kassa, K., and Black, S. E. (1985). Motor impersistance: a right-hemisphere syndrome. *Neurology* 35:662–666.

Kievet, J., and Kuypers, H.G.J.M. (1977). Organization of the thalamo-cortical connections to the frontal lobe in the rhesus monkey. *Exp. Brain Res.* 29:299–322.

Kimura, D. (1967). Function asymmetry of the brain in dichotic listening. *Cortex* 3:163–178.

Kinsbourne, M. (1970). A model for the mechanism of unilateral neglect of space. *Trans. Am. Neurol. Assoc.* 95:143.

Kinsbourne, M. (1974). Direction of gaze and distribution of cerebral thought processes. *Neuropsychologia* 12:270–281.

Kooistra, C. A., and Heilman, K. M. (1989). Hemispatial visual inattention masquerading as hemianopsia. *Neurology* 39:1125–1127.

Kozlowski, M. R., and Marshall, J. F. (1981). Plasticity of neostriatal metabolic activity and behavioral recovery from nigrostriatal injury. *Exp. Neurol.* 74:313–323.

Kuypers, H.G.J.M., and Lawrence, D. G. (1967). Cortical projections to the red nucleus and the brain stem in the rhesus monkey. *Brain Res.* 4:151–188.

Ladavas, E. (1987). Is the hemispatial deficit produced by right parietal damage associated with retinal or gravitational coordinates. *Brain* 110:167–180.

Ladavas, E., Petronio, A., and Umicta, C. (1990). The deployment of visual attention in the intact field of hemineglect patients. *Cortex* 26:307–312.

Lansing, R. W., Schwartz, E., and Lindsley, D. B. (1959). Reaction time and EEG activation under alerted and nonalerted conditions. *J. Exp. Psychol.* 58:1–7.

Lindvall, O., Bjorklund, A., Morre, R. Y., and Stenevi, U. (1974). Mesencephalic dopamine-neurons projecting to the neocortex. *Brain Res.* 81:325–331.

Ljungberg, T., and Ungerstedt, U. (1976). Sensory inattention produced by 6-hydroxydopamine-induced degeneration of ascending dopamine neurons in the brain. *Exp. Neurol.* 53:585–600.

Loeb, J. (1885). Die elementaren storunger eirfacher functionennach oberflachlicher umschriebener Verletzung des Grosshirns Pfluger's. *Arch. Physiol.* 37:51–56.

Lynch, G. S., Ballantine, P., and Campbell, B. A. (1969). Potentiation of behavioral arousal after cortical damage and subsequent recovery. *Exp. Neurol.* 23:195–206.

Lynch, J. C. (1980). The functional organization of posterior parietal association cortex. *Behav. Brain Sci.* 3:485–534.

Mark, V. W., Kooistra, C. A., and Heilman, K. M. (1988). Hemispatial neglect affected by non-neglected stimuli. *Neurology* 38:1207–1211.

Marshall, J. F. (1979). Somatosensory inattention after dopamine-depleting intracerebral 6-OHDA injections: spontaneous recovery and pharmacological control. *Brain Res.* 177:311–324.

Marshall, J. F. (1982). Neurochemistry of attention and attentional disorders. *Annual course 214, Behavioral Neurology*. Presented at the American Academy of Neurology, April 27, 1982.

Marshall, J. F., Richardson, J. S., and Teitelbaum, P. (1974). Nigrostriatal bundle damage and the lateral hypothalamic damage. *J. Comp. Physiol Psychol.* 87:808–830.

Marshall, J. F., Turner, B. H., and Teitelbaum, P. (1971). Sensory neglect produced by lateral hypothalamic damage. *Science* 174:523–525.

McCormick, D. A. (1989). Cholinergic and noradrenergic modulation of thalamocortical processing. *Trends Neurol.* 12:215–221.

McFie, J., Piercy, M. F., and Zangwell, O. L. (1950). Visual spatial agnosia associated with lesions of the right hemisphere. *Brain* 73:167–190.

Meador, K., Hammond, E. J., Loring, D. W., Allen, M., Bowers, D., and Heilman, K. M. (1987). Cognitive evoked potentials and disorders of recent memory. *Neurology* 37:526–529.

Meador, K., Loring, D. W., Lee, G. P., Brooks, B. S., Thompson, W. O., and Heilman, K. M. (1988). Right cerebral specialization for tactile attention as evidenced by intracarotid sodium amytal. *Neurology* 38:1763–1766.

Meador, K., Loring, D. W., Lee, G. P., Brooks, B. S., Nichols, T. T., Thompson, E. E., Thompson, W. O., and Heilman, K. M. (1989). Hemisphere asymmetry for eye gaze mechanism. *Brain* 112:103–111.

Meador, K., Watson, R. T., Bowers, D., and Heilman, K. M., (1986). Hypometria with hemispatial and limb motor neglect. *Brain* 109:293–305.

Mehler, W. R. (1966). Further notes of the center median nucleus of Luys. In *The Thalamus*, D. P. Purpura, and M. D. Yahr (eds.). New York: Columbia University Press, pp. 109–122.

Mesulam, M. M. (1981). A cortical network for directed attention and unilateral neglect. *Ann. Neurol.* 10:309–325.

Mesulam, M., Van Hesen, G. W., Pandya, D. N., and Geschwind, N. (1977). Limbic and sensory connections of the inferior parietal lobule (area PG) in the rhesus monkey: a study with a new method for horseradish perosidase histochemistry. *Brain Res.* 136:393–414.

Meyer, E., Ferguson, S.S.G., Zarorre, R. J., Alivisatos, B., Marrett, S., Evans, A. C., and Hakim, A. M. (1991). Attention modulates somatosensory cerebral blood flow response to vibrotactile stimulation as measured by positron emission tomography. *Ann. Neurol.* 29:440–443.

Mills, R. P., and Swanson, P. D. (1978). Vertical oculomotor apraxia and memory loss. *Ann. Neurol.* 4:149–153.

Milner, B., Taylor, L., and Sperry, R. W. (1968). Lateralized suppression of dichotically presented digits after commissural section in man. *Science* 161:184–186.

Moruzzi, G., and Magoun, H. W. (1949). Brainstem reticular formation and activation of the EEG. *Electroencephalogr. Clin. Neurophysiol.* 1:455–473.

Motter, B. C., and Mountcastle, V. B. (1981). The functional properties of the light sensitive neurons of the posterior parietal cortex studied in waking monkeys: foveal sparing and opponent vector organization. *J. Neurosci.* 1:3–26.

Mountcastle, V. B., Anderson, R. A., and Motter, B. C. (1981). The influence of attentive fixation upon the excitability of the light sensitive neurons of the posterior parietal cortex. *J. Neurosci.* 1:1218–1245.

Mountcastle, V. B., Lynch, J. C., Georgopoulos, A., Sakata, H., and Acuna, C. (1975). Posterior parietal association cortex of the monkey: command function from operations within extrapersonal space. *J. Neurophysiol* 38:871–908.

Nadeau, S. E., and Heilman, K. M. (1991). Gaze-dependent hemianopia without hemispatial neglect. *Neurology* 41:1244–1250.

Nathan, P. W. (1946). On simultaneous bilateral stimulation of the body in a lesion of the parietal lobe. *Brain* 69:325–334.

Neve, K. A., Kozlowski, M. R., and Marshall, J. F. (1982). Plasticity of neostriatal dopamine receptors after nigrostriatal injury: relationship to recovery of sensorimotor functions and behavioral supersensitivity. *Brain Res.* 244:33–44.

Nieoullon, A., Cheramy, A., and Glowinski, J. (1978). Release of dopamine evoked by electrical stimulation of the motor and visual areas of the cerebral cortex in both caudate nuclei and in the substantia nigra in the cat. *Brain Res.* 15:69–83.

Obersteiner, H. (1882). On allochiria—a peculiar sensory disorder. *Brain* 4:153–163.

Olds, J., and Milner, P. (1954). Positive reinforcement produced by electrical stimulation of septal area and other regions of the rat brain. *J. Comp. Physiol. Psychol. 47*:419–427.

Oppenheim, H. (1885). Ueber eine durch eine klinisch bisher nicht verwertete Untersuchungs-methode ermittelte Form der Sensibitats-storung bei einseitigen Erkrankunger des Grosshirns. *Neurol. Zentrabl. 4*:529–533. Cited by A. L. Benton (1956). Jacques Loeb and the method of double stimulation. *J. Hist. Med. Allied Sci. 11*:47–53.

Pandya, D. M., and Kuypers, H.G.J.M. (1969). Cortico-cortical connections in the rhesus monkey. *Brain Res. 13*:13–36.

Pardo, J. V., Fox, P. T., and Raichle, M. E. (1991). Localization of a human system for sustained attention by positron emission tomography. *Nature 349*:61–64.

Paterson, A., and Zangwill, O. L. (1944). Disorders of visual space perception associated with lesions of the right cerebral hemisphere. *Brain 67*:331–358.

Posner, M. I., and Rafal, R. D. (1987). Cognitive theories of attention and rehabilitation of attentional deficits. In *Neuropsychological Rehabilitation*, M. J. Mier, and A. L. Benton, and L. Diller (eds.). Guilford, New York.

Posner, M. I., Walker, J., Friedrich, F. J., and Rafal, R. D. (1984). Effects of parietal lobe injury on covert orienting of visual attention. *J. Neurosci. 4*:163–187.

Poppelreuter, W. L. (1917). *Die psychischen Schadigungen durch Kopfschuss Krieg im 1914–1916: Die Storungen der niederen und hoheren Leistkungen durch Verletzungen des Oksipitalhirns.* Vol. 1. Leipzig: Leopold Voss. Referred to by M. Critchley, (1949). *Brain 72*:540.

Pibram, K. H., and McGuiness, D. (1975). Arousal, activation and effort in the control of attention. *Psychol. Rev. 182*:116–149.

Purpura, D. P. (1970). Operations and processes in thalamic and synaptically related neural subsystemes. In *The Neurosciences, Second Study Program.* F. O. Schmidt (ed.). New York: Rockefeller University Press, pp. 458–470.

Pycock, C. J. (1980). Turning behavior in animals. *Neuroscience 5*:461–514.

Rapcsak, S. Z., Watson, R. T., and Heilman, K. M. (1987). Hemispace-visual field interactions in visual extinction. *J. Neurol. Neurosurg. Psychiatry 50*:1117–1124.

Rapcsak, S. Z., Cimino, C. R., and Heilman, K. M. (1988). Altitudinal neglect. *Neurology 38*:277–281.

Rapcsak, S. Z., Fleet, W. S., Verfaellie, M., and Heilman, K. M. (1989). Selective attention in hemispatial neglect. *Arch. Neurol. 46*:178–182.

Reeves, A. G., and Hagamen, W. D. (1971). Behavioral and EEG asymmetry following unilateral lesions of the forebrain and midbrain of cats. *Electroencephalogr. Clin. Neurophysiol 39*:83–86.

Reider, N. (1946). Phenomena of sensory suppression. *Arch. Neurol. Psychiatry 55*:583–590.

Riddoch, G. (1935). Visual disorientation in homonymous half-fields. *Brain 58*:376–382.

Riddoch, M. J., and Humphreys, G. (1983). The effect of cuing on unilateral neglect. *Neuropsychologia 21*:589–599.

Robinson, D. L., Goldberg, M. E., and Stanton, G. B. (1978). Parietal association cortex in the primate sensory mechanisms and behavioral modulations. *J. Neurophysiol 41*:910–932.

Roeltgen, M. G., Roeltgen, D. P., and Heilman, K. M. (1989). Unilateral motor impersistence and hemispatial neglect from a striatal lesion. *Neuropsychiatry Neuropsychol. Behav. Neurol. 2*:125–135.

Ross, E. D., and Stewart, R. M. (1981). Akinetic mutism from hypothalamic damage: successful treatment with dopamine agonists. *Neurology 31*:1435–1439.

Rossi, P. W. Kheyfets, S., and Reding, M. J. (1990). Fresnel prisms improve visual perception in stroke patients with homonymous hemianopia unilateral visual neglect. *Neurology 40*:1597–1599.

Samuels, I., Butters, N., and Goodglass, H. (1971). Visual memory defects following cortical limbic lesions: effect of field of presentation. *Physiol. Behav.* 6:447–452.

Sato, H., Hata, Y. Hagihara, K., and Tsumoto, T. (1987). Effects of cholinergic depletion on neuron activities in the cat visual cortex. *J. Neurophysiol.* 58:781–794.

Scheibel, M. E., and Scheibel, A. B. (1967). Structural organization of nonspecific thalamic nuclei and their projection toward cortex. *Brain* 6:60–94.

Scheibel, M. E., and Scheibel, A. B. (1966). The organization of the nucleus reticularis thalami: a Golgi study. *Brain Res.* 1:43–62.

Schlag-Rey, M., and Schlag, J. (1980). Eye movement neurons in the thalamus of monkey. *Invest. Ophthalmol. Vis. Sci.* ARVO supplement, 176.

Schrandt, N. J., Tranel, D., and Domasio, H. (1989). The effects of total cerebral lesions on skin conductance response to signal stimuli. *Neurology 39 (Suppl. 1:)*223.

Schwartz, A. S., Marchok, P. L., Kreinick, C. J., and Flynn, R. E. (1979). The asymmetric lateralization of tactile extinction in patients with unilateral cerebral dysfunction. *Brain* 102:669–684.

Segundo, J. P., Naguet, R., and Buser, P. (1955). Effects of cortical stimulation on electrocortial activity in monkeys. *Neurophysiology 1B:*236–245.

Sevush, S., and Heilman, K. M. (1981). Attentional factors in tactile extinction. Presented at a meeting of the International Neuropsychological society, Atlanta, Georgia.

Shelton, P. A., Bowers, D., and Heilman, K. M. (1990). Peripersonal and vertical neglect. *Brain* 113:191–205.

Shute, C.C.D., and Lewis, P. R. (1967). The ascending cholinergic reticular system, neocortical olfactory and subcortical projections. *Brain 90:497–520.*

Singer, W. (1977). Control of thalamic transmission by corticofugal and ascending reticular pathways in the visual system. *Physiol. Rev.* 57:386–420.

Skinner, J. E., and Yingling, C. D. (1976). Regulation of slow potential shifts in nucleus reticularis thalami by the mesencephalic reticular formation and the frontal granular cortex. *Electroencephalogr. Clin. Neurophysiol.* 40:288–296.

Skinner, J. E., and Yingling, C. D. (1977). Central gating mechanisms that regulate event-related potentials and behavior—a neural model for attention. In *Progress in Clinical Neurophysiology*, Vol. 1, J. E. Desmedt (ed.). New York: S. Karger, pp. 30–69.

Sokolov, Y. N. (1963). *Perception and the Conditioned Reflex.* Oxford: Pergmon Press.

Sparks, R., and Geschwind N. (1968). Dichotic listening in man after section of the neocortical commissures. *Cortex* 4:3–16.

Sprague, J. M. (1966). Interaction of cortex and superior colliculus in mediation of visually guided behavior in the cat. *Science* 153:1544–1547.

Sprague, J. M., and Meikle, T. H. (1965). The role of the superior colliculus in visually guided behavior. *Exp. Neurol.* 11:115–146.

Sprague, J. M., Chambers, W. W., and Stellar, E. (1961). Attentive, affective and adaptive behavior in the cat. *Science* 133:165–173.

Stelmack, R. M., Plouffe, L. M., and Winogron, H. W. (1983). Recognition memory and the orienting response. An analysis of the encoding of pictures and words. *Biol. Psychol.* 16:49–63.

Steriade, M., and Glenn, L. (1982). Neocortical and caudate projections of intralaminar thalamic neurons and their synaptic excitation from the midbrain reticular core. *J. Neurophysiol* 48:352–370.

Teitelbaum, P., and Epstein, A. N. (1962). The lateral hypothalamic syndrome: recovery of feeding and drinking after lateral hypothalamic lesions. *Psychol. Rev.* 69:74–90.

Truex, R. C., and Carpenter, M. B. (1964). *Human Neuroanatomy.* Baltimore: Williams and Wilkins.

Ungerstedt, U. (1971a). Striatal dopamine release after amphetamine or nerve degeneration revealed by rotational behavior. *Acta Physiol. Scand.* [*Suppl.*] 82:49–68.

Ungerstedt, U. (1971b). Post-synaptic supersensitivity of 6-hydroxydopamine induced degeneration of the nigro-striatal dopamine system in the rat brain. *Acta. Physiol. Scand.* [*Suppl.*] 82:69–93.

Ungerstedt. U. (1974). Brain dopamine neurons and behavior. In *Neurosciences*, Vol. 3, F. O. Schmidt and F. G. Woren (eds.). Cambridge, Mass.: MIT Press, pp. 695–703.

Vallar, G., Sterzi, R., Bottini, G., Cappa, S., and Rusconi, L. (1990). Temporary remission of left hemianesthesia after vestibular stimulation: A sensory neglect phenomenon. *Cortex* 26:123–131.

Valenstein, E., and Heilman, K. M. (1978). Apraxic agraphia with neglect induced paragraphia. *Arch. Neurol.* 38:506–508.

Valenstein, E., and Heilman, K. M. (1981). Unilateral hypokinesia and motor extinction. *Neurology* 31:445–448.

Valenstein, E., Van den Abell, T., Tankle, R., and Heilman, K. M. (1980). Apomorphine-induced turning after recovery from neglect induced by cortical lesions. *Neurology* 30:358.

Valenstein, E., Van den Abell, T., Watson, R. T., and Heilman, K. M. (1982). Nonsensory neglect from parietotemporal lesions in monkeys. *Neurology* 32:1198–1201.

Valenstein, E., Watson, R. T., Van den Abell, T., Carter, R., and Heilman, K. M. (1987). Response time in monkeys with unilateral neglect. *Arch. Neurol.* 44:517–520.

Velasco, F., and Velasco, M. (1979). A reticulothalamic system mediating proprioceptive attention and tremor in man. *Neurosurgery* 4:30–36.

Vogt, B. A., Rosene, D. L., and Pandya, D. N. (1979). Thalamic and cortical afferents differentiate anterior from posterior cingulate cortex in the monkey. *Science* 204:205–207.

Wagman, I. H., and Mehler, W. R. (1972). Physiology and anatomy of the cortico-oculomotor mechanism. *Prog. Brain Res.* 37:619–635.

Walter, W. G., (1973). Human frontal lobe function in sensory-motor association. In *Psychophysiology of the Frontal Lobes*, K. H. Pribram and A. R. Luria (eds.). New York: Academic Press, pp. 109–122.

Vanderwolf, C. H., and Robinson, T. E. (1981). Reticulo-cortical activity and behavior: a critique of arousal theory and new synthesis. *Behav. Brain Sci.* 4:459–514.

Watson, R. T., and Heilman, K. M. (1979). Thalamic neglect. *Neurology* 29:690–694.

Watson, R. T., Andriola, M., and Heilman, K. M. (1977). The EEG in neglect. *J. Neurol. Sci.* 34:343–348.

Watson, R. T., Heilman, K. M., Cauthen, J. C., and King, F. A. (1973). Neglect after cingulectomy. *Neurology* 23:1003–1007.

Watson, R. T., Heilman, K. M., Miller, B. D., and King, F. A. (1974). Neglect after mesencephalic reticular formation lesions. *Neurology* 24:294–298.

Watson, R. T., Miller, B. D., and Heilman, K. M. (1977). Evoked potential in neglect. *Arch. Neurol.* 34:224–227.

Watson, R. T., Miller, B. D., and Heilman, K. M. (1978). Nonsensory neglect. *Ann. Neurol.* 3:505–508.

Watson, R. T., Valenstein, E., and Heilman, K. M. (1981). Thalamic neglect: the possible role of the medial thalamus and nucleus reticularis thalami in behavior. *Arch. Neurol.* 38:501–507.

Watson, R. T., Valenstein, E., Day, A. L., and Heilman, K. M. (1984). The effects of corpus callosum section on unilateral neglect in monkeys. *Neurology* 34:812–815.

Watson, R. T., Valenstein, E., Day, A., and Heilman, K. M. (in preparation) Posterior neocortical systems subserving awareness and neglect: neglect after superior temporal sucus but not area 7 lesions.

Weinberger, N. M., and Velasco, M., and Lindsley, D. B., (1965). Effects of lesions upon thalamically induced electrocortical desynchronization and recruiting. *Electroencephalogr. Clin. Neurophysiol* 18:369–377.

Weinstein, E. A., and Kahn, R. L. (1955). *Denial of Illness. Symbolic and Physiological Aspects.* Springfield, Ill.: C. C. Thomas.

Weintraub, S., and Mesulam, M. M. (1987). Right cerebral dominance in spatial attention: further evidence based on ipsilateral neglect. *Arch. Neurol.* 44:621–625.

Welch, K., and Stuteville, P. (1958). Experimental production of neglect in monkeys. *Brain* 81:341–347.

Whittington, D. A., and Hepp-Reymond, M. C. (1977). Eye and head movements to auditory targets. *Neurosci. Abstr.* 3:158

Yingling, C. D., and Skinner, J. E. (1975). Regulation of unit activity in nucleus reticularis thalami by the mesencephalic reticular formation and the frontal granular cortex. *Electroencephalogr. Clin. Neurophysiol.* 39:635–642.

Yingling, C. D., and Skinner, J. E. (1977). Gating of thalamic input to cerebral cortex by nucleus reticularis thalami. In *Progress in Clinical Neurophysiology*, Vol. 1, J. E. Desmedt (ed.). New York: S. Karger, pp. 70–96.

Yokoyama, K. Jennings, R., Ackles, P., Hood, P., and Boller, F. (1987). Lack of heart rate changes during an attention demanding task after right hemisphere lesions. *Neurology* 37:624–630.

# 11

# The Callosal Syndromes

JOSEPH E. BOGEN

> In spite of evidence affirming it, the callosal syndrome, whose principal elements
> were magnificently described before 1908, has been discussed, forgotten, rediscov-
> ered, denied, proven, put in doubt; it continues a subject for argument.
>
> Brion and Jedynak (1975)

The corpus callosum is by far the largest of those nerve fiber collections that directly
connect one cerebral hemisphere with the other and are called the cerebral commissures. These include the anterior commissure and the hippocampal commissures. Not
included are the posterior and the habenular commissures as well as other commissures of the spinal cord and brainstem.

When the cerebral commissures have been surgically divided (the "split-brain"
operation), a variety of deficits in interhemispheric communication can be demonstrated. These make up "the syndromes of the cerebral commissures," also known as
"the syndromes of brain bisection" or "the syndrome of hemisphere disconnection"
(Sperry et al., 1969; Gazzaniga, 1970; Sperry, 1982; Bogen, 1987). Many of these same
deficits can occur with only a partial interruption of the commissures (for example,
a portion of the corpus callosum) when this partial disconnection occurs in a setting
of acute, naturally occurring disease, such as a thrombosis (Geschwind, 1965). Earlier
cases were often described as examples of "the anterior cerebral artery syndrome"
(Foix and Hillemand, 1925a; Critchley, 1930; Ethelberg, 1951).

Callosal lesions are often accompanied by damage to neighboring structures. As a
result, neighborhood signs may overshadow signs of callosal disconnection. The situation can also be complicated by nonlocalizing signs, such as meningismus when the
callosal lesion is caused by hemorrhage from an aneurysm, or signs of increased intracranial pressure when the callosal lesion is a tumor. Although any sign after cortical
damage (in a region giving rise to callosal fibers) could be suspected of being partially
callosal in origin, small lesions of the callosum rarely can be reliably correlated with
any behavioral deficit.

This chapter will deal with signs of hemisphere disconnection and neighborhood signs. The first section comments on terminology and etiology. Second is a synopsis of the human split-brain syndrome, to give an overall view of what is to come. Third is an historical account that will help us to understand how the disconnection signs have come to be emphasized. Next are two sections presenting detailed descriptions of the acute and the chronic syndromes that result from complete callosotomy. The sixth section describes clinical testing for callosal signs and symptoms with naturally occurring lesions. The final sections discuss a few examples of ongoing controversy.

## TERMINOLOGY AND ETIOLOGY

The term split-brain has several meanings. Applied to the human, it denotes complete callosal section—with or without anterior commissurotomy—an operation which is usually performed for medically intractable, multifocal epilepsy (Reeves, 1984; Spencer et al., 1987). In the experimental animal, such as the cat or monkey, it usually implies both commissural section *and* a split chiasm; this makes it possible to restrict visual information to one hemisphere merely by covering one eye. In the human with intact chiasm, restriction of visual input to one hemisphere requires restriction of the visual stimuli to one or the other visual hemifield. Our own split-brain patients (Bogen and Vogel, 1962, 1975; Bogen et al., 1965, 1988) had complete cerebral commissurotomy (including anterior commissure, dorsal and ventral hippocampal commissures, and, in some cases, the massa intermedia). But it is now common to use the term split-brain to refer to cases of complete callosotomy alone, since they manifest most of the same signs and symptoms.

The term partial split has come into common usage because some seizure disorders respond well to section of only the anterior half or anterior two-thirds of the callosum. Moreover, partial sections have sometimes been used for surgical approaches: examples are genu section for anterior communicating aneurysm clipping, trunk sections for access to the third ventricle and environs (Apuzzo, 1987), and splenial section for approaching the pineal region. Tumors (usually gliomas) can occur anywhere in the callosum, the best studied being tumors of the genu or of the splenium. Multiple sclerosis can cause disconnection signs. Toxic and/or infectious lesions of the callosum occasionally occur. And from time to time an anterior cerebral artery aneurysm rupture results in hemorrhagic dissection of the callosum. These naturally occurring lesions usually result in eventually subsiding fractions of the complete callosotomy syndrome. Familiarity with the complete syndrome makes it easier to identify the partial or forme fruste varieties. Congenital absence of the corpus callosum (callosal agenesis) has been intensively studied; it is for the most part *not* accompanied by disconnection signs, a perplexity which is discussed in detail further on.

## SYNOPSIS OF THE HUMAN SPLIT-BRAIN SYNDROME

When patients who have had a complete callosotomy have recovered from the acute operative effects and reach a fairly stable state, they manifest a variety of phenomena which can be grouped under four headings.

## Social Ordinariness

One of the most remarkable results is that in ordinary social situations the patients are indistinguishable from normal. Special testing methods, usually involving the lateralization of input, are needed to expose their deficits.

## Lack of Interhemispheric Transfer

A wide variety of situations (to be described below) have been contrived to show that the human subjects are in this respect the same as split-brain cats and monkeys. A typical example is the inability to retrieve with one hand an object palpated with the other.

## Hemispheric Specialization Effects

The hemispheric specialization typical of human subjects results in phenomena not seen in split-brain animals. A typical example is the inability of right-handers to name or describe an object in the left hand, even when it is being appropriately manipulated.

## Compensatory Phenomena

Split-brain subjects progressively acquire a variety of strategies for circumventing their interhemispheric transfer deficits. A common example is for the patient to speak out loud the name of an object palpated in the right hand; because the right hemisphere can recognize many individual words, the object can then be retrieved with the left hand.

These four kinds of phenomena are discussed in detail in the section on the chronic or stabilized syndrome of hemisphere disconnection.

## HISTORICAL BACKGROUND

The history of studies of the corpus callosum can be considered to have six periods:

1. The humoral anatomists
2. The traffic anatomists
3. The classical neurologists
4. The critics
5. The two-brain theorists
6. The revisionists

Contributors not mentioned here are cited in the extensive reviews included in the bibliography.°

## The Humoral Anatomists

By "humoral anatomists" I mean those writers of antiquity whose concepts of brain function emphasized the contents of the brain cavities and the flow of various fluids such as air, phlegm, cerebrospinal fluid, blood, etc. For them, the corpus callosum seemed largely a supporting structure. Even that original Renaissance genius, Vesalius, believed that the corpus callosum served mainly as a mechanical support, maintaining the integrity of the various cavities. In 1543 he wrote:

> There is a part [whose] external surface is gleaming white and harder than the substance on the remaining surface of the brain. It was for this reason that the ancient Greeks called this part "tyloeides" ["callosus" in Latin] and, following their example, in my discourse I have always referred to this part as the corpus callosum. If you look at the right and left brain . . . and also if you compare the front and rear, the corpus callosum is observed to be in the middle of the brain; . . . Indeed, it relates the right side of the cerebrum to the left; then it produces and supports the septum of the right and left ventricles; finally, through that septum it supports and props the [fornix] so that it may not collapse and, to the great detriment of all the functions of the cerebrum, crush the cavity common to the two [lateral] ventricles of the cerebrum. (Clarke and O'Malley, 1968, p. 597)

## The Traffic Anatomists

The "traffic anatomists" took a major step forward. As indicated by Joynt (1974), it was at about the time of Willis (1664) that anatomists began thinking in terms of communication between the more solid parts of the brain. This view became quite explicit in the statement of Viq d'Azyr, who wrote in 1784:

> It seems to me that the commissures are intended to establish sympathetic communications between different parts of the brain, just as the nerves do between different organs and the brain itself. (Clarke and O'Malley, 1968, p. 592)

For over two centuries, beliefs about callosal function consisted almost solely of inferences from its central location, widespread connections, and large size (larger than all those descending and ascending tracts, taken together, which connect the cerebrum with the outside world). Willis, de la Peyronie, and Lancisi, among others, thought the corpus callosum a likely candidate for "the seat of the soul"; or they used some other expression intended to cover that highest or ultimate liaison which brings coherent, vital unity to a complex assemblage.

°Lévy-Valensi, 1910; Mingazzini, 1922; Bremer et al., 1956; Bremer, 1958; Geschwind, 1965; Unterharnscheidt et al., 1968; Bogen and Bogen, 1969; Elliot, 1969; Kuhlenbeck, 1969; Cumming et al., 1970; Doty and Negrào, 1972; Berlucchi, 1972, 1990; Joynt, 1974; Selnes, 1974; Brion and Jedynak, 1975; Pandya, 1975; Reeves, 1984; Innocenti, 1986; Leporé et al., 1986; Harrington, 1987; Berlucchi and Aglioti, 1990; Trevarthen, 1990; Innocenti, 1991.

The observations of the early anatomists have been supported by subsequent anatomic observations, including the large number of callosal fibers, at least 600 million of them.° It seems reasonable to suppose that these fibers which interconnect so much of cerebral cortex, especially that cortex considered associative, have to do with the "highest," most educable, and characteristically human functions of the cerebrum (Bremer, 1958).

Inference of function from observable structure is time honored and productive. However, such inference has its limitations. The physiological evidence has only partially sustained anatomic inference. We now know from various observations (notably the split-brain) that the corpus callosum is indeed an important integrative structure; we also know it is neither sufficient nor indispensable, providing only one of a number of integrative mechanisms. Indeed, the multiplicity of mechanisms mediating between the two hemispheres is a major theme of this chapter.

Behavioral deficits are now easily and clearly demonstrable in individuals who have had surgical section of the cerebral commissures. But these deficits were first recognized, by a number of exceptionally astute clinicians, in patients with vascular disease causing very complex and evolving syndromes.

### The Classical Neurologists

In the closing decades of the nineteenth century (or more broadly construed, in the period between the American Civil War and the First World War), a group of neurologists emerged whose discoveries and formulations are still the core of current clinical knowledge; many issues which they debated remain live issues today. Among them were several, including Wernicke, Liepmann, Dejerine, and Goldstein, who interpreted various neurological symptoms as resulting from disconnection, including interruption of information flow through the corpus callosum.

The concept of apraxia was developed by Liepmann expressly to describe a patient who could carry out commands with one of his hands but not with the other. Liepmann and Maas (1907) described a right-hander whose callosal lesion caused a left apraxia as well as a left-hand agraphia—an inability to write—in the absence of aphasia. These disabilities have subsequently been observed many times. Unilateral apraxia and agraphia are not always present, and they may subside as a stroke victim recovers, but they remain among the cardinal signs of hemisphere disconnection.

Among Liepmann's ideas were two which he considered to be necessarily connected, but whose acceptance, in fact, has waxed and waned independently. We can call them (1) the concept of callosal motor mediation or "the callosal concept" and (2) the concept of left-hemisphere motor dominance or "motor dominance."

According to the first concept, interruption of transcallosal interhemispheric communication results in apraxia. Liepmann considered the corpus callosum instrumental in left-hand responses to verbal command: the verbal instruction was comprehended only by the left hemisphere and the left hand followed instructions which were delivered not by a directly descending pathway which we now call "ipsilateral

°The $2 \times 10^8$ estimate of Tomasch (1954) was based on light microscopy. According to G. Innocenti (personal communication in 1991), electron microscopy will at least triple the old estimate (see also Clarke et al., 1989).

control" (cf. Brinkman and Kuypers, 1973; Jones et al., 1989) but by a route involving callosal interhemispheric tranfer from left to right and then by way of what we now call "contralateral control," that is, by right-hemisphere control of the left hand. Necessarily then, callosal interruption would result in an inability to follow verbal commands with the left hand although there would be no loss of comprehension (as expected from a left-hemisphere lesion). And there would be no weakness or incoordination of the left hand (as would usually result from a right-hemisphere lesion). This view was largely ignored or rejected (particularly in the English-speaking countries) for nearly half a century, although it is now thought to be essentially correct. Correspondingly, we now recognize the notion of spatial or pictorial instructions understood by the right hemisphere and requiring callosally mediated interhemispheric communication for correct right-hand execution. This right-to-left aspect of callosal function was not part of Liepmann's original callosal concept, although, in retrospect, it seems a natural corollary.

Second, there was Liepmann's concept of the left hemisphere as the organizer of complex (particularly learned) motor behavior. Indeed, according to Goldstein (1953), it was Liepmann who made "the important discovery of the dominance of the left hemisphere." Unlike the callosal concept, this idea of motor dominance was readily accepted, along with the already established concept of language dominance by the left hemisphere. Almost everyone came to think of the left hemisphere as *generally* "the dominant hemisphere" (Benton, 1977). The reemergence in the 1960s of interest in the corpus callosum (as described below) was coincidentally accompanied by a recognition of right-hemisphere dominance for certain nonverbal processes and their motor expression. Hence, while Liepmann's callosal concept was regaining popularity, his motor dominance concept was losing some of its appeal. We have here what seems to be an example of how ideas thought by their inventor to be necessarily linked can be separated by the judgments of others. Whether, and in what way, the left hemisphere is dominant for skilled or serially programmed movements generally (and not just those linguistically related) is currently a matter of active controversy (Kimura and Archibald, 1974; Denckla, 1974; Geschwind, 1975; Albert et al., 1976; Zaidel and Sperry, 1977; Haaland et al., 1977; Mateer and Kimura, 1977; Denckla and Rudel, 1978; Zaidel, 1978b; Haaland and Delaney, 1981; Jason 1983a,b; Kimura, 1983; Hampson and Kimura, 1984; Corina et al., 1991; Leonard and Milner, 1991). For a further discussion of apraxia (including callosal apraxia) see Chapter 7.

Meanwhile, Liepmann's callosal concept is now hardly doubted. But this was not always so.

## The Critics

Even during the time of Liepmann, there were critics and doubters; they became progressively more influential in the ensuing decades. In their extensive review, Ironside and Guttmacher (1929) concluded:

> Taking into account the completeness of the case records, our series of tumour cases would lead us to believe that apraxia is not a common symptom of tumours of the corpus callosum.

The symptoms in corpus callosum tumours are largely of the "neighbourhood" type and arise from involvement of, or pressure on, adjacent structures by the growth.

In addition to the criticism of hemisphere disconnection as a cause of symptoms, the situation was clouded by certain distractions which we can consider briefly before returning to the central theme of disconnection.

## MENTAL SYMPTOMS WERE DISPUTED

Distractions arose as a result of attempts to correlate lesions, especially tumors of the corpus callosum, with mental symptoms. For example, a mental callosal syndrome was formulated by Raymond et al. (1906) and their views were widely accepted for many years. They observed a certain loss of connectedness of ideas but no delirium, a difficulty with recent memory, a "bizarreness" of manner, and a lability of mood. One is impressed with the extent to which this resembles symptoms which are now commonly attributed to frontal lobe damage (Botez, 1974; Barbizet et al., 1977; Damasio, 1984; Stuss and Benson, 1986; Fuster, 1989; Levin et al., 1991).

Alpers (1936) redescribed the callosal syndrome emphasizing "imperviousness": a certain indifference to stimuli as if the threshold were elevated, difficulties in concentration, and a lack of elaboration of thought.

After reviewing the relevant literature, and on the basis of personal cases, Brihaye (in Bremer et al., 1956) agreed with the observation of Le Beau (1943) that "there is a certain apathy, that is to say, a clouding without somnolence which is possibly very specific." When we actually read Le Beau, we find that the rest of his sentence is, "but this, in any case, is insufficient to permit more than a clinical suspicion of localization in the corpus callosum. Most of the time, there is nothing of the sort" (p. 1370). And on the very first page of his extensive article, Le Beau says, "The clinical diagnosis of these tumors is hardly possible, because there is no callosal syndrome (p. 1365). And in his summary, "in particular there is no characteristic mental deficit and no apraxia" (p. 1381).

Patients with anterior callosal lesions often do have "a certain apathy." This "imperviousness" occurs in patients with acute or progressive callosal lesions—especially the malignancy that is sometimes called a "butterfly glioma" because it spreads its wings into both frontal lobes. The patient who is impervious to instructions will eventually respond, and often appropriately (but sometimes incompletely), but only after repeated requests and considerable delay. We are now inclined to attribute this symptom not to involvement of the genu of the corpus callosum (which is, to be sure, involved) but rather to involvement of the medial aspects of the frontal lobes including the anterior cingulate gyri. And we suppose the imperviousness to be a milder form of akinesia, often approaching a mute immobility, of a patient who has what is sometimes called the "subfrontal syndrome" consequent to bleeding from an anterior cerebral artery aneurysm, or with a third ventricle tumor. (Also, see Chapters 10 and 12 on the neglect syndrome and the frontal lobes, respectively.)

In any event, imperviousness can be a useful sign of anterior callosal lesions, although it is probably not a result of callosal interruption.

Neighborhood signs have also been noted with posterior callosal lesions, with involvement of the hippocampi. Translating Escourolle et al. (1975):

> A certain number of our tumors of the splenium [twice as common as genu gliomas] were accompanied by memory dysfunction, whereas the anterior tumors were more often manifested by akinetic states with mutism, probably because of bilateral anterior cingulate involvement. (p. 48)

### DISCONNECTION SIGNS WERE NOT OFTEN SEEN

The eclipse of Liepmann's understanding of the corpus callosum was only partly attributable to clouding of the issue with neighborhood signs: mainly it was from an unwillingness to accept as meaningful such disconnection signs as unilateral apraxia, unilateral agraphia, and hemialexia. The objections which were raised included the following six points:

1. *Callosal lesions are rarely if ever isolated, so that deficits attributed to such lesions may well result, at least in part, from associated damage.*

This problem is real enough; the only solution is to obtain a sufficient variety of cases so that one can reasonably attribute to their common anatomic aspects those clinical features which they also have in common. This is reminiscent of the generally accepted attitude among scientists that a belief becomes more secure through the convergence of widely differing lines of evidence.

2. *Signs attributable to callosal lesions often subside or disappear altogether.*

This criticism is correct, especially for younger patients with unimanual dyspraxia and unimanual dysgraphia. But it does not apply to all callosal signs, notably the unilateral anomia and the hemialexia following callosotomy. Even if it did, subsidence does not mean that a sign was without significance, any more than the frequent subsidence of aphasia means that it is not a reliable sign (in right-handers) of a left-hemisphere lesion. Progressive compensation following focal damage is one of the most characteristic features of the brain.

3. *In numerous cases of callosal disease the expected disconnection signs are not elicited.*

This included cases of toxic degeneration of the corpus callosum (such as Marchiafava-Bignami disease) as well as the far more common cases of callosal tumor or callosal infarction. In the massive revised edition of his neurology text, Gowers (1903) reasonably concluded:

> we do not yet know of any symptoms that are the result of the damage to the callosal fibers. (p. 314)

S.A.K. Wilson, in his definitive neurology text (Wilson and Bruce, 1940), reaffirmed, on the basis of tumor cases, much the same conclusion. Wilson mentioned apraxia as an inconstant symptom, emphasized certain mental symptoms such as lack of spontaneity, and concluded:

In fact, the claim might be advanced that all "callosal" symptoms are of a neighboring or distant kind. (p. 1235)

Wilson's discussion refers to studies by Bristowe, Ransom, Tooth, Guillain, Alpers and Grant, Voriz and Adson, Dyke and Davidoff, and the book by Mingazzini (1922), as well as the article by Ironside and Guttmacher (1929) quoted above in the introduction to this subsection on the critics. He does not refer to Liepmann. This insular tradition of disprizing callosal disconnection as a source of symptoms persists (Rudge and Warrington, 1991).

In retrospect, these negative findings can often be attributed to a lack of looking; it is not everyone's routine to look for dysgraphia in the left hand or even for an anomia; and hemialexia in the left half-field can be even more elusive, particularly if no precautions are taken to prevent shift of gaze (such as using a tachistoscope so that stimuli appear, in one visual half-field or the other, for only a fraction of a second). In addition, disconnection signs may not be demonstrable because patients with callosal tumors or toxic degeneration are often too obtunded to be appropriately tested.

When patients with toxic malfunction of the corpus callosum are testable, and appropriately tested, such signs as unilateral anomia and dyspraxia have been found (Lhermitte et al., 1977; Barbizet et al., 1978). Disconnection signs have likewise been found with appropriate testing of tumor/infarction cases, as was so well demonstrated in the now classic paper of Geschwind and Kaplan (1962) (see also Barbizet et al., 1974).

4. *Patients with agenesis of the corpus callosum (and/or callosal lipoma) do not manifest most of the so-called callosal signs.*

Lévy-Valensi (1910) was an ardent admirer of Liepmann, gave him the credit for the concept of apraxia, and said, ". . . apraxia is part of the callosal syndrome." But he, like so many others, was particularly troubled by callosal agenesis and admitted, "The physiologist is no less embarrassed than the anatomist by these disconcerting cases." A sizable number of callosal agenesis patients have been seen in the past few years; and a few deficits in interhemispheric transfer have seemed to be present (Jeeves, 1965, 1991; Lehmann and Lampe, 1970; Dixon and Jeeves, 1970; Kinsbourne and Fisher, 1971; Sadowsky and Reeves, 1975; Milner and Jeeves, 1979; Lassonde et al., 1981; Sauerwein et al., 1981; Milner, 1982).

But there has been no disconnection syndrome typical of the split-brain in such patients. This observation cannot be explained away on methodological grounds since it is true even with the most extensive, systematic testing (Saul and Sperry, 1968; Ettlinger et al., 1974; Ferriss and Dorsen, 1975; Reynolds and Jeeves, 1977; Gott and Saul, 1978; Jeeves, 1979; Lassonde et al., 1988, 1991).

The presence of interhemispheric transfer in spite of callosal agenesis has been attributed to various causes, most notably the use of other commissural systems such as the anterior commissure. There may also be a duplication of function (such as speech in each hemisphere) or the compensatory appearance, during brain development, of unusually effective ipsilateral fiber tracts, or cerebellopetal pathways (Voneida, 1963; Glickstein, 1990).

The anterior commissure explanation is appealing because the available postmortem evidence indicates that individuals with callosal agenesis (if they reach an age sufficient for psychological testing) all have anterior commissures, sometimes larger than normal (Bruce, 1890; Segal, 1935; Reeves and Courville, 1938; Kirschbaum, 1947; Slager et al., 1957; Loeser and Alvord, 1968; Bossy, 1970; Ito et al., 1972; Sheremata et al., 1973; Shoumura et al., 1975; Carleton et al., 1976; Jeret et al., 1987).*

The anterior commissure has been shown in animal experiments to serve visual transfer nearly as well as the splenium (Downer, 1962; Black and Myers, 1964; Doty and Overman, 1977; Sullivan and Hamilton, 1973a; Doty et al., 1986, 1988; Mishkin and Phillips, 1990). And it is now known that in the chronic, stabilized state, the splenium can effect sufficient interhemispheric exchange to avoid signs of disconnection. This conclusion is based on cases having extensive but incomplete commissurotomy, that is, section of the anterior commissure and all of the corpus callosum except for the splenium. Later in this chapter an extensive list of deficits reliably found after a complete commissurotomy is presented; few of these deficits can be found after surgery if the splenium is spared (Gordon et al., 1971; Gazzaniga et al., 1975; Ozgur et al., 1977; Cobben et al., 1978; Benes, 1982; Apuzzo et al., 1982; Greenblatt et al., 1980; Bogen, 1987; Oepen et al., 1988; Purves et al., 1988; Gordon, 1990; Oguni et al., 1991). Certain transfer deficits found with various partial callosal interruptions are discussed at the end of this chapter.

Two points deserve emphasis:

a. An apparent lack of callosal symptoms in cases of long-standing partial lesion (and probably of callosal agenesis) is largely due to the compensatory capabilities of the remaining fibers.
b. Partial lesions are not usually compensated immediately. Hence, disconnection symptoms are more likely to occur after a sudden partial lesion (such as a stroke) or in the presence of progressive lesions (such as tumors) where the deficit is increasing faster than it can be compensated.

The paucity of disconnection deficits in patients with callosal agenesis is not wholly explained by the presence of the anterior commissure. It should be kept in mind that compensation for loss of the splenium, by the anterior commissure, has been imperfect in animal experiments (Butler, 1979; Ringo et al., 1991). Nor does the anterior commissure compensate very well for splenial loss in humans, as shown by the hemialexia usually persisting after splenial section (Trescher and Ford, 1937; Maspes, 1948; Gazzaniga and Freedman, 1973; Iwata et al., 1974; Sugishita et al., 1986).

Interhemispheric transfer of discriminative information via the anterior commissure seems to be, in surgical cases, incomplete (Goldstein and Joynt, 1969; Goldstein et al., 1975). Even if the anterior commissure is responsible for visual transfer in cases of callosal agenesis, how are we to explain the somesthetic transfer in such cases? One consideration is that agenesis cases typically have a large longitudinal bundle of fibers along the medial aspect of each hemisphere (the bundle of Probst, 1973). As pointed out by R. Saul (personal communication) this bundle might make available to the anterior commissure some types of information which it does not ordinarily transfer.

---

*I am aware of only one report, brought to my attention by Dr. Maryse Lassonde, of a person reaching adulthood and at autopsy considered to have absence of the anterior commissure (Harcourt-Webster and Rack, 1965).

In any event, the presence of Probst's bundle fits the view that brains with callosal agenesis differ from normal brains in ways other than disconnection.

Also implying that such a brain is peculiar in its principles of operation is the notion of increased function of ipsilaterally descending or ascending fiber tracts. In this regard, Dennis (1976) confirmed that callosal agenesis is accompanied by deficits within each hemisphere, appearing as a loss of finely differentiated tactile localization and individual finger movements. This loss was attributed to a lack of inhibitory action by the corpus callosum during early development of the brain. The corpus callosum, in this view, oridnarily suppresses information contained in uncrossed pathways. Somewhat related are the suggestions (1) that unilateralization of language (and other engrams) depends on callosal inhibition active at the time of engram acquisition (Doty et al., 1973; but see Temple et al., 1989; Lassonde et al., 1990; Leonard et al., 1991) and (2) that the development of hemispheric specialization depends on competitive interaction between the hemispheres during early childhood (Galin, 1977).

Some reservation is necessary with respect to the interpretation of intrahemispheric deficits in callosal agenesis, since the condition is so often associated with other anomalies. Hence, any deficit in intrahemispheric function might easily be coincidental, not a direct result of the absence of commissures. Further evidence might be expected from animal experiments in which the cerebral commissures are severed shortly after birth (Jeeves and Wilson, 1969; Sechzer et al., 1976; Elberger, 1980; Ptito and Leporé, 1983). Recent results include the finding that callosotomy in kittens seems to interfere with the normal development of a variety of visual functions (Elberger, 1988, 1990).

5. *Callosal section in animal experiments does not produce significant deficits.*

The negative experiments of Zinn (1748); Magendie, Muratow, Roussy, Franck, and Pitres; Koranyi, Dotto, and Pusateri; Lo Monaco; and Baldi were all reviewed by Lévy-Valensi (1910), whose own monkey experiments were (to his dismay) also negative, as were the experiments (cited by Bremer et al., 1956) of Lafora and Prados (1923), Hartmann and Trendelenberg (1927), Seletzky and Gilula (1928), and Kennard and Watts (1934).

In retrospect, these negative results can be attributed to a lack of relevant testing (as will be discussed further on). Besides, the more striking signs and symptoms seen in human patients are attributable to hemispheric specialization which is less evident in rats, cats, dogs, or even monkeys (Warren and Nonneman, 1976; Doty and Overman, 1977; Hamilton, 1977; Stamm et al., 1977; Dewson, 1977; Harnad et al., 1977; Denenberg, 1981; Overman and Doty, 1982; Hamilton and Vermeire, 1982, 1988; Petersen et al., 1984).

6. *Surgical section of the corpus callosum is often asymptomatic.*

Walter Dandy went so far as to say in 1936:

> The corpus callosum is sectioned longitudinally . . . no symptoms follow its division. This simple experiment puts an end to all of the extravagant hypotheses on the functions of the corpus callosum.

Even more persuasive was the negative testing by Akelaitis (1944; 1944–1945) of patients who had callosal section. These results were admitted by Tomasch (1954,

1957), whose interest in the corpus callosum and anterior commissure led him to make his widely known estimates of their fiber content. Of the Akelaitis results he wrote:

> They showed very clearly and in accordance with some earlier authors like Dandy, Foerster, Meagher and Barre, whose material however was not so extensive, that the corpus callosum is hardly connected with any psychological functions at all.

Ethelberg (1951), after an extensive review, concluded:

> It may be premature to consider the recent clinical, surgical, and experimental observations an obituary of Liepmann's concepts as to the role played by the corpus callosum in the development of "true" apraxia. But they certainly suggest the need of some hesitance in accepting them. (p. 117)

About the same time, Fessard (1954) summarized the view which was then generally accepted:

> there is a great deal of data showing [that] sections of important associative white tracts such as the corpus callosum does not seem to affect mental performances. Other similar observations in man or animals are now accumulated in great number and variety. These results are so disturbing that one may be tempted to admit the irrational statement that a heterogeneous system of activities in the nervous system could form a whole in the absence of any identified liaison.

Fessard relied on the foregoing when he emphasized the importance of the brainstem reticular formation not only for wakefulness (Moruzzi and Magoun, 1949; Magoun, 1958) but also as a constituent of Penfield's proposal of a "centrencephalon":

> An area in which those mechanisms are to be found which are prerequisite to the existence of intellectual activity and prerequisite to the initiation of the patterned stream of efferent impulses that produce the planned action of the conscious man. [and] It may be suggested at once that the intralaminar systems of the thalamus and the reticular formation of the brain stem and the non-specific projection systems which have widespread connections with the cortex of both sides satisfy the definition. (Penfield, 1954, pp. 286–287)

When considering this anatomical description, it is well to recall that there are *two* thalami, as well as that the corpus callosum is now known to play an important role in both intellectual activity and planned action. The split-brain observations put a damper on enthusiasm for the "centrencephalon." In 1977, Doty asserted that they "speak quite strongly that the unification of consciousness is not at the brainstem level."

The "centrencephalon" will reemerge later when we consider the revisionists. Meanwhile, we now realize that most of the negative findings after surgical section of the corpus callosum resulted from two sources:

a. As already mentioned, when surgical section of the commissures is incomplete, a remarkable capacity for maintaining cross-communication between the hemispheres may be retained with commissural remnants, particularly when the part remaining is the splenium.

b. Negative findings often result from the use of inappropriate or insensitive testing techniques. What one finds depends on what one looks for; whereas Dandy (1936) said that callosal section produces no observable deficits, among his own patients was the one reported by Trescher and Ford to have hemialexia.

### The Two-Brain Theorists

In the nineteenth century, considering the cerebrum to be a "double brain" was espoused by Wigan (1844), Jackson (1874), and a multitude of others, as described in detail by Harrington (1987). Jackson (1874) advised:

> I use the word brain to include the cerebral hemisphere and the subjacent motor and sensory tract. I use the word encephalon to include all parts of the nervous system within the skull.

But such ideas, along with Liepmann's callosal concept, fell far out of favor by the end of World War I and remained so for many decades. A distinct reversal of opinion occurred during the 1960s, following publication of the "split-brain" experiments, and the concept of a "double brain" again became popular (Dimond, 1972).

Current views on callosal function are attributable in large part to studies, under the aegis of R. W. Sperry, of our patients with surgical section of the cerebral commissures. These patients are indeed without, in Dandy's words, "any deficits" in the ordinary social situation, or even as determined by most of a routine neurological examination (Bogen and Vogel, 1975; Botez and Bogen, 1976). In specially devised testing situations, however, they can be shown to have a wide variety of deficits in interhemispheric communication (Gazzaniga et al., 1962, 1963, 1965, 1967; Gazzaniga, 1970; Sperry, 1968, 1970, 1974, 1982; Sperry and Gazzaniga, 1967; Sperry et al., 1969; Zaidel, 1973, 1983; Bogen, 1987; Zaidel et al., 1990b).

The split-brain humans confirmed in a particularly striking way the importance of commissural fibers for interhemispheric communication. But the essential fact had already been described in animal experiments during the 1950s, initiated by Myers and Sperry (1953, 1958; Myers, 1956). It was found that each hemisphere of a cat or monkey could learn solutions to a problem different from (even conflicting with) the solutions learned by the other hemisphere. This made it clear that effective functioning could occur independently in the two hemispheres. As Sperry (1961) put it:

> Callosum-sectioned cats and monkeys are virtually indistinguishable from their normal cagemates under most tests and training conditions. [But] if one studies such a "split-brain" monkey more carefully, under special training and testing conditions where the inflow of sensory information to the divided hemispheres can be separately restricted and controlled, one finds that each of the divided hemispheres now has its own independent mental sphere or cognitive system—that is, its own independent

perceptual, learning, memory and other mental processes . . . it is as if the animals
had two separate brains. (p. 1749)

It is important to understand that the duality of minds seen after hemisphere disconnection is not an inference solely from certain striking clinical cases, and a handful
of surgical patients, as sometimes said. Split-brain experiments have been carried out
with many different species by hundreds of investigators around the world. They are
virtually unanimous in concluding that each of the disconnected hemispheres can act
independently of the other (Bogen, 1977). Let us consider two examples of variation
on the basic idea that the cerebrum is double.

1. One of the most reliable signs of a bilateral prefrontal lobectomy in monkeys is
   their inability to do delayed-alternation tasks (Jacobsen and Nissen, 1937; Mishkin,
   1957; Iversen and Mishkin, 1970; Pribram et al., 1977; Markowitsch et al., 1980;
   Fuster, 1989; Sawaguchi and Goldman-Rakic, 1991). It was long supposed that this
   inability might be explained as the result of the hyperactivity and/or distractibility which is also characteristic of such monkeys. This supposition can be tested in
   a split-brain monkey, where each hemisphere can function separately. If one
   hemisphere has a prefrontal lobectomy, it performs poorly on the delayed-alternation task. This poor performance by the lobectomized hemisphere is not accompanied by hyperactivity or distractibility. Apparently, the remaining frontal lobe
   keeps the monkey quiet and attentive even though the intact hemisphere is not
   participating in the recognition of various stimuli or the evaluation of their significance (Glickstein et al., 1963).
2. A truly dramatic example occurs when only one hemisphere of a split-brain monkey has had a temporal lobectomy. A bitemporal monkey manifests the Klüver-
   Bucy syndrome, which includes difficulties in the visual identification of objects,
   orality (often mouthing inappropriate objects), hypersexuality, hypomotility, and
   tameness in the presence of humans. When the intact hemisphere can see, the
   split-brain rhesus monkey behaves in the usual rhesus manner, manifesting a fierce
   fear of humans. But if only the temporal lobectomized hemisphere receives the
   visual information, the split-brain animal acts like a Klüver-Bucy monkey, particularly as regards its relative tameness. When this was reported (Downer, 1961),
   1962) it was so amazing that many of us doubted it, although we were already
   convinced of the duality of mind in the split-brain monkey. Little room for doubt
   remains because this finding has, in its essentials, been reported by a number of
   other investigators (Bossom et al., 1961; Barrett, 1969; Horel and Keating, 1972;
   Doty et al., 1971, 1973; Doty and Overman, 1977).

It was knowledge of the split-brain experiments in laboratory animals that alerted
Geschwind and Kaplan (1962) to the possibility of a hemisphere-disconnection syndrome in the human. When a suitable patient appeared, they searched for the disconnection effects. From a complex, evolving picture, they teased out the relevant
phenomena.

One of the first things Geschwind and Kaplan found was that although the patient
wrote clearly with his right hand, he wrote "aphasically" with his left (and was aston-

ished by what he had written). Among other things they found that an object placed in his left hand was handled correctly and was correctly retrieved by feel, but it could not be named; nor could it be retrieved by feel with his right hand. In their words:

> . . . He behaved as if his two cerebral hemispheres were functioning nearly autono-mously. Thus, we found that so long as we confined stimulation and response within the same hemisphere, the patient showed correct performance.

In contrast, the patient performed incorrectly when the stimulus was provided to one hemisphere and the response required from the other. They concluded that the best explanation was to suppose that his hemispheres were disconnected by a lesion of the corpus callosum. Their anatomic prediction was eventually confirmed by autopsy. And their conclusions were soon amply confirmed by the surgical cases whose description we will come to further on.

Liepmann's callosal concept has been resurrected. There is now widespread accep-tance of an idea long ignored. It is an interesting example of what Kuhn (1962) called a paradigm shift. Geschwind (1974) wrote:

> What was astonishing was the fact that this work had been so grossly neglected . . . that important confirmed scientific observations could almost be expunged from the knowledge of contemporary scientists.

As Harrington (1987) put it, ways of thinking about the brain (i.e., laterality and duality) which seem natural enough now had "vanished from the working world view" for nearly 50 years. Chapter 9 of her book is devoted to the causes of this half-century eclipse. These included "neurology's rediscovery of the 'whole'" led by Marie (1906), Head (1926), Goldstein (1939), and, in the laboratory, Lashley (1929, 1951). She is particularly critical of Henry Head, whose highly selective reference to Jackson "borders on intellectual dishonesty." Concurrent was a "trend toward psy-chologism in psychiatry" including the work of Bleuler (1911) and, especially, Freud.

Geschwind has suggested in correspondence that there was a widespread revulsion against attempts to link brain to behavior, associated with the rise of psychoanalysis; and he had another, sociological explanation:

> Henry Head had been shrewd enough to point out that much of the great German growth of neurology had been related to their victory in the Franco-Prussian war. He was not shrewd enough to apply this valuable historical lesson to his own time and to realize that perhaps the decline of the vigor and influence of German neurology was strongly related to the defeat of Germany in World War I and the shift of the center of gravity of intellectual life to the English-speaking world, rather than necessarily to any defects in the ideas of German scholars. (Geschwind, 1964)

But there were other factors. One thing missing was a widespread conviction that the essential facts could be observed repeatedly in humans under controlled, pro-spective circumstances. Such observations (to be described below) are possible with persons who have had a complete cerebral commissurotomy or, short of that, a com-plete callosotomy.

Meanwhile, it is useful to mention briefly some objections to the two-brain view which have been resurrected in the past few years.

### The Revisionists

The two-brain view, recognizing a significant degree of cerebral hemisphere independence (including in cats and monkeys) and conspicuous hemispheric specialization (in most humans) caught the public eye in the 1970s. The media pushed the popularity of the "right brain/left brain" story to fad proportions reaching an almost frenzied peak by 1980. This led not only to simplistic degradation, probably inevitable with popularization, but also to exploitation. Commercially motivated entrepreneurs promised to educate peoples' right hemispheres in short order, sometimes even overnight, ignoring the lengthy, arduous training necessary for *any* mature competence. This was followed by a reaction or backlash which itself served to confuse nonspecialists hoping to distinguish replicable fact from speculation. Much of the reaction involved the debunking of extravagant claims. Some of it, however, was more revisionist. That is, there are some writers who have challenged the basic observations by emphasizing limitations on hemispheric independence and by pointing out the variable degree of hemispheric specialization, as well as by emphasizing the obvious point that for intact individuals, most activities involve hemispheric interaction. A notable example is the recent extreme denigration of hemispheric specialization by Efron (1990).

By now, it may be useful to offer some evaluation of the backlash, concentrating on the revisionist views of a few acknowledged experts who are familiar with the technical details. Such evaluations are presented in the final sections of this chapter. Since they presuppose some familiarity with both clinical and experimental data, these will be presented next.

## THE ACUTE DISCONNECTION SYNDROME FOLLOWING COMPLETE CEREBRAL COMMISSUROTOMY*

During the first few days after complete cerebral commissurotomy, the patients commonly respond reasonably well with their right limbs to simple commands. But they are easily confused by three- or even two-part commands, each part of which is obviously understood. The patients often lie quietly and may seem mildly "akinetic," although cooperating when stimulated. There is sometimes an "imperviousness" resembling that often seen with naturally occurring genu lesions. The patients are often mute even when willing to write short (usually one-word) answers. (Bogen, 1976). The left-sided akinesia to verbal command is usually severe and can be mistaken for hemiplegia. Left-side weakness, or focal clonic seizures, in the first week or so due to edema from retraction of the right hemisphere sometimes confounds the picture. The neurologic status is difficult to evaluate not only because the seemingly flaccid and unresponsive left extremities may exhibit coordinated movements, but

---

* As observed in right-handers operated from the right side.

also because, as the patient improves, there may be competitive movements between the left and right hands. The patients commonly have bilateral Babinski signs as well as bilaterally absent superficial abdominal reflexes, possibly from the diaschistic shock to both hemispheres from the section of so many nerve fibers.

Well-coordinated but repetitive reaching, groping, or grasping with the left hand sometimes resembles a grasp reflex; grasp reflexes may actually be present bilaterally for a day or two. When forced grasping cannot be elicited (by inserting two fingers into the patient's palm from the ulnar side, with some distal stroking), it is nevertheless possible in most cases to demonstrate a proximal traction response (PTR); that is, the patient is unable to relax the hand grip when the examiner pulls so as to exert traction on the elbow and shoulder flexors (Twitchell, 1951). Left-arm hypotonia, left-arm PTR, bilateral Babinski responses, and mutism were regularly observed in our cases. Data from daily observations on some of our patients have been published elsewhere (Bogen, 1987). There is considerable variation from one patient to another. At one extreme was our first patient, (WJ) who had grossly apparent right frontal atrophy, was oldest at the time of brain injury (age 30), the oldest at time of operation (45), and subsequently showed the most severe apraxic and related symptoms. Least affected was LB, a 13-year-old boy (see Bogen et al., 1988, for magnetic resonance imaging (MRI) status). LB had the smoothest postoperative course, relatively little brain damage before surgery, early date of brain injury (birth), was youngest at time of operation, and his left-hand apraxia was minimal. Following a similar operation by others, further variation has been encountered (Wilson et al., 1975, 1977; McKeever et al., 1981; Holtzman et al., 1981; Ferguson et al., 1985; Reeves, 1991; Sass et al., 1988, 1992), but the crucial observations have been the same. The following section describes findings common to split-brain patients subsequent to their recovery from the acute syndrome. (Left-handers are excluded.)

## THE CHRONIC, STABILIZED SYNDROME OF HEMISPHERE DISCONNECTION

The testing of split-brain patients in the psychology laboratory has become progressively more sophisticated in the past three decades. It is often complex, sometimes subtle, and typically unfamiliar, even to otherwise experienced neuropsychologists (Zaidel et al., 1990b). Emphasized here are approaches most readily available to the clinician.

### Overall Effects

Within a few months after operation, the symptoms of hemisphere disconnection tend to be compensated to a remarkable degree. In personality, in social situations, and in most of a routine neurologic exam the patient appears much as before. However, with appropriate tests using lateralized input the disconnected hemispheres can be shown to operate independently to a large extent. Each of the hemispheres appears to have its own learning processes and its own separate memories, many of which are largely inaccessible to the other hemisphere. Certain memory deficits sometimes present after commissural section are discussed further in the final section on remaining problems.

## Visual Effects

Visual material can be presented selectively to a single hemisphere by having the patient fix his gaze on a projection screen or a TV monitor onto which pictures of objects or symbols appear in either right, left, or both visual half-fields, using exposure times of $\frac{1}{10}$ second or less. The patients can read and describe material of various kinds in the right half-field at a level substantially the same as before surgery. When stimuli are presented to the left half-field, however, the patients usually report that they see "nothing" or sometimes "a flash of light."

Simpler procedures often succeed. For example, with the patient fixating on the examiner's nose, different numbers of fingers can be briefly presented in either hemifield; only the hand ipsilateral to that hemifield will consistently respond correctly. As pointed by John Sidtis (personal communication), one can briefly present various hand postures; correct imitation by the left hand (to left hemifield presentation) can occur even though the subject may deny having seen anything.

Inability to describe verbally left half-field stimuli includes hemialexia. That is, the subject cannot read individual words flashed to the left half-field. Hemialexia occurs not only in patients with complete callosotomy but also in patients with section only of the splenium (Trescher and Ford, 1937; Maspes, 1948; Gazzaniga and Freedman, 1973; Damasio et al., 1980; Sugishita et al., 1986; Sugishita and Yoshioka, 1987).

There is some apparent recovery over the years, much of which is attributable to semantic transfer; that is, the word is recognized by the right hemisphere as a symbol for something and this (often diffuse) semantic information transfers to the speaking left hemisphere which can then approximate the stimulus word. Indeed, if the set of stimuli is known and not too numerous, the diffuse semantic information may be used to identify the specific word (Sidtis et al., 1981a; Myers and Sperry, 1985; Cronin-Golomb, 1986b; Sugishita et al., 1986; Zaidel et al., 1990b).

## Auditory Suppression

Following cerebral commissurotomy, the right-handed patient readily identifies single words (and other sounds) if they are presented to one ear at a time. However, if *different* words are presented to the two ears simultaneously (so-called "dichotic listening"), mainly the words presented to the right ear will be reliably reported (Milner et al., 1968; Sparks and Geschwind, 1968; Springer and Gazzaniga, 1975; Gordon, 1975; Cullen, 1975; Zaidel, 1976, 1983; Efron et al., 1977; Henninger-Pechstedt, 1989; Zaidel et al., 1990a).

The large right-ear advantage is usually considered to be the result of two concurrent circumstances: (1) the ipsilateral pathway from the left ear (to the left, speaking, hemisphere) is suppressed by the presence of simultaneous but differing inputs, as it is in intact individuals during dichotic listening (Kimura, 1967; Murray and McLaren, 1990; Asbjørnsen et al., 1990). (2) The contralateral pathway from the left ear (to the right hemisphere) conveys information which ordinarily reaches the left (speaking) hemisphere by the callosal pathway, which has now been severed.

Although left-ear words are poorly reported, their perception by the right hemisphere is occasionally evidenced by appropriate actions of the left hand (Gordon, 1973).

With repeated testing, the ear asymmetry may decrease, particularly if the patient's attention is directed to the left ear or if the information load is reduced (Henninger-Pechstedt, 1986; Corballis and Ogden, 1988). Other relevant variables have been reviewed in detail by Sidtis (1988).

### Motor Function

Immediately after surgery all of our patients showed some left-sided apraxia to verbal commands such as "Wiggle your left toes," or "Make a fist with your left hand." The degree of left-hand (and left-foot) dyspraxia is subject to large individual differences. The left-limb dyspraxia is attributable to the simultaneous presence of two deficits: poor comprehension by the right hemisphere (which has good control of the left hand) and poor ipsilateral control by the left hemisphere (which understands very well). Subsidence of the dyspraxia can therefore result from two compensatory mechanisms: increased right-hemisphere comprehension of words and increased left-hemisphere control of the left hand. The extent of ipsilateral motor control can be tested by flashing to right or left visual half-field sketches of thumb and fingers in different postures, for the subject to mimic with one or the other hand. Responses are poor with the hand on the side opposite the visual input, simple postures such as closed fist or open hand being attainable after further recovery. As recovery proceeds, good ipsilateral control is first attained for responses carried out by the more proximal musculature. After several months, most of the patients can form a variety of hand and finger postures with either hand to verbal instructions, such as, "Make a circle with your thumb and little finger," and the like.

Subsidence of the apraxia continues so that eventually it is hardly in evidence. But even many years later, it can be demonstrated (Zaidel and Sperry, 1977; Trope et al., 1987).

The capacity of either hemisphere, and particularly the left hemisphere, to control the ipsilateral hand varies from one patient to another both in the immediate postoperative period and many years later. This, together with variations in right-hemisphere lexicons, may account for many of the discrepancies in descriptions of the callosal syndromes.

### Somesthetic Effects

The lack of interhemispheric transfer following brain bisection can be demonstrated with respect to somesthesis (including touch, pressure, and proprioception) in a variety of ways.

CROSS-RETRIEVAL OF SMALL TEST OBJECTS

Unseen objects in the right hand are handled, named, and described in normal fashion. In contrast, attempts to name or describe the same objects held out of sight in the left hand consistently fail. Despite the patient's inability to name an unseen object in the left hand, identification of the object by the right hemisphere is evident from appropriate manipulation of the item showing how it is used, or by retrieval of the same object with the left hand from among a collection of other objects screened from sight. Placing the collection of small objects on a paper plate usually works better than putting them into a bag. What distinguishes the split-brain patients from normal is that their excellent same-hand retrieval (with either hand) is *not* accompanied by ability to retrieve with one hand objects felt with the other.

CROSS-REPLICATION OF HAND POSTURES

Specific postures impressed on one (unseen) hand by the examiners cannot be mimicked in the opposite hand. Also, if a hand posture in outline form is flashed by tachistoscope to one visual half-field, it can be copied easily by the hand on that side but usually not by the other hand.

A convenient way to test for lack of interhemispheric transfer of proprioceptive information is as follows: the patient extends both hands beneath the opaque screen (or vision is otherwise excluded) and the examiner impresses a particular posture on one hand. For example, one can put the tip of the thumb against the tip of the little finger and have the other three fingers fully extended and separated (or the other three fingers can be kept close together, as the examiner wishes). The examiner than says, "Now make a fist—good—now put it back the way it was." Then the examiner says, "Keep your hand just the way it is and do exactly the same with your other hand." The patient with complete cerebral commissurotomy cannot mimic with the other hand a posture being held by the first hand. When confirming the presence of hemisphere disconnection, this procedure should be repeated with various postures and in both directions. In this way, one can establish quite clearly (in the absence of malingering) that there is a hemisphere disconnection.

INTERMANUAL POINT LOCALIZATION

After complete cerebral commissurotomy there is a partial loss of the ability to name exact points stimulated on the left side of the body. This defect is least apparent, if at all, on the face, and it is most apparent on the distal parts, especially the fingertips. This deficit is not dependent on language since it can be done in a nonverbal fashion and in both directions (right to left and vice versa). An easy way to demonstrate the deficit is to have the subject's hand extended palm up (again with vision excluded). One touches the tip of one of the four fingers with the point of a pencil, asking the patient to touch the same point with the tip of the thumb of the same hand. Repeating this maneuver many times produces a numerical score, about 100% in normals for either hand. In the absence of a parietal lesion, identification of any of the four fingertips by putting the thumb tip upon the particular finger can be done with great reliability. It can be done at nearly 100% level by the split-brain patient.

One then changes the task so that the fingertip is to be indicated, not by touching it with the thumb of the same hand but by touching the *corresponding* fingertip of the other hand with the thumb of that (other) hand. Sometimes the procedure should be demonstrated with the patient's hand in full view until the patient understands what is required. This cross-localization cannot be done by the split-brain patient at a level much better than chance (25%). Normal adults almost always do better than 90%. This test can be refined (to 12 points) by utilizing the volar surfaces of each of the three phalanges. Another refinement is to use a calibrated esthesiometer (Volpe et al., 1979).

It is of interest that an incompetence to cross-localize or cross-match has been found in young children (Galin et al., 1977, 1979; but cf. Pipe, 1991) possibly because their commissures are not yet fully functioning (Yakovlev and Lecours, 1967; but cf. Brody et al., 1987; Baierl et al., 1988). Immaturity of transcallosal inhibition has been suggested as the source of unnecessary duplication (mirror movements) during simple reaching (Lehman, 1978).

### Right-Hemisphere Verbal Comprehension

Auditory comprehension of words by the disconnected right hemisphere is suggested by the subject's ability to retrieve with the left hand various objects if they are named aloud by the examiner. Visual comprehension of printed words by the right hemisphere is often present, especially short, high-frequency words. For example, after a printed noun is flashed to the left visual half-field, the subjects are typically able to retrieve with the left hand the designated item from among an array of objects hidden from view. Control by the left hemisphere in these tests is excluded because incorrect verbal descriptions given by the subject immediately after a correct response by the left hand show that only the right hemisphere knew the answer.

Right-hemisphere language capabilities in right-handers are distinctly more in evidence when the left hemisphere has been removed. Indeed, if the left hemisphere is removed (or was severely incapacitated) in infancy, these capabilities may seem nearly normal (Smith, 1974; Kohn and Dennis, 1974; Smith and Sugar, 1975; Dennis and Whitaker, 1976). When the left-hemisphere disease appears later in childhood, the language retained is correspondingly less (Gott, 1973a; Patterson et al., 1989). Even after hemispherectomy for tumor of the normally developed, middle-aged adult there can remain a bit of verbal output with excellently articulated repetition of stereotyped phrases, as well as lyrics while singing (Burklund and Smith, 1977).°

When the left hemisphere is present and relatively intact, most linguistic abilities of the disconnected right hemisphere are largely absent, or suppressed. The disconnected right hemisphere's receptive vocabulary can grow considerably over the years, reaching levels comparable with the vocabulary of a 10-year-old or even a 16-year-old. But this impressive single-word comprehension is rarely accompanied by speech. In a broad spectrum of patients, the most extreme cases to date of right-hemisphere language ability in right-handed (and left-hemisphere speaking) split-brain subjects are two (PS and VP, called POV in Ferguson et al., 1985) thought to have right-hemisphere speech. Both VP and PS did not have the anterior commissure cut (LeDoux et al., 1977a; Sidtis et al., 1981a; McKeever et al., 1982; Myers, 1984; Gazzaniga, 1988). Also relevant is that in VP (less likely in PS) there are small callosal remnants (Gazzaniga et al., 1985).

°Particularly convincing is a movie (obtainable from A. Smith) illustrating this point.

In addition to the rarity of speech, right-hemisphere language in the split-brain subject has other limitations, syntactic ability being rudimentary at best (Zaidel, 1973, 1977, 1978a,b). Studying a few cases in great depth for over ten years, Zaidel concluded:

> Whereas phonetic and syntactic analysis seem to specialize heavily in the left hemisphere, there is a rich lexical structure in the right hemisphere. The structure of the right hemisphere lexicon appears to be unique in that it has access to a severely limited short term verbal memory, and it has neither phonetic encoding nor grapheme-to-phoneme correspondence rules. . . . [this] represents the limited linguistic competence that can be acquired by a nonlinguistic, more general purpose (or other purpose) cognitive apparatus. (Zaidel, 1978a)

The language capabilities of the right hemisphere, including right-hemisphere influences on linguistic processing by the left hemisphere have been extensively investigated.[*]

### Right-Hemisphere Dominance

Following commissurotomy, we can test each hemisphere separately. It is thus possible to demonstrate in a positive way those things which each hemisphere can do better than the other, rather than inferring what a hemisphere does from the loss of function when it is injured.

A praxic or "manipulative" superiority of the right hemisphere appeared in the ability of right-handed split-brain patients to do better with their left hands than with their right hands in copying certain geometric figures (Bogen and Gazzaniga, 1965; Bogen, 1969a; Kumar, 1977) or doing block design problems (Bogen and Gazzaniga, 1965; Bogen, 1970; LeDoux et al., 1977b).

Right-hemisphere perceptual superiority was shown in a variety of ways (Levy et al., 1972; Sperry, 1974; Corballis and Sergent, 1988). These included more reliable tactile retrieval of certain shapes not easily nameable (e.g., Milner and Taylor, 1972), the ability to match parts of objects to the entire object (Nebes, 1974), and the ability to use perspective cues to assist in accurate perception (Cronin-Golomb, 1986c). There have also been shown in split-brain patients an apparent right-hemisphere advantage for complex pitch discrimination (Sidtis, 1988) and for an associative auditory function, harmonic progression (Tramo and Bharucha, 1991).

A conceptual superiority of the right hemisphere for geometric invariance was suggested by the results of Franco and Sperry (1977). They found in five patients (LB,

[*]Smith, 1966; Gazzaniga and Sperry, 1967; Gazzaniga and Hillyard, 1971; Levy et al., 1971; Burklund and Smith, 1977; Sasunuma et al., 1977; Kinsbourne, 1971, 1975; Zurif and Ramier, 1972; Teng and Sperry, 1973; Caplan et al., 1974; Glass et al., 1975; Brown and Jaffe, 1975; Carmon et al., 1977; Moscovitch, 1976; Selnes, 1976; Rogers et al., 1977; Winner and Gardner, 1977; Ornstein et al., 1979; Ludlow, 1980; Lassen and Larsen, 1980; Cavalli et al., 1981; Roland et al., 1981; Kimura et al., 1982; Landis et al., 1982; Gazzaniga, 1983; Lecours et al., 1983; Segalowitz, 1983; Myers, 1984; Chernigovskaya and Deglin, 1986; Byrne and Gates, 1987; Landis and Regard, 1988; Ogden, 1988; Papanicokou et al., 1988; Kutas et al., 1988; Patterson et al., 1989; Corina, 1989; Baynes, 1990; Metter et al., 1990; Poizner et al., 1990; E. Zaidel, 1990; Corina et al., 1991; Levin et al., 1989a; Taylor, 1991; Brownell et al., 1992; Anderson et al., 1992; and relatively comprehensive: Code, 1987.

NG, CC, RY, and NW) that as the matching problem shifted successively from Euclidean to affine to projective to topologic invariance, the right-hand performance successively fell off, while the left-hand performance was little affected, maintaining a significant superiority. On a number of tests of abstract thinking, the left hemisphere has been clearly superior (Nass and Gazzaniga, 1987), whereas on others the hemispheres seemed equally proficient (Cronin-Golomb, 1986b).

The hemispheric specialization data from split-brain patients confirmed in a different way many of the conclusions inferred from lateralized lesions, and stimulated in turn extensive testing of intact (i.e., "normal") subjects. For those particularly interested, there is an enormous literature on hemispheric specialization including a number of books and reviews mainly by psychologists (Newcombe, 1969; Milner, 1971, 1975, 1980; Krashen, 1976; Mosidze et al., 1980; Bryden, 1982; Segalowitz, 1983; Bradshaw and Nettleton, 1983; Springer and Deutsch, 1981; Young, 1983; Corballis, 1983, 1991; Trevarthen, 1984; Benson and Zaidel, 1985; Campbell et al., 1986; Butler, 1988; Sugishita, 1990; and reasonably recent and comprehensive: Beaton, 1985).

## CLINICAL TESTING FOR CALLOSAL SIGNS AND SYMPTOMS

Following are some abbreviated descriptions of what one can look for using simple maneuvers in the clinic, when hemisphere disconnection is suspected. The descriptions apply to right-handers. In left-handers the situation is rarely a simple reversal; usually it is quite complex, as can be seen in the case histories described in the literature (Liepmann, 1990; Hécaen and Ajuriaguerra, 1964; Botez and Crighel, 1971; Tzavaras et al., 1971; Heilman et al., 1973; Schott et al., 1974; Michel and Schott, 1975; Aptman et al., 1977; Hirose et al., 1977; Poncet et al., 1978; Herron, 1980; Hécaen et al., 1981; Gur et al., 1984; Joseph, 1986). Probably relevant are variations in size of the callosal isthmus, which seems to be the part of the corpus callosum most apt to vary with respect to sex and/or handedness (Witelson, 1985; O'Kusky et al., 1988; Witelson and Goldsmith, 1990; Habib et al., 1991; Zaidel et al., 1991).

### *History*

Discussions with the patient, relatives, or nursing personnel often disclose sensations or occurrences suggesting hemisphere disconnection. As usual, if one is aware of what can sometimes happen, one is more apt to elicit the relevant report.

DISSOCIATIVE PHENOMENA

If the extracallosal damage is small enough that each hemisphere can retain a capacity for integrative behavior (as distinguished from cases with dense hemiplegia, for example), conflicting actions may occur more or less simultaneously. The commonest of these (which is not very helpful because it often occurs in normal subjects) is a disparity between facial expression and verbalization. More meaningful is a dissociation between what the left hand is doing and what the patient is saying. Or there may be a dissociation between general bodily actions (rising, walking, etc.) and what is being done by either hand or what is being said.

One suspects a conversion hysteria when dissociative phenomena occur. But such dissociations have occurred sufficiently often following callosal section in animals (Trevarthen, 1965) and in humans with cerebral commissurotomy, as well as in naturally occurring cases, that they should arouse suspicion of hemisphere disconnection. Indeed, there may be some substance to the notion that such conative or volitional ambivalence, when it occurs in normal subjects, might be attributable, on some occasions at least, to altered information transfer by anatomically intact commissures (Galin, 1974; Hoppe, 1977; Ross and Rush, 1981).

In contrast with volitional ambivalence, emotional ambivalence (such as the report by the patient of possessing two conflicting internal feelings simultaneously) has not been a symptom of commissurotomy nor of most reported natural cases. Indeed, individuals with cerebral commissurotomy are *less* apt than normal individuals to discuss their feelings, conflicting or otherwise (Hoppe and Bogen, 1977). This condition, callosal alexithymia (TenHouten et al., 1986), suggests a defect in right-to-left callosal conduction (Speedie et al., 1984; Klouda et al., 1988).

*Intermanual conflict.*   The dissociative phenomenon most clearly identifiable with hemisphere disconnection is intermanual conflict, in which the hands act at cross purposes. Almost all of our complete commissurotomy patients manifested some degree of intermanual conflict in the early postoperative period. For example, a few weeks after one patient (RY) underwent surgery, his physiotherapist said, "You should have seen Rocky yesterday—one hand was buttoning up his shirt and the other hand was coming along right behind it undoing the buttons!" The following example is excerpted from my follow-up examination in February 1973 of another patient (AM):

> The most interesting finding in the entire examination is the frequent occurrence of well-coordinated movements of the left arm which are at cross-purposes with whatever else is going on. These sometimes seem to occur spontaneously, but on other occasions are clearly in conflict with the behavior of the right arm. For example, when attempting a Jendrassik reinforcement, the patient reached with his right hand to hold his left but the left hand actually pushed his right hand away. While testing finger-to-nose test (with the patient sitting), his left hand suddenly started slapping his chest like Tarzan.

Similar phenomena have been observed after callosotomy by others (Wilson et al., 1977; Ferguson et al., 1985; Bogen, 1985; Reeves, 1991; Sass et al., 1991) as well as by Akelaitis, (1944–1945) who called it "diagonistic dyspraxia." And the phenomenon has been described in many individual case reports of callosal infarcts or tumors (Fisher, 1963; Schaltenbrand, 1964; Joynt, 1977; Barbizet et al., 1978; Beukelman et al., 1980; Sine et al., 1984; Watson and Heilman, 1983; Levin et al., 1987; Degos et al., 1987; Tanaka et al., 1990; Schwartz et al., 1991; Della Sala et al., 1991).

Intermanual conflict usually subsides soon after callosotomy, probably because of other integrative mechanisms supplementing or replacing commissural function. In rare cases it may persist for years, for reasons as yet poorly understood (Ferguson et al., 1985; Reeves, 1991). When it occurs, the phenomenon is quite striking, and probably pathognomonic.

*The alien hand.* Related to intermanual conflict is what Brion and Jedynak (1972) called, "la main étrangère." This is a circumstance in which one of the patient's hands, usually the left hand in the right-handed patient, behaves in a way which the patient finds "foreign," "alien," or at least uncooperative. Even our youngest patient (LB), who had no long-term appreciable apraxia to verbal command, manifested this alienation three weeks after surgery: while doing the block design test unimanually with his right hand, his left hand came up from beneath the table and was reaching for the blocks when he slapped it with his right hand and said, "That will keep it quiet for a while." Among our patients it has been most persistent in a subject (NW) with a rather flamboyant personality which we believe contributed to her frequent complaints about "my little sister" in referring to whoever or whatever it was that made her left hand behave peculiarly. And it may be that when the "alien hand" accompanies callosal tumors or infacts, some predisposing personality feature could play a part, particularly since so many patients with callosal lesions do not emphasize this problem. However, even Rocky, a rather stolid fellow, complained for several years of an inability to get his left foot to go in the same direction as the rest of him. This may be related to the surgical retraction in his case, since evidence has been steadily accumulating that the alien hand, to be persistent, depends upon mesial frontal cortical dysfunction (Goldberg et al., 1981; McNabb et al., 1988; Banks et al., 1989; Leiguarda et al., 1989; Starkstein et al., 1990; Feinberg et al., 1992; and Tanaka et al., 1990, which includes nine more references in Japanese). Della Sala et al. (1991) point out that such patients rarely deny that the troublesome hand belongs to them; hence, they prefer the term "anarchic hand." They suggest that, in its persistent form, it results from a loss of inhibition originating in mesial frontal cortex (presumably of actions organized or "programmed" elsewhere). This can help us understand anarchic behavior of *either* hand, or even both hands (Mark et al., 1991).

*Autocriticism.* There is a related phenomenon, emphasized by Brion and Jedynak (1975), which they called "l'autocritique interhémisphérique." They refer to the fairly frequent expressions of astonishment by the patient with respect to the capacity of the left hand to behave independently. The patient may say, when the left hand makes some choice among objects, that "my hand did that," rather than taking the responsibility. A patient was described by Sweet (1945) as saying, "Now you want me to put my left index finger on my nose." She then put that finger into her mouth and said, "That's funny; why won't it go up to my nose?" (p. 88).

Split-brain patients soon accept the idea that they have capacities of which they are not aware, such as left-hand retrieval of objects not nameable. They may quickly rationalize such acts, sometimes in a transparently erroneous way (Gazzaniga and LeDoux, 1978). But even many years after operation, the patients will occasionally be surprised when some well-coordinated or obviously well-informed act has just been carried out by the left hand. This is particularly common under conditions of continuously lateralized input (Zaidel, 1977, 1978b; Zaidel and Peters, 1981), but it occurs even in social situations:

In the summer of 1989, LB (then 24 years postop) was having lunch between test-ing sessions with two investigators. One of them asked about his attitude toward his left hand. He replied, "I hardly ever use it." The other (Bogen) then pointed out that he was, at that moment, holding aloft a cup of juice in his left hand and had just taken a drink from the cup. "Sure enough," he said, looking at it, "I guess it is good for something."

*Signs of release from frontal control.*   We can distinguish behaviors of increasing complexity and/or appropriateness in the affected (but nonparetic, nonataxic) upper limb. Relatively simple is forced grasping. However, there may also be groping move-ments which, if followed by grasping upon contact, can be called "impulsive grasp-ing." Visual guidance may give an appearance of purposefulness, as in "magnetic apraxia" (Denny-Brown, 1958) or, when more complex, "utilization behavior" (Lhermitte, 1986; Lhermitte et al., 1986; La Plane et al., 1989; Shallice et al., 1989; Shallice and Burgess, 1991). Frontal infarction (or transient dysfunction), even if insufficient to cause forced grasping, may release synergic effects such as the PTR described above as a feature of the acute syndrome following complete callosotomy. A related but less severe deficit is an inability to keep the thumb extended while exert-ing a forceful grip (Wartenberg, 1953). *Automatic* (i.e., reliably elicited by the exam-iner) actions should be distinguished from well-coordinated behavior which is *auton-omous*, that is, which occurs without obvious external stimulus (i.e., is "spontaneous"). The distinctions "exogenous vs. endogenous" and "induced vs. inci-dental" have also been offered. Behavior that is stereotyped and repetitive can be distinguished from well-directed movement sequences adapted to the surroundings of a particular moment. And any of the foregoing may be accompanied (or not) by verbal denial, simple recognition, elaborate rationalization, or even appreciation.

Forced grasping occurs about equally often with either the right hand or the left hand; it is usually a stereotyped response following regularly and immediately after the adequate stimulation; and it is typically a sign of contralateral frontal lobe dys-function, requiring no direct callosal involvement in the lesion. A nicely coordinated, clearly adaptive, verbally appreciated, autonomous behavior of the nondominant hand (as with the juice cup episode) seems reasonably attributable solely to the cal-losal disconnection. The phenomena between these extremes (including the alien or anarchic hand) depend upon varying combinations of various extents of callosal and mesial frontal damage, of either or both hemispheres.

### Examination

Most naturally occurring cases of hemisphere disconnection are in a process of recov-ery (as with a stroke) or are worsening (as with a tumor) or may be fluctuating (as with remitting vascular disease or fluctuating edema). Findings that are quite clear on one occasion may be doubtful at another time. Hence, repeated examinations at different times are most informative.

Various neighborhood signs can prevent the demonstration of disconnection signs. The imperviousness from certain bifrontal lesions may render the patient insuffi-ciently cooperative. Forced deviation of gaze, not uncommon with unilateral hemispheric involvement, can interfere. The anterior cerebral artery syndrome classically includes a unilateral crural (leg) weakness of the "pyramidal" type and/or a strong grasp reflex, uni- or bilateral. Such an abnormality (especially forced grasping) makes testing for disconnection quite difficult. Most neighborhood signs tend to subside after a stroke, with the emergence of a period during which disconnection signs can be demonstrated for a time, before compensation supervenes.

### UNILATERAL VERBAL ANOSMIA

Following complete cerebral commissurotomy, the patient is unable to name odors presented to the right nostril, even when they can be named quite readily when presented to the left nostril. This is not a defect of smell with the right nostril, since the patient can select, by feeling with the left hand, an object that corresponds to the odor, such as selecting a plastic banana or a plastic fish after having smelled the related odor (Gordon and Sperry, 1969). This has been confirmed in a case (including section of the anterior commissure) from the Dartmouth surgical series (Gazzaniga et al., 1975). Callosotomy without section of the anterior commissure did not affect smell (Risse et al., 1978). Naturally occurring commissural lesion cases await investigation (but see Zatorre and Jones-Gutman, 1991).

### DOUBLE HEMIANOPIA

Most clinicians do not have routinely available a tachistoscope or other means for lateralizing visual information. But the disconnection (if it includes the splenium) can sometimes be demonstrated with simple confrontation testing of the visual field. The patient is allowed to have both eyes open but does not speak, and is allowed to use only one hand (sitting on the other hand, for example). Using the free hand, the subject indicates the onset of a stimulus, such as the wiggling of the examiner's fingers. With such testing there may appear to be a homonymous hemianopia contralateral to the indicating hand (the patient reliably points to the right half-field stimulus with the right hand but not to a left half-field stimulus). When the patient is tested with the *other* hand there seems to be a homonymous hemianopia in the *other* half-field. Occasionally a stimulus in the apparently blind half-field (on the left with the right hand being used) will produce turning of the head and eyes toward the stimulus, and *then* the hand will point.

When the stimuli appear in both fields simultaneously, the patient, if free to do so, will often use both hands simultaneously, but if one hand is restrained, only one half-field will be indicated. This peculiar situation must be distinguished from the much more commonly occurring extinction or hemi-inattention deficits from a hemispheric lesion (commonly right parietal) such that the patient tends to indicate only one stimulus when the stimuli are in fact bilaterally present. An observable difference is that the double hemianopia is a symmetrical phenomenon (the deficit occurs on each side), whereas extinction or hemi-inattention is typically one-sided, more commonly for the left side. Another difference is that the double hemianopia is the result of a sharply defined projection system combined with the commissural disconnection. That is, it is thought to be a relatively primitive sensory loss. In contrast, the phenomenon of hemi-inattention is usually considered to be a higher-order derangement (Heilman and Watson, 1977; Weinstein and Friedland, 1977; Jeannerod, 1987; Bisiach and Vallar, 1988; Chamorro et al., 1990; Feinberg et al., 1990; Spinelli et al., 1990). For a further discussion of hemi-inattention, see Chapter 10, which covers the neglect syndrome.

Each hemisphere can exert a modicum of ipsilateral control, especially for gross arm movements. As a result, stimuli in the right half-field (seen only by the left hemisphere) may be pointed to when the patient is using only the left hand, and similarly for the left half-field stimuli when only the right hand is available. But such pointing is unreliable and inaccurate, as compared with the dependable response and precise localization possible when the patient is using the hand contralateral to the stimulated hemisphere.

Most patients eventually achieve a condition in which no field defect can be demonstrated by a casual confrontation technique. This condition apparently depends mainly upon the ability of each hemisphere to direct the head and eyes. For example, if the patient is instructed to point with the right hand and if the examiner then wiggles the fingers in the patient's left visual half-field, the patient's head and eyes quickly turn to the left and then the right hand points to the correct target.

If turning of the head is prevented, a leftward glance will suffice for the patient's need for a cue. Or the right hand may point to the left visual half-field as soon as it is apparent that there is no suitable stimulus in the right visual half-field. This "cheating" by the left hemisphere can often be detected by providing no stimulus at all. Furthermore, if stimuli are presented simultaneously in both visual half-fields, only the stimulus in the right half-field is described by the patient, that is, by the left hemisphere. There is usually no verbal response to the stimulus in the left visual half-field until the left hemisphere realizes that the patient's left hand is also in action, pointing to the left half-field stimulus.

After a patient has been tested repeatedly, so that the occurrence of bilateral stimuli can be anticipated, both stimuli may be identified by a single hand; if using the right hand, the patient will point first to the right and then to the left half-field. In those patients who have been frequently tested, the appearance of a stimulus in the left visual half-field is occasionally recognized in spite of our attempts to circumvent the various cross-cuing strategies. However, even in our patient who does the best (LB), performance on confrontation testing of visual fields is still distinguishable from normal.

When a patient has a left hemiplegia, one cannot prove that an apparent left hemianopia (when the patient is responding verbally or with right hand) is the result of a commissural lesion; but if threats in the left half-field produce wincing or flinching, failure to point to left half-field stimuli with the right hand is suggestive of a disconnection.

HEMIALEXIA AND ALEXIA WITHOUT AGRAPHIA

When the splenium is affected, it is sometimes possible to demonstrate a hemialexia by the brief presentations of cards, on which are printed letters or short words, in the left half-field. The patient is often unable to read a card presented this way, although he can readily read it when it is presented in the right half-field. Eye movements are usually too active for such simple testing methods; but hemialexia was, in fact, observed by such methods long before its demonstration by tachistoscopic presentation (Trescher and Ford, 1937).

Sometimes the combination of right hemianopia and splenial lesion results not only in alexia but, in addition, an inability to name objects in the left hemifield (Poeck, 1984).

It is necessary to show that the hemialexia is not merely a matter of a left hemianopia, for example by having the patient correctly retrieve objects which are briefly shown in the left half-field. Sometimes a patient can name objects in the left half-field although hemialexic in that half-field and reading normally in the right. Less reliable but suggestive is to see the patient point quickly (with the left hand) to stimuli when they appear in the left half-field, keeping in mind that detection and localization can sometimes occur in the affected hemifield of hemianopics, as a manifestation of "blindsight" (Weiskrantz, 1986; Ptito et al., 1987, 1991; Rafal et al., 1990; Cowey and Stoerig, 1991). Quite often the split-brain patient will manifest normal visual fields by perimetry and tangent screen examination (particularly if permitted to use both hands to indicate the appearance of the stimulus). There may be a partial homonymous defect in the left half-field caused by extension into the right hemisphere of the callosal lesion, but the defect would be insufficient to account for the hemialexia if it were not accompanied by a callosal lesion (Wechsler, 1972). Hemialexia has been intensively studied with both tachistoscopic and computerized techniques by Sugishita and co-workers (1986, 1987, 1991; see also Grüsser and Landis, 1991).

Left hemialexia, when combined with right homonymous hemianopia, results in the syndrome of alexia without agraphia. Stroke patients who can write but are unable to read, even what they have just written correctly to dictation, are not rare. This condition occurs in about 75% of right-handers with left posterior cerebral artery infarcts (De Renzi et al., 1987). This remarkable dissociation of reading from writing has been known for at least a century (Dejerine, 1892). It is usually explained as follows: Since such a patient usually has a right homonymous hemianopia resulting from a left occipital lobe lesion, nothing can be seen, much less read, in the right half-field. Hence, visual information can reach the left-hemisphere language zone only from the left half-field via the right occipital cortex and the splenium. In addition, another (or confluent) splenial lesion (usually present in such cases) has disconnected the right occipital cortex from the left hemisphere. According to this explanation, the left hemisphere still retains a competence to write to dictation but no longer has access to information arriving in the right occipital lobe from the left visual half-field (Foix and Hillemand, 1925b; Geschwind and Fusillo, 1966; Benson and Geschwind, 1969; Geschwind, 1970; Cumming et al., 1970; Assal and Hadj-Djilani, 1976; Ajax et al., 1977; Benson, 1977, 1979; Damasio, 1977).

As its proponents have recognized, there are some difficulties with this explanation. For example, after surgical section of the splenium leaving the anterior commissure intact, patients can often name objects or pictures of objects in the left half-field, showing that information can reach the language zone from left half-field (Iwata et al., 1974). Moreover, alexia without agraphia can sometimes occur without an accompanying loss of the right visual half-field (Ajax, 1967; Heilman et al., 1971; Goldstein et al., 1971; Greenblatt, 1973, 1990; Vincent et al., 1977; Damasio and Damasio, 1983; Henderson et al., 1985). And there occur cases of alexia without agraphia in which the splenium is likely to be largely intact (Wechsler et al., 1972; Hécaen and Gruner, 1975; Greenblatt, 1976; Staller et al., 1978; Holtzman et al., 1978; Bigley and Sharp, 1983; as well as a personal (Bogen) posttraumatic case with CAT scan lesion in the left temporoparietal region).

Some of the problems in explaining alexia without agraphia can be seen in the very first, famous case of Dejerine (1892). A 68-year-old man, "of above-average intelligence and culture," suffered a left occipital infarct. He was followed for four years, during which time he continued to manage his business affairs. During a number of different testing sessions he could write without error entire pages, none of which he could read. An accomplished musician and sight-reader, he readily learned difficult passages by ear following his stroke, but he could no longer read "a single musical note." Nor could he name a single written letter, but he readily named written numbers as well as real objects, and he could do arithmetic problems written on paper. Moreover, his hemianopia was not terribly dense, objects being obscure and gray in his right visual half-field. His callosal (splenial) lesion was quite small and was dismissed by Dejerine as irrelevant to the behavioral deficit.

Over 50 years ago, Nielsen (1946, p. 53) asserted that alexia without agraphia is typically caused by a lesion immediately below the left angular gyrus, "separating its cortex from both calcarine areas." He taught (as I recall from 1955) that neither a callosal lesion nor any field defect was essential.

Alexia without agraphia has been studied for nearly a century; it is still a puzzle. Part of the answer is, among other things, that reading is a multistage process that can be disturbed in a variety of ways (Hécaen and Kremin, 1976; Greenblatt, 1977; Landis et al., 1980; Henderson, 1986; Grüsser and Landis, 1991). This is discussed in Chapter 3.

AUDITORY SUPPRESSION

Following cerebral commissurotomy, the right-ear advantage for verbal stimuli present in most right-handers becomes so great as to be almost complete. Left-ear suppression or extinction also appears after right hemispherectomy or other right-hemisphere ablations or lesions (Curry, 1968; Schulhoff and Goodglass, 1969; Oxbury and Oxbury, 1970; Netley, 1972; Nebes and Nashold, 1980; Michel and Péronnet, 1982; Zaidel, 1983). Left-ear extinction has also been found in patients with lesions of the left hemisphere, if the lesions are fairly deep (where they are apt to interrupt commissural fibers). Since there is usually suppression of the right ear by left-hemisphere lesions, the suppression of the left ear by a left-hemisphere lesion has been called "paradoxical ipsilateral extinction" (Sparks et al., 1970). Further observations support the conclusion that, whether the lesion is in the left or the right hemisphere, if it is close to the midline the suppression of left-ear stimuli is probably attributable to interruption of interhemispheric pathways (Michel and Péronnet, 1975; Damasio and Damasio, 1979; Cambier et al., 1984; Rubens et al., 1985; Rao et al., 1989; Pujol et al., 1991).

Because paracallosal lesions can also result in right-ear extinction for nonverbal material such as complex pitch discrimination, it has been suggested that the so-called paradoxical loss would better be termed "callosal extinction" (Sidtis et al., 1989).

UNILATERAL (LEFT) IDEOMOTOR APRAXIA

Historically, the first described callosal symptom was unilateral ideomotor apraxia, by which we mean that in response to verbal command, the right-handed subject is unable to carry out with the left hand some behavior which is readily executed with the right hand. This ready execution demonstrates that the failure is not ascribable to a lack of understanding. It is also necessary to demonstrate that the inability is not attributable to either weakness (paresis) or incoordination (ataxia) in the left hand (Wilson, 1908; Nielsen, 1946; Denny-Brown, 1958; Hécaen and Gimeno Alava, 1960; Bogen, 1969a,b; Geschwind, 1975; Poeck et al., 1982).

Strength and coordination in the left hand can be demonstrated in various ways. The main problem is not to confuse an ideomotor (also called "ideokinetic") apraxia with the much more commonly occurring loss of dexterity which is called "kinetic dyspraxia" or "limb-kinetic dyspraxia" or "innervatory apraxia" or "melokinetic dyspraxia." Kinetic dyspraxia occurs in the left hand as a result of various right-hemisphere lesions causing a mild weakness, or a release of excessive grasping or groping tendencies that interfere with function. In the words of K. Poeck (personal communication), "There is no apraxia at all!" What many of us, including Poeck (1986), consider the hallmark of apraxia is the appearance of well-executed but incorrect movements. These so-called parapraxias are analogous to the paraphasias (incorrect sounds or entire words) which are so characteristic of much aphasic speech. (For another view, see Chapter 7.)

Nor should ideomotor apraxia be confused with "ideational apraxia" in which a sequence of movements is ineffective to some overall purpose in spite of adequate performance of individual movements. Ideational apraxia can be seen in either or both hands, often in association with linguistic deficit. It can result from a left-hemisphere lesion but usually is caused by diffuse brain disease. (For further discussion, see Chapter 7.)

The best way to demonstrate an absence of weakness or incoordination in the left hand is to see the patient carry out exactly the same behavior (which could not be carried out to verbal instruction) on some other occasion. Such behavior may either occur spontaneously or it may result from some different (nonverbal) instruction. The right-handed patient with callosal disconnection often cannot follow a verbal command such as "pretend you are turning a doorknob" or "pretend you are combing your hair" using the left hand. In contrast, the very same behavior may be readily executed when the patient is actually confronted with a real doorknob to turn, or given (into the left hand) some article whose use is to be demonstrated.

Another way to elicit well-executed movements is to request them to be done bilaterally; this works best if the movements of the two extremities are mirror images. If the examiner first asks the subject to carry out a request with the right hand and immediately thereafter makes the same request of the left hand there is often a correct response (Bogen and Vogel, 1975; Reeves, 1991). As Reeves (1991, p. 295) interpreted it:

> The nondominant hemisphere, perceiving the prosody of a command and the proximal movement of the dominant arm, copies what it has just seen the dominant arm do, leaving the novice examiner with the impression that the nondominant hemisphere has verbal language capability.

This pitfall can be avoided by routinely first requesting the movement of the left hand (in the right-hander).

Left-handed apraxia can sometimes be easily demonstrated simply by requesting a number of individual finger motions such as "stick out your little finger." When the patient is attempting to cooperate with the left hand, such a request may result in a parapraxis, or only in bewilderment on the patient's part; however, the left little finger is adroitly extended when one silently demonstrates the desired action. In the most pronounced cases, the disability may include such relatively crude acts as opening or closing the fist, or even whole arm movements such as saluting, waving goodbye, etc., when they are verbally requested.

A pronounced inability to perform certain movements in the left hand under the circumstances just described is strong evidence for a callosal lesion. One problem is that the dyspraxia is commonly accompanied by some weakness, because the naturally occurring callosal lesions often extend toward one or the other hemisphere. If the dyspraxia is accompanied by paresis or forced grasping, it can nonetheless be quite suggestive, especially when it is out of proportion to any weakness or incoordination simultaneously present.

UNILATERAL (LEFT) AGRAPHIA

Right-handers can write legibly, if not fluently, with the left hand. This ability is commonly lost with callosal lesions, especially (but not always) those which cause a unilateral apraxia (Gersh and Damasio, 1981). An inability to write to dictation is common with left-hemisphere lesions, but these almost always affect the right hand at least as much as they affect the left. The left hand may be dysgraphic because it is affected by a right-hemispheric lesion, such as a frontal lesion causing forced grasping. That the left dysgraphia is not simply attributable to an incoordination or paresis resulting from a right-hemisphere lesion can be established if one can demonstrate some *other* ability in the left hand requiring as much control as would be required for writing. One cannot expect to see spontaneous left-handed writing, since the right hemispheres of most individuals rarely possess sufficient language capacity for this. However, one can sometimes see the left hand doodling spontaneously, or one can ask the patient to use the left hand to copy various designs or diagrams. Here, as elsewhere, it is not so much the presence of a deficit but rather the *contrast* between certain deficits and certain retained abilities that is most informative.

Simple or even complex geometric figures can often be copied by a left hand that cannot write or cannot even copy writing previously made with the patient's own right hand (Bogen and Gazzaniga, 1965; Bogen, 1969a; Kumar, 1977; Zaidel and Sperry, 1977; Della Sala et al., 1991). Copying of block letters may be present when the copying of cursive writing is not; this may not be an example of printing with the left hand but rather a copying of geometric figures that happen also to have linguistic content. (For a further discussion of agraphia, see Chapter 4.)

One of the most convincing ways to demonstrate hemisphere disconnection is to ask the patient to feel with one hand and then to name various small, common objects, such as buttons, coins, large and small paper clips, safety pins, and such. When these are placed in the patient's hand, it is essential that vision be occluded. A blindfold is notoriously unreliable. It is better to have an assistant hold the patient's eyelids closed or to put a pillowcase over the patient's head for the brief testing session. For longer testing sessions, an opaque screen should be used.

Not only is unilateral anomia quite regular in its appearance following callosotomy, but it has also been quite persistent, whenever appropriately tested, for over 25 years. In addition to its regularity and its persistence, the demonstration of this sign requires a minimum of equipment and time, and the interpretation of results is usually quite clear. Of the many maneuvers developed in the laboratory to test split-brain patients, this is the principal one to be adopted as part of a routine neurological examination.

Patients with extensive callosal lesions are commonly unable to name or describe an object held in the left hand although they readily name objects held in the right hand. Sometimes a recovering patient will be able to give a vague description of the object but be unable to name it; in this case there can still be a contrast with the ability to readily name the object when it is placed in the right hand. After a patient with a callosal lesion (e.g., a callosally dissecting hemorrhage) has regained the ability to name objects in the left hand, this ability may extinguish (Mayer et al., 1988) with dichaptic stimulation, i.e., by placing an object in each hand simultaneously (Witelson, 1974).

To establish hemisphere disconnection, it is necessary to exclude other causes of unilateral anomia, particularly astereognosis (or even a gross sensory deficit) as may occur with a right parietal lesion. The best way to exclude astereognosis or tactile agnosia (Caselli, 1991; Tranel, 1991) is to show that the object has in fact been recognized even though it cannot be verbally identified or described. The most certain proof that the object has been identified is for the subject to retrieve it correctly from a collection of similar objects. Such a collection is most conveniently placed in a paper plate about 15 cm in diameter, around which the subject can shuffle the objects with one hand while exploring for the test object. Even without the evidence of correct retrieval, one can often reasonably exclude astereognosis by observing the rapid, facile, and appropriate manipulation of an object in spite of its unavailability to naming or verbal description.

In testing for anomia, one must be aware, in certain clever patients, of strategies for circumventing the defect. For example, the patient may drop an object or may manipulate it in some other way (such as running a fingernail down the teeth of a comb) to produce a characteristic noise by which the object can be identified. In the same vein, a subject may identify a pipe or some other object by a characteristic smell and thus circumvent the inability of the left hemisphere to identify, by palpation alone, an object in the left hand.

UNILATERAL (RIGHT) CONSTRUCTIONAL APRAXIA

By "constructional praxis" we mean the ability to put together a meaningful configuration such as an object (three dimensions) or a complex drawing (two dimensions). Constructional dyspraxia is the inability to organize several parts into a configuration despite a normal ability to handle or draw the individual parts (Benton, 1962; Benton and Fogel, 1962; Warrington, 1969; De Renzi, 1982a). Constructional dyspraxia can occur from lesions in either hemisphere; left lesions may result in an absence of some of the parts and in simplified versions of a model, and right-hemisphere lesions tend to result in inappropriate relationships among the parts, including a loss of perspective in drawings intended to represent three dimensions (Paterson and Zangwill, 1944; Warrington et al., 1966; Benton, 1967; Hécaen, 1969; Hécaen and Assal, 1970; Gainotti et al., 1977). See Chapter 8.)

Constructional apraxia can be quite prominent in the right hand of right-handers with callosal lesions. The simplest way to test for this is to ask the patient to copy with one hand (and subsequently with the other) various geometric figures. It is usually better to proceed from simple squares and triangles to more complex figures, eventually including drawings that represent three-dimensional objects. Drawing with a felt-tip pen is often easier than with a pencil.

Hemisphere disconnection (in a right-hander) is strongly suggested if the patient can copy designs better with the left hand (Yamadori et al., 1983). Of course, if a callosal lesion is accompanied by right-hemisphere involvement, the left hand may be paretic or ataxic so that the patient does no better with the left hand than with the right.

SPATIAL ACALCULIA

Because hemisphere disconnection (or a right-hemisphere lesion) can cause a right-hand disability for spatial forms, such a patient may have difficulties using pencil and paper to solve arithmetic problems (Dahmen et al., 1982; Levin, Goldstein, and Spiers, this volume). In our patients with complete cerebral commissurotomy, we usually observed some difficulty in doing written arithmetic following the operation, a deficit that progressively receded (Bogen, 1969a, p. 92). On a few occasions we were surprised to note that a patient would have difficulty in doing arithmetic on paper, whereas comparable problems could be done by mental calculation. This was a rather elusive phenomenon and was never pursued; that it was, in fact, a sign of hemisphere disconnection is suggested by the report of a similar situation in the case of a 41-year-old woman with a callosal hematoma associated with an (operated) anterior cerebral aneurysm (Brion and Jedynak, 1975).

It is rare to find a patient who can do arithmetic to verbal instruction but cannot do similar problems with pencil and paper despite adequate reading and writing skills; but the phenomenon is sufficiently dramatic and is of sufficient scientific interest that looking for it, in appropriate circumstances, can be worthwhile (Della Sala et al., 1991).

*Lack of somesthetic transfer.*   The foregoing signs of disconnection are mainly dependent upon hemispheric dominance—either left or right, depending upon the particular task. Even more convincing are disconnection signs appearing with tests for which there is little, if any, dominance. These include the transfer of somesthetic information, whether tactile, proprioceptive, or stereognostic. How to test for these was described above.

## THE REVISIONISTS REVIEWED

The section on historical background mentioned briefly the revisionist reaction to a variety of "right brain/left brain" excesses. The larger issues raised can now be discussed in more detail, in the light of the experimental and clinical evidence.

### Does Hemispheric Integration Require a Single, Central Integrator?

One challenge to the two-brain view is based on the normality of split-brain subjects' behaviors in social situations.

Sperry emphasized, as early as his Harvey Lecture (1968), that there continues to be an impressive degree of "mental unity." What are the physiological explanations? Severing the corpus callosum as well as anterior and hippocampal commissures leaves the cerebral hemispheres still multiply connected. In addition to humoral communication (via blood and cerebrospinal fluid) reminiscent of the hormonal integration available to plants, there are substantial neuronal interconnections. These are present in cerebellum, midbrain, pons, and both hypo- and subthalamus. (But direct connections are scarcely present between the thalami [Jones, 1985] which I believe to be a crucial consideration.) Following commissurotomy (and, to a large extent, callosotomy), the functions of other interhemispheric pathways are exposed to investigation; this has been a major focus of split-brain research since the mid 1970s (Trevarthen and Sperry, 1973; Kinsbourne and Smith, 1974; Levy and Trevarthen, 1976; Holtzman et al., 1981; MacKay and MacKay, 1982; Myers and Sperry, 1985; Cronin-Golomb, 1986a; Ramachandran et al., 1986; Luck et al., 1989; Ringo et al., 1991; Lewine et al., 1991; Lambert, 1991; Corballis, 1992).

The experimental results have been interpreted in two major ways: as evidence of interhemispheric communication or as evidence for a centrally located integrative capacity. The latter view has been espoused particularly by Sergent (1986, 1987, 1990, 1991). She reintroduced (1986, p. 368) the concept of a "centrencephalon" and has advocated (1990, p. 563) its "unifying and integrative role" as was proposed by Penfield (1954) and Fessard (1954), whom I have quoted above and to whom she refers. One way to understand the foregoing is to recognize that "interhemispheric communication" is an anatomicophysiologic term whose psychologic correlates need exploration. By contrast, the "centrencephalon" is a psychological construct based, as Fessard (1954, p. 202) put it, on our "experienced [conscious] integration." It is a con-

ception whose anatomicophysiologic bases need exploration; these anatomical con-
stituents clearly include the corpus callosum. One can begin with either the anatomic
or the psychologic, and then can look for answers. Where one starts depends upon
one's preexisting education and philosophy, or theology.

Another psychologically motivated suggestion is that bisecting the cerebrum
coronally rather than midsagittally is equally plausible, leaving an individual with a
posterior sensory mind and an anterior motor mind (Kinsbourne, 1982, 1988, 1991).
Carried further, this view even leads to the possibility of eight or more minds (Kinsbourne, 1991). Related to this are the proposals of Minsky (1988) and Gazzaniga
(1985) urging a multimodular or societal concept of brain, reminiscent of Fodor's
*Modularity of Mind* (1983). According to Fodor (1983), input (sensory) systems are
highly modular, emphasizing that they are "encapsulated," i.e., not subject to "top
down" or other outside influences (p. 66). By contrast, he takes the opposite tack with
respect to cognition saying, "in the case of central processes you get an approach to
universal connectivity" (p. 119) "[where] neural connectivity appears to go every
which way and the form/function correspondence appears to be minimal" (p. 118).
When considering these various modularity proposals it is well to keep in mind the
realities of cerebral anatomy.°

Relevant here is Fodor's (1975) assertion that a scientific psychology need take no
account of brain anatomy, any more than one needs to know the hardwiring of a
computer in order to understand the software. This outlook has been lucidly critized
on philosophical grounds by Churchland (1982). There is little need to detail the
defects of this outlook for neuroscientists. Suffice to note that diagnosing bugs in a
computer system commonly requires knowledge of both software *and* hardware.

Although for some years emphasizing modularity rather than duality, Gazzaniga
recently reaffirmed the opinion he espoused over 20 years ago. He is a co-author of a
paper by Luck et al. (1989) which describes a visual search experiment with two split-
brain humans, leading to the conclusion that "an independent focus of attention was
deployed by each hemisphere."

### Are There Specific Circuits for Consciousness?

The attitude taken toward the two-brain view depends partly upon certain psychological and/or philosophical presuppositions, including the belief that the corpus callosum can perfect hemispheric synchrony. (I have reviewed data elsewhere indicating that it does not; Bogen, 1990.) An important example of psychological
presupposition is the reliance upon introspection as a crucial criterion. Kinsbourne
(1988), having inveighed against such introspection shortly before (p. 248), went on
to assert that, although

> two awarenesses can coexist . . . *the intact individual's unified awareness precludes
> this.* . . . Awareness is a property of [distributed] neural networks, not of any partic-
> ular locus in the brain. (Kinsbourne, 1988, p. 252; italics added)

° An illuminating discussion of modularity is on pages 316–327 of Churchland and Sejnowski (1992).

We have here two different issues, both of long standing (Fessard, 1954). The first is, Is conscious awareness dependent upon specially dedicated circuits? An important example is the role in attention of nucleus reticularis thalami (NRT) for which evidence has steadily accumulated (Scheibel and Scheibel, 1966; Schlag and Waszak, 1970; Yingling and Skinner, 1977; Singer, 1977; Watson et al., 1981; Jones, 1985; Crick, 1984; Sherman and Koch, 1986; Rafal and Posner, 1987; Steriade and Llinás, 1988; La Berge, 1990).

Briefly, a physiologic mechanism for attention is ascribed to NRT because (1) each NRT envelops, in a thin layer, most of the ipsilateral thalamic nuclei, with the thalamocortical fibers passing through NRT, (2) NRT efferents terminate in the immediately underlying thalamic nuclei, and (3) NRT efferents are all GABAergic. The likelihood exists, therefore, that thalamocortical communication can be generally inhibited simultaneously with highly selective noninhibition; such localized gating could thus provide a mechanism for selective attention in cognition (see also Chapter 10).

Rather than specific circuits strategically located, there is the notion that consciousness can arise from sheer numerosity and complexity of neural connections (as in the delightful story by Primo Levi, 1990). The recurrent popularity of this view is no proof of its validity. And it is at odds with the view that specific functions are attributable to specific types of neuronal connections, although not in most cases with circumscribed loci.

In addition to favoring the "distributed" option, Kinsbourne raised a second issue when he expressed faith in "the intact individual's unified awareness." Others of us are less willing to rely on this subjective introspection and prefer a more anatomical view, emphasizing that the crucial anatomy (including NRT) exists in duplicate. Also important, as stressed by Doty (1989), is that the amygdalae have no direct interconnections. That the anatomy for conscious awareness is double is supported by behavior indicating consciousness at a typically human level not only in the right hemispheres of split-brain subjects but also the right hemispheres of individuals rendered globally aphasic and right hemiplegic either by left hemispherectomy in adulthood (Smith, 1966, 1974) or transiently by left carotid barbiturate injection (Rosadini and Rossi, 1967; Lesser et al., 1986; see also Levin et al., 1989).

### How Apt Is the Two-Brain View?

Variable and ambiguous use of the words "language" and "consciousness" has roiled and muddied discussions (and bystanders' understanding) of the human split-brain. But interpretation of the cat and monkey experiments, untrammeled by such verbigeration, remains clear: the cerebrum can sometimes function as if it were two brains, and only two, and only side by side.

The conclusion that conscious cognition could proceed separately, simultaneously, and differently in the two hemispheres of split-brain cats and monkeys incurred little dissent, indeed was generally acclaimed, in the 1960s. Dissent from this conclusion only became emphatic as similar claims were made for human beings, based upon the findings following cerebral commissurotomy for epilepsy. Emphatic dissent in the human case has various motivations. Zangwill (1974) among others has suggested "extrascientific considerations." Such considerations are explicit in Eccles's latest book (Eccles, 1989). He supposes that the nexus (he calls it the "liaison") between brain and the disembodied self occurs by alteration of "the probability field of neurotransmitter release" in cortical columns of the "neo-neocortical areas" of the human (and only human) left hemisphere.

From a theoretical point of view, it is important to keep in mind that there are no phenomena explainable on the one (or "whole") brain view that are not explainable on the two-brain view. In contrast, there are data which fit the two-brain view but are inexplicable on the one-brain view.

From a practical point of view there remains for clinicians the problem of to what extent hemispheric interaction is responsible for some of the deficits consequent to unilateral lesions. When one hemisphere is injured, both hemispheres can undergo readjustment, and so too can the ways in which they interact. When and how is it that a left-hemisphere lesion can cause a greater loss of verbal comprehension and/or a greater degree of orofacial apraxia than that which follows left hemispherectomy (Smith, 1974)? How is it that a right-hemisphere lesion can produce a dramatic denial of left hemispace (or left hemibody) seen neither with right hemispherectomy nor with the disconnected left hemispheres of split-brain patients (Joynt, 1977; Plourde and Sperry, 1984)?[*]

How is it that an individual with a right-hemisphere lesion can reliably choose the more intact of two pictures of houses, the left side of one being on fire, while simultaneously claiming, verbally, that the two pictures are identical (Marshall and Halligan, 1988; Bisiach and Rusconi, 1991)? If such observations could be made in hemispherectomized subjects, the two-brain view would be, for those observations, unnecessary. Meanwhile, the two-brain view, even if only suggestive for the foregoing, appears necessary to explain many of the effects previously described in the sections on split-brain syndromes.

## FURTHER EXAMPLES OF REMAINING PROBLEMS

### *Postcallosotomy Mutism*

Following complete section of the cerebral commissures, there is a mutism of variable duration during which the patient does not talk even when quite cooperative and able to write a word or two. I first thought this was simply a neighborhood sign, a partial form of akinetic mutism (without the akinesia) that resulted from retraction around the anterior end of the third ventricle during section of the anterior commissure (Cairns, 1952; Ross and Stewart, 1981; Lebrun, 1990). In some cases, transient mutism seems related to retraction of medial frontal lobe (Reeves, 1991; Fuiks et al., 1991). A more persistent mutism likely reflects anomalous (including bilateral) speech representation (Bogen and Vogel, 1975; Bogen, 1976; Sussman et al., 1983; Sass et al., 1990) Mutism may well be a disconnection sign, since I have now had a number of

---

[*]Contrasting with this result in humans with callosotomy and (especially) hemispherectomy is the observation that in monkeys the neglect produced by frontal arcuate gyrus ablation was *increased* by callosotomy (Watson et al., 1984).

patients with extensive retraction of either anterior third ventricle or mesial right frontal cortex or both, but whose commissural section spared the splenium and who did *not* have mutism. Rayport et al. (1983; and personal communication from Prof. S. Ferguson in 1991) observed in three of eight cases with staged callosotomy a marked decrease in spontaneous speech without paraphasia or comprehension deficit or inability to sing. Notable was the absence of any mutism after the first stage (rostrum, genu, and most of the trunk). The mutism appeared only after the second stage (splenium and remainder of the trunk). So it appears that one cause of mutism can be an interhemispheric conflict (possibly at a brainstem level) or from a bilateral diaschisis that affects speech much more than writing (Bogen, 1976; Ferguson et al., 1985).

Because of the differences in context, degree, and duration of postoperative mutism, it probably has different causes; I have discussed these in more detail elsewhere (Bogen, 1987). Whatever the various explanations for these postsurgical observations, clinical experience indicates that, when mutism occurs with naturally occurring callosal lesions, the disease process probably involves the anterior cingulate regions bilaterally (above the callosum) or the septal area (below the callosum). These patients, however, are usually also to some extent akinetic (cf. Heilman and Watson, 1991).

### The Anterior Commissure

Another unresolved problem is the role of the anterior commissure, both in the normal state and following callosal injury. Previously mentioned was the compensatory role of the anterior commissure in callosal agenesis and following splenial section. However, most of the syndrome seen after a complete cerebral commissurotomy is also seen (i.e., has not been compensated) after a callosotomy sparing the anterior and hippocampal commissures (Gazzaniga and LeDoux, 1978; McKeever et al., 1981). The lack of compensation is perhaps not surprising since the human anterior commissure is only ¹⁄₁₀₀ the size of the corpus callosum. On the other hand, we can appreciate how significant it might be when we consider the wealth of information conveyed over one optic nerve, the diameter of which is about the same as that of the anterior commissure. This question is complicated by the fact that the anterior commissure, with respect to size, seems to be one of the most variable structures in the brain; it may have as much as three or four times as great a diameter in some people as in others (Yamamoto et al., 1981; Demeter et al., 1988). In addition to these individual differences, there are phylogenetic differences in the anterior commissure; it seems to play a much greater role in interhemispheric transmission in monkeys than in cats (Hamilton, 1982). And one might expect it to be even more important (being larger) in humans, except that it is smaller relative to the corpus callosum (Foxman et al., 1986). The discrepancy between monkeys (transfer of learning by the anterior commissure) and humans (inability to compensate for callosotomy) remains unsettled. It may be the relatively smaller size, the cortical terminations may differ somewhat, and/or there may be postcallosotomy acquisition of function dependent on the tasks used to test monkeys, including the particular types of memory functions involved.

## Postcallosotomy Memory Deficit

It is not yet clear in which respects callosal disconnection contributes to memory deficits that sometimes follow commissural section (Zaidel and Sperry, 1974; LeDoux et al., 1977a; Milner, 1978; Campbell et al., 1981; Huppert, 1981; Gur et al., 1984; Novelly and Lifrak, 1985; Sass et al., 1988; Clark and Geffen, 1989; D. W. Zaidel, 1990; Milner et al., 1990; Reeves, 1991).

Some of the uncertainties are attributable to different kinds of memory testing. More important, I believe is the redundancy of memory circuitry so that several lesions are necessary to produce a severe deficit. An additional consideration is that how well something is remembered often depends upon its emotional significance or "affective load." Hence, dysfunction of regions important for affect such as the amygdalae (LeDoux, 1989, 1992; Aggleton, 1992) could result in memory deficits even if those regions are not directly responsible for either consolidation or recall.

Severe memory deficit in monkeys can be produced by section of the anterior commissure (with corpus callosum left largely intact) if this has been preceded by two other ablations: inferior temporal cortex on one side and amygdala-hippocampus on the other (Mishkin and Phillips, 1990). And section of the (much larger) corpus callosum could well cause memory problems when combined with other lesions, or even without them when good acquisition is dependent upon dual coding (Bryden and Ley, 1983; Paivio, 1990).

Experiments on monkeys have demonstrated *in each hemisphere* complex memory circuits such that multiple or extensive injury to both hemispheres, may be necessary to produce a severe memory deficit (Mishkin, 1982; Zola-Morgan et al., 1982; Zola-Morgan and Squire, 1990; Murray, 1992) (see Chapter 15).

The literature on the fornices (e.g., Garcia-Bengochea and Friedman, 1987) has left me with the impression not only that injury to a single fornix is insufficient to cause perceptible memory loss, but that even bilateral forniceal loss (e.g., Woolsey and Nelson, 1975) can be asymptomatic in the absence of associated lesions. The importance of the fornix was emphasized by Heilman and Sypert (1977). However, this same group (Valenstein et al., 1987) subsequently raised doubts about the importance of fornix lesions, doubts also expressed by Squire and Zola-Morgan (1991).°

When two or three lesions do combine, the results can vary because of the different combinations possible. A detailed discussion of callosotomy and memory deficit was recently provided by D. W. Zaidel (1990).

## Does Cognition in the Disconnected Right Hemisphere Require Right-Hemisphere Possession of Language?

There is an abundance of evidence from various sources that information processing is carried on differently in the right hemisphere than in the left hemisphere, where it commonly appears (in humans) to be intimately associated with language. This has led to the principle of complementary hemispheric specialization (Milner, 1980). The evidence for this principle has come in part from the studies of split-brain patients carried out largely under the supervision of R. W. Sperry, studies which contributed to his sharing of the Nobel Prize for Physiology in 1981 (Sperry, 1974, 1982). Some

°For a contrary view, see Gaffan and Gaffan (1991).

of the split-brain evidence for right hemispheric specialization was briefly described above in the section on the chronic syndrome of hemisphere disconnection. It was contrasted with the poverty of right-hemisphere language, with the implication that specialized right-hemisphere praxis, perception, and certain conceptual abilitites are essentially independent of linguistic competence. Evaluation of the split-brain evidence is further considered here as a remaining problem because the revisionist backlash has included a strong objection to the belief that right-hemisphere cognition is independent of language. (Another major revisionist objection, denial of cerebral duality, was also discussed above.)

We can best consider the necessity of language for right-hemisphere cognition in the form in which it has been argued by Michael Gazzaniga, since he is an oft-cited and widely recognized authority on the split-brain. Gazzaniga once agreed (Wilson et al., 1975, p. 1153) that the block design test was one of "the typical skills of the right hemisphere." However, the same year he wrote:

> I suspect . . . that the claim of laterality in the pure sense is more often an interpretation and hope of the neuropsychologists rather than a true reflection of brain processes. (Gazzaniga, 1975)

In particular, Gazzaniga has often suggested that right-hemisphere cognition requires right-hemisphere language. In 1983, he wrote:

> It could well be argued that the cognitive skills of a normal disconnected right hemisphere without language are vastly inferior to the cognitive skills of a chimpanzee. (Gazzaniga, 1983, p. 536)

This assertion was based on two errors: first, that only five split-brain patients possessed significant (better than an ape) right-hemisphere cognition (NG and LB in our [Vogel-Bogen] series, PS and JW in the Reeves-Wilson [Dartmouth] series, and POV [also called VP] in the Rayport-Ferguson [Toledo] series). The second error is that these five subjects (and only these five) have right-hemisphere linguistic competence.

With respect to the first error, Gazzaniga wrote:

> the vast majority of the cases from all surgical series reveal little cognitive capacity in their right hemispheres. (Gazzaniga, 1987, p. 120)

This may describe the large Dartmouth series available to Gazzaniga (whose case reports are critically reviewed in detail by Myers, 1984) but it has not been the case with most of our patients. The latter have included, in addition to LB and NG who have been most often tested, the patients WJ, CC, AA, NW, RY, and RM who have also been found by us and by visiting investigators to have right-hemisphere superiorities (Bogen and Gazzaniga, 1965; Bogen, 1969a, 1969b, 1976; Nebes, 1974; Levy, 1974; Sperry, 1974; Milner and Taylor, 1972; Zaidel and Sperry, 1973; Franco and Sperry, 1977; Dimond, 1979; Kumar, 1977; Zaidel et al., 1981; Zaidel, 1983; Cronin-Golomb, 1986b,c; Zaidel et al., 1990a).

Gazzaniga's 1983 assertion as to the necessity of right-hemisphere linguistic competence seems not to have fully reflected his beliefs because in the same year he concluded from studies of facial recognition and line orientation that:

> Taken together, these results imply that the right hemisphere possesses some kind of supramodal encoding apparatus that allows it to perform in a superior way in response to stimuli that cannot be fully characterized by a verbal description. (Gazzaniga and Smylie, 1983, p. 537)

He and Smylie went on to say:

> It would appear that there are learned aspects of form perception and that these processes reside in the right hemisphere. [and] This specialized skill is not dependent upon language. (p. 539)

More recently, however, Gazzaniga's assertion regarding right-hemisphere abilities has been reiterated:

> The split-brain patients without right hemisphere language are thus unable to carry out tasks with the right hemisphere that a chimp or monkey could complete. (Nass and Gazzaniga, 1987, p. 722)

The second error, leading to Gazzaniga's somewhat surprising claim for simian superiority, concerns the necessity of language for human thought. Relevant here is the mistaken belief that human consciousness requires language (Popper and Eccles, 1981; Edelman, 1989). These authors evidently lack sufficient experience with the retained capacities of some severely aphasic patients for the recognition and use of personally relevant, nonlinguistic information (Lecours et al., 1983; Van Lancker and Klein, 1990; Van Lancker, 1991; Van Lancker et al., 1991). Is the evidence for persisting cognition in some severely aphasic humans contrary to the split-brain evidence? I think not. Indeed, as I understand the word "language," *none* of our right-handed patients (including the eight just mentioned) has language competence in the disconnected right hemisphere.

Used broadly, the word "language" refers to "the suggestion by objects, actions or conditions, of associated ideas or feelings" (definition 2 in *Webster's Seventh New Collegiate Dictionary*). It is in this sense (characteristic of any symbol system) that one can speak of "the language of the bees" or of music as a "language." But for linguists, language includes:

> the sound system (phonology), the meaningful units (morphemes) and the way they are combined to form words (morphology), the allowable combination of words to form phrases and sentences (syntax), the mental dictionary or lexicon, and the meanings of the lexical units and sentences (semantics).°

(Bloomfield, 1933; Gleason, 1961; Chomsky, 1965; Klima and Bellugi, 1979; Bolinger, 1980; Fromkin and Rodman, 1983; Klima et al., 1988; Poizner et al., 1990; Corina et

---

° With thanks to Prof. V. Fromkin.

al., 1992b). This linguistic view of language means that possession of a collection of meaningful symbols (called a "verbal lexicon" when the symbols are words) does not in itself prove possession of language.

When our right-handed split-brain patients have been tested for right-hemisphere comprehension of single words or for lexical decision (the task of distinguishing words from nonsensical but pronounceable letter strings), they did well. This includes RY, whose brain injury was postpubertal (Bogen, 1969a; Zaidel, 1985a; 1985b; Hamilton et al., 1986).[*]

But none of these right hemispheres possesses to a sufficient degree the phonologic, morphologic, and syntactic capabilities that would constitute language as linguists define it. In this sense, then, the repeated assertion by Gazzaniga is clearly incorrect. However, if "language" be taken in the broadest sense as sometimes used by E. Zaidel (1985a; 1985b; 1990), then Gazzaniga's assertions would be correct but inconsequential, since of our eight right-handed patients repeatedly found to have various right-hemisphere superiorities, seven of them also manifested right-hemisphere "language." (The exception, our first patient, WJ, showed right-hemisphere superiorities without any lexical abilities, but was never tested for "language" with the same sophistication as were subsequent subjects.)

In conclusion, the praxic, perceptual, and conceptual specializations of the disconnected right hemisphere can apparently function independently of significant phonologic, morphologic, or syntactic competence, although they do seem to be accompanied by considerable symbolic (including lexical) ability.

### Callosal Channels

The idea that certain parts of the corpus callosum act as channels for particular kinds of information is suggested by the partial segregation in the callosum of fibers from different cortical regions (Pandya, 1975; Macko and Mishkin, 1985; Pandya and Rosene, 1985; Pandya and Seltzer, 1986; Aboitiz et al., 1992). Some correlations between psychological functions and the cross-sectional area of certain callosal segments have been reported (Zaidel et al., 1990a). Evidence to the same effect has come from observations on patients with incomplete callosal sections (Jeeves et al., 1979; Musick et al., 1981, 1985; Bentin et al., 1984; Geffen et al., 1985; Chen et al., 1990), partial lesions (Lhermitte and Beaurois, 1973; Lhermitte et al., 1975, 1976; Alexander and Warren, 1988), callosal thinning from multiple sclerosis (Rubens et al., 1985; Rao et al., 1989), and post-head-injury callosal thinning (Levin et al., 1989, 1990).

Supporting the concept of callosal channels was an article on the results of incomplete callosotomy by Risse et al. (1989). They found that if only the tip of the splenium was spared, there was good visual transfer while there was a unilateral left anomia, a unilateral left apraxia, deficits in both tactile and kinesthetic transfer, and a large right-ear advantage on dichotic listening. When the entire splenium and some isthmus were spared, there was essentially no anomia, no apraxia (even acutely), nor a

---

[*]Recently reported (Baynes et al., 1992) is another Dartmouth patient (DR) who apparently has "language" but not linguistic ability in her right hemisphere. Her right hemisphere has a verbal lexicon (both visual and auditory) and an apparent ability for lexical decision when responding with her left hand to left half-field stimuli.

kinesthetic deficit. When more (the posterior one-third) of the body was spared along with the splenium, there was no deficit in intermanual point localization but there was still a partial auditory transfer deficit. This last, as noted by Risse et al., is surprising because it is inconsistent with anatomical evidence that superior temporal lobe fibers cross through the callosum posterior to parietal fibers. Still unexplored is the distribution of fibers less specified for sensory modality.

### The Genu Enigma

One of the most striking facts about callosal section is the paucity of deficits following interruption of only the anterior half. Preilowski (1972, 1990) found some deficits in bimanual coordination. After anterior callosotomy there is transient depression bilaterally of frontal lobe metabolism (Yamaguchi et al., 1990). A left-hand apraxia to verbal command is typical, although rapidly subsiding, after *complete* callosotomy. But these three observations do not explain how naturally occurring anterior callosal lesions can cause a unilateral apraxia where surgical section of the same extent does not. Geschwind (1965) once suggested that anterior callosal section could fail to produce apraxia because long-standing epilepsy or other chronic condition could open up alternative pathways. But there has been in the past 25 years a multitude of cases of anterior callosal section without even brief apraxia; these have included patients with widely varying types of epilepsy and many patients with lesions of brief duration and no epilepsy at all. Hence this speculation by Geschwind seems by now to have been disconfirmed.

It is likely that correct left-hand responses to verbal request can be innervated multiply: by anterior callosum, by posterior callosum (Geschwind, 1975)°, by postlesion emergence of ipsilateral control, and possibly by subcerebral (including cerebellar?) pathways. How an anterior callosal stroke can disable all of these simultaneously (whereas anterior section does not) remains a mystery. One might speculate that infarction from anterior cerebral artery ischemia sometimes disables regions which ordinarily suppress the frontal lobe inhibition of post-Rolandic cortex, as well as interrupting anterior callosal conduction.

The role of the genu is likely allied to frontal lobe functions that are still inadequately understood (Stuss and Benson, 1986; Fuster, 1989; Levin et al., 1991). One avenue deserving further intensive investigation appears to have been opened up by the finding of Hamilton and Vermeire (1986) that the anterior half of the corpus callosum can transfer learning sets, i.e., "theories" about the common properties of similar problems.

In the past thirty years, our understanding of callosal function has been greatly enriched and clarified, but significant riddles remain. These include the varieties of alexia without agraphia, the callosal contributions to attention, post-callosotomy mutism, functions of the anterior commissure, post-callosotomy memory deficits, transcallosal contributions to verbal output, plasticity of callosal channels, and the genu

---

°The possibility of a posterior (splenial) pathway for praxis was suggested by Akelaitis (1944). According to Harrington (1987, p. 164), Liepmann and Maas (1907) attributed their patients' "severe apraxia and agraphia [in] the nonparalyzed and nonataxic left upper extremity" to an old lesion in the "rear fourth or fifth" of the corpus callosum.

enigma. Awareness of such ongoing issues, as appropriate cases for study appear, will hasten the pace of discovery.

## REFERENCES

Aboitiz, F., Scheibel, A. B., and Zaidel, E. (1992). The fiber composition of the human corpus callosum. *Proc. Soc. Neurosci. 18*:331.

Aggleton, J. P. (ed.) (1992). *The Amygdala*. New York: Wiley-Liss.

Ajax, E. T. (1967). Dyslexia without agraphia. *Arch. Neurol. 17*:645–652.

Ajax, E. T., Schenkenberg, T., and Kosteljanetz, M. (1977). Alexia without agraphia and the inferior splenium. *Neurology 27*:685–688.

Akelaitis, A. J. (1944–1945). Studies on the corpus callosum. IV: Diagnostic dyspraxia in epileptics following partial and complete section of the corpus callosum. *Am. J. Psychiatry 101*:594–599.

Akelaitis, A. J. (1944). A study of gnosis, praxis and language following section of the corpus callosum and anterior commissure. *J. Neurosurg. 1*:94–102.

Albert, M. L., Silverberg, R., Reches, A., and Berman, M. (1976). Cerebral dominance for consciouness. *Arch. Neurol. 33*:453–454.

Alexander, M. P., and Warren, R. L. (1988). Localization of callosal auditory pathways: a CT case study. *Neurology 38*:802–804.

Alpers, B. J. (1936). The mental syndrome of tumors of the corpus callosum. *Arch. Neurol. Psychiatry 35*:911–912.

Anderson, S. W., Damasio, H., Damasio, A. R., Klima, E., Bellugi, U., and Brandt, J. P. (1992). Acquisition of signs from American sign language in hearing individuals following left hemisphere damage and aphasia. *Neuropsychologia 30*:329–340.

Aptman, M., Levin, H., and Senelick, R. C. (1977). Alexia without agraphia in a left-handed patient with prosopagnosia. *Neurology 27*:533–536.

Apuzzo, M.L.J. (ed.) (1987). *Surgery of the Third Ventricle*. Baltimore: Williams and Wilkins.

Apuzzo, M.L.J., Chikovani, O. K., Gott, P. S., Teng, E. L., Zee, C. S., Giannotta, S. L., and Weiss, M. H. (1982). Transcallosal, interfornicial approaches for lesions affecting the third ventricle: surgical considerations and consequences. *Neurosurgery 10*:547–554.

Asbjørnsen, A., Hugdahl, K., and Hynd, G. W. (1990). The effects of head and eye turns on the right ear advantage in dichotic listening. *Brain Lang. 39*:447–458.

Assal, G., and Hadj-Djilani, M. (1976). Une nouvelle observation d'alexie pure sans hémianopsie. *Cortex 12*:169–174 .

Baierl, P., Förster, C., Fendel, H., Naegele, M., Fink, U., and Kenn, W. (1988). Magnetic resonance imaging of normal and pathological white matter maturation. *Pediatr. Radiol. 18*:183–189.

Banks, G., Short, P., Martinez, A. J., Latchaw, R., Ratcliff, G., and Boller, F. (1989). The alien hand syndrome; clinical and postmortem findings. *Arch. Neurol. 46*:456–459.

Barbizet, J., Degos, J. D., Duizabo, P., and Chartier, B. (1974). Syndrome de déconnexion interhémisphérique de l'origine ischémique. *Rev. Neurol. 130*:127–142.

Barbizet, J., Degos, J. D., Leeune, A., and Leroy, A. (1978). Syndrome de dysconnection interhémisphérique avec dyspraxie diagonistique au cours d'une maladie de Marchafava-Bignami. *Rev. Neurol. (Paris) 134*:781–789.

Barbizet, J., Duizabo, P., Bouchareine, A., Degos, J. D., and Poirier, J. (1977). *Abrégé de Neuropsychologie*. Paris: Masson.

Barrett, T. W. (1969). Studies of the function of the amygdaloid complex in *Macaca mulatta*. *Neuropsychologia 7*:1–12.

Baynes, K. (1990). Language and reading in the right hemisphere: highways or byways of the brain? *J. Cognitive Neurosci.* 2:159–179.

Baynes, K., Tramo, M. J., and Gazzaniga, M. S. (1992). Reading with a limited lexicon in the right hemisphere of a callosotomy patient. *Neuropsychologia* 30:187–200.

Beaton, A. (1985). *Left Side, Right Side: A Review of Laterality Research.* New Haven: Yale University Press.

Benes, V., (1982). Sequelae of transcallosal surgery. *Childs Brain* 9:69–72.

Benson, D. F. (1977). The third alexia. *Arch. Neurol.* 34:327–331.

Benson, D. F. (1979). *Aphasia, Alexia and Agraphia.* New York: Churchill Livingstone.

Benson, D. F., and Geschwind, N. (1969). The alexias. *Hdbk. Clin. Neurol.* 4:112–140.

Benson, D. F., and Zaidel, E. (1985). *The Dual Brain.* New York: The Guilford Press.

Bentin, S., Sahar, A., and Moscovitch, M. (1984). Intermanual information transfer in patients with lesions in the trunk of the corpus callosum. *Neuropsychologia* 22:601–611.

Benton, A. L. (1962). The visual retention test as a constructional praxis task. *Confin. Neurol.* 22:141–155.

Benton, A. L. (1967). Constructional apraxia and the minor hemisphere. *Confin. Neurol.* 29:1–16.

Benton, A. L. (1977). Historical notes on hemispheric dominance. *Arch. Neurol.* 34:127–129.

Benton, A. L., and Fogel, M. L. (1962). Three-dimensional constructional praxis. *Arch. Neurol.* 7:347–354.

Berlucchi, G. (1972). Anatomical and physiological aspects of visual functions of corpus callosum. *Brain Res.* 37:371–392.

Berlucchi, G. (1990). Commissurotomy studies in animals. In *Handbook of Neuropsychology,* Vol. 4, F. Boller and J. Grafman (eds.). Amsterdam: Elsevier.

Berlucchi, G., and Aglioti, S. (1990). Le sindromi da disconnessione interemisferica. In *Manuale di Neuropsicologia,* G. Denes and L. Pizzamiglio (eds.). Bologna: Zanichelli.

Beukelman, D. R., Flowers, C. R., and Swanson, P. D. (1980). Cerebral disconnection associated with anterior communicating artery aneurysm: implications for evaluation of symptoms. *Arch. Phys. Med. Rehabil.* 61:18–23.

Bigley, G. K., and Sharp, F. R. (1983). Reversible alexia without agraphia due to migraine. *Arch. Neurol.* 40:114–115.

Bisiach, E., and Vallar, G. (1988). Hemineglect in humans. In *Handbook of Neuropsychology,* Vol. 1, F. Boller and J. Grafman (eds.). Amsterdam: Elsevier.

Bisiach, E., and Rusconi, M. L. (1991). Breakdown of perceptual awareness in unilateral neglect. *Cortex* 26:643–649.

Black, P., and Myers, R. E. (1964). Visual function of the forebrain commissures in the chimpanzee. *Science* 146:799–800.

Bleuler, E. (1911, republished in 1950 in English translation by J. Zinkin). *Dementia Praecox or The Group of Schizophrenias.* New York: International Universities Press.

Bloomfield, L. (1933). *Language.* New York: Holt.

Bogen, J. E. (1969a). The other side of the brain. I: Dysgraphia and dyscopia following cerebral commissurotomy. *Bull. Los Angeles Neurol. Soc.* 34:73–105.

Bogen, J. E. (1969b). The other side of the brain. II: An appositional mind. *Bull. Los Angeles Neurol. Soc.* 34:135–162.

Bogen, J. E. (1970). The corpus callosum, the other side of the brain, and pharmacologic opportunity. In *Drugs and Cerebral Function,* W. L. Smith (ed.). Springfield, Ill.: C. C. Thomas.

Bogen, J. E. (1976). Language function in the short term following cerebral commissurotomy. In *Current Trends in Neurolinguistics,* H. Avakian-Whitaker and H. A. Whitaker (eds.). New York: Academic Press.

Bogen, J. E. (1977). Further discussion on split-brains and hemispheric capabilities. *Br. J. Philos. Sci.* 28:281–286.

Bogen, J. E. (1985). Concuding overview. In *Epilepsy and the Corpus Callosum*, A. Reeves (ed.). New York: Plenum.

Bogen, J. E. (1987). Physiological consequences of complete or partial commissural section. In *Surgery of the Third Ventricle*, M. L. J. Apuzzo (ed.). Baltimore: Williams and Wilkins.

Bogen, J. E. (1990). Partial hemispheric independence with the neocommissures intact. In *Brain Circuits and Functions of the Mind: Essays in Honor of R. W. Sperry*, C. Trevarthen (ed.). Cambridge: Cambridge University Press.

Bogen, J. E., and Bogen, G. M. (1969). The other side of the brain. III: The corpus callosum and creativity. *Bull. Los Angeles Neurol. Soc.* 34:191–220.

Bogen, J. E., Fisher, E. D., and Vogel, P. J. (1965). Cerebral commissurotomy: a second case report. *J.A.M.A.* 194:1328–1329.

Bogen, J. E., and Gazzaniga, M. S. (1965). Cerebral commissurotomy in man: minor Hemisphere dominance for certain visuospatial functions. *J. Neurosurg.* 23:394–399.

Bogen, J. E., Schultz, D. H., and Vogel, P. J. (1988). Completeness of callosotomy shown by magnetic resonance imaging in the long term. *Arch. Neurol.* 45:1203–1205.

Bogen, J. E., and Vogel, P. J. (1962). Cerebral commissurotomy in man. *Bull. Los Angeles Neurol. Soc.* 27:169–172.

Bogen, J. E., and Vogel, P. J. (1975). Neurologic status in the long term following cerebral commissurotomy. In *Les Syndromes de Disconnexion Calleuse Chez L'Homme*, F. Michel and B. Schott (eds.). Lyon: Hôpital Neurologique.

Bolinger, D. (1980). *Language—The Loaded Weapon*. New York: Longman.

Bossom, J., Sperry, R. W., and Arora, H. (1961). Division of emotional behavior patterns in split-brain monkeys. *Caltech. Biol. Annu. Rep.* p. 127.

Bossy, J. G. (1970). Morphological study of a case of complete, isolated and asymptomatic agnesis of the corpus callosum. *Arch. Anat. Histol. Embryol.* 53:289–340.

Botez, M. (1974). Frontal lobe tumours. *Hdbk. Clin. Neurol.* 17:234–280.

Botez, M. I., and Bogen, J. E. (1976). The grasp reflex of the foot and related phenomena in the absence of other reflex abnormalities following cerebral commissurotomy. *Acta Neurol. Scand.* 54:453–463.

Botez, M. I., and Crighel, E. (1971). Partial disconnexion syndrome in an ambidextrous patient. *Brain* 94:487–494.

Bradshaw, J. L., and Nettleton, N. C. (1983). *Human Cerebral Asymmetry*. Englewood Cliffs, N.J.: Prentice-Hall.

Bremer, F. (1958). Physiology of the corpus callosum. *Res. Publ. Assoc. Res. Nerv. Ment. Dis.* 36:424–448.

Bremer, F., Brihaye, J., and André-Balisaux, G. (1956). Physiologie et pathologie du corps calleux. *Arch. Suisses Neurol. Psychiatr.* 78:31–87.

Brinkman, J., and Kuypers, H.G.J.M. (1973). Cerebral control of contralateral and ipsilateral arm, hand and finger movements in the split-brain rhesus monkey. *Brain* 96:653–674.

Brion, S., and Jedynak, C. P. (1972). Troubles du transfert interhémisphérique (callosal disconnection) à propos de 3 observations de tumeurs du corps calleux: Le signe de la main étrangère. *Rev. Neurol. (Paris)* 126:257–266.

Brion, S., and Jedynak, C. P. (1975). *Les Troubles du Transfert Interhémisphérique*. Paris: Masson.

Brody, B. A., Kinney, H. C., Kloman, A. S., and Gilles, F. H. (1987). Sequence of central nervous system myelination in human infancy. I. An autopsy study of myelination. *J. Neuropathol. Exp. Neurol.* 46:283–301.

Brown, J. W., and Jaffe, J. (1975). Hypothesis on cerebral dominance. *Neuropsychologia* 13:107–110.

Brownell, H. H., Carroll, J. J., Rehak, A., and Wingfield, A. (1992). The use of pronoun anaphora and speaker mood in the interpretation of conversational utterances by right hemisphere brain-damaged patients. *Brain Lang.* 43:121–147.

Bruce, A. (1890). On the absence of corpus callosum in the human brain, with the description of a new case. *Brain* 12:171–190.

Bryden, M. P. (1982). *Laterality: Functional Asymmetry in the Intact Brain.* New York: Academic Press.

Bryden, M. P., and Ley, R. G. (1983). Right-hemisphere involvement in the perception and expression of emotion in normal humans. In *Neuropsychology of Human Emotion,* K. M. Heilman and P. Satz (eds.). New York: Guilford.

Burklund, C. W., and Smith, A. (1977). Language and the cerebral hemispheres. *Neurology* 27:627–633.

Butler, S. R. (1979). Interhemispheric transmission of visual information via the corpus callosum and anterior commissure in the monkey. In *Structure and Function of Cerebral Commissures,* I. S. Russell, M. W. Van Hof, and G. Berlucchi (eds.). Baltimore: University Park Press.

Butler, S. (1988). Alpha asymmetry, hemispheric specialization and the problem of cognitive dynamics. In *The EEG of Mental Activities,* Giannitrapani, and Murri (eds.). Basel: Karger.

Byrne, J. M., and Gates, R. D. (1987). Single-case study of left cereberal hemispherectomy: development in the first five years of life. *J. Clin. Exp. Neuropsychol.* 9:423–434.

Cairns, H. R. (1952). Disturbances of consciousness with lesions of the brainstem and diencephalon. *Brain* 75:109–146.

Cambier, J., Elghozi, D., Graveleau, P., and Lubetzki, C. (1984). Hemisomatagnosie droite et sentiment d'amputation par lésion gauche sous-corticale. Rôle de la disconnexion calleuse. *Rev. Neurol. (Paris)* 140:256–262.

Campbell, A. L., Bogen, J. E., and Smith, A. (1981). Disorganization and reorganization of cognitive and sensorimotor functions in the cerebral commissurotomy. Compensatory roles of the forebrain commissures and cerebral hemispheres in man. *Brain* 104:493–511.

Campbell, R., Landis, T., and Regard, M. (1986). Face recognition and lipreading: a neurological dissociation. *Brain.* 109:509–521.

Caplan, D., Holmes, J. M., and Marshall, J. C. (1974). Word classes and hemispheric specialization. *Neuropsychologia* 12:331–337.

Carleton, C. C., Collins, G. H., and Schimpff, R. D. (1976). Subacute necrotizing encephalopathy (Leigh's disease): two unusual cases. *South. Med. J.* 69:1301–1305.

Carmon, A., Gordon, H. W., Bental, E., and Harness, B. Z. (1977). Retraining in literal alexia: substitution of a right hemisphere perceptual strategy for impaired left hemispheric processing. *Bull. Los Angeles Neurol. Soc.* 42:41–50.

Caselli, R. J. (1991). Rediscovering tactile agnosia. *Mayo Clin. Proc.* 66:129–142.

Cavalli, M., De Renzi, E., Faglioni, P., and Vitale, A. (1981). Impairment of right brain-damaged patients on a linguistic cognitive task. *Cortex* 17:545–556.

Chamorro, A., Sacco, R. L., Ciecierski, K., Binder, J. R., Tatemichi, T. K., and Mohr, J. P. (1990). Visual hemineglect and hemihallucinations in a patient with a subcortical infarction. *Neurology* 40:1463–1464.

Chen, Y. P., Campbell, R., Marshall, J. C., and Zaidel, D. W. (1990). Learning a unimanual motor skill by partial commissurotomy patients. *J. Neurol. Neurosurg. Psychiatry* 53:785–788.

Chernigovskaya, T. V., and Deglin, V. L. (1986). Brain functional asymmetry and neural organization of linguistic competence. *Brain Lang.* 29:141–153.

Chomsky, N. (1965). *Syntactic Structures.* The Hague: Mouton.

Churchland, P. M. (1982). Is thinker a natural kind? *Dialogue* 21:223–238.

Churchland, P. M., and Sejnowski, T. J. (1992). *The Computational Brain.* Cambridge, Mass: MIT Press.

Clark, C. R., and Geffen, G. M. (1989). Corpus callosum surgery and recent memory; a review. *Brain* 112:165–175.

Clarke, E., and O'Malley, C. D. (1968). *The Human Brain and Spinal Cord.* Berkeley: University of California Press.

Clarke, S., Kraftsik, R., Van Der Loos, H., and Innocenti, G. M. (1989). Forms and measures of adult and developing human corpus callosum: is there sexual dimorphism? *J. Comp. Neurol.* 280:213–230.

Cobben, A., Seron, X., Gillet, J., and Bonnal, J. (1978). Absence de signe de déconnexion lors d'un examen neuro-psychologique différé dans quatre cas de lésions callosales antérieures et médianes partielles d'origine vasculaire et neurochirurgicale. *Acta Neurol. Belg.* 78:207–216.

Code, C. (1987). *Language, Aphasia and the Right Hemisphere.* New York: John Wiley and Sons.

Corballis, M. C. (1983). *Human Laterality.* New York: Academic Press.

Corballis, M. C. (1991). *The Lopsided Ape.* New York: Oxford University Press.

Corballis, M. C. (1992). Interhemispheric integration in a commissurotomized subject (in press).

Corballis, M. C., and Ogden, J. A. (1988). Dichotic listening in commissurotomized and hemispherectomy subjects. *Neuropsychologia* 26:565–573.

Corballis, M. C., and Sergent, J. (1988). Imagery in a commissurotomized patient. *Neuropsychologia.* 26:13–26.

Corina, D. P. (1989). Recognition of affective and noncanonical linguistic facial expressions in hearing and deaf subjects. *Brain and Cognition* 9:227–237.

Corina, D. P., Poizner, H., Bellugi, U., Feinberg, T., Dowd, D., and O'Grady-Batch, L. (1992a). Dissociation between linguistic and non-linguistic gestural systems: a case for compositionality. *Brain Lang.* 43:414–447.

Corina, D. P., Vaid, J., and Bellugi, U. (1992b). The linguistic basis of left hemisphere specialization. *Science* 255:1258–1260.

Cowey, A., and Stoerig, P. (1991). *Reflections on Blindsight in the Neuropsychology of Consciousness.* New York: Academic Press.

Crick, F. (1984). Function of the thalamic reticular complex: the searchlight hypothesis. *Proc. Natl. Acad. Sci. U.S.A.* 81:4586–4590.

Critchley, M. (1930). The anterior cerebral artery and its syndromes. *Brain* 53:120–165.

Cronin-Golomb, A. (1986a). Subcortical transfer of cognitive information in subjects with complete forebrain commissurotomy. *Cortex* 22:499–519.

Cronin-Golomb, A. (1986b). Comprehension of abstract concepts in right and left hemispheres of complete commissurotomy subjects. *Neuropsychologia* 24:881–887.

Cronin-Golomb, A. (1986c). Figure-background perception in right and left hemispheres of human commissurotomy subjects. *Perception* 15:95–109.

Cullen, J. K. (1975). Tests of a model for speech information flow. Ph.D. thesis, Louisiana State University.

Cumming, W.J.K., Hurwitz, L. J., and Perl, N. T. (1970). A study of a patient who had alexia without agraphia. *J. Neurol. Neurosurg. Psychiatry* 33:34–39.

Curry, F.K.W. (1968). A comparison of the performances of a right hemispherectomized subject and 25 normals on four dichotic listening tasks. *Cortex 4*:144–153.

Dahmen, W., Hartje, W., Bussing, A., and Sturm, W. (1982). Disorders of calculation in aphasic patients: spatial and verbal components. *Neuropsychologia 20*:145–153.

Damasio, A. R. (1977). Varieties and significance of the alexias. *Arch. Neurol. 34*:325–326.

Damasio, A. R. (1985). The frontal lobes. In *Clinical Neuropsychology*, K. M. Heilman and E. Valenstein (eds.). New York: Oxford University Press.

Damasio, A. R., Chui, H. C., Corbett, J., and Kassel, N. (1980). Posterior callosal section in a non-epileptic patient. *J. Neurol. Neurosurg. Psychiatry 43*:351–356.

Damasio, A. R., and Damasio, H. (1983). The anatomic basis of pure alexia. *Neurology 33*:1573–1583.

Damasio, H., and Damasio, A. (1979). "Paradoxic" ear extinction in dichotic listening: possible anatomic significance. *Neurology 29*:644–653.

Dandy, W. E. (1936). Operative experience in cases of pineal tumor. *Arch. Surg. 33*:19–46.

Degos, J. D., Gray, F., Louarn, F., Ansquer, J. C., Poirier, J., and Barbizet, J. (1987). Posterior callosal infarction. *Brain 110*:1155–1171.

Dejerine, J. (1892). Contributions a l'étude anatomo-pathologique et clinique des différentes variétés de cécité verbale. Comptes rendus des séances et mémoires de la Soc. de Biol. Vol. 44 (vol. 4 of Series 9) (Second section-Mémoires):61–90.

Della Sala, S., Marchetti, C., and Spinnler, H. (1991). Right-sided anarchic (alien) hand: a longitudinal study. *Neuropsychologia 29*:1113–1127.

Demeter, S., Ringo, J. L., and Doty, R. W. (1988). Morphometric analysis of the human corpus callosum and anterior commissure. *Hum. Neurobiol. 6*:219–226.

Denckla, M. B. (1974). Development of motor coordination in normal children. *Dev. Med. Child Neurol. 16*:729–741.

Denckla, M. B., and Rudel, R. G. (1978). Anomalies of motor development in hyperactive boys. *Ann. Neurol. 3*:231–233.

Denenberg, V. H. (1981). Hemispheric laterality in animals and the effects of early experience. *Behav. Brain Sci. 4*:1–49.

Dennis, M. (1976). Impaired sensory and motor differentiation with corpus callosum agenesis: a lack of callosal inhibition during ontogeny? *Neuropsychologia 14*:455–469.

Dennis, M., and Whitaker, H. A. (1976). Language acquisition following hemidecortication: linguistic superiority of the left over the right hemisphere. *Brain Lang. 3*:404–433.

Denny-Brown, D. (1958). The nature of apraxia. *J. Nerv. Ment. Dis. 126*:9–32.

De Renzi, E. (1982a). *Disorders of Space Exploration and Cognition*. New York: Wiley.

De Renzi, E. (1982b). Memory disorders following focal neocortical damage. *Philos. Trans. R. Soc. Lond. [Biol.] 298*:73–83.

De Renzi, E., Zambolin, A., and Crisi, G. (1987). The pattern of neuropsychological impairment associated with left posterior cerebral artery infarcts. *Brain 110*:1099–1116.

Dewson, J. H. III (1977). Preliminary evidence of hemispheric asymmetry of auditory function in monkeys. In *Lateralization in the Nervous System*, S. Harnad et al. (eds.). New York: Academic Press.

Dimond, S. J. (1972). *The Double Brain*. London: Churchill Livingstone.

Dimond, S. J. (1979). Performance by split-brain humans on lateralized vigilance tasks. *Cortex 15*:43–50.

Dixon, N. F., and Jeeves, M. A. (1970). The interhemispheric transfer of movement after effects: a comparison between acallosal and normal subjects. *Psychoneurol Sci. 20(4)*:201–203.

Doty, R. W. (1977). Discussion. *Ann. N. Y. Acad. Sci. 290*:434.

Doty, R. W. (1989). Some anatomical substrates of emotion, and their bihemispheric coordination. In *Emotions and the Dual Brain*, G. Gainotti and C. Caltagirone (eds.). Berlin: Springer-Verlag.

Doty, R. W., and Negrão, N. (1972). Forebrain commissures and vision. In *Handbook of Sensory Physiology*, Vol. VII/3, R. Jung (ed.). Berlin: Springer-Verlag.

Doty, R. W., Negrão, N., and Yamaga, K. (1973). The unilateral engram. *Acta Neurobiol. Exp.* 33:711–728.

Doty, R. W., and Overman, W. H. (1977). Mnemonic role of forebrain commissures in macaques. In *Lateralization in the Nervous System*, S. Harnad et al. (eds.). New York: Academic Press.

Doty, R. W., Ringo, J. L., and Lewine, J. D. (1986). Interhemispheric mnemonic transfer in macaques. In F. Leporé, M. Ptito and H. H Jasper (eds.) *Two Hemispheres--One Brain: Functions of the Corpus Callosum*. New York: Alan R. Liss, Inc.

Doty, R. W., Ringo, J. L., and Lewine, J. D. (1988). Forebrain commissures and visual memory: a new approach. *Behavioural Brain Research.* 29:267-280.

Doty, R. W., Yamaga, K., and Negrão, N. (1971). Mediation of visual fear via the corpus callosum. *Proc. Soc Neurosci.* 1:104.

Downer, J. L. de C. (1961). Changes in visual gnostic functions and emotional behavior following unilateral temporal pole damage in the split-brain monkey. *Nature 191*:50–51.

Downer, J. L. de C. (1962). Interhemispheric integration in the visual system. In *Interhemispheric Relations and Cerebral Dominance*, V. B. Mountcastle (ed.). Baltimore: Johns Hopkins University Press.

Eccles, J. C. (1989). *Evolution of the Brain: Creation of the Self*. New York: Routledge, Chapman and Hall.

Edelman, G. M. (1989). *The Remembered Present: A Biological Theory of Consciousness*. New York: Basic Books.

Efron, R. (1990). *The Decline and Fall of Hemispheric Specialization*. Hillsdale, N.J.: Erlbaum.

Efron, R., Bogen, J. E., and Yund, E. W. (1977). Perception of dichotic chords by normal and commissurotomized human subjects. *Cortex 13*:137-149.

Elberger, A. J. (1980). The effect of neonatal section of the corpus callosum on the development of depth perception in young cats. *Vision Res. 20*:177-187.

Elberger, A. J. (1988). Developmental interactions between the corpus callosum and the visual system in cats. *Behav. Brain Res. 30*:119-134.

Elberger, A. J. (1990). Spatial frequency thresholds of single striate cortical cells in neonatal corpus callosum sectioned cats. *Exp. Brain Res. 82*:617-27.

Elliot, F. A. (1969). The corpus callosum, cingulate gyrus, septum pellucidum, septal area and fornix. *Hdbk. Clin. Neurol. 2*:758-775.

Escourolle, R., Hauw, J. J., Gray, F., and Henin, D. (1975). Aspects neuropathologiques des lésions du corps calleux. In *Les Syndromes de Disconnexion Calleuse Chez L'Homme*, F. Michel and B. Schott (eds.). Lyon: Hôpital Neurologique.

Ethelberg, S. (1951). Changes in circulation through the anterior cerebral artery. *Acta Psychiatr. Neurol. (Suppl.)* 75:3-211.

Ettlinger, G., Blakemore, C. B., Milner, A. D., and Wilson, J. (1974). Agenesis of the corpus callosum: a further behavioral investigation. *Brain 97*:225-234.

Feinberg, T. E., Haber, L. D., and Leeds, N. E. (1990). Verbal asomatognosia. *Neurology 40*:1391-1394.

Feinberg, T. E., Schindler, R. J., Flanagan, N. G., and Haber, L. D. (1992). Two alien hand syndromes. *Neurology 42*:19-24.

Ferguson, S. M., Rayport, M., and Corrie, W. S. (1985). Neuropsychiatric observations on behavioral consequences of corpus callosum section for seizure control. In *Epilepsy and the Corpus Callosum*, M. A. Reeves (ed.). New York: Plenum.

Ferriss, G. D., and Dorsen, M. M. (1975). Agenesis of the corpus callosum: neuropsychological studies. *Cortex* 11:95–122.

Fessard, A. E. (1954). Mechanisms of nervous integration and conscious experience. In *Brain Mechanisms and Consciousness*, J. F. Delafresnaye (ed.). Springfield, Ill.: C. C. Thomas.

Fisher, C. M. (1963). Symmetrical mirror movements and left ideomotor apraxia. *Trans. Am. Neurol. Assoc.* 88:214-216.

Fodor, J. A. (1975). *The Language of Thought*. New York: Crowell.

Fodor, J. A. (1983). *The Modularity of Mind*. Cambridge, Mass.: MIT Press.

Foix, C., and Hillemand, P. (1925a). Les syndromes de l'artère cérèbrale antérieure. *Encéphale* 20:209–232.

Foix, C., and Hillemand, P. (1925b). Role vraisemblable du splenium dans la pathogénie de l'alexie pure par lésion de l'artère cérébrale postérieure. *Bull. Mem. Soc. Med. Hop.* 49:393–395.

Foxman, B. T., Oppenheim, J., Petito, C. K., and Gazzaniga, M. S. (1986). Proportional anterior commissure area in humans and monkeys. *Neurology* 36:1513–1517.

Franco, L., and Sperry, R. W. (1977). Hemisphere lateralization for cognitive processing of geometry. *Neuropsychologia* 15:107–114.

Fromkin, V., and Rodman, R. (1983). *An Introduction to Language*, 3rd ed. New York: Holt, Rinehart and Winston.

Fuiks, K. S., Wyler, A. R., Hermann, B. P., and Somes, G. (1991). Seizure outcome from anterior and complete corpus callosotomy. *J. Neurosurg.* 74:573–578.

Fuster, J. M. (1989). *The Prefrontal Cortex: Anatomy, Physiology and Neuropsychology of the Frontal Lobe*. New York: Raven Press.

Gaffan, D., and Gaffan, E. A. (1991). Amnesia in man following transection of the fornix. *Brain* 114:2611–2618.

Gainotti, G., Miceli, G., and Caltagirone, C. (1977). Constructional apraxia in left brain-damaged patients: a planning disorder? *Cortex* 13:109–118.

Galin, D. (1974). Implications for psychiatry of left and right cerebral specialization. *Arch. Gen. Psychiatry* 31:572–583.

Galin, D. (1977). Lateral specialization and psychiatric issues: speculations on development and the evolution of consciousness. *Ann. N. Y. Acad. Sci.* 299:397–411.

Galin, D., Diamond, R., and Herron, J. (1977). Development of crossed and uncrossed tactile localization on the fingers. *Brain Lang.* 4:588–590.

Galin, D., Johnstone, J., Nakell, L., and Herron, J. (1979). Development of the capacity for tactile information transfer between hemispheres in normal children. *Science* 204:1330–1332.

Garcia-Bengochea, F., and Friedman, W. A. (1987). Persistent memory loss following section of the anterior fornix in humans; a historical review. *Surg. Neurol.* 27:361–364.

Gazzaniga, M. S. (1970). *The Bisected Brain*. New York: Appleton.

Gazzaniga, M. S. (1975). Beyond lateralization. In *Les Syndromes de Disconnexion Calleuse Chez L'Homme*, F. Michel and B. Schott (eds.). Lyon: Hôpital Neurologique.

Gazzaniga, M. S. (1983). Right hemisphere language following brain bisection: a 20-year perspective. *Am. Psychol.* 38:525–537.

Gazzaniga, M. S. (1985). *The Social Brain*. New York: Basic Books.

Gazzaniga, M. S. (1987). Perceptual and attentional processes following callosal section in humans. *Neuropsychologia* 25:119–133.

Gazzaniga, M. S. (1988). Interhemispheric Integration. In *Neurobiology of Neocortex*, P. Rakic and W. Singer (eds.). New York: John Wiley and Sons.

Gazzaniga, M. S., Bogen, J. E., and Sperry, R. W. (1962). Some functional effects of sectioning the cerebral commissures in man. *Proc Natl. Acad. Sci. U.S.A. 48:*1765–1769.

Gazzaniga, M. S., Bogen, J. E., and Sperry, R. W. (1963). Laterality effects in somesthesis following cerebral commissurotomy in man. *Neuropsychologia 1:*209–215.

Gazzaniga, M. S., Bogen, J. E., and Sperry, R. W. (1965). Observations on visual perception after disconnexion of the cerebral hemispheres in man. *Brain 88:*221–236.

Gazzaniga, M. S., Bogen, J. E., and Sperry, R. W. (1967). Dyspraxia following division of the cerebral commissures. *Arch. Neurol. 16:*606–612.

Gazzaniga, M. S., and Freedman, H. (1973). Observations on visual processes after posterior callosal section. *Neurology 23:*1126–1130.

Gazzaniga, M. S., and Hillyard, S. A. (1971). Language and speech capacity of the right hemisphere. *Neuropsychologia 9:*273–280.

Gazzaniga, M. S., Holtzman, J. D., Deck, M. D. F., and Lee, B. C. P. (1985). MRI assessment of human callosal surgery with neuropsychological correlates. *Neurology 35:*1765–1766.

Gazzaniga, M. S., and LeDoux, J. E. (1978). *The Integrated Mind.* New York: Plenum.

Gazzaniga, M. S., Risse, G. L., Springer, S. P., Clark, E., and Wilson, D. H. (1975). Psychologic and neurologic consequences of partial and complete cerebral commissurotomy. *Neurology 25:*10–15.

Gazzaniga, M. S., and Smylie, C. S. (1983). Facial recognition and brain asymmetries: clues to underlying mechanisms. *Ann. Neurol. 13:*536–540.

Gazzaniga, M. S., and Sperry, R. W. (1967). Language after section of the cerebral commissures. *Brain 90:*131–148.

Geffen, G., Nilsson, B., Quinn, K., and Teng, E. L. (1985). The effect of lesions of the corpus callosum on finger localization. *Neuropsychologia 23:*497–514.

Gersh, F., and Damasio, A. R. (1981). Praxis and writing of the left hand may be served by different callosal pathways. *Arch. Neurol. 38:*634–636.

Geschwind, N. (1964). The development of the brain and the evolution of language. In *Monograph Series on Language and Linguistics,* Vol. 17, C. I. J. M. Stuart (ed.). Washington: Georgetown University Press.

Geschwind, N. (1965). Disconnexion syndromes in animals and man. *Brain 88:*237–294, 585–644.

Geschwind, N. (1970). The organization of language and the brain. *Science 170:*940–944.

Geschwind, N. (1974). *Selected Papers on Language and the Brain.* Boston: Reidel.

Geschwind, N. (1975). The apraxias: neural mechanisms of disorders of learned movement. *Am. Sci. 63:*188–195.

Geschwind, N., and Fusillo, M. (1966). Colour-naming defects in association with alexia. *Arch. Neurol. 15:*137–146.

Geschwind, N., and Kaplan, E. (1962). A human cerebral deconnection syndrome: a preliminary report. *Neurology 12:*675–685.

Glass, A., Butler, S. R., and Heffner, R. (1975). Asymmetries in the CNV elicited by verbal and non-verbal stimuli. 10th Int. Cong. Anat., Tokyo.

Gleason, H. A. (1961). *An Introduction to Descriptive Linguistics.* New York: Holt, Rinehart and Winston.

Glickstein, M. E. (1990). Brain pathways in the visual guidance of movement and the behavioral functions of the cerebellum. In *Brain Circuits and Functions of the Mind: Essays in Honor of R. W. Sperry,* C. Trevarthen (ed.). Cambridge: Cambridge University Press.

Glickstein, M., Arora, H. A., and Sperry, R. W. (1963). Delayed/response performance following optic tract section, unilateral frontal lesion, and commissurotomy. *J. Comp. Physiol. Psychol. 56:*11–18.

Goldberg, G., Mayer, N. H., and Toglia, J. U. (1981). Medial frontal cortex infarction and the alien hand sign. *Arch. Neurol.* 38:683–686.

Goldstein, K. (1939). *The Organism.* New York: American Book Co.

Goldstein, K. (1953). Hugo Karl Liepmann. In *The Founders of Neurology*, W. Haymaker (ed.). Springfield, Ill.: C. C. Thomas.

Goldstein, M., and Joynt, R. (1969). Long-term follow-up of a callosal-sectioned patient. *Arch. Neurol.* 20:96–102.

Goldstein, M., Joynt, R. J., and Goldblatt, D. (1971). Word blindness with intact central visual fields. *Neurology* 21:873–876.

Goldstein, M., Joynt, R., and Hartley, R. (1975). The long-term effects of callosal sectioning. *Arch. Neurol.* 32:52–53.

Gordon, H. W. (1973). Verbal and Non-verbal Cerebral Processing in Man for Audition. Thesis, California Institute of Technology.

Gordon, H. W. (1975). Comparison of ipsilateral and contralateral auditory pathways in callosum-sectioned patients by use of a response-time technique. *Neuropsychologia* 13:9–18.

Gordon, H. W. (1990). Neuropsychological sequelae of partial commissurotomy. In *Handbook of Neuropsychology*, Vol. 4, F. Boller and J. Grafman (eds.). Amsterdam: Elsevier.

Gordon, H. W., and Sperry, R. W. (1969). Lateralization of olfactory perception in the surgically separated hemispheres of man. *Neuropsychologia* 7:111–120.

Gordon, H. W., Bogen, J. E., and Sperry, R. W. (1971). Absence of deconnexion syndrome in two patients with partial section of the neocommissures. *Brain* 94:327–336.

Gott, P. S. (1973a). Language after dominant hemispherectomy. *J. Neurol. Neurosurg, Psychiatry* 36:1082–1088.

Gott, P. S. (1937b). Cognitive abilities following right and left hemispherectomy. *Cortex* 9:266–274.

Gott, P. S., and Saul, R. W. (1978). Agenesis of the corpus callosum: limits of functional compensation. *Neurology* 28:1271–1279.

Gowers, W. R. (1903). *A Manual of Diseases of the Nervous System*, Vol. II, 2nd ed. Philadelphia: P. Blakiston's Son and Co., p. 314.

Greenblatt, S. (1973). Alexia without agraphia or hemianopsia. *Brain* 96:307–316.

Greenblatt, S. H. (1976). Subangular alexia without agraphia or hemianopsia. *Brain Lang.* 3:229–245.

Greenblatt, S. H. (1977). Neurosurgery and the anatomy of reading: a practical review. *Neurosurgery* 1:6–15.

Greenblatt, S. H. (1990). Left occipital lobectomy and the preangular anatomy of reading. *Brain Lang.* 38:576–595.

Greenblatt, S. H., Saunders, R. L., Culver, C. M., and Bogdanowicz, W. (1980). Normal interhemispheric transfer with incomplete section of the splenium. *Arch. Neurol.* 37:567–571.

Grüsser, O. J., and Landis, T. (1991). *Visual Agnosias and Other Distrubances of Visual Perception and Cognition.* London: Macmillan Press.

Gur, R. E., Gur, R. C., Sussman, N. M., O'Connor, M. J., and Vey, M. M. (1984). Hemispheric control of the writing hand: the effect of callosotomy in a left-hander. *Neurology* 34:904–908.

Haaland, K. Y., and Delaney, H. D. (1981). Motor deficits after left or right hemisphere damage due to stroke or tumor. *Neuropsychologia* 19:17–27.

Haaland, K. Y., Cleeland, C. S., and Carr, D. (1977). Motor performance after unilateral hemisphere damage in patients with tumors. *Arch. Neurol.* 34:556–559.

Habib, M., Gayraud, D., Oliva, A., Regis, J., Salamon, G., and Khalil, R. (1991). Effects of handedness and sex on the morphology of the corpus callosum: a study with brain magnetic resonance imaging. *Brain Cognition 16*:41–61.

Hamilton, C. R. (1977). Investigations of perceptual and mnemonic lateralization in monkeys. In *Lateralization in the Nervous System*, S. Harnad et al. (eds.). New York: Academic Press.

Hamilton, C. R. (1982). Mechanisms of interocular equivalence. In *Advances in the Analysis of Visual Behavior*, D. Ingle, M. Goodale, and R. Mansfield (eds.). Cambridge, Mass.: MIT Press.

Hamilton, C. R., Nargeot, M. -C., Vermeire, B. A., and Bogen, J. E. (1986). Comprehension of language by the right hemisphere. *Proc. Soc. Neurosci. 12*:721.

Hamilton, C. R., and Vermeire, B. A. (1982). Hemispheric differences in split-brain monkeys learning sequential comparisons. *Neuropsychologia 20*:691–698.

Hamilton, C. R., and Vermeire, B. A. (1986). Localization of visual functions with partially split-brain monkeys. In *Two Hemispheres—One Brain: Functions of the Corpus Callosum*, F. Leporé, M. Ptito and H. Jasper (eds.). New York: Alan R. Liss.

Hamilton, C. R., and Vermeire, B. A. (1988). Complementary hemispheric specialization in monkeys. *Science 242*:1691–1694.

Hampson, E., and Kimura, D. (1984). Hand movement asymmetries during verbal and non-verbal tasks. *Can. J. Psychol. 38*:102–125.

Harcourt-Webster, J. N., and Rack, J. H. (1965). Agenesis of the corpus callosum. *Postgrad. Med. J. 41*:73–79.

Harnad, S., Doty, R. W., Goldstein, L., Jaynes, J., and Krauthamer, G. (1977). *Lateralization in the Nervous System*. New York: Academic Press.

Harrington, A. (1987). *Medicine, Mind, and the Double Brain*. Princeton, N.J.: Princeton University Press.

Head, H. (1926, reprinted in 1963). *Aphasia and Kindred Disorders of Speech*, Vol. I. New York: Hafner.

Hécaen, H. (1969). Aphasic, apraxic and agnosic syndromes in right and left hemisphere lesions. *Handbook Clin. Neurol. 4*:291–311.

Hécaen, H., and Ajuriaguerra, J. (1964). *Left Handedness*. New York: Grune and Stratton.

Hécaen, H., and Assal, G. (1970). A comparison of constructive deficits following right and left hemispheric lesions. *Neuropsychologia 8*:289–303.

Hécaen, H., and Gimeno Alava, A. (1960). L'apraxie idéo-motrice unilatérale gauche. *Rev. Neurol. 102*:648–653.

Hécaen, H., and Gruner, J. (1975). Alexie pure avec intégrité du corps calleux. In *Les Syndromes de Disconnexion Calleuse Chez L'Homme*, F. Michel and B. Schott (eds.). Lyon: Hôpital Neurologique.

Hécaen, H., and Kremin, H. (1976). Neurolinguistic research on reading disorders resulting from left hemisphere lesions: aphasic and pure alexias. In *Studies in Neurolinguistics*, H. Whitaker and H. A. Whitaker (eds.). New York: Academic Press.

Hécaen, H., De Agostini, M., and Monzon-Montes, A. (1981). Cerebral organization in left-handers. *Brain Lang. 12*:261–284.

Heilman, K. M., Coyle, J. M., Gonyear, E. F., and Geschwind, N. (1973). Apraxia and agraphia in a left-hander. *Brain 96*:21–28.

Heilman, K. M., Safran, A., and Geschwind, N. (1971). Closed head trauma and aphasia. *J. Neurol. Neurosurg. Psychiatry 34*:265–269.

Heilman, K. M., and Sypert, G. W. (1977). Korsakoff's syndrome resulting from bilateral fornix lesions. *Neurology 27*:490–493.

Heilman, K. M., and Watson, R. T. (1977). The neglect syndrome: a unilateral defect of the orienting response. In *Lateralization in the Nervous System*, S. Harnad et al. (eds.). New York: Academic Press.

Heilman, K. M., and Watson, R. T. (1991). Intentional motor disorders. In *Frontal Lobe Function and Injury*, H. S. Levin and H. M. Eisenberg (eds.). New York: Oxford University Press.

Henderson, V. W. (1986). Anatomy of posterior pathways in reading: a reassessment. *Brain Lang.* 29:119–133.

Henderson, V. W., Friedman, R. B., Teng, E. L., and Weiner, J. M. (1985). Left hemisphere pathways in reading: inference from pure alexia without hemianopia. *Neurology* 35:962–968.

Henninger-Pechstedt, P. (1986). Suppression of ipsilateral auditory pathways increases with increasing task load in commissurotomy subjects. *Bull. Clin. Neurosci.* 51:73–76.

Henninger-Pechstedt, P. (1989). Commissurotomy subjects show lateralized difference between manual and oral responding. *Cortex.* 325–330.

Herron, J. (ed.) (1980). *Neuropsychology of Left-Handedness.* New York: Academic Press.

Hirose, G., Kin, T., and Murakami, E. (1977). Alexia without agraphia associated with right occipital lesion. *J. Neurol. Neurosurg. Psychiatry* 40:225–227.

Holtzman, J. D., Sidtis, J. J., Volpe, B. T., Wilson, D. H., and Gazzaniga, M. S. (1982). Dissociation of spatial information for stimulus localization and the control of attention. *Brain* 104:861–872.

Holtzman, R.N.N., Rudel, R. G., and Goldensohn, E. S. (1978). Paroxysmal alexia. *Cortex* 14:592–603.

Hoppe, K. D. (1977). Split brains and psychoanalysis. *Psychoanal. Q.* 46:220–244.

Hoppe, K., and Bogen, J. E. (1977). Alexithymia in 12 commissurotomized patients. *Psychother. Psychosom.* 28:148–155.

Horel, J. A., and Keating, E. G. (1972). Recovery from a partial Klüver-Bucy syndrome in the monkey produced by disconnection. *J. Comp. Physiol. Psychol.* 79:105–114.

Huppert, F. A. (1981). Memory in split-brain patients: a comparison with organic amnesic syndromes. *Cortex* 17:303–311.

Innocenti, G. M. (1986). General organization of callosal connections in the cerebral cortex. In *Cerebral Cortex*, Vol. 5, E. G. Jones and A. Peters (eds.). New York: Plenum Press.

Innocenti, G. M. (1991). The development of projections from cerebral cortex. In *Progress in Sensory Physiology*, Vol. 12. [ed.] Berlin-Heidelberg: Springer-Verlag.

Ironside, R., and Guttmacher, M. (1929). The corpus callosum and its tumours. *Brain* 52:442–483.

Ito, M., Yashiki, K., and Hirata, T. (1972). Agenesis of the corpus callosum in man. *Acta Anat. Nippon* 47:391–402.

Iversen, S. D., and Mishkin, M. (1970). Perserverative interference in monkeys following selective lesions of the inferior prefrontal convexity. *Exp. Brain Res.* 11:376–386.

Iwata, M., Sugishita, M., Toyokura, Y., Yamada, R., and Yoshioka, M. (1974). Etude sur le syndrome de disconnexion visuo-linguale après la transection du splénium du corps calleux. *J. Neurol. Sci.* 23:421–432.

Jackson, J. H. (1874). On the nature of the duality of the brain. *Med. Press Circular* 1:19, 41, 63. Reprinted in *Brain*, 1915, and in *Selected Writings of John Hughlings Jackson*, Vol. 2, J. Taylor (ed.). London: Hodder and Stoughton, 1932.

Jacobsen, C. F., and Nissen, H. W. (1937). Studies of cerebral function in primates. IV: The effects of frontal lobe lesions on the delayed alternation habit in monkeys. *J. Comp. Physiol. Psycho.* 23:101–112.

Jason, G. W. (1983a). Hemispheric asymmetries in motor function. I: Left-hemisphere specialization for memory but not performance. *Neuropsychologia* 21:35–45.

Jason, G. W. (1983b). Hemispheric asymmetries in motor function. II: Ordering does not contribute to left-hemisphere specialization. *Neuropsychologia 21*:47–58.

Jeeves, M. A. (1965). Psychological studies of three cases of congenital agenesis of the corpus callosum. In *Functions of the Corpus Callosum*, E. G. Ettlinger (ed.). London: Churchill.

Jeeves, M. A. (1979). Some limits to interhemispheric integration in cases of callosal agenesis and partial commissurotomy. In *Structure and Function of Cerebral Commissures*, I. S. Russell, M. W. van Hof, and G. Berlucchi (eds.). Baltimore: University Park Press.

Jeeves, M. A. (1991). Stereo perception in callosal agenesis and partial callosotomy. *Neuropsychologia 29*:19-34.

Jeeves, M. A., Simpson, D. A., and Geffen, G. (1979). Functional consequences of the transcallosal removal of intraventricular tumors. *J. Neurol. Neurosurg. Psychiatry 42*:134–142.

Jeeves, M. A., and Wilson, A. F. (1969). Tactile transfer and neonatal callosal section in the cat. *Psychoneurol. Sci. 16(5)*:235-237.

Jeannerod, M. (ed.) (1987). *Neurophysiological and Neuropsychological Aspects of Spatial Neglect.* Amsterdam: North-Holland.

Jeret, J., Serur, D., Wisniewski, K. E., and Lubin, R. A. (1987). Clinicopathological findings associated with agenesis of the corpus callosum. *Brain Dev. 9*:255-264.

Jones, E. G. (1985). *The Thalamus.* New York: Plenum.

Jones, R. D., Donaldson, I. M., and Parkin, P. J. (1989). Impairment and recovery of ipsilateral sensory-motor function following unilateral cerebral infarction. *Brain 112*:113-132.

Joseph, R. (1986). Reversal of cerebral dominance for language and emotion in a corpus callosotomy patient. *J. Neurol. Neurosurg. Psychiatry 49*:628-634.

Joynt, R. J. (1974). The corpus callosum: history of thought regarding its function. In *Hemispheric Disconnection and Cerebral Function*, M. Kinsbourne and W. L. Smith (eds.). Springfield, Ill.: C. C. Thomas.

Joynt, R. J. (1977). Inattention syndromes in split-brain man. In *Hemi-Inattention and Hemisphere Specialization*, E. A. Weinstein and R. P. Friedland (eds.). New York: Raven Press.

Kimura, D. (1967). Functional asymmetry of the brain in dichotic listening. *Cortex 3*:163–178.

Kimura, D. (1983). Sex differences in cerebral organization for speech and praxic functions *Can. J. Psychol. 37*:19–35.

Kimura, D., and Archibald, Y. (1974). Motor functions of the left hemisphere. *Brain 97*:337–350.

Kimura, D., Davidson, W., and McCormick, C. W. (1982). No impairment in sign language after right-hemisphere stroke. *Brain Lang. 17*:359–362.

Kinsbourne, M. (1971). The minor cerebral hemisphere as a source of aphasic speech. *Arch. Neurol. 25*:302–306.

Kinsbourne, M. (1975). Minor hemisphere language and cerebral maturation. In *Foundations of Language Development*, H. Lenneberg and E. Lenneberg (eds.). New York: Academic Press.

Kinsbourne, M. (1982). Hemispheric specialization and the growth of human understanding. *Am. Psychol. 37*:411–420.

Kinsbourne, M. (1988). Integrated field theory of consciousness. In *Consciousness in Contemporary Science*, A. J. Marcel and E. Bisiach (eds.). Oxford: Clarendon Press.

Kinsbourne, M. (1991). Discussion on hemispheric integration at the Annual Meeting of The International Neuropsychologic Society, San Antonio, Texas.

Kinsbourne, M., and Fisher, M. (1971). Latency of uncrossed and of crossed reaction in callosal agenesis. *Neuropsychologia 9*:471–473.

Kinsbourne, M., and Smith, W. L. (1974). *Hemispheric Disconnection and Cerebral Function.* Springfield, Ill.: C. C. Thomas.

Kirschbaum, W. R. (1947). Agenesis of the corpus callosum and associated malformations. *J. Neuropathol. Exp. Neurol.* 6:78–94.

Klima, E. S., and Bellugi, V. (1979). *The Signs of Language.* Cambridge, Mass.: Harvard University Press.

Klima, E. S., Bellugi, V., and Poizner, H. (1988). Grammar and space in sign aphasiology. *Aphasiology* 2:319–328.

Klouda, R. V., Robin, D. A., Graff-Radford, N. R., and Cooper, W. E. (1988). The role of callosal connections in speech prosody. *Brain Lang.* 35:154–171.

Kohn, B., and Dennis, M. (1974). Patterns of hemispheric specialization after hemidecortication for infantile hemiplegia. In *Hemispheric Disconnection and Cerebral Function*, M. Kinsbourne and W. L. Smith (eds.). Springfield, Ill.: C. C. Thomas.

Krashen, S. D. (1976). Cerebral asymmetry. In *Studies in Neurolinguistics*, H. Whitaker and H. A. Whitaker (eds.). New York: Academic Press.

Kuhlenbeck, H. (1969). Some comments on the development of the human corpus callosum and septum pellucidum. *Acta Anat. Nippon* 44:245–256.

Kuhn, T. S. (1962). *The Structure of Scientific Revolutions.* Chicago, University of Chicago Press.

Kumar, S. (1977). Short-term memory for a non-verbal tactual task after cerebral commissurotomy. *Cortex* 13:55–61.

Kutas, M., Hillyard, S. A., and Gazzaniga, M. S. (1988). Processing of semantic anomaly by right and left hemispheres of commissurotomy patients. *Brain* 111:553–576.

LaBerge, D. (1990). Thalamic and cortical mechanisms of attention suggested by recent positron emission tomographic experiments. *J. Cog. Neurosci.* 2:358–372.

Lambert, A. J. (1991). Interhemispheric interaction in the split-brain. *Neuropsychologia* 29:941–948.

Landis, T., Graves, R., and Goodglass, H. (1982). Aphasic reading and writing: possible evidence for right hemisphere participation. *Cortex* 18:105–112.

Landis, T., and Regard, M. (1988). The right hemisphere's access to lexical meaning: A function of its release from left-hemisphere control? In C. Chiarello (ed.). *Right Hemisphere Contributions to Lexical Semantics.* New York: Springer-Verlag.

Landis, T., Regard, M., and Serrat, A. (1980). Iconic reading in a case of alexia without agraphia caused by brain tumor: A tachistoscopic study. *Brain and Language* 11:45–53.

LaPlane, D., Levasseur, M., Pillon, B., Dubois, B., Baulac, M., Mazoyer, B., Tran Dinh, S., Sette, G., Danze, F., and Baron, J. C. (1989). Obsessive-compulsive and other behavioural changes with bilateral basal ganglia lesions. *Brain* 112:699–725.

Lashley, K. (1929). *Brain Mechanisms and Intelligence.* Chicago: University of Chicago Press.

Lashley, K. (1951, reprinted in 1967). The problem of serial order in behavior. In L. A. Jeffress (ed.). *Cerebral Mechanisms in Behavior.* New York: Hafner.

Lassen, N. A., and Larsen, B. (1980). Cortical activity in the left and right hemispheres during language-related brain functions. *Phonetica* 37:27–37.

Lassonde, M., and Jeeves, M. A. (eds.) (1992). *Callosal Agenesis: The Natural Split Brain*, New York: Plenum.

Lassonde, M., Bryden, M. P., and Demers, P. (1990). The corpus callosum and cerebral speech lateralization. *Brain and Language.* 38:195–206.

Lassonde, M. C., Lortie, J., Ptito, M., and Geoffroy, G. (1981). Hemispheric asymmetry in callosal agenesis as revealed by dichotic listening performance. *Neuropsychologia* 19:455–458.

Lassonde, M., Sauerwein, H., Chicoine, A., and Geoffroy, G. (1991). Absence of disconnexion syndrome in callosal agenesis and early callosotomy: brain reorganization or lack of structural specificity during ontogeny? *Neuropsychologia* 29:481–495.

Lassonde, M., Sauerwein, H., McCabe, N., Laurencelle, L., and Geoffroy, G. (1988). Extent of limits of cerebral adjustment to early section or congenital absence of the corpus callosum. *Behav. Brain Res.* 30:165–181.

Le Beau, J. (1943) Sur la chirurgie des tumeurs du corps calleux. *Union Med. Can.* 72:1365–1381.

Lebrun, Y. (1990). *Mutism.* London: Whurr.

Lecours, A. R., Lhermitte, F., and Bryans, B. (1983). *Aphasiology.* London: Baillière Tindall.

LeDoux, J. E. (1989). Cognitive-emotional interactions in the brain. *Cognition Emotion* 3:267–289

LeDoux, J. E. (1992). Emotion and the limbic system concept. *Concepts Neurosci.* 2:169–199.

LeDoux, J. E., Risse, G. L., Springer, S. P., Wilson, D. H., and Gazzaniga, M. S. (1977a). Cognition and commissurotomy. *Brain* 100:87–104.

LeDoux, J. E., Wilson, D. H., and Gazzaniga, M. S. (1977b). Manipulo-spatial aspects of cerebral lateralization: clues to the origin of lateralization. *Neuropsychologia* 15:743–750.

Lehman, R.A.W. (1978). The handedness of rhesus monkeys. II: Concurrent reaching. *Cortex* 14:190–196.

Lehmann, H. J., and Lampe, H. (1970). Observations on the interhemispheric transmission of information in nine patients with corpus callosum defect. *Eur. Neurol.* 4:129–147.

Leiguarda, R., Starkstein, S., and Berthier, M. (1989). Anterior callosal haemorrhage: a partial interhemispheric disconnection syndrome. *Brain* 112:1019–1037.

Leonard, G., and Milner, B. (1991). Contribution of the right frontal lobe to the encoding and recall of kinesthetic distance information. *Neuropsychologia* 29:47–58.

Leonard, G., Zatorre, R., and Leblanc, R. (1991). Left-hemisphere language lateralization in a case of agenesis of the corpus callosum. *Neurology* 41:266.

Leporé, F., Ptito, M., and Jasper, H. (1986). *Two Hemispheres—One Brain: Functions of the Corpus Callosum.* New York: Alan R. Liss.

Lesser, R. P., Dinner, D. S., Lüders, H., and Morris, H. H. (1986). Memory for objects presented soon after intracarotid amobarbital sodium injections in patients with medically intractable complex partial seizures. *Neurology* 36:895–899.

Levi, P. (1990) (originally published 1966). For a good purpose. In *The Sixth Day*, R. Rosenthal (trans.). New York: Summit.

Levin, H. S., Eisenberg, H. M., and Benton, A. L. (eds.) (1991). *Frontal Lobe Function and Dysfunction.* New York: Oxford University Press.

Levin, H. S., Gary, H. E., and Eisenberg, H. M. (1989a). Duration of impaired consciousness in relation to side of lesion after severe head injury. *The Lancet* 1001–1003.

Levin. H. S., Goldstein, F. C., Ghostine, S. Y., Weiner, R. L., Crofford, M. J., and Eisenberg, H. M. (1987). Hemispheric disconnection syndrome persisting after anterior cerebral artery aneurysm rupture. *Neurosurgery* 21:831–838.

Levin, H. S., High, W. M., Williams, D. H., Eisenberg, H. M., Amparo, E. G., Guinto, F. C., and Ewert, J. (1989b). Dichotic listening and manual performance in relation to magnetic resonance imaging after closed head injury. *J. Neurol. Neurosurg. Psychiatry* 52:1162–1169.

Levin, H. S., Williams, D. H., Valastro, M., Eisenberg, H. M., Crofford, M. J., and Handel, S. F. (1990). Corpus callosal atrophy following closed head injury: detection with magnetic resonance imaging. *J. Neurosurg.* 73:77–81.

Levy J. (1974). Cerebral asymmetries as manifested in split-brain man. In *Hemispheric Disconnection and Cerebral Function*, M. Kinsbourne and W. L. Smith (eds.). Springfield, Ill.: C. C. Thomas.

Levy, J., Nebes, R. D., and Sperry, R. W. (1971). Expressive language in the surgically separated minor hemisphere. *Cortex* 7:49–58.

Levy, J., and Trevarthen, C. (1976), Metacontrol of hemispheric function in human split-brain patients. *J. Exp. Psychol. (Hum. Percept.)* 2:299–312.

Levy, J., Trevarthen, C., and Sperry, R. W. (1972). Perception of bilateral chimeric figures following hemispheric deconnexion. *Brain* 95:61–78.

Lévy, Valensi, J. (1910). *Le Corps Calleux* (Paris theses 448). Paris: G. Steinheil.

Lhermitte, F. (1986). Human autonomy and the frontal lobes. Part II: Patient behavior in complex and social situations: the "environmental dependency syndrome." *Ann. Neurol.* 19:335–343.

Lhermitte, F., and Beauvois, M. F. (1973). A visual-speech disconnexion syndrome. *Brain* 96:695–714.

Lhermitte, F., Chain, F., and Chedru, F. (1975). Syndrome de déconnexion interhémisphérique: Etude des performances visuelles. In *Les Syndromes de Disconnexion Calleuse Chez L'Homme*, F. Michel and B. Schott, (eds.). Lyon: Hôpital Neurologique.

Lhermitte, F., Chain, F., Chedru, F., and Penet, C. (1976). A study of visual processes in a case of interhemispheric disconnexion. *J. Neurol. Sci.* 28:317–330.

Lhermitte, F., Marteau, R., Serdaru, M., and Chedru, F. (1977). Signs of interhemispheric disconnection in Marchiafava-Bignami disease. *Arch. Neurol.* 34:254.

Lhermitte, F., Pillon, B., and Serdaru, M. (1986). Human autonomy and the frontal lobes. Part I: Imitation and utilization behavior: A neuropsychological study of 75 patients. *Ann. Neurol.* 19:326–334.

Liepmann, H. (1900). Das Krankheitsbild der Apraxie (motorische Asymbolie) auf Grund eines Falles von einseitiger Apraxie. *Monatsschr. Psychiatr. Neurol.* 8:182–197.

Liepmann, H., and Maas, O. (1907). Fall von linksseitiger Agraphie und Apraxie bei rechtsseitiger Lähmung. *J. Psychol. Neurol.* 10:214–227

Loeser, J. E., and Alvord, E. C. (1968). Agenesis of the corpus collosum. *Brain* 91:553–570.

Luck, S. J., Hillyard, S. A., Mangun, G. R., and Gazzaniga, M. S. (1989). Independent hemispheric attentional systems mediate visual search in split-brain patients. *Nature* 342:543–545.

Ludlow, C. L. (1980). Children's language disorders: recent research advances. *Ann. Neurol.* 7:497–507.

MacKay, D. M., and MacKay, V. (1982). Explicit dialogue between left and right half-systems of split brains. *Nature* 295:690–691.

Macko, K. A., and Mishkin, M. (1985). Metabolic mapping of higher-order visual areas in the monkey. In *Brain Imaging and Brain Function*, L. Sokoloff (ed.). New York: Raven Press.

Magoun, W. W. (1958). *The Waking Brain*. Springfield, Ill.: C. C. Thomas.

Mark, V. W., McAlaster, R., and Laser, K. L. (1991). Bilateral alien hand. *Neurology 41(Suppl. 1)*:302.

Marie, P. (1906, reprinted in 1971). The third left frontal convolution plays no special role in the function of Language. *Semaine Med.* 26:241–247. Reprinted in *Pierre Marie's Papers on Speech Disorders*, M. F. Cole and M. Cole (eds.). New York: Hafner.

Markowitsch, H. J., Pritzel, M., Kessler, J., Guldin, W., and Freeman, R. B. (1980). Delayed alternation performance after selective lesions within the prefrontal cortex of the cat. *Behav. Brain Res.* 1:67–91.

Marshall, J. C., and Halligan, P. W. (1988). Blindsight and insight in visuo-spatial neglect. *Nature* 336:766–767.

Maspes, P. E. (1948). Le syndrome expérimental chez l'homme de la section du splénium du corps calleux: alexie visuelle pure hémianopsique. *Rev. Neurol. (Paris)* 80:100–113.

Mateer, C., and Kimura D. (1977). Impairment of nonverbal oral movements in aphasia. *Brain and Language* 4:262–276.

Mayer, E., Koenig, O., and Panchaud, A. (1988). Tactual extinction without anomia: evidence of attentional factors in a patient with a partial callosal disconnection. *Neuropsychologia* 26:851–868.

McKeever, W. F., Sullivan, K. F., Ferguson, S. M., and Rayport, M. (1981). Typical cerebral hemisphere disconnection deficits following corpus callosum section despite sparing of the anterior commissure. *Neuropsychologia* 19:745–755.

McKeever, W. F., Sullivan, K. F., Freguson, S. M., and Rayport, M. (1982). Right hemisphere speech development in the anterior commissure-spared commissurotomy patient: a second case. *Clin. Neuropsychol.* 4:17–22

McNabb, A. W., Carroll, W. M., and Mastaglia, F. L. (1988). "Alien hand" and loss of bimanual coordination after dominant anterior cerebral artery territory infarction. *J. Neurol. Neurosurg. Psychiatry* 51:218–222.

Metter, E. J., Hanson, W. R., Jackson, C. A., Kempler, D., van Lancker, D., Mazziotta, J. C., and Phelps, M. E. (1990). Temporoparietal cortex in aphasia: evidence from positron emission tomography. *Arch. Neurol.* 47:1235–1238.

Michel, F., and Péronnet, F. (1975). Extinction gauche au test dichotique: lésion hémisphérique ou lésion commissurale? In *Les Syndromes de Disconnexion Calleuse Chez L'Homme*, F. Michel and B. Schott (eds.). Lyon: Hôpital Neurologique.

Michel, F., and Péronnet, F. (1982). L'Hémianacousie, un déficit auditif dans un hémisphère. *Rev. Neurol. (Paris)* 138:657–671.

Michel, F., and Schott, B. (eds.). (1975). *Les Syndromes de Disconnexion Calleuse Chez L'Homme*. Lyon: Hôpital Neurologique.

Milner, A. D. (1982). Simple reaction times to lateralized visual stimuli in a case of callosal agenesis. *Neuropsychologia* 20:411–419.

Milner, A. D., and Jeeves, M. A. (1979). A review of behavioural studies of agenesis of the corpus callosum. In *Structure and Function of Cerebral Commissures*, I. S. Russell, M. W. van Hof, and G. Berlucchi (eds.). Baltimore: University Park Press.

Milner, A. D., and Rugg, M. D. (eds.) (1991). *The Neuropsychology of Consciousness*. San Diego: Academic Press.

Milner, B. (1971). Interhemispheric differences in the localization of psychological processes in man. *Br. Med. Bull.* 27:272–277.

Milner, B. (ed.) (1975). *Hemispheric Specialization and Interaction*. Cambridge, Mass.: MIT Press.

Milner, B. (1978). Clues to the cerebral organization of memory. In *Cerebral Correlates of Conscious Experience*, Buser, P. A., and Rougeul-Buser, A.(eds.). Amsterdam: North Holland Publishing Company.

Milner, B. (1980). Complementary functional specializations of the human cerebral hemispheres. In *Nerve Cells, Transmitters and Behavior*, R. Levi-Montalcini (ed.). Rome: Pontifica Academia Scientarium.

Milner, B., and Taylor, L. (1972). Right-hemisphere superiority in tactile pattern-recognition after cerebral commissurotomy: evidence for non-verbal memory. *Neuropsychologia* 10:1–15.

Milner, B., Taylor, L., and Jones-Gotman, M. (1990). Lessons from cerebral commissurotomy: auditory attention, haptic memory, and visual images in verbal associative learning. In *Brain Circuits and Functions of the Mind: Essays in Honour of R. W. Sperry*, C. Trevarthen (ed.). Cambridge: Cambridge University Press.

Milner, B., Taylor, L., and Sperry, R. W. (1968). Lateralized suppression of dichotically presented digits after commissural section in man. *Science* 161:184–186.

Mingazzini, G. (1922) *Der Balken*. Berlin: Springer.

Minsky, M. L. (1988). *The Society of Mind*. New York: Simon and Schuster.

Mishkin, M. (1957). Effects of small frontal lesions on delayed alteration in monkeys. *J. Neurophysiol*. 20:615–622.

Mishkin, M. (1982). A memory system in the monkey. *Philos. Trans. R. Soc. Lond. (Biol.)* 298:85–95.

Mishkin, M., and Phillips, R. R. (1990). A corticolimbic memory path revealed through its disconnection. In *Brain Circuits and Functions of the Mind: Essays in Honour of R. W. Sperry*, C. Trevarthen (ed.). Cambridge: Cambridge University Press.

Moruzzi, G., and Magoun, H. W. (1949). Brain stem reticular formation and activation of the EEG. *EEG Clin. Neurophysiol*. 1:455–473.

Moscovitch, M. (1976). On the representation of language in the right hemisphere of right-handed people. *Brain Lang*. 3:47–71, 590–599.

Mosidze, V. M., Mkheidze, R. A., and Makashvili, M. A. (1980). *Human Brain Asymmetry* (in Russian). Tbilisi: Metsniereba.

Murray, E. A. (1992). Medial temporal lobe structures contributing to recognition memory: the amygdaloid complex versus the rhinal cortex. In *The Amygdala*, J. P. Aggleton (ed.). New York: Wiley-Liss.

Murray, J. E., and McLaren, R. (1990). Recognition of fused dichotic words: an examination of the effects of head-turn and preceived spatial position. *Neuropsychologia* 28:1187–1195.

Musiek, F. E., Reeves, A. G., and Baran, J. A. (1985). Release from central auditory competition in the split-brain patient. *Neurology* 35:983–987.

Musiek, F. E., Wilson, D. H., Reeves, A. G. (1981). Staged commissurotomy and central auditory function. *Arch. Otolaryngol*. 107:233–236.

Myers, J. J. (1984) Right hemisphere language: science or fiction? *Am. Psychol*. 39:315–320.

Myers, J. J., and Sperry, R. W. (1985). Interhemispheric communication after section of the forebrain commissures. *Cortex* 21:249–260.

Myers, R. E. (1956). Function of the corpus callosum in interocular transfer. *Brain* 79:358–363.

Myers, R. E., and Sperry, R. W. (1953). Interocular transfer of visual form discrimination habit on cats after section of the optic chiasma and corpus callosum. *Anat. Rec*. 115:351–352.

Myers, R. E., and Sperry, R. W. (1958). Interhemispheric communication through the corpus callosum: mnemonic carry-over between the hemispheres. *Arch. Neurol. Psychiatry* 80:298–303.

Nass, R. D., and Gazzaniga, M. S. (1987). Cerebral lateralization andspecialization in human central nervous system. In *Handbook of Physiology, Sec. 1: The nervous system*, Vol. V, Pt. 2, V. B. Mountcastle, F. Plum, and S. R. Geiger (eds.). Baltimore: Waverly Press.

Nebes, R. D. (1974). Hemispheric specialization in commissurotomized man. *Psychol. Bull*. 81:1–14.

Nebes, R. D., and Nashold, B. S. (1980). A comparison of dichotic and visuo-acoustic competition in hemispherectomized patients. *Brain Lang*. 9:246–254.

Netley, C. (1972). Dichotic listening performance of hemispherectomized patients. *Neuropsychologia* 10:233–240.

Newcombe, F. (1969). *Missile Wounds of the Brain*. London: Oxford University Press.

Nielsen, J. M. (1946, originally published in 1936). *Agnosia, Apraxia, Aphasia. Their Value in Cerebral Localization*, 2nd ed. New York: Hoeber.

Novelly, R. A., and Lifrak, M. D. (1985). Forebrain commissurotomy reinstates effects of pre-existing hemisphere lesions: an examination of the hypothesis. In *Epilepsy and the Corpus Callosum*, A. G. Reeves (ed.). New York: Plenum.

Oepen, G., Schulz-Weiling, R., Zimmermann, P., Birg, W., Straesser, S., and Gilsbach, J. (1988).

Neuropsychological assessment of the transcallosal approach. *Eur. Arch. Psychiatr. Neurol, Sci.* 237:365–375.

Ogden, J. A. (1988). Language and memory functions after long recovery periods in left-hemispherectomized subject. *Neuropsychologia* 26:645–649.

Oguni, H., Olivier, A., Andermann, F., and Comair, J. (1991). Anterior callosotomy in the treatment of medically intractable epilepsies: a study of 43 patients with a mean follow-up of 39 months. *Ann. Neurol.* 30:357–364.

O'Kusky, J., Strauss, E., Kosaka, B., Wada, J., Li, D., Druhan, M., and Petrie, J. (1988). The corpus callosum is larger with right-hemisphere cerebral speech dominance. *Ann. Neurol.* 24:379–383.

Ornstein, R., Herron, J., Johnstone, J., and Swencionis, C. (1979). Differential right hemisphere involvement in two reading tasks. *Psychophysiology* 16:398–401.

Overman, W. H., and Doty, R. W. (1982). Hemispheric specialization displayed by man but not by macaques for analysis of faces. *Neuropsychologia* 20:113–128.

Oxbury, J. M., and Oxbury, S. M. (1970). Effects of temporal lobectomy on the report of dichotically presented digits. *Cortex* 5:3–14.

Ozgur, M. H., Johnson, T., Smith, A., and Bogen, J. E. (1977). Transcallosal approach to third ventricle tumor: case report. *Bull. Los Angeles Neurol. Soc.* 42:57–62.

Paivio, A. (1990). *Mental Representations: A Dual Coding Approach.* New York: Oxford University Press.

Pandya, D. N. (1975). Interhemispheric connections in primates. In *Les Syndromes de Disconnexion Calleuse Chez l'Homme,* F. Michel and B. Schott (eds.). Lyon: Hôpital Neurologique.

Pandya, D. N., and Rosene, D. F. (1985). Some observations on trajectories and topography of commissural fibers. In *Epilepsy and the Corpus Callosum,* A. G. Reeves (ed.). New York: Plenum.

Pandya, D. N., and Seltzer, B. (1986). The topography of commissural fibers. In *Two Hemispheres—One Brain: Functions of the Corpus Callosum,* F. Leporé., M. Pitito, and H. H. Jasper (eds.). New York: Alan R. Liss.

Papanicolaou, A. C., Moore, B. D., Deutsch, G., Levin, H. S., and Eisenberg, H. M. (1988). Evidence for right-hemisphere involvement in recovery from aphasia. *Arch. Neurol.* 45:1025–1035.

Paterson, A., and Zangwill, O. L. (1944). Disorders of visual space perception associated with lesions of the right cerebral hemisphere. *Brain* 67:331–358.

Patterson, K., Vargha-Khadem, F., and Polkey, C. E. (1989). Reading with one hemisphere. *Brain* 112:39–63.

Penfield, W. (1954). Studies of the cerebral cortex of man—a review and an interpretation. In *Brain Mechanism and Consciousness,* J. F. Delafresnaye (ed.). Springfield, Ill.: C. C. Thomas.

Petersen, M. R., Beecher, M. D., Zoloth, S. R., Green, S., Marler, P. R., Moody, D. B., and Stebbins, W. C. (1984). Neural lateralization of vocalizations by Japanese macaques: communicative significance is more important than acoustic structure. *Behav. Neurosci.* 98:779–790.

Pipe, M. (1991). Developmental changes in finger localization. *Neuropsychologia* 29:339–342.

Plourde, G., and Sperry, R. W. (1984). Left hemisphere involvement in left spatial neglect from right-sided lesions: a commissurotomy study. *Brain* 107:95–106.

Poeck, K. (1984). Neuropsychological demonstration of splenial interhemispheric disconnection in a case of "optic anomia." *Neuropsychologia* 22:707–713.

Poeck, K. (1986). The clinical examination for motor apraxia. *Neuropsychologia* 24:129–134.

Poeck, K., Lehmkuhl, G., and Willmes, K. (1982). Axial movements in ideomotor appraxia. *J. Neurol. Neurosurg. Psychiatry* 45:1125–1129.

Poizner, H., Bellugi, U., and Klima, E. S. (1990). Biological foundations of language: clues from sign language. *Annu. Rev. Neurosci.* 13:283–307.

Poncet, M., Ali Chérif, A., Choux, M., Boudouresques, J., and Lhermitte, F. (1978). Étude neuropsychologique d'un syndrome de déconnexion calleuse totale avec hémianopsie latérale homonyme droite. *Rev. Neurol. (Paris)* 11:633–653.

Popper, K. R., and Eccles, J. C. (1981). *The Self and Its Brain.* Berlin: Springer-Verlag.

Preilowski, B.F.B. (1972). Possible contribution of the anterior forebrain commissures to bilateral motor coordination. *Neuropsychologia* 10:267–277.

Preilowski, B.F.B. (1990). Intermanual transfer, interhemispheric interaction, and handedness in man and monkeys. In *Brain Circuits and Functions of the Mind: Essays in Honor of R. W. Sperry,* C. Trevarthen (ed.). Cambridge: Cambridge University Press.

Pribram, K. H., Plotkin, H. C., Anderson, R. M., and Leong, D. (1977). Information sources in the delayed alternation task for normal and frontal monkeys. *Neuropsychologia* 15:329–340.

Probst, F. P. (1973). Congenital defects of the corpus callosum. *Acta Radiol. (Suppl.)* 331:1–152.

Ptito, A., Lassonde, M., Leporé, F., and Ptito, M. (1987). Visual discrimination in hemispherectomized patients. *Neuropsychologia* 25:869–879.

Ptito, A., Leporé, F., Ptito, M., and Lassonde, M. (1991). Target detection and movement discrimination in the blind field of hemispherectomized patients. *Brain* 114:497–512.

Ptito, M., and Leporé, F. (1983). Interocular transfer in cats with early callosal transection. *Nature* 301:513–515.

Pujol, J., Junqué, C., Vendrell, P., Garcia, P., Capdevila, A., and Marti-Vilalta, J. L. (1991). Left-ear extinction in patients with MRI periventricular lesions. *Neuropsychologia* 29:177–184.

Purves, S. J., Wada, J. A., Woodhurst, W. B., Moyes, P. D., Strauss, E., Kosaka, B., and Li, D. (1988). Results of anterior corpus callosum section in 24 patients with medically intractable seizures. *Neurology* 38:1194–1201.

Rafal, R. D., and Posner, M. I. (1987). Deficits in human visual spatial attention following thalamic lesions. *Proc. Natl. Acad. Sci. U.S.A.* 84:7349–7353.

Rafal, R., Smith, J., Krantz, J., Cohen, A., and Brennan, C. (1990). Extrageniculate vision in hemianopic humans: saccade inhibition by signals in the blind field. *Science* 250:118–121.

Ramachandran, V. S., Cronin-Golomb, A., and Myers, J. J. (1986). Perception of apparent motion by commissurotomy patients. *Nature* 320:358–359.

Rao, S. M., Bernardin, L., Leo, G. J., Ellington, L., Ryan, S. B., and Burg, L. S. (1989). Cerebral disconnection in multiple sclerosis: relationship to atrophy of the corpus callosum. *Arch. Neurol.* 46:918–920.

Raymond, F., Lejonne, P., and Lhermitte, J. (1906). Tumeurs du corps calleux. *Encéphale* 1:533–565.

Rayport, M., Ferguson, S. M., and Corrie, W. S. (1983). Outcomes and indications of corpus callosum section for intractable seizure control. *Appl. Neurophysiol.* 46:47–51.

Reeves, A. G. (ed.) (1984). *Epilepsy and the Corpus Callosum.* New York: Plenum.

Reeves, A. G. (1991). Behavioral changes following corpus callosotomy. In *Advances in Neurology,* Vol. 55, D. Smith, D. Treiman, and M. Trimble (eds.). New York: Raven Press.

Reeves, D. L., and Courville, C. B. (1938). Complete agenesis of the corpus callosum. *Bull. Los Angeles Neurol. Soc.* 3:169–181.

Reynolds, D. McQ., and Jeeves, M. A. (1977). Further studies of tactile perception and motor coordination in agenesis of the corpus callosum. *Cortex* 13:257–272.

Ringo, J. L., Doty, R. W., and Demeter, S. (1991). Bi-versus monohemispheric performance in split-brain and partially split-brain macaques. *Exp. Brain Res.* 86:1–8.

Risse, G. L., Gates, J., Lund, G., Maxwell, R., and Rubens, A. (1989). Interhemispheric transfer in patients with incomplete section of the corpus callosum. *Arch. Neurol.* 46:437–443.

Rogers, L., TenHouten, W., Kaplan, C. D., and Gardiner, M. (1977). Hemispheric specialization of language. An EEG study of bilingual Hopi Indian children. *Int. J. Neurosci.* 8:1–6.

Roland, P. E., Skinhoj, E., and Lassen, N. A. (1981). Focal activations of human cerebral cortex during auditory discrimination. *J. Neurophysiol.* 45:374–386.

Rosadini, G., and Rossi, G. F. (1967). On the suggested cerebral dominance for consciousness. *Brain* 90:101–112.

Ross, E. D., and Rush, A. J. (1981). Diagnosis and neuroanatomical correlates of depression in brain-damaged patients. *Arch. Gen. Psychiatry* 38:1344–1354.

Ross, E. D., and Stewart, R. M. (1981). Akinetic mutism from hypothalamic damage: successful treatment with dopamine agonists. *Neurology* 31:1435–1439.

Rubens, A. B., Froehling, B., Slater, G., and Anderson, D. (1985). Left ear suppression on verbal dichotic tests in patients with multiple sclerosis. *Ann. Neurol.* 18:459–463.

Sadowsky, C., and Reeves, A. G. (1975). Agenesis of the corpus callosum with hypothermia. *Arch. Neurol.* 32:744–776.

Sasanuma, S., Itoh, M., Mori, K., and Kobayashi, Y. (1977). Tachistoscopic recognition of kana and kanji words. *Neuropsychologia* 15:547–553.

Sass, K. J., Novelly, R. A., Spencer, D. D., and Spencer, S. S. (1988). Mnestic and attention impairments following corpus callosum section for epilepsy. *J. Epilepsy* 1:61–66.

Sass, K. J., Novelly, R. A., Spencer, D. D., and Spencer, S. S. (1990). Postcallosotomy language impairments in patients with crossed cerebral dominance. *J. Neurosurg.* 72:85–90.

Sass, K. J., Spencer, S. S., Westerveld, M., and Spencer, D. D. (1992). The neuropsychology of corpus callosotomy for epilepsy. In *The Neuropsychology of Epilepsy*, T. L. Bennett (ed.). New York: Plenum.

Sauerwein, H. C., Lassonde, M. C., Cardin, B., and Geoffroy, G. (1981). Interhemispheric integration of sensory and motor functions in agenesis of the corpus callosum. *Neuropsychologia* 19:445–454.

Saul, R., and Sperry, R. W. (1968). Absence of commissurotomy symptoms with agenesis of the corpus callosum. *Neurology* 18:307.

Sawaguchi, T., and Goldman-Rakic, P. S. (1991). D1 dopamine receptors in prefrontal cortex: involvement in working memory. *Science* 251:947–950.

Schaltenbrand, G. (1964). Discussion in *Cerebral Localization and Organization*, G. Schaltenbrand and C. N. Woolsey (eds.). Madison: University of Wisconsin Press.

Scheibel, M. E., and Scheibel, A. B. (1966). The organization of the nucleus reticularis thalami: a Golgi study. *Brain Res.* 1:43–62.

Schlag, J., and Waszak, M. (1970). Characteristics of unit responses in nucleus reticularis thalami. *Brain Res.* 21:286–288.

Schott, B., Trillet, M., Michel, F., and Tommasi, M. (1974). Le syndrome de disconnexion calleuse chez l'ambidextre et le gaucher. In *Les Syndromes de Disconnexion Calleuse Chez L'Homme*, F. Michel and B. Schott (eds.). Lyon: Hôpital Neurologique.

Schulhoff, C., and Goodglass, H. (1969). Dichotic listening, side of brain injury and cerebral dominance. *Neuropsychologia* 7:149–160.

Schwartz, M. F., Reed, E. S., Montgomery, M., Palmer, C., and Mayer, N. H. (1991). The quantitative description of action disorganisation after brain damage: a case study. *Cognitive Neuropsychol.* 8:381–414.

Sechzer, J. A., Folstein, S. E., Geiger, E. H., and Mervis, R. F. (1976). The split-brain neonate:

a surgical method for corpus callosum section in newborn kittens. *Dev. Psychobiol.* 9:377–388.

Segal, M. (1935). Agenesis of the corpus callosum in man. *S. Afr. J. Med. Sci.* 1:65–74.

Segalowitz, S. J. (1983). *Two Sides of the Brain.* Englewood Cliffs, N.J.: Prentice-Hall.

Selnes, O. A. (1974). The corpus callosum: some anatomical and functional considerations with special reference to language. *Brain Lang.* 1:111–139.

Selnes, O. A. (1976). A note on "On the representation of language in the right hemisphere of right-handed people." Brain Lang. 3:583–589.

Sergent, J. (1986). Subcortical coordination of hemisphere activity in commissurotomized patients. *Brain* 109:357–369.

Sergent, J. (1987). A new look at the human split brain. *Brain* 110:1375–1392.

Sergent, J. (1990). Furtive incursions into bicameral minds: integrative and coordinating role of subcortical structures. *Brain* 113:537–568.

Sergent, J. (1991). Processing of spatial relations within and between the disconnected cerebral hemispheres. *Brain* 114:1025–1043.

Shallice, T., and Burgess, P. W. (1991). Deficits in strategy application following frontal lobe damage in man. *Brain* 114:727–741.

Shallice, T., Burgess, P. W., Schon, F., and Baxter, D. M. (1989). The origins of utilization behaviour. *Brain* 112:1587–1598.

Sheremata, W. A., Deonna, T. W., and Romanul, F. C. A. (1973). Agenesis of the corpus callosum and interhemispheric transfer of information. *Neurology* 23:390.

Sherman, S. M., and Koch, C. (1986). The control of retinogeniculate transmission in the mammalian lateral geniculate nucleus. *Exp. Brain Res.* 63:1–20.

Shoumura, K., Ando, T., and Kato, K. (1975). Structural organization of callosal OBg in human corpus callosum agenesis. *Brain Res.* 93:241–252.

Sidtis, J. J. (1988). Dichotic listening after commissurotomy. In *Handbook of Dichotic Listening: Theory, Methods and Research,* K. Hugdahl (ed.). New York: John Wiley and Sons.

Sidtis, J. J., Sadler, A. E., and Nass, R. D. (1989). Double disconnection effects resulting from infiltrating tumors. *Neuropsychologia* 27:1415–1420.

Sidtis, J. J., Volpe, B. T., Holtzman, J. D., Wilson, D. H., and Gazzaniga, M. S. (1981a). Cognitive interaction after staged callosal section: evidence for transfer of semantic activation. *Science* 212:344–346.

Sidtis, J. J., Volpe, B. T., Wilson, D. H., Rayport, M., and Gazzaniga, M. S. (1981b). Variability in right hemisphere language function after callosal section: evidence for a continuum of generative capacity. *J. Neurosci.* 1:323–331.

Sine, R. D., Soufi, A., and Shah, M. (1984). The callosal syndrome: implications for stroke. *Arch. Phys. Med.* 65:606–610.

Singer, W. (1977). Control of thalamic transmission by corticofugal and ascending reticular pathways in the visual system. *Physiol. Rev.* 57:386–420.

Slager, U. T., Kelly, A. B., and Wagner, J. A. (1957). Congenital absence of the corpus callosum. *N. Engl, J. Med.* 256:1171–1176.

Smith, A. (1966). Speech and other functions after left (dominant) hemispherectomy. *J. Neurol. Neurosurg. Psychiatry* 29:467–471.

Smith, A. (1974). Dominant and nondominant hemispherectomy. In *Hemispheric Disconnection and Cerebral Function,* M. Kinsbourne and L. Smith (eds.). Springfield, Ill.: C. C. Thomas.

Smith, A., and Sugar, O. (1975). Development of above-normal language and intelligence 21 years after left hemispherectomy. *Neurology* 25:813–818.

Sparks, R., and Geschwind, N. (1968). Dichotic listening in man after section of neocortical commissures. *Cortex* 4:3–16.

Sparks, R., Goodglass. H., and Nickel, B. (1970). Ipsilateral versus contralateral extinction in dichotic listening from hemispheric lesions. *Cortex* 6:249–260.

Speedie, L. J., Coslett, H. B., and Heilman, K. M. (1984). Repetition of affective prosody in mixed transcortical aphasia. *Arch. Neurol.* 41:268–270.

Spencer, S. S., Gates, J. R., Reeves, A. R., Spencer, D. D., Maxwell, R. E., and Roberts, D. (1987). Corpus callosum section. In *Surgical Treatment of the Epilepsies,* J. Engel, Jr. (ed.). New York, Raven Press.

Sperry, R. W. (1961). Cerebral organization and behavior. *Science* 133:1749–1757.

Sperry, R. W. (1968). Mental unity following surgical disconnection of the cerebral hemispheres. *Harv. Lect.* 62:293–323.

Sperry, R. W. (1970). Perception in the absence of the neocortical commissures. *Res. Publ. Assoc, Res. Nerv. Ment. Dis.* 48:123–138.

Sperry, R. W. (1974). Lateral specialization in the surgically separated hemispheres. In *Neuroscience 3rd Study Program,* F. O. Schmitt and F. G. Worden (eds.). Cambridge, Mass: MIT Press.

Sperry, R. W. (1982). Some effects of disconnecting the cerebral hemispheres. *Science* 217:1223–1226.

Sperry, R. W., and Gazzaniga, M. S. (1967). Language following surgical disconnection of the hemispheres. In *Brain Mechanisms Underlying Speech and Language,* F. L. Darley (ed.). New York: Grune and Stratton.

Sperry, R. W., Gazzaniga, M. S., and Bogen, J. E. (1969). Interhemispheric relationships: the neocortical commissures; syndromes of hemisphere disconnection. *Hdbk. Clin. Neurol.* 4:273–290.

Spinelli, D., Guariglia, C., Massironi, M., Pizzamiglio, L., and Zoccolotti, P. (1990). Contrast sensitivity and low spatial frequency discrimination in hemi-neglect patients. *Neuropsychologia* 28:727–732.

Springer, S. P., and Deutsch, G. (1981). *Left Brain, Right Brain.* San Francisco: W. H. Freeman and Co.

Springer, S. P., and Gazzaniga, M. S. (1975). Dichotic testing of partial and complete split-brain subjects. *Neuropsychologia* 13:341–346.

Squire, L. R., and Zola-Morgan, S. (1991). The medial temporal lobe memory system. *Science* 253:1380–1386.

Staller, J., Buchanan, D., Singer, M., Lappin, J., and Webb, W. (1978). Alexia without agraphia: an experimental case study. *Brain Lang.* 5:378–387.

Stamm, J. S., Rosen, S. C., and Godotti, A. (1977). Lateralization of functions in the monkey's frontal cortex. In *Lateralization in the Nervous System,* S. Harnad, R. W. Doty, L. Goldstein, J. Jaynes, and G. Krauthamer (eds.). New York: Academic Press.

Starkstein, S. E., Berthier, M. L., Fedoroff, P., Price, T. R., and Robinson, R. G. (1990). Anosognosia and major depression in 2 patients with cerebrovascular lesions. *Neurology* 40:1380–1382.

Steriade, M., and Llinas, R. R. (1988). The functional states of the thalamus and the associated neuronal interplay. *Physiol. Rev.* 68:649–725.

Stuss, D. T., and Benson, D. F. (1986). *The Frontal Lobes.* New York: Raven.

Sugishita, M. (1990). *Right Hemisphere and Left Hemisphere: A Dialogue.* Tokyo: Seidosha (in Japanese).

Sugishita, M., Sakuma, I., and Hamilton, C. R. (1991). Reading aloud letters in and about the fovea of a commissurotomized subject. (submitted).

Sugishita, M., and Yoshioka, M. (1987). Visual processes in a hemialexic patient with posterior callosal section. *Neuropsychologia* 25:329–339.

Sugishita, M., Yoshioka, M., and Kawamura, M. (1986). Recovery from hemialexia. *Brain Lang.* 29:106–118.

Sullivan, M. C., and Hamilton, C. R. (1973a). Interocular transfer of reversed and non-reversed discriminations via the anterior commissure in monkeys. *Physiol. Behav. 10*:355–359.

Sullivan, M. C., and Hamilton, C. R. (1973b). Memory establishment via the anterior commissure in monkeys. *Physiol. Behav. 11*:873–879.

Sussman, N. M., Gur, R. C., Gur, R. E., and O'Connor, M. J. (1983). Mutism as a consequence of callosotomy. *J. Neurosurg. 59*:514–519.

Sweet, W. H. (1945). Seeping intracranial aneurysm simulating neoplasm: syndrome of the corpus callosum. *Arch. Neurol. Psychiatry 45*:86–104.

Tanaka, Y., Iwasa, H., and Yoshida, M. (1990). Diagonistic dyspraxis: case report and movement-related potentials. *Neurology 40*:657–661.

Taylor, L. B. (1991). Neuropsychologic assessment of patients with chronic encephalitis. In *Chronic Encephalitis and Epilepsy: Rasmussen's Syndrome*, F. Andermann (ed.). Boston: Butterworth-Heinemann.

Temple, C. M., Jeeves, M. A., and Vilarroya O. (1989). Ten pen men: rhyming skills in two children with callosal agenesis. *Brain Lang. 37*:548–564.

Teng, E. L., and Sperry, R. W. (1973). Interhemispheric interaction during simultaneous bilateral presentation of letters or digits in commissurotomized patients. *Neuropsychologia 11*:131–140.

TenHouten, W. D., Hoppe, K. D., Bogen, J. E., and Walter, D. O. (1986). Alexithymia: an experimental study of cerebral commissurotomy patients and normal control subjects. *Am. J. Psychiatry 143*:312–316.

Tomasch, J. (1954). Size, distribution, and number of fibres in the human corpus callosum. *Anat. Rec. 119*:7–19.

Tomasch, J. (1957). A quantitiative analysis of the human anterior commissure. *Acta Anat. 30*:902–906.

Tramo, M. J., and Bharucha, J. J. (1991). Musical priming by the right hemisphere post-callosotomy. *Neuropsychologia 29*:313–325.

Tranel, D. (1991). What has been rediscovered in "Rediscovering Tactile Agnosia"? *Mayo Clin. Proc. 66*:210–214.

Trescher, H. H., and Ford, F. R. (1937). Colloid cyst of the third ventricle; report of a case: operative removal with section of posterior half of corpus callosum. *Arch. Neurol. Psychiatry 37*:959–973.

Trevarthen, C. (1965). Motor responses in split-brain animals. In *Functions of the Corpus Callosum*, E. G. Ettlinger (ed.). London: Churchill.

Trevarthen, C. B. (1984). Hemispheric specialization. In *Handbook of Physiology: The Nervous System*, Vol III, Part 2, I. Darion-Smith (ed.). Washington, D.C.: American Physiological Society.

Trevarthen, C. (ed.) (1990). *Brain Circuits and Functions of the Mind: Essays in Honor of R. W. Sperry*. Cambridge: Cambridge University Press.

Trevarthen, C., and Sperry, R. W. (1973). Perceptual unity of the ambient visual field in human commissurotomy patients. *Brain 96*:547–570.

Trope, I., Fishman, B., Gur, R. C., Sussman, N. M., and Gur, R. E. (1987). Contralateral and ipsilateral control of fingers following callosotomy. *Neuropsychologia 25*:287–291.

Twitchell, T. E. (1951). The restoration of motor function following hemiplegia in man. *Brain 74*:443–480.

Tzavaras, A., Hécaen, H., and Le Bras, H. (1971). Troubles de la reconnaissance du visage humain et latéralisation hémisphérique lésionnelle chez les sujets gauchers. *Neuropsychologia 9*:475–477.

Unterharnscheidt, F., Jalnik, D., and Gott, H. (1968). Der balkenmangel. *Monogr. Gesamtgeb. Neurol. Psychiatr. 128*:1–232.

Valenstein, E., Bowers, D., Verfaellie M., Heilman, K. M., Day, A., and Watson, R. T. (1987). Retrosplenial amnesia. *Brain 110*:1631–1646.

Van Lancker, D. (1991). Personal relevance and the human right hemisphere. *Brain and Cognition 17*:64–92.

Van Lancker, D., and Klein, K. (1990). Preserved recognition of familiar personal names in global aphasia. *Brain Lang. 39*:522–529.

Van Lancker, D., Klein, K., Hanson, W., Lanto, A., and Metter, E. J. (1991). Preferential representation of personal names in the right hemisphere. In *Clinical Aphasiology*, Vol. 20, T. Prescott (ed.). Austin, Tex.: Pro-Ed.

Vincent, F. M., Sadowsky, C. H., Saunders, R. L., and Reeves, A. G. (1977). Alexia without agraphia, hemianopia, or color-naming defect: a disconnexion syndrome. *Neurology 27*:689–691.

Volpe, B. T., LeDoux, J. E., Fraser, R. A., and Gazzaniga, M. S. (1979). Spatially oriented movements in the absence of proprioception. *Neurology 29*:1309–1313.

Voneida, T. J. (1963). Performance of a visual conditioned response in split-brain cats. *Exp. Neurol. 8*:493–504.

Warren, J. M., and Nonneman, A. J. (1976). The search for cerebral dominance in monkeys. *Ann. N. Y. Acad. Sci. 280*:732–744.

Warrington, E. K. (1969). Constructional apraxia. *Hdbk. Clin. Neurol. 4*:67–83.

Warrington, E. K., James, M., and Kinsbourne, M. (1966). Drawing disability in relation to laterality of cerebral lesion. *Brain 89*:53–82.

Wartenberg, R. (1953). *Diagnostic Tests in Neurology*. Chicago: Yearbook Publishers.

Watson, R. T., and Heilman, K. M. (1983). Callosal apraxia. *Brain 106*:391-403.

Watson, R. T., Valenstein, E., Day, A. L., Heilman, K. M. (1984). The effects of corpus callosum section on unilateral neglect in monkeys. *Neurology 34*:812–815.

Watson, R. T., Valenstein, E., and Heilman, K. M. (1981). Thalamic neglect: the possible role of the medial thalamus and nucleus reticularis thalami in behavior. *Arch. Neurol. 38*:501–507.

Wechsler, A. F. (1972). Transient left hemialexia. *Neurology 22*:628–633.

Wechsler, A. F., Weinstein, E. A., and Antin, S. P. (1972). Alexia without agraphia. *Bull. Los Angeles Neurol. Soc 37*:1–11.

Weinstein, E. A., and Friedland, R. P. (eds.) (1977). *Hemi-Inattention and Hemisphere Specialization*. New York: Raven Press.

Weiskrantz, L. (1986). *Blindsight*. Oxford: Clarendon Press.

Wigan, A. L. (1844). *The Duality of the Mind*. London: Longman, Brown, Green and Longmans. Republished 1985 by Joseph Simon, Malibu, Calif.

Wilson, D. H., Culver, C., Waddington, M., and Gazzaniga, M. (1975). Disconnection of the cerebral hemispheres. *Neurology 25*:1149–1153.

Wilson, D. H., Reeves, A., Gazzaniga, M., and Culver, C. (1977). Cerebral commissurotomy for control of intractable seizures. *Neurology 27*:708–715.

Wilson, S. A. K. (1908). A contribution to the study of apraxia. *Brain 31*:164–216.

Wilson, S. A. K., and Bruce, A. N. (1940). *Neurology*, Vol. I. Baltimore: Williams and Wilkins.

Winner, E., and Gardner, H. (1977). The comprehension of metaphor in brain-damaged patients. *Brain 100*:717–729.

Witelson, S. F. (1974). Hemispheric specialization for linguistic and nonlinguistic tactual perception using a dichotomous stimulation technique. *Cortex 10*:3–17.

Witelson, S. F. (1985). The brain connection: the corpus callosum is larger in left-handers. *Science 229*:665–668.

Witelson, S. F., and Goldsmith, C. H. (1991). The relationship of hand preference to anatomy of the corpus callosum in men. *Brain Res.* 545:175–182.

Woolsey, R. M., and Nelson, J. S. (1975). Asymptomatic destruction of the fornix in man. *Arch. Neurol.* 32:566–568.

Yakovlev, P. I., and Lecours, A. R. (1967). The myelogenetic cycles of regional maturation of the brain. In *Regional Development of the Brain in Early Life*, A. Minkowski (ed.). Edinburgh: Blackwell.

Yamadori, A., Nagashima, T., and Tamaki, N. (1983). Ideogram writing in a disconnection syndrome. *Brain Lang.* 19:346–356.

Yamaguchi, T., Kunimoto, M., Pappata, S., Chavoix, C., Riche, D., Chevalier, L., Mazoyer, B., Mazière, N., Naquet, R., and Baron, J. (1990). Effects of anterior corpus callosum section on cortical glucose utilization in baboons. *Brain* 113:937–951.

Yamamoto, I., Rhoton, A. L., and Peace, D. A. (1981). Microsurgery of the third ventricle: part 1. *Neurosurgery* 8:334-356.

Yingling, C. D., and Skinner, J. E. (1977). Gating of thalamic input to cerebral cortex by nucleus reticularis thalami. In *Attention, Voluntary Contraction and Event-related Cerebral Potentials*, J. E. Desmedt (ed.). Basel: Karger.

Young, A. W. (ed.) (1983). *Functions of the Right Hemisphere*. London: Academic Press.

Zaidel, D. W. (1990). Memory and spatial cognition following commissurotomy. Im *Handbook of Neuropsychology*, Vol. 4, F. Boller and J. Grafman (eds.). Amsterdam: Elsevier.

Zaidel, D., and Sperry, R. W. (1973). Performance on the Raven Colored Progressive Matrices Test by subjects with cerebral commissurotomy. *Cortex* 9:34–39.

Zaidel, D., and Sperry, R. W. (1974). Memory impairment after commissurotomy in man. *Brain* 97:263–272.

Zaidel, D., and Sperry, R. W. (1977). Some long-term motor effects of cerebral commissurotomy in man. *Neuropsychologia* 15:193–204.

Zaidel, E. (1973). Linguistic competence and related functions in the right hemisphere of man following commissurotomy and hemispherectomy. Ph.D. thesis, California Institute of Technology. *Dissert. Abstr. Int.* 34:3250B.

Zaidel, E. (1976). Language, dichotic listenting, and the disconnected hemispheres. In *BIS Conference Report 42*. D. O. Walter, L. Rogers, and J. M. Finzi-Fried (eds.). Los Angeles: University of California.

Zaidel, E. (1977). Unilateral auditory language comprehension on the token test following cerebral commissurotomy and hemispherectomy. *Neuropsychologia* 15:1–18.

Zaidel, E. (1978a). Lexical organization in the right hemisphere. In *Cerebral Correlates of Conscious Experience*, P. Buser and A. Rougeul-Buser (eds.). Amsterdam: Elsevier.

Zaidel, E. (1978b). Concepts of cerebral dominance in the split-brain. In *Cerebral Correlates of Conscious Experience*, P. Buser and A. Rougeul-Buser (eds.). Amsterdam: Elsevier.

Zaidel, E. (1983). Disconnection syndrome as a model for laterality effects in the normal brain. In *Cerebral Hemisphere Asymmetry: Method, Theory and Application*, J. Hellige (ed.). New York: Praeger.

Zaidel, E. (1985a). Callosal dynamics and right hemisphere language. In *Two Hemispheres— One Brain: Functions of the Corpus Callosum*, F. Leporé, M. Ptito, and H. Jasper (eds.). New York: Alan R. Liss.

Zaidel, E. (1985b). Language in the right hemisphere. In *The Dual Brain: Hemispheric Specialization in Humans*, D. F. Benson and E. Zaidel (eds.). New York: Guilford.

Zaidel, E. (1990). Language functions in the two hemispheres following complete cerebral commissurotomy and hemispherectomy. In *Handbook of Neuropsychology*, Vol. 4, J. Grafman and F. Boller (eds.). Amsterdam: Elsevier.

Zaidel, E., Clarke, J. M., and Suyenobu, B. (1990a). Hemispheric independence: a paradigm case for cognitive neuroscience. In *Neurobiology of Higher Cognitive Functions*, A. B. Scheibel and A. Wechsler (eds.). New York: Guilford.

Zaidel, E., and Peters, A. M. (1981). Phonological encoding and ideographic reading by the disconnected right hemisphere: two case studies. *Brain Lang.* 14:205–234.

Zaidel, E., Zaidel, D. W., and Sperry, R. W. (1981). Left and right intelligence: case studies of Raven's progressive matrices following brain bisection and hemidecortication. *Cortex* 17:167–186.

Zaidel, E., Zaidel, D. W., and Bogen, J. E. (1990b). Testing the commissurotomy patient. In *Neuromethods*, Vol. 17, A. A. Boulton, G. B. Baker, and M. Hiscock (eds.). Clifton, NJ: Humana Press.

Zangwill, O. (1974). Consciousness and the cerebral hemispheres. In *Hemisphere Function in the Human Brain*, S. J. Dimond and J. G. Beaumont (eds.). New York: John Wiley and Sons.

Zatorre, R. J., and Jones-Gutman, M. (1991). Human olfactory discrimination after unilateral frontal or temporal lobectomy. *Brain* 114:71–84.

Zola-Morgan, S., Squire, L. R., and Mishkin, M. (1982). The neuroanatomy of amnesia: amygdala: hippocampus versus temporal stem. *Science* 218:1337–1339.

Zola-Morgan, S., and Squire, L. R. (1990). The neuropsychology of memory: parallel findings in humans and nonhuman primates. *Ann N. Y. Acad. Sci.* 608:434–456.

Zurif, E. B., and Ramier, A. M. (1972). Some effects of unilateral brain damage on the perception of dichotically presented phoneme sequences and digits. *Neuropsychologia* 10:103–110.

# 12
# The Frontal Lobes

ANTONIO R. DAMASIO AND STEVEN W. ANDERSON

Teuber (1964) described the frontal lobes as "a riddle," Luria (1969) described them as "the youngest, the most complex, and the least studied portion of the cerebral hemispheres," and Nauta (1971) referred to the entire region as "the most mystifying of the major subdivisions of the cerebral cortex." The function of the frontal lobes has certainly eluded generations of investigators, and it is also true that the cognitive and behavioral consequences of its damage can defy measurement with the tools of modern neuropsychology. But this state of affairs is changing.

The mystery of the frontal lobes stems, in good part, from their anatomical complexity. The frontal lobes make up over one-third of the human cerebral cortex and have diverse anatomical units, each with distinct connections to other cortical and subcortical regions and to each other. Although we have made progress in elucidating the connectional pattern of some of the subregions in nonhuman primates (see Barbas and Pandya, 1987, 1989; Goldman-Rakic and Friedman, 1991, and below), we are not even close to mapping the equivalent complexity in the human brain. Likewise, although significant advances have been made regarding frontal cortical physiology in nonhuman primates (Fuster, 1989; Goldman-Rakic, 1987; Goldberg and Segraves, 1989), equivalent progress in humans must rely on the lesion method (see the section on experimental studies below), emission tomography (Weinberger et al., 1991), or EEG and evoked potentials (Gevins, 1990; Knight, 1991). Paralleling the challenges presented by the anatomical and functional complexity of the frontal lobes are those which stem from the nature of the signs and symptoms of frontal damage, since they do not lend themselves easily to quantitative analysis in a laboratory setting. Nonetheless, remarkable progress is indeed taking place and the new findings discussed in this text are a good witness to such progress.

This chapter focuses on neuropsychological studies that link the human frontal lobes with cognition and behavior, and gives emphasis to clinically relevant issues.

## NEUROANATOMICAL OVERVIEW

Knowledge of neuroanatomy is necessary to the understanding of frontal lobe functions and a prerequisite for the interpretation of research discussed later in this chapter. For that reason, a brief review of frontal lobe morphology is presented here.

### Frontal Cortex

Inspection of the external surface of the lobe reveals three important natural borders—the rolandic sulcus, the sylvian fissure, and the corpus callosum—and three large expansions of cortex—in the lateral convexity, in the mesial flat aspect that faces the opposite lobe, and in the inferior concave aspect that covers the roof of the orbit. Traditional anatomy has divided this cortex in the following principal regions: the precentral cortex, the prefrontal cortex, and the limbic cortex (Fig. 12-1).

The precentral cortex corresponds to the long gyrus immediately anterior to the rolandic fissure, forming its anterior bank and depth. This area continues over the mesial lip of the lobe, ending in the depths of the cingulate sulcus. Histologically it is a region of agranular cortex and its function as the principal motor area is well known. The presence of Betz cells is a distinguishing feature. In Brodmann's map (Fig. 1-1), it corresponds to field 4. Anterior and parallel to this region lies the premotor cortex, which in humans corresponds to the posterior portion of the three horizontally placed frontal gyri. Histologically, this is a transitional cortex, the function of which is closely related to motor activity. For the most part, this is field 6 in Brodmann's map, but the lower region, which comprises a portion of the third (inferior) frontal gyrus, is referenced as field 44 and presumably corresponds to Broca's area. Field 45 is closely connected to 44, both anatomically and, in all probability, functionally. In the mesial prolongation of the premotor zone which also terminates in the cingulate sulcus, lies the supplementary motor area. Anterior to both the precentral and premotor regions lies the prefrontal cortex, which makes up most of the frontal cortex and encompasses the pole of the lobe. Macroscopically, three major aspects may be distinguished: mesial, dorsolateral, and orbital. Histologically much of this is granular cortex that corresponds in Brodmann's map to fields 8, 9, 10, 11, 12, 47, and 46. This is the enigmatic area that most authors have in mind when they speak of the frontal lobe in relation to behavior. Little is known about the contribution of each of these separate areas, with the exception of field 8, the so-called eye field, which presumably serves a central role in relation to eye and head movements. Limbic system parts of the frontal lobe correspond to areas 24, 25, and 32 (the anterior and subgenual portions of the cingulate gyrus) and to areas 13 and 14 (the posterior parts of the orbitofrontal area and the gyrus rectus). Technically, these are agranular cortices; however, they are probably related in essential ways to both the granular and agranular cortices.

### Frontal Lobe Connections

Understanding the prefrontal lobe depends upon knowledge of the company it keeps, that is, its afferent and efferent connections. Some of these connections are with other neocortical structures, mainly from and to association areas in the temporal, parietal,

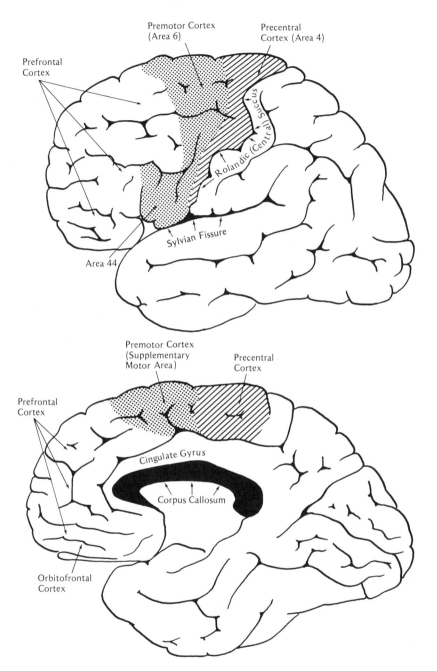

**Fig. 12-1.** Lateral (top) and medial (bottom) views of the human cerebral hemisphere. The diagonal hatching indicates the motor cortex (area 4), and the stippled area the premotor cortex, the inferior and anterior portion of which is area 44 (see Fig. 1-1).

411

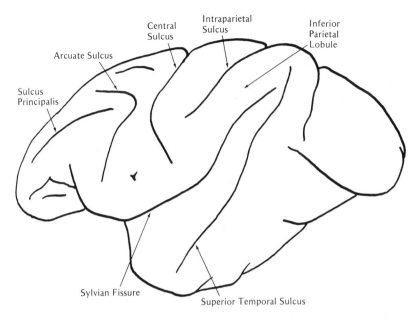

**Fig. 12-2.** Lateral view of the cerebral hemisphere of the rhesus monkey.

and occipital lobes, including special areas of multimodal convergence. The prefrontal cortex is also connected to the premotor region and thus indirectly to motor cortex. There are significant connections with the limbic cortex of the cingulate gyrus and with limbic and motor subcortical structures. Some projections are unidirectional, such as those to the caudate and putamen. Some seem to be bidirectional, such as those with the dorsomedial nucleus of the thalamus. The latter is a particularly important connection, so much so that some authors have defined the prefrontal cortex as that region which is coextensive with projections from the dorsomedial nucleus. The arrangement of projections is quite specific: the orbital aspect is linked with the pars magnocellularis, the dorsolateral cortex with the pars parvocellularis. Other major subcortical connections are with the hippocampus by way of the cingulate and hippocampal gyri, with the amygdala by way of the uncinate fasciculus, and with the hypothalamus, the septum, and the mesencephalon by direct pathways.

The prefrontal cortex thus receives input (by more than one channel) from the sensory association regions of the cortex, it is closely woven with the limbic system, and it can affect the motor system in multiple ways. The functionally central position of the frontal lobe can be made more clear by a brief review of its efferent and afferent connections in nonhuman primates. The frontal lobe of the monkey is roughly comparable to that of humans in shape, limits, connections, and cytoarchitecture. Important differences, other than size, are apparent in the dorsolateral aspect where instead of the three horizontally oriented gyri of the human frontal lobe, there are two fields placed in a dorsal and ventral position in relation to a single sulcus, the principalis (Fig. 12-2). One other major sulcus, the arcuate, arch-shaped and more or less vertically oriented, represents the seam between the monkey's prefrontal and premotor cortex. It is in this transition zone, particularly in the rostral bank of the sulcus, that Brodmann's field 8 is located. Sources used in the following description of subcortical and cortical projections are Ward and McCulloch, 1947; Bailey and Von Bonin, 1951; Pribram and MacLean, 1953; Pribram et al., 1953; Whitlock and Nauta, 1956; Crosby et al., 1962; Nauta, 1962, 1964; Akert, 1964; DeVito and Smith, 1964; Kuypers et al., 1965; Powell et al., 1965; Valverde, 1965; Johnson et al., 1968; Nauta and Haymaker, 1969; Pandya et al., 1969, 1971; Pandya and Kuypers, 1969; Pandya and Vignolo, 1971; Kievit and Kuypers, 1974; Chavis and Pandya, 1976; Rosene et al., 1976; Goldman and Nauta, 1977; Yeterian and Van Hoesen, 1977; Goldman, 1978; Potter and Nauta, 1979; Damasio and Van Hoesen, 1980; Barbas and Mesulam, 1981, 1985; Porrino et al., 1981; Goldman-Rakic and Schwartz, 1982; Porrino and Goldman-Rakic, 1982; Petrides and Pandya, 1984, 1988; Barbas and Pandya, 1987, 1989; Moran et al., 1987; Pandya and Barnes, 1987; Cavada and Goldman-Rakic, 1989; Seltzer and Pandya, 1989; Di Pellegrino and Wise, 1991; and Preuss and Goldman-Rakic, 1991.

## Subcortical Connections

### PROJECTIONS FROM THE HYPOTHALAMUS

Direct projections from the hypothalamus have not been as easy to identify as the ones in the opposite direction, which may possibly reflect a different functional significance. At any rate, there is some evidence that there are such projections to several regions above and below the arcuate sulcus and to the rostral part of the principal sulcus. These projections may be parallel to the monoaminergic projections arising in the mesencephalic tegmentum and may indeed be interwoven with them, since the latter are known to travel in the lateral hypothalamic region.

### PROJECTIONS FROM THE AMYGDALA AND THE HIPPOCAMPUS

There are strong projections from the amygdala and hippocampus to the orbital cortex, particularly in its most posterior and medial region, but the amygdala also projects to the mesial aspect of the frontal lobe, particularly into areas such as the gyrus rectus and the subcallosal portion of the cingulate gyrus and the anterior parts of the cingulate gyrus (Brodmann's areas 25 and 24, respectively). The amygdala, as does the hippocampus, projects to areas of the diencephalon and mesencephalon to which the prefrontal lobe itself strongly projects.

### PROJECTIONS FROM THE THALAMUS

The afferent projections from the thalamus originate mostly in the regions where the efferent projections from the prefrontal cortex terminate, that is, in both the medial and lateral aspects of the dorsomedial nucleus. The medial thalamus thus appears as a transforming station for inputs from the prefrontal regions. Projections of the medial pulvinar to area 8 have also been described, and it is now known that other projections from the thalamic association nuclei, midline nuclei, and intralaminar nuclei exist. These link the prefrontal cortex to ascending reticular, visceral, and autonomic systems.

## PROJECTIONS TO THE AMYGDALA AND HIPPOCAMPUS

The projections to the amygdala and hippocampus arise mostly from the mesial and orbital aspects and partly from the inferior ventral dorsolateral aspect and travel in the cingulum and uncinate fasciculus. Many go directly to the amygdala, although others go to rostral temporal cortex, which in turn projects to the amygdala. Projection to the hippocampus is indirect via the limbic cortex of the cingulate and hippocampal gyri (retrosplenial and perirhinal cortices respectively).

## PROJECTIONS TO THE HYPOTHALAMUS

Direct connections to various hypothalamic nuclei have been mentioned for a long time. These, however, are poorly understood and in need of reinvestigation with modern neuroanatomical tracing procedures. Almost in continuum with the latter, there are projections to the mesencephalic tegmentum, namely, to the anterior half of the periaqueductal gray matter. These are areas to which both the hippocampus and the amygdala send strong projections.

## PROJECTIONS TO THE SEPTUM

In the monkey, projections to the septum probably arise from the upper bank of the sulcus principalis. A reciprocal connection is probably involved. As with hypothalamic projections, further investigations of these potentially important prefrontal efferents are needed.

## PROJECTIONS TO THE THALAMUS

Other than the well-known projections to the nucleus dorsalis medialis, fibers also terminate in the intralaminar thalamic complex and pulvinar.

## PROJECTIONS TO THE STRIATUM

Projections to the caudate and the putamen but not the pallidum have been identified. The projections from the cingulate gyrus and supplementary motor area are especially strong. It was once thought that the frontocaudate projection was limited to the head of the caudate, but it has recently been shown that the prefrontal cortex projects to the whole caudate. Of particular interest is the fact that regions of the cortex with which the frontal lobe is reciprocally innervated, e.g., the parietal lobe, seem to project to the caudate in approximately the same area.

## PROJECTIONS TO THE CLAUSTRUM, SUBTHALAMIC REGION, AND MESENCEPHALON

Projections to the claustrum travel in the uncinate fasciculus and external capsule and originate in the orbital and inferior dorsolateral aspects. Projections to the regions of the subthalamic nucleus and the red nucleus also seem to come primarily from the orbital aspects. Projections to the central gray seem to come from the convexity only.

## Cortical Connections

PROJECTIONS FROM VISUAL, AUDITORY, AND SOMATOSENSORY CORTEX

Practically all areas of the association cortex project to the frontal lobe. In the rhesus monkey these projections have been studied in relation to two distinct regions: the periarcuate cortex, which surrounds the arcuate sulcus, and the prearcuate cortex, which includes all of the frontal pole lying anterior to the former region and which encompasses the region of the sulcus principalis.

Projections terminating in the periarcuate cortex arise from the caudal portion of the superior temporal gyrus, the lateral peristriate belt, the superior parietal lobule, and the anterior portion of the inferior parietal lobule. Projections terminating in the prearcuate cortex arise from the middle region of the superior temporal gyrus, the caudal and inferior temporal cortex, and the middle portion of the interior bank of the intraparietal sulcus.

Direct projections to the orbital cortex come mainly from the anterior region of the superior temporal gyrus, but there are also indirect projections that reach this area by way of the dorsomedial thalamus: they originate in the middle and inferior temporal gyri and share the same route of projections from the olfactory cortex.

Considerable overlap takes place in relation to these connections, for instance, between the first-order visual and auditory projections in the periarcuate region and between second-order visual, auditory, and somatosensory projections in prearcuate cortex.

PROJECTIONS FROM OLFACTORY CORTEX

The piriform cortex projects to the frontal lobe by way of the dorsomedial nucleus of the thalamus. In this way, olfactory information joins that of the other senses to create a convergence absent in the posterior sensory cortex.

PROJECTIONS TO TEMPORAL CORTEX

The temporal cortex receives projections from regions of the sulcus principalis in a well-organized fashion. The anterior third projects mainly to the anterior third of the superior temporal sulcus and the superior temporal gyrus. The middle third connects with both the anterior and the middle portions of the superior temporal sulcus. The posterior third projects mainly to the more caudal region of the superior temporal sulcus. The orbital aspect of the frontal lobe also projects to the rostral area of the temporal lobe and especially the temporal polar cortex.

PROJECTIONS TO POSTERIOR SENSORY CORTEX

The projections to posterior sensory cortex are mainly directed to the inferior parietal lobule and originate in the posterior third of the sulcus principalis and in the arcuate sulcus.

PROJECTIONS TO LIMBIC CORTEX

Both the anterior and middle thirds of the sulcus principalis project to the cingulate gyrus, the latter in a more intense fashion, as do areas in the concavity of the arcuate sulcus. This is an interesting projection that courses all along the cingulate, distributing fibers to the overlying cortex but then continuing as a bundle to reach the hippocampal gyrus.

PROJECTIONS WITHIN THE FRONTAL LOBE

The lower bank of the sulcus principalis is connected to the orbital aspect of the frontal cortex. The region of the arcuate sulcus connects anteriorly to the portions of the frontal pole. In general, however, the intrinsic connections of the frontal lobe are understood poorly in many species, and basic issues such as prefrontal association input to the origin of corticospinal axons in the agranular cortex still remain poorly understood.

## CLINICAL NEUROPSYCHOLOGICAL STUDIES

Evaluation of the consequences of frontal lobe damage is arguably the most challenging task faced by clinical neuropsychologists because the laboratory manifestations of such damage are often subtle. Standard neuropsychological and neurological evaluations may reveal few unequivocal defects, even in patients who are no longer able to behave normally in real life. Nevertheless, comprehensive evaluations can disclose a variety of signs suggestive of dysfunction in frontal cortices. Drawing upon data from our laboratory and from the neuropsychological literature, we describe below the consequences of frontal lobe damage for the basic aspects of cognition assessed in a standard neuropsychological evaluation, and we discuss the more significant neurological signs of frontal lobe dysfunction.

Two problems frequently complicate the evaluation of frontal lobe damage: (1) the concept of a single "frontal lobe syndrome" and (2) the failure to consider the multitude of pathophysiological, individual, and environmental variables that can influence the expression of frontal lobe dysfunction.

The notion that there is a unitary frontal lobe syndrome remains alive, despite the fact that it is not supported by anatomical, clinical, or neuropsychological evidence. The locus of a lesion within the frontal lobe is a crucial factor in the profile of frontal lobe signs. Side of lesion, for instance, is important, as there is evidence that some lesions of the dominant frontal lobe interefere with verbal behavior more so than do corresponding nondominant lesions, and certain emotional changes may also be related to the left-right dichotomy. Bilateral lesions may produce yet a different clinical picture, both quantitatively and qualitatively. The site of damage within a frontal lobe is also relevant to the development of a given syndrome. This regional effect may determine distinctive clinical configurations and allow the prediction of whether the involvement is predominantly mesial or dorsolateral or inferior orbital.

Depth of lesion is also an important variable, probably as much so as surface extent of damage. Many signs of frontal lobe dysfunction result from severed subcortical connections, which a deep lesion has a better chance of destroying.

Analysis of the behavioral effects of different loci of damage must also take account of the nature of the lesion. The clinical presentation of the various pathophysiological processes that can cause damage to the frontal lobes can be quite different from one another. Vascular disorders, tumors, and traumatic injury are among the most common causes of structural damage in the frontal lobes.

The vascular syndromes are the most distinctive, particularly those related to the anterior cerebral artery. Bilateral as well as unilateral involvement is a common cause of mutism with or without akinesia. Personality changes are also frequently found, and a characteristic amnesic syndrome has been identified with lesions in this vascular distribution (Damasio et al., 1985). Damage is predominantly to the ventromedial and mesial aspects of the frontal lobe. The most common cause of those abnormalities is rupture of an aneurysm of the anterior communicating artery or of the anterior cerebral artery itself. In other cases, the frontal branches of the middle cerebral artery may be involved, the more frequent causes being embolism and thrombosis. Damage is almost always unilateral and predominantly affects the dorsolateral aspect of the lobe, giving rise to various speech and language impairments when the dominant hemisphere is involved and to affective and spatial alterations when the nondominant hemisphere is injured.

The syndromes caused by tumors naturally vary with location and histological nature. Extrinsic tumors, such as meningiomas, are frequently located subfrontally or at the cerebral falx, where they involve the mesial aspect of the frontal lobes and often cause bilateral changes. They may also have a more lateral origin and compress the dorsolateral aspect of one frontal lobe only. Intrinsic tumors may show up unilaterally or bilaterally. The distinction often depends on time, as an originally unilateral glioma may invade the corpus callosum and cross to the opposite side.

Not uncommonly, frontal lobe tumors present with major intellectual and affective impairment that justifies the use of the term dementia, so pervasive is the disorganization of normal behavior (e.g., Strauss and Keschner, 1935). For this reason, the diagnosis of frontal lobe tumor should always be considered in the study of a dementia syndrome. Confusional states are also frequently associated with tumors of the frontal lobe, perhaps more so than with tumors anywhere else in the central nervous system (Hécaen, 1964). Disturbances of mood and character, although less frequent than confusion or dementia, were noted almost as frequently in Hécaen's study.

Wounds caused by head injury—whose clinical pictures were vividly described by Kleist (1936) and Goldstein (1948)—may have a preponderant frontal involvement and present with a combination of frontal lobe signs. The orbital surface of the frontal lobes and the frontal poles are particularly susceptible to damage from traumatic head injury, due to contact of these structures with the skull. Although the consequences of head injury typically reflect the combined effects of damage to multiple brain areas, many of the sequelae which prove to be most disruptive are similar to those seen following focal damage in frontal cortex.

The rate of development of a lesion and the time elapsed since peak development are additional factors which interact with lesion type to influence the clinical picture. Worsening, stabilization, or recovery depend on the nature of the underlying pathological process. Most patients with cerebrovascular lesions tend to stabilize and then improve gradually, whereas the course of patients with tumors is a function of the degree of cytological and mechanical malignancy of the tumor and of the type of surgical or medical management adopted. Patients with severe symptomatology from a vascular event or traumatic injury will often have a remarkable remission within a period of weeks. On the other hand, patients with slowly growing tumors that infiltrate neural tissue without grossly disrupting its function may fail to show measurable behavioral defects, in spite of the considerable size of their malignancies (Anderson et al., 1989).

Another important factor is the age at which the dysfunction begins. There is evidence that the effects of lesions starting in childhood or adolescence are different from those caused by lesions starting in adulthood, particularly when they are extensive and bilateral. If these factors are not taken into account it will not be possible to make an adequate clinical evaluation of patients and clinical research may produce paradoxical results.

The results of prefrontal leukotomy and prefrontal lobotomy, which were a source of early information on frontal lobe physiology, have also been a consistent source of controversy. Although Moniz (1936, 1949) was impressed by the lack of pronounced defects of motor, sensory, and language function in cases of frontal lobe lesion, it is clear that he attributed several important functions to the frontal lobe. He reasoned that in cases of schizophrenic thought disorder or of obsessive compulsive disease, "wrongly learned" thinking processes were dependent on frontal lobe function and based on reverberating circuitry connecting the frontal lobe to midline subcortical structures and to the posterior cortical areas. Such "repetitive linkages" called for surgical interruption. He also hypothesized a relation between the aberrant thought process and the accompaning emotional status of the patient and assumed that a lesion that altered one would also alter the other. He recalled the frequent observation of affective indifference in frontal lobe patients, as well as the remarkable affective changes shown in Jacobsen's chimpanzees (Fulton and Jacobsen, 1935) after frontal lobe surgery. As Jacobsen put it, "The animals had joined the happiness cult of the Elder Michaeux and had placed their burdens on the Lord" (Fulton, 1951). It seems that Moniz conceived of the frontal lobes as important for higher cognition and for the regulation of emotion. Far from designing an innocuous intervention, he planned the creation of particular defects which might benefit patients whose previous abnormality was thoroughly incapacitating.

Objective assessment of the results of prefrontal surgery is hard to come by. The original Moniz method, apparently one of the most effective and least damaging, was never used in the United States. Several other surgical methods have been devised involving various amounts of damage to different structures. All cases suffered from preexisting psychiatric disease or intractable pain, generally of considerable severity and duration. Finally, the methods of behavioral assessment have been varied in scope and quality. It is evident, however, that bilateral, surgically controlled frontal lobe damage, particularly when it involves the mesial and inferior orbital cortices or their connections, causes modifications in the affective and emotional sphere. Leaving aside any discussion of the value of this approach in psychiatry, it is important for neuropsychologists to know that even minor psychosurgery may be a factor in their patients' behaivor. For a modern appraisal of the measurable neuropsychologic disturbances associated with leukotomy see Stuss et al. (1981).

## *Personality*

Personality alterations, including changes in social behavior and the high-level cognitive processes that permit appropriate decision making and planning, are the most characteristic changes resulting from frontal lobe damage and certainly the most difficult to evaluate. The assessment of changes at this level of behavior implies a notion of the limits or normal variation of several aspects of human personality. Naturally, only a relative judgment is possible, taking into account the patient's age, educational level, social and cultural group, and previous achievements.

### THE HALLMARK CASE STUDIES

A number of detailed case studies have helped to characterize the personality changes that can result from frontal lobe damage. The famous patient Gage, described by Harlow (1848, 1868), provides the first solid reference to specific injury of the frontal lobes and its relation to disturbances of complex behavior. The other important observations were added in this century. They include the case studies of Brickner (1934, 1936), Hebb (Hebb and Penfield, 1940), Benton (Ackerly and Benton, 1948), and Damasio (Eslinger and Damasio, 1985; Damasio et al., 1991; Saver and Damasio, 1991). For a review of the early history of clinical investigations into frontal lobe damage, see Benton (1991a).

Brickner's patient, known as *A*, was a 39-year-old New York stockbroker who, until one year before surgery, led a normal life. Slowly progressive headaches, which became more and more severe, and finally the sudden onset of mental obtundation brought him to medical attention. A diagnosis of frontal tumor was made, which, at surgery, proved to be a voluminous meningioma of the falx compressing both frontal lobes. The neurosurgeon, Walter Dandy, had to perform an extensive bilateral resection of frontal tissue in two stages. On the left side all the frontal tissue rostral to Broca's area was removed. On the right, the excision was even larger and included all the brain anterior to the motor area. The patient's condition gradually stabilized and no motor or sensory defect could be detected. For months there were frequent periods of restlessness, but akinesia or changes in tone were never noted, nor were there any signs of motor perseveration. Orientation to person, place, and time seemed intact as well as remote and recent memory. *A* was able to understand the circumstances of his illness and the surgical intervention to which he had been subject, and he was aware of the efforts of his family and physician to have him recover as much as possible. The range of his intellectual ability could be inferred from his capacity to play checkers, sometimes at a quick and expert pace, to explain the meaning of proverbs, and, occasionally, to discuss with lucidity the meaning of his predicament for himself, his relatives, and his friends. On the negative side, his behavior had undergone a marked deterioration. He was unable to adjust his emotional reactions appropriately. Furthermore, his affect was shallow. He became boastful, constantly insisting on his professional, physical, and sexual prowess, and showed little restraint, not only in describing his mythical adventures but in verbalizing judgments about people and circumstances surrounding him. His train of thought was hypomanic, with facetious remarks to match, but he could suddenly become aggressive if frustrated. Frequently he tried to be witty, generally at the expense of others. He was particularly nasty toward his wife. Prior to surgery he had always been kind to her, although not unusually considerate. His sex life, which his wife described as normal before the operation, changed radically. He became impotent, and after a few frustrated attempts at intercourse, never again sought her or indeed any other partner, although much of his conversation would revolve around his sexual exploits. Ability to plan daily activity meaningfully had been lost and so had his initiative and creativity. Although he constantly spoke of returning to work, he never made any effort to do so and continued living in close dependence on his relatives. Certain levels of learning ability, however, both verbal and nonverbal, seemed intact. For example, in the face of his constant distractibility and lack of interest, he was taught how to operate proficiently a complex printing machine on which he produced visiting cards. Moreover, when faced with strangers in a reasonably nondemanding situation, he would be charming, display impeccable manners, and be considerably restrained. Independent examiners, including neurologists, would then be unable to detect any abnormality even after fairly long conversations.

Brickner's painstaking description produced different impressions on the readers of the time. The overall view was that the intervention had a crippling effect on A's mental ability, but for Egas Moniz, the enterprising pioneer of frontal leukotomy (1936), A's case was remarkable in that it proved bilateral frontal damage to be compatible with maintenance of major operational abilities and especially because it demonstrated a change in affect and emotional response with pronounced reduction of anxiety. This view is likely to have played a role in the theorization behind the leukotomy project.

In view of the location and size of the tumor, damage to the septal and hypothalamic regions was a possibility, and although the autopsy report on this case (Brickner, 1952) mentioned no such evidence, there may have been microscopic basal forebrain changes. The report is clear in noting that the cortical territory of the anterior cerebral arteries was intact (which might have been predicted from the patient's lack of crural paresis). Nevertheless, the autopsy did becloud the issue by revealing several meningiomas, one of which was of significant size and located in the right occipital area. In retrospect, it seems clear that the latter tumor had not grown yet at the time of operation because the patient developed a new set of symptoms six to seven years after surgery. Such findings should not be used to minimize the significance of this case, as it is unlikely that they played any role in the patient's behavior.

Hebb and Penfield (1940) described an example of relatively successful bilateral removal of frontal tissue with a more straightforward possibility of a clinicoanatomical correlation. This patient had been normal until age 16 and had then sustained a compounded frontal fracture that damaged both frontal lobes, produced the formation of scar tissue, and resulted in a severe convulsive disorder. At age 28, the patient was operated on and the frontal lobes were extensively resected bilaterally, exposing both orbital plates back to the lesser wing of the sphenoid and transecting the frontal horns of the lateral ventricles. The anterior cerebral arteries were spared. At least a third of the frontal lobes was removed. In terms of the anatomical result the intervention was not very different from that of Brickner's patient, but, unlike A, this patient's brain had not been distorted and edematous prior to resection and the ablation took place under optimal surgical circumstances. In the postoperative period, seizures practically stopped and the behavioral disturbances associated with interictal periods disappeared. The authors suggest that the patient's personality actually improved (from the time he had sustained the fracture) and that his intellectual ability was probably better than before the surgical intervention. We take this to mean that comparison with the period of convulsive disorder was favorable. Comparison with the period prior to the initial damage would certainly not be as favorable, as we believe this patient's intellectual and emotional maturation had been considerably affected by his frontal lobe lesion. Even if he is described as relatively independent, socially adequate, and intellectually intact, some observers have felt that his personality development seemed arrested at the age of the accident and a certain resemblance with the patient of Ackerly and Benton has been indicated. In a later study, Hebb (1945) conceded that, in spite of the patient's apparently good adjustment, his long-term planning and initiative were impaired.

The patient of Ackerly and Benton (1948), on the other hand, sustained bilateral frontal lobe damage either at birth or during the perinatal period. A neurosurgical exploration was performed at age 20 and revealed cystic degeneration of the left frontal lobe and absence of the right one, probably as a result of atrophy. This patient's history was marked throughout childhood and adolescence by severe behavioral problems, in school and at home. He could not hold a job, generally because after some days of being an obedient and even charming employee, he would suddenly show bursts of bad temper, lose interest in his activity, and often end up by stealing or being disorderly. He reacted badly to frustration, and departure from routine would easily frustrate him. Except for periods of frustration and catastrophic reaction, his docility, quietness, and polite manners were quite impressive. His general health seems to have been good. His sexual interests were dim, and he never had an emotional invovlement with any partner, although, for a time, he did have occasional sex with prostitutes. As a whole, his behavior was described as stereotyped, unimaginative, and lacking in initiative. He never developed any particular professional skill or hobby. He also failed to plan for the future, either immediate or long range, and reward and punishment did not seem to influence the course of his behavior. His memory was described as capricious, showing at times a remarkable capacity (such as his ability to remember the makes of automobiles) and at other times an inaccurate representatuon of events. There was no evidence of the common varieties of neurotic disorder, of somatization or of deliberate antisocial behavior, or addicitive behaviors. Apparently, he could not be described as being joyful or happy, and it looked like both pleasure and pain were short-lived and directly related to the presence or absence of frustration.

When he was reevaluated 15 years later, there had been no remarkable personality changes except for a higher frustration threshold. Intellectually, however, recent memory deficits were now noticeable and an inability to perform the Wisconsin Card Sorting Test was recorded.

The most recent of the hallmark cases is that of patient EVR (Eslinger and Damasio, 1985). The patient grew up as the oldest of five children, an excellent student, and a role model for many friends and siblings. After high school he married and completed a business college degree in accounting. By age 30, he was the father of two children and a church elder and had come through the ranks of his company to a supervisory post. In 1973 his family and employers began to notice a variety of personality changes. He became unreliable, could not seem to complete his usual work, and experienced marital difficulties. He was suspended from his job. In 1975 a large orbitofrontal meningioma compressing both frontal lobes was removed. After his postoperative recovery, EVR returned to accounting with a small home construction business. He soon established a partnership with a man of questionable reputation and went into busienss, against sound advice. The venture proved catastrophic. EVR had to declare bankruptcy and lost his entire personal investment. Next, he tried several different jobs (warehouse laborer, apartment complex manager, accountant) but was consistently fired from all of them when it became clear that he could not keep reliable standards. His wife left home with the children and filed for a divorce. When he was reevaluated two years later, a CT scan excluded a recurrence of tumor and the neurological examination was normal except for slight incoordination in the left upper extremity and bilateral anosmia. Psychometric evaluation at that time revealed a verbal IQ of 120 (91st percentile), a performance IQ of 108 (70th percentile), and a Wechsler memory quotient of 140. A Minnesota Multiphasic Personality Inventory was valid and entirely within the normal range.

EVR's problems persisted. He was fired from two additional jobs. The reasons given included tardiness and lack of productivity. He remarried within a month after his first divorce, against the advice of his relatives. The second marriage ended in divorce two years later. Further neurological and psychological evaluation of EVR at a private psychiatric institution in September 1981 revealed "no evidence of organic brain syndrome or frontal dysfunction." Assessment with the WAIS disclosed a verbal IQ of 125 (95th percentile) and a performance IQ of 124 (94th percentile). His Wechsler memory quotient was 148, and the Halstead-Reitan battery revealed average to superior ability on every subtest. An MMPI was once again valid with no evidence of psychopathology on the clinical scales. The staff of the psychiatric hospital felt that his "problems are not the result of organic problems or neurological dysfunction . . . Instead they are reflective of emotional and psychological adjustment problems and therefore are amenable to psychotherapy." They believed EVR could return to work by being retrained for employment. The overall evaluation indicated adjustment and dysthymic disorders with a compulsive "personality style."

To this day, EVR's basic neuropsychological test performances remain normal. In many experimental procedures, EVR's performance is also normal (e.g., Saver and Damasio, 1991). We have identified, however, some tasks in which EVR does show a defect (see Damasio et al., 1990).

Neuroanatomical analysis of EVR's neuroimaging studies reveals the structural correlate of his behavioral defect. CT shows clear evidence of bilateral damage to frontal cortices, especially marked in the ventromedial area, and more so on the right than on the left. The dorsolateral sectors, the cingulate gyri, and the motor and supplementary motor regions are intact.

Reflection on these cases is most rewarding. The patients of Hebb and Benton shared a rigid, perseverative attitude in their approach to life, and both had the courteous manner described as "English valet politeness," though in the judgment of several examiners, Hebb's patient led a clearly more productive but not fully independent existence. The evolution of the personality in Hebb's patient seems to have been arrested at the time of his accident, when he was 16, while in Ackerly's patient the defect came early in development. The patients of Brickner and of Damasio, on the other hand, had normal development and sustained frontal lobe damage in adult life. The fact that their lesions came at an age when plasticity of the nervous system was more limited may account for some differences of outcome. Nonetheless, the patients share a number of features: inability to organize future activity and hold gainful employment; tendency to present a favorable view of themselves; stereotyped but correct manners; diminished ability to respond to punishment and experience pleasure; diminished sexual and exploratory drives; lack of motor, sensory, or communication defects; and overall intelligence within expectations based on educational and occupational background. With the exception of Damasio's patient, all patients showed lack of originality and creativity, inability to focus attention, recent memory vulnerable to interference, and a tendency to display inappropriate emotional reactions. The cluster of these features constitutes *one* of the more typical frontal lobe syndromes, and perhaps the one that easily comes to mind when there is a reference to "frontal lobe syndrome." Let us point out again that many patients with frontal lobe damage have no such defects.

The generalizability of the conclusions drawn from the individual case studies is supported by findings from a recent group study. This study also highlights the role of damage to the ventromedial sector of the frontal lobes in the behavioral profile outlined above. Eighteen adult and nonpsychiatric subjects with focal lesions in ventromedial frontal lobe, along with a group of eight subjects with lesions in surrounding regions of the frontal lobes, were studied with standardized neuropsychological and personality measures (Anderson et al., 1992). All subjects with ventromedial frontal damage had alterations of their daily behavior, with impairments in the ability to initiate, organize, and carry through on normal activities. Consequences included financial disaster due to poor decision making and the breakup of previously stable personal relationships. One formerly active subject played solitary card games incessantly unless directed to other activities. The least impaired subjects became docile, occupying themselves with activities initiated by others. Only one subject (with a relatively small unilateral left ventromedial lesion) was able to return to former employment, although with reduced efficiency and with compensatory measures. The subjects with damage to surrounding regions of the frontal lobes showed considerably less behavioral dysfunction, although significant personality alterations were seen in subjects with superior medial lesions and with dorsolateral lesions that extended to the ventral surface.

The most common behavioral descriptors that were applied by relatives to subjects with ventromedial frontal lobe damage included "contented," "dependent," and "talkative." Descriptors that were rated as uncharacteristic inlcuded "cautious," "efficient," and "energetic." Most subjects showed preservation of superficial social graces and lack of insight. Level of eduation did not appear to be related to outcome. However, the extent of psychosocial demands from each subject's environment did appear to affect the manifestation of their behavior disorder. Subjects faced with relatively normal responsibilities and demands for decision making were unable to meet these demands and exhibited a marked decline from premorbid levels of function. In contrast, those subjects living in protected and supportive environments demonstrated dependency on their caretakers, but they generally did not present major behavior management problems.

## AWARENESS

Self-awareness has been described as the highest cognitive attribute of the frontal lobes (Stuss and Benson, 1987). A lack of awareness regarding alterations in behavior, emotions, and thought processes is a common consequence of frontal lobe dysfunction, and one with major implications for assessment and rehabilitation. Interviews with patients may suggest that all is normal, in contrast to descriptions of marked behavioral dysfunction provided by relatives and caretakers. In addition to the lack of appreciation of changes from the premorbid state, frontal lobe damage may impair the ability to gain insight on specific cognitive abilities. For example, Janowsky et al. (1989) found that subjects with frontal lobe lesions were impaired on a "feeling of knowing" task, in which they had to judge the probability that they would recognize the correct answer to a multiple-choice question.

With regard to rehabilitation, patients with limited awareness of impairments tend not to be motivated to improve behavior. A major component of interventions directed at impairments of social behavior, impulse control, and decision making involves training patients to become increasingly aware of their dysfunctional behaviors. These patients often have a more general problem with evaluating the consequences and implications of their own behavior. Patients with frontal lobe damage may fail to see the significance of their decisions for themselves and for those around them. Their behavior suggests an inability to assess the value of each new action, or lack of action, in terms of goals that are not overtly specified in the immediate environment.

## AFFECT

Butter et al. (1963, 1968) observed that monkeys with orbital ablations showed marked and long-lasting changes in emotional behavior that seemed to be related to an increase in aversive reactions and a concomitant decrease in aggressive reactions. They followed these observations with a careful study of aversive and aggressive behaviors in two groups of monkeys, one with orbital lesions, the other with temporal lesions (Butter et al., 1970). The orbital lesions produced a clear reduction in aggressive behaviors, a change that could still be seen after ten months. This reduction seemed to be situational, as there were noticeable differences in the way the animals reacted to different potentially threatening stimuli, and the animals could still demonstrate aggression when brought back to the colony where they had been dominant figures. This suggests that a regulatory mechanism of aggression had been impaired and that the capacity to display aggression had not been eliminated. The authors point out that the dependence on environmental configuration and the variety of possible emotional responses are not consistent with a permanent state of "bluntness of affect" used to describe similar changes in animals or in lobotomized patients, even if superficially the animals are indeed tame in many situations.

Anatomical study of the lesions indicated that damage to the posteromedial sector of the orbital frontal lobe was closely correlated with the reported changes. This area of the cortex is intimately connected to the amygdala, and furthermore, along with the dorsomedial nucleus of the thalamus, the amygdala and posteromedial orbital cortex project to roughly the same regions of the hypothalamus. The combination of behavioral and anatomical data supports the conjecture that these three structures are part of a system involved in certain types of emotional reaction.

The standard descriptions of affective and emotional changes in frontal lobe patients include *witzelsucht*, a term coined by Oppenheim (1889) to describe the facetiousness of these patients, and *moria*, a term coined by Jastrowitz (1888) to denote a sort of caustic euphoric state that is almost inseparable from *witzelsucht*. Phenomena resembling such descriptions are occasionally found, but it should be understood that in no patients are such changes a permanent feature. Indeed, a patient who appears facetious and boastful will look apathetic and indifferent at some later time or else may show a sudden burst of short-lived anger. The instability of humor also applies to the traditional and somewhat misleading descriptions of "tameness" and "bluntness" of emotion, which may be quite changeable and actually give way to unbridled aggressive behavior against a background of flat affect. External circumstances, particularly if they are stressful, as during an examining session, may "set" the patient's emotional tone. Frequently, the reaction will be found inappropriate to the circumstances but not necessarily in a consistent or predictable manner.

When facetiousness is present, it often has a sexual content, but this is kept within verbal limits and rarely does a patient attempt to act according to the wishes or judgments expressed in his profane remarks. The lack of appreciation of social rules is usually quite evident, but even so there is no intentional viciousness associated with this type of behavior. Nor is there any indication that it produces pleasure: indeed, affect tends to be shallow. Inability to enjoy pleasurable stimulation, particularly if it involves social, intellectual, and aesthetic rewards, is probably characteristic of such patients and is in keeping with restricted response to punishment. Both underscore the elementary disorder of affect.

Frontal lobe patients rarely show the concern and preoccupation that depressed patients do. They may appear psychopathic and show expansive, puerile behavior, but they lack the organization of the psychopathic personality. The same applies to the so-called hypomania of frontal lobe disease, which more often consists of an unstable state of exuberance occasionally interrupted by a flare-up of irritation. An interesting discussion of these distinctions is provided by Blumer and Benson (1975).

The association of changes in affect and in emotional control with predominant involvement of a specific region of the frontal lobe is still unsettled. Nonetheless, there

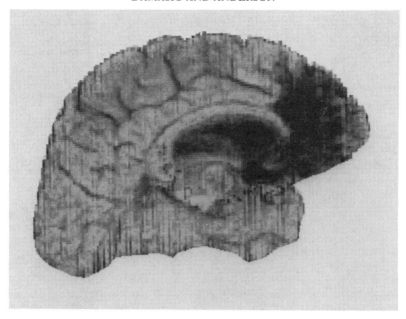

**Fig. 12-3.** Three-dimensional reconstruction of the brain of subject #1445 obtained from thin cut MRI slices using Brainvox (H. Damasio and Frank, 1992). Shown here is a mesial view of the left hemisphere. There is damage to the orbital frontal region, the anterior portion of the cingulate gyrus, and the mesial prefrontal area. [There is comparable, but less extensive, damage to the right hemisphere, not pictured here.]

is little doubt that the orbital aspect of the frontal lobe is especially involved in many patients presenting with emotional changes, particularly if the patient's conflicts are with society rather than intrapersonal. Also, patients with mesial frontal lobe lesions often appear to have blunted emotional responses, as if their affect had been neutralized (Damasio and Van Hoesen, 1983). Yet another interesting fact is that damage to the left dorsolateral frontal cortex is more likely to result in depression than is damage to the right dorsolateral frontal lobe or ventromedial region (Starkstein and Robinson, 1991).

The consequences of ventromedial frontal lobe damage on affect are demonstrated by the following case (#1445) (Fig. 12-3). The patient was a right-handed man who had no history of emotional difficulties or other psychiatric problems. He had been a reliable worker in a steel foundry for nearly 30 years, and was regarded by his wife, children, and co-workers as a well adjusted and emotionally strong individual. At age 47, he underwent resection of a bilateral meningioma arising from the olfactory groove. He demonstrated good recovery of most cognitive abilities over the months following surgery. For example, he obtained IQ scores in the average range, and performed normally on tests of verbal fluency and the Wisconsin Card Sorting Test. However, he developed severe affective changes which remained stable when last seen two years after the surgery.

During social interactions, the patient laughed and giggled frequently in the

**Table 12-1.** WAIS-R Subtest Performances of Patients with Frontal Lobe Damage

| ID # | 318 | 429 | 1065 | 1164 | 1336 | 1331 | 1173 | 534 | 468 | 1198 |
|---|---|---|---|---|---|---|---|---|---|---|
| Age | 49 | 55 | 53 | 70 | 80 | 56 | 67 | 63 | 57 | 31 |
| Education | 16 | 12 | 8 | 12 | 9 | 12 | 8 | 12 | 16 | 12 |
| Occupation | PRO | LAB | LAB | LAB | LAB | LAB | LAB | LAB | PRO | LAB |
| Lesion | BVM | BVM | BVM | BVM | BVM | RDL | RDL | RDL | LDL | LDL |
| *WAIS-R* | | | | | | | | | | |
| Information | 15 | 6 | 8 | 10 | 10 | 13 | 10 | 7 | 14 | 8 |
| Similarities | 17 | 7 | 6 | 11 | 12 | 12 | 9 | 10 | 13 | 9 |
| Arithmetic | 14 | 11 | 8 | 8 | 6 | 11 | 9 | 12 | 11 | 6 |
| Digit span | 13 | 10 | 7 | 10 | 7 | 13 | 11 | 13 | 7 | 4 |
| Block design | 17 | 4 | 10 | 11 | 8 | 9 | 8 | 11 | 12 | 7 |
| Picture arrangement | 13 | 7 | 7 | 8 | 7 | 8 | 7 | 9 | 13 | 8 |
| Digit symbol | 12 | 7 | 7 | 7 | — | 8 | 7 | 13 | 11 | 9 |

PRO = professional; LAB = laborer; BVM = bilateral ventromedial; RDL = right dorsolateral; LDL = left dorso-lateral. WAIS-R scores are age-corrected scaled scores.

absence of humorous stimuli. The laughter occasionally evolved into apparent dysphoria and tears. These outbursts were sudden and would terminate just as quickly. His wife noted that this type of emotional behavior occurred primarily in stressful situations. The patient described his personality and emotions as entirely normal and unchanged from before surgery. When questioned directly while laughing or crying, he denied feeling specifically happy or sad, and appeared quite perplexed when he attempted to gain insight on his emotional state.

## Intelligence

When we consider the role of the frontal lobes in human intellect, it is helpful to distinguish between intelligence as a global capacity to engage in adaptive, goal-directed behavior and intelligence as defined by performance on standard psychometric instruments. It may be stated that the frontal cortices constitute a necessary anatomical substrate for human intelligence as a global adaptive capacity. By contrast, extensive frontal lobe damage may have little or no impact on the abilities measured by intelligence tests.

Although not originally designed as neuropsychological instruments, standardized intelligence tests, and the Wechsler Scales (WAIS and WAIS-R) in particular, are among the most frequently administered measures of cognitive function (Benton, 1991b; Tranel, 1992). There is general agreement that summary IQ scores provide limited information for the purposes of most neuropsychological evaluations (e.g., Lezak, 1988), but the analysis of performances on selected WAIS-R subtests remains a cornerstone of clinical evaluation for neuropsychologists. Early indications that standardized intelligence tests do not address the type of cognitive ability lost by frontal lobe patients were provided by Hebb's patient, who obtained an IQ of 98, and by Brickner's patient *A*, who obtained an IQ of 80 on Terman's revision of the Binet-Simon one year after operation and an IQ of 99 when he was retested 12 months later.

Our findings from patients with focal frontal lobe lesions tested with the Wechsler Scales make the same point. Presented in Table 12-1 are the WAIS-R performances

of ten patients with focal lesions in the frontal lobes (five ventromedial and five dorsolateral). Lesions were caused by either vascular events or surgical resection for
treatment of a meningioma. All subjects were studied at least three months after the
event. The most notable feature of these scores is the consistent preservation of the
cognitive abilities required to perform the various intellectual tasks following frontal
lobe damage.

The preservation of psychometric intelligence in patients with frontal lobe damage
appears to be a consistent finding. For example, Milner (1963) reported a mean loss
of 7.2 IQ points following dorsolateral frontal lobectomies, with mean postoperative
IQ scores remaining in the average range. Likewise, Black (1976) found a mean
WAIS verbal IQ of 99.1 and a mean performance IQ of 99.5 in a group of 44 Vietnam
veterans who had sustained unilateral frontal lobe shrapnel injuries. More recently,
Janowsky et al. (1989) described seven subjects with various focal frontal lobe lesions
who obtained a mean WAIS-R full-scale IQ of 101. In sum, with the exception of
patients who present with confusion or dementia, impairments of cognitive ability
measured by standard intelligence tests are not striking in patients with frontal lobe
lesions, even when bilateral. And yet, as is clearly indicated by the case histories discussed above and others, frontal lobe patients often behave in a most *unintelligent
way.

This mismatch between intelligence measured in a laboratory and intelligence
applied to real-life behaviors remains the most compelling challenge in frontal lobe
research. We believe the mismatch arises because real-life/real-time intelligent
behavior requires more than basic problem-solving rules. Real-life behaviors often
introduce heavy time processing demands. In turn, they require a particular mnestic
and monitoring process known as "working memory" (see below). But real-life problems, unlike most artificial problems posed by neuropsychological tasks, also call for
the participation of a core system of values based on both inherited (drives, instincts)
and acquired (education, socialization) information.

### *Memory*

Since Jacobsen's (1935) demonstration of impairments on a delayed response task by
monkeys with frontal lobe ablations, investigators have been attempting to explicate
the memory defects that follow damage to the frontal lobes. As reviewed earlier, the
anatomical connections of the frontal lobes are certainly consistent with the notion
that the frontal cortices are involved in memory. Bidirectional connections with sensory association cortices, thalamic nuclei, and the amygdalo-hippocampal region provide a framework by which the frontal cortices could play a role in the formation and
activation of stored representations.

Research with nonhuman primates has demonstrated that the dorsolateral frontal
area plays an important role in processing information related to a stimulus after it
has been removed from perception (for reviews, see Goldman-Rakic and Friedman,
1991; Fuster, 1991). This cognitive operation is often referred to as "working memory." Several tasks that require working memory (i.e., the holding of representations
on line while some problem-solving operation is applied to these representations) are

**Table 12-2.** Memory Test Performances

| ID# | 318 | 1065 | 1331 | 468 | 1198 | 770 | 1262 | 414 |
|---|---|---|---|---|---|---|---|---|
| Age | 49 | 53 | 56 | 57 | 31 | 46 | 31 | 40 |
| Education | 16 | 8 | 12 | 16 | 12 | 16 | 16 | 12 |
| *Wechsler Memory Scale* | | | | | | | | |
| MQ | 145 | 112 | 132 | 112 | 86 | 124 | 92 | 103 |
| Paragraph Recall | 31 | 9 | 19 | 20 | 9 | 33 | 20 | 24 |
| Delayed Paragraph Recall | 26 | 7 | 10 | 19 | 10 | 30 | 18 | 24 |
| Paired Associates | 14 | 14 | 8 | 11 | 12 | 14 | 10 | 14 |
| Delayed Paired Associates | 14 | 14 | 6 | 6 | 10 | 14 | 11 | 12 |
| *Rey-AVLT* | | | | | | | | |
| Trial 1 | 9 | 4 | 8 | 4 | 4 | 11 | 5 | 8 |
| Trial 2 | 11 | 11 | 10 | 7 | 7 | 13 | 6 | 9 |
| Trial 3 | 12 | 10 | 8 | 7 | 10 | 14 | 8 | 11 |
| Trial 4 | 12 | 10 | 12 | 10 | 12 | 15 | 12 | 12 |
| Trial 5 | 13 | 12 | 11 | 9 | 11 | 15 | 11 | 13 |
| Delayed Recall | 12 | 8 | 7 | 6 | 11 | 15 | 8 | — |
| Recognition | 30 | 30 | 29 | 28 | 30 | 30 | 30 | — |
| *Benton Visual Retention* | | | | | | | | |
| # Correct | 9 | 4 | 7 | 9 | 7 | 9 | 8 | 4 |
| # Errors | 1 | 9 | 4 | 1 | 5 | 1 | 2 | 11 |
| Complex Figure Delayed Recall | 32 | 15 | 14 | 21 | 14 | 12 | 22 | 20 |

*Note:* All performances are presented as raw scores. The score on WMS Paragraph Recall is the sum of the two paragraphs. The score on Paired Associate Learning is the score on the third trial. Delayed tests were conducted following a 30 minute interval.

also used in human studies, including the Wisconsin Card Sorting Test, the Tower of Hanoi, and the sort of "conditional association" task we will discuss below. There is ample evidence that many frontal lobe patients, though not all, have defects in working memory.

While working memory may be disturbed, so-called "associative" memory is generally not affected. When damage is limited to the frontal lobes, there typically appears to be little or no impairment on most widely used neurospychological memory tests (e.g., Black, 1976; Janowsky et al., 1989; Stuss et al., 1982). To illustrate this point, Table 12-2 contains standardized memory test performances of eight patients with lesions in various aspects of the frontal lobes, including dorsolateral and ventromedial areas, but without involvement of the basal forebrain region or the medial temporal lobe. Lesions were caused by vascular event or surgical excision of a meningioma, and are depicted in Figure 12-4.

It can be seen from the data in Table 12-2 that, although there are occasional isolated scores which are below expectations, the overall profile is consistently one of well-preserved memory abilities.

An important factor to keep in mind when evaluating patients with known or suspected frontal lobe damage is that there may be major dissociations between well-preserved memory capacity (as demonstrated by normal performances on standardized memory tests) and severely impaired utilization of those abilities in real-life situations. A telling example of this dissociation was provided by a patient (#1331)

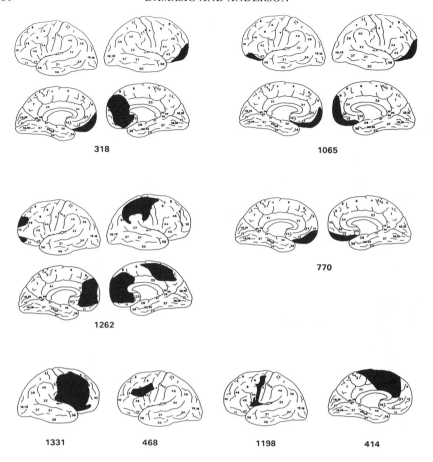

**Fig. 12-4.** The lesions of the subjects included in Table 12-2 were plotted from MR and CT images onto standard templates according to the method of H. Damasio and Damasio (1989), and are presented here in lateral and mesial views. Views that are not shown were normal.

studied in our laboratory following a large right dorsolateral frontal lobe lesion caused by stroke (Fig. 12-5). Six months after the event, this 56-year-old former industrial engineer obtained a Wechsler Memory Scale MQ of 132 and correctly identified 29 of 30 words (15 targets and 15 foils) on a 30 minute delayed recognition version of the Auditory-Verbal Learning Test. However, the patient's wife described him as extremely forgetful in his normal daily activities. In contrast to his formerly conscientious behavior, the patient would now repeatedly misplace his keys and other personal effects, and would regularly leave the television and lights on when he would leave a room. This "failure to remember" remained a constant feature of his behavior. When last seen three years after the stroke, his wife described the following event. The patient had recently driven by himself to a restaurant to dine with some friends. Upon leaving the restaurant after lunch, it was discovered that he had left his car engine running the entire time. These disturbances fall within the confines of working memory.

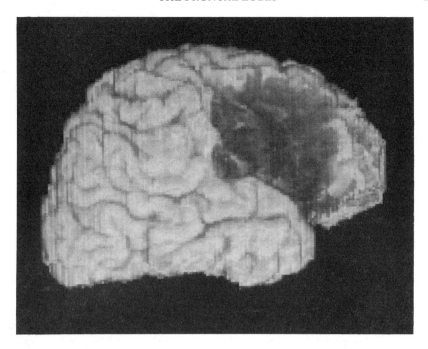

**Fig. 12-5.** Three-dimensional reconstruction of the brain of subject #1331 obtained from thin cut MRI slices using Brainvox (H. Damasio and Frank, 1992).

The distinction of what memory defects are or are not attributable to frontal damage is an important one. For instance, the proximity of the basal forebrain region to the ventromedial frontal lobe makes it likely that both frontal and basal forebrain areas are damaged by the same lesion. The problem is made more difficult by the fact that the basal forebrain region, due to its location and size, is often difficult to visualize. This region contains the largest concentration of cholinergic neurons (including those in the nucleus basalis of Meynert), along with major neurotransmitter projections en route from brainstem to cerebral cortex. Lesions here result in an amnesic syndrome (Damasio et al., 1985). Such lesions are commonly caused by infarcts secondary to rupture of aneurysms on the anterior communicating or anterior cerebral arteries (see also Chapter 15).

There is considerable evidence that one factor which contributes to the memory difficulties of patients with frontal lobe damage is susceptibility to interference (e.g., Malmo, 1942; Milner, 1964; Stuss et al., 1982). Distraction by irrelevant stimuli and failure to inhibit irrelevant responses may have a profound impact on the memory of patients with frontal lobe damage. Other aspects of memory impairment related to frontal lobe dysfunction are discussed below in the section on experimental neuropsychological studies.

### *Response to Changing Contingencies*

Testing for the ability to initiate, stop, and modify behavior in response to changing stimuli has traditionally been part of the evaluation for frontal lobe dysfunction.

Depending on the circumstances, the evaluation may involve observation of performances on bedside "go no go" tasks or more sophisticated psychometric assessment. The Wisconsin Card Sorting Test (WCST) was developed by Berg (1948) and Grant and Berg (1948) to provide a measure of the ability to identify abstract categories and shift cognitive set, and has been widely applied in the assessment of frontal lobe damage. The test requires patients to sort a deck of response cards according to various stimulus dimensions. The patient is not informed of the sorting principles, but rather must infer these from information given by the examiner after each response. Further complicating the patient's task is the fact that the sorting principles change throughout the test without any clue other than the changing pattern of feedback. Although there have been several variations on the original methodology, certain features have remained generally constant (see Heaton, 1981, for a complete description of the test). Each response card contains from one to four identical figures (stars, crosses, triangles, or circles) in one of four colors. These figures provide the basis for the three sorting principles: color, form, and number. At the beginning of the test, four stimulus cards are placed before the patient (one red triangle, two green stars, three yellow crosses, and four blue circles). The patient is instructed to place each consecutive response card in front of one of the stimulus cards, wherever it appears to match best. The patient is not informed of the correct sorting principle, but is told only if each response is right or wrong. After the patient has made ten consecutive correct sorts, the initial sorting principle (color) is changed (to form) without warning. Again, after ten correct sorts, the sorting principle is changed without warning from form to number. This procedure continues until either five shifts of sorting category have been completed, or the two decks of 64 cards have been sorted.

The requirements of the WCST for cognitive abstraction and flexibility in response to changing contingencies make it an attractive instrument for investigating the consequences of frontal lobe damage. In a pioneering study, Milner (1963) documented a consistent and severe impairment on the WCST in patients who had undergone prefrontal lobectomies for treatment of epilepsy. None of her subjects was able to complete more than two shifts of set (three categories). The findings were interpreted as suggesting that the ability to shift from one strategy to another in a sorting task is more compromised by frontal lobe damage than by rolandic or posterior sensory cortex damage. The manifest perseveration that made patients rigidly adhere to one criterion and ignore the examiner's guiding information was interpreted as an inability to overcome an establised response set.

Although some subsequent studies also found that, as a group, frontal lobe damaged subjects tended to perform worse than subjects with focal nonfrontal damage, these investigations showed substantial variability in WCST performance across subjects with frontal lobe damage (Drewe, 1974; Heaton, 1981), and one study using a slightly modified procedure found that patients with posterior lesions performed worse than patients with anterior lesions (Teuber et al., 1951). We recently examined the WCST performance of 91 subjects with focal brain lesions caused by stroke or tumor resection, and found no differences between those subjects with frontal vs. nonfrontal lesions (Anderson et al., 1991). Consistent with most prior studies, there was considerable variability in WCST performances across subjects with frontal damage. Some subjects with extensive frontal lobe damage performed the task with ease and made virtually no errors, while others with comparable lesions were severely defective. Likewise, many subjects with nonfrontal lesions had defective performances. Within the frontal lobe group, performances on the WCST did not appear to be related to the specific area of damage (e.g., dorsolateral vs. ventromedial). Along similar lines, a recent large-scale study of Vietnam war veterans found no difference in WCST performances between subjects with frontal lobe damage vs. posterior damage (Grafman et al., 1990). Regional cerebral blood flow studies have indicated that performance on the WCST is associated with relative increase in physiological activity in the prefrontal area, but that several other areas also show increased activity relative to a resting state (Weinberger et al., 1986). Clearly, scores on the WCST must be interpreted in a broad neuropsychological context. Performances are correlated with age, education, and IQ, and the combined findings of several studies suggest that time since onset is a critical factor, with considerable improvement occurring over time.

The number of perseverative responses or perseverative errors has consistently been found to be the most sensitive WCST score for detection of frontal lobe damage. Perseveration at multiple levels of behavioral organization may be observed in some patients with frontal lobe damage, but the localizing value of perseveration is limited (e.g., Goldberg, 1986).

### Speech and Language

APHASIA

One of the most influential discoveries in the early history of brain-behavior relationships was Paul Broca's (1861) description of an infarction in left posterior inferior frontal cortex in a patient whose speech was limited to repetitive production of a single syllable. It is now known that various sectors of left dorsolateral frontal lobe interface with posterior cortices and subcortical structures to provide the substrate for linguistic formulation and comprehension. The left frontal lobe appears to play an important role in aspects of language processing which involve combinatorial assembly, e.g., the combination of phonemes into morphemes, and of morphemes into sentences (Damasio, 1992). Other frontal regions, namely the cingulate gyrus and supplementary motor area, are involved in the affective and motor control of speech production. Although Broca's aphasia remains the best-known language defect associated with frontal lobe damage, it is becoming increasingly evident that this clinical diagnostic category encompasses various interactions of several dissociable impairments, including defects of linguistic formulation, motor programming, and the initiation and maintenance of output (Alexander et al., 1989). Correspondingly, damage to posterior inferior frontal cortex alone does not produce the full syndrome, but rather Broca's aphasia is caused by extensive and varied damage to several neighboring brain areas (Mohr, 1976; Signoret et al., 1984). Because discussion of Broca's aphasia, transcortical motor aphasia, and speech apraxia are provided elsewhere in this volume (see Chapter 2), we will not go into further detail here. There are, however, several other aspects of frontal lobe involvement in speech and language that warrant comment.

Mutism, generally associated with some degree of both akinesia and bradykinesia, is a frequent sign of frontal lobe dysfunction. It denotes involvement of the mesial cortex of the frontal lobe or of its connections, unilaterally or bilaterally. Current evidence indicates that lesions in the cingulate gyrus or the supplementary motor area (often in both) are crucial for the appearance of mutism and akinesia. Bilateral damage tends to cause longer-lasting changes. Unilateral damage, in vascular cases or in ablations, permits recovery in a matter of weeks. There is no evidence that side of lesion plays a major role here, and dominant as well as nondominant lesions cause much the same results, further evidence that the areas in question are related to affective and motor control but not to linguistic processing, thus being capable of interfering with speech (and all other movement, purposeful or automatic) but not language. The most frequent cause for the lesions that cause mutism is impairment in the blood supply of the anterior cerebral artery territories. Rupture of aneurysms of the anterior communicating or anterior cerebral artery is the usual antecedent event. The patient is mostly silent and motionless or nearly so, but tracking movements of the eyes and blinking are almost always preserved. The ability to walk is maintained in patients who do not have concomitant paraparesis from involvement of the mesial aspect of the motor areas. Often patients make many purposeful movements, such as those needed to adjust clothes or eat. The facial expression is empty, and the patient makes no effort to communicate verbally or by gesture. Rare isolated utterances may be produced, and repetition of single words and short sentences can occasionally be performed under coaxing. Whatever the amount of verbal output, patients do not produce paraphasias and have well-articulated though often hypophonic speech (Damasio and Van Hoesen, 1980, 1983).

The diagnosis of mutism should be made only after careful judgment of accompanying signs and of the whole context of the clinical presentation. Patients with mutism often evoke psychiatric disease, and if it were not for a clarifying previous history, a primarily neurological nature could be unnoticed. Mutism must be distinguished from anarthria and aphemia, conditions in which the inability to speak (or to speak without phonetic errors) is accompanied by a frustrated intent to communicate verbally and in which attempts to communicate by gesture or facial expression are often successful. These features also help distinguish mutism from the transcortical motor aphasias, in which speech is sparse and nonfluent, and in which word and sentence repetition are preserved.

Verbal fluency, as measured by verbal association tests, may also be impaired by frontal lobe damage. This may be noted in the absence of any detectable change in speech output. A curious instance is Brickner's patient A. He spoke fluent and well-articulated speech, often at a high rate, manifesting a free flow of verbal association of almost manic nature. However, when given a certain word, his ability to produce morphologically similar words by changing a letter or letter positions was impaired. This ability is also impaired in many cases of transcortical motor aphasia.

Using Thurstone's Word Fluency Test, Milner (1964) showed that patients with left frontal lobectomies that spared Broca's area scored very poorly in this test, despite there being no evidence of aphasia. Controls with temporal lobectomies performed as well as patients with right frontal lobectomies. Interestingly, both left and right frontals performed at the same level in a task of verbal memory, suggesting the relative independence of the mechanism underlying fluency. The temporal lobe controls did poorly on the verbal memory task.

Benton (1968) arrived at the same conclusions studying a group of patients with left, right, and bilateral frontal damage. The task used to test fluency was an oral version of the Thurstone test, in which the patient is requested to say as many words beginning with a given letter of the alphabet as come to mind. Not only did the left-hemisphere patients do remarkably worse than the right-hemisphere ones, but bilaterally damaged patients also performed more poorly than those with right-hemisphere damage only. The observations of Ramier and Hécaen (1970) were in essential accord with these results.

The findings of Milner and Benton provide empirical confirmation of the classic views of Feuchtwanger (1923) and Kleist (1936), according to which "dominant" frontal lesions, but not "minor" frontal ones, interfere with verbal processes, particularly in respect to spontaneity and the ability to maintain a flow of verbal evocation without actually producing one of the typical aphasias. They are in opposition to the views of Jefferson (1937) and Rylander (1940), who denied any lateralization of defect after frontal lobectomies.

As suggested by Milner's results in the task of verbal memory, the impairment in fluency seems to have an independent mechanism and is not necessarily associated with verbal learning defects. Benton noted that left-hemisphere patients were not worse than right-hemisphere ones in tasks of verbal paired-associate learning.

NONVOCAL LANGUAGE

The role of the frontal lobes in language is not limited to the auditory-vocal channel. Impairments of visuogestural language, reading comprehension, and writing have been documented in patients with focal damage in left premotor and prefrontal cortex. Damage to the left frontal lobe has been shown to result in breakdowns of signed language, which have similarities to the patterns of aphasia in spoken language following damage to this area, with agrammatism and halting, effortful signing (Bellugi et al., 1989).

Damage to the left frontal lobe has long been associated with alexia in the setting of Broca's aphasia (Lichtheim, 1885; Dejerine and Mirallie, 1895; Nielsen, 1938, 1946). Benson (1977) reported that 51 of 61 patients (84%) with Broca's aphasia and no evidence of posterior lesions had at least mild alexia, and that these patients had particular difficulty in decoding words by grapheme to phoneme conversion. It has also been noted that oral reading and reading comprehension of Broca's aphasia may mirror the typical patterns of language breakdown in these patients, in that concrete nouns may be more likely to be read correctly than function words such as conjunctions, prepositions, pronouns, and articles (Gardner and Zurif, 1975; Kaplan and Goodglass, 1981).

Exner (1881) is usually credited with first describing agraphia following lesions in the superior aspect of the left premotor cortex ("Exner's area" in area 6, above areas 44 and 45). Other cases of agraphia associated with left dorsolateral frontal lesions have been described by Gordinier (1899), Penfield and Roberts (1959), and Rapscak et al. (1988). We have studied a case with isolated alexia and agraphia associated with a circumscribed surgical lesion in Exner's area (Anderson et al., 1990). This patient was not aphasic or hemiparetic, but was virtually unable to write any words or letters, with her writing attempts showing severe spatial distortion. Reading of single letters, words, and sentences was also severely impaired, but she could occasionally recognize single words in a gestalt fashion. The impairments of reading and writing were limited to the domain of letters; she could read and write numbers and perform written calculations without difficulty.

Further evidence that Exner's area may be involved in reading is provided by a case of reading epilepsy associated with a focal lesion in this region (A. Rittacio, personal communication). The patient was a 24-year-old college student who underwent removal of a left frontal arteriovenous malformation. He was left without neurologic or cognitive defects except for seizures which occurred only when reading. In a series of controlled laboratory experiments, silent reading while subvocalizing was the most reliable means of eliciting seizure activity. Electrophysiological studies suggested that the epileptogenic zone was just anterior to the postsurgical lesion in Exner's area.

## Motor Function and Visual Perception

Axons from neurons in primary motor cortex and premotor cortex run through the corticospinal tract, providing the major substrate for cortical control of movement. Not surprisingly, lesion studies in humans and monkeys have documented a variety of motor impairments associated with frontal lobe damage, including motor neglect, hypokinesia, motor impersistence, and perseveration (for a review, see Heilman and Watson, 1991). Frontal lobe damage, especially involving the left hemisphere, has long been associated with ideomotor apraxia (Liepmann, 1908), although generally of less severity and less frequently than has parietal lobe damage (e.g., Kolb and Milner, 1981; De Renzi et al., 1983) (See Chapter 7). Benton (1968) demonstrated that patients with right frontal or bilateral frontal lobe lesions were inferior to patients with left frontal lobe lesions on tests of three-dimensional block construction and copying designs. Jones-Gotman and Milner (1977) found that subjects with right frontal lobe damage were impaired relative to subjects with temporal lobe or left frontal lobe damage on a task requiring the rapid generation of original abstract drawings.

Infarction of the middle cerebral artery often results in combined damage to the dorsolateral frontal lobe and the anterior parietal lobe, with a high probability of contralateral neglect if the damage is on the right. Damage limited to the frontal lobes has been shown to cause both contralateral and ipsilateral neglect (Heilman and Valenstein, 1972; Kwon and Heilman, 1991).

In cases of frontal lobe stroke or traumatic injury, considerable recovery of voluntary movement and perception usually occurs in the weeks or months following onset, particularly when the damage is unilateral. Focal frontal lobe damage usually results in little or no long-term impairment on most standardized tests of visual per-

**Table 12-3.** Visual Perception and Constructional Function

| ID# | Facial Recognition | Line Orientation | Complex Figure |
|---|---|---|---|
| 318 | 43 | 30 | 36 |
| 414 | 50 | 22 | 30 |
| 468 | 44 | 30 | 34 |
| 534 | 46 | 21 | 31 |
| 1065 | 43 | 25 | 33 |
| 1173 | 47 | 20 | 32 |
| 1198 | 47 | 22 | 31 |
| 1331 | 50 | 23 | 33 |

*Note:* Data for Facial Recognition and Line Orientation are presented as corrected scores, and data for the Complex Figure are presented as raw scores.

ception or construction. This is illustrated in Table 12-3, which provides the scores of eight subjects with focal damage to various frontal regions, including left and right dorsolateral frontal cortex and bilateral ventromedial areas. The tests include (1) The Facial Recognition Test (Benton et al., 1983), which requires discrimination between black and white photographs of faces which are similar in gender and age, (2) Judgment of Line Orientation (Benton et al., 1983), which requires the matching of lines positioned at the same angle, and (3) the Rey-Osterrieth Complex Figure Test (Lezak, 1983; Spreen and Strauss, 1991), which requires the drawing of an abstract geometric figure from a model. All performances were within normal limits.

### Neurological Findings

CHANGES IN AROUSAL AND ORIENTING RESPONSE

Patients who move little or not at all often pay little or no attention to new stimuli. The possibility that akinesia associated with frontal lobe lesions goes pari passu with severe bilateral neglect is an interesting one. Thus, changes in motor and affective processing may be associated with changes in the mechanisms of arousal. The type of abnormality described by Fisher (1968) as "intermittent interruption of behavior" in cases of anterior cerebral artery infarction is another good example of the coexistence of such changes.

There is little doubt that orienting responses are impaired after dorsolateral and cingulate gyrus damage. The changes generally appear in the setting of neglect to stimuli arriving in the space contralateral to the lesion, with associated hypomobility of the neglected side (Heilman and Valenstein, 1972; Damasio et al., 1980). Lesions in the arcuate region in primates cause unilateral neglect (Kennard and Ectors, 1938; Welch and Stuteville, 1958), not unlike that determined by lesions of multimodal parietal association areas (Heilman et al., 1971), and the same applies to the cingulate gyrus (Watson et al., 1973). Lesions in nonfrontal lobe structures—including the thalamus, hypothalamus, and midbrain—can also cause neglect in both humans and animals (Marshall and Teitelbaum, 1974; Marshall et al., 1971; Segarra and Angelo, 1970; Watson et al., 1974).

## ABNORMAL REFLEXES

The more significant abnormal reflexes are the grasp reflex, the groping reflex, and the snout and sucking reflexes. Traditionally these abnormal responses have been termed "psychomotor signs," calling attention to the fact that they almost invariably appear in the setting of an abnormal mental status.

The most useful of the group is the grasp reflex (the prehension reflex of Kleist, the forced grasping of Adie and Critchley), which may appear unilaterally or bilaterally, in the hands or in the feet. It consists of a more or less forceful prehension of an object that has come into contact with the palm or the sole. It can be elicited by touching or by stroking the skin, particularly in the region between the thumb and index finger. Most maneuvers used to elicit the plantar reflex may produce a grasp reaction of the foot and may even mask an abnormal extensor response, which, in that case, may be obtained from stimulation of the lateral side of the foot. The degree of the grasp reflex varies from patient to patient and is generally more intense in cases with impaired mentation. In more alert states, it is characteristic that the patient cannot release the prehension even if told to do so and even if she or he wishes to do so. The reflex may extinguish after repeated stimulation and reappear after a period of rest. Classic descriptions used to refer to changes in lateralization induced by positioning of the head and body, but such changes are not reliable and should not be used for clinical localization.

The groping reflex is less frequent than the grasp reflex and generally appears in conjunction with the latter. The hand of the patient, as well as the eyes, tend to follow an object or the fingers of the examiner. For a brief period, the patient behaves as if stimulus-bound.

The sucking reflex is elicited by touching the lips of the patient with a cotton swab, and the snout reflex is obtained by tapping the skin of the upper perioral region with finger or hammer. These responses are often present in patients with disease confined to the frontal lobe, but, more so than the grasp reflex, they appear in a wide variety of dementia syndromes associated with more wide-ranging damage. Furthermore, the snout reflex, just like the palmomental reflex, may appear in patients with basal ganglia disorders and even in normal older individuals.

Traditionally, these signs have been interpreted as an indication of release of primitive forms of reflex response, kept in abeyance by normal inhibitory function of frontal lobe structures. This view seems entirely valid.

## ABNORMAL TONE

Patients with lesions in the prefrontal areas often show changes in muscle tone. These may be more closely associated with lesions in the dorsolateral aspect of the frontal lobes, particularly near the premotor regions. The most characteristic sign is Kleist's *Gegenhalten*, also referred to as counterpull, paratonia, opposition, or the Mayer-Reisch phenomenon. This is another of the so-called psychomotor signs and may be wrongly interpreted as a deliberate negative attitude on the part of the patient. When the examiner tries to assess tone by passively moving the arm, he or she may find a sudden resistance to the extension maneuver and note that the counteracting flexion movement actually increases in intensity in an attempt to neutralize the action. The patient may or may not be aware of this development and, as with the grasp reflex, will be unable to suppress the reflex even if desiring to do so. Rigidity may also be present, but since it is not associated with tremor, it will not have "cogwheel" characteristics. The degree of rigidity may show little consistency and may vary between observations. It is best described as plastic. Periodic hypotonia resembling cataplexy is quite rare (Ethelberg, 1949).

ABNORMAL GAIT AND POSTURE

Patients with severe frontal lobe damage often show abnormalities of gait. A wide range of characteristic changes may be present, including walking with short steps but without festination, loss of balance with retropulsion, or inability to walk (as in cases of gait apraxia). The latter may be seen in a variety of conditions, most frequently in the syndrome of normal-pressure hydrocephalus, which is, in effect, a frontal lobe syndrome consequent to periodically raised intraventricular pressure. In diagnosing gait apraxia, an effort should be made to demonstrate that the patient can execute while recumbent all the movements he or she is unable to perform while standing.

The designation "frontal ataxia" probably does not cover a manifestation typical of frontal lobe lesions, as even Bruns admitted when he coined the term. A tendency to fall backward rather than to the side and a predominance of deficits in the trunk rather than in the extremities are evident in some cases.

Abnormalities of posture are possible, though not pathognomic or frequent. In some cases, the examiner is able to place the arms of the patient in various bizarre positions and note the waxy flexibility with which the patient will remain in those unlikely positions. True catalepsy and sudden freezing of posture have also been described but seem rare.

CHANGES IN CONTROL OF EYE MOVEMENT

The control of eye and head movements is part of a highly developed system tuned to orient the organism toward possibly important stimuli and therefore aid perception of the environment. The role of the frontal eye fields, located bilaterally in area 8 of Brodmann, in the control of these movements is still a matter of controversy. The paucity of spontaneous head and eye movement toward new stimuli, which is commonly described in connection with the impairment of orienting responses of frontal lobe patients, is possibly related to eye field function. On the whole, however, the value of eye movement defects in the assessment of higher levels of behavior disturbance is limited.

Frontal seizures, originating in lesions in or near one eye field, may be characterized by a turning of the eye and head away from the side of the lesion. On the other hand, structural damage of one eye field, particularly if acute, produces a turning of eyes and head toward the side lesion.

Clear anomalies of conjugate gaze mechanism have their greatest value in the

440     DAMASIO AND ANDERSON

assessment of the comatose patient, where their relation to a concomitant paresis may decide whether the damage is in the frontal lobe or in the brainstem.

Anatomical and electrophysiological studies in the monkey have suggested that the prefrontal cortex may be involved in qualitative olfactory discrimination (Tanabe et al., 1975a,b; Potter and Nauta, 1979). Potter and Butters (1980) have reported that damage to the orbital region of the frontal lobe can lead to impaired odor-quality discrimination without a significant decrease in odor detection. Projections from the temporal lobe directly to orbitofrontal cortex as well as by way of the thalamus were hypothesized to carry olfactory information in a hierarchial system of "odor-quality analyzers." Damage to thalamic and prefrontal lobe structures has also been found to impair odor-quality discrimination in nonprimates without influencing odor detection (Eichenbaum et al., 1980; Sapolsky and Eichenbaum, 1980). The findings suggest  that selective frontal lobe damage can be associated with deficits in a cognitive task of odor-quality discrimination without decreasing odor-detection ability.

CHANGES IN SPHINCTER CONTROL

It is often noted that patient with frontal lobe damage have disturbances of sphincter control. The patient shows little concern about urinating or even defecating in socially unacceptable situations. Bilateral involvement of the mesial aspect of the frontal lobe is the rule in these cases. Resection of an underlying tumor often improves sphincter disturbances, which tend to recover spontaneously in cases of stroke. Extensive lesions of the white matter may also produce incontinence, as the early techniques of frontal lobotomy demonstrated. This defect is probably the result of loss of the inhibitory action that the frontal lobe presumably exerts over the spinal detrusor reflex.

## EXPERIMENTAL NEUROPSYCHOLOGICAL STUDIES

A comprehensive review of the human and animal experimental research on frontal lobe function is beyond the scope of this chapter. Nevertheless, consideration of some of the major results of this research is in order because of their bearing on clinical issues. In light of the frequent lack of sensitivity of established clinical neuropsychological probes to the cognitive and behavioral defects that result from frontal lobe damage, it is particularly important for the clinician to be aware of experimental findings regarding frontal lobe dysfunction. Attention to this research will not only allow for more sophisticated conceptualizations of the behavioral problems seen in patients with frontal lobe damage, but may also provide clues to help guide development of the next generation of clinical tests.

### Delayed Response Defects

The original findings of Jacobsen (1935; Jacobsen and Nissen, 1937) regarding the impairment in delayed responses in chimpanzees still dominate this area of study.

During the past several decades an impressive number of researchers have replicated Jacobsen's results for both the delayed response and the delayed alternation tasks and extended the verification of the defects to rhesus monkeys, cats, dogs, and rats. Furthermore, within the prefrontal cortex, damage to the region of the sulcus principalis has been identified as the crucial region for the production of the defect (Blum, 1952).

The delayed response procedure consists of the presentation of two or more empty food wells, one of which is baited in front of the animal. The wells are then covered and hidden from view for at least 5 seconds, after which time the animal is again allowed to view the covered wells and requested to retrieve the bait. The number of errors the animal makes reaching for the food is the basis for the score. Jacobsen noted that animals with bilateral removals of the prefrontal lobes did very poorly in this task, unlike animals with bilateral lesions elsewhere in the brain. The initial interpretation was that of an immediate-memory defect, but this hypothesis was abandoned since the same animals that failed the delayed response task passed a visual discrimination procedure, which necessitates the use of immediate memory. If, for instance, one of the food wells was made different by the addition of a specific visual feature, the animal would make a correct choice after the delay. The fact that similar animals would perform normally if left in the dark during the delay suggested that retroactive erasing of traces was at stake. Also, if animals were allowed a rewarded response before the first trial, they would perform normally or with few errors, a finding that pointed to the obvious role of limbic reinforcement in the type of response (Finan, 1942; Malmo, 1942).

The delayed alternation tasks use the same setup, but the procedure is made more complicated by consecutive switching of the bait from one well to the other. Since delayed alternation naturally requires memory in a way that delayed response does not, performance in the two tasks may be dissociated by bilateral lesions of the hippocampus, which compromise delayed alternation but not delayed response (Orbach et al., 1960; Pribram et al., 1962). Destruction of the head of the caudate impairs both, however, in a manner similar to that produced by lesions in the region of the sulcus principalis, and electrical stimulation of the caudate during the trials also impairs the response (Rosvold and Delgado, 1956; Dean and Davis, 1959; Battig et al., 1960). Bilateral stimulation of the region of the sulcus principalis also impairs both tasks (Mishkin and Pribram, 1955, 1956; Pribram, 1961; Stamm, 1961). Furthermore, it has been shown that ablation or stimulation of the middle sector of the sulcus principalis disrupts delayed response or delayed alternation response, whereas ablation or stimulation of the anterior sector does not produce any impairment (Butters and Pandya, 1969; Stamm, 1969). Results of involvement of the posterior sector have been controversial. Finally, only lesions of both the upper and lower banks of the middle third (but not lesions of either upper or lower, in isolation) seem capable of producing the defects (Butters et al., 1971). The suggestion that lesions in the dorsomedial nucleus of the thalamus might impair delayed response (Schulman, 1969) has not been unquestionably verified.

The reason for the failure of nonhuman primates and other animals in the delayed response and delayed alternation tasks has not been unequivocally established. Among the factors that have been proposed are the impairment of processing of temporal and spatial cues and the effect of interference. Several studies tend to support the importance of these factors. For example, evidence that frontal cortices are critical for associating stimuli and responses which are temporally separated comes from single-unit electrophysiological studies of monkeys performing the delayed response task. Fuster (1991) has demonstrated sustained activation in cells in dorsolateral frontal cortex during the delay between stimulus presentation and the opportunity to respond, with some cells showing sustained excitation and others sustained inhibition. In another example, Grueninger and Pribram (1969) showed that the performance of monkeys with dorsolateral lesions is impaired by distraction from the processing of spatial cues, which raises the possibility that changes in spatial information act as distractors in these tasks. Performance on the delayed response and delayed alternation tasks requires formation of stimulus-response relationships that are resistant to distracting stimuli and inappropriate response tendencies (see Stamm, 1987, and Pribram, 1987) for further discussion). It appears likely that an important role of dorsolateral frontal lobe structures is that of an inhibitor of interference. That this inhibitory action might be more marked for spatial than nonspatial information is suggested by the better performance of monkeys with dorsolateral frontal lobe damage in nonspatial and go/no go problems (Mishkin, 1964).

Yet another cause for the delayed response defect may be the lack of "affective tagging" of the stimuli, a circumstance that could arise from the destruction of a frontal region vital to combine external sensory information with information about the somatic state. The fact that (1) the crucial area for delayed response impairment, the sulcus principalis, projects to the limbic system via the cingulate, (2) other areas of the anterior frontal cortex project to the caudate (from which similar defects may be obtained by stimulation), and (3) delayed alternation defects can be obtained from almost anywhere in so-called limbic structures support the view that separating frontal and limbic system processing may play a role in the determination of such defects. Both distractibility and weakness of limbic marking are compatible with Konorski and Lawicka's (1964) interpretation of the defect on the basis of an abnormally rapid decay of the conditioning signal during the delay.

The generalizability of the delayed response and delayed alternation findings from nonhuman primates to humans with frontal lobe dysfunction remains equivocal. Milner et al. (1985) noted that the ability to solve the problems through verbal mediation so alters the task requirements that they may not be appropriate paradigms for human subjects. Consistent with this, Chorover and Cole (1966) did not find impairments on a delayed alternation task in subjects with frontal lobe damage compared to control subjects with lesions outside the frontal lobes. Likewise, Ghent et al. (1962) found no impairment on a delayed response task associated with frontal lesions. Freedman and Oscar-Berman (1986) administered delayed response and delayed alternation tasks to six subjects with frontal lobe damage of various etiologies and found considerable variability in performances on these tasks. Some subjects appeared to perform normally, and the two subjects with the most severe impairments were older and had sustained severe traumatic head injuries.

## Conditional Association Learning

Failure to adjust behavior adequately in response to environmental conditions may play an important role in the cognitive/behavioral defects seen after frontal lobe damage. Socially inappropriate behavior and nonadaptive decisionmaking by patients with frontal lobe damage may reflect dysfunction of the neural system by which the consequences of past actions impact upon the on-line guidance of behavior. It has long been known that monkeys with frontal lobe ablations are unable to make normal adjustments of behavior in response to changing contingencies (Settlage et al., 1948).

Patients with frontal lobe tumors were found to be impaired relative to those with posterior tumors on a task in which they were required to generate hypotheses regarding the relevance of certain stimulus dimensions, and then modify the hypotheses on the basis of repeated feedback (Cicerone et al., 1983). The subjects with frontal lobe tumors showed a tendency to repeat responses despite negative feedback. In a series of studies with nonhuman primates and human subjects with frontal lobe ablations, Petrides has investigated the ability to select, from a number of possible alternative responses, the correct response given the current stimulus. Each of the alternative responses is correct only in the presence of one particular stimulus, and the subject must discover on the basis of information given by the examiner after each response which is the appropriate response for each one of the set of stimuli. Petrides (1985) found that patients with unilateral frontal lobe excisions were impaired, relative to patients with temporal lobe excisions, on tasks that required the subject to point to different locations or display various hand shapes in response to specific stimuli. This basic finding was replicated with a task in which the subjects learned to associate various abstract designs with various colored lights (Petrides, 1990), suggesting that the defect in conditional learning following frontal damage is a general one not limited to situations requiring selection between distinct movements or spatial locations. The subjects involved in these studies had undergone extensive prefrontal lobectomies, with lesions generally involving dorsolateral as well as ventral or medial cortices. However, parallel research with nonhuman primates has suggested that the posterior dorsolateral frontal cortex may be the critical region for performance on the conditional association tasks (Petrides, 1987).

## Temporal Organization of Memory

### RECENCY AND FREQUENCY JUDGMENTS

It was noted earlier that part of the reason for failure on the delayed response and delayed alternation tasks by monkeys with dorsolateral frontal lobe lesions may be related to temporal aspects of the task requirements. Also pointing to a specific role of the frontal lobes in aspects of temporal contextual memory are studies by Milner and her colleagues which have documented impairments of the ability to make judgments of relative recency or frequency (Milner, 1971; Milner et al., 1991; Smith and Milner, 1988). In the recency task, the subject is presented with a series of stimuli (e.g., words or abstract designs). Mixed in with the stimulus items are test items where two stimuli are presented; these are either two stimuli that have been presented previously or one previous item paired with a novel item. The subject is required to judge which of the two items was seen most recently. Subjects with frontal cortical excisions for treatment of epilepsy were able to discriminate between novel and familiar items, but were impaired in the ability to judge the relative recency of two familiar items (Corsi and Milner, reported in Milner, 1971; Milner et al., 1991). In contrast, subjects with unilateral temporal lobectomies show material-specific recognition problems, but normal recency judgments. Impairment of the ability to judge the relative frequency of occurrence of nonverbal items has also been demonstrated in subjects with right frontal lobe damage (Smith and Milner, 1988). The profile of impaired recency and frequency judgments despite good item recognition appears to be specific to patients with frontal lobe damage. Not only did the above studies find normal performances on recency and frequency judgments by control subjects with temporal lobectomies and impairments of item recognition, but it has recently been shown that patient H.M. has relatively preserved recency and frequency judgments despite severely impaired item recognition (Sagar et al., 1990).

PLANNING AND SEQUENCING

The ability to plan short- and long-term future behaviors often seems to be devastated in patients with frontal lobe damage. In our experience, the modal response of these patients to questions regarding plans for the upcoming days or months is a recitation of the activities of the past several days. Consistent with this, their daily behavior often becomes a highly repetitive routine if left to their own devices. Other patients may describe, generally in vague terms, long-term goals that are typically fanciful, unrealistic, or illogical. These verbalizations provide scant evidence of planning, and seem to have little or no impact on the guidance of behavior. Shedding light on the nature of these defects are several experimental studies showing that subjects with frontal lobe damage have impairments on tasks that require the planning and execution of a sequence of responses. For example, Shallice (1982) found that patients with lesions involving the left frontal lobe were impaired on the Tower of London task, which requires the planning of the optimal order of a sequence of simple moves.

Petrides and Milner (1982) contrasted the effect of lesions in the frontal lobe with the effect of lesions in the temporal lobe on four self-ordered tasks that required the organization of the sequence of pointing responses. In these sequential tasks, the subject is free to choose his or her own order of response but is prevented from giving the same response twice. Patients with frontal lobe excisions had significant impairments in all four tasks, whereas the patients with temporal excisions either had no impairment or, when their lesions encompassed the hippocampus, exhibited material-specific deficits. It is of interest that the patients with left frontal lobe excisions were impaired in both verbal and nonverbal tasks whereas the patients with right frontal lobe excisions were impaired only in nonverbal ones. Petrides and Milner (1982) pointed out how this disparity is compatible with the notion of left-hemisphere dominance for the programming of voluntary actions.

Learning to maneuver through a spatial maze requires that a sequence of behaviors be performed in a particular order, and subjects with frontal lobe lesions have been found to be defective in various maze-learning tasks (e.g., Porteus et al., 1944; Milner, 1965; Canavan, 1983). Milner (1965) noted that the frontal lobe subjects repeatedly failed to return to the correct path despite feedback regarding their error. Consistent with this, Karnath et al. (1991) used a computerized maze task to demonstrate that, relative to normal control subjects, subjects with medial frontal lobe lesions showed greater rule-breaking behavior on the second trial through the mazes. The finding that subjects with frontal lobe damage are slower to benefit from experience for the guidance of maze learning is reminiscent of Petrides' findings on learning conditional associations. Additional information regarding the effects of frontal lesions on maze learning comes from a recent study by Winocur and Moscovitch (1990). Rats with bilateral prefrontal lesions were impaired in learning the general skill of maze learning, despite good memory for information regarding the specific maze they had experience with. The opposite pattern was found in rats with bilateral hippocampal lesions.

### Kinesthetic Memory

Teuber's (1964, 1966) contribution to the problem of frontal lobe function is of special interest. At a time when researchers were primarily looking at the sensory aspect of the problem, he emphasized the motor end of the process and introduced the concept of corollary discharge. In brief, this is defined as the preparatory action that the motor system exerts on the sensory system to announce the intention of incoming movement, correct for displacement of perception, and assure smooth perceptual continuity once movement is carried out. Teuber viewed this mechanism as being dependent on frontal lobe structures and considered it to be a basic physiological function of the frontal lobe. In keeping with this idea, he hypothesized that most signs of frontal lobe dysfunction in animals and humans were derived from impairment of the corollary discharge mechanism. Indications of dysfunction as disparate as delayed response deficits in monkeys, perseveration, and the inability to handle sorting tasks were seen as resulting from the absence of a motor sensory alerting signal.

There is no doubt that some mechanism of corollary discharge exists and is essential for the continuity of perception, but it is not clear that frontal lobe structures are indispensable to corollary information processes. Nor does it seem probable that a single impaired mechanism can explain the variety of clinical and experimental signs of frontal lobe damage.

The observations that led Teuber to his concept of corollary discharge were made in patients with penetrating gunshot wounds involving the frontal lobes. Objective evidence of dysfunction in Teuber's patients was reflected in impairment in a series of perceptuomotor tasks that included tests of visuopostural orientation, visual-search, body-orientation, and reversal-of-perspective ability. The visuopostural task (Teuber and Mishkin, 1954) called for the mechanical setting of a brightly luminous rod in the vertical position. The test was conducted in a dark room with the patient under different conditions of body tilt. Frontal lobe subjects did poorly in this task, but if the task was strictly visual and no visuoproprioceptive conflict was established, the subjects performed normally. The visual-search and body-orientation tasks involved active head and eye movement in the search for certain patterns of rapidly shifting left-to-right pointing responses on the patient's body. The reversal-of-perspective task was performed with two Necker cubes with the patient being requested to signify perception of left or right perspective reversal by pressing levers placed to the left and to the right. Since all of these tasks are difficult for a normal person and probably more so for a brain-damaged individual, the strength of the results lies in the verification that patients with nonfrontal brain damage perform consistently better than those with frontal disease. The preliminary results of Teuber and co-workers suggested that this was so.

## Regulation of Arousal and Behavior

Luria's contribution to the study of frontal lobe function encompasses many years of extensive investigation of patients and normals (Luria, 1966, 1969; Luria and Homskaya, 1964). As in so many other studies on the frontal lobe, the importance of the results is somewhat limited by the choice of the subjects for experimentation. Most of the patients studied by Luria and his co-workers had large frontal tumors, some intrinsic and some extrinsic. Some involved subcortical limbic-system structures, such as the septum. Some had associated hydrocephalus and some did not. Most patients had associated nonfrontal dysfunction, due to mass effect or compromise of vascular supply elsewhere in the brain. The location within the frontal lobe was also varied. Nevertheless, Luria's concept of frontal lobe function and dysfunction is quite stimulating.

His interpretation emphasizes the verbally mediated activating and regulatory role of the frontal lobes and their role in problem solving. He suggests that the orienting reaction, as measured by galvanic skin response or suppression of the alpha rhythm in the EEG, cannot be stabilized by verbal stimuli in patients with frontal lobe lesions. In normal subjects, the presentation of verbally meaningful instructions is expected to prevent habituation to stimuli and therefore prevent the orienting response from disappearing (Homskaya, 1966). Apparently nonaphasic patients with tumors, gunshot wounds, or stroke involving the posterior sensory cortex behave as normals in terms of verbal stabilization of the orienting responses even in the presence of praxic and gnosic defects. In patients with frontal lobe lesions, however, the verbal signal does not prevent habituation. Moreover, subjects with damage to the frontal poles and to the mesial and basal aspects of the frontal structures tend to be more affected than those with dorsolateral involvement.

Additional evidence for altered orienting responses in frontal lobe patients comes from studies of visual potentials evoked by verbally tagged stimuli. Stimuli that would have increased the amplitude of visual evoked potentials in normals failed to do so in patients with frontal lobe damage (Simernitskaya and Homskaya, 1966; Simernitskaya, 1970). Animal studies have also supported the idea that frontal lobe damage produces changes in the processing of information by altering the orienting response (Grueninger et al., 1965; Kimble et al., 1965).

Another aspect of frontal lobe dysfunction concerns the possibility of directing the execution of complex actions by verbal mediation. Kaczmarek (1987) documented impairments in several aspects of the linguistic formulations of patients with frontal lobe damage, particularly in the production of propositional statements and descriptions of relationships among objects, and suggested that these impairments may contribute to a defect of regulatory behavior. Several authors have pointed out that frontal lobe patients may be able to repeat correctly the instructions for a given task while making no use whatever of the information in performing a task. Thus, while performing a sorting task, subjects may make perservative sorting errors while verbalizing the correct strategy. The same has been said regarding the utilization of perceived error: patients will verbally admit the mistake but fail to correct it. Luria has repeatedly called attention to this type of defect and considers it one of the hallmarks of frontal lobe dysfunction. He attempted to objectify the defect in a series of experiments in which patients were requested to follow progressively more complex verbal instructions. He noted that patients were able to perform only the more direct and simple commands and would fail to carry out more complex instructions, particularly if they involved some change in principle or some conflict with additional cues provided by the examiner. Since the patient would still be able to repeat the initial verbal instruction, Luria concluded that the primary difficulty was one of verbal guidance of actions (Luria and Homskaya, 1964). Again, the weakness of these studies resides in the subjects used for the observations, i.e., patients with massive bilateral tumors of the frontal lobes. Attempts at replication have met with difficulties (Drewe, 1975). Some defects of the kind reported by Luria were found, but the dissociation between verbal and motor ability was not verified and the author considered it unlikely that a loss of verbal regulatory action was the mechanism underlying impaired performance.

A similar objection may be raised about Luria's description of the changes in problem-solving behavior that attend massive lesions of the frontal lobes. A state of confusion seems to underlie many of the disturbances of planning and calculation exhibited by his patients. Naturally, one can respond to this argument by stating that an element of confusion is part of some frontal lobe syndromes to begin with, but confusion can be caused by central nervous system changes that have little to do with frontal lobe dysfunction, although they may coincide with it and derive from a common cause. Also, confusion is not a necessary accompaniment of frontal lobe damage; it is associated with acute and massive damage of frontal tissue and clearly improves with time as adaptation to the pathological process occurs.

Nonetheless, Luria's observations are very suggestive and his proposals have heurisitic value. The idea that patients have trouble in the choice of programs of action, that their strategy for gathering information necessary for the solution of the problem is impoverished, and that they seldom verify whether their actions meet the original intent are interesting interpretations of defects that can be found often in frontal lobe damage. In addition, it is our impression that even when these defects cannot be demonstrated by an experimental task in the immediate and consistent manner claimed by Luria, one can still encounter them at more complex levels of behavior, for instance, in goal-oriented decision making during long-term planning operations.

### Social Behavior

There has been limited experimental study of the impairment of social behavior shown by patients with frontal lobe damage. However, recent investigations have helped specify the nature of the defect. One possible mechanism for the impairment of social behavior is that frontal lobe damage alters the ability to generate an appropriate array of response options and a satisfactory representation of the future consequences. Another possible mechanism is that these patients are able to conjure up adequate response options and consequences, yet fail to select the most advantageous choice. Saver and Damasio (1991) administered to subject EVR a series of standardized measures designed to examine the manipulation of response options and projected outcomes to social stimuli. EVR demonstrated normal or superior performances on tasks that required the generation of response options to social situations, consideration of the future consequences of pursuing particular responses, and moral reasoning.

Turning to the other possible mechanism, a failure to choose the most advantageous option, Damasio has proposed that the failure may reside with an inability to facilitate the requisite cost-benefit analysis by marking with a *somatic signal* the blatantly disadvantageous future outcomes and thus excluding the options that would lead to them. This theory (see below) calls for an interaction between the physiological process of reactivating a somatic state learned in connection with a particular event and the ability to solve complex problems with varied premises. In favor of this possible mechanism, Damasio et al. (1990) found that subjects with bilateral ventromedial frontal lobe lesions had abnormal autonomic responses to socially meaningful stimuli, despite normal autonomic responses to elementary and unconditioned stimuli. These findings suggest that such stimuli failed to activate somatic states previously associated with specific social situations, and which marked the anticipated outcomes of response options as advantageous or not.

## CONCLUDING REMARKS

The manifestations of frontal lobe dysfunction are varied, ranging all the way from akinesia and mutism to major changes in personality without apparent defects of movement, perception, or intelligence. Depending on cause and location of lesion, a variety of frontal lobe symptom clusters can thus appear. No single frontal lobe syndrome exists.

On the other hand, most frontal lobe syndromes do compromise the ability to guide behavior appropriately and to plan for the future. One might suggest, then, that there is a general role for the vast collection of cerebral cortices collectively known as the frontal lobes.

Elsewhere, one of us has proposed that the frontal cortices have developed to perform a main goal: *to select the responses that are most advantageous for an organism in a complex social environment* (Damasio, 1990). The primary value used to make the selection would be the *state of the soma*, conceived as a combination of the state of viscera, internal milieu, and skeletal musculature. The primary signal used for response selection would be a *somatic marker*, i.e., a somatic state that is temporally correlated with a particular representation that is "marked" by it. The proposal also states that in humans the neural machinery required to perform response selection in a social setting has been co-opted to perform selections in other domains of knowledge, and thus help in general decision making, guidance of multistep tasks, planning, and creativity.

The proposal, which we will refer to as the "theory of somatic markers," draws on the study of patients with damage to prefrontal cortices, especially those with damage to the ventromedial sector (Damasio et al., 1990), and is conceived in the framework of the multiregional retroactivation model (Damasio, 1989a,b). As noted, those previously normal patients develop abnormal social conduct, which repeatedly leads to punishing consequences, in spite of their maintained conventional memory and intelligence. We have proposed that a major factor in the appearance of the disorder (albeit not the only one) is the defective activation of somatic states linked to punishment. Those states ought to have been reenacted in connection with the representation of negative future outcomes related to a given response option. The failure of their reactivation deprives patients of an alarm signal marking the representation of negative consequences for options which might, nonetheless, produce an immediate reward. (Note that positive somatic states may also mark future advantageous outcomes relative to responses that might bring immediate pain.) The activation of somatic markers works at both conscious and nonconscious levels. At the conscious level it draws attention to future negative consequences and promotes the deliberate suppression of the options leading to a negative outcome. At the nonconscious level, somatic markers or signals related to them would trigger inhibition of response states. Subcortical neurotransmitter systems linked to appetitive or aversive behaviors would be involved in this covert level processing.

The neural systems necessary for somatic state activation include the cortices in the ventromedial frontal region, whose damage is the main correlate of these behavioral changes.

There are many reasons, discussed elsewhere, why we place such an emphasis on somatic states. Firstly, and most obvious is that the human acquisition of appropriate behavioral guidance, especially in the social setting, occurs during the process of education and acculturation, under the control of punishment and reward. There are repeated interactions that occur during childhood and adolescence during which social events are paired with somatic states, at both the time of the event and the time at which future consequences take place. Secondly, it is apparent that event/somatic state conjunctions have been important for the behavior of nonhuman species and that those species seem to have an automatic signaling system alerting individuals for immediate potential danger and immediate opportunities for food, sex, and shelter. Such a system has been especially important in those species in which representational capacity and intelligence are limited. We believe there is an equivalent automated device in humans but that it is tuned to future outcomes. The human somatic markers would thus mark future outcome rather than immediate outcome. In subhuman species, the critical conjunction is between response option and immediate outcome and the somatic marker thus tags immediate outcome. We also believe that in humans such an automated decision-making system is then overlaid by cognitive strategy systems that perform cost-benefit analyses but remain connected, neurophysiologically, to the primitive systems. In other words, the systems that humans use for deliberate decision making and planning of the future are rooted in the primitive automated systems that other species have long used for their immediate decision making. The neural architecture of the former is connected to the neural architecture of the latter. When the primitive part of the system fails, superimposed levels cannot operate efficiently.

As indicated above, we view somatic states as one factor in decision-making processes but not the only one. The mechanism of advantageous response selection requires more than somatic markers. For instance, to make a selection among multiple options with myriad possible outcomes, both immediate and future, it is necessary to operate on many premises, some just perceived, some recalled from previous experiences, and some recalled from imagined future scenarios, and it is necessary to mark some of them with the somatic states they trigger. The process of analysis requires the relatively simultaneous holding of numerous sites of neural activity, in widespread regions of the cerebral cortex across long delays of many thousands of milliseconds, i.e., a working memory. Curiously, just as the triggering of somatic states depends on frontal cortices, the neural basis of working memory depends on those frontal cortices too, as the neurophysiological work of Goldman-Rakic has demonstrated (Goldman-Rakic, 1987).

It appears likely that the brain evolved to offer the organism its best chance of survival, and it is no less likely that the prefrontal cortices evolved so that the brain can give the organism its best protection. It is probable that this overall goal was implemented first in simple social environments, dominated by the needs for food, sex, and the avoidance of predators. Many other contingencies in ever more complex environments were later connected with those original contingencies so that the basic neural mechanism for response selection was incorporated in the decision-making mechanisms developed for newer and more complex environments. And in all likelihood, it is out of these higher-order mechanisms that self-consciousness and the abilities to plan and create have emerged.

## ACKNOWLEDGMENT

We thank Hanna Damasio for providing the illustrations and Gary W. Van Hoesen for review of the manuscript and editorial suggestions. Supported by NINDS Program Project Grant NS 19632.

## REFERENCES

Ackerly, S. S., and Benton, A. L. (1948). Report of a case of bilateral frontal lobe defect. *Res. Publ. Assoc. Res. Nerv. Ment. Dis.* 27:479–504.

Akert, K. (1964). Comparative anatomy of frontal cortex and thalamofrontal connections. In *The Frontal Granular Cortex and Behavior*, J. M. Warren and K. Akert (eds.). New York: McGraw-Hill.

Alexander, M. P., Benson, D. F., and Stuss, D. T. (1989). Frontal lobes and language. *Brain and Lang.* 37:656–691.

Anderson, S. W., Damasio, A. R., and Damasio, H. (1990). Troubled letters but not numbers: domain specific cognitive impairments following focal damage in frontal cortex. *Brain* 113:749–766.

Anderson, S. W., Damasio, H., Jones, R. D., and Tranel, D. (1991). Wisconsin Card Sorting Test performance as a measure of frontal lobe damage. *J. Clin. Exp. Neuropsychol.* 13:909–922.

Anderson, S. W., Damasio, H., and Tranel, D. (1989). Neuropsychological profiles associated with lesions caused by tumor or stroke. *Arch. Neurol.* 47:397–405.

Anderson, S. W., Damasio, H., Tranel, D., and Damasio, A. R. (1992). Cognitive sequelae of focal lesions in ventromedial frontal lobe. *J. Clin. Exp. Neuropsychol.* 14:83.

Bailey, P., and Von Bonin, G. (1951). *The Isocortex of Man.* Urbana: University of Illinois Press.

Barbas, H., and Mesulam, M. M. (1981). Organization of afferent input of subdivisions of area 8 in the rhesus monkey. *J. Comp. Neurol. 200:*407–431.

Barbas, H., and Mesulam, M. M. (1985). Cortical afferent input to the principalis region of the rhesus monkey. *Neuroscience* 15:619–637.

Barbas, H., and Pandya, D. N. (1987). Architecture and frontal cortical connections of the premotor cortex (area 6) in the rhesus monkey. *J. Comp. Neurol.* 256:211–228.

Barbas, H., and Pandya, D. N. (1989). Architecture and intrinsic connections of the prefrontal cortex in the rhesus monkey. *J. Comp. Neurol. 286:*353–375.

Battig, K., Rosvold, H. E., and Mishkin, M. (1960). Comparison of the effects of frontal and caudate lesions on delayed response and alternation in monkeys. *J. Comp. Psychol.* 53:400–404.

Bellugi, U., Poizner, H., and Klima, E. S. (1989). Language, modality and the brain. *Trends Neurosci.* 12:380–388.

Benson, D. F. (1977). The third alexia. *Arch. Neurol. 34:*327–331.

Benton, A. L. (1968). Differential behavioral effects in frontal lobe disease. *Neuropsychologia* 6:53–60.

Benton, A. L. (1991a). The prefrontal region: its early history. In *Frontal Lobe Function and Dysfunction,* H. S. Levin, H. M. Eisenberg, and A. L. Benton (eds.). New York: Oxford University Press.

Benton, A. L. (1991b). Basic approaches to neuropsychological assessment. In *Handbook of Schizophrenia,* Vol. 5: *Neuropsychology, Psychophysiology, and Information Processing,* S. R. Steinhauer, J. J. Gruzelier, and J. Zubin (eds.). Amsterdam: Elsevier.

Benton A. L., Hamsher, K., Varney, N. R., and Spreen, O. (1983). *Contributions to Neuropsychological Assessment: A Clinical Manual.* New York: Oxford University Press.

Berg, E. A. (1948). A simple objective technique for measuring flexibility in thinking. *J. Genet. Psychol. 39:*15–22.

Black, F. W. (1976). Cognitive deficits in patients with unilateral war-related frontal lobe lesions. *J. Clin. Psychol. 32:*366–372.

Blum, R. A. (1952). Effects of subtotal lesions of frontal granular cortex on delayed reaction in monkeys. *Arch. Neurol. Psychiatry 67:*375–386.

Blumer, D., and Benson D. F. (1975). Personality changes with frontal and temporal lobe lesions. In *Psychiatric Aspects of Neurologic Disease,* D. F. Benson and D. Blumer (eds.). New York: Grune and Stratton.

Brickner, R. M. (1934). An interpretation of frontal lobe function based upon the study of a case of partial bilateral frontal lobectomy. *Res. Publ. Assoc. Res. Nerv. Ment. Dis.* 13:259–351.

Brickner, R. M. (1936). *The Intellectual Functions of the Frontal Lobes: Study Based upon Observation of a Man After Partial Bilateral Frontal Lobectomy.* New York: Macmillan.

Brickner, R. M. (1952). Brain of patient "A" after bilateral frontal lobectomy: status of frontal lobe problem. *Arch. Neurol. Psychiatry 68:*293–313.

Broca, P. (1861). Remarques sur le siege de la faculte du langage articule, suivies d'une observation d'aphemie (perte de la parole). *Bull. Soc. Anat. 36:*330–357.

Butter, C. M., Mishkin, M., and Mirsky, A. F. (1968). Emotional responses toward humans in monkeys with selective frontal lesions. *Physiol. Behav.* 3:213–215.

Butter, C. M., Mishkin, M., and Rosvold, H. E. (1963). Conditioning and extinction of a food-rewarded response after selective ablations of frontal cortex in rhesus monkeys. *Exp. Neurol. 7*:65–75.

Butter, C. M., Snyder, D. R., and McDonald, J. A. (1970). Effects of orbital frontal lesions on aversive and aggressive behaviors in rhesus monkeys. *J. Comp. Physiol. Psychol. 72*:132–144.

Butters, N., and Pandya, D. (1969). Retention of delayed-alternation: effect of selective lesions of sulcus principalis. *Science 165*:1271–1273.

Butters, N., Pandya, D., Sanders, K., and Dye, P. (1971). Behavioral deficits in monkeys after selective lesions within the middle third of sulcus principalis. *J. Comp. Physiol. Psychol. 76*:8–14.

Canavan, A.G.M. (1983). Stylus-maze performance in patients with frontal-lobe lesions: effects of signal valency and relationship to verbal and spatial abilities. *Neuropsychologia 21*:375–382.

Cavada, C., and Goldman-Rakic, P. S. (1989). Posterior parietal cortex in rhesus monkey: II. Evidence for segregated corticocortical networks linking sensory and limbic areas with the frontal lobe. *J. Comp. Neurol. 287*:422–445.

Chavis, D. A., and Pandya, D. N. (1976). Further observations on corticofrontal connections in the rhesus monkey. *Brain Res. 117*:369–386.

Chorover, S. L., and Cole, M. (1966). Delayed alternation performance in patients with cerebral lesions. *Neuropsychologia 4*:1–7.

Cicerone, K. D., Lazar, R. M., and Shapiro, W. R. (1983). Effects of frontal lobe lesions on hypothesis sampling during concept formation. *Neuropsychologia 21*:513–524.

Crosby, E. C., Humphrey, T., and Lauer, E. W. (1962). *Correlative Anatomy of the Nervous System*. New York: Macmillan.

Damasio, A. R. (1989a). The brain binds entities and events by multiregional activation from convergence zones. *Neural Comput. 1*:123–132.

Damasio, A. R. (1989b). Time-locked multiregional retroactivation: a systems level proposal for the neural substrates of recall and recognition. *Cognition 33*:25–62.

Damasio, A. R. (1990). Synchronous activation in multiple cortical regions: a mechanism for recall. *Semin. Neurosci. 2*:287–296.

Damasio, A. R. (1992). Aphasia. *N. Engl. J. Med. 326*:531–539.

Damasio, A. R., Damasio, H., and Chui, H. C. (1980). Neglect following damage to frontal lobe or basal ganglia. *Neuropsychologia 18*:123–132.

Damasio, A. R., Eslinger, P., Damasio, H., Van Hoesen, G. W., and Cornell, S. (1985). Multimodal amnesic syndrome following bilateral temporal and basal forebrain damage. *Arch. Neurol. 42*:252–259.

Damasio, A. R., Tranel, D., and Damasio, H. (1990). Individuals with sociopathic behavior caused by frontal damage fail to respond autonomically to social stimuli. *Behav. Brain Res. 41*:81–94.

Damasio, A. R., Tranel, D., and Damasio, H. (1991). Somatic markers and the guidance of behavior: theory and preliminary testing. In *Frontal Lobe Function and Dysfunction*, H. S. Levin, H. M. Eisenberg, and A. L. Benton (eds.). New York: Oxford University Press.

Damasio, A. R., and Van Hoesen, G. W. (1980). Structure and function of the supplementary motor area. *Neurology 30*:359.

Damasio, A. R., and Van Hoesen, G. W. (1983). Emotional disturbances associated with focal lesions of the frontal lobe. In *The Neurophysiology of Human Emotion: Recent Advances*, K. Heilman and P. Satz (eds.). New York: Guilford Press.

Damasio, H., and Damasio, A. R. (1989). *Lesion Analysis in Neuropsychology*. New York: Oxford University Press.

Damasio, H., and Frank, R. (1992). Three-dimensional in vivo mapping of brain lesions in humans. *Archives of Neurology 49*:137–143.

Dean, W. H., and Davis, G. D. (1959). Behavior following caudate lesions in rhesus monkey. *J. Neurophysiol. 22*:524–537.

Dejerine, J., and Mirallie, C. (1895). Sur les alterations de la lecture mentale chez les aphasiques moteurs corticaux. *C. R. Seances Mem. Soc. Biol.* (Paris) 10 series, *ii*:523–527.

DeRenzi, E., Faglioni, P., Lodesani, M., and Vecchi, A. (1983). Impairment of left brain-damaged patients on imitation of single movements and motor sequences: frontal and parietal injured patients compared. *Cortex 19*:333–343.

DeVito, J. L., and Smith, O. E. (1964). Subcortical projections of the prefrontal lobe of the monkey. *J. Comp. Neurol. 123*:413.

Di Pellegrino, G., and Wise, S. P. (1991). A neurophysiological comparison of three distinct regions of the primate frontal lobe. *Brain 114*:951–978.

Drewe, E. A. (1974). The effect of type and area of brain lesion on Wisconsin Card Sorting Test performance. *Cortex 10*:159–170.

Drewe, E. A. (1975). An experimental investigation of Luria's theory on the effects of frontal lobe lesions in man. *Neuropsychologia 13*:421–429.

Eichenbaum, H., Shedlack, K. J., and Eckmann, K. W. (1980). Thalamocortical mechanisms in odor-guided behavior. I: Effects of lesions of the mediodorsal thalamic nucleus and frontal cortex on olfactory discrimination in the rat. *Brain Behav. Evol. 17*:225–275.

Eslinger, P. J., and Damasio, A. R. (1985). Severe disturbance of higher cognition after bilateral frontal lobe ablation: patient EVR. *Neurology 35*:1731–1741.

Ethelberg, S. (1949). On "cataplexy" in a case of frontal lobe tumor. *Acta Psychiatr. Neurol. 24*:421–427.

Exner, S. (1881). *Untersuchungen uber die Localisation der Functionen in der Grosshirnrinde des Menschen.* Vienna: W. Braumuller.

Feuchtwanger, E. (1923). Die funktionen des stirnhirns. In *Monographien aus dem Gesamtgebiete der Neurologie und Psychiatrie,* O. Forster and K. Willmanns (eds.). Berlin: Springer.

Finan, J. L. (1942). Delayed response with predelay reinforcement in monkeys after removal of the frontal lobes. *Am. J. Psychol. 55*:202–214.

Fisher, C. M. (1968). Intermittent interruption of behavior. *Trans. Am. Neurol. Assoc. 93*:209–210.

Freedman, M., and Oscar-Berman, M. (1986). Bilateral frontal lobe disease and selective delayed response deficits in humans. *Behav. Neurosci. 100*:337–342.

Fulton, J. F. (1951). *Frontal Lobotomy and Affective Behavior.* New York: Norton.

Fulton, J. F., and Jacobsen, C. F. (1935). The functions of the frontal lobes: a comparative study in monkeys, chimpanzees and man. *Adv. Mod. Biol. (Moscow) 4*:113–123.

Fuster, J. M. (1989). *The Prefrontal Cortex,* 2nd ed. New York: Raven.

Fuster, J. M. (1991). Role of prefrontal cortex in delay tasks: evidence from reversible lesion and unit recording in the monkey. In *Frontal Lobe Function and Dysfunction,* H. W. Levin, H. M. Eisenberg, and A. L. Benton (eds.). New York: Oxford University Press.

Gardner, H., and Zurif, E. (1975). *Bee* but not *be:* oral reading of single words in aphasia and alexia. *Neuropsychologia 13*:181–190.

Gevins, A. (1990). Distributed neuroelectric patterns of human neocortex during simple cognitive tasks. In *The Prefrontal Cortex: Its Structure, Function, and Pathology.* H.B.M. Uylings, C. G. Van Eden, J.P.C. De Bruin, M. A. Corner, and M.G.P. Feenstra (eds.). Amsterdam: Elsevier.

Ghent, L., Mishkin, M., and Teuber, H. L. (1962). Short-term memory after frontal-lobe injury in man. *J. Comp. Physiol. Psychol. 55*:705–709.

Goldberg, E. (1986). Varieties of perseveration: a comparison of two taxonomies. *J. Clin. Exp. Neuropsychol.* 8:710–726.

Goldberg, M. E., and Segraves, M. A. (1989). The visual and frontal cortices. In *The Neurobiology of Saccadic Eye Movements*, R. H. Wurtz and M. E. Goldberg (eds.). New York: Elsevier.

Goldman, P. S. (1978). Neuronal plasticity in primate telencephalon: anomalous projections induced by prenatal removal of frontal cortex. *Science* 202:768–770.

Goldman, P. S., and Nauta, W.J.H. (1977). An intricately patterned prefrontocaudate projection in the rhesus monkey. *J. Comp. Neurol.* 171:369–386.

Goldman-Rakic, P. S. (1987). Circuitry of primate prefrontal cortex and regulation of behavior by representational memory. In *Handbook of Physiology: The Nervous System*, Vol. 5, F. Plum (ed.). Bethesda, Md.: American Physiological Society.

Goldman-Rakic, P. S., and Friedman, H. R. (1991). The circuitry of working memory revealed by anatomy and metabolic imaging. In *Frontal Lobe Function and Dysfunction*, H. S. Levin, H. M. Eisenberg, and A. L. Benton (eds.). New York: Oxford University Press.

Goldman-Rakic, P. S., and Schwartz, M. L. (1982). Interdigitation of contralateral and ipsilateral columnar projections to frontal association cortex in primates. *Science* 216:755–757.

Goldstein, K. (1948). *Aftereffects of Brain Injuries in War.* New York: Grune and Stratton.

Gordinier, H. C. (1899). A case of brain tumor at the base of the second left frontal convolution. *Am. J. Med Sci.* 117:526–535.

Grafman, J., Jonas, B., and Salazar, A. (1990). Wisconsin Card Sorting Test performance based on location and size of neuroanatomical lesion in Vietnam veterans with penetrating head injury. *Percep. Mot. Skills* 71:1120–1122.

Grant, D. A., and Berg, E. A. (1948). A behavioral analysis of degree of reinforcement and ease of shifting to new responses in a Weigl-type card-sorting problem. *J. Exp. Psychol.* 38:404–411.

Grueninger, W. E., and Pribam, K. H. (1969). The effects of spatial and nonspatial distractors on performance latency of monkeys with frontal lesions. *J. Comp. Physiol. Psychol.* 68:203–209.

Grueninger, W. E., Kimble, D. P., Grueninger, J., and Levine, S. E. (1965). GSR and corticosteroid response in monkeys with frontal ablations. *Neuropsychologia* 3:205–216.

Harlow, J. M. (1848). Passage of an iron rod through the head. *Boston Med. Surg. J.* 39:389–393.

Harlow, J. M. (1868). Recovery from the passage of an iron bar through the head. *Publ. Mass. Med. Soc.* 2:327–347.

Heaton, R. K. (1981). *Wisconsin Card Sorting Test Manual.* Odessa, Fla.: Psychological Assessment Resources.

Hebb, D. O. (1945). Man's frontal lobes: a critical review. *Arch. Neurol. Psychiatry* 54:421–438.

Hebb, D. O., and Penfield, W. (1940). Human behavior after extensive bilateral removals from the frontal lobes. *Arch. Neurol. Psychiatry* 44:421–438.

Hécaen, H. (1964). Mental symptoms associated with tumors of the frontal lobe. In *The Frontal Granular Cortex and Behavior*, J. M. Warren and K. Akert (eds.). New York: McGraw-Hill.

Heilman, K. M., Pandya, D. N., Karol, E. A., and Geschwind, N. (1971). Auditory inattention. *Arch. Neurol.* 24:323–325.

Heilman, K. M., and Valenstein, E. (1972). Frontal lobe neglect in man. *Neurology* 22:660–664.

Heilman, K. M., and Watson, R. T. (1991). Intentional motor disorders. In *Frontal Lobe Func-*

*tion and Dysfunction*, H. S. Levin, H. L. Eisenburg, and A. L. Benton (eds.). New York: Oxford University Press.

Homskaya, E. D. (1966). Vegetative components of the orienting reflex to indifferent and significant stimuli in patients with lesions of the frontal lobes. In *Frontal Lobes and Regulation of Psychological Processes*, A. R. Luria and E. D. Homskaya (eds.). Moscow: Moscow University Press.

Jacobsen, C. F. (1935). Functions of the frontal association area in primates. *Arch. Neurol. Psychiatry* 33:558–569.

Jacobsen, C. F., and Nissen, H. W. (1937). Studies of cerebral function in primates. IV: The effects of frontal lobe lesion on the delayed alternation habit in monkeys. *J. Comp. Physiol. Psychol.* 23:101–112.

Janowsky, J. S., Shimamura, A. P., Kritchevsky, M., and Squire, L. R. (1989). Cognitive impairments following frontal lobe damage and its relevance to human amnesia. *Behav. Neurosci.* 103:548–560.

Janowsky, J. S., Shimamura, A. P., and Squire, L. R. (1989). Memory and metamemory: comparisons between patients with frontal lobe lesions and amnesic patients. *Psychobiology* 17:3–11.

Jastrowitz, M. (1888). Beitrage zur Localisation im Grosshirn and uber deren praktische Verwerthung. *Dtsch. Med. Wochenshr.* 14:81.

Jefferson, G. (1937). Removal of right or left frontal lobes in man. *Br. Med. J.* 2:199.

Johnson, T. N., Rosvold, H. E., and Mishkin, M. (1968). Projections from behaviorally defined sectors of the prefrontal cortex to the basal ganglia, septum, and diencephalon of the monkey. *Exp. Neurol.* 21:20.

Jones-Gotman, M., and Milner, B. (1977). Design fluency: the invention of nonsense drawings after focal cortical lesions. *Neuropsychologia* 15:653–674.

Kaczmarek, B.L.J. (1987). Regulatory function of the frontal lobes: a neurolinguistic perspective. In *The Frontal Lobes Revisited*, E. Perecman (ed.). Hillsdale, N.J.: Lawrence Erlbaum Associates.

Kaplan, E., and Goodglass, H. (1981). Aphasia related disorders. In *Acquired Aphasia*, M. T. Sarno (ed.). New York: Academic Press.

Karnath, H. O., Wallesch, C. W., and Zimmerman, P. (1991). Mental planning and anticipatory processes with acute and chronic frontal lobe lesions: a comparison of maze performance in routine and non-routine situations. *Neuropsychologia* 29:271–290.

Kennard, M. A., and Ectors, L. (1938). Forced circling movements in monkeys following lesions of the frontal lobes. *J. Neurophysiol.* 1:45–54.

Kievit, J., and Kuypers, H.G.J.M. (1974). Basal forebrain and hypothalamic connections to frontal and parietal cortex in the rhesus monkey. *Science* 187:660–662.

Kimble, D. P., Bagshaw, M. H., and Pribram, K. H. (1965). The GSR of monkeys during orienting and habituation after selective partial ablations of the cingulate and frontal cortex. *Neuropsychologia* 3:121–128.

Kleist, K. (1936). *Gehirnpatholgie*. Leipzig: Barth.

Knight, R. T. (1991). Evoked potential studies of attention capacity in human frontal lobe lesions. In *Frontal Lobe Function and Dysfunction*, H. S. Levin, H. M. Eisenberg, and A. L. Benton (eds.). New York: Oxford University Press.

Kolb, B., and Milner, B. (1981). Performance of complex arm and facial movements after focal brain lesions. *Neuropsychologia* 19:491–503.

Konorski, J., and Lawicka, W. (1964). Analysis of errors by prefrontal animals on the delayed-response test. In *The Frontal Granular Cortex and Behavior*, J. M. Warren and K. Akert (eds.). New York: McGraw-Hill.

Kuypers, H.G.J.M., Szwarobart, M. K., and Mishkin, M. (1965). Occipitotemporal cortico-cortical connections in the rhesus monkey. *Exp. Neurol. 11*:245.

Kwon, S. E., and Heilman, K. M. (1991). Ipsilateral neglect in a patient following a unilateral frontal lesion. *Neurology 41*:2001–2004.

Lezak, M. D. (1983). *Neuropsychological Assessment*, 2nd ed. New York: Oxford University Press.

Lezak, M. D. (1988). IQ: RIP. *J. Clin. Exp. Neuropsychol. 10*:351–361.

Lichtheim, L. (1885). On aphasia. *Brain 7*:433–484.

Liepmann, H. (1908). *Drei Aufsatze aus dem Apraxiegebiet.* Berlin: Karger.

Luria, A. R. (1966). *Human Brain and Psychological Processes.* New York: Harper and Row.

Luria, A. R. (1969). Frontal lobe syndrome. In *Handbook of Clinical Neurology*, Vol. 2, P. J. Vinkin and G. W. Bruyn (eds.). Amsterdam: North-Holland.

Luria, A. R., and Homskaya, E. D. (1964). Disturbances in the regulative role of speech with frontal lobe lesions. In *The Frontal Granular Cortex and Behavior*, J. M. Warren and K. Akert (eds.). New York: McGraw-Hill.

Malmo, R. B. (1942). Interference factors in delayed response in monkey after removal of frontal lobes. *J. Neurophysiol. 5*:295–308.

Marshall, J. F., and Teitelbaum, P. (1974). Further analysis of sensory inattention allowing lateral hypothalamic damage in rats. *J. Comp. Physiol. Psychol. 86*:375–395.

Marshall, J. F., Turner, B. H., and Teitelbaum, P. (1971). Sensory neglect produced by lateral hypothalamic damage. *Science 174*:523–525.

Milner, B. (1963). Effects of different brain lesions on card sorting. *Arch. Neurol. 9*:90–100.

Milner, B. (1964). Some effects of frontal lobectomy in man. In *The Frontal Granular Cortex and Behavior*, J. M. Warren and K. Akert (eds.). New York: McGraw-Hill.

Milner, B. (1965). Visually-guided maze learning in man: effects of bilateral hippocampal, bilateral frontal, and unilateral cerebral lesions. *Neuropsychologia 3*:317–338.

Milner, B. (1971). Interhemispheric differences in the localisation of psychological processes in man. *Br. Med. Bull. 27*:272–277.

Milner, B., Corsi, P., and Leonard, G. (1991). Frontal-lobe contribution to recency judgments. *Neuropsychologia 29*:601–618.

Milner, B., Petrides, M., and Smith, M. L. (1985). Frontal lobes and the temporal organization of memory. *Hum. Neurobiol. 4*:137–142.

Mishkin, M. (1964). Perseveration of central sets after frontal lesions in monkeys. In *The Frontal Granular Cortex and Behavior*, J. M. Warren and K. Akert, (eds.). New York: McGraw-Hill.

Mishkin, M., and Pribram, K. H. (1955). Analysis of the effects of frontal lesions in monkeys. I: Variations of delayed alternations. *J. Comp. Physiol. Psychol. 48*:492–495.

Mishkin, M., and Pribram, K. H. (1956). Analysis of the effects of frontal lesions in the monkey. II: Variations of delayed response. *J. Comp. Physiol. Psychol. 49*:36–40.

Mohr, J. P. (1976). Broca's area and Broca's aphasia. In *Studies in Neurolinguistics*, Vol. 1, H. Whitaker and H. A. Whitaker (eds.). New York: Academic Press.

Moniz, E. (1936). *Tentatives Operatoires dans le Traitement de Certaines Psychoses.* Paris: Masson et Cie.

Moniz, E. (1949). *Confidencias de um Investigador Cientifico.* Lisbon: Livraria Atica.

Moran, M. A., Mufson, E. J., and Mesulam, M. M. (1987). Neural inputs into the temporopolar cortex of the rhesus monkey. *J. Comp. Neurol. 256*:88–103.

Nauta, W.J.H. (1962). Neural associations of the amygdaloid complex in the monkey. *Brain 85*:505–520.

Nauta, W.J.H. (1964). Some efferent connections of the prefrontal cortex in the monkey. In

*The Frontal Granular Cortex and Behavior*, J. M. Warren and K. Akert (eds.). New York: McGraw-Hill.

Nauta, W.J.H. (1971). The problem of the frontal lobe: A reinterpretation. *J. Psychiatr. Res.* 8:167–187.

Nauta, W.J.H., and Haymaker, W. (1969). *The Hypothalamus.* Springfield, Ill.: Charles C. Thomas.

Nielsen, J. M. (1938). The unsolved problems in aphasia. I. Alexia in motor aphasia. *Bull. Los Angeles Neurol. Soc.* 4:114–122.

Nielsen, J. M. (1946). *Anosia, Apraxia, Aphasia. Their Value in Cerebral Localization.* New York: P. B. Hoeber.

Opppenheim, H. (1889). Zur pathologie der grosshirngeschwulste. *Arch Psychiatr.* 21:560.

Orbach, J., Milner, B., and Rasmussen, T. (1960). Learning and retention in monkeys after amygdala-hippocampal resection. *Arch. Neurol* 3:230–251.

Pandya, D. N., and Barnes, C. L. (1987). Architecture and connections of the frontal lobe. In *The Frontal Lobes Revisited*, E. Perecman (ed.). Hillsdale: N.J.: Lawrence Erlbaum Associates.

Pandya, D. N., Dye, P., and Butters, N. (1971). Efferent cortico-cortical projections of the prefrontal cortex in the rhesus monkey. *Brain Res.* 31:35–46.

Pandya, D. N., Hallett, M., and Mukherjee, S. K. (1969). Intra- and interhemispheric connections of the neocortical auditory system in the rhesus monkey. *Brain Res.* 13:49.

Pandya, D. N., and Kuypers, H.G.J.M. (1969). Cortico-cortical connections in the rhesus monkey. *Brain Res.* 13:13.

Pandya, D. N., and Vignolo, L. A. (1971). Intra- and interhemispheric projections of the precentral, premotor and arcuate areas in the rhesus monkey. *Brain Res.* 26:217–233.

Penfield, W., and Roberts, L. (1959). *Speech and Brain Mechanisms.* Princeton, N.J.: Princeton University Press.

Petrides, M. (1985). Deficits on conditional associative-learning tasks after frontal- and temporal-lobe lesions in man. *Neuropsychologia* 23:601–614.

Petrides, M. (1987). Conditional learning and the primate frontal cortex. In *The Frontal Lobes Revisited*, E. Perecman, (ed.). Hillsdale, N.J.: Lawrence Erlbaum Associates.

Petrides, M. (1990). Nonspatial conditional learning impaired in patients with unilateral frontal but not unilateral temporal lobe excisions. *Neuropsychologia* 28:137–149.

Petrides, M., and Milner, B. (1982). Deficits on subject-ordered tasks after frontal- and temporal-lobe lesions in man. *Neuropsychologia* 20:259–262.

Petrides, M., and Pandya, D. N. (1984). Projections to the frontal cortex from the posterior parietal region in the rhesus monkey. *J. Comp. Neurol.* 228:105–116.

Petrides, M., and Pandya, D. N. (1988). Association fiber pathways to the frontal cortex from the superior temporal region in the rhesus monkey. *J. Comp. Neurol.* 310:507–549.

Porrino, L. J., and Goldman-Rakic, P. S. (1982). Brainstem innervation of prefrontal and anterior cingulate cortex in the rhesus monkey revealed by retrograde transport of HRP. *J. Comp. Neurol.* 205:63–76.

Porrino, L. J., Craine, A. M., and Goldman-Rakic, P. S. (1981). Direct and indirect pathways from the amygdala to the frontal lobe in rhesus monkeys. *J. Comp. Neurol.* 198:121–136.

Porteus, S. D., De Monbrun, R., and Kepner, M. D. (1944). Mental changes after bilateral prefrontal leucotomy. *Genet. Pscyhol. Monogr.* 29:3–115.

Potter, H., and Butters, N. (1980). An assessment of olfactory deficits in patients with damage to prefrontal cortex. *Neuropsychologia* 18:621–628.

Potter, H., and Nauta, W.J.H. (1979). A note on the problem of olfactory associations of the orbitofrontal cortex in the monkey. *Neuroscience* 4:316–367.

Powell, T.P.S., Cowan, W. M., and Raisman, G. (1965). The central olfactory connexions. *J. Anat. 99*:791.

Preuss, T. M., and Goldman-Rakic, P. S. (1991). Ipsilateral cortical connections of the granular frontal cortex in the Strepsirhine primate *Galago*, with comparative comments on anthropoid primates. *J. Comp. Neurol. 310*:507–549.

Pribram, K. H. (1961). A further experimental analysis of the behavioral deficit that follows injury to the primate frontal cortex. *Exp. Neurol. 3*:431–466.

Pribram, K. H. (1987). The subdivisions of the frontal cortex revisited. In *The Frontal Lobes Revisited*, E. Perecman (ed.). Hillsdale, N.J.: Lawrence Erlbaum Associates.

Pribram, K. H., Chow, K. L., and Semmes, J. (1953). Limit and organization of the cortical projection from the medial thalamic nucleus in monkey. *J. Comp. Neurol. 98*:433–448.

Pribram, K. H., and MacLean, P. D. (1953) Neuronographic analysis of medial and basal cerebral cortex. II. Monkey. *J. Neurophysiol. 16*:324–340.

Pribram, K. H., Wilson, W. A., and Connors, J. (1962). Effects of lesions of the medial forebrain on alternation behavior of rhesus monkeys. *Exp. Neurol. 6*:36–47.

Ramier, A. M., and Hécaen, H. (1970). Role respectif des atteintes frontales et de la lateralisation lesionnelle dans les deficits de la "fluence verbale." *Rev. Neurol (Paris) 123*:17–22.

Rapcsak, S. Z., Arthur, S. A., and Rubens, A. B. (1988). Lexical agraphia from focal lesion of the left precentral gyrus. *Neurology 38*:1119–1123.

Rosene, D. L., Mesulam, M. M., and Van Hoesen, G. W. (1976). Afferents to area FL of the medial frontal cortex from the amygdala and hippocampus of the rhesus monkey. In *Neuroscience Abstracts*, Vol. 2, Part 1. Bethesda, Md.: Society for Neuroscience.

Rosvold, H. E., and Delgado, J.M.R. (1956). The effect on delayed-alternation test performance of stimulating or destroying electrically structures within the frontal lobes of the monkey's brain. *J. Comp. Physiol. Psychol. 49*:365–372.

Rylander, G. (1940). *Personality Changes After Operations on the Frontal Lobes*. Copenhagen: Munksgaard.

Sagar, H. J., Gabrieli, J.D.E., Sullivan, E. V., and Corkin, S. (1990). Recency and frequency discrimination in the amnesic patient H.M. *Brain 113*:581–602.

Sapolsky, R. M., and Eichenbaum, H. (1980). Thalamocortical mechanisms in odor guided behavior. II: Effects of lesions of the mediodorsal thalamic nucleus and frontal cortex on odor preferences and sexual behavior in the hamster. *Brain Behav. Evol. 17*:276–290.

Saver, J. L., and Damasio, A. R. (1991). Preserved access and processing of social knowledge in a patient with acquired sociopathy due to ventromedial frontal damage. *Neuropsychologia 29*:1241–1249.

Schulman, J. S. (1969). Electrical stimulation of monkey's prefrontal cortex during delayed response performance. *J. Comp. Physiol. Psychol. 67*:535–546.

Segarra, J., and Angelo, J. (1970). Anatomical determinants of behavioral change. In *Behavioral Change in Cerebrovascular Disease*, A. L. Benton (ed.). New York: Harper and Row.

Seltzer, B., and Pandya, D. N. (1989). Frontal lobe connections of the superior temporal sulcus in the rhesus monkey. *J. Comp. Neurol. 281*:97–113.

Settlage, P., Zable, M., and Harlow, H. F. (1948). Problem solving by monkeys following bilateral removal of the prefrontal areas: VI. Performance on tests requiring contradictory reactions to similar and identical stimuli. *J. Exp. Psychol. 38*:50–65.

Shallice, T. (1982). Specific impairments of planning. *Philos. Trans. R. Soc. London [Biol.] 298*:199–209.

Signoret, J. L., Castaigne, P., Lhermitte, F., Abelenet, R., and Lavorel, P. (1984). Rediscovery of Leborgne's brain: anatomical description with CT scan. *Brain and Language 22*:303–319.

Simernitskaya, E. G. (1970). *Evoked Potentials as an Indicator of the Active Process*. Moscow: Moscow University Press.

Simernitskaya, E. G., and Homskaya, E. D. (1966). Changes in evoked potentials to significant stimuli in normal subjects and in lesions of the frontal lobes. In *Frontal Lobes and Regulation of Psychological Processes*, A. R. Luria and E. D. Homskaya (eds.). Moscow: Moscow University Press.

Smith, M. L., and Milner, B. (1988). Estimation of frequency of occurrence of abstract designs after frontal or temporal lobectomy. *Neuropsychologia 26*:297–306.

Spreen, O., and Strauss, E. (1991). *A Compendium of Neuropsychological Tests*. New York: Oxford University Press.

Stamm, J. S. (1961). Electrical stimulation of frontal cortex in monkeys during learning of an alternation task. *J. Neurophysiol. 24*:414–426.

Stamm, J. S. (1969). Electrical stimulation of monkeys' prefrontal cortex during delayed-response performance. *J. Comp. Physiol. Psychol. 67*:535–546.

Stamm, J. S. (1987). The riddle of the monkey's delayed-response deficit has been solved. In *The Frontal Lobes Revisited*, E. Perecman (ed.). Hillsdale, N.J.: Lawrence Erlbaum Associates.

Starkstein, S. E., and Robinson, R. G. (1991). The role of the frontal lobes in affective disorder following stroke. In *Frontal Lobe Function and Dysfunction*, H. S. Levin, H. M. Eisenberg, and A. L. Benton (eds.). New York: Oxford University Press.

Strauss, I., and Keschner, M. (1935). Mental symptoms in cases of tumor of the frontal lobe. *Arch. Neurol. Psychiatry 33*:986–1007.

Stuss, D. T., and Benson, D. F. (1987). The frontal lobes and control of cognition and memory. In *The Frontal Lobes Revisited*, E. Perecman (ed.). Hillsdale, N.J.: Lawrence Erlbaum Associates.

Stuss, D. T., Kaplan, E. F., Benson, D. F., Weir, W. S., Chiulli, S., and Sarazin, F. F. (1982). Evidence for the involvement of orbitofrontal cortex in memory functions: an interference effect. *J. Comp. Physiol. Psychol. 96*:913–925.

Stuss, D. T., Kaplan, E. F., Benson, D. F., Weir, W. S., Naeser, M. A., and Levine, H. L. (1981). Long-term effects of prefrontal leucotomy: an overview of neuropsychologic residuals. *J. Clin. Neuropsychol. 3*:13–32.

Tanabe, T., Iino, M., and Takogi, S. F. (1975a). Discrimination of odors in olfactory bulb, pyriform-amygdaloid areas, and orbitofrontal cortex of the monkey. *J. Neurophysiol. 38*:1284–1296.

Tanabe, T., Yarita, H., Iino, M., Ooshima, Y., and Takagi, S. F. (1975b). An olfactory projection area in orbitofrontal cortex of the monkey. *J. Neurophysiol. 38*:1269–1283.

Teuber, H. L. (1964). The riddle of frontal lobe function in man. In *The Frontal Granular Cortex and Behavior*, J. M. Warren and K. Akert (eds.). New York: McGraw-Hill.

Teuber, H. L. (1966). The frontal lobes and their function. Further observations on rodents, carnivores, subhuman primates, and man. *Int. J. Neurol. 6*:282–300.

Teuber, H. L., Battersby, W. S., and Bender, M. B. (1951). Performance of complex visual tasks after cerebral lesions. *J. Nerv. Ment. Dis. 114*:413–429.

Teuber, H. L., and Mishkin, M. (1954). Judgment of visual and postural vertical after brain injury. *J. Psychol. 38*:161–175.

Tranel, D. (1992). Neuropsychological assessment. In *Psychiatric Clinics of North America: The Interface of Psychiatry and Neurology*, J. Biller and R. Kathol (eds.). Philadelphia: W. B. Saunders.

Valverde, F. (1965). *Studies on the Piriform Lobe*. Cambridge, Mass.: Harvard University Press.

Ward, A. A., and McCulloch, W. S. (1947). The projection of the frontal lobe on the hypothalamus. *J. Neurophysiol. 10:*309–314.

Watson, R. T., Heilman, K. M., Cauthen, J. C., and King, F. A. (1973). Neglect after cingulectomy. *Neurology 23:*1003–1007.

Watson, R. T., Heilman, K. M., Miller, B. D., and King, F. A. (1974). Neglect after mesencephalic reticular formation lesions. *Neurology 24:*294–298.

Weinberger, D. R., Berman, K. F., and Daniel, D. G. (1991). Prefrontal cortex dysfunction in schizophrenia. In *Frontal Lobe Function and Dysfunction*, H. S. Levin, H. M. Eisenberg, and A. L. Benton (eds.). New York: Oxford University Press.

Weinberger, D. R., Berman, K. F., and Zec, R. F. (1986). Physiologic dysfunction of dorsolateral prefrontal cortex in schizophrenia. *Archives of General Psychiatry, 43:*114–124.

Welch, K., and Stuteville, P. (1958). Experimental production of neglect in monkeys. *Brain 81:*341–347.

Whitlock, D. C., and Nauta, W.J.H. (1956). Subcortical projections from the temporal neocortex in Macaca mulatta. *J. Comp. Neurol. 106:*183–212.

Winocur, G., and Moscovitch, M. (1990). Hippocampal and prefrontal cortex contribution to learning and memory: Analysis of lesion and aging effects on maze learning in rats. *Behavioral Neuroscience 104:*544–551.

Yeterian, E. H., and Van Hoesen, G. W. (1977). Cortico-striate projections in the rhesus monkey. The organization of certain cortico-caudate connections. *Brain Res. 139:*43–63.

# 13

# Emotional Disorders Associated with Neurological Diseases

KENNETH M. HEILMAN, DAWN BOWERS, AND EDWARD VALENSTEIN

In this chapter we will discuss changes in emotional experience and behavior that are caused directly by diseases of the central nervous system. These disorders interfere with brain mechanisms that underlie emotion. There are other ways in which neurological disorders and emotions may interact: patients with neurological diseases may have an emotional response to their illness (e.g., they may get depressed *because* they are disabled); emotional states may enhance neurological symptoms (e.g., anxiety may aggravate tremor); and emotional states may induce neurological symptoms (e.g., stress may cause headaches). Emotional response to disease, emotional enhancement of symptoms, and emotion-induced disorders are not unique to neurology, and are not discussed in this chapter. Finally, it has long been recognized that several disorders traditionally in the realm of psychiatry are probably caused by abnormalities in the brain. Schizophrenia is perhaps the best-documented example of such a disorder, and is discussed in Chapter 14. This chapter is limited to traditional neurological illnesses.

Our approach is anatomic. We first consider emotional changes that result from lesions in the cerebral hemispheres. These may result from interference with specific neocortically mediated cognitive processes, such as stimulus appraisal, or from disruption of cortical modulation of limbic or other subcortical regions. The frontal lobes have particularly strong limbic connections, and frontal lobe lesions can cause prominent emotional changes. These are primarily treated in Chapter 12. After discussing emotional changes resulting from dysfunction of either cerebral hemisphere, we consider changes associated with limbic and basal ganglia disorders. Finally, we discuss the pseudobulbar state, in which inappropriate emotional expression occurs despite appropriate emotional experience.

Throughout this chapter, we emphasize information gained from studies of humans with brain dysfunction because most of our knowledge comes from the investigation of pathological states in humans. We also consider animal studies when they pertain to observations on humans, but we do not attempt to summarize the extensive literature on animals.

## HEMISPHERIC DYSFUNCTION

Hemispheric dysfunction may affect emotion in several ways. There may be receptive and expressive communicative disorders, changes in the viscera and autonomic nervous system, changes in emotional experience and mood, and changes in emotional memory. Each of these will be discussed separately.

### *Communicative Defects: Receptive*

VISUAL NONVERBAL PROCESSES

The development of an appropriate emotional state may depend on perceiving and comprehending visual stimuli such as facial expressions, gestures, and scenes. Gardner and colleagues (1975) found that patients with right-hemisphere disease and those with left-hemisphere disease were equally impaired in selecting the most humorous of a group of cartoons. Patients with left-hemisphere disease, however, performed better on cartoons without captions.

DeKosky et al. (1980) gave facial affective tasks to patients with left- or right-hemisphere lesions as well as to neurologic controls without hemispheric disease. Patients were asked to determine if a pair of neutral faces were the same person or two different people, to name the emotion expressed by a face (happy, sad, angry, indifferent), to select from a multiple-choice array of faces a "target" emotion ("Point to the happy face."), and to determine whether two pictures of the same person's face expressed the same or a different emotion. Patients with right-hemisphere disease were markedly impaired in their ability to discriminate between pairs of neutral faces, as previously reported by Benton and Van Allen (1968). Although both the right- and left-hemisphere-damaged patients had difficulty naming and selecting emotional faces, there was a trend for patients with right-hemisphere disease to perform more poorly on these two tasks than patients with left-hemisphere disease. In addition, patients with right-hemisphere disease were more impaired in making same-different discriminations between emotional faces.

When performance across these various affect tasks was covaried for neutral facial discrimination (a visuoperceptual nonemotional task), differences between the two groups disappeared. This finding suggests that a visuoperceptual disturbance may underlie the poor performance of right-hemisphere-damaged patients' on facial affect tasks. However, the poor facial discrimination by the right-hemisphere group did not entirely correlate with their ability to recognize and discriminate between emotional faces. Retrospective review of the individual cases revealed that about one-third of the patients with right-hemisphere disease performed poorly on both the neutral facial task and the emotional faces tasks, whereas about one-third performed well on both. The remaining patients with right-hemisphere disease, however, performed relatively well on neutral facial discrimination but poorly on the emotional faces tasks. This observation suggests that visuoperceptual deficits do not account for impaired affective processing in all right-hemisphere-damaged patients.

In subsequent research on patients with focal lesions, Bowers and colleagues (1985) addressed several task-specific methodological problems that were inherent in the study by DeKosky et al. (1980). Specifically, some of the facial emotion tasks used by the DeKosky group could be performed by using strategies that involved no knowledge of the emotionality depicted on faces. One such task required subjects to judge whether two faces depicted the same or different emotions. Because the same actor was used for both pictures, subjects could have accurately made this determination merely by deciding whether the two faces had identical physiognomic/structural configurations, without any regard to emotionality on the face. This is what might be referred to as a "perceptual" rather than an "associative" emotion judgment. To circumvent the use of pure perceptual "template matching" in making judgments about the similarity of two facial expressions, two different actors would have to be used, sometimes displaying the same emotion and sometimes displaying different emotions. The faces of two actors have inherently unique physiognomic properties (i.e., faceprints) and therefore must be matched by comparing the similarity of their emotional expressions.

Taking these considerations in mind, Bowers and co-workers (1985) assessed controls and stroke patients with hemispheric lesions across a series of seven "perceptual" and "associative" facial affect tasks. When the patient groups were statistically equated for visuoperceptual ability, the right-hemisphere-damaged group was impaired on three of the facial affect tasks, including naming, selecting, and discriminating facial emotions across two different actors. The critical factor distinguishing these three tasks from those that did not give rise to hemispheric asymmetries was related to the underlying task demand of "categorizing" facial emotions. These findings suggest that the disorders of facial affect recognition among right-hemisphere-damaged patients cannot be solely attributed to defects in visuoperceptual processing, and that a right-hemisphere superiority for processing facial affect exists above and beyond its superiority for processing faces in general.

Investigators from other laboratories have also reported that right-hemisphere-damaged stroke patients are more impaired than their left-hemisphere counterparts in recognizing or categorizing facial emotions (Cicone et al., 1980; Etcoff, 1984; Borod et al., 1986). In general, these defects in identifying facial affect by right-hemisphere-damaged patients are not valence dependent and extend to all categories of emotion (but see Mandel et al., 1991).

In addition to stroke patients, hemispheric asymmetries in the evaluation of nonverbal affect signals have also been described in split-brain patients and in individuals undergoing Wada testing. Benowitz and colleagues (1983) presented filmed facial expressions from the Profile of Nonverbal Sensitivity Test (PONS) to each hemisphere of a split-brain patient. This patient was fitted with special contact lens that restricted visual input to one hemisphere. The patient had no difficulty identifying facial expressions when they were directed to the isolated right hemisphere, but was impaired when the facial expressions were directed to the isolated left hemisphere. Comparable findings have also been reported in patients while undergoing intracarotid sodium amytal procedures (Ahern et al., 1991). Ahern and colleagues found that affective faces were rated as less emotionally intense (as compared to baseline ratings) when they were shown to patients whose nondominant language hemisphere (usually right) was anesthestized. Such an effect was not observed with anesthetization of the language-dominant hemisphere.

Studies of normals have also implicated the right hemisphere in processing affective faces. Tachistoscopic studies have generally found that affective faces are responded to more accurately and/or more quickly when presented to the left visual field (right hemisphere) than to the right visual field (Suberi and McKeever, 1977; Ley and Bryden, 1979; Strauss and Moscovitch, 1981). Reuter-Lorenz and Davidson (1981) reported hemispheric-specific valence effects, in that happy faces were responded to more quickly in the right visual field and sad faces were responded to more quickly in the left visual field. Subsequent investigators have failed to replicate this finding (Duda and Brown, 1984; McLaren and Bryson, 1987; Bryson et al., 1991). Other studies with normals using chimeric and/or composite face stimuli have found that the side of the face on the viewer's left influences judgments of emotionality more than the side of the face on the viewer's right (Campbell, 1978; Heller and Levy, 1981).

Based on these studies with both normal and neurologically impaired subjects, we believe that the right hemisphere is important for perceiving both faces and facial expressions. In particular, we have argued that the right hemisphere may contain a "store of facial emotion icons" or representations (Bowers and Heilman, 1984). Recently, Blonder and colleagues (1991a) found that right-hemisphere-damaged patients were impaired relative to left-hemisphere-damaged and normal controls in identifying the emotion associated with a verbal description of a nonverbal signal. The subjects were read brief sentences describing facial ("his face whitened"), vocal ("she raised her voice"), and gestural signals ("he shook his fist"). Because these signals were described verbally, the poor performance of the right-hemisphere-damaged group could not be attributed to a perceptual disturbance. Further, their poor performance was not due to a general derangement in emotional knowledge in that these patients performed normally on another task in which they had to make inferences about emotions that are linked to various situational contexts (i.e., the children track dirt over your white carpet). Rather, the poor performance of the right-hemisphere-damaged patients in assigning an emotion to a verbally described nonverbal signal is consistent with the view that the right hemisphere normally contains representation of species-typical facial expressions.

Further evidence that the right hemisphere contains representation of species-typical facial expressions comes from a study (Bowers et al., 1991) in which right- and left-hemisphere-damaged patients were evaluated on two imaging tasks. One involved imagery for facial emotional expressions and the other involved imagery for common objects. On both tasks, the subjects were asked to image a target (i.e., frowning face) and were then asked a series of yes-no questions regarding the structural characteristics of the face (i.e., "Are the outer lips pulled down?"). The right-hemisphere-damaged group was more impaired on the facial emotion than on the object imagery task, whereas the left-hemisphere group showed the opposite pattern. The fact that some of these right-hemisphere-damaged patients were also more impaired at recognizing visible facial emotions (i.e., a recognition task, rather than an imagery task) than were the left-hemisphere-damaged group suggests that the right hemisphere contains a hypothetical "store of facial emotional representations" that had been destroyed in these individuals. Unfortunately the storage location for the facial emotion representations in the right hemisphere is not known.

Bowers et al. (1991) also described a patient with a ventral temporal-occipital lesions of the right hemisphere who could recognize emotional faces but could not image them. This case suggests that the mechanism underlying emotion imagery generation is at least in part mediated by the posterior ventral area, and that the facial emotional representations are anatomically distinct from the areas that either generate, display, or immediately inspect the image. Work from Roll's laboratory using single-cell recordings have identified visual neurons in the temporal cortex and amygdala of monkeys that respond selectively to faces and facial expressions (Baylis et al., 1985; Leonard et al., 1985). Similar findings have been reported during intraoperative recordings of awake humans while undergoing epilepsy surgery (Fried et al., 1982).

Bowers and Heilman (1984) described a patient with a category-specific visual verbal discrimination that was confined to facial emotion. The patient had a tumor in the region of the forcepts major (the white matter tract leading into the corpus callosum). This patient was unable both to name emotional facial displays and to point to the emotional faces named by the examiner. In contrast, the patient could determine if two faces displayed the same or different emotions, and performed normally across an array of other affect tasks including prosody, gesture, and narration. It was posited that the tumor induced a callosal disconnection such that the speech and language areas of the left hemisphere were unable to access the emotional facial icons (and vice versa), thus causing a verbal-emotional face disconnection. A similar case has recently been described by Rapscak et al. (1989).

AUDITORY NONVERBAL PROCESSES

Speech may simultaneously communicate propositional and emotional messages. The propositional message is conveyed by a complex code requiring semantic, lexical, syntactic, and phonemic decoding. Although prosody, which includes pitch, tempo, and rhythm, may also convey linguistic content (e.g., declarative vs. interrogative sentences), prosody is more important in conveying emotional content (Paul, 1909; Monrad-Krohn, 1947).

In most individuals, the left hemisphere is superior to the right when decoding the propositional message. We attempted to learn if the right hemisphere was superior to the left in decoding the emotional components of speech. In two studies (Heilman et al., 1975; Tucker et al., 1977), sentences with propositionally neutral content were spoken using four different emotional prosodies (happy, sad, angry, and indifferent) to patients with right-hemisphere infarctions and to aphasic patients with left-hemisphere infarctions. The patients were asked to identify the emotional tone of the speaker based not on what was said, but rather how it was said. Patients with right-hemisphere lesions performed worse on this task than those with left-hemisphere lesions, suggesting that the right hemisphere is more involved in processing the emotional intonations of speech than is the left hemisphere.

Similar findings were reported by Ross (1981), but Schlanger and colleagues (1976) failed to find any differences between right- and left-hemisphere-damaged patients in their comprehension of emotional prosody. Unfortunately, only three of the 20 right-hemisphere patients in the Schlanger et al. study had lesions involving tempo-roparietal areas.

Weintraub et al. (1981) reported that, relative to normal controls, right-hemi-sphere-damaged patients had difficulty determining whether prosodically intoned sentences were statements, commands, or questions. Based on these findings, they suggested that a generalized prosodic disturbance might be associated with right-hemisphere damage. However, a left-hemisphere-damaged group was not tested in this study. Heilman and colleagues (1984) compared right- and left-hemisphere-damaged patients for comprehension of emotional (happy, sad, angry) or nonemo-tional prosody (questions, commands, statements). Compared to normal controls, both the right-hemisphere-damaged and the left-hemisphere-damaged groups were equally impaired on the nonemotional (propositional) prosody task. However, on the emotional prosody task, the right-hemisphere-damaged patients performed signifi-cantly worse than the left-hemisphere-damaged patients. This finding suggests that, whereas both hemispheres may be important in comprehending propositional pros-ody, the right hemisphere plays a dominant role in comprehending emotional pros-ody.

Further evidence for the dominant role of the right hemisphere in comprehending affective intonation comes from studies that demonstrate preserved abilities in patients with left-hemisphere lesions. We examined a patient with pure word deaf-ness (normal speech output and reading but impaired speech comprehension) from a left-hemisphere lesion. In patients with pure word deafness, the left auditory cortex is thought to be destroyed and the right auditory cortex is disconnected from Wer-nicke's area on the left; however, the right auditory area and its connections to the right hemisphere are intact. Although this patient comprehended speech very poorly, he had no difficulty recognizing either environmental sounds or emotional intona-tions of speech.

Using dichotic listening tasks in which two different auditory messages were simul-taneously presented to the right and left ears and subjects were asked to recall what they heard (Kimura, 1967), investigators found that words were recalled best from the right ear (left hemisphere). However, the moods of the speaker, as determined by affective intonation, were better recalled from the left ear (right hemisphere) (Hag-gard and Parkinson, 1971).

The defect underlying the impaired ability of patients with right-hemisphere dis-ease to identify affective intonations in speech is not entirely clear. It may be related to a cognitive disability whereby these patients fail to denote verbally or name stim-uli. It could also be related to an inability to discriminate between different affective intonations in speech. Tucker et al. (1977) attempted to determine whether patients with right-hemisphere disease could in fact discriminate between affective intona-tions of speech without having to verbally classify or denote these intonations. Patients were required to listen to identical pairs of sentences spoken with either the same or different emotional prosody. The patients did not have to identify the emo-tional prosody, but had to tell whether the prosody associated with the sentences sounded the same or different. Patients with right-hemisphere disease performed more poorly on this task than did patients with left-hemisphere disease.

We suspect that the right hemisphere contains not only representations of species-typical facial expressions, but also contains representations of species-typical affective prosodic expressions. Destruction of these representations or an inability to access them could impair both comprehension and discrimination of emotional prosody.

Another possible explanation for the poor performance of right-hemisphere-damaged patients on emotional prosody tasks is that these patients are "distracted" by the propositional semantic message of affectively intoned sentences. In normal conversation and in experimental tasks, emotional prosody is often superimposed on propositional speech. Findings from studies of hemispheric asymmetries of attention in normal adults demosntrate that each hemisphere is more disrupted by stimuli it normally processes (Heilman et al., 1977), the left hemisphere being more disrupted by speech distractors (i.e., running conversation), and the right hemisphere being more disrupted by music distractors.

After right-hemisphere damage, perhaps the "intact" left hemisphere can comprehend emotional prosody, but in our tasks, it is distracted by the propositional semantic message. To test this hypothesis, we presented right- and left-hemisphere-damaged subjects an emotional prosody task that varied in the degree of "conflict" between the emotional message conveyed by the prosody and that conveyed by the propositional content (Bowers et al., 1987). If right-hemisphere-damaged patients were "distracted" by the propositional content, then their comprehension of emotional prosody should be worse when the propositional content and prosody messages are strongly conflicting (i.e., "all the puppies are dead" said in a happy tone of voice). The right-hemisphere-damaged group was more disrupted when the propositional and prosodic emotional messages were highly conflicting than when they were less conflicting. The left-hemisphere-damaged group was unaffected by increasing the discrepancy between the two messages. These results suggest that, at least in part, the defect in comprehending emotional prosody by right-hemisphere-damaged patients is related to "distraction," by which they are "pulled" to the propositional-semantic content of emotionally intoned sentences. However, this distraction defect cannot entirely account for their poor performance, in that right-hemisphere-damaged patients remained impaired in identifying emotional prosody even when the semantic content is rendered completely unintelligible by speech filtering (Bowers et al., 1987).

In summary, these studies suggest that right-hemipshere-damaged patients have both processing and distraction defects that contribute to their poor performance on emotional prosody tasks. The coexistence of these defects might emerge when a right-hemisphere lesion induces defective processing/miscategorization of emotional prosody due to disruption of right-hemisphere prosodic processors. Defective processing of emotional prosody may render the right-hemisphere-damaged patients more susceptible to the distracting effects of propositional semantic stimuli.

VISUAL AND AUDITORY VERBAL PROCESSES

While the preceding sections dealt with the evaluation of nonverbal communicative signals of emotion, the focus here is on emotional meaning that is derived from propositional-semantic messages, i.e., the verbal content. Emotional message can be conveyed at the single word level (i.e., fear, joy) or by sentences and lengthier narratives that describe contextual situations that are associated with specific emotional states. One obvious question concerns whether the right hemisphere plays a critical role in deriving emotional meaning from propositional language, as it appears to do for non-verbal affective signals. Historically, this question has been addressed from three perspectives. The first has involved determining whether laterality effects exist in normals using tachistoscopic presentation of emotional words to the left and right visual fields (Graves et al., 1981). Graves and co-workers found a relative superiority in the left visual field for the recognition of emotional words over nonemotional words. However, Strauss (1983) was unable to replicate these findings.

A second approach has involved looking at the impact of the emotionality of a verbal stimulus on the linguistic competence of aphasic patients with left-hemisphere lesions. Several studies have found that oral reading or auditory comprehension by aphasic left-hemisphere-damaged patients is improved when emotional words or phrases are used (Boller et al., 1979; Landis et al., 1982; Reuterskiold, 1991). Landis and colleagues (1982) reported that emotional words were read and written more accurately than nonemotional words by left-hemisphere-damaged aphasics. Improvements in auditory comprehension have been reported for aphasics with severe comprehension defects when emotional vs. nonemotional words (object names, actions) are presented (Reuterskiold, 1991). While one can interpret such improvements as due to the possible participation of right-hemisphere "semantic emotion" processors, it is more likely that increased arousal that typically accompanies emotional stimuli is the critical factor.

A third and more direct approach to the question of whether the right hemisphere plays a unique role in deriving emotional meaning from propositional language comes from studies that have directly assessed the comprehension of emotional words, sentences, and narratives by patients with right-hemisphere lesions. In general, there is little evidence to suggest that lesions of the right hemisphere disrupt conceptual knowledge about emotions per se. At the single-word level, Morris and colleagues (1992) found no differences between right-hemisphere-damaged and left-hemisphere damaged patients in their ability to comprehend the denotative or connotative meaning of emotional and nonemotional words. Etcoff (1984) presented pairs of emotional words to right- and left-hemisphere-damaged subjects who were required to judge the similarity of the emotional states conveyed by these words. Using multidimensional scaling techniques, she found that right-hemisphere-damaged patients did not differ from controls in their scaling solutions for emotion words, nor in the strategies they described for judging the similarity of the emotions conveyed in words.

Other studies have indicated that right-hemisphere-damaged patients are not impaired in their understanding of the emotionality of short propositional sentences (Heilman et al., 1984; Cicone et al., 1980; Bowers, unpublished data). This is true even when the sentences contain no specific emotion words and the emotional meaning must be derived from the situational context (e.g., the children tracked over your white carpet) (Blonder et al., 1991a). A different pattern of findings emerges when right-hemisphere-damaged patients are presented with lengthier and more complex narratives. Several investigators have found that these patients are impaired in understanding the affective-emotional content of stories and appreciating humor (Gardner et al.; Brownell et al., 1983). Such problems, however, do not appear to be specific to "emotion" per se, but are related to more general difficulties that right-hemisphere-damaged patients have in drawing inferences and logical reasoning (Brownell et al., 1986; McDonald and Wales, 1986; Blonder et al., 1991b) and interpreting figures of speech (Winnar and Gardner, 1977).

Taken together, these studies suggest that lesions of the right hemisphere do not specifically disrupt lexical semantic knowledge about emotions or emotional situations, at least when conveyed by short verbal descriptions. Patients with right-hemisphere lesions appear to have intact conceptual knowledge about emotions that are communicated verbally, as long as this communication does not involve verbal descriptions of nonverbal affect signals (Blonder et al., 1991a) or does not entail higher-level inferential processes (Brownell et al., 1986).

Left-hemisphere-damaged patients, especially those with word deafness or Wernicke's, global, transcortical sensory, or mixed transcortical aphasia, may have defects in comprehending propositional speech. If the development of an appropriate cognitive state is dependent on propositional language, patients with these aphasias would not be able to develop an appropriate cognitive state. Patients with Broca's and conduction aphasia may have difficulty comprehending emotional messages conveyed by propositional speech if these messages contain complex syntax or require a large memory store (see Chapter 2).

Although left-hemisphere-damaged aphasic and word-deaf patients may have difficulty comprehending propositional speech, some of these patients can comprehend emotional intonations, and their comprehension of propositional speech may be aided by these intonations (Heilman et al., 1975; Coslett et al., 1984).

### Communicative Defects: Expressive

SPEECH AND WRITING

We attempted to determine whether patients with right-hemisphere disease can express emotionally intoned speech (Tucker et al., 1977). The patients were asked to say semantically neutral sentences (e.g., "The boy went to the store.") using a happy, sad, angry, or indifferent prosody. These patients were severely impaired. Typically, they spoke the sentences in a flat monotone and often denoted the target affect (e.g., "The boy went to the store and he was sad."). Similar findings have been reported by Borod et al. (1985). Ross and Mesulam (1979) described two patients who could not express affectively intoned speech but could comprehend affective speech. Ross (1981) also described patients who could not comprehend affective intonation but could repeat affectively intoned speech. He postulated that right-hemisphere lesions may disrupt the comprehension, repetition, or production of affective speech in the same manner that left-hemisphere lesions disrupt propositional speech.

Although there is no evidence to suggest that patients with right-hemisphere dysfunction are impaired at expressing emotions using propositional speech or writing, Bloom et al. (1992) reported that right-hemisphere-damaged patients used fewer words when denoting emotions in their spontaneous speech. However, depending on

the type of aphasia, patients with left-hemisphere disease may have difficulty expressing emotions when these emotions are expressed as a spoken or written propositional
message (see Chapter 2). Hughlings Jackson (1932) observed that even nonfluent
aphasics could imbue their simple utterances with emotional content by using affective intonation. In addition, some nonfluent aphasics may be very fluent when using
expletives. Jackson postulated that the right hemisphere may be mediating these
activities. Roeltgen et al. (1983) demonstrated that aphasic patients with agraphia
were able to write emotional words better than nonemotional words. Similar findings
were reported by Landis et al. (1982). However, the role of the right hemisphere in
these cases remain uncertain.

Normally, propositional speech is colored by affective intonation that is governed
by mood. Whereas the left hemisphere is responsible for mediating the propositional
aspect of speech, there is parallel processing in the right hemisphere that is responsible for the emotional prosodic element of speech. Although Ross (1982) posited that
the propositional and prosodic elements are conjoined in the brainstem, Speedie et al.
(1984) provided evidence that this propositional and affective prosodic mixing occurs
interhemispherically.

FACIAL EXPRESSIONS

Although it is well established that lesions of the right hemisphere disrupt the perception and evaluation of nonverbal affective signals, current controversy exists
regarding whether the right hemisphere plays a unique role in communicating or
expressing facial emotions. Some investigators have found that right-hemisphere-
damaged patients are more impaired than left-hemisphere-damaged patients in
expressing facial emotions. In an initial study, Buck and Duffy (1980) reported that
right-hemisphere-damaged patients were less facially expressive than left-hemisphere-damaged patients when viewing slides of familiar people, unpleasant scenes,
and unusual pictures. Subsequent research, much of it from Borod's laboratory, has
replicated these right-left differences in facial expressiveness across a series of studies
with focal lesion stroke patients involving both spontaneous and voluntarily expressed
emotions (Borod et al., 1985, 1986, 1988; Kent et al., 1990; Richardson et al., 1992).
Similar deficits have also been observed in more "naturalistic" settings outside the
laboratory. Blonder and colleagues (Blonder et al., 1991c) videotaped interviews with
patients and their spouses in their homes and found that patients with right-hemisphere damage were rated as less facially expressive than were left-hemisphere-damaged patients and normal controls. A study of deaf signers (Bellugi et al., 1988) found
that right-hemisphere lesions are associated with dramatic impairments in the spontaneous use of affective facial expressions in the context of preserved use of linguistic
facial expressions. The opposite pattern is observed in deaf signers with left-hemisphere lesions.

In contrast, other investigators have reported no differences in facial emotion
expressiveness between right- and left-hemisphere-damaged patients using the facial
action scoring system FACS (Mammucari et al., 1988; Caltagirone et al., 1989). Still
others have found that lesions that extend into the frontal lobes, regardless of whether

the right or left hemispheres are involved, are critical for a reduction of facial expression (Kolb and Milner, 1981; Weddell et al., 1990).

The basis for these discrepant findings is unclear (see Buck, 1990). In part, they may relate to subject factors, intrahemispheric lesion location, as well as the different methods used across laboratories for quantifying facial expressions. Some systems involve scoring the movements of various muscle groups which appear pathognomic of certain emotional facial expressions (i.e., FACS of Ekman and Frisen, 1978), whereas others involve subjective judgments of raters about intended facial expressions, including their intensity and frequency. Another factor may relate to the manner by which facial expressions are elicited. Richardson and colleagues (1992) found that while right-hemisphere-damaged patients were overall less accurate than left-hemisphere-damaged patients and normal control subjects in communicating target facial emotions, their expressive deficits were most salient in response to affective pictures, affective prosody, and other affective faces. There were no differences among the groups in producing facial expressions on "verbal command" or in response to the emotional meaning of sentences. These findings have direct implications for studies that use emotional scenes or films for eliciting spontaneous facial expressions, in that defects in fully evaluating the affective meaning of such stimuli could directly reduce one's responsivity to them. This observation, however, cannot readily account for the diminished facial expressiveness of right-hemisphere-damaged patients in more naturalistic settings (Blonder et al., 1991c) or the asymmetries seen in normal subjects. In general, normals express emotions more intensely on the left side of the face (Sackheim et al., 1978; Campbell, 1978; Heller and Levy, 1981; Moreno et al., 1990).

## Emotional Experience and Mood

CLINICAL DESCRIPTIONS

Babinski (1914) noted that patients with right-hemisphere disease often appeared indifferent or euphoric. Hécaen et al. (1951) and Denny-Brown et al. (1952) also noted that patients with right-hemisphere lesions were often inappropriately indifferent. Gainotti's study (1972) of 160 patients with lateralized brain damage supported these earlier clinical observations: right-hemisphere lesions were often associated with indifference. Terzian (1964) and Rossi and Rosadini (1967) studied the emotional reactions of patients recovering from barbiturate-induced hemispheric anesthesia produced by left or right carotid artery injections (Wada test). They observed that right carotid injections were associated with a euphoric-manic response. Milner (1974), however, was unable to replicate these findings.

In contrast to the flattened emotional response or inappropriate euphoric mood associated with right-hemisphere damage, Goldstein (1948) noted that many patients with left-hemisphere lesions and aphasia appeared anxious, agitated, and sad, which Goldstein called the "catastrophic reaction." Gainotti (1972) confirmed Goldstein's (1948) observations. Terzian (1964) and Rossi and Rosadini (1967) observed that barbiturate injections into the left carotid artery could induce a catastrophic reaction.

Gainotti (1972) thought that the indifference reaction was an abnormal mood associated with denial of illness (anosognosia) but that the catastrophic reaction was a normal response to a serious physical or cognitive deficit.

There are several studies and observations that are incompatible with Gainotti's hypothesis. The Wada test causes only a transient aphasia with hemiparesis and would, therefore, be unlikely to cause a reactive depression in patients who are undergoing a diagnostic test. Anosognosia is the verbal explicit denial of a hemiplegia (see Chapter 10). We see right-hemisphere-damaged patients in the clinic who also appear to be indifferent but do not demonstrate anosognosia. Critchley (1953) has termed this anosodiaphoria. It is not clear if these patients' propensity to be unconcerned about their own illness is related to a general emotional flattening or if anosodiaphoria is a mild form of anosognosia and their indifference is related to defective evaluation of their own illness.

The depressive reaction associated with left-hemisphere disease is usually seen in nonfluent aphasic patients with anterior perisylvian lesions (Benson, 1979; Robinson and Sztela, 1981). As discussed, Hughlings Jackson (1932) noted that left-hemisphere lesions induced deficits in propositional language, and the nonfluent aphasics who could not express themselves with propositional speech could express feelings by using expletives and by intoning simple verbal utterances. Hughlings Jackson postulated that the right hemisphere may be mediating this activity. His postulate was supported by the observations of Tucker et al. (1977) and Ross and Mesulam (1979). Because left-hemisphere-damaged patients are unable to use propositional speech, they may rely more on right-hemisphere nonpropositional affective systems by more heavily intoning their speech and by using more facial expression.

As we discussed, patients with right-hemisphere disease have more difficulty than patients with left-hemisphere disease in comprehending and expressing affectively intoned speech as well as comprehending and expressing emotional facial expressions. Patients with right-hemisphere disease may also have more difficulty comprehending or remembering emotionally charged speech. These perceptual, cognitive, and expressive deficits might underlie and account for the flattened emotional reaction of patients with right-hemisphere lesions (i.e., indifference reactions), as previously described by clinical investigators.

Alternatively, these perceptual, cognitive, and expressive deficits may not reflect the patients' underlying mood. Although defects of affective communication may account for some of the behavioral symptoms discussed by Goldstein (1948), Babinski (1914), and Gainotti (1972), they cannot explain the results of Gasparrini et al. (1978), who administered the Minnesota Multiphasic Inventory (MMPI) to patients with unilateral hemisphere lesions. The MMPI has been widely used as an index of underlying affective experience, and the completion of this inventory does not require the perception of expression of affectively intoned speech or the perception of facial expression. Patients with left-hemisphere disease showed a marked elevation on the depression scale of this inventory, whereas patients with right-hemisphere disease did not. This finding suggests that the differences in emotional reactions of patients after right- vs. left-hemisphere disease cannot be attributed entirely to difficulties in perceiving or expressing affective stimuli.

Starkstein et al. (1987) have studied stroke and depression. They found that about one-third of stroke patients had a major depression and long-lasting depressions were associated with both cortical lesions and subcortical lesions. They also found the left frontal and left caudate lesions were most frequently associated with severe depression. The closer to the frontal pole, the more severe the depression. Many of the patients with depression, and especially those with cortical lesions, were anxious. In contrast, in the acute poststroke period, right frontal lesions were associated with indifference and even euphoria. When patients with right-hemisphere damage had depression, they were more likely to have parietal lesions.

However, not all investigators agree that there are hemispheric asymmetries of depression. House and et al. (1990) believe that depression associated with right-hemisphere disease may be underdiagnosed because right-hemisphere-damaged patients may have an emotional communicative disorder. According to Ross (personal communication), if one examines for vegetative signs of depression such as loss of appetite or sleep, there are no hemispheric asymmetries. Bowers et al. (in preparation) studied right- and left-hemisphere-damaged patients using the Zung Depression Inventory and a Self Assessment Manikin. Whereas we found differences in emotional memory (see the next section), no differences were found in the rate or severity of depression between the groups with left- and right-hemisphere lesions.

PATHOPHYSIOLOGY

If the observation that left-hemisphere-damaged patients are depressed (or anxious) and right-hemisphere-damaged patients are indifferent (or euphoric) is correct, how can these asymmetries be explained? Unfortunately, the brain mechanisms underlying emotional mood and memory have not been entirely elucidated. However, we will briefly review some of the major theories. We will also discuss their relative merits and how well they explain clinical observations.

Theories of emotional experience can be divided into two major types: feedback theories and central theories. Because feedback and central theories both have explanatory value, we will discuss both.

*Feedback theories.* Emotional experiences are also called emotional "feelings." In general, in order to feel something, one must have sensory or afferent input into the brain. Because emotional experience is associated with feelings, emotional experience may also require afferent input. However, emotional feelings are unlike traditional sensory experiences (e.g., visual, tactile, auditory) because they do not rely directly on the physical characteristics of the external stimulus. Rather, they may rely on the pattern of neural activity that the stimulus is eliciting. Emotional feelings may even occur in the absence of an external stimulus, suggesting that afferent activity must have been induced by efferent activity. This efferent activity may not only be important for emotional expression, but feedback of this expression to the brain may be responsible for emotional feelings. There are two major feedback hypotheses: the facial theory of Charles Darwin and the visceral theory of William James. Darwin (1872) noted that the free expression by outward signs of an emotion intensifies it. On the other hand, the repression, as far as possible, of all outward signs softens our emotions. "He who gives violent gesture increases his rage." Darwin also thought that emotional expression is innate. Izard (1977) and Ekman (1969), using cross-cultural studies, provided support for Darwin that emotional expression is innate. Tomkins (1962, 1963) thought that sensory receptors in the face provide afferent activity to the brain and that it was self-perception of the facial expression that induced emotion. Laird (1974) experimentally manipulated facial expression, and subjects felt emotions.

Because patients with right-hemisphere lesions may be impaired in expressing emotions, including facial expression, they may have reduced facial feedback and therefore appear indifferent. However, the facial feedback theory cannot explain why patients with left-hemisphere disease are anxious and depressed. There are many other unresolved problems with the facial feedback theory. If one is feeling a strong emotion (e.g., sadness), one cannot change this emotion to happiness by voluntarily smiling. Therefore, one can express one emotion while feeling another. Patients with pseudobulbar affect (see the final section) may express strong facial emotions that they are not feeling. Although it is possible that feedback is interrupted in these patients, there are other patients who have reduced facial mobility from neuromuscular diseases who report feeling emotions. Therefore, while facial expressions may influence emotions as Darwin suggested, the facial feedback theory cannot alone account for emotional experience.

William James (1890) proposed that emotion-provoking stimuli induced bodily changes and the self-perception of these changes as they occur produce the emotional feeling or experience. James, however, noted that there were also "cerebral" forms of pleasure and displeasure that did not require bodily changes or perception of these changes.

James's model was challenged by Cannon (1927), who argued that the separation of the viscera from the brain does not eliminate emotional feelings. This argument was supported by observations that patients with cervical spinal cord transections continued to experience emotions. However, Hohmann (1966) found that patients with either high or low spinal cord transections experienced emotions, but patients with lower lesions reported stronger emotions than those with high lesions. In addition, because the vagus nerve contains visceral afferents, cord transection at any level may not fully interfere with feedback.

Cannon also noted that pharmacologically induced visceral activation does not produce emotion. Marañon (1924) injected epinephrine into subjects and then inquired whether or not these injections induced an emotion. He found that these injections produced only "as if" feelings. Schachter and Singer (1962) also found that pharmacologically induced visceral activation did not produce an emotion, unless this arousal was accompanied by a cognitive set. Based on his studies, Schachter modified William James's postulate and proposed the "cognitive-arousal" theory of emotions. According to this theory, the experience of emotion involves specific cognitive attributions superimposed on a state of diffuse physiologic arousal; that is, a primary determinant of felt emotion is the environmental context within which arousal occurs.

Cannon also noted that the same visceral responses occur with different emotions. While Schachter's modification of James's theory could also deal with this critique, Ax (1953) and Ekman et al. (1969) have demonstrated that different bodily reactions can be associated with different emotions. It has not been shown, however, that feedback of these different bodily reactions can induce different emotional experiences.

Regarding Cannon's critique that the viscera have insufficient afferent input to the brain, contemporary research has examined the role of autonomic feedback in emotional experience using the heartbeat detection paradigm. Katkin et al. (1982) found that some normal subjects can accurately detect their heartbeats, and it was those individuals who had stronger emotional response to negative slides as determined by self-report (Hantas et al., 1982). Further support for the importance of autonomic feedback comes from other observations. Experiments in animals demonstrate that sympathectomy may retard aversive conditioning (DiGiusto and King, 1972), most likely because sympathectomy reduces fear.

Taken together, not only do Cannon's critiques fail to refute the feedback theory, but there is also increasing evidence that would support a role of visceral feedback in emotional experience. In order for feedback to occur, there must be a means for the viscera and autonomic nervous system to become activated. We will use the term feedforward to refer to the brain's ability to activate the autonomic nervous system and viscera. In humans, the cortex play a critical role in the analysis and interpretation of various stimuli, including those that induce emotional feeling and anatomic visceral responses. Consequently, feedforward systems must exist to enable the cortex to control the autonomic nervous system and hence the viscera such as the heart (visceral efferents). Similarly, if visceral activity can be detected by subjects, there must be neuronal pathways that support the feedback system and bring this information back to the brain (visceral afferents).

As we briefly mentioned, the major nerve that carries visceral afferent information is the vagus. The vagus nerve(s) afferents terminate in the medulla, primarily in the nucleus of the solitary tract. The nucleus of the solitary tract projects to the central nucleus of the amygdala (as well as to several hypothalamic nuclei), which in turn projects to other amygdalar nuclei and to the insula. Electrical stimulation of the vagus nerve also produces excitation of the insula and amygdala. The amygdala and insula project to several cortical areas including temporal, parietal, and frontal regions. It is possible that the vagal–solitary tract nucleus–amygdala–insula cortical pathway may be responsible for visceral feedback.

Emotions can be expressed by both the striated muscles and the autonomic nervous system-controlled viscera. We have already discussed the facial feedback theory. James did not believe that muscle and facial feedback was critical for emotional experience. Viscera, such as the heart, are controlled by the autonomic nervous system. The autonomic nervous system has two major components, the sympathetic and parasympathetic. The sympathetic nerves originate in the spinal cord (intermediolateral). The major parasympathetic nerves that innervate the viscera are the vagus nerves that originate in the brainstem (dorsal motor nucleus). Sympathetic neurons in the spinal cord receive projections from the hypothalamus as well as from cells in the ventrolateral pons and medulla. However, the ventrolateral medulla also receives projections from the hypothalamus (e.g., paraventricular and lateral nuclei). While the hypothalamus receives projections from many "limbic" areas, one of the strongest projections comes from the amygdala. The amygdala not only appears to influence the sympathetic nervous system via the hypothalamus, but also sends direct projections to the nucleus of the solitary tract and the dorsal motor nucleus and, therefore, may also directly influence the parasympathetic system.

While there are more widespread projections from the amygdala to the cortex than vice versa, the amygdala does receive cortical input. The insula also receives projections from the neocortex, and stimulation of the insula induces autonomic and visceral changes. In man, stimuli that induce emotional behavior must be analyzed and interpreted by the cortex, including such areas as the temporoparietal association cortex. Stimuli that induce emotion do cause changes in the autonomic nervous system and the viscera. Although it is not clear which limbic area or areas are critical for transcoding the knowledge gained from the emotional stimuli into changes of the autonomic nervous system and viscera, the amygdala and insula would appear to be ideal candidates.

While the visceral afferent and efferent pathways discussed above are bilateral, several studies suggest that there may be asymmetries both in the control of the autonomic nervous system and in the monitoring of the autonomic nervous system.

Regarding the efferent control of the autonomic nervous system (i.e., feedfoward system), Heilman et al. (1978) studied skin conductance responses (SCR) to mildly noxious stimuli in patients with right- or left-hemisphere lesions. The SCR, which results from phasic changes in eccrine sweat gland activity, is almost entirely mediated by the sympathetic branch of the autonomic nervous system. When compared to both normal controls and subjects with left-hemisphere lesions, those with right-hemisphere damage had decreased SCRs. In contrast, when compared to controls, the left-hemisphere-damaged patients had increased responsivity. While Morrow et al. (1981) also found decreased SCR to emotional stimuli in patients with right-hemisphere damage, they did not find an increased SCR in patients with left-hemisphere damage. Yokoyama et al. (1987) measured heart rate changes in response to an attention-demanding task. These authors found that right-hemisphere-damaged patients had reduced heart rate responses, whereas left-hemisphere-damaged patients had increased responsivity.

The exact parts of the brain that induced these autonomic changes are not known. Although Heilman et al. (1978) suspected the parietal and temporal regions, high-quality CT scans were not available when they did this study. In Yokoyama's study, the lesion loci were noted in the methods section, but no mention is made of the relationship between lesion locus and changes in heart rate. However, Schrandt et al. (1989) reported a study in which they measured SCR to emotional slides. Within the right-hemisphere-damaged group, only those patients whose lesions involved the right parietal lobe showed reduced SCR.

Luria and Simernitskaya (1977) proposed that the right hemisphere may be more important than the left in perceiving visceral changes (i.e., feedback system). To our knowledge, however, visceral perception (e.g., heart rate detection) has not been systematically studied in brain-impaired subjects. There have been several studies in normal subjects that suggest that the right hemisphere may play a special role in visceral perception. For example, Davidson and co-workers (1981) gave a variety of tapping tests to normal individuals in order to assess whether the left or right hand was more influenced by heartbeat. They found that the left hand was more influenced by heart rate than was the right hand, suggesting that the right hemisphere might be superior at detecting heartbeat. However, this left-hand superiority in the detection of heartbeat could not be replicated by other investigators. Hantas et al. (1984) used a signal detection technique to learn if normal subjects could detect their own heartbeat. They also assessed cerebral lateral preference by judging conjugate lateral eye movements and found that left movers (who were "right-hemisphere preferent") were better at detecting their own heartbeat than were those who were right movers.

If the right hemisphere plays a dominant role in visceral autonomic activation, and a dominant role in perceiving visceral changes, and if this feedback is critical to emotional experience, it would follow that right-hemisphere lesions that damage critical cortical and limbic areas should be associated with reduced emotional feeling or indifference even in those patients who are aware of their deficits. Left-hemisphere lesions may not only spare the right-hemisphere feedforward and feedback systems, but the left hemisphere may help regulate or control the feedforward systems such that with left-hemisphere lesions there is increased visceral-autonomic activation (Heilman et al., 1978; Yokoyama et al., 1987). Therefore the heightened autonomic-visceral activity found in patients with left-hemisphere injuries together with their knowledge that they are impaired (e.g., aphasic and hemiparetic) may lead to the anxiety associated with left-hemisphere lesions.

*Central theories.*    One of the first central theories was that of Walter Cannon (1927), who proposed that stimuli that enter the brain by way of the thalamus activate the hypothalamus. The hypothalamus controls the endocrine system and also controls the autonomic nervous system. The endocrine and autonomic nervous systems can induce physiological changes in almost all organ systems. Cannon posited that hypothalamic-induced changes in organ systems are adaptive in that they aid survival. Cannon also thought that the hypothalamus activated the cerebral cortex, and it was this cerebral activation that was responsible for the conscious experience of emotion. Although Cannon believed that the cortex normally inhibits the hypothalamus and a loss of this inhibition was responsible for a loss of appropriate emotional control such as seen in sham rage, he did not suggest a critical role for the cortex in the interpretation of stimuli.

We agree that emotions are adaptive and many of the physiologic changes associated with adaptation are mediated by the hypothalamus. However, as we pointed out earlier in this chapter, it is the cortex, rather than the thalamus or hypothalamus, that appears to be critical in the interpretation of complex stimuli.

In 1878, Broca designated a group of anatomically related structures on the medial wall of the cerebral hemisphere "le grand lobe limbique." Because these structures are in proximity to structures of the olfactory system, it was assumed that they all have olfactory or related functions. In 1901, Ramón y Cajal (1965) concluded on the basis of histological studies that portions of the limbic lobe (the hippocampal-fornix system) had no more than a neighborly relationship with the olfactory apparatus. Papez (1937) postulated that a "circuit" in the limbic lobe (cingulate–hippocampus–fornix–mammillary bodies–anterior thalamus–cingulate) was an important component of the central mechanism subserving emotional feeling and expression. After Bard (1934) demonstrated that the hypothalamus was important in mediating the rage response, Papez (1937) postulated that the hypothalamus was the effector of emotion. In 1948, Yakovlev added the basolateral components (orbitofrontal, insular, and anterior temporal lobe cortex, the amygdala, and the dorsomedial nucleus of the thalamus) to the medial system, and together these were designated as the limbic system (MacLean, 1952).

Although the cortex influences the hypothalamus, both inhibiting and activating it, the cortex does not have strong, direct projections to the hypothalamus. Most of the cortical projections that influence the hypothalamus are mediated by the limbic system. In addition, as we will discuss in a later section, patients who are stimulated in limbic areas or have seizures that emanate from limbic areas may experience an emotion. As demonstrated by Klüver and Bucy (1937), monkeys with a portion of their limbic system ablated (e.g., amygdala) have decreased emotions. Based on these seminal observations, it would appear that Cannon's hypothalamic cortical model is insufficient and at least three systems are important for emotional experience: portions of the cerebral cortex, the limbic system, and the diencephalon including the thalamus, hypothalamus, and reticular system. However, what remains unclear is how these areas mediate different feelings and how they can account for the hemispheric asymmetries we previously discussed.

Schacter and Singer's (1962) cognition-arousal theory was initially tested using peripheral autonomic-visceral activation. However, the cognition-arousal theory could be modified into a central model. According to this central cognitive-arousal model, the cortex appraises and interprets stimuli (emotional cognition) and either activates or inhibits the reticular system. This reticular activation occurs either directly or through the limbic system. When activated, the reticular system activates the cortex. The cerebral arousal in concert with the knowledge of the stimuli's meaning could give rise to emotional feelings. Heilman (1979) posited that the right hemisphere's cortical-limbic-reticular networks are dominant in the control of arousal, both peripherally and centrally. However, the right hemisphere may be inhibited by the left. Therefore, with right-hemisphere disease, in addition to decreased peripheral arousal, there is decreased central arousal and a flattening of emotional experience. With left-hemisphere lesions, there is an increased arousal and anxiety. However, this central cognitive arousal theory cannot explain why patients with left anterior lesions are also sad. One would have relied on Gainotti's explanation that patients with left-hemisphere lesions are aware of their deficit, and those with right-hemisphere disease are unaware. This hypothesis also cannot explain why even in the absence of stimuli patients with focal seizures can experience emotions.

Using electrophysiological studies in normal subjects, Davidson et al. (1981) and Tucker (1981) have suggested that each hemisphere, particularly the frontal regions, makes asymmetric contributions to affective regulation. Greater right than left activation is associated with negative moods (sadness), and greater left than right is associated with positive moods. Fox and Davidson (1984) postulate that there is interhemispheric inhibition such that with left frontal disease there is a release or disinhibition of the right frontal lobe. The right frontal lobe becomes activated and this activation induces sadness. While Fox and Davidson suggest that positive and negative emotions are related to approach (left hemisphere) and avoidance behaviors (right hemisphere), their model does not explain how the two hemispheres are differentially organized such that they make asymmetrical contributions to mood. This theory also does not explain how other emotions are mediated nor does it explain the role of the limbic and subcortical systems.

Tucker and Williamson (1984) also subscribe to the bivalent hemisphere hypothesis but think that the abnormal moods associated with frontal lesion are related to intra-hemispheric (rather than interhemispheric) disinhibition. They believe that hemispheric asymmetries may be related to asymmetries of pharmacologic systems, the left hemisphere being primarily cholinergic and dopaminergic and the right being primarily noradrenergic. Since the time of Hippocrates, it has been postulated that body humors can influence mood. Although there is little question that changes in neurotransmitter systems may have a profound influence on mood and may induce both euphoria and dysphoria, our discussion will be limited to anatomic-physiological models of emotion, the biochemical-pharmacological theories will not be discussed here.

Heller (1990) proposed that feelings are associated with relative patterns of cortical activation of the right and left frontal and parietal regions. As has been discussed, the right parietal lobe appears to play a special role in the mediation of arousal (Heilman, 1979) and the frontal lobes play a special role in emotional valence (Davidson et al., 1979). Therefore when someone is happy, the left frontal and right parietal regions would be more active (high arousal, positive valence) than the right frontal and left parietal regions. When someone is sad (low arousal, negative valence) the opposite would occur (left frontal and right parietal less activated than right frontal and left parietal). Although Heller's model can account for three emotions, it cannot account for other emotions such as anger. It also does not explain the role of the limbic system in emotional experience.

Unfortunately, we do not know the mechanism responsible for emotional experience. We believe that all emotions are primarily adaptive and aid in the organism's and species' survival. Although different emotions may share physiologic features, we propose that the neuronal processes associated with each emotion is unique. The stimulus that induces the emotion, independent of the nature of the induced emotion, is primarily analyzed by the neocortex, and it is the neocortex that determines the meaning of the stimulus.

The neocortex has extensive connections to the limbic systems, including the hippocampus (via the entorhinal cortex). The neocortex also projects to the cingulate gyrus and the amygdala. Whereas the hippocampus and cingulate are part of the Papez circuit, the amygdala is part of the basolateral circuit of Yakovlev. MacLean suggested a critical role for the hippocampus emotional experience. However, ablation of this area appears to induce amnesia rather than a decrease of emotional experience. The cortical projections to either the cingulate gyrus or amygdala may therefore be the critical projections. The limbic system has reciprocal projections to the hypothalamus, and both the cortex and limbic system can influence the reticular system. As discussed, the hypothalamus controls the endocrine and autonomic nervous system, which when activated feed back to the brain. Lastly, associative frontal and temporoparietal cortex also projects to premotor cortex, which has extensive connections with the basal ganglia and motor systems.

We believe that there are four major determinants of emotional experience: (1) emotional cognition, (2) arousal, (3) motor intention-activation, and (4) approach-avoidance. Emotional experience is a "top down" process. Except in conditioned responses where direct thalamic-amygdala connections appear important (Iwata et al., 1986), cognitive interpretation of stimuli helps determine the type of emotion including its valence (positive-negative). The valence decision is based upon whether the stimulus is beneficial (positive) or detrimental (negative) to the well-being of the organism or species. Positive or negative emotions can be associated with high (joy, fear) or low (satisfaction, sadness) arousal. Certain negative emotions are associated with preparation for action (e.g., fear and anger) (increased intention-activation), and others are associated with reduced intention-activation (e.g., sadness). Certain positive emotions may also be associated with preparations for action (joy and surprise) and others may not (satisfaction). The negative emotions that are associated with high arousal are usually associated with action (fear and anger). Anger is also associated with approach behaviors and fear with avoidance. As we have discussed, depending on the nature of the stimulus (e.g., verbal or nonverbal) the left or right hemisphere determines the type of emotion. However, according to Davidson et al. (1979), the frontal lobes play a critical role in the emotional experience associated with valence, the left mediating positive valence, the right negative valence. The right hemisphere and especially the parietal lobe appears to have a strong excitatory role on arousal, and the left hemisphere an inhibitory role (see Chapter 12). The right hemisphere also plays an excitatory role in motor activation or intension (also see Chapter 10). In part, this activation must be mediated by the amygdala. The amygdala influences the hypothalamus, important for hormonal and autonomic nervous system activation. Whereas the right amygdala may influence the arousal and activation associated with negative emotions, the left may be important for positive emotions (Morris et al., 1991). The dorsolateral and medial frontal lobes connect with the striatum and also influence the motor system (see Chapter 12). Denny-Brown suggested that the frontal lobes moderate avoidance behaviors. Patients with frontal and especially orbitofrontal lesions demonstrate approach behaviors including inappropriate anger (Pontius and Yudowitz, 1980). Although one would predict hemispheric asymmetries, most orbitofrontal lesions are bilateral. The orbitofrontal area has close connections with the amygdala and the orbitofrontal cortex may help control the amygdala.

### Emotional Memory

There are several reasons why hemispheric lesions may influence emotional memory. Individuals recall episodes where their affective content was the same as their current mood. For example, depressed patients are more likely to recall events that made them sad. Based on this mood congruence effect, one would expect that if left-hemisphere-damaged patients are depressed, they should recall more sad than happy events, and if right-hemisphere-damaged patients are euphoric or indifferent, they should recall happy or neutral episodes more than sad episodes.

Alternatively, since the right hemisphere appears to mediate arousal and is dominant in the interpretation and expression of nonverbal emotion signals, it may also play a dominant role in emotional memory such that patients with right-hemisphere disease have difficulty recalling emotional memories independent of the valence of the emotion associated with the memory.

Unfortunately, only a limited number of studies have examined the ability of right- and left-hemisphere-damaged patients to recall emotional memories. Weschler

(1973) studied right- and left-hemisphere-damaged patients' ability to recall neutral and emotionally charged stories. The left-hemisphere-damaged patients recalled more portions of the emotional story than they did of the neutral story. The right-hemisphere-damaged patients did not show this enhanced recall. Since the story was sad, this finding was compatible with both the valence-mood congruence and right-hemisphere dominance hypotheses. Cimino and co-workers (1991) examined the ability of right-hemisphere-damaged patients and normal controls to recall personal episodic memories. The autobiographical memories of the right-hemisphere-damaged patients were less emotional and less detailed than the controls. There were no valence effects. Although Cimino et al.'s (1991) findings are compatible with the right-hemisphere dominance hypothesis, Bowers and co-workers (submitted) used a similar paradigm but also examined left-hemisphere-damaged subjects. They not only failed to replicate Cimino et al.'s findings of reduced emotional recall, but found a valence effect in that the left-hemisphere-damaged patients recalled less positive memories. Although these findings would appear to support the valence-mood congruence hypothesis, Bowers et al. (in preparation) did not find that the left-hemisphere-damaged subjects were more depressed than the right, and the mechanism underlying this failure to recall positive episodes remains unknown.

## LIMBIC SYSTEM DYSFUNCTION

### Experimental Observations in Animals

Myriad stimulation and ablation experiments in animals have attempted to define the role of the limbic system in regulating emotion (Valenstein, 1973). Many of these studies have provided confusing and contradictory results. Some of the difficulty undoubtedly results from the complex functional differentiation within each component of the limbic system (Isaacson, 1982). Adding to this is the difficulty of measuring affect in animals; most experiments use techniques such as active or passive avoidance and infer the emotional state from the animal's behavior. Finally, species differences may be significant, even in this phylogenetically older portion of the cerebral hemispheres.

One of the earliest and most important animal observations was that bilateral ablation of the anterior temporal lobe changes the aggressive rhesus monkey into a tame animal (Klüver and Bucy, 1937). Such animals also demonstrated hypersexuality and visual agnosia. Akert et al. (1961) demonstrated that the removal of the temporal lobe neocortex did not produce this tameness. Ursin (1960) stimulated the amygdaloid nucleus and produced a ragelike response and an increase in emotional behavior. Amygdala ablation (Woods, 1956) produced placid animals.

Septal lesions in animals, on the other hand, produced a ragelike state (Brady and Nauta, 1955), and septal stimulation produced an apparently pleasant state in which animals stimulated themselves without additional reward (Olds, 1958). Decortication in animals produces a state of pathological rage ("sham rage"). In a series of experiments, Bard (1934) demonstrated that the caudal hypothalamus was mediating this response. Both the amygdala (a component of the basolateral circuit) and the septal region (a portion of both limbic circuits) have strong input into the hypothalamus (Yakovlev, 1948). MacLean (1952) has proposed that the septal pathway is important for species preservation (that is, social-sexual behavior) and the amygdala circuit is more important for self preservation (fight and flight).

## Lesions

Some of the findings in humans have been analogous to the results reported in animals. In humans, for example, tumors in the septal region have been reported to produce ragelike attacks and increased irritability (Zeman and King, 1958: Poeck and Pilleri, 1961). Bilateral temporal lobe lesions in humans entailing the destruction of the amygdala, uncus, and hippocampal gyrus have been reported to produce placidity (Poeck, 1969). In aggressive patients, stereotactic amygdaloidectomy has been reported to reduce rage (Mark et al., 1972). Anterior temporal lobectomy for seizure disorders has been reported to increase sexuality (Blumer and Walker, 1975). Bilateral hippocampal removal produces a profound and permanent deficit in recent memory (see Chapter 15).

## Inflammation

Several inflammatory and viral diseases have been known to affect the limbic system. Herpes simplex encephalitis has predilection for the orbitofrontal and anterior temporal regions and thus selectively destroys much of the limbic system. Impulsivity, memory loss, and abnormalities of emotional behavior are frequently early manifestations of this infection. Limbic encephalitis may also be associated with carcinoma. There is degeneration and inflammation of amygdaloid nuclei, hippocampi, and cingulate gyri, as well as other structures. Clinically, the picture is similar to that of herpes infection, with memory loss and abnormalities of emotional behavior, including depression, agitation, and anxiety (Corsellis et al., 1968). Rabies, which also has a predilection for limbic structures, such as hippocampus (as well as hypothalamic and brainstem regions) has prominent emotional symptoms including profound anxiety and agitation.

## Seizures

Partial (focal) seizures with complex symptomatology (temporal lobe epilepsy, psychomotor epilepsy) have long been known to produce emotional symptoms. These symptoms may be considered under three headings: ictal phenomena (phenomena directly related to the seizure discharge), postictal phenomena (occurring directly after a seizure), and interictal behavior (occurring between overt seizures).

ICTAL PHENOMENA

One of the strongest arguments supporting the notion that the limbic system is important in mediating emotional behavior is the observation that emotional change as a manifestation of a seizure discharge is highly correlated with foci in or near the limbic system, particularly with foci in the anteromedial temporal lobes.

*Sexuality.*   Currier et al. (1971) described patients who had ictal behavior that resembled sexual intercourse. Undressing and exhibitionism have been described with temporal lobe seizures (Hooshmand and Brawley, 1969; Rodin, 1973). In general, however, ictal sexual behavior is not purposeful. Remillard et al. (1983) reported 12 women with temporal lobe epilepsy who had sexual arousal or orgasm as part of their seizures, and they reviewed 14 other cases. Most cases had right-sided foci, and most were women. Spencer et al. (1983) reported sexual automatisms in four patients with seizure foci in the orbitofrontal cortex. They proposed that sexual experiences were more likely to occur with temporal lobe foci whereas sexual automatisms occurred with frontal foci.

*Gelastic and dacrystic seizures.*   Gelastic epilepsy refers to seizures in which laughter is a prominent ictal event (Daly and Mulder, 1957). Sackeim et al. (1982) reviewed 91 reported cases of gelastic epilepsy and found that, of 59 cases with lateralized foci, 40 were left-sided. Gascon and Lombroso (1971) described ten patients with gelastic epilepsy; five had bilateral synchronous spike and wave abnormalities, and two of these had diencephalic pathology; the other five had right temporal lobe foci. Gascon and Lombroso thought they could differentiate two types of laughter: the diencephalic group appeared to have automatic laughter without affect and the temporal lobe group more affective components (including pleasurable auras).

Crying as an ictal manifestation, termed dacrystic epilepsy (Offen et al., 1976), is much less common than laughing. Of the six cases reviewed by Offen et al., four probably had right-sided pathology, one had left-sided pathology, and in one the site of pathology was uncertain.

*Aggression.*   Ictal aggression is rare. Ashford et al. (1980) documented nonpurposeful violent behavior as an ictal event. The relationship between epileptic seizures and directed, purposeful violence is controversial. Mark and Ervin (1970) are among the strongest proponents of such a relationship, finding a high incidence of epilepsy in a group of violent prisoners. Pincus (1980) reviewed other studies showing a similar relationship; however, Stevens and Hermann (1981) found that controlled studies did not support this view. Many neurologists who have cared for large numbers of temporal lobe epileptics have never seen directed, purposeful violence as an ictal phenomenon. This clinical impression is supported by careful analysis of larger groups of epileptic patients (Delgado-Escueta et al., 1981; Trieman and Delgado-Esqueta, 1983).

*Fear and anxiety.*   Fear is the affect most frequently associated with a temporal lobe seizure (Williams, 1956). Ictal fear may be found equally with right- and left-sided dysfunction (Williams, 1956; Strauss et al., 1982). A prolonged attack of fear has been associated with right-sided temporal lobe status (McLachlan and Blume, 1980).

Although fear responses are usually associated with temporal lobe seizures, they may also be associated with seizures emanating from the cingulate gyrus (Daly,

1958). The amygdala appears to be the critical structure in the induction of the fear response (Gloor, 1972).

*Depression and euphoria.*   Williams (1956) describes patients who became very sad and others who had extreme feelings of well-being.

POSTICTAL PHENOMENA

Many patients are confused, restless, and combative after a seizure and apparently particularly after a temporal lobe seizure. Instances of aggression in this state are common but usually consist only of the patient's struggling with persons who are trying to restrain him or her. Depression may last for several days after a seizure.

INTERICTAL PHENOMENA

The postulate that seizures directly induce interictal behavioral changes has proved to be the most difficult of issues and has yet to be resolved.

*Anxiety, fear, and depression.*   Currier et al. (1971) found that 44% of patients with temporal lobe epilepsy had psychiatric complications. The most common were anxiety and depression. Men with left-sided foci reported more fear than men with right-sided foci. Patients with left-sided foci reported more fear of social and sexual situations (Strauss et al., 1982).

There is an increased risk of suicide in epileptics (Hawton et al., 1980). Flor-Henry (1969) found a relationship between right temporal lobe seizure foci and affective disorders. McIntyre et al. (1976) and Bear and Fedio (1977) also showed that patients with right-hemisphere foci are more likely to show emotional tendencies. However, according to some studies, patients with left-sided foci score higher on depression scales than do patients with right-sided foci (Robertson et al., 1987).

Bear (1979) has suggested that a sensory-limbic hyperconnection may account for interictal behavioral aberrations. Hermann and Chhabria (1980) postulated that classical conditioning might mediate an overinvestment of affective significance. The unconditional stimulus is the firing of limbic focus that induces an emotion (unconditioned response). The conditioned stimulus would be environmental stimuli.

*Sexuality.*   Hyposexuality has been associated with temporal lobe epilepsy (Gastaut and Colomb, 1954). Taylor (1969) studied patients with temporal lobe seizures and found that 72% had a decreased sexual drive. Pritchard (1980) was able to confirm that reduced libido and impotence were associated with temporal lobe seizures. The side of the epileptic focus, drug therapy, and seizure control did not seem to be related to the hyposexuality. The location of the locus did, however, appear important. The mesobasal area of the temporal lobe appears to be the critical area. Increased libido has also been reported (Cogen et al., 1979). The medial temporal lobe structures, including the amygdala, have a close anatomic and physiological relationship with the hypothalamus. Pritchard (1980) found that endocrine changes could be demonstrated, including eugonadotropic, hypogonadotropic, and hypergonadotropic hypogonadism. Herzog et al. (1982) also demonstrated endocrine changes and suggested that hypothalamic-pituitary control of gonadotropin secretion may be altered in patients with temporal lobe epilepsy. Pritchard et al. (1981) found elevation of prolactin following complex partial seizures. Hyperprolactinemia may be associated with impotence in males.

Taylor (1969) and Cogen et al. (1979) noted that temporal lobectomy may restore normal sexual function.

*Aggressiveness.*    Interictal aggressiveness, like ictal aggressiveness, remains controversial and has many medicolegal implications. Taylor (1969) found that about one-third of patients with temporal lobe epilepsy were aggressive interictally. Williams (1969) reviewed the EEGs of aggressive criminals, many of whom had committed acts of violence. Abnormal EEGs were five times more common than in the general population. However, Stevens and Hermann (1981) note that this observation has not been validated by detailed controlled studies. Treiman (1991) notes that interictal violence tends to occur in young men of subnormal intelligence, with character disorders, a history of early and severe seizures, and associated neurological deficits. When patients with psychiatric disorders or subnormal intelligence are removed from a series, there is no increased evidence of violence.

*Other interictal changes.*    Patients with temporal lobe epilepsy are said to have a dramatic, and possibly specific, disorder of personality (Blumer and Benson, 1975). Slater and Beard (1963) described "schizophreniform" psychosis in patients with temporal lobe epilepsy, but they described selected cases and could not comment on the incidence of this disorder in temporal lobe epileptics. Other studies (Currie et al., 1971) have failed to show a higher than expected incidence of psychosis in temporal lobe epileptics, but it can still be maintained that less severe psychiatric abnormalities could have eluded these investigators. Studies that claim to show no difference in emotional makeup between temporal lobe and other epileptics (Guerrant et al., 1962; Stevens, 1966) have been reinterpreted (Blumer, 1975) to indicate that there is, in fact, a difference: temporal lobe epileptics are more likely to have more serious forms of emotional disturbance.

The "typical personality" of the temporal lobe epileptic has been described in roughly similar terms over many years (Blumer and Benson, 1975; Geschwind, 1975, 1977). These patients are said to have a deepening of emotions; they ascribe great significance to commonplace events. This can be manifested as a tendency to take a cosmic view; hyperreligiosity (or intensely professed atheism) is said to be common. Concern with minor details results in slowness of thought and circumstantiality, and can also be manifested by hypergraphia, a tendency of such patients to record in writing minute details of their lives (Waxman and Geschwind, 1974). In the extreme, psychosis, often with prominent paranoid qualities, can be seen (the schizophreniform psychosis noted above, but, unlike schizophrenics, these patients do not have a flat affect and tend to maintain interpersonal relationships. McIntyre et al. (1976) demonstrated that, whereas patients with left temporal lobe foci demonstrate a reflective conceptual approach, patients with right temporal lobe foci are more impulsive.

Bear and Fedio (1977) designed a questionnaire specifically to detect personality features. They found that these personality changes are significantly more common among temporal lobe epileptics than among normal subjects. Patients with right-hemisphere foci are more likely to show emotional tendencies and denial, and patients with left temporal lobe foci show ideational aberrations (paranoia, sense of personal destiny) and dyssocial behavior. Since a control population with seizure foci in other sites was not used, the specificity of these changes to limbic regions can still be questioned. Attempts to replicate Bear and Fedio's findings have failed to define a personality profile specific to temporal lobe epilepsy (Brandt et al., 1985; Hermann and Riel, 1981; Mungas, 1982; Weiser, 1986). Several studies have suggested that patients with limbic temporal lobe foci are more likely to have abnormal personality traits than patients with lateral temporal lobe foci (Nielsen and Kristensen, 1981; Weiser, 1986; Hermann et al., 1982). The literature has recently been reviewed by Strauss (1989).

## BASAL GANGLIA DISORDERS

Basal ganglia disorders are commonly thought to be primarily motor disorders; however, patients with basal ganglia disorders frequently have intellectual and emotional disorders. Parkinson's disease and Huntington's disease are the two most common basal ganglia disorders associated with emotional changes.

### Parkinson's Disease

Parkinson's disease is characterized by akinesia, rigidity, and resting tremor. There may be other associated signs and symptoms, including disorders of gait and intellectual deterioration. Parkinson (1938) noted that his patients were unhappy. Depression has subsequently been found to be a frequent part of the Parkinson's complex. Mayeux et al. (1981), for example, studied well-functioning outpatients. Using the Beck Depression Index, they found that 47% of these patients were depressed. Other investigators have also found a high rate of depression (Warburton, 1967; Mindham, 1970; Celesia and Wanamaker, 1972).

The depression may be reactive or a part of the Parkinsonian syndrome or both. Support for the hypothesis that it is not entirely reactive comes from the observation that the motor impairment and the depression correlate poorly. Patients who are more severely disabled are often less depressed (Robins, 1976), and in many patients depression is noted prior to the onset of motor symptoms (Mindham, 1970; Mayeux et al., 1981).

As might be expected from the poor correlation between depression and motor impairment, the depression in Parkinsonism responds poorly to the drugs that help the motor symptoms. Many of the motor symptoms are primarily induced by deficits in the nigrostriatal dopaminergic system. Although L-dopa replacement therapy improves the motor symptoms, it may not reduce depression (Marsh and Markham, 1973; Mayeux et al., 1981). Parkinson's disease may be associated with cell loss in both the raphe and locus coeruleus. The depression associated with Parkinson's disease may be related to defects in the serotonergic or noradrenergic systems.

Patients with Parkinson's disease may have a masklike face and a voice without prosody. The inability of Parkinson's patients to fully express emotions may be mistaken for apathy. Patients with Parkinson's disease also may have difficulty comprehending affective prosody and faces (Scott et al., 1984; Blonder et al., 1989).

### Huntington's Disease

Huntington's disease, or Huntington's chorea, is characterized by involuntary movements and intellectual decline. Huntington (1872) noted that many patients with this disease have severe emotional disorders and that there is a tendency to suicide. Almost every patient who develops Huntington's disease has emotional or psychiatric signs and symptoms (Mayeux, 1983). Although it is possible that some of the emotional signs and symptoms are a reaction to the disease, in many cases they precede motor and cognitive dysfunction (Heathfield, 1967).

The emotional changes are variable and include mania and depression (Folstein et al., 1979), apathy, aggressiveness, irritability, promiscuity, and irresponsibility. Different emotional symptoms may be manifested at different times during the course of the disease. In general, however, the apathy is usually seen later in the course, when there are signs of intellectual deterioration.

The pathophysiology of the emotional disorders associated with Huntington's disease is unclear. In general, patients have cell loss in the neostriatum and especially in the caudate. There is also cortical cell loss. However, other areas of the brain may also show degenerative changes. Many of the signs displayed by patients with Huntington's disease are similar to those seen with frontal lobe dysfunction (e.g., apathy), and frontal lobe atrophy may be responsible for these signs (see Chapter 12). However, there are profound neurochemical changes associated with Huntington's disease. For example gamma-aminobutyric acid and acetylcholine levels are reduced in the basal ganglia. Unfortunately, it is not known how cellular degenerative and changes in neurotransmitters may account for the profound emotional changes seen in these patients.

Patients with Huntington's disease may also have impaired comprehension of affective prosody (Speedie et al., 1990). The brain mechanism underlying this defect is also not well understood.

## PSEUDOBULBAR PALSY

Wilson (1924) postulated a pontobulbar area responsible for emotional facial expression. Lesions that interrupt the corticobulbar motor pathways bilaterally release reflex mechanisms for facial expression from cortical control. This was called pseudobulbar palsy, to distinguish it from motor deficits (palsy) resulting from lower motor neuron (bulbar) dysfunction, a common occurrence when polio was prevalent.

The syndrome consists of involuntary laughing or crying (or both). As with many forms of release phenomena, this excess of emotional expression is stereotypic and does not show either a wide spectrum of emotions or different degrees of intensity of expression. It can be triggered by a wide variety of stimuli but cannot be initiated or stopped voluntarily. Examination usually shows weakness of voluntary facial movements and increase in the facial and jaw stretch reflexes.

The location of the centers for the control of facial expression is not known, and although Wilson postulated it to be in the lower brainstem, Poeck (1969) has postulated centers in the thalamus and hypothalamus. Although bilateral lesions are usually responsible, the syndrome has been described with unilateral lesions on either side (Bruyn and Gaithier, 1969). Patients with pseudobulbar palsy usually consistently either laugh or cry. Sackeim et al. (1982) noted that, although most patients with pseudobulbar crying or laughing have bilateral lesions, the larger lesion is usually in the right hemisphere when there is laughter and in the left when there is crying.

Patients with this syndrome report feeling normal emotions, despite the abnormality of expression. Commonly, their family and physicians speak of them as being emotionally labile, implying that they no longer have appropriate internal emotional feeling. It is important to make the distinction between true emotional lability (as may be seen with bilateral frontal lobe disturbance) and pseudobulbar lability of emotional expression (with normal inner emotions).

## THERAPY FOR EMOTIONAL CHANGES INDUCED BY NEUROLOGICAL DISEASES

The four major goals of therapy are treatment of underlying disease (when possible), education, alternative strategies, and drug therapy. (The treatment of vascular disease, tumors, trauma, and other processes that may injure the hemisphere is not within the scope of this book.)

A major role of the therapist is educating patients and families. Although patients and families will attribute sensory, motor, and language disorders to brain injury, affective disorders are frequently incorrectly attributed to psychodynamic factors, even though there was a clear temporal relationship between the neurological disease and the emotional changes. When patients and families learn that emotional changes may be related to brain injury, there is often a reduction of guilt, an improvement of interpersonal relations, and a refocusing on the appropriate problems.

In general, there are many alternative strategies available to patients with neurologically induced behavioral deficits. These strategies must be individually tailored. For example, if one has a patient with right temporoparietal injury who cannot comprehend affective intonations, the family should be instructed to use propositional speech to communicate affect. If a patient has a left temporoparietal lesion with decreased comprehension of propositional language, that person may still be able to comprehend affective intonation.

Drug therapy may also be helpful. For example, left-hemisphere depressed patients and patients with depression associated with basal ganglia disease may benefit from antidepressants. Patients with inappropriate aggressiveness may be helped by beta-blockers or anticonvulsants.

# REFERENCES

Ahern, G., Schumer, D., Kleefield, J., Blume, H., Cosgrove, G., Weintraub, S., and Mesalum, M. (1991). Right hemisphere advantage in evaluating emotional facial expressions. *Cortex*, 27:193–202.

Akert, K., Greusen, R. A., Woosley, C. N., and Meyer, D. R. (1961). Kluver-Bucy syndrome in monkeys with neocortical ablations of temporal lobe. *Brain 84*:480–498.

Ashford, J. W., Aabro, E., Gulmann, N., Hjelmsted, A., and Pedersen, H. E. (1980). Antidepressive treatment in Parkinson's disease. *Acta Neurol. Scand. 62*:210–219.

Ashford, J. W., Schulz, C., and Walsh, G. O. (1980). Violent automatism in a partial complex seizure. Report of a case. *Arch. Neurol. 37*:120–122.

Ax, A. F. (1953). The physiological differentiation between fear and anger in humans. *Psychom. Med. 15*:433–442.

Babinski, J. (1914). Contribution à l'etude des troubles mentaux dans l'hemisplegie organique cerebrale (anosognosie). *Revue Neurologique 27*:845–848.

Bard, P. (1934). Emotion. I: The neuro-humoral basis of emotional reactions. In *Handbook of General Experimental Psychology*, C. Murchison, (ed.). Worcester, Mass.: Clark University Press.

Baylis, G., Rolls, E., and Leonard, C. (1985). Selectivity between faces in the responses of a population of neurons in the superior temporal sulcus of the monkey. *Brain Res. 342*:91–102.

Bear, D. M. (1979). Temporal lobe, epilepsy: a syndrome of sensory-limbic hyperconnection. *Cortex 15*:357–384.

Bear, D. M., and Fedio, P. (1977). Quantitative analysis of interictal behavior in temporal lobe epilepsy. *Arch. Neurol. 34*:454–467.

Bellugi, U., Corina, D., Normal, F., Klima, E., and Reilly, J. (1988). Differential specialization for linguistic facial expressions in left and right lesioned deaf singers. Paper presented at the 27th Annual Meeting of the Academy of Aphasia.

Benowitz, L., Bear, D., Mesulam, M., Rosenthal, R., Zaidel, E., and Sperry, W. (1983). Nonverbal sensitivity following lateralized cerebral injury. *Cortex 19*:5–12.

Benson, D. F. (1979). Psychiatric aspects of aphasia. In *Aphasia, Alexia, and Agraphia*, D. F. Benson (ed.). New York: Churchill Livingstone.

Benton, A. L. and Van Allen, M. W. (1968). Impairment in facial recognition in patients with cerebral disease. *Cortex 4*:344–358.

Blonder, L. X., Bowers, D., and Heilman, K. M. (1991a). The role of the right hemisphere on emotional communication. *Brain 114*:1115–1127.

Blonder, L., Bowers, D., and Heilman, K. (1991b). Logical inferences following right hemisphere damage. (Abstract). *J. Clin. Exp. Neuropsychol. 13*:39.

Blonder, L., Burns, A., Bowers, D., Moore, R., and Heilman, K. (1991c). Right hemisphere expressivity during natural conversation. (Abstract) *J. Clin. Exp. Neuropsychol. 13*:85.

Blonder, L. X., Gur, R. E., and Gur, R. C. (1989). The effects of right and left hemiparkinsonism on prosody. *Brain Lang. 36*:193–207.

Bloom, R., Borod, J. C., Obler, L., and Gerstman, L. (1992). Impact of emotional content on discourse production in patients with unilateral brain damage. *Brain and Language 42*:153–164.

Blumer, D. (1975). Temporal lobe epilepsy and its psychiatric significance. In *Psychiatric Aspects of Neurological Disease*, D. F. Benson and D. Blumer (eds.). New York: Grune and Stratton.

Blumer, D., and Benson, D. F. (1975). Personality changes with frontal and temporal lobe lesions. In *Psychiatric Aspects of Neurological Disease*, D. F. Benson and D. Blumer (eds.). New York: Grune & Stratton.

Blumer, D., and Walker, A. E. (1975). The neural basis of sexual behavior. In *Psychiatric Aspects of Neurological Disease*, D. F. Benson and D. Blumer (eds.). New York: Grune and Stratton.

Boller, F., Cole, M., Vtunski, P., Patterson, M., and Kim, Y. (1979). Paralinguistic aspects of auditory comprehension in aphasia. *Brain Lang.* 7:164–174.

Borod, J. C., Koff, E., Lorch, M. P., and Nicholas, M. (1985). Channels of emotional communication in patients with unilateral brain damage. *Archives of Neurology* 42:345–348.

Borod, J., and Koff, E. (1990). Laterlization for facial emotion behavior: a methodological perspective. *Int. J. Psychol.* 25:157–177.

Borod, J., Koff, E., Perlman-Lorch, J., and Nicholas, M. (1986). The expression and perception of facial emotions in brain damaged patients. *Neuropsychologia* 24:169–180.

Borod, J., Koff, E., Perlman-Lorch, M., Nicholas, M., and Welkowitz, J. (1988). Emotional and nonemotional facial behavior in patients with unilateral brain damage. *J. Neurol. Neurosurg. Psychiatry* 51:826–832.

Bowers, D., and Heilman, K. M. (1984). Dissociation of affective and nonaffective faces: a case study. *J. Clin. Neuropsychol.* 6:367–379.

Bowers, D., Bauer, R. M., Coslett, H. B., and Heilman, K. M. (1985). Processing of faces by patients with unilateral hemispheric lesions. I. Dissociation between judgments of facial affect and facial identity. *Brain Cognition* 4:258–272.

Bowers, D., Coslett, H. B., Bauer, R. M., Speedie, L. J., and Heilman, K. M. (1987). Comprehension of emotional prosody following unilateral hemispheric lesions: processing defect vs. distraction defect. *Neuropsychologia* 25:317–328.

Brady, J. V., and Nauta, W. J. (1955). Subcortical mechanisms in control of behavior. *J. Comp. Physiol. Psychol.* 48:412–420.

Brandt, J., Seidman, L. J., and Kohl, D. (1985). Personality characteristics of epileptic patients: a controlled study of generalized and temporal lobe cases. *J. Clin. Exp. Neuropsychol.* 7:25–38.

Broca, P. (1878). Anatomie comparee des enconvolutions cerebrales: le grand lobe limbique et al scissure limbique dans la seire des mammiferes. *Rev. Antrop.* 1:385–498.

Brownell, H., Michel, D., Powelson, J., and Gardner, H. (1983). Surprise but not coherence: sensitivity to verbal humor in right hemisphere patients. *Brain Lang.* 18:20–27.

Brownell, H., Potter, H., and Birhle, A. (1986). Inferences deficits in right brain damaged patients. *Brain Lang.* 27:310–321.

Bruyn, G. W., and Gaither, J. C. (1969). The opercular syndrome. In *Handbook of Clinical Neurology*, Vol. 1, P. J. Vincken and G. W. Bruyn (eds.). Amsterdam: North-Holland.

Bryson, S., McLaren, J., Wadden, N., and Maclean, M. (1991). Differential asymmetries for positive and negative emotions: hemisphere or stimulus effects. *Cortex* 27:359–365.

Buck, R., and Duffy, R. J. (1980). Nonverbal communication of affect in brain damaged patients. *Cortex* 16:351–362.

Buck, R. (1990). Using FACS versus communication scores to measure spontaneous facial expression of emotion in brain damaged patients. *Cortex* 26:275–280.

Caltagirone, C., Ekman, P., Friesen, W., Gainotti, G., Mammucari, A., Pizzamiglio, L., and Zoccolatti, P. (1989). Posed emotional facial expressions in brain damaged patients. *Cortex* 25:653–663.

Campbell, R. (1978). Asymmetries in interpreting and expressing a posed facial expression. *Cortex* 14:327–342.

Cannon, W. B. (1927). The James-Lange theory of emotion: a critical examination and an alternative theory. *Am. J. Psychol.* 39:106–124.

Celesia, G. G., and Wanamaker, W. M. (1972). Psychiatric disturbances in Parkinson's disease. *Dis. Nerv. System* 33:577–583.

Cicone, M., Waper, W., and Gardner, H. (1980). Sensitivity to emotional expressions and situation in organic patients. *Cortex* 16:145–158.

Cimino, C. R., Verfaellie, M., Bowers, D., and Heilman, K. M. (1991). Autobiographical memory with influence of right hemisphere damage on emotionality and specificity. *Brain Cognition* 15:106–118.

Cogen, P. H., Antunes, J. L., and Correll, J. W. (1979). Reproductive function in temporal lobe epilepsy: the effect of temporal lobe lobectomy. *Surg. Neurol.* 12:243–246.

Corsellis, J.A.N., Goldberg, G. J., and Norton, A. R. (1968). Limbic encephalitis and its association with carcinoma. *Brain* 91:481–496.

Coslett, H. B., Brasher, H. R., and Heilman, K. M. (1984). Pure word deafness after bilateral primary auditory cortex infarcts. *Neurology* 34:347–352.

Critchley, M. (1953). *The Parietal Lobes*. London: E. Arnold.

Currie, S., Heathfield, K.W.G., Henson, R. A., and Scott, D. F. (1971). Clinical course and prognosis of temporal lobe epilepsy: a survey of 666 patients. *Brain* 94:173–190.

Currier, R. D., Little, S. C., Suess, J. F., and Andy, O. J. (1971). Sexual seizures. *Arch. Neurol.* 25:260–264.

Daly, D. (1958). Ictal affect. *Am. J. Psychiatry* 115:97–108.

Daly, D. D., and Mulder, D. W. (1957). Gelastic epilepsy. *Neurology* 7:189–192.

Davidson, R. J., Horowitz, M. E., Schwartz, G. E., and Goodman, D. M. (1981). Lateral differences in the latency between finger tapping and heart beat. *Psychophysiology* 18:36–41.

Davidson, R. J., Schwartz, G. E., Saron, C., Bennett, J., and Goldman, D. J. (1979). Frontal versus parietal EEG asymmetry during positive and negative affect. *Psychophysiology* 16:202–203.

DeKosky, S., Heilman, K. M., Bowers, D., and Valenstein, E. (1980). Recognition and discrimination of emotional faces and pictures. *Brain Lang.* 9:206–214.

Delgade-Escueta, A. V., Mattson, R. H., King, L., Goldensohn, E. S., Spiegel, H., Madsen, J., Crandall, P., Dreifus, F., and Porter, R. J. (1981). The nature of aggression during epileptic seizures. *N. Engl. J. Med.* 305:711–716.

Denny-Brown, D., Meyer, J. S., and Horenstein, S. (1952). The significance of perceptual rivalry resulting from parietal lesions. *Brain* 75:434–471.

Darwin, C. (1872). *The Expression of Emotion in Man and Animals*. London: John Murray.

DiGuisto, E. L., and King, M. G. (1972). Chemical sympathectomy and avoidance learning. *Natl. J. Comp. Physiol. Psychol.* 81:491–500.

Duda, P., and Brown, J. (1984). Lateral asymmetry of positive and negative emotions. *Cortex* 20:253–261.

Ekman, P., Sorenson, E. R., and Friesen, W. V. (1969). Pancultural elements in facial displays of emotions. *Science* 164:86–88.

Ekman, P., and Friesen, W. V. (1978). *Facial Action Coding System*. Palo Alto, CA: Consulting Psychologists Press.

Etcoff, N. (1984). Perceptual and conceptual organization of facial emotions. *Brain Cognition* 3:385–412.

Flor-Henry, P. (1969). Psychosis and temporal lobe epilepsy: a controlled investigation. *Epilepsia* 10:363–395.

Folstein, S. E., Folstein, M. F., and McHugh, P. R. (1979). Psychiatric syndromes in Huntington's disease. *Adv. Neurol.* 23:281–289.

Fox, N. A., and Davidson, R. J. (1984). Hemispheric substrates for affect: a developmental model. In *The Psychobiology of Affective Development*, N. A. Fox and R. J. Davidson (eds.). Hillsdale, N.J.: Erlbaum.

Fried, I., Mateer, C., Ojemann, G., Wohns, R., and Fedio, P. (1982). Organization of visuospatial functions in human cortex. *Brain 105*:349–371.

Gainotti, G. (1972). Emotional behavior and hemispheric side of lesion. *Cortex 8*:41–55.

Gardner, H., Ling, P. K., Flam, I., and Silverman, J. (1975). Comprehension and appreciation of humorous material following brain damage. *Brain 98*:399–412.

Gascon, G. G., and Lombroso, C. T. (1971). Epileptic (gelastic) laughter. *Epilepsia 12*:63–76.

Gasparrini, W. G., Spatz, P., Heilman, K. M., and Coolidge, F. L. (1978). Hemispheric asymmetries of affective processing as determined by the Minnesota multiphasic personality inventory. *J. Neurol. Neurosurg. Psychiatry 41*:470–473.

Gaustaut, H., and Colomb, H. (1954). Etude du comportment sexuel chez les ipieptiques psychomoteurs. *Ann. Med. Psychol. (Paris) 112*:659–696.

Geschwind, N. (1975). The clinical setting of aggression in temporal lobe epilepsy. In *The Neurobiology of Violence*, W. S. Fields and W. H. Sweets (eds.). St. Louis: Warren H. Green.

Geschwind, N. (1977). Behavioral changes in temporal lobe epilepsy. *Arch. Neurol. 34*:453.

Gloor, P. (1972). Temporal lobe epilepsy. In *Advances in Behavioral Biology*, Vol. 2, B. Eleftheriou (ed.). New York: Plenum, pp. 423–427.

Goldstein, K. (1948). *Language and Language Disturbances*. New York: Grune and Stratton.

Graves, R., Landis, T., and Goodglass, H. (1981). Laterality and sex differences for visual recognition of emotional and nonemotional words. *Neuropsychologia 19*:95–102.

Guerrant, J., Anderson, W. W., Fischer, A., Weinstein, M. R., Janos, R. M. and Deskins, A. (1962). *Personality in Epilepsy*. Springfield, Ill.: Charles C. Thomas.

Haggard, M. P., and Parkinson, A. M. (1971). Stimulus and task factors as determinants of ear advantages. *Quart. J. Exp. Psychol. 23*:168–177.

Hantas, M., Katkin, E. S., and Blasovich, J. (1982). Relationship between heartbeat discrimination and subjective experience of affective state. *Psychophysiology 19*:563.

Hantas, M., Katkin, E. S., and Reed, S. D. (1984). Heartbeat discrimination training and cerebral lateralization. *Psychophysiology 21*:274–278.

Hawton, K., Fagg, J., and Marsack, P. (1980). Association between epilepsy and attempted suicide. *J. Neurol. Neurosurg. Psychiatry 43*:168–170.

Heathfield, K.W.G. (1967). Huntington's chorea. *Brain 90*:203–232.

Hécaen, H., Ajuriagurra, J., and de Massonet, J. (1951). Les troubles visuoconstuctifs par lesion parieto-occipitale droit. *Encephale 40*:122–179.

Heilman, K. M. (1979). Neglect and related syndromes. In *Clinical Neuropsychology*, K. M. Heilman and E. Valenstein (eds.). New York: Oxford University Press.

Heilman, K. M., Bowers, D., Rasbury, W., and Ray, R. (1977). Ear asymmetries on a selective attention task. *Brain Lang. 4*:390–395.

Heilman, K. M., Schwartz, H., and Watson, R. T. (1978). Hypoarousal in patients with the neglect syndrome and emotional indifference. *Neurology 28*:229–232.

Heilman, K. M., Bowers, D., Speedie, L., and Coslett, B. (1984). Comprehension of affective and nonaffective speech. *Neurology 34*:917–921.

Heilman, K. M., Scholes, R., and Watson, R. T. (1975). Auditory affective agnosia: disturbed comprehension of affective speech. *J. Neurol. Neurosurg. Psychiatry 38*:69–72.

Heller, W. (1990). The neuropsychology of emotion: developmental and complications for psychopathology. In *Psychological and Biological Approaches to Emotion*, N. L. Stein, B. Leventhal, and T. Trebasso (eds.). Hillsdale, N.J.: Lawrence Erlbaum.

Heller, W., and Levy, J. (1981). Perception and expression of emotion in right handers and left handers. *Neuropsychologia 19*:263–272.

Hermann, B. P., and Chhabria, S. (1980). Interictal psychopathology in patients with ictal fear: examples of sensory-limbic hyperconnection? *Arch. Neurol. 37*:667–668.

Hermann, B. P., Dikmen, S., and Wilensky, A. (1982). Increased psychopathology associated with multiple seizure types: fact or artifact? *Epilepsia* 23:587–596.

Hermann, B. P., and Riel, P. (1981). Interictal personality and behavioral traits in temporal lobe and generalized epilepsy. *Cortex* 17:125–128.

Herzog, A. G., Russell, V., Vaitukatis, J. L., and Geschwind, N. (1982). Neuroendocrine dysfunction in temporal lobe epilepsy. *Arch Neurol.* 39:133–135.

Hohmann, G. (1966). Some effects of spinal cord lesions on experimental emotional feelings. *Psychophysiology* 3:143–156.

Hooshmand, H., and Brawley, B. W. (1969). Temporal lobe seizures and exhibitionism. *Neurology* 19:119–124.

House, A., Dennis, M., Warlow, C., Hawton, K., and Molyneux, A. (1990). Mood disorders after stroke and their relation to lesion location. *Brain* 113:1113–1129.

Hughlings Jackson, J. (1932) *Selected Writings of John Hughlings Jackson*, J. Taylor (ed.). London: Hodder and Stoughton.

Huntington, G. W. (1872). On chorea. *Med. Surg. Rep.* 26:317–321.

Isaacson, R. L. (1982). *The Limbic System*, 2nd ed. New York: Plenum Press.

Iwata, J., LeDoux, J. E., Meeley, M. P., Arneric, S., and Reis, D. J. (1986). Intrinsic neurons in the amygdaloid field projected to by the medial geniculate body mediate emotional responses conditioned to acoustic stimuli. *Brain Res.* 383:195–214.

Izard, C. E. (1977). *Human Emotions*. New York: Plenum Press.

James, W. (1890, reprinted 1950). *The Principles of Psychology*, Vol. 2. New York: Dover Publications.

Katkin, E. S., Morrell, M. A., Goldband, S., Bernstein, G. L., and Wise, J. A. (1982). Individual differences in heartbeat discrimination. *Psychophysiology* 19:160–166.

Kent, J., Borod, J. C., Koff, E., Welkowitz, J., and Alpert, M. (1988). Posed facial emotional expression in brain-damaged patients. *International Journal of Neuroscience* 43:81–87.

Kimura, D. (1967). Functional asymmetry of the brain in dichotic listening. *Cortex* 3:163–178.

Klüver, H., and Bucy, P. C. (1937). "Psychic blindness" and other symptoms following bilateral temporal lobe lobectomy in rhesus monkeys. *Am. J. Physiol.* 119:352–353.

Kolb, B., and Milner, B. (1981). Observations on spontaneous facial expression after focal cerebral excisions and after intracarotid injection of sodium amytal. *Neuropsychologia* 19:505–514.

Laird, J. D. (1974). Self-attribution of emotion: the effects of expressive behavior on the quality of emotional experience. *J. Pers. Soc. Psychol.* 29:475–486.

Landis, T., Graves, R., and Goodglass, H. (1982). Aphasic reading and writing: possible evidence for right hemisphere participation. *Cortex* 18:105–122.

Leonard, C., Rolls, E., and Wilson, A. (1985). Neurons in the amygdala of the monkey with responses selective for faces. *Behav. Brain Res.* 15:159–176.

Ley, R., and Bryden, M. (1979). Hemispheric differences in recognizing faces and emotions. *Brain and Language* 1:127–138.

Luria, A. R., and Simernitskaya, E. G. (1977). Interhemispheric relations and the functions of the minor hemisphere. *Neuropsychologia* 15:175–178.

MacLean, P. D. (1952). Some psychiatric implications of physiological studies of the frontotemporal portion of the limbic system (visceral brain). *EEG Clin. Neurophysiol.* 4:407–418.

Mammucari, A., Caltagirone, C., Ekman, P., Friesen, W., Gainotti, G., Pizzamiglio, L., and Zoccolatti, P. (1988). Spontaneous facial expression of emotions in brain damaged patients. *Cortex* 24:521–533.

Mandel, M., Tandon, S., and Asthana, H. (1991). Right brain damage impairs recognition of negative emotions. *Cortex* 27:247–253.

Marañon, G. (1924). Contribution a l'entude de l'action emotive de l'adrenaline. *Rev. Fr. Endo-crinol.* 2:301–325.

Mark, V. H., and Ervin, F. R. (1970). *Violence and the Brain.* New York: Harper and Row.

Mark, V. H., Sween, W. H., and Ervin, F. R. (1972). The effect of amygdalectomy on violent behavior in patients with temporal lobe epilepsy. In *Psychosurgery*, E. Hitchcock, L. Laitinen, and K. Vernet (eds.). Springfield, Ill.: Charles C. Thomas.

Marsh, G. G., and Markham, C. H. (1973). Does levodopa alter depression and psychopathology in parkinsonism patients? *J. Neurol. Neurosurg. Psychiatry* 36:935.

Mayeux, R. (1983). Emotional changes associated with basal ganglia disorders. In *Neuropsychology of Human Emotion*, K. M. Heilman and P. Satz (eds.). New York: Guilford Press.

Mayeux, R., Stern, Y., Rosen, J., and Leventhal, J. (1981). Depression, intellectual impairment, and Parkinson disease. *Neurology 31*:645–650.

McDonald, S., and Wales, R. (1986). An investigation of the ability to process inferences in language following right hemisphere brain damage. *Brain Lang.* 29:68.

McIntyre, M., Pritchard, P. B., and Lombroso, C. T. (1976). Left and right temporal lobe epileptics: a controlled investigation of some psychological differences. *Epilepsia 17*:377–386.

McLachlan, R. S., and Blume, W. T. (1980). Isolated fear in complex partial status epilepticus. *Ann. Neurol.* 8:639–641.

McLaren, J., and Bryson, S. (1987). Hemispheric asymmetry in the perception of emotional and neutral faces. *Cortex 23*:645–654.

Milner, B. (1974). Hemispheric specialization: Scope and limits. In *The Neurosciences: Third Study Program*, F. O. Schmitt and F. G. Worden (eds.).Cambridge, Mass.: MIT Press.

Mindham, H. S. (1970). Psychiatric syndromes in Parkinsonism. *J. Neurol. Neurosurg. Psychiatry 30*:188–191.

Monrad-Krohn, G. (1947). The prosodic quality of speech and its disorders. *Acta Psychol. Scand.* 22:225–265.

Moreno, C. R., Borod, J., Welkowitz, J., and Alpert, M. (1990). Lateralization for the expression and perception of facial emotion as a function of age. *Neuropsychologia 28*:119–209.

Morris, M., Bowers, D., Verfaellie, M., Blonder, L., Cimino, C., Bauer, R., and Heilman, K. (1992). Lexical denotation and connotation in right and left hemisphere damaged patients. (Abstract). *J. Clin. Exp. Neuropsychol. 14*:105.

Morris, M. K., Bradley, M., Bowers, D., Lang, P. J., and Heilman, K. M. (1991). Valence-specific hypoarousal following right temporal lobectomy. Presented at the 19th Annual Meeting of the International Neuropsychology Society, San Antonio.

Morrow, L., Vrtunski, P. B., Kim, Y., and Boller, F. (1981). Arousal responses to emotional stimuli and laterality of lesions. *Neuropsychologia 19*:65–71.

Mungas, D. (1982). Interictal behavior abnormality in temporal lobe epilepsy: a specific syndrome or nonspecific psychopathology? *Arch. Gen. Psychiatry 39*:108–111.

Nielsen, H., and Kristensen, O. (1981). Personality correlates of sphenoidal EEG foci in temporal lobe epilepsy. *Acta Neurol. Scand.* 64:289–300.

Offen, M. L., Davidoff, R. A., Troost, B. T., and Richey, E. T. (1976). Dacrystic epilepsy. *J. Neurol. Neurosurg. Psychiatry 39*:829–834.

Olds, J. (1958). Self-stimulation of the brain. *Science 127*:315–324.

Papez, J. W. (1937). A proposed mechanism of emotion. *Arch. Neurol Psychiatry 38*:725–743.

Parkinson, J. (1938). An essay of the shaking palsy, 1817. *Med. Classics 2*:964–997.

Paul, H. (1909). *Principien der Sprachgeschichte*, 4th ed. Niemeyer.

Pincus, J. H. (1980). Can violence be a manifestation of epilepsy? *Neurology 30*:304–307.

Poeck, K. (1969). Pathophysiology of emotional disorders associated with brain damage. In *Handbook of Neurology*, Vol. 3, P. J. Vinken and G. W. Bruyn (eds.). New York: Elsevier.

Poeck, K., and Pilleri, G. (1961). Wutverhalten and pathologischer Schlaf bei Tumor dervor-
deren Mitellinie. *Arch. Psychiatr. Nervenkr. 201*:593–604.

Pontius, A. A., and Yudowitz, B. S. (1980). Frontal lobe system dysfunction in some criminal
actions as shown in the Narratines text. *J. Nerv. Ment. Dis. 168*:111–117.

Pritchard, P. B. (1980). Hyposexuality: a complication of complex partial epilepsy. *Trans. Am.
Neurol. Assoc. 105*:193–195.

Pritchard, P. B., Wannamaker, B. B., Sagel, J., and deVillier, C. (1981). Post-ictal hyperprolactinemia in complex partial epilepsy. *Ann. Neurol. 10*:81–82.

Ramón y Cajal, S. (1965). *Studies on the Cerebral Cortex (Limbic Structures)*, L. M. Kraft
(trans.). London: Lloyd-Luke.

Rapscak, S., Kasniak, A., and Rubins, A. (1989). Anomia for facial expressions: evidence for a
category specific visual verbal disconnection. *Neuropsychologia 27*:1031–1041.

Remillard, G. M., Andermann, F., Testa, G. F., Gloor, P., Aube, M., Martin, J. B., Feindel, W.,
Guberman, A., and Simpson, C. (1983). Sexual manifestations predominate in a woman
with temporal lobe epilepsy: a finding suggesting sexual dimorphism in the human brain.
*Neurology 33*:3–30.

Reuter-Lorenz, P., and Davidson, R. (1981). Differential contributions of the two cerebral
hemispheres for perception of happy and sad faces. *Neuropsychologia 19*:609–614.

Reuterskiold, C. (1991). The effects of emotionality on auditory comprehension in aphasia.
*Cortex 27*:595–604.

Richardson, C., Bowers, D., Eyeler, L., and Heilman, K. (1992). Asymmetrical control of facial
emotional expression depends on the means of elicitation. Presented at the meeting of the
International Neuropsychology Society, San Diego.

Robertson, M. M., Trimble, M. R., and Townsend, H. R. (1987). Phenomenology of depression
in epilepsy. *Epilepsia 28*:364–72.

Robins, A. H. (1976). Depression in patients with Parkinsonism. *Br. J. Psychol. 128*:141–
145.

Robinson, R. G., and Sztela, B. (1981). Mood change following left hemisphere brain injury.
*Ann. Neurol. 9*:447–453.

Rodin, E. A. (1973). Psychomotor epilepsy and aggressive behavior. *Arch. Gen. Psychiatry
28*:210–213.

Roeltgen, D. P., Sevush, S., and Heilman, K. M. (1983). Ponological agraphia: writing by the
lexical semantic route. *Neurology 33*:755–765.

Ross, E. D. (1981). The aprosodias: functional-anatomic organization of the affective components of language in the right hemisphere. *Ann. Neurol. 38*:561–589.

Ross, E. D., and Mesulam, M. M. (1979). Dominant language functions of the right hemisphere? Prosody and emotional gesturing. *Arch. Neurol. 36*:144–148.

Rossi, G. S., and Rodadini, G. (1967). Experimental analysis of cerebral dominance in man. In
*Brain Mechanisms Underlying Speech and Language*, C. Millikan and F. L. Darley
(eds.). New York: Grune & Stratton.

Sackeim, H., Gur, R., and Saucy, M. (1978). Emotions are expressed more intensely on the left
side of the face. *Science 202*:434–436.

Sackeim, H. A., Greenberg, M. S., Weiman, A. L., Gur, R. C., Hungerbuhler, J. P., and Geschwind, N. (1982). Hemispheric asymmetry in the expression of positive and negative
emotion: neurologic evidence. *Arch. Neurol. 39*:210–218.

Schacter, S., and Singer, J. E. (1962). Cognitive, social, and physiological determinants of emotional state. *Psychol. Rev. 69*:379–399.

Schlanger, B. B., Schlanger, P., and Gerstmann, L. J. (1976). The perception of emotionally
toned sentences by right-hemisphere damaged and aphasic subjects. *Brain Lang. 3*:396–
403.

Schrandt, N. J., Tranel, D., and Damasio, H. (1989). The effects of total cerebral lesions on skin conductance response to signal stimuli. *Neurology 39 (Suppl.) 1*:223.

Scott, S., Caird, B. I., and Williams, B. (1984). Evidence of apparent sensory speech disorder in Parkinson's disease. *J. Neurol. Neurosurg. Psychiatry 47*:840–843.

Slater, E., and Beard, A. W. (1963). The schizophrenia-like psychoses of epilepsy. *Br. J. Psychiatry 109*:95–150.

Speedie, L. J., Broke, N., Folstein, S. E., Bowers, D., and Heilman, K. M. (1990). Comprehension of prosody in Huntington's disease. *J. Neurol. Neurosurg. Psychiatry 53*:607–610.

Speedie, L. J., Coslett, H. B., and Heilman, K. M. (1984). Repetition of affective prosody in mixed transcortical aphasia. *Arch. Neurol. 41*:268–270.

Spencer, S. S., Spencer, D. D., Williamson, P. D., and Mattson, R. H. (1983). Sexual automatisms in complex parital seizures. *Neurology 33*:527–533.

Starkstein, S., and Robinson, R. (1990). Depression following cerebrovascular lesions. *Semin. Neurol. 10*:247

Starkstein, S. E., Robinson, R. G., and Price, T. R. (1987). Comparison of cortical and subcortical lesions in the production of poststroke mood disorders. *Brain 110*:1045–1059.

Stevens, J. R. (1966). Psychiatric implications of psychomotor epilepsy. *Arch. Gen. Psychiatry 14*:461–471.

Stevens, J. R., and Hermann, B. P. (1981). Temporal lobe epilepsy, psychopathology and violence: the state of evidence. *Neurology 31*:1127–1132.

Strauss, E. (1983). Perception of emotional words. *Neuropsychologia 21*:99–103.

Strauss, E. (1989). Ictal and interictal manifestations of emotions in epilepsy. In *Handbook of Neuropsychology*, Vol. 3, F. Boller and J. Grafman (eds.). Amsterdam: Elsevier, pp. 315–344.

Strauss, E., Risser, A., and Jones, M. W. (1982). Fear responses in patients with epilepsy. *Neurology 39*:626–630.

Suberi, M., and McKeever, W. (1977). Differential right hemisphere memory storage of emotional and nonemotional faces. *Neuropsychologia 15*:757–768.

Taylor, D. C. (1969). Aggression and epilepsy. *J. Psychiatr. Res. 13*:229–236.

Tomkins, S. S. (1962). *Affect, Imagery, Consciousness*, Vol. 1, *The Positive Affect*. New York: Springer.

Tomkins, S. S. (1963). *Affect, Imagery, Consciousness*, Vol. 2, *The Negative Affects*. New York: Springer.

Terzian, H. (1964). Behavioral and EEG effects of intracarotid sodium amytal injections. *Acta Neurochirugica* (Vienna) *12*:230–240.

Trieman, D. M. (1991). *Psychobiology of Ictal Aggression*, D. Smith, D. Treiman, and M. Trimble (eds.). New York: Raven Press, p. 341.

Trieman, D. M., and Delgado-Escueta, A. V. (1983). Violence and epilepsy: a critical review. In *Recent Advances in Epilepsy*, Vol. 1, T. A. Pedley and B. S. Meldrum (eds.). London: Churchill Livingstone, pp. 179–209.

Tucker, D. M. (1981). Lateral brain function, emotion and conceptualization. *Psychol. Bull. 89*:19–46.

Tucker, D. M., Watson, R. T., and Heilman, K. M. (1977). Affective discrimination and evocation in patients with right parietal disease. *Neurology 17*:947–950.

Tucker, D. M., and Williamson, P. A. (1984). Asymmetric neural control in human self-regulation. *Psychol. Rev. 91*:185–215.

Ursin, H. (1960). The temporal lobe substrate of fear and anger. *Acta Psychiatr. Scand. 35*:378–396.

Valenstein, E. S. (1973). *Brain Control: A Critical Examination of Brain Stimulation and Psychosurgery*. New York: Wiley-Interscience.

Wapner, W., Harby, S., and Gardner, H. (1981). The role of the right hemisphere in the apprehension of complex linguistic stimuli. *Brain Cognition* 14:15–33.

Warburton, J. W. (1967). Depressive symptoms in Parkinson patients referred for thalamotomy. *J. Neurol. Neurosurg. Psychiatry* 30:368–370.

Waxman, S. G., and Geschwind, N. (1974). Hypergraphia in temporal lobe epilepsy. *Neurology* 24:629–636.

Wechsler, A. F. (1973). The effect of organic brain disease on recall of emotionally charged versus neutral narrative texts. *Neurology* 23:130–135.

Weddell, R., Miller, R., and Trevarthen, C. (1990). Voluntary emotional facial expressions in patients with focal cerebral lesions. *Neuropsychologia* 28:49–60.

Weintraub, S., Mesulam, M. M., and Kramer, L. (1981). Disturbances in prosody. *Arch. Neurol.* 38:742–744.

Wieser, H. G. (1986). Selective amygdalohippocampectomy: indication, investigative technique and results. *Adv. Techn. Stand. Neurosurg.* 13:39–133.

Williams, D. (1956). The structure of emotions reflected in epileptic experiences. *Brain* 79:29–67.

Williams, D. (1969). Neural factors related to habitual aggression. *Brain* 92:503–520.

Wilson, S.A.K. (1924). Some problems in neurology. II: Pathological laughing and crying. *J. Neurol. Psychopathol.* 16:299–333.

Winnar, E., and Gardner, H. (1977). The comprehension of metaphor in brain damaged patients. *Brain* 100:711–729.

Woods, J. W. (1956). Taming of the wild in Norway rat by rhinocephalic lesions. *Nature* 170:869.

Yakovlev, P. I. (1948). Motility, behavior and the brain: stereodynamic organization and neural coordinates in behavior. *J. Nerv. Ment. Dis.* 107:313–335.

Yokoyama, K., Jennings, R., Ackles, P., Hood, P., and Boller, F. (1987). Lack of heart rate changes during an attention-demanding task after right hemisphere lesions. *Neurology* 37:624–630.

Zeman, W., and King, F. A. (1958). Tumors of the septum pellucidum and adjacent structures with abnormal affective behavior: an anterior midline structure syndrome. *J. Nerv. Ment. Dis.* 127:490–502.

# 14
# The Neuropsychology of Schizophrenia

CHRISTOPHER RANDOLPH, TERRY E. GOLDBERG, AND DANIEL R. WEINBERGER

If it should be confirmed that the disease attacks by preference the frontal areas of the brain, the central convolutions and the temporal lobes, this distribution would in a certain measure agree with our present views about the site of the psychic mechanisms which are principally injured by the disease.

Kraepelin (1913)

Despite Kraepelin's anatomical speculations, neuropathologists throughout this century have met with a distinct lack of success in locating the schizophrenic "lesion." Indeed, the numerous claims and counterclaims that characterized the anatomic research on schizophrenia during the first half of this century led to its being called the "graveyard of neuropathology." The ascendancy of psychodynamic theories, in conjunction with the failure to identify a distinctive neuropathology, resulted in a shift away from brain-based explanations for the etiology of schizophrenia. This trend led to a greater emphasis on descriptive psychopathology than neuropsychological deficits.

Over the past 15 years, however, evidence from neuropsychological, neuropathological, and neuroimaging studies has revived interest in schizophrenia as a neuropsychiatric disease with a putatively identifiable neuropathophysiology. We will review this evidence with a focus on the neuropsychological literature. The first section of the chapter provides a brief overview of the clinical phenomenology and epidemiology of schizophrenia. The second section reviews the results of standardized neuropsychological testing ,and the third section discusses experimental neuropsychological approaches to "mapping" dysfunctional systems in schizophrenia. The final section will attempt a synthesis of these data, arriving at some conclusions which suggest that Kraepelin's early clinical-pathological formulation was remarkably prescient with respect to currently evolving hypotheses of the neuropsychology of schizophrenia.

499

## DIAGNOSIS, EPIDEMIOLOGY, AND CLINICAL PHENOMENOLOGY

The essential features of schizophrenia are the presence of bizarre delusions and/or complex hallucinations, disturbances of the content and form of thought, and deterioration from a previous level of functioning. These features must not be attributable to a diagnosable neurological or other psychiatric disorder. The DSM III-R (American Psychiatric Association, 1987) requires that at least some of these symptoms be present continuously for six months to establish a diagnosis of schizophrenia.

The incidence of schizophrenia in the United States and Europe has been estimated at 0.3–0.6/1000, with a prevalence between 0.25% and 1.0% (Hare, 1987). There is minimal geographic variability in prevalence (Torrey, 1980). Age of onset is most common in the third decade, and is rare prior to the age of 10 or after 40. Males tend to have an earlier age of onset than females (Stromgren, 1987). Incidence is increased among individuals of lower socioeconomic status in urban environs (Saugstad, 1989). The cause/effect relationship underlying this observation is unclear; increased incidence of schizophrenia in lower socioeconomic levels may be attributable to a social "downward drift" phenomenon, or to increased environmental stress (Dohrenwend and Dohrenwend, 1974). Schizophrenic patients have higher mortality rates from a variety of illnesses (Allebeck, 1989) as well as increased suicide rates (Tsuang, 1978). Men and women are at equal risk for schizophrenia. Relatives of probands with schizophrenia, even the biologic relatives who were adopted at birth, are at significantly greater risk for the development of schizophrenia, strongly suggesting a genetic influence on susceptibility for this disorder (Kendler et al., 1985; Kety, 1988). The economic cost of schizophrenia is enormous; schizophrenics occupy 25% of all the hospital beds in the United States (Davies and Drummond, 1990). The loss of productivity is also substantial, as disease onset is typically in early adulthood and often consists of a disabling, chronic course. The total annual cost of schizophrenia in the United States, including direct and indirect costs, has been estimated at approximately 50 billion dollars (Torrey, 1988).

A number of attempts have been made to subtype schizophrenia. All of these rest on purely phenomenological grounds. The DSM III-R recognizes five subtypes: disorganized (previously hebephrenic), catatonic, paranoid, undifferentiated, and residual. The utility of this subtyping scheme with respect to treatment or prognosis has been limited, at best, and family studies do not suggest a genetic determination for subtype manifestation (Kendler et al., 1988).

Recently, it has been popular to divide schizophrenic patients into groups on the basis of "positive" and "negative" symptoms. The distinction between positive symptoms, which include hallucinations, delusions, and disordered thought processes, and negative symptoms such as flattened affect, cognitive impairment, and social withdrawal is not new, having been appreciated by both Kraepelin (1913) and Bleuler (1911). In fact, this distinction was perhaps first made by Hughlings Jackson (1894), who viewed positive symptoms as release phenomena, or "evolution" of intact brain systems, whereas negative symptoms were the direct result of brain "dissolution," or degeneration. Crow (1980) was the first, however, to propose that this distinction could form the basis of a clinical typology, describing syndrome categories that he called type I and type II. Crow suggested that type I patients have prominent positive symptomatology, normal brain structure, and relatively good response to treatment. In type II schizophrenia, negative symptoms dominate the clinical picture, cognitive function is impaired, structural brain abnormalities (e.g., enlarged cerebral ventricles) are more likely to be observed on in vivo scans, and there is a poorer response to treatment.

Attempts to validate this typology have met with limited success. Establishing criteria for reliably classifying patients into these two groups has proved to be problematic (Andreasen et al., 1990), which immediately limits the utility of this distinction. The inadequacy of a dichotomous classification scheme is also evident from the results of recent factor analytic studies of symptomatology in schizophrenia, which suggest that more than two factors are necessary to account for symptom variance in this disorder (Arndt et al., 1991; Bilder et al., 1985; Liddle, 1987). Although there have been reports supporting the hypothesis that patients with more negative symptoms have larger cerebral ventricles than those with predominantly positive symptoms, more recent studies have been unable to replicate these findings, and a few investigators have reported the opposite relationship (see Marks and Luchins, 1990, for a review). The stability of the positive/negative classification over time is still unclear, and the utility of this distinction in predicting neuroleptic response has been reported to be poor (Kay and Singh, 1989). In general, the only consistent findings in the effort to establish the validity of the positive/negative distinction are that patients with more negative symptoms tend to exhibit a greater degree of cognitive impairment, poorer premorbid function, and lower educational achievement (e.g., Andreasen et al., 1990; Kay et al., 1986). Since negative symptoms by definition include cognitive impairment, these findings to some extent represent a tautology. It has become increasingly evident from studies over the past decade that the clinical phenomenology of schizophrenia is too complex for a dichotomous classification scheme to be heuristically useful.

### Course of Illness

The natural history of schizophrenia is still undergoing investigation. Kraepelin established the notion of a progressively deteriorating course with an ultimately poor outcome as typical for this disease. Although subsequent outcome studies are often difficult to interpret because of differences in diagnostic criteria, sample selection, and outcome variables, they generally agree that Kraepelin's notion is *incorrect* for the majority of patients. Perhaps 25% of schizophrenic patients achieve apparent complete remission after one or more psychotic episodes, and while the course of illness is variable in chronic schizophrenia, most patients appear to function at a relatively static level after the first few years of their disease, with a small percentage exhibiting some improvement later in life (Ciompi, 1987). There is some evidence that the advent of neuroleptic treatment has increased the likelihood of an improved long-term course (Wyatt, 1991). Factors associated with a more favorable outcome include later age of onset, acute onset with obvious precipitating factors, good premorbid social and occupational history, and the absence of a family history of schizophrenia (McGlashan, 1986; Kay and Lindenmayer, 1987).

The development and course of cognitive deficits in patients with schizophrenia remain to be completely elucidated, but the bulk of evidence to date suggests that deficits appear at the time of onset of diagnostic schizophrenic symptoms, and remain relatively stable thereafter. There are a few older studies that have compared pre-morbid performance on military classification tests to performance following the onset of schizophrenia (Kingsley and Streuning, 1966; Lubin et al., 1962; Schwartzman and Douglas, 1962). These studies have concluded that the onset of schizophrenia is associated with the loss of what would be roughly equivalent to ten IQ points. This is consistent with the IQ discrepancy between monozygotic twins discordant for schizophrenia reported by Goldberg et al. (1990). There is also a larger series of studies that have compared the performance of schizophrenic patients shortly after initial hospitalization to their performance from 1 to 14 years later (e.g., Haywood and Modelis, 1963; Klonoff et al., 1970; Martin et al., 1977; Moran et al., 1962). Overall, these studies have reported generally stable neuropsychological status across test sessions. If anything, slight improvement is sometimes observed; this may be attributable to practice effects, but it does suggest at least that most patients do not experience progressive *decline* in neuropsychological function following the initial onset of their illness. The final type of evidence supporting this interpretation is derived from a cross-sectional analysis performed by Heaton and Drexler (1987). They reviewed 100 studies that contained neuropsychological data from patients in various age groups, and concluded that there was no increased incidence of impairments in the older patients when compared to the younger patients. This result again suggests that deficits are relatively stable across time. Although these various approaches have been consistent in their findings thus far, it must be noted that most of these studies are older, and it is still unclear whether these conclusions are equally true for all neuropsychological functions or are tenable over very long periods of time. Moreover, it remains to be determined what, if any, neuropsychological deficits predate the onset of psychotic symptomatology.


## STANDARDIZED NEUROPSYCHOLOGICAL TESTING

### *Evolution of Neuropsychological Approaches*

Although Kraepelin discussed impairments of attention and memory in his textbook on clinical psychiatry, he revised his impression of the memory impairment in schizophrenia from the 7th to the 8th edition of his text. In the 7th edition, he states that there is "a characteristic and progressive, but not profound, impairment of memory from the onset of the disease" (1902), and goes on to distinguish between retrograde memory, which he felt was intact, and anterograde memory, to which the above quotation refers. By the 8th edition, however, he revised this opinion, stating, "Memory is comparatively little disordered" (1913). In this, the final edition of his classic text, he attributed poor performance on experimental tests of memory to impairments of attention. The increasing influence of psychodynamic theory in the first half of this century compounded this trend to downplay the significance of cognitive deficits in schizophrenia. This resulted in the implicit assumption by many researchers that the deficits displayed on formal neuropsychological testing by schizophrenics were secondary to disordered thought processes or impaired motivation. Early application of neuropsychological testing in the assessment of psychiatric disorders, including schizophrenia, was therefore to "rule out" an organic basis for psychiatric symptomatology.

By the late 1970s, however, it had been repeatedly reported that patients with schizophrenia were the one psychiatric group that could not be reliably discriminated from brain-damaged populations on the basis of neuropsychological test scores (Goldstein, 1978; Heaton et al., 1978; Malec, 1978). This suggested the possibility of an underlying neuropathological process that was intrinsic to schizophrenia. Nevertheless, many researchers still questioned the role of motivational factors, thought disorder, medication effects, and institutionalization in the production of these deficits (e.g., Heaton et al., 1979). A variety of subsequent studies, however, failed to confirm a substantive role for any of these variables in the expression of neuropsychological deficits (vide infra), strengthening the interpretation that the deficits reflect "real" cerebral dysfunction.

The advent of in vivo imaging techniques for examining brain structure and function provided additional impetus to this view (Seidman, 1983). First, it became apparent from early CT studies that patients with schizophrenia had larger cerebral ventricles than normal controls (see Shelton and Weinberger, 1986, for a review). This finding was followed by a number of MRI studies, which have firmly established the presence of structural brain abnormalities in patients with schizophrenia (for a review see Zigun and Weinberger, 1992). While not invariably the case, a number of studies have also reported a correlation between ventricular size and the degree of impairment on neuropsychological testing, with larger ventricles being associated with poorer performance (e.g., Lawson et al., 1988). Impairment of cognitive functions in schizophrenia has also been associated with hypofrontality on functional brain imaging (Buchsbaum et al., 1990). Moreover, one form of cognitive impairment (i.e., poor performance on the Wisconsin Card Sorting Test) has been directly linked to impaired activation of prefrontal cortex in regional cerebral blood flow studies (Weinberger et al., 1988).

There is currently broad agreement in the field of schizophrenia research that schizophrenia is a brain disease that reliably results in some impairment of neuropsychological function. Perhaps the clearest evidence for this is derived from a series of studies on a group of monozygotic twins who were discordant for schizophrenia. The affected twins were found to have larger ventricles and smaller hippocampi (Suddath et al., 1990), perform more poorly on a variety of neuropsychological tests (Goldberg et al., 1990), and exhibit less task-specific regional cerebral blood flow activation in prefrontal cortex (Berman et al., in press) than their unaffected cotwin (see Fig. 14-1). The most compelling aspect of these data was that the differences between the twins on each of these measures was evident even when the affected twin's values *were well within the normal range.* This suggests that although the neuroanatomical, neurophysiological, and neuropsychological concomitants of schizophrenia may be subtle (and seemingly insignificant in some cases), they almost invariably represent a change from the baseline state.

One persistent controversy in the neuropsychology of schizophrenia is the notion that this disorder is characterized by a "generalized deficit," in which all neuropsy-

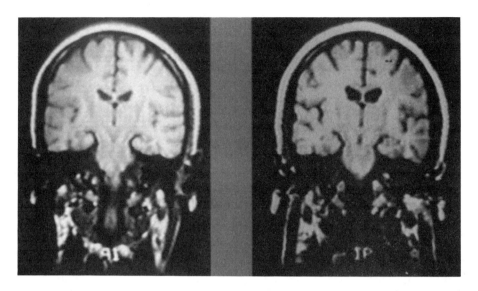

MONOZYGOTIC TWINS DISCORDANT FOR SCHIZOPHRENIA

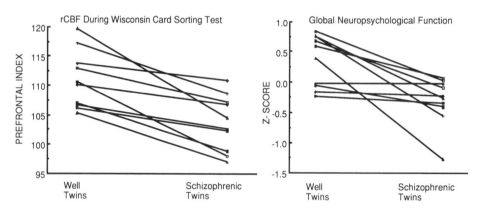

**Fig. 14-1.** This figure illustrates the relatively subtle changes in neuroanatomical, neurophysiological, and neuropsychological measures that were identified in studies of monozygotic twins discordant for schizophrenia. A coronal MRI slice depicts ventriculomegaly in a schizophrenic twin (right) that is apparent only in comparison to her well co-twin (left) (see Suddath et al., 1990). Affected twins also displayed consistent hypofrontality on an index of prefrontal cerebral blood flow during performance of the WCST (see Berman et al., in press). A global neuropsychological measure was computed by first transforming scores from a variety of tests to z-scores and then averaging the z-scores (see Goldberg et al., 1990, for tests administered).

chological functions are equally affected. This may be a holdover from the notion that the cognitive deficits in this disorder do not reflect real cerebral dysfunction, but are secondary to motivational defects or disordered thought processes. It is true that patients with schizophrenia usually do perform worse than controls across a wide variety of neuropsychological measures. On the other hand, this is also true of other neuropsychiatric disorders that result in significant compromise of cognitive function (e.g., Huntington's disease), and yet the generalized deficit notion is rarely (if ever) invoked in interpreting the neuropsychological performance of these patients. Such a conclusion regarding schizophrenia is premature and scientifically uninformative.

In a larger sense, the current state of the art in neuropsychology does not permit the derivation of a valid, empirically based differential deficit profile from standardized tests for any disorder (vide infra). As a result, a hypothetical profile can only be based on the consistency with which particular deficits are reported, in the context of clinical judgment as to the severity of these deficits. With this caveat in mind, we will review three areas of cognitive function which have been repeatedly implicated in studies of schizophrenia: attention, memory, and executive functions.

## Applications and Limitations of Neuropsychological Testing

### REVIEW OF THE CORE DEFICITS

*Attention.* That patients with schizophrenia exhibit deficits in attention is evident even from the most casual clinical contact with these patients, and was recognized as a central feature of the disorder by Kraepelin (1913). Attentional functions were also the focus of the early application of experimental psychology to the study of schizophrenia. In his tenure as chief of the Laboratory of Psychology at the National Institute of Mental Health during the 1950s and 1960s, David Shakow developed a seminal theory of segmental set, based on a series of reaction time experiments (Shakow, 1963, 1979). This was the notion that schizophrenics lack the capacity to perceive and respond to situations objectively, due to their inability to achieve a "major set." A major set, according to Shakow, includes receptivity to external stimuli, appropriate attentional adjustment to the environment, and the capacity to identify and inhibit irrelevant stimuli. He postulated that schizophrenia is characterized by "segmental set," in which response preparation is compromised due to an inappropriate focus on minor or irrelevant aspects of the stimulus array. Although this theory evolved from cognitive psychology perspective, a neuropsychological interpretation might conclude that the deficits identified by Shakow were indicative of an impairment of complex attentional functions.

This early experimental focus on attentional function in schizophrenia has been followed by a number of studies comparing schizophrenic patients and at-risk individuals to normal subjects on a variety of attentional measures. Unfortunately, attention is an ill-defined construct, subsuming a number of cognitive processes that overlap to varying degrees, and there is as yet no established consensus for the definition of these individual processes. Subsequently, the precise nature of the attentional defect in schizophrenia remains to be determined.

It seems likely, however, that this impairment will prove to be broad-based, given the number of paradigms in which schizophrenic patients have exhibited deficits. These include immediate serial recall tasks, span of apprehension, reaction time, dichotic listening, backward masking, and continuous performance tests. These tests involve short-term memory, sensory storage and readout, sustained attention, and selective attention.

Immediate serial recall simply involves repeating a string of numbers or digits in order. Schizophrenics have been reported to be worse than controls on these tasks with or without the presence of an additional distractor condition, indicating impairment of simple attentional/short-term memory functions (Oltmanns and Neale, 1975; Frame and Oltmanns, 1982). The span-of-apprehension task involves searching a tachistoscopically presented array of items for a particular target item. Schizophrenic patients perform more poorly than controls on this task as the size of the to-be-searched array increases, suggesting slowed processing from sensory storage (Davidson and Neale, 1974). Backward masking tasks involve perceptual identification of tachistoscopically presented stimuli, which are then "masked" with a another stimulus. Studies involving patients with schizophrenia have suggested that they require an abnormally long interval between the target stimulus and the mask in order to correctly identify the target (e.g., Braff and Saccuzzo, 1981). This again suggests an impairment in processing sensory information. Schizophrenic patients have also exhibited deficits on simple reaction time (RT) tasks in which subjects are required to make a button-press response to either a visual or an auditory stimulus (Nuechterlein, 1977). The RT crossover effect in schizophrenia reflects an inability of these patients to benefit from predictable interstimulus intervals on these tasks at longer intervals. The crossover refers to a crossing of the lines depicting average RT for predictable vs. unpredictable intervals, as the intervals increase in length. For short interstimulus intervals, patients with schizophrenia (like normals) are faster when the intervals are predictable. Unlike normals, however, as the predictable intervals increase in length, schizophrenic performance declines, eventually dropping below their level for unpredictable delays of the same average duration (Nuechterlein and Dawson, 1984). This is usually attributed to an inability to sustain attention (readiness to respond across time). Selective attention has also been demonstrated to be impaired in schizophrenia, through the use of dichotic listening paradigms. In these tasks subjects listen through headphones to verbal stimuli, with different messages being delivered to each ear simultaneously. They are required to attend to one message and ignore the other. Patients with schizophrenia usually make more errors of omission than controls, indicating an increased susceptibility to distraction (e.g., Helmsley and Richardson, 1980). Finally, the attentional paradigm that has been studied most frequently in schizophrenia is the continuous performance test (CPT). This task requires sustained vigilance and consists of a continuous presentation of stimuli, usually letters or numbers. Subjects are asked to make a response following the appearance of a certain stimulus or specific combination of stimuli, and the stimuli on some versions of this task are degraded, making identification more difficult. Schizophrenics have been reported to be impaired relative to normals on a variety of CPT paradigms (e.g., Wohlberg and Kornetsky, 1973; Walker, 1981).

Perhaps the most intriguing aspect of the investigation of the various information processing and attentional functions in schizophrenia is that a number of these deficits have also been identified in populations at risk (see Nuechterlein and Dawson, 1984, for a review). These include the relatives of schizophrenics as well as normals with schizophrenic-like profiles on the MMPI or other scales specifically designed to measure schizophrenic-like thinking (e.g., anhedonia scales; Chapman et al., 1976). Thus, certain attentional abnormalities may reflect a vulnerability to schizophrenia (Mirsky, 1988).

Unfortunately, in addition to the ill-defined nature of attention as a cognitive ability, the neural structures that have been implicated in the control of attentional functions are also widely distributed (Mesulam, 1985) (see also Chapter 10). They include prefrontal cortex, inferior parietal cortex, cingulate cortex, reticular formation, striatum, and thalamus. It is currently unclear what the contribution of these various structures is to the various components of attention. The broad-based deficits of attention in schizophrenia are therefore of little utility in providing a clue as to the neuropathophysiology of the disorder.

The suggestion that attentional abnormalities may precede the onset of schizophrenic symptoms is of interest from another perspective, however. As previously mentioned, older studies of premorbid function on standardized tests have indicated that cognitive deficits in schizophrenia are probably acquired contemporaneously with the onset of symptoms (cf. Heaton and Drexler, 1987). Additional support for this hypothesis is derived from the use of measures of academic achievement (e.g., reading pronunciation) as indicators of premorbid level of function. Comparisons of reading ability to IQ data in schizophrenic patients provide an estimate of acquired impairment which averages about ten full-scale IQ points (Goldberg et al., 1990), which is consistent with the results of the older studies. While there is reasonably good evidence that significant cognitive impairment is acquired sometime around the onset of psychotic symptomatology, only attentional deficits have been implicated as possibly preceding the clinical manifestation of schizophrenic illness. Additional prospective studies are needed to delineate the natural history of neuropsychological impairments in schizophrenia. These may provide some clues as to what type of neuropathology may predate the onset of the illness.

*Memory.*   Studies of memory function in schizophrenia have taken on greater significance since a number of studies have implicated the medial temporal lobe as a putative site of pathology in this illness (Bogerts et al., 1985; Jakob and Beckmann, 1986; Suddath et al., 1990). As with attention, there is a relatively broad literature supporting the hypothesis that schizophrenia is characterized by a significant impairment of memory functions. Kolb and Whishaw (1983) reported schizophrenics to be impaired relative to controls on both verbal and visual portions of the Wechsler Memory Scale (Wechsler, 1945). More recently, Gold et al. (in press) have reported that schizophrenic patients perform significantly worse on the Wechsler Memory Scale-Revised (Wechsler, 1987) than on the Wechsler Adult Intelligence Scale-Revised (Wechsler, 1981). Approximately 30% of the patients tested in their sample had a general memory index that was 15 points or more below their full-scale IQ. Again, both visual and verbal indexes were equally impaired. Performance across all five indexes of this memory battery was impaired to about the same degree in the schizophrenic patients, and the percentage of information retained across the delay for the logical memory and visual reproduction sections was poor. In another recent study, involving monozygotic twins discordant for schizophrenia, Goldberg et al. (in press) reported a difference of 23 points between the mean Wechsler Memory Scale performance of the schizophrenic twins and that of their well co-twins. This indicates a substantial impairment of memory associated with the presence of schizophrenia in these twin pairs which cannot be accounted for by possible "risk" factors, such as genetic or socioeconomic endowment.

Some of the earlier studies of memory in schizophrenia suggested that the schizophrenic memory deficit was due primarily to inefficient encoding strategies (e.g., Bauman and Murray, 1968; Koh et al., 1973). This conclusion was based on findings of "preserved" recognition performance and the ability to benefit from specific encoding instructions. These studies involved samples of schizophrenics who were comparatively young, nonchronic patients, and some of the recognition tasks that were used were confounded by ceiling effects. Later studies using more representative samples have concluded that the memory deficit in schizophrenia is broad-ranging, involving all aspects of encoding, retrieval, and recognition (Calev et al., 1983; Calev, 1984; Gold et al., 1992; Koh and Kayton, 1974).

More recently, memory impairments have reached such prominence in the neuropsychology of schizophrenia that it has even been referred to as an "amnesic syndrome" (McKenna et al., 1990) and as a "selective impairment" that is relatively more severe than other neuropsychological deficits (Saykin et al., 1991). While these conclusions are probably overstated and must be tempered by psychometric scaling problems (vide infra), the bulk of recent data suggest that memory deficits are a core feature of the neuropsychological profile of schizophrenia. In addition, virtually all of the studies to date have suggested that the memory impairments in schizophrenia are not material specific, strongly suggesting bilateral dysfunction of medial temporal lobe systems involved in mnemonic processing.

*Executive functions.*    A major impetus for the study of executive, or "prefrontal" functions in schizophrenia has been the behavioral similarities between chronic schizophrenia and patients with frontal lobe disease. Poor planning abilities, impaired social judgment and insight, aspontaneity or lack of initiative, anhedonia, and affective flattening are behavioral features shared by these two patient groups (Goldberg, 1989; Weinberger, 1988). Unfortunately, the behavioral manifestations of prefrontal dysfunction do not translate into discrete neuropsychological impairments, making the psychometric assessment of this neurobehavioral syndrome difficult (Damasio, 1985).

Nevertheless, it has been repeatedly demonstrated that patients with schizophrenia exhibit deficits on tasks that have been shown to be sensitive (if not specific) to frontal lobe dysfunction. Fey (1951) and Stuss et al. (1983) demonstrated that chronic schizophrenics performed quite poorly on the Wisconsin Card Sorting Test (WCST) (Heaton, 1981). Goldberg et al. (1987) demonstrated that this deficit persisted even after attempts to teach the task to chronic schizophrenic patients. In addition, patients with schizophrenia have been reported to exhibit deficits on word fluency (Kolb and Whishaw, 1983; Goldberg et al., 1988), as well as design fluency (Kolb and Whishaw,

1983). Impairments on the Halstead Category Test, which involves abstraction and hypothesis testing, have also been noted (Golden, 1977; Goldberg et al., 1988; Goldstein and Halperin, 1977; Heaton et al., 1978).

The lack of standardized neuropsychological instruments that are both sensitive to and relatively specific for prefrontal dysfunction limits the conclusions that can be drawn from these studies regarding the likelihood of prefrontal neuropathology in schizophrenia. This likelihood is strengthened, however, by the behavioral similarities between schizophrenic patients and patients with frontal lobe disease. In addition, a recent series of experimental paradigms (vide infra) has provided direct evidence of physiological dysfunction of dorsolateral prefrontal cortex in schizophrenia. This convergence of neuropsychological, neurobehavioral, and neurophysiological data strongly suggests that executive functions, mediated primarily by prefrontal cortices, comprise a core deficit in schizophrenia.

POSSIBLE SOURCES OF VARIANCE IN TEST PERFORMANCE

The interpretation of neuropsychological test results in schizophrenia is complicated by a variety of issues that are, to some degree, unique to this disorder. These include the effects of medication, psychiatric symptomatology, and long-term institutionalization.

*Medication effects.*    Three relatively recent reviews have addressed the issue of medication effects on cognitive function (King, 1990; Medalia et al., 1988; Spohn and Strauss, 1989). These are in general agreement that the effects of neuroleptic medication on neuropsychological test performance in patients with schizophrenia are minimal overall. There is some evidence that neuroleptic treatment may result in a slight improvement in attentional functions, as well as in some slowing of psychomotor speed. Memory performance may be adversely affected by the intrinsic anticholinergic activity of some neuroleptics, an effect which can be compounded by the addition of anticholinergic medication to control extrapyramidal side effects (Fayen et al., 1988; Hitri et al., 1987; Tune et al., 1982). The proportion of the memory deficit routinely exhibited by schizophrenic patients that is attributable to a medication effect is probably clinically insignificant, but is deserving of further investigation. Although there is little data regarding the effects of medication on executive functions, at least one study did not identify changes on WCST performance in patients as a result of medication (Berman et al., 1986).

*Effects of symptoms.*    Another issue that has been raised with respect to the interpretation of neuropsychological testing in schizophrenia is the effect of psychotic symptomatology (i.e., thought disorder, hallucinations) on performance. The literature on this topic is mixed, with some investigators reporting a significant correlation between the severity of positive symptoms or thought disorder and impairment on cognitive tests while others have not been able to identify such a relationship (see Gold et al., 1991b, for a review). This literature is somewhat difficult to interpret, due to inconsistencies in task selection, symptom ratings, and subject selection. There is one very compelling line of evidence, however, which suggests that it is unlikely that positive symptomatology exerts an appreciable effect on neuropsychological test performance. This is that cognitive deficits measured prior to the initiation of neuroleptic treatment remain unchanged posttreatment, despite significant reductions in positive symptoms (e.g., Frame and Oltmanns, 1982; Gold and Hurt, 1990; Goldberg et al., in press). In the Goldberg et al. study, chronic schizophrenic patients who had not shown adequate response to typical neuroleptics were treated with clozapine. Despite striking improvements in psychiatric symptoms in a portion of the sample as a result of clozapine treatment, neuropsychological functions remained unchanged. When psychotic symptoms respond dramatically to neuroleptic treatment and cognitive deficits do not change, as these studies have reported, the hypothesis that neuropsychological deficits are consequent to psychotic symptomatology becomes untenable.

*Effects of long-term institutionalization.* A final potential confound in the neuropsychological assessment of patients with schizophrenia is the possibly deleterious effect of long-term institutionalization on cognitive functioning. This issue was addressed directly in a study by Harrow et al. (1987), in which they compared a group of continuously hospitalized chronic schizophrenics to a matched group of intermittently hospitalized chronic schizophrenics on measures of intelligence and abstract thinking. There was no significant difference between the groups on any measure, suggesting that hospitalization per se does not have a negative influence on cognitive functioning. This finding is similar to the results of an earlier cross-sectional study (Johnstone et al., 1981), which did not find evidence for increased impairment on a brief mental status test as a function of the duration of hospitalization. In a recent study, neuropsychological data from 245 schizophrenic patients were analyzed to determine the effects of age, education, and length of hospitalization on performance (Goldstein et al., 1991). Hospitalization was not found to account for a significant proportion of the variance in test performance, after age and education were entered into the regression analyses. The results of these investigations are consistent in their failure to identify any contributory effects of hospitalization to neuropsychological deficits. The results of earlier longitudinal studies (discussed in the first section of this chapter), which did not find evidence for progression of impairments in chronic schizophrenics over a period of years, lend additional support to this conclusion.

In sum, then, the effects of medication, positive symptomatology, and long-term institutionalization on the neuropsychological performance of patients with schizophrenia appear to be minimal. The cognitive deficts associated with this disorder are, for the most part, present at the onset of psychotic symptoms, are relatively stable over time, and do not remit with neuroleptic treatment, even when such treatment is effective in eliminating other symptoms.

SELECTIVITY OF DEFICITS? THE DIFFERENTIAL DEFICIT PROBLEM

As mentioned above, schizophrenic patients are likely to perform below the level of normals on a wide variety of tests. This creates a problem for the derivation of a differential deficit profile. Unfortunately, there is no way to empirically determine whether a patient's performance on a test of memory, for example, is worse than his performance on the WCST, *when both are below normal levels*. This is because neu-ropsychological tests vary in their sensitivity to brain dysfunction in general. The WCST is not a very sensitive neuropsychological test, insofar as the distribution of the brain-damaged population is not very different from that of normals. Even patients with large lesions of the frontal lobes do not score much more than two standard devi-ations (SDs) below normal on WCST measures (Heaton, 1981). On many memory tests, however, memory-impaired patients routinely score many SDs below normal. One cannot, therefore, conclude that a score which is three SDs below normal on the California Verbal Learning Test (CVLT), for example, represents a relatively greater deficit than a score that is two SDs below normal on the WCST.

This is a continuing problem for attempts to define relative impairments in a single group of patients, compared to normal controls. Attempts to circumvent this problem have included the use of tasks which are psychometrically matched in a normal sam-ple or the application of a regression equation to predict performance on one task from another, again derived from the relationship between the two tasks in the nor-mal population (Chapman and Chapman, 1989). Unfortunately, both of these tech-niques fail to account for the unique nature of neuropsychological tasks, which is their variable sensitivity to *nonspecific* brain dysfunction. Using the example outlined above, performance on the WCST and the CVLT might have similar distribution characteristics in the normal population. In the brain-damaged population, however, the distribution of scores for the WCST would probably be of a similar shape to the normal distribution, but shifted slightly. On the other hand, the distribution for the CVLT would be shifted to a greater degree and be much broader. Under almost all circumstances, including relatively "equivalent" degrees of damage to prefrontal and medial temporal systems, the Chapman and Chapman (1989) techniques would conclude that the patient group of interest had relatively more impairment of mem-ory function (these two tests were used merely as hypothetical examples; for a further discussion of this problem in referencing neuropsychological tests to one another see Russell, 1987).

Therefore, while the weight of evidence to date suggests a primary involvement of attentional, mnemonic, and executive functions in schizophrenic illness, this conclu-sion rests more upon clinical judgment than empirically derived dissociation of def-icits, since other functions are affected to some degree as well. In defense of this for-mulation, it could be argued that a combination of these deficits would be likely to at least slightly disrupt performance on other measures which are not primarily depen-dent on these functions, and that this slight disruption would often be sufficient for a statistically significant difference to emerge in comparison to controls. In addition, it should be noted that the neuropsychological tests on which schizophrenic patients *do* sometimes perform normally are usually tests of visuospatial perception, linguistic, or constructional functions (e.g., Kolb and Whishaw, 1983).

Additional elucidation of the pattern of neuropsychological deficits in schizophre-nia may require the direct comparison of schizophrenics to other patient groups on both standardized and experimental tests. This approach has been fruitful in identi-fying differential deficit patterns in dementing disorders (e.g., Delis et al., 1991; Heindel et al., 1989; Troster et al., 1989) and is as yet a relatively untapped method for determining the specificity of the deficit pattern in schizophrenia.

## EXPERIMENTAL NEUROPSYCHOLOGICAL APPROACHES

In addition to the use of standardized neuropsychological instruments in the investigation of schizophrenia, experimental approaches have provided some useful insights into the nature of this disorder. These approaches have involved not only the use of hypothesis-driven cognitive tasks to more fully characterize deficits identified on standardized tests, but also the coupling of neuropsychological assessment to brain-imaging techniques, in order to "map" dysfunctional neural systems.

### The Use of Experimental Techniques to More Fully Characterize Deficits

Attention is somewhat unique among neuropsychological constructs to the extent that, for many aspects of attentional function, there are no widely used standardized instruments. This is particularly true for measures of sustained attention and freedom from distractibility, which may be of particular interest in the neuropsychological assessment of schizophrenia. The parameters of the continuous performance tests used to assess these functions have varied from laboratory to laboratory. As a result, much of the literature to date on attentional function in schizophrenia is derived from what are essentially experimental techniques. Continuing evolution of our understanding of the neural mechanisms underlying the various components of attention will allow a more complete characterization of the neuropsychology of attention in schizophrenia.

A recent study by Posner et al. (1988) represents a step in this direction. Using an experimental paradigm for which performance data had been previously obtained from patients with focal lesions, these authors concluded that the pattern of performance exhibited by schizophrenic patients indicated difficulty in disengaging attention, and linked this deficit to left-hemisphere dysfunction. While attempts to replicate this finding have been largely unsuccessful (Gold et al., 1992a; Strauss et al., 1991), this type of approach represents a level of analysis that is potentially more informative from a neuropsychological perspective than much of the earlier work in this field, which has been primarily concerned with the identification of an attentional "marker" for schizophrenia rather than an elucidation of specific brain-behavior relationships.

The study of memory function in schizophrenia has also been enriched by the use of experimental paradigms, which have been useful in more completely elaborating the nature of this impairment. For example, the early belief that the schizophrenic memory impairment was attributable entirely to inefficient encoding strategies was disconfirmed as a result of the use of matched recall/recognition tasks (Calev, 1984), systematic variation of encoding conditions (Calev et al., 1983; Gold et al., 1992b), and the demonstration that schizophrenics exhibit deficits on noneffortful, or "automatic" memory functions, such as frequency estimation (Gold et al., 1992b) and recency estimation (Schwartz et al., 1991).

Another experimental paradigm recently employed with a schizophrenic sample is the Wickens release from proactive interference (PI) modification of the Brown-Peterson task (Randolph et al., 1992). Failure to release from PI on this task had previously been demonstrated only in patient groups with evidence of both frontal lobe pathology *and* memory impairments (e.g., Korsakoff's syndrome). The schizophrenic patients in this study also exhibited impaired release from PI, providing further evidence for the involvement of prefrontal and medial temporal systems in this disorder.

Prefrontal function in schizophrenia has received somewhat less attention with respect to the use of experimental paradigms, partly as a result of the relative paucity of such paradigms. One approach to the development of such tasks is to rely upon the animal literature, in which the effects of prefrontal lesions have been more systematically studied than in humans. Recently, we developed a task that is an analogue of the animal delayed response task, with the addition of a component requiring response alternation. Performance on the delayed response task in monkeys has been shown to be selectively disrupted following lesions of the prefrontal cortex (Goldman and Rosvold, 1970). In a preliminary study using this new task, a group of schizophrenic patients was compared to matched controls. The patients were significantly impaired in their ability to learn this relatively simple task, as well as in their ability to perform it following explicit instructions and training (Gold et al., 1991a). The validity of this task as a measure of prefrontal integrity was supported by a parallel experiment that examined regional cerebral blood flow patterns through PET in normal subjects during the performance of the task, finding increased activation of prefrontal cortex.

### The Coupling of Neuropsychological Tasks and Brain-Imaging Techniques to "Map" Dysfunctional Systems

One final approach to delineating the neuropsychology of schizophrenia has been to directly examine the relationship between neuropsychological performance and brain structure or function in schizophrenic patients. For the most part, attempts to relate structural changes on CT or MRI scan to neuropsychological deficit have involved global measures of deficit and limited, or nonspecific measures of brain structure (e.g., cerebral ventricular size). As a result, no consistent relationships between brain structure and *specific* neuropsychological impairments have emerged, although patients with obviously abnormal scans tend to exhibit a greater degree of overall impairment (cf. Zec and Weinberger, 1986).

A more rewarding strategy has involved the examination of patterns of regional cerebral blood flow activation in patients and normal controls while engaged in neuropsychological tasks presumed to activate specific brain systems. In a series of such experiments, Weinberger and his colleagues have accrued compelling evidence for the existence of a task-specific prefrontal dysfunction in schizophrenia (Weinberger et al., 1988).

The majority of these studies have involved examining cerebral blood flow activation during the WCST, in comparison to a control task used to account for the sensory and motor aspects of performing the WCST. Normal control subjects exhibit a significant activation of prefrontal cortex during WCST performance, relative to the control task. Unlike the normals, patients with schizophrenia do not exhibit prefrontal activation during the WCST. This finding has been observed in two different medication-free samples (Weinberger et al., 1986, 1988), as well as in patients undergoing treatment with neuroleptics (Berman et al., 1986). In addition, in a study of monozygotic twins discordant for schizophrenia, there were no consistent differences between the twins during resting or control task conditions, but during the WCST, every ill twin was hypofrontal compared to his or her well co-twin (Berman et al., in press).

Convergent validity for the hypothesis that schizophrenia may be characterized by a failure to normally activate prefrontal systems in response to cognitive tasks requiring this activation is derived from studies employing other tasks designed to activate prefrontal regions. These have included tasks involving auditory attention (Cohen et al., 1987), visual attention (Buchsbaum et al., 1990), and eye tracking (Volkow et al., 1986). In all of these paradigms, the normal response of increased frontal activation in response to the task demands was attenuated or absent in patients with schizophrenia. To date, cognitive "activators" for these functional imaging studies have involved only measures of attention or putative tasks of prefrontal function. Memory tasks have not yet been employed for this purpose; in part this may be due to difficulty in imaging medial temporal regions with earlier technologies. It is interesting to note, however, that patients with schizophrenia have been reported to demonstrate normal patterns of increased posterior cerebral blood flow activation in response to a cognitively demanding task that involves visuospatial problem solving, i.e., Raven's Progressive Matrices (Berman et al., 1988). This supports the hypothesis that the failure of prefrontal activation is related to the regionally specific demand of the task and not to nonspecific factors such as attention, motivation, effort, etc. Finally, the possibility that prefrontal hypoactivity (a putative explanation for deficits in "executive" functions in schizophrenia) and temporal-limbic neuropathology (a putative explanation for memory deficits) are related is suggested by further data from the NIMH study of discordant monozygotic twins. In this sample, the difference within a twin pair in volume of the pes hippocampus on MRI strongly predicted the difference within the same pair in prefrontal activation during the WCST (Weinberger et al., 1992).

## CONCLUSIONS

The renaissance of neuroscience in the study of schizophrenia that began in the 1970s has, to some degree, brought us full circle to the early clinical-pathological formulations of Kraepelin. Neuropsychological investigations have repeatedly concluded that this disorder is characterized by deficits in attention, memory, and executive functions. Recent neuroimaging and postmortem studies have suggested the existence of neuropathological changes in the medial temporal lobe structures of schizophrenic patients. Functional imaging studies have consistently reported a pattern of hypofrontality in response to cognitive demands which normally produce activation of this neocortical region. Together, these lines of evidence implicate medial temporal and dorsolateral prefrontal cortical systems in the pathophysiology of schizophrenia.

Although the studies reviewed here have now provided some direct empirical support for this recycled hypothesis, there are a number of essential features of this disorder which are largely beyond the scope of this chapter, but must be incorporated into any neurobehavioral understanding of schizophrenia. These include the role of brain dopamine systems, which are of obvious importance in the medical treatment of schizophrenic symptoms, the neuropathophysiology of positive symptoms, and the natural history of the disease. Evidence is accumulating, however, to suggest a mechanism that may link these diverse features. Pycock et al. (1980) demonstrated that a lesion of the prefrontal cortex in the rat can result in disinhibition of mesolimbic dopaminergic systems, producing chronic subcortical dopamine hyperactivity. Other studies have elaborated on the cortical regulation of limbic dopamine activity, demonstrating that projections not only from the prefrontal cortex (Jaskiw et al., 1991) but also from the rostral hippocampus participate in this regulation (Lipska et al., 1992). It is therefore possible that hypofunction of prefrontal and/or hippocampal regions, whether due to intrinsic dysfunction or functional deafferentation, can lead to overactivity of mesolimbic systems that have been implicated in the production of positive symptoms in schizophrenia. Weinberger (1987) has suggested that the late maturation of prefrontal cortical areas may interact with an earlier fixed "lesion" to produce a dysfunctional state that becomes clinically evident only as these prefrontal systems come "on line." Evidence for this hypothesis is derived from the finding that dorsolateral prefrontal cortical lesions in infant monkeys do not impair performance on delayed response tasks. When these early-lesioned monkeys reach early adulthood, however, they "lose" the ability to perform this task (Goldman, 1974).

The nature of the putative early "lesion" or developmental dysplasia or hypoplasia which may interact with adolescent brain maturational processes remains speculative. It is possible that a disruption of mesocortical dopaminergic systems could produce this effect. Such a deafferentation of dorsolateral prefrontal cortex could account for findings of premorbid attentional dysfunction, and theoretically impede the normal development of corticolimbic circuitry. Subsequently, the failure of the prefrontal cortex to adequately respond to stress could lead to mesolimbic hyperactivity, resulting in the onset of clinical symptoms (cf. Weinberger, 1987; Grace, 1991). How this series of neural events could also result in worsening neuropsychological function is unclear, although Goldman's (1974) finding clearly suggests that it is possible. This hypothesis would also account for the cerebral blood flow literature, in which hypofunction is only reliably identified in response to specific cognitive activation, and not at rest or during nonspecific tasks (cf. Berman and Weinberger, 1991). This pattern of findings is more consistent with pathology that is extrinsic to the prefrontal cortex, resulting in a functional deafferentation that is only evident under conditions which normally recruit this area to participate in cognition. This possibility is supported by the finding that differences in hippocampal size between monozygotic twins discordant for schizophrenia were predictive of differences in cerebral blood flow activation during the WCST (Weinberger et al., 1992).

Although these deliberations on the neural mechanisms underlying the pathogenesis and neuropsychology of schizophrenia are preliminary and highly speculative, they have generated a series of testable hypotheses that promise to move the focus of this research from a broad-based emphasis on demonstrating the existence of some form of neuropathology to a theoretically driven analysis of the role of specific brain systems in this disorder. Neuropsychology has played a pivotal role in the reemergence of schizophrenia as a brain disease, and will continue to be of primary importance in clinical evaluation, treatment planning, and research into this devastating illness.

# REFERENCES

Allebeck, P. (1989). Schizophrenia: a life-shortening disease. *Schizophr. Bull.* 15:81–89.

American Psychiatric Association. (1987). *Diagnostic and Statistical Manual of Mental Disorders*, 3rd ed. Washington, D.C.: APA.

Andreasen, N. C., Flaum, M., Swayze, V. W., Tyrell, G., and Arndt, S. (1990). Positive and negative symptoms in schizophrenia. *Arch. Gen. Psychiatry* 47:615–621.

Arndt, S., Alliger, R. J., and Andreasen, N. C. (1991). The distinction of positive and negative symptoms: the failure of a two-dimensional model. *Br. J. Psychiatry* 158:317–322.

Bauman, E., and Murray, D. J. (1968). Recognition versus recall in schizophrenia. *Can. J. Psychol.* 22:18–25.

Berman, K. F., Illowsky, B. P., and Weinberger, D. F. (1988). Physiological dysfunction of dorsolateral prefrontal cortex in schizophrenia: IV. Further evidence for regional and behavioral specificity. *Arch. Gen. Psychiatry* 45:616–622.

Berman, K. F., Torrey, E. F., Daniel, D. G., and Weinberger, D. R. (in press). Regional cerebral blood flow in monozygotic twins concordant and discordant for schizophrenia. *Arch. Gen. Psychiatry*

Berman, K. F., and Weinberger, D. R. (1991). Functional localization in the brain in schizophrenia. In A. Tasman and S. M. Goldfinger (eds.). *American Psychiatric Press Review of Psychiatry*, Washington, D. C.: American Psychiatric Press.

Berman, K. F., Zec, R. F., and Weinberger, D. R. (1986). Physiological dysfunction of dorsolateral prefrontal cortex in schizophrenia: II. Role of neuroleptic treatment, attention, and mental effort. *Arch. Gen. Psychiatry* 43:126–135.

Bilder, R. M., Mukherjee, S., Rieder, R. O., and Pandurangi, A. K. (1985). Symptomatic and neuropsychological components of defect states. *Schizophr. Bull.* 11:409–417.

Bleuler, E. (1911; reprinted in 1950). *Dementia Praecox, or the Group of Schizophrenias*, J. Zinken (trans.). New York: International Universities Press.

Bogerts, B., Meertz, E., and Schonfeldt-Bausch, R. (1985) Basal ganglia and limbic system pathology in schizophrenia. *Arch. Gen. Psychiatry* 42:784–791.

Braff, D. L., and Saccuzzo, D. P. (1981). Information processing dysfunction in paranoid schizophrenia: a two-factor deficit. *Am. J. Psychiatry* 138:1051–1056.

Buchsbaum, M. S., Nuechterlein, K. H., Haier, R. J., Wu, J., Sicotte, N., Hazlett, E., Asarnow, R., Potkin, S., and Guich, S. (1990). Glucose metabolic rate in normals and schizophrenics during the continuous performance test assessed by positron emission tomography. *Br. J. Psychiatry* 156:216–227.

Calev, A. (1984). Recall and recognition in mildly disturbed schizophrenics: the use of matched tasks. *Psychol. Med.* 14:425–429.

Calev, A., Venables, P. H., and Monk, A. F. (1983). Evidence for distinct verbal memory pathologies in severly and mildly disturbed schizophrenics. *Schizophr. Bull.* 9:247–264.

Chapman, L. J., and Chapman, J. P. (1989). Strategies for resolving the heterogeneity of schizophrenics and their relatives using cognitive measures. *J. Abnorm. Psychol.* 98:357–366.

Chapman, L. J., Chapman, J. P., and Raulin, M. L. (1976). Scales for physical and social anhedonia. *J. Abnorm. Psychol.* 85:374–382.

Ciompi, L. (1987). Review of follow-up studies on long-term evolution and aging in schizophrenia. In *Schizophrenia and Aging*, N. E. Miller and G. D. Cohen (eds.). New York: Guilford Press, pp. 37–51.

Cohen, R. M., Semple, W. E., Gross, M., Nordahl, T. E., DeLisi, L. E., Holcomb, H. H., King, A. C., Morihisa, J. M., and Pickar, D. (1987). Dysfunction in a prefrontal substrate of sustained attention in schizophrenia. *Life Sci.* 40:2031–2039.

Crow, T. J. (1980). Molecular pathology of schizophrenia: more than one disease process? *Br. Med. J. 280*:66–68.

Damasio, A. (1985). The frontal lobes. In *Clinical Neuropsychology*. K. M. Heilman and E. Valenstein (eds.). New York: Oxford University Press, pp. 339–402.

Davidson, G. S., and Neale, J. M. (1974). The effects of signal-noise similarity on visual information processing of schizophrenics. *J. Abnorm. Psychol. 83*:683–686.

Davies, L. M., and Drummond, M. F. (1990). The economic burden of schizophrenia. *Psychiatr. Bull. 14*:522–525.

Delis, D. C., Massman, P. J., Butters, N., Salmon, D. P., Cermak, L. S., and Kramer, J. H. (1991). Profiles of demented and amnesic patients on the California Verbal Learning Test: implications for the assessment of memory disorders. *Psychol. Assess. 3*:19–26.

Dohrenwend, B. P., and Dohrenwend, B. S. (1974). Social and cultural influences on psychopathology. *Annu. Rev. Psychol. 24*:417–452.

Fayen, M., Goldman, M. B., Moulthrop, M. A., and Luchins, D. J. (1988). Differential memory impairment with dopaminergic versus anticholinergic treatment of drug-induced extrapyramidal symptoms. *Am. J. Psychiatry 145*:483–486.

Fey, E. T. (1951). The performance of young schizophrenics and young normals on the Wisconsin Card Sorting Test. *J. Consult. Psychol. 15*:311–319.

Frame, C. L., and Oltmanns, T. F. (1982). Serial recall by schizophrenic and affective patients during and after psychotic episodes. *J. Abnorm. Psychol. 91*:311–318.

Gold, J. M., Berman, K. F., Randolph, C., Goldberg, T. E., and Weinberger, D. R. (1991a). PET validation and clinical application of a novel prefrontal task. *J. Clin. Exp. Neuropsychol. 13*:81.

Gold, J. M., Goldberg, T. E., Kleinman, J. E., and Weinberger, D. R. (1991b). The impact of symptomatic state and pharmacological treatment on cognitive functioning of patients with schizophrenia and mood disorders. In *Handbook of Clinical Trials. The Neurobehavioral Approach*, E. Mohr and P. Brouwers (eds.). Amsterdam: Swets, pp. 185–216.

Gold, J. M., and Hurt, S. (1990). The effects of haloperidol in thought disorder and IQ in schizophrenia. *J. Pers. Assess. 54*:390–400.

Gold, J. M., Randolph, C., Carpenter, C. J., Coppola, R. M., Goldberg, T. E., and Weinberger, D. R. (1992a). Visual orienting in schizophrenia. *Schizophrenia Research. 7*:203–209.

Gold, J. M., Randolph, C., Carpenter, C. J., Goldberg, T. E., and Weinberger, D. R. (in press, b). The performance of patients with schizophrenia on the Wechsler Memory Scale-Revised. *Clin. Neuropsychol.*

Gold, J. M., Randolph, C., Carpenter, C. J., Goldberg, T. E., and Weinberger, D. R. (1992b). Forms of memory failure in schizophrenia. *J. Abnorm. Psychol. 101*:487–494.

Goldberg, E. (1989). Neuropsychology in the studies of psychopathology. In *Contemporary Approaches to Psychological Assessment*, M. Katz and S. Wetzler (eds.). New York: Brunner-Mazel, pp. 213–235.

Goldberg, T. E., Greenberg, R. D., Griffin, S. J., Gold, J. M., Kleinman, J. E., Pickar, D., Shulz, S., and Weinberger, D. R. (in press). The impact of clozapine on cognition and psychiatric symptoms in patients with schizophrenia. *Br. J. Psychiatry.*

Goldberg, T. E., Kelsoe, J. R., Weinberger, D. R., Pliskin, N. H., Kirwin, P. D., and Berman, K. F. (1988) Performance of schizophrenic patients on putative neuropsychological tests of frontal lobe function. *Int. J. Neurosci. 42*:51–58.

Goldberg, T. E., Ragland, J. D., Torrey, E. F., Gold, J. M., Bigelow, L. B., and Weinberger, D. R. (1990). Neuropsychological assessment of monozygotic twins discordant for schizophrenia. *Arch. Gen. Psychiatry 47*:1066–1072.

Goldberg, T. E., Weinberger, D. R., Berman, K. F., Pliskin, N. H., and Podd, M. H. (1987).

Further evidence for dementia of the prefrontal type in schizophrenia? *Arch. Gen. Psychiatry* 44:1088–1014.

Golden, C. J. (1977). Validity of the Halstead-Reitan neuropsychological battery in a mixed psychiatric and brain injured population. *J. Consult. Clin. Psychol.* 45:1043–1051.

Goldman, P. S. (1974). An alternative to developmental plasticity: heterology of CNS structures in infants and adults. In *Plasticity and Recovery of Function in the Central Nervous System*, D. G. Stein, J. J. Rosen, and N. Butters (eds.). New York: Academic Press, pp. 149–174.

Goldman, P. S., and Rosvold, H. E. (1970). Localization of function within the dorsolateral prefrontal cortex of the rhesus monkey. *Exp. Neurol.* 27:291–304.

Goldstein, G. (1978). Cognitive and perceptual differences between schizophrenics and organics. *Schizophr. Bull.* 4:160–185.

Goldstein, G., and Halperin, K. M. (1977). Neuropsychological differences among subtypes of schizophrenia. *J. Abnorm. Psychol.* 86:34–40.

Goldstein, G., Zubin, J., and Pogue-Geile, M. F. (1991). Hospitalization and the cognitive deficits of schizophrenia. The influences of age and education. *J. Nerv. Ment. Dis.* 179:202–205.

Grace. A. A. (1991). Phasic vs tonic dopamine release and the modulation of dopamine system responsivity: a hypothesis for the etiology of schizophrenia. *Neuroscience* 41:1–24.

Hare, E. H. (1987). Epidemiology of schizophrenia and affective psychoses. *Br. Med. Bull.* 43:514–430.

Harrow, M., Marengo, J., Pogue-Geile, M., and Pawelski, T. J. (1987). Schizophrenic deficits in intelligence and abstract thinking: influence of aging and long-term institutionalization. In *Schizophrenia and Aging*, N. E. Miller and G. D. Cohen (eds.). New York: Guilford Press, pp. 133–144.

Haywood, H. C., and Modelis, I. (1963). Effect of symptom change on intellectual function in schizophrenia. *J. Abnorm. Soc. Psychol.* 67:76–78.

Heaton, R. K. (1981). *Wisconsin Card Sorting Test Manual.* Odessa, Fla: Psychological Assessment Resources.

Heaton, R. K., Boade, L. E., and Johnson, K. L. (1978). Neuropsychological test results associated with psychiatric disorders in adults. *Psychol. Bull.* 85:141–162.

Heaton, R. K., and Drexler, M. (1987). Clinical neuropsychological findings in schizophrenia and aging. In *Schizophrenia and Aging*, N. E. Miller and G. D. Coles (eds.). New York: Guilford Press, pp. 145–161.

Heaton, R. K., Vogt, A. T., Hoehn, M. M., Lewis, J. A., Crowley, T. J., and Stallings, M. A. (1979). Neuropsychological impairment with schizophrenia vs. acute and chronic cerebral lesions. *J. Clin. Psychol.* 35:46–53.

Heindel, W. C., Salmon, D. P. and Butters, N. (1989). Neuropsychological differentiation of memory impairments in dementia. In *Memory, Aging, and Dementia*, G. Gilmore, P. Whitehouse, and M. Wyke (eds.). New York: Springer, pp. 112–139.

Helmsley, D. R., and Richardson, P. H. (1980). Shadowing by context in schizophrenia. *J. Nerv. Ment. Dis.* 168:141–145.

Hitri, A., Craft, R. B., Fallon, J., Sethi, R., and Sinha, D. (1987). Serum neuroleptic and anticholinergic activity in relationship to cognitive toxicity of antiparkinsonian agents in schizophrenic patients. *Psychopharmacol. Bull.* 23:33–37.

Jackson, J. H. (1894). The factors of the insanities. *Med. Press Circular* ii:615. Reprinted in *Selected Writings of John Hughlings Jackson*. London: Hodder and Stoughton, 1932.

Jakob, H., and Beckmann, H. (1986). Prenatal developmental disturbances in the limbic allocortex in schizophrenia. *J. Neural Transm.* 65:303–326.

Jaskiw, G. E., Weinberger, D. R., and Crawley, J. N. (1991). Microinjection of apomorphine into the prefrontal cortex of the rat reduces dopamine metabolite concentrations in micro-dialysate from the caudate nucleus. *Biol. Psychiatry* 29:703–706.

Johnstone, E. C., Cunningham Owens, D. G., Gold, A., Crow, T. J., and MacMillan, J. F. (1981). Institutionalization and the defects of schizophrenia. *Br. J. Psychiatry* 139:195–203.

Kay, S. R., Opler, L. A., and Fiszbein, A. (1986). Significance of positive and negative syndromes in chronic schizophrenia. *Br. J. Psychiatry* 149:439–448.

Kay, S. R., and Lindenmayer, J. P. (1987). Outcome predictors in acute schizophrenia. Prospective significance of background and clinical dimensions. *J. Nerv. Ment. Dis.* 175:152–160.

Kay, S. R., and Singh, M. M. (1989). The positive-negative distinction in drug-free schizophrenic patients. Stability, response to neuroleptics, and prognostic significance. *Arch. Gen. Psychiatry* 46:711–718.

Kendler, K. S., Gruenberg, A. M., and Tsuang, M. T. (1988). A family study of the subtypes of schizophrenia. *Am. J. Psychiatry* 145:57–62.

Kendler, K. S., Gruenberg, A. M., and Tsuang, M. T. (1985). Psychiatric illness in first degree relatives of schizophrenic and surgical control patients. *Arch. Gen. Psychiatry* 42:770–779.

Kety, S. S. (1988). Schizophrenic illness in the families of schizophrenic adoptees: findings from the Danish national sample. *Schizophr. Bull.* 14:217–222.

King, D. J. (1990). The effects of neuroleptics on cognitive and psychomotor function. *Br. J. Psychiatry* 157:799–811.

Kingsley, L., and Streuning, E. L., (1966). Changes in intellectual performance of acute and chronic schizophrenics. *Psychol. Rep.* 18:791–800.

Klonoff, H., Fibiger, C. H., and Hutton, G. H. (1970). Neuropsychological patterns in chronic schizophrenia. *J. Nerv. Ment. Dis.* 150:291–300.

Koh, S. D., and Kayton, L. (1974). Memorization of "unrelated" word strings by young nonpsychotic schizophrenics. *J. Abnorm. Psychol.* 83:14–22.

Koh, S. D., Kayton, L., and Berry, R. (1973). Mnemonic organization in young nonpsychotic schizophrenics. *J. Abnorm. Psychol.* 81:299–310.

Kolb, B., and Whishaw, I. Q. (1983). Performance of schizophrenic patients on tests sensitive to left or right frontal, temporal, or parietal function in neurological patients. *J. Nerv. Ment. Dis.* 171:435–443.

Kraepelin, E. (1902; English translation by A. R. Diefendorf, 1907). *Clinical Psychiatry.* New York: Macmillan.

Kraepelin, E. (1913; English transalation by R. M. Barclay, 1919). *Dementia Praecox and Paraphrenia.* Edinburgh: E&S Livingstone.

Lawson, W. B., Walsman, I. V., and Weinberger, D. R. (1988). Schizophrenic dementia. Clinical and computed axial tomography correlates. *J. Nerv. Ment. Dis.* 176:207–212.

Liddle, P. F. (1987). Schizophrenic syndromes, cognitive performance and neurological dysfunction. *Psychol. Med.* 17:49–57.

Lipska, B. K., Jaskiw, G. E., Karoum, F., Chrapusta, S., and Weinberger, D. R., (1992). Ibotenic acid lesion of the ventral hippocampus differentially affects dopamine and its metabolites in the nucleus accumbens and prefrontal cortex in the rat. *Brain Research* 585:1–6.

Lubin, A., Gieseking, C. F., and Williams, H. L. (1962). Direct measurement of cognitive deficit in schizophrenia. *J. Consult. Psychol.* 26:139–143.

Malec, J. (1978). Neuropsychological assessment of schizophrenia versus brain damage: a review. *J. Nerv. Ment. Dis.* 166:507–516.

Marks, R. C., and Luchins, D. J. (1990). Relationship between brain imaging findings in schizophrenia and psychopathology: a review of the literature relating to positive and negative symptoms. In *Modern Problems of Pharmacopsychiatry: Positive and Negative Symptoms and Syndromes*, N. C. Andreasen (ed.). Basel: S. Karger, pp. 89-123.

Martin, J. P., Friedmeyer, M. H., Sterne, A. L., and Brittain, H. M. (1977). IQ deficit in schizophrenia: a test of competing theories. *J. Clin. Psychol. 33*:667-672.

McGlashan, T. H. (1986). The prediction of outcome in chronic schizophrenia. IV. The Chesnut Lodge follow-up study. *Arch. Gen. Psychiatry 43*:167-176.

McKenna, P. J., Tamlyn, D., Lund, C. E., Mortimer, A. M., Hammond, S., and Baddely, A. D. (1990). Amnesic syndrome in schizophrenia. *Psychol. Med. 20*:967-972.

Medalia, A., Gold, J. M., and Merriam, A. (1988). The effects of neuroleptics on neuropsychological test results of schizophrenics. *Arch. Clin. Neuropsychol. 3*:249-271.

Mesulam, M.-M. (1985). Attention, confusional states, and neglect. In *Principles of Behavioral Neurology*, M.-M. Mesulam (ed.). Philadelphia: F. A. Davis, pp. 125-168.

Mirsky, A. F. (1988). Research on schizophrenia in the NIMH laboratory of psychology and psychopathology, 1954-1987. *Schizophr. Bull. 14*:151-156.

Moran, L. J., Gorham, D. R., and Holtzman, W. H. (1962). Vocabulary knowledge and usage of schizophrenic subjects: a six-year follow-up. *J. Abnorm. Soc. Psychol. 61*:246-254.

Nuechterlein, K. H. (1977). Reaction time and attention in schizophrenia: a critical evaluation of the data and the theories. *Schizoph. Bull. 3*:373-428.

Nuechterlein, K. H., and Dawson, M. E. (1984). Informational processing and attentional functioning in the developmental course of schizophrenic disorders. *Schizophr. Bull 10*:160-203.

Oltmanns, T. F., and Neale, J. M. (1975). Schizophrenic performance when distractors are present: attentional deficit or differential task difficulty? *J. Abnorm. Psychol. 84*:205-209.

Posner, M. I., Early, T. S., Reiman, E., Pardo, P. J., and Dhawan, M. (1988). Asymmetries in hemispheric control of attention in schizophrenia. *Arch. Gen. Psychiatry 45*:814-821.

Pycock, C. J., Kerwin, R. W., and Carter, C. J. (1980). Effects of lesion of cortical dopamine terminals on subcortical dopamine in rats. *Nature 286*:74-77.

Randolph, C., Gold, J. M., Carpenter C. J., Goldberg, T. E., and Weinberger, D. R. (1992). Release from proactive interference: determinants of performance and neuropsychological correlates. *J. Clin. Exp. Neuropsychol. 14*:785-800.

Russell, E. W. (1987). A reference scale method for constructing neuropsychological test batteries. *J. Clin. Exp. Neuropsychol. 9*:376-392.

Saugstad, L. F. (1989). Social class, marriage, and fertility in schizophrenia. *Schizophr. Bull. 15*:9-43.

Saykin, A. J., Gur, R. C., Gur, R. E., Mozley, P. D., Mozley, L. H., Resnick, S. M., Kester, D. B., and Stafniak, P. (1991). Neuropsychological impairment in schizophrenia: selective impairment in memory and learning. *Arch. Gen. Psychiatry 48*:618-624.

Schwartz, B. L., Deutsch, L. H., Cohen, C., Warden, D., and Deutsch, S. I. (1991). Memory for temporal order in schizophrenia. *Biol. Psychiatry 29*:329-339.

Schwartzman, A. E., and Douglas, V. I. (1962). Intellectual loss in schizophrenia: part I. *Can. J. Psychol. 16*:1-10.

Seidman, L. J. (1983). Schizophrenia and brain dysfunction: an integration of recent neurodiagnostic findings. *Psychol. Bull. 94*:195-238.

Shakow, D. (1963). Psychological deficit in schizophrenia. *Behav. Sci. 8*:275-305.

Shakow, D. (1979). *Adaptation in Schizophrenia: The Theory of Segmental Set*. New York: John Wiley and Sons.

Shelton, R. C., and Weinberger, D. R. (1986). X-ray computerized tomography studies of schizophrenia: a review and synthesis. In *The Neurology of Schizophrenia*, H. A. Nasrallah and D. R. Weinberger (eds.). Amsterdam: Elsevier, pp. 325–348.

Spohn, H. E., and Strauss, M. E. (1989). Relation of neuroleptic and anticholinergic medications to cognitive functions in schizophrenia. *J. Abnorm. Psychol.* 98:367–380.

Strauss, M. E., Novakovic, T., Tien, A. Y., Bylsma, F., and Pearlson, G. D. (1991). Disengagement of attention in schizophrenia. *Psychiatry Res.* 37:139–146.

Stromgren, E. (1987). Changes in the incidence of schizophrenia? *Br. J. Psychiatry* 150:1–7.

Stuss, D. T., Benson, D. F., Kaplan, E. F., Weir, W. S., Naeser, M. A., Lieberman, I., and Ferrill, D. (1983). The involvement of orbito-frontal cerebrum in cognitive tasks. *Neuropsychologia* 21:235–249.

Suddath, R. L., Christison, G. W., Torrey, E. F., Casanova, M. F., and Weinberger, D. R. (1990). Anatomical abnormalities in the brains of monozygotic twins discordant for schizophrenia. *N. Engl. J. Med.* 322:789–794.

Torrey, E. F. (1980). *Civilization and Schizophrenia*. New York: Jason Aronson.

Torrey, E. F. (1988). *Surviving Schizophrenia*. New York: Harper and Row.

Troster, A. I., Jacobs, D., Butters, N., Cullum, C., and Salmon, D. P. (1989). Differentiating Alzheimer's disease from Huntington's disease with the Wechsler Memory Scale-Revised. *Clin. Geriatr. Med.* 5:611–632.

Tsuang, M. T. (1978). Suicide in schizophrenics, manics, depressives, and surgical controls. A comparison with general population suicide mortality. *Arch. Gen. Psychiatry* 35:153–155.

Tune, L. E., Strauss, M. E., Lew, M. F., Breitlinger, E. B. and Coyle, J. T. (1982). Serum levels of anticholinergic drugs and impaired recent memory in chronic schizophrenic patients. *Am. J. Psychiatry* 139:1460–1462.

Volkow, N. D., Brodie, J. D., Wolf, A. P., Gomez-Mont, F., Cancro, R., Van Gelder, P., Russell, J.A.G., and Overall, J. (1986). Brain organization in schizophrenia. *J. Cerebral Blood Flow Metab.* 6:441–446.

Walker, E. (1981). Attentional and neuro-motor functions of schizophrenics, schizoaffectives, and patients with other affective disorders. *Arch. Gen. Psychiatry* 38:1355–1358.

Wechsler, D. (1945). A standardized memory scale for clinical use. *J. Psychol.* 19:87–95.

Wechsler, D. (1981). *Wechsler Adult Intelligence Scale-Revised*. New York: The Psychological Corporation.

Wechsler, D. (1987). *Wechsler Memory Scale-Revised*. New York: The Psychological Corporation.

Weinberger, D. R. (1987). Implications of normal brain development for the pathogenesis of schizophrenia. *Arch. Gen. Psychiatry* 44:660–669.

Weinberger, D. R. (1988). Schizophrenia and the frontal lobe. *Trends Neurosci.* 11:367–370.

Weinberger, D. R., Berman, K. F., and Illowsky, B. P. (1988). Physiological dysfunction of dorsolateral prefrontal cortex in schizophrenia. *Arch. Gen. Psychiatry* 45:609–615.

Weinberger, D. R., Berman, K. F., Suddath, R. L., and Torrey, E. F. (1992). Evidence for dysfunction of a prefrontal-limbic network in schizophrenia: an MRI and regional cerebral blood flow study of discordant monzygotic twins. *Am. J. Psychiatry* 149:890–897.

Weinberger, D. R., Berman, K. F., and Zec, R. F. (1986). Physiologic dysfunction of dorsolateral prefrontal cortex in schizophrenia: I. Regional cerebral blood flow evidence. *Arch. Gen. Psychiatry* 43:114–124.

Wohlberg, G. W., and Kornetsky, C. (1973). Sustained attention in remitted schizophrenics. *Arch. Gen. Psychiatry* 28:533–537.

Wyatt, R. J. (1991). Neuroleptics and the natural course of schizophrenia. *Schizophr. Bull.* 17:325–351.

Zec, R. F., and Weinberger, D. R. (1986). Relationship between CT scan findings and neuropsychological performance in chronic schizophrenia. *Psychiatr. Clin. North Am.* 9:49–61.

Zigun, J. R., and Weinberger, D. R. (1992). In vivo studies of brain norphology in schizophrenia. In *New Biological Vistas on Schizophrenia*, J. P. Lindenmaer and S. R. Kay (eds.). New York: Brunner-Mazel, pp. 57–81.

# 15

# Amnesic Disorders

RUSSELL M. BAUER, BETSY TOBIAS, AND EDWARD VALENSTEIN

Over the past four decades, our understanding of disorders of memory has advanced remarkably. In 1950 very little was known about the localization of brain lesions causing amnesia. Despite a few clues in earlier literature, it came as a complete surprise in the early 1950s that bilateral medial temporal resection caused amnesia. The importance of the thalamus in memory was hardly suspected until the 1970s and the basal forebrain was an area virtually unknown to clinicians before the 1980s. An animal model of the amnesic syndrome was not developed until the 1970s.

During this same period, the neuropsychological characteristics of amnesia were better defined. As a result, we no longer consider memory to be unitary. The typical amnesic syndrome does not affect all kinds of memory, and patients who do not qualify as typically amnesic (e.g., patients with frontal lobe lesions) may have qualitatively different memory disturbances. The idea that there is a core "amnesic syndrome" can also be called into question, but we will use this term to describe the memory disturbances that typically follow medial temporal lobe destruction and the substantially similar disorders associated with diencephalic and basal forebrain lesions. We begin this chapter by summarizing the most salient features of this syndrome and by briefly describing the methods for evaluating amnesia in the clinic. The neuropsychological mechanisms underlying the amnesic syndrome, and those underlying memory functions typically spared in the amnesic syndrome, are then discussed in some detail. The evidence for the anatomic localization of amnesia is reviewed. In the section on amnesia subtypes we consider the possibility that there is more than one "amnesic syndrome" depending upon the locus of the lesion. The next sections briefly consider the disorders that commonly present with amnesia, and the chapter concludes with the principles of memory rehabilitation.

## CLINICAL CHARACTERISTICS OF THE AMNESIC SYNDROME

The amnesic syndromes caused by different diseases, or by lesions in different parts of the brain, have in common characteristics that are considered to comprise the "amnesic syndrome." It is possible to date the onset of many of the disorders that cause amnesia. Loss of memory for events occurring after the onset of the disorder is called anterograde amnesia. In addition, however, most amnesics have difficulty recalling some events that occurred prior to the onset of their amnesia. This has been called retrograde amnesia. Finally, patients with the amnesic syndrome should have preservation of many cognitive abilities, and these preserved abilities also help to define the syndrome.

## Anterograde Amnesia

The hallmark of the amnesic syndrome is a profound defect in new learning called anterograde amnesia. In some studies, the deficit is described as involving "recent" or "long-term" memory; the essential feature of the deficit is the impairment in the conscious, deliberate recall of information initially learned after illness onset. The defect is disclosed in practically any situation in which the recall burden exceeds the immediate memory span, or in which there is sufficient distraction between information exposure and the memory test to prevent rehearsal. Anterograde memory loss prevents the patient from establishing new memories from the time of illness onset. Amnesic patients are severely impaired in everyday life and their learning deficit is apparent on even casual observation. Such patients may fail to learn the names of hospital staff and will fail to recognize newly encountered persons after brief delays. They may appear disoriented in place or time because they have failed to learn their location or have lost the ability to monitor and keep track of ongoing events. Amnesic patients are frequently capable of maintaining adequate conversation and interaction, but their deficit may become obvious when they are asked to recall an event that occurred only hours or minutes before. Instructions to remember such events for later recall rarely result in measurable improvement. Although such deficits are apparent in the patient's everyday behavior, they may be more precisely documented by traditional tests of delayed free recall, cued recall, and recognition.

## Retrograde Amnesia

In addition to defects of new learning, the amnesic patient usually also has difficulty recalling events that occurred prior to illness onset. In many cases, this impairment is worse for relatively recent events than for events that occurred in the very remote past. Retrograde amnesia typically involves both "autobiographical" information from the patient's specific past (e.g., the circumstances surrounding an important relative's death) as well as more "public" information (such as which American president helped negotiate the Arab-Israeli peace accord).

Among amnesic subjects, three patterns of retrograde amnesia have been described in the literature: (1) An impairment that is temporally limited, involving primarily the few years prior to the onset of amnesia with complete or near complete sparing of more remote time periods. This has been documented in the famous temporal lobe amnesic H.M. (Milner et al. 1968; Marslen-Wilson and Teuber, 1974; Corkin, 1984) and in patients receiving electroconvulsive therapy for depression (Squire et al. 1975; Squire and Fox, 1980). (2) An impairment that is temporally graded, affecting all time periods, with greater impairment of memories derived from recent time periods is said to be typical of patients with alcoholic Korsakoff's syndrome (Albert et al. 1979; Meudell et al., 1980; Cohen and Squire, 1981; Seltzer and Benson, 1974; Squire and Cohen, 1984; Squire et al., 1989a). (3) A decade-nonspecific impairment affecting all time periods equally has been described in patients surviving herpes simplex encephalitis (Cermak and O'Connor, 1983; Butters et al., 1984; Damasio et al., 1985a) and certain other amnesic subjects (Sanders and Warrington, 1971), as well as in patients with Huntington's disease (Albert et al. 1981).

### Other Characteristics of the Amnesic Syndrome

Amnesic patients, despite significant impairments in new learning and remote memory, characteristically score normally or near normally on psychometric tests of intelligence (e.g., the Wechsler Adult Intelligence Scale—Revised (WAIS-R)) and perform normally on measures of immediate memory, provided that the amount of information they are required to learn is within their attention span (Drachman and Arbit, 1966). Thus, amnesia cannot be explained on the basis of poor attention span, or by other cognitive deficits. However, other cognitive deficits can be seen in some amnesic patients, and may contribute to their deficits in memory. A good example is the patient with alcoholic Korsakoff's syndrome, in whom visuospatial and visuoperceptual deficits (Kapur and Butters, 1977) and impairment on so-called frontal lobe tests like the Wisconsin Card Sorting Test (cf. Moscovitch, 1982; Squire, 1982b) are commonly found.

As classically defined, the anterograde and retrograde deficits that characterize the amnesic syndrome are multimodal. Such a pattern likely results from bilateral or midline involvement of a memory system which is not itself organized in a modality-specific way. However, modality-specific impairments in new learning have been described in patients with circumscribed vascular lesions affecting cortico-cortical pathways linking sensory association cortices with the medial temporal memory system (Ross, 1980a,b). Also, patients with unilateral lesions may have a modality-independent amnesia that is nevertheless *material specific:* patients with left-hemisphere lesions typically have more difficulty with verbal than nonverbal memory, and the reverse tends to be true of patients with right-hemisphere lesions.

Finally, even densely amnesic patients show certain spared memory capacities in addition to their spared attentional and intellectual skills. When memory is indexed by changes in performance rather than by direct, conscious recollection, amnesics often show remarkably normal new learning capacity. These intact capabilities have been documented in two general areas: (1) the acquisition of new motor, perceptual, and cognitive skills (e.g., Cohen and Squire, 1980) and (2) an intact ability to show normal facilitation ("priming") of performance (as measured by increased accuracy or response speed) when specific stimuli, or stimulus contexts, are repeated after initial presentation (e.g., Cermak et al., 1985).

## EVALUATING THE AMNESIC PATIENT

The two main goals of memory assessment in amnesic patients are (1) to establish the severity of the memory defect in the context of other cognitive complaints and (2) to characterize the nature of the memory impairment and its basis in encoding, storage, and retrieval operations.

The first goal is best achieved by embedding memory testing in a comprehensive mental status or neuropsychological examination that includes assessment of general intellectual capacity, language functions, visuoperceptual/visuospatial skill, frontal executive skills, motor functions, and an evaluation of psychopathology and emotional dysfunction.

The second goal is achieved by assessing memory functions relevant to the diagnostic/descriptive task faced by the clinician. Historically, there have been two general approaches to the neuropsychological examination of memory deficits. The "global achievement model" (Delis, 1989) is primarily designed to quantify the severity of a memory deficit by subjecting a patient to a variety of tests and by representing the patient's performance in terms of a single overall score. For example, the original Wechsler Memory Scale (WMS; Wechsler, 1945) yielded an overall memory quotient (MQ) which was conceptually and psychometrically intended as an omnibus index of memory ability that could be compared with the IQ. This approach has been criticized because, in representing performance by a single numerical score, it fails to account for qualitative differences among patients who achieve about the same level (Kaplan, 1983). The second approach, called the "cognitive science model" by Delis (1989), applies methods of memory assessment derived from the cognitive information processing literature to the clinical evaluation of memory-disordered patients. As such, this endeavor essentially represents an intersection between cognitive psychology and psychometrics. Which of these two approaches is used depends, to some extent, on the goals of memory assessment. In some clinical settings, where the goal is to detect rather than to characterize a memory defect, a global achievement approach with a valid (sensitive and selective) measure may be quite appropriate. In other settings, however, more specific information about the nature of a patient's memory disorder is needed; in this case, an extended assessment with a flexible battery of memory tests may be required.

Such a battery should broadly evaluate immediate, recent, and remote memory, should incorporate different types of material (e.g., verbal and nonverbal), should evaluate the manner in which the patient learns complex material (e.g., word lists), and should test for memory using a variety of testing formats (e.g., free recall, cued recall, recognition). A detailed description of the various clinical memory tests available is given in Lezak (1983), and other reviews of the memory assessment enterprise include Loring and Papanicolaou (1987) and Russell (1981).

## Immediate Memory Span

As indicated above, the classic amnesic subject performs normally on tasks that require the repetition of information immediately after it is presented. Normal performance, however, is not characteristic of patients with impaired attention secondary to psychiatric illness or dementia. The main purpose of giving a test of immediate memory span is to determine whether a patient's memory impairment can be explained by attentional disturbance. The most widely used span tests are the Digit Span subtests of the Wechsler Intelligence Scales and the Wechsler Memory Scale.

These tests are actually two tests in one: a digits forward and a digits backward test. The latter probably places more demand on effort, vigilance, and mental control, and may also involve a visual scanning component (Weinberg et al. 1972). Separate scores for digits forward and digits backward are available on the Wechsler Memory Scale-Revised (WMS-R; Wechsler, 1987). Nonverbal pointing span can be evaluated with a recent modification of the Corsi Blocks (Kaplan et al., 1991). Memory tests for increasingly long sequences of words (Miller, 1973) or sentences (Benton and Hamsher, 1976) are also avaiable.

## Tests of Anterograde Learning

MEMORY FOR WORD LISTS AND STORIES

By far the most widely used clinical memory tests are those that require the patient to verbally recall or recognize information presented in list or story format. The most useful tests are those that include both immediate- and delayed-recall probes. Prominent examples of list-learning tasks include the Rey Auditory Verbal Learning Test (RAVLT; Lezak, 1983), the California Verbal Learning Test (CVLT; Delis et al., 1987), and the Selective Reminding Procedure (Bushke and Fuld, 1974). Examples of story recall tests include the WMS-R Logical Memory subtest (Wechsler, 1987), the Babcock-Levy Story (Babcock, 1930), and the Randt Memory Test (Randt and Brown, 1983). The Warrington Recognition Memory Test (RMT; Warrington, 1984) provides a relatively sensitive test of verbal (word) and nonverbal (face) recognition using a forced-choice format. It seems useful for documenting material specificity (e.g., verbal vs. nonverbal memory deficits) in memory performance after unilateral brain lesions.

The CVLT is particularly useful in documenting the manner in which the patient goes about learning a superspan list. It consists of sixteen shopping items, arranged into four categories (fruits, tools, spices/herbs, clothing). The items are randomly presented to the subject, who must recall as many as possible in any order. After five repetitions of the list, a second list is introduced and recall is probed once. Free and cued recall for the first list is then obtained immediately and after a 20-minute delay. Finally, yes-no recognition is measured. Normative data on a variety of learning and memory variables, including consistency of item recall across trials, the strength of primacy and recency effects, vulnerability to retroactive and proactive interference, retention of information across delays, enhancement of recall performance by category cuing and recognition testing, and frequency of error types (intrusions, perseverations, and false positives) are provided.

NONVERBAL MEMORY TESTS

A variety of tests using nonverbal stimuli are also available. Some of these tests— Visual Reproduction subtest of the WMS and WMS-R, Benton Visual Retention Test (VRT; Benton, 1974), and Rey-Osterrieth Complex Figure (Lezak, 1983)—test nonverbal memory by requiring a drawing-from-memory response. The patient's approach to the Rey-Osterrieth test can be evaluated for the degree of organization

(Binder, 1982) and, if the separate details of the figure are considered as a "list," delayed recall after 20 minutes can be evaluated for primacy and recency effects. It should be emphasized that deficits on drawing-from-memory tests may reflect memory impairment, constructional disability, visuoperceptual dysfunction, or a complex combination of deficits (Kaplan, 1983). For this reason, it is important to test nonverbal memory by including additional tests that do not require a drawn memory reproduction. Benton et al. (1983) and Kaplan (cf. Milberg et al. 1986) provide multiple-choice alternatives for the Benton VRT and the WMS figures, respectively. The WMS-R also provides a visual paired-associate learning subtest which requires the subject to match a series of figures with one of six colors until perfect performance is achieved. The Continuous Visual Memory Test (Trahan and Larrabee, 1986) provides a "recurring figures" type of recognition test with excellent normative data, a visuoperceptual check, and a method for calculating response bias in recognition performance.

## Tests for Retrograde Amnesia

The patient's ability to recall information acquired before the onset of amnesia can be assessed informally by planning an interview containing both autobiographical and public-domain questions. Including the former type of material obviously requires the cooperation of a knowledgeable informant, and poses some difficulty regarding quantification of the severity and temporal parameters of any deficit that emerges. Alternatively, a number of more formal, well-normed assessments of remote memory are available. The Boston Remote Memory Battery (Albert et al. 1979) assesses memory for public events and famous faces, and contains both easy and difficult items from the 1930s to the 1970s. A recent extension of the test into the 1980s has been completed and is available from Marilyn Albert. The test, and others like it, has been used extensively in clinical and experimental research documenting patterns of remote memory impairment in various clinical populations described above. One problem with such tests is that, since many items (and faces) are widely accessible to the general public, it is difficult to determine when knowledge about a specific public event or famous personality was actually acquired; this makes interpretation of temporal parameters of retrograde memory loss very difficult. In an attempt to deal with this problem, Squire and colleagues (Squire et al. 1975) developed a test that assesses memory for television shows that were broadcast for only one season. This test has been periodically updated and has been used in a variety of studies in Squire's lab and elsewhere.

It should be recognized that tests of retrograde amnesia present substantial methodological and conceptual complexity (cf. Sanders and Warrington, 1971; Squire and Cohen, 1982; Squire et al. 1989a). Most of these tests make two important assumptions: (1) that relevant information was experienced and learned at about the time it occurred (e.g., that the patient learned in early 1960 about John Glenn and his earth orbit) and (2) that all items were learned with approximately equal strength, and that forgetting of specific details has proceeded at approximately the same rate since original learning. Although a discussion of these complexities is beyond the scope of this chapter, it is important to recognize that results may be difficult to interpret in younger patients, because such tests evaluate memory for events that span several decades.

## Specialized Tests of Information Processing

If precise characterization of a patient's memory deficit is desired, several experimental memory tests are available which are designed to evaluate specific aspects of memory-relevant information processing. Tests relevant to *encoding* ability include Wickens's release from proactive interference (PI) procedure (Wickens, 1970) and variations of the levels-of-processing approach of Craik and Lockhart (1972), in which orienting questions at the point of learning direct processing to particular aspects of target stimuli; these may be further analyzed by comparing recall and recognition performance on categorized vs. uncategorized lists. Rate of forgetting from long-term memory may be evaluated with a variety of recognition paradigms based on the Huppert and Piercy (1979) procedure. The key feature of this approach is to equate initial learning in some meaningful way with a control group, and then periodically to probe recognition accuracy at specified delays after original learning. Retrieval processes are usually evaluated by manipulating cues available during the memory test; comparisons between free recall and recognition, as well as between free and cued recall are relevant to retrieval explanations of memory disorder. It should be kept in mind, however, that better performance on recognition testing compared to recall may not specifically implicate retrieval processes; such a finding is also characteristic of "weak" memory due to poor initial encoding or a long study-test interval. Other relevant tasks include tests that evaluate memory for temporal order and recency, metamemory, and source amnesia described below.

Effort should also be devoted to documenting domains of spared memory in amnesic patients. "Semantic" memory can be assessed with general information questions (e.g., WAIS-R Information subtest; Wechsler, 1981) and with tests of controlled word association (Benton et al., 1983). Performance on "indirect" tests of memory can be assessed using variants of word-stem completion priming (Graf et al., 1984), perceptual identification (Jacoby and Dallas, 1981), motor skill learning (Milner et al. 1968), and other procedures relevant to the specific case.

One issue is how to quantify the severity of amnesia in the individual patient. This is important in scientific and clinical communication in order to compare a given patient with others described in the literature. A commonly used convention is to specify a discrepancy (usually one standard deviation or 15 points) between an omnibus test of memory (e.g., Wechsler Memory Scale MQ) and a similarly scaled measure of overall cognitive ability (e.g., Wechsler Adult Intelligence Scale IQ) (Squire and Shimamura, 1986). One problem with this approach is that the MQ is comprised of a number of subtests, only some of which measure abilities impaired in amnesia (cf. Lezak, 1983; Erickson and Scott, 1977). This practice is further complicated by the fact that the Wechsler Memory Scale-IQ discrepancy was originally formulated at a time when earlier versions of the Wechsler Intelligence Scale were in wide use. The Revised Wechsler Memory Scale is now available, and yields multiple memory indices rather than a single MQ. Given all of these options, there is as yet no widely accepted convention for quantitatively representing amnesia severity across laboratories, though the suggestion of Squire and Shimamura (1986) to use a variety of measures with a range of difficulty represents a useful first step. If the lessons of the past are to be learned appropriately, it is important, when advancing a particular view of amnesia, to rule out alternative interpretations of the patient's deficit by sufficiently broad neuropsychological analysis. In the least, it is important, in documenting amnesia severity, to take the various restandardizations of the available tests into account when calculating discrepancy scores.

## NEUROPSYCHOLOGICAL ANALYSES OF AMNESIC SYNDROMES: I. FUNCTIONS IMPAIRED IN AMNESIA

In this section we discuss information processing models of anterograde and retrograde amnesia (cf. Klatzky, 1982). Regardless of the psychological function it wishes to model, any information processing approach assumes that complex abilities (e.g., memory) can be subdivided into distinct and more fundamental subprocesses (cf. Klatzky, 1982). This emphasis on "process" rather than "product" has stimulated a whole generation of experimental evaluations of the nature of amnesia, often in hopes of disclosing a singular "core" defect that might account for the range of observed impairments.

Information processing accounts of amnesia can be grouped into three broad types: (1) those that characterize the defect as impairment in the *acquisition* of new information, (2) those that invoke impaired *maintenance and storage* of information during the retention interval, and (3) those that assert that the amnesic patient has impaired *retrieval* of information when formally tested (see Squire and Cohen, 1984, for an extensive review). Proponents of each of these views have tended to rely on certain restricted features of the overall syndrome and have tended, in advancing their view, to draw largely from a specific patient population. Studies favoring an encoding deficit have largely relied on the performance of alcoholic Korsakoff patients, while studies invoking storage deficits have usually studied patients with medial temporal lesions.

Researchers who assert that amnesia is the result of an impairment in a specific information processing ability incur certain formidable responsibilities. As Squire and Cohen (1984) indicate, doing so requires a demonstration that such a defect is a cause, rather than a consequence, of amnesia (cf. Mayes et al. 1981). Similarly, when one asserts that amnesia results from the impairment of some information processing capacity, it is necessary to show that amnesics are differentially affected by manipulations designed to affect that process (the "law of differential deficits"). This has proved to be a demanding task. For example, retrieval explanations of amnesia have relied extensively on the idea that the performance of amnesics on memory tests is influenced more by the method of testing (e.g., cued vs. free recall) than by the method of study. Many studies comparing amnesics to normals on cued recall (Squire et al. 1978; Mayes and Meudell, 1981) and recognition (Mayes et al. 1980) have shown that the pattern exhibited by amnesics was also shown by normals during the course of natural forgetting. Such findings favor a "weak memory" interpretation of amnesia: amnesics have a weakened, but structurally normal memory, rather than a disproportionate impairment in retrieval. Because of such complexities, growing discomfort has emerged regarding any view that asserts that amnesia results from "nothing but ..." encoding, retention, and/or retrieval deficits. Attempts to fractionate amnesic defects have been extremely valuable, not as ultimate explanations, but as *heuristics* in specifying the important dimensions on which amnesic syndromes may vary.

### Amnesia as an Encoding Deficit

The postulate that amnesia reflects a deficit that occurs at the time of learning derives mainly from studies showing that certain amnesics, when faced with a memory task, do not organize or encode to-be-learned information in a normal way (cf. Butters and Cermak, 1980). Such studies, mainly involving analysis of the performance of alcoholic Korsakoff patients, have suggested that these patients have difficulty in engaging in "deeper," more elaborative levels of information processing, resulting in impoverished stimulus analysis.

Evaluations of encoding deficits as a causative factor in amnesia were stimulated by the "levels-of-processing" approach to memory introduced by Craik and Lockhart (1972). These authors asserted that memory is the natural result of cognitive operations applied to stimuli at the point of learning, and that "deeper," meaning-based, semantic analysis would lead to superior retention than would analysis of the "superficial" (orthographic or phonemic) characteristics of stimuli. Talland (1965) asserted that the alcoholic Korsakoff patient engaged in a "premature closure of activation" that affected the dynamic processing required for full encoding of to-be-learned stimuli. This laid a foundation for considering Korsakoff amnesia within the context of the levels-of-processing framework. Studies conducted within this tradition (Cermak and Butters, 1972; Cermak et al. 1973a, 1974, 1976) demonstrated that amnesic Korsakoff patients spontaneously analyze only those features of verbal information that represent superficial levels of processing.

Support for the idea that superficial analysis leads to poor retrieval comes from results of a study (Cermak et al., 1974) using Wickens's (1970) release from PI technique. In this procedure, three words from the same semantic category are presented. After 20 seconds of distraction, subjects are asked to recall the words. On each subsequent trial, three more words from the same semantic category are presented. As trials proceed, practically all subjects recall fewer and fewer words, until on a later trial, the category to which the words belong is changed. According to Wickens (1970), when a category shift improves performance, this is evidence that the subject must have been encoding information along the shifted dimension (e.g., semantic category membership). When a category switch occurs, normals typically improve their performance because PI is reduced. When this task is given to alcoholic Korsakoff patients, however, the amount of PI release varies with the nature of to-be-learned information. In the Cermak et al. (1974) study, normal release was seen when numbers were used as stimuli, but a failure to release from PI was seen with words. Cermak et al. concluded that their retrieval deficit was a direct result of the amnesics' inability to spontaneously analyze words on the basis of their semantic features.

More recent investigations of "encoding deficits" theory have shown that, even when alcoholic Korsakoff patients are directed toward semantic analysis via appropriate orienting questions, their retention remains far below normal. This finding, and subsequent results using a variant of Thomson and Tulving's (1970) encoding specificity procedure, have led to a recent modification of the original encoding deficits theory (Cermak et al., 1980; cf. Verfaellie and Cermak, 1991). In this modification, encoding is redefined as a product of analysis in which subjects cognitively manipulate those features of the information they just analyzed in order to permit differential storage. By this modified view, amnesics may be able to semantically analyze information, but may not be able to profit from the results of such analysis because they fail to encode its products. Verfaellie and Cermak (1991) assert that this view of encoding (as manipulation and organization of features of information into a more permanent memory) bridges the gap between theories of amnesia that focus on encoding, consolidation, and retrieval deficits. Common to all these theories is the idea that amnesics cannot store new material because they cannot cognitively manipulate the features of the material to permit assimilation into a general knowledge system.

One problem with the encoding deficit theory, even as modified, is that the abnormal performances it seeks to explain (e.g., failure to release from PI; subnormal performance even when orienting questions direct attention toward semantic features) are not found in all amnesics. For example, normal release from PI after a shift in semantic category has been found in patient N.A. (with traumatic lesions in the diencephalon), patients undergoing bilateral electroconvulsive therapy (ECT) (Squire, 1982b), postencephalitic amnesics (Cermak, 1976), and a patient with amnesia secondary to a left retrosplenial lesion (Valenstein et al., 1987). Also, other studies have suggested that alcoholic Korsakoff patients may show a release from PI effect if they are provided with repeated exposure to the new category members (Kinsbourne and Wood, 1975) or if they are forewarned of the impending shift (Winocur et al. 1981).

### Amnesia as a Retention Deficit

Theories that postulate a retention deficit as responsible for amnesia propose a "postencoding" deficit in which memory representations are poorly maintained or elaborated with the passage of time. One such theory was advanced by Milner (1962, 1966), who described a postencoding process called "consolidation" that was presumed to mediate the transition of memory from an unstable short-term memory store to a more permanent and stable long-term store. Retention deficit views have been based on two main findings: (1) that at least some forms of amnesia show an abnormally rapid rate of forgetting in recognition paradigms and (2) the same patients tend to display a temporally limited retrograde defect, affecting only those time periods immediately preceding the onset of amnesia.

While encoding deficit theories have primarily relied on alcoholic Korsakoff patients for supportive data, theories that postulate a deficit in retention/storage have drawn supportive findings primarily from research with patients with damage to medial temporal structures. Huppert and Piercy (1979) published an influential paper demonstrating abnormally rapid forgetting in the temporal lobe amnesic H.M.

In this study, H.M. was shown 120 slides of colored magazine photographs and was asked to remember them. His performance was equated to that of normals by allowing him increased study time. Yes-no recognition was probed ten minutes, one day, and seven days after initial learning, each probe using a different subset of targets. Although H.M. performed equally to the control groups at the ten-minute test, his retention scores at the one-day and seven-day probes suggested that he forgot the material more rapidly than two matched normal controls. In a second experiment, using different but equivalent stimuli, Huppert and Piercy demonstrated that H.M. forgot more rapidly than alcoholic Korsakoff patients, scoring 1.61 standard deviations below their mean at one day and $-2.55$ standard deviations at seven days. Squire (1981) reported similar results with bilateral ECT patients, whose transient posttreatment deficits are due to putative medial temporal dysfunction. Zola-Morgan and Squire (1982) found that monkeys with medial temporal ablations displayed abnormally rapid forgetting when assessed after a 24-hour delay on a delayed non-matching-to-sample procedure, while monkeys with diencephalic lesions showed a normal rate of forgetting.

Although the apparent association of rapid forgetting with damage to the medial temporal region initially led to the suggestion that forgetting rates (and the retention defect they seemed to indicate) might serve to differentiate medial temporal from diencephalic forms of amnesia (cf. also Squire, 1982a), more recent studies have generally failed to provide support for the view that links medial temporal damage to abnormally rapid forgetting (Freed et al. 1987; Kopelman, 1985; McKee and Squire, 1992). These studies will be reviewed in detail below when we consider the possibility that distinct subtypes of amnesia exist.

Squire et al. (1984a) suggested that the temporally limited retrograde amnesia said to be typical of patients with medial temporal lobe lesions may result from a defect in *consolidation* of information. They proposed that consolidation is a gradual process, lasting for months or even years. When this process is interrupted by brain impairment, premorbid memories will be affected, but only for a limited period of time. According to this view, the medial temporal system initially stored. After a time, the storage sites are capable of being autonomously activated in a coordinated fashion, after which the medial temporal system is not involved in memory retrieval. If one supposes that this process takes place gradually (over a period of years), then retrieval of very remote memories is normal in medial temporal amnesia because they are fully consolidated and no longer depend upon the activity of the medial temporal system (Squire et al. 1984a). This view predicts a strong relationship between temporally limited retrograde amnesia and anterograde amnesia because it suggests that the same mechanism (impairment in the ability of the medial temporal system to mediate time-locked information retrieval prior to the point at which consolidation is complete) may be responsible for both (Squire and Cohen, 1984).

Limited support for the idea that the hippocampus is needed for consolidation of memories comes from animal studies. Zola-Morgan and Squire (1990b) trained monkeys to make 20 object discriminations each at 16, 12, 8, 4, and 2 weeks prior to bilateral hippocampal and parahippocampal gyrus (H+) lesions (for a total of 100 object pairs). Whereas control monkeys recalled recently presented objects (the pairs learned at weeks 2 and 4) better than discriminations learned earlier, lesioned animals performed worse at the more recently learned discriminations. After 12 to 16 weeks, hippocampal lesions made no difference in recall, presumably because consolidation was complete.

## Amnesia as a Retrieval Deficit

The view that amnesia reflects a deficit in information retrieval is based on two main findings: (1) that manipulating testing procedures by providing aids to retrieval in the form of cues or prompts can dramatically improve the memory performance of some amnesic patients and (2) that all amnesics exhibit some form of retrograde memory loss.

### RETRIEVAL DEFICITS IN ANTEROGRADE AMNESIA

Warrington and Weiskrantz (1968, 1970) proposed a retrieval deficit model of amnesia, basing their view on findings from what has become known as the "partial information technique." In their initial experiments, amnesic subjects were presented on each of five learning trials with a series of stimuli that were increasingly less fragmented until they could identify the stimulus. When the stimuli were re-presented after a one-day delay, amnesic subjects identified them sooner (i.e., when more fragmented) than on the initial presentation, implying that something was retained from the initial stimulus exposure. Despite this facilitation, amnesics showed little evidence of retention on conventional recall and recognition tests. Based on these findings, Warrington and Weiskrantz concluded that retention by amnesics depended more on the method of retrieval than on the method of acquisition. They explained the amnesic deficit as resulting from abnormal susceptibility to interference from competing responses at the point of recall. Because of this, their view has also been referred to as the "retrieval interference" model of amnesia.

To provide further support for the presumed effects of interference during retrieval, Warrington and Weiskrantz (1974, 1978) performed a series of experiments using a reversal learning paradigm. In these experiments, subjects learned two different word lists constructed so that each word on one list began with the same three letters as a word on the second list. Subjects studied list 1 once and had multiple trials to learn list 2. After each trial, retention was assessed with a cued recall paradigm in which the first three letters of target words were provided. For normal controls, initial learning of list 2 was markedly inferior to list 1 recall, though performance improved on repeated trials. Like controls, amnesics performed well on list 1 and experienced considerable interference from list 1 when attempting to recall list 2 words. However, amnesics continued, despite repeated exposure to list 2, to exhibit a high incidence of list 1 intrusions. Since amnesics gave such a high incidence of list 1 intrusions, Warrington and Weiskrantz argued that storage of list 1 had occurred, and that it continued to interfere with retrieval of list 2 words through a process of response competition.

In a subsequent study (Warrington and Weiskrantz, 1978), several problems with a strict retrieval interference interpretation of this data became apparent. First, amnesics did not show *more* susceptibility to interference than normals on the initial list 2 trial, violating the principle of differential deficits. Second, an attempt was made to reduce response competition by creating word lists in which each pair of words (one from list 1 and one from list 2) were the only English words beginning with those initial letters. Unfortunately for the retrieval interference interpretation, this manipulation had no effect on performance. These results led Warrington and Weiskrantz to modify their view and to suggest that list 1 responses were so domineering as to actually impede the *learning* of list 2 words. This was an important statement, since it represents the first time that a retrieval deficit theorist admitted the possibility of a deficit in acquisition into their model. As a consequence, it represents the beginning of an eventual merger between retrieval deficit and encoding deficit theories (Cermak, 1982; Winocur et al. 1981; Verfaellie and Cermak, 1991) that characterizes present-day theory.

RETRIEVAL DEFICITS IN RETROGRADE AMNESIA

Retrieval deficits are more securely invoked in explaining retrograde amnesia. Although temporally limited retrograde amnesia has been attributed to defects in consolidation (see above), this clearly cannot be the case in patients whose retrograde amnesia recovers. Thus, the retrograde amnesia that follows closed head injury, which recovers as the posttraumatic anterograde amnesia improves, must be attributed to a retrieval deficit, since memories of events prior to the injury must be present during the amnesia if they are to be recalled afterward. Similarly, patients with transient global amnesia may forget that a relative has died months or years ago, but recall this clearly after their anterograde deficit has improved.

Retrieval deficits may also explain some of the extensive, temporally graded retrograde amnesia seen in patients with alcoholic Korsakoff's syndrome. It has been argued, however, that this retrograde amnesia may in fact be an artifact of progressively severe learning deficits seen in non-Korsakoff alcoholics (Albert et al. 1980; cf. Squire and Cohen, 1984). The severity of anterograde learning defects in detoxified non-Korsakoff alcoholics is correlated with the duration of alcohol abuse (Ryan and Butters, 1980a,b). The temporal gradient in the retrograde amnesia of Korsakoff patients may thus reflect the fact that more recent information was never effectively learned. In support of this idea, studies of amnesic patients with acute-onset diencephalic pathology (e.g., stroke, trauma) generally report relatively mild retrograde amnesia (Winocur et al. 1984; Cohen and Squire, 1981). However, Korsakoff patients, compared to alcoholic controls, tend to be impaired at *all decades*, even those that predated the onset of abuse-related anterograde amnesia (Albert et al. 1980; Cohen and Squire, 1981).

More convincing evidence for a true retrograde amnesia in Korsakoff patients comes from a single case study reported by Butters and Cermak (1986). These authors studied the Korsakoff patient P.Z., an eminent scientist who had published an autobiography three years prior to the acute onset of Wernicke's encephalopathy in 1982. On Albert et al.'s remote memory test, P.Z., like other Korsakoff patients, had significant impairment *across all time periods*, with some relative sparing of the ability to recognize famous faces from the 1930s and 1940s. Butters and Cermak then devised a remote memory test based on information derived from his autobiography. They found a rather striking temporal gradient in his memory of autobiographical events, with dramatic and complete impairment of information taken from the 1960s and 1970s and relative (though not complete) sparing of very remote memories. The fact that all questions were taken from his own autobiography eliminates the possibility that this information was never learned, though the possibility remains that it was somehow "less stable," and therefore more difficult to retrieve, for more recent time periods.

These findings led Butters and Miliotis (1985) to propose that the temporally graded retrograde memory impairment in Korsakoff's syndrome is the product of two separate factors: (1) an increasingly severe anterograde learning deficit that is gradually acquired through years of alcohol abuse and (2) an impairment of memory retrieval, appearing acutely with the Wernicke stage of the illness, that affects all time periods equally. These two superimposed deficits result in a temporally graded retrograde amnesia affecting all time periods.

A retrieval deficit also may explain decade-nonspecific retrograde amnesia, since there is no a priori basis to suppose that a generalized retrieval deficit would favor certain time periods over others. Such an explanation has, in fact, been advanced to explain retrograde amnesia in Huntington's disease (Albert et al., 1981).

STATE-DEPENDENT LEARNING

Another phenomenon that may illustrate a specific retrieval deficit is state-dependent memory. This denotes the enhanced ability to recall information when the subject is in the same physiological state that accompanied learning. For example, the retrieval of information encoded while inebriated may be better recalled after subsequent alcohol ingestion than when sober (Goodwin et al., 1969). This subject has been reviewed by Eich (1989).

## Summary

Although encoding, retention, and retrieval views all have their merits, it is clear that any view that postulates one (and only one) deficient stage of memory processing cannot explain the variety of deficits seen in amnesia. Instead, it may be better to view encoding, retention, and retrieval as dimensions (or sources of variance) that all contribute in every situation to the strength of a memory trace and which contribute unequally, and in a complex way, to different memory assessment tasks.

## NEUROPSYCHOLOGICAL ANALYSES OF AMNESIC SYNDROMES: II. MEMORY FUNCTIONS SPARED IN AMNESIA

The studies and formulations just described have largely been designed to explain what is "wrong" with amnesics; i.e., what they cannot do. In the course of examining the scope and limits of these defects, it has become clear that amnesics are not impaired on all memory-related tasks. This behavioral selectivity has obvious implications for how memory is organized, and has had significant impact on theoretical accounts devised to explain the nature of memory dysfunction in amnesia. In the past two decades, a substantial literature has developed in the area of "memory dissociations": dissociations between a class of tasks amnesics can perform and a class of tasks they cannot perform (cf. Roediger et al., 1989; Schacter, 1987a, 1989; Squire, 1987, for reviews). In this section we first review findings of spared memory function in amnesia, and then discuss theoretical accounts advanced to explain such dissociations.

## Preserved Preillness Memory

Although amnesics generally have some form of impairment in memory for events that occurred prior to onset of amnesia, this loss of memory is not complete. If it was, amnesics would be like newborn babies, having to relearn everything anew. In fact, most amnesics remember more from the time prior to onset of their illness than they forget. This preserved preillness memory can take several forms: intact knowledge structures, preservation of skills, and retained preferences.

### INTACT KNOWLEDGE STRUCTURES

The amnesic patient retains substantial intellectual, linguistic, and social skill despite profound impairments in the ability to recall specific information encountered in prior learning episodes. Performance on standard intellectual tests is frequently normal or near normal. Social graces are almost always intact, and linguistic skill typically reveals no gross abnormalities. That is, amnesics appear to be able to use "general knowledge" at the same time they have significantly impaired memory and learning skills. One important characteristic of general knowledge that distinguishes it from the type of memory usually impaired in amnesia is that general knowledge is generally "context free"; i.e., its content is generally devoid of autobiographical information about the time and place in which the information was originally learned. Thus, for example, social and linguistic knowledge is accessed and used without reference to the situation in which it was originally learned. This is in contrast to the type of memory manifested in conventional tests of recall and recognition, which refers specifically to a learning experience and involves a directed "readout" of information learned at that time.

### MOTOR AND COGNITIVE SKILLS

In addition to a sparing of intellectual, social, and linguistic skill, amnesics frequently show relatively good retention of previously acquired motor and cognitive skills such as how to ride a bike, drive a car, play the piano, or use appliances. Evidence that a previously acquired skill can be spared after the onset of amnesia comes from work by Schacter (1983) and Squire et al. (1984b). Schacter (1983) provides a fascinating case study of an amnesic who retained his skill at golf, but who became unable to accurately remember his score, or his immediately preceding shots, on each hole. Moments after teeing off he would begin to tee another ball, forgetting that he had just taken a shot. (Similar impairments are widely recognized in the general golfing population, with errors tending toward flagrant underestimations of actual scores!) Squire and colleagues taught a mirror-reading skill to depressed psychiatric inpatients prior to a scheduled course of ECT. After treatment was completed, the skill was retained despite marked retrograde amnesia for the training procedure itself.

PREFERENCES

Although very little empirical data are available regarding the effects of memory impairment on emotional functioning, Johnson et al. (1985) suggest that feelings and preferences may be spared in amnesics to the extent that they are based on memory for general sensory and perceptual features of stimuli as opposed to specific autobiographical memories which are often impaired in amnesics. Indeed, anecdotal evidence suggests that many amnesics continue to exhibit *personal* preferences for such things as favorite color, certain clothes, and food. They continue to like and dislike the people they liked and disliked before, even though they may not remember the specific reasons for these feelings. They also retain *general* evaluative responses and emotional reactions. They remember that fire is dangerous and will respond physiologically to fearful stimuli, just as they will appropriately express sadness and joy in response to sad or happy stimuli. Very little is known about the relationship of these responses to more general emotional functioning. The relationship between emotional functioning and memory remains an interesting area for future inquiry.

## Preserved New Learning Capacities

Most amnesics are capable of learning a wide range of information, even though they have no conscious recollection for the experience upon which the learning is based. Memory for such information has been called *implicit* memory, and is distinguished from *explicit* memory, which requires a conscious, deliberate attempt to retrieve target information. In amnesic patients, implicit memory is typically spared, while explicit memory is typically impaired (Schacter, 1987a; Squire, 1987).

Implicit memory is measured using *indirect* (Johnson and Hasher, 1987; Richardson-Klavehn and Bjork, 1988) or *incidental* (Jacoby, 1984) tasks, which make no reference to prior learning episodes at the time of retrieval. Explicit memory is tested with *direct* (or intentional) tasks, which make specific reference to prior exposure (e.g., "Was this word on the list you were shown?"). There is no guarantee, however, that the subject will have the requisite state of mind to make all indirect tasks dependent upon implicit memory (the normal subject may recall the learning episode and use conscious recall) or all direct tasks measures of explicit memory (the subject may make "guesses" that depend upon nonconscious recollection of prior exposures).

Studies of implicit memory include (1) investigations of skill learning, (2) studies of repetition priming, (3) studies of physiologic responses, and (4) studies of preferences.

SKILL LEARNING

Most amnesics are capable of learning new perceptual, cognitive, and motor skills despite a nearly total lack of explicit recall of experiences that lead to such learning

(Milner, 1962; Cermak et al., 1973b; Brooks and Baddeley, 1976; for reviews see Baddeley, 1982; Cohen, 1984; Moscovitch 1982; Squire and Cohen, 1984; Weiskrantz, 1985). Like other psychological processes and procedures, *how* a skill is learned or performed is not thought to be accessible to consciousness, even in individuals with intact explicit memory (Kihlstrom, 1984; Kinsbourne and Wood, 1982; Nisbett and Wilson, 1977). Similarly, changes in these processes are thought to be inaccessible to conscious inspection (Cohen, 1984; Schacter, 1987a); thus, gradual acquisition of cognitive, perceptual, or motor skills through repetition can be seen as largely unconscious or implicit.

Skill learning in amnesics was first investigated by Milner and colleagues in patient H.M. He demonstrated consistent learning in rotary pursuit and bimanual tracking tasks (Corkin, 1968). Similar results have been documented with other amnesics (Eslinger and Damasio, 1986; Starr and Phillips, 1970). H.M. also improved in daily performance on a mirror-tracing task (Milner, 1962), and he was able to learn a short visual maze and showed significant saving during relearning when tested at one-, two-, and three-, and six-day intervals (Milner et al., 1968). Other amnesics have shown practice effects on a variety of relatively complex cognitive skills such as assembling jigsaw puzzles (Brooks and Baddeley, 1976), solving the Tower of Hanoi puzzle (Cohen, 1984; Squire and Cohen, 1984; but see Butters et al., 1985), applying numerical rules (Wood et al., 1982), and learning serial patterns (Nissen and Bullemer, 1987). Gardner (1975) described an amnesic who was able to learn to play a melody on the piano and retain this ability over time, despite his failure to explicitly recall the learning session. Numerous studies have demonstrated that amnesics can gain facility at mirror reading, even though they lack explicit memory of the material (Cohen and Squire, 1980; Verfaellie et al., 1991). Normals show similar degrees of improvement with unfamiliar material, but greater gains with texts that they have seen before, presumably because, unlike the amnesics, they can also use explicit memory. When masking is used to prevent the use of explicit strategies, normals and amnesics perform comparably (Moscovitch et al., 1986).

In most cases, practice effects on skill learning tend to be relatively enduring, persisting up to three months on mirror reading tasks (Cohen and Squire, 1980) and over a year on the Tower of Hanoi puzzle (Cohen, 1984).

REPETITION PRIMING

In a seminal series of studies, Warrington and Weiskrantz (1968, 1970, 1974, 1978) demonstrated that amnesics who were greatly impaired on traditional tests of recall and recognition could show learning and retention of new information in a long-term store, equivalent to normal controls, when cued with partial information such as stimulus fragments or word-stems. Although they interpreted their findings as support for a retrieval deficit account of amnesia, these results can be construed as the first evidence of intact priming in amnesics.

Direct or repetition priming is the facilitation in the processing of a stimulus that occurs following a previous exposure to that stimulus (Schacter, 1987a). Priming tasks can be considered implicit or indirect because subjects are generally not referred to the learning episode during testing. Although Warrington and Weiskrantz (1968) did refer subjects to the learning episode, there is evidence that the subjects had such poor memory that they abandoned explicit strategies and treated the task as a "guessing game." It has subsequently been demonstrated that amnesics perform like normals only when indirect instructions are specifically utilized (e.g., "read this word," "generate the first word that comes to mind," etc.). When direct instructions are given, performance by normals may be boosted by use of explicit strategies and amnesics may refuse to guess (Squire et al., 1978; Graf et al., 1984, 1985).

Amnesics have demonstrated facilitated processing of stimuli following a previous exposure in a number of ways: (1) They have shown decreased latency in making decisions regarding the status of previously exposed stimuli as words or nonwords in *lexical decision* tests (Moscovitch, 1982) and in the case of novel geometric shapes, as possible or impossible objects (Schacter et al., 1991). (2) They have shown increased accuracy and speed in processing previously exposed stimuli on *perceptual identification* tasks which require the identification of words or pictures at very brief exposure durations (Cermak et al., 1985, 1988; Verfaellie et al., 1991), or from degraded representations (Warrington and Weiskrantz, 1968; Milner et al., 1968). Increased speed and accuracy is also seen on speed reading tests (Musen et al., 1990). (3) They have shown a normal tendency to generate previously exposed stimuli in response to nominal cues on *stem completion* (MOT———) and *fragment completion* (—A—IN—) tasks (Diamond and Rozin, 1984; Graf and Schacter, 1985; Graf et al., 1985; Shimamura and Squire, 1984; Shimamura, 1986; Squire et al., 1985). In all of these cases, they have been found to be greatly impaired on comparable direct or explicit memory tests.

While performance of the foregoing priming tests tends to rely on retention of perceptual information regarding the stimuli, a number of studies indicate that amnesics can process and retain more conceptual features of stimuli, such as meaning or category membership. This is evidenced by an increased tendency to generate previously studied items on free association or category generation tests following study of closely related word pairs (e.g., table-chair; Shimamura and Squire, 1984), common idioms (e.g., "small potatoes"; Schacter, 1985), or categorized word lists (Gardner et al., 1973), in spite of greatly impaired performance on comparable cued recall tests. In a clever study by Jacoby and Witherspoon (1982), amnesics demonstrated a tendency to select the less frequent spelling of homophones following biasing orienting questions (e.g., "A reed instrument is a—?"), despite severely impaired recognition performance for the same items (for reviews see Schacter and Graf, 1986b; Shimamura, 1986).

PSYCHOPHYSIOLOGICAL RESPONSES

The foregoing studies provide examples of changes in overt behavior as a result of prior exposure to stimuli in the absence of a subjective report of remembering. This dissociation between behavioral responses (e.g., generating target items) and conscious verbal cognition (e.g., report of remembering target items) is analogous to the desynchrony noted among response systems in emotion (Hodgson and Rachman, 1974; Rachman, 1978; Rachman and Hodgson, 1974; Tobias et al., 1992). Lang (1968, 1971) proposed a multiple-system theory of emotions, in which subjective, behavioral, and physiological indices were only imperfectly coupled, particularly under states of low arousal.

In the mid-1980s it was noted that prosopagnosics showed a reliably stronger electrodermal response (EDR) (skin conductance) to familiar faces relative to unfamiliar foils in a multiple-choice paradigm. This occurred despite their inability to consciously recognize the faces as familiar (Bauer, 1984a; Tranel and Damasio, 1984; see Chapter 9). Schacter et al. (1988) noted intriguing conceptual similarities between spared implicit memory in amnesia and spared recognition abilities in agnosia and hemianopia. Bauer et al. (1992) hypothesized that EDR recognition may provide another index of this unconscious form of memory.

In support of this hypothesis, Verfaellie et al. (1991) demonstrated that an amnesic patient with a left retrosplenial-fornix lesion showed normal electrodermal response to targets despite greatly impaired overt recognition. Verbal recognition and EDR recognition were statistically independent. Similar effects have been demonstrated by Tranel and Damasio (1987) in a postencephalitic patient and by Bauer et al. (1992) in alcoholic Korsakoff and early Alzheimer's disease patients.

Is this form of recognition truly "unconscious" or does it depend on variables that affect more direct forms of memory? Studies by Bauer and colleagues (cf. Bauer and Verfaellie, 1992) indicate that certain variables known to affect direct recognition memory do not affect EDR such as levels of processing and retention interval (effects persisted up to four weeks and in fact were augmented as verbal recognition declined), lending support for the hypothesis that EDR recognition more closely resembles implicit phenomena. On the other hand, the EDR in learning and memory paradigms has been linked to constructs such as orienting, significance detection, and cognitive effort (e.g., EDR recognition is augmented under conditions of uncertainty), which may correlate with aspects of explicit memory. Understanding the relationship of EDR to overt recollection and to other implicit memory phenomena will likely increase our understanding of the neuropsychological mechanism responsible for amnesia and spared learning, and provde a potentially rich domain of behavior and set of tasks for exploring unconscious forms of memory.

EVALUATIVE RESPONSES

Both anecdotal and formal experimental evidence indicate that emotional responses can be preserved as implicit memories in amnesic patients, in the absence of explicit memory for the experiences on which these responses are based. The earliest accounts come from observations of alcoholic Korsakoff patients. Korsakoff (1889) observed that a patient expressed fear at the sight of a case for a shock apparatus and thought that the doctor had "probably come to electrify him," even though he was unable to consciously remember that he had previously been shocked by the apparatus (cf. Schacter, 1987, p. 512). Korsakoff interpreted this comment to reflect a memory trace that was "too weak to enter consciousness." Claparede (1911) surprised a patient by pricking her with a pin hidden in his hand. She later refused to shake hands with him, even though her memory for their previous encounter was very vague and she could explain her behavior only by stating that "pins are sometimes held in hands." He interpreted the problem as a dissociation between the "me-ness" of an experience and the memory trace.

Recent studies have confirmed that amnesics can have preferences despite having no explicit recollection of the reasons for the preferences. Johnson et al. (1985) explored this idea formally. Their first study was based on the "mere exposure" effect documented by Zajonc (1968). Repeated exposure to an object tends to increase judgments of likability, even if there is no substantive information presented that would support such attitudinal change. This phenomenon occurred even when explicit perception and therefore overt recognition of the items was precluded by use of subliminal exposure (Zajonc, 1980). Both Korsakoff patients and controls preferred Korean melodies that had been presented at the outset of an experiment to new Korean melodies when later asked to choose which of two melodies they preferred. Although normals and amnesics showed equivalent preferences, Korsakoff patients were significantly impaired in their ability to recognize the old melodies.

In a second study, amnesic and control subjects were presented with pictures of two faces, accompanied by fictional biographical information that depicted one individual positively and the other negatively. When asked which of the two they preferred 20 days later, both groups showed a strong preference for the "good guy." Control subjects made this choice 100% of the time and always reported that their judgment was made on the basis of explicit memory for the accompanying descriptive information. The patients were unable to recall any of this biographical information, but also showed a strong preference for the "good guy," choosing him 78% of the time. They reported vague reasons for their choice, usually based on the pictured person's physical appearance. This preference was maintained at one-year follow-up.

Damasio et al. (1989) reported a similar experiment with the postencephalitic patient Boswell. It had been observed that Boswell demonstrated some consistency in seeking out certain staff members for certain purposes (e.g., he would go to generous staff members when he wanted treats), despite a profound inability to recognize people. To examine whether Boswell was able to form new preferences, the experimenters set up an extended series of positive, negative, and neutral encounters between Boswell and three different confederates. When asked on a forced-choice recognition test to whom he would go for treats, he strongly preferred the "good" confederate over the "bad" one, with the neutral confederate falling in between. This occurred despite his inability to recall anything about any of the people or to demonstrate familiarity with them in any way. These preferences were maintained over a period of years.

These two studies suggest that amnesics can learn new "emotional" associations of a conceptual nature that persist over long periods of time. They also suggest that emotional responses as reflected by fairly complex behavioral interactions can serve as another measure of spared memory function. This line of research may provide insights on emotional functioning in memory-impaired individuals, about which little is currently known (for a review of emotion and implicit memory, see Tobias et al., 1992).

OTHER DOMAINS OF NEW LEARNING

Many other types of behavior may be affected by and thus serve as measures for implicit memory. Amnesics can learn fictional facts (e.g., Bob Hope's father was a fireman) despite being unable to state the source of this information (Schacter et al., 1984). Amnesics show facilitation in spotting hidden figures after a prior exposure (Crovitz et al., 1979b). Weiskrantz and Warrington (1979) demonstrated classical eyelid conditioning in amnesic patients despite the patients' inability to recollect anything about the conditioning episode. A number of experiments have demonstrated that amnesics can learn new computer skills and technical language by use of implicit strategies. With the vanishing cue method, the amnesic is given increasingly shorter versions of a rule such as "to save your file press F10," or of a word such as "delete" (e.g., dele___), until they are able to perform the function or can recall the word without the cue (Glisky and Schacter, 1987; Glisky et al., 1986a,b; Schacter and Glisky, 1986).

## Interpreting Memory Dissociations: Some Cautions

Even though it is tempting to interpret selectively spared and impaired memory performance in amnesics as indicative of separate memory systems, some cautions are in order in view of our limited understanding of the anatomic and behavioral substrates underlying such dissociations. One key issue is that, although implicit and explicit memories appear dissociable, they can interact substantially in traditional tasks of memory (Jacoby et al., 1989; Jacoby and Dallas, 1981). Implicit memory may be more likely to contribute to direct memory performances under conditions of low confidence or very poor explicit memory, particularly in situations where guessing is required. Explicit memory is more likely to contribute to indirect memory performance when explicit memory is intact and the subject is aware that use of explicit strategies can facilitate performance. Even though a test superficially seems to evaluate explicit memory, performance on it may in part reflect the operation of implicit or unconscious processes. For example, Jacoby and Dallas (1981) argued that performance on recognition tests can be based on two relatively independent processes: direct (explicit) recollection, and an unconscious, or implicit, feeling of facilitated processing termed "perceptual fluency." Thus, one may select an item on forced-choice recognition because it is directly remembered or because it seems to "jump off of the page" as a result of perceptual priming. Because both explicit and implicit memory operate in the same direction (i.e., both would increase the probability of selecting a target item), it has been difficult to specify the relative contribution each has to recognition memory in normals and amnesics. Only recently have methods been developed for measuring the separate and interacting contributions of recollection and "fluency" (Jacoby and Kelly, 1992). Such methods may lead to a greater understanding of the ways such abilities become dissociated in amnesic states, and may provide useful data on the relative merits of available theoretical accounts of implicit-explicit dissociations.

## Theoretical Accounts of Spared vs. Impaired Learning

A number of theories have been generated to account for the differences between spared and impaired memory functions in amnesia. The most influential of these viewpoints will be discussed below.

### THRESHOLD ACCOUNTS

Originally, implicit memory was thought to represent a memory trace that was too weak to enter consciousness (Korsakoff, 1889; Prince, 1914; Leibniz, 1916). In this view, implicit and explicit memory are qualitatively the same; implicit memory traces are simply not strong enough to reach the threshold of activation necessary for explicit memory, just as some traces are strong enough to support recognition but not recall. If this theory is correct, variables that affect explicit memory performance should have parallel effects on implicit memory, only at a different level of performance.

The idea that explicit and implicit memory differ only in sensitivity is contradicted by numerous studies showing that, in both normals and amnesics, explicit and implicit memory are "functionally independent" (see Schacter, 1987a; Richardson-Klavehn and Bjork, 1988; Lewandowsky et al., 1989, for reviews). For example, increased study time or elaborative processing increases explicit memory but often has little effect on indirect tests such as repetition priming (e.g., Jacoby and Dallas, 1981; Graf and Mandler, 1984). Conversely, manipulations that change perceptual or surface features of stimuli, such as letter case, typeface, or modality of presentation, reduce repetition priming effects but have little effect on explicit memory (e.g., Jacoby, 1983b; Blaxton, 1985; Roediger and Weldon, 1987; Winnick and Daniel, 1970). Other variables, including interference effects (Graf and Schacter, 1987; but see Booker, 1992) and retention intervals (Tulving et al., 1982) have different effects on direct and indirect tests of memory.

In addition, several studies have demonstrated that priming effects in word-fragment completion and mirror reading are statistically ("stochastically") independent of comparable direct memory tests (Tulving et al., 1982; Squire et al., 1987). When individual items are analyzed, the stimuli yielding evidence of explicit memory are often different from those yielding evidence of implicit recognition. This is contrary to a threshold account, which would predict that explicitly recognized stimuli would always be implicitly recognized as well. Because of this, a threshold interpretation of implicit-explicit dissociations is no longer regarded as a viable explanation of memory dissociations.

### MULTIPLE MEMORY SYSTEMS ACCOUNTS

By far the most popular approach to explaining spared and impaired memory function in amnesia is to postulate the existence of two (or more) memory "systems," each handling a different type of memory function and operating according to different parameters (cf. Roediger et al., 1989; Sherry and Schacter, 1987). The "episodic" vs. "semantic" memory distinction (Tulving, 1972, 1983) has been frequently invoked to explain the fact that amnesics, despite profound learning deficits, generally retain capacities reflecting general knowledge. Two additional distinctions, the "declarative" vs. "procedural" (more recently, "declarative" vs. "nondeclarative") memory distinction (Cohen and Squire, 1980) and the "explicit" vs. "implicit" memory distinction (Graf and Schacter, 1985; Schacter and Graf, 1986a,b), evolved to explain dissociations between amnesic performance on the direct and indirect tests of memory reviewed above.

*Episodic vs. semantic memory.* As indicated above, the amnesic patient retains substantial intellectual, linguistic, and social skill despite profound impairments in the ability to recall specific information encountered in prior learning episodes. Tulving's (1972, 1983) distinction between "episodic" memory (an "autobiographical" form of memory for contextually specific events) and "semantic" memory (general-world knowledge, linguistic skill, vocabulary), appears in many important ways to account for such a dissociation (Cermak, 1984; Kinsbourne and Wood, 1975; Martin and Fedio, 1983; Weingartner et al., 1983). Many authors have argued that amnesia involves a selective impairment in episodic memory, leaving semantic memory largely intact.

Kinsbourne and Wood (1975) were among the first to formally suggest that amnesia could be accounted for in terms of a distinction between episodic and semantic memory. They asked amnesic patients to define common objects (e.g., "railroad ticket") and to then recall an event from their past in which such an object had been used. They found that the amnesics could provide adequate definitions, but were impaired in recalling specific autobiographical events. Similar findings were reported by Cermak (1984) in a postencephalitic patient.

Cermak (1984) has suggested that the episodic/semantic distinction may explain temporally graded retrograde amnesia. As biographical material ages, it becomes progressively more semantic. Through retelling it becomes incorporated into personal history, a part of personal or family "folklore." More recent memories, however, are less likely to have been repeatedly retold and elaborated, and thus may remain within episodic memory. If amnesia reflects a relatively selective impairment in episodic memory, then more remote memories would be selectively spared, because they have become more semantic. This resembles the consolidation theory of memory, but suggests that cognitive operations, rather than automatic physiologic processes, result in the storage of memories in a form ("semantic store") that remains accessible to amnesic patients.

But there is recent empiric evidence that many amnesics suffer impairments of semantic as well as episodic memory (Cermak et al., 1978; Butters et al., 1987; Cohen and Squire, 1981; Zola-Morgan et al., 1983). For example, Cermak et al. (1978) found that Korsakoff patients had difficulty generating words from what Collins and Loftus (1975) called "conceptual" semantic memory ("name a fruit that is red"). Butters and colleagues (1987) similarly found Korsakoff amnesics deficient on a semantic (verbal fluency) task. These results suggest that amnesia (at least the type seen in Korsakoff's syndrome) is not accurately described as an exclusively episodic deficit.

A more fundamental problem is that episodic and semantic memories are not easily dissociable. Not only do they interact in complex ways (for example, episodic learning can have a stimulating effect on semantic search rate (Loftus and Cole, 1974)), but there is no agreement on exactly what makes a memory episodic rather than semantic. Squire (1987) suggests reserving the term "episodic" for acts of remembering that are specifically autobiographical. In this sense, amnesics clearly suffer from an episodic memory defect. However, if one defines as "episodic" any learning experience that leaves a direct, experience-specific trace in the memory system, then it is clear that amnesics are capable of some forms of new episodic learning. The episodic-semantic distinction has been criticized for these and other reasons (see, for example, Anderson and Ross, 1980; McKoon et al., 1986), and its relevance for explaining the pattern of spared and impaired abilities in amnesia has been questioned (Shimamura and Squire, 1987).

*Declarative vs. procedural memory.*    Cohen and Squire (1980), borrowing from the literature of artificial intelligence (Winograd, 1975) and cognitive psychology (Anderson, 1976), suggested that two separate memory systems existed: a *declarative* memory system dedicated to knowing *that* something was learned, and a *procedural* memory system, dedicated to knowing *how* to perform a skill. Declarative memory includes "the facts, lists, and data of conventional memory experiments and everyday remembering" (Squire, 1987, p. 158), and as such comprises both episodic and semantic material. Skill learning has been discussed above. More recently, the term "nondeclarative" has been used in place of "procedural" (cf. Squire, 1987) to include skills, priming, and evaluative responses (e.g., preferences), in general agreement with the classification system proposed earlier by Cermak et al. (1985). Thus nondeclarative memory has come to mean much the same thing as implicit memory.

The declarative-nondeclarative distinction does not account for the ability of amnesics to learn new facts and acquire new vocabulary (albeit at a much slower rate), a function specifically reserved for the declarative system (Glisky et al., 1986a; Schacter et al., 1984).

*Implicit vs. explicit memory.*    The distinction between explicit and implicit memory (cf. Schacter, 1987a; Sherry and Schacter, 1987) has been discussed above. Sherry and Schacter (1987) suggested that separate memory systems have evolved to perform functionally incompatible memory processes. The purpose of explicit memory is to preserve specific contextual details of events so as to promote conscious, unique recollection of individual experiences; it is highly context dependent (Sherry and Schacter, 1987; Tulving and Pearlstone, 1966). In contrast, the purpose of implicit memory (which encompasses skill learning, priming, and other so-called "indirect" effects) is to preserve those aspects of learning situations that tend to recur across specific instances (i.e., it is dedicated to preserving "invariances" between learning situations). Its operation can explain why perceptual and motor skills transfer to different situations.

ACTIVATION ACCOUNTS

Activation accounts of memory dissociations have suggested that normal performance on indirect memory tests such as word-stem completion result from temporary, automatic activation of preexisting memory representations (Graf and Mandler, 1984). By this view, explicit memory requires additional (effortful, elaborative) processing that is largely impaired in amnesia. This view is relevant to the episodic-semantic distinction in that spared memory (e.g., priming) is thought to reflect activation of representations residing within semantic memory. This explanation was originally advanced to account for the relatively short-lived nature of repetition priming effects (Cermak et al., 1985; Graf et al., 1984) and for early findings that, in normals and amnesics, priming did not occur for stimuli that had no preexisting memory representations (e.g., nonwords) (Bentin and Moscovitch, 1988; Cermak et al., 1985; Diamond and Rozin 1984; Kersteen-Tucker 1991; Scarborough et al. 1977).

Two general findings have recently challenged the activation account. First, primary effects sometimes persist over several weeks or longer (Jacoby and Dallas, 1981; Schacter and Graf, 1986a), which pushes the concept of "activation" to unacceptable limits. Second, recent studies have shown normal priming of novel material (e.g., nonwords, novel line patterns and objects) in both normals (Cermak et al., 1985, 1991; Feustel et al., 1983; Jacoby, 1983a; Jacoby and Dallas, 1981; Rueckl, 1991; Musen and Triesman, 1990; Schacter et al., 1990) and amnesics (Gabrieli et al., 1990; Haist et al., 1991; Musen and Squire, 1991; Schacter et al., 1991). Haist et al. (1991) found that amnesics showed entirely normal priming for both words and studied nonwords. These findings suggest the acquisition of new memories, not simply the activation of preexisting representations.

Further evidence that new learning may underlie at least some forms of priming is provided by a recent experiment that showed long-lasting priming of novel solutions to complex sentence puzzles (McAndrews et al., 1987). In this study, a mixed group of "severely amnesic" subjects were presented with difficult-to-comprehend sentences like "The person was unhappy because the hole closed." Subjects were instructed that the sentence would become comprehensible if they could think of a specific key word or phrase (in this case, "pierced ears"). They had to come up with a solution within one minute and, if they did not, the experimenter presented the solution and asked the subject to explain it. Subsequent testing revealed that amnesics were able to generate the key word/phrase needed to solve the sentence puzzles for periods up to one week, after only one exposure to the problem. This convincingly demonstrates that amnesics can implicitly remember the meaning of novel sentences, and suggests that new episodic representations of the sentence-solution relationship can be formed after only a single exposure. Findings by Johnson et al. (1985) that amnesics can form preferences for pictured faces that are congruent with previously associated positive and negative biographical material that they can no longer explicitly remember is also evidence of the ability of amnesics to form new associations which are relatively enduring.

Finally, Graf and Schacter (1985) and Schacter and Graf (1986a) exposed amnesics to unrelated word pairs like "window-reason." In a subsequent test, subjects were presented with the stem of the target word (second word) preceded either by the word it was studied with (e.g., window-rea___), or a different word (e.g., officer-rea___). Subjects were asked to complete the stem with the first word that came to mind and were told that the preceding word might help them think of a completion. Amnesics with relatively mild memory problems (but not severely amnesic patients) demonstrated more priming when the stem was preceded by the word it was originally studied with than when it was preceded by a different word, thus demonstrating memory for a new association. Although this result only obtained when items were semantically elaborated at time of study, explicit memory could not account for the effect because subjects were unable to use the cues to explicitly recall the studied words. These findings are difficult to accommodate within an activation framework, since they strongly suggest that amnesic subjects are capable of showing priming that is based on the establishing of new meaningful relationships which did not exist in semantic memory prior to experimental exposure.

TRANSFER-APPROPRIATE PROCESSING

Processing views of implicit-explicit memory explain the striking dissociations observed between these two types of memory by suggesting that indirect (e.g., repetition priming) and direct (e.g., free recall) tests generally demand different cognitive processes. By this view, memory performance benefits to the extent that the cognitive operations applied at test overlap with the encoding operations performed during original learning (Blaxton, 1989; Roediger et al., 1989; Roediger and Blaxton, 1987; Witherspoon and Moscovitch, 1989). Most tests of explicit recall allegedly rely on elaborative, semantic encoding, and have been referred to as reflecting "conceptually driven" processing (Jacoby, 1983a, b). In contrast, most tests of implicit memory (e.g., stem completion, perceptual identification) rely on the perceptual match between study and test, and have been referred to as reflecting "data-driven" processing. The resulting account of amnesia suggests that amnesics are capable of extensive data-driven processing, but are impaired in elaborative, conceptually driven processing. Unlike the activation view, the transfer-appropriate processing (TAP) approach views implicit memory effects as exclusively *episodic* in origin, rather than as based on activation of semantic memory representations.

Support for the TAP account has been furnished in a series of experiments by Jacoby (1983a, b) and by Roediger and colleagues (Blaxton, 1985, cited in Roediger et al., 1989; Roediger and Blaxton, 1987; Roediger and Weldon, 1987; see Roediger, 1990, for review). Blaxton (1985) found that the relative strength of word-fragment completion and free recall depended upon the activities engaged in during the study interval. Better word-fragment completion was seen when subjects simply read words (XXXX-COLD), and better free recall was seen when they generated the words from associative cues (hot-????). The TAP approach thus emphasizes what has come to be known as "study-test correspondence," and suggests that explicit-implicit dissociations can be understood within the general framework of encoding specificity (Tulving and Pearlstone, 1966).

The TAP approach has encouraged greater specificity regarding the cognitive demands imposed by direct and indirect tests of memory. Although direct tests typically utilize conceptual processes whereas indirect tasks rely heavily on data-driven processes, both tests can have data-driven and conceptually driven components. For example, Blaxton (1985) has shown that certain direct/explicit memory tests (e.g., graphemic cued recall, where subjects are cued for a target word [SUNRISE] with a graphically similar word [SURMISE]) are heavily data driven, while certain indirect/implicit tests (e.g., having subjects study word pairs like ESPIONAGE-treason, then asking "For what crime were the Rosenbergs executed?") are conceptually driven. Thus, studies that demonstrate parallel effects on explicit and implicit memory may be the result of the inclusion of conceptual material in indirect tasks, or perceptual (data-driven) material in direct tasks.

The TAP approach is able to account for findings that priming is sometimes long-lasting and that amnesics can acquire new associations and show priming of novel material. It also accounts for many of the dissociations and parallel effects found in the normal literature. However, it has difficulty explaining why some amnesics do not show priming of novel information and why some priming effects dissipate rapidly.

The main difficulty with the TAP approach is in accounting for the fact that amnesics are able to perform well on both data-driven and conceptually driven indirect tasks, but are greatly impaired on both types of direct tasks (cf. Schacter, 1987a; Richardson-Klavehn and Bjork, 1988).

COMBINED APPROACHES

It is important to recognize that activation and processing theories are not necessarily mutually exclusive. It is possible that some types of implicit memory rely more heavily on activation of preexisting knowledge, whereas others are the result of laying down of new memory traces based on processing similarities between study and test. The ability to perform indirect tasks requiring the laying down of new memory traces may depend on severity of amnesia (cf. Schacter, 1987a), while the ability to display "activation" effects may be more independent of amnesia severity. In any case, there are clear instances in which amnesics demonstrate priming that depends on the laying down of new traces. To the extent that new traces are laid down, the strength of the nominal cue and type of measure may be critical in determining the duration of the effect.

Important distinctions have been noted between certain classes of behavior described under the rubric of "implicit memory." For example, patients with severe memory loss attributable to Parkinson's disease have been found to be deficient in some types of motor learning, but demonstrate intact repetition priming, whereas patients' suffering from Alzheimer's disease show the opposite effect (Heindel, et al., 1989; cf. Butters et al., 1990). In addition to demonstrating differences among subgroups of amnesics, these findings suggest that implicit memory may be divisible into independent subsystems (cf. Witherspoon and Moscovitch, 1989).

Schacter (1990) has proposed the existence of multiple memory systems, including a perceptual representation system with subsystems for "word form" and "structural description" processing that could account for much of the perceptually based or data-driven priming effects observed. He suggests that a separate system or systems would be needed to account for conceptually based priming. He also postulates linkages with a variety of memory systems, depending on the particular task used and domain of knowledge being tapped. In this sense, he incorporates processing accounts into a multiple memory system framework.

While a combination of theoretical accounts covers more of the existing data, this approach is somewhat unsatisfying in that it is nonparsimonious and its explanatory

power is diluted since it is unclear what approach to take in confirming or disconfirm-
ing the theory and how new data will be accounted for within the theory. Inquiry
into implicit and explicit memory phenomena is still in its infancy, and these alternative theoretical approaches provide a basis to begin asking new questions that may
lead to greater understanding of the complexity of memory processes. What is clear
from this body of research is that memory is not a unitary process and we must go
beyond standard tests of recognition and recall in assessing the nature and extent of
preserved and impaired memory functioning in individual patients.

## ANATOMIC CORRELATES OF AMNESIA

### Temporal Lobe

Although there were previous reports of temporal lobe lesions in amnesic patients
(von Bechterew, 1900; Grünthal 1947; Glees and Griffith, 1952), recognition of the
importance of the temporal lobes in memory followed reports of severe and permanent amnesia after bilateral resections of the medial aspects of the temporal lobes in
humans (Scoville, 1954; Scoville and Milner, 1957). The aim of surgery was either to
ameliorate psychotic behavior or to treat intractable focal epilepsy. H.M., who was
treated for epilepsy, is the best studied of such patients: he continues to this day to
participate in neuropsychological studies of his memory disorder. His intended
lesions extend 8 to 9 centimeters back from the temporal poles, and include the uncus,
amygdala, periamygdalar and perirhinal cortex, hippocampus, and parahippocampal gyrus (Fig. 15-1).

THE HIPPOCAMPUS

Subsequent studies attempted to determine which of these areas is important for
memory. Scoville and Milner (1957) reviewed the effects of medial temporal resection on ten patients with medial temporal lesions (Scoville's original two patients, plus
seven with bilateral temporal lobectomies for psychosis and one with medial temporal lobe damage and resection after tentorial herniation). Removal of the uncus and
amygdala (in one patient) caused no memory loss, but resections that extended more
posteriorly to involve the hippocampus and parahippocampal gyrus were associated
with amnesia. The amnesia was more severe with more extensive resections. The relationship between the extent of resection and the severity of amnesia also held for the
selective verbal or nonverbal amnesias that followed, respectively, left or right temporal resections (Milner, 1972, 1974; Smith, 1989). Scoville and Milner concluded that
amnesia would not occur unless the surgery extended far enough back to involve the
hippocampus. The importance of the hippocampus was also supported by Penfield
and Milner (1958), who reported two patients with amnesia following *unilateral* temporal resections. They speculated that preexisting contralateral hippocampal damage
explained the severe amnesia after unilateral resection. This speculation was confirmed when one of the patients (P.B.) was found at autopsy to have hippocampal
sclerosis in the unoperated temporal lobe, but no damage to other temporal cortical
structures or to the amygdala (Penfield and Mathieson, 1974).

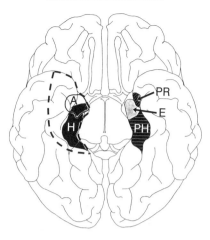

**Fig. 15-1.** The inferior surface of the brain, with the approximate locations of important medial temporal structures indicated. On the left, two deep structures, the amygdala (A) and the hippocampus (H), are shown. On the right, medial cortical structures indicated include the perirhinal cortex (PR), the entorhinal cortex (E) and the parahippocampal gyrus (PH). (See Squire and Zola-Morgan (1991, figure 1) for a similar view of the monkey brain.) On the left the heavy dashed line indicates the area ablated in patients, such as HM with medial temporal lesions. (Of course, in HM the lesions were bilateral.)

Although this experience strongly suggested that the hippocampus was necessary for memory, by the 1970s there was still very little support for this supposition from the experimental literature. Twenty years after Scoville and Milner's influential report, there were only a handful of papers suggesting a role of the hippocampus in memory (see, for example, Correll and Scoville, 1965) and scores more that failed to demonstrate learning problems in animals with bilateral hippocampal ablations (see Horel, 1978). Several alternative explanations were advanced. One was that the hippocampus was *not* important in memory. Surgical excisions always included structures other than the hippocampus: parahippocampal gyrus, amgydala, periamygdaloid and perirhinal and entorhinal cortices, and variable amounts of temporal neocortex and deep temporal lobe white matter. Horel (1978) concluded that the anterior temporal neocortex, the amygdala, and white matter connections of these structures in the temporal stem to the medial thalamus and brainstem were the critical areas affected. The experimental literature (as summarized by Horel) suggested that lesions of the hippocampus impaired spatial discriminations (Mahut, 1971) but not memory.

A second explanation was that human memory differed from nonhuman memory: the cognitive structure humans could impose on information (e.g., verbal mediation) made the human memory process not comparable to memory in animals.

A third explanation has received much support in the past two decades: experimental paradigms for testing memory in animals had simply not been adequate to demonstrate the amnesia that in fact had resulted from medial temporal resections in animals. Gaffan (1972, 1974) proposed that testing animals with trial-unique stimuli was necessary in order to demonstrate deficits in recognition memory on a delayed matching-to-sample (DMS) task, and Mishkin and Saunders (1979) used a delayed nonmatching-to-sample (DNMS) task with trial-unique stimuli to demonstrate amnesia in monkeys with medial temporal lesions. In the DNMS, on each trial a new object is shown to the monkey. After a variable delay, during which the stimuli are hidden, the monkey is shown this object paired with another unfamiliar but readily discriminable object. The monkey must choose the *new* object (nonmatching) to receive a reward. Gaffan (1974) and Mishkin and Petri (1984) pointed out that recognition memory tests using trial-unique stimuli more nearly approximate the tasks that present problems for human amnesics. Tests that use repeated trials with the same stimuli and enable response habits to be formed can be performed well both by human amnesics and by animals with medial temporal resections (Mishkin and Petri, 1984). Similarly, both human amnesics (as extensively discussed above) and monkeys with medial temporal lesions can learn new skills (Zola-Morgan and Squire, 1983, 1984). Human amnesics have been tested with the DMS task (Sidman et al., 1968) and the DNMS task (Oscar-Berman and Bonner, 1985; Squire et al., 1988; Zola-Morgan and Squire, 1990a), which they do not perform as well as normals. Other tasks have also been developed that are sensitive to medial temporal lesions in monkeys and that present difficulties for human amnesics (Squire et al., 1988; Zola-Morgan and Squire, 1990a).

The development of a primate model of human amnesia allowed for a more direct way to test the relative importance of various temporal lobe structures in memory. Zola-Morgan, Squire, and colleagues refer to medial temporal lesions involving the hippocampus and neighboring parahippocampal cortex as H+ lesions, amygdala and neighboring perirhinal and anterior entorhinal cortex as A+ lesions, and combined lesions as A+H+ lesions. A+H+ lesions cause amnesia, whereas lesions of the temporal stem white matter do not (Zola-Morgan et al., 1982). H+ lesions also cause amnesia that is less severe than H+A+ lesions, and lesions confined to the hippocampus amnesia that is significant, but less severe than that caused by H+ lesions (Zola-Morgan and Squire, 1986; Squire and Zola-Morgan, 1991). The importance of the hippocampus in memory was also supported by the moderately severe and permanent amnesia following hypoxic-ischemic encephalopathy in humans (Cummings et al., 1984; Zola-Morgan et al., 1986; Victor and Agamanolis, 1990). In a particularly well-studied case, Zola-Morgan et al. (1986) demonstrated that temporal lobe damage was restricted to the CA1 field of the hippocampus (see below). There were no lesions in amygdala, mammillary bodies, medial thalamus, or basal forebrain. The patient had careful neuropsychological documentation of anterograde amnesia over a period of five years prior to his death. Global ischemia in the monkey causes similar lesions, with scores on memory tasks comparable to those of monkeys with surgical lesions restricted to the hippocampus (Squire and Zola-Morgan, 1991).

*Internal hippocampal circuits.*   The internal anatomy of the hippocampus helps us to understand how lesions affecting only one group of hippocampal neurons may be able to produce a deficit comparable to removal of the entire structure. The hippocampal formation comprises the fields of Ammon's horn (CA1, CA2, and CA3), the dentate gyrus (including CA4), and the subicular complex (Fig. 15-2). The internal

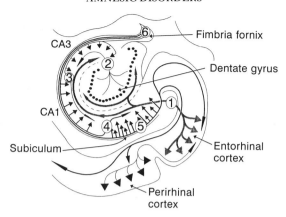

**Fig. 15-2.** The internal structure of the hippocampus (adapted from Van Hoesen, 1985). The numbered pathways include the perforant pathway (1), the projections from dentate to CA3 (2), from CA3 to CA1(3), from CA1 to the subiculum (4), from the subiculum to the entorhinal and perirhinal cortices (5), and the subcortical projections of CA3, CA1 and the subiculum via the fibria fornix (6).

connections of the hippocampus were identified by Ramón y Cajal and his student Lorrente de Nó (cited by Van Hoesen, 1985), who first described the trisynaptic circuit. Neurons of the entorhinal cortex, the gateway for the majority of information reaching the hippocampus, project via the perforant pathway to synapse on dendrites of granule cells in the dentate gyrus. Granule cell axons project to the dendrites of pyramidal cells in the CA3 region of Ammon's horn (mossy fiber projection). These pyramidal cells have axons that bifurcate, one branch projecting subcortically via the fimbria fornix and the other to CA1 (Shaffer collateral pathway). CA1 neurons project subcortically via the fimbria, but also to the subiculum (a fact not appreciated by the early anatomists). The subiculum is the major source of hippocampal efferent projections (Rosene and Van Hoesen, 1977). Efferent fibers from the subiculum project either to subcortical targets (via the fimbria and fornix) or to other cortical regions. The subiculum also projects back to the entorhinal cortex, completing an intrinsic hippocampal circuit. This orderly progression of information through the hippocampus helps explain how lesions restricted to CA1 (Zola-Morgan et al., 1986) or to the entorhinal cortex (Hyman et al., 1984) may critically interfere with hippocampal function.

Hippocampal physiology may provide clues to the cellular mechanisms of memory. High-frequency stimulation of the perforant path enhances transmission at synapses in the dentate gyrus. This enhancement can last weeks (Lomo, 1971; Bliss and Lomo 1973; Bliss and Gardner-Medwin, 1973), and has been called long-term potentiation. Weak stimulation of one pathway, combined with stimulation of nearby excitatory synapses, can also induce long-term potentiation, both in the dentate gyrus and in CA1 neurons. This could be a mechanism by which two coincident stimuli are associated (see Kennedy, 1989). Further studies have identified some of the cellular mechanisms underlying long-term potentiation (see Gustaffsson and Wigstrom, 1988;

Kennedy, 1989; Matthies et al., 1990). In the experimental setting, drugs that block specific kinds of glutamate receptors may interfere with both long-term potentiation and memory (see Izquierdo, 1991). Although the existence within a neuroanatomic structure of a mechanism to preserve records of associations does not ensure that damage to the structure will cause amnesia (and, indeed, long-term potentiation has been identified in many regions of the nervous system, including subcortical sites not directly implicated in human amnesia), the extrinsic connections of the hippocampus suggest that this structure is particularly suited to preserve associations of the seemingly limitless variety of occurrences that comprise declarative memory.

*Cortical connections.*    Papez (1937) had suggested that the cingulate gyrus provided a means for cortically processed information to reach the hippocampus. Indeed, the cingulate cortex has since been shown to have extensive neocortical connections (Baleydier and Mauguiere, 1980; Pandya et al., 1981). Fibers from the cingulate gyrus and retrosplenial cortex travel in the cingulate bundle and terminate in the subiculum and caudal entorhinal cortex (Mufson and Pandya, 1984; Insausti et al., 1987a), and thus have access to the hippocampus itself (Van Hoesen and Pandya, 1975). The entorhinal cortex also funnels information from many other regions of the cerebral cortex to the hippocampus. It receives afferents from neighboring regions of the temporal lobe, including perirhinal, pre-, and parasubicular cortices, and with areas TF-TH of the parahippocampal gyrus (Rosene and Van Hoesen, 1977; Van Hoesen et al., 1979; Irle and Markowitsch, 1982; Insausti et al., 1987a). It is also connected either directly or by the above-mentioned neighboring cortices with orbitofrontal cortex, superior temporal cortex, and other high-order sensory and frontal association cortices (Amaral et al., 1983; Insausti et al., 1987a; Van Hoesen et al., 1972; Van Hoesen, 1985). Thus the hippocampus has access to highly processed information in unimodal and polymodal association cortex. These neocortical-hippocampal connections are reciprocated. The subiculum projects to many of the same areas that project to it and to entorhinal cortex (Rosene and Van Hoesen, 1977).

*Subcortical connections of the hippocampus.*    Cortical-hippocampal connections are necessary, but not sufficient, to maintain normal memory function, since subcortical lesions can also result in amnesia. The pyramidal cells of Ammon's horn (fields CA3 and CA1 in Fig. 15-2) project via the precommissural fornix to the lateral septal area (Swanson and Cowan, 1979). Other subcortical projections of the hippocampus arise in the subiculum (also the origin of cortical efferents mentioned above) and project via the fornix to the septal area, the anterior nuclear complex of the thalamus, and the mammillary bodies (Swanson and Cowan, 1979; Van Hoesen, 1985). There are also projections to the amygdala, nucleus accumbens and other regions in the basal forebrain, and the ventromedial hypothalamus (Swanson and Cowan, 1979; Amaral and Insausti, 1990).

The hippocampal → postcommissural fornix → mammillary body projection is evident upon gross inspection of the brain, and was part of the "circuit" described by Papez in 1937 to explain how emotional expression and feeling, mediated by the hypothalamus, could be coordinated with cognition, mediated by the cortex. As noted

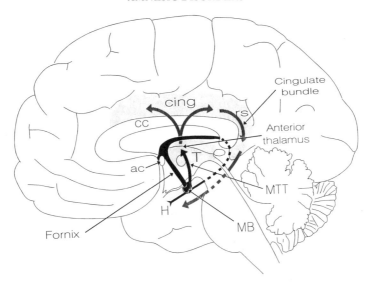

**Fig. 15-3.** The Papez circuit (see text). ac = anterior commissure; cc = corpus callosum; cing = cingulate gyrus; H = hippocampus; MB = mammillary body; MTT = mammillothalamic tract; rs = retrosplenial cortex; T = thalamus. The fornix, projecting from the hippocampus to the mammillary body, is shown in black. It divides at the anterior commissure, the anterior (pre-commissural) division destined for the septal nuclei (not shown).

above, Papez assumed that cortical input to the hippocampus arrived principally from the cingulate cortex via the cingulate bundle (cingulum). The hippocampus projected to the mamillary bodies, which, in turn, projected (via the mammillothalamic tract) to the anterior nuclei of the thalamus. The thalamic projection to the cingulate gyrus completed the circuit (see Fig. 15-3).

There are also direct subcortical projections to the hippocampus and entorhinal cortex. These arise in the basal forebrain (medial septal nucleus and the nucleus of the diagonal band of Broca) from midline, anterior, and laterodorsal thalamic nuclei, and from amygdala, hypothalamus, and brainstem, including the central grey, ventral tegmental area, raphe nuclei, and locus coeruleus (Amaral and Cowan, 1980; Amaral and Insausti, 1990; Insausti et al., 1987b; Herkenham, 1978; Van Hoesen, 1985).

The importance of these subcortical regions in memory will be considered below in the sections on diencephalic amnesia, the dual system theory, and the basal forebrain.

TEMPORAL NEOCORTEX

We previously mentioned that lesions of the hippocampus and overlying cortex (H+) induce more severe amnesia than lesions confined to the hippocampus (H). This implies that the overlying cortex (entorhinal and parahippocampal gyrus) contributes to memory independent of its close connections with the hippocampus. Zola-

Morgan et al. (1989b) found that lesions that spare the hippocampus, but involve both perirhinal and parahippocampal cortex (PRPH lesions), cause severe memory impairment in the monkey. Interestingly, monkeys with this lesion had *more* severe deficits than monkeys with the hippocampal and parahippocampal gyrus (H+) lesion. Again, this suggests that the perirhinal cortex not only conveys information to the entorhinal cortex and thus to the hippocampus, but that it contributes to memory in its own right.

The contribution of temporal neocortex to memory remains controversial. The concept has been advanced that a cascade from primary sensory cortex to increasingly higher-order (unimodal and then polymodal) association cortex to limbic cortex underlies the progressive elaboration of sensory information into complex perceptions and constructs, which then can be remembered by virtue of their interaction with limbic structures of the medial temporal lobe. Analagous, but separate, pathways are described for visual, tactile, and auditory modalities (Turner et al., 1980; Ungerleider and Mishkin, 1982). Interruption of these pathways could therefore result in a modality-specific amnesia. Ross (1980a,b) describes such "fractional" amnesias in two patients, and a similar visual amnesia has been described by Bauer (1982, 1984a).

It has also been argued that anterior temporal neocortex has a role in memory independent of its connections to limbic cortex. Lesions of anterior temporal neocortex (temporal pole and portions of the inferotemporal cortex) in monkeys impair performance on DNMS (Spiegler and Mishkin, 1981) and DMS (Horel, et al. 1984; Cirillo et al., 1989; George et al., 1989).[*] Horel and colleagues provide evidence that this cannot be accounted for by impairment in visual discrimination, and they argue that anterior and inferior temporal neocortex contribute to memory (George et al., 1989; see also Horel, 1978). Some patients with anterior unilateral temporal lobectomies sparing the hippocampus have been reported to demonstrate limited memory deficits (Ojemann and Dodrill, 1985; Smith, 1989). Damasio and colleagues (Damasio et al., 1985a; 1985b; 1987, 1989) suggest that the temporally extensive retrograde amnesia of their postencephalitic patient, Boswell, might be attributed to anterior temporal neocortical destruction. Boswell's severe retrograde amnesia distinguished him from H. M., whose lesions spared most temporal neocortical areas. Damasio and colleagues propose that anterior temporal neocortex is an area of "convergence zones" in which the unique saptiotemporal complexity of specific events is encoded. Without these convergence zones, Boswell could not reconstruct previous memories, or lay down a record to preserve new memories. They suggest that his deficit would have been just as great had the medial temporal structures been spared (Damasio et al., 1989). This, however, is speculative, and it is possible that the severity of his retrograde amnesia reflects instead the co-occurrence of temporal with frontal and/or basal forebrain lesions. Severe retrograde amnesia with lesions restricted to antteror temporal neocortex has not been reported.

[*] The DMS and DNMS are similar, but not equivalent. In the DMS task, the animal is rewarded for choosing the object previously seen. In the DNMS task, it is rewarded for choosing the new object. Animals have a tendency to choose the novel stimulus; thus the DMS is more difficult, and entails the animal's need to suppress a natural response. This may explain why lesions in dorsolateral frontal lobes impair performance on DMS, but not on DNMS.

THE AMYGDALA

The amygdala is situated anterior to the hippocampus, and deep to the periamygdaloid and perirhinal cortices. It can be broadly conceived as having two parts: a large basolateral group of nuclei, with extensive connections to limbic and association cortex and to dorsomedial thalamus, and a smaller corticomedial segment, which extends into the basal forebrain and has extensive connections with basal forebrain, hypothalamus, and brainstem (DeOlmos, 1990; Heimer and Alheid, 1991; Scott et al., 1991). In a very general sense, the connections of amygdala and hippocampus are similar: both are strongly interconnected with frontal and temporal limbic cortex, and thus have indirect access to polymodal and supramodal neocortical association areas (Herzog and Van Hoesen, 1976; Rosene and Van Hoesen, 1977). Both project to basal forebrain and hypothalamus. The amygdala and hippocampus also have direct interconnections (Insausti et al, 1987b; Saunders et al., 1988; Polettia, 1986).

But there are also striking anatomic differences. Although in the brains of higher mammals the amygdala is adjacent to the hippocampus, it differs radically from the hippocampus in structure and derivation. The amygdala is a largely subcortical structure, intimately related with the basal forebrain, and considered by some to be one of the basal ganglia. The amygdala is more closely related to limbic and neocortical regions that are of paleocortical derivation, whereas the hippocampus is archicortical and is more closely related to cortex of archicortical derivation (Pandya and Yeterian 1990). Thus, the amygdala is more closely related to orbitofrontal and anterior temporal cortex (Porrino et al., 1981), and the hippocampus is more closely related to cingulate cortex. It is of interest that abnormalities in emotional responsiveness and social interactions are associated not only with amygdala, but also with anterior temporal and orbitofrontal lesions (Butter and Snyder, 1972).

Another difference in cortical connectivity has less clear behavioral consequences. The amygdala, but not the hippocampus, receives direct input from unimodal sensory association cortex (Turner et al., 1980; Aggleton et al., 1980). Murray and Mishkin (1985) suggested that the amygdala may be important in cross-modal recognition. Monkeys with amygdala lesions, but not monkeys with hippocampal lesions, had difficulty performing a nonmatching-to-sample task in which the test stimulus was provided in one modality, and the response stimulus in another. Lee et al. (1988) could not demonstrate this deficit in a patient with bilateral amygdalectomy.

The subcortical connections of the amygdala also differ from those of the hippocampus. Whereas the hippocampus is related through the Papez circuit with the mammillary bodies and the anterior thalamic nuclei, the amygdala has projections to the dorsomedial nucleus of the thalamus (Nauta, 1961). Basal forebrain connections also differ: the hippocampus is related to more ventral portions of the septal nuclei, and the amygdala has more extensive connections with the bed nucleus of the stria terminalis. Cholinergic projections to the amygdala are from the nucleus basalis of Meynert, whereas the hippocampus receives input from the septal region and diagonal band of Broca (Mesulam et al., 1983). Finally, the amygdala has connections with brainstem autonomic centers (nucleus of the tractus solitarius), providing a direct pathway for limbic-autonomic interaction.

The behavioral consequences of amygdalar and hippocampal lesions are also very different. Amygdala lesions in nonhuman primates have been associated with impairments in stimulus-reward association (Jones and Mishkin, 1972; Speigler and Mishkin, 1981) and the association of affect with neutral stimuli (LeDoux, 1987; Iwata et al., 1986; Gaffan and Harrison, 1987; McGaugh et al., 1990) and with defects in social and emotional behavior (Kling and Stecklis, 1976; Zola-Morgan et al., 1989a). In humans, stimulation of the amygdala is particularly likely to result in emotional experiences (Gloor, 1986; see also Chapter 13). Hippocampal lesions appear to have no effect on the emotional behavior of nonhuman primates (Squire and Zola-Morgan, 1991).

Whereas the importance of the hippocampus for memory is no longer controversial, the role of the amygdala remains uncertain. Mishkin and his colleagues provided indirect evidence that the amygdala is involved in memory. They resected the hippocampus and neighboring parahippocampal gyrus in one group of monkeys and the amygdala and adjacent cortex in another group (Mishkin, 1978; Mishkin and Saunders, 1979). They found that deficits on the DNMS task were very mild in both groups and that combined lesions (A + H +, in Zola-Morgan's terminology) were required to demonstrate a severe deficit. They suggested that in both humans and monkeys, severe amnesia, as seen in H. M., required lesions affecting both the hippocampus and amygdala and that Penfield's patient P. B. (described above) had a milder amnesia than H. M. because P. B. had one functioning amygdala (Mishkin et al., 1982).

The contribution of the amygdala to performance on standard tests of memory has been carefully studied in monkeys by Zola-Morgan, Squire, and colleagues. They suggest that memory deficits attributed to amygdala damage actually resulted from damage to the overlying perirhinal cortex. The perirhinal cortex provides a major input to the entorhinal cortex (Insausti et al., 1987a), which is, in turn, the major gateway to the hippocampus (Van Hoesen and Pandya, 1975) (see Fig. 15-1). Zola-Morgan et al. (1989b) found that lesions of the perirhinal and parahippocampal gyri (including entorhinal area), their PRPH lesion, produced amnesia as severe as the full medial temporal resection (H + A +), even though damage to fibers destined for the amygdala was minimal. Furthermore, stereotactic lesions of the amygdala (which spared perirhinal cortex) did not add to the memory deficit of animals with hippocampal and parahippocampal gyrus lesions (Zola-Morgan et al., 1989a). These studies suggested that the amygdala did not contribute to performance on the memory tasks used in these experiments.

The literature on human amnesia also sheds little light on the amygdala's function in memory. Narabayashi et al. (1963) reported a series of patients with unilateral or bilateral stereotactic amygdalectomies, many of whom were severely impaired prior to surgery. Although these patients were thought to be free of memory loss postoperatively, specific memory testing was not reported. Milner (1966) reported no deficits in patients with anterior temporal lobe resections that included the amygdala but spared the hippocampus; Andersen (1978) reported inconsistent and relatively mild memory deficits in patients with unilateral stereotactic amygdalotomies. Lee et al. (1988) found no deficits in a patient with bilateral stereotactic amygdalectomies on a cross-modal memory task. Tranel and Hyman (1990) reported memory deficits in a patient with bilateral amygdala calcifications secondary to lipoid proteinosis (Urbach-Wiethe disease); however, microscopic involvement of hippocampus, which may not have been apparent on MR scanning, has been reported in this illness (Holtz, 1962). Thus the contention that amgydala lesions contribute to amnesia in humans remains to be conclusively demonstrated.

It appears, then, that the amygdala is more important for emotion than memory, whereas (despite Papez's prediction) the reverse is true of the hippocampus. Could the amygdala be important in mediating aspects of emotional memory? Although this is an attractive possibility, it is clear from the case of Boswell described by Damasio et al. (1989) that implicit memory of preferences for individuals who treated Boswell poorly or well was possible despite bilateral destruction of the amygdalae. It is also known that EDRs to affective stimuli are preserved in amygdalectomized patients (Lee et al., 1988).

### Diencephalon (Mammillary Bodies and Thalamus)

The history of the localization of lesions responsible for Wernicke's encephalopathy and Korsakoff's psychosis (now recognized to be one disorder due to thiamine deficiency, and called the Wernicke-Korsakoff syndrome) is detailed in the monograph by Victor et al. (1971). Although cortical lesions were often blamed for the amnesia, Gamper found no cortical lesions, and attributed amnesia to lesions in the mammillary bodies. A diencephalic localization (either mammillary bodies or thalamus) became favored as cases of amnesia associated with tumors in the walls of the third ventricle became recognized (Foerster and Gagel, 1933; Grünthal, 1939; Lhermitte et al., 1937; Sprofkin and Sciarra, 1952; Williams and Pennybacker, 1954). Victor et al. (1971) studied 245 patients with Wernicke-Korsakoff disease, practically all of them alcoholics. In 43 cases the dorsomedial nucleus and the mammillary bodies were examined at autopsy. Five of these patients had suffered Wernicke's encephalopathy but had recovered without evidence of memory loss. All five had mammillary body lesions, but none of them had dorsomedial thalamic lesions. In the 38 remaining cases (all with memory loss), both the mammillary bodies and the dorsomedial thalamic nucleus were involved. In addition, the medial portion of the pulvinar of the thalamus was also frequently involved. On the basis of these findings, these authors concluded that memory loss could not be attributed to the mammillary bodies, and was more likely to be associated with dorsomedial and perhaps medial pulvinar lesions.

Not all patients with alcoholic Korsakoff's syndrome, however, have been found to have dorsomedial thalamic lesions. Mair et al. (1979) and Mayes et al. (1988) each report two cases of Wernicke-Korsakoff syndrome with lesions in the thalamus restricted to a thin band of gliosis adjacent to the third ventricle that affected the midline nuclei, but not the dorsomedial nucleus. Mair et al. (1979) suggested that the mammillary body lesions (present in each of these patients) may be important. Lesions restricted to the mammillary bodies, however, have not been associated with deficits on memory tasks in monkeys (Aggleton and Mishkin, 1985) or rats (Aggleton et al, 1991), although memory deficits have been described in a patient with magnetic resonance (MR) evidence of mammillary body lesions following a penetrating injury from a snooker cue (Dusoir et al., 1990).

If mammillary body lesions are not in themselves sufficient to cause severe amnesia, it is possible that a combination of lesions are needed (Mair et al., 1979; Mayes et al.,

1988). Several regions have been mentioned as possibly important. Damage to midline thalamic nuclei (parataenial, anterior paraventricular, centralis medialis, and reuniens nuclei) could influence the hippocampal system, since they have connections with the hippocampus (Amaral and Cowan, 1989; Herkenham, 1978, Insausti et al., 1987b; Van Hoesen, 1985). Cell loss in cholinergic neurons of the basal forebrain (Arendt et al., 1983) has led some to suggest that cholinergic deficits could contribute to the amnesia of Korsakoff's syndrome (Butters, 1985; Butters and Stuss, 1989). Claims have also been made for the importance of noradrenergic systems, because of associated atrophy in locus coeruleus (Mayes et al., 1988), as well as the (possibly nonspecific) benefits of adrenergic agents (McEntee and Mair, 1978, 1980). Quantitative computed tomographic (CT) studies suggest both diencephalic and frontal involvement in many patients with alcoholic Korsakoff's syndrome (Shimamura et al., 1988; Jernigan et al., 1991). Becker et al. (1990) report a nonalcoholic patient who developed Wernicke-Korsakoff syndrome from malabsorption. Behavioral and radiologic tests failed to reveal evidence of prominent frontal pathology, though many of the behavioral manifestations of the syndrome were similar to that seen in alcoholic Korsakoff patients. In summary, the variability of extramammillary lesions in Wernicke-Korsakoff disease, as well as the presence of similar pathology in some alcoholic patients without symptoms of Wernicke-Korsakoff disease (Lishman, 1986; Harper and Finlay-Jones, 1986), makes behavioral-anatomic correlations difficult (Mayes et al., 1988; Butters and Stuss, 1989).

Another proposal is that thalamic lesions may disconnect areas important in memory. Warrington (Warrington and Weiskrantz, 1982; Warrington, 1985) proposed that restricted thalamic lesions found in their cases of Wernicke-Korsakoff disease (Mair et al., 1979) might disconnect mediodorsal-frontal connections important for coordinating posterior cortical regions subserving semantic memories with frontal structures that impose cognitive structure upon these memories. Kooistra and Heilman (1988) also suggested that thalamo-frontal disconnections might contribute to amnesia.

The advent of CT and MR imaging has made it possible to correlate memory deficits with restricted thalamic lesions in patients with thalamic strokes. Although initial reports pointed to the dorsomedial nucleus as the major site of damage in amnesic patients, subsequent studies cast doubt upon this. Thus, early reports suggested that N.A., a patient who became amnesic after a fencing foil passed through his nose into the brain (Teuber et al., 1968), had a relatively restricted lesion involving the left dorsomedial thalamic nucleus on CT scan (Squire and Moore, 1979) and that amnesic patients with thalamic strokes had CT evidence of dorsomedial lesions (Choi et al., 1983; Speedie and Heilman, 1982; Bogousslavsky et al., 1986). High-resolution imaging in N.A., however, revealed that his lesion affected only the ventral aspect of the dorsomedial nucleus, but severely damaged the intralaminar nuclei, mammillothalamic tract, and internal medullary lamina (Squire et al., 1989). N.A. also had lesions affecting the postcommissural fornix, mammillary bodies, and the right temporal tip. More restricted lesions in patients with thalamic infarctions suggest that thalamic amnesia best correlates with lesions affecting the internal medullary lamina and mammillothalamic tract (von Cramon et al., 1985; Gentilini et al., 1987; Graff-Radford et al., 1990; Malamut et al., 1992). More posterior lesions that involve portions of the dorsomedial nucleus but spare the internal medullary lamina and mammillothalmic tract are not associated with amnesia (von Cramon et al, 1985; Kritchevsky et al., 1987; Graff-Radford et al., 1990).

The mammillothalamic tract is a component of the Papez circuit that connects the mammillary bodies with the anterior group of thalamic nuclei (Fig. 15-3). The anterior thalamic nuclei project to the cingulate and retrosplenial cortices, among other locations. The lateral dorsal nucleus (considered to be one of the anterior thalamic nuclei) projects strongly to retrosplenial cortex, and shows specific degeneration in Alzheimer's disease (Xuereb et al., 1991). It is not known if lesions restricted to the anterior thalamic nuclei will cause amnesia in humans.

Lesions in the internal medullary lamina may disrupt the ventral amygdalofugal pathway, connecting the amygdala with the dorsomedial nucleus (von Cramen et al., 1985; Graff-Radford et al., 1990; Malamut et al., 1992). Graff-Radford et al. (1990) provided a clear anatomic demonstration in the monkey of the juxtaposition of these two pathways. These findings have been interpreted as supporting a dual system theory of amnesia, proposed by Mishkin and colleagues.

## The Dual System Theory of Amnesia

The data summarized above can be used to suggest that lesions affecting either the amygdala or the dorsomedial nucleus, to which it projects, do not result in clinically apparent amnesia. Mishkin and colleagues have pointed out, however, that this does not necessarily mean that these structures have nothing to do with memory. As noted above, Mishkin (1978, 1982; Mishkin and Saunders, 1979; Mishkin et al., 1982) argued that severe amnesia would result from medial temporal lesions *only* if the lesions involved both the amygdala and the hippocampus (see Zola-Morgan et al., 1989a,b, for a different interpretation, discussed above). Mishkin and colleagues suggested that this reasoning applied not only to the amygdala and hippocampus, but also to their subcortical projections. In a series of experiments, they provided evidence to suggest that two telencephalic/diencephalic systems were involved in memory, and that for amnesia to be severe, *both* systems had to be damaged. The systems were the two limbic circuits described above: the Papez circuit and the lateral limbic circuit involving the anterior temporal cortex and amygdala, dorsomedial thalamus, and orbitofrontal cortex. Thus lesions that interrupt both the fornix (disrupting the Papez circuit) and the ventral amygdalofugal pathways (disrupting the lateral circuit) cause severe amnesia, whereas lesions restricted to either pathway cause little or no memory disturbance (Bachevalier et al., 1985a,b). Lesions that affect either the posteromedial or anteromedial aspect of the thalamus cause little memory disturbance; but severe amnesia, comparable to that associated with medial temporal ablations, occurs only when *both* anterior and posterior medial thalamic regions are involved (Aggleton and Mishkin, 1983). Finally lesions that affect the frontal projections of both the Papez circuit (anterior cingulate gyrus) or the lateral circuit produce a greater memory loss than lesions of either alone (Bachevalier and Mishkin, 1986). This series of studies on primates suggests (1) that structures within each memory system are highly interdependent, since damage to different parts of each system can cause apparently equivalent deficits, and (2) that each system can, to a large extent, carry on the function of the other, since lesions affecting only one system result in little or no memory loss.

The fact that significant amnesia in humans attends damage restricted to the hippocampus partly contradicts the dual system theory; however, it is possible that, at least in humans, the contribution of the hippocampal system is greater, but that very severe amnesia may still require damage to both systems. Because isolated hippocampal damage causes amnesia, the dual system theory might predict that lesions to other components of the Papez circuit might cause comparable degrees of amnesia. The evidence, however, remains inconclusive. We have already summarized the data on mammillary body and mammillothalamic tract lesions. This leaves us to consider lesions of the fornix, anterior thalamus, cingulate gyrus, and cingulum.

In both humans and primates, lesions of the fornix have been reported without (Dott, 1938; Cairns and Mosberg, 1951; Garcia Bengochea et al., 1954; Woolsey and Nelson, 1975) and with (Sweet et al., 1959: Hassler and Riechert, 1957; Grafman et al., 1985; Gaffan, 1974; Owen and Butler, 1981; Moss et al., 1981; Carr, 1982; Bachevalier et al., 1985 a,b) memory loss. The memory loss that sometimes follows section of the corpus callosum has been attributed to incidental damage to the fornix (see Clark and Geffen, 1989). Recent memory may not be affected by section of the columns of the fornix (sometimes performed to gain access to the third ventricle), but more posterior lesions of the fornix may cause amnesia. It has been suggested (Heilman and Sypert, 1977) that posterior lesions affect fibers in the fornix that connect the hippocampus with the basal forebrain, and also disrupt direct hippocampal-thalamic connections. These fibers leave the fornix at the level of the anterior commissure, so section of the columns of the fornix beneath this level will only affect projections to the mammillary bodies.

Amnesia from a lesion that involves the anterior nuclei but spares the mammillothalamic tract and internal medullary lamina has not been reported. Anterior cingulate lesions in man have not been documented to cause amnesia, but lesions affecting the poster cingulate/retrosplenial regions have been reported to cause amnesia (Heilman and Sypert, 1977; Valenstein et al. 1987; Rudge and Warrington, 1991). Lesions in this region could affect the posterior cingulate and retrosplenial cortex and the underlying cingulate bundle, but also could possibly affect the fornix, hippocampal commissure, and the posterior extent of the hippocampus and parahippocampal gyrus, so it remains uncertain if the amnesia can be attributed entirely to interruption of the cingulate → hippocampus limb of the Papez circuit.

The dual system theory also predicts that lesions of white matter structures should have as devastating an effect as lesions of nuclear or cortical structures. This appears to be confirmed by the finding of exquisitely small thalamic lesions affecting the internal medullary lamina (and thus the mammillothalamic tract and ventral amygdalofugal pathway) that cause severe amnesia (Graff-Radford et al., 1990; Malamut et al., 1992; Winoucur et al., 1984). Kooistra and Heilman (1988) reported a patient with amnesia following infarction affecting the inferior aspect of the posterior limb of the internal capsule. They attributed the memory loss to interruption of pathways connecting the dorsomedial nucleus with the amygdala and frontal lobes; however, they point out that the lesion probably also affected the basal nucleus of Meynert (basal forebrain). Memory disturbances are common in multiple sclerosis, where multiple lesons affect white matter pathways in the hemispheres (Rao et al., 1984, 1991; Carroll et al., 1984). Correlations of lesion location in this disorder with specific behavioral abnormalities have been poor, probably because lesions are multiple and not all visualized on CT or even MR scans.

Finally, the contribution of the frontal lobes to memory function should be briefly addressed in this context. As noted above, Bachevalier and Mishkin (1986) proposed that if their dual system theory was correct, lesions that affected the frontal connections of both the anterior thalamic nuclei (the anterior cingulate gyrus) and the dorsomedial nucleus (the posterior orbitofrontal cortex) should cause amnesia, whereas lesions affecting either one alone should not. Although their experiment supported their hypothesis, large frontal lobe lesions in humans that spare the basal forebrain are not associated with the typical amnesic syndrome (Eslinger and Damasio, 1985). Interestingly, memory deficits have been reported after dorsolateral frontal lesions (sparing both regions directly associated with the two limbic circuits), but these frontal amnesias are arguably different from the typical amnesic syndrome described in this chapter. Coslett et al. (1991) describe an interesting patient who had clinically significant memory deficits thought to be due to defects in the controlled search for phonological information. Frontal lobe damage may also cause deficits in judgment of temporal order, resulting in "source amnesia." This is discussed below (see also Chapter 12).

To summarize, the dual system theory predicts that lesions affecting both the hippocampal and amygdalar systems are required for there to be severe amnesia. The theory is supported by a body of experimental work in monkeys. It helps explain why lesions in monkeys and humans confined to one system do not always result in amnesia. It allows for lesions in one system to cause *some* memory disturbance, so long as it is not as severe as lesions affecting both systems. It predicts that white matter lesions should be equally as damaging as nuclear or cortical lesions. It is consistent with the finding that lesions in the diencephalon can produce a long-lasting disruption of memory, which may not be readily distinguishable from the disorder produced by medial temporal lesions (see below for further discussion of this issue). Despite these many attractions, the theory does not explain why lesions affecting the hippocampal system in primates and humans cause definite amnesia, whereas lesions confined to the amygdalar system have not caused appreciable memory loss. Furthermore, the relative roles of the two systems in memory is not specified.

### The Basal Forebrain

The basal forebrain is at the junction of the diencephalon and the cerebral hemispheres, and has, at minimum, the following components: the septal area, diagonal band of Broca, nucleus accumbens septi, olfactory tubercle, substantia innominata (containing the nucleus basalis of Meynert), bed nucleus of the stria terminalis, and preoptic area (Fig. 15-4). It is the third major region, after the temporal lobes and diencephalon, to be considered essential for normal memory function in man. It was known for many years that some patients developed memory loss after hemorrhage from aneurysms, particularly after rupture of anterior communicating artery aneurysms (Linqvist and Norlen, 1966; Talland et al., 1967); however, the pathogenesis of

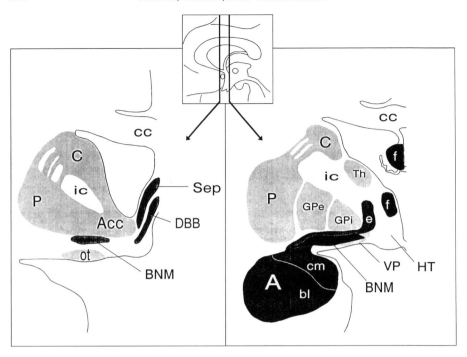

**Fig. 15-4.** The basal forebrain. Two coronal sections are shown through the basal forebrain, at levels indicated in the inset. A = amygdala; Acc = nucleus accumbens septi; bl = basolateral division of the amygdala; BNM = basal nucleus of Meynert; C = caudate nucleus; cc = corpus callosum; cm = corticomedial division of the amygdala; DBB = diagonal band of Broca; e = extended amygdala; f = fornix (transected twice in the posterior section); GPe = external globus pallidus; GPi = internal globus pallidus; HT = hypothalamus; ic = internal capsule; P = putamen; Sep = septal nuclei; Th = thalamus (anterior); VP = ventral pallidum.

this amnesia was not understood. Several lines of evidence suggested that cholinergic neurons in the basal forebrain were involved in memory. Lewis and Shute (1967) documented a cholinergic projection from the medial septal region of the basal forebrain to the hippocampus. For many years, scopolamine, a centrally acting anticholinergic agent, had been used in obstetrics, in conjunction with analgesics, to induce a "twilight" state, after which women would have little recall of their deliveries. Drachman and Leavitt (1974) demonstrated that normal subjects had difficulty with free recall of words when given scopolamine and that this effect was reversed by physostigmine, a centrally acting anticholinesterase agent that prevents inactivation of acetyl choline. Mesulam and Van Hoesen (1976) documented a cholinergic projection from the basal nucleus of Meynert, and in subsequent studies Mesulam and his colleagues (Mesulam et al., 1983; Mesulam and Mufson, 1984) defined the connections of basal forebrain cholinergic neurons. Neurons in the medial septal nucleus and diagonal band of Broca project strongly to the hippocampus, as had been documented by Lewis and Shute (1967). Cholinergic neurons in the substantia innominata (nucleus basalis of Meynert), however, project widely to limbic and neocortex. In 1981, Whitehouse et al. documented selective loss of neurons in the nucleus basalis of Meynert in patients with Alzheimer's disease. All of these lines of evidence suggested a role for the basal forebrain in memory, and more specifically, suggested that the cholinergic projections of the basal forebrain may be of particular importance.

This "cholinergic hypothesis" (Bartus et al., 1985; Kopelman, 1986) has generated a large volume of research, but the cholinergic hypothesis itself remains to be established (cf. Fibiger, 1991). The hope that acetyl choline replacement would substantially improve memory in patients with Alzheimer's disease has not been fulfilled: the benefits of pharmacotherapy are so modest as to be clinically insignificant (Peters and Levin, 1982; Johns et al., 1983; Thal et al., 1983) (see also Chapter 16). This is not surprising, since patients with Alzheimer's disease have degeneration in many other areas thought to be of importance to memory, including the target areas of basal forebrain cholinergic projections (the hippocampus, amygdala, and neocortex).

The complexity of basal forebrain anatomy makes it difficult to arrive at firm conclusions about the pathophysiology of amnesia associated with basal forebrain lesions. In addition to the structures that harbor cholinergic neurons (the substantia innominata [basal nucleus of Meynert], diagonal band of Broca, and the septal nuclei), the basal forebrain encompasses pathways and systems that could conceivably participate in memory. The anterior commissure crosses the midline just posterior to the septal nuclei. The columns of the fornix descend near the basal forebrain on their way to the hypothalamus. Part of the ventral amygdalofugal pathway projects to the basal forebrain, and part traverses it on its way to the thalamus. Thus basal forebrain lesions, if properly situated, may disrupt both the hippocampal (fornix) and amygdalar systems. The medial forebrain bundle, which interconnects brainstem, hypothalamic, and forebrain structures, travels in the lateral hypothalmus and through the basal forebrain. Recently, two other systems have been identified in the basal forebrain. The extended amygdala refers to groups of neurons within the basal forebrain, including neurons in the bed nucleus of the stria terminalis and portions of the nucleus accumbens septi, that are anatomically considered to be related to the corticomedial amygdala, with which they are laterally confluent (Heimer and Alheid, 1991.) The core of the nucleus accumbens and the olfactory tubercle closely resemble the caudate-putamen, and form the ventral striatum, which, in turn, projects to the region of basal forebrain beneath the globus pallidus (the ventral pallidum). It is not known if these areas contribute to memory function. The preoptic area receives projections from amygdala, hippocampus, and other areas of the basal forebrain. It is thought to be of most importance in self-regulatory and species-specific behaviors (Swanson, 1987). It is unkown if it has a role in memory.

Most basal forebrain lesions reported in human cases of amnesia have been large, and probably affect all or many of the above structures. Often, they also involve areas outside the basal forebrain, such as the orbitofrontal and medial frontal cortices. Morris et al. (in press) recently reported a patient with amnesia following removal of a very small glioma in the lamina terminalis, just posterior to the right gyrus rectus. Postoperative MR scans demonstrated a lesion restricted to the diagonal band of Broca, anterior commissure, nucleus accumbens, and preoptic area. They postulated that destruction of the cholinergic projection to the hippocampus, most of which originates in the nucleus of the diagonal band of Broca, probably accounted for the amnesia, but they could not rule out contributions from other damaged areas.

### Laterality of Lesions Causing Amnesia in Humans

Many of the best-studied patients with amnesia have bilateral lesions. When unilateral temporal lobectomy for epilepsy causes severe amnesia, it is usually assumed that there has been damage to the contralateral hippocampus. Otherwise, memory deficits are relatively mild, and often are material specific (verbal for left-sided lesions; visuospatial for right-sided lesions). More severe memory disturbances have been described, however, with unilateral lesions. Most often these are left-sided and cause more verbal than nonverbal memory disturbance. This has been reported for left posterior cerebral artery infarctions affecting the medial temporal region, for left retrosplenial lesions (Valenstein et al., 1987), and for left thalamic lesions (Speedie and Heilman, 1982; Goldenberg et al., 1983; Graf-Radford et al., 1984; Mori et al., 1986). Less often, lesions causing relatively severe amnestic disturbances are right-sided (Graf-Radford et al., 1984; Morris et al., in press). There are no comparable findings in animals.

### Summary of the Anatomy of Memory

It is important to point out that the areas discussed above that are known to be important for normal memory function may not actually contain entire "memory traces." Memories are not stored in the hippocampus, diencephalon, or basal forebrain, the way goods are stored in a warehouse. These regions of the brain, however, provide the ability to access information that is probably stored elsewhere. It is considered likely that the parts of the brain that process the information as it is acquired also retain fragmentary traces of experience (Fuster, 1984; Damasio, 1989; Damasio et al., 1989, 1990). Whereas primary sensory and first-order unimodal sensory association cortices may encode purely sensory aspects of events, higher-order cortices probably build up more complex images and constructs that may transcend modalities. Damasio (1989) suggests that these "convergence zones" do not themselves contain the code to reproduce a complex memory, but rather, that they retrogradely activate the primary cortical areas that originally processed the material of which the memory consists. The hippocampal system, in his view, contributes by recording the context of events in relation to each other and to the person, such that the unique properties can be recalled. Thus patients with medial temporal lesions retain general knowledge, but fail to recall the context of these general memories, so that the amnesic's memories lack contextual complexity, definitions of uniqueness, or connection to autobiography (Damasio, 1989). Activation of the hippocampus allows for temporally coordinated "retroactivation" of convergence zones, which in turn simultaneously activate specifically those neuronal ensembles, widely distributed in primary cortices, that were involved in the original experience. Damasio suggests that only with such retroactivation is a memory brought to consciousness. The hippocampus has a limited capacity, and eventually such records are lost or consolidated in different brain areas, so that the hippocampal system is not required for retrieval of remote memories.

It remains unclear how subcortical regions interact with this cortical memory system; but clearly subcortical centers in the basal forebrain and thalamus are critical, since diencephalic amnesics appear not to be able to use their temporal lobes effectively for memory. Highly divergent systems, such as the basal forebrain cholinergic projection system, may nonspecifically activate the hippocampal-neocortical system. Subcortical structures may also provide critical pathways for memory processing, as suggested by the dual system theory, but the unique contributions of different diencephalic and basal forebrain regions to memory function remain to be elucidated. It is hoped that careful study of patients with well-localized lesions may help define subtypes of amnesia that will elucidate the contribution of specific areas to memory function.

## AMNESIA SUBTYPES: SIMILARITIES AND DIFFERENCES AMONG AMNESICS

Anatomic considerations indicate considerable heterogeneity within the amnesic population. Qualitative performance differences among patients with lesions in different areas would imply that the neuroanatomic regions contribute to memory function in different ways. In the last two decades, these behavioral and anatomic facts fueled speculation that there may be several subtypes of amnesia (Huppert and Piercy, 1979; Lhermitte and Signoret, 1972; Squire, 1981).

### *Bitemporal vs. Diencephalic Amnesia*

Historically, two subtypes have received the most attention: Bitemporal amnesia, as exemplified by patient H.M., and diencephalic amnesia, as represented by patients with alcoholic Korsakoff's disease (Butters, 1985; Butters and Cermak, 1989; Victor et al., 1971, 1989) and other patients with discrete thalamic or mammillary body lesions (Squire and Moore, 1979; Speedie and Heilman, 1982, 1983; Winocur et al., 1984; Mair et al., 1979). A third subtype, basal forebrain amnesia, has received less study, and will be considered separately.

   A key question has been whether these anatomic-descriptive subtypes can be distinguished on behavioral grounds. Data on this issue have come from two main sources: studies evaluating rates of forgetting from long-term memory in diencephalic and bitemporal amnesics and studies evaluating cognitive deficits specific to diencephalic amnesia, particularly Korsakoff's syndrome.

RATE OF FORGETTING FROM LONG-TERM MEMORY

One frequently evaluated behavioral dimension is the rate at which information is forgotten once it has been initially learned to some criteriorn. Using retention intervals from ten minutes to seven days, several studies have shown that bitemporal amnesics (H.M., herpes encephalitic, bilateral ECT, and, more controversial, early Alzheimer's patients) may show a more rapid rate of forgetting than diencephalic amnesics (Korsakoff, N. A.) or controls (Huppert and Piercy, 1979; Squire, 1981; Martone et al., 1986). In most of these studies, diencephalic patients are given longer stimulus exposures than are controls or bitemporals in order to achieve comparable recognition performance at the shortest delays. This, coupled with faster forgetting for bitemporals, initially led to the conclusion that bitemporal amnesia involves a defect in "consolidation," while diencephalic amnesia involves an earlier defect in stimulus "registration" (Huppert and Piercy, 1979; Squire, 1982a; Winocur, 1984). Once this latter defect is circumvented, however, by increased exposure to the stimuli, the normal forgetting in diencephalic amnesics has been taken to mean that their consolidation ability is intact.

The widely held view that bitemporal amnesia is distinctively characterized by abnormally rapid forgetting has been questioned by the results of two recent studies. Freed et al., (1987) retested H.M.'s recognition memory over intervals of 10 minutes, 24 hours, 72 hours, and one week with two recognition paradigms, taking pains to precisely equate his 10-minute recall with that of normals. The first was a modified Huppert and Piercy (1979) rate-of-forgetting paradigm in which H.M. was given increased exposure to pictorial stimuli (10 seconds compared to 1 second for controls) and in which yes-no recognition was probed at the four retention intervals. H.M.'s performance was normal after 10 minutes, but dropped significantly below controls after 24 hours and remained at that level through the one-week recognition probe. The normal controls continued to forget over the entire week such that their recognition performance declined to H.M.'s level, and was not significnatly better than it at 72 hours or one week. Freed et al. suggested that their findings indicated a "normal rate of forgetting over a 1-week delay interval," though as Crosson (1992) has indicated, an alternative explanaton of these results is that H.M.'s lowest level of performance for the one-week interval was raised above previous levels reported by Huppert and Piercy (1979) by virtue of additional stimulus exposure. That is, although Freed et al. focused on the equivalence between H.M. and normals at the 72-hour and one-week delays, the fact that H.M.'s performance leveled off more rapidly than controls may, in fact, be taken to support, rather than refute, the notion that bitemporal amnesics forget at an abnormally rapid rate (Crosson, 1992). In the second task reported by Freed et al., forgetting rate was assessed at the same intervals by a forced-choice recognition test rather than a yes-no recognition test. On this task, H.M.'s performance was not significantly different from controls at any interval, and in fact was slightly above that of the controls at 72 hours and one week. This is a more convincing demonstration that abnormally rapid forgetting does not necessarily characterize bitemporal amnesia.

Whereas Freed et al. compared H.M. and normals, a more recent study by McKee and Squire (1992) directly compared rate of forgetting from long-term memory in bitemporal and diencephalic amnesics equated for amnesia severity. Both groups of amnesics received eight seconds of exposure to each of 120 target pictures, while normal controls received one second of exposure. Ten minutes, two hours, and 30–32 hours after study, subjects were tested with four different recognition memory tests. On the first, subjects were asked to respond "yes" to a previously studied (old) item and "no" to a new item. The second test required subjects to respond "yes" to a new item and "no" to an old item. In the third test, subjects were asked to point to the one old item in a laterally presented pair (DMS), while in the fourth test, subjects were asked to point to the one new item (DNMS). There were no group differences for any of the recognition tests at any retention interval. Thus, although initial studies differentiated bitemporal and diencephalic amnesia on the basis of long-term forgetting rate, recent studies have tended to emphasize the similarities, rather then the differences, in rate of forgetting in these two groups. McKee and Squire (1992) suggest that, although it is reasonable to suppose that the medial temporal lobe and diencephalic systems should have different contributions to normal memory, "each region might also be an essential component of a larger functional system such that a similar amnesia might result from damage to any portion of that system." The emerging notion that bitemporal and diencephalic amnesia may be more similar than different is consistent with anatomic data comprising the dual system theory described above.

## RETROGRADE AMNESIA

Squire (1984) suggested that temporally limited retrograde amnesia was due to a defect in consolidation and was specifically related to dysfunction of the hippocampus (Zola-Morgan and Squire, 1990b). Squire et al. (1989a), however, using an updated version of Squire and Cohen's (1984) remote faces and events tests, found extensive, temporally limited retrograde amnesia in both Korsakoff patients (n = 7) and a group of patients with presumed medial temporal pathology secondary to anoxia or ischemia (n = 3). Although there were differences in the specific pattern exhibited by individual patients, their retrograde amnesia spanned a period of about 15 years and was not detectable in the more remote time periods. Gade and Mortensen (1990) found graded retrograde memory loss, supposedly typical of patients with bitemporal amnesia, in patients with basal forebrain and diencephalic amnesia (including five patients with Korsakoff's syndrome). It is thus unlikely that differences in the degree of retrograde amnesia will reliably distinguish among basal forebrain, diencephalic, or medial temporal amnesics.

## DEFICITS SPECIFIC TO KORSAKOFF'S SYNDROME

Despite the apparent failure of forgetting rate to consistently distinguish between bitemporal and diencephalic amnesia, other data suggest that certain cognitive abilities might be differentially impaired in diencephalic amnesia, particularly patients with Korsakoff's syndrome. As we shall see, a key issue is whether such impairments are an obligatory part of the amnesia seen in these patients.

### Defects in spatiotemporal aspects of memory

*Memory for temporal order.* One such ability concerns the judgment of the temporal order of events; that is, to discriminate when a target item occurred in the study sequence (Hirst and Volpe, 1982; Huppert and Piercy, 1976; McAndrews and Milner, 1991). In a typical temporal-order judgment paradigm, subjects are given a list discrimination task in which a target list of stimuli is initially shown, followed after a brief delay by a second target list. During subsequent testing, subjects are asked whether they had seen each stimulus before (recognition judgment) and, if so, whether it belonged to the first or second list (temporal order judgment). In an early study of this phenomenon, Squire et al. (1981) examined temporal order judgments in bilateral ECT patients, patient N.A., and controls. They found that, though impairments in temporal order judgments were seen in both, their recognition judgments were also poor. When recognition performance was subsequently equated with normals, no temporal ordering deficit remained. Thus, in these patients, impaired temporal order judgments appeared to be due to poor recognition memory.

However, the impairment in temporal order judgments exhibited by a different amnesic population, patients with alcoholic Korsakoff's syndrome, cannot be accounted for on the basis of their poor recognition performance (Meudell et al., 1985; Squire, 1982b). Several authors (Moscovitch, 1982; Schacter, 1987b; Squire, 1982b) have attributed the temporal ordering impairment in these patients to concomitant frontal lobe pathology known to coexist with diencephalic damage (Jernigan et al., 1991). Two facts support this interpretation: (1) nonamnesic patients with left frontal lesions (Corsi, cited in Milner et al., 1991) and basal ganglia disease (Sager et al., 1988) also show impairment in temporal order judgments and (2) deficits in temporal order judgments in amnesics correlate significantly with neuropsychological tests putatively sensitive to frontal pathology such as the Wisconsin Card Sort (Squire, 1982b). Although the link to frontal lobe damage has been relatively consistent, there are two reasons to keep the book open on this issue. First, the Wisconsin Card Sort may not be as specifically sensitive to frontal lobe pathology as originally thought (Anderson et al., 1991). Second, a recent case study of T.R., a densely amnesic patient with a left retrosplenial lesion, suggests that a defect in temporal ordering can exist independently of both recognition ability and frontal lobe function (Bowers et al., 1988). Interestingly, T.R. was dramatically impaired in temporal order judgments for newly acquired information, but had no difficulty judging the temporal order of remote events. He performed normally on tests of frontal lobe function. These findings provide an initial clue that it may be important to distinguish between two kinds of temporal ordering deficits: (1) one which is a part of a more general, frontally mediated strategic deficit (as in Korsakoff's syndrome) and (2) another which reflects an anterograde impairment in "time tagging" new information (as in T.R.).

*Source monitoring and source amnesia.* As indicated above, successful retrieval from episodic memory has an autobiographical quality and is characterized by direct recollection of both the content and source of remembered information. The phenomenon of source amnesia illustrates that such characteristics are potentially dissociable. Source amnesia refers to a situation in which one remembers some fact or piece of information, but forgets the source of the information. For example, we might remember specific information about a book or movie, but be unable to recollect where that information was learned. Source attributions differentiate autobiographical event memories from more general knowledge, and source amnesia has been described as a form of memory impairment for spatiotemporal context since it reflects recollection of content devoid of the context (temporal and situational factors) that gives rise to the memory (Johnson et al., 1992; Shimamura, 1989). Schacter et al. (1984) used a paradigm first introduced by Evans and Thorn (1966) to study source amnesia in memory-disordered patients with Alzheimer's disease, closed head injury, and encephalitis. They presented bogus facts (e.g., Bob Hope's father was a fireman) to their patients and then gave a recall test. If a fact was recalled, patients were asked where they had learned it. Many patients demonstrated recall of at least some of the facts, but frequently asserted that they had known them before the experimental session. This finding could not be explained by poor memory, since normal subjects whose recall was lowered by a one-week study-test interval did not commit source errors. Shimamura and Squire (1987) taught obscure (true) facts to a group of Korsakoff patients (n = 6) and a group of patients with amnesia secondary to anoxia (n = 3). Severe source amnesia, in which recall was attributed to sources other than the experiment, was observed in three of the Korsakoff patients and in one of the anoxic patients. The level of fact memory performance did not predict the degree of source amnesia. Not only do control subjects whose fact memory is reduced by a long delay not exhibit source errors, but patients with bitemporal amnesia, including H.M., perform *better* at tests of recency and temporal order than do frontal patients (Milner et al., 1991; Sager et al., 1990).

Some evidence suggests that the severity of source amnesia varies as a function of frontal lobe impairment in amnesic and nonamnesic subjects (Schacter et al., 1984; Janowsky et al., 1989), though some authors (see Johnson et al., 1992) are not willing to rule out important contributions from diencephalic and medial temporal regions. One way of understanding the relative contributions of these various regions is to suggest that source monitoring tasks make variable demands on cognitive estimation (Shallice and Evans, 1978), reality monitoring (Johnson, 1991), attribution (Jacoby et al., 1989), and temporal order memory (Olton, 1989; Hirst and Volpe, 1982). It may be that different populations of amnesics are differentially impaired depending on the specific test used to test source monitoring. If this is so, then more precise development of source monitoring assessments may provide a future basis on which such subpopulations may be differentiated (Johnson et al., in press).

*Metamemory and "feeling of knowing."* Another cognitive domain that appears differentially impaired in alcoholic Korsakoff's syndrome has been referred to as metamemory. Metamemory involves knowledge about (1) one's own memory capabilities, (2) the memory demands of particular tasks or situations, and (3) potentially useful strategies relevant to given tasks or situations (Flavell and Wellman, 1977; Gruneberg, 1983). It encompasses people's beliefs (e.g., "I will [or will not] be able to remember these words.") as well as their knowlege about the memory system (e.g., rehearsal strategies that enhance recall). Hirst and Volpe (cited in Hirst, 1982) were among the first to report differentially impaired metamemory in Korsakoff patients when compared to other etiologies of amnesia. Based on interviews, they found that Korsakoff patients had less knowledge of mnemonic strategies than did patients with amnesia from other causes.

The most widely studied metamemorial capacity in amnesic patients is the feeling-of-knowing (FOK) phenomenon (cf. Hart, 1965, 1967; Gruneberg and Monks, 1974; Nelson et al., 1982, 1984). In a typical FOK experiment, subjects are asked to freely recall the answers to general informaton questions of varying difficulty (e.g., "What is the tallest mountain in South America?") until a certain number of failures occurs. For these unrecalled items, subjects are then asked to judge the likelihood that they would be able to recognize the correct answer if it was presented along with other likely but incorrect choices. FOK predictions are then validated by a subsequent recognition test. The general finding in normals is that recognition performance is better for questions eliciting strong FOK than for questions eliciting weak or no FOK.

Simamura and Squire (1986) evaluated FOK judgments, and their ability to predict subsequent recognition performance, in patients with Korakoff's syndrome, psychiatric patients undergoing bilateral ECT, a mixed group of amnesics which included N.A., and controls. Using general information questions (study 1) and a sentence memory paradigm that assessed newly learned information (study 2), they found that only the Korsakoff patients displayed an impairment in making FOK judgments. From these results, it appears that metamemory dysfunction is not an obligatorty aspect of amnesia, since amnesia can occur without any measurable impairment in FOK. The authors speculated that the disturbed FOK in Korsakoff patients might be a function of their frontal pathology, which would be expected to impair their ability on a variety of judgment and planning tasks.

*Summary.*   It is important to emphasize that deficits in temporal order judgments, source amnesia, and metamemory have frequently been interpreted in the context of frontal lobe pathology, and more generally have been used to distinguish between groups of amnesics with (diencephalic) and without (bitemporal) associated frontal lobe deficits. This distinction has had two very different potential meanings (cf. Schacter, 1987b). The first is that there is a "core" amnesic syndrome upon which frontal deficits might be nonspecifically superimposed. If this is true, then an important task for neuropsychological research is to distinguish that which is "core" and that which is "ancillary" to amnesia. Arguments of this type are frequently invoked when a cognitive deficit (e.g., failure to release from proactive interference) thought to reflect the nature of the memory disorder in Korsakoff patients turns out to exist in nonamnesic patients with frontal lobe lesions (cf. Moscovitch, 1982). If this is true, such frontal impairments become more of a "nuisance" to the amnesia researcher than a topic worthy of primary concern. Alternatively, one could suppose that frontal lobe systems have specific memory-related functions (Petrides, 1989). If this is the case, then it becomes important to recognize that patients with frontal-related memory impairment represent a type of amnesic syndrome that differs from the amnesia associated with other anatomic lesions—a syndrome that is equally significant to our understanding of memory disorders. Indeed, there is growing evidence that the frontal lobes play an important, specific role in mediating temporal context (Goldman-Rakic, 1984; McAndrews and Milner, 1991; Milner et al., 1984, 1991; Stuss et al., 1982; Schacter, 1987b), and memory for self-generated responses (Petrides and Milner, 1982), and may contain specific regions that mediate working memory (Goldman-Rakic, 1992). These findings strongly suggest that specific frontally mediated memory deficits should be admitted, finally, into the domain of impairments worthy of study by amnesia researchers.

### Basal Forebrain Amnesia

Studies of patients with amnesia from basal forebrain lesions suggest that it is clinically distinctive. As noted above, this form of amnesia most commonly results from vascular lesion or aneurysm surgery in the region of the anterior communicating artery (Okawa et al., 1980; Volpe and Hirst, 1983; Vilkki, 1985; Gade, 1982; Alexander and Freedman, 1983; Damasio et al., 1985b; Phillips et al., 1987; DeLuca and

Cicerone, 1989). After basal forebrain damage, the patient exhibits extensive antero-grade but variable retrograde amnesia. Temporal gradients similar to that seen in Korsakoff's syndrome have been described (Lindqvist and Norlen, 1966; Gade and Mortensen, 1990). Some authors have also described an impairment in placing mem-ories in proper chronological order (Lindqvist and Norlen, 1966; Damasio et al., 1985b; Talland et al., 1967). Free, and sometimes wild, confabulation appears to be characteristic, particularly in the acute period (Alexander and Freedman, 1983; Damasio et al., 1985b; Okawa et al., 1980; Lindqvist and Norlen, 1966; Logue et al., 1968; Talland et al., 1967) and may relate to the extent of concomitant orbitofrontal involvement existing along with the memory impairment (Vikki, 1985; Damasio et al., 1985b; Phillips et al., 1987; DeLuca and Cicerone, 1989). Some patients have dif-ficulty distinguishing reality from dreaming. Although these behavioral abnormali-ties are distinctive, they may not be functionally related to the amnesia; often, basal forebrain amnesia persists after dream-waking confusion and confabulation have subsided.

Cuing seems to differentially improve memory performance in these patients, and anecdotal evidence suggests that many of these patients can recall specific informa-tion in one retrieval attempt, but not the next; these data have led to the general idea that these patients suffer from a problem in accessing information that does exist in long-term memory. However, further data are needed before accepting this propo-sition confidently. It has frequently been noted that these patients appear apathetic and unconcerned about their memory impairment (Alexander and Freedman, 1983; Phillips et al., 1987; Talland et al., 1967). Interestingly, Talland et al. regarded basal forebrain amnesics to show striking behavioral similarities to patients with Korsa-koff's syndrome, and Graff-Radford et al. (1990) saw similarities between these amnesics and those suffering memory loss secondary to paramedian thalamic infarc-tions. It may be that such similarities arise because the large vascular lesions that char-acterize this case material also involve structures or pathways destined for compo-nents of the medial temporal or diencephalic memory systems (Gade, 1982; Crosson, 1992). Although these anatomic considerations are compelling, there are as yet insuf-ficient behavioral data on which to formally compare basal forebrain amnesics with amnesics of diencephalic or bitemporal origin.

## CLINICAL PRESENTATION OF DISORDERS ASSOCIATED WITH AMNESIA

Memory loss is a common problem encountered in patients seen by physicians and psychologists. As discussed above, it has considerable localizing significance. It is also a helpful diagnostic finding, since it is a distinguishing feature of several neurological disorders. It is beyond the scope of this book to discuss these illnesses in detail; how-ever, we will comment on some of the more important disorders.

### Age-Associated Memory Impairment and Benign Senescent Forgetfulness

Kral (1962) used the term benign senescent forgetfulness to describe adults whose memory was poorer than their peers, but who had no other evidence of progressive dementia. Such patients, however, may be difficult to distinguish from patients with early Alzheimer's disease (Welsh et al., 1991). Memory deteriorates with increasing age in normal persons. Normal 70- and 80-year-old persons perform at levels that are 50% below that of young adults on tests of learning and memory (Larrabee et al., 1988). The term age-associated memory impairment refers to healthy persons over 50 who are not depressed or demented and who score at least one standard deviation below the mean for young adults on tests of memory (Crook et al., 1986, 1991). These normal adults may complain of memory loss, particularly if they are in intellectually demanding positions.

### Degenerative Disorders

Many of the degenerative dementias (such as Pick's, Huntington's, and Parkinson's disease) eventually affect memory (see Chapter 16), but Alzheimer's disease typically first manifests with amnesia (Damasio et al., 1989). As discussed above, nearly all of the areas thought to be important in memory are affected by Alzheimer's disease, including the medial temporal lobe (Hyman et al., 1984, 1986; Scott et al., 1991), the basal forebrain (Whitehouse et al., 1981), the thalamus (Xuereb et al., 1991), and the neocortex. The memory impairment in advancing Alzheimer's disease affects not only new learning, but also results in the gradual loss of knowledge structures and semantic memory stores. Eventually, other cognitive domains such as language, visuospatial/perceptual ability, personality, and affect become involved. Thus, the memory loss found in cortical dementia is not as "pure" as in other forms of amnesia, but takes place in the context of widespread cognitive decline.

Amnesia is a feature of fatal familial insomnia, a disease characterized by insomnia, autonomic disturbances, ataxia, and myoclonus (Lugaresi et al., 1986). Atrophy of the anterior and dorsomedial thalamic nuclei is seen in all cases, in addition to variable extrathalamic pathology (Manetto et al., 1992). A mutation in the prion protein gene has been identified (Medori et al., 1992).

### Vascular Disease

Stroke will manifest with amnesia when critical areas are infarcted. The deficits associated with strokes affecting the posterior cerebral artery territory (posterior medial temporal lobe and retrosplenial cortex) (Benson et al., 1974) and the thalamic penetrating arteries have been discussed above, as has basal forebrain amnesia from anterior communicating artery aneurysm hemorrhage or surgery. In these cases, the onset of amnesia is abrupt. Improvement is variable, and often patients are left with serious permanent deficits, even following small infarctions (for example, of the thalamus).

### Cerebral Anoxia

Depending upon the degree and duration of ischemia and/or hypoxia, neuronal loss may be widespread or very focal. We have already discussed amnesia following cardiac arrest in which the only pathological feature identified was loss of neurons in field CA1 of the hippocampus (Zola-Morgan et al., 1986).

## Wernicke-Korsakoff Syndrome

Alcoholic Korsakoff's syndrome typically develops after years of conjoint alcohol abuse and nutritional deficiency (Butters and Cermak, 1980; Butters, 1984; Victor et al., 1989). Patients first undergo an acute stage of the illness, Wernicke's encephalopathy, in which symptoms of confusion, disorientation, oculomotor dysfunction, and ataxia are present. After this resolves, amnesia can persist as a permanent symptom. Severe anterograde amnesia and an extensive, temporally graded retrograde amnesia are characteristic. Although usually associated with chronic alcohol abuse, Korsakoff's syndrome can occur in nonalcoholic patients who suffer chronic avitaminosis secondary to malabsorption syndromes (cf. Becker et al., 1990). Lesion location and neuropsychological features related to amnesia are discussed in detail above.

## Herpes Simplex Encephalitis

Herpes simplex encephalitis causes inflammation and necrosis particularly in the orbitofrontal and inferior temporal regions. It thus involves limbic structures, including the hippocampus, parahippocampal gyrus, amygdala and overlying cortex, the polar limbic cortex, cingulate gyrus, and the orbitofrontal cortex (Damasio et al., 1989). Patients may present with personality change, confusion, headache, fever, and seizures, and they are often amnestic. Prompt treatment with antiviral agents can control the illness, and full recovery is possible; however, damage to the aforementioned structures often leaves the patient with severe anterograde and retrograde amnesia. The amnesic syndromes in patient D.R.B. (also known as Boswell) (Damasio et al., 1985a) and patient S.S. (Cermak, 1976; Cermak and O'Connor, 1983) have been particularly well characterized.

## Limbic Encephalitis

Limbic encephalitis occurs as a remote effect of carcinoma and, like herpes encephalitis, affects limbic structures at the base of the forebrain (Corsellis et al., 1968). Patients present with personality change, agitation, and amnestic dementia. Amnesia has also been reported in association with Hodgkin's disease (Duyckaerts et al., 1985), probably on the same basis.

## Trauma

Following closed head injury, patients may have an acute anterograde and retrograde amnesia, the duration of which correlates with the severity of the injury, as measured by the Glasgow Coma Scale, or the duration of unconsciousness (Levin, 1989). The retrograde amnesia typically improves along with improvement in anterograde amnesia, providing evidence that a retrieval deficit is responsible for the portion of the retrograde memory loss that recovers. Residual memory impairment is usually a feature of broader cognitive and attentional impairment, but it can be prominent with severe injuries (Russell and Nathan, 1946; Whitty and Zangwill, 1977). Pathological changes are variable and widespread. Memory dysfunction may be caused by anterior temporal lobe contusions, by temporal lobe white matter necrosis, or by more diffuse axonal disruption (Levin, 1989).

## Transient Global Amnesia

Transient global amnesia is a distinctive form of amnesia that begins suddenly and typically resolves within a day (Fisher and Adams, 1964; Kritchevsky, 1987, 1989; Kritchevsky et al., 1988; Caplan, 1985). A severe impairment in new learning and patchy loss of information learned prior to onset is seen. The patient often asks repetitive questions and may be aware of the memory deficit. Fifteen percent complain of headache. After resolution, neuropsychological testing is normal except for amnesia for the episode (Kritchevsky, 1989). Evidence suggests that an episode of transient global amnesia does not increase the risk of developing more permanent memory dysfunction. In a recent review, Kritchevsky (1989) considered the possible etiologic role played by epilepsy (Fisher, 1982; Fisher and Adams, 1958), emotional stress (Olesen and Jørgensen, 1986), occlusive cerebrovascular disease (Heathfield et al., 1973; Shuping et al., 1980), migranous vasospasm (Caplan et al., 1981; Haas and Ross, 1986; Hodges and Warlow, 1990), and vertebrobasilar dyscontrol (Caplan, 1985). He found no specific etiology to be convincingly associated with the syndrome, but suggested that transient disturbance in medial temporal and/or diencephalic brain structures appeared to be involved. Importantly, although some form of cerebrovascular disease is frequently invoked to explain transient global amnesia, it has no greater incidence in the affected population than in an age-matched control group (Miller et al., 1987; Hodges and Warlow, 1990), and patients with this form of amnesia are equally or *less* likely to have strokes than a control population (Hodges and Warlow, 1990).

## Electroconvulsive Therapy

Electroconvulsive therapy used for relief of depression can produce severe anterograde and temporally limited retrograde amnesia (cf. Miller and Marlin, 1979; Squire, 1984). More severe impairment is seen after bilateral than after unilateral application. The anterograde defect is related in severity to the number of treatments and is characterized by rapid forgetting and poor delayed recall (Squire, 1984). Substantial, often complete recovery takes place in the few months after treatment ends (Squire and Chace, 1975; Squire and Slater, 1983). The retrograde amnesia appears to be temporally limited, involving only the few years prior to treatment onset. It, too, recovers almost completely in the months after treatment (Squire et al, 1976, 1981). The extent of memory loss appears unrelated to therapeutic efficacy (Small et al., 1981; Welch, 1982). Though the data are by no means clear, some authors have suggested that memory loss induced by ECT models bilateral temporal lobe disease (Squire, 1984; Inglis, 1970), and several studies have used ECT patients as a contrast for patients with diencephalic pathology.

## Functional Amnesias

Functional amnesias have been reviewed by Schacter and Kihlstrom (1989) and Kihlstrom (1980). They may be normal, as in amnesia for events of childhood and for events during sleep, or they may be pathological, as in the amnesias associated with dissociative states, with multiple personality, or with simulated amnesia. A striking loss of autobiographical memory is a hallmark of functional amnesia, and amnesia for one's own name (in the absence of aphasia or severe cognitive dysfunction in other spheres) is seen exclusively in this form of memory loss. Retrograde loss is often disproportionate to anterograde amnesia (cf. Schacter and Tulving, 1982) and some patients will demonstrate loss of skills or other procedural memories typically retained by organic amnesic patients.

## REHABILITATION OF MEMORY DISORDERS

Recently, increased neurobehavioral interest has been devoted to the rehabilitation of patients with memory disorders (cf. Volpe and McDowell, 1990). Historically, the field of memory rehabilitation has been guided by practical, rather than theoretical concerns, although there are important recent attempts to formulate an underlying theoretical basis for therapeutic interventions (cf. Baddeley, 1984; Parente and DiCesare, 1991; Sohlberg and Mateer, 1989; Wilson, 1987). As Glisky and Schacter (1987) point out, most rehabilitative interventions have attempted to directly improve memory performance through repetitive practice or exercises (cf. Prigatano et al., 1984) or through the teaching of mnemonic strategies. They refer to this as the "restorative" approach, since its goal is to restore a certain degree of memory skill in these patients, thus improving functional adaptation in real life. Depending on severity of the memory loss and the nature of material to be learned, some studies have suggested the beneficial effect of rehearsal strategies (Schacter et al., 1985), organizational techniques (Gianutsos and Gianutsos, 1979), and imagery mnemonics (Crovitz et al., 1979a; Patten, 1972). Although such techniques have proved useful in individual cases, large-scale empirical group investigations of the efficacy of well-controlled rehabilitative techniques have not yet been performed. As a result, there is as yet little empirical evidence that such approaches are applicable to the range of memory-disordered patients without extensive individual modification. More importantly, there is little evidence that such techniques lead to substantial generalization outside the laboratory (Bauer, 1984b). Despite this, clinical practitioners are frequently called upon to provide assistance to individual patients in their attempts to regain functional memory capacity at work and at home. Interested readers should consult recent reviews of cognitive rehabilitation and memory therapy (Glisky and Schacter, 1986; Kreutzer and Wehman, 1991; Meier et al., 1987; Sohlberg and Mateer, 1989; Uzzell and Gross, 1986; Wilson and Moffat, 1984; Wilson, 1987) for information regarding empirical results and specific techniques that may be useful in working with the individual memory-disordered patient.

As an alternative to the restorative approach, Schacter and Glisky (1986) have attempted to capitalize on the relatively spared ability of the amnesic patient to learn specific skills or procedures, and have been relatively successful in teaching memory-disordered patients a computer-related vocabulary using a variant of word-stem completion they call the "method of vanishing cues" (Glisky et al., 1986b). In related studies, Glisky and colleagues have shown that, using an approach based on skill/procedural learning, memory-disordered patients can be taught functional use of a microcomputer (Glisky et al., 1986a), and that, when enhanced with extensive repetition and direct cuing, such learning could generalize to a real work environment (Glisky and Schacter, 1987). Though such procedures appear relatively labor intensive, and may not lead to extensive explicit memory, they do demonstrate that it is possible to obtain generalization of a newly acquired skill to the natural environment; perhaps with further refinement of the technique, such generalization might be made to occur more efficiently. It is important to recognize that the goal of this approach is not to restore or improve memory in any general sense; instead, it is designed to teach a specific skill in hopes of preparing the patient for gainful employment. Glisky and Schacter (1987; cf. also Schacter and Glisky, 1986) have called this the "domain-specific" approach to distinguish it from the larger body of restorative techniques. In our view, it represents a promising area for future clinical and experimental investigation.

## CONCLUSION

Experimental studies of the amnesic syndrome have provided important information about how memory is normally organized in the brain and have generated new approaches to the clinical study of memory disorders. The sparing of many memory functions has led to structural ("systems") and functional ("process") distinctions between different types of memory which are only now receiving anatomic verification. In the next decade, studies of amnesia are likely to benefit substantially from continued interdisciplinary collaboration, owing to the growing availability of sensitive and specific assessment tools and to the development of exciting new technologies.

What are the likely foci of such collaborative activity? The first focus concerns the question of whether the "amnesic syndrome" is a singular entity. Significant debate continues regarding the notion of a "core" amnesic syndrome and whether the diverse causes of amnesia share a common underlying basis. We have considered information processing views which place the locus of the amnesic deficit at the level of encoding, retention, or retrieval, and have found evidence suggesting the existence of different amnesic subtypes. Just how distinct these subtypes are is being questioned on behavioral and anatomic grounds. For example, recent data suggest that the distinction between bitemporal and diencephalic amnesia, which once held promise for elucidating the anatomy of storage and encoding/retrieval, may not be as sharp as once thought, suggesting that the medial temporal and diencephalic regions participate in a larger, more complex memory system. This leaves open the question of whether the characteristics of this system are such that an underlying "core" amnesic deficit will be found.

Another focus concerns the continuing question of necessary and sufficient deficits in amnesia. Since amnesic disorders can result from diverse disease processes and may be seen in the context of a variety of cognitive deficits, it seems reasonable to attempt to distinguish between what is causative (central) and what is ancillary to the underlying memory disorder. A prominent example of how this issue complicates contemporary amnesia research is the controversy regarding the role of frontal lobe deficits in the memory impairment of diencephalic (and, perhaps, basal forebrain) amnesics. Traditionally, frontal contributions to memory have been considered to be relatively "nonspecific," producing complex disturbances in attention and strategy formation that affect various domains of neuropsychological functioning in addition to memory. However, recent research has revealed that the frontal lobes play specific mnemonic roles and may mediate complex processes such as working memory and memory for self-generated responses. Thus, frontal contributions to memory are receiving renewed attention, not as "nuisance variables," but as aspects of memory functioning worthy of assuming a central place in amnesia research.

A third issue involves how to best understand distinctions between spared and impaired memory abilities in amnesia. We have considered various ways of viewing these distinctions (e.g., multiple memory systems vs. transfer-appropriate processing) and have suggested that much of the data can be considered as supportive of both approaches. That is, viewing memory dissociations as supportive of the idea of multiple memory systems as opposed to considering such dissociations as based on differences in cognitive processes applied at study and test are not necessarily mutually exclusive. More stringent empirical criteria for distinguishing among such views would seem to be an important priority. It will also be important to better understand how "implicit" phenomena (e.g., "priming" and "perceptual fluency") contribute to performances on traditional (explicit) tests of recall and recognition. New strategies for empirically and statistically separating effects of direct recollection (e.g., recall) from the indirect effects of prior stimulus exposure (e.g., perceptual fluency and familiarity) hold significant promise in facilitating this understanding in normals and amnesics (cf. Jacoby and Kelly, 1992).

In the past few years, exciting new technologies have become available which will undoubtedly inform us further about the anatomic, metabolic, and behavioral substrate of memory and its disorders. New "functional imaging" techniques such as PET and SPECT allow evaluation of time-locked, regional brain activity during the performance of memory tasks. As such, these new techniques arguably represent a real alternative to traditional neurobehavioral investigations of brain-impaired patients conducted largely within the ablation tradition. Whether these new technologies will be able to resolve the many controversies discussed in this chapter, or whether they will bring with them new and different controversies, remains to be seen. However, they do represent new tools which, if used appropriately and in combination with tried-and-true methods developed within behavioral neurology and neuropsychology, provide exciting new prospects and challenges for the interdisciplinary study of memory and amnesia.

# REFERENCES

Aggleton, J. P., Burton, M. J., and Passingham, M. E. (1980). Cortical and subcortical afferents to the amygdala of the rhesus monkey. *Brain Res. 190*:347–368.

Aggleton, J. P., Keith, A. B., and Sahgal, A. (1991). Both fornix and anterior thalamic, but not mammillary, lesions disrupt delayed non-matching-to-position memory in rats. *Behav. Brain Res. 44*:151–161.

Aggleton, J. P., and Mishkin, M. (1983). Memory impairments following restricted medial thalamic lesions in monkeys. *Exp. Brain Res. 52*:199–209.

Aggleton, J. P., and Mishkin, M. (1985). Mamillary-body lesions and visual recognition in monkeys. *Exp. Brain Res. 58*:190–197.

Albert, M. S., Butters, N., and Brandt, J. (1980). Memory for remote events in alcoholics. *J. Stud. Alcohol 41*:1071–1081.

Albert, M. S., Butters, N., and Brandt, J. (1981). Patterns of remote memory in amnesic and demented patients. *Arch. Neurol. 38*:495–500.

Albert, M. S., Butters, N., and Levin, J. (1979). Temporal gradients in the retrograde amnesia of patients with alcoholic Korsakoff's disease. *Arch. Neurol. 36*:211–216.

Alexander, M. P., and Freedman, M. (1983). Amnesia after anterior communicating artery rupture. *Neurology 33 (Suppl 2)*:104.

Amaral, D. G., and Cowan, W. M. (1980). Subcortical afferents to the hippocampal formation in the monkey. *J. Comp. Neurol. 189*:573–591.

Amaral, D. G., and Insausti, R. (1990). Hippocampal formation. In *Human Nervous System*, G. Paxinos (ed.). San Diego: Academic Press, pp. 711–755.

Amaral, D. G., Insausti, R., and Cowan, W. M. (1983). Evidence for a direct projection from the superior temporal gyrus to the entorhinal cortex in the monkey. *Brain Res. 275*:263–277.

Andersen, R. (1978). Cognitive changes after amygdalotomy. *Neuropsychologia 16*:439–451.

Anderson, J. R.(1976). *Language, Memory, and Thought*. Hillsdale, N.J.: Lawrence Erlbaum.

Anderson, J. R., and Ross, B. H. (1980). Evidence against a semantic-episodic distinction. *J. Exp. Psychol. [Hum. Learn.] 6*:441–465.

Anderson, S. W., Damasio, H., Jones, R. D., and Tranel, D. (1991). Wisconsin Card Sorting Test performance as a measure of frontal lobe damage. *J. Clin. Exp. Neuropsychol. 13*:909–922.

Arendt, T., Bigl, V., and Arendt, A. (1983). Loss of neurons in the nucleus basalis of Meynert in Alzheimer's disease, paralysis agitans and Korsakoff's disease. *Acta Neuropathol. 61*:101–108.

Babcock, H. (1930). An experiment in the measurement of mental deterioration. *Arch. Psychol. 117*:105.

Bachevalier, J., and Mishkin, M. (1986). Visual recognition impairment follows ventromedial but not dorsolateral prefrontal lesions in monkeys. *Behav. Brain Res. 20*:249–261.

Bachevalier, J., Parkinson, J. K., and Mishkin, M. (1985a). Visual recognition in monkeys: effects of separate vs. combined transection of fornix and amygdalofugal pathways. *Exp. Brain Res. 57*:554–561.

Bachevalier, J., Saunders, R. C., and Mishkin, M. (1985b). Visual recognition in monkeys: effects of transection of the fornix. *Exp. Brain Res. 57*:547–553.

Baddeley, A. (1982). Implications of neuropsychological evidence for theories of normal memory. In *Philosophical Transactions of the Royal Society of London*, D. E. Broadbent and L. Weiskrantz (eds.). London: The Royal Society, pp. 59–72.

Baddeley, A. D. (1984). Memory theory and memory therapy. In *Clinical Management of*

*Memory Disorders*, B. A. Wilson and N. Moffat (eds.). Rockville, Md.: Aspen Publications, pp. 5–27.

Baleydier, C., and Mauguiere, F. (1980). The duality of the cingulate gyrus in monkey. Neuroanatomical study and functional hypothesis. *Brain 103*:525–554.

Bartus, R. T., Dean, R. L., Beer, B., Ponecorvo, M. J., and Flicker, C. (1985). The cholinergic hypothesis: an historical overview, current perspective, and future directions. *Ann. N.Y. Acad. Sci. 444*:332–358.

Bauer, R. M. (1982). Visual hypoemotionality as a symptom of visual-limbic disconnection in man. *Arch. Neurol. 39*:702–708.

Bauer, R. M. (1984a). Autonomic recognition of names and faces in prosopagnosia: a neuropsychological application of the Guilty Knowledge Test. *Neuropsychologia 22*:457–469.

Bauer, R. M. (1984b). State of the art (not yet "science") of cognitive rehabilitation. *Contemp. Psychiatry 3*:41–43.

Bauer, R. M., and Verfaellie, M. (1992). Memory dissociations: a cognitive psychophysiological perspective. In *Neuropsychology of Memory*, 2nd ed., L. R. Squire and N. Butters (eds.). New York: Guilford Press, pp. 58–71.

Bauer, R. M., Verfaellie, M., Rediess, S., Bowers, D., and Watson, R. T. (1992). Autonomic recognition of newly learned information in alcoholic Korsakoff and Alzheimer's disease patients. Submitted for publication.

Becker J. T., Furman, J.M.R., Panisset, M., and Smith, C. (1990). Characteristics of the memory loss of a patient with Wernicke-Korsakoff's syndrome without alcoholism. *Neuropsychologia 28*:171–179.

Benson, D. F., Marsden, C. D., and Meadows, J. C. (1974). The amnesic syndrome of posterior cerebral artery occulusion. *Acta Neurol. Scand. 50*:133–145.

Bentin, S., and Moscovitch, M. (1988). The time course of repetition effects for words and unfamiliar faces. *J. Exp. Psychol. [Gen.] 117*:148–160.

Benton, A., Hamsher, K., Varney, N. R., and Spreen, O. (1983). *Contributions to Neuropsychological Assessment*. New York: Oxford University Press.

Benton, A. L. (1974). *The Revised Visual Retention Test*, 4th Ed. New York: Psychological Corporation.

Benton, A. L., and Hamsher, K. deS. (1976). *Multilingual Aphasia Examination*. Iowa City: University of Iowa Press.

Binder, L. M. (1982). Constructional strategies on complex figure drawings after unilateral brain damage. *J. Clin. Neuropsychol. 4*:51–58.

Blaxton, T. A. (1985). Investigating dissociations among memory measures: support for a transfer-appropriate processing framework. Ph.D. thesis, Purdue University.

Blaxton, T. A. (1989). Investigating dissociations among memory measures: support for a transfer-appropriate processing framework. *J. Exp. Psychol. [Learn. Mem.] 15*:657–668.

Bliss, T.V.P., and Gardner-Medwin, A. R. (1973). Long-lasting potentiation of synaptic transmission in the dentate area of the unanesthetized rabbit following stimulation of the perforant path. *J. Physiol. 232*:357–374.

Bliss, T.V.P., and Lomo, T. (1973). Long-lasting potentiation of synaptic transmission in the dentate area of the anesthetized rabbit following stimulation of the perforant path. *J. Physiol. 232*:331–356.

Bogousslavsky, J., Regli, F., and Assal, G. (1986). The syndrome of tuberothalamic artery territory infarction. *Stroke 17*:434–441.

Booker, J. (1992). Unpublished dissertation. University of Arizona.

Bowers, D., Verfaellie, M., Valenstein, E., and Heilman, K. M. (1988). Impaired acquisition of temporal order information in amnesia. *Brain Cognition 8*:47–66.

Brooks D. N., and Baddeley A. (1976). What can amnesics learn? *Neuropsychologia* 14:111–122.

Bushke, H., and Fuld, P. A. (1974). Evaluating storage, retention, and retrieval in disordered memory and learning. *Neurology* 11:1019–1025.

Butter, C. M., and Snyder, D. R. (1972). Alterations in aversive and aggressive behaviors following orbital frontal lesions in rhesus monkeys. *Acta Neurobiol. Exp.* 32:525–565.

Butters, N. (1984). Alcoholic Korsakoff's syndrome: an update. *Semin. Neurol.* 4:226–244.

Butters, N. (1985). Alcoholic Korsakoff syndrome: some unresolved issues concerning etiology, neuropathology, and cognitive deficits. *J. Clin. Exp. Neuropsychol.* 7:181–210.

Butters, N., and Cermak, L. S. (1980). *Alcoholic Korsakoff's Syndrome: An Information Processing Approach to Amnesia.* New York: Academic Press.

Butters, N., and Cermak, L. S. (1986). A case study of the forgetting of autobiographical knowledge: implications for the study of retrograde amnesia. In *Autobiographical Memory*, D. Rubin (ed.). New York: Cambridge University Press, pp. 253–272.

Butters, N., and Miliotis, P. (1985). Amnesic disorders. In *Clinical Neuropsychology*, 2nd ed. K. M. Heilman and E. Valenstein (eds.). New York: Oxford University Press, pp. 403–451.

Butters, N., and Stuss, D. T. (1989). Diencephalic amnesia. In *Handbook of Neuropsychology*, Vol. 3, F. Boller and J. Grafman (eds.). Amsterdam: Elsevier, pp. 107–148.

Butters, N., Heindel, W. C., and Salmon, D. P. (1990). Dissociation of implicit memory in dementia: neurological implications. *Bull. Psychonom. Soc.* 28:359–366.

Butters, N., Miliotis, P., Albert, M. S., and Sax, D. S. (1984). Memory assessment: evidence of the heterogeneity of amnesic symptoms. In *Advances in Clinical Neuropsychology*, Vol. 1, G. Goldstein (ed.). New York: Plenum Press, pp. 127–159.

Butters, N., Granholm, E. Salmon, E., Grant, I., and Wolfe, J. (1987). Episodic and semantic memory: a comparison of amnesic and demented patients. *J. Exp. Clin. Neuropsychol.* 9:479–497.

Butters, N., Wolfe, J., Martone, M., Granholm, E., and Cermak, L. S. (1985). Memory disorders associated with Huntington's disease: Verbal recall, verbal recognition and procedural memory. *Neuropsychologia* 23:729–743.

Cairns, H., and Mosberg, W. H. (1951). Colloid cyst of the third ventricle. *Surg. Gynecol. Obstet.* 92:545–570.

Caplan, L., Chedru, F., Lhermitte, F., and Mayman, C. (1981). Transient global amnesia and migraine. *Neurology* 31:1167–1170.

Caplan, L. B. (1985). Transient global amnesia. In *Handbook of Clinical Neurology*, Vol. 1(45), J.A.M. Frederiks (ed.). Amsterdam: Elsevier, pp. 205–218.

Carr, A. C. (1982). Memory deficit after fornix section. *Neuropsychologia* 20:95–98.

Carroll, M., Gates, R., and Roldan, F. (1984). Memory impairment in multiple sclerosis. *Neuropsychologia* 22:297–302.

Cermak, L. S. (1976). The encoding capacity of patients with amnesia due to encephalitis. *Neuropsychologia* 14:311–326.

Cermak, L. S. (1982). The long and short of it in amnesia. In *Human Memory and Amnesia*, L. S. Cermak (ed.). Hillsdale, N.J.: Lawrence Erlbaum.

Cermak, L. S. (1984). The episodic-semantic distinction in amnesia. In *Neuropsychology of Memory*, L. Squire and N. Butters (eds.). New York: Guilford Press, pp. 55–62.

Cermak, L. S., Blackford, S., O'Connor, M., and Bleich, R. (1988). The implicit memory ability of a patient with amnesia due to encephalitis. *Brain Cognition* 7:145–156.

Cermak, L. S., and Butters, N. (1972). The role of interference and encoding in the short-term memory deficits of Korsakoff patients. *Neuropsychologia* 10:89–96.

Cermak, L. S., Butters, N., and Gerrein, J. (1973a). The extent of the verbal encoding ability of Korsakoff patients. *Neuropsychologia* 11:85–94.

Cermak, L. S., Butters, N., and Moreines, J. (1974). Some analyses of the verbal encoding deficit of alcoholic Korsakoff patients. *Brain Lang.* 1:141–150.

Cermak, L. S., Lewis, R., Butters, N., and Goodglass, H. (1973b). Role of verbal mediation in performance of motor tasks by Korsakoff patients. *Percept. Mot. Skills* 37:259–262,

Cermak, L. S., Naus, M., and Reale, L. (1976). Rehearsal and organizational strategies of alcoholic Korsakoff patients. *Brain Lang.* 3:375–385.

Cermak, L. S., and O'Connor, M. (1983). The anterograde and retrograde retrieval ability of a patient with amnesia due to encephalitis. *Neuropsychologia* 21:213–234.

Cermak, L. S., Reale, L., and Baker, E. (1978). Alcoholic Korsakoff patients' retrieval from semantic memory. *Brain Lang.* 5:215–226.

Cermak, L. S., Talbot, N., Chandler, K., and Wolbarst, L. R. (1985). The perceptual priming phenomenon in amnesia. *Neuropsychologia* 23:615–622.

Cermak, L. S., Uhly, B., and Reale, L. (1980). Encoding specificity in the alcoholic Korsakoff patient. *Brain Lang.* 11:119–127.

Cermak, L. S., Verfaellie, M., Milberg, W., Letourneau, L., and Blackford, S. (1991). A further analysis of perceptual identification priming in alcoholic Korsakoff patients. *Neuropsychologia* 29:725–736.

Choi, D., Sudarsky, L., Schachter, S., Biber, M., and Burke, P. (1983). Medial thalamic hemorrhage with amnesia. *Arch. Neurol.* 40:611–613.

Cirillo, R. A., Horel, J. A., and George, P. J. (1989). Lesions of the anterior temporal stem and the performance of delayed match-to-sample and visual discriminations in monkeys. *Behav. Brain Res.* 34:55–69.

Claparede, E. (1911). Recognition and "me-ness." *Arch. Psychol.* 11:79–90. Reprinted in *Organization and Pathology of Thought*, D. Rapaport (ed.). New York: Columbia University Press, 1951, pp. 58–75.

Clark, C. R., and Geffen, G. M. (1989). Corpus callosum surgery and recent memory. A review, *Brain* 112:165–175.

Cohen, N. J. (1984). Preserved learning capacity in amnesia: evidence for multiple memory systems. In *Neuropsychology of Memory*, L. Squire and N Butters (eds.). New York: Guilford Press, pp. 83–103.

Cohen, N. J., and Squire, L. R. (1980). Preserved learning and retention of pattern analyzing skill in amnesia: dissociation of knowing how and knowing that. *Science* 210:207–209.

Cohen, N. J., and Squire, L. R. (1981). Retrograde amnesia and remote memory impairment. *Neuropsychologia* 19:337–356.

Collins, A. M., and Loftus, E. F. (1975). A spreading-activation theory of semantic processing. *Psychol. Rev.* 82:407–428.

Corkin, S. (1968). Acquisition of motor skill after bilateral medial temporal lobe excision. *Neuropsychologia* 6:225–265.

Corkin, S. (1984). Lasting consequences of bilateral medial temporal lobectomy: clinical course and experimental findings in H.M. *Semin. Neurol.* 4:249–259.

Correll, R. E., and Scoville, W. B. (1965). Effects of medial temporal lesions on visual discrimination performance. *J. Comp. Physiol. Psychol.* 60:360–367.

Corsellis, J.A.N., Goldberg, G. J., and Morton, A. R. (1968). Limbic encephalitis and its association with carcinoma. *Brain* 91:481–496.

Coslett, H. B., Bowers, D., Verfaellie, M., and Heilman, K. M. (1991). Frontal verbal amnesia: phonological amnesia. *Arch. Neurol.* 48:949–955.

Craik, F.I.M., and Lockhart. R. S. (1972). Levels of processing: a framework for memory research. *J. Verb. Learn. Verb. Behav.* 11:671–684.

Crook, T., Bartus, R. T., Ferris, S. H., Whitehouse, P., Cohen, G. D., and Gershon, S. (1986). Age-associated memory impairment: proposed diagnostic criteria and measures of clinical change. Report of a National Institute of Mental Health work group. *Dev. Neuropsychol.* 2:261–276.

Crook, T. H., Tinglenberg, J., Yesavage, J., Petrie, W., Nunzi, M. G., and Massari, D. C. (1991). Effects of phosphatidylserine in age-associated memory impairment. *Neurology 41*:644–649.

Crosson, B., (1992). *Subcortical Functions in Language and Memory.* New York: Guilford Press.

Crovitz, H. F., Harvey, M. T., and Horn, R. W (1979a). Problems in the acquisition of imagery mnemonics: three brain-damaged cases. *Cortex 15*:225–234.

Crovitz, H. F., Harvey, M. T., and McClanahan, S. (1979b). Hidden memory: a rapid method for the study of amnesia using perceptual learning. *Cortex 17*:273–278.

Cummings, J. L., Tomiyasu, U., Read, S., and Benson, D. F. (1984). Amnesia with hippocampal lesions after cardiopulmonary arrest. *Neurology 42*:263–271.

Damasio, A. R. (1989). Time-locked multiregional retroactivation: a systems-level proposal for the neural substrates of recall and recognition. *Cognition 33*:25–62.

Damasio, A. R., Damasio, H., Tranel, D., Welsh, K., and Brandt, J. (1987). Additional neural and cognitive evidence in patient DRB. *Soc. Neurosci. 13*:1452.

Damasio, A. R., Eslinger, P. J., Damasio, H., Van Hoesen, G. W., and Cornell, S. (1985a). Multimodal amnesic syndrome following bilateral temporal and basal forebrain damage. *Arch. Neurol. 42*:252–259.

Damasio, A. R., Graff-Radford, N. R., Eslinger, P. J., Damasio, H., and Kassell, N. (1985b). Amnesia following basal forebrain lesions. *Arch. Neurol. 42*:263–271.

Damasio, A. R., Tranel, D., and Damasio, H. (1989). Amnesia caused by herpes simplex encephalitis, infarctions in basal forebrain, Alzheimer's disease, and anoxia/ischemia. In *Handbook of Neuropsychology,* Vol. 3. F. Boller and J. Grafman (eds.). Amsterdam: Elsevier, pp. 149–166.

Damasio, A. R., Tranel, D., and Damasio, H. (1990). Face agnosia and the neural substrates of memory. *Annu. Rev. Neurosci. 13*:89–109.

Delis, D. C. (1989). Neuropsychological assessment of learning and memory. In *Handbook of Neuropsychology,* Vol. 3, F. Boller and J. Grafman (eds.). Amsterdam: Elsevier, pp. 3–33.

Delis, D. C., Kramer, J. H., Kaplan, E., and Ober, B. A. (1987). *California Verbal Learning Test,* Research Edition, Manual. San Antonio: The Psychological Corporation, Harcourt Brace Jovanovich.

DeLuca, J., and Cicerone, K. (1989). Cognitive impairments following anterior communicating artery aneurysm. *J. Clin. Exp. Neuropsychol. 11*:47.

DeOlmos, J. S. (1990). Amygdala. In *The Human Nervous System,* G. Paxinos (ed.). San Diego: Academic Press, pp. 583–710.

Diamond, R., and Rozin, P. (1984). Activation of existing memories in the amnesic syndrome. *J. Abnorm. Psychol. 93*:98–105.

Dott, N. M. (1938). Surgical aspects of the hypothalamus. In *The Hypothalamus: Morphological, Functional, Clinical and Surgical Aspects,* W. E. le G. Clark, J. Beattie, G. Riddoch, and N. M. Dott (eds.). Edinburgh: Oliver and Boyd, pp. 131–185.

Drachman, D. A., and Arbit, J. (1966). Memory and the hippocampal complex. *Arch. Neurol. 15*:52–61.

Drachman, D. A., and Leavitt, J. (1974). Human memory and the cholinergic system. A relationship to aging? *Arch. Neurol. 30*:113–121.

Dusoir, H., Kapur, N., Byrnes, D. P., McKinstry, S., and Hoare, R. D. (1990). The role of diencephalic pathology in human memory disorder. Evidence from a penetrating paranasal brain injury. *Brain 113*:1695–1706.

Duyckaerts, C., Derouesne C., Signoret, J. L., Gray, F., Escourolle, R., and Castaigne, P. (1985).

Bilateral and limited amygdalohippocampal lesions causing a pure amnesic syndrome. *Ann. Neurol. 18*:314–319.

Eich, E. (1989). Theoretical issues in state dependent memory. In *Varieties of Memory and Consciousness: Essays in Honour of Endel Tulving*, H. L. Roediger and F.I.M. Craik (eds.). Hillsdale, N.J.: Lawrence Erlbaum, pp. 331–354.

Erickson, R. C., and Scott, M. L. (1977). Clinical memory testing: a review. *Psychol. Bull. 84*:1130–1149.

Eslinger, P. J., and Damasio, A. R. (1985). Severe disturbance of higher cognition after bilateral frontal lobe ablation: patient EVR. *Neurology 35*:1731–1741.

Eslinger, P. J., and Damasio, A. R. (1986). Preserved motor learning in Alzheimer's disease: implications for anatomy and behavior. *J. Neurosci. 6*:3006–3009.

Evans, F. J., and Thorn, W.A.F. (1966). Two types of posthypnotic amnesia: recall amnesia and source amnesia. *Int. J. Clin. Exp. Hypn. 14*:162–179.

Feustel, T. C., Shiffrin, R. M., and Salasoo, A. (1983). Episodic and lexical contributions to the repetition effect in word identification. *J. Exp. Psychol. [Gen.] 112*:309–346.

Fibiger, H. C. (1991). Cholinergic mechanisms in learning, memory and dementia: a review of recent evidence. *Trends Neurosci. 14*:220–223.

Fisher, C. M. (1982). Transient global amnesia: precipitating activities and other observations. *Arch. Neurol. 39*:605–608.

Fisher, C. M., and Adams, R. D. (1958). Transient global amnesia. *Trans. Am. Neurol. Assoc. 83*:143–145.

Fisher, C. M., and Adams, R. D. (1964). Transient global amnesia. *Act. Neurol. Scand. 40* (Suppl. 9.):1–83.

Flavell, J. H., and Wellman, H. M. (1977). Metamemory. In *Perspectives on the Development of Memory and Cognition*, R. V. Kail and J. W. Hagen (eds.). Hillsdale, N.J.: Lawrence Erlbaum, pp. 3–33.

Foerster, O., and Gagel, O. (1983). Ein Fall von Ependymcyste des III Ventrikels. Ein Beitrag zur Frage der Beziehungen psychischer Störungen zum Hirnstamm. Z. *Gesamte Neurol. Psychiar. 149*:312–344.

Freed, D. M., Corkin, S., and Cohen, N. J. (1987). Forgetting in H.M.: a second look. *Neuropsychologia 25*:451–471.

Fuster, J. M. (1984). The cortical substrate of memory. In *Neuropsychology of Memory*, L. R. Squire and N. Butters (eds.). New York: Guilford Press, pp. 279–286.

Gabrieli, J.D.E., Milberg, W., Keane, M. M., and Corkin, S. (1990). Intact priming of patterns despite impaired memory. *Neuropsychologia 28*:417–427.

Gade, A. (1982). Amnesia after operations on aneurysms of the anterior communicating artery. *Surg. Neurol. 18*:46–49.

Gade, A., and Mortensen, E. L. (1990). Temporal gradient in the remote memory impairment of amnesic patients with lesion in the basal forebrain. *Neuropsychologia 28*:985–1001.

Gaffan, D. (1972). Loss of recognition memory in rats with lesions of the fornix. *Neuropsychologia 10*:327–341.

Gaffan, D. (1974). Recognition impaired and association intact in the memory of monkeys after transection of the fornix. *J. Comp. Physiol. Psychol. 86*:1100–1109.

Gaffan, D., and Harrison, S. (1987). Amygdalectomy and disconnection in visual learning for auditory secondary reinforcement by monkeys. *J. Neurosci. 7*:2285–2292.

Garcia Bencochea, F., De La Torre, O., Esquivel, O., Vieta, R., and Fernandec, C. (1954). The section of the fornix in the surgical treatment of certain epilepsies: a preliminary report. *Trans. Am. Neurol. Assoc. 79*:176–178.

Gardner, H. (1975). *The Shattered Mind*. New York: Knopf.

Gardner, H., Boller, F., Moreines, J., and Butters, N. (1973). Retrieving information from Korsakoff patients: effects of categorical cues and reference to the task. *Cortex* 9:165–175.

Gentilini, M., DeRenzi, E., and Crisi, G. (1987). Bilateral paramedian thalamic artery infarcts: report of eight cases. *J. Neurol. Neurosurg. Psychiatry* 50:900–909.

George, P. J., Horel, J. A., and Cirillo, R. A. (1989). Reversible cold lesions of the parahippocampal gyrus in monkeys result in deficits on the delayed match-to-sample and other visual tasks. *Behav. Brain Res.* 34:163–178.

Gianutsos, R., and Gianutsos, J. (1979). Rehabilitating the verbal recall of brain-damaged patients by mnemonic training: an experimental demonstration using single-case methodology. *J. Clin. Neuropsychol.* 1:117–135.

Glees, P., and Griffith, H. B. (1952). Bilateral destruction of the hippocampus (cornu ammonis) in a case of dementia. *Psychiatr. Neurol. Med. Psychol.* 123:193–204.

Glisky, E. L. and Schacter, D. L. (1986). Remediation of organic memory disorders: current status and future prospects. *J. Head Trauma Rehabil.* 1:54–63.

Glisky, E. L., and Schacter, D. L. (1987). Acquistion of domain specific knowledge in organic amnesia: training for computer-related work. *Neuropsychologia* 25:893–906.

Glisky, E. L., Schacter, D. L., and Tulving, E. (1986a). Learning and retention of computer-related vocabulary in memory-impaired patients: method of vanishing cues. *J. Clin. Exp. Neuropsychol.* 8:292–312.

Glisky, E. L., Schacter, D. L., and Tulving, E. (1986b). Computer learning by memory-impaired patients: acquisition and retention of complex knowledge. *Neuropsychologia* 24:313–328.

Gloor, P. (1986). Role of the human limbic system in perception, memory, and affect: lessons from temporal lobe epilepsy. In *The Limbic System: Functional Organization and Clinical Disorders*, B. K. Doane and K. E. Livingston (eds.). New York: Raven Press, pp. 159–169.

Goldenberg, G., Wimmer, A., and Maly, J. (1983). Amnesic syndrome with a unilateral thalamic lesion: a case report. *J. Neurol.* 229:79–86.

Goldman-Rakic, P. S. (1984). Modular organization of the prefrontal cortex. *Trends Neurosci.* 7:419–424.

Goldman-Rakic, P. S. (1992). Prefrontal cortical dysfunction in schizophrenia: the relevance of working memory. In *Psychopathology and the Brain*, B. Carroll (ed.). New York: Raven Press.

Goodwin, D. W., Powell, B., Bremer, D., Hoine, H., and Stern, J. (1969). Alcohol and recall: state dependent effects in man. *Science* 163:1358–1360.

Graf, P., and Mandler, G. (1984). Activation makes words more accessible, but not necessarily more retrievable. *J. Verb. Learn. Verb. Behav.* 23:553–568.

Graf, P., and Schacter, D. L. (1985). Implicit and explicit memory for new associations in normal and amnesic subjects. *J. Exp. Psychol. [Learn. Mem.]* 11:501–518.

Graf, P., and Schacter D. L. (1987). Selective effects of interference on implicit and explicit memory for new associations. *J. Exp. Psychol. [Learn. Mem.]*13:45–53.

Graf, P., Shimamura, A. P., and Squire, L. R. (1985). Priming across modalities and priming across category levels: extending the domain of preserved function in amnesia. *J. Psychol. Learn. Mem.* 11:385–395.

Graf, P., Squire, L. R., and Mandler, G. (1984). The information that amnesic patients do not forget. *J. Exp. Psychol. [Learn. Mem.]* 10:164–178.

Graff-Radford, N. R., Eslinger, P. J., Damasio, A. R., and Yamada, T. (1984). Nonhemorrhagic infarction of the thalamus: behavioral, anatomic, and physiologic correlates. *Neurology* 34:14–23.

Graff-Radford, N. R., Tranel, D., Van Hoesen, G. W., and Brandt, J. P. (1980). Diencephalic amnesia. *Brain* 113:1–25.

Grafman, J., Salazar, A. M., Weingartner, J., Vance, S. C., and Ludlow, C. (1985). Isolated impairment of memory following a penetrating lesion of the fornix cerebri. *Arch. Neurol.* 42:1162–1168.

Gruneberg, M. M. (1983). Memory processes unique to humans. In *Memory in Animals and Man*, A. Mayes (ed.). London: Van Nostrand, pp. 253–281.

Gruneberg, M. M., and Monks, J. (1974). Feeling of knowing and cued recall. *Acta Psychol.* 41:257–265.

Grünthal, E. (1939). Über das Corpus mamillare und den Korsakowshcen Symptomenkomplex. *Confin. Neurol.* 2:64–95.

Grünthal, E. (1947). Über das klinische Bild nach umschriebenem beiderseitigem Ausfall der Ammonshornrinde. *Monatsschr. Psychiatr. Neurol.* 113:1–6.

Gustafsson, B., and Wigstrom, H. (1988). Physiological mechanisms underlying long-term potentiation. *Trends Neurosci.* 11:156–162.

Haas, D. C., and Ross, G. S. (1986). Transient global amnesia triggered by mild head trauma. *Brain* 109:251–257.

Haist, F., Musen, G., and Squire, L. R. (1991). Intact priming of words and nonwords in amnesia. *Psychobiology* 19:275–285.

Harper, C., and Finlay-Jones, R. (1986). Clinical signs in the Wernicke-Korsakoff complex: a retrospective analysis of 131 cases diagnosed at necropsy. *J. Neurol. Neurosurg. Psychiatry* 49:341–345.

Hart, J. T. (1965). Memory and the feeling-of-knowing experience. *J. Educ. Psychol.* 56:208–216.

Hart, J. T. (1967). Memory and the memory-monitoring process. *J. Verb. Learn. Verb. Behav.* 6:685–691.

Hassler, R., and Riechert, T. (1957). Über einen Fall von doppelseitiger Fornicotomie bei sogenannter temporaler Epilepsie. *Acta Neurochir.* 5:330–340.

Heathfield, K.W.G., Croft, P. B., and Swash, M. (1973). The syndrome of transient global amnesia. *Brain* 96:729–736.

Heilman, K. M., and Sypert, G. W. (1977). Korsakoff's syndrome resulting from bilateral fornix lesions. *Neurology* 27:490–493.

Heimer, L., and Alheid, G. F. (1991). Piecing together the puzzle of basal forebrain anatomy. In *The Basal Forebrain*, T. C. Napier, P. W. Kalivas, and I. Hanin (eds.). New York: Plenum Press.

Heindel, W. C., Salmon, D. P., Shults, C. W., Walicke, P. A., and Butters, N. (1989). Neuropsychological evidence for multiple memory systems: a comparison of Alzheimer's, Huntington's, and Parkinson's disease patients. *J. Neurosci.* 9:582–587.

Herkenham, M. (1978). The connections of the nucleus reuniens thalami: evidence for a direct thalmo-hippocampal pathway in the rat. *J. Comp. Neurol.* 177:589–610.

Herzog, A. G., and Van Hoesen, G. W. (1976). Temporal neocortical afferent connections to the amygdala in the rhesus monkey. *Brain Res.* 115:57–69.

Hirst, W. (1982). The amnesic syndrome: descriptions of explanations. *Psychol. Bull.* 91:435–462.

Hirst, W., and Volpe, B. T. (1982). Temporal order judgements with amnesia. *Brain Cognition* 1:294–306.

Hodges, J. R., and Warlow, C. P. (1990). The aetiology of transient global amnesia. A case control study of 114 cases with prospective follow-up. *Brain* 113:639–657.

Hodgson, R., and Rachman, S. (1974). II. Desynchrony in measures of fear. *Behav. Res. Ther.* 12:319–326.

Holtz, K. H. (1962). Über Gehirn- und Augenveränderunge bei Hyalinosis cutis et mucosae (lipoid Proteinose) mit Autopsiebefund. *Arch. Klin. Exp. Dermatol. 214*:289–306.

Horel, J. A. (1978). The neuroanatomy of amnesia. A critique of the hippocampal memory hypothesis. *Brain 101*:403–445.

Horel, J. A., Voytko, M. L., and Salsbury, K. (1984). Visual learning suppressed by cooling of the temporal lobe. *Behav. Neurosci. 98*:310–324.

Huppert, F. A., and Piercy, M. (1976). Recognition memory in amnesic patients: effect of temporal context and familiarity of material. *Cortex 12*:3–20.

Huppert, F. A., and Piercy, M. (1979). Normal and abnormal forgetting in organic amnesia: effect of locus of lesion. *Cortex 15*:385–390.

Hyman, B. T., Van Hoesen, G. W., Damasio, A. R, and Barnes, C. L. (1984). Alzheimer's disease: cell-specific pathology isolates the hippocampal formation. *Science 225*:1168–1170.

Hyman, B. T., Van Hoesen, G. W., Kromer, J. J., and Damasio, A. R. (1986). Perforant pathway changes and the memory impairment of Alzheimer's disease. *Ann. Neurol. 20*:472–481.

Inglis, J. (1970). Shock, surgery, and cerebral asymmetry. *Br. J. Psychiatry 117*:143–148.

Insausti, R., Amaral, D. G., and Cowan, W. M. (1987a). The entorhinal cortex of the monkey: II. Cortical afferents. *J. Comp. Neurol. 264*:356–395.

Insausti, R., Amaral, D. G., and Cowan, W. M. (1987b). The entorhinal cortex of the monkey: III. Subcortical afferents. *J. Comp. Neurol. 264*:396–408.

Irie, E., and Markowitsch, H. J. (1982). Widespread cortical projections of the hippocampal formation in the cat. *Neuroscience 7*:2637–2647.

Iwata, J., LeDoux, J. E., Meeley, M. P., Arneric, S., and Reis, D. J (1986). Intrinsic neurons in amygdaloid field projected to by the medial geniculate body mediate emotional responses conditioned to acoustic stimuli. *Brain Res. 383*:195–214.

Izquierdo, I. (1991). Role of NMDA receptors in memory. *Trends Pharmacol. Sci. 12*:128–129.

Jacoby, L. L. (1983a). Perceptual enhancement: persistent effects of an experience. *J. Exp. Psychol. [Learn. Mem.] 9*:21–38.

Jacoby, L. L. (1983b). Analysing interactive processes in reading. *J. Verb. Learn. Verb. Behav. 22*:485–508.

Jacoby, L. L. (1984). Incidental versus intentional retrieval: remembering and awareness as separate issues. In *Neuropsychology of Memory*, L. R. Squire and N. Butters (eds.). New York: Guilford Press. pp. 145–156.

Jacoby, L. L., and Dallas, M. (1981). On the relationship between autobiographical memory and perceptual learning. *J. Exp. Psychol. [Gen.] 3*:306–340.

Jacoby, L. L., and Kelly, C. (1992). Unconscious influences of memory: dissociations and automaticity. In *Consciousness and Cognition: Neuropsychological Perspectives*, D. Milner and M. Rugg (eds.). San Diego: Academic Press.

Jacoby, L. L., Kelly, C. M., and Dywan, J. (1989). Memory attributions. In *Varieties of Memory and Consciousness: Essays in Honour of Endel Tulving*, H. L. Roediger and F. I. M. Craik (eds.). Hillsdale N.J.: Lawrence Erlbaum. pp. 391–422.

Jacoby, L. L., and Witherspoon, D. (1982). Remembering without awareness. *Can. J. Psychol. 36*:300–324.

Janowsky, J. S., Shimamura, A. P., and Squire, L. R. (1989). Memory and metamemory: comparisons between patients with frontal lobe lesions and amnesic patients. *Psychobiology 17*:3–11.

Jernigan, T. L., Schafer, K., Butters, N., and Cermak, L. S. (1991). Magnetic resonance imaging of alcoholic Korsakoff patients. *Neuropsychopharmacology. 4*:175–186.

Johns, C. A., Greenwald, B. S., Mohs, R. C., and Davis, K. L. (1983). The cholinergic treatment strategy in ageing and senile dementia. *Psychopharmacol. Bull. 19*:185–197.

Johnson, M. K. (1991). Reality monitoring: evidence from confabulation in organic brain disease patients. In *Awareness of Deficit After Brain Injury*, G. Prigatano and D. L. Schacter (eds.). New York: Oxford University Press, pp. 176–197.

Johnson, M. K., and Hasher, L. (1987). Human learning and memory. *Annot. Rev. Psychology* 38:631–668.

Johnson, M. K., Hashtroudi, S., and Lindsay, D. S. (1992). Source monitoring. Manuscript submitted for publication.

Johnson, M. K., Kim, J. K., and Risse, G. (1985). Do alcoholic Korsakoff's syndrome patients acquire affective reactions? *J. Exp. Psychol. [Learn. Mem.]* 11:27–36.

Jones, B., and Mishkin, M. (1972). Limbic lesions and the problem of stimulus-reinforcement associations. *Exp. Neurol.* 36:362–377.

Kaplan, E. (1983). Process and achievement revisited. In *Toward a Holistic Developmental Psychology*, S. Wapner and B. Kaplan (eds.). Hillsdale, N.J.: Lawrence Erlbaum, pp. 143–156.

Kaplan, E. F., Fein, D., Morris, R., and Delis, D. C. (1991). *Manual for the WAIS-R as a Neuropsychological Instrument (WAIS-R-NI)*. New York: The Psychological Corporation.

Kapur, N., and Butters, N. (1977). Visuoperceptive deficits in long-term alcoholics with Korsakoff's psychosis. *J. Stud. Alcohol* 38:2025–2035.

Kennedy, M. B. (1989). Regulation of synaptic transmission in the central nervous sytem: long-term potentiation. *Cell* 59:777–787.

Kersteen-Tucker, Z. (1991). Long-term repetition priming with symmetrical polygons and words. *Memory Cognition* 19:37–43.

Kihlstrom, J. F. (1980). Posthypnotic amnesia for recently learned materials: Interactions with "episodic" and "semantic" memory. *Cognitive Psychology* 12:227–251.

Kihlstrom, J. F. (1984). Conscious, subconscious, unconscious: a cognitive view. In *The Unconscious Reconsidered*, K. S. Biowers and D. Meichenbaum (eds.). New York: Wiley-Interscience, pp. 149–211.

Kinsbourne, M., and Wood, F. (1975). Short-term memory processes and the amnesic syndrome. In *Short-Term memory*, D. Deutsch and J. A. Deutsch (eds.). New York: Academic Press, pp. 258–291.

Kinsbourne, M., and Wood, F. (1982). Theoretical considerations regarding the episodic-semantic memory distinction. In *Human Memory and Amnesia*, L. S. Cermak (ed.). Hillsdale, N.J. Lawrence Erlbaum, pp. 195–217.

Klatzky, R. L. (1982). *Human Memory*, 2nd. ed. San Francisco: W. H. Freeman.

Kling, A., and Steklis, H. D. (1976). A neural substrate for affiliative behavior in non-human primates. *Brain Behav. Evol.* 13:216–238.

Kooistra, D. A., and Heilman, K. M. (1988). Memory loss from a subcortical white matter infarct. *J. Neurol. Neurosurg. Psychiatry* 51:866–869.

Kopelman, M. D. (1985). Rates of forgetting in Alzheimer-type dementia and Korsakoff's syndrome. *Neuropsychologia* 23:623–638.

Kopelman, M. D. (1986). The cholinergic neurotransmitter system in human memory and dementia: a review. *Q. J. Exp. Psychol.* 38A:535–573.

Korsakoff, S. S. (1889). Etude medico-psychologique sur une forme des maladies de la memoire. *Rev. Philos.* 28:501–530.

Kral, V. A. (1962). Senescent forgetfulness: benign and malignant. *J. Can. Med. Assoc.* 86:257–260.

Kreutzer, J. S., and Wehman, P. H. (eds.) (1991). *Cognitive Rehabilitation for Persons with Traumatic Brain Injury*. Baltimore: Paul H. Brooks Publishing Company.

Kritchevsky, M. (1987). Transient global amnesia: when memory temporarily disappears. *Postgrad. Med.* 82:95–100.

Kritchevsky, M. (1989). Transient global amnesia. In *Handbook of Neuropsychology*, Vol. 3, F. Boller and J. Grafman (eds.). Amsterdam: Elsevier, pp. 167–182.

Kritchevsky, M., Graff-Radford, N. R., and Damasio, A. R. (1987). Normal memory after damage to medial thalamus. *Arch. Neurol. 44*:959–962.

Kritchevsky, M., Squire, L. R., and Zouzounis, J. A. (1988). Transient global amnesia: characterization of anterograde and retrograde amnesia. *Neurology 38*:213–219.

Lang, P. J. (1968). Fear reduction and fear behavior: problems in treating a construct. In *Research in Psychotherapy*, J. M. Schein (ed.). Washington, D.C.: American Psychological Association, pp. 90–103.

Lang, P. J. (1971). The application of psychophysiological methods to the study of psychotherapy and behavior modification. In *Handbook of Psychotherapy and Behavior Change: An Empirical Analysis*, A. E. Bergin and S. L. Garfield (eds.). New York: Wiley, pp. 75–125.

Larrabee, G. J., Trahan, D. E., Curtiss, G., and Levin, H. S. (1988). Normative data for the Verbal Selective Reminding Test. *Neuropsychology 2*:173–182.

LeDoux, J. E. (1987). Emotion. In *Handbook of Physiology*, Vol. 5, V. B. Mountcastle, F. Plum, and S. R. Geiger (eds.). Bethesda, Md.: American Physiological Society, pp. 419–460.

Lee, G. P., Meador, K. J., Smith, J. R., Loring, D. W., and Flanigin, H. F. (1988). Preserved crossmodal association following bilateral amygdalotomy in man. *Int. J. Neurosci. 50*:47–55.

Leibniz, G. W. (1916). *New Essays Concerning Human Understanding*. Chicago: Open Court.

Levin, H. S. (1989). Memory deficit after closed head injury. In *Handbook of Neuropsychology*, Vol. 3, F. Boller and J. Grafman (eds.). Amsterdam: Elsevier, pp. 183–207.

Lewandowsky, S., Dunn, J. C., and Kirsner, K. (1989). *Implicit Memory: Theoretical Issues*. Hillsdale, N.J.: Lawrence Erlbaum.

Lewis, P. R., and Shute, C.C.D. (1967). The cholinergic limbic system: projections of the hippocampal formation, medial cortex, nuclei of the ascending cholinergic reticular system, and the subfornical organ and supra-optic crest. *Brain 90*:521–540.

Lezak, M. D. (1987). *Neuropsychological Assessment*, 2nd. ed. New York: Oxford University Press.

Lhermitte, J., Doussinet, and de Ajuriaguerra, J. (1937). Une observation de la forme Korsakowienne des tumeurs du 3ᵉ ventricule. *Rev. Neurol. (Paris) 68*:709–711.

Lhermitte, F., and Signoret, J. L. (1972). Analyse neuropsychologique et differenciation des syndromes amnesiques. *Rev. Neurol. (Paris) 126*:161–178.

Lindqvist, G., and Norlen, G. (1966). Korsakoff's syndrome after operation on ruptured aneurysm of the anterior communicating artery. *Acta Psychiatr. Scand. 42*:24–34.

Lishman, W. A. (1986). Alcoholic dementia: a hypothesis. *Lancet I*:1184–1186.

Loftus, E. F., and Cole, W. (1974). Retrieving attribute and name information from semantic memory. *J. Exp. Psychol. 102*:1116–1122.

Logue, V., Durward, M., Pratt, R.T.C., Piercy, M., and Nixon, W.L.B. (1968). The quality of survival after rupture of an anterior cerebral aneurysm. *Br. J. Psychiatry 114*:137–160.

Lomo, T. (1971). Patterns of activation in a monsynaptic cortical pathway: the perforant path input to the dentate areas of the hippocampal formation. *Exp. Brain Res. 12*:18–45.

Loring, D. W., and Papanicolaou, A. C. (1987). Memory assessment in neuropsychology: theoretical considerations and practical utility. *J. Clin. Exp. Neuropsychol. 9*:340–358.

Lugaresi, E., Medori, R., Montagna, P., Baruzzi, A., Cortelli, P., Lugaresi, A., Tinuper, P., Zucconi, M., and Gambetti, P. (1986). Fatal familial insomnia and dysautonomia with selective degeneration of thalamic nuclei. *New Engl. J. Med. 315*:997–1003.

Mahut, H. (1971). Spatial and object reversal learning in monkeys with partial temporal lobe ablations. *Neuropsychologia 9:*409–424.

Mair, W.G.P., Warrington, E. K., and Weiskrantz, L. (1979). Memory disorder in Korsakoff's psychosis: a neuropathological and neuropsychological investigation of two cases. *Brain 102:*749–783.

Malamut, B. L., Graff-Radford, N., Chawluk, J., Grossman, R. I., and Gur, R. C. (1992). Memory in a case of bilateral thalamic infarction. *Neurology 42:*163–169.

Manetto, V., Medori, R., Cortelli, P., Montagna, P., Tinuper, P., Baruzzi, A., Rancurel, G., Hauw, J.-J., Vanderhaeghen, J.-J., Mailleux, P., Bugiani, O., Tagliavini, F., Bouras, C., Rizzuto, N., Lugaresi, E., and Gambetti, P. (1992). Fatal familial insomnia: Clinical and pathologic study of five new cases. *Neurology 42:*312–319.

Marslen-Wilson, W. D., and Teuber, H.-L. (1974). Memory for remote events in anterograde amnesia: recognition of public figures from news photographs. *Neuropsychologia 13:*353–364.

Martin, A., and Fedio, P. (1983). Word production and comprehension in Alzheimer's disease: the breakdown of semantic knowledge. *Brain Lang. 19:*124–141.

Martone, M., Butters, N., and Trauner, D. (1986). Some analyses of forgetting pictorial material in amnesic and demented patients. *J. Clin. Exp. Neuropsychol. 8:*161–178.

Matthies, H., Frey, U., Reymann, K., Krug, M., Jork, R., and Schroeder, H. (1990). Different mechanisms and multiple stages of LTP. In *Excitatory Amino Acids and Neuronal Plasticity*, Ben-Ari, Y (ed.). New York: Plenum Press, pp. 359–368.

Mayes, A., Meudell, P., amd Som, S. (1981). Further similarities between amnesia and normal attenuated memory: effects of paired-associate learning and contextual shifts. *Neuropsychologia 18:*655–664.

Mayes, A. R., and Meudell, P. (1981). How similar is immediate memory in amnesic patients to delayed memory in normal subjects? A replication, extension and reassessment of the amnesic cueing effect. *Neuropsychologia 19:*647–654.

Mayes, A. R., Meudell, P. R., and Neary, D. (1980) Do amnesics adopt inefficient encoding strategies with faces and random shapes? *Neuropsychologia 18:*527–540.

Mayes, A. R., Meudell, P. R., Mann, D., and Pickering, A. (1988). Location of lesions in Korsakoff's syndrome: neuropsychological and neuropathological data on two patients. *Cortex 24:*367–388.

McAndrews, M. P., and Milner, B. (1991). The frontal cortex and memory for temporal order. *Neuropsychologia 29:*849–859.

McAndrews, M. P., Glisky, E. L., and Schacter, D. L. (1987). When priming persists: longlasting implicit memory for a single episode in amnesic patients. *Neuropsychologia 25:*497–506.

McEntee, W. J., and Mair, R. G. (1978). Memory impairments in Korsakoff's psychosis: a correlation with brain noradrenergic activity. *Science 202:*905–907.

McEntee, W. J., and Mair, R. G. (1980). Memory enhancement in Korsakoff's psychosis by clonidine: further evidence for a noradrenergic defect. *Ann. Neurol. 7:*466–470.

McGaugh, J. L., Introini-Collison. I. B., Nagahara, A. H., Cahill, L., Brioni, J. D., and Castellano, C. (1990). Involvement of the amygdaloid complex in neuromodulatory influences on memory storage. *Neurosci. Biobehav. Rev. 14:*425–431.

McKee, R. D., and Squire, L. R. (1992). Both hippocampal and diencephalic amnesia result in normal forgetting for complex visual material. *J. Clin. Exp. Neuropsychol. 14:*103.

McKoon, G., Ratcliff, R., and Dell, G. S. (1986). A critical evaluation of the semantic-episode distinction. *J. Exp. Psychol. [Learn. Mem.] 12:*295–306.

Medori, R., Tritschler, H.-J., LeBlanc, A., Villare, F., Manetto, V., Chen, H. Y., Xue, R., Leal, S., Montagna, P., Cortelli, P., Tinuper, P., Avioni, P., Mochi, M., Baruzzi, A., Hauw, J. J.,

Ott, J., Lugaresi, E., Autilio-Gambetti, L., and Gambetti, P. (1992). Fatal familial insomnia, a prion disease with a mutation at codon 178 of the prion protein gene. *New Engl. J. Med.* 326:444–449.

Meier, M. J., Benton, A. L., and Diller, L. (eds.). (1987). *Neuropsychological Rehabilitation.* New York: Guilford Press.

Mesulam, M.-M., Mufson, E. J., Levey, E. J., and Wainer, B. H. (1983). Cholinergic innervation of cortex by the basal forebrain: cytochemistry and cortical connections of the septal area, diagonal band nuclei, nucleus basalis (substantia innominata) and hypothalmus in the rhesus monkey. *J. Comp. Neurol.* 214:170–197.

Mesulam, M.-M., and Mufson, E. J. (1984). Neural inputs into the nucleus basalis of the substantia innominata (Ch4) in the rhesus monkey. *Brain* 107:253–274.

Mesulam, M.-M., and Van Hoesen, G. W. (1976). Acetylcholinesterase containing basal forebrain neurons in the rhesus monkey project to neocortex. *Brain Res.* 109:152–157.

Meudell, P. R., Mayew, A. R., Ostergaard, A., and Pickering, A. (1985). Recency and frequency judgements in alcoholic amnesics and normal people with poor memory. *Cortex* 21:487–511.

Meudell, P. R., Northern, B., Snowden, J. S., and Neary, D. (1980). Long-term memory for famous voices in amnesic and normal subjects. *Neuropsychologia* 18:133–139.

Milberg, W. P., Hebben, N., and Kaplan, E. (1986). The Boston process approach to neuropsychological assessment. In *Neuropsychological Assessment of Neuropsychiatric Disorders*, I. Grant and K. Adams (eds.). New York: Oxford University Press. pp. 65–86.

Miller, E. (1973). Short- and long-term memory in patients with presenile dementia. *Psychol. Med.* 3:221–224.

Miller, J. W., Petersen, R. C., Metter, E. J., Millikan, C. H., and Yanagihara, T. (1987). Transient global amnesia: clinical characteristics and prognosis. *Neurology* 37:733–737.

Miller, R. R., and Marlin, N. A. (1979). Amnesia following electroconvulsive shock. In *Functional Disorders of Memory*, J. F. Kihlstrom and F. J. Evans (eds.). Hillsdale, N.J.: Lawrence Erlbaum, pp. 143–178.

Milner, B. (1962). Les troubles de la memoire accompagnant des lesions hippocampiques bilaterales. In *Physiologie de l'Hippocampe*, P. Passouant (ed.). Paris: Centre National de la Recherche Scientifique.

Milner, B. (1966). Amnesia following operation on the temporal lobes. In *Amnesia*, C.W.M. Whitty and O. L. Zangwill (eds.). London: Butterworths.

Milner, B. (1972). Disorders of learning and memory after temporal lobe lesions in man. *Clin. Neurosurg.* 19:421–446.

Milner, B. (1974). Hemispheric specialization: scope and limits. In *The Neurosciences: Third Study Program*, F. O. Schmitt and F. G. Worden (eds.). Boston: MIT Press, pp. 75–89.

Milner, B., Corkin, S., and Teuber, H.-L. (1968). Further analysis of the hippocampal amnesic syndrome: 14-year follow-up study of H.M. *Neuropsychologia* 6:215–234.

Milner, B., Corsi, P., and Leonard, G. (1991). Frontal-lobe contributions to recency judgements. *Neuropsychologia* 29:601–618.

Milner, B., Petrides, M., and Smith, M. L. (1984). Behavioural effects of frontal-lobe lesions in man. *Trends Neurosci.* 7:403–407.

Mishkin, M. (1978). Memory in monkeys severely impaired by combined but not separate removal of the amygdala and hippocampus. *Nature* 273:297–298.

Mishkin, M. (1982). A memory system in the monkey. *Phil. Trans. R. Soc. Lond.* 298:85–95.

Mishkin, M., and Petri H. L. (1984). Memories and habits: some implications for the analysis of learning and retention. In *Neuropsychology of Memory*, L. R. Squire and N. Butters (eds.). New York: Guilford Press, pp. 287–296.

Mishkin, M., and Saunders, R. C. (1979). Degree of memory impairment in monkeys related to amount of conjoint damage to amygdaloid and hippocampal systems. *Soc. Neurosci. Abstr.* 5:320.

Mishkin, M., Spiegler, B. J., Saunders, R. C., and Malamut, B. L. (1982). An animal model of global amnesia. In *Alzheimer's Disease: A Report of Progress*, S. Corkin, K. L. Davis, J. H. Growdon, E. Usdin, and R. J. Wurtman (eds.). New York: Raven Press, pp. 235–247.

Mori, E., Yamadori, A., and Mitani, Y. (1986). Left thalamic infarction and disturbance of verbal memory: a clinicoanatomical study with a new method of computed tomographic stereotaxis lesion localization. *Ann. Neurol.* 20:671–676.

Morris, M. K., Bowers, D., Chatterjee, A., and Heilman, K. M. (in press). Amnesia following a discrete basal forebrain lesion. *Brain.*

Moscovitch, M. (1982). Multiple dissociations of function in amnesia. In *Human Memory and Amnesia*, L. S. Cermak (ed.). Hillsdale, N.J.: Lawrence Erlbaum, pp. 337–370.

Moscovitch, M., Winocur, G., and McLachlan, D. (1986). Memory as assessed by recognition and reading time in normal and memory-impaired people with Alzheimer's disease and other neurological disorders. *J. Exp. Psychol [Gen.]* 115:331–347.

Moss, M., Mahut, H., and Zola-Morgan, S. (1981). Concurrent discrimination learning of monkeys after hippocampal, entorhinal, or fornix lesions. *J. Neurosci.* 1:227–240.

Mufson, E. J., and Pandya, D. N. (1984). Some observations on the course and composition of the cingulum bundle in the rhesus monkey. *J. Comp. Neurol.* 225:31–43.

Murray, E. A., and Mishkin, M. (1985). Amygdalectomy impairs crossmodal association in monkeys. *Science* 228:604–606.

Musen, G., Shimamura, A. P., and Squire, L. R. (1990). Intact text-specific reading in amnesia. *J. Exp. Psychol. [Learn. Mem.]* 16:1068–1076.

Musen, G., and Squire, L. R. (1991). Nonverbal priming in amnesia. Manuscript submitted for publication.

Musen, G., and Triesman, A. (1990). Implicit and explicit memory for visual patterns. *J. Exp. Psychol. [Learn. Mem.]* 16:127–137.

Narabayashi, H., Nagao, T., Saito, Y., Yoshida, M., and Nagahata, M. (1963). Stereotaxic amygdalotomy for behavior disorders. *Arch. Neurol.* 9:1–16.

Nauta, W.J.H. (1961). Fibre degeneration following lesions of the amygdaloid complex in the monkey. *J. Anat.* 95:515–531.

Nelson, T. O., Gerler, D., and Narens, L. (1984). Accuracy of feeling-of-knowing judgements for predicting perceptual identification and relearning. *J. Exp. Psychol. [Gen.]* 113:282–300.

Nelson, T. O., Leonesio, R. J., Shimamura, A. P., Landwehr, R. F., and Narens, L. (1982). Overlearning and the feeling of knowing. *J. Exp. Psychol. [Learn. Mem.]* 8:279–288.

Nisbett, R. E., and Wilson, T. D. (1977). Telling more than we can know: verbal reports on mental processes. *Psychol. Rev.* 84:231–259.

Nissen, M. J., and Bullemer, P. (1987). Attentional requirements of learning: evidence from performance measures. *Cognitive Psychol.* 19:1–32.

Ojemann, G. A., and Dodrill, C. B. (1985). Verbal memory deficits after left temporal lobectomy for epilepsy. *J. Neurosurg.* 62:101–107.

Okawa, M., Maeda, S., Nukui, H., and Kawafuchi, J. (1980). Psychiatric symptoms in ruptured anterior communicating aneurysms: social prognosis. *Acta Psychiatr. Scand.* 61:306–312.

Olesen, J., and Jorgensen, M. B. (1986). Leao's spreading depression in the hippocampus explains transient global amnesia: a hypothesis. *Acta Neurol. Scand.* 73:219–220.

Olton, D. S. (1989). Inferring psychological dissociations from experimental dissociations: the temporal context of episodic memory. In *Varieties of Memory and Consciousness: Essays in Honour of Endel Tulving*, H. L. Roediger and F.I.M. Craik (eds.). Hillsdale, N.J.: Lawrence Erlbaum, pp. 161–177.

Oscar-Berman, M., and Bonner, R. T. (1985). Matching- and delayed matching-to-sample performance as measures of visual processing, selective attention, and memory in aging and alcoholic individuals. *Neuropsychologia* 23:639-651.

Owen, M. J., and Butler, S. R. (1981). Amnesia after transection of the fornix in monkeys: long-term memory impaired, short-term memory intact. *Behav. Brain Res.* 3:115-123.

Pandya, D. N., Van Hoesen, G. W., and Mesulam, M.-M. (1981). Efferent connections of the cingulate gyrus in the rhesus monkey. *Exp. Brain Res.* 42:319-330.

Pandya, D. N., and Yeterian, E. H. (1990). Architecture and connections of cerebral cortex: implications for brain evolution and function. In *Neurobiology of Higher Cognitive Function*, A. B. Scheibel and A. F. Wechsler (eds.). New York: Guilford Press.

Papez, J. W. (1937). A proposed mechanism of emotion. *Arch. Neurol. Psychiatry* 38:725-743.

Parente, R., and DiCesare, A. (1991). Retraining memory: theory, evaluation, and applications. In *Cognitive Rehabilitation for Persons with Traumatic Brain Injury*, J. S. Kreutzer and P. H. Wehman (eds.). Baltimore: Paul H. Brooks Publishing Company, pp. 147-162.

Patten, B. M. (1972). The ancient art of memory. *Arch. Neurol.* 26:25-31.

Penfield, W., and Mathieson, G. (1974). Memory. Autopsy findings and comments on the role of hippocampus in experiential recall. *Arch. Neurol.* 31:145-154.

Penfield, W., and Milner, B. (1958). Memory deficit produced by bilateral lesions in the hippocampal zone. *Arch. Neurol. Psychiatry* 79:475-497.

Peters, B. H., and Levin, H. S. (1982). Chronic oral physostigmine and lecithin administration in memory disorders of aging. In *Alzheimer's Disease: A Report of Progress in Research* S. Corkin, J. H. Davis, E. Growdon, and R. J. Writman (eds.). New York: Raven Press, pp. 421-426.

Petrides, M. (1989). Frontal lobes and memory. In *Handbook of Neuropsychology*, Vol. 3, F. Boller, and J. Grafman (eds.). Amsterdam: Elsevier, pp. 75-90.

Petrides, M., and Milner, B. (1982). Deficits on subject-ordered tasks after frontal- and temporal-lobe lesions in man. *Neuropsychologia* 20:249-262.

Phillips, S., Sangalang, V., and Sterns, G. (1987). Basal forebrain infarction: a clinicopathologic correlation. *Arch. Neurol.* 44:1134-1138.

Poletti, C. E. (1986). Is the limbic system a limbic system? Studies of hippocampal efferents: their functional and clinical implications. In *The Limbic System: Functional Organization and Clinical Disorders*, B. K. Doane and K. E. Livingston (eds.). New York: Raven Press, pp. 79-94.

Porrino, L. J., Crane, A. M., and Goldman-Rakic, P. S. (1981). Direct and indirect pathways from the amygdala to the frontal lobe in rhesus monkeys. *J. Comp. Neurol.* 198:121-136.

Prigatano, G. P., Fordyce, D. J., Zeiner, H. K., Roueche, J. R., Pepping, M., and Wood, B. C. (1984). Neuropsychological rehabilitation after closed head injury in young adults. *J. Neurol. Neurosurg. Psychiatry* 47:505-513.

Prince, M. (1914). *The Unconscious*. New York: Macmillan.

Rachman, S. (1978). Human fears: a three systems analysis. *Scand. J. Behav. Ther.* 7:237-245.

Rachman, S., and Hodgson, R. (1974). I. Synchrony and desynchrony in fear and avoidance. *Behav. Res. Ther.* 12:311-318.

Randt, C. T., and Brown, E. R. (1983). *Randt Memory Test*. Bayport, Life Science Associates.

Rao S. M., Hammeke, T. A., McQuillen, M. P., Khatri, B. O., and Lloyd, D. (1984). Memory disturbance in chronic progressive multiple sclerosis. *Arch. Neurol.* 41:625-631.

Rao, S. M., Leo, G. J., Bernardin, L., and Unverzagt, M. S. (1991). Cognitive dysfunction in multiple sclerosis. I. Frequency, patterns, and prediction. *Neurology* 41:685-691.

Richardson-Klavehn, A., and Bjork, R. A. (1988). Measures of memory. *Ann. Rev. Psychol.* 39:475-543.

Roediger, H. L. (1990). Implicit memory: retention without remembering. *Am. Psychol.* 45:1043–1056.

Roediger, H. L., and Blaxton, T. A. (1987). Effects of varying modality, surface features, and retention interval on priming in word fragment completion. *Memory Cognition* 15:379–388.

Roediger, H. L., and Weldon, M. S. (1987). Reversing the picture superiority effect. In *Imagery and Related Mnemonic Processes: Theory, Individual Differences, and Applications*, M. A. McDaniel and M. Pressley (eds.). New York: Springer, pp. 151–174.

Roediger, H. L., Weldon, M. S., and Challis, B. H. (1989). Explaining dissociations between implicit and explicit measures of retention: a processing account. In *Varieties of Memory and Consciousness: Essays in Honour of Endel Tulving*, H. L. Roediger and F.I.M. Craik (eds.). Hillsdale, N.J.: Lawrence Erlbaum, pp. 3–41.

Rosene, D. L., and Van Hoesen, G. W. (1977). Hippocampal efferents reach widespread areas of cerebral cortex and amygdala in the rhesus monkey. *Science* 198:315–317.

Ross, E. D. (1980a). Sensory-specific and fractional disorders of recent memory in man. I: Isolated loss of visual recent memory. *Arch. Neurol.* 37:193–200.

Ross, E. D. (1980b). Sensory-specific and fractional disorders of recent memory in man. II. Unilateral loss of tactile recent memory. *Arch. Neurol.* 37:267–272.

Rudge, P., and Warrington, E. K. (1991). Selective impairment of memory and visual perception in splenial tumours. *Brain* 114:349–360.

Rueckl, J. G. (1991). Similarity effects in word and pseudoword repetition priming. *J. Exp. Psychol.* [*Learn. Mem.*] 16:374–391.

Russell, E. W. (1981). The pathology and clinical examination of memory. In *Handbook of Clinical Neuropsychology*, S. B. Filskov and T. J. Boll (eds.). New York: John Wiley and Sons, pp. 287–319.

Russell, W. R., and Nathan, P. W. (1946). Traumatic amnesia. *Brain* 69:290–300.

Ryan, C., and Butters, N. (1980a). Further evidence for a continuum of impairment encompassing male alcoholic Korsakoff patients and chronic alcoholic men. *Alcoholism Clin. Exp. Res.* 4:190–197.

Ryan, C., and Butters, N. (1980b). Learning and memory impairments in young and old alcoholics: evidence for the premature-aging hypothesis. *Alcoholism Clin. Exp. Res.* 4:288–293.

Sagar, H. J., Gabrieli, J.D.E., Sullivan, E. V., and Corkin, S. (1990). Recency and frequency discrimination in the amnesic patient H.M. *Brain* 113:581–602.

Sagar, H. J., Sullivan, E. V., Gabrieli, J.D.E., Corkin, S., and Growdon, J. H. (1988). Temporal ordering and short-term memory deficits in Parkinson's disease. *Brain* 111:525–539.

Sanders, H. I., and Warrington, E. K. (1971). Memory for remote events in amnesic patients. *Brain* 94:661–668.

Saunders, R. C., Rosene, D. L., and Van Hoesen, G. W. (1988). Comparison of the efferents of the amygdala and the hippocampal formation in the rhesus monkey: II. Reciprocal and nonreciprocal connections. *J. Comp. Neurol.* 271:185–207.

Scarborough, D. L., Cortese, C., and Scarborough, H. S. (1977). Frequency and repitition effects in lexical memory. *J. Exp. Psychol.* [*Hum. Percept.*] 3:1–17.

Schacter, D. L. (1983). Amnesia observed: remembering and forgetting in a natural environment. *J. Abnorm. Psychol.* 92:236–242.

Schacter, D. L. (1985). Priming of old and new knowledge in amnesic patients and normal subjects. *Ann. N.Y. Acad. Sci.* 444:41–53.

Schacter, D. L. (1987a). Implicit memory: history and current status. *J. Exp. Psychol.* [*Learn. Mem.*] 13:501–518.

Schacter, D. L. (1987b). Memory, amnesia, and frontal lobe dysfunction: a critique and interpretation. *Psychobiology* 15:21–36.

Schacter, D. L. (1989). On the relation between memory and consciousness: Dissociable interactions and conscious experience. In *Varieties of Memory and Consciousness: Essays in Honour of Endel Tulving*, H. L. Roediger and F.I.M. Craik (eds.). Hillsdale, N.J.: Lawrence Erlbaum, pp. 355–389.

Schacter, D. L. (1990). Perceptual representation systems and implicit memory: toward a resolution of the multiple memory systems debate. *Ann. N.Y. Acad. Sci.* 608:543–571.

Schacter, D. L., Cooper, L. A., and Delaney, S. M. (1990). Implicit memory for unfamiliar objects depends on access to structural descriptions. *J. Exp. Psychol. [Gen.]* 11:5–24.

Schacter, D. L., Cooper, L. A., Tharan, M., and Rubens, A. B. (1991). Preserved priming of novel objects in patients with memory disorders. *J. Cognitive Neurosci.* 3:118–131.

Schacter, D. L., and Glisky, E. L. (1986). Memory remediation: restoration, alleviation, and the acquisition of domain-specific knowledge. In *Clinical Neuropsychology of Intervention*, B. Uzzell and Y. Gross (eds.). Boston: Martinus Nijhoff.

Schacter, D. L., and Graf, P. (1986a). Effects of elaborative processing on implicit and explicit memory for new associations. *J. Exp. Psychol. [Learn. Mem.]* 12:432–444.

Schacter, D. L., and Graf, P. (1986b). Preserved learning in amnesic patients: perspectives from research on direct priming. *J. Clin. Exp. Neuropsychol.* 8:727–743.

Schacter, D. L., Harbluck, J., and McLachlan, D. (1984). Retrieval without recollection. An experimental analysis of source amnesia. *J. Verb. Learn. Verb. Behav.* 23:593–611.

Schacter, D. L., and Kihlstrom, J. F. (1989). Functional amnesia. In *Handbook of Neuropsychology*, F. Boller and J. Grafman (eds.). Amsterdam: Elsevier, pp. 209–231.

Schacter, D. L., McAndrews, M. P., and Moscovitch, M. (1988). Access to consciousness: dissociations between implicit and explicit knowledge in neuropsychological syndromes. In *Thought Without Language*, L. Weiskrantz (ed.). Oxford: Oxford University Press, pp. 242–278.

Schacter, D. L., Rich, S. A., and Stampp, M. S. (1985). Remediation of memory disorders: experimental evaluation of the spaced retrieval technique. *J. Clin. Exp. Neuropsychol.* 7:79–96.

Schacter, D. L., and Tulving, E. (1982). Memory, amnesia, and the episodic/semantic distinction. In *The expression of knowledge*, R. L. Isaacson and N. E. Spear (eds.). New York: Plenum Press, pp. 33–65.

Scott, S. A., DeKosky, S. T., and Scheff, S. W. (1991). Volumetric atrophy of the amygdala in Alzheimer's disease: quantitative serial reconstruction. *Neurology* 41:351–356.

Scoville, W. B. (1954). The limbic lobe in man. *J. Neurosurg.* 11:64–66.

Scoville, W. B., and Milner, B. (1957). Loss of recent memory after bilateral hippocampal lesions. *J. Neurol. Neurosurg. Psychiatry* 20:11–21.

Seltzer, B., and Benson, D. F. (1974). The temporal pattern of retrograde amnesia in Korsakoff's disease. *Neurology* 24:527–530.

Shallice, T., and Evans, M. E. (1978). The involvement of the frontal lobes in cognitive estimation. *Cortex* 14:294–303.

Sherry, D. F., and Schacter, D. L. (1987). The evolution of multiple memory systems. *Psychol. Rev.* 94:439–454.

Shimamura, A. P. (1986). Priming effects in amnesia: evidence for a dissociable memory function. *Q. J. Exp. Psychol.* 38A:619–644.

Shimamura, A. P. (1989). Disorders of memory: the cognitive science perspective. In *Handbook of Neuropsychology*, Vol. 3, F. Boller and J. Grafman (eds.). Amsterdam: Elsevier pp. 35–73.

Shimamura, A. P., Jernigan, T. L., and Squire, L. R. (1988). Korsakoff's syndrome: radiologic (CT) findings and neuropsychological correlates. *J. Neurosci.* 8:4400–4410.

Shimamura, A. P., and Squire, L. R. (1984). Paried-associate learning and priming effects in amnesia: a neuropsychological study. *J. Exp. Psychol.* [*Gen.*] 113:556–570.

Shimamura, A. P., and Squire, L. R. (1986). Memory and metamemory: a study of the feeling-of-knowing phenomenon in amnesic patients. *J. Exp. Psychol.* [*Learn. Mem.*] 12:452–460.

Shimamura, A. P., and Squire, L. R. (1987). A neuropsychological study of fact memory and source amnesia. *J. Exp. Psychol.* [*Learn. Mem.*] 13:464–473.

Shuping, J. R., Rollinson, R. D., and Toole, J. F. (1980). Transient global amnesia. *Ann. Neurol.* 7:281–285.

Sidman, M., Stoddard, L. T., and Mohr, J. P. (1968). Some additional observations of immediate memory in a patient with bilateral hippocampal lesions. *Neuropsychologia* 6:245–254.

Small, I. F., Milstein, V., and Small, J. G. (1981). Relationship between clinical and cognitive change with bilateral and unilateral ECT. *Biol. Psychiatry* 16:793–794.

Smith, M. L. (1989). Memory disorders associated with temporal-lobe lesions. In *Handbook of Neuropsychology*, Vol. 3, F. Boller and J. Grafman (eds.). Amsterdam: Elsevier, pp. 91–106.

Sohlberg, M. M., and Mateer, C. A. (1989). *Introduction to Cognitive Rehabilitation: Theory and Practice.* New York: Guilford Press.

Speedie, L., and Heilman, K. M. (1982). Amnesic disturbance following infarction of the left dorsomedial nucleus of the thalamus. *Neuropsychologia* 2:597–604.

Speedie, L., and Heilman, K. M. (1983). Anterograde memory deficits for visuospatial material after infarction of the right thalamus. *Arch. Neurol.* 40:183–186.

Spiegler, B. J., and Mishkin, M. (1981). Evidence for the sequential participation of inferior temporal cortex and amygdala in the acquisition of stimulus-reward associations. *Behav. Brain Res.* 3:303–317.

Sprofkin, B. E., and Sciarra, D. (1952). Korsakoff's psychosis associated with cerebral tumors. *Neurology* 2:427–434.

Squire, L. R. (1981). Two forms of human amnesia: an analysis of forgetting. *J. Neurosci.* 1:635–640.

Squire, L. R. (1982a). The neuropsychology of human memory. *Annu. Rev. Neurosci.* 5:241–273.

Squire, L. R. (1982b). Compairson between forms of amnesia: some deficits are unique to Korsakoff syndrome. *J. Exp. Psychol.* [*Learn. Mem.*] 8:560–571.

Squire, L. R. (1984). ECT and memory dysfunction. In *ECT: Basic Mechanisms*, B. Lerer, R. D. Weiner, and R. H. Belmaker (eds.). Washington, D.C.: American Psychiatric Press, pp. 156–163.

Squire, L. R. (1987). *Memory and Brain.* New York: Oxford University Press.

Squire, L. R., Amaral, D. G., Zola-Morgan, S., Kritchevsky, M., and Press, G. (1989b). Description of brain injury in the amnesia patient N.A. based on magnetic resonance imaging. *Exp. Neurol.* 105:23–35.

Squire, L. R., and Chase, P. M. (1975). Memory functions six to nine months after electroconsulsive therapy. *Arch. Gen. Psychiatry* 32:1157–1164.

Squire, L. R., Chace, P. M., and Slater, P. C. (1976). Retrograde amnesia following electroconsulvisve therapy. *Nature* 260:775–777.

Squire, L. R., and Cohen, N. J. (1982). Remote memory, retrograde amnesia and the neuropsychology of memory. In *Human Memory and Amnesia*, L. S. Cermak (ed.). Hillsdale, N.J.: Lawrence Erlbaum, pp. 275–304.

Squire, L. R., and Cohen, N. J. (1984). Human memory and amnesia. In *Neurobiology of*

*Learning and Memory*, G. Lynch, J. L. McGaugh, and N. M. Weinberger (eds.). New York: Guilford Press, pp. 3–64.

Squire, L. R., Cohen, N. J., and Nadel, L. (1984a). The medial temporal region and memory consolidation: a new hypothesis. In *Memory Consolidation*, H. Weingartner and E. Parker (eds.). Hillsdale, N.J.: Lawrence Erlbaum.

Squire, L. R., Cohen, N. J., and Zouzounis, J. A. (1984b). Preserved memory in retrograde amnesia: sparing of a recently acquired skill. *Neuropsychologia 22*:145–152.

Squire, L. R., and Fox, M. M. (1980). Assessment of remote memory: validation of the television test by repeated testing during a seven-day period. *Behav. Res. Methods Instrument. 12*:583–586.

Squire, L. R., Haist, F., and Shimamura, A. P. (1989a). The neurology of memory: a quantitative assessment of retrograde amnesia in two groups of amnesic patients. *J. Neurosci. 9*:828–839.

Squire, L. R., and Moore, R. Y. (1979). Dorsal thalamic lesion in a noted case of chronic memory dysfunction. *Ann. Neurol. 6*:503–506.

Squire, L. R., Nadel, L., and Slater, P. C. (1981a). Anterograde amnesia and memory for temporal order. *Neuropsychologia 19*:141–145.

Squire, L. R., and Shimamura, A. P. (1986). Characterizing amnesic patients for neurobehavioral study. *Behav. Neurosci. 100*:866–877.

Squire, L. R., Shimamura, A. P., and Graf, P. (1985). Independence of recognition memory and priming effects: A neuropsychological analysis. *J. Exp. Psychol. Learn. Mem. Cognition II*:37–44.

Squire, L. R., Shimamura, A. P., and Graf, P. (1987). Strength and duration of priming effects in normal subjects and amnesic patients. *Neuropsychologia 25*:195–210.

Squire, L. R., and Slater, P. C. (1983). Electroconvulsive therapy and complaints of memory dysfunction: a prospective three-year study. *Br. J. Psychiatry 142*:1–8.

Squire, L. R., Slater, P., and Chace, P. M. (1975). Retrograde amnesia: temporal gradient in very long-term memory following electroconsulsive therapy. *Science 187*:77–79.

Squire, L. R., Slater, P. C., and Miller, P. (1981b). Retrograde amnesia following ECT: long-term follow-up studies. *Arch. Gen. Psychiatry 38*:89–95.

Squire, L. R., Wetzel, C. D., and Slater, P. C. (1978). Anterograde amnesia following ECT: an analysis of the beneficial effect of partial information. *Neuropsychologia 16*:339–347.

Squire, L. R., and Zola-Morgan, S. (1991). The medial temporal lobe memory system. *Science 253*:1380–1386.

Squire, L. R., Zola-Morgan, S., and Chen, K. (1988). Human amnesia and animal models of amnesia: performance of amnesic patients on tests designed for the monkey. *Behav. Neurosci. 102*:210–211.

Starr, A., and Phillips, L. (1970). Verbal and motor memory in the amnesic syndrome. *Neuropsychologia 8*:75–88.

Stuss, D. T., Kaplan, E. F., Benson, D. F., Weir, W. S., Chiulli, S., and Sarazin, F. F. (1982). Evidence for the involvement of orbitofrontal cortex in memory functions: an interference effect. *J. Comp. Physiol. Psychol. 96*:913–925.

Swanson, L. (1987). The hypothalmus. In *Handbook of Chemical Neuroanatomy: Integrate Systems of the CNS. Part I — Hypothalamus, Hippocampus, Amygdala, Retina*, Vol. 5, A. Bjorklund, T. Hokfelt, and L. Swanson (eds.). Amsterdam: Elsevier, pp. 1–124.

Swanson, L. W., and Cowan, W. M. (1979). An autoradiographic study of the organization of the efferent connections of the hippocampal formation in the rat. *J. Comp. Neurol. 172*:49–84.

Sweet, W. H., Talland, G. A., and Ervin, F. R. (1959). Loss of recent memory following section of fornix. *Trans. Am. Neurol. Assoc. 84*:76–82.

Talland, G. (1965). *Deranged Memory*. New York: Academic Press.

Talland, G. A., Sweet, W. H., and Ballantine, H. T. (1967). Amnesic syndrome with anterior communicating aneurysm. *J. Nerv. Ment. Dis. 145*:179–192.

Teuber, H.-L, Milner, B., and Vaughan, H. G. (1968). Persistent anterograde amnesia after stab wound to the basal brain. *Neuropsychologia 6*:267–282.

Thal, L. J., Fuld, P. A., Masur, D. M., and Sharpless, N. S. (1983). Oral physostigmine and lecithin improves memory in Alzheimer's disease. *Ann. Neurol. 113*:491–496.

Thomson, D. M., and Tulving, E. (1970). Associative encoding and retrieval: weak and strong cues. *J. Exp. Psychol. 86*:255–262.

Tobias, B. A., Kihlstrom, J. F., and Schacter, D. L. (1992). Emotion and implicit memory. In *Handbook of Emotion and Memory*, S.-A. Christianson (ed.). Hillsdale, N.J.: Lawrence Erlbaum.

Trahan, D. M., and Larrabee, G. (1986). *Continuous Visual Memory Test*. Odessa, Fla.: Psychological Assessment Resources.

Tranel, D., and Damasio, A. R. (1985). Knowledge without awareness: an automatic index of facial recognition by prosopagnosics. *Science 228*:1453–1454.

Tranel, D., and Damasio, A. R. (1987). Evidence for covert recognition of faces in a global amnesiac patient. *J. Clin. Exp. Neuropsychol. 9*:15.

Tranel, D., and Hyman, B. T. (1990). Neuropsychological correlates of bilateral amygdala damage. *Arch. Neurol. 47*:349–355.

Tulving, E. (1972). Episodic and semantic memory. In *Organization of Memory*, E. Tulving and W. Donaldson (eds.). New York: Academic Press, pp. 381–403.

Tulving, E. (1983). *Elements of Episodic Memory*. New York: Oxford University Press.

Tulving, E., and Pearlstone, Z. (1966). Availability versus accessability of information in memory for words. *J. Verb. Learn. Verb. Behav. 5*:381–391.

Tulving, E., Schacter, D. L., and Start, H. A. (1982). Priming effects in word-fragment completion are independent of recognition memory. *J. Exp. Psychol. [Learn. Mem.] 8*:336–342.

Turner, B. H., Mishkin, M., and Knapp, M. (1980). Organization of the amygdalopetal projections from modality-specific cortical association areas in the monkey. *J. Comp. Neurol. 191*:515–543.

Ungerleider, L. G., and Mishkin, M. (1982). Two cortical visual systems. In *The Analysis of Visual Behavior*, D. J. Ingle, R.J.W. Mansfield, and M. A. Goodale, (eds.). New York: Academic Press.

Uzzell, B., and Gross, Y. (eds.). (1986). *Clinical Neuropsychology of Intervention*. Boston: Martinus Nijhoff.

Valenstein, E., Bowers, D., Verfaellie, M., Heilman, K. M., Day, A., and Watson, R. T. (1987). Retrosplenial amnesia. *Brain 110*:1631–1646.

Van Hoesen, G. W. (1985). Neural systems of the non-human primate forebrain implicated in memory. *Ann. N.Y. Acad. Sci. 444*:97–112.

Van Hoesen, G. W., and Pandya, D. N. (1975). Some connections of the entorhinal (area 28) and perirhinal (area 35) cortices of the rhesus monkey. I. Temporal lobe afferents. *Brain Res. 95*:25–38.

Van Hoesen, G. W., Pandya, D. N., and Butters, N. (1972). Cortical afferents to the entorhinal cortex of the rhesus monkey. *Science 175*:1471–1473.

Van Hoesen, G. W., Rosene, D. L., and Mesulam, M.-M. (1979). Subicular input from temporal cortex in the rhesus monkey. *Science 205*:608–610.

Verfaellie, M., Bauer, R. M., and Bowers, D. (1991). Autonomic and behavioral evidence of "implicit" memory in amnesia. *Brain Cognition 15*:10–25.

Verfaellie, M., and Cermak, L. S. (1991). Neuropsychological issues in amnesia. In *Learning* and Memory: A Biological View, J. L. Martinez and R. P. Kesner (eds.). San Diego: Academic Press, pp. 467–497.

Victor, M., Adams, R. D., and Collins, G. H. (1971). The Wernicke-Korsakoff Syndrome. Philadelphia: F. A. Davis.

Victor, M., Adams, R. D., and Collins, G. H. (1989). The Wernicke-Korsakoff Syndrome and Related Neurologic Disorders Due to Alcoholism and Malnutrition, 2nd ed. Philadelphia: F. A. Davis.

Victor, M., and Agamanolis, D. (1990). Amnesia due to lesions confined to the hippocampus: a clinical-pathologic study. J. Cognitive Neurosci. 2:246–257.

Vilkki, J. (1985). Amnesic syndromes after surgery of anterior communicating artery aneurysms. Cortex 21:431–444.

Volpe, B. T., and Hirst, W. (1983). Amnesia following the rupture and repair of an anterior communicating artery aneurysm. J. Neurol. Neurosurg. Psychiatry 46:704–709.

Volpe, B. T., and McDowell, F. H. (1990). The efficacy of cognitive rehabilitation in patients with traumatic brain injury. Arch. Neurol. 47:220–222.

von Bechterew, W. (1900). Demonstration eines Gehirns mit Zerstörung der vorderen und inneren Theile der Hirnrinde beider Schläfenlappen. Neurologish. Zentralbl. 19:990–991.

von Cramon, D. Y., Hebel, N. and Schuri, U. (1985). A contribution to the anatomical basis of thalamic amnesia. Brain 108:993–1008.

Warrington, E. K. (1985). A disconnection analysis of amnesia. Ann. N.Y. Acad. Sci. 444:72–77.

Warrington, E., K. (1984). Recognition Memory Test. Windsor, Berkshire: NFER-Nelson Publishing Company.

Warrington, E. K., and Weiskrantz, L. (1968). New method of testing long-term retention with special reference to amnesic patients. Nature 217:972–974.

Warrington, E. K., and Weiskrantz, L. (1970). The amnesic syndrome: consolidation or retrieval? Nature 228:628–630.

Warrington, E. K., and Weiskrantz, L. (1974). The effect of prior learning on subsequent retention in amnesic patients. Neuropsychologia 12:419–428.

Warrington, E. K., and Weiskrantz, L. (1978). Further analysis of the prior learning effect in amnesic patients. Neuropsychologia 16:169–177.

Warrington, E. K., and Weiskrantz, L. (1982). Amnesia: a disconnection syndrome? Neuropsychologia 20:233–248.

Weingartner, H., Grafman, J., Boutelle, W., Kaye, W., and Martin, P. (1983). Forms of cognitive failure. Science 221:380–382.

Wechsler, D. (1945). A standardized memory scale for clinical use. J. Psychol. 19:87–95.

Wechsler, D. (1981). Manual for the Wechsler Adult Intelligence Scale—Revised. New York: The Psychological Corporation.

Wechsler, D. (1987). Wechsler Memory Scale—Revised. New York: The Psychological Corporation.

Weinberg, J., Diller, L., Gerstman, L., and Schulman, P. (1972). Digit span of right and left hemiplegics. J. Clin. Psychol. 28:361.

Weiskrantz, L. (1985). On issues and theories of the human amnesic syndrome. In Memory Systems of the Brain, N. Weinberger, J. L. McGaugh, and G. Lynch (eds.). New York: Guilford Press, pp. 380–415.

Weiskrantz, L., and Warrington, E. K. (1979). Conditioning in amnesic patients. Neuropsychologia 17:187–194.

Welch, C. A. (1982). The relative efficacy of unilateral nondominant and bilateral stimulation. Psychopharmacol. Bull. 18:68–70.

Welsh, K., Butters, N., Hughes, J., Mohs, R., and Heyman, A. (1991). Detection of abnormal memory decline in mild cases of Alzheimer's disease using CERAD neuropsychological measures. *Arch. Neurol.* 48:278–281.

Whitehouse, P. J., Price, D. L., Clark, A. W., Coyle, J. T., and DeLong, M. R. (1981). Alzheimer disease: evidence for selective loss of cholinergic neurons in the nucleus basalis. *Ann. Neurol.* 10:122–126.

Whitty, C. D., and Zangwill, O. L. (eds.). (1977). *Amnesia.* London: Butterworths.

Wickens, D. D. (1970). Encoding strategies of words: an empirical approach to meaning. *Psychol. Rev.* 22:1–15.

Williams, M., and Pennybacker, J. (1954). Memory disturbances in third ventricle tumours. *J. Neurol. Neurosurg. Psychiatry* 17:115–123.

Wilson, B. A. 91987). *Rehabilitation of Memory.* New York: Guilford Press.

Wilson, B. A., and Moffat, N. (eds.) (1984). *Clinical management of Memory Problems.* Rockville, Md.: Aspen Publications.

Winnick, W. A., and Daniel, S. A. (1970). Two kinds of response priming in tachistoscopic recognition. *J. Exp. Psychol.* 84:74–81.

Winocur, G. (1984). Memory localization in the brain. In *Neuropsychology of Memory*, L. R. Squire and N. Butters (eds.). New York: Guilford Press, pp. 122–133.

Winocur, G., Kinsbourne, M., and Moscovitch, M. (1981). The effect of curing on release from proactive interference in Korsakoff amnesic patients. *J. Exp. Psychol.* [*Hum. Learn.*] 7:56–65.

Winocur, G., Oxbury, S., Roberts, R., Agnetti, V., and Davis, C. (1984). Amnesia in a patient with bilateral lesions to the thalamus. *Neuropsychologia* 22:123–143.

Winograd, T. (1975). Understanding natural language. In *Representation and Understanding*, D. Bohrow and A. Collins (eds.). New York: Academic Press.

Witherspoon, D., and Moscovitch, M. (1989). Stochastic independence between two implicit memory tests. *J. Exp. Psychol.* [*Learn. Mem.*] 15:22–30.

Wood, F., Ebert, V., and Kinsbourne, M. (1982). The episodic-semantic memory distinction in memory and amnesia: clinical and experimental observations. In *Human Memory and Amnesia*, L. S. Cermak (ed.). Hillsdale, N.J.: Lawrence Erlbaum, pp. 167–194.

Woolsey, R. M., and Nelson, J. S. (1975). Asymptomatic destruction of the fornix in man. *Arch. Neurol.* 32:566–568.

Xuereb, J. H., Perry, R. H., Candy, J. M., Perry, E. K., Marshall, E., and Bonham, J. R. (1991). Nerve cell loss in the thalamus in Alzheimer's disease and Parkinson's disease. *Brain* 114:1363–1379.

Zajonc, R. B. (1968). Attitudinal effects of mere exposure. *J. Pers. Soc. Psychol. Monogr.* 9:1–28.

Zajonc, R. B. (1980). Feeling and thinking: preferences need no interferences. *Am. Psychol.* 35:151–175.

Zola-Morgan, S., Cohen, N. J., and Squire, L. R. (1983). Recall of remote episodic memory in amnesia. *Neuropsychologia* 21:487–500.

Zola-Morgan, S., and Squire, L. R. (1982). Two forms of amnesia in monkeys: rapid forgetting after medial temporal lesions but not diencephalic lesions. *Soc. Neurosci. Abstr.* 8:24.

Zola-Morgan, S., and Squire, L. R. (1983). Intact perceptuo-motor skill learning in monkeys with medial temporal lobe lesions. *Soc. Neurosci. Abstr.* 9:27.

Zola-Morgan, S., and Squire, L. R. (1984). Preserved learning in monkeys with medial temporal lesions: sparing of motor and cognitive skills. *J. Neurosci.* 4:1072–1085.

Zola-Morgan, S., and Squire, L. R. (1986). Memory impairment in monkeys following lesions limited to the hippocampus. *Behav. Neurosci.* 100:155–160.

Zola-Morgan, S., and Squire, L. R. (1990a). The neuropsychology of memory. Parallel findings in humans and nonhuman primates. *Ann. N. Y. Acad. Sci. 608*:434–450.

Zola-Morgan, S., and Squire, L. R. (1990b). The primate hippocampal formation: evidence for a time-limited role in memory storage. *Science 250*:288–290.

Zola-Morgan, S., Squire, L. R., and Amaral, D. G. (1986). Human amnesia and the medial temporal region: enduring memory impairment following a bilateral lesion limited to field CA1 of the hippocampus. *J. Neurosci. 6*:2950–2967.

Zola-Morgan, S., Squire, L. R., and Amaral, D. G. (1989a). Lesions of the amygdala that spare adjacent cortical regions do not impair memory or exacerbate the impairment following lesions of the hippocampal formation. *J. Neurosci. 9*:1922–1936.

Zola-Morgan, S., Squire, L. R., and Mishkin, M. (1982). The neuroanatomy of amneisa: amygdala-hippocampus versus temporal stem. *Science 218*:1337–1339.

Zola-Morgan, S., Squire, L. R., Amaral, D. G., and Suzuki, W. A. (1989b). Lesions of perirhinal and parahippocampal cortex that spare the amygdala and hippocampal formation produce severe memory impairment. *J. Neurosci. 9*:4355–4370.

# 16

# Dementia

PETER J. WHITEHOUSE, ALAN LERNER, AND PETER HEDERA

In the early 1800s, the term dementia began to be used to describe acquired global cognitive impairments that were differentiated from mental retardation, delirium, and primary disorders of affect and thought content (Albert and Albert, 1984; Lipowski, 1981; Prichard, 1837). With the increase in average human life expectancy from less than 50 years at the turn of the century to close to 80 years now, the growing impact of age-related dementias on individuals, families, caregivers, professionals, and society is being recognized. A mind-robbing, body-sparing condition, dementia has been called the funeral that never ends. As a major cause of disability and death in developed countries, dementia accounts for a large share of health-care expenses (Cross and Gurland, 1986). The elderly, particularly the so-called "oldest old," over the age of 85, are most at risk for the most common causes of dementia, such as Alzheimer's disease (AD), and as their percentage in our population increases, so too will the effect of what has been called the epidemic of the century (Plum, 1979).

## DEFINITIONS AND CRITERIA

Dementia is a clinical syndrome characterized by loss of function in multiple cognitive abilities in an individual with previously normal (or at least higher) intellectual abilities and occurring in clear consciousness. Several different but overlapping diagnostic criteria have been offered for dementia (see Table 16-1). Whereas there is general agreement on the criteria of dementia, several ambiguities exist. The term dementia does not imply a specific underlying cause, progressive course, or irreversibility, though it has sometimes been misused in these ways. The distinction between delirium and dementia is made difficult because, although the delirious patient is often characterized as stuporous and inattentive, hypervigilant delirium can occur, and attention difficulties have been described in dementia.

Moreover, dementia and delirium frequently coexist. Although involvement of multiple domains of cognitive function is required to differentiate dementia from conditions that cause more discrete focal syndromes such as amnesias or aphasias, how

**Table 16-1.** DSM-III-R Diagnostic Criteria for Dementia

A. Demonstrable evidence of impairment in short- and long-term memory. Impairment in short-term memory (inability to learn new information) may be indicated by inability to remember three objects after five minutes. Long-term memory impairment (inability to remember information that was known in the past) may be indicated by inability to remember past personal information (e.g., what happened yesterday, birthplace, occupation) or facts of common knowledge (e.g., past Presidents, well-known dates).

B. At least one of the following:
    (1) impairment in abstract thinking, as indicated by inability to find similarities and differences between related words, difficulty in defining words and concepts, and other similar tasks;
    (2) impaired judgment, as indicated by inability to make reasonable plans to deal with interpersonal, family, and job-related problems and issues;
    (3) other disturbances of higher cortical function, such as aphasia (disorder of language), apraxia (inability to carry out motor activities despite intact comprehension and motor function), agnosia (failure to recognize or identify objects despite intact sensory function), and "constructional difficulty" (e.g., inability to copy three-dimensional figures, assemble blocks, or arrange sticks in specific designs);
    (4) personality change, i.e., alteration or accentuation of premorbid traits.

C. The disturbance in A and B significantly interferes with work or usual social activities or relationships with others.

D. Not occurring exclusively during the course of delirium.

E. Either (1) or (2):
    (1) there is evidence from the history, physical examination, or laboratory tests of a specific organic factor (or factors) judged to be etiologically related to the disturbance;
    (2) in the absence of such evidence, an etiologic organic factor can be presumed if the disturbance cannot be accounted for by any nonorganic mental disorder, e.g., major depression accounting for cognitive impairment.

From the American Psychiatric Association, 1987.

many areas of cognitive impairment are required to fulfill the criteria for dementia is unclear. Should psychiatric symptoms such as depression or changes in personality be regarded as impairments appropriate to meet criteria? Is a deficit in memory required, or is this just one of the more common cognitive manifestations of dementia? Finally, it is often difficult to delineate the boundaries between early dementia and normal age-related memory changes. Although controversy surrounds the term age-associated memory impairment, the concept represents a reasonable attempt to define more precisely what was previously called benign senile forgetfulness (Crook et al., 1986).

## DIFFERENTIAL DIAGNOSIS

Evaluation of the patient with a dementia syndrome begins with history taking, searching for symptoms of specific causes of dementia. An attempt to detect symptoms of depression, hysteria, or major psychosis must be included. The medical history should be explored for possible stroke, seizures, head injury, infections, alcohol or drug abuse, risk factors for AIDS, endocrine dysfunction, anemia, vitamin deficiency, and cancer. Particular attention should be paid to prescribed and over-the-counter medications. Occasionally, home or occupational exposure to heavy metals or solvents may be relevant. The history should also include an assessment of the functional impact of the disease on patient and family life, including activities of daily living and the family as a whole. A family genetic history is essential, as several dementias can be inherited.

A general physical examination should include searching for signs of metabolic abnormalities such as endocrine dysfunction, particularly hypo- and hyperthyroidism, and other systemic illnesses that may contribute to the cognitive impairment. The neurological examination should focus on specific diagnostic signs, particularly of the treatable dementias. Examination of the mental status should include a comprehensive survey of different areas of cognitive performance, including memory, language, perception, praxis, and executive functions such as planning and attention. The presence of psychiatric features, such as change in personality, hallucinations, delusions, affective disorder, anxiety, agitation, and sleep disturbance, should be sought. Elementary neurological examination is necessary to screen for signs of pathology in extrapyramidal (basal ganglia and cerebellum) and pyramidal or voluntary motor systems, as well as cranial and peripheral nerves.

Ancillary laboratory studies are also an important part of the evaluation, although recently the need for extensive metabolic screens, and even neuroimaging, has been questioned (Larson et al., 1985, 1986a; Smith and Kiloh, 1981). A recent NIH consensus conference (Office of Medical Applications of Research, Consensus Conference on Dementia, National Institutes of Health, 1987) on the diagnosis of dementia suggested the inclusion of a complete blood cell count, electrolyte panel, screening metabolic panel, thyroid function tests, vitamin $B_{12}$ and folate levels, tests for syphilis (and depending on history, human immunodeficiency viral antibodies), urinalysis, electrocardiogram, and chest x-ray. Most of these studies will produce normal results, particularly in neurology referral situations. Some believe that vitamin $B_{12}$ and folate levels are unnecessary in the absence of an anemia and that urinalysis, electrocardiogram, and chest x-rays should be done only if other signs on the history and physical point to their need.

Lumbar puncture, which used to be considered a routine part of the evaluation of dementia, is not necessary unless the history suggests an infectious process because of systemic manifestations, fever, or meningismus (Hammerstrom and Zimmer, 1985). It may be undertaken in cases in which the clinical presentation is unusual such as dementia in a young adult or a rapidly progressive course. Attempts to find cerebrospinal fluid (CSF) markers for degenerative dementias have so far been unsuccessful. Although changes in neurotransmitter markers for acetylcholine in AD and proteins associated with pathological features, e.g. beta-amyloid protein, in AD have been reported, a consistent pattern of CSF alterations has not been found (VanGool and Bolhuis, 1991). Rarely, cerebral biopsy may be indicated in younger patients with unusual presentation (Hulette et al., 1992).

Electroencephalography (EEG) is useful in selected cases, such as in differentiating dementia and depression, and searching for features of specific dementing illnesses, such as those associated with seizures of Creutzfeldt-Jakob disease (CJD). Evoked potentials are abnormal in dementia (Patterson et al., 1988; Syndulko et al., 1982), but are not yet helpful in the differential diagnosis.

Structural brain imaging, either computerized tomography (CT) or magnetic resonance imaging (MRI), is usually considered part of the general evaluation of the patient with dementia, although rarely will one find lesions not suspected on clinical grounds. CT without contrast is probably appropriate unless other signs and symptoms suggest the need for contrast, e.g., headache possibly due to a low-growing tumor. Brain atrophy is the usual finding in AD and related primary dementias; it is also found, although to a lesser, but overlapping, degree, in healthy aged individuals. Multi-infarct dementia (MID) can be confirmed by CT. MRI is probably not necessary except in selected rare cases in which one suspects small infarcts, white matter pathology, or abnormalities in the posterior fossa. MRI is more sensitive than CT at discovering abnormal areas of decreased signal, so-called bright spots or unidentified bright objects (Rezek et al., 1987). These lesions may be associated with multi-infarct dementia, but may also be found in normal aging. In AD, the term leukoaraiosis (Hachinski et al., 1987) has been used to describe this white matter pathology, although it bears an unclear relationship to the severity of dementia (Diaz et al., 1991; Mirsen et al., 1991).

Functional brain imaging, such as single photon emission tomography and positron emission tomography (PET), offers some hope to provide an improved diagnostic test. Attempts are being made to develop specific biological markers for different diseases. AD causes predominately posterior temporal parietal hypometabolism (Duara et al., 1986; Friedland et al., 1983), and the severity of symptoms correlates with the reduction in glucose metabolism (Friedland et al., 1983). Nevertheless, the pattern of cerebral metabolic alteration overlaps among different degenerative disorders and also to an extent with normal aging. These limitations and the high current cost make it difficult to predict how useful such tests will be in routine diagnostic evaluation of patients with dementia.

Neuropsychological testing can be an important part of the differential diagnostic process in dementia, although it does not have to be performed routinely. Standardized tests offer an opportunity to detect subtle cognitive abnormalities and differentiate early dementia from normal aging. Nevertheless, even with the most sophisticated evaluations, it will not be clear in many patients' first examination whether a small degree of cognitive impairment represents early dementia, so that follow-up examinations are often necessary. Neuropsychological examinations can also help differentiate dementia syndromes such as AD from cognitive impairment associated with psychopathology, such as depression. Moreover, some neuropsychologists find it useful to counsel patients and families concerning the pattern of cognitive deficits and how specific disabilities may affect the patient's activities of daily living.

Once the patient has been diagnosed as having a dementia syndrome, the differential diagnosis process must establish, as clearly as possible, the cause of the cognitive impairment. As shown in Table 16-2, dementia can be caused by a number of different illnesses. Unfortunately, neurological and medical causes that are potentially reversible are rare. Thus, at the end of a diagnostic evaluation, many patients will not be found to have a specifically identifiable cause of dementia and will be labeled through a process of diagnosis by exclusion as having a primary degenerative dementia, most likely probable AD. Degenerative diseases, particularly AD, account for most patients with dementia in community hospital and clinic surveys of dementia

**Table 16-2.** Conditions Causing Dementia

| | |
|---|---|
| Degenerative disorders of the central nervous system | Cerebrovascular disease |
|   Alzheimer's disease |   Single large strokes |
|   Pick's disease |   Multiple small infarcts (multi-infarct dementia) |
|   Huntington's disease |   Binswanger's multifocal leukoencephalopathy |
|   Parkinson's disease |   Vasculitis |
|   Progressive supranuclear palsy |   Arteriovenous malformations |
|   Striatonigral degeneration | Deficiency disorders |
|   Cortical-basal ganglionic degeneration |   Wernicke-Korsakoff syndrome |
|   Spinocerebellar degenerations |   Pellagra |
|   Progressive myoclonic epilepsy (Kuf's disease) |   Marchiafava-Bignami disease |
|   Gerstmann-Straussler syndrome |   Combined systems disease of $B_{12}$ deficiency |
|   Progressive subcortical gliosis | Toxins/drugs |
|   Amyotrophic lateral sclerosis (ALS) |   Alcohol-related syndromes |
|   ALS-parkinsonism-dementia complex |   Heavy metals |
|   Dementia lacking distinctive histology |   Carbon monoxide |
|   Frontal lobe degeneration |   Medication(s) |
|   Neuronal intranuclear inclusion disease | Brain tumors |
| Inherited metabolic disorders |   Direct effect |
|   Mitochondrial disorders |   Paraneoplastic effects |
|   Adrenoleukodystrophy | Trauma |
|   Metachromatic leukodystrophy |   Sequelae of both open and closed head injury |
|   Lipomembranous polycystic osteodysplasia | Infections |
|   Cerebrotendinous xanthomatosis |   Brain abscess |
|   $GM_2$ gangliosidosis |   Bacterial, fungal, and other forms of meningitis |
|   Gaucher's disease |   Postviral encephalitic syndromes |
|   Niemann–Pick's disease (type II-C) |   Progressive multifocal leukoencephalopathy |
|   Choreoacanthocytosis |   Subacute sclerosing panencephalitis |
|   Subacute necrotizing encephalomyelitis |   Syphilis |
|   Acute intermittent porphyria |   Human immunodeficiency virus |
|   Fabry's disease |   Whipple's disease |
|   Hallervorden-Spatz disease |   Creutzfeldt-Jakob disease |
|   Adult polyglucosan body disease |   Kuru |
| Metabolic disorders | Psychiatric syndromes |
|   Hypoxia |   Affective disorders |
|   Prolonged hypoglycemia |   Schizophrenic disorders |
|   Hepatic encephalopathy |   Hysterical disorders |
|   Cushing's syndrome | Other |
|   Hypopituitarism |   Normal pressure hydrocephalus |
|   Uremia |   Multiple sclerosis |
|   Hyperthyroidism |   Muscular dystrophy |
|   Hypothyroidism |   Sarcoidosis |
| |   Behcet's syndrome |

(Larson et al., 1985; Marsden and Harrison, 1972). MID and mixed AD/MID are probably the next most common causes of dementia. Some patients will be found to have medical or psychological factors that may contribute to producing some cognitive impairment. The treatment of these reversible factors, which contribute to what has been called excess disability, is important; but, unfortunately, when these conditions are treated, the primary dementia remains.

In the remainder of this chapter, we will review specific causes of dementia, present some general principles of management, and conclude by discussing issues important to the care of demented patients in the future.

## DEGENERATIVE DEMENTIAS

Although broader conceptions have been offered (Dyken and Krawiecki, 1983), the term degenerative dementia is usually reserved for those causes of progressive cognitive impairment that are associated with neuronal death, often with specific pathological stigmata, but without typical signs of diseases of known cause, such as signs of inflammation or infection. The term degeneration links these diseases with theories of aging developed in the last century. These dementias are more common in individuals later in life and often share some clinical and biological features found, albeit to a lesser degree, in intellectually intact older individuals. Clinical characteristics of the primary degenerative dementias include insidious onset in an individual who was previously normal or at a static level of dysfunction and gradual progression. Their etiologies are often unclear, although a genetic component is frequently present. The degenerative disorders can be categorized by whether or not the dementia is associated with other neurological signs. In this section, we will consider those degenerative dementias that occur without additional clinical pathology, as well as those with signs of disturbance in the basal ganglia, cerebellum, or corticospinal motor neurons.

### *Dementias Without Other Neurological Signs*

ALZHEIMER'S DISEASE

*Epidemiology and etiology.*   Estimates for the prevalence and incidence of AD vary, but perhaps 5% to 10% of individuals over the age of 65 suffer from the disorder (Rocca et al., 1986). With advancing age, one's risk of suffering from the disease increases, and a recent study in East Boston (Evans et al., 1989) demonstrated that almost 50% of individuals over the age of 85 may suffer from this disease. This study illustrated how using broader criteria to include cases of early dementia led to an increase in estimates of prevalence. In general, AD has been reported in all populations around the world, although variations may occur in different populations. In addition to advancing age, genetic factors have been demonstrated to contribute to AD (Folstein and Powell, 1984). Clear-cut autosomal dominant inheritance is found, and St. Georgy-Hyslop et al. (1987) demonstrated that the gene that causes the disease in some families is located on chromosome 21. Recently, specific amino acid substitutions in the gene that produces the amyloid precursor protein (APP) from which the major protein associated with senile plaques (SP) (beta-amyloid, see below) forms have been linked with AD (Goate et al., 1991; Murrell et al., 1991). That these point mutations cause the disease in these families seems likely but is not completely certain. This exciting connection between genetics and neuropathology is clearly a major advance in our understanding of the pathogenesis of AD. In other cases of familial

AD (FAD), however, other genes, perhaps located on chromosome 19, may play a role (Pericak-Vance et al., 1991). Modifying genes and environment probably also affect the phenotype, such as age of onset, even in autosomal dominant cases.

Other risk factors that have been fairly consistently associated with AD include family history of Down syndrome and female gender (Rocca et al., 1986). Some studies have shown an effect of head injury, increased mother's age at subject's birth, later position in the birth order, and history of thyroid disease. Smoking history has been negatively associated with AD in several case-control studies (Graves et al., 1991).

Despite the exciting work in elucidating the infectious and genetic origins of CJD, no transmissible agent has been demonstrated in AD (Prusiner, 1987). Moreover, early studies (Crapper et al., 1973) that demonstrated increased aluminum in the brains of patients with AD have not been confirmed (Markesbery et al., 1981). Epidemiological studies suggesting association between aluminum exposure and dementia (Martyn et al., 1989) and intervention studies suggesting that chelation therapy with desferrioxamine (Crapper-McLachlin et al., 1991) may slow the progression of the disease have been criticized (Whitehouse and Kennedy, 1991).

*Clinical features.*    Clinical features of AD are shown in Table 16-3 and include progressive loss of memory and other cognitive functions over time, a relatively intact level of consciousness, and the absence of other systemic or central nervous system processes that can account for the cognitive deterioration. A consensus group (McKhann et al., 1984) indicated that the diagnosis of definite AD can be made only at autopsy or biopsy; but when their clinical criteria are used in research centers, diagnostic accuracy can be as high as 90% (Tierney et al., 1988).

*Neuropsychology.*    Because AD can affect almost any sphere of cognitive activity, a broad neuropsychological assessment is appropriate. Memory can be distinguished in terms of the *nature* of the material to be remembered (i.e., verbal or nonverbal) and the *type* of memory (i.e., for event or motor or perceptual skills). Patients with AD show difficulty with short-term memory (Corkin, 1982), but more with explicit memory, rather than implicit learning, where the patient is unaware that learning is occurring and being assessed. Remote memory is relatively more preserved in AD than recent memory, but may deteriorate as the disease progresses (Sagar et al., 1988). Language deficits occur in AD, particularly later in the disorder (Hier et al., 1985) and include impairments in speech content, comprehension, and naming. Semantic knowledge is relatively more affected than syntactic knowledge. Studies of communication pattern, such as discourse analysis, show profound difficulty with communication between AD subjects and their caregivers (Ripich et al., 1991).

The so-called executive functions, such as concept formation, problem solving, and set shifting, such as on the Wisconsin Card Sorting Test (Berg, 1988), are impaired in AD as well as in other dementias. Visuospatial function is also impaired, particularly later in the disease (Mendez et al., 1990). Impairment on constructional visuospatial tasks may be associated with right parietal temporal pathology in AD (Brun and Englund, 1981).

Although patients with AD are generally alert and do not suffer from impairments of consciousness, i.e., delirium, these individuals may have deficits in selective atten-

**Table 16-3.** NINCDS ADRDA Criteria for Clinical Diagnosis of Alzheimer's Disease

I. The criteria for the clinical diagnosis of probable Alzheimer's disease include:
   (1) dementia established by clinical examination and documented by the Mini-Mental Test, Blessed Dementia Scale, or some similar examination, and confirmed by neuropsychological tests;
   (2) deficits in two or more areas of cognition;
   (3) progressive worsening of memory and other cognitive functions;
   (4) no disturbance of consciousness;
   (5) onset between ages 40 and 90, most often after age 65;
   (6) absence of systemic disorders or other brain diseases that in and of themselves could account for the progressive deficits in memory and cognition.

II. The diagnosis of probable Alzheimer's disease is supported by:
   (1) progressive deterioration of specific cognitive functions such as language (aphasia), motor skills (apraxia), and perception (agnosia);
   (2) impaired activities of daily living and altered patterns of behavior;
   (3) family history of similar disorders, particularly if confirmed neuropathologically;
   (4) laboratory results of:
       a. normal lumbar puncture as evaluated by standard techniques,
       b. normal pattern or nonspecific changes in EEG, such as increased slow-wave activity,
       c. evidence of cerebral atrophy on CT with progression documented by serial observation.

III. Other clinical features consistent with the diagnosis of probable Alzheimer's disease, after exclusion of causes of dementia other than Alzheimer's disease, include:
   (1) plateaus in the course of progression of the illness;
   (2) associated symptoms of depression, insomnia, incontinence, delusions, illusions, hallucinations, catastrophic verbal, emotional, or physical outbursts, sexual disorders, and weight loss;
   (3) other neurologic abnormalities in some patients, especially with more advanced disease and including more signs such as increased muscle tone, myoclonus, or gait disorder;
   (4) seizures in advanced disease;
   (5) CT normal for age.

IV. Features that make the diagnosis of probable Alzheimer's disease uncertain or unlikely include:
   (1) sudden, apoplectic onset;
   (2) focal neurologic findings such as hemiparesis, sensory loss, visual-field deficits, and incoordination early in the course of the illness;
   (3) seizures or gait disturbances at the onset or very early in the course of the illness.

V. Clinical diagnosis of possible Alzheimer's disease:
   (1) may be made on the basis of the dementia syndrome, in the absence of other neurologic, psychiatric, or systemic disorders sufficient to cause dementia, and in the presence of variations in the onset, in the presentation, or in the clinical course;
   (2) may be made in the presence of a second systemic or brain disorder sufficient to produce dementia, which is not considered to be the cause of the dementia;
   (3) should be used in research studies when a single, gradually progressive severe cognitive deficit is identified in the absence of other identifiable cause.

VI. Criteria for diagnosis of definite Alzheimer's disease are:
   (1) the clinical criteria for probable Alzheimer's disease;
   (2) histopathologic evidence obtained from a biopsy or autopsy.

VII. Classification of Alzheimer's disease for research purposes should specify features that may differentiate subtypes of the disorder, such as:
   (1) familial occurrence;
   (2) onset before age 65;
   (3) presence of trisomy-21;
   (4) coexistence of other relevant conditions such as Parkinson's disease.

From McKhann et al., 1984.

610

tion. Reaction time tests, particularly those with complex choices, show abnormal slowing (Pirozzolo et al., 1981).

*Neurobiology.* Generalized atrophy is associated with cell loss in specific neuronal populations, including cortex, hippocampus, amygdala, cholinergic basal forebrain, locus coeruleus, and raphe nuclei. Numerous other structures are also variably affected. In association with the cell death, there are four pathological hallmarks: neurofibrillary tangles (NFT), SP, granulovacuolar degeneration, and Hirano bodies. NFTs are intracellular accumulations of straight and paired helical filaments that are likely composed primarily of microtubule-associated protein, tau, as well as other proteins, such as ubiquitin. SPs are spherical structures consisting of glia and distorted nerve cell processes surrounding extracellular deposits of amyloid. Beta-amyloid protein ($\beta$-AP), a 40–43 amino acid peptide produced from several forms of a larger (approximately 700 amino acid) membrane-associated precursor protein ($\beta$-APP), is the predominant protein in the SP core. Hirano bodies are rod-shaped neuronal inclusions, and granulovacuolar degeneration occurs primarily in the hippocampus. In association with the neuropathological factors, many aspects of neuronal function deteriorate. For example, loss of synapses occurs and has been shown to correlate with indices of cognitive decline (Terry et al., 1991). Moreover, concentrations of neurotransmitter-specific markers are reduced in association with neuronal loss. For example, choline acetyltransferase, acetylcholinesterase, and nicotinic cholinergic receptors are lost in cerebral cortex, likely as a result of dysfunction in the cholinergic basal forebrain, which includes the septal nuclei, nucleus of the diagonal band, and nucleus basalis of Meynert (Whitehouse et al., 1982). Other neurotransmitter systems affected in AD include noradrenaline (Zweig et al., 1988), serotonin, and several peptides including corticotropin releasing factor and somatostatin (Whitehouse and Unnerstall 1988; Gottfries, 1990). The strongest association between dementia and cell degeneration occurs with dysfunction in cholinergic neurons. This correlation has led to considerable effort to develop therapeutic interventions based on enhancing cholinergic function, i.e., the use of cholinesterase inhibitors, muscarinic cholinergic receptor agonists, and acetylcholine release promoting agents. An application was recently submitted to the Food and Drug Administration for approval of Tacrine, a long-acting cholinesterase inhibitor that shows minimal positive effects on cognition and, unfortunately, causes liver toxicity.

PICK'S DISEASE

Pick's disease is associated with early personality and behavioral, or so-called frontal lobe clinical features. Neuropathologically, neuronal loss is associated with gliosis, and in most cases, the presence of argentophilic intracellular Pick bodies. Pick's disease is rare, occurring perhaps one twenty-fifth as commonly as AD (Wechsler et al., 1982).

It is difficult to differentiate Pick's disease from AD in life, but the typical clinical picture of disinhibited behavior with abnormalities in executive functions in association with asymmetrical frontal or temporal atrophy and a normal EEG late in the course of the illness makes the diagnosis likely.

OTHER DEMENTIAS WITHOUT MOTOR OR OTHER NEUROLOGICAL SIGNS

Over the past several years, a number of different groups have reported their autopsy series of demented patients, which indicate that approximately 10% to 15% of cases suspected to be AD in life have another variant of degenerative dementia. Unfortunately, in the different series, the miscellaneous category seems to be composed of a wide variety of degenerative diseases with nonspecific pathological features (Clark et al., 1986). Brun (1987), for example, has characterized frontal lobe degeneration of the non-Alzheimer type. These cases are characterized by frontal and anterior temporal lobe pathology which perhaps overlap in some cases with Pick's disease, progressive subcortical gliosis, and the ALS–dementia complex. Knopman and colleagues (1990) define a condition called dementia lacking distinctive histology. The criteria for this diagnosis includes neocortical cell loss and gliosis, subcortical cell loss involving at least the substantia nigra, and the absence of specific stigmata, such as SPs, NFTs, Pick or Lewy bodies. Braak and Braak (1989) have reported cases of clinically apparent AD without SPs and NFTs showing abnormal silver staining positive granules.

## Dementia with Extrapyramidal Motor Signs

HUNTINGTON'S DISEASE

Huntington's disease (HD) is a rare degenerative disorder that is invariably autosomal dominant and affects approximately five out of 100,000 patients (Folstein, 1989). In addition to dementia, it is characterized by abnormal choreiform movements, slow voluntary movements, and psychiatric disturbances, particularly affective disorder, most notably manic depressive illness. The gene causing HD was isolated in 1983 and localizes to the short arm of chromosome 4 (Gusella et al., 1983). All HD families tested so far have shown linkage to the same locus, and the mutation rate is very low (perhaps zero), helping to lead to the availability of an accurate presymptomatic diagnostic test for HD within affected families (Lanska and Whitehouse, 1989; Meissen et al., 1988).

*Clinical features.* The presentation of HD can be quite variable, with either neurological or psychiatric manifestations occurring first. Subtle alterations in personality, memory, and motor coordination are often the initial signs. Eventually, fully developed chorea, oculomotor disturbances, and disorders in voluntary movement are accompanied by a progressive dementia. A small percentage of patients, particularly young males with an affected father, may have parkinsonian features as their clinical features.

The cognitive symptoms of HD include disturbances in concentration, attention, and executive abilities (Brandt and Butters, 1986; Brandt et al., 1988; Butters et al., 1978; Jason et al., 1988). Memory disorder is prominent and may be due to difficulties with information storage and retrieval. Language praxis and gnosis are usually spared early but become affected later in the disorder, although testing may be difficult because of dysarthria and behavioral abnormalities (Wallesch and Fehrenbach,

1988). Affective disorders are the most common psychiatric disturbances, affecting perhaps one-half of patients during their illness (Folstein, 1989). Diagnosis of HD is not difficult if a positive family history is associated with typical clinical features. The absence of a positive family history must make one consider the possibility of false paternity, but also Wilson's disease, choreoacanthocytosis or other conditions with chorea. Occasionally, senile chorea needs to be differentiated from true HD. In HD, CT or MRI usually shows caudate atrophy, although this may not occur until late in the disorder.

*Neurobiology.* The basal ganglia are atrophic due to losses of populations of spiny, medium-size neurons associated with losses of choline acetyltransferase, somatostatin, GABA, and corticotropin releasing factor (DeSouza, 1987; Folstein, 1989). Neuro-pathology may also occur in the subthalamic nuclei, which may relate to the chorea. The pathological substrate for the dementia in HD is uncertain; cortical neuronal loss also occurs. Experimental models suggest that excitatory amino acides may be responsible for inducing cell death (reviewed in Choi, 1990).

PARKINSON'S DISEASE

The most common cause of dementia associated with extrapyramidal dysfunction is Parkinson's disease (PD). PD affects one out of 100 people over the age of 65. The frequency of cognitive and psychiatric disturbances in PD is somewhat controversial. Clinically diagnosable dementia probably occurs in 30% of patients. Most studies demonstrate that PD does not appear to be inherited. The human and animal models of PD due to exposure to 1-methyl-4-phenyl-1,2,3,6-tetrahydropyridine (MPTP) (Langston et al., 1983) raises the possibility that exposure to environmental toxins may play a role in all PD.

*Clinical features.* Bradyphrenia or mental slowing may occur early and in a large percentage of patients with PD. Just as in HD, some have used the label subcortical dementia to characterize the particular patterns of cognitive disabilities found in PD. The patients suffer from memory problems, attention difficulties, and bradyphrenia unassociated with cortical cognitive disturbances, such as aphasia and apraxia. Although there are undoubtedly a considerable number of heterogeneous patterns of cognitive impairment in different dementias, it is not clear that all dementias can be grouped into two categories, cortical and subcortical, which are somewhat vague and arbitrary terms (Whitehouse, 1986). Visuospatial deficits are, in fact, quite prominent in PD, and later in the illness, naming and other language problems may occur. Depression is common in PD, occurring in perhaps 30% of patients.

*Neurobiology.* Neuronal loss occurs in the substantia nigra, associated with Lewy bodies which are spherical, intracellular inclusion bodies. The recognition of reduc-tions in striatal dopamine concentration led to effective therapies being developed to treat PD. Other neurochemical abnormalities occur, for example, reductions in cor-tical choline acetyltransferase, which may underlie the cognitive impairment and corticotropin releasing factor (Whitehouse et al., 1987). Reduced levels of brain serotonin may be associated with other clinical changes, such as depression (Mayeux et al., 1986).

Several different degenerative dementias involve involuntary movement disorders and pathology in basal ganglia. Striatonigral degeneration produces dementia and parkinsonism, but the pathology in the basal ganglia is more extensive than that found in idiopathic PD. Lack of response to L-dopa, early autonomic dysfunction, and absence of rest tremor suggests the diagnosis clinically, although these findings can also be found in the various syndromes grouped under the term multiple system atrophy.

Progressive supranuclear palsy (PSP) similarly has features in common with PD, but in addition to prominent extrapyramidal rigidity, axial dystonia, and lability of affect, the disorder affects brainstem nuclei causing swallowing difficulties and supranuclear ophthalmoplegia. Dementia probably occurs in 60% to 80% of patients with PSP (Mayeux et al., 1986). The term subcortical dementia was originally used to describe this condition, although the overlap with frontal lobe pathology led to the term fronto-subcortical dementia being proposed, as well (Albert, 1978). Pathological changes include neuronal loss associated with gliosis and NFTs which are primarily composed of straight, rather than paired, helical filaments, as in AD. Abnormalities in a variety of neurotransmitter systems, including dopamine and acetylcholine, occur.

Hallervorden-Spatz disease is a rare autosomal recessive condition with late childhood or adolescent onset. Clinical features include dementia with spasticity and rigidity, dystonia, or chorea (Dooling et al., 1974). It is characterized by the accumulation of iron in the blood vessels and cells of the basal ganglia. Neurons in affected areas show swollen axonal fragments. MRI is sensitive to iron accumulation and has increased antemortem recognition of this disease (Schaffert et al., 1989). There is no effective therapy.

Wilson's disease is an autosomal recessive disorder, with a prevalence of one case per 30,000 individuals and peak onset in the second decade of life. The hepatic and central nervous system dysfunction is due to abnormalities in copper metabolism. Neurologic or psychiatric signs may predominate and include tremor, rigidity, dysarthria, psychosis, and dementia. The diagnosis can be confirmed by the presence of Kayser-Fleischer rings in the cornea and a low serum ceruloplasmin. Urinary copper excretion will usually be elevated. Liver biopsy demonstrating high copper content is an early pathological marker. Recognition of Wilson's disease is essential, since it is a fatal disorder without treatment with D-penicillamine. Early treatment can prevent disease progression and reverse both hepatic and neurological manifestations.

### Dementias Associated with Degenerative Disorders of the Cerebellum

Progressive ataxia associated with neuronal loss in the cerebellum is often associated with dementia, although the pathology in these cases is not usually confined to the cerebellum. The role of the cerebellum itself in cognition is unknown (Schmahmann, 1991), and classification of the degenerative disorders of the cerebellum is difficult. Syndromes that can be associated with dementia include olivopontocerebellar atrophies (Konigsmark and Weiner, 1970), some forms of hereditary cerebellar ataxias (Holmes, 1907; Gilman et al., 1981), and Friedrich's ataxia.

### Dementias Associated with Motor Neuron Disease

Loss of motor neurons and resultant clinical weakness is associated with dementia in several different conditions including ALS-parkinsonism-dementia complex of Guam (Hirano et al., 1966), the amyotrophy–dementia complex (Mitsuyama et al., 1985), and familial ALS/dementia (Hudson, 1981). Moreover, loss of motor neurons may occur in other neurodegenerative conditions, including HD, Pick's disease, PD, and spinocerebellar degeneration (Rosenberg, 1982). Study of the ALS-parkinsonism-dementia complex of Guam has been particularly valuable in attempting to elucidate the environmental factors that may cause this mixed condition, which apparently is now disappearing. Dementia in this condition is associated with striking bradykinesia and rigidity. Neuronal loss and depigmentation occurs in the substantia nigra without Lewy bodies, although NFTs are present. Sporadic cases of a combination of motor neuron disease and dementia have been reported (Morita et al., 1987; Sam et al., 1991). These patients are often described as frontal type and have features that overlap considerably with the cognitive symptoms found in Pick's disease (Montgomery and Erickson, 1987; Gallassi et al., 1989).

### Adult-Onset Biochemical Disorders

It is important to remember that adult-onset forms of inherited metabolic dementias can occur, although they are rare. Dyken and Krawiecki (1983) characterized these disorders into leukoencephalopathies, polioencephalopathies, corencephalopathies, and diffuse encephalopathies. Leukoencephalopathies affect primarily subcortical white matter, whereas polioencephalopathies affect gray matter. Corencephalopathies are syndromes in which the principal pathology occurs in deep telencephalic, diencephalic, or mesencephalic structures, including both gray and white matter. Diffuse encephalopathies affect all these different areas. The presence of prominent early motor signs, seizures, blindness, or peripheral neuropathy should lead the neurologist to consider some of these rarer conditions.

## NONDEGENERATIVE CAUSES OF DEMENTIA

### Vascular Dementia

The concept of vascular dementia has a rich history, confusing present and uncertain future. Beginning in the late nineteenth and continuing into the early twentieth century, a variety of vascular causes of dementia were described. In fact, until the second part of this century, arteriosclerotic processes were thought to be the major cause of dementia rather than AD. Today, in the Western countries, dementia associated with vascular pathology is probably the second most common dementing disorder after AD, and mixed cases of multi-infarct dementia and AD are common.

### MULTI-INFARCT DEMENTIA

The finding study of Tomlinson and colleagues (1968) and Hachinski and co-workers (1974) led to an understanding that multiple small infarcts could cause dementia. Problems with nosology have made it difficult to precisely define the numbers of cases of MID. Neuroimaging has increased the reliability of diagnosis, although MRI, because of its ability to detect so-called unidentified bright objects, which may or may not in particular cases represent vascular lesions, has made the interpretation of this disease even more complicated. There is also confusion as to whether an individual with cognitive impairment in more than one intellectual domain due to a single stroke should be considered demented. Many individuals with dementia are found to have small strokes on neuroimaging, and yet it is not clear that those strokes are adequate to explain the cognitive impairment, and patients such as these frequently get diagnosed as mixed AD/MID. In examining a patient with possible MID, discovery and treatment of risk factors are essential, including hypertension and other risk factors for cerebrovascular disease such as abnormal lipid levels, smoking, diabetes, and obesity.

The clinical presentation of MID depends on the location and number of infarcts. Moreover, patients with cerebrovascular disease frequently have coronary vascular disease, and may have had episodes of coronary insufficiency with associated systemic hypotension leading to more diffuse brain damage. In addition to specific clinical features associated with lesions in certain locations, episodes of confusion, pseudobulbar palsy, gait disturbance, and other clinical features may be associated with strokes.

The Hachinski scale (Hachinski et al., 1975) (Table 16-4) is useful as an aide in distinguishing MID from primary degenerative dementias, such as AD. Key differentiating factors include abrupt onset, stepwise progression, focal neurological symptoms and signs in a setting of risk factors for vascular disease (Rosen et al., 1980).

The pathogenesis of MID is uncertain. It is likely the primary cause of the dementia

Table 16-4. The Hachinski Scale

| | Modified Ischemia Score | |
| --- | --- | --- |
| | Absent | Present |
| Abrupt onset | 0 | 2 |
| Stepwise deterioration | 0 | 1 |
| Somatic complaints | 0 | 1 |
| Emotional incontinence | 0 | 1 |
| History or presence of hypertension | 0 | 1 |
| History of strokes | 0 | 2 |
| Focal neurological signs | 0 | 2 |
| Focal neurological symptoms | 0 | 2 |

Modification of Hachinski Ischemia scale by Rosen et al., 1980.

is the actual loss of brain tissue rather than lowered cerebral blood flow (CBF). Dementia may be greater if there are multiple bilateral strokes (Ladurner et al., 1982). Although MID is usually associated with elevated blood pressure and concomitant damage to small blood vessels, embolic strokes can also cause a similar clinical picture. A variant of MID is Binswanger's disease (Babikian and Ropper, 1987), where strokes are limited to white matter. The clinical features are similar to MID affecting gray matter. MRI is useful in delineating the distribution of the white matter pathology, but again, high-signal areas can be seen in white matter in nondemented normal-aged individuals.

VASCULITIS

Vasculitic dementia may be caused by inflammation of cranial arteries often in association with systemic illness, such as giant cell arteritis, systemic lupus erythematosus, and polyarteritis nodosa (Feinglass et al., 1976; Asheron et al., 1987; Moore and Cupps, 1983). The rare condition granulomatous angiitis (Moore and Cupps, 1983) presents as a vasculitis limited to the central nervous system. Cerebral amyloid angiopathy frequently causes hemorrhages, but can be manifested as dementia (Vinters, 1987).

## Infectious Causes of Dementia

VIRAL DEMENTIAS

Viral infections of the central nervous system can result in dementia through several mechanisms. Some viruses, for example, herpes simplex, cause an acute encephalitis with a residual dementia due to damage of specific populations of neurons in hippocampus and temporal lobe. Infections disturb neuronal functions such as neurotransmission (Oldstone, 1984) but do not actually lead to cell death and may also lead to dementia. Chronic inflammatory meningoencephalitis, such as occurs in subacute sclerosing panencephalitis, can cause dementia. Other mechanisms include subcortical demyelination associated with progressive multifocal leukoencephalopathy and noninflammatory cortical neuronal death as in slow virus disease such as CJD.

The recognition that a virus may be involved in the dementia depends on historical and laboratory features. The appearance of the illness in association with a particular season or epidemic is important. The presence of certain risk factors, such as a history of intravenous drug use, receipt of blood products, or homosexual activity, should suggest the human immunodeficiency virus (HIV) infection. Laboratory testing can be useful; serial serological analysis may be helpful if the acute illness is being observed. CSF studies are, by themselves, rarely diagnostic. Imaging studies may be helpful in localizing infections such as herpes simplex or in exclusion of structural lesions, such as an abscess. Some selected viral causes of dementia are reviewed below to illustrate general principles.

*Postinfectious encephalomyelitis.* A variety of viral illnesses, including measles as well as vaccinia, varicella, and rubella, may be associated with an infectious dementia syndrome that shares clinical and pathological similarities with experimental allergic encephalomyelitis. An autoimmune mechanism is thought to underlie the pathogenesis of these conditions.

*Human immunodeficiency virus type I encephalopathy.*    Patients with HIV infection develop cognitive impairment and many a frank dementia (Navia et al., 1986; Levy et al., 1985). Twenty to 60% of patients with acquired immune deficiency syndrome (AIDS) are demented by the time of death, and over 90% of patients dying with AIDS show evidence in the brain of a subacute encephalitis. Typically, HIV encephalopathy occurs in the later stages of AIDS in association with marked immunodeficiency. Typical clinical presentations include alterations in mood, including apathy, depression, and withdrawal. Early symptoms can be confused with psychological reactions to the disease and depression. Later on, psychomotor slowing, memory disturbance, and visuospatial abnormalities occur. The course of the disease is rapid in that the interval between first symptoms and death in one series was less than six months (McArthur, 1987). Cerebral atrophy is associated with microglial nodules which are scattered throughout the brain.

The most important differential diagnosis includes infection with other agents such as toxoplasmosis, syphilis, fungus, *Cryptococcus*, and tuberculosis, or tumors such as primary central nervous system lymphoma. All patients with AIDS who develop change in cognition require a full evaluation for dementia, looking for these and other treatable causes.

*Subacute sclerosing panencephalitis.*    This rare complication of measles usually occurs in childhood but has been known to occur in early adulthood. The progressive dementia is frequently associated with myoclonic jerks and fairly characteristic EEG changes. Eventually, other signs of corticospinal and extrapyramidal motor system dysfunction occur and death occurs within three years of onset (ter Meulen et al., 1983).

*Progressive multifocal leukoencephalopathy.*    Progressive multifocal leukoencephalopathy is due to an opportunistic infection that occurs in individuals whose immunological systems are compromised because of infections or treatment for cancer. As the name suggests, neurological signs occur in many different systems, and they include motor weakness, speech disturbances, seizures, gait disturbances, and dementia (Walker, 1985). Neuropathological examination shows primarily a subcortical pattern of demyelination in association with abnormal astrocytes. The disease is now known to be due to several viruses including SV40 (Padgett and Walker, 1983).

*Creutzfeldt-Jakob disease.*    CJD is another rare condition that affects perhaps one individual per million population per year (Brown, 1980). The presentation is that of a rapidly progressive degenerative dementia, and although the first symptoms are often subtle, cognitive deterioration usually develops rapidly over weeks to months, and is frequently associated with cerebellar and visual complaints (Brown et al., 1987). In the end stages, myoclonus and typical EEG findings, including periodic complexes of a triphasic or burst suppression pattern, are present. Occasionally, slowly progressive forms of CJD are difficult to distinguish from AD.

CJD is a form of subacute spongiform encephalopathy that is characterized microscopically by neuronal loss and astrocytosis associated with vacuoles in the cytoplasm of both of these types of cells. Although CJD is clearly a transmissible disorder, it is not associated with the usual histopathological findings of viral diseases including inflammation and inclusion bodies. Experiments with animal models have led to tremendous advances in the molecular understanding of these etiological agents which are caused by novel infectious agents. Prusiner (1987) believes that the etiological agent may be a protein and has labeled these prions (proteinaceous infectious particles). Mutations in the gene for the prion protein lead to a variety of neurological conditions including Gerstmann-Straussler-Scheinker syndrome, which is autosomally dominantly inherited. These disorders are challenging our current notions of the relationships among genes, infectious agents, and disease out of proportion to the frequency with which they cause human disease.

BACTERIAL, FUNGAL, AND PARASITIC CAUSES OF DEMENTIA

Many nonviral agents can also cause progressive and cognitive impairment, and are frequently reversible if treated appropriately and rapidly. Nevertheless, because these conditions are rare, the clinician should only perform an extensive evaluation for the possibility of an infectious cause of dementia in the appropriate clinical circumstances. A patient who presents with rapid intellectual decline in association with a systemic manifestation of an infection, including fever and signs of other focuses of inflammation elsewhere in the body, should be evaluated carefully. Delirium, headaches, nausea, focal neurological deficits, and seizures should also suggest the possibility of an infectious process. Particular attention should be paid to patients who are immunosuppressed, or for other reasons more susceptible to infectious processes. In addition to history and physical examination, neuroimaging and lumbar puncture are essential to establish the diagnosis (Booss and Thornton, 1986; Becker et al., 1985). As with the viral causes of dementia, there are many different mechanisms by which bacteria, fungi, and parasites can cause dementia.

*Residual dementia due to bacterial meningitis.* Many survivors of bacterial meningitis are left with significant mental impairment. However, in children, subtle signs that manifest as difficulties in school may be the only manifestation of the damage due to nervous system pathology (Dodge, 1986; Klein et al., 1986). In addition to damage to the brain itself, associated vascular inflammation and increased intracranial pressure may contribute to cognitive impairment.

*Neurosyphilis.* Untreated syphilis leads to symptomatic neurosyphilis in approximately 10% of cases (Simon, 1985). With the apparent increase in incidence of primary syphilis, which may go untreated, physicians need to be vigilant for these particular syndromes. After a period of asymptomatic neurosyphilis, patients may develop meningovascular syphilis which manifests as multiple strokes and associated dementia. General paresis usually manifests later, 10 to 20 years after the primary infection, and presents insidiously with changes in personality. Psychosis may appear, although the classic delusions of grandeur are less common than previously thought. Examination of CSF can lead to a definitive diagnosis in many cases which, in turn, can lead to appropriate antibiotic treatment.

*Tuberculous meningitis.*   Another infectious disease that appears to be increasing in frequency in the United States and is still a major problem in underdeveloped nations is tuberculosis. Tuberculous meningitis can cause dementia, although frequently other neurological signs are present, and the course of the illness is over a matter of months, leading to death if adequate treatment is not instituted. Elderly patients with tuberculosis meningitis may not present in the classic fashion, and may have fewer signs of meningismus and more signs of progressive mental change (Dixon et al., 1984).

*Lyme disease.*   Lyme disease is caused by the spirochete *Borrelia burgdorferi*, which is endemic, particularly in the northeastern United States, but also is found in other areas of the country. Fifteen percent of patients may develop neurological involvement in the early stages (Pachner et al., 1989), but occasional patients develop persistent infections and dementia (Logigian et al., 1990). Polyneuropathy and other neurological signs due to meningopolyneuritis or myelitis usually allow the diagnosis to be made especially if associated with appropriate skin and joint involvement. However, history of arthropod bite or the classic rash of erythema chronicum migrans are frequently absent. Laboratory tests including serum and CSF serologies may be helpful, although in the late persistent diseases, the diagnosis may be difficult.

*Brain abscess.*   Abscesses present with a combination of features suggesting infection and a structural lesion. They are frequently associated with infection in the ears or mastoids, which spread to brain or hematogenous spread from other foci in the body. Anaerobic organisms are the most common organisms found, often without a single predominant organism. Head trauma can be also associated with brain abscesses. Dementia or at least some mental status changes occur in perhaps 50% of cases, with the symptoms of cognitive impairment depending on the location of the abscess. CT scan will usually determine the nature of the problem, and a combination of surgery and antibiotics are often required. Permanent neurological sequela frequently occurs resulting in cognitive impairment in perhaps 20% of patients (Chun et al., 1986).

*Fungal infections.*   Many different fungi can cause meningitis, which can present as chronic dementia. The most common is cryptococcal meningitis. This infection frequently occurs in the setting of the immunodeficiency associated with cancer, corticosteroid therapy, or now most commonly, HIV infection. Neurocysticercosis is now seen worldwide because of changes in migration, for example in the southwestern United States in Hispanics. This condition is caused by the cestode pork tapeworm. The clinical symptoms are caused by the degeneration of brain cysts producing inflammation. Seizures are common. Dementia as initial presentation occurs in about 3% (Sandyk et al., 1987).

*African trypanosomiasis.* This African sleeping sickness is caused by a hemoflagellate that is transmitted through the bite of a tsetse fly. This is an exceedingly common cause of progressive nervous system deterioration, particularly dementia, in Africa, and is seen in this country in travelers to endemic foci (Greenwood and Whittle, 1980).

### Sarcoidosis

Sarcoidosis is a multisystem granulomatous disease of unknown etiology with neurological involvement in perhaps 5% of cases. Symptomatology depends on the location of the lesions, but cranial neuropathies, hypothalamic dysfunction, hydrocephalus, aseptic meningitis, seizures, neuropathy, and myopathy are most common (Stern et al., 1985). Dementia mimicking AD with progressive memory problems, poor concentration, disorientation, personality changes, and hallucinations has been reported (Cordingley et al., 1981). Although sarcoidosis may be restricted to the nervous system, most cases show evidence of multisystem involvement, either clinically or at autopsy. CSF examination is almost always abnormal, characterized by lymphocytic pleocytosis and high protein and low glucose concentrations. Neuroimaging can detect hydrocephalus, mass lesions, and contrast enhancement of the meninges. Treatment with corticosteroids is recommended after exclusion of infectious disorders which can present with similar syndromes.

### Metabolic Causes of Dementia

Metabolic dementias are caused by diffuse dysfunction of brain at the molecular-chemical level. A fixed dementia can be due to intellectual impairment due to a single metabolic insult, such as hypoxia, whereas progressive dementia may be due to chronic insufficiency of the metabolic support of the brain (Gershell, 1981). Many elderly suffer from systemic disorders that may contribute to mental impairment (Cummings et al., 1984) (see Table 16-5). A frequent cause of reversible metabolic dementia is the use of over-the-counter or prescribed medications. Since a variety of biochemical conditions can cause metabolic dementia, extensive diagnostic procedures should be used selectively. Table 16-6 suggests a scenario for the selective use

**Table 16-5.** Causes of Metabolic Dementia in Elderly Patients with Symptoms for at Least Three Months

| | |
|---|---|
| Medications | 9.5% |
| Hypothyroidism | 3.0% |
| Hyperparathyroidism | 1.0% |
| Hypoglycemia° | 1.0% |
| Hyponatremia† | 1.0% |

The values reflect the percentage of 200 patients evaluated with dementia. The remainder of the 200 patients had other causes of dementia. (Adapted from Larson et al., 1986b.)
°Due to insulin.
†Due to diuretics

**Table 16-6.** An Extensive Potential Testing
Battery for the Evaluation of the Demented
Patient

CT scan or MRI
Thyroid screen
Serum and urine drug screen
SMA-16
Complete blood count and differential
Arterial blood gas
Syphilis serology
Vitamin $B_1$ and $B_{12}$ and folate levels
EEG
Lumbar puncture
Isotope cisternography
Erythrocyte sedimentation rate
ANA, lupus anticoagulant
Cerebral angiography
Brain biopsy
PET
HIV titer

From Feldmann and Plum, 1992.

of these metabolic screens. Nevertheless, most patients with dementia should have included in their evaluation a thyroid screen, vitamin $B_{12}$ determination, as well as complete blood count and screening chemistries (Cummings and Benson, 1983). The mechanisms by which these metabolic insults cause dementia are varied and frequently relate to the alterations in oxygen and glucose support which lead to a failure of energy metabolism. In this chapter, we cannot review all the causes of metabolic dementia, but once again, will review selected examples.

EXOGENOUS TOXINS

Potentially harmful chemical agents are used in our society, either as therapies or foods, or related to industrial exposure. Sedatives, alcohol, and psychotropic medications, such as antidepressants, lithium, and major tranquilizers, are probably the most common causes of reversible metabolic dementia (Larson et al., 1986b). Other medications which are not designed to have a primary effect on the central nervous system, including digitalis, antihypertensive agents, antineoplastic agents, and anticonvulsants are also common causes of cognitive impairment. Exposure to heavy metals and a variety of other industrial compounds can also be, in the appropriate clinical circumstances, a consideration for the patient who presents with progressive dementia.

## Systemic Illness

ENDOCRINE DYSFUNCTION

A variety of medical illnesses can cause chronic cognitive impairment, including disturbances of the endocrine system. Disturbances of the endocrine system are particularly important to consider because they are frequently treatable with hormone replacement. Thyroid disease is common, and may present with changes in personality as well as changes in intellectual abilities (Swanson et al., 1981). Particularly in the elderly, hyperthyroidism can also present as cognitive retardation. Addison's disease and Cushing's disease can both present as cognitive impairment (Swanson et al., 1981; Martin and Reichlin, 1987). Parathyroid disease, by altering serum calcium levels (Cummings and Benson, 1983), can be associated with dementia and changes in the personality in perhaps as many as 12% of cases. Similarly, hypocalcemia may also be associated with cognitive impairment. Patients with panhypopituitarism may suffer from intellectual impairment from multisystem hormonal failure.

CARDIOPULMONARY DYSFUNCTION

Cardiovascular and pulmonary failure may also lead to cognitive impairment, either acutely or chronically. Multiple episodes of hypoxia may contribute to a pattern of stepwise deterioration. Alterations in blood components, such as anemia or hyperviscosity, can also contribute to cognitive impairment.

HEPATIC DYSFUNCTION

Mental impairment can be associated with many different causes of hepatic dysfunction, probably due to elevated levels of ammonium. Five percent of patients with cirrhosis may develop encephalopathy (Cooper and Plum, 1987). With every episode of liver failure, a dementia syndrome may be left as a static deficit. Motor symptoms are frequently associated with the dementia, including dysarthria and ataxia.

RENAL DYSFUNCTION

Any cause of chronic renal failure can result in cognitive impairment if uremic or other metabolic imbalances occur (Cummings and Benson, 1983). Dementia has been associated with dialysis itself (Teschan and Arrief, 1985).

## Deficiency States

Absence of a variety of nutritional substances required for metabolic support of the brain can lead to dementia, including glucose (Martin and Reichlin, 1987), thiamine (Victor et al., 1989), niacin (Martin and Reichlin, 1987), and vitamin $B_{12}$ deficiency (Blass and Plum, 1983). Whether there is a specific association of mental impairment with reduced folate levels is unclear (Weinger, 1981).

## Psychiatric Causes

Cognitive impairment can be associated with a number of psychiatric syndromes (Rabins et al., 1992). Clear-cut conceptual and other clinical distinctions between what diseases are neurological and what are psychiatric (or what has been called organic and functional disorders) are not posible. The term pseudodementia was first used in 1952 (Madden et al., 1952) and popularized by Kiloh to refer to cognitive impairment occurring in patients with "psychiatric" disease such as depression (Kiloh, 1961). Nevertheless, most people now believe that the dementia associated with psychiatric conditions is not false; therefore, it should not be labeled as such. Rarely in most practices will one see a case of hysteria or malingering in which the cognitive impairment might more appropriately be lateled a pseudodementia, although again, the nosological issues surrounding the use of these labels are difficult.

AFFECTIVE DISORDER

The most common source of concern to clinicians regarding to differential diagnosis has to do with separating depression from mild dementia. Depression can present as a progressive cognitive impairment, and patients with dementia can be depressed, so that a number of different relationships exist between the affective symptoms and the cognitive impairment (Reiffler, 1986; McAllister and Price, 1982). Approximately 30% of patients with dementia may be depressed during some part of the illness. Moreover, depression can be the earliest manifestation of the dementing illness. (Reading et al., 1985; Reynolds et al., 1986).

A variety of criteria have been proposed to differentiate depression from primary degenerative disorders such as AD (Wells, 1979; 1982). Rabins et al. (1983) have summarized these criteria and proposed a scheme by which one can distinguish these two conditions (Table 16-7). Unfortunately, the dexamethasone suppression test did not prove to be successful because it lacks specificity (Spar and Gerner, 1982). Research on sleep EEG studies may provide answers to diagnostic dilemmas in the future (Fleming, 1989).

**Table 16-7.** Validated Criteria That Identify Reversible Dementia

| Wells, 1979 | Rabins et al., 1983 | Reding et al., 1985 | Reynolds et al., 1986 |
|---|---|---|---|
| Patient complains frequently of memory loss | Past history of depression | Lack of cerebrovascular, extrapyramidal, or spinocerebellar disease | MMSE >21 |
| Patient emphasizes disability | Subacute onset (<6 months) | Modified HIS <4 | HDRS >21 |
| Memory loss for recent and remote events is equally severe | Delusions of guilt, self-blame, hopelessness | MSQ >8 | Sleep efficiency <75% |
| Memory loss for specific period or events | Appetite loss | Haycox <7 | |
| | Reports depressed mood | Not delirious on TCA | |

MMSE = Mini-Mental State Exam; HDRS = Hamilton Depression Rating Scale; HIS = Hachinski Ischemic Score; MSQ = Mental Status Questionaire; TCA = Tricyclic antidepressant. (From Rabins et al., 1992).

Schizophrenia is a common cause of psychosis which frequently begins in adolescence or early adulthood. Psychotic symptoms are spoken of belonging to two groups—positive symptoms, such as delusions, hallucinations, and thought disorder, and negative symptoms, which include apathy and impoverishment of emotional relationships. The negative symptoms may emerge later and be associated with a dementia (Ciompi, 1987; Heaton and Drexler, 1987). Schizophrenic patients can usually be differentiated from patients with primary degenerative dementia because of the earlier age of onset and initial presentation with hallucinations and delusions. The nature of the late-onset schizophrenia, which has been called paraphrenia in Europe, is still being explored (Bridge and Wyatt, 1980) (see also Chapter 14).

## Miscellaneous Causes of Dementia

A variety of conditions that do not fit naturally into other neurological categories are reviewed below.

HYDROCEPHALUS

Obstructive hydrocephalus, due to a tumor or bleeding, has been known to cause acute confusional states as well as progressive dementia. Normal-pressure hydrocephalus (NPH) was described in 1965 (Adams et al., 1965) and is characterized clinically by dementia, gait disturbance, and urinary incontinence. Unfortunately, the clinical presentation is nonspecific. It has been estimated that NPH occurs in 4–7% of all cases of dementia (Anderson, 1986). It is most frequently due to a known cause, such as subarachnoid hemorrhage or head injury. Although some patients respond to CSF shunting, it has been difficult to identify those patients who are likely to respond to this intervention.

DEMYELINATING DISEASES

Multiple sclerosis (MS) is the most common demyelinating disease of young adults with a prevalence of 50 to 60 per 100,000 individuals, with peak onset in the third and fourth decades (Rao, 1986). It is classically diagnosed by the presence of central nervous system lesions disseminated in location and time (Schumacher et al., 1965), although new criteria using neuroimaging and other laboratory tests are now in use (Poser et al., 1983). The course of MS may be either as a relapsing-remitting illness or a chronic progressive decline in function. The accumulation of neurological deficits eventually results in cognitive dysfunction in a majority of patients (Peyser et al., 1990), but does not necessarily correlate with other neurological findings, severity or duration of illness (Van den Burg et al., 1987; Rao et al., 1991). Rarely, dementia has been an early and prominent feature (Filley et al., 1989). The dementia of MS may be seen in either form of the disease. It may be manifest primarily as a deficit in attention (Filley et al., 1989). Significant deficits in recent memory, sustained attention, verbal fluency, conceptual reasoning, and visuospatial perception occur most commonly (Rao et al., 1991). Great difficulties with recall and recognition suggest to some that retrieval mechanisms are the primary problem underlying the memory difficulties (Rao, 1986).

A variety of affective disorders are also common in MS. These include euphoria, pathological laughing and crying, depression, and bipolar disorder. Depression appears to be more common than can be explained by the presence of a chronic illness alone (Minden and Schiffer, 1990).

Recent studies have correlated neuropsychological findings with measures of disease activity or location. MRI can visualize demyelinated areas, and total lesion area correlates well with degree of cognitive impairment (Rao et al., 1989; Baumhefner et al., 1990). The degree of atrophy of the corpus callosum correlates with performance on tasks requiring sustained attention (Franklin et al., 1988; Rao et al., 1991). Patterns of demyelination may relate to patterns of dysfunction in structures subserving relatively focal functions.

HEAD TRAUMA

Posttraumatic dementia is one of the most debilitating sequelae of head traumas, accounting for approximately 2% of all dementias (Smith and Kiloh, 1981). Head injuries can result in different behavioral and cognitive residuals and we will discuss only global cognitive deficit after severe head injury. The residual deficit correlates with the severity and mechanism of trauma and with the localization of brain damage. Duration and grading of coma are important for predicting functional outcome (Uzzel et al., 1987).

Dementia should be evaluated only after the acute symptoms have subsided. The range of residual deficit usually stabilizes within six to eight months after the accident, and compensatory adaptation can little improve the trauma outcome (Bond, 1986).

The most common type of head trauma is closed head injury. Several mechanisms can be involved in the pathophysiology of cognitive deficit: diffuse axonal injury, contusion, intracerebral hemorrhage (Feher et al., 1988). Clinical symptoms include deficit in attention, concentration, and memory and are often accompanied with focal signs as aphasia, agnosia, etc.

Cognitive deficit can also develop after repeated minor head blows, such as typically occurs in boxing, which is known as dementia pugilistica. Characteristic clinical features include extrapyramidal, cerebellar, and pyramidal symptoms (Roberts, 1969).

Secondary complications following the head traumas are epilepsy and NPH, both of which can be associated with a dementia. Head injuries have also been reported as a possible risk factor for AD (see above).

NEOPLASMS

Neoplastic process can influence cognitive functions as intracranially localized tumors (either primary brain tumors or metastatic tumors) or as extracranial neoplastic disorder (paraneoplastic syndrome). Interventions to treat the neoplasm may also adversely affect mentation.

Dementia is only one of the variety of symptoms caused by brain tumors (Haase, 1977). Behavioral changes are the earliest symptoms and may occur in the absence of other focal neurological deficits. Dementia is commonly observed with tumors located in frontal or temporal lobes or in the diencephalon. Apathy, decreased psychomotor activity, and impaired executive abilities are the most typical manifestations of frontally located neoplasms (Holmes, 1931). Patients with temporal lobe tumors may have impaired memory and orientation, and often experience hallucinations. Language involvement is common in temporal lobe tumors located in the dominant hemisphere (Strobos, 1974). Dementia in thalamic and hypothalamic tumors is often accompanied by neuroendocrinologic and autonomic disturbances and may mimic psychiatric disorder (Malamud, 1967). Behavioral and cognitive changes are associated with indirect manifestations of intracranial expansion (increased intracranial pressure or noncommunicating hydrocephalus). Remote effects of extracranial carcinoma can also result in dementia. The pathophysiology of paraneoplastic syndromes is still uncertain (Henson and Ullrich, 1982). Limbic encephalitis, most commonly associated with small cell lung carcinoma, is characterized by rapidly progressive deterioration of intellect, often accompanied with seizures. The primary tumor may be found only at autopsy (Palma, 1987). Other forms of paraneoplastic syndromes include polio-like encephalomyelitis with dementia and cerebellar degeneration, which can be profound and often the presenting symptom of a cancer. Ectopic hormonal production by carcinomas may cause dementia, which has similar features similar to primary endocrine dementias due to hyperparathyroidism and increased production of antidiuretic hormone. Dementias associated with a paraneoplastic syndrome have less favorable prognosis and may often persist after the primary neoplasm has been removed or treated (Palma, 1987).

Exposure to radiotherapy can cause dementia by demyelinization; concurrent chemotherapy increases the risk for developing of leukoencephalopathy (DeAngelis et al., 1989).

EPILEPSY

Epilepsy is a common neurological disorder, affecting 1–2% of the United States population. It is a heterogeneous disorder, with more than 30 seizure types and 20 epileptic syndromes being recognized (International League Against Epilepsy, 1981, 1985). Only a small percentage of epileptics have dementia (Lesser et al., 1986), often associated with multifactorial etiologies. The major causes for dementia associated with epilepsy are heredity, preexisting brain damage, effects from the seizures themselves (Guberman et al., 1986), and sedative drugs. More recent studies have looked at the relation of seizure type and frequency, demographic features, anticonvulsant medication, and past medical history, especially head injury, in determining risk of dementia in epilepsy. Patients with generalized seizures have more attentional difficulties and lower IQ scores than those with partial seizures (Petersen and Dam, 1986; Trimble, 1987). Memory deficits in patients with temporal lobe discharges may depend on hemispheric laterality, with verbal memory affected more with left temporal discharges and visuospatial memory in patients with right-hemisphere discharges (Trimble and Thompson, 1986). The role of seizure frequency in cognitive deterioration is complex. Some studies have found positive correlations between seizure frequency and IQ scores (Dikmen and Matthews, 1977; Dodrill and Troupin, 1976). A longitudinal study of epileptics with declines in IQ scores did not find consistent relationships to disease duration (Trimble, 1984). This same study found a correlation between history of head injury and type of medication used, and decline in intellectual function.

Anticonvulsants used to treat epilepsy can cause cognitive dysfunction. This may be a direct effect of the medication, or mediated through other metabolic changes, such as phenytoin-induced folate deficiency (Trimble, 1987). A recent study comparing phenobarbital to phenytoin and carbamazepine found more cognitive effects with phenobarbital than with the other medications (Meador et al., 1990). A condition termed "Dilantin dementia" has been described, mostly affecting children with pre-existing mental retardation, frequent seizures, increased CSF protein, and cerebellar atrophy.

## BIOLOGICAL MANAGEMENT

Our knowledge of the biological nature of dementias, particularly the primary degenerative dementias such as AD, remains limited. This lack of understanding of pathological mechanisms in many dementias has limited our therapeutic success in the more common dementias. However, in some of the metabolic dementias, such as hypothyroidism, those associated with vitamin $B_{12}$ deficiency, and benign tumors, reversal of cognitive impairments can occur, particularly if the disease has been detected early. Moreover, the treatment of patients with MID with stroke-prevention regimens and antihypertensives may slow the progression of the disease, although there are no empirical studies to support this claim.

Recent advances in understanding the neural substrates of behavior and plasticity in the nervous system are enabling more rational approaches with greater hope for success in the future for treating degenerative dementias. Currently, treatment of degenerative dementias has focused on ameliorating the symptoms, although basic and clinical studies are under way to try to slow the disease progression as well. In the future, we hope to be able to prevent the onset of the disease, or cure dementia, as our understanding of the basic pathogenesis increases dramatically.

The first group of therapeutic approaches to be considered focuses on controlling the behavioral symptoms found in dementia. Effective treatment of agitation, depression, hallucinations, and sleep disorders can provide significant relief, not only for the patients, but for the caregivers as well. Such palliative treatment must consider all the principles of careful drug administration, especially in elderly patients, such as defining target symptoms, monitoring carefully for positive and negative effects, starting with low doses, adjusting doses slowly, and watching carefully for drug interactions (i.e., polypharmacy). Antidepressants and neuroleptics with significant anticholinergic side effects should be avoided (Crimson, 1990, Larson et al., 1984). More empirical studies are needed of current generation psychoactive drugs, and the future looks bright in this area because of the development of novel antianxiety, antidepressant, and antipsychotic agents with side-effect profiles that may make them more valuable for elderly patients with dementia.

Most current experimental studies of symptomatic treatment in AD have focused on the treatment of cognitive abnormalities and are based primarily on the understanding of the neurotransmitter pathology that occurs in AD (Ferris, 1990; Haroutunian et al., 1990). The reductions of markers for cholinergic neurotransmission associated with dysfunction in cells in the cholinergic basal forebrain (Whitehouse et al., 1982) have been the major stimulus to develop drugs to improve cognition. Cholinoactive agents have consistent effects on memory in human subjects and animals. Reductions of cholinergic markers in AD and other dementias, such as PD, correlate with the severity of cognitive decline.

Many different mechanisms have been used to try to enhance cholinergic transmission including increasing the availability of acetylcholine precursors (e.g., choline), administration of acetylcholinesterase inhibitors, directly stimulating postsynaptic muscarinic cholinergic receptors, or enhancing the release of acetylcholine (e.g., DUP996) (see Table 16-8). (Nordberg, 1990). Most studies in late phases of development involve cholinesterase inhibitors. A limited treatment IND (investigational new drug) application has recently been approved by the FDA for tetrahydroaminoacridine (THA), or Tacrine, a long-acting cholinesterase inhibitor of uncertain clinical efficacy, which has shown some minimal positive effects on cognition as well as liver toxicity (Francis and Bowen, 1989; Freeman and Dawson, 1991). Longer-acting acetylcholinesterase inhibitors without liver toxicity may be more useful. A variety of subtypes of muscarinic and nicotinic cholinergic receptors have been described, and many current development efforts are focusing on finding an ideal drug that stimulates the appropriate receptors to improve cognition and minimize

**Table 16-8.** Current Drug Trials in Alzheimer's Disease: Phase II/ III, III, and Investigational New Drug (IND)

| | |
|---|---|
| *Cholinergic Drugs* | |
| Acetyl-L-carnitine (Alcar/Sigma-Tau) | Phase III |
| Choline-L-alfoscerate (Sandoz) | Phase III |
| Bros (Fidia) | Phase III |
| Ceranapril (Bristol-Myers Squibb) | Phase III |
| Ebiratide (Hoechst) | Phase II/III |
| Linopirdine (Dupont/Merck) | Phase III |
| Physostigmine (Synapton/Forrest Lab) | Phase III |
| Tacrine (Cognex/Warner-Lambert) | IND |
| Velnacrine (Mentane/Hoechst-Roussel) | Phase III |
| *Noncholinergic Drugs* | |
| Granisetron (Kytril/SmithKline Beecham) | Phase III |
| Ondansetron (Zofran/Glaxo) | Phase III |
| Tropisperon (Navoban/Sandoz) | Phase III |
| Selegiline (Sandoz/Somerset) | Phase III |
| Bretanezil (Roche) | Phase III |
| FG-7516 (Novo-Nordix/Schering) | Phase III |
| Nimodipine (Miles) | Phase III |

side effects. For example, stimulating the postsynaptic M-1 cholinergic receptors, while antagonizing the inhibitory M-2 presynaptic cholinergic receptor, might be a viable strategy (Whitehouse, 1991). One problem with the strategy to stimulate post-synaptic receptors is that there is some evidence of uncoupling of the M-1 receptor from its second messenger system (G protein) in AD (Flynn et al., 1991).

Other symptomatic treatments to attempt to improve cognition are based on an understanding of the abnormalities in other neurotransmitter systems in AD, such as the loss of noradrenergic cells in the locus coeruleus and serotonergic cells in raphe nuclei. The role of these systems in animals and man to support cognition are not clear, and it is also possible that alterations in monoaminergic systems may underlie some of the psychiatric symptoms, such as depression, psychosis, and agitation (Zweig et al., 1988). The selective inhibition of monoamine oxidase B with Deprenyl and blocking serotonergic reuptake with Citalopram have provided benefits in behavioral symptoms (Goad et al., 1991; Gottfries, 1990).

Several neuropeptides are affected in AD including somatostatin and corticotropin releasing factor (DeSouza et al., 1988; Beal and Martin, 1986). The relationship between alteration of neuropeptides and cognitive impairment remains unknown. Attempts to treat AD with vasopressin, angiotensin-converting enzyme inhibitors, and Naloxone (an opiate antagonist) have not demonstrated convincing proof of their benefit (Volger, 1991).

Intermediate strategies to slow the progression of the disease can be based on an understanding of the mechanisms that promote neuronal viability. Stimulation of excitatory amino acid receptors may contribute to cell death by enhancing calcium influx (Rothman and Olney, 1987). Milacemide, a glycine agonist that may enhance an inhibition of the glutamate NMDA receptor, is currently being tested as are calcium channel blockers. The role of these systems in AD is uncertain (Greenamyre and Young, 1989), and there may be more evidence for the role of excitatory amino acid damage in HD and possibly PD (Plaitakis, 1990; Perry and Hanson, 1990).

A large number of trophic factors have been described in the central nervous system, including nerve growth factor (NGF), which was originally described in the 1960s as having growth-promoting effects on the peripheral nervous system. Cholinergic basal forebrain neurons have specific receptors for NGF, and NGF has been used to enhance the viability of these cells in animals with experimental lesions and to improve learning and memory in these animals (Bond et al., 1989; Hefti et al., 1989). A variety of proteins related to NGF, including brain-derived neurotrophic factors, have also been described and may have therapeutic benefit in AD (Hefti and Schneider, 1991).

Clinical trials with NGF have been proposed in the United States, and a single patient in Sweden has been given intraventricular NGF by implanted infusion pump with unclear results (Olson, 1990). Although we do not have direct evidence supporting a pivotal role for NGF or related growth factors in AD, administration of NGF or the development of an analogue that crosses the blood-brain barrier may, nevertheless, slow the progression of the disease by preventing neuronal death (Phelps et al., 1989; Hefti et al., 1989).

Ultimately, a better understanding of the pathophysiology of AD could lead to treatments that prevent the onset of the disease or actually cure the disorder. The understanding of molecular mechanisms that lead to the deposition of amyloid and SPs and NFTs is of particular interest. Patients with FAD have been reported to have point mutations on chromosome 21 in the amyloid precursor gene (Goate et al., 1991). Repairing such a gene deficit or developing molecular strategies to prevent the proteolysis that allows the accumulation of beta-amyloid in SPs may lead to more effective therapies based on a rational understanding of the pathogenesis of the disorder.

## BEHAVIORAL MANAGEMENT

Because there are few curative medical interventions available for many people with dementia, especially those with AD (see the section on biological management), a sense of nihilism has pervaded the medical community regarding clinical care for these patients. However, this negativism overlooks both the hope for better drug treatments in the future and current behavioral, psychosocial, and environmental interventions that may improve quality of life for both patient and family (Mace and Rabins, 1981; Mace, 1990). Moreover, new innovations in health care, such as dementia-specific day care and special dementia units in nursing homes, are being developed.

Behavior management of a patient with demential begins with a comprehensive medical examination (Patterson and Whitehouse, 1990), accompanied by assessment of activities of daily living, home safety, and practical care issues. Nurses are particularly valuable in providing assessments of activities of daily living and the impact of the disease on family function in addition to educating families about the disease. An assessment of safety in the home and driving is a key part of this assessment. A social worker can assess family dynamics, community services, and financial resources. Often, a summary conference attended by the patient, caregiver and other family members, and the clinicians can be effective in providing an integrated diagnostic and prognostic view. When the diagnosis is made early in the course, the patient can participate in legal, financial, and long-term care planning. Since the course of dementing illnesses varies widely, and families differ in their ability to accept a changing situation, individualized plans should be crafted to suit the clinical circumstances. Knowledge of community resources (legal advice, community-based respite care such as home care, day care, and institutional care, e.g., nursing homes) is critical to planning for the future. The physician and other health workers can encourage early and appropriate use of services to prevent caregiver burnout. Appropriate attention to financial aspects of care, Medicaid and Medicare coverage and eligibility, as well as assessing private long-term care insurance is key.

Patients and families should be reassessed at regular intervals, or when a significant change in functioning occurs. Patients with dementia are especially vulnerable to conditions that cause excess disability, i.e., more cognitive impairment than can be explained by the primary disease itself (Martin and Whitehouse, 1990). Appropriate diagnosis and treatment of intercurrent medical and psychiatric disorders will ensure that the patient functions as well as possible throughout the illness (see Table 16-9).

Management of problem behaviors often consumes a large portion of caregiver time and energy and is often the cause for seeking medical attention. Psychiatric

**Table 16-9.** Excess Disability in Patients with Dementia: Causes, Examples, and Associated Behavioral Symptoms

| Cause | Examples | Associated Behavioral Symptoms |
|---|---|---|
| Illness | Upper respiratory infection | Delirium |
| | Urinary tract infection | Lethargy |
| | | Increased agitation |
| Pain | Constipation | Increased agitation |
| | Arthritis | Stubbornness |
| | Muscle cramp | Screaming, moaning |
| | Compression fracture | |
| Medications | Neuroleptics | Delirium |
| | | Akathisia |
| | | Dystonia |
| | | Tardive dyskinesia |
| | | Parkinsonian symptoms |
| | | Hypotension |
| | Minor tranquilizers | Depression |
| | | Delirium |
| | Antidepressants | Tremor |
| | | Dry mouth |
| | | Difficulty with urination |
| | | Delirium |
| | | Hypotension |
| Poor hearing | | Paranoia |
| Poor vision | | Illusions |
| | | Hallucinations |

From Mace et al., 1992.

symptoms including depression, hallucinations, delusions, paranoia, or insomnia are common in dementia (Patterson et al., 1990). Other symptoms such as wandering, repetitive actions, or intermittent agitation do not fit into standard psychiatric diagnostic categories but are a major cause of caregiver burden.

The first goal of management is to focus on elucidating the scope and impact of the problem behavior on the patient and family (Patterson and Whitehouse, 1990). The exact circumstances under which the behaviors manifest will often help identify precipitating factors. This process will usually suggest interventions, especially those requiring nonpharmacologic intervention. Medications should be reserved for situations where specific therapeutic goals can be identified (Mace, 1990), since psychoactive medications tend to further cloud cognition and may cause serious side effects, such as akinesia, or paradoxically akathisia, or increased agitation, especially in the elderly.

### Caregivers and Families

The caregiver and family need to provide an ever-increasing amount of support and structure to maintain the patient's well-being. This so-called "informal" care system provides 80–90% of all care (U.S. Congress Office of Technology Assessment, 1987).

The capacity of individuals in families to provide care varies widely, and is determined by factors such as relation to patient, gender, health status, and culture. Role conflict is frequent and may be a major contributor to caregiver stress. Psychological and physical abuse by caregivers has been recognized and may occur because caregivers do not understand the illness or are under severe stress (Haley et al., 1987b).

Support groups can provide families with information and an opportunity to share the positive and negative experiences associated with caregiving. The National Alzheimer's Association and affiliated local chapters can be a major source of support and information. While it is important to make caregivers aware of the appropriate illness-specific support groups, attendance may be less than 20% (U.S. Congress Office of Technology Assessment, 1987), due to the pressures of care and other demands. Studies evaluating the effect of support groups have found them generally to be a positive experience, and one study found that participation reduced the likelihood of patients requiring institutional care (Greene and Monahan, 1987; Haley et al., 1987a). More research is needed on ways to deliver support to caregivers and on the specific benefits of participation in support group activities.

## CONCLUSIONS

The study of dementia has had a brief history, enjoys an exciting present, and unfortunately faces an extended future. We conclude this chapter by reviewing our expectations of the challenges clinicians and researchers will face in the years to come.

### *Clinical Challenges*

In the future, a greater emphasis will be paid in our health-care systems to assessing the impact clinicians make on the quality of lives on individuals with diseases, particularly chronic diseases such as most dementias. Clinicians as well as researchers will be called on to demonstrate that their activities use resources effectively and will have a positive effect on individual patients and families as well as on society as a whole. Medicare and Medicaid pay for considerable amounts of acute and institutional chronic care, but community services that provide respite to families are relatively underfunded. The provision of home- and community-based services, such as day care, will likely increase. Targeting services to those most likely to use and benefit from them will be key.

In the future, the clinician caring for patients with dementia will also be called upon to address more systematically the ethical issues involved in the care of these patients. How can we encourage patients to, when competent, write advance directives to guide care during the later stages of terminal care? Should we condone passive euthanasia or allow active euthanasia? How do we balance the health-care needs of demented patients with those of nondemented and younger patients, including children. What are the roles of different disciplines in addressing the health-care needs of demented patients?

## Research Challenges

Just as the clinical care of cognitively impaired patients requires an interdisciplinary approach, so too do the many unanswered questions about dementia, involving fields spanning molecular biology to ethics.

### BIOLOGY

The major biological question in AD is why do cells die prematurely? Major advances are being made in understanding the formation of amyloid, but the connections between the abnormal processing of APP in AD and the process of neuronal death are as yet unclear. In familial AD, the selective vulnerability of specific neuronal populations needs to be explained given the abnormal gene is contained in all neurons. The specific characteristics of the neurons affected in the disease need to be better understood from a systems level, rather than just a molecular level. More concentrated efforts to relate basic neuroscience to the development of better diagnostic tests and therapeutic interventions need to be made. The degenerative dementias also challenge us to understand the molecular biology of normal aging and its relationship to these dementing illnesses.

### NEUROPSYCHOLOGY

Considerable clinical as well as biological variability occurs in different dementing illnesses. Dysfunction in specific neuronal populations is characteristic of many dementias, allowing opportunities to relate this specific pathology to specific clinical features. In addition to providing clues to understanding the biological substrates of intellectual activities, the behavioral disturbances in AD and related disorders may provide clues to understanding the biological basis of psychiatric symptoms, such as psychosis and depression. Functional neuroimaging studies in dementia should allow us unique vistas into understanding brain function and behavior.

We will be challenged in the future to go beyond the paper and pencil characterization of the cognitive deficits to understanding the relationships between these laboratory-assessed difficulties and the patient's functional abilities in activities of daily living. New assessment protocols are needed to help us make difficult decisions about how effective drugs should be in AD before we, as a society, approve them.

### SOCIOLOGICAL

At a time of constrained resources and strong societal pressures to improve our healthcare system, research on the impact of disease on family and community will become more important. The development of demonstration programs to improve the complex flow of patients and information among different organizations in our healthcare system will be emphasized. For example, the National Chronic Care Consortium represents 14 providers around the country that are trying to build bridges between acute and long-term care services for the frail elderly, such as those with dementia.

In sum, the challenges of dementia will only grow in the future. Taking on these challenges will be important, not only for patients with dementia, but also for other individuals with chronic disease. What we learn about the biology of AD, we will undoubtedly contribute to our understanding of other age-related diseases and aging itself. How we manage to improve the quality of care for patients and their families with these diseases will, similarly, provide leads to improving the health system for others with chronic illness. Thus, dementia, an important clinical problem in its own right, is also a lead issue for meeting other clinical and research challenges as well.

## ACKNOWLEDGMENTS

The authors acknowledge the support of the National Institute on Aging Alzheimer Disease Research Center grant (AG08012 01) and the Ohio Department of Aging Alzheimer Disease Research Center grant (ADR-2), and would also like to thank Cheryl Cowan for her help in preparing the manuscript.

## REFERENCES

Adams, R. D., Fisher, C. M., Hakim, S., Ojemann, R. G., and Sweet, W. H. (1965). Symptomatic occult hydrocephalus with "normal" cerebrospinal fluid pressure. *N. Engl. J. Med.* 273:117–126.

Albert, M. L. (1978). Subcortical dementia. In *Alzheimer's Disease, Senile Dementia and Related Disorders,* R. Katzman, R. D. Terry, and K. L. Bick (eds.). New York: Raven Press, pp. 173–180.

Albert, P. C., and Albert, M. L. (1984). History and scope of geriatric neurology. In *Clinical Neurology of Aging,* M. L. Albert (ed.). New York: Oxford University Press, pp. 3–8.

American Psychiatric Association (1987). *Diagnostic and Statistical Manual of Mental Disorders,* 3rd ed. Washington, D.C.: American Psychiatric Association.

Anderson, M. (1986). Normal pressure hydrocephalus. *Br. Med. J. 293:*837–838.

Asherson, R. A., Mercey, D., Phillips, G., Sheehan, N., Gharavi, A. E., Harris, E. N., and Hughes, G.R.V. (1987). Recurrent stroke and multi-infarct dementia in systemic lupus erythematosus: association with antiphospholipid antibodies. *Ann. Rheum. Dis. 46:*605–611.

Babikian, V., and Ropper, A. H. (1987). Binswanger's disease: a review. *Stroke 18:*2–12.

Baumhefner, R. W., Touirtellotte, W. W., Syndulko, K., Waluch, V., Ellison, G. W., Meyers, L. W., Cohen, S. N., Osborne, M., and Shapshak, P. (1990). Quantitative multiple sclerosis plaque assessment with magnetic resonance imaging. *Arch. Neurol. 47:*19–26.

Beal, M. F., and Martin, B. E. (1986). Neuropeptides in neurological disease. *Ann. Neurol. 20:*547–565.

Becker, P. M., Fensoner, J. R., Mulrow, C. D., Williams, B. C., and Vokaty, K. A. (1985). The role of lumbar puncture in the evaluation of dementia: the Veterans Association/Duke University Study. *J. Am. Geriatr. Soc. 33:*392–396.

Berg, L. (1988). Mild senile dementia of the Alzheimer type: diagnostic criteria and natural history. *Mt. Sinai J. Med. (N.Y.)* 55:87–96.

Blass, J. P., and Plum, F. (1983). Metabolic encephalopathies in older adults. In *Neurology of Aging,* R. Katzman and R. Terry (eds.). Philadelphia: F. A. Davis, pp. 189–214.

Bond, M. R. (1986). Neurobehavioral sequelae of closed head injury. In *Neuropsychological*

*Assessment of Neuropsychiatric Disorders*, I. Gran and K. H. Adams (eds.) New York: Oxford University Press, pp. 248–373.

Bond, N. W., Walton, J. and Pruss, J. (1989). Restoration of memory following septo-hippocampal grafts: a possible treatment for Alzheimer's disease. Biol. Psychol. 28:67–87.

Booss, J., and Thornton, G. F. (1986). *Infectious Diseases of the Central Nervous System.* Philadelphia: W. B. Saunders.

Braak, H., and Braak, E. (1989). Cortical and subcortical argyrophilic grains characterize a disease associated with adult onset dementia. *Neuropathol. Appl. Neurobiol. 15:*13–26.

Brandt, J., and Butters, N. (1986). The neuropsychology of Huntington's disease. *Trends in Neuroscience 9:*118–120.

Brandt, J., Folstein, S. E., Folstein, M. F. (1988). Differential cognitive impairment in Alzheimer's disease and Huntington's disease. *Ann. Neurol. 23:*555–561.

Bridge, T. P., and Wyatt, R. J. (1980). Paraphrenia: paranoid states of late life. I. European research. *J. Am. Geriatr. Soc. 28:*193–200.

Brown, P. (1980). An epidemiologic critique of Creutzfeldt-Jakob disease. *Epidemiol. Rev. 2:*113–135.

Brown, P., Cathala, F., Raubertas, R. F., Gajdusek, D. C., and Castainge, P. (1987). The epidemiology of Creutzfeldt-Jakob disease: conclusion of a 15-year investigation in France and review of the world literature. *Neurology 37:*895–904.

Brun, A. (1987). Frontal lobe degeneration of non-Alzheimer type. I. Neuropathology. *Arch. Gerontol. Geriatr. 6:*193–208.

Brun, A., and Englund, E. (1981). Regional pattern of degeneration in Alzheimer's disease: neuronal loss and histopathological grading. *Histopathology 5:*549–564.

Butters, N., Sax, D., Montgomery, K., and Tarlow, S. (1978). Comparison of the neuropsychological deficits associated with early and advanced Huntington's disease. *Arch. Neurol. 35:*585–589.

Choi, D. W. (1990). The role of glutamate neurotoxicity in diseases: hypoxic-ischemic neuronal death. *Annu. Rev. Neurosci. 13:*171–182.

Chun, C. H., Johnson, J. D., Hofstetter, M., and Raff, M. J. (1986). Brain abscess: a study of 45 consecutive cases. *Medicine 65:*415–431.

Ciompi, L. (1987). Review of follow-up studies on long-term evolution and aging in schizophrenia. In *Schizophrenia and Aging*, N. E. Miller and G. D. Cohen (eds.). New York: Guilford Press, pp. 37–51.

Clark, A. W., White, C. L. 3rd, Manz, H. J., Parhad, I. M., Curry, B., Whitehouse, P. J., Lehmann, J. and Coyle, J. T. (1986). Primary degenerative dementia without Alzheimer pathology. *Can. J. Neurol. Sci. 13*(Suppl. 4):462–470.

Cooper, A.J.L., and Plum, F. (1987). Biochemistry and physiology of brain ammonia. *Physiol. Rev. 67:*440–519.

Cordingley, G., Navarro, C., Brust, J.C.M., and Healton, E. B. (1981). Sarcoidosis presenting as senile dementia. *Neurology 31:*1148–1151.

Corkin, S. (1982). Some relationships between global amnesias and the memory impairments in Alzheimer's disease. In *Alzheimer's Disease: A Report of Progress in Research,* S. Corkin, K. L. Davis, J. H. Growdon, and E. Usdin (eds.). New York: Raven Press, pp. 149–164.

Crapper, D. R., Krishnan, S. S., and Dalton, A. J. (1973). Brain aluminum distribution in Alzheimer's disease and experimental neurofibrillary degeneration. *Science 180:*511–513.

Crapper-McLachlan, D. R., Dalton, A. J., Kruck, T.P.A., Bell, M. Y., Smith, W. L., Kalow, W., and Andrews, D. F. (1991). Intramuscular desferrioxamine in patients with Alzheimer's disease. *Lancet 337:*1304–1308; erratum published in *Lancet 337:*1618.

Crimson, M. L. (1990). Psychotropic drugs in the elderly: principles of use. *Am. Pharm. 30*:57–63.

Crook, T., Bartus, R. T., Ferris, S. H., Whitehouse, P., Cohen, G. D., and Gershon, S. (1986). Age-associated memory impairment: proposed diagnostic criteria and measures of clinical change—report of a National Institute of Mental Health Work Group. *Dev. Neuropsychol. 2*:261–276.

Cross, P. S., and Gurland, G. J. (1986). The epidemiology of dementing disorders. Contract report prepared for the Office of Technology Assessment, U.S. Congress.

Cummings, J. L., and Benson, D. F. (1983). *Dementia: A Clinical Approach*. Boston: Butterworths.

Cummings, J. L., Tomiyasu, V., Read, S., and Benson, D. F. (1984). Amnesia with hippocampal lesions after cardiopulmonary arrest. *Neurology 34*:679–681.

DeAngelis, L., Delattre, J.-Y., and Posner, J. B. (1989). Radiation-induced dementia in patients cured of brain metastasis. *Neurology 39*:789–796.

Desouza, E. B., Whitehouse, P. J., Folstein, S. E., Price, D. L. and Vale, W. W. (1987). Corticotropin-releasing hormone (CRH) is decreased in the basal ganglia in Huntington's disease. *Brain Res. 437*:355–359.

Desouza, E. B., Whitehouse, P. J., Price, D. L. and Vale, M. W. (1988). Abnormalities in Corticotropin-releasing hormone (CRH) in Alzheimer's disease and other human disorders. In *Corticotropin-Releasing Factor: Basic and Clinical Studies of a Neuropeptide*, E. B. Desouza and C. Nemeroff (eds.). Annals of the New York Academy of Sciences (Proceedings of the Hypothalamic-Pituitary-Adrenal Axis Revisited), CRC Press, Boca Raton, pp. 237–247.

Diaz, J. F., Merskey, H., Hachinski, V. C., Lee, D. H., Boniferro, M., Wong, C. J., Mirsen, T. R., and Fox, H. (1991). Improved recognition of leukaraiosis and cognitive impairment in Alzheimer's disease. *Arch. Neurol. 48*:1022–1025.

Dikmen, S., and Matthews, C. G. (1977). Effect of major motor seizure frequency upon cognitive-intellectual functions in adults. *Epilepsia 18*:21–29.

Dixon, P. E., Cayley, A.C.D., and Hoey, C. (1984). Tuberculous meningitis in the elderly. *Postgrad. Med. J. 6*:586–588.

Dodge, P. R. (1986). Sequelae of bacterial meningitis. *Pediatr. Infect. Dis. 5*:618–620.

Dodrill, C. B., and Troupin, A. S. (1976). Seizures and adaptive abilities. A case of identical twins. *Arch. Neurol. 33*:604–607.

Dooling, E. C., Schoene, W. C., and Richardson, E. P. (1974). Hallovorden-Spatz syndrome. *Arch. Neurol. 30*:70–83.

Duara, R., Grady, C., Haxby, J., Sundaram, M., Cutler, N. R., Heston, L., Moore, A., Schlageter, N., Larson, S., and Rapoport, S. I. (1986). Positron emission tomography in Alzheimer's disease. *Neurology 36*:879–887.

Dyken, P., and Krawiecki, N. (1983). Neurodegenerative diseases of infancy and childhood. *Ann. Neurol. 13*:351–364.

Evans, D. A., Funkenstein, H. H., Albert, M. S., Scherr, P. A., Cook, N. R., Chown, M. J., Hebert, L. E., Hennekens, C. H., and Taylor, J. O. (1989). Prevalence of Alzheimer's disease in a community population of older persons: higher than previously reported. *J.A.M.A. 262*:2551–2556.

Feher, E. P., Inbody, S. B., Nolan, B., and Pirozzolo, F. J. (1988). Other neurologic diseases with dementia as a sequelae. *Clin. Geriatr. Med. 4*:799–814.

Feinglass, E. J., Arnett, F. C., Dorsch, C. A., Zizic, T. M., and Stevens, M. B. (1976). Neuropsychiatric manifestations of systemic lupus erythematosus. *Medicine (Baltimore) 55*:323–339.

Ferris, S. H. (1990). Therapeutic strategies in dementia disorder. *Acta Neurol. Scand. Suppl.* *129*:23–26.

Feldman, E., and Plum, F. (1992). Metabolic dementia. In *Dementia*, P. J. Whitehouse (ed.). Philadelphia: F. A. Davis.

Filley, C. M., Heaton, R. K., Nelson, L. M., Burks, J. S., and Franklin, G. M. (1989). A comparison of dementia in Alzheimer's disease and multiple sclerosis. *Arch. Neurol. 46*:157–161.

Fleming, J. (1989). Sleep architecture changes in depression: interesting finding or clinically useful? *Prog. Neuropsychopharmacol. Biol. Psychiatry 13*:419–429.

Flynn, D. D., Weinstein, D. A., and Mash, D. C. (1991). Loss of high-affinity agonist binding to M1 muscarinic receptors in Alzheimer's disease: implication for the failure of cholinergic replacement therapies. *Ann. Neurol. 29*:256–262.

Folstein, M. F., and Powell, D. (1984). Is Alzheimer's disease inherited? A methodological review. *Integrative Psychiatry 2*:163–176.

Folstein, S. E. (1989). *Huntington's Disease: A Disorder of Families*. Baltimore: Johns Hopkins University Press.

Francis, P. T., and Bowen, D. M. (1989). Tacrine, a drug with therapeutic potential for dementia: Post-mortem biochemical evidence. *Can. J. Neurol. Sci. 16*:504–510.

Franklin, G. M., Heston, R. K., Nelson, L. M., Filley, C. M., and Seibert, C. (1988). Correlation of neuropsychological and MRI findings in chronic/progressive multiple sclerosis. *Neurology 38*:1826–1829.

Freeman, S. E., and Dawson, R. M (1991). Tacrine: a pharmacological review. *Prog. Neurobiol. 36*:257–277.

Friedland, R. P., Budinger, T. F., Ganz, E., Yano, Y., Mathis, C. A., Koss, B., Ober, B., Huesman, R. H., and Deezo, S. E. (1983). Regional cerebral metabolic alterations in dementia of the Alzheimer type: positron emission tomography with 18-F-fluorodeoxyglucose. *J. Comput. Assist. Tomogr. 7*:590–598.

Gallassi, R., Montagna, P., Morreale, A., Lorusso, S., Tinuper, P., Daidone, R., and Lugaresi, E. (1989). Neuropsychological electroencephalogram and brain computed tomography findings in motor neuron disease. *Eur. Neurol. 25*:115–120.

Gershell, W. J. (1981). Psychiatric manifestations and nutritional deficiencies in the elderly. In *Neuropsychiatric Manifestations of Physical Disease in the Elderly*, A. J. Levinson and R.C.W. Hall (eds.). New York. Raven Press, 119–124.

Gilman, S., Bloedel, J. R., and Lechtenberg, R. (1981). *Disorders of the Cerebellum*. Philadelphia: F. A. Davis.

Goad, D. L., Davis, C. M., Liem, P., Fusilier, C. C., McCormack, J. R., and Olsen, K. M. (1991). The use of selegiline in Alzheimer's patients with behavioral problems. *J. Clin. Psychiatry 52*:342–345.

Goate, A., Chartier-Harlin, M.-C., Mullan, M., Brown, J., Crawford, F., Fidani, L., Giuffra, L., Haynes, A., Irving, N., James, L., Mant, R., Newton, P., Rooke, K., Roques, P., Talbot, C., Pericak-Vance, M., Roses, A., Williamson, R., Rossor, M., Owen, M., and Hardy, J. (1991). Segregation of a missense mutation in the amyloid precursor protein gene with familial Alzheimer's disease. *Nature 349*:704–706.

Gottfries, C. G. (1990). Neurochemical aspects of dementia disorders. *Dementia 1*:56–64.

Graves, A. B., van Duijn, C. M., Chandra, V., Fratiglioni, L., Heyman, A., Jorm, A. F., Kokmen, E., Kondo, K., Mortimer, J. A., Rocca, W. A., Shalat, S. L., Soininen, H., and Hofman, A. (1991). Alcohol and tobacco consumption as risk factors for Alzheimer's disease: a collaborative re-analysis of case-control studies. *Int. J. Epidemiol. 20 (Suppl. 2)*:48–57.

Greenamyre, J. T., and Young, A. B. (1989). Excitatory amino acids and Alzheimer's disease. *Neurobiol. Aging 10*:593–602.

Greene, V. L., and Monahan, D. J. (1987). The effect of a professionally guided caregiver support and education group on institutionalization of care receivers. *Gerontologist* 27:716–721.

Greenwood, B. M., and Whittle, H. C. (1980). The pathogenesis of sleeping sickness. *Trans. Soc. Trop. Med. Hyg.* 74:716–25.

Guberman, A., Cantu-Reyna, G., Stuss, D., and Broughton, F. (1986). Nonconvulsive generalized status epilepticus: Clinical features, neuropsychological testing, and long-term follow-up. Neurology 36:1284–1291.

Gusella, J. F., Wexler, N. S., Conneally, P. M., Naylor, S. J., Anderson, M. A., Tanzi, R. E., Wathins, P. C., Ottina, K., Wallace, M. R., Sakaguchi, A. Y., Young, A. B., Shoulson, I., Bonilla, E., and Martin, J. B. (1983). A polymorphic DNA marker genetically linked to Huntington's disease. *Nature 306*:134–238.

Haase, G. R. (1977). Diseases presenting as dementia. In *Dementia*, C. E. Wells (ed.). Philadelphia: F. A. Davis, 27–67.

Hachinski, V. C., Lassen, N. A., and Marshall, J. (1974). Multi-infarct dementia: a case of mental deterioration in the elderly. *Lancet 2*:207–210.

Hachinski, V. C., Iliff, L. D., Zilkha, E., duBoulay, G. H., McAllister, V. L., Marshall, J., Ross-Russell, R. W., and Symon, L. (1975). Cerebral blood flow in dementia. *Arch. Neurol. 32*:632–637.

Hachinski, V. C., Potter, P., and Merskey, H. (1987). Leukoaraiosis. *Arch. Neurol. 44*:21–23.

Haley, W. E., Brown, S. L., and Levine, E. G. (1987a). Experimental evaluation of the effectiveness of group intervention for dementia caregivers. *Gerontologist 27*:376–382.

Haley, W. E., Levine, E. G., Brown, S. L., Berry, J. W., and Hughes, G. H. (1987b). Psychosocial, social, and health consequences of caring for a relative with senile dementia. *J. Am. Geriatr. Soc. 35*:405–411.

Hammerstrom, D. C., and Zimmer, B. (1985). The role of lumbar puncture in the evaluation of dementia: the University of Pittsburgh study. *J. Am. Geriatr. Soc. 33*:397–400.

Haroutunian, V., Santuci, A. C., and Davis, K. L. (1990). Implication of multiple transmitter system lesions for cholinergic therapy in Alzheimer's disease. *Prog. Brain Res. 84*:333–346.

Heaton, R. K., and Drexler, M. (1987). Clinical neuropsychological findings in schizophrenia and aging. In *Schizophrenia and Aging*, N. E. Miller and G. D. Cohen (eds.). New York: Guilford Press.

Hefti, F., Hartikka, J., and Knusel, B. (1989). Function of neurotrophic factors in the adult and aging brain and their possible use in the treatment of neurodegenerative diseases. *Neurobiol. Aging 10*:515–533.

Hefti, F., and Schneider, L. S. (1991). Nerve growth factor and Alzheimer's disease. *Clin. Neuropharmacol. 14*:S62–S76.

Henson, R. A., and Ulrich, H. (1982). *Cancer and the Nervous System: The Neurological Manifestation of Systemic Malignant Disease.* Oxford: Blackwell.

Hier, B., Hagenlocker, K., and Shindler, A. G. (1985). Language disintegration in dementia: effects of etiology and severity. *Brain Lang. 25*:117–133.

Hirano, A., Malamud, N., Elizan, T. S., and Kurland, L. T. (1966). Amyotrophic lateral sclerosis and parkinsonism-dementia complex on Guam. *Arch. Neurol. 15*:35–51.

Holmes, G. (1907). A form of familial degeneration of the cerebellum. *Brain 30*:466–489.

Holmes, G. (1931). Discussion on the mental symptoms associated with cerebral tumors. *Proc. R. Soc. Med. 24*:65–71.

Hudson, A. J. (1981). Amyotrophic lateral sclerosis and its association with dementia, parkinsonism, and other neurological disorder: a review. *Brain 104*:217–247.

Hulette, C. M., Earl, N. L., and Crain, B. J. (1992). Evaluation of cerebral biopsies for the diagnosis of dementia. *Arch. Neurol. 49*:28–31.

International League Against Epilepsy, Commission on Classification and Terminology (1981). Proposal for revised clinical and electroencephalographic classification of epileptic seizures. *Epilepsia 22*:489–501.

International League Against Epilepsy, Commission on Classification and Terminology (1985). Proposal for classification of epilepsis and epileptic syndromes. *Epilepsia 26*:268–278.

Jason, G. W., Pajurkova, E. M., Suchowersky, O., Hewitt, J., Hilbert, C., Reed, J., and Hayden, M. R. (1988). Pre-symptomatic neuropsychological impairment in Huntington's disease. *Arch. Neurol. 45*:769–773.

Kiloh, L. C. (1961). Pseudo-dementia. *Acta Psychiatr. Scand. 37*:336–351.

Klein, J. O., Feigin, R. D., and McCracken, G. H. (1986). Report of the task force on diagnosis and management of meningitis. *Pediatrics 78 (Suppl.)*:955–982.

Knopman, D. S., Mastri, A. R., Frey, W. H., Sung, J. H., and Rustan, T. (1990). Dementia lacking distinctive histologic features: a common non-Alzheimer degenerative dementia. *Neurology 40*:251–256.

Konigsmark, B. W., and Weiner, L. P. (1970). The olivopontocerebellar atrophies: a review. *Medicine 49*:227–241.

Ladurner, G., Iliff, L. D., and Lechner, H. (1982). Clinical factors associated with dementia in ischemic stroke. *J. Neurol. Neurosurg. Psychiatry 45*:97–101.

Langston, J. W., Bollard, P., Tetrud, J. W., and Irwin, I. (1983). Chronic parkinsonism in humans due to a product of meperidine-analog synthesis. *Science 219*:979–980.

Lanska, D. J., and Whitehouse, P. J. (1989). Huntington's disease. *Neurol. Neurosurg. Update. 8(11)*:1–8.

Larson, E. B., Kukull, W. A., Buchner, D., and Reifler, B. V. (1984). Adverse drug reactions associated with global cognitive impairment in elderly persons. *Ann. Intern. Med. 100*:417–423.

Larson, E. B., Reifler, B. V., Sumi, A. M., Canfield, C. G., and Chinn, N. M. (1985). Diagnostic evaluation of 200 outpatients with suspected dementia. *Gerontology 40*:536–543.

Larson, E. B., Reifler, B. V., Sumi, A. M., Canfield, C. G., and Chinn, N. M. (1986a). Diagnostic tests in the evaluation of dementia: a prospective study of 200 elderly outpatients. *Arch. Intern. Med. 146*:1917–1922.

Larson, E. B., Reifler, B. V., Suni, S. M., Canfield, C. G., and Chinn, N. M. (1986b). Features of potentially reversible dementia in elderly outpatients. *West. J. Med. 145*:488–492.

Lesser, R. P., Luders, H., Wyllie, E., Dinner, D. S., and Morris, H. H. III (1986). Mental deterioration in epilepsy. *Epilepsia 27(2)*:S105–S123.

Levy, R. M., Bredesen, D. E., and Rosenblum, M. L. (1985). Neurological manifestations of the acquired immunodeficiency syndrome (AIDS): experience at UCSF and review of the literature. *J. Neurosurg. 62*:475–495.

Lipowski, Z. J. (1981). Organic mental disorders: their history and classification with special referecent to DSM-III. In *Aging*, N. E. Miller and G. D. Cohen (eds.). New York: Raven Press, pp. 37–45.

Logigian, E. L., Kaplan, R. F., and Steere, A. C. (1990). Chronic neurologic manifestations of Lyme disease. *N. Engl. J. Med. 323*:1438–1444.

Mace, N. L. (1990). Management of problem behaviors. In *Dementia Care: Patient, Family and Community*, N. L. Mace (ed.). Baltimore: Johns Hopkins University Press. pp. 74–112.

Mace, N. L., and Rabins, P. V. (1981). *The Thirty-Six Hour Day: A Family Guide to Caring for Persons with Alzheimer's Disease, Related Dementing Illnesses and Memory Loss in Later Life*. Baltimore: Johns Hopkins University Press.

Madden, J. J., Lohan, J. A., Kaplan, L. A., and Manfredi, M. M. (1952). Nondementing psychoses in older persons. *J.A.M.A.* 150:1567–1570.

Malamud, N. (1967). Psychiatric disorders with intracranial tumors of the limbic system. *Arch. Neurol.* 17:113–123.

Markesbery, W. R., Ehmann, W. D., Hossain, T.I.M., Alauddin, M., and Goodin, D. T. (1981). Instrumental neutron activation analysis of brain aluminum in Alzheimer's disease and aging. *Ann. Neurol.* 10:511–516.

Marsden, C. D., and Harrison, M.J.G. (1972). Outcome of investigation of patients with presenile dementia. *Br. Med. J.* 2:249–252.

Martin, J. B., and Reichlin, S. (1987). *Clinical Neuroendocrinology*, 2nd ed. Philadelphia: F. A. Davis.

Martin, R. M., and Whitehouse, P. J. (1990). The clinical care of patients with dementia. In *Dementia Care: Patient, Family, and Community*, N. L. Mace (ed.). Baltimore: Johns Hopkins University Press.

Martyn, C. N., Barker, D.J.P. Osmond, C., Harris, E. C., Edwardson, J. A., and Lacey, R. F. (1989). Geographical relationship between Alzheimer's disease and aluminum in drinking water. *Lancet* i:59–62.

Mayeux, R., Stern, Y., and Williams, J.B.W. (1986). Clinical and biochemical features of depression in Parkinson's disease. *Am. J. Psychiatry* 143:756–759.

McAllister, T. W., and Price, T.R.P. (1982). Severe depressive pseudodementia with and without dementia. *Am. J. Psychiatry* 139:626–629.

McArthur, J. C. (1987). Neurologic manifestations of AIDS. *Medicine* 66:407–437.

McKhann, G., Drachman, D., Folstein, M., Katzman, R., Price, D., and Stadian, E. (1984). Clinical diagnosis of Alzheimer's disease: report of the NINCDS-ADRDA work group under the auspices of Department of Health and Human Services Task Force on Alzheimer's Disease. *Neurology* 34:939–944.

Meador, K. J., Loring, D. W., Huh, K., Gallagher, B. B., and King, D. W. (1990). Comparative cognitive effects of anticonvulsants. *Neurology* 40:391–394.

Meissen, G. J., Meyers, R. H., Mastromauro, C. A., Koroshetz, W. J., Klinger, K. W., Farrer, L. A., Watkins, P. A., Gusella, J. F., Bird, E. D., and Martin, J. B. (1988). Predictive testing for Huntington's disease with use of a linked DNA marker. *N. Engl. J. Med.* 318:535–542.

Mendez, M. F., Mendez, M. A., Martin, R., Smyth, K. A., and Whitehouse, P. J. (1990). Complex visual disturbances in Alzheimer's disease. *Neurology* 40:439–443.

Minden, S. L., and Schiffer, R. B. (1990). Affective disorders in multiple sclerosis. Review and recommendations for clinical research. *Arch. Neurol.* 47:98–104.

Mirsen, T. R., Lee, D. H., Wong, C. J., Diaz, J. F., Fox, A. J., and Hachinski, V. C. (1991). Clinical correlates of white matter changes on magnetic resonance imaging scans of the brain. *Arch. Neurol.* 48:1015–1021.

Mitsuyama, Y., Kogoh, H., and Ata, K. (1985). Progressive dementia with motor neuron disease: an additional case report and neuropathological review of 20 cases in Japan. *Eur. Arch. Psychiatr. Neurol. Sci.* 235:1–8.

Montgomery, G. K., and Erickson, L. M. (1987). Neuropsychological perspectives in amyotrophic lateral sclerosis. *Neurol. Clin.* 5:61–81.

Moore, P. M., and Cupps, T. R. (1983). Neurological complications of vasculitis. *Ann. Neurol.* 14:155–167.

Morita, K., Halya, H., Ikeda, T., and Namba, M. (1987). Presenile dementia combined with amyotrophy: a review of 34 Japanese cases. *Arch. Gerontol. Geriatr.* 6:263–277.

Murrell, J., Farlow, M., Ghetti, B., and Benson, M. D. (1991). A mutation in the amyloid precursor protein associated with hereditary Alzheimer's disease. *Science* 254:97–99.

Navia, B. A., Jordan, B. D., and Price, R. W. (1986). The AIDS dementia complex: I. Clinical features. *Ann. Neurol. 19:*517–524.

Nordberg, A. (1990). Pharmacological modulation of transmitter activity in Alzheimer's brains—an experimental model. *Acta Neurol. Scand. [Suppl] 129:*17–20.

Office of Medical Applications of Research, Consensus Conference on Dementia, National Institutes of Health (1987). Differential diagnosis of dementing diseases. *J.A.M.A. 258:*3411–3416.

Oldstone, M.B.A. (1984). Viruses can alter cell function without causing cell pathology: disordered function leads to imbalance of homeostasis and disease. In *Concepts in Viral Pathogenesis*, A. L. Notkins and M.B.A. Oldstone (eds.) New York: Springer-Verlag.

Olson, L. (1990). Grafts and growth factors in CNS. Basic science with clinical promise. *Stereotact. Funct. Neurosurg. 54:*250–267.

Pachner, A. R., Duray, P., and Steere, A. C. (1989). Central nervous system manifestations of Lyme disease. *Arch. Neurol. 46:*790–795.

Padgett, B. L., and Walker, D. L. (1983). Urologic and serologic studies of progressive multifocal leukoencephalopathy. *Prog. Clin. Biol. Res. 105:*107–117.

Palma, G. (1987). Paraneoplastic syndromes of the nervous system. *West. J. Med. 142:*787–796.

Patterson, J. V., Michalewski, H. J., and Starr, A. (1988). Latency variability of the components of auditory event-related potentials to infrequent stimuli in aging, Alzheimer-type dementia, and depression. *Electroencephalogr. Clin. Neurophysiol. 71:*450–460.

Patterson, M. B., Schnell, A., Martin, R. J., Mendez, M. F., Smyth, K., and Whitehouse P. J. (1990). Assessment of behavioral and affective symptoms in Alzheimer's disease. *J. Geriatr. Psychiatry Neurol. 3:*21–30.

Patterson, M. B., and Whitehouse, P. J. (1990). The diagnostic assessment of patients with dementia. In *Dementia Care: Patient, Family, and Community*, N. L. Mace (ed.). Baltimore: Johns Hopkins University Press, pp. 3–21.

Pericak-Vance, M. A., Bebout, J. L., Gaskell, P. C., Yamaoka, L. N., Hung, W.-Y., Alberts, M. J., Walker, A. P., Bartlett, R. J., Haynes, C. A., Welsh, K. A., Earl, N. L., Heyman, A., Clark, C. M., and Roses, A. D. (1991). Linkage studies in familial Alzheimer's disease: evidence for chromosome 19 linkage. *Am. J. Hum. Genet. 48:*1034–1050.

Perry, T. L., and Hansen, B. A. (1990). What neurotoxin kills striatal neurons in Huntington's disease? Clues from neurochemical studies. *Neurology 40:*20–24.

Petersen, B., and Dam, M. (1986). Memory disturbances in epileptic patients. *Acta Neurol. Scand 74 [Suppl. 109]:*11–14.

Peyser, J. M., Rao, S. M., LaRocca, N. C., and Kaplan, E. (1990). Guidelines for neuropsychological research in multiple sclerosis. *Arch. Neurol. 47:*94–97.

Phelps, C. H., Gage, F. H., Growdon, J. H., Hefti, F., Harbaugh, R., Johnston, M. V., Khachaturian, Z. S., Mobley, N. C., Price, D. L., and Raskind, M. (1989). Potential use of nerve growth factor to treat Alzheimer's disease. *Neurobiol. Aging 10:*205–207.

Pirozzolo, F. J., Christense, K. J., Ogl, K. M., Hansch, E. C., and Thompson, W. E. (1981). Simple and choice reaction time in dementia: clinical implications. *Neurobiol. Aging 2:*113–117.

Plaitakis, A. (1990). Glutamate dysfunction and selective motor neuron degeneration in amyotrophic lateral sclerosis: a hypothesis. *Ann. Neurol. 28:*3–8.

Plum, F. (1979). Dementia: an approaching epidemic. *Nature 279:*372–373.

Poser, C. M., Paty, D. W., Scheinberg, L., McDonald, W. I., Davis, F. A., Ebers, G. C., Johnson, K. P., Sibley, W. A., Silberberg, D. H., and Tourtellotte, W. W. (1983). New diagnostic criteria for multiple sclerosis: guidelines for research protocols. *Ann. Neurol. 13(3):*227–231.

Prichard, J. C. (1837). *A Treatise on Insanity*. Philadelphia: Haswell, Barrington, and Haswell.

Prusiner, S. B. (1987). Prions and neurodegenerative diseases. *N. Engl. J. Med. 317*:1571–1581.

Rabins, P. V., Merchant, A., and Nestadt, G. (1983). Criteria for diagnosing reversible dementia caused by depression: validation by 2-year follow up. *Br. J. Psychiatry 144*:488–492.

Rabins, P. V., Pearlson, G., and Strauss, M. (1992). Cognitive impairment in psychiatric syndromes. In *Dementia*, P. J. Whitehouse (ed.). Philadelphia: F. A. Davis.

Rao, S. M. (1986). Neuropsychology of multiple sclerosis: a critical review. *J. Clin. Exp. Neuropsychol. 8*:503–542.

Rao, S. M., Leo, G. J., Bernardin, L., and Unverzagt, F. (1991). Cognitive dysfunction in multiple sclerosis. I. Frequency, patterns, and prediction. *Neurology 41*:685–691.

Rao, S. M., Leo, G. J., Haughton, V. M., St. Aubin-Faubert, P., and Bernardin, L. (1989). Correlation of magnetic resonance imaging with neuropsychological testing in multiple sclerosis. *Neurology 39*:161–166.

Reding, M., Haycox, J., and Blass, J. (1985). Depression in patients referred to a dementia clinic. *Arch. Neurol. 42*:894–896.

Reiffler, B. V. (1986). Mixed cognitive-affective disturbances in the elderly: a new classification. *J. Clin. Psychiatry 47*:354–356.

Reynolds, C. F., Kupfer, D. J., Hoch, C. C., Stack, J. A., Houck, P. R., and Sewitch, D. E. (1986). Two-year follow up of elderly patients with mixed depression and dementia. *J. Am. Geriatr. Soc. 34*:793–799.

Rezek, D. L., Morris, J. C., Fulling, K. H., and Gado, M. H. (1987). Periventricular white matter lucencies in senile dementia of the Alzheimer type and in normal aging. *Neurology 37*:1365–1368.

Ripich, D. N., Vertes, D., Whitehouse, P., Fulton, S., and Ekelman, B. (1991). Turn-taking and speech act patterns in the discourse of senile dementia of the Alzheimer's type patients. *Brain Lang. 40*:330–342.

Roberts, A. H. (1969). *Brain Damage in Boxers*. London: Pitman.

Rocca, W. A., Amaducci, L. A., and Schoenberg, B. S. (1986). Epidemiology of clinically diagnosed Alzheimer's disease. *Ann. Neurol. 19*:415–424.

Rosen, W. G., Terry, R. D., Fuld, P. A., Katzman, R., and Peck, A. (1980). Pathological verification of ischemic score in differentiation of dementias. *Ann. Neurol. 7*:486–488.

Rosenberg, R. N. (1982). Amyotrophy in multisystem genetic diseases. In *Human Motor Neuron Diseases*, L. P. Rowland (ed.). New York: Raven Press. pp. 149–157.

Rothman, S. M., and Olney, J. W. (1987). Excitotoxicity and the NMDA receptor. *Trends Neurosci. 7*:299–302.

Sagar, H. J., Cohen, N. J., Sullivan, E. G., Corkin, S., and Growdon, J. H. (1988). Remote memory function in Alzheimer's disease and Parkinson's disease. *Brain 111*:185–206.

Sam, M., Gutmann, L., Schochet, S. S. Jr., and Doshi, H. (1991). Pick's disease: a case clinically resembling amyotrophic lateral sclerosis. *Neurology 41*:1831–1833.

Sandyk, R., Bamford, C., Iacono, R. P., and Gillman, M. A. (1987). Cerebral cysticercosis presenting as progressive dementia. *Int. J. Neurosci. 35*:251–254.

Schaffert, D. A., Johnsen, S. D., Johnson, P. C., and Drayer, B. P. (1989). Magnetic resonance imaging in pathologically proven Hallovorden-Spatz disease. *Neurology 39*:440–442.

Schmahmann, J. D. (1991). An emerging concept: the cerebellar contribution to higher function. *Arch. Neurol. 48*:1178–1187.

Schumacher, G. A., Beebe, G., Kibler, R. F., Kurland, L. T., Kurtzke, J. F., McDowell, F., Nagler, B., Sibley, W. A., Tourtellotte, W. W., and Willmon, T. L. (1965). Problems of experimental trials of therapy in multiple sclerosis: report by the panel on the evaluation of experimental trials of therapy in multiple sclerosis. *Ann. N.Y. Acad. Sci. 122*:552–568.

Simon, R. P. (1985). Neurosyphilis. *Arch. Neurol. 42*:606–613.

Smith, J. S., and Kiloh, L. G. (1981). The investigation of dementia: results in 200 consecutive admissions. *Lancet* 2:824–827.

Spar, J. E., and Gerner, R. (1982). Does the dexamethasone suppression test distinguish dementia from depression? *Am. J. Psychiatry* 139:238–240.

Stern, B. J., Krumholz, A., Johns, C., Scott, P., and Nissim, J. (1985). Sarcoidosis and its neurological manifestations. *Arch. Neurol.* 42:909–917.

St. George-Hyslop, P. H., Tanzi, R. E., Polinsky, R. J., Haines, J. L., Nee, L., Watkins, P. C., Meyers, R. H., Feldman, R. G., Pollen, D., Drachman, E., Growdon, J., Bruni, A., Foncin, J. F., Salmon, G., Fromeld, P., Amaducci, L., Sorgi, S., Placentini, S., Stewart, G. D., Hobbs, W., Conneally, P. M., and Gusella, J. F. (1987). The genetic defect causing familial Alzheimer's disease maps on chromosome 21. *Science* 235:885–890.

Strobos, R. J. (1974). Temporal lobe tumors. In *Handbook of Clinical Neurology: Tumors of the Brain and Skull, Pt II*, Vol. 17, P. J. Vinken and G. W. Bruyn (eds.). Amsterdam: North Holland Publishing Co., pp. 281–295.

Swanson, J. W., Kelly, J. J., and McConahey, W. M. (1981). Neurologic aspects of thyroid dysfunction. *Mayo Clin. Proc.* 56:504–512.

Syndulko, K., Hansch, E. C., Cohen, S. N., Pearce, I. W., Goldberg, Z., Montan, B., Tourtellotte, W. W., and Potrin, A. R. (1982). Long-latency event related potentials in normal aging and dementia. In *Clinical Application of Evoked Potentials in Neurology*, J. Courjon, F. Maugierer, and M. Revol (eds.). New York: Raven Press, pp. 279–285.

ter Meulen, V., Stephenson, J. R., and Kreth, W. H. (1983). Subacute sclerosing panencephalitis. In *Virus-Host Interactions: Receptors, Persistence, and Neurological Disease*, H. Fraekel-Conrat and R. R. Wagner (eds.). New York: Plenum Press, pp. 766–769.

Terry, R. D., Maslia, H., Salmon, D. P., Butters, N., DeTeresa, R., Hill, R., Hansen, L. A., and Katzman, R. (1991). Physical basis of cognitive alterations in Alzheimer's disease: synapse loss is the major correlate of cognitive impairment. *Ann. Neurol.* 30:572–580.

Teschan, P. E., and Arrief, A. I. (1985). Uremia and dialysis encephalopathies. In *Cerebral Energy Metabolism and Metabolic Encephalopathy*, D. W. McCandless (ed.). New York: Plenum, pp 268–285.

Tierney, M. C., Fisher, R. H., Lewis, A. J., Zorzitto, M. L., Snow, W. G., Reid, D. W., and Nieuwstraten, P. (1988). The NINCDS-ADRDA work group criteria for the clinical diagnosis of probable Alzheimer's disease: a clinicopathologic study of 57 cases. *Neurology* 38:359–364.

Tomlinson, B. E., Blessed, G., and Roth, M. (1968). Observations on the brains of non-demented old people. *J. Neurol. Sci.* 7:205–242.

Trimble, M. R. (1984). Dementia in epilepsy. *Acta Neurol. Scand.* 99 [Suppl.]:99–104.

Trimble, M. R. (1987). Anticonvulsant drugs and cognitive function: a review of the literature. *Epilepsia* 28 (Suppl. 3):537–545.

Trimble, M. R., and Thompson, P. J. (1986). Neuropsychological aspects of epilepsy. In *Neuropsychological Assessment of Neuropsychiatric Disorders*, I. Grant and K. H. Adams (eds.). New York: Oxford University Press, pp. 321–346.

U.S. Congress, Office of Technology Assessment (1987). *Losing a Million Minds: Confronting the Tragedy of Alzheimer's Disease and Other Dementias*, OTA-BA-323, Washington, D.C.: U.S. Government Printing.

Uzzel, B. P., Langfitt, T. W., and Dolinskas, C. A. (1987). Influence of injury severity on quality of survival after head injury. *Surg. Neurol.* 27:419–429.

Van den Burg, W., Van Zomeran, A. H., Minderhound, J. M., Prange, A. J., and Meijer, N.S.A. (1987). Cognitive impairment in patients with multiple sclerosis and mild physical disability. *Arch. Neurol.* 44:494–501.

VanGool, W. A., and Bolhuis, P. A. (1991). Cerebrospinal fluid markers of Alzheimer's disease. *J. Am. Geriatr. Assoc. 39*:1025–1039.

Victor, M., Adams, R. D., and Collins, G. H. (1989). *The Wernicke-Korsakoff Syndrome*, 2nd ed. Philadelphia: F. A. Davis.

Vinters, V. (1987). Cerebral amyloid angiopathy. A critical review. *Stroke 18*:311–324.

Volger, B. W. (1991). Alternatives in the treatment of memory loss in patients with Alzheimer's disease. *Clin. Pharm. 10*:447–456.

Walker, D. L. (1985). Progressive multifocal leukoencephalopathy. In *Handbook of Clinical Neurology*, Vol. 47: *Demyelinating Diseases*, P. J. Vinken, G. W. Bruyn, H. L. Klawans, and J. C. Koetsier (eds.). Amsterdam, Elsevier, pp. 503–524.

Wallesch, C. W., and Fehrenbach, R. A. (1988). On the neurolinguistic nature of language abnormalities in Huntington's disease. *J. Neurol. Neurosurg. Psychiatry 51*:367–373.

Wechsler, A. F., Verity, M. A., Rosenschein, S., Fried, I., and Scheibel, A. B. (1982). Pick's disease: a clinical, computed tomographic, and histologic study with Golgi impregnation observations. *Arch. Neurol. 39*:287–290.

Weinger, R. S. (1981). Psychiatric manifestations of hepatopoietic system disease. In *Neuropsychiatric Manifestations of Physical Disease in the Elderly*, Levinson, A. J. and R.C.W. Hall (eds.). New York: Raven Press, pp. 83–91.

Wells, C. E. (1979). Pseudodementia. *Am. J. Psychiatry 136*:894–896.

Wells, C. E. (1982). Refinements in the diagnosis of dementia. *Am. J. Psychiatry 139*:621–626.

Whitehouse, P. J. (1986). The concept of cortical and subcortical dementia: another look. *Ann. Neurol. 19*:1–6.

Whitehouse, P. J. (1991). Biochemical and morphological aspects of pathologic brain aging. In: Crook, T. Gershon S. (eds): Diagnosis and treatment of adult-onset cognitive disorders. Psymark Communication, 1991, pp. 1–11.

Whitehouse, P. J., and Kennedy, J. S. (1991). Intramuscular desferroxiamine in Alzheimer's disease. *ACP Journal Club* (A supplement to *Annals of Internal Medicine*) 115:44.

Whitehouse, P. J., Price, D. L., Struble, R. G., Clark, A. W., Coyle, J. T., and DeLong, M. R. (1982). Alzheimer's disease and senile dementia: loss of neurons in the basal forebrain. *Science 215*:1237–1239.

Whitehouse, P. J., and Unnerstall, J. R. (1988). Neurochemistry of dementia. *Eur. Neurol.* 28 (Suppl. 1):36–41.

Whitehouse, P. J., Vale, W. W., Zweig, R. M., Singer, H. S., Mayeux, R., Kuhar, M. J., Price, D. L., and Desouza, E. B. (1987). Reductions in corticotropin releasing factor-like immunoreactivity in cerebral cortex in Alzheimer's disease, Parkinson's disease, and progressive supranuclear palsy. *Neurology 37*:905–909.

Zweig, R. M., Ross, C. A., Hedreen, J. C., Steele, C., Cardillo, J. E., Whitehouse, P. J., Folstein, M. F., and Price, D. L. (1988). The neuropathology of aminergic nuclei in Alzheimer's disease. *Ann. Neurol. 24*:233–242.

# 17

# Recovery and Treatment

ANDREW KERTESZ

The study of neurobehavioral recovery is more than just a practical consideration for the clinician in providing a prognosis or baseline for therapy. It is also important because of the theoretical implications for cerebral reorganization. The study of recovery from central nervous system (CNS) lesions in humans has been difficult because it requires that patients be followed for months or years. Clinicians observing patients in the acute state often do not have the opportunity to follow them this long, and rehabilitation specialists rarely see them during the early stages of their illness. Assessing the efficacy of treatment is complicated by the difficulty of finding matching controls to determine the extent of spontaneous recovery. Those interested primarily in clinical and pathological diagnosis often disregard changes in performance and tend to view the neuropsychological deficit as stable. Despite these pitfalls, a considerable body of information has accumulated on the recovery of cognitive functions. There are several recent reviews of various aspects of recovery, mostly from a biological point of view (Waxman, see Kertesz, 1988; Finger and Stein, 1982). In this chapter, I will attempt to cover the recovery of cognitive function in human brain damage. The mechanisms underlying recovery of cognitive, or for that matter, other CNS functions are incompletely understood. Before discussing the patterns of recovery in specific clinical situations, it is worthwhile to review, briefly, the major theories proposed to explain recovery of function, as well as some of the experimental evidence supporting these theories.

## THEORETICAL MECHANISMS OF RECOVERY

### *First-Stage Recovery*

Recovery from brain damage due to stroke or trauma can be divided into two stages. The first stage is related to recovery from the acute effects of metabolic and membrane failure, ionic and transmitter imbalance, hemorrhage, cellular reaction, and edema. The reestablishment of the circulation in the "ischemic penumbra" (Kohlmeyer, 1976; Astrup et al., 1981) or reperfusion after thrombolysis (Zivin et al., 1985) are possible early mechanisms of recovery. The ischemic threshold of cerebral perfusion for membrane failure is around 8 ml/100 g/min. Therefore, damage can be reversed if blood flow can be increased. Rapid recovery from neurological deficit after a stroke is often attributed to recovery of function by the cells in this area of partial ischemia or ischemic penumbra.

Alterations in tissue water and electrolytes are responsible for some of the early changes in the first stage of recovery. The initial pharmacologic treatment of trauma includes attempts to control cerebral edema. Corticosteroids are controversial in trauma and contraindicated in stroke edema, although undoubtedly valuable in brain tumor. Hyperosmolar agents, such as mannitol and glycerol, reduce brain volume and increase cerebral blood flow, but most of the acutely effective drugs unfortunately have only a temporary effect, and some even produce rebound edema.

One of the important electrolyte changes in acute ischemia and trauma is the increase of intracellular calcium, which inhibits mitochondrial respiration. Calcium activates phospholipase and other lysosomal enzymes, destroying mitochondria and the cytoskeleton. Impaired membrane permeability increases calcium influx, which seriously interferes with neuronal functioning. Calcium channel antagonists not only inhibit calcium influx, but also prevent the postischemic reduction of cerebral blood flow and reduce mortality in experimental animals. Some excitatory amino acids, particularly glutamate, influence calcium channels, and since calcium influx is considered a major mechanism of injury, pharmacological agents inhibiting the glutamate cascade and calcium channels may promote early recovery (Gelmers et al., 1988; Stevens and Yaksh, 1990). Another mechanism of damage is the accumulation of free radicals. Agents, called Lazaroids, that mop up free radicals may promote early recovery (Tazaki et al., 1988). The restoration of high-energy phosphates depleted by ischemia also contributes to early recovery (Argentino et al., 1989).

The first few days and weeks after the onset of a stroke may be a time of critical regrowth, when partially damaged neurons start to regenerate and other neurons form new connections to compensate for ones that have been lost. Feeney and Sutton (1987) suspected that a depression of the catecholamine neurotransmitter system might contribute to behavioral deficits after a stroke. Amphetamines, which increase catecholamine transmission, produced a lasting improvement in their study.

### Second-Stage Recovery

This chapter will focus on the second stage of recovery of cognitive function that takes place months, even years, after injury. Its mechanisms remain largely unknown. A significant amount of physiological and functional recovery in this stage is probably related to intact structures compensating for the functional loss. Axonal regrowth and collateral sprouting are important mechanisms in the peripheral nervous system, and in certain instances, also in the CNS. However, in the large lesions in humans that cause focal cognitive or language loss, compensation is likely effected by (1) ipsilateral cortical structures physiologically and anatomically connected to damaged structures, (2) contralateral homologous cortical areas, or (3) subcortical systems hierarchically and physiologically related to the damaged structures. Some of the theories of how cognitive recovery takes place will be summarized below.

THEORY OF EQUIPOTENTIALITY AND THE EMBRYOGENETIC ANALOGY

The repeated observation that recovery occurs after destruction of a brain area leads to the conclusion that a particular function cannot be localized to a portion of the brain and contradicts the idea of rigid localization of function in the nervous system. Flourens (1824), one of the earliest opponents of cortical localization, demonstrated recovery after ablative experiments in pigeons and chickens. Lashley (1938) based his well-known theory of equipotentiality on similar extensive ablations in rats. He also found 18 cases in the clinical literature in which he could correlate the degree of recovery from motor aphasia with the estimated magnitude of lesions in the frontal lobe. He considered this analogous to the finding that learning in brain-lesioned animals was positively correlated with the amount of remaining intact cortical tissue, and negatively with the extent of ablation. Lashley compared the plasticity of cerebral cortex to the embryogenetic capacity of the organism to develop fully from a fertilized ovum. In this view, recovery would represent a continuation of the growth capacity of the organism that it has manifested in its earlier development. Lashley also reviewed the evidence that there are certain basic areas of the cerebral cortex that are required to remain intact for compensation to take place. One of the prime examples of the concept of essential cortex is the visual striate cortex in man.

REDUNDANCY VICARIOUS FUNCTIONING

A somewhat different theory implies that there is a biological protective mechanism built into the organism, anticipating injury. This assumes a redundancy of structures that can substitute for the damaged areas. The idea that some neuronal structures can take over functions that they were not associated with previously is called "vicarious functioning." This theory was first proposed by Fritsch and Hitzig (1870) and subsequently promoted by Munk (1881), who thought that regions of the brain previously "not occupied" could assume certain functions. Pavlov also argued for vicarious functioning and a large factor of redundancy stating that there were many potential conditioned reflex paths that are never used by the normal organisms. Lashley (1938), on the other hand, thought that preservation of a part of a system concerned with the same function is necessary. Bucy (1934) performed "reverse ablations," removing areas first that were shown previously to be necessary for recovery and finding no deficits, which indicated that areas needed for recovery do not necessarily contribute to normal function. Clinically, it is evident that right-hemisphere lesions do not cause aphasia in most people, even though the right hemisphere subserves some language functions and may play a role in recovery.

HEMISPHERIC SUBSTITUTION

Fritsch and Hitzig (1870) observed dogs after unilateral cortical lesions and proposed that the opposite hemisphere was taking over motor function for the injured hemisphere. In adult animals, however, destruction of an analogous area in the opposite hemisphere did not interrupt recovery. In humans, observations of patients with hemispherectomies (Smith, 1966) and callosal sections (Gazzaniga, 1970) provided evidence that the right hemisphere is capable of assuming some speech functions, such as comprehension (nouns better than verbs) and automatic nonpropositional speech. Kinsbourne (1971) argued that the right hemisphere may be the source of some aphasic speech since intracarotid sodium amytol injection on the right produced aphasia again in patients who had recovered from aphasia caused by left-hemisphere strokes. In the adult, however, the extent to which this recovery occurs is finite, both in cases of hemispherectomy and in global aphasics. The behavior of hemispherectomized adult patients is very similar to the behavior of global aphasics with extensive perisylvian infarction, suggesting that remaining language function in global aphasia is probably subserved entirely by the right hemisphere. That the restitution of speech is often due to the activity of the opposite hemisphere is known as Henschen's axiom. Henschen (1922) gave credit to Wernicke and other contemporaries for this principle. Nielsen (1946) further advocated the idea that the variable extent of recovery is related to the variable capacity of the right hemisphere to subserve speech. Geschwind (1969) also believed there is a considerable amount of individual variation in hemispheric substitution. Some people can make use of certain commissural connections and can activate some cortical mechanisms in the right hemisphere more than others. Recent studies of cerebral blood flow with xenon 133 also revealed right-hemisphere hypometabolism in aphasic strokes, the extent of which correlated with recovery to a modest degree (Knopman et al., 1984). Positron emission tomography (PET) studies of cerebral metabolism showed a great deal of hypometabolism surrounding, but also remote from cerebral infarcts, thus suggesting that not only surrounding areas but also homologous areas in the contralateral hemisphere play a role in compensation (Metter et al., 1981).

HIERARCHICAL REPRESENTATION

Jackson (1873) promoted the idea that the nervous system is organized hierarchically, with higher levels controlling lower ones. Function is represented at several levels. Damage at a higher levels releases lower ones from inhibition and leads to "compensation." Geschwind (1974) cited examples of neuronal systems that could take over function when released by destruction of higher centers: the spinal cord innervation of the diaphragm, which occurs when brainstem structures are damaged, is one such system. The most frequently mentioned examples of hierarchical representation are the multiplex cortical sensory systems (Woolsey and Van der Loos, 1970) and the cortical and subcortical (collicular and thalamic) visual systems.

DIASCHISIS

Monakow (1914), who established the principle of diaschisis to explain second-stage recovery, used aphasia as the most obvious model for studying recovery. His theory of diaschisis stipulated that acute damage to the nervous system, such as in stroke, deprives the surrounding, functionally connected tissues from innervation; therefore, they become inactivated, similar to the previously well-known phenomenon of "spinal shock." As innervation is regained from somewhere else, function returns to otherwise undamaged structures. The phenomenon of diaschisis has been widely accepted and subsequently elaborated, with biochemical and physiological supporting evidence.

Even before Monakow's diaschisis theory, it was noted that sudden lesions produced more deficit than slowly growing ones. Dax (1865) suggested that left-hemisphere lesions may not result in aphasia if the lesion develops gradually. Modern animal experimentation confirmed this "serial lesion" effect (Ades and Raab, 1946).

## REGENERATION

For quite some time it was thought that regeneration occurred only in the peripheral nervous system. Recent studies have shown quite a significant amount in the CNS. Axonal regrowth has been demonstrated in ascending catecholaminergic fibers; growing zones tend to invade vacant terminal spaces (Schneider, 1973). In addition, neighboring neurons may sprout and send collateral fibers to synapse on vacant terminals (Liu and Chambers, 1958). Both regenerative and collateral sprouting have been demonstrated by Moore (1974) in the mammalian nervous system. Collateral sprouting appears to be more important, whether from intact axons or from collaterals of the damaged axons. Denervation hypersensitivity may explain why some central structures become more responsive to stimulation after damage (Stavraky, 1961). The remaining fibers from the damaged area may produce a greater effect on the denervated region, thereby promoting recovery. The opposite effect, however, has also been argued. The initial hypersensitivity could induce inhibition of function (diaschisis), and the appearance of collateral sprouting might reduce the denervation and the accompanying inhibition (Goldberger, 1974).

## FUNCTIONAL COMPENSATION

Functional compensation explains recovery with a behavioral rather than a neural model. Instead of rerouting connections, the brain-damaged organism develops new solutions to problems using residual structures. Substitute maneuvers or tricks have been observed in various experimental situations. Luria (1970) formulated the theory of retraining, which claims that the dynamic reorganization of the nervous system is promoted by specific therapy.

Motivational factors, which effect postlesion behavior in animals, are even more important in humans. The experiments of Franz and Oden (1917), where subjects were forced to use paralyzed limbs, provided evidence that intense motivation is effective. Stoicheff (1960) demonstrated the effect of positive and negative verbal comments on the performance of aphasics. Improvement was promoted by positive reinforcement, and worsening was observed with negative reinforcement. Many patients develop functional disorders superimposed on their organic deficit. A passive attitude and depression are particularly likely to impede recovery (Robinson and Benson, 1981).

# RECOVERY FROM APHASIA

## Factors Affecting Recovery from Aphasia

Initially, most long-term studies of aphasic patients concerned patients in therapy. Vignolo (1964) was the first to include the objective assessment of untreated patients at various intervals. Subsequent studies of spontaneous recovery have been performed by Culton (1969), Sarno et al. (1970a,b), Sarno and Levita (1971), Hagen (1973), Basso et al. (1975), and Kertesz and McCabe (1977). These studies are difficult to compare, because the methods of evaluation differed. The patient populations were not comparable, since some authors restricted their study to severe aphasics (Sarno et al., 1970a,b; Sarno and Levita, 1971) whereas others tried to look at an unselected population (Kertesz and McCabe, 1977). Different classification systems were used to group patients. Hagen (1973), for example, used Schuell's system (Schuell et al., 1964), whereas Basso et al. (1975) divided their patients into only two categories—Broca's aphasics and Wernicke's aphasics. Some studies only dealt with the recovery of certain symptoms rather than the overall aphasic deficits (Selnes et al., 1983; Knopman et al., 1983). The interval between follow-up examinations and the methods of assessment differed from study to study. In spite of these diversities, several important factors in the recovery of treated and untreated patients emerge.

ETIOLOGY

Recovery and prognosis depend to some extent on etiology. Patients with posttraumatic aphasia recover better than patients with aphasia following stroke (Butfield and Zangwill, 1946; Wepman, 1951; Marks et al., 1957; Godfrey and Douglass, 1959; Luria, 1970). Complete recovery was seen in more than half of our posttraumatic cases (Kertesz and McCabe, 1977). Dramatic spontaneous recovery, such as global aphasia improving to a mild anomic state, occurred after closed head injury, but not in patients with vascular lesions with a similar degree of initial impairment. Even though traumatic aphasia recovers quickly compared to stroke lesions, severe persisting dysarthria often disrupts communication. Levin et al. (1982) have provided data concerning the relationship of the duration of posttraumatic coma and the prognosis in closed head injury. Penetrating head injury behaves somewhat differently again, because of the variation in the speed and path of the missiles and the associated concussion; therefore, posttraumatic aphasia is even more heterogeneous than the vascular type. Nevertheless, a recent study by Ludlow et al. (1986), on Vietnam veterans, showed that the lesions that produced persisting asyntactic or Broca's aphasia are large, involving subcortical structures and the parietal area in addition to Broca's area, very much the same conclusion that is reached studying stroke recovery.

Aphasias resulting from subarachnoid hemorrhage showed a wide variation in rate of recovery (Kertesz and McCabe, 1977). This variability was presumably related to the extent of hemorrhage and to the variable presence of infarction or tissue destruction. To some extent, the prognosis was predictable from the initial severity of the aphasia. It is of interest that some of the worst jargon and global aphasias were seen following ruptured middle cerebral artery aneurysms. Rubens (1977) pointed out the dramatic recovery from thalamic hemorrhage in one patient was explained by the deficit being caused by distortion of neural structures by the hemorrhage rather than by their destruction. Although hemorrhages can initially be devastating the subsequent recovery can be rapid and suprisingly complete.

APHASIA TYPE

Head (1926) recognized that some types of aphasia improve more rapidly than others. Weisenburg and McBride (1935), Butfield and Zangwill (1946), Messerli et al. (1976), and Kertesz and McCabe (1977) considered Broca's or "expressive" aphasics to improve most. Vignolo (1964) considered expressive disorders to have a poor prognosis, but he did not separate Broca's from global aphasics, and the severely affected global patients influenced the results. Basso et al. (1975) did not find any difference between the recovery of fluent and nonfluent aphasic patients. The variability of conclusions, in part, reflects problems in classification. For example, an expressive disorder is found in many different kinds of aphasias, and the expressive-receptive dichotomy by itself is misleading.

We assessed the prognosis of 47 patients with aphasia following stroke who had both an initial examination with the Western Aphasia Battery (WAB) (Kertesz and Poole, 1974) in the acute stages of illness and a follow-up test performed three months, six months, and one year later. The outcome was categorized on the basis of the aphasia quotient (AQ), a summary score of the WAB at one year poststroke (Table 17-1). Many of the global aphasics remained severely impaired. Although some regain comprehension, they remain nonfluent. Broca's and Wernicke's aphasics showed a wider range of outcome. Some patients with Wernicke's aphasia retain fluent jargon for many months. After a while, however, they lose their phonemic paraphasias and their language deficit consists of verbal substitutions and anomia. Broca's aphasics have an intermediate outlook, just about evenly divided between fair and good recovery. Anomic, conduction, and transcortical aphasics have a uniformly good prognosis, the majority of cases showing excellent spontaneous recovery. Some of the completely recovered patients were not even included in this analysis because they were not tested again after their three-month repeat scores were normal (as were

**Table 17-1.** Final Outcome of Aphasia

| Group | N | Percentile 0-25 (poor) | 25-50 (fair) | 50-75 (good) | 75-100 (very good) |
|---|---|---|---|---|---|
| Global | 16 | 13 | 2 | 0 | 1 |
| Broca's | 12 | 0 | 6 | 6 | 1 |
| Conduction | 6 | 0 | 1 | 1 | 4 |
| Wernicke's | 13 | 4 | 6 | 3 | 0 |
| Isolation | 1 | 0 | 1 | 0 | 0 |
| Transcortical motor | 2 | 0 | 0 | 2 | 0 |
| Transcortical sensory | 3 | 0 | 0 | 1 | 2 |
| Anomic | 13 | 0 | 0 | 3 | 10 |
| Total | 67 | 17 (25.4%) | 16 (23.9%) | 16 (23.9%) | 18 (26.9%) |

almost half of the anomic aphasia patients' scores). To define recovery from aphasia, we used an arbitrary cutoff AQ of 93.8, which was the actual mean score of a standardization group of brain-damaged patients who were judged clinically not to be aphasic (Kertesz and Poole, 1974). Final AQs indicated that 12 anomic, 5 conduction, 2 transcortical sensory, and 1 transcortical motor aphasic reached the criterion of recovery. Although this represents only 21% of the 93 patients having aphasias with various etiologies (Kertesz and McCabe, 1977), it represents 62.5% of the conduction, 50% of the transcortical, and 48% of the anomic patients. The overall prognosis, regardless of aphasia type, for the 47 patients followed for a year was as follows: poor for 28%, fair for 19%, good for 13%, and excellent for 40%.

We have also studied the evolution of aphasic syndromes, documenting the patterns of transformation from one clinically distinct aphasic type to another, as defined by subscores on subsequent examinations using the WAB (Kertesz and McCabe, 1977). We found that anomic aphasia is a common end-stage of evolution, in addition to being a common aphasic syndrome de novo. Four of 13 Wernicke's, 4 of 8 transcortical, 4 of 17 Broca's, 2 of 8 conduction, and 1 of 22 global aphasias evolved into anomic aphasia. Reversal of the usual direction of evolution of aphasic patterns should make the clinician suspect that a new lesion has appeared, such as from an extension of a stroke or a tumor. Thus, for example, an anomic aphasic of a vascular etiology should not in the course of recovery become nonfluent, nor should the patient develop fluent paraphasic or neologistic jargon. The dissolution of language in dementia, however, may produce this kind of reversal of the pattern of evolution in vascular aphasia. Some patients with Alzheimer's disease initially have anomic aphasia and subsequently develop a picture of transcortical sensory or Wernicke's aphasia (Kertesz et al., 1986a). Leischner (1976) also studied the transformation of aphasic syndromes three months after stroke. A significant number of patients with total aphasia and mixed aphasia evolved toward motor-amnestic aphasia.

## SEVERITY

The initial severity of the aphasia is closely tied in with the type of aphasia, and it is considered to be highly predictive of outcome (Godfrey and Douglass, 1959; Schuell et al., 1964; Sands et al., 1969; Sarno et al., 1970a,b; Gloning et al., 1976; Kertesz and McCabe, 1977). Unfortunately, it is not always considered in studies of recovery. The most severely affected patients show poor outcome, whether treated or not (Sarno et al., 1970a). Mildly affected patients, on the other hand, more often recovery completely (Kertesz and McCabe, 1977). Initial severity affects recovery rates in a complex paradoxical fashion, because patients with initially low scores may have more room to improve than those with high scores, who have reached "ceiling." Treated patients tend to be selected from the less severe groups and unless initial severity is controlled, studies of treatment should not be considered reliable. There are various methods of controlling for initial severity, such as analysis of covariance, or using outcome measures instead of recovery rates, or the change expressed as percentage of initial severity, or comparing patients who have the same degree of impairment.

## AGE

The influence of age on recovery is controversial. There is a clinical impression that younger patients recover better (Eisenson, 1949; Wepman, 1951; Vignolo, 1964). Some of these studies include younger posttraumatic patients, contaminating the age factor with etiology. We demonstrated an inverse correlation between age and initial recovery rates (from 0 to 3 months), but when we excluded the posttraumatic group whose mean age was well below that of the patients with infarction, the trend just missed being significant (Kertesz and McCabe, 1977). Others have failed to show any correlation between age and recovery in etiologically homogenous populations such as stroke patients (Culton, 1971; Sarno and Levita, 1971; Smith et al., 1972).

Transfer of function occurs more easily in the immature nervous system. Kennard (1936) demonstrated that unilateral precentral lesions in immature animals have minimal effects when compared with similar lesions in adults. In children, recovery from aphasia acquired before the age of 10 to 12 is excellent (Basser, 1962; Hécaen, 1976). Maturation of the left hemisphere appears to inhibit the language abilities of the right hemisphere. Lesions in the left speech area early in life occur before this inhibition can develop and prevent transfer of function (Milner, 1974). It has been proposed that the functional plasticity of the young may depend on the adaptability of Golgi type II cells (Hirsch and Jacobson, 1974). These cells remain adaptive, whereas cells with long axons responsible for the major transmission of information in and out of the CNS are under early and exacting genetic specification and control. In humans, the flexibility of these neurons may be terminated in the teens by hormonal changes. This may explain the age limit on the functional plasticity of the brain. It is of interest that acquisition of a foreign language without an accent also appears to be limited by puberty. Although comparisons between species are risky, there appears to be an analogous effect of hormone levels on bird song acquisition (Nottebohn, 1970).

## SEX AND HANDEDNESS

Findings by Subirana (1969) and Gloning et al. (1969) indicate that left-handers recover better from aphasias than right-handers. Gloning et al. (1969) also suggested that left-handers are likely to become aphasic regardless of which hemisphere is damaged. Right-handers with a history of left-handedness among parents, siblings, or children were said to recover better than right-handers without such a family history (Geschwind, 1974). The evidence for this is largely anecdotal. We looked at the few left-handers in our population and they showed a variable rate of recovery, not significantly different from the right-handed group.

## ANATOMICAL AND FUNCTIONAL VARIATIONS

The anatomy of the speech areas is variable, so that lesions of similar size may affect language differently in different patients. In addition, there may be some variability in the degree to which language is lateralized. Some studies, discussed above, assumed that left-handers are more likely to have language function in both hemispheres. Recently, attempts were made to correlate the in vivo measurement of anatomical asymmetries particularly of language areas with functional differences (Kertesz et al., 1990). Anatomical asymmetries, as measured on CT scans, were correlated with recovery (Pieniadz et al., 1983). Global aphasics who had atypical asymmetries, indicating more bilateral or reverse distribution of language function, appeared to recover better. We have studied a wider range of fluent and nonfluent aphasics and could not confirm these observations (Kertesz et al., 1986b; Kertesz, 1988). Anatomical asymmetries are complex variables interacting with the multifactorial recovery phenomenon, and more sophisticated multivariate analysis will be required to detect any effect. It could be that anatomical asymmetries, as we measure them, relate more to a handedness variable rather than language distribution, as suggested by some of our studies in normals (Kertesz et al., 1990), and this is why we are not seeing an effect on language recovery. The individual variations in the intra- and interhemispheric distibution of various functional components may contribute to an important extent to the ability of the mature brain to compensate after a single nonprogressive lesion.

TIME COURSE FOR RECOVERY

There is a considerable amount of agreement about the time course of recovery. A large number of stroke patients recover a great deal in the first two weeks (Kohlmeyer, 1976). The greatest amount of improvement from aphasia occurs in the first two or three months after onset (Vignolo, 1964; Culton, 1969; Sarno and Levita, 1971; Basso et al., 1975; Kertesz and McCabe, 1977). After six months, the rate of recovery significantly drops (Butfield and Zangwill, 1946; Vignolo, 1964; Sands et al., 1969; Kertesz and McCabe, 1977). In the majority of cases, spontaneous recovery does not seem to occur after a year (Culton, 1969; Kertesz and McCabe, 1977); however, there are reports of improvement in cases under therapy many years after the stroke (Marks et al., 1957; Schuell et al., 1964; Smith et al., 1972; Broida, 1977).

LINGUISTIC FEATURES OF RECOVERY

Various language components recover differently, contributing to the differences in clinical course between patients with different aphasia types. Alajouanine (1956) distinguished four stages of recovery in severe expressive aphasia: (1) differentiation by intonation, (2) decreased automatic utterances, (3) less rigid stereotypic utterances, and (4) volitional, slow, agrammatical speech. Kertesz and Benson (1970) pointed out the predictable pattern of linguistic recovery in jargon aphasia. Copious neologistic or phonemic jargon is replaced by verbal paraphasias or semantic jargon, and eventually anomia, or more rarely a "pure" word deafness, develops. The fact that overproduction of jargon is replaced by anomic gaps or circumlocutions indicates that there is recovery of regulatory or inhibitory systems. There are numerous language features that have been tested longitudinally. Kreindler and Fradis (1968) found that naming, oral imitation, and comprehension of nouns showed the most improvement. In the study of Broca's aphasics by Kenin and Swisher (1972), gains were greater in comprehension than in expressive language, but no such difference was found by Sarno and Levita (1971). Hagen (1973) found improvement in language formulation, auditory retention, visual comprehension, and visual motor abilities in a three- to six-month period after the onset of symptoms. Ludlow (1977) detected greatest improvement in digit repetition reverse, identification by sentence, and word fluency in fluent aphasics, while digit repetition forward, sentence comprehension, and tactile naming improved most in Broca's aphasics. Both groups showed the greatest gains in mean sentence length, grammaticability index, and sentence production index in the second month after onset of symptoms. We studied various language components in four groups of 31 untreated aphasics (Lomas and Kertesz, 1978). Comprehension of yes-no questions, sequential commands, and repetition were the most improved components, and word fluency improved least. In fact, word fluency remained impaired while all other language factors improved, indicating that word fluency measures a nonlanguage factor in addition to language-related factors. This is corroborated by the observation that word fluency is often impaired in nonaphasic demented subjects (Kertesz et al., 1986a). The highest overall recovery scores were attained by the low-fluency, high-comprehension group (mostly Broca's aphasia). The groups with low initial comprehension showed recovery in yes-no comprehension and repetition tasks, and patients with high comprehension recovered in all tasks except word fluency.

LESION SIZE AND LOCATION IN RECOVERY

The importance of lesion size was discussed above in conjunction with theories of equipotentiality. Clinicians have repeatedly observed that recovery is proportional to lesion size (Kertesz et al., 1979; Selnes et al., 1983; Knopman et al., 1983). However, lesion size by itself does not account for all the variability in recovery; lesion location is also a major factor that interacts with lesion size.

Our studies demonstrated the importance of structures that surround the lesion areas in the recovery process. Those left-hemisphere structures that are connected sequentially with the opercular and anterior insular regions play a crucial role in recovery from Broca's aphasia (Kertesz, 1988). Patients with damage to adjacent areas, especially the inferior portion of the precentral gyrus and the anterior parietal region, recover less than those in whom these areas are spared.

Similarly, in Wernicke's aphasia the second temporal gyrus, the insular region, and the supramarginal gyrus that surround the superior temporal area are instrumental in recovery (Kertesz et al., 1989). Damage to these areas results in persisting Wernicke's aphasia. Larger posterior lesions may also destroy access to a potential right-hemisphere comprehension process. Certain subcortical white matter structures, such as the temporal isthmus and the arcuate fasciculus, are often involved in Wernicke's aphasia, and temporal isthmus involvement correlated significantly with outcome in our study. Naeser et al. (1987) also found the temporal isthmus to be significant, but not the posterior structures. Selnes et al. (1983) concluded that reversible suppression of left posterior temporal and inferior parietal region function by transsynaptic mechanisms appeared to be the most plausible explanation for recovery of auditory comprehension.

Lesion size is undoubtedly the most significant factor in the extent of recovery.

However, important exceptions are seen when lesions affect crucial areas in the left hemisphere. Motor and premotor phonemic assembly mechanisms are elaborated by a cortical/subcortical network that can be damaged partially with good recovery. However, if both cortical and subcortical components of the network are impaired, recovery is much less likely. A similar complex integration of various structures takes place for the mechanisms of language comprehension, although interhemispheric connections seem to be playing a larger role in comprehension than in motor output. It seems that a restricted deficit in the dominant-hemisphere auditory association area, the posterior superior temporal gyrus, and the planum temporale can be compensated for by the opposite or homologous hemispheric structures, or by surrounding structures in the temporal and inferior parietal regions and in the insula. However, when either of these compensating structures is affected, or when the lesion is large and precludes right-hemisphere access, recovery is not as likely.

OTHER FACTORS

Darley (1972) considered premorbid intelligence, health, and social milieu to have significant influence on recovery. Although intellectual and educational level influence what the patient and family consider recovery to be, Keenan and Brassel's (1974) study indicated that health, employment, and age had little, if any, prognostic value when compared with factors such as listening and motor speech (comprehension and fluency). Sarno et al. (1970b) similarly showed that recovery in severe aphasia was not influenced by age, sex, education, occupational status, preillness language proficiency, or current living environment. Other pathological variations, such as repeated stroke insults, cerebral atrophy, intercurrent latent dementia, etc., remain factors to be considered or even studied directly, although they are usually controlled by exclusion in most studies.

## Recovery from Alexia

Recovery from alexia is scantily documented. Newcombe et al. (1976) drew recovery curves for the performance of two patients who were followed—one for six months and one for four years—after removal of occipital lesions (abscess and meningioma). Without language therapy, the rate of recovery of the ability to read word lists was maximal initially and decelerated until eight to ten weeks after surgery, at which time a lower rate was achieved. Object-naming curves showed that the patient with an abscess recovered more slowly and retained more residual errors than a posttraumatic patient, who exhibited better recovery of naming. Newcombe et al. (1976) classified linguistic errors as (1) visual confusions (beg → leg), (2) failure of grapheme-phoneme translation (of → off), (3) semantic substitutions (berry → grape), and (4) combinations of these. "Pure dyslexics" tended to make visual errors, and patients with dysphasic symptoms showed more grapheme-phoneme mistranslations; semantic errors were rare. Mixed errors were numerous initially, with many neologistic errors. In the residual phase the visual errors seemed independent of the syntactic class of words, but in cases of persistent aphasia, syntax had a marked effect: nouns were easier to read than verbs or adjectives. Recovery from writing is described later in the therapy section.

### Recovery of Nonverbal Function in Aphasics

Studies of aphasic patients have shown that performance on nonverbal intelligence tests is also impaired, with some interesting dissociations. Culton (1969) used Raven's Standard Progressive Matrices in testing aphasics and found that considerable recovery of nonverbal performance occurred after two months; no further recovery occurred after 11 months. Our own analysis of Raven's Coloured Progressive Matrices (RCPM) performance in aphasic patients suggested that, of all the subtests in the aphasia battery, language comprehension correlated best with performance on the RCPM (Kertesz, 1979).

## RECOVERY OF FUNCTION IN NONAPHASIC BRAIN-DAMAGED PATIENTS

### Neglect

Lawson (1962) emphasized that unawareness of left unilateral neglect retards recovery and that active treatment is needed to overcome it. Campbell and Oxbury (1976) examined the performance of right-hemisphere-damaged patients three to four weeks (and then six months) after a stroke on verbal and nonverbal tasks, including block design and matrices. Those who demonstrated neglect on the initial drawing tests remained impaired on visuospatial tests six months later, in spite of the resolution of neglect. Other reports describe unilateral neglect remaining up to 12 years after onset. Visual neglect and the inability to scan the environment have been targets of rehabilitation therapy (Weinberg et al., 1977). This was a controlled study of right-hemisphere stroke patients using reading, written arithmetic, cancellation of letters, matching of faces, double simultaneous stimulation, and the performance subtest of the WAIS. The rehabilitation efforts included anchoring points on the left side, encouraging leftward head turning, decreasing the density of stimuli, and pacing visual tracking to prevent drifts to the right. The pharmacotherapy of neglect is based on the reversal of neglect by dopamine agonists such as apomorphine in animals. Fleet et al. (1987), in an open trial in humans, demonstrated that neglect was reduced by dopamine agonist therapy. Levine et al. (1986) found that recovery of neglect correlated negatively with sulcal atrophy. Although they did not find one particular area of the right hemisphere responsible for recovery, they thought that any of multiple critical areas may have limited the duration of neglect (see also Chapter 10).

### Cortical Blindness and Visual Agnosia

Recovery from cortical blindness and related syndromes of the parietal and occipital lobes has been described by Gloning et al. (1968). There appear to be regular stages of progression from cortical blindness through visual agnosia and partially impaired perceptual function to recovery. Sometimes syndromes of visual agnosia remain persistent (Kertesz, 1979).

## Recovery of Memory

The etiology of the most frequently studied memory loss is trauma. The prognosis of posttraumatic memory impairment has been correlated with the duration of posttraumatic amnesia by Russell (1971): 82% of his patients returned to full duty, 92% of these in less than three weeks. Learning capacity may continue to be impaired after the acute amnesia has subsided (the postconcussional syndrome). The phenomenon of shrinking retrograde amnesia, seen with head trauma (Russell and Nathan, 1946; Benson and Geschwind, 1967), suggests that during the amnestic period memories are not lost but rather cannot be activated (retrieved).

Memory loss secondary to alcoholic, postinfectious, and toxic causes, when severe, tends to persist (Talland, 1965), whereas electro-convulsive therapy (ECT)-induced memory loss is rarely permanent (Williams, 1966). The acute amnestic confabulatory syndrome (Wernicke's encephalopathy) often subsides within weeks, becoming a more chronic state of Korsakoff's psychosis. Korsakoff was optimistic about the prognosis but did not have reliable reports beyond the acute stage. Later clinicians denied seeing complete remissions. Victor and Adams (1953) arrived at a more hopeful conclusion but noted that "complete restoration of memory is . . . unusual when the defect is severe." Amnestic symptoms from unilateral infarctions subside in a few months, but more lasting deficit occurs with bilateral posterior cerebral artery involvement (Benson et al., 1975). Recent monographs on memory rehabilitation reflect the increase in the treatment of head-injured adults, funded by compensation schemes in industrialized countries (Sohlberg and Mateer, 1989; Prigitano, 1985).

## Recovery from Hemiplegia

Even though hemiplegia is not covered by this book, the parallels between recovery of neuropsychological function and of motor function cannot be ignored. There is an extensive body of information on this subject. The testing of hemiplegia is a more uniform procedure than the testing of neuropsychological disorders, and despite the variability of recovery, there is general agreement about many aspects. For example, recovery of the upper extremity is not as good as that of the lower extremity. Motion begins proximally and then spreads to the more distal portions of the arm. The initial motion occurs one to six weeks after the stroke. A study by Van Buskirk (1955) showed that restitution of function occurs chiefly in the first two months and appears to be a spontaneous process. When full recovery occurs, initial motion begins within two weeks and full motion occurs within three months. About 45% recover full motion, 40% recover partial motion, and 15% do not recover function of the upper extremity (when followed for more than seven months). The role of cerebral dominance was examined in the recovery of ambulation. Right hemiplegics recover independent ambulation more often and faster than left hemiplegics. The spatial-perceptual deficiencies of left hemiplegics were considered to be more resistant to recovery and hampered recovery of ambulation (Cassvan et al., 1976). Newman (1972) suggested that much of the early recovery (especially in the upper limb) could be due to return of circulation to ischemic areas. Transfer of function to undamaged neurons is suggested as the mechanism underlying late recovery (especially in the lower limbs).

## LANGUAGE THERAPY

The treatment of aphasics is an established practice, even though only a few studies have accounted for spontaneous recovery in assessing the efficacy of therapy. The first systematic study of treatment (Butfield and Zangwill, 1946) did not use untreated controls, but an attempt was made to describe the method of therapy—mainly the use of oral drills and transmodal cues. Gains after six months were attributed to therapy, assuming that further spontaneous recovery was not significant at that time. Vignolo (1964) studied treated and untreated patients and did not find a significant difference between these groups; nevertheless, he suggested that therapy between the second and sixth months may be beneficial. Sarno et al. (1970a) compared global aphasics who underwent stimulation therapy and programmed instruction with untreated controls and found no significant difference.

A few studies using untreated controls have provided evidence that therapy is effective. Hagen (1973) compared ten treated aphasics matched for severity and type (sensorimotor type III of Schuell) with ten untreated aphasics and found significantly better recovery in language formulation, speech production, reading comprehension, spelling, and arithmetic in the treated group. Most improvement occurred during the first six months of treatment. Auditory comprehension, auditory retention, visual comprehension, and visuomotor abilities improved equally in the treated and control group. All patients were included in the study at three months, and treatment began at six months after the stroke. Basso et al. (1975) studied 91 treated aphasics and 94 controls who could not come for therapy for personal or logistic reasons. The control group was significantly older than the treated group. They were not matched for severity. A minimum of six months of therapy was shown to significantly affect the oral expression of aphasics; the longer the duration of aphasia before therapy began, the less effective the therapy. This retrospective study, instead of controlling the time of inclusion after the onset, examined the effect of this variable on improvement. This, in fact, allowed patients seen soon after their stroke, with more spontaneous recovery, to be overrepresented in the treatment group and patients, seen at a later stage when recovery is less likely to occur, to be overrepresented in the untreated group.

A comparison of language-oriented, stimulation therapy by speech therapists and supportive therapy by untrained therapists revealed no significant differences (Shewan and Kertesz, 1984). Patients were admitted to treatment at two weeks poststroke and had a least three hours of therapy per week, if possible, for one year. Because of attrition, the average duration of treatment was about 20 weeks. The WAB was used to follow patients on entry at 3, 6, 12, and 18 months poststroke. A nonrandomized, untreated group, which happened to be less severely affected, showed less recovery in writing and other performance scores rather than the treated groups. The oral language scores also showed less improvement in this untreated (by default) group, but the difference did not reach significance. David et al. (1982) reported a multicenter trial comparing therapy for 155 stroke patients by either speech therapists or untrained volunteers. They used the Functional Communication Profile as a basic measure. Patients were entered after three weeks postonset and were randomized to the two treatment groups. Treatment was only for 30 hours over 15 to 20 weeks. The study concluded that there was no significant difference between the treatment groups. These workers felt that the improvement was the result of the support and stimulation provided by speech therapist and volunteer alike. Lincoln et al. (1984) assigned patients randomly to treatment and nontreatment groups. A comparison after 24 weeks of therapy indicated no differences, but this study was criticized subsequently because it included patients with mixed etiologies and multiple episodes, and a variable amount of treatment was received.

A multicenter study of aphasia therapy by Wertz et al. (1981) compared stroke patients undergoing stimulus-response speech therapy and "social interaction" group therapy. There were significant gains in both groups, with individually treated patients doing slightly better. Maximum improvement occurred in the first three months. Further significant improvement occurred between 26 and 48 weeks, and it was assumed that spontaneous recovery was not operational at that time. Another large multicenter study of aphasia therapy by the same investigators used a crossover design of treated and untreated groups and showed significant gains in both treated groups compared to the untreated ones in both early and late phases of the study (Wertz, 1983). Prins et al. (1989) assigned patients randomly to either a systematic treatment program for auditory language comprehension or stimulation therapy. A self-selected nontreatment group had reached their limits of recovery according to their speech therapists. Comparison of groups posttreatment indicated no significant differences. These results are very similar to the Shewan and Kertesz (1984) study mentioned earlier.

Poeck et al. (1989) studied treatment retrospectively and found it effective beyond spontaneous recovery. They did not use randomized controls but compared their patients to another population.

To design a study of treatment of aphasia, it is essential to match patients for initial severity, type, etiology, and time from onset; these criteria have rarely been met. To determine efficacy, randomized controls would be ideal, but this has proved to be difficult.

Therapy itself is complex and difficult to standardize. It is said that there are as many varieties of aphasia treatment as there are therapists. Speech therapists tailor therapy to the needs of the individual and are reluctant to follow rigidly prescribed treatment programs. The content of therapy and the methods differ considerably, creating overlapping categories. Lately, the contribution of psycholinguistic principles to the content of therapy has been increasing, and old methods are redesigned and relabeled according to the theoretical constructs they are based upon. Brookshire (1977) attempted to analyze the relationship between clinical behavior and patient behavior. He has called for a system for recording and coding events during therapy. His statement sets the standard that is difficult to achieve in reality: "a definite study of the effects of treatment on recovery from aphasia will be impossible without some means of describing objectively and unambiguously the exact nature of the treatment program or programs employed in the study." In the following sections, varieties of aphasia treatment are described as a clinical guide.

## Stimulation Approach

Wepman (1951) recognized that aphasics are, in fact, stimulated rather than educated during treatment. Familiar materials relevant to the individual patient are used. The patient is not pressured: every response is accepted and the correct ones are reinforced. Schuell et al.'s (1964) approach has been used widely: (1) use intensive auditory stimulation, i.e., meaningful patterns and high-frequency words, adjusting the rate, loudness, and length of presentation to the needs of each patient; (2) use highly repetitive stimulation; (3) elicit, rather than force, some response to every stimulus; (4) stimulate more responses rather than correct errors; and (5) use different language modalities for facilitation: spelling aloud to help writing, writing to help auditory retention, etc. Various forms of the specific stimulation approach were defined by Taylor (1964): (1) association approach: attempting to elicit associated words by structuring sessions around families of words, using the maximum possible word environments for each target word; (2) situational approach: everyday situations are acted out, facilitating learning functionally useful vocabulary or statements; and (3) minimal differences approach: similarly sounding words and similar-looking written material are used as stimuli for teaching.

Other varieties of stimulation are less structured. These are variously called (1) environmental stimulation: everybody talks to the patient as much as possible; (2) rapport approach: a warm relationship is established between the clinician and the patient without regard to the content and method of contact; (3) socialization approach: individual or group sessions include informal "fun" activities; (4) interest approach: subjects related to the patient's previous group or individual word activities and interests are discussed; and (5) psychotherapeutic approach: problems of anxiety and loss of self-esteem are focused upon.

## Programmed Instruction

The desired language behavior is defined and programs to reach it are constructed. Martha Taylor Sarno and associates defined and developed this approach (Taylor, 1964). Many individual steps, from preverbal programs to practicing syntax, are used to achieve the desired language behavior (Sarno et al., 1970a). Although repeatable and quantifiable, it is very difficult to design and persist in such a program. When careful attention is directed to the rules of language and the language deficit itself, programmed instruction is also called the psycholinguistic approach. Language-oriented therapy, as described by Shewan and Bandur (1986), considers the language modalities of training and the level at which the patient shows a deficit. Criteria for moving from one level to another are predetermined. The purpose is to teach strategies rather than responses. Other systematic linguistic approaches were described in Germany (Springer and Weniger, 1980; Weniger et al., 1980) and in Belgium (Seron, 1987). The psycholinguistic or structural approach is also called a didactic method because the training materials resemble the exercises used in second-language learning. It is difficult to demonstrate stabilization and generalization effect after a period of training. Most of the detailed reports represent single case studies. In a structural approach, the patient is instructed to practice syntactic units in a stepwise fashion of increasing inherent difficulties (Helm-Estabrooks and Ramsberger, 1986).

## Deblocking Method and Facilitation

Weigl (1968) described a special kind of stimulation that uses an intact channel of communication to eliminate a block in understanding or expression via other channels. A response is evoked in an intact channel (e.g., recognition of a printed word) just before presenting the same stimulus to a blocked channel (auditory comprehension). This is similar to Schuell's intermodality facilitation. Auditory prestimulation with the target word was more effective than semantically related words in naming (Podraza and Darley, 1977). Contextual knowledge facilitated comprehension of surface markers of agent-object relationship. An experimental analysis of facilitation of word retrieval used the pictorial semantic system to retrieve items from the phonological verbal lexicon (Howard et al., 1985). Other terms, used more recently for deblocking and facilitation, are priming of targets by using structurally or semantically similar items or cuing techniques between related units (Huber, 1991).

## Preventive Method

The preventive method is a specific application of a linguistic theory by Beyn and Shokhor-Trotskaya (1966). Instead of object naming, patients work on expressions as a whole, preventing the occurrence of telegraphic speech. The treatment of aphasic perseveration is aimed to inhibit these responses by the patient once they can be made conscious of them (Helm-Estabrooks et al., 1987).

## Compensatory Approach

The compensatory approach encourages patients to use their own compensatory strategies. Patients with word-finding difficulty are encouraged to circumlocute (Holland, 1977). Goda (1962) advocated using the patient's own spontaneous speech to design programs and drill material. This approach sometimes is called the strategy approach. Instead of setting targets in terms of linguistic units, the patients are encouraged to concentrate on the remaining strength of their communication. Compensatory strategy for writing disorders has been described by Hatfield (1989). Most therapies have, at one time or another, utilized the strategy of optimizing the preserved processes, since working with impaired processes is much more frustrating for patient and therapist alike. Often the patients themselves discover compensatory strategies. Patients with agrammatism are asked to concentrate on thematic elements rather than grammar (Kearns, 1990).

## Teaching Machines and Microcomputers

Operant conditioning with automated teaching machines has been described by Keith and Darley (1967). Patients seemed to prefer human contact according to these authors. Microcomputers, however, have been used with increasing frequency (Katz, 1986; Stachowiak, 1987; Burton et al., 1988). Sentence-level auditory comprehension (SLAC) treatment is a structured method, utilizing language master tapes.

Bruce and Howard (1987) used computer-generated phonemic cuing to aid naming in aphasics. Katz and Wertz (1990) assigned patients randomly to computerized reading treatment, computer stimulation (nonlinguistic cognitive tasks and computer games), and no-treatment groups. At the end of a six-month treatment trial, the computerized reading treatment group made significantly more improvement than both the computer stimulation and the no-treatment groups. There was no significant difference between the computer stimulation and the no-treatment groups.

## Pragmatics and PACE Therapy

PACE is an acronym for "promoting aphasics' communicative effectiveness" (Davis and Wilcox, 1981). PACE therapy emphasizes pragmatic rather than linguistic parameters. The patient is encouraged to convey a message by using any verbal or nonverbal means available. For example, the patient has to identify drawings of objects unknown to the therapist. Communicative effectiveness is judged by the therapist's understanding of the message. The effectiveness of PACE therapy compared favorably with the traditional stimulation approach in a study using an ABCBC time-series design in a single patient (Chin Li et al., 1988). A modified PACE approach (Springer et al., 1991) introduced linguistic tasks.

## Melodic Intonation Therapy (MIT)

Singing was recommended for the rehabilitation of expressive deficits by Vargha and Gereb (1953). MIT was initially described by Sparks et al. (1974), based on the widespread knowledge that many severely affected aphasics can sing words better than they speak and that musical, tonal abilities are subserved by the right hemisphere. The patient intones a melody for simple statements. MIT was initially thought to be successful with global aphasias, but the applicability of the method, particularly its transfer to practical day-to-day communicative situations, is very limited. Certain parameters such as syllable duration of the stimulus items have been further analyzed (Laughlin et al., 1979).

## Visual Communication

Nonverbal symbols are used to train global aphasics to express themselves, since there has been a successful demonstration that chimpanzees can be taught a nonverbal communication system (Glass et al., 1973). Gardner et al. (1976) (Helm-Estabrooks, et al., 1982) taught patients to recognize and manipulate symbols in order to respond to commands, answer questions, describe their actions, and express desires and feelings. A similar approach is the use of hand signals to teach global aphasics basic communication (Eagleson et al., 1970). Amerind (American Indian sign language) has been successfully used to aid patients' language expression (Skelly et al., 1974) and comprehension (Heilman et al., 1979). A computer-based visual communication has also been successfully used with aphasic patients (Steele et al., 1989).

### Drug Treatment

Drugs have been used to treat aphasia—including dexamethasone, sodium amytal, priscol, meprobamate, and hyperbaric oxygen—with unimpressive results (Darley, 1975). Recently, bromocriptine has been found to improve spontaneous speech in a case of transcortical motor aphasia (Albert et al., 1987). Apparently, language deteriorated to baseline after cessation of therapy.

### Psychotherapy

At times, psychotherapy has been considered useful in reducing the emotional problems of aphasics and in facilitating recovery. Therapy may be aimed at the family (Wahrborg and Bornstein, 1989) or specifically at the depression of certain aphasics (Robinson and Benson, 1981). The therapeutic effect of laughter may be mediated through relaxation or stimulating right-hemisphere mechanisms to compensate (Potter and Goodman, 1983). The psychosocial approach takes into account the reentry of the aphasic patient into the community on both social and occupational levels (Pachalska, 1991).

### Specific Target Therapies

Therapies for various specific modalities have been developed, for example, therapies for correcting "verbal apraxia" (Rosenbeck et al., 1973), for retraining of writing (Hatfield and Weddell, 1976; Hatfield, 1989), or for treating agrammatism (Helm-Estabrooks and Ramsberger, 1986; Davis and Tan, 1987; Byng, 1988; Kearns, 1990). Training agrammatic aphasics with questions resulted in negligible generalization (Wambaugh and Thompson, 1989).

### Cognitive Therapy

Recently cognitive neuropsychological models have been applied to therapy (Lesser, 1987; Howard and Patterson, 1989). Some of the methods are quite similar to more conventional approaches, except that the component language processes are renamed in information processing terminology. For instance, in a description of correcting the access deficit from the semantic system to the phonological output lexicon (word-finding difficulty in the older terminology), patient RS was asked to read semantically related words aloud to match them to pictures (Marshall et al., 1990). This resembles the previous therapies described under deblocking and facilitation. Improvement in word finding in RS and similar patients after relatively brief therapy sessions remains uncontrolled and anecdotal. Other single case studies in similar cognitive modes used a period before therapy as a control base-time to which the results of therapy were compared. Some used untreated deficits as controls. However, when untreated areas improve, generalization from therapy is often invoked. Advocates of the method claim that response to therapy may clarify the nature of language deficit (Byng, 1988). Despite the emphasis on individual case designs that are by necessity different from each other, a call has gone out to replicate the case reports in order to establish the generalizability of the method (Lesser, 1987).

## REFERENCES

Ades, H. W., and Raab, D. H. (1946). Recovery of motor function after two-stage extirpation of area 4 in monkeys. *J. Neurophysiol. 9*:55–60.

Alajouanine, T. (1956). Verbal realization in aphasia. *Brain 79*:1–28.

Albert, M. L., Bachman, D., Morgan, A., and Helm-Estabrooks, N. (1987). Pharmacotherapy for aphasia. *Neurology 37*:175.

Argentino, C., Sacchetti, M. L., Toni, D., Sauoini, G., D'Arcangelo, E., Erminio, F., Federico, F., Milone, F. F., Galli, V., Gambi, D., Mamoli, A., Ottonello, G. A., Ponari, O. Rebucci, G., Senin, V., and Fieschi, C. (1989). GM$_1$ ganglioside therapy in acute ischemic stroke. *Stroke 20*:1143–1149.

Astrup, J., Siesjo, B. K., and Symon, L. (1981). Thresholds in cerebral ischemia—the ischemia penumbra. *Stroke 12*:723–725.

Basser, L. S. (1962). Hemiplegia of early onset and the faculty of speech with special reference to the effects of hemispherectomy. *Brain 85*:427–460.

Basso, A., Faglioni, P., and Vignolo, L. A. (1975). Etude controlee de la reeducation of language dans l'aphasie: Comparaison entre aphasiques traites et non-traitee. *Rev. Neurol. (Paris) 131*:607–614.

Benson, D. F., and Geschwind, N. (1967). Shrinking retrograde amnesia. *J. Neurol. Neurosurg. Psychiatry 30*:539–544.

Benson, D. F., Marsden, C. D., and Meadows, J. C. (1975). The amnesic syndrome of posterior cerebral artery occlusion. *Acta Neurol. Scand. 50*:133–145.

Beyn, E. S., and Shokhor-Trotskaya, M. K. (1966). The preventive method of speech rehabilitation in aphasia. *Cortex 2*:96–108.

Broida, H. (1977). Language therapy effects in long term aphasia. *Arch. Phys. Med. Rehab. 58*:248–253.

Brookshire, R. H. (1977). A system for recording events in patient-clinician interactions during aphasia treatment sessions. In *Rationale for Adult Aphasia Therapy*. Lincoln: University of Nebraska Medical Center.

Bruce, C., and Howard, D. (1987). Computer-generated phonemic cues: an effective aid for naming in aphasia. *Br. J. Disord. Commun. 22*:191–201.

Bucy, P. C. (1934). The relation of the premotor cortex to motor activity. *J. Nerv. Ment. Dis. 79*:621–630.

Burton, E., Burton, A., and Lucas, D. (1988). The use of microcomputers with aphasic patients. *Aphasiology 2*:479–491.

Butfield, E., and Zangwill, O. L. (1946). Re-education in aphasia. A review of 70 cases. *J. Neurol. Neurosurg. Psychiatry 9*:75–79.

Byng, S. (1988). Sentence processing deficits: theory and therapy. *Cognitive Neuropsychol. 5*:629–676.

Campbell, D. C., and Oxbury, J. M. (1976). Recovery from unilateral visuospatial neglect. *Cortex 12*:303–312.

Cassvan, A., Ross, P. L., Dyer, P. R., and Zane, L. (1976). Lateralization in stroke syndromes as a factor in ambulation. *Arch. Phys. Med. Rehabil. 57*:583–587.

Chin Li, E., Kitselman, K., Dusatko, D., and Spinelli, C. (1988). The efficacy of PACE in the remediation of naming deficits. *J. Commun. Dis. 21*:491–503.

Culton, G. L. (1969). Spontaneous recovery from aphasia. *J. Speech Hear. Res. 12*:825–832.

Culton, G. L. (1971). Reaction to age as a factor in chronic aphasia in stroke patients. *J. Speech Hear. Disord. 36*:563–564.

Darley, F. L. (1972). The efficacy of language rehabilitation in aphasia. *J. Speech Hear. Disord. 30*:3–22.

Darley, F. L. (1975). Treatment of acquired aphasia. In *Advances in Neurology*, Vol. 7, *Current Reviews of Higher Nervous System Dysfunction*, W. S. Friedlander (ed.). New York: Raven Press.

David, R., Enderby, P., and Bainton, D. (1982). Treatment of acquired aphasia: speech therapists and volunteers compared. *J. Neurol. Neurosurg. Psychiatry 45*:957–961.

Davis, G. A., and Tan, L. L. (1987). Stimulation of sentence production in a case with agrammatism. *J. Commun. Disord. 20*:447–457.

Davis, G. A., and Wilcox, M. J. (1981). Incorporating parameters of natural conversation aphasia treatment. In *Language Intervention Strategies in Adult Aphasia*, R. Chapey (ed.). Baltimore, Williams and Wilkins.

Dax, M. (1865). Lesions de la moitie gauche de l'encephale coincivant avec l'oubli des signes de la pensee. *Gaz. Hebd. Med. Chir. 2-ieme serie, 2.*

Eagleson, H. M., Vaugh, G. R., and Knudson, A.B.C. (1970). Hand signals for dysphasia. *Arch. Phys. Med. Rehabil. 51*:111–113.

Eisenson, J. (1949). Prognostic factors related to language rehabilitation in aphasic patients. *J. Speech Hear. Disord. 14*:262–264.

Feeney, D. M., and Sutton, R. L. (1987). Pharmacotherapy for recovery of function after brain injury. *CRC Crit. Rev. Neurobiol. 3*:135–197.

Finger, S., and Stein, D. F. (1982). *Brain Damage and Recovery*. New York: Plenum Press.

Fleet, W. S., Valenstein, E., Watson, R. T., and Heilman, K. M. (1987). Dopamine agonist therapy for neglect in humans. *Neurology 37*:1765–1771.

Flourens, P. (1824). *Recherches Experimentales sur les Proprietes et les Fonctions du Systeme Nerveux dans les Animaux vertebres.* Paris: Cervot.

Franz, S. I., and Oden, R. (1917). On cerebral motor control: the recovery from experimentally produced hemiplegia. *Psychobiology 1*:3–18.

Fritsch, G., and Hitzig, E. (1870). Uber die electrische Erregbarkeit des Grosshirns. *Arch. Anat. Physiol. 37*:300–332.

Gardner, H., Zurif, E. B., Berry, T., and Baker, E. (1976). Visual communication in aphasia. *Neuropsychologia 14*:275–292.

Gazzaniga, M. S. (1970). *The Bisected Brain*. New York: Appleton.

Gelmers, H. J., Gorter, K., DeWeerdt, C. J., and Wiezer, H.J.A. (1988). A controlled trial of nimodopine in acute ischemic stroke. *N. Engl. J. Med. 318*:203–207.

Geschwind, N. (1969). Problems in the anatomical understanding of the aphasias. In *Contributions to Clinical Neuropsychology*, A. Benton (ed.). Chicago: Aldine.

Geschwind, N. (1974). Late changes in the nervous system: an overview. In *Plasticity and Recovery of Function in the Central Nervous System*, D. Stein, J. Rosen, and N. Butters (eds.). New York: Academic Press.

Glass, A. V., Gazzaniga, M. S., and Premack, D. (1973). Artificial language training in global aphasics. *Neuropsychologia 11*:95–103.

Gloning, I., Gloning, K., and Haff, H. (1968). *Neuropsychological Symptoms and Syndromes in Lesions of the Occipital Lobes and Adjacent Areas*. Paris: Gauthier-Villars.

Gloning, I., Gloning, K., Haub, G., and Quatember, R. (1969). Comparison of verbal behavior in right-handed and non-right-handed patients with anatomically verified lesion of one hemisphere. *Cortex* 5:43–52.

Gloning, K., Trappl, R., Heiss, W. D., and Quatember, R. (1976). *Prognosis and Speech Therapy in Aphasia in Neurolinguistics*, Vol. 4. *Recovery in Aphasics*. Amsterdam: Swets and Zeitlinger.

Goda, S. (1962). Spontaneous speech: a primary source of therapy material. *J. Speech Hear. Disord.* 27:190–192.

Godfrey, C. M., and Douglass, E. (1959). The recovery process in aphasia. *Can. Med. Assoc. J.* 80:618–624.

Goldberger, M. E. (1974). Recovery of movement after CNS lesions in monkeys. In *Plasticity and Recovery of Function in the Central Nervous System*, D. Stein, J. Rosen, and N. Butters (eds.). New York: Academic Press.

Hagen, C. (1973). Communication abilities in hemiplegia: effect of speech therapy. *Arch. Phys. Med. Rehabil.* 54:454–463.

Hatfield, F. (1989). Aspects of acquired dysgraphia and implications for reeducation. In *Aphasia Therapy. Studies in Disorders of Communication*, 2nd ed, C. Code and D. J. Muller (eds.). London: Whurr.

Hatfield, F., and Weddell, R. (1976). Re-training in writing in severe aphasia. in *Neurolinguistics*, Vol. 4, *Recovery in Aphasics*. Amsterdam: Swets and Zeitlinger.

Head, H. (1926). *Aphasia and Kindred Disorders of Speech*. Cambridge: Cambridge University Press.

Hécaen, H. (1976). Acquired aphasia in children and the ontogenesis of hemispheric functional specialization. *Brain Lang.* 3:114–134.

Heilman, K. M., Rothi, L.J.G., Campanella, D., and Wolfson, S. (1979). Wernicke's and global aphasia without alexia. *Arch. Neurol.* 36:129–133.

Helm-Estabrooks, N., Emery, P., and Albert, M. L. (1987). Treatment of aphasic perseveration (TAP) program: a new approach to aphasia therapy. *Arch. Neurol.* 44:1253–1255.

Helm-Estabrooks, N., Fitzpatrick, P. M., and Barresi, B. (1982). Visual action therapy for global aphasia. *J. Speech Hear. Disord.* 47:385–389.

Helm-Estabrooks, N., and Ramsberger, G. (1986). Treatment of agrammatism in long term Broca's aphasia. *Br. J. Disord. Commun.* 21:39–45.

Henschen, S. E. (1922). *Klinische und anatomische Beitrage zur Pathologie des Gehirns*, Vols 5–7. Stockholm: Nordiska Bokhandelin.

Hirsch, H.V.B., and Jacobson, M. (1974). The perfect brain. In *Fundamentals of Psychobiology*, M. S. Gazzaniga and C. B. Blakemore (eds.). New York: Academic Press.

Holland, A. L. (1977). Some practical considerations in aphasia rehabilitation. In *Rationale for Adult Aphasia Therapy*, M. Sullivan and M. S. Kommers (eds.). Lincoln: University of Nebraska Medical Center.

Howard, D., Patterson, K., Franklin, S., Orchard-Lisle, V., and Morton, J. (1985). The facilitation of picture naming in aphasia. *Cognitive Neuropsychol.* 2:49–80.

Howard, D., and Patterson, K. (1989). Models for therapy. In *Cognitive Approaches in Rehabilitation*, T. Seron and G. DeLoche (eds.). Hillsdale, N.J.: Lawrence Erlbaum Associates, pp. 39–63.

Huber, W., Poeck, K., and Springer, L. (1991), *Sprachstorungen*. Stuttgart: TRIAS.

Jackson, J. H. (1873). On the anatomical and physiological localization of movements in the brain. *Lancet* 1:84–85, 162–164, 232–234.

Katz, R. C. (1986). *Aphasia Treatment and Microcomputers*. London: Taylor and Francis.

Katz, R. C., and Wertz, R. T. (1990). Computerized hierarchical reading treatment in aphasia. Paper presented at the Fourth International Aphasia Rehabilitation Congress, Edinburgh, Scotland.

Kearns, K. P. (1990). Broca's aphasia. In *Aphasia and Related Neurogenic Language Disorders*, L. L. LaPointe (ed). New York: Thieme.

Keenan, S. S., and Brassel, E. G. (1974). A study of factors related to prognosis for individual aphasic patients. *J. Speech Hear. Disord. 39:*257–269.

Keith, R. L., and Darley, F. L. (1967). The use of a specific electric board in rehabilitation of the aphasic patient. *J. Speech Hear. Disord. 32:*148–153.

Kenin, M., and Swisher, L. (1972). A study of pattern of recovery in aphasia. *Cortex 8:*56–68.

Kennard, M. A. (1936). Age and other factors in motor recovery from precentral lesions in monkeys. *Am. J. Physiol. 115:*138–146.

Kertesz, A. (1979). *Aphasia and Associated Disorders: Taxonomy, Localization and Recovery.* New York: Grune and Stratton.

Kertesz, A. (1988). What do we learn from aphasia? In *Advances in Neurology*, Vol. 47: *Functional Recovery in Neurological Disease*, S. G. Waxman (ed.). New York: Raven Press, pp. 277–292.

Kertesz, A., Appell, J., and Fisman, M. (1986a). The dissolution of language in Alzheimer's disease. *Can. J. Neurol. Sc. 13:*415–418.

Kertesz, A., Black, S. E., Polk, M., and Howell, J. (1986b). Cerebral asymmetries on magnetic resonance imaging. *Cortex 22:*177–227.

Kertesz, A., and Benson, D. F. (1970). Neologistic jargon: a clinicopathological study. *Cortex 6:*362–387.

Kertesz, A., Dennis, S., Polk, M., and McCabe, P. (1989). The structural determinants of recovery in Wernicke's aphasia. *Neurology 39 (Suppl. 1):*177.

Kertesz, A., Harlock, W., and Coates, R. (1979). Computer tomographic localization, lesion size and prognosis in aphasia. *Brain Lang. 3:*34–50.

Kertesz, A., and McCabe, P. (1977). Recovery patterns and prognosis in aphasia. *Brain 100:*1–18.

Kertesz, A., Polk, M., Black, S. E., and Howell, J. (1990). Sex, handedness, and the morphometry of cerebral asymmetries on magnetic resonance imaging. *Brain Res. 530:*40–48.

Kertesz, A., and Poole, E. (1974). The aphasia quotient: the taxonomic approach to measurement of aphasic disability. *Can. J. Neurol. Sc. 1:*7–16.

Kinsbourne, M. (1971). The minor cerebral hemisphere as a source of aphasic speech. *Arch. Neurol. 25:*302–306.

Knopman, D. S., Rubens, A. B., Selnes, O. R., Klassen, A. C., and Meyer, M. W. (1984). Mechanisms of recovery from aphasia: evidence from serial xenon 133 cerebral blood flow studies. *Ann. Neurol. 15:*530–535.

Knopman, D. S., Selnes, O. A., Niccum, N., Rubens, A. B., Yock, D., and Larson, D. (1983). A longitudinal study of speech fluency in aphasia: CT correlates of recovery and persistent nonfluency. *Neurology 33:*1170–1178.

Kohlmeyer, K. (1976). Aphasia due to focal disorders of cerebral circulation: some aspects of localization and of spontaneous recovery. In *Neurolinguistics*. Vol. 4. *Recovery in Aphasics*. Amsterdam: Swets and Zeitlinger.

Kreindler, A., and Fradis, A. (1968). *Performances in Aphasia: A neurodynamical, Diagnostic and Psychological Study*. Paris: Gauthier-Villars.

Lashley, K. S. (1938). Factors limiting recovery after central nervous lesions. *J. Nerv. Ment. Dis. 88:*733–755.

Laughlin, S. A., Naeser, M. A., and Gordon, W. P. (1979). Effects of three syllable durations using the melodic intonation therapy technique. *J. Speech Hear. Res. 22:*311–320.

Lawson, I. R. (1962). Visual-spatial neglect in lesions of the right cerebral hemisphere: a study in recovery. *Neurology* 12:23–33.

Leischner, A. (1976). Aptitude of Aphasics for Language Treatment. *Neurolinguistics.* Vol. 4. *Recovery of Aphasics,* Y. Lebrun and R. Hoops (eds.). Amsterdam: Swets and Zeitlinger.

Lesser, R. (1987). Cognitive neuropsychological influences of aphasia therapy. *Aphasiology* 1:189–200.

Levin, H. S., Benton, A. L., and Grossman, R. G. (1982). *Neurobehavioral Consequences of Closed Head Injury.* Oxford: Oxford University Press.

Levine, D. N., Warach, J. D., Benowitz, L., and Calvanio, R. (1986). Left spatial neglect: effects of lesion size and premorbid brain atrophy on severity and recovery following right cerebral infarction. *Neurology* 36:362–366.

Lincoln, N. B., McGuirk, E., Mulley, G. P., Lendrum, W., Jones, A. C., and Mitchell, J. R. (1984). Effectiveness of speech therapy for aphasic stroke patients. *Lancet* 1:1197–1200.

Liu, C. N., and Chambers, W. W. (1958). Intraspinal sprouting of dorsal root axons. *Arch. Neurol.* 79:46–61.

Lomas, J., and Kertesz, A. (1978). Patterns of spontaneous recovery in aphasic groups: a study of adult stroke patients. *Brain Lang.* 5:388–401.

Ludlow, C. (1977). Recovery from aphasia: a foundation for treatment. In *Rationale for Adult Aphasia Therapy,* M. A. Sullivan and M. S. Kommers (eds.). Lincoln: University of Nebraska Medical Center.

Ludlow, C., Rosenberg, J., Fair, C., Buck, D., Schesselman, S., and Salazar, A. (1986). Brain lesions associated with nonfluent aphasia fifteen years following penetrating head injury. *Brain* 109:55–80.

Luria, A. R. (1970). *Traumatic Aphasia.* Hague: Mouton.

Marks, M. M., Taylor, M. L., and Rusk, L. A. (1957). Rehabilitation of the aphasic patient: a survey of three years' experience in a rehabilitation setting. *Neurology* 7:837–843.

Marshall, J., Pound, D., White-Thomson, M., and Pring, T. (1990). The use of picture/word matching tasks to assist word retrieval in aphasic patients. *Aphasiology* 4:167–184.

Messerli, P., Tissot, A., and Rodrigues, J. (1976). Recovery from aphasia: some factors of prognosis. In *Neurolinguistics.* Vol. 4. *Recovery in Aphasics,* Y. Lebrun and R. Hoops (eds.). Amsterdam: Swets and Zeitlinger.

Metter, E. J., Wasterlain, C. G., Kuhl, D. E., Hanson, W. R., and Phelps, M. E. (1981). FDG positron emission computed tomography in a study of aphasia. *Ann. Neurol.* 10:173–183.

Milner, B. (1974). Hemispheric specialization: scope and limits. In *The Neurosciences: Third Study Program,* F. O. Schmitt and F. G. Worden (eds.). Cambridge, Mass.: MIT Press.

Monakow, C. von (1914). *Die localisation im Grosshirn und der Abbau funktionen durch corticale Herde.* Wiesbaden: Bergmann.

Moore, R. Y. (1974). Central regeneration and recovery of function: the problem of collateral reinnervation. In *Plasticity and Recovery of Function in the Central Nervous System,* D. Stein, J. J. Rosen, and N. Butters (eds.). New York: Academic Press.

Munk, H. (1881). *Ueber die Funktionen der Grosshirnrinde, Gesammelte Mitteilungen aus den Jahren 1877–1880.* Berlin: Hirshwald.

Naeser, M. A., Helm-Estabrooks, N., Haas, G., Auerbach, S., and Srinivasan, M. (1987). Relationship between lesion extent in Wernicke's area on computed tomographic scan and predicting recovery of comprehension in Wernicke's aphasia. *Arch. Neurol.* 44:73–82.

Newcombe, F., Hions, R. W., and Marshall, J. C. (1976). Acquired dyslexia: recovery and retraining. In *Neurolinguistics.* Vol. 4. *Recovery in Aphasics,* Y. Lebrun and R. Hoops (eds.). Amsterdam: Swets and Zeitlinger.

Newman, M. (1972). The process of recovery after hemiplegia. *Stroke* 3:702–710.

Nielsen, J. M. (1946). *Agnosia, Apraxia, Aphasia.* New York: Hoeber.

Nottebohn, F. (1970). Ontogeny of bird song. *Science* 167:950–956.

Pachalska, M. (1991). Group therapy for aphasia patients. *Aphasiology* 5:541–554.

Pieniadz, J. M., Naeser, M. A., Kloff, E., and Levine, H. L. (1983). CT scan cerebral hemispheric asymmetry measurements in stroke cases with global aphasia: atypical asymmetries associated with improved recovery. *Cortex* 19:371–391.

Podraza, B. L., and Darley, F. L. (1977). Effect of auditory prestimulation on naming in aphasia. *J. Speech Hear. Res.* 20:669–683.

Poeck, K., Huber, W., and Willmes, K. (1989). Outcome of intensive language treatment in aphasia. *J. Speech Hear. Disord.* 54:471–479.

Potter, R. E., and Goodman, N. J. (1983). The implementation of laughter as a therapy facilitator with adult aphasics. *J. Commun. Disord.* 16:41–48.

Prigitano, G. (1985). *Neuropsychological Rehabilitation After Brain Injury.* Baltimore: Johns Hopkins University Press.

Prins, R. S., Schoonen, R., and Vermeulen, J. (1989). Efficacy of two different types of speech therapy for aphasic stroke patients. *Appl. Psycholing.* 10:85–123.

Robinson, R. G., and Benson, D. F. (1981). Depression in aphasic patients: frequency, severity and clinical pathological correlations. *Brain Lang.* 14:610–614.

Rosenbeck, J. C., Lemme, M. L., Ahern, M. B., Harris, E. H., and Wertz, R. T. (1973). A treatment for apraxia of speech in adults. *J. Speech Hear. Disord.* 38:462–472.

Rubens, A. (1977). The role of changes within the central nervous system during recovery from aphasia. In *Rationale for Adult Aphasia Therapy*, M. A. Sullivan and M. S. Kommers (eds.). Lincoln: University of Nebraska Medical Center.

Russell, W. R. (1971). *The Traumatic Amnesias.* London: Oxford University Press.

Russell, W. R., and Nathan, P. W. (1946). Traumatic amnesia. *Brain* 69:280–300.

Sands, E., Sarno, M. T., and Shankweiler, D. (1969). Long-term assessment of language function in aphasia due to stroke. *Arch. Phys. Med. Rehabil.* 50:202–222.

Sarno, M. T., and Levita, E. (1971). Natural course of recovery in severe aphasia. *Arch. Phys. Med. Rehabil.* 52:175–179.

Sarno, M. T., Silverman, M., and Levita, E. (1970a). Speech therapy and language recovery in severe aphasia. *J. Speech Hear. Res.* 13:607–623.

Sarno, M. T., Silverman, M., and Levita, E. (1970b). Psychosocial factors and recovery in geriatric patients with severe aphasia. *J. Am. Geriat. Soc.* 18:405–409.

Schneider, G. E. (1973). Early lesions of superior colliculus: factors affecting the formation of abnormal retinal projections. *Brain Behav. Evol.* 8:73–109.

Schuell, A., Jenkins, J. J., and Jiménez-Pabón, E. (1964). *Aphasia in Adults.* New York: Harper and Row.

Selnes, O. A., Knopman, D. S., Niccum, N., and Rubens, A. B. (1983). CT scan correlates of auditory comprehension deficits in aphasia: a prospective recovery study. *Ann. Neurol.* 13:558–566.

Seron, X. (1987). Operant procedures and neuropsychology rehabilitation. In *Neuropsychological Rehabilitation*, M. J. Meier, A. L. Benton, and L. Diller (eds.). Edinburg: Churchill Livingstone.

Shewan, C. M., and Bandur, D. L. (1986). *Treatment of Aphasia. A Language-Oriented Approach.* London: Taylor and Francis.

Shewan, C. M., and Kertesz, A. (1984). Effects of speech and language treatment on recovery from aphasia. *Brain Lang.* 23:272–299.

Skelly, M., Schinsky, L., Smith, R., and Fust, R. (1974). American Indian sign (Amerind) as a facilitator of verbalization for the oral apraxic. *J. Speech Hear. Disord.* 39:445–456.

Smith, A. (1966). Speech and other functions after left (dominant) hemispherectomy. *J. Neurol. Neurosurg. Psychiatry* 29:467–471.

Smith, A., Chamoux, R., Leri, J., London, R., and Muraski, A. (1972). *Diagnosis, Intelligence and Rehabilitation of Chronic Aphasics*. Ann Arbor: University of Michigan Department of Physical Medicine and Rehabilitation.

Sohlberg, M., and Mateer, C. (1989). *Introduction to Cognitive Rehabilitation*. Mississauga, Ontario: Gilford Press.

Sparks, R., Helm, N., and Albert, M. (1974). Aphasia rehabilitation resulting from melodic intonation therapy. *Cortex 10*:303–316.

Springer, L., Glindemann, R., Huber, W., and Willmes, K. (1991). How efficacious is PACE therapy when "Language Systematic Training" is incorporated. *Aphasiology 5*:391–401.

Springer, L., and Weniger, D. (1980). Aphasietherapie aus logopadisch-linguistischer Sicht. In *Therapie der Sprach-, Sprech- und Stimmstorungen*, G. Bohme (ed.). Stuttgart: Fischer.

Stachowiak, F.-J. (1987). Computer als Werkzeug der Sprachtherapie. *Neurolinguistik 1*:57–94.

Stavraky, G. W. (1961). *Supersensitivity Following Lesions of the Nervous System*. Toronto: University of Toronto Press.

Steele, R. D., Weinrich, M., Wertz, R. T., Kleczewska, M. K., and Carlson, G. S. (1989). Computer-based visual communication in aphasia. *Neuropsychologia 27*:409–426.

Stevens, M. K., and Yaksh, T. L. (1990). Systemic studies on the effects of the NMDA receptor antagonist MK-801 on cerebral blood flow and responsivity, EEG, and blood-brain barrier following complete reversible cerebral ischemia. *J. Cerebral Blood Flow Metab. 10*:77–88.

Stoicheff, M. L. (1960). Motivating instructions and language performance of dysphasic subjects. *J. Speech Hear. Res. 3*:75–85.

Subirana, A. (1969). Handedness and cerebral dominance. In *Handbook of Clinical Neurology*, P. J. Vinken and G. W. Bruyn (eds.). Amsterdam: North Holland.

Talland, G. A. (1965). *Deranged Memory*. New York: Academic Press.

Taylor, M. L. (1964). Language therapy. In *The Aphasic Adult: Evaluation and Rehabilitation*, H. G. Burr (ed.). Charlottesville, Va.: Wayside Press.

Tazaki, Y., Sakai, F., Otomo, E., Kutsuzawa, T., Kameyama, M., Omae, T., Fujishima, M., and Sakuma, A. (1988). Treatment of cerebral infarction with a choline precursor in a multicenter double blind placebo-controlled study. *Stroke 19*:211–216.

Van Buskirk, C. (1955). Prognostic value of sensory defect in rehabilitation of hemiplegics. *Neurology (Minneap.) 5*:407–411.

Vargha, M., and Gereb, G. (1953). *Aphasie Therapie*. Jena: V.E.B. Fisher.

Victor, M., and Adams, R. D. (1953). The effect of alcohol on the nervous system. *Proc. Assoc. Res. Nerv. Ment. Dis. 32*:526–573.

Vignolo, L. A. (1964). Evolution of aphasia and language rehabilitation. A retrospective exploratory study. *Cortex 1*:344–367.

Wahrberg, P., and Borenstein, P. (1989). Family therapy in families with an aphasic member. *Aphasiology 3*:93–98.

Wambaugh, J. L., and Thompson, C. K. (1989). Training and generalization of agrammatic aphasic adults' Wh-interrogative productions. *J. Speech Hear. Disord. 54*:509–525.

Weigl, E. (1968). On the problem of cortical syndromes. In *The Reach of Mind*, M. L. Simmel (ed.). New York: Springer.

Weinberg, J., Diller, L., Gordon, W. A., Gerstman, L. J., Lieberman, A., Lakin, P., Hodges, G., Ezrachi, M. A. (1977). Visual scanning training effect on reading-related tasks in acquired right brain damage. *Arch. Phys. Med. Rehabil. 58*:479–486.

Weisenburg, T., and McBride, K. E. (1935). *Aphasia: A Clinical and Psychological Study*. New York: Commonwealth Fund.

Weniger, D., Huber, W. H., Stachowiak, F. J., and Poeck, K. (1980). Treatment of aphasia on a linguistic basis. In *Aphasia: Assessment and Treatment*, M. T. Sarno and O. Hook (eds.). Stockholm: Almquist and Wiksell.

Wepman, J. M. (1951). *Recovery from Aphasia.* New York: Ronald Press.

Wertz, R. T. (1983). Language intervention context and setting for the aphasic adult: when? In *Clinical Management of Neurogenic Communicative Disorders*, D. F. Johns (ed.). Boston: Little, Brown, pp. 1–102.

Wertz, R. T., Collins, M. J., Weiss, D. G., Kurtzke, J. F., Friden, T., Brookshire, R. H., Pierce, J., Holtapple, P., Hubbard, D. J., Porch, B. E., West, J. A., Davis, L. A., Matouitch, V. Morely, G. K., and Ressurection, E. (1981). Veterans Administration cooperative study on aphasia: a comparison of individual and group treatment. *J. Speech Hear. Res. 24*:580–594.

Williams, M. (1966). Memory disorders associated with electroconvulsive therapy. In *Amnesia*, C.W.M. Whitby and O. L. Zangwill (eds.). London: Butterworths.

Woolsey, T., and Van der Loos, H. (1970). The structural organization of layer IV in the somatosensory region (S1) of mouse cerebral cortex. *Brain Res. 17*:205–242.

Zivin, J. A., Fisher, M., DeGirolami, J., Hemenway, C. C., and Stashak, J. A. (1985). Tissue plasminogen activator reduces neurological damage after cerebral embolism. *Science 230*:1289–1292.

# Index of Authors Cited

# Subject Index